Frommer's®

EUROPE
FROM $50 A DAY

Here's what the critics say about Frommer's:

"Amazingly easy to use. Very portable, very complete."
—*Booklist*

♦

"The only mainstream guide to list specific prices. The Walter Cronkite of guidebooks—with all that implies."
—*Travel & Leisure*

♦

"Complete, concise, and filled with useful information."
—*New York Daily News*

♦

"Hotel information is close to encyclopedic."
—*Des Moines Sunday Register*

♦

"The best series for travelers who want one easy-to-use guidebook."

—*U.S. Air Magazine*

Other Great Guides for Your Trip:

Frommer's Paris from $70 a Day

Frommer's London from $70 a Day

Frommer's England from $60 a Day

Frommer's Italy from $60 a Day

Frommer's Ireland from $50 a Day

Frommer's Greece from $50 a Day

For even more guides, see the "Other Frommer's Titles" section at the beginning of each city chapter.

Frommer's® 99

EUROPE
FROM $50 A DAY

The Ultimate Guide to
Comfortable Low-Cost Travel

MACMILLAN • USA

MACMILLAN TRAVEL

A Simon & Schuster Macmillan Company
1633 Broadway
New York, NY 10019

Find us online at **www.frommers.com**

Copyright © 1999 by Simon & Schuster, Inc.
Maps copyright © by Simon & Schuster, Inc.

ISBN 0-02-862245-6
ISSN 0730-1510

Editor: Ron Boudreau
Special thanks to Jeff Soloway, Bob O'Sullivan, and Marie Morris
Production Editor: Michael Thomas
Photo Editor: Richard Fox
Design by Michele Laseau
Digital Cartography by Roberta Stockwell and Ortelius Design
Page Creation by Tammy Ahrens, Toi Davis, Natalie Hollifield, and Terri Sheehan

SPECIAL SALES

Bulk purchases (10+ copies) of Frommer's and selected Macmillan travel guides are available to corporations, organizations, mail-order catalogs, institutions, and charities at special discounts, and can be customized to suit individual needs. For more information write to Special Sales, Macmillan General Reference, 1633 Broadway, New York, NY 10019.

Manufactured in the United States of America

Contents

14   Geneva & Bern   405

by Nikolaus Lorey

15   Innsbruck & Environs   430

by Beth Reiber

16   Lisbon & Environs   452

by Herbert Bailey Livesey

17 London, Bath & Environs 483

by Richard Jones

18 Madrid & Environs 537

by Herbert Bailey Livesey

28 Vienna & Environs 950

by Beth Reiber

Appendix 995

Index 1006

List of Maps

An Invitation to the Reader

In researching this book, we discovered many wonderful places—hotels, restaurants, shops, and more. We're sure you'll find others. Please tell us about them, so we can share the information with your fellow travelers in upcoming editions. If you were disappointed with a recommendation, we'd love to know that, too. Please write to:

Frommer's Europe from $50 a Day '99
Macmillan Travel
1633 Broadway
New York, NY 10019

An Additional Note

Please be advised that travel information is subject to change at any time—and this is especially true of prices. We therefore suggest that you write or call ahead for confirmation when making your travel plans. The authors, editors, and publisher cannot be held responsible for the experiences of readers while traveling. Your safety is important to us, however, so we encourage you to stay alert and be aware of your surroundings. Keep a close eye on cameras, purses, and wallets, all favorite targets of thieves and pickpockets.

What the Symbols Mean

✪ Frommer's Favorites

Our favorite places and experiences—outstanding for quality, value, or both.

The following abbreviations are used for credit cards:

AC	Access	ER	enRoute
AE	American Express	EURO	EuroCard
CB	Carte Blanche	JCB	Japan Credit Bank
DC	Diners Club	MC	MasterCard
DISC	Discover	V	Visa

Find Frommer's Online

Arthur Frommer's Outspoken Encyclopedia of Travel (www.frommers.com) offers more than 6,000 pages of up-to-the-minute travel information—including the latest bargains and candid, personal articles updated daily by Arthur Frommer himself. No other Web site offers such comprehensive and timely coverage of the world of travel.

Enjoying Europe
on a Budget

by Reid Bramblett

Americans have such a love affair with Europe that more than 8 million of us cross the Atlantic every year to trace our roots, explore its cities, discover its countryside, and soak up the incomparable culture, history, art, and architecture. And that's not mentioning all the other travelers to Europe and within Europe.

This guide will prepare you for your travels and serve as your trusty handbook so that you can get the most out of Europe on a budget, providing all the hints, advice, practical information, and historical background you'll need—whether your goal is to see all the Renaissance museums in Florence, ponder life at a sidewalk table of a Parisian cafe, bask in the baroque beauty of Prague, explore the hill towns of Andalusia, or hit the theaters of London's West End.

ABOUT THE $50-A-DAY PREMISE   Times—and most definitely prices—have changed since Arthur Frommer himself published the first edition of this book in 1957. This 42nd edition, *Europe from $50 a Day,* has been completely revised for 1999, yet it retains the dependable Frommer's emphasis: *great value for your money.*

This book is *not* about just barely scraping by but rather about traveling comfortably on a reasonable budget. Spend too little and you suck all the fun out of travel; you shortchange yourself, your vacation, and your experiences. Spend too much and you insulate yourself from the local side of Europe and some of the best travel memories.

Frommer's Europe from $50 a Day takes you down the middle road, where the joys and experiences of Europe open wide to let you in. Traveling frugally provides rewarding opportunities for you to mingle with Europeans on their own turf—in plazas and parks, pubs and cafes, trains and buses, and sometimes even homes.

Doing Europe "from $50 a day" means that $50 is the average starting amount per person you'll need to spend on accommodations and meals *only;* transportation, sightseeing, shopping, souvenirs, entertainment, and other expenses are *not* included. Expect to use a little over half your $50 each day on accommodations. Obviously, two people can travel within this budget more easily than one—$60 for a double room and $20 each for meals.

Of course, since our budget is *from* $50 a day, we don't limit our hotel and restaurant recommendations to only rock-bottom places. You'll also find moderately priced choices as well as more expensive options for those who'd like to splurge here and there.

Europe

Norwegian Sea

North Atlantic Ocean

Bergen

NORWAY

North Sea

GRAMPIAN
Aberdeen
TAYSIDE
Perth
Edinburgh

Belfast

DENMARK

IRELAND
Dublin

DINGLE
PENINSULA
KERRY
COUNTY

Liverpool

THE
NETHERLANDS

Hamburg

U. K.
COTSWOLDS Oxford
Bath
STONEHENGE
Salisbury

London

Amsterdam

Bruges
BELGIUM
Brussels Liège
LUX.

GERMANY
Bonn
Frankfurt
Rothenburg
ob der Tauber
Augsburg

English Channel

Le Havre

Paris

LOIRE VALLEY

FRANCE

Strasbourg

Munich
BAVARIAN
Bern Innsbruck
SWITZERLAND
BERNER
OBERLAND

Bay of Biscay

Bordeaux

Geneva

Milan

Bilbao

Arles **PROVENCE**
Marseille Nice

MONACO
Florence

Côte d'Azur

ANDORRA

Porto

PORTUGAL
Lisbon

Madrid

Barcelona

CORSICA

TUSCANY

SPAIN
Córdoba
Valencia

ALGARVE
Seville **ANDALUSIA**
Malaga Granada
Costa del Sol

SARDINIA Cagliari

Mediterranean Sea

0 ⊢ 250 km
155 mi
N

E-0001

2

SWEDEN

rondheim

Sundsvall •

Gulf of Bothnia

Oslo

Gavle •

Stockholm •

Göteborg

Copenhagen

Baltic Sea

Berlin •

FINLAND

• Tampere

Helsinki •

• Tallinn

ESTONIA

• Riga

LATVIA

LITHUANIA

Vilnius •

• Tver

Gdansk

• Poznan

• Warsaw

POLAND

St. Petersburg

RUSSIA

Moscow •

• Minsk

BELARUS

Karlovy Vary
(Carlsbad)
• Prague

CZECH
REPUBLIC

KITZBÜHEL ALPS

Salzburg

AUSTRIA

Ljubljana

SLOVENIA

Venice

ITALY

• Rome

Naples
■ POMPEII

Tyrrhenian Sea

Palermo

SICILY

MALTA

• Krakow

SLOVAKIA

Vienna

Bratislava

DANUBE
VALLEY

• Budapest

HUNGARY

Lake Balaton

Zagreb

CROATIA

BOSNIA

Sarajevo

SERBIA

MONTENEGRO

Titograd •

• Tirana

ALBANIA

• Lvov

UKRAINE

• Kiev

MOLDOVA

Chisinau • • Odessa

Cluj-Napoca •

ROMANIA

Constanta •

Bucharest •

Varna •

BULGARIA

• Sofiya

Skopje •

MACEDONIA

Belgrade •

Adriatic Sea

Black Sea

Istanbul •

TURKEY

GREECE

Aegean Sea

Delphi •

Athens •

CYCLADES

PELOPONNESE

CYPRUS

Ionian Sea

CRETE

3

These first three chapters will show you how to squeeze the most out of your budget in Europe. Refer to the individual city chapters for specifics, such as when to go, where to stay, what to do, and how to save money once you arrive. And be sure to check out the many **valuable coupons** at the back of this book.

1 Money-Saving Strategies

For city-specific tips, see the "Getting the Best Deal" boxes throughout this guide.

GETTING THE BEST DEAL ON ACCOMMODATIONS

Most tourist offices, some travel agents, and often a hotel reservation booth at foreign train stations can provide listings of B&Bs, inns, rooms for rent, farmhouses, and small hotels where a couple might spend only $20 to $30 each for a double. Besides the more traditional options below, creative travel alternatives where lodging costs nothing or next to nothing include home exchanges and educational vacations (see "Educational & Volunteer Vacations" in chapter 3).

BRINGING THE RATES DOWN   Keep prices low by traveling off-season and off the beaten track. In cities, seek out local, not touristy, neighborhoods, or those frequented largely by students. Small family-run B&Bs, inns, and pensione tend to be cheaper—not to mention friendlier—than larger hotels. In fact, though you'll find more and more properties in Europe sporting the familiar titles of American chain hotels, these are almost always standardized business hotels with a price tag two to four times as high as the same chain charges in the States.

Getting a good rate at any hotel is an exercise in trade-offs. You can get lower prices by looking for hotels away from the center of town or opting for a smaller room, one without a private bath, or one without a TV or other amenities. Ask to see different rooms—they'll often try to move the most expensive or least appealing ones first, so let them know you're a smart shopper who'll only stay in a room you approve of and that's at a fair price. Politely negotiate the rates, especially off-season and if you sense that the hotel has plenty of empty rooms—you might pay 25% less. Always ask about discounts for stays of 3 or more days, over the weekend, or for students or seniors.

Be pleasant, not pushy. Call around to a few hotels before you begin visiting them to gauge how full the city's inns seem to be. If there are plenty of extra rooms in town, you've got more bargaining leverage. If one proprietor isn't easily persuaded to give you a worthwhile deal, try elsewhere. If, however, hotels in town seem booked, bed down in the first reasonable place and hope for better bargaining luck next time.

OVERNIGHT TRAINS   One of the great European deals is the overnight train couchette, where for only about $20 (second class) you get a reserved bunk for the night in a shared sleeping compartment (four to six people). You can sleep for free by taking your chances on finding an empty sitting couchette where you can slide down the seat backs to make a bed. When you wake up, you've gotten where you're going without wasting your daylight hours on a train, plus you've saved yourself one night's hotel charges.

PACKAGE TOURS   Airlines and tour operators offer package tours that, unlike fully escorted guided tours, get you great rates on air transportation and hotels but leave the sightseeing up to you. It's a good mix of the joys and freedom of independent travel at the cut rates of a tour. See "Taking a Tour" in chapter 3 for more details.

RENTING   If you rent a room, an apartment, a cottage, or a farmhouse, you can live life like a European, if only for a few days or weeks. In cities, rental rooms and

A Note on Special Rates

In several chapters of this book you'll see that some hotels offer special rates "for Frommer's readers." The hotel owners request that you please make it clear on booking or arrival (or both) that you're a Frommer's reader to avoid confusion regarding those special rates. Note that the actual rates may have changed by the time you plan your trip, but the hotels will still offer our readers a discount.

apartments can often be brokered through the tourist office or some other privately run accommodations service in the train station. Rooms for rent usually offer great rates (much cheaper than a hotel) even for the single traveler staying just one night, though some may require a minimum stay of a few nights. Apartments start making economic sense when you have three or more people and are staying in town for a week or longer.

Renting villas, cottages, farmhouses, and the like is a much trickier business, with a wide range of rates—and of quality. It can be a downright budget option (usually, again, for small groups of more than three or four renting for a few weeks), or it can be a hedonistic splurge on an overpriced historic castle. Shop around. Contact local tourist offices before leaving home; they may have lists or catalogs of available properties. Or read through travel magazines and newspaper supplements for ads. Or you can try **Europa-Let/Tropical In-Let,** 92 N. Main St., Ashland, OR 97520 (☎ **800/ 462-4486** or 541/482-5806; fax 541/482-0660), which represents about 100,000 European properties, many off the beaten path. Imagine living for a week in a studio apartment in London for $500 to $600 or in a cottage in France for $450 to $600. Book as early as possible.

HOSTELS   One of the least expensive ways to keep a roof over your head and meet other travelers is to stay in hostels. What were once "youth hostels" are increasingly popular with travelers of all ages—though in many you pay a bit more if you're over 26. They're plentiful in Europe and charge about $10 to $25 per night for what's usually a bunk in a dorm (often sex-segregated) sleeping anywhere from 4 to 50. There are lockers for your bags, and you often must bring your own sleep-sack (basically a sheet folded in half and sewn up the side) or buy one on-site. For many, you'll need an HI membership card (see below); at some, the card is required for you to stay there, at others it'll get you a discount, and at some hostels you can "buy" the card by staying a few nights. There's usually a lockout from morning to mid-afternoon and an evening curfew. Be warned that in summer especially, they fill up early each morning, often with high school and college students partying their way through Europe.

Membership in **Hostelling International/American Youth Hostels (HI-AYH),** 733 15th St. NW, Suite 840, Washington, DC 20005 (☎ **202/783-6161;** www. hiayh.org), an affiliate of the International Youth Hostel Federation (IYH), costs $25 per year for people 18 to 54, $15 for those 55 and older, and $10 for those 17 and younger. Family memberships cover parents and children 16 and under and cost $35. Kids as young as 5 or 6 are generally welcome at hostels. You can book hostel accommodations worldwide up to 6 months in advance by calling the above number or the hostel itself. HI sells the *Hostelling International Budget Accommodations You Can Trust, Vol. I: Europe and the Mediterranean,* for $13.95.

Also check out *Frommer's Complete Hostel Vacation Guide to England, Wales & Scotland* ($14.95), the first-ever guide to the 300-plus hostels in those countries. You'll find more hostel information on the **Internet Guide to Hostelling** at **www.hostels.com.**

GETTING THE BEST DEAL ON DINING

Some hotels include dinner or breakfast in their rates or offer them as extras. For dinner, this will sometimes be a good price and a fine meal, but you can almost always eat just as cheaply—and find considerably more variety—by dining at local restaurants. **Hotel breakfasts**—with the exception of the cholesterol-laden minifeasts of the British Isles—are invariably overpriced. A "continental breakfast" means a roll with jam and coffee or tea, occasionally with some sliced ham, cheese, or fruit to justify the $4 to $15 price. Some hotels include breakfast in the rates, but if there's any way you can get out of paying for it, do so. You can pick up the same food at the corner cafe or bar for $2 to $3.

When it comes to **choosing your restaurant,** a local bistro, trattoria, taverna, or pub will not only be cheaper than a fancier restaurant but will also offer you the opportunity to rub elbows with Europeans. Ask locals you meet for recommendations of places they like, not places they think you'd like. Pick restaurants that are packed with locals, not abandoned or filled only with tourists; if the folks in the neighborhood stay away, there's usually a good reason. At any restaurant, the **house table wine** will usually be just fine, if not excellent.

The **fixed-price menu** is a budget option at many eateries that gets you a semi-full meal at a cheaper price—but a much more limited selection—than if you ordered each dish from the full menu. The best deals include wine (a glass or quarter-carafe) or beer, coffee, and dessert along with a choice for first and second courses.

If you love fine food, but not huge bills, consider patronizing **top restaurants at lunch.** Outstanding places may serve the same or similar dishes at both meals, but with lunch prices two-thirds to one-half those at dinner. Plus, lunch reservations are easier to come by. In Britain and Ireland, indulge in afternoon tea, in Spain do a tapas bar crawl, and in Italy nibble during the evening *passeggiata* stroll—all inexpensive popular customs that'll cut your appetite for a huge meal later. Wherever you eat, be sure to check the menu and ask your waiter to see if a **service charge** is automatically included; don't tip twice by accident.

In the **bars and cafes** of many European countries, the price on any item consumed while standing at the bar is lower (sometimes by as much as half) than the price you'd pay sitting at a table and three times lower than the price charged at the outdoor tables.

If your day is filled with sightseeing, lunch can be as quick as local cheeses and salamis, ripe fruit, a loaf of freshly baked bread, and a bottle of wine or mineral water eaten on the steps of the cathedral, a park bench, or in your hotel room. **Picnic** ingredients in Europe, from outdoor markets and tiny neighborhood shops, are ultrafresh and so cheap you usually won't spend more than $5 to $10 per person.

GETTING THE BEST DEAL ON SIGHTSEEING

You've heard that the best things in life are free. Well, some of the best things in sightseeing are too. You can't get much better than strolling through Paris's Luxembourg Gardens or spending an afternoon in London's Tate Gallery. And how about exploring Barcelona's medieval quarter or relaxing on a St-Tropez beach? Often a city's tourist office will offer a free booklet of walking tours so that you can explore the city on foot. Also note that Frommer's publishes *Memorable Walks in Paris* and *Memorable Walks in London* (both $9.95).

Visit the tourist office and pump them for free information, brochures, and museum lists—everything you need to sightsee on your own. Find out if some museums offer free entry on a particular day or reduced admission after a certain hour and go then (but be prepared for crowds). Keep in mind that many European museums are closed on Monday and open just a half day on Sunday, so check the schedule before you go.

GETTING THE BEST DEAL ON SHOPPING

GETTING YOUR VAT REFUND   First the bad news: All European countries charge a **value-added tax (VAT)** of 15% to 33% on goods and services—it's like a sales tax that's already included in the price. Rates vary from country to country, though the goal in EU countries is to arrive at a uniform rate of about 15%.

Now the good news: Non-EU citizens are entitled to have some or all of the VAT refunded on purchases if you spend more than a certain amount at any one store (how much ranges from as low as $80 in England—though some stores, like Harrods, require as much as $150—up to $200 in France or Italy).

Request a VAT refund invoice from the cashier when you make your purchase, and bring this and your receipts to the customs office at the airport of the last EU country you'll be in to have it stamped. In other words, if you're flying home from England, bring all your slips from Italy, France, Germany, and so on to the airport in London and allow a good 30 to 45 extra minutes to get it all done. Once back home and within 90 days of the purchase, mail all stamped invoices back to the stores, and they'll send you a refund check in a few weeks or months or will credit your account if you paid with plastic.

CUSTOMS   For U.S. Citizens   You can bring back into the United States $400 worth of goods (per person) without paying a duty on them. There are a few restrictions on amount: 1 liter of alcohol (you must be over 21), 200 cigarettes, and 100 cigars. Antiques over 100 years old and works of art are exempt from the $400 limit, as is anything you mail home. Once per day, you can mail yourself $200 worth of goods duty-free; mark them "for personal use." You can also mail to other people up to $100 worth of goods per person, per day; label each "unsolicited gift." Any package must state on the exterior a description of the contents and their values. You cannot mail alcohol, perfume (it contains alcohol), or tobacco products.

You pay a flat 10% duty on the first $1,000 worth of goods over $400. Beyond that, it works on an item-by-item basis. For more information on regulations, check out the **U.S. Customs Service** Web site at **www.customs.ustreas.gov** or write to P.O. Box 7407, Washington, DC 20044, to request the free "Know Before You Go" pamphlet.

To prevent the spread of diseases, you can't bring into the U.S. any plants, fruits, vegetables, meats, or other foodstuffs. This includes even cured meats like salami (no matter what the shopkeeper in Europe says). You may bring in the following: bakery goods, all but the softest cheeses (the rule is vague, but if the cheese is at all spreadable, don't risk confiscation), candies, roasted coffee beans and dried tea, fish (packaged salmon is okay), seeds for veggies and flowers (but not for trees), and mushrooms. Check out the USDA's Web site at **www.aphis.usda.gov/oa/travel.html** for more information.

For U.K. Citizens   You can bring home *almost* as much as you like of any goods from any EU country (theoretical limits run along the lines of 90 liters of wine). If you're returning home from a non-EU country or if you buy your goods in a duty-free shop, you're allowed to bring home 200 cigarettes, 2 liters of table wine, plus 1 liter of spirits or 2 liters of fortified wine. Get in touch with **Her Majesty's Customs and Excise Office,** New King's Beam House, 22 Upper Ground, London SE1 9PJ (☎ 0171/620-1313), for more information.

DUTY-FREE SHOPS   Until July 1, 1999, when duty-free shopping will be abolished in all EU countries, you can avoid the VAT right from the get-go. "Duty-free" means that a shop sells an item to you without the VAT added in (the assumption is that you're on your way out of the country and would be applying for a VAT refund on the spot anyway). It's available in airports; on planes, ferries, and cruise ships; at international border crossings; and in some downtown stores (technically, this last one is called "Tax Free Shopping for Tourists" and what happens is that you get a form and a check to bring to the Tax Free Shopping booth at the airport for an instant refund).

Most of us patronize duty-free shops in the airport simply as a way to get rid of foreign currency at the end of a trip. To take best advantage of duty-free—and of European shopping in general—**know the at-home price** of any item you're thinking about purchasing. If you're saving only a couple of bucks, it's hardly worth it to lug the stuff home. Know that lately the prices at many duty-free shops have been creeping up to equal, if not more than, the prices at regular stores—and since the store's not paying the government VAT, they're pocketing the difference. Remember: The duty you're avoiding is the local tax on items, *not* the duty on imports you may have to pay the Customs office upon reentering your home country (see below).

BARGAINING   Bargaining may be more prevalent in parts of the world other than Europe, but it's still done in Spain, Portugal, Greece, and to some degree Italy. In other countries, store prices are pretty set, but you'll run across the opportunity to haggle in flea markets.

These tips will help ease the process along: Never appear too interested or too anxious; offer only a third of the original asking price and slowly work your way up from there (the price should never jump up—it should inch up, so take the time to inch it properly); tantalize with cash and have the exact amount you want to pay in your hand. Finally, don't take bargaining, the vendor, or yourself too seriously. The seller will act shocked, hurt, or angry, but he or she isn't really; it's all just part of the ritual. Ideally, bargaining should be fun for both parties.

GETTING THE BEST DEAL ON AFTER-DARK ENTERTAINMENT

If you're interested in the theater, ballet, or opera, ask at the tourist office if discount or last-minute tickets are available and where to get them (at the theater itself or a special booth). Some theaters sell standing-room or discount seats on the day of the performance, and students and seniors may qualify for special admission.

Nightclubs tend to be expensive, but you might be able to avoid a cover charge by sitting or standing at the bar rather than taking a table. If you decide to splurge, keep a lid on your alcohol intake; that's where the costs mount up astronomically. If you've arrived during a public holiday or festival, there may be abundant free entertainment, much of it in the streets.

For more leads on stretching your entertainment dollar, check "Deals & Discounts" and "After Dark" in each city chapter.

GETTING THE BEST DEAL ON PHONE CALLS & E-MAIL

LOCAL CALLS   In most European countries these days, public phones work with prepaid **phonecards**—many don't even take change anymore—sold at train stations, post offices, and newsstands. Calls cost the same whether made with coins or cards. If you'll be in town a while, phonecards pay off in convenience. If you're just in a country for a few days, you probably won't use up an entire card, so don't bother to buy one.

OVERSEAS CALLS   If you can avoid it, never pay European rates for a transcontinental call; American ones are cheaper. AT&T, MCI, and Sprint all have local (usually) free numbers in each country that'll link you directly to an American operator, who can place a collect call or take your calling card number.

Number, Please: Europe's Country Codes & City Codes

To call Europe from the United States, dial 011, followed by the country code, then the city code. Note that most city codes start with a "0" (in Spain, with a 9; in France, Copenhagen, Monaco, and now Italy, the city code is built into the number itself). You dial this initial 0 only when calling from another city within that country; when calling from anywhere outside that country, you must drop the city code's 0. Except for Italy—when calling Italy from outside the country, you need to dial the 0 as well.

The following are the codes for the countries and major cities covered in this guide. For more specific information, see "Telephone" under the "Fast Facts" section at the beginning of each city chapter.

Austria	**43**		**Ireland**	**353**
Innsbruck	0512		Dublin	01
Salzburg	0662		**Italy**	**39**
Vienna	1		Florence	055
Belgium	**32**		Rome	06
Brussels	02		Venice	041
The Czech Republic	**420**		**Monaco**	**377**
Prague	02		Monte Carlo	none
Denmark	**45**		**The Netherlands**	**31**
Copenhagen	none		Amsterdam	020
England	**44**		**Portugal**	**351**
London	0171 or 0181		Lisbon	01
France	**33**		**Scotland**	**44**
Nice	04		Edinburgh	0131
Paris	01		**Spain**	**34**
Germany	**49**		Barcelona	93
Berlin	030		Madrid	91
Munich	089		Seville	95
Greece	**30**		**Sweden**	**46**
Athens	01		Stockholm	08
Hungary	**36**		**Switzerland**	**41**
Budapest	01		Geneva	22

Calling cards, not to be confused with phonecards, are like credit cards for phone calls and usually offer the easiest and cheapest way for you to call home (or even call ahead to the next country on your itinerary to reserve a hotel room). They're issued by major long-distance carriers like AT&T, MCI, and Sprint and come with a wallet-size list of those local numbers around the world; since the rates and calling plans change regularly, shop around to find out which one is currently offering the best deal on Europe-to-the-U.S. rates.

Avoid making *any* **calls from European hotels.** They charge exorbitant rates—especially for transatlantic calls, but even for a local call like ringing up a nearby restaurant for reservations—and they often add a "surcharge" on top of that, sometimes bringing the total to over 200% above what the same call would cost from a pay phone. If you have to place the call from the hotel, have your party call you right back.

Again, calling cards are the cheapest way to call home, but if for some reason you choose to travel without one, you have two choices. Since phonecards (see above) come in a variety of increments, you can buy a few of the more expensive phonecards and call abroad by feeding them into a pay phone, one after the other, as they get used up. Or go to a big-city post office where you can call home from a little booth on a toll phone, then pay when you're done.

E-MAIL   Cybercafes (www.easynet.co.uk/pages/cafe/ccafe.htm) have popped up all over Europe faster than you could say "le e-mail." You can stop at them in most cities, check your e-mail, and send virtual postcards to your friends back home for around 10¢ to 30¢ per minute. Most also offer temporary mailboxes you can rent for the day, week, or month if you'll be sticking around town for a while.

2   Getting Around Without Going Broke

BY TRAIN

In Europe, the shortest—and cheapest—distance between two points is lined with rail tracks. European trains are less expensive than those in the United States, far more advanced in many ways, and certainly more extensive, with over 100,000 miles of track. Modern high-speed trains make the rails faster than the plane for short journeys, and **overnight trains** get you where you're going without wasting valuable daylight hours—and you save money on lodging to boot (a reserved bunk in a second-class couchette, shared with five others and with a lock on the door, costs about $20).

You can get much more information about train travel in Europe, and receive automated schedule information by fax, by contacting **Rail Europe** at ☎ **800/438-7245** or **www.raileurope.com.** Or buy the **Thomas Cook European Timetable** ($27.95 from travel specialty stores or order it at ☎ **800/FORSYTH**). Each country's national rail Web site—with schedules and fare information, occasionally in English—are hotlisted at **mercurio.iet.unipi.it/misc/timetabl.html.** For sample ticket prices and detailed train schedules, see the Appendix.

CLASSIFICATIONS   Europe has a rainbow of train classifications ranging from local milk runs that stop at every tiny station to high-speed bullet trains that cruise at 130 mph between major cities.

The most useful of the international high-speed trains is the **Eurostar,** which ducks under the Channel Tunnel to whisk you from London to Paris (or Brussels) and cuts the old train-ferry-train odyssey of 10 hours down to an easy 3. (See "Getting to the Continent from the U.K." in chapter 3 for details.)

The difference between **first- and second-class** seats on European trains is small—a matter of 1 or 2 inches of extra padding and a bit more elbow room at most.

SUPPLEMENTS & RESERVATIONS   Many high-speed trains throughout Europe, including the popular EC (EuroCity), IC (InterCity), and EN (EuroNight), require that you pay a **supplement** of $5 to $15 in addition to the ticket. It's included when you buy regular tickets but not in any railpass, so check at the ticket window before boarding; otherwise, the conductor will sell you the supplement on the train and assess you a small fine.

Reservations are required on some of the speediest of the high-speed runs—most trains marked with an "R" on a schedule. Reservations range from $15 up beyond $50 (when a meal is included). You can almost always reserve a seat within a few hours of the train's departure, but play it safe by booking a few days in advance at the station's ticket windows. You'll also need to reserve any sleeping couchette or sleeping berth.

With two exceptions, there's no need to buy individual train tickets or make these reservations before you leave home, where travel agents will book for you but also charge for the service. However, when buying the required supplement on the high-speed "Artesia" run (Paris–Turin and Milan), you can get a substantial discount if you have a railpass—but only if you buy the supplement in the States along with the pass itself. It's also wise to reserve a seat on the Chunnel's *Eurostar* train, as England's frequent "bank holidays" (long weekends) book the train solid with Londoners taking a short vacation to Paris.

RAILPASSES

The greatest value in European travel has always been the railpass, a single ticket that allows you unlimited travel—or a certain number of days—within a set period of time. On trips where you cover countless kilometers on the rails and range all over Europe by train, a pass will end up costing you considerably less than buying individual tickets. Plus it gives you the freedom to hop on a train whenever you feel like it, making day-tripping out of town easy and cheap, and there's no waiting in ticket lines. For more focused trips, you may want to look into national or regional passes, or just buy individual tickets as you go.

Tips for Riding the Rails

- Use your time on the train wisely. Read about your next destination in this guide, begin practicing the foreign phrases, make up daily itineraries, choose your hotels and pick out a few restaurants to try, have a picnic, write postcards, catch up on your journal, or nap.
- Many countries, such as Italy, require you to stamp the ticket in a little box on the platform before boarding the train (unnecessary for railpasses), so search these out or ask when you buy your ticket. Hold onto your ticket until the ride is over and you're out of the final station (on rare occasions, security guards may ask to see it).
- Track assignments may change suddenly. Seek out a conductor on the indicated platform and ask before stepping onto the train, then triple-check with passengers on-board who look like they take this train every day.
- Make sure you get on the right *car*, not just the right train. Each car may very well be splitting off down the line and joining a train headed to a different destination.
- Don't drink the water on trains. Not even to rinse your mouth. It's for handwashing only. Trains, especially overnighters, dehydrate you quickly, so make sure you bring bottled water to sip throughout the night and to rinse your mouth and your toothbrush the next morning.
- Trains are relatively safe, but take a few sensible precautions. On overnighters, always lock your couchette door from the inside. Remember, you're sharing a room with up to five strangers, so don't flash anything valuable. Secure your bag to the luggage rack by buckling a few of the straps around the guardrail (if a potential thief can't tug it down in one quick motion, he'll be unlikely to stick around and unstrap it all). Keep your money belt on all night under your pants (in fact, many people go into the train bathroom and restrap it around their upper thigh so that light-fingered crooks don't unzip you to extract your cash and documents).

Countries Honoring Train Passes

Eurail Countries: Austria, Belgium, Denmark, Finland, France, Germany, Greece, Hungary, Ireland, Italy, Luxembourg, the Netherlands, Norway, Portugal, Spain, Sweden, Switzerland.
Europass Core Countries: France, Germany, Switzerland, Italy, Spain.
Europass Add-on "Zones": Austria/Hungary, Belgium/Netherlands/
Luxembourg, Greece (including the ferry from Brindisi, Italy), Portugal.
Note: Great Britain isn't included in any pass.

The granddaddy of passes is the **Eurailpass,** covering 17 countries (most of Western Europe *except* Britain), and the whirlwind, pan-European tour's single best investment. It has recently been joined by its nephew the **Europass** (5–12 countries depending on what sort of version you buy, also not including England, mainly for travelers who are going to stay within the heart of Western Europe), and their various **rail-and-drive** and **partner-pass** cousins (details on all to follow).

There are also **national passes** of various kinds, as well as **regional passes** such as **ScanRail** (Scandinavia), **BritRail** (covering Great Britain), and the **European East Pass** (good in Austria, Czech Republic, Slovakia, Hungary, and Poland). Some types of national passes you have to buy outside of Europe, some you can get on either side of the Atlantic, and still others you must purchase in Europe itself. Remember: Seniors, students, and youths can usually get discounts on European trains—in some countries just by asking, in others by buying a discount card good for a year (or whatever). Rail Europe or your travel agent can fill you in on all the details.

Railpasses come in two main flavors: consecutive-day or flexipass (in which you have, say, 2 months in which to use 10 days of train travel). **Consecutive-day** passes are best for those taking the train very frequently (every few days), covering a lot of ground, and making many short train hops. **Flexipasses** are for folks who want to range far and wide but plan on taking their time over a long trip and intend to stay in each city for a while.

PASSES AVAILABLE IN NORTH AMERICA   If you're under 26, you can opt to buy a regular first-class pass or a second-class **youth pass;** age 26 and over, you're stuck buying a first-class pass. Passes for kids 4 to 11 are half price, and children under 4 travel free. The rates quoted below are for 1998, and they'll rise each year.

- **Eurailpass**—Consecutive-day Eurailpasses at $538 for 15 days, $698 for 21 days, $864 for 1 month, $1,224 for 2 months, or $1,512 for 3 months.
- **Eurail Flexipass**—Good for 2 months of travel, within which you can train it for 10 days (consecutive or not) at $634 or 15 days at $836.
- **Eurail Saverpass**—If you're traveling with buddies, you can save 15% each as long as you ride together. The "saverpass" for 2 to 5 people costs, *per person,* $458 for 15 days, $594 for 21 days, $734 for 1 month, $1,040 for 2 months, or $1,286 for 3 months.
- **Eurail Saver Flexipass**—The flexipass is for groups. You must travel together (2 to 5 people) and each pays $540 for 10 days within 2 months or $710 for 15 days within 2 months.
- **Eurail Youthpass**—The second-class ticket to Europe on the cheap, perfect for summer vacations and whirlwind tours: $376 for 15 days, $489 for 21 days, $605 for 1 month, $857 for 2 months, or $1,059 for 3 months.
- **Eurail Youth Flexipass**—On a study abroad program? This may be the pass for you, since it allows 10 days of travel within 2 months for $444 or 15 days in

2 months for $585—just right for long weekends and vacations between classes.

- **Europass**—If your trip focuses on the core of Western Europe (see above for the countries), Eurail is wasteful spending. Go for the Europass—you've got 2 months in which you can take 5 days of train travel. The add-on "zones" let you expand the scope of your trip to other countries. The base pass is $326, $386 with 1 zone added, $416 with 2 zones, $436 with 3 zones, or $446 with all 4 zones. You can also add up to 10 extra days (for 15 days total) at $42 per day (do some math to see if adding zones and days brings your total high enough that Eurail makes more sense).

- **Europass Partner**—This isn't actually a different pass, but rather a way for one traveling companion to get a 40% discount on his or her own Europass. You must travel together and each pay 20% less than going solo: $261 each for the basic pass, $309 with 1 zone, $333 with 2 zones, $349 with 3 zones, $357 with all 4 zones, and $34 each for each extra day.

- **Europass Youth**—Same deal as the Europass (no partner pass version), only in second class and for under 26 only. The base pass costs $216, $261 with 1 zone, $286 with 2 zones, $301 with 3 zones, $309 with all 4 zones, and $29 for each extra day.

- **EurailDrive Pass**—The best of both worlds, mixing train travel and rental cars (Hertz or Avis) for less money than it would cost to do them separately (and one of the only ways to get around the high daily car rates in Europe when you rent for less than a week). You get 4 rail days and 3 car days within a 2-month period. Prices (for 1 adult/2 adults each) vary with the class of the car: $435/$350 economy class, $495/$380 compact, $525/$395 midsize. You can add up to 5 extra rail and/or car days. Extra rail days are $55 each; car days cost $58 each for economy class, $78 compact, and $88 midsize. You have to reserve the first car day a week before leaving home but can make other reservations as you go (subject to availability). If there are more than 2 adults, the extra passengers get the car portion free but must buy the 4-day railpass for about $268.

- **Eurodrive Pass**—Similar deal, but for Europass countries only (no add-on zones) and for shorter trips. It's good for 3 rail days and 2 car days within a 2-month period. Prices (1 adult/2 adults each) are $315/$265 economy class, $355/$280 compact, and $370/$290 midsize. You can add up to 9 extra rails days at $42 each, and unlimited extra car days for $55 to $85, depending on the class of car.

Again, you have to buy Eurail and its offshoots outside Europe (they're available from some major European train stations but are up to 50% more expensive). You can buy railpasses from most travel agents, but the biggest supplier is **Rail Europe** (☎ 800/438-7245; www.raileurope.com). It also sells most national passes save a few minor British ones.

My recommendation is to contact **Rick Steves's Europe Through the Back Door** (☎ 425/771-8303; www.ricksteves.com). He doesn't tack on the $10 handling fee that all other agencies do. He also sells all Europe-wide and all national railpasses, and sends a free video and guide on how to use railpasses with every order. **BritRail** (☎ 800/BRITRAIL; www.britrail.com/us/ushome.htm) specializes in Great Britain, and **DER Tours** (☎ 800/782-2424; www.dertravel.com) is a Germany specialist that also sells other national passes (except French and British ones).

PASSES AVAILABLE IN THE U.K. Many railpasses are available in the United Kingdom for travel in Britain and Europe.

The **InterRail Card** is the most popular rail ticket for anyone who has lived in Europe at least 6 months and is 26 or under (an over-26 version exists but offers discounts in fewer countries). It costs £279, is valid for 1 month, and entitles you to unlimited second-class travel in 28 European countries. It also gives you a 34% discount on rail travel in Britain and Northern Ireland, plus an up-to-50% discount on the rail portion of travel from London to various continental ports, plus special rates on *Eurostar* trains. You'll also get a reduction (30% to 50%) on most sailings to Europe and a variety of other shipping services around the Mediterranean and Scandinavia. If you're not planning to travel in 28 countries, you can purchase a lower-price card. The 28 countries have been divided up into zones. A card for one zone is £189.

Another good option for travelers 26 and under, **Eurotrain** tickets are valid for 2 months and allow you to choose your own route to a final destination and stop off as many times as you like along the way. **Eurotrain "Explorer"** tickets are slightly more expensive but allow you to travel to your final destination along one route and back on another. The price includes round-trip ferry crossing as well as round-trip rail travel from London to the port.

For help in determining the best option for your trip and to buy tickets, stop in at the **International Rail Centre,** in Victoria Station London SW1V 1JY (☎ **0990/ 848-848**); **Wasteels,** also in Victoria Station (☎ **0171/834-7066**), adjacent to Platform 2; or **Campus Travel,** 52 Grosvenor Gardens, London SW1W 0AG (☎ **0171/730-3402**).

BY CAR

Getting around by car in Europe may not be the pricey endeavor you imagine. True, rental rates can be quite high and gasoline costs as much as three times higher than in the States (the price may look lower, but remember it's quoted in liters; there are 3.8 liters in 1 U.S. gallon; in Britain, the Imperial gallon is the equivalent of 1.2 U.S. gallons).

But after all the math is done, three or more people traveling together can actually go cheaper by car than by train (even with railpasses). Many rental companies grant discounts if you reserve in advance (usually 48 hours), and it's always cheaper to reserve from your home country. Weekly rentals are usually less expensive than day rentals.

In addition, driving is the best way to explore the rural and small-town side of Europe, like France's Riviera, Italy's Tuscany, and southern Spain's Andalusia. You might want to mix-and-match train travel to get between cities and the occasional rental car to explore a region or two; if so, look into the rail/drive versions of railpasses (see "By Train").

TAXES & INSURANCE   When you reserve a car, be sure to ask if the price includes the value-added tax (VAT), personal accident insurance (PAI), collision-damage waiver (CDW), and any other insurance options. If not, ask what they'll cost, because at the end of your rental they can make a big difference in your bottom line. Some rental companies may require that you purchase a theft-protection policy in Italy.

CDW costs around $10 per day. It can add up but can also buy you great peace of mind, allowing you to walk away from a totaled rental car without owing a cent. CDW and other insurance may be covered by your credit card if you use it to pay for the rental; check with the card issuer. **Travel Guard International,** 1145 Clark St., Stevens Point, WI 54481-9970 (☎ **800/826-1300;** www.travel-guard.com), offers CDW for $5 per day.

RENTAL AGENCIES   The main car-rental companies include **Avis** (☎ 800/ 331-1212; www.avis.com); **Budget** (☎ 800/527-0700; www.budgetrentacar. com); **Dollar** (known as Europcar in Europe; ☎ 800/800-6000; www.dollarcar.com);

Hertz (☎ 800/654-3131; www.hertz.com); and **National** (☎ 800/227-7368; www.nationalcar.com).

U.S.-based companies that specialize in European car rentals are **Auto-Europe** (☎ 800/223-5555; www.autoeurope.com); **Europe by Car** (☎ 800/223-1516, 800/252-9401 in California, or 212/581-3040 in New York; www.europebycar.com); and **Kemwel** (☎ 800/678-0678; www.kemwel.com).

SOME ROAD RULES   Driving on the right is standard, except in Great Britain and Ireland. Roads are marked in kilometers (km), one of which equals 0.62 miles. Except for the German autobahn, most highways do indeed have speed limits of around 60 to 80 mph (100 to 135 kph). Self-service gas stations are readily available, and prices tend to be lower off the freeway. European drivers tend to be more aggressive than their American counterparts, and gas is generally expensive. Never leave anything of value in the car overnight and nothing visible any time you leave the car (this goes doubly in Italy, triply in Seville).

PERMITS & HIGHWAY STICKERS   Though a valid U.S. state driver's license usually suffices, it's wise to carry an **International Driving Permit,** which costs $10 from any AAA branch.

Some countries, like Austria and Switzerland, require that cars riding the national highways have special stickers. If you rent within the country, the car already has one, but if you're crossing a border, check at the crossing station to see whether you need to purchase a sticker on the spot for a nominal fee.

BY BUS

Bus transportation is readily available throughout Europe; it sometimes is less expensive than train travel and covers a more extensive area but can be slower and much less comfortable. European buses, like the trains, outshine their American counterparts, but they're perhaps best used only to pick up where the extensive train network leaves off.

BY PLANE

Though the train remains the cheapest and often easiest way to get around Europe, air transport options have improved drastically in the last few years. Intense competition with rail and ferry companies has slowly forced airfares into the bargain basement. British Airways and other scheduled airlines now fly regularly to Paris for only £75 to £60 ($96 to $136) round-trip, depending on the season. Lower fares usually apply to midweek flights.

The biggest news in Europe is the rise of the **no-frills airline,** modeled on American upstarts like Southwest. They keep their overheads down by using electronic ticketing, forgoing meal service, and flying from less popular airports and thus are able to offer low, low fares. Look out for: in England, **Debonair** (☎ 44-541/500-300) and **EasyJet** (☎ 44-1582/700-004; www.easyjet.com); in Ireland, **Ryanair** (☎ 353/1609-7800); in Spain, **Air Europa** (☎ 071/178-191); in Italy, **Air One** (☎ 39-1478/48-880 or 39-6/488-800; www.air-one.com); in Belgium, **Virgin Express** (☎ 32-2/752-0505; www.virgin-express.com), an offshoot of Virgin Air. Be aware, though, that these small airlines are often economically vulnerable and can fail. Still, as quickly as one disappears, another will take off.

Lower airfares are also available throughout Europe on **charter flights** rather than on regularly scheduled ones. Look in local newspapers to find out about them. **Consolidators** cluster in cities like London and Athens.

2

Before Leaving Home

by Reid Bramblett

The secret to enjoying a great hassle-free trip to Europe is advance planning. This chapter provides all the information on what you'll need to do before leaving and all the tips you'll need to make the wisest choices.

1 Sources of Visitor Information

TOURIST OFFICES

Start with the **European tourist offices** in the United States, Canada, the United Kingdom, or sometimes Australia. If you live in New York or London, you're especially fortunate because often you can visit national tourist offices in person; otherwise, you'll have to write, phone, or e-mail for information. For a complete list of tourist offices and their Web sites and e-mail addresses, see the Appendix.

If you aren't sure about which countries you want to visit, send for the free *Planning Your Trip to Europe,* an information-packed booklet revised annually by the 27-nation **European Travel Commission,** European Planner, P.O. Box 1754, New York, NY 10185 (☎ **800/816-7530;** www.visiteurope.com).

THE INTERNET

The Internet can provide lots of travel information. **Yahoo** (www.yahoo.com), **Excite** (www.excite.com), **Lycos** (www.lycos.com), **Infoseek** (www.infoseek.com), and the other major indexing sites have subcategories for travel, country/regional information, and culture—click on all three for links to travel-related sites. One of the best hotlists is Excite's **City.Net** (www.city.net).

Other good clearinghouse sites are Microsoft's **Expedia** (expedia.msn.com), **Travelocity** (www.travelocity.com), **Internet Travel Nework** (www.itn.com), **TravelWeb** (www.travelweb.com), **TheTrip.Com** (www.thetrip.com), and **Discount Tickets** (www.discount-tickets.com).

Of the many on-line travel magazines (the above sites will point you to them), two of the best are **Condé Nast's Epicurious** (www.epicurious.com), based on articles from the company's glossy magazines *Traveller* and *Bon Appétit;* and **Arthur Frommer's Outspoken Encyclopedia of Travel** (www.frommers.com), written and updated by the guru of budget travel himself. Through this site you can order the new *Arthur Frommer's Budget Travel* magazine, costing $14.95 per year for four full-color issues packed with deals and discounts.

The Best of Budget Travel from the King of Budget Travel

Forget the usual travel magazines: They generally focus on high-end vacations, and even when they boast about "deals" the savings they claim are really negligible. However, now there's ***Arthur Frommer's Budget Travel,*** a quarterly available for $14.95 per year. This full-color magazine is filled with all the details concerning "vacations for real people." In the premiere issue were articles like "The Cheapest Places on Earth" and "This Spring's 40 Best Bargain Vacations." You can find individual issues on the shelves (beware, though—it sells out fast), or you can order a subscription by calling ☎ **800/829-9121** or by checking out Arthur Frommer's Web site (see above).

That covers some of the top general Web sites. As often as possible throughout this chapter I've included specific Web sites along with phone numbers and addresses, and the Appendix includes the Web sites of individual counties' tourist offices.

TRAVEL AGENTS

Travel agents can save you plenty of time and money by hunting down the best airfare for your route and arranging for railpasses and rental cars. For the time being, most travel agents still charge you nothing for their services—they're paid through commissions from the airlines and other agencies they book for you. However, a number of airlines have begun cutting commissions down, and increasingly agents are finding they have to charge a fee in order to hold the bottom line—or the unscrupulous ones will give you only options that bag them the juiciest commissions. Shop around and ask hard questions.

If you decide to use one, make sure the agent is a member of good standing with the **American Society of Travel Agents (ASTA),** 1101 King St., Alexandria, VA 22314 (☎ **703/739-8739;** www.astanet.com). If you send a self-addressed stamped envelope, ASTA will mail you the free *Avoiding Travel Problems* booklet.

NEWSLETTERS

Many **travel newsletters** are ripoffs, but there are a few good ones. One favorite, of course, is the monthly ***Frommer's Travel Update,*** 240 Frisch Court, Paramus, NJ 07652 (☎ **914/265-5211;** fax 914/265-5212; E-mail: frommer_travel@prenhall. com), packed with money-saving tips and the latest travel offerings. An annual subscription is just $19.95. Also good are the monthly ***Travel Smart,*** 40 Beechdale Rd., Dobbs Ferry, NY 10522 (☎ **800/327-3633** or 914/693-8300), with an introductory subscription of $37; and the monthly ***Consumer Reports Travel Letter,*** Circulation Department, P.O. Box 53629, Boulder, CO 80322 (☎ **800/234-1970;** www. ConsumerReports.org), costing $39 annually.

TRAVEL BOOKSTORES

If you live outside a large urban area, you can order maps or travel guides from bookstores specializing in mail- or phone-order service. Some of these are **The Traveller's Bookstore,** 22 W. 52nd St., New York, NY 10019 (☎ **800/755-8728** or 212/664-0995; www.travellersbookstore.com); **Book Passage,** 51 Tamal Vista Blvd., Corte Madera, CA 94925 (☎ **800/321-9785** or 415/927-0960; www.bookpassage.com); and **Forsyth Travel Library,** 1780 E. 131st St., P.O. Box 480800, Kansas City, MO 64148-0800 (☎ **800/FORSYTH;** www.forsyth.com).

Canadians can contact **Ulysses Bookshop,** 4176 rue St-Denis, Montréal, PQ H2M5 (☎ **514/843-9447**), or 101 Yorkville Ave., Toronto, ON M5R 1C1 (☎ **416/**

323-3609). In London, try **The Travellers Bookshop,** 25 Cecil Court (☎ 0171/836-9132).

2 Passports

Citizens of non-EU countries need a **passport** to enter any European country. Keep your passport in a safe place like a money belt while you travel, and if you loose it, visit the nearest consulate of your home country as soon as possible to have it replaced. Passport applications are downloadable from the Internet sites listed below.

Note: Countries covered in this guide don't require **visas** for U.S. or Canadian citizens for stays shorter than 90 days.

U.S. CITIZENS   If you're applying for a first-time passport, you need to do it in person at one of 13 passport offices throughout the States or at a federal or state court, probate court, or a major post office (not all accept applications; call the number below to find the ones that do). You need to bring a certified birth certificate as proof of citizenship, and bringing along your driver's license, state or military ID, and social security card is wise. You also need two *identical* passport-size photos (2 in. by 2 in.), taken at any corner photo shop (*not* the strip photos from one of those photo-vending machines).

For people over 15, a passport is valid 10 years and costs $60 ($45 plus a $15 handling fee); for those 15 and under, it's valid 5 years and costs $40. If you're over 15 and have a valid passport issued within the past 12 years, you can renew it by mail and bypass the $15 handling fee. Allow plenty of time before your trip to apply; processing takes an average of 3 weeks but can run longer in busy periods (especially spring). For more information and to find your regional passport office, call the **National Passport Information Center** at ☎ 900/225-5674 or get on the Web at **www.travel. state.gov.**

CANADIANS   You can pick up a passport application at one of 28 regional passport offices or most travel agencies. The passport is valid 5 years and costs $60. Children under 16 may be included on a parent's passport but need their own passport to travel unaccompanied by the parent. Applications, which must be accompanied by two identical passport-size photographs and proof of Canadian citizenship, are available at travel agencies throughout Canada or from the central **Passport Office,** Department of Foreign Affairs and International Trade, Ottawa, Ont. K1A 0G3 (☎ 800/567-6868; www.dfait-maeci.gc.ca/passport). Processing takes 5 to 10 days if you apply in person or about 3 weeks by mail.

U.K. CITIZENS   As a member of the European Union, you need only an **identity card,** not a passport, to travel to other EU countries. However, if you already possess a passport, it's always useful to carry it. To pick up an application for a regular 10-year passport (the Visitor's Passport has been abolished), visit your nearest passport office, major post office, or travel agency or contact the **London Passport Office** at ☎ 0171/271-3000 or on the Web at **www.open.gov.uk/ukpass/ukpass.htm.**

IRISH CITIZENS   You can apply for a 10-year passport, costing IR£45, at the **Passport Office,** Setanta Centre, Molesworth Street, Dublin 2 (☎ 01/671-1633; www.irlgov.ie/iveagh/foreignaffairs/services). Those under age 18 and over 65 must apply for a IR£10 3-year passport. There's another office at 1A South Mall, Cork (☎ 021/272-525). You can also apply over the counter at most main post offices.

AUSTRALIAN CITIZENS   Apply at your local post office or passport office or contact toll-free ☎ 131-232 or the Web at **www.dfat.gov.au/passports/pp_home.html.** Passports for adults are A$126 and for those under 18 A$63.

NEW ZEALAND CITIZENS   You can pick up a passport application at any travel agency or Link Centre. For more information, contact the **Passport Office,** P.O. Box 805, Wellington (☎ **0800/225-050;** inform.dia.govt.nz/internal_affairs/businesses/doni_pro/pports_home.html). Passports for adults are NZ$80 and for those under 16 NZ$40.

3 Money

Traveler's checks, while still the safest way to carry money, are going the way of the dinosaur. The aggressive evolution of international computerized banking and consolidated ATM networks has led to the triumph of plastic throughout Europe—even if cold cash is still the most trusted currency. Odds are you can saunter up to an ATM in the dinkiest Tuscan village with your bank card or PIN-enabled Visa and get lire out of it just like at home.

Never rely on credit cards and ATMs alone, however. Though you should be safe in most hotels and many restaurants, smaller towns and cheaper places are still wary, and occasionally the phone lines and computer networks used to verify your plastic can go down and render your cards useless. Always carry some local currency and some traveler's checks for insurance.

ATMs

At the ATMs of many European banks, you can withdraw money, in local currency, directly from your home checking account via the Plus or Cirrus network. This is the fastest, easiest, and least expensive way to change money. You take advantage of the bank's bulk exchange rate (better than anything you'll get on the street) and, unless your home bank charges for using a nonproprietary ATM, it's commission-free. Make sure the PINs on your bank cards and credit cards will work in Europe; you usually need a four-digit code (six digits often won't work).

Both the **Cirrus** (☎ **800/424-7787;** www.mastercard.com/atm) and **Plus** (☎ **800/843-7587;** www.visa.com/atms) networks have automated ATM locators listing the banks in each country that will accept your card. Or just search out any machine with your network's symbol emblazoned on it. Europe is getting to be like America—a bank on virtually every corner, and increasingly, most are globally networked.

You can also get a cash advance through Visa or MasterCard (contact the issuing bank to enable this feature and get a PIN), but note that the credit-card company will begin charging you interest immediately. American Express card cash advances are usually available only from AMEX offices, which exist in every European city (see the "Fast Facts" sections in this book for locations).

CREDIT CARDS

Most hotels, restaurants, and shops in Europe, especially middle-bracket moderate places and above, accept major credit cards—American Express, Diners Club, MasterCard, and Visa (not Discover). As for budget places, increasingly more are accepting credit cards, but some still don't. The most widely accepted are Visa and MasterCard—especially among smaller budget-oriented places—but it pays to carry American Express as well.

TRAVELER'S CHECKS

Most large banks sell traveler's checks, charging fees of 1% to 2% the value of the checks. AAA members can buy American Express checks commission-free. Traveler's checks are great insurance since if you lose them—and have kept a list of their

The World's Greatest Financial Merger: The Euro

The adoption of a single European currency, called the **euro,** is a contentious move within Europe. Even though most of Western Europe has been closely interconnected as an economic and trade unit for years, the actual official merger of its national currencies and economies is another matter. Each nation is fighting to get the best deal for itself as union draws ever closer.

As this book goes to press, they've finally settled on which countries will adopt the euro: Austria, Belgium, Finland, France, Germany, Ireland, Italy, Luxembourg, the Netherlands, Portugal, and Spain. Several countries have opted out from switching over just yet, including Britain, Denmark, and Sweden; Greece never made the economic requirements to join.

However, as a visitor, you needn't worry about dealing with the euro for a while. Though slated to take effect on paper on January 1, 1999—at which time the exchange rates of participating countries will be locked in together and will fluctuate against the dollar in synch—this change will apply mostly to financial transactions between businesses in Europe. The euro itself won't be issued as banknotes and coins until January 1, 2002, and it won't fully replace national currencies until July 1, 2002. Since you'll still be juggling marks, lire, francs, and pesetas until then, prices in this book will remain quoted in the local national currencies.

numbers (and record of which ones were cashed) in a safe place separate from the checks themselves—you can get them replaced at no charge. Hotels and shops usually accept them, but you'll get a lousy exchange rate. Use traveler's checks to exchange for local spending money from banks or American Express offices. Note that personal checks are next to useless in Europe.

American Express (☎ 800/221-7282; www.americanexpress.com) is one of the largest issuers of traveler's checks, and theirs are the most commonly accepted. They'll also sell checks to holders of certain types of American Express cards at no commission. **Thomas Cook** (☎ 800/223-7373 in the U.S./Canada, 0171/480-7226 in London, or 609/987-7300 collect from everywhere else; www.thomascook.com) issues MasterCard traveler's checks. **Citicorp** (☎ 800/645-6556 in the U.S./Canada, or 813/623-1709 collect from everywhere else; www.citicorp.com) and many other banks issue checks under their own name or under MasterCard or Visa. Checks issued in dollar amounts (as opposed to, say, French francs) are the most widely accepted abroad.

WIRE SERVICES

American Express's **MoneyGram,** Wadsworth St., Englewood, CO 80155 (☎ 800/926-9400), will allow friends back home to wire you money in an emergency in less than 10 minutes. Senders should call AMEX to learn the address of the closest outlet that handles MoneyGrams. Cash, credit card, and the occasional personal check (with ID) are acceptable forms of payment. AMEX's fee is $40 for the first $500, with a sliding scale for larger sums. The service includes a short telex message and a 3-minute phone call from sender to recipient. The beneficiary must present a photo ID at the outlet where the money is received.

CURRENCY EXCHANGE

It's more expensive to purchase foreign currency in your own country than it is once you've reached your destination. But a bit of primer cash will make arriving anywhere

Exchange Rate Updates

Though currency conversions in this guide were accurate at press time, European exchange rates fluctuate. For up-to-date rates, look in the business pages of a newspaper, check on-line at the **Universal Currency Converter** (www.xe.net/currency/table.htm), or call **Thomas Cook** (see "Traveler's Checks").

---

in Europe a lot smoother—and allow you to buy the bus or metro ticket that will get you from the bad exchange rates of the airport to the better rates of downtown banks. So bring along about $30 to $50 in the local currencies of every European city you'll be visiting (call around to the major branches of local banks in your hometown to find the best rate).

While traveling, **convert your money** at banks whenever possible, as they invariably give better rates than tourist offices, hotels, travel agencies, or exchange booths. Shop around for the best rate and be sure to factor in the commission: Sometimes it's a flat fee, sometimes a percentage. You lose money every time you make a transaction, so it's often better to convert large sums at once (especially in flat-fee transactions). The rates on traveler's checks are usually better than those for cash, but you get the best rates by withdrawing money from an ATM with your bank card or credit card.

4 Health & Insurance

HEALTH

You'll encounter few health problems in Europe. The tap water is generally safe to drink (except on trains and elsewhere it's marked as nondrinking water), the milk is pasteurized, and health services are good to superb. You will, however, be eating foods and spices your body isn't used to, so bring along Pepto-Bismol tablets in case sour stomach, indigestion, or diarrhea strikes.

Carry any prescriptions written in generic, not brand-name form, and take all prescription medications in their original labeled vials. For minor problems, visit the local pharmacy; European druggists are usually highly trained and skilled at their trade.

Many European **hospitals** are partially socialized, and you'll usually be taken care of speedily, often at no charge for simple ailments. If you have to be admitted, most **health insurance plans and HMOs** will cover, at least to some extent, out-of-country hospital visits and procedures. However, most make you pay the bills up front at the time of care, and you'll get a refund after you've returned and filed all the paperwork. Members of **Blue Cross/Blue Shield** can now use their cards at select hospitals in most major cities worldwide (☎ **800/810-BLUE** or www.bluecares.com/blue/bluecard/wwn for a list of hospitals). For independent travel health insurance providers, see below under "Insurance."

If you suffer from a **chronic illness,** talk to your doctor before taking the trip. For conditions like epilepsy, diabetes, or a heart condition, wear a **Medic Alert Identification Tag** (☎ **800/825-3785;** www.medicalert.org), which will immediately alert doctors to your condition and give them access to your records through Medic Alert's 24-hour hotline. Membership is $35, plus $15 annually.

For tips on travel and health concerns in the countries you'll be visiting, plus lists of local English-speaking doctors, contact the **International Association for Medical Assistance to Travelers (IAMAT)** (☎ **716/754-4883** or 416/652-0137; www.sentex.net/~iamat). The **United States Centers for Disease Control and Prevention** (☎ **404/332-4559;** www.cdc.gov) provides up-to-date information on necessary vaccines and health hazards by region or country (by mail, their booklet is $20; on the Internet, it's free). When you're abroad, any local consulate can provide a list of area doctors who speak English.

INSURANCE

The differences between travel assistance and insurance are often blurred, but in general the former offers on-the-spot assistance and 24-hour hotlines (mostly oriented toward medical problems), while the latter serves more to reimburse you for travel problems (medical, travel, or otherwise) after you get home and file the paperwork.

Comprehensive insurance programs, covering basically everything—from trip cancellation to lost luggage, to medical coverage abroad and accidental death—are offered by the following: **Access America,** 6600 W. Broad St., Richmond, VA 23230 (☎ **800/284-8300**); **Columbus Travel Insurance,** 279 High St., Croydon CR0 1QH (☎ **0171/375-0011** in London; www2.columbusdirect.com/columbusdirect); **International SOS Assistance,** P.O. Box 11568, Philadelphia, PA 11916 (☎ **800/ 523-8930** or 215/244-1500), strictly an assistance company; **Travelex Insurance Services,** P.O. Box 9408, Garden City, NY 11530-9408 (☎ **800/228-9792**); **Travel Guard International,** 1145 Clark St., Stevens Point, WI 54481-9970 (☎ **800/ 826-1300;** www.travel-guard.com); **Travel Insured International,** P.O. Box 280568, East Hartford, CT 06128-0568 (☎ **800/243-3174**).

Medicare only covers U.S. citizens traveling in Mexico and Canada. For Blue Cross/Blue Shield coverage abroad, see "Health" above. Companies specializing in accident and medical care are **MEDEX International,** P.O. Box 5375, Timonium, MD 21094-5375 (☎ **888/MEDEX-00** or 410/453-6300; fax 410/453-6301; www. medexassist.com); **Travel Assistance International** (Worldwide Assistance Services, Inc.), 1133 15th St. NW, Suite 400, Washington, DC 20005 (☎ **800/821-2828** or 202/828-5894; fax 202/828-5896).

5   Tips for Travelers with Special Needs

FOR FAMILIES

Europeans expect to see families traveling together. Europe is a multigenerational continent, and you'll sometimes see the whole clan—from grandmothers to babes in arms—caravaning around. And Europeans tend to love kids. You'll often find that a child guarantees you an even warmer reception at hotels and restaurants than you'd normally receive.

Ask waiters for a half portion to fit junior's appetite. With small children, three- and four-star hotels may be your best bet—baby-sitters are on call and they have a better general ability to help visitors access the city and its services, which may outweigh the cost factors. But even cheaper hotels can usually find you a sitter, and in small family-run places there'll often be a family member who'll watch your kids.

Traveling with a pint-size person usually entails pint-size rates. An extra cot in the room won't cost more than 30% extra—if anything—and most museums and sights offer reduced-price or free admission for children under a certain age (ranging from 6 to 18). Kids also almost always get discounts on plane and train tickets.

Adventuring with Children (Foghorn Press) and Lonely Planet's *Travel with Children* are both loaded with specific advice on dealing with everyday family situations—especially where infants are concerned—that become superhuman chores when they pop up on the road.

Family Travel Times is published 10 times a year by **TWYCH (Travel with Your Children),** 40 Fifth Ave., New York, NY 10011 (☎ **212/477-5524**), and includes a weekly call-in service for subscribers. Subscriptions are $40 a year for quarterly editions. A free publication list and a sample issue are available by calling or sending a request to the above address.

Families Welcome!, 92 N. Main, Ashland, OR 97520 (☎ **800/326-0724** or 541/482-6121), a travel company specializing in worry-free vacations for families, offers "City Kids" packages to certain European cities.

The University of New Hampshire runs **Familyhostel** (☎ **800/733-9753;** www.learn.unh.edu), an educational/intergenerational alternative to standard guided tours. You live on a European college campus for the 2- or 3-week program, attend lectures and seminars, go on lots of field trips, and get in all the sightseeing—all guided by a team of experts and academics. It's designed for children 8 to 15, parents, and grandparents.

FOR STUDENTS

The best resource for students is the **Council on International Educational Exchange (CIEE)** (☎ **800/2COUNCIL;** www.ciee.org). It can set you up with an ID card (see below) and its travel branch, **Council Travel Service (CTS),** is the biggest student travel agency in the world. It can get you discounts on plane tickets, railpasses, and the like. Ask for a list of CTS offices in major European cities so that you can keep the discounts flowing and aid lines open as you travel. In Canada, **Travel CUTS,** 187 College St., Toronto, ONT M5T 1P7 (☎ **888/838-CUTS** or 416/798-2887; www.travelcuts.com), offers similar services. **Campus Travel,** 52 Grosvenor Gardens, London SW1W 0AG (☎ **0171/730-3402;** www.campustravel.co.uk), opposite Victoria Station, is Britain's leading specialist in student and youth travel.

From CIEE (or its Canadian or British counterparts) you can obtain the student traveler's best European friend, the $18 **International Student Identity Card (ISIC).** It's the only officially acceptable form of student ID, good for cut rates on railpasses and plane tickets and other discounts. It also provides basic health and life insurance and a 24-hour help line. If you're no longer a student but are still under 26, you can get a **GO 25 card** from the same people; it'll get you the insurance and some of the discounts (but not student admissions in museums).

If you enjoy meeting other young travelers on the road—and to save big on hotel expenses—consider staying in **hostels.** Though only those in Bavaria still enforce an under 26 age limit, hostels are primarily student stomping grounds. For details on hostels, see "Getting the Best Deal on Accommodations" in chapter 1.

FOR SENIORS

Many senior discounts are available, but some require membership in a particular association. Members of **AARP (American Association of Retired Persons),** 601 E St. NW, Washington, DC 20049 (☎ **800/424-3410;** www.aarp.org), get discounts on some car rentals and chain hotels.

Most **major airlines** offer discount programs for seniors; be sure to ask whenever you book a flight. Of the big **car-rental agencies,** only National currently gives an AARP discount (10%), but the many rental dealers who specialize in Europe—Auto-Europe, Kemwel, Europe-by-Car—offer seniors 5% off. In most **European cities,** people over 60 or 65 get reduced admission at theaters, museums, and other attractions, and they can often get discount fares or cards on public transport and national rail systems. Carrying ID with proof of age can pay off in all these situations.

Grand Circle Travel (☎ **800/221-2610;** www.gct.com), besides publishing the free booklet "101 Tips for the Mature Traveler," is one of the literally hundreds of

travel agencies specializing in vacations for seniors. But beware: Many packages are of the tour-bus variety. Seniors seeking more independent travel should probably consult a regular travel agent. **SAGA International Holidays,** 222 Berkeley St., Boston, MA 02116 (☎ **800/343-0273;** www.sagaholidays.com), has 40 years of experience running all-inclusive tours and cruises for those 50 and older. It also sponsors the more substantial **Road Scholar Tours** (☎ **800/621-2151**), which are fun-loving but with an educational bent.

If you want something more than the average vacation or guided tour, try **Interhostel** (☎ **800/733-9753;** www.learn.unh.edu) and **Elderhostel** (☎ **617/426-8056;** www.elderhostel.org), both variations on educational travel. The tours, around $2,000 to $3,500, are hosted by foreign universities, and the days are packed with seminars, lectures, field trips, and sightseeing, all led by academic experts. For Elderhostel you must be over 55 (a spouse or companion of any age can accompany you), and it offers programs from 1 to 4 weeks. Interhostel participants must be over 50 (any companion must be over 40), and it offers 2- and 3-week programs.

Though all the specialty books currently on the market are U.S. focused, three do provide good general advice and contacts for the savvy senior traveler. Thumb through *The 50+ Traveler's Guidebook* (St. Martin's Press), *The Seasoned Traveler* (Country Roads Press), or *Unbelievably Good Deals and Great Adventures That You Absolutely Can't Get Unless You're Over 50* (Contemporary Books). Also check out the magazine shelf for the quarterly *Travel 50 & Beyond.*

If you'd like an extended stay abroad in the off-season at huge discounts, consult **Sun Holidays,** 7280 W. Palmetto Park Rd., Suite 301, Boca Raton, FL 33433 (☎ **800/422-8000** or 561/367-0105; www.sun-holidays.com).

FOR GAY & LESBIAN TRAVELERS

Much of Europe has grown to accept same-sex couples over the past few decades, and in most countries homosexual sex acts are legal. To be on the safe side, do a bit of research and test the waters for acceptability in any one city or area. As you might expect, smaller towns tend to be less accepting than cities. Gay centers include parts of London, Paris, Amsterdam, Berlin, Milan, and Greece.

The **International Gay & Lesbian Travel Association (IGLTA),** P.O. Box 4974, Key West, FL 33041 (☎ **800/448-8550** or 305/292-0217; www.iglta.com), is your best all-around resource. Members get a newsletter, advice on specialist travel agencies, and a membership directory. General gay and lesbian travel agencies include **Our Family Abroad** (☎ **212/459-1800**), **Islanders/Kennedy Travels** (☎ **212/242-3220**), and **Yellowbrick Road** (☎ **800/642-2488**).

There are also two good biannual English-language gay guidebooks, both focused on gay men but including information for lesbians as well. You can get the *Spartacus International Gay Guide* or *Odysseus* from most gay and lesbian bookstores or order them from **Giovanni's Room** (☎ **215/923-2960**) or **A Different Light Bookstore** (☎ **800/343-4002** or 212/989-4850; www.adlbooks.com). The *Ferrari Guides* (www.q-net.com) is another very good series of gay and lesbian guidebooks.

However, as of early 1999 Frommer's will publish its first guidebook specifically for gays and lesbians. *Frommer's Gay & Lesbian Europe* covers every aspect—from hotels and restaurants to sights, shopping, and nightlife—of the hottest cities and resorts in France, England, Italy, and more.

Out and About, 8 W. 19th St., Suite 401, New York, NY 10011 (☎ **800/929-2268** or 212/645-6922), is a monthly newsletter packed with good information on the global gay and lesbian scene. A year's subscription is $49. *Our World,* 1104 N. Nova

Rd., Suite 251, Daytona Beach, FL 32117 (☎ **904/441-5367**), is a slicker monthly magazine promoting and highlighting travel bargains and opportunities. Annual subscription rates are $35 in the United States and $45 outside the States.

FOR PEOPLE WITH DISABILITIES

While Europe won't win any medals for handicap accessibility (especially in cities like Amsterdam and Venice), in the past few years its big cities have made an effort to accommodate the disabled, and a handicap shouldn't stop anybody from traveling. There are numerous organizations to help you out with planning and specific advice before you go.

The **Moss Rehab Hospital** (☎ **215/456-9600**) has been providing phone advice and referrals to disabled travelers for years. The **American Foundation for the Blind,** 11 Penn Plaza, Suite 300, New York, NY 10001 (☎ **800/232-5463** or 212/502-7600), can fill you in on travel in general and how to get your seeing-eye dog into Europe. Travelers with a hearing impairment should contact the **American Academy of Otolaryngology,** 1 Prince St., Alexandria, VA 22314 (☎ **703/836-4444** or 703/ 519-1585 TTY).

You can join the **Society for the Advancement of Travel for the Handicapped (SATH),** 347 Fifth Ave., Suite 610, New York, NY 10016 (☎ **212/447-7284;** fax 212/725-8253), for $45 annually to gain access to their information sheets on travel destinations, network of travel industry connections, and referrals to specialized tour operators. Their quarterly magazine *Open World for Accessible Travel* is full of good information and resources. A year's subscription is $13 ($21 outside the United States).

Mobility International, P.O. Box 10767, Eugene, OR 97440 (☎ **541/343-1284** V/TDD; fax 541/343-6812; www.miusa.org), is a worldwide organization promoting international disability rights, hosting international exchanges, and providing reference sheets on travel destinations for people with disabilities. Their *A World of Options* book has resources on everything from biking trips to scuba outfitters for disabled travelers. Annual membership is $25 or $15 just to receive their quarterly *Over the Rainbow* newsletter. For more personal assistance, call the **Travel Information Service** at ☎ **215/456-9603** or 215/456-9602 TTY.

You might consider joining a **guided tour** that caters to the disabled. One of the best operators is **Flying Wheels Travel** (☎ **800/535-6790**). It offers various escorted tours and cruises, as well as private tours in minivans with lifts. Other reputable specialized tour operators are **Access Adventures** (☎ **716/889-9096**), **Accessible Journeys** (☎ **800/846-4537**), **Directions Unlimited** (☎ **800/533-5343**), and **Wheelchair Journeys** (☎ **206/885-2210**). In addition, the **Information Center for Individuals with Disabilities** (☎ **800/462-5015**) provides lists of travel agents who specialize in tours for the handicapped.

FOR U.K. CITIZENS   The **Royal Association for Disability and Rehabilitation (RADAR),** Unit 12, City Forum, 250 City Rd., London EC1V 8AF (☎ **0171/ 250-3222**), publishes three holiday "fact packs." The first provides general information, including planning and booking a holiday, insurance, finances, and useful organization and holiday providers. The second outlines transportation and rental equipment options. The third deals with specialized accommodations.

Also good is the **Holiday Care Service,** Imperial Building, 2nd Floor, Victoria Rd., Horley, Surrey RH6 7PZ (☎ **01293/774-535;** fax 01293/784-647), a national charity that advises on accessible accommodations for the elderly and persons with disabilities. Annual membership is £30 ($50).

6   Some Practical Concerns

CAMERAS & FILM

Figure on shooting about a roll a day, then throw in two to three more rolls per week for good measure. Film can be twice as expensive in foreign countries as it is at home, so bring all your film with you. Also bring several spare batteries. Processing is even more expensive abroad, and the quality is generally better at home anyway. If you do have to buy film or other equipment in Europe, search out a camera shop or department store.

Throw out the film's cardboard boxes and stick the plastic containers into see-through plastic sandwich bags so that you can have the security people at the airport glance at them and pass them around the potentially harmful X-rays (the higher the film speed, the more likely multiple exposures to X-rays will fog the film). If you have film in your camera, pass it around the X-ray machine as well.

If you're traveling with a new camera, test out a few rolls at home to see how the camera behaves in different lighting situations and so on (shooting and developing a few test rolls may cost a couple of bucks, but it's much less expensive than returning home with a dozen rolls of underexposed pictures).

MAIL & MESSAGES

Post offices work pretty much the same the world over. When you write to an address in the States, end it with a big "USA" under the city/state/ZIP code line. Write "Par Avion" on any letter or postcard to ensure it goes airmail (that French term is used internationally).

For writing letters, you can buy tissue paper–like stationery to cut down on weight (and hence cost) or get the nifty blue airmail letter/envelopes, which you write on, fold up, lick, and seal—the letter itself becomes the envelope (widely available at stationery stores). Mail can take anywhere from a few days to a few months (the latter not uncommon for mail from Italy) but usually finds its way across the ocean in 2 to 6 weeks.

Save letters to mail from countries with low **postage rates**—Germany charges $2.15 for letters to America, but England charges only 67¢. Other expensive lands are the Netherlands and Austria. Cheapies include Greece, Ireland, and Spain. Italy's postal system is notoriously slow but the Vatican's isn't, so when in Rome, mail everything from St. Peter's (same prices, different stamps).

To **receive mail in Europe,** there are two options. The best is open only to American Express cardholders. Just have your mail addressed to: Your Name/Client's Mail/Full Postal Address of the AMEX office in whatever city you'll be staying. The local AMEX office will hold it for 30 days after they receive it, and the service is free (again, it may take 5 days or 6 weeks for the letter to cross the ocean).

Post offices offer the same service; just address the letter to: Your Name/Poste Restante/Address of the Post Office. Bring ID to the post office to claim your mail. The charge for picking up such held mail ranges from a few dimes to a few bucks.

Try not to receive mail on the road unless absolutely necessary. With the unpredictable postal systems, you'll miss more letters than you'll receive, plus via cybercafes (see "Getting the Best Deal on Phone Calls & E-Mail" in chapter 1) you can communicate much more easily and quickly with home.

ELECTRICITY

American current runs 110V, 60 cycles, and Europe's 210–220V, 50 cycles. You can't plug an American appliance into a European outlet without frying your appliance and/or blowing a fuse. Hair dryers are the worst culprits; many hotels now have built-in dryers in the baths, or you can just spend a few weeks towel- and air-drying.

You need a **currency converter or transformer** to bring the voltage down and the cycles up. In addition, American plugs won't fit into European outlets (most Continental plugs have two round metal flanges; in Britain they often have three flat prongs). You can get small **plug adapters,** *but these aren't currency converters.* You still need to go through a transformer to get the electrical current running properly.

For shaving, stick with a razor unless you have a battery-operated **electric shaver.** However, most hotels have a special plug for low-wattage shavers *and shavers only.* Such outlets are usually identified by an icon of a half-shaven face. Plug nothing else in there or you may blow a fuse.

There are travel-size versions of popular items like **hair dryers,** irons, and shavers that are "dual voltage," which means they have built-in converters (usually you have to turn a switch to go back and forth). Most contemporary **laptop computers** automatically sense the current and adapt accordingly (check the manuals, bottom of the machine, or manufacturer first to make sure).

Plug adapters and converters are available at most travel, luggage, electronics, and hardware stores. Or call the **Franzus Corporation** at ☎ **203/723-6664** for a copy of its pamphlet "Foreign Electricity Is No Deep Dark Secret" (complete with an order form for adapters and converters).

Airlines request that you don't have your computer, personal tape deck, CD player, or other electronic device turned on during takeoff and landing on the chance that the waves emitted by these items might interfere with the computerized guidance systems.

EUROPEAN TIME ZONES, DATES & HOURS

Based on U.S. eastern standard time, Britain, Ireland, and Portugal are 5 hours ahead of New York City; Greece is 7 hours ahead of New York. The rest of the countries in this book are 6 hours ahead of EST. For instance, when it's noon in New York, it's 5pm in London and Lisbon, 6pm in Paris and Rome, and 7pm in Athens.

Europeans usually use the 24-hour clock, also known as "military time." That means they write 1pm as 13:00 and midnight as 24:00. If the number is over 12, just subtract 12 and add a "pm"—so 20:00 would be 8pm. Spoken, they might use either the 24-hour-clock number or a 12-hour-clock number (at 3pm, they may say "15 o'clock" or "3 in the afternoon"). Additionally, Europeans numerically abbreviate dates as day/month/year, not month/day/year as Americans do.

3

Getting to Europe Without Going Broke

by Reid Bramblett

This chapter explores the various options for getting to Europe. A round-trip plane ticket from the United States can run into the thousands of dollars or can be as cheap as $179. Now that last price is the sort of deal you'll run across only occasionally, but there's no need to pay more than $500 even on a regularly scheduled flight. You just have to know how to find such fares, and that's what I'm going to show you. I'll go into not only the obvious choices but also some you may not have thought of, like rebators, flying courier, and the Internet's E-Savers programs.

1 Getting There by Plane

Most major airlines charge competitive fares to European cities, but price wars break out regularly and fares can change overnight. Tickets tend to be cheaper if you fly midweek or off-season. High season on most routes is June to early September—the most expensive and most crowded time to travel. Shoulder season is April to May, mid-September to October, and December 15 to 24. Low season—with the cheapest fares—is November to December 14 and December 25 to March.

You can get the best fares simply by planning ahead and buying low-cost **advance-purchase (APEX) tickets.** Usually, you must buy APEX tickets 7 to 21 days in advance and must stay in Europe 7 to 30 days. The downside is that APEX locks you into those dates and times, with penalties for trying to change them.

A more flexible but more expensive option is the **regular economy fare,** which allows for a stay shorter than the 7-day APEX minimum. You're also usually free to make last-minute changes in flight dates and to have unrestricted stopovers.

THE BEST DEALS THE AIRLINES HAVE TO OFFER

CONSOLIDATORS Consolidators, also known as bucket shops, act as clearinghouses for blocks of tickets, on regularly scheduled flights, that airlines discount during slow periods.

One of the biggest U.S. consolidators is **Travac,** 989 Sixth Ave., New York, NY 10018 (☎ **800/TRAV-800** or 212/563-3303; www.travac.com). Also try **TFI Tours International,** 34 W. 32nd St., 12th Floor, New York, NY 10001 (☎ **800/745-8000**); **Euram Tours,**

1522 K St. NW, 4th Floor, Washington, DC 20005 (☎ **800/848-6789** or 202/789-2255; www.flyeuram.com); and **Travel Avenue,** 10 S. Riverside Plaza, Suite 1404, Chicago, IL 60606 (☎ **800/333-3335** or 312/876-6866; www.travelavenue.com).

In addition, **Cheap Tickets** (☎ **800/377-1000**), **1-800/FLY-4-LESS,** and **1-800/FLY-CHEAP** all specialize in finding the lowest fares out there. You can often get discounted fares on short notice without all the advance-purchase requirements.

In the United Kingdom, **Trailfinders** (☎ **0171/937-5400** in London) is a consolidator that offers access to tickets on major European carriers. There are many bucket shops around Victoria and Earls Court in London. **CEEFAX,** an information service included on many home and hotel TVs, runs details of package holidays and flights to continental Europe and beyond.

CHARTER FLIGHTS   In a strict sense, charters book a block of seats (or an entire plane) months in advance and then resell the tickets to consumers. Always ask about restrictions: You may have to purchase a tour package and pay far in advance and pay a stiff penalty (or forfeit the ticket entirely) if you cancel. Charters are sometimes canceled when the plane doesn't fill. In some cases, the charter company will offer you an insurance policy in case you need to cancel for a legitimate reason (hospitalization, death in the family).

Council Travel, 205 E. 42nd St., New York, NY 10017 (☎ **800/226-8624** or 212/822-2800; www.ciee.org), arranges charter seats on regularly scheduled aircraft. One of the biggest charter operators is **Travac** (see "Consolidators"). For Canadians, good charter deals are offered by **Martinair** (☎ **800/627-8462;** www.martinair.com) and **Travel CUTS** (☎ **888/838-CUTS;** www.travelcuts.com), which also has an office in London (☎ **0171/255-1944**).

REBATORS   To confuse the situation even more, rebators compete in the low-airfare market. These outfits pass along to you part of their commission, though many also assess a fee. Most discounts run 10% to 25%, minus a $25 handling fee. Rebators aren't travel agents, but they sometimes offer services like land arrangements and car rentals.

Specializing in clients in the Midwest, **Travel Avenue** (see "Consolidators") offers cash rebates on every ticket over $375. Another major rebator is **The Smart Traveller,** 3111 SW 27th Ave. (P.O. Box 330010), Miami, FL 33133 (☎ **800/448-3338** or 305/448-3338), offering discounts on packaged tours.

FLYING STANDBY   If your plans are flexible, try **Airhitch,** 2641 Broadway, 3rd Floor, New York, NY 10025 (☎ **212/864-2000;** www.airhitch.org). You give them a window of 5 days during which you can leave from one of five U.S. regions to fly to a European region, and they'll call you a few days in advance to let you know what date and city you're flying out of and where you're landing. They try and fly you to and from cities of your choice within the regions, but there are no guarantees. Typical one-way fares to Europe are $169 from the Northeast, $229 from the Midwest, $249 from the West Coast, and $209 from the Southeast.

With the exception of E-Savers (see "Using the Internet"), waiting until the last minute to buy those "unfilled seats" is *not* the best way to get a great fare. Though such deals do exist, you run the chance of not finding anything, and the savings are often not much better than a regular APEX fare. If you want to give it a try, call the **Last Minute Travel Club** (☎ **800/527-8646** or 617/267-9800).

GOING AS A COURIER   Travelers who are flexible and willing to travel with only carry-on luggage can save a lot of money. The courier company handles the check-in and pickup of packages at each airport, and all you have to do is give up your checked-baggage allowance. Expect to meet someone at the airport before departure to get the manifest of the checked items; on arrival, you deliver the baggage-claim tag to a waiting courier agent. It sounds like a spy thriller, but it's really mundane, serving companies that need to transport time-sensitive materials like film or documents for banks and insurance firms.

The drawbacks: the restricted baggage allowance (sometimes you get the luggage space on the return trip); you have to travel alone, since only one person can take advantage of any given flight (they'll try to get partners flights on consecutive days); and your stay is often a fixed one of about 1 week.

Two major companies offer frequent courier service to Europe: **Now Voyager,** 74 Varick St., Suite 307, New York, NY 10013 (☎ **212/431-1616;** www.nowyoyager-travel.com), which flies about 18 couriers to Europe per day; and **Halbart Express,** 147-05 176th St., Jamaica, NY 11434 (☎ **718/656-8189;** fax 718/244-0559; open Mon–Fri 9am–3pm).

Most flights depart from New York City, so you may have to tack on the extra cost to get to the gateway city. Prices change all the time, from immediate, emergency runs where you could travel for as little as $99 round-trip, to the more common range of $299 to $359. They'll book flights up to 2 to 3 months in advance, but call the 24-hour number for last-minute departure specials.

For current information about courier travel, subscribe to the monthly newsletter *Travel Unlimited,* P.O. Box 1058, Allston, MA 02134. The cost is $25 per year ($35 outside the U.S.) or $5 per single issue. Or sign up for the newsletter of the **Air Courier Association** (☎ **800/822-0888;** www.aircourier.org), costing $45 per year.

USING THE INTERNET   The number of virtual travel agents on the Web has exploded in recent years. A few of the better-respected ones are **Travelocity** (www.travelocity.com), which also advertises last-minute deals; **Microsoft Expedia** (www.expedia.com), which will e-mail you weekly with the best fares for a chosen destination; and **Yahoo's Flifo Global** (travel.yahoo.com/travel), whose "Fare Beater" compares airlines to find the best going rate. For most, just enter your dates and cities and the computer looks for the lowest fares. **Preview Travel**'s (www.reservations.com) Best Fare Finder will search the Apollo computer reservations system for the three lowest fares for any route on any days of the year.

Great last-minute deals are often available directly from many airlines through a free service called **E-Savers.** Each week, the airline sends you an e-mail list of discounted flights, usually leaving the upcoming Thursday to Saturday and returning the following Monday to Wednesday. You can sign up at any airline's Web site (see below).

THE MAJOR AIRLINES
NORTH AMERICAN AIRLINES   North American carriers with frequent service and flights to Europe are **Air Canada** (☎ 800/776-3000 in the U.S., 800/555-1212 in Canada; www.aircanada.ca), **American Airlines** (☎ 800/433-7300; www.americanair.com), **Canadian Airlines** (☎ 800/426-7000 in the U.S., 800/665-1177 in Canada; www.cdnair.ca), **Continental Airlines** (☎ 800/231-0856; www.flycontinental.com), **Delta Airlines** (☎ 800/241-4141; www.delta-air.com), **Northwest Airlines** (☎ 800/447-4747; www.nwa.com), **Tower Air** (☎ 800/221-2500; www.towerair.com), **TWA** (☎ 800/892-4141; www.twa.com), and **U.S. Airways** (☎ 800/622-1015; www.usairways.com).

For the latest on airline Web sites, check **airlines-online.com** or **www.itn.com.**

EUROPEAN NATIONAL AIRLINES Not only will the national carriers of European countries offer the greatest number of direct flights from the United States (and can easily book you through to cities beyond the major hubs), but since their entire U.S. market is to fly you to their home country, they often run more competitive deals than most North American carriers. In fact, the competition between British Airways and Virgin Atlantic leads them to offer incredible deals to London, already the cheapest European gateway.

Major national and country-affiliated European airlines include the following:

- **Austria:** Austrian Airlines. *In the U.S. and Canada:* 800/843-0002. *In the U.K.:* 0171/434-7300. *In Australia:* 02/9241-4277. *Web site:* www.aua.com.
- **Belgium:** Sabena. *In the U.S. and Canada:* 800/955-2000. *In the U.K.:* 0171/494-2629. *Web site:* www.sabena-usa.com.
- **Czech Republic:** CSA Czech Airlines. *In the U.S. and Canada:* 800/223-2365. *In the U.K.:* 0171/255-1898. *In Australia:* 02/9247-6196. *Web site:* www.csa.cz.
- **France:** Air France. *In the U.S.:* 800/237-2747. *In Canada:* 514/847-1106. *In the U.K.:* 0181/742-6600. *In Australia:* 02/9321-1000. *In New Zealand:* 068/725-8800. *Web site:* www.airfrance.com.
- **Germany:** Lufthansa. *In the U.S.:* 800/645-3880. *In Canada:* 800/563-5954. *In the U.K.:* 0345/737-747. *In Australia:* 02/9367-3888. *In New Zealand:* 09/303-1529. *Web site:* www.lufthansa.com.
- **Greece:** Olympic Airways. *In the U.S.:* 800/223-1226, or 212/735-0200 in New York State. *In Canada:* 514/878-3891 (Montréal) or 416/920-2452 (Toronto). *In the U.K.:* 0171/409-2400. *In Australia:* 02/9251-2044. *Web site:* agn.hol.gr/info/olympic1.htm
- **Hungary:** Malev Hungarian Airlines. *In the U.S.:* 800/262-5380. *In Canada:* 416/9440-093. *In the U.K.:* 0171/439-0577. *In Australia:* 02/9321-9111. *In New Zealand:* 09/379-4455. *Web site:* www.malev-airlines.com.
- **Ireland:** Aer Lingus. *In the U.S.:* 800/IRISH-AIR. *In the U.K.:* 0181/899-4747 in London, 0645/737-747 in all other areas. *In Australia:* 02/9321-9123. *In New Zealand:* 09/379-4455. *Web site:* www.aerlingus.ie.
- **Italy:** Alitalia. *In the U.S.:* 800/223-5730. *In Canada:* 514/842-8241 (Montréal) or 416/363-1348 (Toronto). *In the U.K.:* 0181/745-8200. *In Australia:* 02/9247-1307. *In New Zealand:* 09/379-4457. *Web site:* www.alitalia.com.
- **The Netherlands:** KLM Royal Dutch Airlines. *In the U.S.:* 800/374-7747. *In Canada:* 514/939-4040 (Montréal) or 416/204-5100 (Toronto). *In the U.K.:* 0990/750-9900. *In Australia:* 02/9231-6333. *In New Zealand:* 09/309-1782. *Web site:* www.klm.nl.
- **Portugal:** TAP Air Portugal. *In the U.S.:* 800/221-7370. *In the U.K.:* 0171/828-0262. *Web site:* www.tap-airportugal.pt.
- **Scandinavia (Denmark, Norway, Sweden):** SAS Scandinavian Airlines. *In the U.S.:* 800/221-2350. *In the U.K.:* 0171/734-6777. *In Australia:* 02/9299-6688. *Web site:* www.flysas.com.
- **Spain:** Iberia. *In the U.S.:* 800/772-4642. *In Canada:* 800/363-4534. *In the U.K.:* 0171/830-0011. *In Australia:* 02/9283-3660. *In New Zealand:* 09/379-3076. *Web site:* www.iberia.com.
- **Switzerland:** Swissair. *In the U.S. and Canada:* 800/221-4750. *In the U.K.:* 0171/434-7300. *In Australia:* 02/9232-1744. *Web site:* www.swissair.com.
- **United Kingdom:** (1) British Airways. *In the U.S. and Canada:* 800/247-9297. *In the U.K.:* 0181/897-4000 or 034/522-2111. *In Australia:* 02/9258-3300. *Web site:* www.british-airways.com. (2) Virgin Atlantic Airways. *In the U.S. and Canada:*

800/862-8621. *In the U.K.:* 01293/747-747. *In Australia:* 02/9352-6199. *Web site:* www.fly.virgin.com.

2 Getting to the Continent from the U.K.

BY TRAIN

Many railpasses and discounts are available in the United Kingdom for travel in continental Europe. Stop in at the **International Rail Centre,** Victoria Station, London SW1V 1JY (☎ **0990/848-848**), or **Wasteels,** opposite Platform 2 in Victoria Station (☎ **0171/834-7066**), to find the best option for your trip.

There are a number of choices for travelers under 26. **Inter-Rail** and **EuroYouth passes** entitle the holder to unlimited second-class travel in 26 European countries. **Eurotrain "Explorer" tickets** allow passengers to move leisurely from London to Rome, for example, with as many stopovers as desired, and return by a different route for £195 round-trip (£160 without stopovers). All travel must be completed within 2 months of the departure date. **Campus Travel,** 52 Grosvenor Gardens, London SW1W OAG (☎ **0171/730-3402**), and **Wasteels** (see above), can both help with youth travel.

Wasteels also sells a **Rail Europe Senior Pass** for £5 that entitles the holder to discounted tickets on many European rail lines. Purchasers must be U.K. residents over 60 and hold a British Senior Citizen rail card, available for £16 at any BritRail office.

THE CHUNNEL TRAIN   The *Eurostar* train shuttles between London and Paris or Brussels in less than 3 hours (compared to 10 hours on the traditional train-ferry-train route). The 1998 one-way costs range from $299 (first class, with meal) to $99 (standard class, without meal). You can bring that lowest price down with the discount you get by having a railpass—Eurail, Europass, BritRail, French, or Benelux. Your pass must be validated to get the discount.

Eurostar trains arrive and depart from Waterloo Station in London, Gare du Nord in Paris, and Central Station in Brussels. For reservations, call ☎ **0990/300-003** in London, **01-44-51-06-02** in Paris, or in the U.S. RailEurope at ☎ **800/EUROSTAR** or **800/94-CHUNNEL.** Or you can reserve on the Web at **www.eurostar.com** or **www.raileurope.com**.

BY FERRY OR HOVERCRAFT

Brittany Ferries (☎ **01705/892-200**) is the largest British ferry/drive outfit, sailing from the southern coast of England to Spain and France. From Portsmouth, sailings reach St-Malo and Caen; from Poole, Cherbourg; from Plymouth, Santander in Spain.

P&O Channel Lines (☎ **0990/980-980**) operates car and passenger ferries between Portsmouth and Cherbourg (three departures a day; 5 to 7 hours); Portsmouth to Le Havre (three a day; 5½ hours); and Dover to Calais (25 a day; 75 minutes).

P&O's major competitor is **Stena Sealink** (☎ **01233/615-455**), which carries both passengers and vehicles and is represented in North America by BritRail (☎ **800/677-8585,** or 212/575-2667 in New York). Stena offers ferryboat service between Newhaven and Dieppe (four departures daily; 4 hours), but the car ferries between Dover and Calais are more popular (20 a day; 90 minutes). One-way fares for a car with driver and one passenger are $134 to $255, depending on the season; passengers without cars cost $40 in any season.

Unless you're interested in a leisurely sea voyage, foot passengers might be better off using the quicker, slightly cheaper, **Hoverspeed** (☎ **01304/240-241**). Within North

America, contact BritRail (see above). Hoverspeeds make the 35-minute crossings 12 times daily for only $39.

Scandinavia Seaways (☎ **0171/491-7256**) offers sea links to Germany and all the Scandinavian countries. From England, the Norway route is the most popular. Fares are reduced on "Flag Days"; ask about these when booking.

BY CAR

Many rental companies won't let you rent a car in Britain and take it to the Continent, so always check ahead. There are many drive-on/drive-off car-ferry services across the Channel; see above. There are also Chunnel trains that run a drive-on/drive-off service every 15 minutes (once an hour at night) for the 35-minute ride between Ashford and Calais.

BY COACH

Though considerably slower and less comfortable than the trains, on a budget you may opt for one of **Eurolines'** regular departures from London's Victoria Coach Station to destinations throughout Europe. Contact them at 52 Grosvenor Gardens, Victoria, London SW1W OAU (☎ **0171/730-8235** or 01582/404511). A one-way ticket from London to Rome, for example, is £89 to £95 ($147 to $157), depending on the season, for the 34-hour trip (departures twice weekly).

3 Taking a Tour

With this book, you have everything you need to travel on your own in Europe on a budget and love it. If, however, you want to take advantage of the airfare and hotel bargains offered by a packager or like the we'll-take-care-of-all-the-details attitude of a group-escorted tour, this section will give you the lowdown on getting a good deal. And since even diehard independent travelers might want to hook up with the odd bike tour through Tuscany, classical music cruise down the Danube, language school in Paris, or archaeological dig on a Greek island, the final sections deal with specialized active and educational tours.

PACKAGE TOURS

Package tours aren't the same thing as escorted tours. They're simply a way of buying your airfare and accommodations—and sometime rental cars through a "fly/drive" package—at the same time and getting an excellent rate on all. Your trip is your own. In many cases, a package that includes airfare, hotel, and transportation to and from the airport will cost less than just that hotel if you tried to book it yourself.

However, packages tend to book only large international-style hotels, and though they get you great rates on those rooms, with a little bit of searching (and the listing in this book), you can often find even cheaper digs in a small European-style hotel, pensione, or private home.

All **major airlines** flying to Europe sell independent vacation packages. The best places to start looking for packagers are the travel section of your local Sunday newspaper and national travel magazines. **Central Holidays** (☎ **800/611-1139;** www.centralholidays.com) is one of the best and most reputable. **Liberty Travel** (many locations; check your local directory, since there's not a central 800 number; www.libertytravel.com) is one of the biggest packagers in the Northeast and usually boasts a full-page ad in Sunday papers. **American Express Vacations,** P.O. Box 1525, Fort Lauderdale, FL 33302 (☎ **800/241-1700;** www.americanexpress.com/travel), and **Kemwel** (☎ **800/678-0678;** www.kemwel.com) are both reputable options.

Moment's Notice (☎ 718/234-6295; www.moments-notice.com) is technically a travel club and only members ($25 a year) can book air tickets and hotel packages, but anyone can call the hotline (☎ 212/873-0908) to learn what options are available. On the Internet, head to **Preview's Travel** (www.vacations.com), where you can check out the latest package deals by clicking on Hot Deals.

GROUP & ESCORTED TOURS

With a good group tour, you'll know ahead of time just what your trip will cost and won't have to worry about transportation, luggage, hotel reservations, communicating in foreign languages, and other basic requirements of travel—an experienced guide will take care of all that and will lead you through all the sightseeing. The downside of a guided tour is that you trade a good deal of the freedom and personal free time that independent travel grants you, and you often see only the canned, postcard-ready side of Europe through the tinted windows of a giant bus.

Two of the top operators are **Kemwel** and **American Express Vacations,** which offer the most comprehensive tours to Europe (for both, see "Package Tours"). If you want a tour that balances independent-style travel and plenty of free time with all the pluses of a guided tour, try the very popular itineraries offered by **Europe Through the Back Door,** 120 Fourth Ave. North, P.O. Box 2009, Edmonds, WA 98020-2009 (☎ 425/771-8303; www.ricksteves.com), run by Rick Steves, of public TV's *Travels in Europe* fame.

Other reputable operators are **Bennett Tours,** 342 Madison Ave., New York, NY 10073 (☎ 800/221-2420 or 212/697-1092 in New York), and **Norvista Travel Services,** 228 E. 45th St., New York, NY 10017 (☎ 800/677-6454 or 212/832-8989; fax 212/818-0585). Specialists in group motorcoach tours of Europe are **Travcoa,** P.O. Box 2630, Newport Beach, CA 92658 (☎ 800/992-2003 or 714/476-2800); **Tauck Tours,** 276 Post Rd. W., Westport, CT 06880 (☎ 800/468-2825 or 203/226-6911); **Maupintour,** P.O. Box 807, Lawrence, KS 66044 (☎ 800/255-4266 or 913/843-1211); and **Caravan Tours,** 401 N. Michigan Ave., Chicago, IL 60611 (☎ 800/227-2826 or 312/321-9800).

OUTDOOR & ADVENTURE VACATIONS

BICYCLING   Cycling is the best way to see Europe at your own pace. You can rent at many train stations or private agencies in just about any city or town. You can often pick up a bike in one train station and drop it off at another. In parts of Germany, Scandinavia, and especially the pancake-flat Netherlands, biking is a way of life and the opportunities and resources for pedalers are extensive. In fact, in Copenhagen, thousands of rickety old free bikes are scattered at racks throughout town; just grab one, pop in a few coins to unlock it (they'll be refunded when you reattach the bike to another rack), and pedal away.

Avid cyclists who plan to tour a whole region by bike will probably want to bring their own. Neophytes might want to try a short trip at home first to learn the basics

---

A Tour Warning

Before you sign up with any tour, check on its quality and business practices. Ask the operator if you can see surveys and observations filled out by past participants. Check any tour company with the local **Better Business Bureau** and/or with the **U.S. Tour Operators Association (USTOA),** 342 Madison Ave., Suite 1522, New York, NY 10173 (☎ 212/750-7371), which keeps tabs on its members.

and figure out the essential gear. Some airlines charge extra to bring a bike; many count it as one of your pieces of checked luggage. Either way, your bicycle must be properly boxed—remove the pedals and front wheel; buy the box at a bike shop or the airport for around $10. You can take a bike onto just about any train, but on many you'll have to pay a fee ranging from nominal to ridiculously high (up to 75% the cost of your own ticket).

To sign up for a bike tour, try the following: **Holland Bicycling Tours, Inc.,** P.O. Box 6485, Thousand Oaks, CA 91359 (☎ **800/852-3258;** fax 805/495-8601), leads 8-day bicycle tours throughout Europe (not just in the Netherlands). **Experience Plus** (☎ **800/685-4565;** www.xplus.com) runs bike tours across Europe, and **Cicilsmo Classico,** 13 Marathon St., Arlington, MA 02174 (☎ **800/866-7314;** fax 781/ 641-1512; www.ciclismoclassico.com), is an excellent outfit running tours of Ireland, France, Switzerland, and especially Italy.

The best tour resource is the annual December **Tourfinder** issue of *Bicycle USA.* A copy costs $7 from the League of American Bicyclists, 1612 K St. NW, Suite 401, Washington, DC 20006 (☎ **202/822-1333**). Membership is $30 per year and includes the Tourfinder and the annual Almanac with information on European bicycling organizations.

In England, try **Bike Tours Ltd.,** 82 Walcot St., Bath, BA1 5BD (☎ **01225/ 310-859;** fax 01225/480-132), which offers a variety of tours in Britain, France, Portugal, Italy, Spain, the Czech Republic, and Hungary. Britain's national **Cyclists' Touring Club** (☎ **01483/417-217**) has a membership fee of £25 for adults and £12.50 for children and runs trips to most European countries.

HIKING & WALKING   Most European countries have associations geared toward aiding hikers and walkers. In England it's the **Ramblers' Association,** 1–5 Wandsworth Rd., London SW8 2XX (☎ **0171/339-8500**); in Italy contact the **Club Alpino Italiano,** 7 via E. Fonseca Pimental, Milan 20127 (☎ **02/2614-1378**); for Austria, try the **Österreichischer Alpenverein (Austrian Alpine Club),** Wilhelm-Greil-Strasse 15, Innsbruck, A-6020 (☎ **0512/595470**).

Wilderness Travel, 1102 9th St., Berkeley, CA 94710 (☎ **800/368-2794,** ext. 113; www.wildernesstravel.com), specializes in walking tours, treks, and inn-to-inn hiking tours of Europe, as well as less strenuous walking tours. Two long-established, somewhat upscale walking-tour companies are **Butterfield & Robinson,** 70 Bond St., Suite 300, Toronto, ON M5B 1X3 (☎ **800/678-1147;** fax 416/864-0541; www.butterfield.com), and **Country Walkers,** P.O. Box 180, Waterbury, VT 05676-0180 (☎ **800/464-9225;** fax 802/244-5661; www.countrywalkers.com).

In the United Kingdom, **Sherpa Expeditions,** 131A Heston Rd., Hounslow, Middlesex, England TW5 ORD (☎ **0181/577-2717**), offers both self-guided and group treks through off-the-beaten-track regions of Europe.

WILDERNESS & ADVENTURE TRAVEL   The least expensive of the adventure companies is the **Adventure Center,** 1311 63rd St., Suite 200, Emeryville, CA 94608 (☎ **800/227-8747** or 510/654-1879; www.adventure-center.com). Its slow-paced, flexible trips range from hiking in Tuscany to canoeing the Danube, sailing along the Turkish coast, or taking a wildlife hike through Romania.

Other adventure travel operators featuring European trips are **Above the Clouds,** P.O. Box 398, Worcester, MA 01602-0398 (☎ **800/233-4499** or 508/799-4499; fax 508/797-4779); **Overseas Adventure Travel,** 625 Mt. Auburn St., Cambridge, MA 02138 (☎ **800/221-0814** or 617/876-0533); and **Mountain Travel–Sobek,** 6420 Fairmount Ave., El Cerrito, CA 94350 (☎ **888/687-6235;** fax 510/525-7710; www.MTSobek.com).

In the United Kingdom, try **Waymark Holidays,** 44 Windsor Rd., Slough SL1 2EJ (☎ **01753/516-477**); **Sherpa Expeditions** (see "Hiking & Walking" above); or **HF Holidays,** Imperial House, Edgware Road, Colindale, London NW9 5AL (☎ **0181/905-9388;** fax 0181/205-0506).

EDUCATIONAL & VOLUNTEER VACATIONS

ARCHAEOLOGICAL DIGS   Earthwatch, 680 Mount Auburn St. (P.O. Box 9104), Watertown, MA 02272-9104 (☎ **617/926-8200;** www.earthwatch.org), and **Earthwatch Europe,** 57 Woodstock Rd., Delsyre Court, Oxford, England 0X2 6HU (☎ **01865/311-600**), offer education-packed participation in worldwide archaeological digs and other opportunities to engage in academic fieldwork.

HOME EXCHANGES   Intervac U.S., P.O. Box 590504, San Francisco, CA 94159 (☎ **800/756-HOME** or 415/435-3497; www.intervac.com), is part of the largest worldwide home-exchange network, with a special emphasis on Europe. It publishes four catalogs a year, listing homes in more than 36 countries. Members contact each other directly. The cost is $65 plus postage, which includes three of the catalogs, plus your own listing in one catalog. A fourth catalog is an extra $25.

EDUCATIONAL & STUDY TRAVEL   The best—and one of the most expensive—of the escorted cultural tour operators is **IST Cultural Tours (☎ **800/ 833-2111;** www.ist-tours.com), whose tours are first class all the way and are accompanied by a certified expert in whatever field the trip focuses on.

If you missed out on study abroad in college, the brainy **Smithsonian Study Tours** (☎ **202/357-4700;** www.si.edu/tsa/sst) may be just the ticket, albeit a pricey one. The cheaper alternative is **Smithsonian Odyssey Tours** (☎ **800/258-5885**), run by Saga International Holidays (they save mainly by staying in three- or four-star hotels rather than deluxe). Also contact your **alma mater** or **local university** to see if they offer summer tours open to the public and guided by a professor specialist.

The **National Registration Center for Studies Abroad (NRCSA),** P.O. Box 1393, 823 N. 2nd St., Milwaukee, WI 53203 (☎ **414/278-7410;** www.NRCSA.com), and the **American Institute for Foreign Study (AIFS),** 102 Greenwich Ave., Greenwich, CT 06830 (☎ **800/727-2437** or 203/869-9090; www.AIFS.com), can both help you arrange study programs and summer programs abroad.

The biggest organizations dealing with higher education in Europe are the **Council on International Educational Exchange (CIEE),** 205 E. 42nd St., New York, NY 10017-5706 (☎ **888/COUNCIL;** www.ciee.org), and the **Institute of International Education,** 11 E. Brooks (P.O. Box 371), Annapolis Junction, MD 20701-0371 (☎ **800/445-0443;** www.ciee.org).

A clearinghouse for information on European-based language schools is **Lingua Service Worldwide,** 211 E. 43rd St., Suite 1303, New York, NY 10017 (☎ **800/ 394-LEARN** or 212/867-1225; fax 212/983-2590; www.itctravel.com).

Amsterdam, Delft & Environs

4

by Jeanne Oliver

Amsterdam has never entirely shed its reputation as a hippie haven of peace, love, pot, and tulips, even with an economy that has become the envy of Europe. Fueled more by free trade than free love, prosperity has settled over the graceful cityscape of canals and 17th-century town houses. The city center recalls Amsterdam's golden age as the command post of a vast colonial empire, when wealthy merchants built narrow gabled homes along neatly laid-out canals. Now a new generation of entrepreneurs is revitalizing old neighborhoods like the Jordaan and often turning the distinctive houses into bustling shops, cafes, hotels, and restaurants.

Yet Amsterdam's delicious irony is that the placid 17th-century structures also host brothels, smoke shops, and Europe's wildest nightlife. The Dutch are proud of their live-and-let-live stance, which is based on pragmatism as much as on the country's long history of tolerance. Deciding to control what they cannot effectively outlaw, they permit prostitution in the Red Light District and the sale of marijuana and hashish in designated "coffee shops."

Don't think that Amsterdammers are drifting around in a drug-induced haze, however. They're far too busy whizzing around on bikes, jogging through Vondelpark, feasting on an array of ethnic dishes, or watching the parade of street life from a cafe's terrace. Between dips into the trove of Amsterdam's artistic and historical treasures, take time out to absorb the freewheeling spirit of Europe's most vibrant city.

REQUIRED DOCUMENTS   Citizens of the United States, Canada, the United Kingdom, Australia, and New Zealand need only a valid passport for stays of less than 3 months.

OTHER FROMMER'S TITLES   For more on Amsterdam, see *Frommer's Amsterdam; Frommer's Belgium, Holland & Luxembourg; Frommer's Irreverent Guide to Amsterdam; Frommer's Gay & Lesbian Europe;* or *Frommer's Europe.*

1 Amsterdam Deals & Discounts

SPECIAL DISCOUNTS
FOR EVERYONE   One of the best all-around discounts is the **Museumkaart (National Museum Card),** giving free admission to

---

Budget Bests

Amsterdam's best deal by far is simply **strolling along the shady canals** with their bridges and beautiful 17th-century houses. Few cities have so many buildings of this vintage still standing. While strolling, you'll likely see many **street performers,** from marionettes to five-piece rock bands. The entertainment costs as much as you wish to toss into the hat.

---

more than 350 museums all over the Netherlands for 1 year for 45DFL ($23) adults, 25DFL ($13) 18 and under, and 32.50DFL ($16) 65 and over. If you plan to visit more than five or six museums in Amsterdam, you'll save money with this card, available from museum ticket windows and at the Tourist Information Office in front of Centraal Station. You'll need a passport-size photo to attach to it, which you can get in photo booths at Centraal Station. Note that the Anne Frankhuis, one of Amsterdam's most popular museums, doesn't honor this card.

A **Culture & Leisure Pass** for 33.60DFL ($17) includes 31 coupons offering free admission to four museums and discounts on several others, a free canal cruise, and discounts on selected restaurants, shops, and transport. It's available at all tourist offices.

For getting around on Amsterdam's public transit system—which includes trams, buses, and a subway—you'll need to buy either a **dagkaart (day card)** for 12DFL ($6) or a 15-strip **strippenkaart** for 11.50DFL ($6). The dagkaart is good for 1 day's unlimited travel in the city, and the strippenkaart is good for as many as seven trips with no time limit. A dagkaart is available from bus and tram drivers, in Metro stations, and at the ticket office located in front of Centraal Station; the strippenkaart is available only in tobacco shops, at the ticket office located in front of Centraal Station, and at post offices.

FOR STUDENTS & THOSE UNDER 26   If you're under 26 and not necessarily a student, you can buy a **Cultureel Jongeren Passport (CJP)** or Cultural Youth Passport, entitling you to free admission to many of the city's museums, as well as to discounts on theater performances, concerts, and other events. It costs only 20DFL ($10) and is good for 1 year. You can get a CJP at the Amsterdam Tourist Information Office on Centraal Station Square, on Leidseplein, and on Stadionplein. Be sure to bring your passport and a passport-size photo of yourself.

If you're under 25, you can also get a **National Museum Card,** good for 1 year, for only 25DFL ($13). This card allows you free admission to most of Amsterdam's major museums.

FOR SENIORS   Almost all Amsterdam museums have reduced admission for seniors, and there's also a senior citizens' **National Museum Card,** available for 32.50DFL ($16).

WORTH A SPLURGE

Amsterdam is a city of canals—in fact, there are more here than in Venice. It would be a shame to visit this watery city without staying in a hotel overlooking one of the canals, especially since these **canal-house hotels** are generally in 300-year-old buildings. So if you really want to experience Amsterdam, splurge a bit, even if it's only for 1 night, and stay at one of the canal-house hotels.

The other Amsterdam splurge you won't want to miss is an **Indonesian rijsttafel dinner.** This dining extravaganza includes 15 to 20 courses and will cost you between 40DFL and 60DFL ($20 and $30).

What Things Cost in Amsterdam	U.S. $
Taxi from airport to city center	30.00
Train from airport to city center	3.10
Metro from Centraal Station to Waterloopein	1.50
Local telephone call	.25
Double room at Amsterdam Hilton (deluxe)	257.50
Double room at Hotel Seven Bridges (moderate)	120.00
Double room at the Hotel Pax (budget)	40.00
Lunch for one at Sama Sebo (moderate)	22.50
Lunch for one at Broodje van Kootje (budget)	4.50
Dinner for one, without wine, at Haesje Claes (moderate)	14.25
Glass of beer	2.00
Cup of coffee in a cafe	1.10
Roll of ASA 100 color film, 36 exposures	6.50
Admission to Rijksmuseum	7.50
Movie ticket	8.50
Theater ticket to Concertgebouw	7.50–105.00

2 Essentials

ARRIVING

BY PLANE   If you fly into Amsterdam, you'll arrive at the efficient **Schiphol Airport** (☎ **06/350-34-050**), 11 miles from the city, where the runways are 16 feet below sea level, on the floor of what was once a large lake. For many years, Schiphol has been voted the best airport in Europe, in part because of its massive duty-free shopping center.

Making Schiphol even more convenient is the **train** connecting the airport with Amsterdam's Centraal Station. Leaving directly from the air terminal, it costs 6.25DFL ($3.10) one-way in second class and takes about 20 minutes. It's also possible to catch trains to other European cities directly from the airport. **Taxis** are available at the airport, but since you'll pay about 60DFL ($30) this isn't a viable budget option unless you have tons of luggage or are with several people to split the cost.

BY TRAIN   Whether you fly into Amsterdam or take a train from another city in Europe, you'll find yourself at massive **Centraal Station,** built a little over 100 years ago on a man-made island. Inside the terminal you'll find a currency exchange counter, a railway information center, and the Amsterdam Tourist Information Office. Directly in front of the station is another branch of the Amsterdam Tourist Information Office, a Metro station, and a ticket office where you can buy a strippenkaart or dagkaart for use on the trams and buses (see below). These cards are less expensive here than when bought from tram and bus drivers. Many tram and bus stops are also in front of Centraal Station.

VISITOR INFORMATION

At Schiphol Airport you can go to **Holland Tourist Information** (☎ **31-6/340-340-66** if you call from abroad) in Schiphol Plaza to make hotel reservations and get information. It's open daily 7am to 10pm.

The **Amsterdam Tourist Information Office,** Stationsplein 10 (☎ **0900/400-40-40,** or 31-6/340-340-66 if you call from abroad; fax 020/625-28-69), is in front of Centraal Station in a small white building that also contains a coffee shop and boat dock. It's open daily 9am to 5pm (to 4:30pm November to March). There's another office in the train station that's open Monday to Saturday 8am to 8pm and Sunday 8:30am to 4:30pm. Both offices provide maps and information about the city, plus reserve hotels and tours; there's also a window for buying theater and concert tickets. An information center on Leidseplein is open Monday to Saturday 9am to 8pm and Sunday 9am to 5pm.

If you arrive in town without a hotel reservation, the best place to head is the **Dutch Tourist Information Office,** Damrak 35 (☎ **020/638-28-00;** fax 020/625-09-74). Hotels with unsold rooms often sell them at the last minute through this office at a substantial discount, and the reservation fee is 2.50DFL ($1.25) per person. There's also a service to buy theater tickets, rent cars, and book excursions. The office is open Monday to Saturday 8am to 10pm and Sunday 9am to 10pm.

Be sure to pick up a copy of *What's On in Amsterdam* for 3.50DFL ($1.75). This small magazine is full of details about the month's art exhibits, concerts, and theater performances and lists bars, dance clubs, and restaurants. The yellow **Visitors Guide,** free at any tourist office, has a wealth of practical information. A great source for the young and budget conscious is the *Use-It* guide, costing 2.50DFL ($1.25) at the private Tourist Information Office at the Arena Budget Hotel, s'Gravesandestraat 51.

For more details on cultural events or to make reservations, stop by the **Amsterdam Uit Buro (AUB),** on Leidseplein, open Monday to Saturday 10am to 6pm.

CITY LAYOUT

When you step out of Centraal Station's main entrance, you're facing the center of Amsterdam. Using this point as a reference, you'll see the city is laid out along five concentric semicircles of canals: **Singel, Herengracht, Keizersgracht, Prinsengracht,** and the outermost, **Singelgracht** (*gracht* means "canal"). It was along these canals that wealthy 17th-century merchants built their elegant homes, which are still standing. The largest and most stately of the canal houses are along Herengracht. Within these canals are many smaller canals radiating out from the center. The area within Singelgracht is known as the Old City.

Damrak is a busy tourist street leading from Centraal Station to **Dam Square,** location of the former dam on the Amstel River that gave Amsterdam its name. To the left is Amsterdam's famous **Red Light District,** where government-licensed prostitutes sit in their windows with red lights glowing, waiting for customers. One block to the right of Damrak is **Nieuwendijk** (which becomes **Kalverstraat** when it crosses Dam Square), a pedestrian-only shopping street. If you follow Kalverstraat to the end, you'll find yourself at **Muntplein** (*plein* means "square") beside the old Mint Tower. Cross Singel and continue in the same direction and you'll reach **Rembrandtplein,** one of Amsterdam's main nightlife areas.

The other main nightlife area is **Leidseplein,** on the last of Amsterdam's concentric canals, Singelgracht (not to be confused with Singel, the first of the concentric canals). Leidseplein is at the end of **Leidsestraat,** a pedestrian shopping street that leads from Singel to Singelgracht. Leidsestraat is reached from Kalverstraat by Heiligeweg, another short pedestrian shopping street.

Museumplein, where you'll find Amsterdam's three most famous museums—the Rijksmuseum, Vincent van Gogh Museum, and Stedelijk Museum of Modern Art—is a 5-minute walk along Singelgracht from Leidseplein.

One other area worth mentioning is the **Jordaan,** a quickly developing old neighborhood now filled with inexpensive restaurants, unusual shops, and small galleries. The Jordaan is between Prinsengracht and Singelgracht in the area bounded by Rozengracht and Brouwersgracht. To reach this area, turn right off Damrak at any point between Centraal Station and Dam Square. When you cross Prinsengracht, you're in the Jordaan.

GETTING AROUND

When looking at a map of Amsterdam, you might think that the city is too large to explore on foot. This isn't true. In fact, it's possible to see almost every important sight on a 4-hour walk. One important thing to remember is that cars and bikes have the right of way when turning. Don't step in front of one thinking it's going to stop for you.

BY SUBWAY, BUS & TRAM   Amsterdam's subway system, the **Metro,** unfortunately doesn't serve most areas visitors want to visit. You can, however, use it to reach Waterlooplein or the Amstel Station from Centraal Station. Both these stops are within Zone 1 and require two boxes on a strippenkaart (see below).

Sixteen **tram** lines and 30 **bus** lines serve Amsterdam. The buses and trams are the most convenient means of getting around, though they can be slow during rush hours. Tram nos. 1, 2, 4, 5, 9, 13, 16, 17, 24, and 25 and bus nos. 18, 21, 32, 33, 34, 35, 39, and 67 originate at Centraal Station. The public transport system begins at about 6:30am, and the last tram leaves around midnight. After that, there are infrequent night buses.

You should also know about the **circle tram,** a special tram line that makes 30 stops at most of the important museums and attractions as well as Centraal Station. Prices are the same as the dagkaarts (see below), and a circle tram ticket is valid for all other transport. You can buy tickets from the ticket office opposite Centraal Station, circle-tram conductors, and tourist information offices. It runs from 9am to 6pm and is a convenient option for a heavy sightseeing day.

Should you be considering not paying the fare, keep in mind that inspectors, sometimes undercover, may demand to see your ticket at any time. If you haven't paid the proper fare, you'll be fined 60DFL ($30) plus the fare for the ride.

Tickets & Passes   The fare system is complex, with a baffling array of combinations. You can buy passes, **dagkaarts,** good for unlimited travel in all zones for up to 9 days. A 1-day card is 12DFL ($6) and is available on buses and trams as well as at tobacco shops, newsstands, and post offices. At the ticket office at Centraal Station it's only 10DFL ($5). You can also buy 2- to 9-day dagkaarts for 15DFL to 43DFL ($8 to $22), but these aren't available on buses or trams. You need to take a lot of trams for a dagkaart to be worthwhile, but if you're staying outside the town center a day or multiday pass may be your best bet.

You can also buy a **strippenkaart,** which you have stamped according to the number or zones you're traveling through. (Most attractions are in the central zone.) Strippenkaarts come in denominations of 2, 3, 8, 15, and 45 boxes. Before boarding a bus or tram, consult the map posted at every stop to determine how many zones you'll be traversing. Fold your strippenkaart so that one more box than the number of zones you're traveling through is facing up and stick this end into the yellow box near the door as you enter. The machine will stamp your card. On buses, have the driver stamp your card. The ticket includes transfers to other tram, bus, and Metro lines within 1 hour. If you don't have a strippenkaart, you can buy 2-, 3-, and 8-strip cards from the driver, but this is a more expensive option.

A Transport Pass Tip

If you're staying more than a couple of days and your hotel is in the town center, the most economical solution is to buy a **15-strip strippenkaart** for 11.50DFL ($6) from the ticket office outside Centraal Station or at a tobacco shop, newsstand, or post office. The card has no time limit, is good for up to seven rides in the town center, and can be used by any number of people.

BY BICYCLE   Of the approximately 700,000 Amsterdammers, around 550,000 own bikes. You'll see children barely old enough to walk, their great-grandparents, and even businesswomen in high heels pedaling through the city in any weather. A bicycle is one of the best ways to get around in this flat city where too many cars clog the narrow streets. There are two things to remember: Watch out for unpredictable drivers and always lock your bike—theft is a common problem.

You can rent bikes all over town, but the following offer good rates: **Take a Bike,** in the basement of Centraal Station, to the right of the main entrance as you face the station (☎ **020/624-83-91**), charges only 8DFL ($4) per day plus a passport and a 200DFL ($100) deposit; and **MacBike,** Mr. Visserplein 2 (☎ **020/620-09-85**), or Marnixstraat 220 (☎ **020/626-69-64**), charges 12.50DFL ($6) per day, plus a passport and a 50DFL ($25) deposit.

Amsterdam has another pedal-powered means of transport—**canal bikes.** These are small pedal boats for two to four that are available on Leidseplein, near the Rijksmuseum, on Westerkerk and the Anne Frankhuis, and on Keizersgracht near Leidsestraat. Canal bikes are available daily 10am to 4pm in spring and autumn (to 10pm in summer). Rates are 25DFL ($13) per hour for a two-person boat and 40DFL ($20) per hour for a four-person boat. There's also a 50DFL ($25) refundable deposit.

BY TAXI   You can get a taxi in front of any major hotel or at Leidseplein, Rembrandtplein, or Centraal Station. To phone for a cab, call ☎ **020/677-77-77.** Rates start at 5.80DFL ($2.95) and increase by 2.80DFL ($1.40) per kilometer.

BY RENTAL CAR   Though a car is a good way to see the nearby countryside, I strongly advise against driving in Amsterdam. In an ongoing struggle against air pollution, the city has adopted a series of measures to make driving as difficult as possible. Several major axes have been closed to cars or turned into one-way streets, and the limited parking spaces are expensive. Also be aware that car break-ins aren't uncommon, especially at night.

All the major car-rental agencies have offices in Amsterdam, and a number of smaller companies offer rates as low as 63DFL ($32) per day for very economical subcompacts that include the first 125 miles, insurance, and tax. You pay 51 Dutch cents (25¢) for each additional mile. Try **Diks,** van Ostadestraat 278–280 (☎ **020/662-33-66**), or **Budget,** van Ostadestraat 232–234 (☎ **020/671-70-66**).

BY BOAT   One last means of getting around is by boat. The best option is the **Museumboat** (☎ **020/622-21-81**), which stops near virtually all Amsterdam's museums and attractions. The boats leave from behind the Tourist Information Office in front of Centraal Station every 30 minutes daily 10am to 5pm. Tickets are available at the Lovers Canal Cruises counter near the dock. A 1-day ticket is 22.50DFL ($11) adults and 15DFL ($8) after 1pm for seniors or age 13 and under. The ticket also allows reduced admission at most of the museums. There are English-speaking guides on the boats.

There are also **water taxis,** but these are quite expensive. If you feel like a splurge, call ☎ **020/622-21-81.**

The **Canal Bus** (☎ 020/623-98-86), a boat operating on a fixed route, stops at the Rijksmuseum, Leidseplein, Leidesestraat/Keizersgracht, Westerkerk/Anne Frankhuis, Centraal Station, and City Hall/Rembrandthuis. A ticket costs 19.50DFL ($10) adults and 15DFL ($8) children and is good all day.

FAST FACTS: Amsterdam

American Express   The offices are at Damrak 66 (☎ 020/520-77-77) and Van Baerlestraat 39 (☎ 020/673-85-50), open Monday to Friday 9am to 5pm and Saturday 9am to noon.

Banks   Two convenient banks are **ABN–Amro Bank,** Rokin 82 (☎ 020/624-25-90), open Monday to Friday 9am to 4pm; and **ABN–Amro Bank,** Rokin 16 (☎ 020/520-66-66), open Monday to Friday 9am to 5pm.

Business Hours   Most **banks** are open Monday to Friday 9am to 4 or 5pm, occasionally later on late-night shopping evenings. **Shops** are generally open Monday to Friday 8:30 or 9am to 5:30 or 6pm and Saturday 8:30 or 9am to 4 or 5pm. Many shops don't open until 1pm Monday and stay open to 9pm Thursday or Friday. Shops in the Magna Plaza mall and some of the large department stores are open on Sunday noon to 5pm and shops in the museum quarter are open every first Sunday of the month.

Consulates   The Hague is the seat of government of the Netherlands, and that's where all embassies are located. But there are a few consulates in Amsterdam, including those of the **United States,** Museumplein 19 (☎ 020/575-53-09), open Monday to Friday 8:30am to noon and 1:30 to 3:30pm; and the **United Kingdom,** Konigslaan 44 (☎ 020/676-43-43), open Monday to Friday 9am to noon and 2 to 4pm.

Currency   The Netherlands **guilder** (abbreviated **DFL** for Dutch florin, the old name of the currency) is the basic monetary unit. The guilder is divided into 100 cents, and there are coins of 5, 10, and 25 cents, as well as 1, 2.50, and 5 guilders. Paper-note denominations include 5, 10, 25, 50, 100, 250, and 1,000 guilders.

Currency Exchange   When changing money, be absolutely sure to ask the exchange rate and service charge. Rarely will a currency exchange office give you the official rate, so shop around. Banks are usually best, followed by windows in train stations and tourist offices. American Express and Thomas Cook also offer good rates and can be found at several locations in Amsterdam. Cirrus and Plus cardholders get the best rate from the numerous ATMs throughout the city.

Emergencies   For 24-hour **doctor and dentist** referrals, call ☎ 0900/503-20-42. In an emergency, call ☎ 112 for **police,** an **ambulance,** or the **fire department.** For nonurgent police matters, call ☎ 020/559-91-11. Before and after regular **pharmacy** hours (Monday to Friday 9am to 5:30pm), call ☎ 0900/503-20-42 for info on where you can get a prescription filled.

Holidays   Public holidays in Amsterdam include New Year's Day (January 1), Good Friday, Easter Monday, Queen's Day (April 30), Ascension Day, Whit Sunday and Monday, Christmas Day (December 25), and Boxing Day (December 26).

Hospitals   The following hospitals have a first-aid department: **Academisch Medisch Centrum,** Meibergdreef 9 (☎ 020/566-33-33 or 020/566-91-11);

The Dutch Guilder

For American Readers At this writing, $1 was approximately 2DFL (or 1DFL = 50¢), and this was the rate of exchange used to calculate the dollar values given in this chapter (rounded to the nearest dollar if over $5).

For British Readers At this writing, £1 was approximately 3.30DFL (or 1DFL = 30p), and this was the rate of exchange used to calculate the pound values in the table below.

Note: Exchange rates fluctuate from time to time and may not be the same when you travel to Holland.

DFL	U.S.$	U.K.£	DFL	U.S.$	U.K.£
1	.50	.34	10	5	3.45
2	1	.69	20	10	6.90
3	1.50	1.03	30	15	10.34
4	2	1.38	40	20	13.79
5	2.50	1.72	50	25	17.24
6	3	2.07	75	37.50	25.86
7	3.50	2.41	100	50	34.48
8	4	2.76	125	62.50	43.10
9	4.50	3.10	150	75	51.72

and **Onze Lieve Vrouwe Gasthuis,** Oosterparkstraat 179 1e (☎ **020/599-91-11**).

Laundry & Dry Cleaning Most wasserettes are open daily 7 or 8am to 9 or 10pm and cost about 13DFL ($7) for 6 kilos (13 pounds) of laundry. Convenient locations include Oudebrugsgracht 22, between Damrak and Nieuwendijk; Ferdinand Bolstraat 9, near the Heineken brewery; and Rozengracht 59, on the edge of the Jordaan. Get your dry cleaning done at the **Clean Center,** Ferdinand Bolstraat 9 (☎ **020/662-71-67**), near the Heineken brewery.

Mail The **PTT–Main Post Office,** Singel 256, at the corner of Raadhuisstraat, is open Monday to Friday 9am to 6pm (to 8pm on Thursday) and Saturday 9am to 3pm. Branch offices are open Monday to Friday 9am to 5pm. A letter or postcard to the United States will cost 1.60DFL (80¢).

Police For police emergencies, dial ☎ **112.**

Tax Look for the HOLLAND TAX-FREE SHOPPING sign in shop windows around Amsterdam. These shops will provide you with the form you need for recovering the **VAT (value-added tax)** when you leave the European Union. Refunds are available only when you spend more than 300DFL ($150) in a store. For more information, see "Shopping," later in this chapter.

Telephone A **local phone call** costs .50DFL (25¢) for 3 minutes, but watch out for numbers that begin with 06 or 0900 as they can be more expensive. Telephone instructions are in English and, though some machines accept coins, most will accept only phonecards. For **international phone calls,** you can use any of the phone booths spread all over town, by using plastic phonecards selling for 5DFL ($2.50), 10DFL ($5), or 25DFL ($13) at post offices and newsstands. You

Networks & Resources

STUDENTS   Student activities don't revolve around a university because the city's main university has relocated many miles outside central Amsterdam and is no longer convenient to the places young people frequent. However, classes are still held in various buildings around the city, and you'll find students gathering at two restaurants: **The Atrium,** Grimburgwal 237, on the Voorburgwal canal, open Monday to Friday noon to 2pm and 5 to 7pm; and **The Agora,** a short walk from Waterlooplein at Roeterstraat 11–13, open daily noon to 7:30pm, with a cafe that stays open to 1am.

For information about cultural events, visit the **AUB,** on Leidseplein at Marnixstraat. If you're under 26, you can pick up a CJP (Cultural Youth Pass) here for 20DFL ($10). The CJP is good for free admission to most museums and discounts on most cultural events. The AUB is open Monday to Saturday 10am to 6pm (to 9pm on Thursday). If you're young and in trouble or just want someone to talk to, contact the **JAC (Youth Help Center),** Amstel 30 (☎ **020/624-29-49**), along the river near Rembrandtplein.

GAYS & LESBIANS   To find out more about the gay and lesbian scenes, stop by **COC,** Rozenstraat 14 (☎ **020/623-40-79**), 2 blocks off Westerkerk. It houses a coffee shop open Monday to Saturday 11pm to 4am as well as a disco. On Friday the disco is for men and on Saturday for women. Sunday attracts an older mixed crowd. You can also call the **Gay and Lesbian Switchboard** (☎ **020/623-65-65**), open daily 10am to 10pm, for information and advice.

Gay News Amsterdam is a new monthly newspaper in English that covers the gay scene, including news on nightlife, special events, and gay issues. It's available free in gay establishments throughout Amsterdam. The ***Best Gay Guide,*** available at the W. H. Smith bookstore on Kalverstraat, provides a thorough introduction to the city's gay life. Also see "Gay & Lesbian Bars" under "Amsterdam After Dark," later in this chapter.

A must-see is the ***Homomonument,*** three pink triangles dedicated in memory of those gays and lesbians killed during World War II and also to those who have died of AIDS. You'll find it along Keizersgracht, at Westermarkt, near the Westerkerk and the Anne Frankhuis. This area becomes a huge outdoor disco on Queen's Day (April 30).

can also reach an AT&T operator by dialing 06 (wait for the tone), then 022-9111.

Tipping   In almost all restaurants, a service charge is included in the price of the meals, so it's not necessary to leave any tip. However, if service is exceptionally good, you may want to leave a small tip, depending on the price of the meal. Taxi fares include a service charge, but drivers expect a small tip as well.

Country & City Codes

The **country code** for the Netherlands is **31.** The **city code** for Amsterdam is **20;** use this code when you're calling from outside the Netherlands. If you're within the Netherlands but not in Amsterdam, use **020.** If you're calling within Amsterdam, simply leave off the code and dial only the regular phone number.

3 Accommodations You Can Afford

There was a time when the canal-house hotels were quite cheap, but most of them have raised their rates beyond the budget range (though you'll still find a few listed here). They make a great splurge choice. Even if you don't stay in a canal house, you'll most likely stay in a building built 250 to 350 years ago during Amsterdam's golden age.

If you arrive in Amsterdam without a reservation, consult any of the room-finding services listed under "Visitor Information" earlier in this chapter.

In most cases a large Dutch breakfast is included with the room rate. These hearty repasts usually include ham, cheese, a boiled egg, several types of bread, butter, milk, and sometimes chocolate sprinkles, which are very popular.

If you plan to stay in a hostel or student hotel in summer, it's imperative that you look for a room early in the day—by late afternoon hostels are usually full. Try to avoid arriving after dark since this will make finding a place to stay very difficult. B&B accommodations are available by contacting **Bed & Breakfast Holland,** Theophile de Bockstraat 3, 1058 TV Amsterdam (☎ **020/615-75-27;** fax 020/669-15-73). Prices per person range from 37.50DFL to 62.50DFL ($19 to $31), depending on amenities and location. Breakfast is included, and there's a 2-night minimum stay.

Note: You can find most of the lodging choices below plotted on the map included in "Seeing the Sights" later in this chapter.

NEAR DAM SQUARE & CENTRAAL STATION

Amstel Botel. Oosterdokskade 2–4, Amsterdam 1011 AE. ☎ **020/626-42-47.** Fax 020/639-19-52. 176 units, all with bathroom (shower). TV TEL. 135DFL ($68) single; 153DFL ($77) double; 190DFL ($95) triple. Buffet breakfast 10DFL ($5). AE, DC, EURO, MC, V. 24-hour parking 25DFL ($13).

This boat-hotel is moored 250 yards off Centraal Station, with 352 beds in 176 cabins on four decks, connected by an elevator. The boat was built in 1993 as a hotel and has never sailed on the open sea. The Amstel is Amsterdam's only floating hotel and has become quite popular, largely because of its location and rates. To find it, leave Centraal Station and turn left, passing the bike rental—it's painted white and directly in front of you. Public parking is on the street. There's no curfew.

✪ **Bob's Youth Hostel.** Nieuwezijds Voorburgwal 92, Amsterdam 1012 SG. ☎ **020/623-00-63.** Fax 020/675-64-46. 6 units, all with bathroom (tub); 200 dorm beds. 125DFL ($63) apt for 2–4; 25DFL ($13) dorm bed, plus refundable 25DFL ($13) deposit for locker key. Rates include continental breakfast and showers. Dinner (summer only) 8DFL ($4). No credit cards. Tram: 1, 2, 5, 13, or 17 from Centraal Station to the second stop.

Conveniently located halfway between Centraal Station and Dam Square, this hostel is open all year. Guests are accommodated in dorms with 4 to 16 bunk beds. Sheets and blankets are furnished, and there's a 3am curfew. The reception and breakfast room is a few steps below street level. The atmosphere is international; 50% of the

A Canal House Warning

Be prepared to climb hard-to-navigate stairways if you want to save money on lodging in Amsterdam. Narrow and steep as ladders, these stairways were designed to conserve space in the narrow houses along the canals. Today they're an anomaly that'll make your stay even more memorable. If you have difficulty climbing stairs, ask for a room on a low floor.

customers are from English-speaking countries. Users of alcohol and drugs are definitely barred. Bob's also has an annex around the corner at Spui 47, renting six modern apartments with kitchenettes and color TVs for two to four guests—one of the best deals in town.

Eben Haezer. Bloemstraat 179, Amsterdam 1016 LA. ☎ **020/624-47-17.** Fax 020/627-61-37. E-mail: the0eb@globalxs.nl. 114 dorm beds. 20DFL ($10) dorm bed; locker 1 DFL (50¢) plus refundable 10DFL ($5) deposit for locker key. Rates include full breakfast. No credit cards. Tram: 13 or 17 to Marnixstraat.

The nicer of the two Christian Youth Hostels, the Eben Haezer is on the edge of the Jordaan, a 10-minute walk from Dam Square. The beds are bright red bunks in large dorms with huge windows. There's a curfew (midnight Sunday to Thursday and 1am Friday and Saturday), and the dorms are closed for cleaning daily 10am to 2pm. New showers, central heating, a small lounge, a large dining hall serving three meals a day, and a peaceful patio all add up to a great deal if you don't mind sleeping in a dorm.

Hotel de Westertoren. Raadhuisstraat 35B, Amsterdam 1016 DC. ☎ **020/624-46-39.** 8 units, 4 with bathroom (shower). 55DFL ($28) single without bathroom; 95DFL ($48) double without bathroom, 105DFL ($53) double with bathroom. Rates include full breakfast. AE, DC, EURO, MC, V. Tram: 13 or 17 to Westermarkt.

Perhaps the best of the hotels on this block is the recently renovated Westertoren. The two rooms in the front with balconies are attractive but tend to be a bit noisy; the quieter rooms in back are large and bright. Breakfast is served in the rooms, and proprietors Tony and Chris van der Veen, who speak English, will share a wealth of information about the city.

Hotel Pax. Raadhuisstraat 37, Amsterdam 1016 DC. ☎ **020/624-97-35.** 8 units, none with bathroom. TEL. 50DFL ($25) single; 80DFL ($40) double. AE, DC, MC, V. Tram: 13 or 17 to Westermarkt.

Most rooms here are large, and all are simply furnished and clean; two have small balconies overlooking the street. Room 19, with four beds and plenty of space, is particularly well suited to students or young people traveling together. Mr. Veldhuizen has been in business for nearly 30 years.

Winston Hotel. Warmoesstraat 123–129. ☎ **020/623-13-80.** Fax 020/639-23-08. E-mail: winston@xs4all.nl. 67 units, 33 with bathroom (shower or tub). 93DFL ($47) single without bathroom; 124DFL ($62) double without bathroom; 158DFL ($79) double with bathroom (shower); 169DFL ($84) with bathroom (tub); 195DFL ($98) triple with bathroom (shower), 213DFL ($106) triple with bathroom (tub); 238DFL ($119) quad with bathroom (shower); 282DFL ($141) quint with bathroom (shower); 334DFL ($167) six-bed dorm with bathroom (shower); 54DFL ($27) bed in 8-bed dorm with bathroom (shower). Rates include continental breakfast. AE, DC, MC, V. Tram: 4, 9, 16, 24, or 25 to Dam Square.

More stylish than most backpacker hotels, the Winston is moving upscale by asking local artists to hand-paint the halls, rooms, and doors. Though not yet completed, the project is bringing some whimsy to a rather bland place that at least is equipped with an elevator. The sparsely furnished rooms vary in size but are clean and well maintained; the bathrooms are small. The downstairs bar is a lively meeting place and offers live music on weekends.

NEAR THE RIJKSMUSEUM & LEIDSEPLEIN

Euphemia Budget Hotel. Fokke Simonszstraat 1, Amsterdam 1017 TD. ☎ and fax **020/622-90-45.** E-mail: euphjm@pi.net. Internet: www.channels.nl/amsterdam/euphemia. 27 units, 15 with bathroom (tub). TV. 110DFL ($55) double without bathroom, 150DFL ($75) double with bathroom; 45DFL ($23) per person triple/quad without bathroom. Continental breakfast 6DFL ($3). AE, DC, MC, V. Tram: 16, 24, or 25 to Weteringcircuit.

A 5-minute walk from the Rijksmuseum, the Euphemia is popular with students and young travelers. It's a clean and inexpensive place, with ground-floor rooms that are wheelchair accessible. In addition to the color TV in most rooms, there's a TV and VCR in the breakfast room; you can even rent videos here. Inexpensive snacks are sold during the afternoon and evening.

Hotel Asterisk. Den Texstraat 14–16, Amsterdam 1017 ZA. ☎ **020/624-17-68.** Fax 020/638-27-90. 29 units, 24 with bathroom (21 with tub, 3 with shower). TV TEL. 70DFL ($35) single without bathroom, 85DFL ($43) single with bathroom; 115DFL ($58) double without bathroom, 170DFL ($85) double with bathroom; 195DFL ($98) triple with bathroom. Rates include full breakfast. MC, V. Tram: 16, 24, or 25 to Weteringcircuit.

This is the nicer of the Texstraat options. All the rooms come with new carpets and furniture, and a buffet Dutch breakfast, with at least five types of bread as well as meats and cheeses, is served in the bright breakfast room; over the years visitors from all over the world have tacked pieces of their own money on the wall. There are a few rooms on the ground floor, an elevator, and baby-sitters available, making this good for older travelers and families.

Hotel Bema. Concertgebouwplein 19B, Amsterdam 1071 LM. ☎ **020/679-13-96.** Fax 020/662-36-88. 7 units, 4 with bathroom (shower). 65DFL ($33) single without bathroom; 95DFL ($48) double without bathroom, 125DFL ($63) double with bathroom; 125DFL ($62.50) triple without bathroom, 150DFL ($75) triple with bathroom; 185DFL ($92.50) quad with bathroom. Rates include full breakfast. V. Tram: 5 or 16 to Concertgebouwplein.

American ownership/management and an enviable location across from the Concertgebouw make this a popular budget choice, albeit with younger visitors. The rooms are large, though a bit worn, and many still show the original ornate plasterwork. If peace and quiet are important, ask for a room overlooking the garden. Breakfast is served in the rooms.

Hotel Casa-Cara. Emmastraat 24, Amsterdam 1075 HV. ☎ **020/662-31-35.** 9 units, 6 with bathroom (tub). TEL. 60DFL ($30) single without bathroom, 95DFL ($48) single with bathroom; 75DFL ($38) double without bathroom, 105DFL ($53) double with bathroom; 130DFL ($65) triple with bathroom; 150DFL ($75) quad with bathroom. Rates include full breakfast. No credit cards. Tram: 2 or 16 to Emmastraat. Bus: 197 from airport.

A 10-minute walk from the Rijksmuseum, the Casa-Cara is another good choice. A marble floor in the entry hall and contemporary black furniture in the breakfast room lend an air of sophistication. The guest rooms are spacious and clean, with large windows and high ceilings.

Hotel de Leydsche Hof. Leidsegracht 14, Amsterdam 1016 CK. ☎ **020/623-21-48.** 10 units, 4 with bathroom (shower). 85DFL ($43) double without bathroom, 95DFL ($47.50) double with bathroom; 135DFL ($97.50) triple with bathroom; 170DFL ($85) quad with bathroom. No credit cards. Tram: 1, 2, or 5 to Keizersgracht.

Built in 1665 overlooking Leidsegracht, this has long been an excellent budget hotel. The rooms vary in size, the larger ones with high ceilings and big windows. Many have wood paneling that makes them look a bit like saunas, but the original plasterwork and old (unused) fireplaces in some rooms hint at the building's past. If you need a firm mattress, though, you may want to look elsewhere. The most interesting feature of the hotel is its intricately carved stairway railing.

Hotel Kap. Den Texstraat 5B, Amsterdam 1017 XW. ☎ **020/624-59-08.** 17 units, 4 with bathroom (1 with shower, 3 with tub). 60DFL ($30) single without bathroom; 90DFL ($45) double without bathroom, 140DFL ($70) double with shower only; 190DFL ($95) triple with bathroom; 230DFL ($115) quad with bathroom. Rates include full breakfast. AE, MC, V. Tram: 16, 24, or 25 to Weteringcircuit.

Across from the Asterisk (above), this hotel has several large family rooms as well as smaller ones. Simply furnished and decorated, they're clean and comfortable. A dark wooden table and chairs fill the breakfast room.

Hotel Museumzicht. Jan Luykenstraat 22, Amsterdam 1071 CN. ☎ **020/671-29-54.** Fax 020/671-35-97. 14 units, 3 with bathroom (shower). 70DFL ($35) single without bathroom; 115DFL ($58) double without bathroom, 150DFL ($75) double with bathroom; 150DFL ($75) triple without bathroom, 180DFL ($90) triple with bathroom. Rates include full breakfast. AE, EURO, MC, V. Tram: 2 or 5 to Hobbemastraat.

This hotel is ideal for museum-goers since it's across from the back of the Rijksmuseum. The breakfast room commands an excellent view of the museum with its numerous stained-glass windows. Robin de Jong, the proprietor, has filled the rooms with an eclectic furniture collection, from 1930s English wicker to 1950s modern.

Hotel P. C. Hooft. P. C. Hooftstraat 63, Amsterdam 1071 BN. ☎ **020/662-71-07.** Fax 020/675-89-61. 16 units, 3 with bathroom (shower). TV. 75DFL ($37.50) single with bathroom; 95DFL ($48) double without bathroom, 105DFL ($52.50) double with bathroom. Rates include full breakfast. MC, V. Tram: 1, 2, or 5 to Leidseplein.

Imagine staying on Amsterdam's most upscale shopping street, amid the chic boutiques and classy restaurants, for no more than you'd pay in any other budget hotel in town. That's what you get at the P. C. Hooft, though you'll have to climb quite a few stairs to enjoy your stay. Most of the rooms have been recently updated with contemporary furnishings and new carpets, and there are plans to add full baths to some. The breakfast room is painted wild shades of orange and blue, guaranteed to wake you up.

✪ **Hotel Wynnobel.** Vossiusstraat 9, Amsterdam 1071 AB. ☎ **020/662-22-98.** 12 units, none with bathroom. 70DFL–80DFL ($35–$40) single; 110DFL–140DFL ($55–$70) double; 150DFL–180DFL ($75–$90) triple; 190DFL–210DFL ($95–$105) quad. Rates include full breakfast. No credit cards. Tram: 1, 2, or 5 to Leidseplein; then cross the canal, turn left, and watch for the street on the far side of the Vondelpark entrance.

The Wynnobel is around the corner from the chic boutiques of P. C. Hooftstraat and a few minutes' walk from the Rijksmuseum. It overlooks part of Vondelpark and is run by friendly Pierre Wynnobel and his wife, who sees to it that the hotel is kept clean. If you can convince Mr. Wynnobel to play the piano in the lobby, you'll have an added treat. The large rooms are furnished with old or antique furniture, and a large breakfast is served in your room. A beautiful central stairway winds around to the four floors, and the first floor is only a short climb. A stay here is always pleasant.

✪ **Kooyk Hotel.** Leidsekade 82, Amsterdam 1017 PM. ☎ **020/623-02-95** or 020/622-67-36. Fax 020/638-83-37. 19 units, none with bathroom. TV. 75DFL ($38) single; 115DFL ($58) double; 165DFL ($83) triple; 195DFL ($98) quad. Rates include full breakfast. MC, V (add 4% to rates). Tram: 1, 2, or 5 to Leidseplein.

Most rooms at the Kooyk have been refurnished and redecorated; several are wheelchair accessible. A huge four-bed room in front overlooks Singelgracht canal. Reproductions of Dutch paintings, old photographs of Amsterdam, and photos of American movie stars hang on the breakfast room walls.

Van Ostade Bicycle Hotel. Van Ostadestraat 123, Amsterdam 1072 SV. ☎ **020/679-34-52.** Fax 020/671-52-13. 16 units, 8 with bathroom (shower). TV. 90DFL ($45) single without bathroom; 115DFL ($58) double without bathroom, 150DFL ($75) double with bathroom. Rates include continental breakfast. No credit cards. Tram: 24 or 25 to Ceintuurbaan (9th stop).

The young owners have hit on an interesting idea: They cater to visitors who wish to explore Amsterdam on bikes. Their guests can rent bikes for only 7.50DFL ($3.75) per day, no deposit. They're also helpful in planning biking routes. The recently renovated rooms feature new carpets and comfortable modern furnishings; some have kitchenettes and small balconies, and there are large rooms for families. The hotel is a few blocks from the popular Albert Cuypstraat Market. An old bike hangs on the facade, and there are always bikes parked in front. For long stays, "selected tourists" can rent two doubles with kitchenettes in an annex near Rembrandtplein. The atmosphere is friendly and easygoing.

✪ **Vondelpark.** Zandpad 5, Amsterdam 1054 GA. ☎ **020/589-89-99.** Fax 020/589-89-55. E-mail: vondelpark@njhc.org. Internet: www.njhc.org/vondelpark. 9 units, all with bathroom (shower); 485 dorm beds. 100DFL ($50) double; 168DFL ($84) quad; 36.50DFL ($18) dorm bed for IYHF members. Nonmembers pay 5DFL ($2.50) extra for first 6 nights. Rates include sheets and full breakfast. No credit cards. Tram: 1, 2, or 5 to Leidseplein.

The hostel is in an imposing old school building, with its own entrance gate from Vondelpark. The dorms are outfitted with six to eight double-decker bunks. The new furnishings and carpets and the cleanliness make this an exceptional deal. A few doubles and quads are available. Other amenities are sturdy lockers for 5DFL ($2.50) per day (refunded), a self-service kitchen, a bar with a small dance floor, a no-smoking reading room, and a covered bike shed.

IN & NEAR THE JORDAAN

Hotel Acacia. Lindengracht 251, Amsterdam 1015 KH. ☎ **020/622-14-60.** Fax 020/638-07-48. 16 units, 2 houseboats, all with bathroom (tub). TV TEL. 100DFL ($50) single; 135DFL ($68) double; 175DFL ($88) triple; 210DFL ($105) quad; 150DFL ($75) studio; 175DFL ($88) houseboat for 1, 239DFL ($120) houseboat for 4. Rates include full breakfast. MC, V (add 5% to rates). Bus: 18 to Nieuwe Willems Straat.

This unusual triangular corner building faces a picturesque small canal. The young Dutch owners, Hans and Marlene van Vliet, are proud of their hotel. All rooms are furnished with modern beds, small tables, and chairs, as well as attractive new carpets. The large front-corner rooms sleep as many as five and have windows on three sides. On the ground floor is a cozy Old Dutch breakfast room where a full breakfast is served at long wooden tables. There are also a couple of studios with tiny kitchenettes, plus a spacious houseboat moored in the canal across the street.

Hotel de Bloiende Ramenas. Haarlemmerdijk 61, Amsterdam 1013 KB. ☎ and fax **020/624-60-30.** 10 units, none with bathroom. 45DFL ($23) per person. No credit cards. Bus: 11 or 18 from Centraal Station to Oranjestraat (3rd stop).

On a street lined with all sorts of shops on the edge of the Jordaan, this hotel (no elevator) is a good choice for readers traveling in small groups. Most of the spacious rooms have up to five beds. The hotel, whose name means the Blooming Radish, is on three floors in a 17th-century building, with a street-level coffee shop and bar; it has been open for more than 100 years. Don't expect more than average comfort, but the location and price are excellent.

✪ **Hotel van Onna.** Bloemgracht 102–104 and 108, Amsterdam 1015 TN. ☎ **020/626-58-01.** 39 units, 30 with bathroom (shower). 55DFL ($27.50) per person without bathroom, 70DFL ($35) per person with bathroom. Rates include full breakfast. No credit cards. Tram: 13, 14, or 17 to Westermarkt.

Consisting of three canal houses (two old and one new), this hotel has grown over the years, but genial owner Loek van Onna continues to keep his prices reasonable. Mr. van Onna has lived here since he was a boy and will gladly tell you of the building's history. Accommodations in the three buildings vary considerably, with the best rooms in the new building. However, the oldest and simplest rooms also have a great deal of charm. Whichever building you wind up in, ask for a room in front overlooking the canal.

Getting the Best Deal on Accommodations

- Stick to the hotels listed in this book or recommended by the Amsterdam Tourist Information Office in front of the train station. Politely decline the offers of young men and women in the train stations who'll want to take you to a hotel.
- Be aware that hotels near the Jordaan and Leidseplein offer great deals.
- Take advantage of discounts often offered in winter. Even if the rates haven't been lowered, it's often possible to get a few guilders off the quoted price.
- Note that advance reservations are extremely important in summer, when Amsterdam is the youth vacation capital of Europe.
- Consider taking a room without a private bath. Hallway showers and toilets are usually well maintained, and the price reduction is substantial.

NEAR REMBRANDTPLEIN

Arena Budget Hotel. s'Gravesandestraat 51, Amsterdam 1092 AA. ☎ **020/ 694-74-44.** Fax 020/663-26-49. 600 beds, 38 units, all with bathroom (shower); 330 dorm beds. 110DFL ($55) double; 140DFL ($70) triple; 25DFL ($12.50) dorm bed. Breakfast 8DFL ($4). No credit cards. Metro: Weesperplein. Tram: 9 or 14 to Tropenmuseum.

This is no doubt the happiest hostel in town. In a massive red-brick house built in 1890 as a hospital, the hotel is today not only a place to sleep but also a cultural center. The large dorms have 60 beds each; eight smaller dorms have 6 to 8 bunk beds each. There are also 34 doubles, 4 triples, and an apartment with 6 beds. The hotel features an information center, a concert hall, and a TV/video lounge, plus a restaurant and a garden. Bike rentals are offered. In summer, pop concerts, dance parties, and film showings liven up the atmosphere.

Hotel Adolesce. Nieuwe Kiezersgracht 26, Amsterdam 1018 DS. ☎ **020/626-39-59.** Fax 020/627-42-49. 23 units, 10 with bathroom (shower). 120DFL ($60) double without bathroom, 150DFL ($75) double with bathroom; 150DFL ($75) triple without bathroom; 180DFL ($90) quad without bathroom. Rates include full breakfast. MC, V. Closed Nov–Mar. Metro: Waterlooplein.

Quilts and parrots are the themes here. You'll find live parrots in the lobby and parrot prints decorating the rooms and halls. Likewise, old quilts are displayed throughout. All guest rooms are outfitted with new furnishings. The breakfast room, which includes a small bar, a patio garden, and a TV lounge, is in the basement but is made bright with large skylights. This six-story building has steep stairs and no elevator, but a few rooms are on the ground floor, including two off the back patio.

✪ **Hotel Agora.** Singel 462, Amsterdam 1017 AW. ☎ **020/627-22-00.** Fax 020/627-22-02. 15 units, 13 with bathroom (11 with shower, 2 with tub). TV TEL. 120DFL ($60) single without bathroom, 180DFL ($90) single with bathroom; 145DFL ($73) double without bathroom, 210DFL ($105) double with bathroom; 275DFL ($138) triple with bathroom; 325DFL ($163) quad with bathroom. Rates include full breakfast. AE, DC, EURO, MC, V. Tram: 1, 2, 5, or 11 to Koningsplein–Singel.

Two houses built in 1735 have been fully restored to create this fine hotel, steps from the floating flower market. Two rooms fall within our budget, and the 13 others (with bath) are worth the extra money. All the rooms are carpeted and attractively furnished with new beds and a few antiques. The large family room has three windows overlooking the Singel canal. The hotel is efficiently run and well maintained by friendly Yvo Muthert and Els Bruijnse, and breakfast is served in the ground-floor breakfast room.

Hotel Barbacan. Plantage Muidergracht 89, Amsterdam 1018 TN. ☎ **020/623-62-41.** Fax 020/627-20-41. 20 rms, 18 with bathroom (shower). TV TEL. 90DFL ($45) single without bathroom; 115DFL ($58) double without bathroom, 100DFL–157DFL ($50–$79) double with bathroom. Rates include full breakfast. AE, EURO, MC, V. Tram: 9 to Artis Zoo.

You can't miss the Barbacan—it's the building with all the flags out front. Inside you'll find a collection of police memorabilia and a lobby gift shop. The rooms are clean, modern, and quiet, with new carpets and contemporary furnishings. There are even safes in all rooms.

Hotel Keizershof. Keizersgracht 618, Amsterdam 1017 ER. ☎ **020/622-28-55.** Fax 020/624-84-12. 6 units, 2 with shower only, 1 with bathroom (shower). 75DFL ($38) single without bathroom; 125DFL ($63) double without bathroom, 135DFL ($68) double with shower only, 150DFL ($75) double with bathroom. Rates include full breakfast. MC, V. Tram: 16, 24, or 25 to Keizersgracht.

This hotel, in a large old canal house, is run by the genial Mrs. de Vries, her son Ernest, and her daughter Hanneke. The rooms are named after movie stars, and there are several other special touches that make a stay here memorable. You enter through a street-level door, and to reach the upper floors you must climb a wooden spiral staircase built from a ship's mast. The ceilings of most rooms have exposed beams. Breakfast is served in the ground-floor breakfast room.

✪ **Hotel Prinsenhof.** Prinsengracht 810, Amsterdam 1017 SL. ☎ **020/623-17-72** or 020/627-65-67. Fax 020/638-33-68. 10 units, 2 with bathroom (shower). 85DFL ($43) single without bathroom; 120DFL–125DFL ($60–$63) double without bathroom, 160DFL–165DFL ($80–$83) double with bathroom; 175DFL ($88) triple without bathroom, 210DFL ($105) triple with bathroom; 290DFL ($145) quad with bathroom. Rates include full breakfast. AE, MC, V. Tram: 4 to Keizersgracht.

One of the best deals in Amsterdam, the Prinsenhof isn't far from the Amstel River in a renovated canal house. Most rooms are large, with beamed ceilings, and the front rooms look onto Prinsengracht, where colorful boats are docked. The large breakfast is served in an attractive blue-and-white dining room. The friendly proprietors, André van Houten and Mark Bakker, take pride in the hotel's quality and will make you feel at home. A pulley will haul your bags to the upper floors.

A GAY & LESBIAN HOTEL
Hotel New York. Herengracht 13, Amsterdam 1015 BA. ☎ **020/624-30-66.** Fax 020/620-32-30. 38 units, all with bathroom (32 with shower, 6 with tub). TV TEL. 150DFL ($75) single with shower; 200DFL ($100) double with shower, 250DFL ($125) double with tub; 275DFL ($137.50) triple with tub. Rates include full breakfast. AE, DC, MC, V. Tram: 1, 2, 5, 11, or 13 from Centraal Station.

On one of the most beautiful canals, overlooking the Milk Maid's Bridge, this is one of Amsterdam's most popular gay hotels. It occupies four floors (no elevator) in three connected 17th-century houses and is managed by a Frenchman named Philippe. The rooms are spacious, with modern furniture, hair dryers, and safes, and the facilities include a cocktail lounge and same-day laundry service. Three gay bars are within easy walking distance—just ask at the desk.

WORTH A SPLURGE
✪ **Hotel de Filosoof.** Anna van den Vondelstraat 6, 1054 GZ Amsterdam. ☎ **020/683-30-13.** Fax 020/685-37-50. 25 units, all with bathroom. TV TEL. 155–185DFL ($78–$93) double. Rates include breakfast. AE, MC, V. Tram: 1 to Constantine Huygenstraat.

On a quiet street of brick houses near Vondelpark, this extraordinary hotel is an open challenge to cookie-cutter rooms. One of the owners is a philosophy professor who has expressed her passion for ideas in the most imaginatively decorated rooms you could ever find. Posters, painted ceilings, framed quotes, and unusual objects in each room are carefully chosen representations of philosophical or cultural themes. You can ponder the meaning of life in rooms dedicated to thinkers like Goethe, Wittgenstein, Nieztsche, Marx, and Einstein or rooms based on motifs like Eros, the Renaissance, astrology, or women. To help you out of any existential crisis, you can even consult your private bookshelf of philosophical works or join in one of the weekly philosophy roundtables. The rooms are larger in the annex across the street and some open onto a private terrace. Creature comforts aren't forgotten either. The bathrooms vary in size but are well equipped, and the beds are firm.

✪ **Hotel Seven Bridges.** Reguliersgracht 31, Amsterdam 1017 LK. ☎ **020/623-13-29.** 11 rms, 6 with bathroom (shower). 115DFL ($58) single without bathroom, 200DFL ($100) single with bathroom; 150DFL ($75) double without bathroom, 240DFL ($120) double with bathroom. Rates include full breakfast. AE, MC, V. Tram: 16, 24, or 25 to Keizersgracht.

This may be the best hotel value in all of Amsterdam. If you're going to splurge for a room with a bath, this is the place to do it. Each huge room is unique, with antique furnishings, plush carpets, and reproductions of modern art on the walls; one room even has a bath with a skylight and wooden walls similar to those in a sauna. The front rooms overlook a small canal, and the rear rooms overlook a garden. Some rooms have a TV, and all bathrooms have hair dryers. Your large breakfast will be served in your room at the time you request. Proprietors Pierre Keulers and Gunter Glaner are extremely helpful. An added bonus is that the hotel is only 2 blocks from busy Rembrandtplein.

4 Great Deals on Dining

In Amsterdam you'll find not only plenty of traditional Dutch restaurants but also dozens of ethnic places serving everything from Argentine to Tunisian food. Indonesian food is extremely popular, notably the *rijsttafel.* These ethnic places generally offer hearty and delicious meals at very reasonable prices. Two great areas for discovering new restaurants are around Leidseplein and in the Jordaan.

Amsterdam's favorite lunch is a *broodje,* a small sandwich made with a soft roll or French bread and filled with meat or fish. You'll find these inexpensive tasty sandwiches in restaurants and at street stands around the city. An especially popular street food is *broodje haring,* raw herring and onions in a soft bun for around 5DFL ($2.50). The traditional method for eating herring is to tip your head back and lower the fish head-first into your mouth. Another traditional Dutch lunch is *uitsmijters* (pronounced *out*-smayters): two pieces of toast topped with ham or cheese and two fried eggs, often served with a small salad.

If you want to experience Amsterdam conviviality at its finest, head to one of the city's hundreds of brown cafes, local bars that get their name from the interior's predominantly brown coloring. Why are the interiors brown? Hundreds of years of thick tobacco smoke have stained the walls and furniture—and continue to do so today.

If you have a sweet tooth, be sure to try some traditional Dutch desserts, like *poffertjes* (miniature pancakes), *oliebollen* (like powdered sugar–covered doughnut holes), or pancakes. All these come with various fillings or toppings, many of which contain a liqueur of some sort. Traditional *poffertje* restaurants are garish affairs that look as though they've run away from the circus. You'll find one on the Nieuwendijk pedestrian shopping street and another on the Weteringcircuit near Leidseplein.

As in most European cities, you'll find that the best meal bargains are the offerings of the most recent immigrants. In Amsterdam's case the Turkish snack bars and Surinamese fast-food restaurants offer the cheapest meals. The former specialize in *shwarma* and *falafel* and can be found around Leidseplein and Rembrandtplein; the latter are known for their *chicken roti* and can be found in the vicinity of Albert Cuyp-straat, the site of a popular daily market. About 6DFL to 8DFL ($3 to $4) will get you a filling meal in either type of restaurant.

NEAR DAM SQUARE & CENTRAAL STATION

The Atrium. Oudezijds Achterburgwal 237. ☎ **020/525-39-99.** Meals 7DFL–9DFL ($3.50–$4.50). No credit cards. Mon–Fri noon–2pm and 5–7pm. Tram: 1, 2, 24, or 25 to Spui. DUTCH.

This spectacular facility is the self-service student restaurant on the grounds of Amsterdam's old university. A courtyard between four restored buildings has been covered with a glass roof that lets in plenty of light all year. To reach the food lines, walk up the stairs just inside the door and cross the pedestrian bridge.

Another university cafeteria, **Agora,** is at Roeterstraat 11–13, near Waterlooplein. The hours and prices are similar. This latter place also houses a more upscale dining room and a cafe.

Cafe de Pilserlj. Gravenstraat 10. ☎ **020/625-00-14.** Meals 10DFL–25DFL ($5–$12.50). No credit cards. Mon–Fri noon–midnight, Sat noon–8:30pm. Tram: 10 to Dam Square. DUTCH.

This high-ceilinged cafe/bar may look as though it has been here forever, but not too long ago it was a stationery store. Inside you'll find tables in front and back, with hanging plants adding a bit of color to the dark interior. Old jazz recordings are a favorite with the bartender. Behind the Nieuwekerk and only steps from the Nieuwendijk pedestrian shopping street, this atmospheric cafe is an excellent place to try a traditional Dutch lunch of *uitsmijters.*

Calypso Sandwich Shop. Zoutsteeg 3–5. ☎ **020/626-33-88.** Meals 5DFL–12DFL ($2.50–$6). No credit cards. Sun–Wed and Fri 8am–7pm, Sat 8am–5pm. Tram: 16 to Dam Square. DUTCH (BROODJES).

If you're looking for an inexpensive place for a quick *broodje* or two while strolling along Nieuwendijk, duck into one of the many little alleys that lead toward Damrak—there are at least two or three sandwich shops on most alleys. This is one of the nicest, with 30 seats. It serves a wide selection of *broodjes, uitsmijters,* and cro-quettes.

David & Goliath. Kalverstraat 92. ☎ **020/623-67-36.** Meals 10DFL–30DFL ($5–$15); tourist menu 27.50DFL ($14). No credit cards. Daily 10am–5pm (to 6pm in summer). Tram: 4, 9, or 16 to Dam Square. DUTCH.

At the entrance to the Amsterdam Historisch Museum and affiliated with the museum, David & Goliath is popular with well-to-do older Amsterdammers. The meals are well-prepared Dutch standards, such as *broodjes, uitsmijters,* and solid meat-and-potatoes hot meals, but the real reason to eat here is the decor. A "life-size" wooden statue of David and Goliath, carved in 1650 for a local amusement garden, stands in one corner of the high-ceilinged dining room. The immense ogre watching over diners is an Amsterdam artwork not to be missed.

✪ **Haesje Claes.** Spuistraat 273–275. ☎ **020/624-99-98.** Meals 15DFL–42DFL ($8–$21); tourist menu 28.50DFL ($14). AE, DC, MC, V. Daily noon–10pm. Tram: 1, 2, or 5 to Spui. DUTCH.

Dark wood paneling, low-beamed ceilings, and stained-glass windows create just the right atmosphere for traditional Dutch food. The meals are hearty and the portions large enough to satisfy even the hungriest person. The 250-seat restaurant is popular with executives and shoppers from nearby Kalverstraat as well as tour groups, who fill

Great Deals on Dining 55

A True Amsterdam Dining Experience

Even if you're on a tight budget, try to have at least one Indonesian *rijsttafel* dinner, a traditional "rice table" banquet of as many as 20 succulent and spicy foods served in tiny bowls. Pick and choose from among the bowls and add your choice to the pile of rice on your plate. It's almost impossible to eat all the food set on your table, but give it a shot—it's delicious. For an abbreviated version served on one plate, try *nasi rames*. At lunch, the standard Indonesian fare is *nasi goreng* (fried rice with meat and vegetables) or *bami goreng* (fried noodles prepared in the same way).

the small tables in the two dining rooms. They come for the delicious food and reasonable prices.

Kam Yin. Warmoesstraat 6. ☎ **020/625-31-15.** Meals 8.50DFL–13.50DFL ($4.25–$6). No credit cards. Daily noon–midnight. Tram to Centraal Station. SURINAMESE/CHINESE.

Though the neon-and-tile interior may remind you of the waiting room in a bus station, this restaurant is extremely popular with budget-conscious Amsterdammers. The constant turnover keeps the cooks busy all day, ensuring that your meal is freshly prepared. Heaping mounds of rice and noodles are topped with fish, meat, or vegetables blending Chinese, Indonesian, and South American flavors. Try the *moksi meti,* a hearty plate of mixed meats with noodles or rice, as a main meal or inexpensive *broodjes* as a snack. Another outlet is around the corner at Nieuwebrugsteeg 10–12 (☎ **020/420-45-63**).

Keuken Van 1870. Spuistraat 4. ☎ **020/624-89-65.** Meals 8.50DFL–16.50DFL ($4.25–$8). AE, DC, MC, V. Mon–Fri 12:30–8pm, Sat–Sun 4–9pm. Tram: 1, 2, 5, 13, 17, or 20 to Martelaarsgracht. DUTCH.

In business for more than 125 years, this restaurant is one of Amsterdam's cheapest. At one time the place was primarily for feeding the poor, but today it's frequented by working people, students, and shoppers from Nieuwendijk 2 blocks away, all of whom line up for the inexpensive meals. The spotless large dining area seats more than 100.

La Place. Rokin 160. ☎ **020/622-01-71.** Meals 10DFL ($5). AE, MC, V. Mon–Sat 9:30am–8pm, Sun 11am–8pm. Tram: 4, 9, 14, 16, 24, or 25 to Muntplein. DUTCH.

This vast multilevel food depot offers something for everyone. The ground floor is devoted to the bread family, offering thick slabs of quiche, an assortment of pizzas, and delicious fresh breads (the cheese-onion loaf is a meal in itself). The airy glass-topped cafeteria covers the three upstairs floors. Main dishes include a meat or fish of the day, often with a vaguely Indonesian touch, along with vegetables and potatoes. Vegetarians will love the soup and salad selection, and there's an assortment of freshly squeezed fruit juices—all at a reasonable price.

Nam Kee. Zeedijk 111–113. ☎ **020/624-34-70.** Meals 10DFL–30.50DFL ($5–$15). AE, MC, V. Daily noon–12:30am. Metro: Nieuwmarkt. CHINESE.

Stylish it isn't, but this modest place attracts throngs of locals in search of cheap, authentic Chinese dishes. Even with another outlet at Geldersekade 117 (☎ **020/639-28-48**), it's popularity often entails lines out to the street. Whether your taste is for sweet-and-sour prawns, sliced pork, or stir-fried vegetables, your choice is guaranteed to be fresh and filling. The noodle soups are a one-dish meal at 10DFL ($5). My favorite is the *bami soep goulash,* a peppery soup with huge chunks of beef.

Ovidius. At the corner of Spuistraat and Raadhuisstraat. ☎ **020/620-89-77.** Meals from 15.50DFL ($7). AE, MC, V. Daily 9:30am–8pm (Thurs to 11pm). Tram: 13 or 17 to Dam Square. INTERNATIONAL.

Cheap Eats

For the cheapest food in Amsterdam, stop by one of the city's many *automatieks,* snack bars reminiscent of the Automats that long ago disappeared from the American scene. Walls of little glass boxes display croquettes, *broodjes,* and other snacks. Just drop your coins in the slot and take your pick. Croquettes are 2DFL ($1) and *broodjes* 2.50DFL ($1.25). And for 3DFL ($1.50) you get a large container or cone of delicious fries with your choice of ketchup or the Dutch mayonnaise-like sauce that's traditionally served on fries here. **Febo,** the best-known automatiek, is at Stadionplein 20, Linnaeusstraat 24, and Reguliersbreestraat 38.

Judging by the brass railings, wood floors, mirrors, and massive crystal chandelier, you'd expect the prices here to reflect the elegant decor, but this cafe/brasserie is surprisingly reasonable. It's located in the stylish shopping mall Magna Plaza. The menu touches all parts of the globe, offering an array of snacks and light meals—broodjes with brie, Caesar salad, tapas, tortilla chips, pasta, chicken saté, muffins, croissants, and excellent coffee.

✪ **Seafood.** Kalverstraat 122. ☎ **020/623-73-37.** Meals 6.30DFL–11.75DFL ($3.15–$6). No credit cards. Mon–Sat 9:30am–6:30pm, Sun noon–4:30pm. Tram: 1, 2, 4, 5, 9, 14, 16, 20, 24, or 25 to Spui. DUTCH/SEAFOOD.

If you're walking down crowded Kalverstraat and your eyes are suddenly drawn to a most colorful sandwich display, you've undoubtedly stumbled on the Nordsee. The herring, mackerel, shrimp, tuna, and crab are delicious.

NEAR THE RIJKSMUSEUM & LEIDSEPLEIN

Bojo. Lange Leidsedwarsstraat 51. ☎ **020/622-74-34.** Main courses 15DFL–22DFL ($8–$11). No credit cards. Mon–Thurs 5pm–2am, Fri–Sat noon–2am. Tram: 1, 2, or 5 to Leidseplein. INDONESIAN.

This excellent Indonesian restaurant is inexpensive and conveniently located near Leidseplein, and it's also open all night on weekends. So if hunger strikes after a late night on the town, drop in for a flavorful *longtong rames* special (served with chewy rice cakes). If it looks too crowded, be sure to check the adjoining dining room, with a separate entrance.

Broodje Van Kootje. Leidseplein 20. ☎ **020/623-20-36.** Meals 4DFL–9DFL ($2–$4.50). No credit cards. Sun–Thurs 9:30am–1am, Fri–Sat 9:30am–3am. Tram: 1, 2, or 5 to Leidseplein. DUTCH (BROODJES).

This is basically a Dutch-style fast-food place. Brightly lit, with only a few tables, Broodje van Kootje is popular with Amsterdammers on the go. If you can't stomach the idea of eating a raw herring from a street vendor, maybe it'll seem more palatable here. A specialty is the creamy croquette broodje. There's an equally popular branch at Spui 28 (☎ **020/623-74-51**).

De Blauwe Hollander. Leidsekruisstraat 28. ☎ **020/623-30-14.** Meals 17DFL–40DFL ($9–$20); tourist menu 24DFL ($12). No credit cards. Daily 5–10pm. Tram: 1, 2, or 5 to Leidseplein. DUTCH.

The atmosphere here is casual and relaxed, and it's popular with the younger set who are on their way out for a night of bar-hopping around nearby Leidseplein. Along the front window is a long table piled with magazines in several languages for you to read over tea, coffee, or a beer or while you wait for your meal. Best of all, the special tourist menu may include pea soup, ribs, bacon, black bread and butter, or meatballs, potatoes, and a salad or vegetable.

✪ **De Boemerang.** Weteringschans 171. ☎ **020/623-42-51.** Meals 17.50DFL–38DFL ($8–$19). AE, EURO, MC, V. Mon–Tues and Thurs–Fri noon–9:30pm, Sat–Sun 4–9:30pm. Tram: 16, 24, or 25 to Meteringschans. MUSSELS/STEAK.

If you like mussels, this legendary restaurant, which opened in 1915, is the place to go. The decor is old and eclectic—notice the 500 paper banknotes hanging from the ceiling behind the counter and the huge copper teakettle above the main door. The selection on the jukebox is 40 years old (corresponding to the term of the current owner), but you don't come here for the atmosphere—you come for the succulent mussels, served in huge pots in a quantity that's almost impossible to finish. Choose from among a number of dipping sauces, all delicious. It's a favorite of various airline pilots and staff, which is an additional recommendation. (The owner named the place after a boomerang, in hopes that his customers would return just as the Australian hunting weapon does.)

Hot Potato. Leidsestraat 44 (near the corner of Keizersgracht). ☎ **020/623-23-01.** Baked potato platters 3DFL–7.50DFL ($1.50–$3.25); hot dogs 4.50DFL ($2.25). No credit cards. Mon–Fri 8:30am–1pm, Sat 9am–1:30pm, Sun 10am–10pm. Tram: 1, 2, or 5 to Leidseplein. DUTCH/AMERICAN.

This restaurant serves up 30 varieties of baked potato platters, ranging from one with butter or cream to a deluxe spud prepared with crabmeat. It's a tiny place, with only stools (no chairs), but it's a good value—especially for those fed up with chips and burgers.

IN & NEAR THE JORDAAN

Cafe de Jaren. Nieuwe Doelenstraat 20–22. ☎ **020/625-57-71.** Meals 19DFL–30DFL ($10–$15); dinner menu 28DFL ($14). No credit cards. Daily 10am–1am. Tram: 9 or 14 to Muntplein. DUTCH/CONTINENTAL.

This is one of Amsterdam's largest cafe/restaurants, with 300 seats in the spacious high-ceilinged dining rooms, plus 150 more on a terrace. Anyone who likes picturesque surroundings will love this place. Many students eat lunch here (it's near the university). Supposedly Rembrandt lived and worked in this house more than 300 years ago.

De Bolhoed Restaurant. Prinsengracht 60–62. ☎ **020/626-18-03.** Meals 15DFL–30DFL ($8–$15). No credit cards. Daily noon–10pm. Tram: 13 or 17 to Westerkeirk. VEGETARIAN/HEALTH FOOD.

You may be hesitant to enter this restaurant when you see how badly it's leaning (a common problem in a city built on wooden pilings), but the owner assured me that the building has been that way for hundreds of years. High ceilings, large windows, and blond hardwood floors give this place a bright and airy feel. Live piano music is often offered in the evenings.

✪ **Hostaria.** Tweed Egelantiersdwarsstraat 9. ☎ **020/626-00-28.** Reservations essential. Meals 18DFL–56DFL ($9–$28). No credit cards. Tues–Sun 6:30–10pm. Tram: 3 or 10 to Marnixplein. ITALIAN.

Abandon all thoughts of factory-made pasta drowning in gloppy tomato sauce. Owners Marjolein and Massimo Pasquinoli have transformed this tiny space into a showcase for the kind of cuisine Italian mothers only wish they could equal. When you sit down, Marjolein brings you a dish of garlicky tapenade and warm bread. As an appetizer you might then select a perfectly balanced fish soup with a slice of salmon or lightly grilled eggplant slices with fresh herbs. You also have a choice of wonderful pastas—the tagliatelle with arugula and truffles is a particular treat. An appetizer and pasta with a glass of wine is a great little meal for only about 35DFL

($18), but a full menu of Italian classics is available for heartier appetites (and thicker wallets).

Moeder's Pot. Vinkenstraat 119. ☎ **020/623-76-43.** Meals 15DFL–35DFL ($8–$18). No credit cards. Mon–Fri 5–10pm, Sat 5–9:30pm. From Centraal Station, walk up Haarlemstraat, cross a bridge, and turn left. DUTCH.

This restaurant close to Haarlemer Square is small, but the meals it serves are huge. The daily specials of typical Dutch food are a particularly good deal. Moeder's Pot, managed since 1970 by the friendly Mr. Cor, has been around for years and is a popular neighborhood hangout. You'll find it especially convenient if you're staying at the Hotel Acacia or Hotel de Bloiende Ramenas.

Pancake Bakery. Prinsengracht 191. ☎ **020/625-13-33.** Pancakes 7.95DFL–18.95DFL ($3.95–$9). AE, V. Daily noon–9:30pm. Tram: 1, 2, or 5 to Spui or 13, 14, or 17 to Westermarket. PANCAKES.

In the basement of a 17th-century canal warehouse (near the Anne Frankhuis) is this long, narrow restaurant serving some of the most delicious and unusual pancakes you'll ever taste. There are several dozen varieties, almost all of which are a full meal. Choices include salami and cheese, cheese and ginger, honey nuts and whipped cream, and *advokaat* (a Dutch eggnog-like cocktail). One of the best-sellers is what they call the American pancake: with fried chicken, sweet corn, peppers, carrots, Cajun sauce, and salad. In summer, a few tables are placed in front overlooking the canal.

Speciaal. Nieuwe Leliestraat 142. ☎ **020/624-97-06.** Meals 21.50DFL–60DFL ($11–$30); *rijsttafel* 50DFL ($25). AE, EURO, MC, V. Daily 5:30–11pm. Tram: 13, 14, or 17 to Rozengracht. INDONESIAN.

For an Indonesian meal in the Jordaan, try this tiny restaurant. The woven bamboo walls are hung with framed batiks and photos of Indonesia; the tablecloths are also batik. Besides the standard Indonesian dishes, they have some unusual offerings for those already familiar with Indonesian food.

NEAR REMBRANDTPLEIN

Eethuisje Cantharel. Kerkstraat 377 (off Utrechterstraat). ☎ **020/626-64-00.** Reservations recommended in the evening. Meals 14.95DFL–24.95DFL ($7–$12); daily specials 15DFL–17DFL ($8–$9). AE, DC, MC, V. Daily 5–10pm. Tram: 4 to Utrechterstraat. DUTCH.

Small and dark, this restaurant is a classic Dutch eatery that's been serving up hearty meals for years. Meat and potatoes are the order of the day, but the choices can be surprising—from liver and onions to schnitzel paprikasaus, marinated spareribs to chicken cordon bleu. You'll find Eethuisje Cantharel across from the old wooden church (one of the only wooden buildings left in Amsterdam).

PICNICKING

You can pick up almost anything you might want for a picnic, from cold cuts to a bottle of wine, at the **Albert Heijn supermarket,** at the corner of Leidsestraat and Koningsplein, near Spui, open Monday to Friday 9am to 8pm and Saturday 9am to 6pm. Then head over to **Vondelpark,** only a 15-minute walk. If it's summer, you might even catch a free concert at the outdoor theater.

WORTH A SPLURGE

✪ **D'Vijff Vlieghen.** Spuistraat 294–302. ☎ **020/624-83-69.** Reservations recommended. Fixed-price menu 60DFL ($30) for 3 courses, 77.50DFL–147.50DFL ($39–$74) for 4 courses. DC, EURO, MC, V. Daily 5:30–10pm. Tram: 1, 2, 5, or 11 to Dam Square. DUTCH.

Touristy? Yes, but this is one of Amsterdam's most famous restaurants, and the food is authentic stick-to-the-ribs Dutch fare. The menu offers a selection of seasonal fish and

Getting the Best Deal on Dining

- Save money by grabbing a quick lunch from an *automatiek* (like an Automat).
- For lunch, try those Dutch favorites *broodjes* and *uitsmijters*, both tasty and inexpensive.
- Sample Dutch cheese—it's wonderful and makes an ideal picnic food.
- Note that a cone of hot fries can be a filling and inexpensive snack—not to mention delicious.
- Look for fixed-price or tourist menus—the selection of dishes is limited, but you can eat at restaurants that would normally be out of our price range.

game often marinated with fresh herbs and served with unusual vegetables like chard, wild spinach, and brussels sprout leaves. If you're feeling adventurous, try the wild boar with sweet chestnuts and gin sauce. Occupying five canal houses, the restaurant is a kind of Dutch theme park boasting seven dining rooms decorated with artifacts from Holland's golden age. Don't miss the four original Rembrandt etchings in the Rembrandt Room and the collection of handmade glass in the Glass Room.

Sama Sebo. P. C. Hooftstraat 27. ☎ **020/662-81-46.** Meals 25DFL–45DFL ($13–$23); *nasi rames* or *bami rames* lunch 22.50DFL ($11); *rijsttafel* 45DFL ($23). AE, DC, EURO, MC, V. Mon–Fri noon–3pm and 6–10pm, Sat to 11pm. Tram: 2 or 5 to Hobbemastraat. INDONESIAN.

Sama Sebo serves the best *bami goreng* and *nasi goreng* in Amsterdam (only at lunch). A meal here is a worthwhile splurge. When you order either of the two lunch specials, you get a heaping mound of food that's really a *nasi rames* or *bami rames* (one-plate *rijsttafel*). The restaurant has two sections: the main dining room with its Indonesian motif and the bar area for more casual dining.

5 Seeing the Sights

SIGHTSEEING SUGGESTIONS

IF YOU HAVE 1 DAY   The first thing you should do in Amsterdam is take a **boat tour** of the canals. Then head to the **Rijksmuseum** and see several Rembrandts and the large collection of paintings by 17th-century Dutch masters. After lunch, visit the **Vincent van Gogh Museum** and finish your day at the **Museum Het Rembrandthuis;** not only will you get a look at virtually all the prints that Rembrandt made but also you'll get to see inside the restored 17th-century house where he once lived.

IF YOU HAVE 2 DAYS   For Day 1, follow the above. On Day 2, visit the famous **Anne Frankhuis,** where the Jewish Frank family hid from the Nazis during World War II. Then stroll around the **Jordaan,** an old section that has been restored in the past few years. Have lunch at one of the many restaurants in the Jordaan, then head for the **Amsterdam Historisch Museum** on Kalverstraat. This excellent museum covers several hundred years of local Amsterdam history. When you leave, be sure to take a stroll around the **Begijnhof,** a peaceful courtyard surrounded by old houses. Since you're on **Kalverstraat,** Amsterdam's busiest pedestrian shopping street, you might want to get in a bit of shopping.

IF YOU HAVE 3 DAYS   After your canal tour, spend the rest of Day 1 on Museumplein. Visit the **Rijksmuseum,** the **Vincent van Gogh Museum,** and the **Stedelijk Museum of Modern Art.**

A Museum Tip

I'd advise museum buffs to buy a **Museumkaart (National Museum Card)**—for details, see "Amsterdam Deals & Discounts" at the beginning of this chapter.

On Day 2, visit the **Museum Het Rembrandthuis** and the **Jewish Historical Museum,** only a few blocks away. While you're in this area, you can stroll around the **Waterlooplein flea market.** If you're interested, this would be a good time, and much safer than at night, to stroll through Amsterdam's famous **Red Light District,** where the women sit in their windows. Take precautions if you visit this district—night or day. In the afternoon, visit the **Amsterdam Historisch Museum** and the **Begijnhof.**

On Day 3, visit the nearby museum village of **Zaanse Schans** in the morning. Working windmills and Dutch artisans are two of the attractions in this beautiful little village only 20 minutes from the city. In the afternoon, visit the **Anne Frankhuis** and tour the **Jordaan.**

IF YOU HAVE 5 DAYS   Spend Days 1 to 3 as above. On Day 4, get up early and take the bus to **Aalsmeer,** the world's largest flower auction. Back in town, visit the **Tropenmuseum,** Amsterdam's museum of the tropics. To continue your exotic journey, visit the **Albert Cuypstraat market** next. It's lined with vendors selling all manner of goods, from fresh fish to Japanese electronics. You might even be able to catch a tour of the **Heineken Brewery** if you time things well.

On Day 5, try an all-day excursion to Enkhuizen's **Zuiderzee Museum,** a restored village featuring more than 100 houses and other buildings from around the former Zuiderzee. An alternative to this is a trip to **Haarlem** for a taste of life in a traditional Dutch village, or **Delft,** a lovely city laced with canals that's famous for its porcelain.

THE TOP MUSEUMS

The Netherlands calls itself Museum Land, and Amsterdam, with 42 museums, is its de facto capital. These museums range from the grandiose 200-plus-room Rijksmuseum to the fascinating little Amstelkring, also known as "Our Lord in the Attic."

There's a new Web site for a large group of Dutch museums: **www.hollandmuseums.nl**.

✪ **Rijksmuseum.** Stadhouderskade 42. ☎ **020/673-21-21.** Admission 15DFL ($8) adults, 7.50DFL ($3.25) seniors/ages 6–18, free for age 5 and under. Mon–Sat 10am–5pm. Closed Jan 1. Tram: 2, 5, or 20 to Museumplein.

This is the Netherlands's largest and most important collection of art, focusing, of course, on the Dutch masters: Rembrandt, Vermeer, Frans Hals, Jan Steen, and others. In addition, there are large collections of sculpture and applied arts, Asian art, prints and drawings, and Dutch antiquities.

The museum was founded in 1798 as the National Art Gallery located in The Hague. The steady growth of the collection of paintings and prints necessitated several moves: In 1808 Louis Napoléon had it moved to the Royal Palace in Amsterdam and renamed it the Royal Museum (the name Rijksmuseum—State Museum—dates from 1815). Then in 1816 it was moved to a large residence called the Trippenhuis. However, that building soon proved too small and another was sought.

After years of negotiations, architect P. J. H. Cuypers designed the core of the present museum, and this monumental neo-Gothic building opened in 1885. Since then, many additions have been made to the collections and the building so that the museum now encompasses five departments: Painting, Print Room, Sculpture and Decorative Arts, Dutch History, and Asiatic Art.

The World's Smallest Art Museum

The world's smallest art museum is now in Amsterdam, at Weteringschans, opposite the Rijksmuseum (☎ **020/627-28-32**). It's only 13.2 square meters and displays 1,500 miniature paintings, graphics, sculptures, and pictures, including works by Picasso, Lichtenstein, Oldenburg, and Christo. Admission is free, and it's open Tuesday to Saturday 10am to 6pm.

Although the museum has literally hundreds of rooms full of art, first-time visitors invariably head for *The Night Watch,* Rembrandt's most famous masterpiece. Painted in 1642 and, since 1947, correctly titled *The Shooting Company of Captain Frans Banning Cocq and Lieutenant Willem van Ruytenbuch,* this large canvas was commissioned as a group portrait to hang in a guild hall. In the two small rooms directly preceding *The Night Watch* room are several of Rembrandt's most beautiful paintings, including *The Jewish Bride* and *Self-portrait as the Apostle Paul.* Rembrandt was a master of chiaroscuro (light and shadow), and these paintings from late in his life are some of his finest. In the rooms to the left are more works by Rembrandt and other 17th-century Dutch masters.

The long-closed South Wing (now called the New Wing) was reopened in 1996. It exhibits a variety of art objects from Asia, like jewelry, Buddha sculptures, and weapons.

Note: In early 1998, the Rijksmuseum introduced an ARIA, an interactive multimedia system, so you can learn more about the museum's collections. By touching a screen, you can access information about more than 1,200 artworks, including text, illustrations, video, and animation.

✪ **Vincent van Gogh Museum.** Paulus Potterstraat 7. ☎ **020/570-52-00.** Admission 12.50DFL ($6) adults, 5DFL ($2.50) seniors/age 17 and under; recorded audio tours, 7.50DFL ($3.25). Daily 10am–5pm (ticket office closes at 4pm). Closed Jan 1. Tram: 2, 5, or 16 to Museumplein.

This modern museum houses the world's largest collection of the works—200 paintings and 500 drawings—of the 19th century's most important Dutch artist. It gives both a chronological and a thematic presentation of van Gogh's Dutch and French periods and includes his private collection of Japanese prints, magazine illustrations, and books. The museum also displays works by contemporaries who both influenced him and in turn were influenced by him; the periods before he was born and after his death are represented as well. As you view the paintings, you'll see van Gogh's early, gloomy style slowly change to one of vibrant colors and his brush strokes getting bolder as he developed his unique style.

Note: This museum will be closed for renovations from September 1998 to April 1999. Meanwhile, part of the collection will be shown at the Rijksmuseum.

Stedelijk Museum of Modern Art. Paulus Potterstraat 13. ☎ **020/573-29-11.** Admission 9DFL ($4.50) adults, 4.50DFL ($2.25) seniors/children. Daily 11am–5pm. Closed Jan 1. Tram: 2, 5, or 16 to Museumplein.

Focusing on modern art from 1850 to the present, the Stedelijk is Amsterdam's most innovative major museum. Virtually all its extensive permanent collection—including works by Chagall, Picasso, Monet, Manet, Cézanne, Mondrian, Matisse, Dubuffet, De Kooning, Appel, and Rauschenberg—is on display every summer. In winter many works are put into storage to make way for temporary exhibits and installations by artists from the current scene. The most recent trends in European and American art are well represented, so be prepared for cutting-edge works. In addition to the

The Rijksmuseum

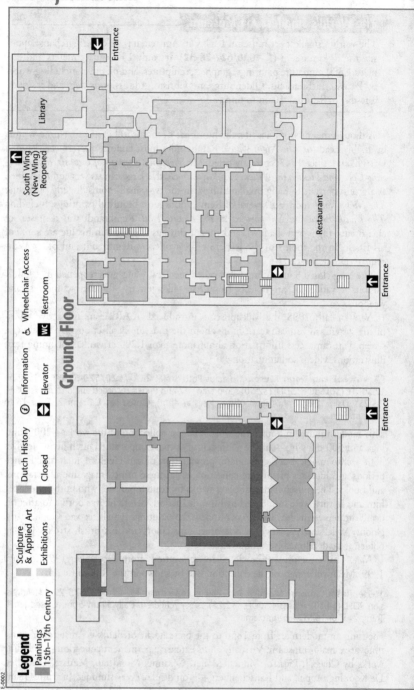

Ground Floor

Legend

Paintings
15th–17th Century

Sculpture
& Applied Art

Exhibitions

Dutch History

Closed

ⓘ Information

Elevator

♿ Wheelchair Access

WC Restroom

Library

South Wing
(New Wing)
Reopened

Entrance

Restaurant

Entrance

Entrance

E-0002

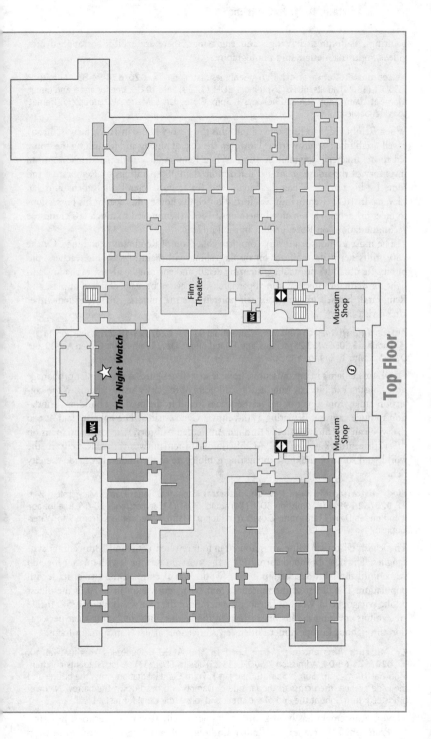

The Night Watch

Film Theater

Museum Shop

Museum Shop

Top Floor

paintings, sculptures, drawings, and engravings, there are exhibits of applied arts, videos, industrial design, and photography.

Museum Het Rembrandthuis. Jodenbreestraat 4–6. ☎ **020/624-94-86.** Admission 7.50DFL ($3.25) adults, 6DFL ($3) seniors, 5DFL ($2.50) ages 10–15, free for age 9 and under. Mon–Sat 10am–5pm, Sun and holidays 1–5pm. Closed Jan 1. Metro: Waterlooplein. Tram: 9 to Waterlooplein.

When Rembrandt van Rijn moved into this three-story house in 1639, he was already a well-established wealthy artist. However, the cost of buying and furnishing the house led to his financial downfall in 1656. When Rembrandt was declared insolvent, an inventory of the house's contents listed more than 300 paintings by Rembrandt and some by his teacher, Pieter Lasteman, and his friends Peter Paul Rubens and Jan Lievens. In 1640, Rembrandt was forced to sell the house and most of his possessions to meet his debts. He remained there until 1660, then moved to much less grandiose accommodations on Rozengracht, in the Jordaan.

The museum houses a nearly complete collection of Rembrandt's etchings. Of the 280 prints he made, 250 are on display, along with paintings by his teachers and pupils. Rembrandt's prints show amazing detail, and you can see his use of shadow and light for dramatic effect. Wizened patriarchs, emaciated beggars, children at play, and Rembrandt himself in numerous self-portraits are the subjects you'll long remember after a visit here.

Amsterdam Historisch Museum. Kalverstraat 92. ☎ **020/523-18-22.** Admission 11DFL ($6) adults, 5.50DFL ($2.25) seniors/age 16 and under. Daily 11am–5pm. Closed Apr 30 and Dec 25. Tram: 1, 2, 4, or 5 to Spui.

Of all Amsterdam's many museums, none is so well designed as this former orphanage now housing exhibits covering nearly 700 years of the city's history. Items in the collection range from a pair of old leather shoes found in the mud of a building foundation to huge canvases depicting 17th-century Civic Guards. The halls are laid out so that you can go chronologically through Amsterdam's history, with the main focus on the 17th century's golden age. At this time, Amsterdam was the richest city in the world, and some of the most interesting exhibits are of the trades that made the city rich.

Joods Historisch Museum (Jewish Historical Museum). Jonas Daniel Meiyjerplein 2–4. ☎ **020/626-99-45.** Admission 8DFL ($4) adults, 2DFL ($1) seniors/ages 10–16, free for age 9 and under. Daily 11am–5pm. Closed Yom Kippur. Metro: Waterlooplein. Tram: 9 to Waterlooplein.

The Jewish Historical Museum is housed in four restored 17th- and 18th-century synagogues. The neighborhood surrounding the museum was the Jewish quarter for 300 years, until the Nazi occupation during World War II emptied the city of its Jewish population. The oldest of the museum's four synagogues, built in 1670, is the oldest public synagogue in Western Europe; the newest of the four was built in 1752. Inside are exhibits covering the history of Jews in the Netherlands, including their persecution throughout Europe under Hitler. Jewish religious artifacts are a major focus.

✪ **Museum Amstelkring ("Our Lord in the Attic").** Oudezijds Voorburgwal 40. ☎ **020/624-66-04.** Admission 7.50DFL ($3.25) adults, 6DFL ($3) seniors/students/children. Mon–Sat 10am–5pm, Sun 1–5pm. Closed Jan 1. From Centraal Station, cross the bridge and the wide avenue, then cross to the far side of Damrak and head down the narrow Nieuwe-brugsteeg; turn right at the end of the street and follow the canal for half a block.

Though Amsterdam has been known as a tolerant city for many centuries, just after the Protestant Reformation the Roman Catholics fell into disfavor. Forced to worship in secret, they devised ingenious ways of gathering for Sunday services. In an

---

Getting the Best Deal on Sightseeing

- Take advantage of the free admission to Vondelpark, 120 acres of trees, ponds, flower beds, and picnic grounds, where in summer concerts and all kinds of open-air activities are held. Call ☎ 020/644-42-16 to find out what's going on.
- Seek out the best panoramic views of Amsterdam by climbing up the tower of the Westerkerk, Prinsengracht 279, near the Anne Frankhuis (costing 3DFL/$1.50), or by walking up the steep stairs of the Oude Kerk, Kerksplein 23. For a free view, take the elevator to the top of the Okura Hotel, Ferdinand Bolstraat 333, a few blocks south of the Rijksmuseum.
- Remember that the best (and cheapest) way to see Amsterdam is by wandering its streets and along its canals. You really can't get lost—if you're unsure where you are, just ask a passerby for directions (in English) or board any tram marked CENTRAAL STATION to return to the city center.
- The Culture and Leisure Pass offers 31 coupons worth 160DFL ($80) for only 33.60DFL ($17). Though some of the attractions may not interest you, if you use it to visit three major museums and take a canal cruise the card is a worthwhile investment.

---

otherwise ordinary-looking 17th-century canal house in the middle of the Red Light District is the most amazing of these clandestine churches, known to the general public as "Our Lord in the Attic." The three houses comprising this museum were built in the 1660s by a wealthy Catholic merchant specifically to house a church. Today they're furnished much as they would've been in the mid–18th century. Nothing prepares you for the minicathedral you come upon when you climb the last flight of stairs into the attic. A large baroque altar, religious statuary, pews to seat 150, an 18th-century organ, and an upper gallery complete this miniature church.

Tropenmuseum. Linnaeusstraat 2. ☎ **020/568-82-00.** Admission 10DFL ($5) adults, 5DFL ($2.50) seniors/ages 6–17, free for age 5 and under. Mon–Fri 10am–5pm, Sat–Sun and holidays noon–5pm. Closed Jan 1, Apr 30, May 5, and Dec 25. Tram: 9 to Linnaeusstraat. Bus: 22 from Centraal Station to Linnaeusstraat.

One of Amsterdam's finest and most unusual museums is dedicated to presenting the tropics to people living in a far different climate. On the three floors surrounding the spacious main hall are numerous life-size tableaux depicting life in tropical countries. Though there are displays of beautiful handcrafts and antiquities from these regions, the main focus is the life of the people today. There are hovels from the ghettos of Calcutta and Bombay, as well as mud-walled houses from the villages of rural India. Bamboo huts from Southeast Asia and crowded little shops no bigger than closets show you how people today live in such areas as Southeast Asia, Latin America, and Africa. Sound effects play over hidden speakers: Dogs bark, children scream, car horns blare, frogs croak, and vendors call out their wares. In the main hall and in separate halls the museum offers temporary exhibits, events, and dance and music workshops. In the Children's Museum, youngsters 6 to 12 can explore and participate in all sorts of activities.

Anne Frankhuis. Prinsengracht 263–265. ☎ **020/556-71-00.** Admission 10DFL ($5) adults, 5DFL ($2.50) students/ages 10–17, free for age 9 and under. MC, V. Apr–Aug daily 9am–9pm; Sept–May 9am–5pm. Closed Jan 1, Yom Kippur, and Dec 25. Tram: 13 or 17 to Westermarkt.

Central Amsterdam

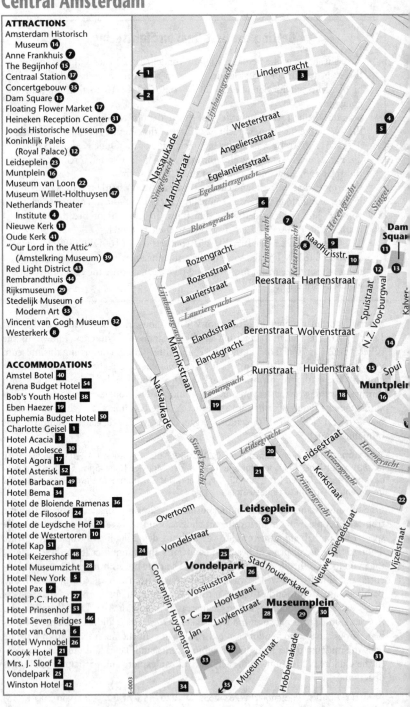

E-0003

66

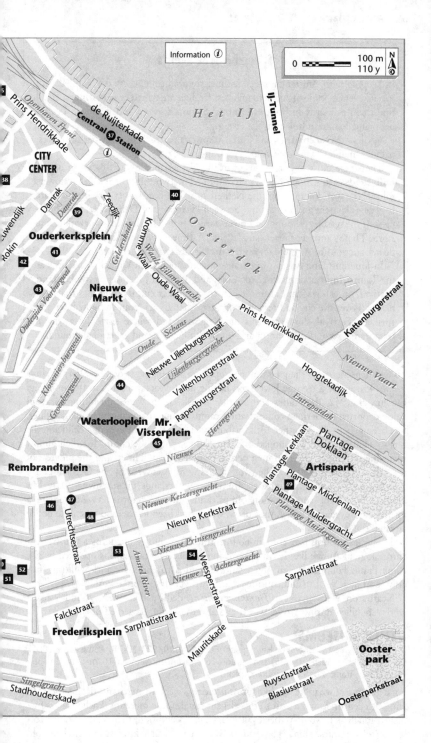

Special & Free Events

In keeping with Amsterdammers' enthusiasm about life, every day is filled with special events. Some of Amsterdam's best freebies are its **street performers.** You'll find them primarily in front of Centraal Station during the day and on Leidseplein and Rembrandtplein in the evening.

April 30 is **Queen's Day,** and the city crowds the streets to enjoy performances, parades, markets, and general merrymaking.

The single most important event in the Netherlands is the **flowering of the bulb fields** each spring from March to mid-May. Two-thirds of all the cut flowers sold in the world come from the Netherlands. The best flower-viewing areas are between Haarlem and Leiden and between Haarlem and Den Helder. The highlight of the season is the annual **flower parade** from Haarlem to Noorwijk in late April. There's another flower parade from Aalsmeer (home of the world's largest flower auction) to Amsterdam on the first Saturday in September.

In June, July, and August, **open-air concerts** are held in Vondelpark. Check at the Tourist Information Office for times and dates. In June, there's the **Holland Festival,** an extravaganza of music, dance, and other cultural offerings that take place all over the city and feature a different theme each year. In September, the **Jordaan Festival** showcases this old neighborhood where small, inexpensive restaurants, secondhand shops, and unusual boutiques and galleries are found.

Today there are more than 13 million copies in 50 languages of *The Diary of Anne Frank,* written by a teenage Jewish girl during her 2 years of hiding in this building. On July 6, 1942, the Franks and another Jewish family went into hiding to avoid being deported to German concentration camps. Anne, the youngest Frank daughter, had been given a diary for her 13th birthday in 1942. With the eyes of a child and the literary skills of a girl who hoped one day to be a writer, she chronicled their almost silent life in hiding, the continued persecution of Jews by Hitler, and the progress of the war. On August 4, 1944, the two families were discovered by the German police and deported on the last transport from the Netherlands to Auschwitz. Only Mr. Frank survived the concentration camps, and when he returned to Amsterdam a former employee gave him Anne's diary, which had been left behind when the police arrested the family.

Though the rooms here contain no furniture, the exhibits, including a year-by-year chronology of Anne's life, fill in the missing details. The museum is operated by the Anne Frank Foundation, an organization founded to eliminate anti-Semitism, fascism, and neo-Naziism and continue Anne's struggle for a better world.

Nearby on Westermarkt is *Homomonument,* dedicated to the gays and lesbians who were killed during World War II and also those who have died of AIDS.

OTHER MUSEUMS

Museum Willet-Holthuysen. Herengracht 605. ☎ **020/523-18-70.** Admission 7.50DFL ($3.75) adults, 5.50DFL ($2.25) seniors/age 16 and under. Mon–Fri 10am–5pm, Sat–Sun 11am–5pm. Tram: 4 or 9 to Rembrandtplein.

For a glimpse of what life was like for Amsterdam's wealthy merchants during the 18th and 19th centuries, pay a visit to this elegant canal-house museum. Each room is furnished much as it would've been 200 years ago. In addition, there's an extensive collection of ceramics, china, glass, and silver. Of particular interest are the large old kitchen and the formal garden in back.

Checking Out the Red Light District

The warren of streets around Oudezijds Achterburgwal and Oudezijds Voorburgwal by the Oude Kerk is the **Red Light District (Walletjes),** one of the most famous features of Amsterdam sightseeing (take tram no. 9 or 14 to Mr. Visserplein or the Metro to Waterlooplein). It's extraordinary to see women of all nationalities dressed in exotic underwear and perched in windows waiting for customers. With radios and TVs blaring, they knit, brush their hair, or just slink enticingly in their seats.

The Red Light District has now become a major attraction not only for customers of storefront sex but also for sightseers. If you choose to go, though, you need to exercise some caution. Avoid the area at night and watch out for pickpockets at all times. In a neighborhood where anything seems permissible the one no-no is taking pictures: Violate this rule and your camera could be removed from you and broken.

Koninklijk Paleis (Royal Palace). Dam Square. ☎ **020/624-86-98.** Admission 5DFL ($2.50) adults, 3DFL ($1.50) seniors/ages 13–18, 2DFL ($1) age 12 and under. June–Aug daily 12:30–5pm; Sept–May Tues–Thurs 1–4pm. To get here, walk down Damrak from Centraal Station.

Built in the 17th century on top of 13,659 wooden pilings to prevent it from sinking into the soft Amsterdam soil, the Royal Palace was originally the Town Hall. At the time it was built, the building was referred to as the Eighth Wonder of the World because of its immense size (it was the largest town hall ever built) and the fact that it used so many pilings to support it. In 1808, the building was converted into a palace. The dazzling interior is filled with sculptures, frescoes, and furniture. In summer (occasionally in other months as well), conducted tours are given.

Theater Institute Nederland. Herengracht 168. ☎ **020/551-33-00.** Admission 7.50DFL ($3.25) adults, 4DFL ($2) seniors. Tues–Fri 11am–5pm, Sat–Sun 1–5pm. Tram: 13, 14, or 17 to Dam Square.

Splendid marble corridors, wall and ceiling frescoes, and ornate plasterwork make this patrician canal house one of the city's most beautiful. Richly ornamented roof gables of different styles were a sign of wealth during Amsterdam's golden age, and crowning this building is the oldest extant example of an ornate neck gable. Although it's worth visiting this museum simply to see how the wealthy once lived, there are also many interesting exhibits pertaining to theater in the Netherlands over the centuries. Be sure to press the buttons of the miniature stage sets: You'll see how waves once rolled across the stage and other equally dramatic effects.

CHURCHES

Nieuwe Kerk. Dam Square. ☎ **020/638-69-09.** Admission and opening hours vary depending on the exhibit or event. To get here, walk down Damrak from Centraal Station.

This church across from the Royal Palace is new in name only. Construction on this Late Gothic structure was begun about 1400, but much of the interior, including the organ, dates from the 17th century. Since 1815, all Dutch kings and queens have been crowned here. Today the church is used primarily as a cultural center where special art exhibits are held. Regular performances on the church's huge organ are held in summer.

Oude Kerk. Oudekerksplein 1. ☎ **020/624-91-83.** Admission 5DFL ($2.50) adults, 3.50 ($1.75) seniors/students. Mon–Sat 11am–5pm, Sun 1–5pm. Walk 3 blocks from Damrak to the middle of the Red Light District.

This Gothic church from the 13th century is the city's oldest. Its many stained-glass windows are particularly beautiful. Inside are monumental tombs, including that of Rembrandt's wife, Saskia van Uylenburg. The organ, built in 1724, is played regularly in summer; many connoisseurs believe it has the best tone of any organ in the world. During summer you can climb the 230-foot-high tower for an excellent view of Old Amsterdam.

Westerkerk. Prinsengracht 279. ☎ **020/624-77-66.** Church, free; tower, 3DFL ($1.50); concerts, about 25DFL ($13) depending on the artist. May 15–Sept 15 Mon–Sat 10am–4pm. Closed Sept 16–May 14. Tram: 13 or 17 to Westermarkt.

Built between 1620 and 1630, this church is a masterpiece of Dutch Renaissance style. At the top of the 275-foot-high tower is a giant replica of the imperial crown of Maximilian of Austria. Somewhere in this church (no one knows where) is Rembrandt's grave. During summer, regular organ concerts are played on a 300-year-old instrument. Also in summer you can climb the tower.

OTHER ATTRACTIONS

The Begijnhof. Spui. Free admission. Daily 8am–8pm. Tram: 1, 2, or 5 to Spui.

Only steps from Amsterdam's busiest pedestrian shopping street is the city's most tranquil spot. Hidden behind a nondescript facade is a courtyard ringed with restored almshouses. Since the 14th century the Begijnhof has been home to poor widows and lay nuns of the order of the Beguines (Begijns in Dutch; *Begijnhof* means Beguine Court). The oldest and one of the last remaining wooden houses in Amsterdam is here at no. 34, built in 1475. In the center of the courtyard are a clandestine Roman Catholic church and an English Presbyterian church.

Artis Zoo. Plantage Kerklaan 40. ☎ **020/523-34-00.** Admission (including zoo, children's farm, planetarium, and zoological museum) 23.50DFL ($12) adults, 15.50DFL ($8) age 10 and under. Daily 9am–5pm. Tram: 7, 9, or 14 to Artis Zoo.

Great for all ages, this zoo was established in 1838, making it the oldest in the Netherlands. It houses over 6,000 animals and features a children's farm, a planetarium, an aquarium, and a geological/zoological museum.

PARKS & GARDENS

When the sun shines in Amsterdam, people head for the parks. The most popular and conveniently located of Amsterdam's 20 parks is **Vondelpark,** only a short walk from Leidseplein. Covering 122 acres, its lakes, ponds, and streams are surrounded by meadows, trees, and colorful flowers. This park, open daily 8am to sunset, is extremely popular in summer with young people from all over the world.

Farther from the city center are many more large parks, such as the huge **Amsterdamse Bos,** covering more than 2,000 acres and providing hiking, biking, and horseback-riding trails, as well as picnic areas and campgrounds. Closer to the city center are **Rembrandtpark, Artis Zoo,** and **Oosterpark.**

EXPLORING THE CANAL HOUSES

The fascinating narrow **canal houses** and warehouses built primarily during the 17th century are not only beautiful to look at (and best viewed from a boat cruising the canals) but also great places to stay. All the canal-house hotels listed earlier feature steep narrow stairways and other original period touches. You'll have to crane your neck a bit to appreciate the beauty of these old houses fully since their most striking features are their gables. The largest are on Herengracht, but the smaller houses on other canals (especially in the Jordaan) are more interesting architecturally.

To see the inside of some restored canal houses other than hotels, visit the **Theater Institute Netherlands,** Herengracht 168 (☎ **020/623-51-04**); and the **Museum Willet-Holthuysen,** Herengracht 605 (☎ **020/523-18-70**)—see above for hours and admission—or the **Museum van Loon,** Keizersgracht 672 (☎ **020/624-52-55**). An interesting contrast to these grand mansions is Amsterdam's narrowest house (only a yard wide) at Singel 7.

ORGANIZED TOURS

WALKING TOURS   Though you could see most of Amsterdam's important sights in one long walking tour, it's best to break the city into smaller tours. Luckily, the Tourist Information Office has done that. For 3.50DFL ($1.75) you can buy a brochure outlining one of four walking tours: *Voyage of Discovery Through Amsterdam, A Walk Through Jewish Amsterdam, A Walk Through the Jordaan,* or *A Walk Through Maritime Amsterdam.*

BUS TOURS   For a much faster tour that covers much of the same ground as the walking tours, try one of the 3-hour guided bus tours offered by **NZH Travel,** Damrak between Centraal Station and the Victoria Hotel (☎ **020/625-07-72**), or **Lindbergh Excursions,** Damrak 26 (☎ **020/622-27-66**). The basic tour costs 27.50DFL ($14), but for 45DFL ($23) you get a visit to a diamond cutter, a canal cruise, and a ticket to the Rijksmuseum.

BOAT TOURS   Gazing up from a boat on a canal is the best way to view the old houses and warehouses. If you have to choose among a walking tour, a bus tour, and a boat tour, definitely take a boat. This is a city built on the shipping trade, so it's only fitting you should see it from the water, just as the merchants of the 17th century's golden age saw their city.

The city is filled with canal-boat docks, all of which have signs stating the time of the next tour. Tours last 1 hour and cost 12DFL to 15DFL ($6 to $8). The greatest concentration of canal-boat operators is along Damrak, a block from Centraal Station. Since the tours are all basically the same, simply pick the one that's most convenient for you.

A BREWERY TOUR   The **Heineken Brewery Museum,** Stadhouderskade 78 (☎ **020/523-96-66**), is a short walk along Singelgracht from the Rijksmuseum. Tours are held Monday to Friday at 9:30 and 11am (also at 1 and 2:30pm June to September 15), and the only charge is a 2DFL ($1) donation given to several charities. Heineken opened its first Amsterdam brewery in 1864, and over the years it expanded as its beer gained popularity. The guides take you on a "history of beer" tour explaining the brewing process (highlighting the Heineken story) and show you the characteristic copper brew house, the horse stables, and many other facilities traditionally used in beer brewing. After watching a film on the company's history, you'll be invited to sample the beer, served with snacks, in a large room overlooking the city.

DIAMOND FACTORY TOURS   For more than 400 years Amsterdam has been associated with diamonds, and while you're here be sure to take a tour of a diamond-cutting and -polishing facility. Tours are offered daily at many of the largest companies. The tours show you how the rough stones are cut and polished, a process that reduces 50% of every stone to diamond dust. There's no pressure to buy stones or jewelry when you're taken to the company's showroom as part of the tour. Here your guide will show you the different cuts and how to determine the quality of a diamond. Diamond cutting is a very specialized skill and is still done by hand.

Diamond factories offering free individual and small-group tours include the **Amsterdam Diamond Center,** Rokin 1 (☎ **020/624-57-87**), just off Dam Square, down Damrak from Centraal Station, open daily 10am to 5:30pm (to 8:30pm Thursday); **Coster Diamonds,** Paulus Potterstraat 2–6 (☎ **020/676-22-22**), reachable by tram nos. 1, 2, or 5 to Museumplein, open daily 9am to 5pm; and **Van Moppes Diamonds,** Albert Cuypstraat 2–6 (☎ **020/676-12-42**), near the Albert Cuypstraat stop on tram nos. 16, 24, or 25, and open daily 9:30am to 6pm.

6 Shopping

Strolling Amsterdam's streets, you could get the impression that the city is one giant outdoor shopping mall. Everywhere you look are stores ranging in price and variety from the Jordaan's used clothing shops and bookstores to P. C. Hooftstraat's designer boutiques. Alas, most stores offer little in the way of bargains. However, many typically Dutch souvenirs and gift items might appeal to you and can be real bargains if you shop around.

The **main shopping areas** are Nieuwendijk and Kalverstraat. On these streets you'll find inexpensive clothing stores, plus many souvenir shops—recommendable is **Delftware,** Nieuwendijk 24 (☎ **020/627-39-74**), with friendly owners who accept all credit cards. Amsterdam's upscale shopping area is **P. C. Hooftstraat,** near Museumplein, a street lined with designer boutiques and expensive restaurants. For secondhand goods, wander the streets of the **Jordaan,** and for pricey antiques, try **Nieuwe Spiegelstraat,** which leads to the Rijksmuseum.

Magna Plaza, a splendid three-story shopping mall, is at the corner of Nieuwezijds Voorburgwal and Raadhuisstraat, a 1-minute walk from Dam Square. Here you can find almost everything there is to buy in Amsterdam—except food. You'll find paperbacks by the thousand at **W. H. Smith,** Kalverstraat 152, at the corner of Spui (☎ **020/638-38-21**). British travelers will find a taste of home at **Marks & Spencer,** Kalverstraat 66 (☎ **020/620-00-06**). And two of Amsterdam's largest department stores, the **Bijenkorf** and **C&A,** face each other on Damrak near Dam Square.

Most shops that deal with tourists will be happy to **ship your purchases home** for an additional charge. If you want to ship something yourself, go to the Main Post Office, where there's a special counter selling boxes and packing materials. They'll also provide you with the necessary Customs forms to fill out.

Watch for the TAX FREE FOR TOURISTS signs in shop windows. These stores will provide you with a form for claiming a **refund of the VAT (value-added tax).** This refund amounts to 14.9% of the total cost of purchases here and throughout the Netherlands. However, before you can get a refund you'll have to make a purchase of at least 300DFL ($150) in a participating store. When you're leaving the European Union by air, you must present the form and the goods to Customs. After Customs has stamped your form, you mail it directly from Customs. Your refund will be mailed to you within 10 days or credited to your credit card account. You can also claim an immediate cash refund at any Grens Wissel Kantoor (GWK) office and in Schiphol Airport at the ABN–Amro bank.

MARKETS

Amsterdam's two most famous markets are the **Waterlooplein flea market** and the **Albert Cuypstraat open-air market.** Both generally sell the same sorts of goods, but you can still find a few antiques and near-antiques on Waterlooplein. The flea market surrounds the modern Muziektheater building. Most of what's offered these days is used and cheap clothing. On Albert Cuypstraat you'll find more cheap clothing than you'd ever want to look at, plus fresh fish, Asian vegetables, fresh-cut flowers, electronics, cosmetics, and all the assorted people who buy and sell such an array of products. Both markets are open Monday to Saturday 9am to 5pm.

Other Amsterdam markets are the **Sunday Antiques Market,** by the Weigh House on Nieuwmarkt, open May to October 10am to 4pm. The ✪ **Floating Flower Market** is along Singel between Muntplein and Leidsestraat, open Monday to Saturday 9am to 5pm. There's a **flea market** on Noordermarkt in the Jordaan on Monday morning and a farmer's market on Saturday 10am to 3pm. The **book market** on Oudemanhuispoort, between Oudezijds Voorburgwal and Kloveniersburgwal on the edge of the Red Light District, is held Monday to Saturday 10am to 4pm; another is held on the Spui on Friday 10am to 6pm. On Sunday 10am to 5pm there's an **art market** on the Spui.

7 Amsterdam After Dark

Since **Leidseplein** and **Rembrandtplein** are Amsterdam's nightlife centers, you'll find dozens of bars, nightclubs, cafes, dance clubs, and movie theaters around these two squares. However, more cultured evening entertainment is to be found in various parts of the city.

For listings of the week's performances in the many theaters and concert halls, consult *What's On in Amsterdam,* a magazine available for 3.50DFL ($1.75) at the Tourist Information Office in front of Centraal Station or on Leidseplein. At these locations you can also make reservations and buy tickets for shows at many venues. *Uitkrant* is a monthly free paper in Dutch that has an even more thorough listing of events. It's available in various clubs around town as well as any tourist information office.

THE PERFORMING ARTS

THEATER & CLASSICAL MUSIC   The **Royal Carré Theatre,** Amstel 115–125 (☎ **020/622-52-25;** Metro: Weesperplein), a huge old domed theater on the Amstel River near the Skinny Bridge, occasionally presents touring plays from New York's Broadway or London's West End. The box office is open Monday to Saturday 10am to 7pm and Sunday 1 to 7pm. Tickets go for 25DFL to 115DFL ($13 to $58).

The world-famous ✪ **Concertgebouw,** Concertgebouwplein 2–6 (☎ **020/671-83-45;** Tram: 2, 3, 5, 12, or 16), with its ornate Greek Revival facade, is said to have some of the best acoustics of any hall in the world. Performances, including those by the renowned **Royal Concertgebouw Orchestra,** are held almost every night in the building's two halls. There are free concerts on Wednesday at 12:30pm. The box office is open daily 10am to 7pm. Tickets range from 15DFL to 210DFL ($8 to $105). The impressive **Beurs van Berlage,** Damrak 243 (☎ **020/627-04-66;** Tram: 1, 2, 4, 5, 9, 16, or 24), was once the Amsterdam stock exchange, but a few years ago it was converted into two concert halls that host frequent symphony performances. The box office is open Tuesday to Friday 12:30 to 6pm and Saturday noon to 5pm. Tickets are 12DFL to 55DFL ($6 to $28). The recently rebuilt **Koepelkerk church,** Kattengat 1 (☎ **020/616-77-91;** Tram: Centraal Station), has begun offering Sunday jazz and classical concerts. Try to see a concert on the famous Baetz organ. Ticket prices depend on the performance but generally run 25DFL ($13).

OPERA & DANCE The ultramodern 1,600-seat **Het Muziektheater,** Amstel 3 (☎ **020/625-54-55;** Tram: 9 or 14), caused quite a stir when it was built, for Amsterdammers thought the architecture clashed with the neighborhood. The innovative **Netherlands Opera,** the famed **Netherlands Dance Theater,** and the **Dutch National Ballet** perform here. The box office is open Monday to Saturday 10am to 8pm and Sunday 11:30am to 6pm. Tickets cost 20DFL to 100DFL ($10 to $50).

The 1894 **Stadsschouwburg,** Leidseplein 26 (☎ **020/624-23-11;** Tram: 1, 2, or 5), Amsterdam's former opera and ballet theater, is neoclassical with Dutch Renaissance features. Performances include plays in Dutch and English, plus music and dance performances by international companies. The box office is open daily 10am to 6pm. Tickets are 15DFL to 75DFL ($8 to $42).

LIVE-MUSIC CLUBS

Listed here are some of Amsterdam's biggest and most popular clubs, booking up-and-coming acts and always charging admission. However, plenty of smaller clubs showcase local bands and charge no admission.

Check out the **Bamboo Bar,** Lange Leidsedwarstraat 64 (☎ **020/624-39-93**), and the **Café Alto,** Korte Leidsedwarstraat 115 (☎ **020/626-32-49**), for nightly live jazz; and the funky **Bourbon Street,** Leidsekruisstraat 6–8 (☎ **020/623-34-40**), for nightly blues and rock. All three clubs are near Leidseplein. **De IJsbreker,** Weesperzijde 23 (☎ **020/668-18-05;** Metro: Weesperplein), is a pleasant cafe on the banks of the Amstel that offers an interesting mix of contemporary classical music and avant-garde jazz. Admission runs 15DFL to 25DFL ($8 to $13).

The world beat music scene is very much alive in cosmopolitan Amsterdam, and **Akhnaton,** Nieuwezijds Kolk 25 (☎ **020/624-33-96;** Tram: 1, 2, 5, 13, or 17), is the most popular club for ethnic rhythms. There might be a night of Latin dance music, hip-hop block jam, African drumming, and Persian music. It's generally open Wednesday to Sunday 9pm to 3am, but hours are irregular, so call ahead. The cover is 10DFL to 15DFL ($5 to $8). Housed in an old canalside warehouse, ✪ **Bimhuis,** Oude Schans 73–77 (☎ **020/623-13-61;** Metro: Waterlooplein), is Amsterdam's premier jazz club. Music workshops are on Tuesday at 8pm (no admission), and during the rest of the week jazz musicians from all over Europe perform. It's open Monday to Saturday 8pm to 3am. The cover is 15DFL to 25DFL ($8 to $13).

Melkweg, Lijnbaangracht 234A, just off Leidseplein behind the Stadsschouwburg (☎ **020/624-17-77;** Tram: 1, 2, or 5), is very popular, with activities starting at 8pm and continuing until the early hours. You can see films, dance to recorded music, hang out in the restaurant or cafe, view the changing art exhibits, hear a live band, or watch art videos. It's open Wednesday to Sunday 2pm to midnight. The cover is 10DFL to 35DFL ($5 to $18). In a former church, **Paradiso,** Weteringschans 6–8, near Leidseplein (☎ **020/626-45-21;** Tram: 1, 2, or 5), is an Amsterdam landmark. In addition to regular rock, pop, and jazz concerts, there are political forums, lectures, and festivals. It's open daily with hours that vary depending on the program. The cover is 10DFL to 35DFL ($5 to $18), plus 4.50DFL ($2.25) for a monthly membership.

BARS & BROWN CAFES

Particularly old and traditional bars often earn the appellation of **brown cafe.** The name is said to have been derived as much from the preponderance of wood furnishings as from the browning of the walls from years of dense tobacco smoke. To experience Amsterdam conviviality, head to one of these cafes (be prepared for thick smog when you walk through the doors). Here you'll encounter a warm and friendly atmosphere where you can sit and sip a glass of beer or a mixed drink and even get a cheap meal.

There are countless bars in Amsterdam, most around Leidseplein and Rembrandt-plein. They don't start to get busy until at least 10pm, though they usually open at noon and stay open all day. In both the cafes and the bars, the most popular drink is draft Heineken served in small glasses with two fingers of head on top for around 4DFL ($2). Also popular is *genever* (Dutch gin) available in *jonge* (young) and *oude* (old) varieties—oude is quite a bit stronger in taste and alcoholic content. Genever shots start at 4DFL ($2) as well.

Most cafes and bars are open Sunday to Thursday noon to 1am and Friday and Saturday noon to 2am. On Sunday from about 6pm on, you'll find live traditional Dutch music in several bars on Rembrandtplein.

Cafe Papeneiland, Prinsengracht 2, at the corner of Brouwersgracht (☎ 020/624-19-89; Bus: Haarlemmer Houttuinen), is Amsterdam's oldest cafe: Since 1600 or thereabouts, folks have been dropping by for shots of genever and glasses of beer. The walls near the huge front windows are covered with blue-and-white tiles, and there's an old woodstove. If you have a feeling of déjà vu while here, it's probably because you saw the same view in a painting in the Amsterdam Historisch Museum.

Originally a tasting house where people could try liqueurs distilled and aged on the premises, ✪ **De Drie Fleschjes,** Gravenstraat 18, between the Nieuwe Kerk and Nieuwendijk (☎ 020/624-84-43; Tram: 13 or 17), has been in business for more than 300 years. One wall is lined with old wood aging barrels. De Drie Fleschjes is popular with businesspeople and journalists, who stop by to sample the wide variety of oude and jonge genevers. It's open Monday to Saturday noon to 8:30pm and Sunday 3 to 7pm.

Though you'll see signs for Hoppe genever in front of most cafes, there's only one **Cafe Hoppe,** Spui 18–20 (☎ 020/420-44-20; Tram: 1, 2, or 5)—one of Amsterdam's oldest, most traditional, and most popular brown cafes. The dark walls, low ceilings, and old wooden furniture have literally remained unchanged since the cafe opened in 1670.

In the Jordaan, **De Twee Zwaantjes,** Prinsengracht 114 (☎ 020/625-27-29), is a small brown cafe popular with locals and visitors alike for its weekend sing-alongs. Late in the evening the musical instruments begin to show up, and once everyone has had enough Heineken and genever, the old music begins. You're welcome to join in and learn a few traditional Amsterdam favorites while the accordion wheezes away.

The concept of the "Grand Cafe" has recently taken Amsterdam by storm. New Amsterdammers, tired of cramped and crowded brown cafes, have been flocking to these new large cafes. One of the best is **De Kroon Royal Cafe,** Rembrandtplein 15 (☎ 020/625-20-11; Tram: 4, 9, or 14). On the second floor of a building over-looking Rembrandtplein, it features such unusual decor as old display cabinets of stuffed animals and human anatomy models. Whether you're in jeans or theater attire, you'll feel comfortable here.

Another comfortable hangout is ✪ **Café Schuim,** Spuistraat 189 (☎ 020/638-93-57; Tram: 1, 2, or 5). Flea market tables, armchairs left over from the 1970s, and rotating exhibits of rather puzzling artwork have made this large space the cafe of the moment in the Dam Square neighborhood. The rumpled surroundings attract an assortment of creative types who debate and discuss during the week and try to avoid being crushed by mobs on weekend nights.

On summer evenings trendies head to the terrace of **Vertigo Café,** Vondelpark 3 (☎ 020/612-30-21; Tram: 1), in the middle of Vondelpark for the liveliest scene in town. Inside, the low arched ceilings, subtle lighting, and unobtrusive music set a mood of casual sophistication. The pricey menu is nouveau Italian, with exotic pasta combinations, salads, bruschetta, and carpaccio.

GAY & LESBIAN BARS

Amsterdam bills itself as the gay capital of Europe, proud of its open and tolerant attitude toward homosexuality. There are lots of bars and dance clubs for gay men all over the city but far fewer lesbian spots. Generally you'll find the trendier spots around **Rembrandtplein,** a more casual atmosphere on **Kerkstraat** near Leidseplein, and leather bars on **Warmoesstraat.**

Some of the more popular places for men are **Exit,** Reguliersdwarsstraat 42 (☎ 020/624-77-78), a disco that attracts a younger crowd; **iT,** Amstelstraat 24 (☎ 020/625-01-11), Amsterdam's most famous and flamboyant disco; **Cockring,** Warmoesstraat 96 (☎ 020/623-96-04), a popular disco; **Argos,** Warmoesstraat 95 (☎ 020/622-65-72), Europe's oldest leather bar; and **Cosmos,** Kerkstraat 42 (☎ 020/624-77-78), a late-night bar. **Saarein,** Elandstraat 119 (☎ 020/623-49-01), near Leidseplein, is a women-only bar. **Vive la Vie,** Amstelstraat 7 (☎ 020/624-01-14), on the edge of Rembrandtplein, is a lively lesbian bar that hosts periodic parties.

DANCE CLUBS

You'll find dozens of large and small clubs around **Leidseplein** and **Rembrandtplein.** They tend to rise and fall in popularity, so ask someone in a cafe what the current favorite is.

Arena, s'Gravesandestraat 51 (☎ 020/625-87-88; Tram 3, 6, 7, or 10), is part of the popular hostel (see above). The club offers house, garage, and techno on Friday and classic rock on Saturday. The cover is 12.50DFL ($6). **Escape,** Rembrandtplein 11 (☎ 020/625-20-11; Tram: 4, 9, or 14), is large and popular. Here you have a choice of several dance floors, all with flashing lights and a great sound system. It's open Thursday 10pm to 4am and Friday and Saturday 10pm to 5am. The cover is 10DFL to 20DFL ($5 to $10), free for students on Thursday.

Odeon, Singel 460 (☎ 020/624-97-11; Tram: 1, 2, 5, or 11), is a three-floor dance club with different music on each floor—house music for young people, golden oldies from the 1960s and 1970s for nostalgic baby-boomers, and a pop/jazz mellow mood on the top floor. The cover is 5DFL to 12.50DFL ($2.50 to $6). The ✪ **Roxy,** Singel 465 (☎ 020/620-03-54; Tram: 1, 2, 5, or 11), a huge multilevel club (space for 450) created from an old movie theater near the flower market, has for many years been the place to go dancing. The place stays packed on weekends despite a draconian door policy that excludes all but the most glamorous. It's open Wednesday, Thursday, and Sunday 11pm to 4am and Friday and Saturday 11pm to 5am. Wednesday is "hard" night for gay men only. The cover is 10DFL to 20DFL ($5 to $10).

8 Side Trips: Dikes, Windmills & Villages

If Amsterdam is your only stop in the Netherlands, try to make at least one excursion into the countryside. Dikes, windmills, and some of Holland's quaintest villages await you just beyond the city limits.

ZAANSE SCHANS

If you have time for only one excursion, make this the one. ✪ **Zaanse Schans** is a beautiful little village on the banks of the river Zaan 15 miles north of Amsterdam. Along the riverbank are six windmills, two of which are still operating and can be visited. Surrounding the village are pastures where cows graze, and the nearby cocoa factory fills the air with the smell of chocolate.

The windmill museum in Zaanse Schans is open daily April to November 1, on weekends only during the rest of the year. The best way to get here is by **train** from Amsterdam's Centraal Station. There are departures every 30 minutes and the trip takes 15 minutes. Take a train bound for Alkmaar that makes local stops and get off at the Koog–Zaandijk station; from the station, follow the signs. It's about an 8-minute walk. The round-trip fare is 8.75DFL ($4.35). A railway excursion ticket, for 25DFL ($13), includes round-trip rail fare, a 45-minute cruise on the river, coffee and a pancake in the De Krai pancake restaurant, and admission to the Zaandam Clockwork Museum. For information, call ☎ **075/16-82-18.** If you're **driving,** take A10 in the direction of Zaanstad, then A7 in the direction of Leeuwarden, following the signs to Zaanse Schans.

DELFT

Yes, **Delft,** 38 miles south of Amsterdam, is the city of the famous blue-and-white earthenware. And, yes, you can visit the factory of De Porceleyne Fles, as long as you realize it's only a visit to a showroom and not the painting studios and other workrooms. But don't let Delftware be your only reason to visit. Not only is this one of the prettiest small cities in Holland but also Delft is important as a cradle of the Dutch Republic and the traditional burial place of the royal family. Plus, it was the birthplace (and inspiration) of the 17th-century master of light and subtle emotion, painter Jan Vermeer. Delft remains a quiet little town, with flowers in its flower boxes and linden trees bending over its gracious canals.

ARRIVING   For **bus** information, call ☎ **020/651-27-93.** There are **several** trains per hour from Amsterdam's Centraal Station. The trip takes about 1 hour and 10 minutes and costs 32DFL ($16) round-trip. If you're **driving,** take A13 in the direction of The Hague and watch for the Delft exit.

SEEING THE SIGHTS   The house where Vermeer was born, lived, and painted is long gone from Delft, as are his paintings. Instead, you can visit the **Oude Kerk,** at Roland Holstlaan 753, where he's buried; it's open April to October, Monday to Saturday 10am to 5pm. You might want to visit the **Nieuwe Kerk,** on Markt near the VVV office, where Prince William of Orange and all other members of the House of Orange–Nassau are buried. It's open Monday to Saturday 11am to 5pm; its tower is open May to September, Tuesday to Saturday 10am to 4:30pm.

The **Prinsenhof Museum,** Sint-Agathaplein 1 (☎ **015/260-23-58**), on the nearby Oude Delft canal, is where William I of Orange (William the Silent) lived and had his headquarters in the years during which he helped found the Dutch Republic. It's also where he was assassinated in 1584 (you can still see the musket-ball holes in the stairwell). Today, however, the Prinsenhof is a museum of paintings, tapestries, silverware, and pottery. It's open Tuesday to Saturday 10am to 5pm and Sunday 1 to 5pm. Admission is 5DFL ($2.50) adults and 2.50DFL ($1.75) ages 12 to 16.

In the same neighborhood you can see a fine collection of old Delft tiles displayed in the wood-paneled setting of a 19th-century mansion museum called **Lambert van Meerten,** at Oude Delft 199 (☎ **015/260-23-58**); it's open Tuesday to Saturday 10am to 5pm and Sunday 1 to 5pm and charges an admission of 3.50DFL ($1.75). Or to see brand-new Delftware and a demonstration of the art of hand-painting it, visit the showroom of **De Porceleyne Fles,** Rotterdamseweg 196 (☎ **015/256-92-14**). April to October, it's open Monday to Saturday 9am to 5pm and Sunday 9:30am to 4pm; November to March, the hours are Monday to Saturday 9am to 5pm. Admission is free.

ACCOMMODATIONS Delft isn't chock full of budget accommodations, but in a pinch you could try the pensions near the train station. They tend to fill up fast in summer, however. Another possibility is **'T Raedthuys,** Markt 38 (☎ **015/ 212-5115;** fax 015/213-6069), with 9 rooms (some with bath). Doubles are 95DFL ($48) without a bathroom and 125DFL ($63) with a bathroom, breakfast included. American Express, Diners Club, MasterCard, and Visa are accepted. Also in the town center and slightly more expensive is **De Koophandel,** Beestenmarkt 30 (☎ **015/214-2302;** fax 015/214-0674), which has 14 rooms, all with bathroom (tub or shower) for 140DFL ($70), breakfast included. American Express, Diners Club, MasterCard, and Visa are accepted.

DINING Delft has a full panoply of Dutch and international restaurants. The best is **Spijshuis de Dis,** Beestenmarkt 36 (☎ **015/213-1782**), where a meal is about 35DFL ($18). Although the specialty is steak, the pork filet with vegetables and the lamb filet are delicious. Try the homemade mushroom soup. It's open Thursday to Tuesday 5 to 9:30pm and accepts American Express, Diners Club, MasterCard, and Visa. **Stadsherberg de Mol,** Molslaan 104 (☎ **015/212-1343**), is a large, fun place with live music and dancing that offers a 39DFL ($20) fixed-price menu. The food is served medieval style in wooden bowls, and you eat with your hands. It's open Tuesday to Sunday 6 to 11pm and accepts Visa and MasterCard.

AALSMEER FLOWER AUCTION

The Netherlands is the world's largest exporter of cut flowers, and nearly 50% of the flowers that leave the country are sold at the massive **Aalsmeer Flower Auction.** Nothing could adequately prepare you for the sight of these acres of cut flowers stacked three tiers high on moving carts. In two auction halls, hundreds of buyers compete for the best flowers at the lowest prices. The auction is open Monday to Friday 7:30 to 11am. Admission is 7.50DFL ($3.25).

To reach the auction in Aalsmeer, take **bus no. 172** from in front of the Victoria Hotel across the square from Centraal Station. The trip will take five strips on your strippenkaart. For further information, call ☎ **0297/39-00-62.** If you're **driving,** take A4 and follow the signs to Aalsmeer.

ALKMAAR

One of the most popular summer excursions is to the **open-air cheese market** in Alkmaar, 28 miles north of Amsterdam. Held between mid-April and September, Friday 10am to noon, the cheese market attracts thousands of picture-taking visitors to this historic old town. Huge piles of yellow cheese cover the paving stones of Alkmaar's main square while men in white suits and red, yellow, green, or blue hats rush about carrying wooden platforms stacked with still more rounds. When the auction is over, be sure to take time to explore the town. For more information, call ☎ **072/511-42-84.**

Trains leave regularly from Amsterdam's Centraal Station for the 45-minute trip to Alkmaar. A round-trip ticket is 19.25DFL ($10). If you're **driving,** take A10 and follow the signs to A9 north.

HAARLEM

Haarlem, 13 miles west of Amsterdam, is a graceful town of winding canals and medieval neighborhoods that also boasts several fine museums. The best time to visit is Saturday, for the market in Grote Markt, or in tulip season (March to mid-May), when the city explodes with flowers.

Haarlem is only an hour from Amsterdam by **train,** and a train leaves every hour from Centraal Station. A round-trip ticket is 10.50DFL ($5). There are also frequent **buses;** call ☎ 0900/92-92 for information. If you go by **car,** take route A16.

Haarlem is where Frans Hals, Jacob van Ruysdael, and Pieter Saenredam were living and painting their famous portraits, landscapes, and church interiors while Rembrandt was living and working in Amsterdam. It's also a city to which both Handel and Mozart made special visits just to play the magnificent organ of the **Church of St. Bavo,** also known as Grote Kerk, Oude Groenmarkt 23. Look for the tombstone of painter Frans Hals and for a cannonball that has been embedded in the wall ever since it came flying through a window during the 1572–73 siege of Haarlem. And, of course, don't miss seeing the famous **Christian Muller Organ,** built in 1738. You can hear it at one of the free concerts given on Tuesday and Thursday April to October. It has 5,068 pipes and is nearly 98 feet tall. The woodwork was done by Jan van Logteren. Mozart played the organ in 1766 when he was just 10 years old. St. Bavo's is open Monday to Saturday 10am to 4pm.

From St. Bavo's, it's an easy walk to the oldest and perhaps the most unusual museum in Holland, the **Teylers Museum,** Spaarne 16 (☎ 023/531-90-10). It contains a curious collection: drawings by Michelangelo, Raphael, and Rembrandt; fossils, minerals, and skeletons; instruments of physics and an odd assortment of inventions, including the largest electrostatic generator in the world (1784) and a 19th-century radarscope. It's open Tuesday to Saturday 10am to 5pm and Sunday noon to 5pm. Admission is 7.50DFL ($3.25) adults, 5DFL ($2.50) seniors, and 3.50DFL ($1.75) ages 5 to 15.

Saving the best for last, visit the **Frans Halsmuseum,** Groot Heiligeland 62 (☎ 023/516-42-00), where the galleries are the halls and furnished chambers of a former pensioners' home, and the famous paintings by the masters of the Haarlem school hang in settings that look like the 17th-century homes they were intended to adorn. It's open Monday to Saturday 11am to 5pm and Sunday 1 to 5pm. Admission is 7.50DFL ($3.75) adults and 3.50DFL ($1.75) ages 10 to 18, free for age 9 and under.

DINING   You'll find reasonably priced meals at **Café Mephisto,** Grote Markt 29 (☎ 023/532-97-42). At the comfortable brown cafe, the decor is Jugendstil (Dutch art nouveau) and the music leans toward classic jazz. Broodjes cost from 6.50DFL to 8.50DFL ($3.25 to $4.25), and the kitchen turns out a respectable chicken saté for 18.50DFL ($9). It opens daily at 9am (meals begin at noon) and closes at 2am on weekdays and at 3am on weekends. No credit cards are accepted.

5

Athens & Delphi

by Sherry Marker

Athens is the city Greeks love to hate, complaining that it's too expensive, too crowded, too polluted. Some 40% of Greece's population lives here, making the city burst at the seams, with 5 million inhabitants, a rumored 17,000 taxis (but try to find one that's empty), and streets so congested you'll suspect that each of those 5 million Athenians has a car. Meanwhile, work proceeds at a snail's pace on the new Metro (subway line), with the tunneling disrupting traffic in much of central Athens and turning lovely Sýntagma Square into a construction site. So, why are you here? Because you too will probably soon develop a love-hate relationship with Athens, snarling at the traffic and gasping in wonder at the Acropolis, fuming at the taxi driver who tries to overcharge you and marveling at the stranger who realizes that you're lost and walks several blocks out of his way to take you where you're going.

Even though you've probably come here to see the "glory that was Greece"—perhaps best symbolized by the Parthenon and the superb statues and vases in the National Archaeological Museum—allow some time to make haste slowly in Athens. Your best moments may come at a small cafe, sipping a tiny cup of the sweet sludge Greeks call coffee, or getting hopelessly lost in the Pláka, only to find yourself in the shady courtyard of an old church. With a little planning, you should find a pleasant, inexpensive hotel, eat well in convivial restaurants, and leave Athens planning to return, as the Greeks say, *Tou Chrónou* (next year).

REQUIRED DOCUMENTS   Citizens of the United States, Canada, New Zealand, and Australia need only a valid passport for stays up to 3 months. British subjects need only an identity card.

OTHER FROMMER'S TITLES   For more on Athens, see *Frommer's Greece, Frommer's Greece from $50 a Day, Frommer's The Greek Islands, Frommer's Gay & Lesbian Europe,* or *Frommer's Europe.*

1 Athens Deals & Discounts

SPECIAL DISCOUNTS
With an **International Student Identification Card (ISIC),** students receive a substantial discount—usually 50%—on entrance fees to archaeological sites and museums and to most artistic events, theater performances, and festivals. If you have documents proving you're a

Budget Bests

From hotels and restaurants to transportation and sights (many museums and monuments are free on Sunday), Athens remains one of the least expensive European capitals. With the dollar currently worth 270Dr, the meticulous budget traveler can live comfortably on $50 a day.

If you're here in winter, you may be able to take advantage of one of the astonishing bargains sometimes offered at expensive hotels like the **Hilton** (☎ **800/445-8667** or 01/725-0201), **Grande Bretagne** (☎ **800/325-3535** or 01/331-5555), and **Electra Palace** (☎ **01/324-1410**).

And remember that at most **Greek cafes,** you're perfectly welcome to sit as long as you wish and enjoy the passing scene for the price of a coffee. When you feel like stretching your legs, head into the **National Garden,** where you can stroll through the former royal gardens free.

---

student, you can obtain a student card at the **International Student and Youth Travel Service** (☎ **01/323-3767**), on the second floor of 11 Níkis St., 2 blocks southeast of Sýntagma Square. It's open Monday to Friday 9am to 5pm and Saturday 9am to 1pm. Those under 26, student or not, can purchase international rail tickets for up to 40% below official prices here.

Most museums also grant 30% to 50% ticket discounts to **seniors**—women over 60 and men over 65.

WORTH A SPLURGE

If it's hot and you're tired (but dressed for the occasion), treat yourself to **afternoon tea** at the Grande Bretagne or Hilton (see "Budget Bests," above). For about $10 you'll have an elegant snack and see how the other half lives. Then have the doorman get you a taxi and journey on in style.

Consider getting tickets to a concert or opera at Athens's handsome new **Megaron Mousikis Concert Hall.** After the performance, enjoy a wickedly rich Black Venus sundae or a snifter of brandy at the city's best-known cafe, **Zonar's,** 9 Panepistimiou St., a block off Sýntagma Square.

2 Essentials

ARRIVING

BY PLANE   Athens's **Ellinikón International Airport** is 7 miles south of Sýntagma (Constitution) Square. Most visitors arrive at the **East Air Terminal,** on the eastern side of the runways. It offers a few convenient facilities, including branches of the major Greek banks (usually open 24 hours). You can change money while waiting for your luggage to arrive in the baggage area or after you clear Customs in the main airport. Luggage carts are 200Dr (75¢), a managed taxi rank is outside to the right, and buses are to the left. The information desk, slightly to the left as you come out of Customs, usually has pamphlets on Athens, and for a small fee its staff will book you into a hotel in your price range. For flight information, call ☎ **01/969-4466.**

All domestic and international flights of the national airline, Olympic Airways, arrive at the newer **West Air Terminal.** For flight information about incoming Olympic flights, call ☎ **01/926-9111.** Alas, this number is often busy and information isn't always updated. Bank offices are in the arrivals area and are open 7am to 11pm, with ATMs usually operating after hours. Olympic has an information booth,

What Things Cost in Athens	U.S. $
Taxi from the airport to Sýntagma Square	10.00
Taxi from Larissa train station to hotel	3.30
Public transportation (bus or Metro)	.30
Local telephone call	.10
Double room at the Athenian Inn (superior)	104.00
Double room at the Hotel Neféli (moderate)	60.00
Double room at the Hotel Tempi (budget)	28.00–32.00
Continental breakfast	5.50
Meal for one, with beverage, at To Kafeneio (splurge)	25.00
Meal for one, with beverage, at Restaurant Kentrikón (moderate)	12.00
Meal for one, with beverage, at Thanasis (budget)	5.00
Half-liter of beer	2.60
Half-liter of retsína (house wine)	2.50
Coca-Cola in a restaurant	2.00
Cup of coffee in a restaurant with table service	1.50
Roll of ASA 100 color film, 36 exposures	9.50
Admission to the Acropolis	7.40
Movie ticket	5.00

and the Tourist Police have a corner office in the building across from the terminal entrance.

Many charter flights now use the **Charter Terminal,** south of the East Air Terminal.

If you arrive at one of these terminals and have to make connections at another, you can either take the **shuttle bus** service (200Dr/74¢) or a **taxi.** The shuttle bus service officially runs once an hour 8:30am to 8:30pm but actually runs on an erratic schedule. If you decide to take a taxi, ask an airline official or a police officer what the fare should be and let the taxi driver know you've been told the official rate before you begin your journey.

If you're heading into Athens, a **cab** into the center *(kentro)* of town from any of the three terminals should cost about 2,500Dr to 3,000Dr ($7 to $11), double that between midnight and 5am.

Bus nos. 91 and 101 run from the East and West Terminals into central Athens (200Dr/74¢). Again, schedules are erratic, with both buses officially running 6am to 9pm, and no. 91 continuing service until midnight. In addition, bus no. 101 runs from the West Terminal to Athens and continues to Piraeus; the official schedule for service is hourly 8am to midnight (100Dr/37¢). There's sometimes hourly express bus service to Athens and continuing on to Piraeus. In short, all bus schedules are erratic, and schedules posted at the airport are often months out of date. Due to ongoing road work between Athens and Piraeus, journey times and routes are subject to change.

BY TRAIN　Trains from the west, including Eurail connections via Pátra, arrive at the **Peloponnese Station (Stathmós Peloponníssou),** about a mile northwest of Omónia Square. Trains from the north arrive about 3 long blocks north on the opposite side of the tracks at the **Larissa Station (Stathmós Laríssis).** If you're making connections from one station to the other, allow 10 to 15 minutes for the walk. Both stations have currency exchange offices that are usually open daily 8am to 9:15pm and luggage storage offices that charge 300Dr ($1.10) per bag per day, open 6:30am to 9:30pm. A **taxi** into the center of town should cost about 1,000Dr ($3.35).

BY BOAT   Athens's main seaport, **Piraeus,** 7 miles southwest, is a 15-minute subway ride from Monastiráki and Omónia squares. The subway runs about 5am to midnight and costs 75Dr (30¢), with a surcharge of 75Dr after Omónia.

VISITOR INFORMATION

The **Greek National Tourist Organization (EOT,** also known as the Hellenic Tourism Organization) has closed its central office in Sýntagma Square. The new office on the ground floor at 2 Amerikís St. (☎ **01/331-0437** or 01/331-0561), 2 blocks west of Sýntagma between Stadiou and Venizélou, is open Monday to Friday 9am to 7pm and Saturday 9:30am to 2pm (closed Sunday and holidays). Information about Athens, free city maps, transportation schedules, hotel lists, and other booklets on many regions of Greece are available in Greek, English, French, and German.

CITY LAYOUT

Central Athens is based on an almost equilateral triangle, with points at **Sýntagma (Constitution) Square, Omónia (Harmony) Square,** and **Monastiráki (Little Monastery) Square,** near the **Acropolis.** All three are now construction sites for a new line of the Metro (subway). This area is defined as Athens's commercial center, from which cars are banned (in theory, if not in practice) except for several cross streets. Most Greeks consider Omónia the city center, but most visitors take their bearings from Sýntagma, where the House of Parliament is. Omónia and Sýntagma squares are connected by the parallel **Stadíou Street** and **Panepistimíou Street,** also called Elefthériou Venizélou. West from Sýntagma Square, ancient **Ermoú Street** and broader **Mitropóleos Street** lead slightly downhill to Monastiráki Square. Here you'll find the flea market, the **Ancient Agorá (Market)** below the Acropolis, and the **Pláka,** the oldest neighborhood, with many street names and a scattering of monuments from antiquity. From Monastiráki Square, **Athinás Street** leads north past the modern market (aka Central Market) to Omónia Square.

In general, finding your way around Athens is relatively easy, except in the Pláka, the labyrinth of narrow, winding streets at the foot of the Acropolis that can challenge even the best navigators. Don't panic: The Pláka is small enough that you can't go far astray, and its side streets, with small houses and churches, are so charming you won't mind being lost. One excellent map may help: the **Historical Map of Athens,** produced by the Greek Archaeological Service, which has a map of the Pláka in addition to a map of the city center showing the major archaeological sites. The map (about 500Dr/$1.85) is sold at many bookstores, museums, ancient sites, and newspaper kiosks.

GETTING AROUND

BY BUS, TROLLEY BUS & METRO (SUBWAY)   The **blue-and-white buses** run regular routes in Athens and its suburbs every 15 minutes from 5am to midnight. (For the more distant suburbs, you may need to change buses at a transfer station.) The **orange electric trolley buses** serve areas in the city center from 5am to midnight. The **green buses** run between the city center and Piraeus every 20 minutes from 6am to midnight, then hourly until 6am. Tickets cost 75Dr (30¢) and must be purchased in advance, usually in groups of 10, from any news kiosk or special bus ticket kiosks at the main stations.

When you board, validate your ticket in the automatic machine. Hold onto your ticket: Uniformed and plainclothes inspectors periodically check tickets and can levy fines of 1,500Dr ($6) on the spot.

The Athens map distributed by the Greek National Tourist Organization indicates major public transportation stops and routes. Keep in mind that the buses are usually very crowded and their schedules are erratic.

The **Metro** currently links Piraeus, the seaport of Athens, and Kifissiá, an upscale northern suburb. (A second line is under construction and should be finished before the 2004 Olympics in Athens.) In the city center the trains run underground, and the main stops are **Monastiráki, Omónia,** and **Viktorías (Victoria).** Trains run about every 5 to 15 minutes from 5am to midnight. Tickets cost 75Dr (30¢), with a 75Dr surcharge after Omónia. Validate your ticket in the machine as you enter the waiting platform or risk a fine. Metro and bus tickets are not interchangeable.

BY TAXI   It's rumored that there are 17,000 taxis in Athens, but finding one is almost never easy. Especially if you have travel connections to make, it's a good idea to reserve a **radio taxi** (see below). Fortunately, taxis are inexpensive, and most drivers are honest men trying to wrest a living by maneuvering through Athens's endemic gridlock. However, some drivers, notably those working Piraeus, the airports, and popular tourist destinations, can't resist trying to overcharge foreigners. When you get into a taxi, check to see the meter is turned on and set on "1" rather than "2"; the meter should be set on "2" (double fare) only between midnight and 5am or if you take a taxi outside the city limits. (If you plan to do this, try to negotiate a flat rate in advance.) Unless your cab is caught in very heavy traffic, a trip to the center of town from the airport between 5am and midnight shouldn't cost more than 4,000Dr ($15). Don't be surprised if your driver picks up other passengers en route; he'll work out everyone's share, and the worst that probably will happen is that you'll get less of a break on the shared fare than you would if you spoke Greek.

At press time, the minimum fare is 200Dr (75¢), and the "1" meter rate is 62Dr (22¢) per kilometer. Surcharges include 150Dr (55¢) for service from a port or rail or bus station, 300Dr ($1.10) for service from the airport, and a luggage fee of 50Dr (20¢) for every bag over 10kg (22 lb.). If you suspect you've been overcharged, ask for help at your hotel or other destination before you pay the fare. Keep in mind that your driver may have difficulty understanding your pronunciation of your destination. If you're taking a taxi from your hotel, a staff member can assist you by telling the driver your destination or writing down the address for you to show him. If you carry a business card from your hotel with you, you can show it to the driver when you return.

There are about 15 radio taxi companies, including **Aris** (☎ 01/346-7137), **Express** (☎ 01/993-4812), **Kosmos** (☎ 01/801-9000), **Parthenon** (☎ 01/581-4711), and **Piraeus** (☎ 01/413-5888). If you're trying to make travel connections or traveling during rush hours, the service will be well worth the 300Dr ($1.10) surcharge. Again, your hotel can make the call for you and make sure that the driver knows where you want to go. Most restaurants will call a taxi for you without charge.

The Greek National Tourist Organization's pamphlet "Helpful Hints for Taxi Users" has information on taxi fares as well as a complaint form, which you can send to the Ministry of Transport and Communication, 13 Xenophondos, 101 91 Athens. Replies to complaints are infrequent but not unknown.

BY CAR & MOPED   Parking is so difficult and traffic so heavy in Athens that you should use a car only for trips outside the city. Keep in mind that on any day trip (to Sounion or Eleusis, for example), you'll spend at least several hours leaving and reentering central Athens.

Not far south of Sýntagma Square, **Avis,** 48 Amalías Ave. (☎ **01/322-4951**), charges about 16,000Dr ($60) per day with unlimited mileage, including insurance and tax. A little farther south, **AutoEurope,** 29 Hatzihrístou St., right off Syngroú (☎ **01/924-2206**), charges about 12,500Dr ($46); **Budget,** 8 Syngroú Ave. (☎ **01/921-4711**), charges about 14,000Dr ($52); and **Eurodollar,** 29 Syngroú Ave. (☎ **01/922-9672**), charges about 12,500Dr ($46). You can usually reduce the price considerably by booking from outside Greece; sometimes, especially in the off-season, on-the-spot bargaining is effective. Most companies add, and don't always mention, the hefty surcharge for airport pickup or drop-off.

You can rent mopeds from **Meintanis,** 4 Dionysíou Areopayítou St., near the inter-section with Amalías Avenue, Pláka (☎ **01/323-2346**), at the foot of the Acropolis, for about 4,500Dr ($17) per day, tax included. You'll receive a 20% discount if you rent for a week.

FAST FACTS: Athens

American Express   The office at 2 Ermoú St., near the southwest corner of Sýntagma Square (☎ **01/324-4975**), offers currency exchange and other services Monday to Friday 8:30am to 4pm and Saturday 8:30am to 1:30pm.

Banks   Banks are generally open Monday to Thursday 8am to 2pm and Friday 8am to 1:30pm. Most have currency exchange counters that use the rates set daily by the government; this rate is usually more favorable than that offered at unofficial exchange bureaus. It's worth doing a little comparison shopping for the best rate of exchange: For example, many hotels offer rates (usually only for cash) that are better than the official bank rate. **ATMs** are increasingly common in Athens, and the National Bank of Greece operates a 24-hour ATM on Sýntagma Square. It's *not* a good idea to rely on using ATMs exclusively in Athens, because the machines are often out of service when you need them most: on holidays or during bank strikes.

Business Hours   In winter, shops are generally open Monday and Wednesday 9am to 5pm; Tuesday, Thursday, and Friday 10am to 7pm; and Saturday 8:30am to 3:30pm. In summer, shops are generally open Monday, Wednesday, and Saturday 8am to 3pm; and Tuesday, Thursday, and Friday 8am to 1:30pm and 5:30 to 10pm. Note that many shops geared to visitors keep especially long hours, and some close about 2 to 5pm. Most food stores and the Central Market are open Monday and Wednesday 9am to 4:30pm, Tuesday 9am to 6pm, Thursday 9:30am to 6:30pm, Friday 9:30am to 7pm, and Saturday 8:30am to 4:30pm.

Currency   The **drachma (Dr)** is the Greek national currency. Coins are issued in 5, 10, 20, 50, and 100Dr; bills are denominated in 50, 100, 500, 1,000, 5,000, and 10,000Dr. At press time, there were 270Dr to the dollar.

Embassies/Consulates   Australia, 37 Dimitríou Soútsou Ave. (☎ **01/ 644-7303**); **Canada,** 4 Ioánnou Yenadíou St. (☎ **01/723-9511** or 725-4011); **New Zealand** (consulate), 9 Semitelou St. (☎ **01/771-0112**); **United Kingdom,** 1 Ploutárchou St. (☎ **01/723-6211**); **United States,** 91 Vasilíssis Sofías Ave. (☎ **01/721-2951**). Embassies are usually closed on their own impor-tant national holidays and sometimes on Greek holidays as well.

Emergencies   In an emergency, dial ☎ **100** for fast police assistance and ☎ **171** for the Tourist Police (see "Police," below). Dial ☎ **199** to report a fire

The Greek Drachma

For American Readers   At this writing, $1 = approximately 270Dr; this was the rate of exchange used to calculate the dollar values in this chapter.
For British Readers   At this writing, £1 = approximately 445Dr.
Note: Exchange rates fluctuate and may not be the same when you travel to Greece.

Dr	U.S.$	U.K.£	Dr	U.S.$	U.K.£
100	.37	.22	1,000	3.70	2.22
200	.74	.44	1,500	5.55	3.33
300	1.11	.66	2,000	7.40	4.44
400	1.48	.88	2,500	9.25	5.55
500	1.85	1.10	5,000	18.52	11.10
600	2.22	1.32	7,500	27.78	16.67
700	2.59	1.54	10,000	37.04	22.20
800	2.96	1.76	15,000	55.55	33.33
900	3.33	1.98	20,000	74.08	44.40

and ☎ **166** for an ambulance and hospital. If you need an English-speaking doctor or dentist, call your embassy for advice or try **SOS Doctor** (☎ **331-0310** or 331-0311). The English-language *Athens News* lists some American- and British-trained doctors and hospitals offering emergency services. Most of the larger hotels have doctors whom they can call for you in an emergency.

Holidays   Major public holidays in Athens include New Year's Day (January 1), Epiphany (January 6), Ash Wednesday, Independence Day (March 25), Good Friday, Easter Sunday and Monday (Orthodox Easter can coincide with or vary by 2 weeks from Catholic and Protestant Easter), Labor Day (May 1), Assumption Day (August 15), National Day (October 28), and Christmas (December 25 and 26). It is not unusual for some shops and offices to close for at least a week at Christmas and Easter.

Laundry   The self-service **launderette** at 10 Angélou Yerónda St., off Kidathenéon Street, Pláka, is open daily 8:30am to 7pm; it charges 2,000Dr ($7) for wash, dry, and soap. The **National Dry Cleaners and Laundry Service,** 17 Apóllonos St. (☎ **01/323-2226**), next to the Hermes Hotel, is open Monday and Wednesday 7am to 4pm and Tuesday, Thursday, and Friday 7am to 8pm; laundry costs 1,500Dr ($6) per kilo. Hotel chambermaids will often do laundry for you at a reasonable price.

Mail   The main **post offices** in central Athens are at 100 Eólou St., just south of Omónia Square, and in Sýntagma Square on the corner of Mitropóleos Street. They're open Monday to Friday 7:30am to 8pm, Saturday 7:30am to 2pm, and Sunday 9am to 1pm. The two post offices at the East and West Air Terminals keep the same hours. Oddly, mail posted at the air terminals almost always takes longer to arrive than mail posted in Athens itself.

   All the post offices can accept parcels. The **parcel post office,** 4 Stadíou St., inside the arcade (☎ **01/322-8940**), is open Monday to Friday 7:30am to 8pm. It sells cardboard shipping boxes in four sizes. Parcels must be open for inspection before you seal them at the post office.

Country & City Codes

The **country code** for Greece is **30.** The **city code** for Athens is **1;** use this code when you're calling from outside Greece. If you're within Greece but not in Athens, use **01.** If you're calling within Athens, simply leave off the code and dial only the regular phone number.

You can receive correspondence in Athens in care of **American Express,** 2 Ermoú St., 102 25 Athens, Greece (☎ **01/324-4975**), near the southwest corner of Sýntagma Square. The office is open Monday to Friday 8:30am to 4pm and Saturday 8:30am to 1:30pm. If you have an American Express card or traveler's checks, the service is free; otherwise, each article costs a steep 600Dr ($2.20).

Pharmacies   Pharmakía, identified by green crosses, are scattered throughout Athens. Hours are usually weekdays 8am to 2pm. In the evening and on weekends most are closed but usually post a notice listing the names and addresses of pharmacies that are open or will open in an emergency. Newspapers, including the *Athens News,* list the pharmacies open outside regular hours.

Police   In an emergency, dial ☎ **100.** For help dealing with a troublesome taxi driver, hotel, restaurant, or shop owner, call the Tourist Police at ☎ **171.**

Tax   **Value-added tax (VAT)** is included in the price of all goods and services in Athens, ranging from 4% on books to 36% on certain luxury items.

Telephone   Many of the city's public phones now accept only **phonecards,** available at newsstands and OTE (the state-owned telephone company) offices in several denominations starting at 1,700Dr ($6). The card works for 100 short local calls (or briefer long-distance or international calls). Some kiosks still have **metered** phones; you pay what the meter records. Local phone calls cost 20Dr (8¢).

You can also use your phonecard to place an international call. If you don't want to phone from a public call box and don't want to be slapped with a steep hotel surcharge, try the **Telephone Office (OTE),** 15 Stadíou St., 3 blocks from Sýntagma Square. It's open Monday to Friday 7am to midnight and Saturday, Sunday, and holidays 8am to midnight and is usually very crowded. North Americans can phone home directly through **AT&T** (☎ **00/800-1311**), **MCI** (☎ **00/800-1211**), or **Sprint** (☎ **00/800-1411**); calls can be collect or billed to your phone charge card.

Tipping   Restaurants include a service charge in the bill, but many visitors add a 10% tip. Most Greeks don't give a percentage tip to taxi drivers but often round out the fare to the nearest 1,000Dr.

3 Accommodations You Can Afford

To avoid settling for a bad or expensive room, you should reserve in advance or arrive with a considerable reserve of time and energy. You can book a room at the tourist information booth at the West Air Terminal, run by a private tourist agency and open 7am to 1am; the agency charges a small fee. Or head into town and drop your baggage (300Dr/$1.10 per day) at **Pacific Ltd.,** 26 Níkis St. (☎ **01/324-1007**), 2 blocks southwest of Sýntagma Square. Its official hours are Monday to Saturday 7am to 8pm and Sunday 7am to 2pm, but phone first to make sure it's open.

The **Greek National Tourist Organization** (EOT, also known as the Hellenic Tourism Organization), on the ground floor at 2 Amerikís St. (☎ **01/331-0437** or 331-0561), 2 blocks west of Sýntagma between Stadiou and Venizéliou, will sometimes help you book a hotel room. The office is open Monday to Friday 9am to 7pm and Saturday 9:30am to 2pm (closed holidays).

Many budget hotels are on small side streets that can be difficult to find or are 5 to 15 minutes on foot from the main public transport hubs of Omónia or Sýntagma Square, so consider taking a taxi to your hotel if you have a lot of luggage.

Virtually all Greek hotels are clean, though few are charming or elegant. In short, don't expect frills at your budget hotel: Most rooms are rather spartan, furnished with old beds and bureaus. If shower and tub facilities are important to you, be sure to have a look at the bathroom before you take a room; many Greek tubs are tiny and the showers are handheld. You may decide that location is most important. The Pláka, with its labyrinthine lanes and small houses at the foot of the Acropolis, is the first choice for most budget travelers, but because of its popularity an affordable room may be hard to find. Try hotels adjacent to the Pláka between Monastiráki Square and Sýntagma Square, on the south side of the Acropolis in Makriyánni, or farther south in Koukáki—but keep in mind that if you stay in Koukáki, you'll spend a lot of time getting to and from most places that you want to go.

Note: You can find most of the lodging choices below plotted on the map included in "Seeing the Sights," later in this chapter.

IN THE PLÁKA

Acropolis House Hotel. 6–8 Kodroú St., 105 58 Athens. ☎ **01/322-2344.** Fax 01/324-4143. 29 units, 19 with bathroom. A/C TEL. 10,000Dr ($37) single without bathroom; 15,000Dr ($56) double without bathroom, 18,000Dr ($66) double with bathroom; 35,000Dr ($130) suite. Rates include continental breakfast. Air-conditioning 4,000Dr ($15). No credit cards. Walk 2 blocks out of Sýntagma Sq. on Mitropóleos St. and turn left on Voulís, which becomes pedestrianized Kodroú St.

This small hotel in a handsomely restored 150-year-old villa retains many of its original classical architectural details and offers the convenience of a central location in the heart of the Pláka. It's a 5-minute walk from Sýntagma Square, with the charm of a quiet pedestrianized side street. The newer wing (only 60 years old) isn't architecturally special, but it's just as clean, and the toilets (one for each room, but across the hall) are fully tiled and acceptably modern. There's a book-swap spot and a washing machine (for a small fee, free after a 4-day stay). If the Acropolis House is full, try the Adonis or Kouros, both also on Kodroú Street (see below).

Byron Hotel. 19 Vyronos St., 105 58 Athens. ☎ **01/325-3554.** Fax 01/323-0327. 20 units, all with bathroom. TEL. 18,000Dr ($67) single; 22,000Dr ($82) double. Rates include breakfast. No credit cards. From Sýntagma Sq., walk south on Amalías Ave. past Hadrian's Arch, stay right, and turn right on Dionysíou Areopayítou St.; Vyronos (Byron in Greek) is 2nd street on right, and hotel (with a portrait of Lord Byron by the door) is on right.

The Byron is in a convenient and reasonably quiet Pláka location. You can negotiate having the TV in the lobby cafe turned off (or on) at breakfast. The small rooms here are pleasant if spare, and the ones in the back overlooking apartments and gardens are usually quieter than the six in front (but lack balconies and partial views of the Acropolis). Eight rooms have air-conditioning and cost 2,500Dr ($9) extra.

Hotel Adonis. 3 Kodroú St., 105 58 Athens. ☎ **01/324-9737.** Fax 01/323-1602. 26 units, all with bathroom. TEL. 10,000Dr ($37) single; 15,000Dr ($56) double; 18,000Dr ($67) suite. Rates include breakfast. No credit cards. Walk 2 blocks out of Sýntagma Sq. on Mitropóleos St., turn left on Voulís, and continue along pedestrians-only extension.

A Hotel Warning

I no longer recommend hotels near Omónia Square, which has become a hangout for petty criminals. Some hotels have become the haunts of Russian prostitutes. There are, however, still some good hotels north of Omónia near Exárchia Square and the National Archaeological Museum—a good place to stay if you plan to spend time exploring this extraordinary collection of ancient art.

The architecturally undistinguished Adonis has plain, well-maintained units with small balconies in an appealing location just off Kidathenéon Street. Though you might not have chosen the tan-and-brown wallpaper for your home, you'll enjoy the view from the rooftop garden overlooking the Acropolis and Lykavitós Hill.

✪ **Hotel Neféli.** 16 Iperídou St., 105 58 Athens. ☎ **01/322-8044.** 18 units, all with bathroom. TEL. 14,000Dr ($52) single; 16,000Dr ($60) double. Rates include breakfast. AE, V. Walk 2 blocks west from Sýntagma Sq. on Mitropóleos St., turn left (south) on the 2nd street, Voulís, cross Nikodímou St., and turn right on Iperídou.

The charming little Neféli ("cloud"), steps from the Cultural Center of the Municipality of Athens, is very quiet considering its central location. The rooms (some with old-fashioned ceiling fans, others with air-conditioning) are small but comfortable, with the quietest overlooking pedestrianized Angelikís Hatzimiháli Street. I found the staff courteous and helpful. To make a reservation, send a deposit for 1 night well in advance of your arrival and request a reply.

Kouros Hotel. 11 Kodroú St., 105 58 Athens. ☎ **01/322-7431.** 10 units, none with bathroom. 5,000Dr ($19) single; 8,000Dr ($30) double. No credit cards. Walk 2 blocks west from Sýntagma Sq. on Mitropóleos St., turn left (south) on the 2nd street, Voulís, and continue along pedestrians-only extension.

Like the Adonis and the Acropolis House, the Kouros has a fine location on pedestrianized Kodroú Street, just off Kidathenéon Street in the heart of the Pláka. From the street, the Kouros is charming: a 200-year-old house with nice architectural details and three attractive balconies. Alas, the small rooms are gloomy (the three with balconies get more light but also more street noise)—and so is the staff. Many guests tend to stay out late and come back at hours when those less fond of nightlife may be trying to sleep.

Student and Travelers' Inn. 16 Kidathenéon St., 105 58 Athens. ☎ **01/324-4808** or 01/324-8802. 45 units, none with bathroom. 6,500Dr ($24) single; 8,500Dr ($32) double; 4,000Dr ($15) dorm bed. No credit cards. Follow Filellínon St. south from southwest corner of Sýntagma Sq.; Kidathenéon is 4th street on right.

Although it's often noisy at night, this hostel/hotel offers a great deal on inexpensive accommodations in the heart of the Pláka for the young at heart (and those who remember to travel with ear plugs). The nicest feature: the appealing back garden, with a shady arbor where you can have breakfast and take a break from sightseeing. The rooms are what you'd expect: very spare, with four beds to each dorm. There's a 1:30am curfew, not always enforced.

NEAR SÝNTAGMA SQUARE

Hotel Achilléas. 21 Lekká St., 105 62 Athens. ☎ **01/323-3197.** Fax 01/324-1092. 34 units, all with bathroom. A/C TEL. 16,000Dr ($60) single; 22,000Dr ($82) double. Rates include breakfast. AE, DC, EURO, MC, V. With Hotel Grande Bretagne on your right, walk 2 blocks west out of Sýntagma Sq. on Karayióryi Servías, turn right up Lekká; the hotel is on left.

Getting the Best Deal on Accommodations

- Try to avoid Athens in July and August, when the city is hot and crowded. You can get a better deal in other months (especially January to March), when rates are reduced about 30%, and it's more of a buyer's market.
- If you ask to see a room before you take it, you're more likely to be shown a better room. You might also check out several rooms and ask for a lower price for a smaller, less attractive, or less convenient room.
- Take a room without a private bath. Most rooms have a washbasin, and common bath facilities are usually clean and shared by only two or three rooms. If the kind of tub or shower you have is important, ask to see the room. Many Greek tubs are cramped; many showers are flimsy.
- Ask for the reduced rate for a stay over 3 nights.

The Achilléas (Achilles), on a relatively quiet side street steps from Sýntagma Square, was fully renovated in 1995. Although the off-street entrance lacks charm, this hotel's central location and fair prices make it a good choice. The pleasant bedrooms are good-sized, cheerful, and light; some rear rooms have small balconies. Breakfast is served in the first-floor dining room, which has lots of green plants.

Hotel Diomía. 5 Diomías St., 105 62 Athens. ☎ **01/323-8034.** Fax 01/323-8034. 71 units, all with bathroom. A/C TV TEL. 18,000Dr ($67) single; 22,000Dr ($82) double. AE, DC, MC, V.

The Diomía's location can't be beat: The front rooms overlook a pedestrianized street off Sýntagma Square, and back rooms on the top two floors look out across buildings to the Acropolis. The Diomía repainted most of its rooms in 1996, and though they still lack charm, the fresh paint (mostly pastels) certainly helps. The baths retain their original inconveniences, such as minuscule shower curtains, ancient tubs (usually without plugs), and handheld showers. The staff is either exceptionally helpful or amazingly unhelpful. Breakfast (supplement) is uninteresting; it makes much better sense to head out to one of the many nearby coffee shops. That said, the barman can usually fix you a snack like an omelet at almost any hour.

NEAR MONASTIRÁKI SQUARE

Attalos Hotel. 29 Athinás St., 105 54 Athens. ☎ **01/321-2801.** Fax 01/324-3124. 80 units, all with bathroom. A/C TEL. 15,000Dr ($56) double; 18,000Dr ($67) triple. Air-conditioning 2,000Dr ($7). Rates include buffet breakfast. AE, V. Walk about 1½ blocks north from Monastiráki Sq. on Athinás St.; hotel (large sign) is on left.

One of the pleasures of staying at the six-story (with elevator) Attalos is taking in the frenzied street life of the nearby Central Market. Things quiet down at night, though the market opens around 5am, making the early morning lively. The recently repainted rooms are plain, but many have framed color photos of archaeological sites and antiquities. The roof garden has fine views of the city and the Acropolis. The Attalos provides free luggage storage and often offers a discount for Frommer's readers.

✪ **Hotel Tempi.** 29 Eólou St., 105 51 Athens. ☎ **01/321-3175.** Fax 01/325-4179. 24 units, 8 with shower only. 5,200Dr ($19) single without shower; 7,500Dr ($28) double without shower, 8,500Dr ($32) double with shower. AE, MC, V. From Monastiráki Sq., walk 1 block east (toward Sýntagma Sq.) on Hermou St. and turn left (north) up Eólou; hotel is on left just after church of Agia Irini.

A very good value choice, this three-story hotel is across from the flower market on a basically pedestrians-only street. It has very simply furnished rooms with firm beds, high ceilings, and (usually) hot showers. Ten rooms have balconies from which, if you lean, you can see the Acropolis. There's a rooftop lounge, laundry facilities, free luggage storage, and a book exchange that includes a number of travel guides.

Jason Inn Hotel. 12 Ayíon Assómaton St., 105 53 Athens. ☎ **01/325-1106.** Fax 01/523-4786. 57 units, all with bathroom. A/C TV TEL. 12,000Dr ($44) single; 16,500Dr ($61) double. Rates include American buffet breakfast. From Monastiráki Sq., head west on Ermoú, turn right (north) at Thisío Metro station, pass small below-ground-level church, and bear left; hotel is on right.

This newly renovated hotel (admittedly on a dull street) offers attractive, comfortable rooms with modern amenities and double-paned windows. If you don't mind walking a few more blocks to Sýntagma, this is one of the best values in Athens, with an eager-to-help staff. If the Jason Inn is full, the staff may be able to find you a room in one of their other hotels: the similarly priced Adrian, on busy Hadrian Street in the Pláka, or the slightly less expensive King Jason or Jason, both a few blocks from Omónia Square.

IN MAKRIYÁNNI & KOUKÁKI

With all the Makriyánni and Koukáki hotels, you'll be doing some extra walking (and having to cross busy Dionysíou Areopayítou Street) to get to most places you want to visit.

Art Gallery Hotel. 5 Erechthíou St., Koukáki, 117 42 Athens. ☎ **01/923-8376.** Fax 01/923-3025. 22 units, all with bathroom. TEL. 12,000Dr ($44) single; 15,000Dr ($56) double. No credit cards. Follow Dionysíou Areopayítou St. around south side of Acropolis to Odeum of Heródes Atticus and turn left on Erechthíou; Art Gallery is 3 blocks down on right.

As you might expect, this small hotel—in a half-century-old house that has been home to several artists—has an artistic flair (and a nice old-fashioned cage elevator). The rooms are plain but comfortable, with polished hardwood floors and ceiling fans.

✪ **Marble House Pension.** 35 A. Zinní St., Koukáki, 117 41 Athens. ☎ **01/923-4058.** 17 units, 9 with bathroom. TEL. 6,960Dr ($26) single without bathroom, 5,600Dr ($21) single with bathroom; 10,680Dr ($40) double without bathroom, 11,800Dr ($44) double with bathroom. Monthly rate 70,000Dr ($260) available Oct–May. No credit cards. Take orange trolley bus no. 1, 5, or 9 from Sýntagma Sq., get off at Olympic office, walk 2 blocks up, and turn left after church.

Named for its marble facade, which is usually covered by bougainvillea, this place is famous among budget travelers (including many teachers) for its friendly, helpful staff. The rooms, with wood-frame beds, stone floors, and ceiling fans, boast balconies overlooking the residential neighborhood. If you're spending more than a few days in Athens and don't mind being out of the center, this is a fine base for sightseeing. Luggage storage is free.

Parthenon. 6 Makri St., 115 27 Athens. ☎ **01/923-4594.** Fax 01/644-1084. 79 units, all with bathroom. TEL. 15,000Dr ($56) single; 19,200Dr ($71) double. MC, V. Follow Amalías Ave. into Dionysíou Areopayítou St.; cross at light by Vyronos Street to reach Makri.

This recently refurbished modern hotel is in an excellent location just across from the Pláka and the Acropolis. The good-size lobby is more glitzy than that at many moderately priced hotels, and there's a bar, restaurant, and small garden. The rooms (some with TVs) are carpeted, with bright, cheerful bedspreads and decent-size baths. The Parthenon is one of a group of four hotels; if it's full, the management will try to get you a room in the Christina, a few blocks away, or at the Riva or Alexandros, near the Mégaron (the concert hall).

Tony's Pension. 26 Zaharítsa St., 117 42 Athens. ☎ **01/923-0561.** 15 units, all with bathroom; 11 studios. TV TEL. 9,200Dr ($34) single; 10,900Dr ($40) double; 16,500Dr ($61) studio. V. Follow Dionysíou Areopayítou St. around south side of Acropolis to Propiléon St., turn left, and walk downhill 5 blocks to its end; zig right, then zag left to Zaharítsa.

This pension has a common kitchen and TV lounge on each floor. Students, fashion models, and singles dominate the scene at Tony's, and if it's full, Tony or his multilingual wife, Charo, will contact their pension peers and try to accommodate the overflow. Tony's also has 11 studios with kitchenettes available for short stays or long-term rent. Air-conditioning and minibars are available only in the studios.

NEAR THE NATIONAL ARCHAEOLOGICAL MUSEUM & EXÁRCHIA SQUARE

Hotel Exarchion. 55 Themistokléous St., 106 83 Athens. ☎ **01/360-1256.** Fax 01/360-3296. 49 units, all with bathroom. TEL. 8,000Dr ($30) single; 9,250Dr ($34) double. No credit cards. Themistokléous leads northeast from Panepistimíou St., 2 blocks east of Omónia Sq.; Exárchia Sq. is 7 blocks up.

The modern Hotel Exarchion has comfortable, decent-size rooms, most of which have a balcony. The lobby is decorated with handsome photographs of classical sites, and there's a large rooftop where you can drink and snack while you watch—and, when there are demonstrations, hear until the wee hours—University of Athens students debating in the square below.

Museum Hotel. 16 Bouboulínas St., 106 82 Athens. ☎ **01/360-5611.** Fax 01/380-0057. 58 units, all with bathroom. TEL. 6,300Dr ($23) single; 9,200Dr ($34) double. Rates include breakfast. AE, DC, V.

This venerable hotel is so close to the National Archaeological Museum that all its balconies overlook the museum's relatively quiet tree-filled park. The rooms are bland and could use sprucing up, but they're comfortable and average in size. It's a good value in a good location, though the traffic here is, as almost everywhere in Athens, pretty steady.

A YOUTH HOSTEL

The **Greek Youth Hostel Federation,** at 4 Dragatsaníou St., 105 59 Athens (☎ 01/323-4107), operates several hostels in the country.

Athens International Youth Hostel. 16 Victor Hugo, 104 38 Athens. ☎ **01/523-4170.** Fax 01/523-4115. 138 beds. 2,500Dr ($9) per person. Rates include breakfast. No credit cards. Walk west from Omónia Sq. 3 blocks on Ayiou Konstantinou and turn right (north) on Koumoundoúrou St.; Victor Hugo is 2 blocks up and across street, and hostel is on right.

This is easily the best hostel in Athens. The completely renovated rooms sleep two to four people in decent beds and have private showers and lockers. You must join the IYHF—3,000Dr ($11)—or pay an additional 500Dr ($1.85) daily. There's a shared kitchen for use by members, a laundry facility, and no curfew.

WORTH A SPLURGE

Athenian Inn. 22 Háritos St., Kolonáki, 106 75 Athens. ☎ **01/723-8097.** Fax 01/724-2268. 28 units, all with bathroom. A/C. 18,900Dr ($70) single; 28,200Dr ($104) double; 35,150Dr ($130) triple. Rates include breakfast. AE, DC, V. From Sýntagma Sq., go east on Vasilíssis Sofías Ave. 5 blocks, turn left on Koumbári, and find square 1 block up; continue northeast of square to Iródotou, turn left, then turn right 1 block up.

Kolonáki is a fashionable residential and shopping neighborhood northeast of Sýntagma at the foot of Mount Likavitós. The Athenian Inn's quiet location 3 blocks from Kolonáki Square is a blessing, as are the clean accommodations and friendly staff.

(A quote from the guest book: "At last the ideal Athens hotel, good and modest in scale but perfect in service and goodwill.") Many of the balconies look out on Lykavitós Hill. Breakfast is served in the small ground-floor lounge, which has a fireplace, piano, and (when I was there last) TV.

Hotel Pláka. Mitropóleos and 7 Kapnikareas St., 105 56 Athens. ☎ **01/322-2096.** Fax 01/322-2412. 67 units, all with bathroom. A/C TV TEL. 15,000Dr ($56) single; 25,000Dr ($93) double. Rates include breakfast. AE, EURO, MC, V. Follow Mitropóleos St. out of Sýntagma Sq. past Cathedral and turn left onto Kapnikareas.

This cheerful 10-year-old hotel—popular with Greeks, who prefer its modern conveniences to the old-fashioned charms of most other hotels in the Pláka area, as well as with gays—has a terrific location and fair prices. Most rooms have bedspreads and rugs in blue and white, the Greek national colors, and many have balconies. Rooms on the fifth and sixth floors in the rear (where it's usually quieter) have views of the Pláka and the Acropolis, also splendidly visible from the roof garden (which has a snack bar).

4 Great Deals on Dining

Athens has an astonishing number of restaurants and tavérnas (and a growing number of fast-food joints) offering everything from good, cheap Greek food in plain surroundings to fine Greek, French, Asian, and other international cuisines served in luxurious settings. Budget travelers may not experience the top of the line, but they can eat very well in Athens. Here are a few pointers.

You may have heard that there's a substantial difference between restaurants and tavérnas. True, there was a time when a restaurant *(estiatórion)* served food cooked ahead of time and was usually fancier than a tavérna, which prepared grilled food to order. Today, the distinction has all but disappeared, but you may want to keep in mind that in all but the best Greek eateries, prepared-in-advance dishes are made in the morning and are fresher at lunch than at dinner.

Most restaurants have menus printed in both Greek and English, but many don't keep their printed (or handwritten) menus up to date. If a menu is not in English, there's almost always someone working at the restaurant who will either translate or rattle off suggestions for you in English. That may mean that you'll be offered some fairly repetitive suggestions, because restaurant staff members tend to suggest what most tourists request. In Athens, that means *moussaká* (baked eggplant casserole, usually with ground meat), *souvláki* (chunks of beef, chicken, pork, or lamb grilled on a skewer), *pastítsio* (baked pasta, usually with ground meat and béchamel sauce), or *dolmadákia* (grape leaves, usually stuffed with rice and ground meat). Although all these dishes can be delicious—you may have eaten them outside of Greece and looked forward to enjoying the real thing here—the truth is that you may end up cherishing your memories. All too often, restaurants catering heavily to tourists tend to serve profoundly dull moussaká and unpleasantly chewy souvláki. I hope that the places we're suggesting do better, but I have to confess that I only order moussaká at places I know very well—and souvláki has to be *very* chewy to disconcert me.

To avoid the ubiquitous favorites-for-foreigners, you may prefer to indicate to your waiter that you'd like to have a look at the food display case, often positioned just outside the kitchen, and then point out what you'd like to order. Many restaurants are perfectly happy to have you take a look in the kitchen itself, but it's not a good idea to do this without checking first. Not surprisingly, you'll get the best value and the tastiest food at establishments serving a predominantly Greek, rather than a transient tourist, clientele.

Mezédes (appetizers served with bread) are one of the great delights of Greek cuisine, and often can be enjoyed in lieu of a main course. Some perennial favorites include *tzatzíki* (garlic, cucumber, dill, and yogurt dip), *melitzanosaláta* (eggplant dip), *skordaliá* (garlic dip), *taramosaláta* (fish roe dip), *keftédes* (crispy meatballs), *kalamária* (squid), *yigántes* (large white beans in tomato sauce), *loukánika* (little sausages), and octopus. *A few warnings:* Virtually all the squid served in Greece is frozen, and many restaurants serve dreadful keftédes and taramosaláta, and melitzanosaláta made with more bread than any other ingredient. That's the bad news. The good news is that the bad news leaves you free to order things you may not have had before—grilled green or red peppers or a tasty snack of *kokoretsi* (grilled entrails)—or something you probably have had (Greek olives), but never with such variety and pizzazz.

When it's not being used as filler, fresh Greek bread is generally tasty, substantial, nutritious, and inexpensive. If you're buying bread at a bakery, ask for *mavro somí* ("black bread"). It's almost always better than the blander white stuff. An exception is the white bread in the *kouloúria* (pretzel-like rolls covered with sesame seeds) you'll see Greeks buying on their way to work in the morning from street vendors carrying wooden trays of the bracelet-shaped snacks.

If you're wondering what to wash all this food down with, you'll want to know that the most popular Greek wine is *retsína,* usually white, although often rosé or red, flavored with pine resin. In theory, the European Common Market now controls the amount of resin added, so you're less likely to come across the harsh retsína that some compare to turpentine. If you don't like the taste of retsína, try *aretsínato* (wine without resin). The best-known Greek beer is Amstel, and you'll also find many European brands (Henniger is especially popular).

When it comes time for dessert, or a midafternoon infusion of sugar, Greeks usually head to a *zaharoplastíon* (sweet shop). Consequently, most restaurants don't offer a wide variety of desserts. Almost all restaurants do serve fruit (stewed in winter, fresh in season). If you're in Athens when cherries, apricots, peaches, and melon are in season, you might try an assortment for dessert—or a light meal. Increasingly, many restaurants do serve sweets such as *baklavá* (pastry and ground nuts with honey), *halvá* (sesame, chopped nuts, and honey), and *kataífi* (shredded wheat with chopped nuts and lots of honey). All these sweets are seriously sweet. If you want coffee with your dessert, keep in mind that for Greeks, regular coffee usually includes a mere teaspoon of sugar. Sweet coffee seems to be about a 50–50 mixture of coffee and sugar. If you've never had Greek coffee before, you may find it tastes a bit like espresso. Watch out for the grounds in the bottom of the cup.

Greek brandy is a popular after-dinner drink (though a bit sweet for non-Greek tastes), but the most popular Greek hard drink is *oúzo,* an anise-flavored liqueur. In fact, there are many cafes *(ouzerí)* where oúzo, wine, and a selection of mezédes are served from breakfast to bedtime. Oúzo is taken either straight or with water, which turns it cloudy white. You may see Greek men drinking quarter- and even half-bottles of oúzo with their lunch; if you do the same, you'll find out why the after-lunch siesta is so popular.

IN THE PLÁKA

Some of the most charming old restaurants in Athens are in the Pláka—and so are some of the worst tourist traps. Here are a few things to keep in mind when you head out for a meal.

Some Pláka restaurants station waiters outside who don't just urge you to come in and sit down but virtually pursue you down the street with an unrelenting sales pitch.

Getting the Best Deal on Dining

- Snack on a *koulouria* (round pretzel-like roll covered with sesame seeds), which costs about 100Dr (37¢).
- For a cheap and tasty meal, buy a *gyro* (sliced lamb served in píta bread), *souvlákia* (usually grilled bits of pork, lamb, or chicken) with píta, *tyrópitta* (cheese pie), *spanokópita* (spinach-and-cheese pie), or a sandwich at a *souvlakatzídiko* (souvlákia stand), *zaharoplastíon* (confectioner), or other sandwich shop. If you're not exhausted from sightseeing, get it to go: Table service costs more. See the "Quick Bites" box below for suggestions.
- Buy water and other drinks at a grocery store or kiosk, where they can cost a fourth of what you'll be charged at a restaurant.
- Be aware that seafood isn't a good choice in Athens; it's always expensive and its freshness is often questionable.
- Try a few *mezédes* (appetizers), usually about 500Dr to 1,000Dr ($1.85 to $3.70) a portion; if you're eating with friends, all the better: You can order a variety, share, and find out what you like best.
- Note that *krasí* (wine, whether retsína or nonresinated), and oúzo are generally less expensive than beer and soft drinks. Check to see whether a restaurant has its own wine from the barrel. Many restaurants have both a resinated and a nonresinated house wine, but customarily suggest the more expensive bottled wines to foreigners.
- Domestic beer, such as Amstel, is usually much less expensive than imported beer.

The hard sell is almost always a giveaway that the place caters to tourists. (That said, it's worth noting that calling out what's for sale is not invariably a ploy reserved for tourists. If you visit Athens's Central Market, you'll see and hear stall owners calling out the attractions of their meat, fish, and produce to passersby—and even waving particularly tempting fish and fowl in front of potential customers.)

If you're lucky enough to be in Athens in the winter, you'll see the Pláka as it once was: thronged with Greek families. In high summer, Greeks tend to abandon the Pláka to the tourists. In general, it's a good idea to avoid Pláka places with floor shows; many are clip joints that charge outrageous amounts (and levy surcharges not always openly stated on menus) for drinks and food. If you do get burned, stand your ground, phone the Tourist Police (☎ 171), and pay nothing before they arrive. Often the mere threat of calling the Tourist Police has the miraculous effect of causing a bill to be lowered.

Damigos (The Bakaliarakia). 41 Kidathinéon St. ☎ **01/322-5084.** Main courses 1,000–2,000Dr ($3.70–$7). No credit cards. Daily 7pm to anywhere from 11pm to 1am. Usually closed part of Aug and Sept. From Sýntagma Sq., head south on Filellínon St. or Níkis St. to Kidathinéon; Damigos is on the left just before Adrianoú St. GREEK/CODFISH.

Damigos has been serving delicious deep-fried codfish and eggplant, as well as chops and stews for inveterate meat-eaters, since 1865. It's a basement tavérna with enormous wine barrels in the back room and an ancient column supporting the roof in the front room. The wine comes from the family vineyards, and there are few pleasures greater than sipping some retsína while you watch the cook—who manages to look genial while never smiling—turn out unending meals in his absurdly small kitchen. Don't miss the delicious skordaliá (garlic sauce), which is equally good with cod, eggplant, bread—well, you get the idea.

Eden Vegetarian Restaurant. 12 Lissíou St. ☎ **01/324-8858.** Main courses 1,200–2,500Dr ($4.44–$9). No credit cards. Daily noon–midnight. From Adrianoú St. take Mnissikléos up 2 blocks toward Acropolis to Lissíou St. VEGETARIAN.

You can find vegetarian dishes at almost every Greek restaurant, but if you want to experience soy (rather than eggplant) moussaká, mushroom pie with a sturdy whole-wheat crust, freshly squeezed juices, and salads with bean sprouts, join the young Athenians and European students who patronize the Eden. You may or may not be amused to watch Greeks tucking into their healthy fare while smoking nonstop. The prices here are reasonable, if not cheap, and the decor, with 1920s-style prints and mirrors, and wrought-iron lamps, is engaging.

Koúklis Ouzerí (To Yeráni). 14 Tripódon St. ☎ **01/324-7605.** Appetizers 500–1,000Dr ($1.85–$3.70). No credit cards. Daily 11am–2am. Take Kidathinéon to Théspidos and climb toward Acropolis; Tripódon is 1st street on right after Adrianoú. GREEK.

Besides Koúklis Ouzerí and To Yeráni ("geranium"), Greeks also call this popular old favorite "Skolarío" because of the nearby school. Find a seat, and a waiter will present a large tray with about a dozen plates of mezédes—appetizer portions of fried fish, beans, grilled eggplant, taramosaláta, cucumber-and-tomato salad, olives, fried cheese, sausages, and other seasonal specialties. Accept the ones that appeal to you. If you don't order all 12, you can enjoy a tasty and inexpensive meal, washed down with the house *krasí* (wine).

Plátanos Tavérna. 4 Dioyénous St. ☎ **01/322-0666.** Main courses 1,600–3,000Dr ($6–$11). No credit cards. Mon–Sat noon–4:30pm and 8pm–midnight. From Adrianoú St., take Mnissikléos up 1 block toward Acropolis and turn right on Dioyénous. GREEK.

This traditional tavérna on a quiet pedestrian square near the Tower of the Winds has tables outdoors in good weather beneath a spreading *plátanos* (plane tree). Inside, where locals usually congregate to escape the summer sun at midday and the tourists in the evening, you can enjoy looking at the old paintings and photos on the walls. The Plátanos has been serving good *spitiko fageto* (home cooking) since 1932 and has managed to keep steady customers happy while enchanting visitors. If artichokes or spinach with lamb are on the menu, you're in luck: They're delicious. The house wine is tasty and there's a wide choice of bottled wines from many regions of Greece.

Tavérna Xinos. 4 Agelou Geronta St. (just off Kidathenéon St., and signposted in the cul-de-sac). ☎ **01/322-1065.** Meals 2,000–4,000Dr ($7–$15). No credit cards. Daily 8pm to anywhere from 11pm to 1am; sometimes closed Sun, usually closed part of July and Aug. GREEK.

Despite the forgivable lapse in spelling, Xinos's business card says it best: "In the heart of old Athens there is still a place where the traditional Greek way of cooking is upheld." In summer, there are tables outside in the courtyard; in winter, you can warm yourself by the coal-burning stove and admire the frescoes showing Greek soldiers, gypsies, and what appears to be a camel. While the strolling musicians may not sound as good as the Three Tenors, they do sing wonderful Greek golden oldies, accompanying themselves on the guitar and bouzouki. (If you are serenaded, you may want to give the musicians a small tip. If you want to hear the theme from "Never on Sunday," ask to hear "Ena Zorbas.") Most evenings, tourists predominate until around 10, when locals begin to arrive, as they have since Xinos opened in 1935.

NEAR SÝNTAGMA SQUARE

Neon. 3 Mitropóleos St. (southwest corner of Sýntagma Sq.). ☎ **01/322-8155.** Snacks 200–650Dr (75¢–$2.41); sandwiches 450–900Dr ($1.70–$3.35); main courses 1,000–3,000Dr ($3.70–$11). No credit cards. Daily 9am–midnight. GREEK/INTERNATIONAL.

Quick Bites

The **Apollonion Bakery,** 10 Níkis St. (near Sýntagma Square), and the **Elleniki Gonia,** 10 Karayióryis tis Servías St., are among a number of places around Sýntagma that make sandwiches to order and sell croissants, both stuffed and plain. **Ariston** is a small chain of zaharoplastía (confectioners), with a branch at the corner of Karayióryis tis Servías and Voulís streets (just off Sýntagma), that sells snacks as well as pastries. **Floca** is another excellent chain of pastry shops with 14 branches; there's one in the arcade on Panepistimíou Street near Sýntagma and another just south of the Center for Acropolis Studies, at Makriyánni and Hatzihrístou; as always, you pay extra to be served at a table. For the quintessential Greek sweet *loukoumades* (round doughnut-center-like pastries deep-fried and then drenched with honey and topped with powdered sugar and cinnamon), nothing beats **Doris,** 30 Praxiteles St., a continuation of Lekká Street, a few blocks from Sýntagma. If you're still hungry, Doris serves hearty stews and pasta dishes for absurdly low prices daily except Sunday until 3:30pm. **Everest** is another chain worth trying; there's one a block north of Kolonáki Square at Tsakálof and Iraklítou. Also in Kolonáki Square, **To Kotopolo** ("the Chicken Place") serves succulent grilled chicken to take out or eat in. In the Pláka, you'll find excellent coffee and sweets at the **K. Kotsolis Pastry Shop,** 112 Adrianoú St., an oasis of old-fashioned charm in the midst of the souvenir shops. The **Center of Hellenic Tradition,** opening onto both 36 Pandrossou St. and 59 Mitropóleos St., near the flea market, has a small cafe with a spectacular view of the Acropolis where you can revive yourself with a cappuccino and snack on pastries.

This new addition to the Neon chain is convenient, though not as charming as the original restored kafeníon on Omónia Square or the Kolonáki Neon (see below). You're sure to find something to your taste—maybe a Mexican omelet, a salad, spaghetti bolognese, choices from the salad bar, or sweets ranging from Black Forest cake to tiramisú.

Restaurant Kentrikón. 3 Kolokotróni St. ☎ **01/323-2482.** Main courses 1,500–5,000Dr ($6–$19). AE, DC, EURO, MC, V. Mon–Fri noon–5 or 6pm. Walk 1 block up Stadíou and turn left. GREEK/INTERNATIONAL.

The Kentrikón has been here for decades, setting up tables outside in the arcade in the summer, and serving indoors (with air-conditioning in the summer) year-round. Its central location and reasonable prices make it popular with local workers and businesspeople as well as tourists. The large interior room can be terribly noisy, and service seems to alternate between rushed and desultory. This is definitely not the place for a romantic meal. The lamb ragout with spinach, chicken with okra, and the Kentrikón's special macaroni are often on the menu.

NEAR MONASTIRÁKI SQUARE

✪ **Abyssinia Cafe.** Plateia Abyssinia, Monastiráki. ☎ **01/321-7047.** Appetizers and main courses 600–2,000Dr ($2.20–$7). No credit cards. Mon–Sat 10:30am to anywhere from 10pm to 1am. Sometimes closed part of Jan and Feb. Abyssinia Square is off Ifaistou (Hephaistos) St., which is parallel to Adrianoú, almost directly opposite entrance to Ancient Agorá. GREEK.

This small cafe in a ramshackle building has a nicely restored interior featuring lots of gleaming dark wood and polished copper. It faces a lopsided square where furniture restorers ply their trade and you can buy anything from gramophones to hubcaps in "antiques" shops. You can sit indoors or outside and have just a coffee, but it's tempting to snack on *saganaki* (fried cheese), fried eggplant, or keftédes (meatballs).

Tavérna Ipiros (Epirus). 15 Ayíou Philíppou Sq. ☎ **01/324-5572.** Main courses 1,200–2,000Dr ($4.44–$7). No credit cards. Daily noon–midnight. From Monastiráki Metro station, walk 2 blocks southwest on Ermoú to Ayiou Philíppou. GREEK.

This is a great budget spot on a crowded little square in the heart of the flea market. The food is standard Greek fare, the portions generous, and the prices fair. Be sure to take a table that belongs to unpretentious little Ipiros, rather than to a nearby competitor taking advantage of this place's reputation.

✪ **Thanasis.** 69 Mitropóleos St. (just off the northeast corner of Monastiráki Sq.). ☎ **01/324-4705.** Main courses 500–2,500Dr ($1.85–$9). No credit cards. Daily 9am–2am. GREEK.

Thanasis serves souvlákia and píta and exceptionally good french fries, both to go and at its outdoor and indoor tables; as always, prices are higher if you sit down to eat. On weekends, it often takes the strength and determination of an Olympic athlete to get through the door and place an order. It's worth the effort: This is both a great budget choice and a great place to take in the local scene.

IN MAKRIYÁNNI & KOUKÁKI

Meltemi Ouzerí. 26 Zinní St. ☎ **01/902-8230.** Appetizers and entrees 600–2,150Dr ($2.20–$8). No credit cards. Mon–Sat noon–1:30am. Walk 3 blocks up (west) from Olympic Airways office on Syngroú Ave. and turn right. GREEK.

If you're arriving at or leaving from the Olympic Airways office on Syngroú, this nearby ouzerí is the obvious place for a light meal and drink. In summer, trees and big white umbrellas shade the blue chairs and tables outdoors. The mezédes (appetizers), including homemade sausages (loukánika) and various eggplant dishes, are excellent, and you may simply want to order the assorted platter. There's usually a variety of salads, rather than just the inevitable "country salad," as well as daily specials.

Socrates' Prison. 20 Mitséon St. ☎ **01/922-3434.** Main courses 1,250–2,700Dr ($4.60–$10). V. Mon–Sat 7pm–1am. Closed Aug. Cross to non-Acropolis side of Dionysíou Areopayítou St., walk west (away from Temple of Zeus) 1 block, and turn left; it's halfway down block on left. GREEK/CONTINENTAL.

This place is a favorite with both Greeks and American and European expatriates living in Athens, who lounge at tables outdoors in good weather and in the pleasant indoor rooms year-round. Some long tables are communal, and there are also tables for four. The food here is noticeably more imaginative than average Greek fare (try the veggie croquettes), and includes continental dishes such as pork roll stuffed with vegetables, and salade Niçoise. The retsína is excellent, and there's a wide choice of bottled wines and beers. This is a good place to head if you don't want to eat in the Pláka but enjoy strolling through it on your way to or from dinner.

NEAR THE NATIONAL ARCHAEOLOGICAL MUSEUM & OMÓNIA SQUARE

Athinaikon. 2 Themistokléous St. ☎ **01/383-8485.** Main courses 2,000–4,000Dr ($7.40–$16). No credit cards. Mon–Sat 10am–midnight. Closed Aug. Themistokléous St. intersects Panepistimoú St. at Omonía Sq. GREEK.

This is a favorite haunt of lawyers and businesspeople working in the Omónia Square area. You can have just some appetizers (technically, this is an ouzerí) or a full meal.

Obviously, the way to have a reasonably priced snack is to stick to the appetizers and pass on the grilled shrimp or swordfish.

Neon. 1 Dorou, Omónia Sq. ☎ **01/522-9939.** Snacks 200–650Dr (75¢–$2.41); sandwiches 450–900Dr ($1.66–$3.35); main courses 1,000–3,000Dr ($3.70–$11). No credit cards. Daily 8am–midnight or later. GREEK/INTERNATIONAL.

In a handsome 1920s building, the Neon serves up cafeteria-style food, including cooked-to-order pasta, omelets, and grills, as well as salads and sweets. Equally good for a meal or a snack, the Neon proves that fast food doesn't have to be junk food.

Restaurant Kostoyannis. 37 Zaími St. (2 blocks behind the National Archaeological Museum). ☎ **01/822-0624.** Main courses 2,400–6,000Dr ($9–$22). No credit cards. Mon–Sat 8pm–2am. GREEK/SEAFOOD.

It's not easy to simply walk into Kostoyannis and sit down: Just inside the entrance is a show-stopping display of shrimp, mussels, fresh fish, seemingly endless appetizers, tempting stews *(stifada)* in ceramic pots, and yards of chops that could almost make a dedicated vegetarian fall off the wagon. You can choose the items you'd like to sample, and you may decide to make an entire meal just from the mezédes (appetizers), which I think are even better than the entrees. Don't be put off by this restaurant's slightly out-of-the-way location on a rather uninteresting street: It's well worth the trip.

Taygetos. 4 Satovriandou St. ☎ **01/523-5352.** Main courses 1,000–2,000Dr ($3.70–$7). No credit cards. Mon–Sat 9am–1am. GREEK/SOUVLAKIA.

This is a great place to stop on your way to or from the National Archaeological Museum. Service is swift, and the souvlákia and fried potatoes are excellent, as are the grilled lamb and chicken (priced by the kilo). The menu sometimes also includes delicious *kokoretsi* (grilled entrails). The Ellinikon Restaurant next door is also a good value.

IN KOLONÁKI

Neon. 6 Tsakálof St., Kolonáki Sq. ☎ **01/364-6873.** Snacks 200–650Dr (75¢–$2.41); sandwiches 450–900Dr ($1.66–$3.35); main courses 1,000–3,000Dr ($3.70–$11). No credit cards. Daily 8am–midnight or later. GREEK/INTERNATIONAL.

The Kolonáki Neon serves the same food as the Sýntagma and Omónia branches, but the fair prices are especially welcome in this expensive neighborhood. Tsakálof is a shady pedestrian arcade, and you can usually sit indoors or outdoors.

Rhodia. 44 Aristipou St. ☎ **01/722-9883.** Main courses 2,000–3,500Dr ($7–$13). No credit cards. Mon–Sat 8pm–2am. GREEK.

This well-established tavérna in a handsome old Kolonáki house has tables in its small garden in good weather—although the interior, with its tile floor and old prints, is so charming that you may be tempted to eat indoors. The Rhodia is a favorite of visiting archaeologists from the nearby British and American Schools of Classical Studies, as well as of local residents. It may not sound like just what you'd always hoped to have for dinner, but the octopus in mustard sauce is terrific, as are the perhaps less intimidating veal or dolmades (stuffed grape leaves) in egg-lemon sauce. The house wine is excellent, as is the halvah, which manages to be both creamy and crunchy.

WORTH A SPLURGE

To Kafeneio. 26 Loukianou St. ☎ **01/722-9056.** Main courses 1,800–4,200Dr ($7–$16). No credit cards. Mon–Sat 11am–midnight or later. From Kolonáki Sq., follow Patriarkou Ioakim St. several blocks to Loukianou and turn right to Kafeneio. GREEK/INTERNATIONAL.

This is hardly a typical rough-and-ready Kafeneio (coffee shop/cafe): There are pictures on the walls, pink tablecloths, and a clientele of ladies who lunch and staff members from the many embassies in Kolonáki. In short, a great people-watching place. If you relax you can easily run up a substantial tab ($50 for lunch or dinner for two is easy), but you can also eat more modestly and equally elegantly. If you have something light, like the artichokes à la polita, leeks in crème fraîche, or onion pie, washed down with draft beer or the house wine, you can finish up with profiteroles and not put too big a dent in your budget. This is an especially congenial spot if you're eating alone.

Vlassis. 8 Paster St. (off Plateia Mavili). ☎ **01/646-3060.** Main courses 1,500–3,000Dr ($5.55–$11). No credit cards. Reservations necessary. Mon–Sat 8pm–1am.

Greeks call this kind of food *paradisiako*—traditional, but paradisical is just as good a description. This is traditional food fit for the gods: delicious fluffy vegetable cro-quettes, eggplant salad that tastes like no other eggplant salad, hauntingly tender lamb in egg-lemon sauce. It's a sign of Vlassis's popularity with Athenians—the last time I ate there, I was the only obvious foreigner in the place—that there's not even a dis-creet sign announcing its presence in a small apartment building on hard-to-find Paster Street. Figure the price of a taxi (no more than $10) into your meal tab; you may feel so giddy with delight after eating that you won't mind the half-hour walk back to Sýntagma Square.

5 Seeing the Sights

SIGHTSEEING SUGGESTIONS

IF YOU HAVE 1 DAY Try to be at the **Acropolis** as soon as it opens so that you can take in the site and enjoy seeing the **Parthenon** and the **Acropolis Museum** before the crowds arrive. Afterward, walk downhill to visit the **Ancient Agorá,** and then head into **Monastiráki** and the **Pláka,** where you can window-shop and relax over lunch or dinner.

IF YOU HAVE 2 DAYS On Day 1, follow the above. It's worth spending several hours of Day 2 at the **National Archaeological Museum** (again, try to arrive the minute it opens to beat the crowds). Then visit some of Athens's **smaller museums**— or, if you need a change of pace, head up **Mount Lykavitós,** on the funicular that leaves from the top of Ploutárchou Street (500Dr/$1.85, 8am to 10pm, about every 20 minutes in summer). If the *néfos* (smog) isn't too bad, you'll have a wonderful view of Athens, Piraeus, and the Saronic Gulf. If you have an extra hour, take one of the paths from the summit and stroll down Lykavitós, enjoying the scent of the pine trees and the changing views of the city.

IF YOU HAVE 3 DAYS OR MORE For Days 1 and 2, follow the above. For the rest of your stay, visit more of the museums below or consider a **day trip** to one of the great sights of antiquity, such as **Delphi** or **Sounion;** a day excursion to **Corinth, Mycenae,** and **Epidauros** (best done on a bus tour); or a visit to the Byzantine **monasteries** of Dafní or Kaisarianí. (See "Side Trips: Delphi & More," below). If you don't want to go home without seeing one of the "isles of Greece," take a day trip by boat from Piraeus to one or more of the islands of the Saronic Gulf. **Aegina (Égina), Póros, Hydra (Idra), Salamis,** and **Spetsai** are all feasible day trips—but best not done the day before you leave Athens, lest bad weather strand you on an island. Whatever you do, be sure to give yourself time to sit in cafes and watch the world go by.

A Warning

Strikes that close museums and archaeological sites can occur without warning. Decide what you most want to see and go there as soon as possible after your arrival. The fact that something is open today says nothing about tomorrow. If you're here in the off-season, check with the **Greek National Tourist Organization** (☎ **01/331-0437**) for the abbreviated winter hours of sites and museums.

THE ACROPOLIS & ANCIENT AGORÁ

✪ **The Acropolis.** ☎ **01/321-0219.** Admission 2,000Dr ($7) adults, 1,500Dr ($6) seniors, 1,000Dr ($3.70) students with ID. Free Sun. Admission includes entrance to the Acropolis Museum, which sometimes closes earlier than the site. Summer, Mon–Fri 8am–6pm, Sat–Sun and holidays 8:30am–3pm; check winter hours with Greek National Tourist Organization (☎ **01/331-0437**). Follow Dionysíou Areopayítou St., Theorías St., or path up through Ancient Agorá to reach path to ticket booth and Acropolis entrance.

When you climb up the Acropolis—the heights above the city—you'll realize why people seem to have lived here as long ago as 5000 B.C. The sheer sides of the Acropolis make it a superb natural defense, just the place to avoid enemies and to be able to see invaders coming across the sea or the plains of Attica. And, of course, it helped that in antiquity there was a spring here.

In classical times, when Athens's population had grown to around 250,000, people lived on the slopes below the Acropolis, which had become the city's most important religious center. Athens's civic and business center, the Agorá, and its cultural center, with several theaters and concert halls, bracketed the Acropolis; when you peer over the sides of the Acropolis at the houses in the Pláka and the remains of the ancient Agorá and the Theater of Dionysos, you'll see the layout of the ancient city. Sýntagma and Omónia squares, the heart of today's Athens, were well out of the ancient city center.

Even the Acropolis's superb heights couldn't protect it from the Persian invasion of 480 B.C., when most of its monuments were burned and destroyed. You may notice some immense column drums built into the Acropolis's walls. When the great Athenian statesman Pericles ordered the monuments of the Acropolis rebuilt, he had the drums from the destroyed Parthenon built into the walls lest Athenians forget what had happened—and so that they would remember that they had rebuilt what they had lost. Pericles's rebuilding program began about 448 B.C.; the new Parthenon was dedicated 10 years later, but work on other monuments continued for a century.

The Parthenon, dedicated to Athena Parthénos (the Virgin), patron goddess of Athens, was, of course, the most important religious shrine here, but there were shrines to many other gods and goddesses on the Acropolis's broad summit. As you climb up to the Acropolis, passing first through the Beulé Gate, built by the Romans and named for the French archaeologist who discovered it in 1852, and then through the *Propylaia,* the monumental 5th-century B.C. entranceway, you'll notice the little temple of Athena Nike (Athena of Victory) perched above the Propylaia. This beautifully proportioned Ionic temple was built in 424 B.C. and restored in the 1930s. Off to the left of the Parthenon is the Erechtheion, which the Athenians honored as the tomb of Erechtheus, a legendary king of Athens. A hole in the ceiling and floor of the northern porch indicates the spot where Poseidon's trident struck to make a spring (symbolizing control of the sea) gush forth during his contest with Athena to be the city's chief deity. Athena countered with an olive tree (symbolizing control of the rich Attic plain); the olive tree planted beside the Erechtheion reminds visitors of her

Getting the Best Deal on Sightseeing

- Take advantage of free admission to many sites and museums every Sunday. Admission is always free at the Center for Acropolis Studies (see below); the Center of Folk Art and Tradition (also known as the Cultural Center of the Municipality of Athens), 6 Angelikís Hatzimiháli St.; the Children's Museum, 14 Kidathinéon St.; the Jewish Museum, 39 Níkis St.; the Museum of Greek Costume, 7 Dimókritou St.; the Museum of Greek Popular Musical Instruments, 1–3 Diogenous St., and several other small museums.

- If you're a student, your current student ID may net you a discount; if you run into trouble, take documentation to the International Student and Youth Travel Service (see "Special Discounts" under "Athens Deals & Discounts," earlier in this chapter). It can issue a student card entitling you to half-price admission to most archaeological sites and museums, as well as discounts on many performances and events.

- If you're studying archaeology, art history, or the classics, obtain a free pass to museums and sites by writing to the Museum Section, Ministry of Science and Culture, 14 Aristídou St., 105 59 Athens, where you should be able to collect your pass when you produce a copy of your letter and documentation. Apply several weeks in advance and include verification from your college or university.

- If you arrive an hour or so before closing, some sites and museums will stamp your entrance ticket so that you can make a free return visit the next day.

victory. Give yourself a little time to enjoy the delicate carving on the Erechtheion, and be sure to see the original caryatids in the Acropolis Museum.

However charmed you are by these elegant little temples, you're probably still heading resolutely toward the Parthenon, and you may be disappointed to realize that visitors are not allowed inside, both to protect the monument and to allow restoration work to proceed safely. If you find this frustrating, keep in mind that in antiquity only priests and honored visitors were allowed in to see the monumental—some 36 feet tall—statue of Athena designed by the great Phidias, who was in charge of Pericles's building program. Nothing of this huge gold-and-ivory statue remains, but there's a small Roman copy in the National Archaeological Museum—and horrific renditions on souvenirs ranging from T-shirts to oúzo bottles. Admittedly, the original statue was not understated; the 2nd-century A.D. traveler Pausanias, one of the first guidebook writers, recorded that the statue stood "upright in an ankle-length tunic with a head of Medusa carved in ivory on her breast. She has a Victory about 8 feet high, and a spear in her hand and a shield at her feet, with a snake beside the shield, possibly representing Erechtheus." The floor of the room in which the statue stood was covered in olive oil so that the gold and ivory reflected through the dimly lit room.

If you look over the edge of the Acropolis toward the Temple of Hephaistos in the ancient Agorá, and then back up at the Parthenon, you can't help but be struck by how much lighter, how much more graceful, the Parthenon is than the Theseion, as the Temple of Hephaistos is known today. Scholars tell us that this is because Iktinos, the architect of the Parthenon, was something of a magician of optical illusions: The columns and stairs—the very floor—of the Parthenon all appear straight because they are minutely curved. The exterior columns, for example, are slightly thicker in the middle (a device known as *entasis*), which makes the entire column appear straight.

The Acropolis & Ancient Agorá

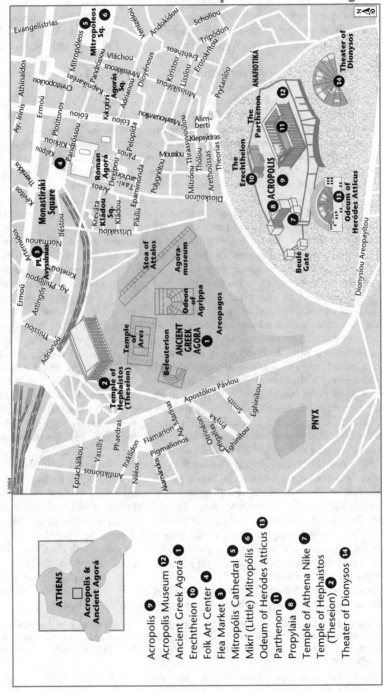

ATHENS

Acropolis & Ancient Agorá

Acropolis **9**
Acropolis Museum **12**
Ancient Greek Agorá **1**
Erechtheion **10**
Folk Art Center **4**
Flea Market **3**
Mitrópolis Cathedral **5**
Mikrí (Little) Mitropólis **6**
Odeum of Heródes Atticus **13**
Parthenon **11**
Propylaia **8**
Temple of Athena Nike **7**
Temple of Hephaistos (Theseion) **2**
Theater of Dionysos **14**

That's why the Parthenon, with 17 columns on each side and 8 at each end (creating a peristyle, or exterior colonnade, of 46 relatively slender columns), looks so graceful, while the Theseion, with only 6 columns at each end and 13 along each side, seems so stolid.

Of course, one reason that the Parthenon looks so airy is that it is, literally, open to the air. The entire roof and much of the interior were blown to smithereens in 1687, when a party of Venetians attempted to take the Acropolis from the Turks. A shell fired from nearby Mouseion Hill struck the Parthenon—where the Turks were storing gunpowder and munitions—and caused appalling damage to the building and its sculptures. Most of the remaining sculptures were carted off to London by Lord Elgin in the first decade of the 19th century. Those surviving sculptures—known as the Elgin Marbles—are on display in the British Museum, causing ongoing pain to generations of Greeks, who continue to press for their return.

The Parthenon originally had sculpture in both its pediments, as well as a frieze running around the entire temple. The frieze was made up of alternating triglyphs (panels with three incised grooves) and *metopes* (sculptured panels). The east pediment showed scenes from the birth of Athena, the west pediment Athena and Poseidon's contest for possession of Athens. The long frieze showed the battle of the Athenians, led by the hero Theseus, against the Amazons; scenes from the Trojan War; and the struggles of the Olympian gods against giants and centaurs. The message of most of this sculpture was the triumph of knowledge and civilization (read: Athens) over the forces of darkness and barbarians. An interior frieze showed scenes from the Panathenaic Festival each August, when citizens processed through the streets, bringing a new *peplos* (tunic) for the statue of Athena. Only a few fragments of any of the sculptures remain in place, and every visitor will have to decide whether it's a good or a bad thing that Lord Elgin removed so much before the *néfos* (smog) spread over Athens and ate away at the remaining sculpture here.

If you're lucky enough to visit the Acropolis on a smog-free and sunny day, you'll see the golden and cream tones of the Parthenon's handsome Pentelic marble at their most subtle. It may come as something of a shock to realize that the Parthenon, like most other monuments here, was painted in antiquity, with gay colors that have since faded, revealing the tones of the natural marble.

The Acropolis Archaeological Museum hugs the ground to detract as little as possible from the ancient monuments. Inside, you'll see the four original caryatids from the Erechtheion that are still in Athens (one disappeared during the Ottoman occupation, and one is in the British Museum). Other delights here include sculpture from the Parthenon burned by the Persians, statues of *korai* (maidens) dedicated to Athena, figures of *kouroi* (young men), and a wide range of finds from the Acropolis.

Those interested in learning more about the Acropolis should visit the **Center for Acropolis Studies,** on Makriyánni Street just southeast of the Acropolis (☎ **01/923-9381**). It's open daily 9am to 2:30pm; admission is free. On display are artifacts, reconstructions, photographs, drawings—and plaster casts of the Elgin Marbles that Greeks hope will someday return to Athens and be put on display here.

Ancient Agorá. Below the Acropolis on the edge of Monastiráki (entrance on Adrianoú St., near Ayíou Philíppou Sq., east of Monastiráki Sq.). ☎ **01/321-0185.** Admission (includes museum) 1,200Dr ($4.45) adults, 900Dr ($3.35) seniors, 600Dr ($2.20) students. Tues–Sun 8:30am–3pm.

The Agorá was Athens's commercial and civic center, with buildings used for a wide range of political, educational, philosophical, theatrical, and athletic purposes—which may be why what remains seems such a jumble. This is a nice place to wander and enjoy the views up toward the Acropolis, take in the herb garden and flowers planted around the 5th-century B.C. Temple of Hephaistos and Athena (the Theseion), and admire the 2nd-century B.C. Stoa of Attalos, totally reconstructed by American archaeologists in the 1950s. The museum in the Stoa's ground floor has finds from 5,000 years of Athenian history, including sculpture and pottery, as well as a voting machine and a child's potty seat, all with labels in English. The museum closes 15 minutes before the site.

THE TOP MUSEUMS

✪ National Archaeological Museum. 44 Patissíon St. ☎ **01/821-7717.** Admission 2,000Dr ($7) adults, 1,000Dr ($3.70) students. Mon 12:30–5pm, Tues–Fri 8am–5pm, Sat–Sun and holidays 8:30am–3pm. Walk about a third of a mile (10 minutes) north of Omónia Sq. on the road officially named October 28 Ave. but usually called Patissíon. Or take trolley bus no. 2, 4, 5, 9, 11, 12, 15, or 18 from the east side of Amalías Ave., 3 blocks south of Sýntagma Sq.

This is an enormous and enormously popular museum; try to arrive as soon as it opens so that you can see the exhibits, and not just other visitors' backs. Early arrival should give you at least an hour before most tour groups turn up. Don't miss the stunning gold masks, cups, dishes, and jewelry unearthed from the site of Mycenae by Heinrich Schliemann in 1876—on display in the first room—and the elegant marble Cycladic figurines (ca. 2000 B.C.) in the adjacent room. Other stars of the collection include the monumental bronzes (especially the mid-5th-century B.C. figure variously identified as Zeus or Poseidon), both the black and the red figure vases, and the restored 3500 B.C. frescoes from the island of Santorini.

Goulandris Museum of Cycladic and Ancient Greek Art. 4 Neophytou Douká St. ☎ **01/722-8321.** Admission 800Dr ($3) adults, 250Dr (90¢) students. Mon and Wed–Fri 10am–4pm, Sat 10am–3pm. From Sýntagma Sq., walk 7 blocks east along Vasilíssis Sofías Ave., then half a block north on Neophytou Douká; museum is on right.

This handsome new museum houses the largest collection of Cycladic art outside the National Archaeological Museum, with some 230 stone and pottery vessels and figurines from the 3rd millennium B.C. on display. See if you agree with those who have compared the faces of the Cycladic figurines to the work of Modigliani. Be sure to go through the courtyard into the museum's newest acquisition: an elegant 19th-century house with some of its original furnishings, and visiting exhibits.

Benáki Museum. 1 Koumbári St. (at Vasilíssis Sofías Ave., Kolonáki, 5 blocks east of Sýntagma Sq.). ☎ **01/361-1617.**

The Benáki Museum has been closed for major alterations. If it has reopened by the time you're here, you're in luck. The costume collection is superb, and the relics of Greece's 1821 War of Independence, including Lord Byron's writing desk and pen, are fascinating.

Byzantine Museum. 22 Vasilíssis Sofías Ave. (at Vassiléos Konstandínou Ave.). ☎ **01/723-1570** or 01/721-1027. Admission 500Dr ($1.85) adults, 250Dr (90¢) students. Tues–Sun 8:30am–3pm. From Sýntagma Sq., walk along Queen Sophias Ave. (aka Venizelou Ave.) for about 15 minutes; museum will be on your right, on same side of street as National Garden.

As its name makes clear, this museum, in a 19th-century Florentine-style former villa, is devoted to the art and history of the Byzantine era (roughly the 4th to the 15th centuries A.D.). Greece's most important collection of icons and religious art— along with sculptures, altars, mosaics, religious vestments, bibles, and a small-scale reconstruction of an early Christian basilica—are exhibited on several floors around a courtyard.

Greek Folk Art Museum. 17 Kidathenéon St., Pláka. ☎ **01/322-9031.** Admission 500Dr ($1.85) adults, 400Dr ($1.50) seniors, 300Dr ($1.10) students. Tues–Sun 10am–2pm.

Athens

ATTRACTIONS
Acropolis Museum 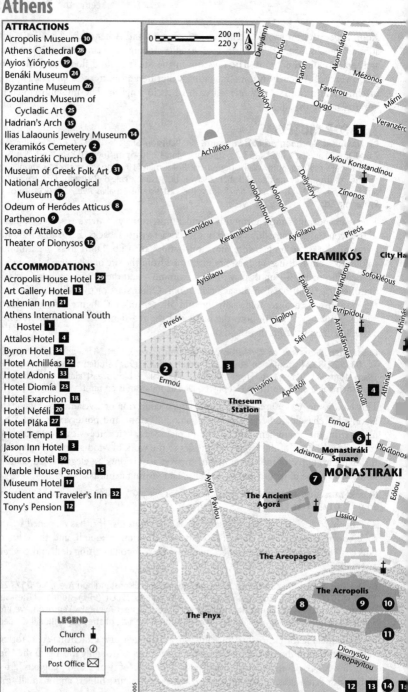10
Athens Cathedral 28
Ayios Yióryios 19
Benáki Museum 24
Byzantine Museum 26
Goulandris Museum of
  Cycladic Art 25
Hadrian's Arch 35
Ilias Lalaounis Jewelry Museum 14
Keramikós Cemetery 2
Monastiráki Church 6
Museum of Greek Folk Art 31
National Archaeological
  Museum 16
Odeum of Heródes Atticus 8
Parthenon 9
Stoa of Attalos 7
Theater of Dionysos 12

ACCOMMODATIONS
Acropolis House Hotel 29
Art Gallery Hotel 13
Athenian Inn 21
Athens International Youth
  Hostel 1
Attalos Hotel 4
Byron Hotel 34
Hotel Achilléas 22
Hotel Adonis 33
Hotel Diomía 23
Hotel Exarchion 18
Hotel Neféli 20
Hotel Pláka 27
Hotel Tempi 5
Jason Inn Hotel 3
Kouros Hotel 30
Marble House Pension 15
Museum Hotel 17
Student and Traveler's Inn 32
Tony's Pension 12

LEGEND
Church ✝
Information ⓘ
Post Office ✉

E-0005

(Map of Athens showing streets including Delifánni, Chíou, Psarón, Akominátou, Mézonos, Favíerou, Márni, Veranzérou, Deliyóryi, Ougó, Achilléos, Ayíou Konstandínou, Zínonos, Kolokynthoús, Kolonoú, Deliyóryi, Leonídou, Keramikoú, Ayísilaou, Pireós, KERAMIKÓS, City Ha..., Menándrou, Sofokléous, Epikoúrou, Evripídou, Pireós, Ayísilaou, Dipílou, Aristofánous, Athinás, Sári, Thissíou, Apostóli, Miaoúli, Athinás, Ermoú, Theseum Station, Ermoú, Adrianoú, Monastiráki Square, Ploútonos, MONASTIRÁKI, The Ancient Agorá, Lissíou, Eólou, Ayíou Pávlou, The Areopagos, The Acropolis, The Pnyx, Dionysíou Areopayítou; numbered markers 1, 2, 3, 4, 5, 6, 7, 8, 9, 10, 11, 12, 13, 14, 15)

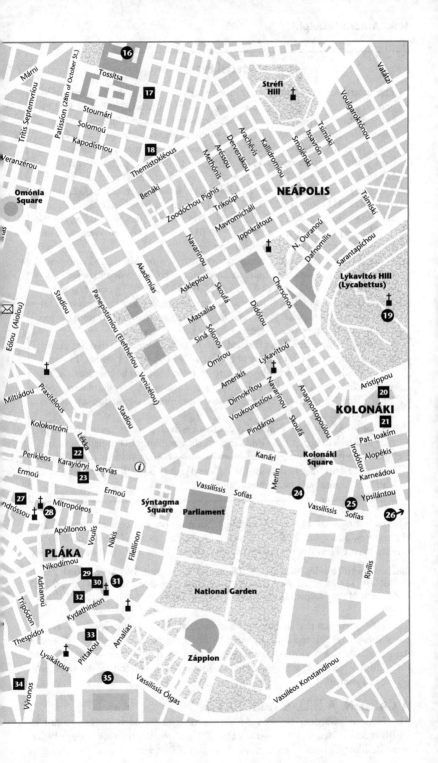

Special Events

The annual **Athens Festival,** early June to early October, is the city's main celebration of the arts. The Odeum *(Odíon)* of Heródes Atticus, built in A.D. 174,
is the setting for performances by well-known Greek and foreign orchestras,
ballet companies, singers, and dancers; offerings also include opera and classical
Greek tragedies and comedies. The only drawbacks are that the stone seats are
hard, with thin foam cushions, and there are no backrests. Tickets cost about
5,000Dr to 12,000Dr ($19 to $44). Find out what's playing in the English-
language press or at the Athens Festival Office, 4 Stadíou St. (☎ **01/322-1459**
or 01/322-3111 to 01/322-3119, ext. 137). It's open Monday to Saturday
8:30am to 2pm and 5 to 7pm, Sunday 10am to 1pm. If they're available, tickets
can also be purchased at the Odeum (☎ **01/323-2771**) on the evening of the
show. Performances usually begin at 9pm.

The **Lykavitós Festival,** an outdoor event held atop Mount Lykavitós each
summer, features more contemporary entertainers. For schedule and ticket information, contact the Lykavitós Theater (☎ **01/322-1459**). You can buy tickets
at the Athens Festival box office or at the gate. Ask about free transportation for
ticket holders. Otherwise, you'll need to take a taxi or the funicular from the top
of Ploutárchou Street (see "Sightseeing Suggestions," above).

The annual **Daphni Wine Festival** runs from mid-August to mid-September
on the grounds of the Monastery of Daphni, 6¼ miles west of Athens. Entrance
costs 2,000Dr ($7), which allows you to go from booth to booth sampling the
wines. Check with the Athens Festival box office for more information. (See
"Side Trips: Daphní & Eleusis," below, for more information about the
monastery and directions.)

Beyond Athens, the annual **Epidauros Festival** presents performances of
ancient Greek drama at the world's most perfect amphitheater, usually from late
June to early September. Special buses (about 2,000Dr/$7) run from Athens
during the festival. Check with the Athens Festival box office (see above) for
schedules, tickets, and more information.

This endearing small museum has dazzling embroideries and costumes from all over
the country, and a small room with zany frescoes of gods and heroes done by the
eccentric artist Theofilos Hadjimichael, who painted in the early part of this century.

Ilias Lalaounis Jewelry Museum. 12 Kalispéri (at Karyátidon). ☎ **01/922-1044.** Admission 800Dr ($3). Mon and Wed 9am–9pm, Thurs–Sat 9am–3pm, Sun 10am–3pm. Walk 1
block south of the Acropolis between the Theater of Dionysos and the Odeum of Heródes
Atticus.

The 3,000 pieces on display here are so spectacular that even non-jewelry lovers will
enjoy this glitzy new museum, founded by one of Greece's most successful jewelry
designers. The first floor has a boutique and small workshop. The second and third
floors display pieces inspired by ancient, Byzantine, and Cycladic designs, as well as by
plants and animals.

A GARDEN, A HILL & A MONASTERY

The **National Garden,** between Amalías Avenue and Iródou Attikoú, south of
Vasilíssis Sofías Avenue, was originally the garden of the Royal Palace (today's Parliament Building). The 40 acres contain more than 500 varieties of plants and trees, as

well as duck ponds and a small, rather sad, zoo, with some peacocks. There are several cafes tucked away in the garden, and you can also picnic here—or just escape from the summer heat by sheltering on one of the benches under shade trees. The large neo-classical exhibition and reception hall was built by the brothers Zappas and so is known as the Záppion. The garden is officially open daily 7am to 10pm and admission is free.

Mount Lykavitós (Lycabettus), which dominates the northeast of the city, is a favorite retreat for Athenians and a great place to get a bird's-eye view of Athens and its environs—if the *néfos* (smog) isn't too bad. Even when the *néfos* is bad, sunsets can be spectacular here. On top, there's a small chapel of Ayios Yióryios (St. George), whose name day is celebrated on April 23. Nearby are the Lykavitós Theater, an important venue for summer music performances, as well as a couple of overpriced cafes. You can take the funicular from the top of Ploutárchou Street (500Dr/$1.85, 8am to 10pm, about every 20 minutes in summer) or walk up from Dexamení Square, which is the route preferred by young lovers and the energetic.

The **Kessariani Monastery,** just 4¼ miles east on the cool, forested slope of Mount Imittós (Hymettus), is another lovely place to escape Athens's noise and *néfos* (smog). The monastery is open Tuesday to Sunday 8:30am to 3pm; admission is 800Dr ($3). The small church was built in the 5th century, probably over an ancient temple; its pretty frescoes date from the 16th century. Bus no. 224 leaves from Panepistimíou Street and Vasilíssis Sofías Avenue, northeast of Sýntagma Square, about every 20 minutes.

ORGANIZED TOURS

You can book tours of Athens through most hotels or any travel agency. A half-day tour of city highlights should cost about 8,000Dr ($30). Night tours can include a sound-and-light show, Greek folk dancing at the Dóra Strátou Dance Theater, or dinner and Greek dancing; they range from about 8,000Dr to 12,000Dr ($30 to $44).

Educational Tours & Cruises, 1 Artemídos St., Glyfáda (☎ **01/898-1741**), can arrange tours in Athens and throughout Greece, including individual tours with an emphasis on historical and educational aspects. **CHAT Tours,** 4 Stadíou St. (☎ **01/322-3137**); **GO Tours,** 31–33 Voulís St. (☎ **01/322-5951**); and **Key Tours,** 4 Kaliroïs St. (☎ **01/923-3166**) are all reliable long-established companies that offer tours of Athens and various day trips to destinations such as the temple of Apollo at Sounion; Delphi and the Byzantine monastery of Osios Loukas; and the Peloponnese (usually taking in Corinth, Mycenae, and Epidauros). Tours are often no more expensive, and considerably less stressful, than renting a car for the day and driving yourself.

6 Shopping

If you want to pick up retro clothes or old copper, try the **flea market,** a daily spectacle between the Pláka and Monastiráki Square. It's most lively on Sunday, but you can find the usual touristy trinkets, copies of ancient artifacts, jewelry, sandals, and various handmade goods, including embroideries, any day. Keep in mind that not everything sold as an antique is genuine, and that it's illegal to take antiquities and icons more than 100 years old out of the country without a hard-to-obtain export license.

In the Pláka–Monastiráki area, several shops with nicer than usual arts and crafts and fair prices include **Stavros Melissinos,** the Poet-Sandalmaker of Athens, 89 Pandrossou St. (☎ **01/321-9247**); **Iphanta,** the weaving workshop, 6 Selleu St. (☎ **01/322-3628**); **Emanuel Masmanidis' Gold Rose Jewelry** shop, 85 Pandroussou St.

(☎ 01/321-5662); the **Center of Hellenic Tradition,** 59 Metropoleos and 36 Pandrossou sts. (☎ 01/321-3023), which has a lovely cafe; and the **Hellenic Folk-Art Gallery,** 6 Ipatias and Apóllonos sts., Pláka (☎ 01/324-0017). A portion of the gallery's proceeds goes to the National Welfare Organization, which encourages traditional crafts. Also, don't forget that most museums have excellent shops.

Clothes in Greece are expensive, and it isn't a good place to add to your wardrobe, unless you happen to hit the January or August sales. If you need to get something, try the moderately priced shops in the Omónia–Sýntagma–Monastiráki squares triangle—and avoid the boutiques around Kolonáki Square. The city's three major department stores are all near Omónia Square: **Athenee,** 33 Stadíou St.; **Lambropouli Bros.,** Eólou and Lykoúrgos streets; and the largest, **Minion,** Patissíon (a continuation of Eólou) and Veranzérou streets. **BHS (British Home Stores),** Athinás and Efpolídos streets, 2 blocks south of Omónia, has a handy self-service restaurant (open 9am to 8:30pm) on the eighth floor, with indoor and outdoor seating and a great view.

To see top-of-the-line goods, including designer wear—not at bargain prices— wander around the smaller streets near **Kolonáki Square,** between Sýntagma Square and Lykavitós Hill. Keep in mind that almost all of the shops are seriously expensive.

The biggest foreign-language bookstore in Athens is **Eleftheroudákis,** which has a branch at 4 Níkis St. (☎ 01/322-2255) and a new headquarters at 17 Panepistimíou St. (☎ 01/331-4480). The new location has eight stories filled with a full range of subjects, plus a cafe and a music shop, and stages a series of small concerts and readings by local authors.

Compendium, 28 Níkis St., on the edge of Pláka near Sýntagma Square (☎ 01/322-1248), is a good English-language bookstore, selling new and used fiction and nonfiction, plus magazines and maps. **Reymondos,** 18 Voukourestíou St., a pedestrianized street just off Sýntagma Square (☎ 01/364-8189), has a good selection in English, including some dazzling photo books on Greece, and is often open after usual shop hours. On your way there, you can ogle the window displays at **Zolotas,** 10 Panepistimíou St. (☎ 01/361-3782) and **Lalounis,** 6 Panepistimíou St. (☎ 01/362-1371), Greece's two finest jewelers, which have branches at the foot of Voukourestíou Street.

7 Athens After Dark

Greeks enjoy their nightlife so much that they take an afternoon nap to rest up for it. The evening often begins with a leisurely *vólta* (stroll); you'll see it happening in many neighborhoods, including the Pláka and Kolonáki Square. Most Greeks don't think of dinner until at least 9pm—and even then there's no hurry. Around midnight the party may move on to a club for music and dancing. Feel free to try places on your own, although you may feel like the odd man out, because Greeks seldom go anywhere alone. If you're a woman on your own and wish to be left alone, you'll probably find hitting the bars and dance clubs uncongenial.

Check the daily *Athens News,* sold at most major newsstands, for current cultural and entertainment events, including films, lectures, theater, music, and dance. The weekly *Hellenic Times* and *Athenscope* and the monthly *Now in Athens* have good lists of nightspots, restaurants, movies, theater, and much else.

THE PERFORMING ARTS

The acoustically marvelous new **Mégaron Mousikís Concert Hall,** 89 Vasilíssis Sofías Ave. (☎ 01/729-0391 or 01/728-2333), hosts a wide range of classical music programs that include quartets, operas in concert, symphonies, and recitals. The box

In case you want to be welcomed there.

We're here to see that you're always welcomed at establishments everywhere. That's why millions of people carry the American Express® Card – for peace of mind, confidence, and security, around the world or just around the corner.

do more

AMERICAN
EXPRESS

Cards

And just in case.

We're here with American Express® Travelers Cheques and Cheques *for Two*.® They're the safest way to carry money on your vacation and the surest way to get a refund, practically anywhere, anytime. Another way we help you...

do more ®

Travelers Cheques

office is open weekdays 10am to 6pm, Saturday 10am to 2pm, and Sunday 6 to 10:30pm on performance nights. Tickets run 1,000Dr to 20,000Dr ($3.70 to $74), depending on the performance. The Mégaron has a limited summer season, but is in full swing the rest of the year.

Most major jazz and rock concerts, as well as some classical performances, are held at the **Pallas Theater,** 1 Voukourestíou St. (☎ **01/322-8275**).

English-language theater and American-style music are performed at the **Hellenic American Union Auditorium,** 22 Massalías St., between Kolonáki and Omónia squares (☎ **01/362-9886**); you can usually get a ticket for around 3,000Dr ($11). Arrive early and check out the art show or photo exhibition at the adjacent gallery. The **Greek National Opera** performs at the **Olympia Theater,** 59 Akadimías St., at Mavromiháli (☎ **01/361-2461**).

The **Dóra Strátou Folk Dance Theater,** which performs on Philopáppos Hill, is the best known of the traditional dance troupes. Various regional dances are performed in costume with appropriate musical accompaniment nightly at 10:15, with additional shows at 8:15pm on Wednesday and Sunday. You can buy tickets from 8am to 2pm at the box office, 8 Scholío St., Pláka (☎ **01/924-4395,** or 01/921-4650 after 5:30pm); prices are 2,000Dr to 3,500Dr ($7 to $13).

LIVE-MUSIC CLUBS

Walk the streets of the Pláka on any night and you'll find lots of tavérnas offering pseudo-traditional live music and a few offering the real thing. **Tavérna Mostrou,** 22 Mnissikléos St. (☎ **01/324-2441**), is one of the largest, oldest, and best known for traditional Greek music and dancing. Shows begin about 11pm and usually last until 2am. The entrance cost of 5,000Dr ($19) includes a fixed-menu supper. À la carte fare is available but expensive. Nearby, **Palia Tavérna Kritikou,** 24 Odós Mnissikléos (☎ **01/322-2809**), is another lively open-air tavérna with music and dancing. Other reliable tavérnas with live traditional music include **Neféli,** 24 Pános St. (☎ **01/ 321-2475**); **Dioyenis,** 3 Séllei (Shelley) St. (☎ **01/324-7933**); **Stamatopoulou,** 26 Lissíou St. (☎ **01/322-8722**); and **Xinos,** 4 Agelou Geronta St. (☎ **01/322-1065**).

For more intimate and unusual entertainment, climb Mnissikléos toward the Acropolis, turn right on Thólou, and find **Apanemia** and **Esperides,** two smoky little cafes usually filled with hip young Athenians nursing drinks (from 1,500Dr/$6) and enjoying music that's both traditional and innovative, sometimes even humorous.

For Greek pop music, try **Zoom,** 37 Kidathinéon St., in the heart of the Pláka (☎ **01/322-5920**). Performers, who are likely to have current hit albums, are showered with carnations by adoring fans. The minimum order is 5,000Dr ($19). If you want to check out the local rock and blues scene along with small doses of metal, Athenian popsters play at **Memphis,** 5 Ventíri St., near the Hilton Hotel east of Sýntagma Square (☎ **01/722-4104**); it's open Tuesday to Friday 10:30pm to 2:30am.

Those interested in authentic *rebétika* (music of the urban poor and dispossessed) should consult their hotel receptionist or the current issue of *Athenscope* magazine to find out which clubs are featuring the best performers. Shows usually don't start until nearly midnight, and though there's usually no cover charge, drinks can cost as much as 4,000Dr ($15). Most clubs are closed during the summer, and many are far from the center of town, so budget another 2,500Dr to 5,000Dr ($9 to $19) for round-trip taxi fare. Among the more distant upscale bouzoúkia are the **Dioyenis Palace,** 259 Syngroú (☎ **01/942-4267**)—a lot farther out than you might think—and **Posidonio,** 18 Posidónos, Ellinikó, near the airport (☎ **01/894-1033**).

One of the more central clubs is the **Stoa Athanaton,** 19 Sofokléous, in the Central Meat Market (☎ **01/321-4362**), which has live rebétika Monday to Saturday

3 to 6pm and after midnight and serves good food; minimum is 2,500Dr ($9). **Taximi,** 29 Odós Isávron, Exárchia (☎ **01/363-9919**), is consistently popular; drinks cost 3,500Dr ($11). It's closed Sunday and July and August. **Frangosyriani,** 57 Odós Aráchovis, Exárchia (☎ **01/360-0693**), specializes in the music of rebétika legend Markos Vamvakaris; it's closed Tuesday and Wednesday. The downscale, smoke-filled **Rebétiki Istoría,** in a neoclassical building at 181 Ippókratous St. (☎ **01/642-4937**), features old-style rebétika music, played to a mixed crowd of older regulars and younger students and intellectuals. The music usually starts at 11pm, but arrive earlier to get a seat.

GAY & LESBIAN BARS

The gay scene is fairly low-key; get-togethers are sometimes advertised in the English-language press. Among bars, **Granazi,** 20 Lebési St. (☎ **01/325-3979**), is popular, as is **E . . . Kai?** ("So What?"), just off Syngroú at 12 Iossíf ton Rogón (☎ **01/922-1742**). In upscale Kolonáki, **Alexander's,** 44 Anagnostopoúlou (☎ **01/364-6660**), is more sedate, with more variety. There's usually a lively nighttime transvestite cruising scene along Syngroú Avenue in Makriyánni.

DANCE CLUBS

Hidden on the outskirts of the Pláka, **Booze,** 57 Kolokotróni St., second floor (☎ **01/324-0944**), blasts danceable rock to a hip student crowd. There's art on every wall, jelled stage lights, and two bars. Admission is 1,500Dr ($6), plus 800Dr ($3) per drink. If it's disco you're craving, head east to **Absolut,** 23 Filellínon St. (no phone). If you feel a bit too old there, head north to the **Wild Rose,** in the arcade at 10 Panepistimíou St. (☎ **01/364-2160**). Up the street, **Mercedes Rex,** 48 Panepistimíou St. (☎ **01/361-4591**), has even more diversity.

8 Side Trips: Delphi & More

Whether you're planning to take a boat from the port of Piraeus to a Greek island, or to travel somewhere by train or bus, you'll probably want to stop first at the **Greek National Tourist Organization,** 2 Amerikís St., off Sýntagma Square (☎ **01/331-0437**), to get an up-to-date ferry, bus, or train schedule. The English-language *Athens News* usually prints a partial schedule of popular island boat destinations in its weekend edition. For flight information, check at any Olympic Airways office or travel bureau. For car-rental suggestions, see "Getting Around," earlier in this chapter.

Several words of advice: Getting in and out of Athens by car, especially if you haven't driven here before, can eat up a lot of your day. You could make a day trip by public bus to any one of the famous sites I suggest, but to visit more than one in a day, you'll need to take a tour or rent a car. And remember that island boat (and air) schedules are always subject to weather conditions and are often delayed. To be sure that you won't miss your flight home, don't plan to arrive back in Athens less than 24 hours before your departure.

DELPHI

Many tour groups offer day trips here, stopping at the Byzantine Monastery of Osios Loukas (see "Organized Tours," above). Public buses leave for Delphi five times daily from Bus Terminal B (☎ **01/831-7096**), some distance north of Omónia Square; the trip takes about 3 hours. The address is given as 260 Liossíon St., which is actually where you get off the local bus; turn right onto Gousíou Street and you'll see the terminal at the end of the road.

Delphi Site Plan

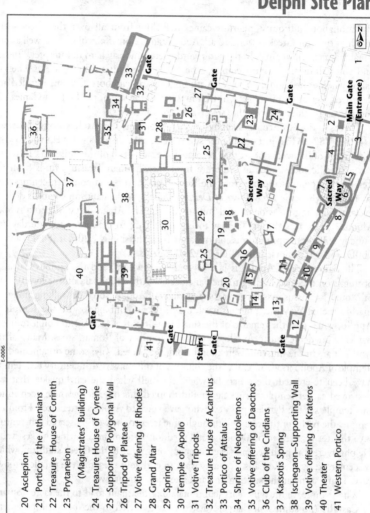

1 Roman Agorá (Marketplace)
2 Votive offering of Corfu ("Bull")
3 Votive offering of Athens
   ("Victory at Marathon")
4 Votive offering of
   Lacedaemonians
5 Votive offering of Argos
   ("Seven Against Thebes")
6 Votive offering of Argos
   ("Descendants")
7 Votive offering of Argos
   ("The King of Argos")
8 Votive offering of Taras
9 Treasure House of Sikyon
10 Treasure House of Siphnos
11 Treasure House of Megara
12 Treasure House of Thebes
13 Treasure House of Boeotia
14 Treasure House of Potidaea
15 Treasure House of Athens
16 Bouleuterion (Council House)
17 Treasure House of Cnidus (Knidos)
18 Rock of Sibylla
19 Naxian Column

20 Asclepion
21 Portico of the Athenians
22 Treasure House of Corinth
23 Prytaneion
   (Magistrates' Building)
24 Treasure House of Cyrene
25 Supporting Polygonal Wall
26 Tripod of Plateae
27 Votive offering of Rhodes
28 Grand Altar
29 Spring
30 Temple of Apollo
31 Votive Tripods
32 Treasure House of Acanthus
33 Portico of Attalus
34 Shrine of Neoptolemos
35 Votive offering of Daochos
36 Club of the Cnidians
37 Kassotis Spring
38 Ischegaon–Supporting Wall
39 Votive offering of Krateros
40 Theater
41 Western Portico

Throughout antiquity, pilgrims came to Delphi from all over the Greek—and much of the non-Greek—world to ask Apollo's advice on affairs of state as well as personal matters. Unfortunately, the god's words were famously hard to interpret. "Invade and you will destroy a great empire," the oracle told Lydian King Croesus when he asked whether he should go to war with his Persian neighbors. Croesus invaded and destroyed a great empire: his own. Delphi was also the site of the Pythian Games, the most famous athletic festival in Greece after the Olympics.

There's a lot to see at Delphi; if you begin at the **Archaeology Museum** (☎ 0265/82-1313), just outside the site entrance, the displays will help you to visualize many of the works of art that decorated the site. Each of the museum's 13 rooms has a specific focus, such as sculpture from the Siphnian Treasury, finds from the Temple of Apollo, sculpture from the Roman era, and the famous 5th-century B.C. bronze known as the *Charioteer of Delphi.* Don't miss the handsome youth's delicate eyelashes shading his wide enamel-and-stone eyes. The Archaeology Museum is open Monday 11am to 5:30pm, Tuesday to Friday 7:30am to 6:30pm, and Saturday and Sunday 8:30am to 3pm. Admission (separate from the site) is 1,200Dr ($4.45) adults, 900Dr ($3.35) seniors, and 600Dr ($2.20) students.

The **Sanctuary of Apollo** is just beyond the museum, and the famous Castalian Spring is on the road leading to the Sanctuary of Athena Pronaia on the lower slopes of Mount Parnassus. As you enter the Sanctuary of Apollo, you'll be walking along the marble **Sacred Way** that pilgrims used in antiquity. Climbing toward the **Temple of Apollo,** you'll pass the remains of the small treasuries that Greek cities built to house works of art dedicated to Apollo, as well as a number of Roman stoas. Many of the works of art in the museum were found along the Sacred Way; some ornamented the Temple of Apollo itself. Several of the columns of this massive 4th-century B.C. temple have been re-erected; the others lie where they fell when the earthquakes that had destroyed earlier temples struck again and toppled this one. Somewhere deep inside this temple sat the Pythian priestess who gave voice to Apollo's utterances. From the temple, the path continues uphill through pine trees to the well-preserved 4th-century B.C. **theater** that seated 5,000 and is still used for performances during the Festival of Delphi. Here, the path becomes even steeper, continuing to the Greek **stadium,** which was enlarged by the Romans. You may want to curl your toes into the parallel grooves carved into stone at the starting line and attempt a lap or two.

When you leave the Sanctuary, continue along the main road to the sacred **Spring of Castalia** (no admission charge), tucked away in a cleft in the rocks behind a bend in the road. This is where Apollo planted a laurel he brought from the beautiful Vale of Tempe, and where poets drank from the spring in search of inspiration. Alas, the spring is now off-limits because of the threat of falling rocks, and the sacred spring shows signs of becoming an unattractive cesspool. Across from the spring, farther along the road, you'll see the entrance to the **Sanctuary of Athena Pronaia** (Athena the Guardian of the Temple). This area is also known as the *Marmaria* because of all the marble found here, much of which was hacked up and carted off to build buildings after the Sanctuary lost its power during the early Christian era. The antiquities here, including sections of two temples and a gymnasium, are poorly preserved, and you may prefer just to peer down at the elegant 4th-century *Tholos* (a round building of unknown function), whose slender Doric columns are easy to spot. The archaeological site is open weekdays 7:30am to 6:30pm and Saturday, Sunday, and holidays 8:30am to 3pm; admission is 1,200Dr ($4.45) adults, 900Dr ($3.35) seniors, and 600Dr ($2.20) students.

ACCOMMODATIONS & DINING   If at all possible, spend the night in Delphi so that you're less rushed and can take in the spectacular scenery of Mount Parnassus and the plain of olives stretching below Delphi to the sea. The small family-owned **Hotel Varonos,** 27 Pavlou and Frederikis (Delphi's main street), 330 54 Delphi (☎ **0265/82-345**), has nine rooms with spectacular views out over the plain and reasonable rates (14,000Dr/$52 double). American Express, MasterCard, and Visa are accepted.

Most Delphi restaurants serve bland tourist fare; prices at the **Tavérna Vakchos,** 31 Apóllonos St. (☎ **0265/82-448**), are about as good as you'll get (dinner for two is about 4,000Dr/$15). You'll eat better and escape the tourists if you take a bus or cab to the village of **Arachova,** 6 miles north of Delphi. You can sit in the little town square, drink glasses of the water that gushes from freshwater springs, and eat modestly but well at either the **Tavérna Karathanassi** or the **Tavérna Dasargyri** (dinner for two is about 4,000Dr/$15). No credit cards are accepted at these restaurants, and all are open daily approximately noon to midnight.

THE TEMPLE OF POSEIDON AT SOUNION

Probably the most popular day trip from Athens is to the 5th-century B.C. **Temple of Poseidon** at Cape Sounion, an hour's bus ride outside Athens. It's possible to visit the temple, dramatically perched high above the sea, have a swim in the sea below, and grab a snack at one of the overpriced restaurants. (Better yet, bring a picnic.) This is a good place *not* to go on Sunday, when it is very crowded and the traffic to and from beaches outside Athens is very heavy. Fifteen columns of the Doric temple are still standing; try to find the one where Lord Byron carved his name. The archaeological site (☎ **0292/39-363**) is open daily 10am to sunset. Admission is 800Dr ($3) adults, 600Dr ($2.20) seniors, and 400Dr ($1.50) students. Buses to Sounion leave hourly on the half hour 6:30am to 6:30pm from the station at 14 Mavromatéon St. (☎ **01/821-3203**), at the southwest corner of Areos Park, well north of Omónia Square (best reached by taxi).

PIRAEUS

If you're taking a boat to the Greek islands (**Aegina, Salamis, Hydra, Poros,** and **Spetsai** are all possibilities for a day trip), you'll probably leave from Piraeus, and you might want to take a few hours to look around. You can whiz down to Piraeus on the Athens Metro (about 15 minutes), hopping on at Monastiráki or Omónia squares. Keep in mind that Piraeus isn't a good place to explore alone at night. That said, the main harbor area is always bustling and energetic, and the **Maritime Museum** at Akti Themistokléous (☎ **01/451-6264**), near the departure pier for the Flying Dolphin hydrofoils, has handsome models of ancient, medieval, and modern ships. The museum is open Tuesday to Friday 9am to 2pm and weekends 9am to 1pm; admission is 400Dr ($1.50). The nearby **Archaeological Museum,** 32 Harilaou Trikoupi St. (☎ **01/452-1598**), is open Tuesday to Sunday 8:30am to 3pm, and also costs 400Dr ($1.50). The stars of the museum are the three superb monumental bronzes: a youth and the goddesses Artemis and Athena. If you have time for only one museum, you'll probably find the Maritime Museum a pleasant departure from what you've seen in other archaeological museums.

DINING   If you plan to visit Piraeus in the evening, you might fast all day and then gorge on the 15-dish fixed-price feast (4,000Dr/$15) at **Vasilainas,** 72 Etolikou, Ayia Sophia (☎ **01/461-2457**), a 10-minute cab ride from the harbor. Most harborside restaurants in Piraeus are overpriced and not very good. The fish restaurants on the shore at Microlimani are sometimes excellent but very expensive, and best avoided unless you're going with Greek friends who know the ropes.

DAPHNÍ & ELEUSIS

You can visit both the recently restored 11th-century **Daphní Monastery** (☎ 01/581-1558) and **Eleusis,** site of an important ancient cult of the Mysteries, on a day trip. Daphní, 6¼ miles west of Athens on the Athens–Corinth highway, is one of the finest examples of Byzantine architecture in Greece, with exquisite mosaics. It's open daily 8:30am to 3pm; admission is 800Dr ($3) adults, 600Dr ($2.20) seniors, and 400Dr ($1.50) students. Take bus no. 860 or 880 from Panepistimíou Street north of Siná (behind the university) or bus no. 853, 862, 873, or 880 from Elefthería Square off Piréos Street (northwest of Monastiráki).

From Daphní, you can continue by bus to the **Sanctuary of Eleusis** (☎ 01/554-6019), the site of the most famous and revered of all the ancient Mysteries. The unknown and the famous were initiated into the sacred rites here, yet we know almost nothing about the Eleusinian Mysteries, which commemorated the abduction of Demeter's daughter Persephone by the god of the underworld, Hades (Pluto).

Despite its substantial remains and glorious past—this was already a religious site in Mycenaean times—the Sanctuary's present surroundings in the industrial city of Eleusis are so grim that it's not easy to warm to the spot. You'll see remains of several temples, a 2nd-century A.D. Roman *Propylaia* (monumental entrance), and triumphal arches dedicated to the Great Goddesses and to the emperor Hadrian. (Hadrian's Arch inspired the Arc de Triomphe, on the Champs-Elysées in Paris.)

There's also a small **museum,** with finds from the site, including the greater part of a famous Demeter by Agoracritis. The Sanctuary and museum are open Tuesday to Sunday and holidays 8:30am to 3pm; admission is 500Dr ($1.85), free on Sunday. You can get there by taking bus no. 853 or no. 862 from Elefthería, a square off Piréos Avenue (northwest of Monastiráki), or bus no. A15, marked Elefsina, from Sachtouri Street, southeast of Elefthería Square. When you get into Eleusis, tell the bus driver that you want to see *"ta archaia"* (the antiquities).

THE PELOPONNESE

Many tour companies offer day trips into the Peloponnese—to **Corinth,** with its famous Doric temple and Greek and Roman ruins; **Mycenae,** the city of Agamemnon, with the ruins of the royal citadel and the eerie "beehive" tombs where Mycenaean royalty were buried; and **Epidauros,** where you can visit the Sanctuary of the healing god Asclepios and the best-preserved ancient theater in Greece, which seats 14,000 and is still used each summer for performances in the Festival of Epidauros. If you want to see a show, try to find a tour company that gets you here early so that you can visit the site before the performance begins.

Buses for these and other destinations on the Peloponnese Peninsula leave from Bus Terminal A, 100 Kifissioú St. (☎ 01/512-9233). To reach it, take local bus no. 051 at Zinónos and Menándrou streets, 3 blocks southwest of Omónia Square.

Contact the **Greek National Tourist Organization (EOT),** 2 Amerikís St. (☎ 01/331-0437 or 01/331-0561), for more information on other day trips from Athens.

Barcelona & Environs

by Herbert Bailey Livesey

Barcelona just keeps getting better—the astonishing improvements made for the 1992 Summer Olympics have never really stopped. Since the Games, a major new contemporary art museum has opened and the city's port has been redeveloped, adding a new aquarium. A sparkling satellite city has materialized where abandoned warehouses and rail yards stood but a few years ago. Barcelona remains comfortable with both its heritage and the approach of the millennium.

In part, Barcelona's topography was its destiny. It's cradled in a great half bowl, open to the Mediterranean on one side but contained by a brooding hill called Montjuïc at the harbor's southwest edge and backed up to the north by a massif dominated by Tibidabo's peak. Apart from church steeples and a few misguided efforts at skyscraper modernity, most of man-made Barcelona tops out at under eight stories. It rises gently from the sea and climbs its slopes and elevations with admirable respect for the land.

In A.D. 874, Barcelona was nicknamed La Ciudad Condal for the counts who negotiated its independence. In the 13th and 14th centuries, it was the capital of the Kingdom of Catalunya and Aragón, whose colonial influence extended into southern France, down to Valencia, and over to Sicily and Greece. It's still the Mediterranean's third largest port—and, arguably, its Queen City. Long Spain's most progressive and "European" city, Barcelona was the country's first industrial force, emerging in the mid–19th century.

From the Gothic cathedral to Sagrada Família to the new National Theater, Barcelona celebrates its flair for eye-catching architecture. And with parlays like Picasso to Miró to Tàpies, the city has fostered more than its share of artistic genius. Now eager to be a key player in the European Union and the world beyond, Barcelona has everything going for it.

REQUIRED DOCUMENTS   See chapter 18 on Madrid.

OTHER FROMMER'S TITLES   For more on Barcelona, see *Frommer's Spain; Frommer's Madrid, Barcelona & Seville; Frommer's Gay & Lesbian Europe;* or *Frommer's Europe.*

1 Barcelona Deals & Discounts

SPECIAL DISCOUNTS
FOR EVERYONE   Ask about **special promotions** offered by Iberia (☎ 800/772-4642), the national airline. U.K. travelers will also want to check British Airways for special promotions or charters.

Budget Bests

At lunch—and at dinner in some restaurants—the three-course *menú del día* is usually a bargain. Make that the main meal and stick to snacks, sandwiches, pizza, or *tapas* (assorted bar snacks) at other times.

January, February, and July are **sale months,** when signs on almost every type of store shriek ¡REBAIXES! (Catalan) or ¡REBAJAS! (Spanish). Toward the end of these months prices hit rock-bottom.

Most three- to five-star hotels have adopted the North American practice of sharply **reduced weekend rates,** often including extras not provided during the week, such as breakfast and a morning newspaper. Booklets of **discount coupons** on tours, meals, shopping, clubs, casinos, car rentals, concerts, and museum admissions are frequently offered. These lowered rates aren't necessarily volunteered, so always ask if less expensive rooms are available Friday to Sunday. For details and reservations, contact the **Centre d'Informació,** Plaça de Catalunya, 08015 Barcelona (☎ **93/423-18-00;** fax 93/423-26-49).

Also available at that office is the **Barcelona Card,** which permits discounts of 30% to 50% off admission to museums and other attractions and smaller discounts at a selection of shops and restaurants. Cards are good for periods of 24, 48, or 72 hours, and cost 2,500P ($17), 3,000P ($21), and 3,500P ($24), respectively.

FOR STUDENTS   Students with appropriate ID enjoy reduced or free admission to most of the city's museums and monuments. The Youth Card issued by the Generalitat de Catalunya makes it easy and cheap for young people to get the most out of their stay. The **Youth Card** guide lists almost 8,000 places offering discounts. Contact the **Punt d'Informació Juvenil,** Secretaria General de Joventut, Calabria 147, 08001 Barcelona (☎ **93/483-83-84**), open Monday to Friday 10am to 8pm.

WORTH A SPLURGE

Tickets for performances at the **Palau de la Música Catalana** give top value, if only to view that remarkable interior. Sampling Catalunya's fine *cavas* (wines made by the champagne method) in a sophisticated *xampanyeria* or nursing a pricey beer in one of the city's celebrated **designer bars** make for memorable evenings.

2 Essentials

ARRIVING

BY PLANE   Newly expanded and modern **El Prat Airport** is about 8 miles from the center city. A **train** runs from the airport every 30 minutes 6am to 10:15pm, taking about 20 minutes to Estació Sants and continuing to the more central Praça de Catalunya; it costs 300P ($2.05) Monday to Friday and 345P ($2.35) Saturday, Sunday, and holidays. **Aerobuses** run between the three terminals at the airport and Plaça de Catalunya (with intermediate stops) Monday to Friday every 15 minutes 6am to 11pm and Saturday and holidays every 30 minutes 6:30am to 10:50pm. The trip takes 25 to 35 minutes and costs 450P ($3.10). Tickets are sold on the bus, which is air-conditioned and has a low-level entry without steps. A **taxi** into town is 2,000P to 2,500P ($14 to $17), depending on traffic and destination.

BY TRAIN   National and international trains arrive at the **Estació Sants** or **Estació de França,** both slightly outside the city center but linked to the municipal Metro network. Many trains also stop at the Metro station at **Plaça de Catalunya.**

What Things Cost in Barcelona	U.S. $
Taxi from the airport to the Regencia Colón	22.00–25.00
Metro fare	.95
Local telephone call	.10
Double room at the Claris (deluxe)	235.15
Double room at the Duques de Bergara (moderate)	113.10
Double room at the Neutral (budget)	36.90
Continental breakfast	6.90
Lunch for one, without wine, at El Gran Café (moderate)	9.25
Lunch for one, without wine, at Self Naturista (budget)	6.10
Dinner for one, without wine, at Neichel (deluxe)	49.65
Dinner for one, without wine, at Set Portes (moderate)	22.20
Dinner for one, without wine at Pitarra (budget)	9.60
Small beer (una caña)	.70–1.30
Coca-Cola in a restaurant	.95
Cup of coffee	.80
Roll of ASA 100 color film, 36 exposures	5.15
Movie ticket	5.15
Concert ticket	4.50–23.15 and up

BY BUS   Not all bus lines use it, but the principal terminal is the **Estació del Nord,** at Ali-bei 80 (☎ **93/265-65-08;** Metro: Arc d'Triomf), not far from the Old Town and Plaça de Catalunya. Some companies stop near the **Estació Sants,** which has a Metro station.

BY CAR   Despite all the new roads and beltways, traffic is heavy and often chaotic, especially in the Eixample and on the Old Town's narrow streets. Obtaining a detailed street map in advance is wise, and once at your destination seriously consider garaging the car until departure. Do not leave possessions in the car, not even in the trunk. If your hotel has no garage, there are usually nearby lots or facilities. One of the easiest to find is the garage beneath the plaza in front of the cathedral.

VISITOR INFORMATION

The most central and helpful of the information offices is the subterranean **Centre d'Informació** (☎ **93/304-31-35;** Metro: Catalunya), under the southeast corner of Plaça Catalunya, open daily 9am to 9pm. Its multilingual attendants can provide free street maps, answer questions, change money, and make hotel reservations. There's also a shop selling books and souvenirs.

In addition, these **tourist offices** offer maps, brochures, and schedules of exhibits, concerts, and other cultural events: **Estació Sants,** open Monday to Friday 8am to 8pm and Saturday, Sunday, and holidays 8am to 2pm; and the **airport information office,** open Monday to Saturday 9:30am to 8pm and Sunday and holidays 9:30am to 3pm. For information on Barcelona and the entire region of Catalunya, try the **Oficina de Informació Turística,** Gran Vía C.C. 658 (☎ **93/301-74-43;** Metro: Catalunya), open Monday to Friday 9am to 7pm and Saturday 9am to 2pm.

During summer, over 100 young people known as **Red Jackets** (for their crimson-and-white uniforms) roam the principal tourism areas offering assistance in various languages. In addition, five mobile **tourist information booths** are set up in such locations as Plaça de Catalunya, La Rambla, and the Barri Gòtic. They're open daily 9am to 9pm.

For **information** on what's happening in Barcelona, dial ☎ **010** Monday to Friday 7am to 11pm and Saturday 9am to 2pm. English-speaking attendants are available. Barcelona is in the process of providing multilingual phone lines for information. See the brochure *Facil parlar,* free at any tourist office.

CITY LAYOUT

Barcelona took shape under the Romans and later expanded from a walled medieval core at the water's edge. Between the harbor and the ordered grid of the 19th-century Eixample district lies the **Ciutat Vella (Old Town),** bordered by the Parc de la Ciutadella to the northeast and the fortress-topped hill of Montjuïc to the southwest. Its focal point is the **Barri Gòtic (Gothic Quarter),** which once contained the Call, a medieval Jewish neighborhood.

To the east is the **Barri de la Ribera,** focal point of Barcelona's 13th- and 14th-century colonial and commercial expansion. Below the Parc de la Ciutadella and enclosing the east end of the harbor is **Barceloneta,** originally home to the city's mariners and fishermen and now known primarily for its seafood restaurants. It connects to the southwestern edge of the **Vila Olímpica,** the former Olympic Village that's part of **Poble Nou,** an urbanized satellite of the central city. A long beach recently reopened to the public runs from the tip of Barceloneta to the **Port Olímpic** and beyond.

At the Barri Gòtic's western edge, bisecting the Old Town, is **La Rambla,** a boulevard (made up of five individually named sections) curving a little over a mile from the port to Plaça de Catalunya. On the other side, down by the port, is the notorious **Barri Xinés (Chinese Quarter),** a potentially dangerous neighborhood best avoided at night. Above the Barri Xinés, roughly north of the street called Nou de la Rambla, is the residential **El Raval** district, currently enjoying a measure of rejuvenation.

To the north of Plaça de Catalunya is the **Eixample,** a grid of wide streets that's the product of Barcelona's growing prosperity in the late 19th century. North of the Eixample are **Gràcia,** an area of small squares and lively bars and restaurants that was once a separate village, and **Tibidabo,** Barcelona's tallest mountain.

GETTING AROUND

The several important districts of the city are accessible by Metro (subway), bus, funicular, cable car, taxi, train, or on foot. Given persistent traffic congestion, the Metro and walking are quickest. Note that public transportation fares are slightly higher on weekends and holidays. Call ☎ **93/412-00-00** Monday to Friday 7:30am to 8:30pm and Saturday 8am to 2pm for general public transport information.

BY METRO (SUBWAY)   The Metro and integrated commuter train lines (called FF.CC. de la Generalitat) operate Monday to Thursday 5am to 11pm; Friday, Saturday, and weekend holidays 5am to 1am; weekday holidays 6am to 11pm; and Sunday 6am to midnight.

The one-way fare is 135P (95¢), but two types of **10-trip cards** save you money. **Tarjeta T-1,** at 740P ($5), entitles you to travel by bus, Metro, *tramvía blau,* the Montjuïc funicular, and the FF.CC. de la Generalitat within the city limits. **Tarjeta T-2,** at 720P ($4.95), is for the Metro only. **Special 1-day passes** *(abono temporales),* at 500P ($3.45), permit unlimited travel on the Metro and buses. Remember to keep tickets or passes until after leaving the Metro or bus or face the possibility of a stiff fine. Passes are sold at these TMB (Transports Metropolita de Barcelona) offices:

Barcelona Metro

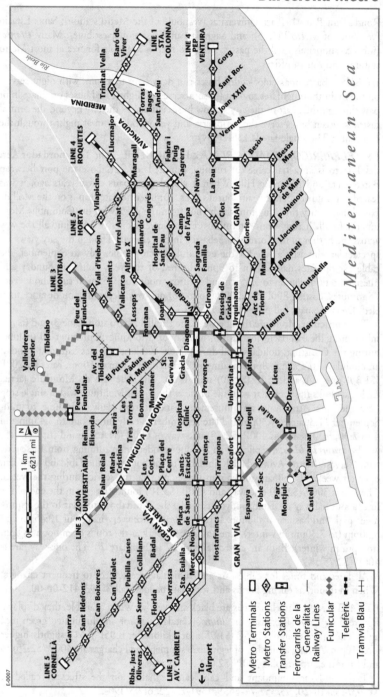

121

Ronda Sant Pau 41; Plaça Universitat (vestibule of the Metro station); Sants Estació (vestibule of Metro Line 5); and Sagrada Família station (vestibule). Many *estancos* (tobacco shops) also sell the passes. A Metro map is available for free at most Metro stations and tourist offices.

BY BUS Barcelona's color-coded buses run daily 5am to 11pm, with night service on the main thoroughfares to 4am (in some cases all night). Red buses originate in or pass through the heart of the city; yellow buses cut across the city beyond the central districts; green buses serve the periphery; and yellow buses run at night through the city center. The single fare is 135P (95¢).

BY *TELEFÉRICO, TRAMVÍA BLAU* & FUNICULAR The **Transbordador Aeri del Puerto** is an aerial cable car running hundreds of feet above the port between Barceloneta and Montjuïc Hill. When it closed for repairs a few years ago, it was feared it wouldn't operate again, but it's back. An intermediate stop is on the Moll de Barcelona, a jetty thrusting into the harbor from the plaza with the Columbus Monument. In all, it runs from a terminus on the lower slopes of Montjuïc all the way across the harbor to the Torre Sant Sebastià, in Barceloneta. Though the city views are spectacular, this isn't a ride for the even mildly acrophobic. July to September, the cable car operates daily 11am to 9pm; the rest of the year, hours are Sunday and Tuesday to Friday noon to 5:45pm and Saturday noon to 6:15pm. It runs about every 15 minutes, costing 800P to 1,200P ($6 to $8) one-way, depending on distance traveled. Everyone pays full price except infants.

The **Funicular Montjuïc** runs between the Parallel Metro stop (Line 3) and its terminus near the Fundació Joan Miró, halfway up Montjuïc. September 30 to June, during the Christmas holidays, and during Holy Week, it operates Saturday, Sunday, and holidays 10:45am to 8pm; in summer, it runs daily 11am to 10pm. Fares are 200P ($1.35) one-way and 350P ($2.40) round-trip. The **Teleféric de Montjuïc** (aerial cable car) links the funicular with the castle at the top of Montjuïc, with a single stop near the Parc Atraccions, an amusement park. It runs daily: mid-June to mid-September 11:30am to 9:30pm and late September to early June 11am to 2:45pm and 4 to 7:30pm. The fare is 400P ($2.75) one-way or 600P ($4.15) round-trip.

The ***tramvía blau,*** a replica of an antique wooden tram running from Passeig de Sant Gervasi (Metro: Avinguda del Tibidabo) to the bottom of the Tibidabo funicular, operates weekends 7:05am to 9:55pm (buses provide the service during the week). The fare is 300P ($2.05) one-way and 450P ($3.10) round-trip. From the end of the line, about halfway up Tibidabo, you can take the **Tibidabo funicular** to the amusement park and basilica at the top. It runs at least once every half hour 10:45am and 8:30pm (to 7:30pm in winter). The amusement park at the top is open noon to 8pm (to 7pm in winter). Both are closed January 27 to February 28. The one-way fare is 400P ($2.75).

All fares and times for cable cars and funiculars are subject to frequent changes. When in doubt, as during fiestas and seasonal changes, call ☎ **93/412-00-00.**

BY TAXI Most Barcelona taxis are black and yellow. When available, they display a sign reading *"libre"* (Spanish) or *"lliure"* (Catalan) and/or an illuminated green roof light. The initial charge is 285P ($1.95); each kilometer is 95P (65¢), slightly higher after 10pm. Among a number of legitimate supplemental charges are 400P ($2.75) to and from the airport, plus 300P ($2.05) for luggage.

Taxi stands are abundant and cabs can be hailed on the street or called at ☎ **93/433-10-20,** 93/357-77-55, 93/391-22-22, or 93/490-22-22.

BY RENTAL CAR Having a car here is a burden, and I strongly recommend that you use one only for out-of-town excursions. Spain has one of the worst traffic fatality rates in Europe, almost five times that of Holland, the safest country in that regard. Renting a car is expensive, but if one is a necessity, an airline fly/drive package may be the most economical solution. Otherwise, shop for the best deal among these agencies with town and airport offices: **Atesa,** Balmes 141 (☎ **93/237-81-40,** or 93/302-28-32 at the airport); **Avis,** Aragó 235 (☎ **93/487-87-54,** or 93/379-40-26 at the airport); **Europcar,** Av. Marques de l'Argentera 6 (☎ **93/319-50-36,** or 93/379-92-051 at the airport); and **Hertz,** Tuset 10 (☎ **93/217-80-79,** or 93/ 370-58-11 at the airport).

FAST FACTS: Barcelona

Addresses   In Spain, street numbers follow street names and the ° sign indicates the floor. The Spanish first floor (1°) is the American second. The Catalan words for "street," "avenue," "boulevard," and "plaza" are *carrer, avinguda, passeig,* and *plaça,* respectively.

American Express   The office at Passeig de Gràcia 101 (☎ **93/217-00-70;** Metro: Passeig de Gràcia) is open Monday to Friday 9:30am to 6pm and Saturday 10am to noon. They'll hold mail for holders of their cards or traveler's checks for up to 1 month free. In addition to a currency exchange during business hours, there's a 24-hour ATM.

Baby-sitters   Concierges in the larger hotels have lists of persons available to provide child care. In the smaller hotels and pensions this service is less certain, but in family-run places teenage children of the managers can sometimes be hired.

Business Hours   Hours at **banks** vary, though usually are Monday to Friday 8:30am to 2pm and Saturday 9am to 1pm (closed Saturday June to September). Typical **office** hours are Monday to Friday 9am to 1:30pm and 4 to 7pm, but in some offices summer hours are 8am to 3pm. **Shop** hours vary widely, but the norm is Monday to Friday 10am to 1:30pm and 5 to 8pm and Saturday 10am to 1:30pm.

Consulates   The **United States** consulate is at Passeig Reina Elisenda 23 (☎ **93/280-22-27;** Metro: Reina Elisenda); the consulate of **Canada** is at Traveserra de les Corts 265 (☎ **93/410-66-99;** Metro: Plaça Molina); the consulate of the **United Kingdom** is at Av. Diagonal 477 (☎ **93/419-90-44;** Metro: Hospital Clinic); the consulate of **Ireland** is at Gran Via Carles III 94 (☎ **93/491-50-21;** Metro: María Cristina); the consulate of **Australia** is at Gran Via Carles III 98 (☎ **93/330-94-96;** Metro: **María Cristina**); and the consulate of **New Zealand** is at Travessera de Gràcia 64 (☎ **93/209-03-99;** Metro: none nearby).

Crime   The street crime for which Barcelona once drew unwanted attention has diminished, due in part to an increased police presence and new lighting along once dark streets in the old city. A measure of wariness is still required, however. A favorite maneuver of street criminals is to spill or spray a messy substance on a victim, and while one member of the team offers to "help," another relieves the distracted target of valuables. While men are more likely to suffer this ploy, women are often the victims of simple purse snatchings. Visitors are prime targets, so be particularly alert in the Old City and around popular attractions. Assistance from bystanders can't be anticipated, at least not until after the fact. Take the usual urban precautions, including utilizing hotel safes for jewelry, traveler's checks, extra credit cards, and any cash not required for each excursion.

Operated 24 hours by the municipal police, **Tourist Attention,** La Rambla 43 (☎ **93/301-90-60;** Metro: Liceu), has English-speaking attendants who can aid crime victims in reporting losses and obtaining new documents.

Currency See "Fast Facts: Madrid" in chapter 18.

Currency Exchange You can change money and traveler's checks at any bank advertising a *cambio.* A set commission is nearly always charged, which makes cashing small amounts expensive. When banks are closed, you can change money at the Estació Sants daily 8am to 10pm or at the airport daily 7am to 11pm.

Only in a pinch, there are Chequepoint offices on La Rambla and near the cathedral where you can change money or traveler's checks daily 9am to midnight. They don't charge a commission, but their exchange rate is significantly lower than the rates prevailing at banks. There are also exchange machines at Banco Santander, on Plaça San Jaume (at the corner of C. Fernando), and at Plaça de Gràcia 5.

ATMs are located throughout the city. Some Stateside banks charge excessive fees for this service and others charge little or nothing, so check that out before you leave.

Dentist Call ☎ **415-9922.**

Doctor Call ☎ **061.** Consulates keep lists of English-speaking physicians, as do most hotel concierges.

Drugstores Pharmacies stay open late in rotation—*farmàcias de guardia.* They're listed in the daily newspapers and have signs on their front doors giving the location of the nearest *farmàcia* that's open late.

Emergencies In a **medical emergency,** call ☎ **061.** For the **police,** call ☎ **092.** In the event of **fire,** call ☎ **080.**

Holidays See the "Special & Free Events" box later in this chapter. Other holidays include New Year's Day (January 1), Epiphany (January 6), Good Friday, Easter Monday, Pentecost (May 1), St. John's Day (June 24), Feast of the Assumption (August 15), Fiesta of the Hispanic Nations (October 12), All Saints Day (November 1), Constitution Day (December 6), Feast of the Immaculate Conception (December 8), and Christmas (December 25 and 26).

Hospitals Three have emergency departments *(urgencias):* **Hospital Clínic i Provincial,** Casanova 143 (☎ **93/454-60-00;** Metro: Hospital Clinic); **Hospital Creu Roja de Barcelona,** Dos de Maig 301 (☎ **93/433-15-51;** Metro: Hospital de Sant Pau); and **Hospital de la Santa Creu I de Sant Pau,** Sant Antoni Maria Claret 167 (☎ **93/347-31-33;** Metro: Hospital de Sant Pau), a landmark modernista structure designed by Lluis Domènech i Montaner.

Language Catalan, the indigenous language of Catalunya, is the official language of the region, and most signs appear either solely in Catalan or in both Catalan and Spanish. Catalan is a separate language, not a dialect, and is related to *langue d'oc* and *provençal,* spoken across the Pyrénées in southern France. To the casual ear, spoken Catalan sounds like a mix of French and Spanish.

Laundry Clothing sent out to be laundered in a hotel comes back with a nasty shock—the bill. Even in moderately priced hotels, the cost will be three to four times that charged by independent shops. One of the latter in Ciutat Vella is **Lavanderia C. Roca** (☎ **93/302-24-87;** Metro: Liceu), at Carrer Roca 3, on a side street between Plaça del Pi and La Rambla.

Country & City Codes

The **country code** for Spain is **34**. The **city code** for Barcelona is **3**; use this code when you're calling from outside Spain. If you're within Spain but not in Barcelona, use **93**. If you're calling within Barcelona, simply leave off the code and dial only the regular phone number.

Luggage Storage/Lockers   The two main rail stations, Estació Sants and Estació França, have small and large lockers for rent for 400P to 600P ($2.75 to $4.15). Most hotels will store baggage for a day or two for free, sometimes for longer periods for a fee.

Mail   Post offices *(correos)* are generally open Monday to Friday 9am to 2pm. Most will hold mail addressed to you and labeled *lista de correos*. Take along your passport when collecting mail. The **central post office** in Plaça Antoni López (☎ **93/318-38-31;** Metro: Jaume I) is open Monday to Friday 8am to 9pm and Saturday 8am to 2pm. Letters and postcards to the United States cost 95P (65¢). Stamps *(sellos* or *estampillas)* can also be purchased at tobacco stores *(estanco* or *estanc)*. Mailboxes are yellow and are identified by the word *correos* or *correu.* When mailing or receiving packages, it's best to use one of the familiar international shippers—Federal Express, DHL, or UPS. Parcel delivery through the Spanish postal service is painfully slow.

Police   In an emergency, call ☎ **092** or **291-5092.**

Rest Rooms   Lavatories in train and Metro stations are unappealing and potentially unsafe, and there are as yet only a handful of the sophisticated new coin-operated electronic booths installed on streets, notably on the Plaça Catalunya. Rely on the rest rooms in bars, restaurants, and museums, or, in desperation, the nearest large hotel.

Telephone   If you're calling long distance from a hotel or hostal, expect a hefty surcharge. Most **public phone** *cabinas* provide clear instructions in English. Place at least 25 pesetas' worth of coins in the rack at the top for a local call—they'll roll in as required.

To make an **international call,** dial ☎ **07,** wait for the tone, and dial the country code, the area code, and the number. Note that an international call from a phone booth requires stacks and stacks of 100P coins.

As an alternative, purchase **phone cards** worth 1,000P or 2,000P ($7 or $14) and use them to make international calls from specially equipped booths, which are clearly identified. Phone cards are available in tobacco shops, at the post office, and at other authorized outlets. Some phones are also equipped to take American Express and Diners Club. Or you can make calls and pay for them after completion at the currency exchange booth at La Rambla 88, open Monday to Saturday 10am to 11pm and Sunday 10am to 1:30pm. Contact MCI at ☎ **900/99-00-14** or AT&T at ☎ **900/99-00-11** directly from any phone.

Tipping   While tipping for certain services is customary, large amounts aren't expected. A bellhop should get at least 100P (70¢) per bag. Taxi drivers usually get 10%. Virtually all restaurants include a service charge in the bill, so a 5% to 10% tip usually suffices. Ushers in cinemas and theaters and at the bullring get about 75P (50¢).

Transit Information   Call ☎ **93/412-00-00.**

Water   Tap water is perfectly safe, but because of minerals and chemical treatments it doesn't taste very good. Bottled water is widely available, and restaurant patrons routinely order a bottle with meals, either fizzy *(con gas)* or still *(sin gas)*.

3 Accommodations You Can Afford

Budget accommodations (good ones, at any rate) have never been abundant in Barcelona, and the 1992 Olympics helped lessen their number, for many hostelries upgraded to capitalize on that flood of visitors. A few economical hostals and pensions were opened at that time, however, and while renovations enhanced the facilities of some old reliables, they didn't necessarily propel them out of their relatively low-priced categories. (Note that hostals aren't youth hostels in the conventional sense, though they are popular with young travelers. While they don't have all the conveniences of a conventional hotel, they're usually family-run and more personal.)

Most of these inexpensive digs are in the Old Town, a block or two to either side of La Rambla, with a few scattered around the Eixample. Rooms without a shower or tub usually at least have washbasins. Though most places make at least modest increases in their rates from year to year, the long advance in the strength of the dollar over the past 2 years has minimized, even reversed, the effect.

Unless otherwise indicated, the rates below don't include breakfast or tax (IVA in Spain).

Note: You can find most of the lodging choices below plotted on the map included in "Seeing the Sights," later in this chapter.

IN THE BARRI GÒTIC

Call. Arc de Sant Ramón del Call 4 (2 blocks west of Plaça Sant Jaume off Carrer del Call), 08002 Barcelona. ☎ **93/302-11-23.** Fax 93/301-34-86. 26 units, all with bathroom. TEL. 3,210P ($22) single; 4,600P ($32) double; 5,700P ($39) triple. MC, V. Metro: Liceu.

This renovated hostal, in what used to be the Jewish quarter of medieval Barcelona, combines basic comfort and function with a central location ideal for exploring the Old City. The cathedral and La Rambla are only minutes away.

Cataluña. Carrer de Santa Anna 24 (about 1 block east of the upper Rambla), 08002 Barcelona. ☎ **93/301-91-50.** Fax 93/302-78-70. 50 units, all with bathroom. TV TEL. 5,460P ($38) single; 8,960P ($62) double; 12,260P ($85) triple. Rates include breakfast and IVA. AE, DC, MC, V. Metro: Plaça de Catalunya.

This long popular budget choice is more desirable than ever since it undertook renovations (including adding new baths) and held the line on its rates. Admittedly a second choice to the Cortés, its sibling across the street, its rooms (including 16 singles) are simply furnished but well maintained. Next to the streetside lobby is the cafe where breakfast is served. Guests at either hotel get a 10% discount on meals in their restaurants.

✪ Cortés. Carrer de Santa Anna 25, 08002 Barcelona. ☎ **93/317-91-12.** Fax 93/302-78-70. 46 units, all with bathroom. TV TEL. 5,460P ($38) single; 8,960P ($62) double; 12,260P ($85) triple. Rates include breakfast and IVA. AE, DC, MC, V. Metro: Plaça de Catalunya.

Across from the Cataluña (above) and under the same ownership, the Cortés is favored by American students on youth tours. The ground-floor lobby is inviting, with an adjoining restaurant where the three-course *menú del día* is 1,325P ($9). Guests receive a 10% discount on meals in the restaurant. The recently renovated rooms have modern tile baths, and English is spoken.

Getting the Best Deal on Accommodations

- Note that some lodgings offer reductions if you pay in cash rather than with a credit card.
- Be aware that discounts are often available for stays of a week or more.
- Don't accept the first rate quoted. Ask for a cheaper room—especially off-season.
- Ask if there's a surcharge for local or long-distance phone calls. Usually there is and it can be as high as 40%. Make calls at the nearest telephone office instead.
- Inquire if service is included or will be added to the final bill. Likewise, ask if all taxes are included or will be billed extra.

Dalí. Carrer de Boquería 12 (east of La Rambla), 08002 Barcelona. ☎ and fax **93/318-55-80.** 57 units, 40 with bathroom. 2,400P ($17) single without bathroom, 3,400P ($23) single with bathroom; 3,400P ($23) double without bathroom, 4,400P ($30) double with bathroom. AE, DC, MC, V. Metro: Liceu.

The sculptured door frame (check out the man in the top hat on the right) is the best decorative feature of the otherwise bland *modernista* building. However, this pension is unusually large, so rooms are often available when other places are full. Recent repainting has made it less gloomy. In warmer months many groups stay here, particularly students. At other times a little bargaining can get a discount. The room configurations and sizes vary substantially, so check before accepting. Some English is spoken.

Inglés. Carrer de Boquería 17, 08001 Barcelona. ☎ **93/317-37-70.** Fax 93/302-78-70. 28 units, all with bathroom. TEL. 4,350P ($30) single; 7,225P ($50) double. Rates include IVA. AE, MC, V. Metro: Liceu.

On a narrow, busy side street off La Rambla, this four-floor hotel (with elevator) offers surprisingly quiet rooms, especially those in back. The furnishings are utilitarian, the floors vinyl tile, and the baths marble, with handheld showerheads. English is spoken. Next to the lobby is a bar/restaurant with several special fixed-price meals, including a paella with sangría for only 1,300P ($9).

Jardí. Plaça Sant Joseo Oriol 1 (1 block from the middle of La Rambla), 08001 Barcelona. ☎ **93/301-59-00** or 93/301-59-58. Fax 93/318-36-64. 38 units, all with bathroom. TEL. 4,000P ($28) single; 5,500P or 6,600P ($38 or $46) double; 6,200P or 9,200P ($43 or $63) triple. Rates include IVA. MC, V. Metro: Liceu.

The Jardí overlooks the enchanting plazas that embrace the 14th-century Santa María del Pi church. Down below is a favorite bar of the district's artists and students. The routinely furnished rooms vary significantly in size and layout, and some doubles overlooking the plaza have been renovated (they go for the higher rates). Breakfast is available, but you can get a cheaper one at bars on or near the plaza.

Rey Don Jaime I. Carrer Jaume I 11, 08002 Barcelona. ☎ and fax **93/310-62-08.** 30 units, all with bathroom. TEL. 3,900P ($27) single; 5,900P ($41) double. Extra person 1,000P ($7). No credit cards. Metro: Jaume I.

A solid choice east of Plaça Sant Jaume, the main plaza of the Barri Gòtic, this unassuming hotel (with elevator) has three floors of renovated rooms, most with writing desks and some with small balconies. Since the hotel is on a busy street, the rooms in back are quieter. There's a TV salon on the first floor.

IN THE EIXAMPLE

Ciudad Condal. Carrer Mallorca 255 (between Passeig de Gràcia and Rambla de Catalunya), 08008 Barcelona. ☎ **93/487-04-59.** 11 units, all with bathroom. TEL. 4,500P ($31) single; 6,500P ($45) double; 8,500P ($59) triple. AE, DC, MC, V. Metro: Passeig de Gràcia or Diagonal.

Sharing an Eixample block with two of the city's better first-class hotels, the basically furnished Ciudad Condal is in a late 19th-century *modernista* structure. Rooms facing the street have balconies, while interior rooms look down on a garden rather than the usual air shaft. The hostal is three flights up (no elevator).

Neutral. Rambla de Catalunya 42 (at the corner of Carrer de Consell de Cent), 08007 Barcelona. ☎ **93/487-63-90** or 93/487-68-48. 28 units, 10 with shower only, 18 with bathroom. TEL. 3,000P ($21) single with shower only, 4,450P ($31) single with bathroom; 4,450P ($31) double with shower only, 5,350P ($37) double with bathroom; 5,100P ($35) triple with shower only, 6,200P ($43) triple with bathroom. MC, V. Metro: Passeig de Gràcia.

An economy choice in a luxury area, the Neutral has an entrance one flight up, on the mezzanine. Antique floor tiling helps brighten the small but high-ceilinged rooms, furnished with assorted odds and ends, the better ones with easy chairs. All have room safes and most have balconies. The breakfast room boasts an impressive coffered ceiling, and the adjacent TV room is spacious. English is spoken by the two owners.

Oliva. Passeig de Gràcia 32 (at the corner of Carrer Diputación), 08007 Barcelona. ☎ **93/488-01-62.** 16 units, 9 with bathroom. 3,100P ($21) single without bathroom; 5,700P ($39) double without bathroom, 6,700P ($46) double with bathroom. Rates include IVA. No credit cards. Metro: Passeig de Gràcia.

The Oliva is in a fine Eixample building above a tony clothing store, with a beautiful vintage elevator that ascends in stately manner to the fourth floor. It boasts high-ceilinged rooms with tile floors, lace curtains, and sinks. Most have views of the Passeig de Gràcia but are nevertheless quiet. Some are cramped, though.

Universal. Carrer Aragó 281 (near Carrer de Pau Claris), 08009 Barcelona. ☎ **93/487-97-62.** Fax 93/487-40-28. 18 units, all with bathroom. A/C TV TEL. 4,300P ($30) single; 5,850P ($40) double; 7,150P ($49) triple. AE, MC, V. Metro: Passeig de Gràcia.

An elevator from the empty, well-lit entry hall takes you to the narrow second-floor lobby. Beer and soft drinks are served in the adjacent sitting room. The rooms are sparse, usually with built-in desks and twin beds. This is a good bet for those who want to be near the center of the pricey Eixample. It's a step up from the Neutral (above), which is under the same ownership.

✪ Windsor. Rambla de Catalunya 84, 08008 Barcelona. ☎ **93/215-11-98.** 15 units, 11 with bathroom. 3,500P ($24) single without bathroom, 4,300P ($30) single with bathroom; 5,900P ($41) double without bathroom, 7,100P ($49) double with bathroom. No credit cards. Metro: Passeig de Gràcia or Provença.

The carpeted rooms, though small, are cozily quiet; some have balconies. As befits this upscale neighborhood, the hostal's lobby, halls, and TV room are elegantly outfitted, and all areas have recently been repainted. Rooms without a bath share a bath with just one other room. There's an elevator, but the hostal is only one flight up. English is spoken by some of the staff.

ON LA RAMBLA

Continental. La Rambla 138 (at the corner of Carrer Boqueria), 08002 Barcelona. ☎ **93/301-25-70.** Fax 93/302-73-60. 35 units, all with bathroom. A/C TV TEL. 6,950P ($48) single; 9,900P–11,250P ($68–$78) double; 12,000P ($83) triple. Rates include breakfast. AE, DC, MC, V. Metro: Liceu or Plaça de Catalunya.

Try not to be put off by the unpromising entrance or lobby with its clanging colors and patterns. This is now a three-star hotel offering considerable value for its price range. The two floors of rooms have new baths, ceiling fans, and refrigerators (unstocked)—as well as a certain goofy charm. Nine have balconies. The rooms overlooking La Rambla are more expensive. The windows are double-paned, reducing street noise to a murmur. The salon is a gathering place where drinks and an ample buffet breakfast are offered. Some of the staff speak English.

Internacional. La Rambla 78–80, 08002 Barcelona. ☎ **93/302-25-66.** Fax 93/317-61-90. 60 units, all with bathroom. TEL. 6,800P ($47) single; 9,900P ($68) double. Rates include breakfast and IVA. AE, DC, MC, V. Metro: Liceu.

This is a unit of the HUSA chain (which recently bought the luxurious Ritz and renamed it the Palace), across from the Liceu opera house. The functional rooms are of good size, with ample baths. Some sleep three or four, providing a substantial savings over renting two separate rooms. The bright breakfast room overlooks La Rambla, where the hotel also runs an alfresco balcony cafe in summer. Show this book and the management promises a 10% discount.

Mare Nostrum. Carrer Sant Pau 2 (directly on La Rambla), 08001 Barcelona. ☎ and fax **93/318-53-40** or 93/412-30-69. 30 units, 21 with bathroom. A/C TV TEL. 4,000P ($28) single without bathroom, 5,200P ($36) single with bathroom; 5,000P ($35) double without bathroom, 7,000P ($48) double with bathroom; 6,000P ($41) triple without bathroom, 8,000P ($55) triple with bathroom. AE, DC, MC, V. Metro: Liceu.

In 1992, this old building was stripped down and spruced up with comforts not often found at this price level. Though the air-conditioning isn't essential much of the year, it's a relief in a humid July. The most attractive room is the breakfast salon, with a wide window displaying the pageant of La Rambla. Many rooms have balconies, and five have double beds (not easy to find). There's a laundry service, which is also rare. Apart from a slightly haphazard quality to the architecture and the administration, this represents good value. Discounts are often given to guests who mention that they read about this hotel in *Frommer's*.

IN EL RAVAL

✪ **España.** Carrer Sant Pau 9–11 (1 block west of La Rambla), 08002 Barcelona. ☎ **93/318-17-58.** Fax 93/317-11-34. 90 units, all with bathroom. TEL. 4,350P ($30) single; 8,260P ($57) double. AE, MC, V. Metro: Liceu.

Since seeing the inside of a *modernista* building (most of which are still in private hands) is rare, it's almost an honor to pass an hour or two in one of the dining rooms here. This 1904 hotel was designed by Domènech i Montaner, an equal of Antoni Gaudí. A mural in one dining room was painted by Ramón Casas, one of the most prominent artists of his time, and the fantastical limestone fireplace in another was carved by Eusebi Arnau, who did the proscenium sculptures in Domènech's Palau de la Música. It's difficult to maintain a landmark at these prices, though, so the facilities look a bit worn. The fact that a large part of their business is rambunctious student tour groups doesn't help. The rooms are of varying sizes, with clean tile baths, ceiling fans, and safes. Fixed-price meals of so-so quality in those superb dining rooms go for 1,000P to 1,450P ($7 to $10).

Lleó. Carrer de Pelai 22 (about midway between the University and Plaça de Catalunya), 08001 Barcelona. ☎ **93/318-13-12.** Fax 93/412-26-57. 80 units, all with bathroom.

A/C MINIBAR TV TEL. 9,000P ($62) single; 12,500P ($86) double. AE, DC, MC, V. Metro: Universitat.

While the guest rooms don't quite deliver on the promise of the gleaming streetside lobby, they have comforts and conveniences not seen in many hotels costing only a few pesetas less. Not least among these are the firm mattresses, room safes, and a substantial buffet breakfast at 975P ($7). The 19th-century building was renovated for the Olympics and has held up pretty well.

Mesón Castilla. Carrer Valdoncella 5, 08001 Barcelona. ☎ **93/318-21-82.** Fax 93/412-40-20. 56 units, all with bathroom. MINIBAR TV TEL. 8,250P ($57) single; 11,750P ($81) double. AE, MC, V. Metro: Universitat.

After dark, they keep the front door locked, but if you appear harmless the person at the desk buzzes it open. The hotel is on a largely residential square not far from Plaça de Catalunya and the Museu d'Art Contemporani. Substantial redecorating and the installation of new light-wood paneling have banished the former gloom of the lobby. The upstairs rooms and restaurant are less old-fashioned than they once were. The large breakfast buffet is a plus. Some staff members speak English.

✪ **San Agustín.** Plaça San Agustín 3 (1 block west of La Rambla, near Carrer Hospital), 08001 Barcelona. ☎ **93/318-16-58.** Fax 93/317-29-28. 80 units, all with bathroom. A/C TV TEL. 5,800P ($40) single; 8,900P ($61) double; 10,100P ($70) triple; 13,900P ($96) suite. Rates include breakfast. AE, MC, V. Metro: Liceu.

Now a three-star hotel, this is Barcelona's top value. On a square shaded by plane trees, it was built as a convent in 1740 and converted to a hotel in 1840, making it the city's oldest (according to the management). The attractive lobby makes effective use of ancient stone-and-brick arches and windows overlooking the plaza. No two rooms are the same—some ceilings soar; hand-hewn wood beams in other sections are head-knockers. The marble-sheathed baths have hair dryers. Particularly good for families are the two-room suites with two baths. The new attic rooms (nos. 401 to 408) are very desirable, and the commendable restaurant offers three-course fixed-price lunch and dinner. The manager and some staffers speak English.

NEAR THE MUSEU PICASSO

Layetana. Plaça Ramón Berenguer el Gran 2 (Via Laietana), 08002 Barcelona. ☎ **93/319-20-12.** 20 units, 14 with bathroom. 2,300P ($15.85) single without bathroom; 3,600P ($25) double without bathroom, 5,200P ($36) double with bathroom. No credit cards. Metro: Jaume I.

Several flights up by creaky elevator (press the "H"), this hostal overlooks a small park next to an imposing section of the old Roman wall. Its rooms, all with sinks, are somewhat larger than those at other lodgings in its price category. Beer and soft drinks are available in the TV lounge. Breakfast isn't served, but there are several cafes on the ground floor and around the corner.

WORTH A SPLURGE

For reservations at either of the following hotels, contact **Marketing Ahead,** 433 Fifth Ave., New York, NY 10016 (☎ **212/686-9213**).

Duques de Bergara. Bergara 11, 08002 Barcelona. ☎ **93/301-51-51.** Fax 93/317-34-42. 54 units, all with bathroom. A/C MINIBAR TV TEL. 14,850P ($102) single; 16,400P ($113) double. AE, DC, MC, V. Metro: Universitat.

It's rare that a hotel given the four-star rating comes within hailing distance of budgeteers in the mood for a splurge. Here's one, and it throws in the visual exuberance of an 1898 mansion. The *modernista* details have been retained and restored in the lobby and staircase, while the bar/lounge/restaurant is sleekly contemporary. The halls are constricted to allow for relatively spacious rooms, many with separate seating and desk areas. The location is a bonus, off Plaça de Catalunya, between the Old City and the Eixample. There's a no-smoking floor. Some of the staff are multilingual.

✪ **Regencia Colón.** Sangristans 13–17, 08002 Barcelona. ☎ **93/318-98-58.** Fax 93/317-28-22. 55 units, all with bathroom. A/C MINIBAR TV TEL. 7,900P ($55) single; 14,000P ($97) double. AE, DC, MC, V. Metro: Jaume I.

With the cathedral only a block away, this is a great location for exploring the Barri Gòtic. Behind the exterior of brick and rusticated stone, the lobby is pleasantly old-fashioned, with comfortable seating groups and a bar/restaurant. The rooms were redecorated for the Olympics, but the carpets are overdue for cleaning. Units vary widely in appointments and size, so speak up if you don't care for the room you're assigned. The *conserjes,* a helpful group, are usually accommodating.

4   Great Deals on Dining

Eating well in Barcelona is easy. Eating inexpensively is only a bit more challenging. The city's restaurants offer a wealth of dishes, primarily Mediterranean in their ingredients—olive oil, almonds, garlic, aromatic herbs, and tomatoes. Sausages (like the traditional *butifarra*), robust game, delicate seafood, savory rice dishes and stews, and myriad treatments of mushrooms are mainstays of the Catalan repertoire, often in such unusual combinations as fruit with poultry or shellfish with game. Look for *fideos* (*fideus* in Catalan), a form of paella made with thin noodles instead of rice. The highest concentrations of low-priced eateries are in Ciutat Vella.

There are many ways to keep food costs down, without relying on the ubiquitous fast-food emporia or fly-specked cafes in the more forbidding neighborhoods. A heightened Catalan enthusiasm for *tapas* (*tapes* in Catalan), the bar snacks for which other parts of Spain have long been noted, has resulted in the opening of big, gleaming places boasting long bars laden with platters of appetizing foods. Dished up in small *tape* servings or in larger *ración* (*racció*) portions, two or three can constitute a meal. Just be sure to check the prices, for many kinds of shellfish and the delicacy *angulas* (baby eels boiled in oil) can do severe damage to a food budget.

Also often found in *tapas* bars are meal-sized treats called *tostadas* (*torrades* in Catalan). Similar to Italian *crostini,* they're slabs of toasted or grilled bread rubbed with garlic and tomato, drizzled with olive oil, then topped with any of dozens of ingredients, including *xorico* sausage, beef tartar, mushrooms, slices of pork loin, cheese, anchovies, or sardines. One or two can make a lunch. Smaller versions of *torrades* are *montaditos.*

If you arrive at any of the restaurants below before 2pm for lunch or 10pm for dinner, you'll almost certainly be seated quickly without a reservation. After those times, lines form at the more popular places. This will be true at all but the most exclusive (expensive) restaurants. A tax of 7% is added to every bill.

IN THE BARRI GÒTIC

El Gallo Kirko. Carrer Avinyó 19 (south of Carrer Ferran). ☎ **93/412-48-38.** Main courses and *plats combinats* 450P–700P ($3.10–$4.80). MC, V. Daily noon–midnight. Metro: Liceu or Jaume I. PAKISTANI/SPANISH.

Nearly all Barcelona restaurants with non-Spanish cuisines feel the need to cater to local preferences; thus, the appearance of *arroz con pollo* alongside tandoori chicken. The curry dishes are more successful than those replicating Spanish recipes—hardly surprising since the owners are Pakistani. Further flinging authenticity aside, they have

---

Getting the Best Deal on Dining

- Take advantage of the three-course *menú del día* offered at lunch in most restaurants and at dinner in some.
- Order the *plat combinat* offered at many restaurants—it's a one-dish meal usually of meat, fish, or chicken joined by fried potatoes and a salad or vegetable. Bread and a beverage are often included. The price rarely exceeds 1,200P ($8) and can be much less.
- Try eating or drinking standing up. Many places have two prices: *taula* (table) and *barra* (bar).
- Enjoy a truly Spanish meal in a *tapas* bar. Two or three *tapes* or larger *racció* portions can constitute a great inexpensive meal.

---

a number of non-Pakistani couscous plates that are very popular. Skip the salads. The food is often slow in coming, but it's good value.

El Gran Café. Carrer Avinyo 9 (1 block south of Carrer Ferran). ☎ **93/318-79-86.** Main courses 975P–1,850P ($7–$13); *menús del día* 975P and 1,200P ($7 and $8). AE, DC, MC, V. Mon–Sat noon–3pm and 8:30–11:30pm. Metro: Liceu or Jaume I. SPANISH.

The tobacco-brown ceiling is high enough to accommodate 15-foot windows and a dining balcony over the service bar. The building is 19th century, and the restaurant has been given a belle époque appearance. A piano player adds to the mood in the evening, when the crowd tends to have a polished look. Fish and game dominate the menu but are changed frequently, a sign that the chef follows the market. A fast-moving staff wastes not a step bringing his creations to the table.

La Fonda. Carrer dels Escudellers 10 (east of La Rambla). ☎ **93/301-75-15.** Main courses 450P–990P ($3.10–$7); *menú del día* 950P ($7). V. Tues–Sun 1–3:30pm and 8:30–11:30pm. Metro: Liceu. SPANISH/CATALAN.

A block east of La Fonda is the atmospheric but overpraised Los Caracoles. Knowledgeable locals leave that ancient *taberna* to the tourists, lining up at this spiffy two-tiered place framed behind high-arched windows (there's another floor downstairs). Casually stylish and mostly under 35, especially in the evening, they come to check each other out and enjoy paella at 685P ($4.70) and other rice dishes and meat-and-fruit combos for as little as 450P ($3.10). Even with appetizers and desserts, meals can be kept under 1,500P ($10), but live it up with a carafe of robust Catalan wine. The prices, quality, and ambiance make up for the distracted, sometimes grumpy service. Arrive early, as it fills up quickly.

Le Pineda. Carrer del Pi 16 (near Plaça del Pi). ☎ **93/302-43-93.** Meals under 1,500P ($10). No credit cards. Mon–Sat 9am–8pm. Metro: Liceu. SPANISH.

The windows of this *charcutería* are draped with loops of sausages and whole hams, its interior enclosed by dark beams, cracked tiles, and shelves and cabinets lined with bottles. This kind of atmosphere isn't planned but just happens, and La Pineda has had most of this century to let it. Take a small marble-topped table at the back. A usual order (there's no menu) is *jamón, queso, pan,* and *tinto*—air-cured ham, Manchego cheese, bread, and a tumbler of red wine. Don't put too much faith in the above hours, as they're flexible.

Les Quinze Nits. Plaça Reial 6 (east of La Rambla). ☎ **93/317-30-75.** Main courses 425P–1,195P ($2.95–$8); *menú del día* (lunch) 950P ($7). AE, MC, V. Daily 1–3:45pm and 6:30–11:45pm. Metro: Liceu. SPANISH/CATALAN.

Choose recklessly from the à la carte menu and a meal can fly past budget parameters, so stick with the fixed-price deals, as most people do. The large front room overlooks the plaza, with tables under the loggia most of the year. A smaller, quieter room in back suits couples who don't need to be seen (the place attracts chic nightbirds). An earnest, if not always precise, young staff swiftly brings dishes like spinach-filled cannelloni under melted cheese and tender beef filet with shoestring potatoes. A half carafe of one of the palatable house wines is only 275P ($1.90).

✪ **Pitarra.** Carrer d'Avinyó 56 (south of Carrer Ferran). ☎ **93/301-16-47.** Main courses 600P–1,800P ($4.15–$12); *menú del día* 1,100P ($8). DC, MC, V. Mon–Sat 1–4pm and 8:30–11pm. Closed Aug. Metro: Liceu or Jaume I. SPANISH.

Pitarra occupies the former home and watch shop of prolific and much honored Catalan playwright/poet Federic Soler Hubert (pseudonym Pitarra). The atmosphere is friendly, the service swift, and the food hearty. Look for game dishes in winter, such as the platter of hare with wild mushrooms. The *menú* price includes a beverage and IVA. While this renovated place offers good value, its location deep in the Barri Gòtic means you might prefer to come here for lunch rather than dinner.

✪ **Self Naturista.** Carrer de Santa Anna 13–15 (just east of the upper Rambla). ☎ **93/318-23-88.** Main courses 280P–645P ($1.95–$4.45); *menú del día* 885P ($6). No credit cards. Mon–Sat 11:30am–10pm. Closed holidays. Metro: Plaça de Catalunya. VEGETARIAN.

This crisp self-service restaurant is as good as it gets in quality and price. The munificent selection of salads, main courses, and desserts varies daily, and there's a healthy choice of fresh fruit juices. Seating is McDonald's style, in a large dining room with windows on the street.

IN THE EIXAMPLE

Cerveseria d'Dor. Consell de Cent 339 (at the corner of Rambla Catalunya). ☎ **93/216-02-41.** Meals under 1,500P ($10). AE, MC, V. Mon–Sat 8am–1am. Metro: Passeig de Gràcia. SPANISH.

This reliable *tapas* bar/cafe has a long list of *plats combinats*, filling one-dish meals at 675P to 920P ($4.65 to $6). Among the tastier tidbits on the bar are crispy nuggets of creamy potatoes, zippy pork brochettes called *pintxos morunos*, and *empañadillas*, slabs of chicken or tuna pie. German beers are featured, several on draft. There are outdoor tables in good weather.

✪ **El Café de Internet.** Gran Vía C.C. 656. ☎ **93/412-19-14.** Main courses 410P–1,600P ($2.80–$11); *menú del día* 900P or 1,050P ($6 or $7). DC, MC, V. Mon–Sat 10am–midnight. Metro: Passeig de Gràcia. SPANISH.

It was inevitable that the first cybercafe (www.cafeinternet.es) in Spain would open in progressive Barcelona. Pop in, have a meal, then nip upstairs and surf the Net at one of a dozen computers. A half hour online is 600P ($4.15), and since about 80% of the Internet is in English, the attendant and users speak it too. Gimmicks aside, the food is quite good, featuring fresh ingredients and ample servings. Grilled salmon and tender pork loin in tomato sauce are often featured. Sandwiches and salads are also available.

Qu Qu (Quasi Queviures). Passeig de Gràcia 24. ☎ **93/317-45-12.** Meals under 1,500P ($10). AE, MC, V. Daily 8:30am–1am. Metro: Passeig de Gràcia. SPANISH.

This is one of the new breed of updated *tapas* bars showing up in Barcelona's better quarters. On the left is a takeout counter for meats, salads, and pastas and on the right a bar for sampling the delectable *tapes;* in back is a sit-down section for light meals. *Plats combinats* run 405P to 715P ($2.80 to $4.95). Funky jazz and alternative rock on the stereo proclaim this isn't your grandpa's *tapes* joint.

Tapa Tapa. Passeig de Gràcia 44. ☎ **93/488-33-69.** *Tapes* 260P–605P ($1.80–$4.15); *racciós* 405P–960P ($2.80–$6.60). AE, MC, V. Mon–Fri 8am–1am, Sat 9am–2am, Sun 11am–2am. Metro: Plaça de Catalunya. TAPAS.

Slick and contemporary, this wildly popular *tapes* emporium sets the pace for a new breed of restaurants. With its sidewalk tables under big umbrellas, twin long bars open to the street, and large elevated dining room, it's perfect for drop-in meals and snacks. Expect a wait, though. The place claims to offer 80 *tapes*, with daily specials.

WEST OF LA RAMBLA

Egipte. Carrer Jerusalem 3. ☎ **93/317-74-08.** Main courses 780P–2,100P ($5–$15); *menú del día* 950P ($7). AE, DC, MC, V. Mon–Sat 1–4pm and 8pm–midnight. Closed holidays. Metro: Liceu. CATALAN/SPANISH.

Not to be confused with the bar down the street or the more expensive restaurant on La Rambla, this Egipte has nothing to do with the Middle East. Its food is Spanish, with a few idiosyncratic touches—a cherry on the mashed potatoes for one. The bilevel space fills to the walls most nights, with not only bargain-seekers but also businesspeople and suburbanites who love its comfort food. Among the favorites are gazpacho, chicken with mustard-herb sauce, and veal scallops with mushrooms. A portion of *arroz negro* (rice and seafood cooked in squid ink) is 925P ($6). Prices on à la carte dishes have risen, but they've held the line on the *menù del día*, which includes IVA and beverage.

El Turia. Carrer Petxina 7 (off La Rambla). ☎ **93/317-95-09.** Main courses 1,000P–1,400P ($7–$10); *menú del día* 1,300P ($9) Mon–Fri, 1,500P ($10) Sat. MC, V. Mon–Sat 1–4pm and 8:30–11pm. Closed Aug 16–Sept 15 and for dinner on holidays. Metro: Liceu. SPANISH.

Especially lively at lunch, this restaurant is a family affair: The father tends the zinc-topped bar, the mother works the stove, and the daughter runs the dining room. It's frequented by actors and writers, many of whom are gay and who live and work nearby, and they come for the simple food featuring grilled meats. Daily *plats combinats* are about 900P ($6), so even with an appetizer and a glass of wine, lunch needn't be more than 1,750P ($12). Find El Turia down the pedestrian street just below La Boquería.

La Garduña. Carrer Morera 17–19. ☎ **93/302-43-23.** Main courses 850P–1,850P ($6–$13); *menú del día* 1,375P ($10). AE, MC, V. Mon–Sat 1–5pm and 8–11pm, Sun 1–4:30pm. Metro: Liceu. SPANISH.

To get to this Barcelona institution, enter the market at the doorway off La Rambla and walk all the way to the back, bearing slightly left. Identify it by the claustrophobic glassed-in bar in front, walking down into the lower dining room or upstairs. Autographed photos of Catalan notables crowd the walls. The close quarters and paper table coverings signal that this is the kind of place where you keep the same cutlery through all the courses. The first can be *escalibada con butifarra*, which is roast peppers and eggplant with a link of Catalan sausage; the second, one of several fishes *à la plancha*, which, in the case of the twin thin salmon steaks, arrives charred and crispy from the grill. Value and informality reign.

✪ **Pollo Rico.** Carrer Sant Pau 31 (2 blocks west of La Rambla). ☎ **93/441-31-84.** Main courses 450P–1,750P ($3.10–$12); *menú del día* 775P ($5). No credit cards. Thurs–Tues 1pm–midnight. Metro: Liceu. SPANISH.

Every budgeteer seeks out this place sooner or later—the word of mouth is that intense. The ground-floor windows are covered with gaudy colors and cartoons, nearly masking the display of golden birds turning slowly on their spits. This "rich chicken" refers to the taste, not the cost. A half chicken comes with various trimmings, but a typical deal includes soup, good greasy fries, bread, water, and a glass of sparkling *cava* for 950P ($7). *Plats combinats* run as little as 325P to 900P ($2.25 to $6), or do a mild splurge on paella for two with sangría for only 2,800P ($19). The service and surroundings are strictly rough-and-ready, with a long counter on the ground floor and wooden booths in the tile-dadoed upstairs room.

NEAR THE MUSEU PICASSO

El Xampanyet. Carrer Montcada 22. ☎ **93/319-70-03.** *Tapas* 165P–430P ($1.15–$2.95). No credit cards. Tues–Sun noon–4pm and 6:30pm–midnight. Metro: Jaume I. SPANISH.

As long as anyone can remember, a sign stating "Hay sidra fresca" ("We have fresh cider") has hung on the door frame of this 1929 bodega. They do, of the alcoholic Asturian variety, but the primary tipple is a sweetish wine with a *cava*-like spritz called Ca l'Esteve, the former name of the bar. A relentlessly cheerful family greets every new patron as a great friend, and while the *tapas* are limited to anchovies, tortillas, and a selection of canned fish, people stay on just to bask in the friendly glow. Antique tile dadoes, large dark casks, and bottles black with decades of tobacco smoke provide the setting.

Euskal Etxea. Placeta Montcada 1–3. ☎ **93/310-21-85.** *Menú del día* 1,175P ($8). No credit cards. Tues–Sat 12:30–4pm and 7:30–midnight, Sun 7:30–midnight. Metro: Jaume I. BASQUE/SPANISH.

A short walk down Carrer Montcada from the Picasso Museum, this neighborhood favorite is billed as a Basque "Cultural Center" but is at least as popular for tapas called *pintxos* set out on the bar at opening time. Here, the drill is to take a plate and heap on as many tapas as you wish. Individually, they cost 120P (80¢). This is on the honor system, so you report your consumption after the fact. Go early, for when the initial supply at each session is gobbled up, they don't make more. There are tables in back for sit-down meals.

✪ **La Pizza Nostra.** Carrer Montcada 29. ☎ **93/319-90-58.** Pizzas 750P–1,350P ($5–$9); pastas 975P–1,275P ($7–$9); *menú del día* 1,300P ($9). AE, DC, MC, V. Tues–Sun 1:30–4pm and 8:45–11:30pm (Fri–Sat to midnight). Metro: Jaume I. ITALIAN.

Within the walls of a medieval mansion on the same block as the Picasso Museum, throngs enjoy some of the best pizza in town. These are of the knife-and-fork variety, partly because that's the way Spaniards eat almost everything, but more because the pizzas are piled with all manner of topping. Some of these are conventional (sausage or shrimp) while others are unlike American versions (spinach with béchamel sauce, squid, or bits of cod). A plate of pasta or an 8-inch pizza should satisfy most appetites, especially when they're accompanied by sangría or a respectable René Barbier wine. Salads are also available. Despite the museum's proximity, the patrons are mostly young locals rather than tourists. The service is rushed but pleasant enough.

Little Italy. Carrer Rec 30 (near Passeig Born). ☎ **93/319-79-73.** Main courses 715P–1,480 ($4.95–$10). AE, DC, MC, V. Mon–Fri 1:30–4pm and 9–midnight, Sat 9pm–2am. Metro: Jaume I. ITALIAN.

New streetlamps have made this a more approachable after-dark choice in the resurgent Born area. Once trendy, it has settled into middle age, making it more comfortable for those who aren't pale, underweight, and artistic. The wait staff is still dressed in black and the crowd mostly on the sunny side of 35, apart from the occasional blond thing with a man who only *looks* like her father. Pasta offerings are all under 950P ($7), so a good way to keep the tab within reason is to have one of them preceded by soup or salad. The two levels are framed by stone walls and 19th-century iron beams and pillars. Given the name, it hardly surprises that Sinatra is a near-constant on the stereo.

THE CHAINS

Pans & Company has branches throughout the city, three on La Rambla alone. It specializes in inventive sandwiches using freshly baked French-style baguettes. Most are open Monday to Saturday 9am to midnight and Sunday 10am to midnight. You can eat well for under 800P ($6), with a sandwich, salad, and drink. **Bocatta** claims, in four languages, to make the "Best Sandwiches in Town." **Pastafiore** specializes in pizzas and pastas, **Pokin's** is a McDonald's clone, and **Farggi** has a tearoom character, serving crêpes and ice creams.

PICNICKING

Found in almost every neighborhood, *xarcuterias* (*charcuterías* in Spanish) specialize in sausages, meats, and cheeses and usually have bottles of wine and stocks of canned goods that can comprise a memorable picnic. One of the most appetizing is **L. Simo,** Passeig de Gràcia 46, opposite the modernist Block of Discord. It makes sandwiches to eat in or take out, and a glass case is filled with cheeses, smoked fish, pâtés, and various salads. **La Pineda,** above, is another possibility. Or stock up on everything at the incomparable **La Boquería** market on La Rambla.

Wherever you load up on supplies, head for the **Parc de la Ciutadella,** the **Barceloneta** beach, or the park at the Montjuïc end of the **Transbordador del Puerto** to enjoy your picnic.

WORTH A SPLURGE

Set Portes (Siete Puertas). Passeig Isabel II 14. ☎ **93/319-30-33.** Reservations required weekends. Main courses 1,450P–2,350P ($10–$16). AE, DC, V. Daily 1pm–1am. Metro: Barceloneta. CATALAN/SPANISH.

This is Barcelona's oldest restaurant, with over 150 years behind it, and still one of the most popular. These "seven doors" open onto as many rooms, with smaller salons on the second floor. Cloth-covered hanging lamps provide a peachy glow for the crowd of businesspeople, trendies, families, and visitors, served by an efficient staff. House specialties are rice dishes, including paella, and Catalan combinations of fruit with seafood or meats. Careful selection (avoiding costly shellfish and crustaceans) can keep your meal near budget level. Most nights, a piano player enhances the jovial mood.

5 Seeing the Sights

SIGHTSEEING SUGGESTIONS

Even if you don't have time to visit a single museum or monument, be sure to take a stroll along **La Rambla.** The flamboyant spectacle is ever-changing street theater, coursing with families, sailors, transvestites, mimes, lovers, lowlifes, sketch artists, punks, models, "living statues," beggars, buskers, and political activists at all hours.

IF YOU HAVE 1 DAY   In the morning, stroll down from Plaça de Catalunya along **La Rambla.** It flows from the sublime to the seedy, taking in the eye-filling La Boquería market, midway down the promenade, and the under-reconstruction opera house, and then continuing down to the Columbus Monument and the newly busy harbor. In the afternoon, head for the **cathedral** and the **Museu Picasso.** (If it's the first Sunday of the month, admission will be free; if it's Wednesday, it'll be half price.)

A Museum Note

All Barcelona's municipal museums are free for those under 18 and students with international IDs. They're closed January 1 and 6, April 12 and 19, May 1 and 31, June 24, September 11 and 24, October 12, November 1, and December 6, 8, and 25. Nearly all museums are closed on Monday, but many now stay open through the afternoon siesta on other days, when most stores are closed.

IF YOU HAVE 2 DAYS   Spend Day 1 as above. On the morning of Day 2, visit **La Sagrada Família** (skipping the expensive admission and the museum is no great loss and saves you $5). Then stroll along **Passeig de Gràcia** to see masterpieces of *modernista* architecture. In the afternoon, head for the top of **Montjuïc** and visit the fortress overlooking the city and harbor, the **Museu d'Art de Catalunya, Fundació Joan Miró,** and **Poble Espanyol.**

IF YOU HAVE 3 DAYS   Spend Days 1 and 2 as above. On the morning of Day 3, head north to the **Museu-Monestir de Pedralbes** and **Museu de Cerámica** and spend the afternoon wandering around the **Barri Gòtic** and visiting the **Saló del Tinell, Capilla de Santa Agueda, Museu d'Historia de la Ciutat,** and **Museu Frederic Marès.**

IF YOU HAVE 5 DAYS   Spend Days 1 to 3 as above. On Day 4, explore the **Ribera** barrio, visiting its **Santa Maria del Mar Church,** then stroll over to the **Parc de la Ciutadella** and visit the zoo. Have lunch in Barceloneta and, weather permitting, take to the **beach** or stroll along the waterfront's **Moll de la Fusta** over to the new Moll d'Espanya and its aquarium. A trip on one of *Las Golodrinas* (harbor sightseeing boats) caps the afternoon.

On Day 5, tour the **Eixample** to see the results of the Catalan *modernisme* movement and pay a visit to **Parc Güell** in the morning. From there, go up **Tibidabo** for a late lunch at one of the restaurants near the funicular and spend the afternoon enjoying the views and the amusement park.

THE TOP MUSEUMS

✪ **Museu Picasso.** Carrer de Montcada 15–19. ☎ **93/319-63-10.** Admission 600P ($4.15) adults (1,000P/$7 for both regular and temporary exhibits), 300P ($2.05) seniors/ students ages 12–16, free for age 11 and under. Free for everyone first Sun of every month. Tues–Sat and holidays 10am–8pm, Sun 10am–3pm. Metro: Jaume I.

Barcelona's most popular attraction, this museum reveals much about the artist whose long, prolific career extended well beyond cubism. Most of the paintings, drawings, engravings, and ceramics relate to the artist's earliest years, when he lived and studied in Barcelona and spent summers in Catalan hill towns. If you expect to see anything more than hints of Picasso's most famous works, you may be disappointed. The museum is housed in three adjoining Renaissance mansions that are nearly as interesting as the artworks they contain. The new terraced cafe is popular.

✪ **Fundació Joan Miró.** Av. Miramar 71–75, Parc de Montjuïc. ☎ **93/329-19-08.** Admission 600P ($4.15) adults, 400P ($2.75) students, free for age 13 and under. Tues–Wed and Fri–Sat 11am–7pm, Thurs 11am–9:30pm, Sun and holidays (Mon holidays too) 10:30am–2:30pm. Bus: 61 from Plaça de Espanya.

A tribute to Catalan lyrical surrealist Joan Miró, this contemporary museum reminiscent of Bauhaus dicta follows his work from 1914 to 1978 and includes many of his sculptures, paintings, and multimedia tapestries. Even the roof boasts his whimsical

Barcelona

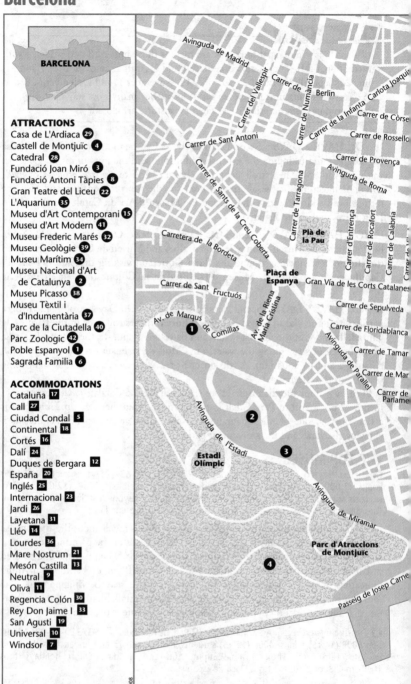

E-0008

138

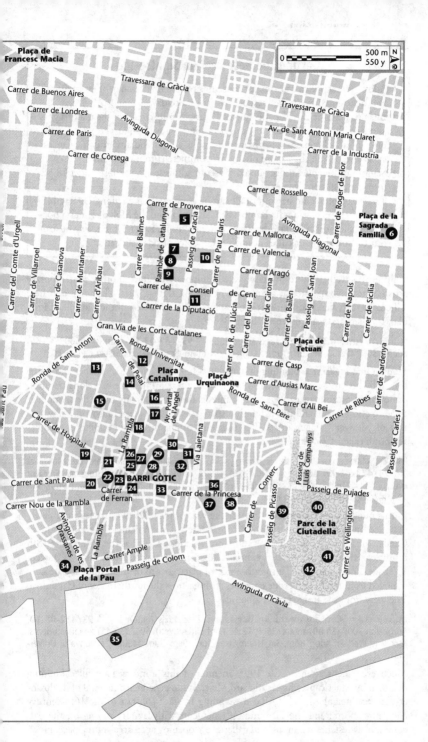

Getting the Best Deal on Sightseeing

- Admission is free to most major museums on the first Sunday of every month and discounted every Wednesday that isn't a holiday.
- Bus no. 100, the Bus Turístic, makes 17 stops on its circuit of the major sights and neighborhoods, and you can get off and on as often as you wish for the price of a 1-day pass. With free guidebooks and attendants, this is a far less expensive option than those offered by commercial tour companies.
- Seniors are eligible for discounted museum admission, and those under 18 get into many museums free.
- The best sightseeing bargain of all can be people-watching along La Rambla, its northerly extension the Rambla de Catalunya, and the Moll de la Fusta bordering the port. All have benches scattered around to relax on, or you can nurse a soft drink or coffee at one of the scores of sidewalk cafes.

sculptures as well as impressive city vistas. Temporary exhibits of other contemporary artists, often two or three at a time, are held on a regular basis. The restaurant here adheres to high standards but isn't too expensive. From the top of the Montjuïc funicular, turn left and walk down to the museum.

Fundació Antoni Tàpies. Carrer d'Aragó 255. ☎ **93/487-03-15.** Admission 500P ($3.45) adults, 300P ($2.05) seniors/students. Tues–Sun 11am–8pm. Metro: Passeig de Gràcia.

Housed in a *modernista* building designed by Lluís Domènech i Montaner and refurbished by his great-grandson in 1989, this museum continues the Barcelona tradition of honoring prominent native artists. Tàpies is thought by many to be the living heir to Miró and Picasso, and this exhibition space rotates examples of his work, as well as that of younger Catalan artists. The tangle of tubing atop the building is a Tàpies sculpture called *Chair and Cloud.*

Museu Nacional d'Art de Catalunya. In the Palau Nacional, Parc de Montjuïc. ☎ **93/423-71-99.** Admission 800P ($6) adults, 400P ($3.10) seniors/students. Free for everyone first Thurs of the month. Tues–Wed and Fri–Sat 10am–7pm, Thurs 10am–9pm, Sun 10am–2:30pm. Metro: Espanya.

In this building—meant to last only for the year of the 1929 World's Fair and newly designed inside by controversial Italian architect Gae Aulenti—is a collection of Catalan art from the Romanesque and Gothic periods as well as the 16th to the 18th centuries, along with works by high-caliber non-Catalan artists like El Greco, Velázquez, Zurbarán, and Tintoretto. Pride of place goes to the sculptures and frescoes removed from the Romanesque churches strung across the northern tier of Catalunya. The view from the front steps is a bonus.

Museu d'Art Contemporàni de Barcelona. Plaça deis Angels 1. ☎ **93/412-08-10.** Admission 700P ($4.80) adults (350P/$2.40 nonholiday Wed), 500P ($3.45) seniors/students. Mon and Wed–Fri noon–8pm, Sat 10am–8pm, Sun 10am–3pm. Metro: Catalunya or Universitat.

Much excitement attended the 1995 opening of this stunning light-filled building designed by American architect Richard Meier. It has generated a renewal of its down-at-the-heels neighborhood, El Raval, standing in stark contrast to the 16th-century convent opposite and the surrounding tenements with laundry drying on the balconies. New restaurants, shops, and galleries are opening at an accelerating pace. However, the permanent collection of about 1,100 paintings and sculptures is relatively small, and critical assessments of the museum will depend on the future acquisitions and the success of the temporary exhibits, which have so far proved to be on the cutting edge. In the meantime, see it for the architecture. Walk 5 blocks west from the upper Rambla along Carrer Bonsucces, which changes to Elisabets. After a visit, you might want to check out the **Centre de Cultura Contemporania** next door, which combines a modern glass wing with a former monastery and mounts provocative exhibits and installations.

THE TOP CHURCHES

✪ **Templo de la Sagrada Família.** Carrer de Mallorca 401. ☎ **93/455-02-47.** Admission: Templo, free; museum, 750P ($5) adults, 500P ($3.45) seniors, free for age 9 and under; elevator, 200P ($1.35). Apr–Aug daily 9am–8pm; Mar and Sept daily 9am–7pm; Oct–Feb daily 9am–6pm. Metro: Sagrada Família. Bus: 19, 34, 43, 50, 51, or 54.

An ambitious work in progress, this *modernista* rendition of a cathedral will, when and if finished, be Europe's largest. Work began on the Church of the Holy Family in 1882; 2 years later architect Antoni Gaudí y Cornet took over and projected a temple of immense proportions—the central dome is slated to be 525 feet high. His vision, as seen in other of his commissions around the city, amounts to a flamboyant surrealism with extensive stone carving, ceramics, and intricate ironwork. At the pinnacles of the completed towers, for example, are vivid mosaic sunbursts of gold and crimson. Controversy swirls around the cathedral's completion: Since Gaudí died in 1926 leaving no detailed plans, construction has continued by fits and starts, and the style and direction of recent additions—especially the inept sculptures on the west facade—aren't to everyone's liking. One of the towers has an elevator that takes you up to a magnificent view. The **Museu del Templo** in the crypt chronicles the cathedral's structural evolution, but it may not be worth the hefty admission for those with scant interest in the nuts and bolts of architecture.

Catedral de Barcelona (La Seu). Plaça de la Seu. ☎ **93/315-35-55.** Admission: Cathedral and cloister, free; Museu de la Catedral, 55P (35¢). Cathedral, daily 8am–1:30pm and 4–7:30pm; museum, daily 11am–1pm. Metro: Jaume I. Bus: 16, 17, 19, 22, or 45.

Begun in the late 13th century and completed in the mid-15th (except for the main facade, from the late 19th), this Gothic cathedral attests to the splendor of medieval Barcelona. Its main points of interest are the central choir; the crypt of Santa Eulàlia, whose alabaster sepulcher is of 14th-century Italian craftsmanship; and the *Cristo de Lepanto,* whose twisted torso allegedly dodged a bullet during the naval battle of the same name. A popular feature is the adjoining **cloister,** which encloses palm trees, magnolias, medlars, a fountain erupting from a moss-covered rock, and a gaggle of live geese, said to be reminders of the Roman occupation (or the Apostles or the virtuous St. Eulàlia, depending on various writers and guides).

Try not to miss the cathedral exterior when it's illuminated, usually Friday, Saturday, and Sunday evenings, though the schedule isn't consistent. On the steps at Sunday noon, a band with ancient instruments plays the eerily haunting *sardana,* the music of the classic Catalan folk dance.

OTHER MUSEUMS

Museu d'Art Modern de Catalunya. Plaça de les Armes, Parc de la Ciutadella. ☎ **93/319-57-28.** Admission 500P ($3.45) adults (250P/$1.70 Thurs 6–9pm), 250P ($1.70) seniors/students. Tues–Sat 10am–7pm, Sun 10am–2:30pm. Metro: Arc de Triomf.

Despite its name, this museum focuses somewhat narrowly on the work of Catalan painters and sculptors who worked in the *modernista* period (1880–1930), along with

---

Special & Free Events

Locals gather regularly to **dance the sardana,** a sedate, precisely choreographed Catalan folk dance. People of all ages and aptitudes form circles to perform its deceptively complex steps. Watch them in front of the cathedral on Saturday at 6:30pm and Sunday at noon, at Plaça Sant Jaume on Sunday and holidays at 7pm in summer and 6:30pm in winter, at Plaça Sant Felip Neri the first Saturday of the month at 6pm, and at Plaça de la Sagrada Família on Sunday at noon.

On the night of June 23, Barcelona celebrates the **Verbena de Sant Joan** with bonfires in the streets and plazas. It's customary to eat coca, a special sweet made from fruit and pine nuts, and festivities held on Montjuïc culminate in an impressive fireworks display.

During the week of September 24 are the celebrations of the **fiestas de la Mercé,** Barcelona's most important popular festival. Concerts and theatrical performances animate Plaças Sant Jaume, de la Seu, del Rei, Sot del Migdia, Escorxador, and Reial, and giants, devils, dragons, and other fantastic creatures parade through the Old Town. At the end of it all is a music pageant and fireworks. The days-long pre-Lenten **Carnaval** has grown in importance in recent years, with a parade and elaborately costumed citizens partying all night in the streets and clubs.

During November the **Festival Internacional de Jazz de Barcelona** takes place in the Palau de la Música Catalana.

---

some fine examples of furniture and decorative arts by like-minded craftspeople and designers of the time. Eventually, the collection is supposed to move to the Museu Nacional d'Art de Catalunya, so call before making a special trip.

Museu de Ceramicà/Museu de les Arts Decoratives. Av. Diagonal 686. ☎ **93/280-34-21.** Admission to both museums 500P ($3.45); free first Sun of each month. Tues–Sun 10am–3pm. Metro: Palau Reial.

In a 1920s palace, this collection traces the history of Spanish ceramics from the 13th century to the present. It's one of the most important museums of its kind in Europe, and included are a few rare Moorish pieces as well as plates executed by Picasso and Miró. Also contained in the palace is the less interesting Museu de les Arts Decoratives. The building sits on attractive parklike grounds that are worth a visit by themselves, if you're in the neighborhood.

Museu Marítim. Plaça Portal de la Pau 1 (Av. de les Drassanes). ☎ **93/301-18-71.** Admission 800P ($6) adults, 400P ($2.75) seniors/age 15 and under. Free for everyone first Sun each month. Daily 10am–7pm (winter to 6pm, Sun 10am–3pm). Metro: Drassanes.

Installed in the Drassanes, the 14th-century royal shipyards, this museum's superb collection of maritime vessels and artifacts is distinguished by a full-size replica of Don Juan of Austria's galleon. The marvelously baroque flagship of the Spanish and Italian fleet defeated a naval force of the Ottoman Empire in the 1571 Battle of Lepanto. There are also humbler fishing boats, many intricate ship models, and a map owned by Amerigo Vespucci.

Museu-Monestir de Pedralbes. Baixada del Monestir 9. ☎ **93/203-92-82** for monastery, or 93/280-14-34 for Sala Thyssen. Monastery and Sala Thyssen, 600P ($4.15) adults, 350P ($2.40) seniors, free for age 15 and under. Tues–Sun 10am–2pm. Closed holidays. FF.CC.: Line Sarrià–Reina Elisenda to the Reina Elisenda stop. Bus: 22 or 64.

(**world wonder**)

xploring lost cultures? Take along an **AT&T Direct**® Service wallet guide. It's a list of access numbers you need to call

ome fast and clear from around the world, using an AT&T Calling Card or credit card. What an amazing planet we live on.

For a list of **AT&T Access Numbers,** take the attached wallet guide.

t's all within your reach.

For Travelers who want more than the Official Line

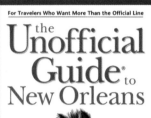

For Travelers Who Want More Than the Official Line

the Unofficial Guide to New Orleans

The Guides with More Than 2.5 Million Copies in Print!

the Unofficial Guide to Walt Disney World®

The Series with More Than **2.5 Million** Copies Sold!

♦ Save Time & Money
♦ Hotels & Restaurants Candidly Rated & Ranked
♦ Insider Tips & Warnings

...ve Zibart with Bob Sehlinger

♦ Tips & Warnings
♦ Save Money & Time
♦ All Attractions Ranked & Rated
♦ Plus Disney's New Animal Kingdom

Bob Sehlinger

For Travelers Who Want More Than the Official Line

the Unofficial Guide to Las Vegas

The Series with More Than **2.5 Million** Copies Sold!

♦ Save Time & Money
♦ Insider Gambling Tips
♦ Casinos & Hotels Candidly Rated & Ranked

Bob Sehlinger

Macmillan Publishing USA

Also Available:

- The Unofficial Guide to Branson
- The Unofficial Guide to Chicago
- The Unofficial Guide to Cruises
- The Unofficial Disney Companion
- The Unofficial Guide to Disneyland
- The Unofficial Guide to the Great Smoky & Blue Ridge Mountains
- The Unofficial Guide to Miami & the Keys
- Mini-Mickey: The Pocket-Sized Unofficial Guide to Walt Disney World
- The Unofficial Guide to New York City
- The Unofficial Guide to San Francisco
- The Unofficial Guide to Skiing in the West
- The Unofficial Guide to Washington, D.C.

This 14th-century monastery, with impressive stained-glass windows, was founded by Queen Elisenda de Montcada, whose sepulcher is inside the Early Gothic church. The cloisters provide glimpses of several monks' cells, an apothecary, a kitchen that was in use until recently, a 16th-century infirmary, and St. Michael's Chapel, which features 14th-century murals. A newly renovated wing has over 80 medieval paintings and sculptures from the Thyssen–Bornemisza collection, the bulk of which is now housed in its own museum in Madrid (see chapter 18).

Museu Tèxtil i d'Indumentària. Carrer de Montcada 12–14. ☎ **93/319-76-03.** Admission 300P ($2.05), 150P ($1.05) on nonholiday Wed. Tues–Sat 10am–8pm, Sun and holidays 10am–3pm. Metro: Jaume I. Bus: 16, 17, or 45.

Occupying two 13th-century Gothic palaces opposite the Museu Picasso (above), this museum contains a collection of textiles spanning ancient times to the 20th century. The manufacture of textiles was central to Barcelona's part in the Industrial Revolution. A pleasant courtyard cafe invites lingering.

MORE ATTRACTIONS

L'Aquàrium. On the Moll d'Espanya, at the harbor. ☎ **93/412-19-14.** Admission 1,300P ($9) adults, 950P ($7) seniors/ages 4–12. Daily 9:30am–9pm (Sat–Sun to 9:30pm). Metro: Drassanes.

The crowning touch of the new wharf that juts into the harbor (see below), this attractive and carefully conceived aquarium is said to be the largest in Europe. Opened in September 1995, it exhibits over 8,000 marine creatures of 300 species in 21 tanks. The rainbow-hued fishes and spectacular invertebrates are each identified by their Catalan, Spanish, Latin, and English (which is to say, British) names. A highlight is the Perspex tunnel that allows you to walk through a tank stocked with prowling sharks and gliding rays.

Monument à Colom (Columbus Monument). Plaça Portal de la Pau. ☎ **93/302-52-24.** Admission 200P ($1.35) adults, 100P (70¢) seniors/ages 4–12, free for age 3 and under. Late June to late Sept daily 9am–9pm; late Sept to late June Tues–Sun 9:30am–8pm. Elevator operates Mon–Fri 10am–1:30pm and 3:30–6:30pm, Sat–Sun 10am–6:30. Metro: Drassanes.

This waterfront landmark, erected for the 1888 Universal Exhibition, commemorates Columbus's triumphant return after his first expedition to the New World. After sailing into Barcelona, he delivered news of his discoveries to Queen Isabel and King Fernando. A 25-foot-high bronze statue of the explorer surmounts the Victorian-era monument. Oddly, it has been positioned so that he's pointing vaguely off to Africa, rather than toward the New World. Inside the iron column on which he stands is a creaking elevator that ascends to a panoramic view.

Las Golondrinas. Moll de les Drassanes. ☎ **93/412-59-44.** Tickets 440P ($3.05) adults, 225P ($1.55) ages 4–10. Harbor cruises depart daily at 11am and 1, 4:30, and 6:30pm. Metro: Drassanes.

Both kids and adults enjoy the 30-minute round-trip boat ride from the Portal de la Pau, near the Monument à Colom, to the harbor breakwater and back. This minivoyage bestows close-up views of the harbor traffic and the skyline. While room has been made for pleasure craft, this is a working harbor, with tugs, cranes off-loading freighters, dry docks, and shipyards. The company also offers 2-hour cruises to the Olympic Port and back for 1,250P ($9) adults, 875P ($6) seniors/ages 11 to 18, and 525P ($3.60) ages 4 to 10. To save some pesetas on the 30-minute cruise, go to the north end of the harbor, where smaller boats do the same thing for as little as 350P ($2.40).

Moll d'Espanya, Port Vell (Old Port). At the harbor. Metro: Drassanes.

The final phase of a long-term rehabilitation effort, this comma-shaped wharf with palm trees and lawns thrusts from the northeast corner into the center of the harbor. It carves out packed marinas of working and pleasure boats while providing for **Maremagnum,** a complex of shops, eating places, an IMAX theater, and an eight-screen cineplex. The development, along with the rejuvenated Moll de la Fusta that borders the shore, has brought vibrant life to an area that was once dark and ominous. A footbridge connects the tip of the wharf with the traffic circle ringing the Columbus monument at the foot of La Rambla.

Poble Espanyol. Av. Marqués de Comillas, Montjuïc. ☎ **93/325-78-66.** Admission 950P ($7) adults, 500P ($3.45) seniors/students/ages 7–14, free for age 6 and under. Mon 9am–8pm, Tues–Thurs and Sun 9am–2am, Fri–Sat 9am–4pm. Metro: Plaça de Espanya, then bus no. 61 or the free double-decker Poble Espanyol shuttle bus (on the half hour).

This consolidated village of examples of the varied architectural styles found throughout Spain was conceived and executed for the 1929 World's Fair. After substantial renovations and alterations in operational philosophy, it's now much more than an open-air museum. It has become almost a village in its own right, with working artisans, dozens of craft shops, restaurants, and assorted nightclubs and bars, a few of which are much in vogue.

PARKS & GARDENS

The **Parc de la Ciutadella** occupies the former site of a detested 18th-century citadel, some remnants of which remain. Here, too, are found the Museu d'Art Modern, the Museu de Zoología, the Museu de Geología, the regional Parliament, the zoo, and an ornate fountain that's in small part the work of the young Gaudí.

    Parc Güell, on the northern rim of the Gràcia section, was to be an upper-crust development of 60 homes with a full complement of roads, markets, and schools. Financed by Eusebi Güell and designed by Gaudí, the project was aborted after only two houses and a few public areas were built. One of the two houses is now the Casa–Museu Gaudí. Don't miss the ceramic mosaic lizard at the park's entrance stairway, the Hall of a Hundred Columns, and the view from the plaza above. Admission is free.

STROLLING AROUND THE BARRI GÒTIC

This suggested walk passes the quarter's most important sites and should take under 2 hours. Begin at **Plaça Nova,** to the right of the cathedral as you face it, where there are remnants of the Roman wall. Walk up the ramp between the cylindrical towers that were once a gateway to the Old City. Emerge into Carrer del Bisbe and the first building on your left is the **Casa de l'Ardiaca (Archbishop's House).** Its 18th-century portal opens onto an attractive courtyard with Romanesque details below and Gothic above. At the top of the stairway is a patio with a 13th-century mural and a splendid coffered ceiling. The courtyard is open daily 10am to 1:30pm.

    Opposite on Carrer Santa Llúcia is the Romanesque doorway to the **Capilla de Santa Llúcia** (open daily 8am to 1:30pm and 4 to 7:30pm), a vestige of the 11th-century cathedral that preceded the current one. Walk through the chapel and exit at the far side, entering the cathedral cloisters. After a circuit of the cloisters, enter the cathedral proper and walk through it and out the main entrance.

    Turn right, then right again, and proceed up Carrer dels Comtes (look up to see some classic Gothic gargoyles); make yet another right along Carrer de la Pietat behind the cathedral. Leading off to the left is Carrer Paradís, where inside the **Centre**

Excursionista de Catalunya (no. 10) are surviving columns of the city's largest Roman temple, which honored Augustus. Return to Carrer de la Pietat and continue to the left behind the cathedral.

Turn left on Carrer del Bisbe Irurita and walk to Plaça de Sant Jaume. On the right is the **Palau de la Generalitat,** seat of the regional Catalan government; its main 16th-century Renaissance facade faces the plaza and the **Casa de la Ciutat (City Hall),** whose 19th-century neoclassical facade supersedes a Gothic one. To the left off Carrer de la Ciutat runs the narrow Carrer d'Hercules, leading into **Plaça de Sant Just.** Notice the 18th-century mansions with the sgraffito decoration and the Sants Just i Pastor Church.

Now turn left onto Carrer Daguería, cross Carrer Jaume I and Carrer de la Llibrería, and continue along Carrer Frenería. Turn right onto the Baixada de Santa Clara and in a few yards enter the enclosed **Plaça del Rei.** At that corner is the **Palau Reial Major,** the former residence of the counts of Barcelona and the kings of Aragón. The staircase with semicircular risers at the opposite corner leads up to (on the left) the **Saló del Tinell,** where Isabel and Fernando are said to have received Columbus on his return from the New World, and (on the right) the **Capilla de Santa Agata,** built atop the Roman wall and featuring a handsome 15th-century retablo.

Turn right on Carrer del Veguer to the entrance of the **Museu de l'Historia de la Ciutat** (☎ **93/315-11-11**), open Tuesday to Saturday 10am to 8pm and holidays 10am to 2pm from June to September. (The rest of the year it closes 2 to 4pm.) Admission is 500P ($3.45) or 250P ($1.70) on nonholiday Wednesdays. Housed in a 15th-century mansion that was moved here stone by stone from Carrer Mercaders, several blocks away, the museum features excavations of Roman and Visigothic remains belowground and up above a gallimaufry of sculptures, weapons, ceramics, household implements, and more—a sort of municipal attic.

Returning to the Baixada de Santa Clara, turn right on Carrer dels Comtes. Alongside the cathedral in Plaça de Sant Iu is the **Museu Frederic Marès** (☎ **93/310-58-00**), open Tuesday to Saturday 10am to 5pm and Sunday and holidays 10am to 2pm; admission is 300P ($2.05) adults and 150P ($1.05) seniors/students; free for under age 12 and for everyone the first Sunday of the month. It houses the eclectic antiquities and curios of benefactor Mares, a Catalan sculptor. At the far end of the peaceful exterior courtyard is a section of the Roman wall.

BUS TOURS

From late March to early January, take advantage of the bargain **Bus Turístic.** A single ticket permits unlimited travel on these special buses, many of them open-topped double-deckers, as well as on the Montjuïc funicular and cable car, and Tibidabo's *tramvía blau.* Originating at Plaça de Catalunya, the red bus no. 100 makes a sweep of the city, driving north along Passeig de Gràcia, over by La Sagrada Família, along Avinguda del Tibidabo and Avinguda Diagonal, by the Estació Sants, through the Parc de Montjuïc, along the Passeig de Colom to Parc de la Ciutadella and back up La Rambla past the Barri Gòtic. It makes 17 stops along its 2½-hour route, and you can get off and reboard as often as you please. The 6 to 10 buses in service run daily, about every 15 minutes in summer and every 30 minutes the rest of the year, from 9am to 9:30pm. An all-day ticket is 1,400P ($10) and a ticket good for 2 consecutive days is 1,800P ($12). You can buy tickets on the bus, and they come with a guidebook in six languages and vouchers that provide discounts on entrance to such attractions as the zoo and the Poble Espanyol. Multilingual guide-conductors announce stops and answer questions.

6 Shopping

Barcelona's **value-added tax** (**IVA** in Spain) is now 7% for most items and services, but 16% for those defined as luxury goods. IVA recovery is possible for residents of countries outside the European Union, but only on purchases of more than 15,000P ($103) from stores with the "Tax-Free" sticker displayed. Obtain a certificate at the store and cash it in at airport Customs.

The **main shopping streets** in the Old Town are Avinguda Portal de l'Angel, Carrer Portaferrissa, Carrer del Pi, Carrer de la Palla, and Carrer Pelai. In the Eixample, they're Passeig de Gràcia and Rambla de Catalunya; in the northern reaches of town, Avinguda de la Diagonal, Via Augusta, Travessera de Gràcia, Carrer de Balmes, and Carrer Muntaner. **El Corte Inglés** is Spain's most prominent department store, its main branch at Plaça de Catalunya 14 (☎ **93/302-12-12**). It stays open through the siesta period and has a pleasant cafe with views on the top floor.

Barcelona's strengths are fashion and design, examples of which are nearly always costly. **Vinçon,** Passeig de Gràcia 96 (☎ **93/215-60-50**), carries the latest gadgets and home furnishings. A number of shops offer authentic ceramics from prominent regions of the country, as well as from Morocco. Three worthwhile choices are **La Caixa de Frang,** on Carrer Freneria (no phone), behind the cathedral; **Itaca,** on Carrer Ferrán, near Plaça Sant Jaume (☎ **93/301-3044**); and **Molsa,** on Plaça Sant Josep Oriol (☎ **93/302-3103**). A larger space with individual stalls and a potter at work is **ART Escudellers,** at Carrer Escudellers 23–25 (☎ **93/412-68-01**). For the handmade espadrilles seen on dancers of the sardana, the best shop is **La Manual Alpargatera,** Avinyo 7 (☎ **93/301-01-72**), which has many styles and also sells hats and some folk art.

Several stores carry English-language volumes, but **Come In Bookshop,** Provença 203 (☎ **93/453-12-04**), specializes in British and American travel guides, novels, and nonfiction. Two other possibilities are **Documenta,** Cardenal Casañas 4 (☎ **93/317-25-27**), and **Cómplices,** Cervantes 2 (☎ **93/412-72-83**), which offers gay and lesbian publications as well as providing information about local bars and dance clubs.

La Boquería, officially the Mercat de Sant Josep, is Spain's cleanest, most extensive, and most fascinating market, purveying fresh produce, meats, cheeses, fish, and every imaginable edible. For teas and spices, and especially good prices on expensive thread saffron, try **Angel Jobal** on Carrer Princesa 38, a block past the turn for the Picasso Museum. Antiques lovers will enjoy the open-air **Mercat Gòtic de Antigüedades** by the cathedral, held every Thursday 9am to 8pm (except August). Other days, stroll down nearby Carrer de la Palla, which has at least 18 shops and galleries.

7 Barcelona After Dark

Barcelona's nightlife runs from the campy burlesque of El Molino to the bizarre opulence of the Palau de la Música Catalana. For the latest information on concerts and other musical events, call the **Amics de la Música de Barcelona** at ☎ **93/302-68-70** (Monday to Friday 10am to 1pm and 3 to 8pm). For information on the **Ballet Contemporáneo de Barcelona,** call ☎ **93/322-10-37.** For a comprehensive list of evening activities, pick up a copy of the weekly *Guía del Ocio* or the entertainment guide offered with the Thursday edition of *El País.* For a guide to the gay and lesbian scene, pick up a map of gay Barcelona at **Sex Tienda,** Carrer Raurich 11 (☎ **93/ 532-73-70**).

The **Gran Teatre del Liceu,** on La Rambla, the traditional home to opera and ballet, suffered a devastating fire in 1994 but might reopen before you arrive. That projection may prove to be too optimistic, however, so check.

THE PERFORMING ARTS

A magnificent *modernista* concert hall, the **Palau de la Música Catalana,** Amadeu Vives 1 (☎ 93/268-10-00 for reservations; Metro: Urquinaona), is the work of the Catalan architect Lluís Domènech i Montaner, a rival of Gaudí. Its distinctive facade is a tour de force of brick, mosaic, and glass. However, the drama and elegance within are what set it apart from its peers. The interplay of ceramic mosaics, stained glass, and a central skylight build to the stunning crescendo of massive carvings framing the stage. It's home to the Orquestra Simfònica de Barcelona, directed by an American, Lawrence Foster, and hosts a variety of classical and jazz concerts and recitals. Tickets cost 650P to 5,250P ($4.50 to $36).

A favored venue for ballet and modern dance, the **Teatre Victòria,** Av. Parallel 65 (☎ 93/329-91-89; Metro: Espanya), is picking up some of the slack brought about by the destruction of the Gran Teatre del Liceu. And at a recycled former market, the **Mercat de les Flors,** Lleida 59 (☎ 93/426-21-02; Metro: Pole Sec), dance, theatrical productions, and occasional musical events are on the menu. Ticket prices vary with the attraction at both venues.

LIVE-MUSIC CLUBS

At nightfall, the **Poble Espanyol** switches from museum village to entertainment complex, offering everything from jazz and flamenco to dance clubs and designer bars. The rage here has been the **Torres de Avila** (☎ 93/424-93-09), a multifloor bar/disco conceived by the designers Marisol and Arribas and installed in one of the fake fortified towers near the main entrance. On warm nights, head for the open-air roof for a spangled city view. The place is open daily 10pm to 4am.

Also on site is **El Tablao de Carmen,** Poble Espanyol, Arcs 9 (☎ 93/325-68-95), the best place in Barcelona to see flamenco. That isn't much of a compliment, for the passionate dance of Andalucia is seen to better advantage in Madrid or Seville (see chapters 18 and 25). Admission is 7,000P ($48) for dinner and the first show or 4,000P ($28) for the first show and one drink. Dinner begins at 9pm; the first show is at 10:30pm, the second at 1am.

A reliable venue for top-drawer jazz performers, **La Cova del Drac (Cave of the Dragon),** Carrer Vallmajor 33 (☎ 93/200-70-32; Metro: Muntaner or La Bonanova), is in a less intimidating neighborhood than the Harlem Jazz Club (below), with many other fun spots on nearby blocks. It's open daily 8pm to 3am, with no cover.

The **Harlem Jazz Club,** Comtessa Sobradiel 8 (☎ 93/310-07-55; Metro: Jaume I), is a Barri Gòtic hideaway on a surprising tree-lined street, but it fills with aficionados who come for the music, not the setting. With no cover, it's open Tuesday to Sunday 7pm to 3am; live performances are Tuesday to Thursday at 10 and 11:30pm, Friday and Saturday at 11pm and midnight, and Sunday at 9:30 and 11pm.

BARS & DANCE CLUBS

In summer, the lower end of **Rambla de Catalunya** blossoms with outdoor cafe/bars. The bars of **Carrer Santaló,** near Plaça de Francesc Macià on the Diagonal, are popular with the younger crowd. **Passeig del Born,** near the Museu Picasso, has several low-key "bars of the night."

Over in **Poble Nou,** near the Parc de la Ciutadella, the two skyscrapers marking the location of the former Olympic Village also point the way to the site of the latest frenetic bar scene. The artificial harbor that was the launch point for the Olympic sailing competition is now lined on three sides with over 50 bars and cafes that pound on toward dawn. Among the headliners are **Dreams, Garatage Club,** and **Zeleste.** It's also one of the safest nightlife districts.

The following are standouts among the "designer" bars and the larger disco/bar/restaurants sometimes known as *multispacios:*

Nick Havanna, Rosselló 208 (☎ **93/215-65-91;** Metro: Provença or Diagonal), bills itself, in English, as the "Ultimate Bar." That's a stretch, but it was one of the first designer bars. One feature is a bank of video monitors bouncing with MTV-like images. It's open nightly 11pm to 4am. **Oliver & Hardy,** Diagonal 593 (☎ **93/419-31-81;** Metro: Maria Cristina), offers upscale facilities and prices to match its slightly older crowd, about 25 to 40. Diners can move from the outdoor terrace to the piano bar and wind up in the dance club. There's jazz Wednesday night, and it's open Monday to Saturday 8pm to 5am.

Conjure an abandoned county jail or a two-story parking garage—that'll give you a foretaste of the ambiance at **Otto Zutz,** Lincoln 15 (☎ **93/238-07-22;** Metro: Plaça Molina). Go early to avoid the restrictive entrance policy. It's open Tuesday to Saturday midnight to 4am or later, and the cover is 2,000P ($14), which includes the first drink. In a *modernista* structure, **Velvet,** Balmes 161 (☎ **93/217-67-14;** Metro: Diagonal), has a dance floor and two bars lined with buttocks-shaped stools. Don't miss the bathrooms. The music is mostly British and American rock from the 1960s, older than most of the patrons. It's open daily 7:30pm to 5am.

GAY & LESBIAN BARS

Gays have a number of beguiling bars and dance clubs to choose from, but lesbians very few. **Café de la Calle,** Vic 11 (☎ **93/218-38-63;** Metro: Diagonal), caters to both and is often used as a place to meet before embarking on a night out; it's open daily 6pm to 3am. A relatively new venue is **Distrito Maritimo,** on the Moll de la Fusta in the Port Vell (☎ **93/221-56-61;** Metro: Barceloneta). The music is mostly house and techno, and it's open weekends midnight to 5am. Women may want to check out the curiously named **Daniel's,** Plaça Cardona 7 (no phone; Metro: Fontana), open daily 6pm to 3am. Habitués are happy to reveal what's hot in town this very nanosecond.

For the latest on the nightlife scene, also check out **Cómplices** (see "Shopping," earlier in this chapter).

PUBS

Newly popular alternatives for those nightcrawlers seeking relief from designer bars are more or less accurate replications of Irish pubs. Featuring pints of Guinness Stout and Irish folk music, these three have opened over the last few years: At **The Quiet Man,** Marquès de Barberà 11 (☎ **93/412-12-19;** Metro: Liceu), Irish expatriates and visitors mingle with nearly equal numbers of locals. It's an oasis in the disreputable Barri Xines, west of the lower La Rambla, open Sunday to Thursday 6pm to 2am and Friday and Saturday 6pm to 3am.

An offshoot of a growing European chain, **Kitty O'Shea's,** Nau Santa Maria 5, just east of Carrer Numancia (☎ **93/280-36-75;** Metro: Maria Cristina), draws eaters as well as drinkers, with a menu that offers Irish-style mixed grills, roast beef, smoked salmon, and an exotic item called Dublin coddle. There's live music on Wednesday, and it's open daily midnight to 3am. **Flann O'Brien's,** Casanova 264 (☎ **93/201-16-06**), is known for its superior sound system. The three Irish owners named their pub after a popular newspaperman, and samples of his writings are part of the decor. It's open daily 6pm to 3am.

XAMPANYERIAS

These places specialize in *cavas,* the sparkling wines of Catalunya made by the *méthode champenoise.* **La Cava del Palau,** Verdaguer i Callis 10 (☎ **93/310-09-38;** Metro: Urquinaona), stocks over 40 regional *cavas,* 40 French champagnes, and some 350 appellation wines from Spain, France, and Chile. Champagne connoisseurs will want to try the *brut natures,* the driest and most natural of all *cavas.* To accompany the libations, there's a selection of cheese, pâtés, and salmon for 1,200P to 2,000P ($8 to $14) per *ración* (larger than a *tapas* portion). A glass of *cava* averages about 600P ($4.15). It's open Monday to Saturday 7pm to 3am, with live piano music starting at 11:30pm. **Xampu Xampany,** Gran Via 702 (☎ **93/265-04-83;** Metro: Girona), is a spacious enterprise with a good sound system and highly eclectic music programs to go with a few score *cavas.* Apt accompaniments are the smoked salmon and caviar nibbles. It's open daily 6pm to 2:30am (to 4am weekends).

COCTELERIAS

More than any other Spanish city, Barcelona enjoys its cocktail lounges. Typically open from early evening to the small hours, they're meeting places before dinner or for nightcaps; little or no food is served. Many are named for their specialties—like **El Dry Martini,** Aribau 166 (☎ **93/217-50-72;** Metro: Provença), and **Gimlet,** Rec 24 (☎ **93/310-10-27;** Metro: Jaume I)—or have English names, like Blue Moon, Snooker, Derby, and Pep's Corner.

Probably the oldest of the breed is **Boadas,** Tallers 1 (☎ **93/318-88-26;** Metro: Catalunya), just off La Rambla. The tight triangular room, sheathed in mahogany, dates to the 1930s. The bartenders can mix just about anything, though a Long Island Iced Tea is probably beyond their ken. It's open daily noon to 2am (later in season). Off Praça Sant Jaume is a tranquil spot with sinuous *modernista*-style decor, **El Paraigua,** Pas de l'Ensenyança 2 (☎ **93/302-11-31;** Metro: Jaume I). Since it doesn't attract a rowdy crowd, it's a great place for a heart-to-heart with a buddy or lover.

An exceptional retreat that eclipses all the rest for elegance and panache is the **Palau Dalmases,** Carrer Montcada 20 (☎ **93/310-06-73**), a 16th-century mansion a few doors down from the Picasso Museum. You enter at the end of an enclosed courtyard. Multiple archways and ancient stone walls are hung with large copies of florid Baroque paintings; candles are lit on the marble-topped tables when you sit down. Vivaldi and Bach provide the stereo underscore for murmured confidences and romantic intimacies. Magicians perform Wednesday at 11:30pm and opera singers appear Thursday at 11pm. On those nights, the cover charge (including first drink) is 2,500P ($17). No food is served. It's open Tuesday to Saturday 7pm to 2am and Sunday 5 to 10pm.

CAFES

The Spanish tradition of the *tertulia,* a semiformalized debate/conversation, is carried on at a handful of smoke-filled turn-of-the-century cafes, notably the **Café de l'Opera,** La Rambla 74 (☎ **93/317-75-85;** Metro: Liceu). It remains a good lookout on the often eyebrow-raising doings on La Rambla, best for breakfast or an afternoon caffeine reinforcement. Another choice is **Els Quatre Gats,** Montsió 5 (☎ **93/302-41-40;** Metro: Catalunya). For a brief burst of time in the first decade of this century, this "Four Cats" was *the* gathering place for the artists, designers, and poets (including Picasso) who were making Barcelona a creative hot spot. You can eat there, but skip the food and go for a drink to take in the atmosphere. A dark Disney doppleganger looks to have been at work at **Bosc de les Fades,** Pasaje de la Banca 7 (no phone; Metro: Drassanes). It attempts to evoke a woodland dell, fairy-tale style, with fake twisted tree trunks and dangling faux branches. Twentysomethings constitute most of the crowd dawdling over sandwiches, drinks, and smokes. Find it down the alley to the right of the entrance to the wax museum, at the harbor end of La Rambla.

8 Side Trips: Beaches, Wine & Dalí

MONTSERRAT MONASTERY

The vast **Montserrat Monastery** complex, 32 miles northwest of Barcelona, has a basilica with a venerated Black Virgin, a museum, hotels and eating places, and an abundance of souvenir shops and food stalls.

The monastery—a 19th-century structure that replaced one leveled by Napoléon's army in 1812—is situated 2,400 feet up Montserrat. Its name refers to the serrated peaks of the massif, bulbous, elongated formations that provided shelter for 11th-century Benedictine monks. One of the noted institutions of the Monastery is the **Boys' Choir,** begun in the 13th century. Composed of 50 boys, the choir sings at 1 and 6:45pm. Its performances are thrilling to the faithful and curious alike and are the best reason for a visit. Second on that list is the newly constituted subterranean **Museu de Montserrat** (☎ 93/835-02-51), near the entrance to the basilica. It brings together artworks once scattered around the complex, including gold and silver liturgical objects, archaeological artifacts from the Holy Land, and paintings of both the Renaissance and the 20th century. Admission is 300P ($2.05), and it's open Monday to Friday 10am to 6pm and Saturday, Sunday, and holidays 9:30am to 6pm. Numerous **funiculars** and **paths** lead to hermitages and shrines higher up the mountain.

Heavily touted and touristed, the monastery may be best saved as a stopover on a **driving tour** of the region, rather than seen on a special trip. The least expensive transport to Montserrat from Barcelona is the **train** from Plaça de Espanya, costing 1,560P ($11). It leaves five times daily for the Aeri de Montserrat station, where a **funicular** carries you to the mountaintop for another 750P ($5) round-trip. Several tour companies offer daily **bus tours** all year, but they cost upward of 5,000P ($35). Families, in particular, can find better ways to spend their money.

ACCOMMODATIONS & DINING   One strategy to avoid the worst of the crowds, especially in summer, is to check into the central **Hotel Abat Cisneros** (☎ 93/828-40-06) in late afternoon in time to hear the choir. The units (all with bathrooms) are comfortable enough, with doubles at 5,100P to 8,360P ($35 to $58), and the kitchen and dining room staffs are quite capable; full lunch or dinner is 2,430P ($17).

SITGES

A popular beach destination 25 miles south of Barcelona, **Sitges** really swings in summer, especially with young Barcelonans and gays. By mid-October it goes into hibernation, but its scenic charms and museums may be motive enough for a winter visit. Things pick up with Carnaval in late February, a riotously turbulent event with costumed revelers partying for days.

The beaches here have showers, bathing cabins, and stalls. Kiosks rent items like air cushions and motorboats. Those beaches on the eastern end and those inside the town center are the most peaceful, like **Aiguadoiç** and **Els Balomins. Playa San Sabestián, Playa Fregata,** and **"Beach of the Boats"** (under the church, next to the yacht club) are the family beaches. Most young people go to the **Playa de la Ribera,** in the west.

The **Museu Cau Ferrat,** Fonollars (☎ **93/894-03-64**), is the legacy of wealthy Catalan painter Santiago Rusinyol, a leading light of belle époque Barcelona. His 19th-century house, fashioned of two 16th-century fishermen's homes, contains a collection not only of his works but also several pieces by Picasso and El Greco, much ornate wrought iron (a Catalan specialty), folk art, and archaeological finds. Next door is the **Museu Maricel de Mar** (☎ **93/894-03-64**), the legacy of Dr. Pérez Rosales, whose impressive accumulation of furniture, porcelain, and tapestries draws largely from the medieval, Renaissance, and Baroque periods. Both museums are open Tuesday to Sunday 9:30am to 2pm and 4 to 6pm. Admission to each is 300P ($2.05).

Trains run daily to Sitges from the Estació Sants. The round-trip fare is 600P ($4.15).

THE WINE COUNTRY

The wineries in Sant Sadurní d'Anoia, 25 miles from Barcelona off the A2 *autopista* (toll highway), produce Catalunya's estimable *cavas*. **Freixenet** (☎ **93/891-07-00**) and **Codorniu** (☎ **93/891-01-25**) offer the best tours and tastings. Call for hours.

Trains run daily to Sant Sadurní d'Anoia (the station is right next to Freixenet) from the Estació Sants. The round-trip fare is 600P ($4.15). A **car** is all but essential to visit Codorniu, as taxis from the Sant Sadurní d'Anoia train station are unreliable.

That reservation applies as well to a visit to **Vilafranca del Penedès,** about 10 miles beyond Sant Sadurní d'Anoia. This is the center of the Penedés wine district, a rival to the better-known Rioja region in north-central Spain. It may be instructive to think of Penedés as Spain's Burgundy and of Rioja as its Bordeaux, for the wines they produce share characteristics with the ones made in those French wine-producing regions. The best-known winery is **Miguel Torres,** Carrer Comercio 22 (☎ **93/890-01-00**), which offers tours and tastings.

DALÍ LAND

Irrepressibly eccentric and enormously skilled at self-promotion, surrealist Salvador Dalí traveled widely, especially to the United States, but he always returned to his home territory of northeastern Catalunya.

With the recent opening of two of Dalí's former residences, not far from his museum in Figueres, near the French border, a more fully rounded picture of his complex life and enthusiasms has emerged. The only difficulty is that while Figueres and Girona, the region's main city, can be reached by bus and train from Barcelona, the much smaller towns of Púbol and Port Lligat require a car. You won't need it for more than a day, though more extended touring of this lovely region easily justifies a 2- or 3-day rental.

ARRIVING   A logical scheme is to travel first to Girona by **bus** or **train** or by the A-7 *autopista* (toll highway) from Barcelona, a distance of 60 miles. Buses stop near the **tourist information office** (☎ **972/41-94-19**) at Rambla de la Libertat 1, and there's also a branch office in the rail station (☎ **972/21-62-96**). Girona deserves at least a 2- or 3-hour exploration. The Old Town is on the other side of the Onyar river from the main *turismo* and can be taken in easily on foot.

Several car-rental agencies are around the train station. From there, drive north about 2½ miles to pick up Route 255 heading east toward La Bisbal. In 15 miles, watch for signs directing to the small village of Púbol.

SEEING THE SIGHTS   Dalí's favorite model and lifelong enamorata was Gala, another man's wife when he met her in 1929. They ran away to Paris and led a tempestuous life together and apart, through their mutual experimentations in art and sexuality. He bought her a mansion in Púbol and vowed he wouldn't come there unless she specifically invited him, in writing. This was fortunate, since she had a steady stream of young lovers from the village, though she didn't move in until she was in her 70s. In 1996, the **Casa–Museu Castell Gala Dalí** (☎ 72/51-18-00) was opened to the public. It houses a fascinating collection of antiques, tapestries, and Dalí's inimitable contributions, including a stuffed horse and a painting of two radiators on a panel covering two real ones. March 15 to June 30, it's open Tuesday to Sunday 10:30am to 5:30pm (to 6:30pm July 1 to September 30). Admission is 600P ($4.15).

From Púbol, pick up Route 252 north, which arrives in central Figueres in about 27 miles. Signs point the way to the artist's **Teatre–Museu Dalí** (☎ 72/51-19-76). It's said to attract more visitors than any other museum in Spain, save for Madrid's Prado. Opened in 1974, the museum was designed outside and in by the artist himself, who installed his works and those of a select few friends over four floors. They titillate, amuse, and baffle in varying proportions. In the atrium, for example, his mural-sized painting of a row of armless Venuses incorporates a near-hidden representation of the famous matador Manolete (the right breast of the second Venus is his nose, her stomach his mouth). A certain symmetry is established when it's learned that the artist lived out his last years in the museum's tower, dying there in 1989. It's open daily: October to June 10:30am to 6pm and July to September 9am to 8pm. Admission is 700P ($4.80) adults and 500P ($3.45) seniors/students in low season and 1,000P ($7) and 800P ($6), respectively, in high season.

If the experience leaves you in the mood for a modest splurge, one of the best restaurants in the region is about 2 miles away: the **Hotel Empordà** (☎ 72/50-05-62) on the Antiga Carretera de França (s/n). Inventive Catalan cuisine is solemnly and efficiently brought to the table, with fixed-price meals at 3,400P or 4,900P ($23 or $34). Simple double rooms upstairs go for 11,400P ($79). It's open daily 1 to 3:30pm and 8:30 to 11:30pm. American Express, Diners Club, MasterCard, and Visa are accepted.

The last corner of this Dalí triangle, a cluster of cottages on the shore of the fishing village of Port Lligat, was the most recent (1997) of the artist's habitations to be opened. From his museum in Figueres, drive east on Route 260 about 20 miles toward Cadaqués. On a protected cove a couple of miles north of that town, the connected white stucco structures that became Dalí's home nudge a beach banked with heaps of seaweed and crowded with working boats and Zodiacs. Called the **Casa–Museu Dalí Port Lligat** (☎ 72/25-80-63), the rambling house contains his studio with a motorized easel, a roaring stuffed bear, and an extensive library (albeit with fake books replacing the originals). English-speaking docents are on duty in most of the rooms, nudging you along to the next room after your brief inspection. The tour ends out on the patio, where parents may not wish to point out that the long pool with bulges at each end outline the shape of a phallus. At this writing, the museum is open only July to September daily 10:30am to 7:30pm; March 15 to June and October Tuesday to Sunday 10:30am to 5:30pm. Visits must be reserved in advance, a task best accomplished by a hotel *conserje*. Admission is 1,200P ($8) adults and 700P ($4.80) seniors/students.

Berlin & Potsdam

7

by Beth Reiber

The history of Berlin this century—particularly given the events of the late 1980s—is one of Europe's most compelling stories. Even in the mid-1980s, who'd have imagined the Wall would come tumbling down, communism would be defeated throughout Eastern Europe, and the two Germanys would reunite, with Berlin as the new capital?

Ironically, Berlin began as a divided city in the 13th century, when two settlements were founded on opposite banks of the Spree River. These settlements grew and merged. Berlin served as capital of Prussia under the Hohenzollerns and then as capital of the German nation. After the turn of this century, Berlin began to challenge Munich as the cultural capital, attracting artists like Max Liebermann, Lovis Corinth, and Max Slevogt. Max Reinhardt took over as director of the Deutsches Theater, Richard Strauss became conductor at the Royal Opera, and Albert Einstein was director of physics at what became the Max Planck Institute.

After the German defeat in World War II, Germany and its former capital were carved into four sections: Soviet, American, French, and British. Berlin, deep in the Soviet sector, was divided into East and West, with East Berlin serving as the capital of East Germany. In 1961, after a series of disputes and standoffs, a 13-foot-high wall was erected around West Berlin, in part to stop a mass exodus of East Germans to the West. Three million had already fled, most of them young, draining East Germany of many of its brightest and most educated. How ironic that in 1989 it was another exodus from the East to the West that triggered the Wall's sudden demise.

Today Berlin is changing so rapidly it's impossible to keep abreast of everything, particularly in eastern Berlin, where new development has transformed it into the world's largest construction site. Though with the rest of the nation it has felt economic recession and ideological differences between eastern and western Germans, Germany's largest city (pop. 3.5 million) is one of Europe's most exciting, with some of the best museums, a thriving nightlife, and a rich cultural legacy.

REQUIRED DOCUMENTS Citizens of the United States, Canada, Australia, and New Zealand need only a valid passport, which allows stays of up to 3 months. Visitors from the United Kingdom need only an identity card. Students should be sure to bring an International Student Identity Card (ISIC) as well.

OTHER FROMMER'S TITLES For more on Berlin, see *Frommer's Germany, Frommer's Gay & Lesbian Europe,* or *Frommer's Europe.*

1 Berlin Deals & Discounts

SPECIAL DISCOUNTS

Students can obtain cheaper admission to most museums by presenting an **International Student Identity Card (ISIC).** In addition, some theaters and live-music venues offer student reductions.

If you've arrived without an ISIC and can show proof of current student status, you can get the card at **Kilroy Travels,** Hardenbergstrasse 9, a travel agency in the technical university district not far from Bahnhof Zoologischer Garten. It also offers discount plane fares. The agency is open Monday to Friday 10am to 6pm and Saturday 11am to 2pm. Other branches are Georgenstrasse 3 in Berlin-Mitte and Takustrasse 47 in Dahlem. For more information, call ☎ **030/20 39 030.**

WORTH A SPLURGE

For an evening of grand entertainment, it's worth forking over the extra marks to see an opera at the **Deutsche Oper Berlin, Staatsoper Unter den Linden,** or **Komische Oper.** If you're lucky enough to get a ticket, it's also worth the money to see the **Berlin Philharmonic.** If you can't get tickets, console yourself with a cocktail or two high above the city in the **Telecafe of the Fernsehturm.** Though the ride on the elevator adds to the cost, the view is the best in Berlin.

2 Essentials

ARRIVING

BY PLANE　If you're flying to Berlin on Lufthansa or any of the other airlines serving Berlin from Frankfurt, Munich, Western Europe, or the United States, most likely you'll arrive at **Tegel Airport** (☎ **030/41 01-1**), 5 miles from the city center. Be sure to stop by the Airport Service Center for a city map, directions to your hotel, and sightseeing information. The best and easiest way to get into town, particularly if your destination is one of the hotels on or around Kurfürstendamm, is on **city bus no. 109,** departing about every 10 to 15 minutes from outside the arrivals hall. The fare is 3.60DM ($2.05) one-way. The bus travels to Stuttgarter Platz and along Kurfürstendamm to Bahnhof Zoologischer Garten (Berlin's main train station, usually called Bahnhof Zoo) in about 30 minutes. **Bus X9** travels a more direct route, with fewer stops, between Tegel Airport and Bahnhof Zoo in less than 20 minutes for the same fare. The trip by **taxi** from Tegel Airport to Bahnhof Zoo costs about 30DM ($17).

Schönefeld Airport (☎ **030/60 91-0**), which once served as East Berlin's major airport, is the destination for most flights from Russia, Asia, and the Middle East. The easiest way to get from Schönefeld to Bahnhof Zoo and the center of Berlin is via **S-Bahn S-9** from Schönefeld Station (a 5-minute walk from the airport), which also stops at Alexanderplatz and Savignyplatz. The fare is 3.60DM ($2.05).

Finally, because of Berlin's sudden rise in status to capital of Germany, **Berlin–Templehof Airport** (☎ **030/69 51-0**) has been resurrected for commercial use, serving flights from Basel, Brussels, Copenhagen, Prague, and several cities in Germany. Transportation from the airport is either **bus no. 119,** which travels the length of Kurfürstendamm, or via **U-Bahn** from the Platz der Luftbrücke station. In either case, the fare is 3.60DM ($2.05).

BY TRAIN　If you're arriving by train from Western Europe, including Amsterdam, Munich, and Paris, you'll probably end up at the city center **Bahnhof Zoologischer**

Budget Bests

If you're on a tight budget but love museums, note that Berlin's state-owned museums offer **free admission** the first Sunday of every month, including the cluster of museums in Dahlem, on Museumsinsel (Museum Island), and in the Tiergarten. Included are Berlin's most famous: the Pergamon, the Gemäldegalerie, the Egyptian Museum, and the Berggruen Sammlung.

You can save money on both public transport and sightseeing by purchasing the WelcomeCard for 29DM ($16), which allows unlimited travel throughout Berlin for 3 days and discounts on selected museums, guided tours, and the performing arts.

Another bargain is Berlin's **theaters, operas,** and **concerts,** particularly those offering up to 50% off unsold tickets for that evening's performance. As for dining, your ticket to cheap meals is the *Imbiss,* a streetside food stall or tiny locale serving food for takeout or dining standing at chest-high counters. Sausages, Berliner boulettes, hamburgers, french fries, pizza by the slice, Turkish pizza, döner kebab, and other finger foods are common fare, as well as beer and soft drinks. You can easily dine for less than 8DM ($5). You'll find Imbisse along side streets of the Ku'damm, as well as on Alexanderplatz, Wittenbergplatz, Savignyplatz, and many other thoroughfares and squares throughout Berlin, and at major train and S-Bahn stations.

Garten, Berlin's main train station (called Bahnhof Zoo), not far from Kurfürstendamm with its hotels and nightlife. Both the subway and the bus system connect the train station to the rest of the city. A post office, money exchange counter, and English-language information office for train travel and local sightseeing are in the station.

If you're arriving from Eastern Europe, including Prague and Budapest, you'll probably arrive at **Berlin–Lichtenberg** station, where you'll find S-Bahn connections to take you on to your final destination. S-Bahn S-5 or S-7 will take you to Bahnhof Zoologischer Garten (make sure you board the S-Bahn traveling the correct direction—otherwise you'll end up going in the opposite direction from Bahnhof Zoo). *A money-saving tip:* If you arrive at Berlin–Lichtenberg station, your train ticket (or Eurailpass) is valid for onward travel via S-Bahn to Bahnhof Zoo, Savignyplatz, or Charlottenburg, thus saving you the cost of an S-Bahn ticket. It's not valid, however, for transportation on Berlin's U-Bahn or bus systems.

For information on train schedules, call ☎ **194 19.**

VISITOR INFORMATION

If you're arriving at Bahnhof Zoologischer Garten, the most convenient stop for information on Berlin, including how to get to your hotel, is **EurAide,** on the ground floor, between the Reisezentrum and Jebensstrasse exit. Though its main function is to provide English-speaking visitors with information on train travel, it will also answer questions on local sightseeing. It's open Monday to Saturday 8am to noon and 1 to 4:30pm. If you're arriving at Tegel Airport, stop by the **Airport Service Center,** in the Haupthalle (Main Hall), open daily 5am to 10:30pm.

Otherwise, Berlin's main tourist information office, **Tourist Info Berlin,** is in the Europa-Center, with its entrance on Budapester Strasse, a 4-minute walk from Bahnhof Zoo. Besides stocking maps (1DM/55¢), souvenirs, and brochures and dispensing sightseeing advice, the tourist office will book a room for you for 5DM ($2.85). It's open Monday to Saturday 8am to 10pm and Sunday 9am to 9pm.

Another convenient tourist office is at **Brandenburger Tor,** open daily 9:30am to 6pm.

For more information or hotel reservations, call the **Berlin Hotline** at ☎ **030/25 00 25** or fax 030/25 00 24 24. Further information is also available on the Internet at **www.berlin.de.** The e-mail address for information is **information@btm.de;** for hotel reservations it's **reservation@btm.de.**

Otherwise, your best bet on what's happening, including concerts, plays, operas, and special events, is *Berlin* (published in German and English every 3 months), available at the Tourist Info Berlin for 3.50DM ($2). It also contains a city map and a subway map. Though printed only in German, the most thorough publication of what's happening is *Berlin Programm,* available at the tourist office and at magazine kiosks for 2.80DM ($1.60). Other German publications are the city magazines *tip* (4.50DM/$2.55) and *zitty* (4DM/$2.30), which come out on alternate weeks with information on fringe theater, film, rock, folk, and all that's happening on the alternative scene.

CITY LAYOUT

Berlin forms both a city and a federal state and consists of 23 precincts. The 1990s has been a decade of tremendous change here. Indeed, the city is being transformed by one of the most extensive and ambitious urban-renewal plans ever undertaken, particularly in former East Berlin and in the vast swath of land once occupied by the Wall and its surrounding no-man's-land. There are probably more cranes towering above Berlin than above any other city in the world.

Still, one of the most famous streets in Berlin remains **Kurfürstendamm,** affectionately called the **Ku'damm.** About 2½ miles long, it starts at the Kaiser-Wilhelm Gedächtniskirche (Memorial Church), a ruined church that's been left standing as a permanent reminder of the horrors of war. Near the Memorial Church is the Bahnhof Zoologischer Garten (a main train station), a large park called the Tiergarten (complete with a zoo), and the Europa-Center, a 22-story building with shops, restaurants, bars, and the Tourist Info Berlin. Along the Ku'damm are many of the city's smartest boutiques, as well as many hotels and pensions. Note that the numbering system of buildings runs on one side of the Ku'damm all the way to the end, then jumps to the other side of the street and runs all the way back. For example, across from Ku'damm 11 is Ku'damm 230. It's a bit complicated, but numbers for each block are posted on street signs.

Nearby **Wilmersdorfer Strasse** is where most of the natives shop. A pedestrian street near a U-Bahn station of the same name, it boasts several department stores and numerous boutiques and restaurants. Not far away is Charlottenburg Palace and a cluster of fine museums, including the Egyptian Museum (with the famous bust of Nefertiti), the Berggruen Sammlung (with its many Picassos), and the Bröhan Museum (with its art nouveau collection). This area around the Ku'damm is part of Charlottenburg, western Berlin's most important precinct.

Berlin's other well-known street—and historically much more significant—is **Unter den Linden,** in a precinct called **Berlin-Mitte.** This was the heart of Old Berlin before World War II, its most fashionable and lively street, and thereafter was part of East Berlin. The Brandenburg Gate is the most readily recognized landmark, and buildings along the tree-lined street have been painstakingly restored. Unter den Linden leads past **Friedrichstrasse,** which will soon surpass the Ku'damm for its smart shops and boutiques; past Museumsinsel (Museum Island), which boasts the outstanding Pergamon; to the drab, modern square called **Alexanderplatz,** once the heart of East

Berlin and easily found with its tall TV tower. Nearby is the **Nikolai Quarter,** a reconstructed neighborhood of shops, bars, and restaurants built to resemble Old Berlin.

Berlin's other important museum districts, **Tiergarten** and **Dahlem,** are within easy reach of the city center by subway or bus. Spread along the city's southwestern edge and accessible by S-Bahn are Berlin's most famous woods, the **Grünewald,** and waterways, the **Havel** and **Wannsee.** In the east, the **Spreewald** is a huge refuge of waterways and woods.

GETTING AROUND

Berlin has an excellent public transport network, including the U-Bahn (underground), the S-Bahn (inner-city railway), buses, and, in eastern Berlin, trams. All are run by the **Public Transport Company Berlin–Brandenburg (BVG)** (☎ **030/19 449**), which maintains a booth outside Bahnhof Zoo on Hardenbergplatz. Open daily 8am to 10pm, it provides details on how to reach destinations and the various ticket options available and also sells tickets.

BUYING TICKETS Though Greater Berlin is divided into three fare zones, A, B, and C (you'll find zone maps posted at all U-Bahn and S-Bahn stations), you needn't worry about which ticket to buy because most destinations of interest to visitors require purchase only of the **AB Einzelfahrausweis** single ticket, costing 3.60DM ($2.05) and covering zones A and B. Using this ticket, you can travel all of Berlin's U-Bahn system, most of its S-Bahn network, and buses and trams, including travel to Berlin's three airports and its major attractions. The only notable exception is Potsdam, for which you must buy a three-zone ABC Einzelfahrausweis for 3.90DM ($2.25).

If you're traveling only a short distance (six stops by bus or three by subway), you have the option of buying a **Kurzstreckenkarte** for 2.50DM ($1.40). Note that this ticket is good only for a single journey and is valid for only 2 hours.

If you don't want to hassle with individual tickets and plan to travel a lot on a given day, consider purchasing a **Tageskarte** (day ticket) for 7.50DM ($4.25), which covers zones A and B. If you're going to Potsdam, purchase the 8.50DM ($4.85) Tageskarte valid for all three zones.

However, if you're going to be in Berlin at least 3 days and plan to do a lot of sightseeing and traveling back and forth, your best bet is the **WelcomeCard,** available at all tourist offices, most hotels, and transportation ticket offices in major S-Bahn stations. Costing 29DM ($17), it allows one adult and up to three children 13 and under unlimited travel for 72 hours throughout all three zones (including Potsdam), as well as 25% to 50% reductions on guided sightseeing tours, performing arts (including the Komische Oper and Staatsoper Unter den Linden), and admission to a limited selection of museums and attractions in Berlin and Potsdam over a 3-day period (major attractions aren't included). The tourist office has brochures listing the participating places; be sure to check whether the discounted museums and attractions include those you're interested in.

Finally, if you're going to be in Berlin for at least a week, an excellent value is the **7-Tage-Karte** (7-day ticket) for 40DM ($23), valid for any 7 consecutive days you wish to travel in zones A and B. The 7-day ticket for all three zones is 45DM ($26).

Tickets are available from automatic machines at U-Bahn and S-Bahn stations, ticket windows, bus drivers, and even some automatic machines at bus stops (most common at bus stops on the Ku'damm). Once you purchase a ticket, you must validate it yourself by inserting it into one of the red machines at the entrance to S-Bahn and U-Bahn platforms and on buses.

A Transportation Tip

The best thing about Berlin's public-transportation system is that both types of Einzelfahrausweis tickets are valid for up to 2 hours, allowing transfers to all lines, round-trips, or even trip interruptions (you could, for example, go to Dahlem for an hour and then return to the city center with the same ticket).

BY U-BAHN & S-BAHN   The U-Bahn (underground) has 10 lines with more than 130 stations. Lines run about 5am to midnight or 1am (except for lines U-9 and U-12, which run all night on weekends). The S-Bahn (inner-city railway) stretches throughout Greater Berlin and is useful for trips to Wannsee and even Potsdam. If you have a valid Eurailpass, you can use it on the S-Bahn but not the U-Bahn.

BY BUS   Many of Berlin's buses are double-deckers, affording great views of the city. You can purchase only a single ticket from the bus driver; otherwise, use one of the other ticket options above. If you're transferring, simply show the driver your ticket. Apart from the normal day services, there are special night buses (Nachtbussen, marked with an "N" before the route number) that run all night. You can pick up the schedule at the BVG office in front of the Bahnhof Zoo. Bus no. 100, a double-decker, travels 24 hours between Bahnhof Zoo and Prenzlauer Berg. It travels through the Tiergarten and Brandenburg Gate and continues along Unter den Linden with its Museum Island on its way to Alexanderplatz and Prenzlauer Berg, making this an interesting ride between the eastern and western parts of the city.

BY TRAM   East Berlin's most popular form of transportation during the Cold War has been overhauled with new streetcars and improved service. Though tickets purchased for buses and the underground are valid on trams, you'll find the U-Bahn and S-Bahn more useful.

BY BICYCLE   Riding a bike in Berlin can be a hair-raising experience, but with almost 500 miles of bicycle paths, there are parts of the city and parks that are pleasant for cycling. **Fahrradstation/Berlin by Bike** rents city and mountain bikes beginning at 20DM ($11) for 1 day or 70DM ($40) for 1 week; students receive a 15% discount. Maps and recommended cycling routes are dispensed for free, and organized bike tours are also offered. Rental bikes are available from a number of locations, most convenient of which is probably Zoologischer Garten train station (☎ **030/29 74 93 19**), open daily 6am to 11pm. Other Fahrradstation locations are bike shops at Möckernstrasse 92 in Kreuzberg (☎ **030/16 91 77**) and in a complex called Die Hackeschen Höfe at Rosenthaler Strasse 40–41 in Berlin-Mitte (☎ **030/285 99 895**), open Monday to Friday 10am to 7pm (opens 1pm in winter) and Saturday 10am to 4pm.

BY TAXI   You shouldn't have to take a taxi, but if you do, there are several companies with the following numbers: ☎ 030/690 22, 030/26 10 26, 030/21 01 01, 030/96 44, or 030/21 02 02. The meter starts at 4DM ($2.30), then increases according to a complicated tariff system. Taxis ordered by phone start at 6DM ($3.40). For short distances of up to 2 kilometers (1.24 miles), a standard rate of 5DM ($2.85) is charged.

BY RENTAL CAR   Several well-known agencies have offices in Berlin. **Avis** has a counter at Tegel Airport (☎ **030/410 13 148**), as well as an office near Bahnhof Zoo at Budapester Strasse 41 (☎ **030/23 09 37-0**), open Monday to Friday 7am to 8pm and Saturday 8am to 2pm. **Hertz** has a counter at Tegel Airport (☎ **030/410 13 315**) and at Budapester Strasse 39 (☎ **030/261 10 53**). The downtown office is open Monday to Friday 7am to 6:30pm and Saturday 8am to 2pm. Though prices vary, expect to spend about 119DM ($68) for a 1-day rental of a VW Polo or Ford Fiesta, including 16% tax and unlimited mileage. It's cheaper to rent a car over the weekend, when the rate falls as low as 125DM ($71) for the entire period noon Friday to 9am Monday.

FAST FACTS: Berlin

American Express   There are two offices in Berlin. One is at Bayreuther Strasse 37 (☎ **030/21 49 83-0**), catercorner from KaDeWe department store across Wittenbergplatz, open Monday to Friday 9am to 6pm and Saturday 10am to 1pm. The other is in Berlin-Mitte at Friedrichstrasse 172 (☎ **030/20 17 40 12**), across from Galeries Lafayette, open Monday to Friday 9am to 6pm and Saturday 10am to 1pm. You can cash American Express traveler's checks here without paying a commission. If you have American Express traveler's checks or its card, you can have your mail sent here free.

Banks   Banks are open Monday to Friday 9am to 1 or 3pm, with slightly longer hours 1 or 2 days a week, depending on the bank. If you need to **exchange money** outside bank hours, your best bet is the Reise Bank (☎ **030/881 71 17**), the exchange office just outside Bahnhof Zoo with an entrance on Hardenbergplatz. It's open daily 7:30am to 10pm. For transactions using credit cards, you'll find **ATMs** (*Geldautomat* in German) open 24 hours throughout the city, including the Reise Bank at Bahnhof Zoo and banks up and down the Ku'damm. Though transaction fees are high, the exchange rate is better than that offered at banks, making it useful for exchanging large amounts of money.

Business Hours   Downtown **businesses** and **shops** open Monday to Friday at about 9 or 10am. While some of the smaller boutiques may close at 6pm, larger stores and department stores remain open to 8pm. On Saturday shops are generally open 9am to 4pm.

Consulates   The consulate of the **United States** is in Dahlem at Clayallee 170 (☎ **030/238 51 74**). It's open for Americans who have lost their passports Monday to Friday 8:30am to noon, while its visa section (☎ **030/832 40 87**) is open Monday to Friday 8:30 to 11:30am. The consulate of **Canada** is at Friedrichstrasse 95 (☎ **030/261 11 61**), open Monday to Friday 8:30am to 12:30pm and 1:30 to 5pm. The consulate of the **United Kingdom** is at Unter den Linden 32–34 (☎ **030/201 84-0**), open Monday to Friday 9am to noon and 2 to 4pm. The embassy of **Australia,** with a consular section, is at Kempinski Plaza, Uhlandstrasse 181–183 (☎ **030/880 08 80**), and is open for general business Monday to Thursday 8:30am to 1pm and 2 to 5pm and Friday 8:30am to 1pm and 2 to 4:15pm. Since various departments have different open hours, call ahead.

Currency   The **deutsche mark (DM)** is divided into 100 **pfennig.** Coins come in 1, 2, 5, 10, and 50 Pfennig, and 1, 2, and 5 Marks. Notes are issued in 5, 10, 20, 50, 100, 200, 500, and 1,000 Marks.

Dentists & Doctors   The Tourist Info Berlin in the Europa-Center has a list of English-speaking doctors and dentists in Berlin. In addition, the American Hotline (☎ **0177-814 15 10**) has a free medical referral service. If you need a doctor in the middle of the night or on the weekend, call ☎ **31 00 31;** for

Berlin U-Bahn & S-Bahn

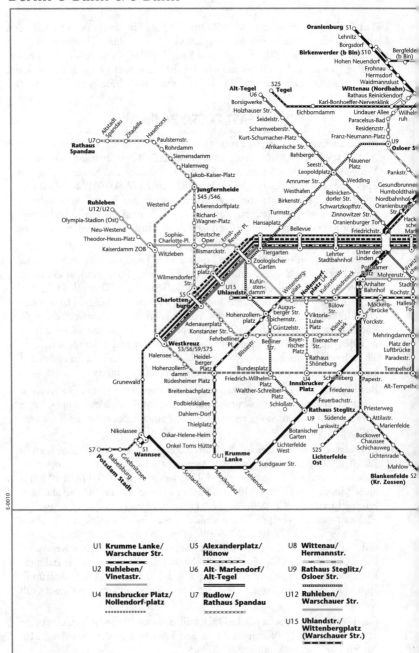

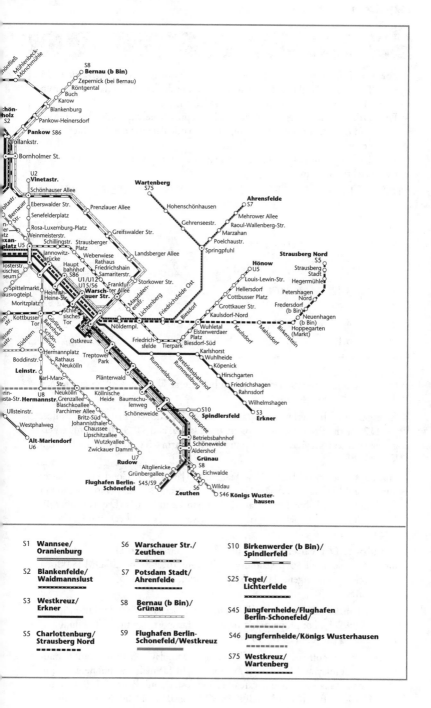

The German Mark

For American Readers   At this writing $1 = approximately 1.75DM (or 1DM = 57¢), and this was the rate of exchange used to calculate the dollar values given in this chapter (rounded to the nearest dollar if more than $5).

For British Readers   At this writing £1 = approximately 2.90DM (or 1DM = 34p), and this was the rate of exchange used to calculate the pound values in the table below.

Note: Exchange rates fluctuate from time to time and may not be the same when you travel to Germany.

DM	U.S.$	U.K.£	DM	U.S.$	U.K.£
1	.57	.34	10	5.70	3.45
2	1.14	.69	15	8.55	5.17
3	1.71	1.03	20	11.40	6.89
4	2.28	1.38	30	17.10	10.34
5	2.85	1.72	40	22.80	13.79
6	3.42	2.07	50	28.50	17.24
7	3.99	2.41	75	42.75	25.86
8	4.56	2.75	100	57.00	34.48
9	5.13	3.10	150	85.50	51.72

life-threatening emergencies, call an ambulance at ☎ **112.** Call an emergency dentist at ☎ **890 04-333.**

Emergencies   In Berlin, important numbers include ☎ **110** for the **police,** ☎ **112** for the **fire** department or an **ambulance,** and ☎ **31 00 31** for **emergency medical service.** To find out which **pharmacies** are open nights, call ☎ **011 89.**

Holidays   Berlin celebrates New Year's Day (January 1), Good Friday, Easter Sunday and Monday, Ascension Day, Whitsunday and Monday (variable dates in April and May), Labor Day (May 1), German Reunification Day (October 3), Day of Prayer and Repentance (third Wednesday in November), and Christmas (December 25 and 26).

Laundry & Dry Cleaning   Ask the staff of your pension or hotel where the most convenient self-service laundry is. You can expect to spend 7DM ($4) for a wash cycle with detergent, 1DM (55¢) for a spin, and 1DM (55¢) for a dryer for 10 minutes.

Lost & Found   Berlin's general lost-property office is at Platz der Luftbrücke 6 (☎ **030/699-5**). For property lost on public transport, call the BVG Fundburo, Lorenzweg 5 (☎ **030/25 62 30 40**).

Mail   The post office in Bahnhof Zoo is open Monday to Saturday 6am to midnight and Sunday and holidays 8am to midnight for mail and phone calls. You can have your mail sent here in care of Hauptpostlagernd, Postamt 120, Bahnhof Zoo, D-10623 Berlin 12 (☎ **030/313 97 99** or 030/311 00 20 for inquiries). Mailboxes in Germany are yellow.

Air-mail letters to North America cost 3DM ($1.70) for the first 20 grams, while postcards cost 2DM ($1.15). If you want to mail a package, you'll have to

Country & City Codes

The **country code** for Germany is **49.** The **city code** for Berlin is **30;** use this code if you're calling from outside Germany. If you're within Germany but not in Berlin, use **030.** If you're calling within Berlin, simply leave off the code and dial only the regular phone number.

go to one of the city's larger post offices, like that at Goethestrasse 2–3 or Marburger Strasse 12–13, near the Europa-Center. At these post offices you can buy boxes, complete with string and tape. Boxes come in six sizes and range from 2.90DM to 5.50DM ($1.65 to $3.15). Like most post offices, both these offices are open Monday to Friday 8am to 6pm and Saturday 8am to 1pm.

Police   The emergency number for police is ☎ **110.**

Tax   Germany's 16% **government tax** is included in the price at restaurants and hotels, including all the locales in this chapter. You can recover part of the 16% **value-added tax (VAT)** added to most goods—for more information, check "Shopping," later in this chapter.

Telephone   A **local telephone call** costs 20 pfennig (10¢) for the first 90 seconds; restaurants and shops usually charge more for the use of their public phones, generally 50 pfennig (30¢). To make sure you're not cut off, insert more coins than you think you'll need—unused coins will be returned.

If you're going to make a lot of phone calls or wish to make an international call from a phone booth, you'll probably want to purchase a **telephone card.** For sale at post offices, they come in values of 12DM and 50DM ($7 and $29). Simply insert them into the phone slot. Telephone cards are becoming so popular in Germany that many public phones no longer accept coins.

Another option for making **international calls** is to look for a phone booth that accepts major credit cards—there's one outside the tourist office in the Europa-Center on Budapester Strasse. Finally, you can also make international calls at post offices. The main post office at Bahnhof Zoo is open to midnight. Due to recent deregulation of Germany's telephone industry and Telecom's loss of monopoly over domestic phone service, competition among telephone companies is expected to lower long-distance rates, especially for private lines. At press time, it costs 7.20DM ($4.10) to make a 3-minute long-distance call to the United States from a post office.

For **information** on telephone numbers in Berlin (those in the east are slowly being changed), call ☎ **011 8 33.**

Incidentally, if you come across a number with a dash, the number following the dash is the extension, which you reach directly simply by dialing the entire number.

Tipping   Service is already included in hotel and restaurant bills, so you're not obliged to tip. However, it's customary to round up restaurant bills to the nearest mark; if a meal costs more than 10DM ($6), most Germans add a 10% tip. For taxi drivers, add a mark. Porters receive 5DM ($2.85) for two pieces of baggage.

3 Accommodations You Can Afford

Most of Berlin's pensions and hotels are clustered along and around one of its best-known streets, Kurfürstendamm (Ku'damm for short). Even those places farther away aren't very far, usually a 5- or 10-minute subway ride to Zoologischer Garten.

A pension is usually a small place with fewer rooms and lower prices than a hotel, though sometimes there's only a fine line between the two. Continental or buffet breakfast is sometimes optional in the lower-priced places. If you like breakfast, however, you're probably better off opting for the meal, especially if it's buffet style, allowing you to eat as much as you want, thereby perhaps saving on lunch.

Keep in mind that though I've made every effort to be accurate, prices for rooms may go up during the lifetime of this edition. After the fall of the Wall, Berlin's popularity grew and room rates shot upward, with the demand for rooms sometimes exceeding the supply. At the same time, Berlin real estate skyrocketed, making it difficult for small pension owners to make ends meet. In the past few years, however, tourism has leveled off, with the result that room rates have remained rather constant.

However, there are peak times—primarily during major trade fairs *(Messe)* held in March, May, June, September, and October—when many hotels and pensions raise their rates and when it may be difficult to find a room. Be sure to confirm the exact rate when making your reservation. The prices below reflect both low- and peak-season rates.

Note: You can find most of the lodging choices below plotted on the map included in "Seeing the Sights," later in this chapter.

NEAR THE KU'DAMM & BAHNHOF ZOO

✪ **Alexandra.** Wielandstrasse 32, 10629 Berlin. ☎ **030/881 21 07.** Fax 030/885 77 818. 12 units, 2 with shower only, 9 with bathroom. TV TEL. 70DM–85DM ($40–$48) single without bathroom, 95DM–135DM ($54–$77) single with shower only, 110DM–155DM ($63–$88) single with bathroom; 120DM–145DM ($68–$83) double with shower only, 125DM–185DM ($71–$105) double with bathroom. Rates include buffet breakfast. Weekend discounts available. AE, DC, MC, V. S-Bahn: Savignyplatz, then a 5-minute walk. U-Bahn: Adenauerplatz, then a 5-minute walk. Bus: 109 from Tegel Airport or Bahnhof Zoo to Olivaer Platz, then a 2-minute walk.

Just a stone's throw from the Ku'damm, this pension, owned by the friendly English-speaking Frau Kuhn (who's happy to give sightseeing tips), offers spotless rooms decorated with either modern or antique furniture and equipped with radios, curtains that can block sunlight, and shaving/makeup mirrors and hair dryers in rooms with bathrooms. The stucco-ceilinged breakfast room with antique lighting sets the mood—it's lined with pictures of Old Berlin and has flowers on the tables. Unusual for a pension this size, laundry service and baby-sitting are available. You'll find the reception on the second floor, while most rooms are on the third (there's an elevator). The wide range of prices reflects the seasons, making it a bargain off season but pricey during major trade fairs—Frau Kuhn does, however, offer a 10% discount to readers of this book who reserve directly with the pension.

Alpenland. Carmerstrasse 8 (near Savignyplatz), 10623 Berlin. ☎ **030/312 48 98** or 030/313 39 70. Fax 030/313 84 44. 40 units, 10 with shower only, 20 with bathroom. 75DM–90DM ($43–$51) single without bathroom, 95DM–110DM ($54–$63) single with shower only, 110DM–140DM ($63–$80) single with bathroom; 100DM–120DM ($57–$68) double without bathroom, 130DM–190DM ($74–$108) double with bathroom. Extra bed 50DM–65DM ($29–$37). Rates include buffet breakfast. MC, V. S-Bahn: Savignyplatz, then a 3-minute walk. Bus: 109 to Uhlandstrasse, then a 5-minute walk (or a 10-minute walk from Bahnhof Zoo).

North of the Ku'damm, this simple hotel occupies a 100-year-old building, with rooms spread over four floors (no elevator). Decorated with Scandinavian-style wood furniture, most rooms are equipped with phones, TVs, room safes, and tiny bathrooms, and those facing the back are quieter (though the view is duller). The cheapest doubles with bathroom are small, with a full-size bed. The highest rates are charged

Getting the Best Deal on Accommodations

- Try to time your visit to Berlin when there aren't any major trade fairs (these are in March, May, June, September, October), when rates are usually lower.
- Book reservations directly with the hotel, saving yourself the 5DM fee ($2.85) charged by the tourist office for the service.
- Save money by taking a room without a private bath. In Berlin (unlike in Munich's cheaper accommodations), you rarely have to pay extra for taking a shower in the communal bathroom down the hall.
- When quoted a price for a room, ask whether it's the cheapest room available.
- Note that you can find inexpensive lodging in the heart of town, thus saving on transportation costs.
- Take advantage of winter discounts; always ask whether one is available.
- Inquire whether breakfast is included in the room rate—if it's buffet style, you can eat as much as you wish.
- Before dialing, check to see what the surcharge is on local and long-distance phone calls made from the lodging.

during Messe (major trade fairs). Its one restaurant, with outdoor seating in summer, serves German food.

Arco. Geisbergstrasse 30, 10777 Berlin. ☎ **030/235 14 80.** Fax 030/211 33 87. E-mail: arco-hotel@t-online.de. 22 units, 1 with shower only, 21 with bathroom. TV TEL. 100DM–120DM ($57–$68) single with bathroom; 130DM ($74) double with shower only, 140DM–170DM ($80–$97) double with bathroom. Rates include buffet breakfast. AE, DC, MC, V. U-Bahn: Wittenbergplatz, Augsburger Strasse, or Spichernstrasse, all within a 4-minute walk.

On a tree-shaded residential street minutes from the Ku'damm and KaDeWe department store, this hotel is a turn-of-the-century renovated building, complete with an outdoor garden serving breakfast in summer, a rarity in downtown Berlin. Breakfast is served until 11am, making it a hit with the many repeat guests. The attractive rooms offer satellite TVs with English programs, radios, and safes. Two even have closets built into the extra-wide doors, a unique feature, and two double rooms boast a balcony. All in all, you can't go wrong staying here.

✪ **Bogota.** Schlüterstrasse 45, 10707 Berlin. ☎ **030/881 50 01.** Fax 030/883 58 87. E-mail: hotel.bogota@t-online.de. 125 units, 12 with shower only, 65 with bathroom. TEL. 79DM–82DM ($45–$47) single without bathroom, 90DM–105DM ($51–$60) single with shower only, 110DM–130DM ($63–$74) single with bathroom; 110DM–130DM ($63–$74) double without bathroom, 145DM–155DM ($83–$88) double with shower only, 160DM–190DM ($91–$108) double with bathroom. Rates include continental breakfast. Extra bed 40DM–45DM ($23–$26). AE, DC, MC, V. U-Bahn: Adenauerplatz, then a 6-minute walk. Bus: 109 from Tegel Airport or Bahnhof Zoo to Bleibtreustrasse.

Just off the Ku'damm, this older hotel with personality is well maintained and has a friendly staff. Built in 1911 as an apartment house and boasting a colorful history captured in old photographs, it has lobbies on each floor that are reminiscent of another era and rooms that are each unique. There's a cozy TV room where you can spend a quiet evening; otherwise, you can request cable TV in your room for 5DM ($2.85) per day.

✪ **Crystal.** Kantstrasse 144 (off Savignyplatz), 10623 Berlin. ☎ **030/312 90 47** or 030/312 90 48. Fax 030/312 64 65. 33 units, 7 with shower only, 21 with bathroom. TEL. 70DM ($40) single without bathroom, 80DM ($46) single with shower only, 80DM–120DM

($46–$68) single with bathroom; 90DM ($51) double without bathroom, 110DM ($63) double with shower only, 130DM–150DM ($74–$86) double with bathroom; 170DM–190DM ($97–$108) triple with bathroom. Rates include continental breakfast. Cribs available. AE, MC, V. S-Bahn: Savignyplatz, then a 1-minute walk. Bus: 109 from Tegel Airport to Bleibtreustrasse or 149 from Bahnhof Zoo to Savignyplatz (2 stops).

A 5-minute walk north of the Ku'damm, this hotel is housed in an early 1900s building with an updated facade. Yet the interior seems like a relic from the 1950s: outdatedly old-fashioned, comfortable, and endearingly German. Owners John and Dorothee Schwarzrock (John is American) are real characters—friendly, outgoing, and happy to see U.S. guests. The rooms (with just the basics) are spotless, and TVs are available. All employees speak English, and a small bar open only to guests has cable TV. The rooms with bathrooms are among the cheapest in the city center, making the Crystal highly recommended.

Fischer. Nürnberger Strasse 24a (near the Europa-Center), 10789 Berlin. ☎ **030/218 68 08.** Fax 030/213 42 25. 10 units, 6 with shower only, 2 with bathroom. 60DM ($34) single without bathroom, 70DM ($40) single with shower only; 80DM ($46) double without bathroom, 90DM–100DM ($51–$57) double with shower only, 130DM ($74) double with bathroom; 130DM–150DM ($74–$86) triple with shower only. Breakfast 10DM ($6). V. U-Bahn: Augsburger Strasse, then a 1-minute walk. Bus: 109 from Tegel Airport to Joachimstaler Strasse (or a 7-minute walk from Bahnhof Zoo).

Each spacious room has large windows and an old-fashioned tiled stove, the kind that once heated all German homes. The doubles with shower have their own refrigerators; some also have radios. There's also a communal refrigerator in the hall, a public phone, a vending machine with cold drinks, and an automatic machine for coffee or hot chocolate. The pleasant breakfast room has plants and flowers and a TV. Reception is on the second floor (no elevator).

Funk. Fasanenstrasse 69, 10719 Berlin. ☎ **030/882 71 93.** Fax 030/883 33 29. 14 units, 4 with shower only, 7 with bathroom. TEL. 65DM–80DM ($37–$46) single without bathroom, 80DM–95DM ($46–$54) single with shower only, 100DM–120DM ($57–$68) single with bathroom; 100DM–120DM ($57–$68) double without bathroom, 125DM–140DM ($71–$80) double with shower only, 140DM–170DM ($80–$97) double with bathroom. Rates include buffet breakfast. Extra bed 45DM ($26). AE, MC, V. U-Bahn: Uhlandstrasse. Bus: 109 from Tegel Airport or Bahnhof Zoo to Uhlandstrasse (or an 8-minute walk from Bahnhof Zoo).

Take the sweeping white-marble staircase up to the first floor of this grand turn-of-the-century building, where you'll find this pension reminiscent of a past era, formerly the home of the silent-film star Asta Nielsen. The rooms are large, with authentic Jugendstil (German art nouveau) or reproduction Chippendale furnishings and updated modern bathrooms; most have tall stucco ceilings. Two rooms with bath even boast balconies overlooking Fasanenstrasse, one of Berlin's most charming residential streets.

Imperator. Meinekestrasse 5, 10719 Berlin. ☎ **030/881 41 81** or 030/882 51 85. Fax 030/885 19 19. 11 units, 7 with shower only, 2 with bathroom. 80DM ($46) single without bathroom, 100DM ($57) single with shower only, 110DM ($63) single with bathroom; 140DM ($80) double without bathroom, 160DM–170DM ($91–$97) double with shower only, 180DM ($103) double with bathroom; 190DM–200DM ($108–$114) triple with shower. Breakfast 12DM–20DM ($7–$11). Off-season discounts available. No credit cards. U-Bahn: Uhlandstrasse or Kurfürstendamm, then a 2-minute walk. Bus: 109 from Tegel Airport to Uhlandstrasse.

A stone's throw off the Ku'damm and an 8-minute walk from Bahnhof Zoo, this small pension is on the second floor of a turn-of-the-century building, reached via an ornate gilded entry and elevator. A pension since 1926, it has a variety of mostly large rooms, all with tall ceilings and wooden floors and modern or antique furniture. One room even has the luxury of a sunroom (called a winter garden in German). Since all rooms face an inner courtyard, they're quieter than what you'd expect from the busy location. Original artwork decorates the walls, and a pleasant breakfast room has the extras of a TV and sofa, but you can have breakfast delivered to your room until a civilized 1pm.

Knesebeck. Knesebeckstrasse 86, 10623 Berlin. ☎ **030/312 72 55.** 12 units, 5 with shower only. 65DM–75DM ($37–$43) single without shower, 80DM–90DM ($46–$51) single with shower; 110DM–120DM ($63–$68) double without shower, 130DM–140DM ($74–$80) double with shower; 180DM ($103) triple without shower; 200DM ($114) quad without shower; 225DM ($128) quint without shower. Rates include buffet breakfast. V. S-Bahn: Savignyplatz, then a 3-minute walk. Bus: X9 from Tegel Airport or Bahnhof Zoo to Ernst-Reuter-Platz (or a 7-minute walk from Bahnhof Zoo).

Having only recently acquired this older pension, Brigitte Kalinowski has been busy taking English lessons but makes up for any shortcomings with a gracious personality. The breakfast room, with cable TV, is lined with photos of Berlin's most historic recent event, the fall of the Wall, and a washing machine and dryer are available for guest use. Newly painted and carpeted, most rooms feature tall stucco ceilings and face a quiet inner courtyard. In addition to singles and doubles, rooms sleeping three, four, and five are available, including two with a balcony. Cable TVs are available on request for 5DM ($2.85) per day. You can't go wrong here.

Nürnberger Eck. Nürnberger Strasse 24a, 10789 Berlin. ☎ **030/235 17 80.** Fax 030/23 51 78 99. 8 units, 5 with bathroom. TV TEL. 80DM ($46) single without bathroom, 100DM ($57) single with bathroom; 130DM ($74) double without bathroom, 150DM–160DM ($86–$91) double with bathroom. Rates include continental breakfast. MC, V. U-Bahn: Augsburger Strasse, then a 1-minute walk. Bus: 109 from Tegel Airport to Joachimstaler Strasse (or a 7-minute walk from Bahnhof Zoo).

Fresh flowers decorate the hall of this first-floor pension (no elevator), and the pleasant rooms have comfortable Biedermeier-style furniture. The huge doors and stucco ceilings are typical of Old Berlin, making it look like a set for the movie *Cabaret*.

Peters. Kantstrasse 146 (just east of Savignyplatz), 10623 Berlin. ☎ **030/312 22 78.** Fax 030/312 35 19. 8 units, 5 with shower. TV. 70DM–90DM ($40–$51) single without shower, 90DM–110DM ($51–$63) single with shower; 100DM ($57) double without shower, 120DM–140DM ($68–$80) double with shower. Rates include buffet breakfast. Children under 12 stay free in parents' room. AE, DC, MC, V. S-Bahn: Savignyplatz, then a 2-minute walk. Bus: 109 from Tegel Airport to Uhlandstrasse or 149 from Bahnhof Zoo to Savignyplatz (2 stops).

Owned by Annika and Christoph Steiner, a friendly English-speaking Swedish painter and her art-historian German husband, this inexpensive pension is within a 10-minute walk of Bahnhof Zoo and a 5-minute walk from the Ku'damm. It occupies the second floor (no elevator) of an 1890 building, with cheerfully renovated white-walled rooms of various sizes, some with stucco ceilings. One of the singles without bath has a sofa bed—if you're counting every pfennig and don't mind cramped quarters, two of you can room here for 80DM ($46). The Steiners have children, so baby-sitting is available, as are a crib and high chair.

Viola Nova. Kantstrasse 146 (east of Savignyplatz), 10623 Berlin. ☎ **030/313 14 57.** Fax 030/312 33 14. 15 units, 2 with shower only, 4 with bathroom. TEL. 90DM ($51) single without bathroom, 120DM ($68) single with shower only, 140DM ($80) single with bathroom; 120DM ($68) double without bathroom, 150DM ($86) double with shower only, 160DM ($91) double with bathroom. Buffet breakfast 9.50DM ($5). Extra bed 30DM ($17).

AE, DC, MC, V. S-Bahn: Savignyplatz, then a 2-minute walk. Bus: 109 from Tegel Airport to Uhlandstrasse or 149 from Bahnhof Zoo to Savignyplatz (2 stops).

About a 5-minute walk from the Ku'damm and a 10-minute walk from Bahnhof Zoo, this updated pension has a cheerful, modern breakfast room and reception area on the ground floor, complete with changing artwork for sale. It offers bright rooms, several of which sleep three to four, with sleek black furniture, modern lighting, and tall stucco ceilings. TVs are provided in some rooms and are available for rent in others.

West-Pension. Kurfürstendamm 48–49, 10707 Berlin. ☎ **030/881 80 57** or 030/881 80 58. Fax 030/881 38 92. 33 units, 8 with shower only, 15 with bathroom. TEL. 70DM ($40) single without bathroom, 90DM ($51) single with shower only, 100DM ($57) single with bathroom; 120DM ($68) double without bathroom, 140DM ($80) double with shower only, 160DM–200DM ($91–$114) double with bathroom. Extra bed 40DM ($23). Buffet breakfast 13DM ($7). MC, V. U-Bahn: Uhlandstrasse, then a 3-minute walk. Bus: 109 from Tegel Airport or Bahnhof Zoo to Bleibtreustrasse.

Right on the Ku'damm, this pension (with elevator) occupies the second floor of a beautiful turn-of-the-century building that boasts an old-world atmosphere and interesting architectural details like wainscoting, stucco, chandeliers, and gilded mirrors. Facilities include a comfortable bar, a pleasant breakfast room, and rooms furnished with antiques or modern pieces. Some of the doubles with shower face the Ku'damm; the rest face the back and are quieter. Units with bathrooms have TVs. Since a variety of rooms is available, specify what you want when making your reservation.

Zimmer des Westens. Tauentzienstrasse 5, 10789 Berlin. ☎ **030/214 11 30.** Fax 030/214 34 50. 11 units, 4 with bathroom. TV. 70DM ($40) single without bathroom, 85DM ($48) single with bathroom; 100DM ($57) double without bathroom, 120DM ($68) double with bathroom. Rates include continental breakfast. Extra bed 30DM ($17). No credit cards. U-Bahn: Wittenbergplatz, then a 1-minute walk (or about a 7-minute walk from Bahnhof Zoo).

This clean and pleasant pension, owned by Doris Simsek, is tucked away in a quiet inner courtyard on busy Tauentzienstrasse, up three flights of rickety stairs. This is a good value in a great location that can't be beat, across from KaDeWe department store.

NEAR GÜNTZELSTRASSE STATION

✪ **München.** Güntzelstrasse 62, 10717 Berlin. ☎ **030/85 79 12-0.** Fax 030/85 79 12-22. 8 units, 4 with bathroom. TV TEL. 66DM ($38) single without bathroom, 110DM ($63) single with bathroom; 85DM–90DM ($48–$51) double without bathroom, 125DM–130DM ($71–$74) double with bathroom. Extra person 35DM ($20). Breakfast 9DM ($5). AE, DC, MC, V. U-Bahn: Güntzelstrasse, then a 3-minute walk.

This third-floor pension (with elevator) is about a 20-minute walk south of the Ku'damm or two stops on the U-Bahn. You'll be able to tell immediately that it's run by an artist: Original works by Berlin artists adorn the walls, flowers fill the vases, and everything is tastefully done. Frau Renate Prasse, the charming proprietor, is a sculptor (her work decorates the hall), and her rooms are bright white and spotless, with firm beds.

IN BERLIN-MITTE

✪ **Scheunenviertel.** Oranienburger Strasse 38, 10117 Berlin. ☎ **030/282 21 25** or 030/283 08 310. Fax 030/282 11 15. 18 units, all with bathroom. TV TEL. 120DM–130DM ($68) single; 140DM–150DM ($80–$86) double; 180DM ($103) triple. Rates include buffet breakfast. AE, MC, V. S-Bahn: Oranienburger Strasse, then a 1-minute walk. U-Bahn: Oranienburger Tor, then a 1-minute walk.

Opened in 1996, this is by far the best reasonably priced lodging in fast-changing Berlin-Mitte. In the heart of Berlin's former Jewish quarter not far from a newly restored synagogue, it's surrounded by some of Berlin's hippest alternative nightlife venues and avant-garde galleries and is a 5-minute walk from Museum Island. Upbeat and modern with comfortable rooms, it attracts both business types and well-heeled younger travelers. A young staff cultivates a laid-back atmosphere, evidenced by the fact that breakfast is served open-end for all those late-night revelers.

IN KREUZBERG

Die Fabrik. Schlesische Strasse 18, 10997 Berlin. ☎ **030/611 71 16** or 030/617 51 04. Fax 030/618 29 74. 41 units, none with bathroom; 15 dorm beds. 66DM ($38) single; 94DM ($54) double; 120DM ($68) triple; 144DM ($82) quad; 30DM ($17) dorm bed. No credit cards. U-Bahn: Schlesisches Tor, then a 3-minute walk.

In a century-old five-story brick building that once served as a factory, this place opened in 1995 and offers cheerful rooms with modern furnishings, tall arched ceilings, and large windows facing quiet inner courtyards. Facilities include modern tiled communal bathrooms, lockers, and a cafe that offers breakfast for 10DM ($6) and stays open to midnight. The majority of rooms are doubles and triples at very reasonable prices, though for truly budget travelers there's one dorm for both sexes with 15 beds.

Kreuzberg. Grossbeerenstrasse 64, 10963 Berlin. ☎ **030/251 13 62.** Fax 030/251 06 38. 13 units, none with bathroom. 75DM ($43) single; 95DM ($54) double; 130DM ($74) triple; 160DM ($91) quad. Rates include buffet breakfast. No credit cards. U-Bahn: U-9 from Bahnhof Zoo to Berliner Strasse, then U-7 from Berliner Strasse to Mehringdamm, then a 5-minute walk. Bus: 119 or 219 from the Ku'damm to Grossbeerenstrasse or 109 from Tegel Airport to Adenauerplatz and then 119 from Adenauerplatz to Grossbeerenstrasse.

In a turn-of-the-century former tenement with character, this 50-year-old pension on the second floor (no elevator) is owned by energetic young people who renovated the place themselves. The breakfast room is cheerful and bright, and the rooms are perfectly acceptable, especially for younger backpackers. This is one of Berlin's best values.

✪ Transit. Hagelberger Strasse 53–54, 10965 Berlin. ☎ **030/789 047-0.** Fax 030/789 047-77. 30 units, all with shower only; 100 dorm beds. 90DM ($51) single; 105DM ($60) double; 140DM ($80) triple; 170DM ($97) quad; 33DM ($19) dorm bed. Rates include buffet breakfast. AE, MC, V. U-Bahn: U-9 from Bahnhof Zoo to Berliner Strasse, then U-7 from Berliner Strasse to Mehringdamm. Bus: 119 or 219 from the Ku'damm to Mehringdamm or 109 from Tegel Airport to Adenauerplatz and then 119 from Adenauerplatz to Mehringdamm.

This great place for young travelers opened in 1987 in a converted tobacco factory. It's in the inner courtyard of an old brick building, on the fourth floor reached via elevator. The singles and doubles are a bit expensive, but the economical dorms that sleep six are perfect for the truly frugal. All rooms are painted white, a bit stark, but they have huge windows, high ceilings, photos of Berlin, and modern furniture. The airy breakfast room features a buffet offering as much coffee or tea as you want, and there's a bar open around the clock with cable TV.

NEAR BAHNHOF CHARLOTTENBURG

✪ Charlottenburger Hof. Stuttgarter Platz 14, 10627 Berlin. ☎ **030/32 90 70.** Fax 030/323 37 23. 45 units, 42 with bathroom. TV TEL. 75DM–80DM ($43–$46) single without bathroom, 90DM–120DM ($51–$68) single with bathroom; 90DM–110DM ($51–$63) double without bathroom, 110DM–150DM ($63–$86) double with bathroom; 180DM–240DM ($113–$150) quad with bathroom. Discounts available in winter and for longer stays. AE, MC, V. S-Bahn: Charlottenburg, then a 1-minute walk. Bus: 109 from Tegel Airport or Bahnhof Zoo to Charlottenburg.

This is one of Berlin's most modern budget hotels, complete with laundry facilities, a small lounge with a big-screen cable TV and free coffee, and a friendly young staff. Its white rooms trimmed with primary colors are spread over three floors (no elevator) and come with modern furniture and colored bedsheets; posters of the works of Miró, Kandinsky, van Gogh, or Picasso; safes; soundproof windows; and hair dryers. Several rooms are large enough for three or four and have the advantage of two sinks and shower separate from the toilet, perfect for families. For breakfast, you may want to go to the adjoining 24-hour Café Voltaire, where breakfast is 6DM to 9DM ($3.40 to $5).

YOUTH HOSTELS & HOTELS

Though catering largely to young backpackers and youth groups, **youth hotels** will take individual travelers of any age when there's room. In addition to singles and doubles, they offer multibed dorms. To stay at Berlin's **youth hostels,** you must have a youth hostel card, available at youth hostels for 36DM ($21). Or you can pay an extra 6DM ($3.40) per night for a "guest card"; after 6 nights it becomes a regular youth hostel card. There's no age limit (though "seniors," those older than 27, pay more), but keep in mind that the curfew is midnight.

Jugendgästehaus Berlin. Kluckstrasse 3, 10785 Berlin. ☎ **030/261 10 97.** Fax 030/265-03 83. 364 beds. 34DM ($19) per person for "juniors" (26 and under), 43DM ($25) per person for "seniors" (27 and older). Rates include breakfast and sheets. Dinner 9DM ($5). No credit cards. U-Bahn: Kurfürstenstrasse, then a 12-minute walk. Bus: 109 from Tegel Airport to Bahnhof Zoo and then 129 from Bahnhof Zoo to Kluckstrasse.

This is Berlin's most conveniently located hostel. A white-and-black modern building not far from the Kurfürstenstrasse U-Bahn station, it's so popular that between February and November you should write a month in advance to reserve a bed. All rooms have four to six beds, and everyone gets a locker with a key.

Studenten-Hotel Berlin. Meininger Strasse 10 (near John F. Kennedy Platz and Rathaus Schsneberg), 10823 Berlin. ☎ **030/784 67 20** or 030/784 67 30. Fax 030/788 15 23. 20 units, none with bathroom; 120 dorm beds. 64DM ($37) single; 88DM ($50) double; 40DM ($23) dorm bed. Rates include breakfast and sheets. No credit cards. U-Bahn: Schöneberg. Bus: 109 from Tegel Airport or Bahnhof Zoo and then 146 from Bahnhof Zoo to JFK Platz.

Although this is called a student hotel, you don't have to be a student to stay here—any age is welcome—and there's no curfew. It has 20 double rooms you can rent for single or double occupancy; the remaining rooms contain four or five beds each. The games room is outfitted with a pool table, soccer game, and pinball machine.

WORTH A SPLURGE

Hansablick. Flotowstrasse 6, 10555 Berlin. ☎ **030/39 04 80-0.** Fax 030/392 69 37. 23 units, all with bathroom. MINIBAR TV TEL. 135DM ($77) single; 150DM–215DM ($86–$123) double. Rates include buffet breakfast. Extra bed 55DM ($31). Free parking. AE, DC, MC, V. S-Bahn: Tiergarten, then a 3-minute walk. U-Bahn: U-9 to Hansaplatz, then a 5-minute walk.

Of all my recommendations, this hotel-pension has the most idyllic location: on a quiet residential street beside the Spree River, lined with willows. And yet it's very centrally located, just a few minutes' walk from the sprawling Tiergarten and one stop by S-Bahn from Bahnhof Zoo. The rooms themselves, in a turn-of-the-century building (without elevator), are a tasteful blend of the antique and modern, with wood floors, stucco ceilings, high-tech lighting, and smart-looking modern furniture that hints at art deco. The rooms (with all the comforts, including hair dryers and magnifying mirrors) come in varying sizes. The best are those with views of the Spree, the largest of which even has a balcony. Facilities and services include a small bar, rental bikes (20DM/$11 per day), laundry service, baby-sitting, and theater bookings.

✪ **Tiergarten Berlin.** Alt-Moabit 89, 10559 Berlin. ☎ **030/399 89 6.** Fax 030/393 86 92. 40 units, all with bathroom. MINIBAR TV TEL. 180DM ($103) single; 210DM ($120) double. Rates include buffet breakfast. Winter and weekend discounts available. Extra person 35DM ($20). Children 11 and under stay free in parents' room. AE, DC, MC, V. U-Bahn: U-9 to Turmstrasse, then a 3-minute walk.

This intimate hotel (with elevator) possesses all the makings of a first-rate place: polite and efficient staff, turn-of-the-century charm and elegance, and light and airy rooms sporting tall stucco ceilings. The bathrooms are modern and spotless, complete with a magnifying mirror for shaving or applying makeup. Even the breakfast room with its great buffet is something to write home about. In short, this is the kind of place that appeals to both business and pleasure travelers; it's certainly one of my favorites in Berlin.

4 Great Deals on Dining

Berlin has an estimated 6,000 restaurants and bars, a great many of which serve international cuisine—which isn't surprising, considering Berlin's large foreign population. Even young Germans are more likely to go out for Greek or Italian than they are for their own heavier cuisine. What's more, ethnic restaurants are often cheaper than their German counterparts.

You'll find many restaurants clustered along the Ku'damm, as well as on the pedestrians-only Wilmersdorfer Strasse and around Savignyplatz. The cheapest of these is the *Imbiss,* a stand-up eatery where everything from sausages to fish sandwiches might be offered. Many of the cheaper restaurants also offer takeout.

Most main dishes served in a German restaurant come with side dishes like potatoes and/or sauerkraut. One of Berlin's best-known specialties is *eisbein* (pig's knuckle), usually served with sauerkraut and potatoes or puréed peas. *Kasseler rippenspeer* is smoked pork chops, created by a butcher in Berlin named Kassel. *Bockwurst,* also created in Berlin, is a super-long sausage, and *boulette* is a type of meatball. Other foods you might encounter on a menu are sauerbraten (marinated beef in sauce), *leberkäs* (a Bavarian specialty, a type of meat loaf), and schnitzel (breaded veal cutlet). In any case, since most main dishes in a German restaurant include one or two side dishes, that's all you'll need to order. And by all means, try a *Berliner weisse*—a draft beer with a shot of raspberry.

In addition to the restaurants below, several nightspots in "Berlin After Dark," later in this chapter, offer food. In fact, a few of the bars specialize in breakfast for those who stay out all night.

LOCAL BUDGET BESTS: DEPARTMENT STORES

✪ **Le Buffet.** In Hertie Bei Wertheim. Kurfürstendamm 231. ☎ **030/88 20 61.** Meals 11DM–16DM ($6–$9). No credit cards. Mon–Fri 9:30am–7:30pm, Sat 9am–3:30pm. U-Bahn: Kurfürstendamm. GERMAN.

This is my pick for an inexpensive meal with a view. Located on the top (sixth) floor of this centrally located department store (on the Ku'damm across from the Kaiser Wilhelm Memorial Church), Le Buffet is a self-service restaurant with various counters offering salads, vegetables, vegetarian dishes, daily specials of typical German food ranging from *schnitzel* to *eisbein,* juices, and desserts. A glass facade overlooks the rooftops of Berlin, and there's a no-smoking section. This is a great place for a meal, a quick snack, or just a cup of coffee.

✪ **Wintergarten.** In KaDeWe. Wittenbergplatz. ☎ **030/212 10.** Meals 10DM–25DM ($6–$14). No credit cards. Mon–Fri 9:30am–7:30pm, Sat 9am–3:30pm. U-Bahn: U-1, U-2, or U-3 to Wittenbergplatz. INTERNATIONAL.

KaDeWe is short for Kaufhaus des Westens, and on the fifth floor of this large department store is the biggest food department in continental Europe. It's so amazing that it may be worth coming to Berlin just to see it—sausages galore (the Germans must make more types than anyone else), cheeses, teas, breads, jams, sweets, vegetables, coffees, spices, wines, salads, meats (including more cuts of pork than I could count), live fish, and much more. And one floor up is the Wintergarten, a glass-enclosed self-service restaurant that's almost like dining in a greenhouse, with plants galore, piped-in bird songs, and the rush of running water. Its food selections are more sophisticated than what's normally offered by cafeterias, with counters devoted to steaks, Chinese food, pasta, salads, fish, Berlin specialties, desserts, and more. A smart-looking bar occupies one end of the restaurant, and there's a no-smoking section.

ON OR NEAR THE KU'DAMM

Ano Kato. Leibnizstrasse 70 (just south of Kantstrasse). ☎ **030/313 04 70.** Meals 16DM–23DM ($9–$13). No credit cards. Daily 5pm–12:30am. S-Bahn: Savignyplatz. GREEK.

About a 7-minute walk north of the Ku'damm, this unpretentious Greek restaurant with its white tablecloths, candles, and cheerful Greek music is a popular choice for a casual meal, which can range from moussaka, souvlaki, lamb, and gyros to calamari. And, of course, everything tastes better with a glass of retsina.

Ashoka. Grolmanstrasse 51 (just north of Savignyplatz). ☎ **030/313 20 66.** Meals 6DM–13DM ($3.40–$7). No credit cards. Daily 11am–midnight. S-Bahn: Savignyplatz. INDIAN.

This tiny hole-in-the-wall restaurant has an open kitchen that takes up half the place. It's popular with area students and features more than a dozen vegetarian dishes—the Gemüseplatte Benares, a vegetarian platter, is a bargain at 10DM ($6). Good for a hot-and-spicy fix, it even has outdoor seating.

Asia-Quick. Lietzenburgerstrasse 96. ☎ **030/882 15 33.** Meals 9DM–15DM ($5–$9). No credit cards. Mon–Fri 11:30am–11:30pm, Sat–Sun 2–11:30pm. U-Bahn: Uhlandstrasse. CHINESE.

This simple place is, as its name implies, quick to serve soups and dishes of fish, pork, beef, chicken, rice, and noodles, as well as vegetarian selections. The meat dishes come with a choice of several sauces, including chop suey and sweet and sour. With a TV in the corner (as in most restaurants in Asia), it's too bright and sterile to be cozy; if you don't want to eat here, order takeout. It's a 2-minute walk south of the Ku'damm, near Bleibtreustrasse.

Avanti. Rankestrasse 2. ☎ **030/883 52 40.** Meals 8DM–17.50DM ($4.55–$10). No credit cards. Daily 11am–2am. U-Bahn: Kurfürstendamm. ITALIAN.

I wouldn't be surprised to hear that there are more self-service Italian cafeterias than any other ethnic restaurant in Berlin (with the exception of Turkish *Imbisse*). This one is just off the Ku'damm near the Gedächtniskirche and the Hertie Bei Wertheim department store. It's clean and modern, with contemporary art on the walls and an ice-cream/cocktail/espresso bar. Pizzas and pastas are priced under 12DM ($7), and there's a salad bar and daily specials.

Cafe Hardenberg. Hardenbergstrasse 10. ☎ **030/312 26 44.** Main courses 9DM–15DM ($5–$9). No credit cards. Daily 9am–midnight. U-Bahn: Ernst-Reuter-Platz. GERMAN/INTERNATIONAL.

In the technical university district, across from the Mensa student cafeteria and less than a 5-minute walk from Bahnhof Zoo, this cafe is always packed with students and

---

Getting the Best Deal on Dining

- Take advantage of the stand-up food stalls called *Imbisse,* many in the area of the Ku'damm and Friedrichstrasse Station.
- Ask about the daily special *(tageskarte),* which may not be on the menu.
- Eat at the Mensa, a student cafeteria open also to nonstudents, with some of the cheapest meals served in Berlin.
- An especially good value in Berlin are department-store food counters and restaurants, like those at KaDeWe.
- Try one of the coffee-shop chains, such as Tschibo, where coffee costs 3DM ($1.70) a cup.
- Ask whether there's a charge for an extra piece of bread or whether your entree comes with side dishes.

---

people who work nearby. The portions of the daily specials (ranging from schnitzel to spaghetti) are hearty, there's an English menu, breakfast is served all day, and the place is decorated with museum posters, plants, and ceiling fans. If you want, come just for a cup of coffee. Classical music can be heard to 4pm, when it's replaced by 20th-century music. In the evening the atmosphere is more like that of a bar—beer and cocktails are served in addition to dinner. In summer you can sit outside.

Einhorn. Wittenbergplatz 5–6. ☎ **030/213 75 49.** Meals 12DM–17DM ($7–$10). AE, MC, V. Mon–Sat 9am–11pm. U-Bahn: Wittenbergplatz. VEGETARIAN/INTERNATIONAL.

This simple but pleasant restaurant, on the opposite end of the square from KaDeWe, with outdoor seating in fine weather, specializes in a changing daily menu of vegetarian and international cuisine. Past dishes have ranged from salmon tortellini to spaghetti al pesto and turkey with rice. Available to 3pm, the three daily specials for 15DM ($9) come with a soft drink, beer, or glass of wine. Beside the restaurant is a natural-foods shop of the same name, which offers ready-made vegetarian dishes that always include three main dishes, a couple of pasta dishes, and a self-service counter with salads and warm vegetables. You can eat here for less than 14DM ($8) at one of its stand-up counters or take your food and sit on one of the benches lining the square.

Good Friend. Kantstrasse 30. ☎ **030/313 26 59.** Main dishes 16DM–26DM ($9–$15). AE, MC, V. Daily noon–2am. S-Bahn: Savignyplatz. CHINESE.

This large, bustling Cantonese restaurant, on the corner of Kantstrasse and Schlüterstrasse about a 6-minute walk north of the Ku'damm, includes many Chinese among its regular customers, always a good sign. Service by the Chinese staff is quick, abrupt, and matter-of-fact. There are more than 100 items on the English menu, with an additional 17 choices available for weekday lunch to 3pm, priced below 15DM ($9).

✪ **Hardtke.** Meinekestrasse 27 a/b. ☎ **030/881 98 27.** Main courses 15DM–30DM ($9–$17). No credit cards. Daily 11am–11:30pm. U-Bahn: Uhlandstrasse, then less than a 2-minute walk. GERMAN.

Just off the Ku'damm, this typical German eatery has been here more than 40 years and is popular with older German visitors. It has its own butcher shop, ensuring the freshest cuts; its sausages are excellent. Though you can spend up to 30DM ($17) for a dinner of *eisbein, schnitzel,* and *schweinebraten* on a splurge, you can also dine on sausages for 10.50DM ($6) until 6pm; afterward, the price increases to 15DM ($9). Alternatively, you can order one of three set-priced meals available weekdays to 5pm for 15.50DM to 17.90DM ($9 to $10). Either way, you're in for a treat.

Jimmy's Diner. Pariser Strasse 41 (at the corner of Sächsische Strasse). ☎ **030/882 31 41.** Meals 8DM–15DM ($4.55–$9). No credit cards. Sun–Thurs noon–3am, Fri–Sat noon–4am. U-Bahn: Uhlandstrasse, then a 10-minute walk. Bus: 109, 119, or 129 to Bleibtreustrasse. AMERICAN/MEXICAN.

Come here for a bit of 1950s Americana. It looks like a diner, with blood-red furniture, chrome, and old ads on the wall. Its English menu is eclectic, from corn on the cob and Aunt Mary's chicken salad to huge hamburgers with fries, sandwiches, spareribs, spaghetti, tacos, enchiladas, burritos, and chili con carne, most under 13DM ($7). Purists will be disappointed in the German presentations of Mexican food—you're better off sticking to the burger. A 5-minute walk south of the Ku'damm, this place is popular with young students and has been joined in recent years by several other restaurants specializing in Mexican and American food.

Karavan. Kurfürstendamm 11. ☎ **030/881 50 05.** Meals 4DM–12DM ($2.30–$7). No credit cards. Daily 9am–midnight. U-Bahn: Kurfürstendamm or Bahnhof Zoologischer Garten. TURKISH.

Across the plaza from the Kaiser Wilhelm Memorial Church, this is a tiny Turkish takeout where you can sample ethnic food at low prices. I recommend the Turkish pizza, which has a thick soft crust with a thin spread of meat and spices; the kofti burger, a Turkish-style burger; or the Spinat-tasche, a spinach-filled pastry. There are also lamb, chicken, and vegetarian dishes, and sandwiches and salads. Since all the food is visible behind the glass counter, you can just choose and point. There are a few bar stools along a counter, or you can sit on one of the benches in the square and watch the human parade.

✪ **Marché Mövenpick.** Kurfürstendamm 14–15. ☎ **030/882 75 79.** Main courses 8DM–15DM ($4.55–$9). AE, MC, V. Daily 8am–midnight. U-Bahn: Kurfürstendamm. INTERNATIONAL.

This is one of my favorite places on the Ku'damm. A cafeteria, it imitates the neighborhood market, with various stands of fresh meals—most prepared in front of you. There's a salad bar, a vegetable stand, and counters offering meat dishes, soups, pastas, salads, daily specials, cakes, ice cream, desserts, and more. Simply grab a tray and walk around to the various counters. It's a good place to load up on veggies; there are also freshly squeezed fruit and vegetable juices. A meal here will run between 13DM and 20DM ($7 and $11).

✪ **Mensa.** Technische Universität, Hardenbergstrasse 34. ☎ **030/3140.** Meals 4DM–8DM ($2.30–$4.55). No credit cards. Mon–Fri 11:15am–2:30pm. U-Bahn: Ernst-Reuter-Platz. GERMAN.

This student cafeteria serves fixed-price meals and is by far the cheapest place to eat near the Ku'damm, a 5-minute walk from Bahnhof Zoo. You'll find it up the stairs to the left, along with a display case showing the four main courses of the day, which may include *schnitzel* with noodles and vegetables or spaghetti with salad, along with choices of other side dishes and desserts. Decide which meal you want, then head to the appropriate counter. Prices for meals are generally 3.50DM to 4DM ($2 to $2.30), with nonstudents (under the heading *Mitarbeiter*) paying slightly more. For more relaxed dining, head to the top-floor restaurant to the right (follow the signs). While not an aesthetic place for a meal (it looks like the student place it is), it offers a slightly more expansive menu from self-service counters, giving you the chance to point at what you want.

Piccola Taormina Tavola Calda. Uhlandstrasse 29. ☎ **030/881 47 10.** Pizza and pasta 5.50DM–11DM ($3.15–$6). No credit cards. Daily 10:30am–1:30am. U-Bahn: Uhlandstrasse. ITALIAN.

Afternoon Coffee & Cake

As the British crave their afternoon tea, the Germans love their afternoon coffee, which naturally requires a slice of cake to accompany it. If you're a caffeine addict, the cheapest place for a cup is **Tschibo,** a chain that sells both the beans and the brew. A cup of coffee or a cappuccino costs 3DM ($1.70), which you can drink at one of the stand-up counters. You can find Tschibo shops at Ku'-damm 11 (across the plaza from the Kaiser Wilhelm Memorial Church) and Wilmersdorfer Strasse 117.

Another place for afternoon coffee is one of the department-store restaurants (above). But if you want to splurge, go to **Café Kranzler,** Kurfürstendamm 18–19 (☎ **030/882 69 11**), which first opened in 1825 on Unter den Linden and relocated here after World War II in a classic 1950s building. It's the favored people-watching spot on the Ku'damm, and in summer you can sit outside. Coffee starts at 3.70DM ($2.10), with cakes costing more.

In eastern Berlin, the place to go is the opulent **Operncafe,** Unter den Linden 5 (☎ **030/20 26 83**). One of Berlin's most celebrated cafes, it's on the ground floor of the Opernpalais, built in 1733, destroyed during World War II, then rebuilt. Coffee here costs 3.50DM ($2), but the main attraction is the more than 40 tortes, prepared daily. In warm weather an outdoor *Imbiss* sells coffee, drinks, and snacks.

This is one of the cheapest places for Italian pizza, pasta, and risotto. The menu is written on the wall: After deciding what you want, place your order at the counter opposite. These guys—all Italian—are fast and will have your food ready in no time. You can take out your meal (a slice of pizza is only 2DM/$1.15) or sit at one of the wooden tables. As for the food, the crowd at this usually packed eatery a 2-minute walk south of the Ku'damm speaks for itself. Beer and wine are available.

San Marino. Savignyplatz 12. ☎ **030/313 60 86.** Pizzas and pasta 8DM–18.50DM ($4.55–$12). AE, MC, V. Daily 11am–midnight. S-Bahn: Savignyplatz. ITALIAN.

Most of the pizza and pasta dishes, which is all you need order, are priced under 15DM ($9), but if you feel like splurging you can also order the much higher-priced steaks and seafood from the English menu. Even better, order one of the four daily fixed-price meals for less than 20DM ($11), available until midnight Monday to Friday and until 7pm Saturday and Sunday. A 4-minute walk north of the Ku'damm, the restaurant is upscale and artsy; in summer you can sit outside with a view of Savignyplatz.

IN BERLIN-MITTE

For several choices in fast-food dining under one roof, head for **Carre,** on Alexander-platz near the S-Bahn station and behind the Kaufhof department store. McDonald's, Nordsee, Ihre Frisch-Backstube, and other chains have concessions here, open daily about 10am to as late as 8pm or even midnight.

Kartoffel-Laube. Probststrasse 1. ☎ **030/241 56 81.** Main courses 15DM–25DM ($9–$14). AE, DC, MC, V. Daily 11am–11pm. U-Bahn/S-Bahn: Alexanderplatz. GERMAN.

The potato in all its glory is the star of this antiques-filled restaurant in the restored Nikolai Quarter, not far from Alexanderplatz. An English menu covers pretty much all the different ways Germans love their staple, including fried with onions, ham, or other ingredients; baked with toppings; in casseroles; and served as dumplings, salads, and soups. In summer, you can sit outside with a view of the Nikolai Church.

✪ **Oren.** Oranienburger Strasse 28. ☎ **030/282 82 28.** Meals 14DM–26DM ($8–$16). No credit cards. Mon–Thurs noon–midnight, Fri noon–1am, Sat 10am–1am, Sun 10am–midnight. S-Bahn: Oranienburger Strasse. KOSHER/VEGETARIAN.

About a 5-minute walk north of Museum Island, next to a towering gold-domed synagogue, this is the former East Berlin's first modern kosher restaurant. Decorated like a 1920s Berlin coffeehouse and catering to an intellectual crowd, it offers excellent food, with an interesting menu that draws inspiration from Asia, the Middle East, and international vegetarian cuisine. Perhaps start with the Russian borscht or falafel with hummus and pita, followed by grilled fish, vegetarian lasagna, or one of the daily specials. The Orient Express is an assortment of Middle Eastern vegetarian food, including hummus, tahina, falafel, tabbouleh, eggplant salad, and pita.

✪ **Restaurant/Casino.** In the Staatsbibliothek, Unter den Linden 8. ☎ **030/2015 13 10.** Meals 5.50DM–10DM ($3.15–$6). No credit cards. Mon–Fri 9am–6pm, Sat 10am–4pm. Bus: 100 or 157 to the Staatsoper stop. GERMAN.

Casino means "canteen" in German, and the only gamble here is whether you'll be able to find an empty seat at lunch. This inexpensive cafeteria in a public library offers a limited chalkboard menu of soups, stews, salads, and daily specials. Offerings may include *schnitzel* with fries and salad, rump steak, chicken, or fish. Coffee is a cheap 1.50DM (85¢) per cup. This place is convenient for jaunts along Unter den Linden and to Museum Island. Just be sure to clear away your own tray after eating and note that smoking is prohibited noon to 2pm.

Self-Service Terrace of Opernpalais. Unter den Linden 5. ☎ **030/200 22 69.** Meals 4DM–7DM ($2.30–$4). No credit cards. Summer daily noon–midnight (to 6pm in winter). U-Bahn: Französische Strasse. Bus: 100 to the Staatsoper stop. GERMAN/SNACKS.

The Opernpalais, on eastern Berlin's famous boulevard not far from Museum Island, contains one of the city's best-known restaurants and coffeehouses. Prices inside are well over our budget (good for a splurge, though), but outside the cafe, in a pretty tree-shaded square, is a self-service *Imbiss* selling *würste* (sausages), *boulette*, soups, coffee, beer, and other drinks. Eat your purchase at one of the tables beside the *Imbiss*—but don't wander to the tables on the terraces, as these are reserved for coffeehouse customers.

T. G. I. Fridays. Karl-Liebknecht-Strasse 5. ☎ **030/2382 79 66.** Meals 16DM–32DM ($9–$18). AE, DC, MC, V. Daily noon–midnight. S-Bahn: Alexanderplatz or Hackescher Markt. Bus: 100 to Spandauer Strasse. AMERICAN.

Just like home—and in the heart of former East Berlin. Opened in 1994, this member of the well-known American chain just a stone's throw from Museum Island is one of the city's best places for bar food, cocktails (more than 400 mind-boggling concoctions), and a variety of American cuisine. Buffalo wings, potato skins, nachos, fajitas, fettuccine Alfredo, baby-back ribs, steak, blackened Cajun tuna, burgers, club sandwiches, and salads are some choices on the English menu. There's also a children's menu. The staff is enthusiastic, and in summer there's dining beside the Spree River with a view of the Berliner Dom.

Zur Letzten Instanz. Waisenstrasse 14–16. ☎ **030/242 55 28.** Meals 17DM–22DM ($10–$13). AE, DC, MC, V. Mon–Sat noon–midnight, Sun noon–10pm. U-Bahn: Klosterstrasse, then about a 2-minute walk. GERMAN.

Open since 1621, this tiny restaurant claims to be Berlin's oldest *gaststätte* (neighborhood pub). Its rooms are rustic, with plank floors, wainscoting, and a few antiques. Its

English menu offers very traditional Berlin specialties, including *boulette,* grilled herring with onions, grilled pork knuckles, roast pork with an herb crust, and braised beef, all served with side dishes like dumplings, potatoes, or red cabbage. Be sure to save room for Berlin's famous dessert, *rote grütze* (cooked fruits with vanilla sauce). In summer tables are placed outside. It's about a 5-minute walk from Alexanderplatz, behind the Rathaus.

NEAR CHARLOTTENBURG PALACE

✪ **Luisen-Bräu.** Luisenplatz 1. ☎ **030/341 93 88.** Meals 10DM–20DM ($6–$11). No credit cards. Sun–Thurs 9am–1am, Fri–Sat 9am–2am. Bus: 109, 121, 145, or 204. GERMAN.

Southeast of Charlottenburg Palace on the corner of Spandauer Damm, Luisen-Bräu brews its own beer on the premises (you can see the stainless-steel tanks) and sells German dishes to go along with it. The buffet-style food changes daily but may include *spiessbraten* (skewered meat and vegetables), *kasseler rippenspeer* (pork chops), *schweienbraten* (pot-roasted pork), *boulette* (a meatball), salads, and stews. Dining is at long wooden tables (which includes conversation with neighbors) or, in summer, outside. This place is convenient if you're visiting the palace or the many area museums. And it's a good place for just a beer, served in a tiny mug for 2.80DM ($1.60).

NEAR WILMERSDORFER STRASSE & BAHNHOF CHARLOTTENBURG

Ty Breizh Savoie Rire. Kantstrasse 75. ☎ **030/323 99 32.** Main courses 18.50DM–28.50DM ($11–$16). No credit cards. Mon–Fri 5pm–1am, Sat 6pm–1am. S-Bahn: Charlottenburg. U-Bahn: Wilmersdorfer Strasse. FRENCH.

This rather eccentric-looking cozy place, with an odd mix of clutter and antiques, is owned by the gregarious Patrick Matteï, who speaks English, Italian, French, German, and Finnish. He puts on quite a show—singing chansons and hand-drawing colored bills. His specialties are an appetizer of mushrooms with shrimp and cheese, housemade pâté, cheeses imported from Savoie, and fish soup. Other dishes are avocado with shrimp, orange duck with pepper sauce, lamb cutlet, beef cooked in burgundy sauce with onions, seafood, and a couple of vegetarian choices, including an eggplant-and-zucchini ratatouille. Daily specials may include couscous, lamb, duck, or mussels. A good—and unique—place for French food on a budget.

STREET EATS & PICNICKING

There are a number of food stalls, *Imbisse,* up and down the Ku'damm and clustered around Friedrichstrasse Station selling *würste,* fries, Turkish specialties, and beer. Prices are generally under 4DM ($2.30). In addition, a number of restaurants above—Piccola Taormina Tavola Calda, Einhorn, Asia-Quick, Ashoka, and Karavan—sell takeout food at low prices.

All the **department stores** have large food departments (especially KaDeWe) and counters serving prepared meats, salads, and takeout food. You can also buy takeout at the stand-up places above. As for a place to consume your picnic, the most convenient green space is the huge **Tiergarten** just northwest of Bahnhof Zoo, packed with families enjoying cookouts on summer weekends. For people-watching, sit on one of the benches or stairs in the shadow of the Kaiser Wilhelm Memorial Church on the Ku'damm.

WORTH A SPLURGE

Lutter & Wegner. Schlüterstrasse 55. ☎ **030/881 34 40.** Reservations recommended. Meals 30DM–36DM ($17–$21). AE, DC, MC, V. Daily 6pm–midnight. S-Bahn: Savignyplatz. AUSTRIAN/GERMAN.

A wine bar/restaurant, Lutter & Wegner dates from 1811, when it opened as a wine cellar in East Berlin. Moving to West Berlin after World War II, it still exudes an old-world charm, simple and unpretentious, yet refined and civilized, with dark-paneled wainscoting, candles on white tablecloths, and changing art exhibits. It caters to a professional and artistic crowd, and despite the fact that the tables are too close together in the tiny restaurant—or perhaps because of it—the atmosphere is convivial, as though all the diners were invited guests. In summer, tables are set up on the sidewalk. In addition to a standard menu, there's a handwritten daily menu, with offerings like tafelspitz, Wiener schnitzel, and fish.

✪ **Zitadelle.** Am Juliusturm, Spandau. ☎ **030/334 21 06.** Reservations required. Fixed-price banquet 78.50DM ($45). AE, DC, MC, V. Tues–Sun 7–11pm. U-Bahn: Zitadelle. GERMAN.

Imagine sitting in the bowels of a 700-year-old fortress with stone walls and an open fireplace and eating fish or skewered grilled meat much as people did centuries ago. The Zitadelle is such a fortress, offering a medieval banquet every evening except Monday with ballad singing and special entertainment; it's best to make a reservation. Meals include a welcoming drink in a bull's horn, bread, an appetizer, a main dish like *spiessbraten,* and several other dishes. Although Spandau is on the outskirts of Berlin and was its own city until incorporated in 1920, you can easily reach it by subway.

5 Seeing the Sights

Berlin has four museum centers: **Charlottenburg,** with its palace and three significant museums, including the Ägyptisches Museum (Egyptian Museum); **Museumsinsel (Museum Island),** with its cluster of excellent museums, including the world-famous Pergamon Museum; the **Tiergarten,** a newly developed center for European art, including the Gemäldegalerie; and **Dahlem,** with its museums of non-European art and ethnology. It makes sense to cover Berlin section by section—saving time and money on transportation.

SIGHTSEEING SUGGESTIONS

Berlin is compact, with an efficient public transport system, so you can see quite a lot of it in a few days. To help you get the most out of your visit, here are some suggestions to guide you to the most important attractions. Keep in mind that most museums are closed on Monday.

IF YOU HAVE 1 DAY   By 9am you should be at the **Ägyptisches Museum** in Charlottenburg, where the legendary beauty Nefertiti holds court. Across the street is the **Berggruen Collection** with its extensive Picasso collection. Here, too, is the beautiful baroque **Schloss Charlottenburg,** where you can visit the Historical Rooms, Knobelsdorff Flügel, and Schinkel Pavilion for a look at how Prussian royalty lived. Be sure to stroll its lovely gardens. Have lunch at the nearby **Luisen-Bräu.**

In the afternoon, head for the **Brandenburger Tor,** built in the 1780s as the finishing touch to **Unter den Linden,** one of Berlin's most famous boulevards. When the Berlin Wall fell, it was here that many Berliners gathered to rejoice. Take a stroll down Unter den Linden to the **Pergamon Museum** with its incredible Pergamon Altar, on Museumsinsel.

Round out your eastern Berlin experience with a trip to the **Museum Haus am Checkpoint Charlie,** which opened in 1961 with the sole purpose of documenting the Berlin Wall and the many attempts of East Berliners to escape to the West. Today it's the best place in the city to gain an understanding of what Berlin was like during the decades of division. Finish off the day with a leisurely evening stroll along the **Ku'-damm** and a meal in a German restaurant.

IF YOU HAVE 2 DAYS   Devote the entire first morning to Charlottenburg as above, where there's also the wonderful **Bröhan Museum** with its art deco and Jugendstil (art nouveau) decorative arts collection. Have lunch at the nearby **Luisen-Bräu.**

In the afternoon, head for the Ku'damm, where you can visit the **Kaiser Wilhelm Memorial Church** and the **Käthe-Kollwitz-Museum** with its powerful drawings, have coffee at a sidewalk cafe, and stroll and window-shop on Berlin's most fashionable boulevard. Include a visit to the **KaDeWe,** the largest department store on the European continent.

On Day 2, go to eastern Berlin, starting at **Brandenburg Gate** and walking along the famous tree-lined **Unter den Linden** to Museumsinsel with the **Pergamon Museum** and the **Berliner Dom.** Then walk to **Alexanderplatz,** once the heart of East Germany's capital, where you can take an elevator to the top of the Fernsehturm (TV Tower) for refreshments and a bird's-eye view of Berlin. Have dinner at the nearby **Nikolai Quarter,** a small neighborhood of restored buildings. At the end of the day, head for the **Museum Haus am Checkpoint Charlie** (open to 10pm) with its important collections documenting the history of the Wall.

IF YOU HAVE 3 DAYS   Spend Days 1 and 2 as above. On Day 3, head for the **Tiergarten,** where you'll find the **Gemäldegalerie,** one of Berlin's most significant museums with masterpieces from the 13th to the 18th centuries. Here too are the **Neue Nationalgalerie,** with its extensive collection of German and European 20th-century art, and the **Kunstgewerbe Museum,** devoted to European applied arts from the Middle Ages to the present.

Spend the rest of the day according to your special interests: perhaps the **zoo,** next to Bahnhof Zoo, the **Ku'damm** and **Wilmersdorfer Strasse** for shopping, or the **Hamburger Bahnhof** with its Museum for Contemporary Art. You might also consider going to **Dahlem,** which boasts museums for Indian and Far Eastern art, as well as an ethnological museum with an outstanding international collection and a German ethnological museum that illustrates what life was like for middle- and lower-class Germans in centuries past.

IF YOU HAVE 5 DAYS   Spend Days 1 to 3 as above. If possible, be sure to include a visit to the **flea market** held every Saturday and Sunday on Strasse des 17 Juni near the Tiergarten. If you're in Berlin on a Tuesday or Friday afternoon, consider visiting the **Turkish Market** with its colorful stands of fruits, vegetables, and exotic spices and food. On Day 4, take an excursion to **Lake Wannsee** or **Havel,** where you can swim or take a boat trip and spend a relaxing day, or take an excursion to **Lübbenau** in the Spreewald, where you can board a punt for a ride through this magical countryside. On Day 5, visit **Potsdam** in eastern Germany with its palace and park of Sanssouci.

IN CHARLOTTENBURG

To reach these sights, take city bus no. 109 from the Ku'damm, getting off at Luisen-platz/Schloss Charlottenburg, or bus no. 145 from Bahnhof Zoo to Schloss Charlottenburg. Or take U-Bahn U-2 to Sophie-Charlotte-Platz, then walk 10 minutes up Schlossstrasse to Spandauer Damm. Most of the museums are on the corner of Schlossstrasse and Spandauer Damm.

An 8DM ($4.55) *Tageskarte* bought at either the Ägyptisches Museum or the Sammlung Berggruen entitles entry to both these museums, as well as the Galerie der

---

Getting the Best Deal on Sightseeing

- Take advantage of free admission to most state museums on the first Sunday of every month, including the Pergamon, the Ägyptisches Museum, and the Gemäldegalerie.
- Note that the 8DM ($4.55) *Tageskarte* admission to the Pergamon, Ägyptisches Museum, Sammlung Berggruen, Gemäldegalerie, Neue Nationalgalerie, and Museum for Contemporary Art at the Hamburger Bahnhof allows entry to all other state-owned museums that same day. Make sure your first visit of the day is to one of the above museums, where you'll then find a printed list of all other museums you're entitled to visit free.
- Be aware that the Berlin WelcomeCard, costing 29DM ($17) and valid for 72 hours, offers unlimited transportation throughout the city and as much as 50% off the admission price to a limited selection of museums and attractions.
- Take a ride on public bus no. 100, the best sightseeing deal in Berlin. It travels day and night from Bahnhof Zoo through Tiergarten and Brandenburger Tor, continuing along Unter den Linden to Alexanderplatz and Prenzlauer Berg.
- Seek out churches for music virtually every day of the week, either for free or for a small fee.

Romantik in Charlottenburg Palace. Not included, however, are the Historical Rooms or the other attractions of the palace.

✪ **Schloss Charlottenburg (Charlottenburg Palace).** Spandauer Damm. ☎ **030/ 32 09 11.** Combination ticket (Sammelkarte) to everything, 15DM ($9) adults, 10DM ($6) students/children. Individual tickets: Nering-Eosander Building with guided tour of the Historical Rooms, 8DM ($4.55) adults, 4DM ($2.30) students/children; Nering-Eosander Building (upper floor only) without guided tour, 3DM ($1.70) adults, 2DM ($1.15) students/children; Knobelsdorff Flügel, 5DM ($2.85) adults, 3DM ($1.70) students/children; Schinkel Pavilion and Belvedere, each 3DM ($1.70) adults, 2DM ($1.15) students/children; Mausoleum, 2DM ($1.15) adults, 1DM (50¢) students/children. Galerie der Romantik (not included in combination ticket), 4DM ($2.30) adults, 2DM ($1.15) students/children. Nering-Eosander Building, Tues–Fri 9am–5pm, Sat–Sun 10am–5pm; Knobelsdorff Flügel and Galerie der Romantik, Tues–Fri 10am–6pm, Sat–Sun 11am–6pm; Schinkel Pavilion, Tues–Sun 10am–5pm; Belvedere, Tues–Sun noon–4pm, Sat–Sun noon–5pm. Mausoleum closed Nov–Mar. U-Bahn: U-2 to Sophie-Charlotte-Platz, then a 10-minute walk. Bus: 109 or 145 to Luisenplatz/Schloss Charlottenburg.

Berlin's most beautiful Baroque building, Charlottenburg Palace was built in 1695 for Sophia Charlotte, the very popular wife of the future king of Prussia, Frederick I. Later it was expanded and served as the summer residence of the Prussian kings, the Hohenzollerns. Badly damaged during World War II and since restored, it consists of one main building and several outlying structures, surrounded by a beautiful park.

Straight ahead as you enter the main gate is the **Nering-Eosander Building,** which contains the **Historical Rooms** on the ground floor, once the private quarters of Sophia Charlotte and her husband. Of these, the Porcelain Cabinet is the most striking (and kitschy), filled with about 2,000 pieces of porcelain. You have to join a guided tour conducted only in German to visit the Historical Rooms, but English descriptions of what you'll see are available at the ticket office. Alternatively, you can skip the tour but head to the upper floor of the Nering-Eosander, where you can wander on your own through rooms containing tapestries, goblets, swords, portraits, and other royal possessions, including the Hohenzollern insignia and a stunning silver place setting completed in 1914 but never used by the family because of the outbreak of World War I. If you join the guided tour, a visit to these rooms is included in your ticket.

To the right of the Nering-Eosander Building is the **Knobelsdorff Flügel (New Wing)**, where you can wander on your own through more royal quarters, the state dining hall, and the elaborate ballroom, as well as through the **Galerie der Romantik** with its 19th-century romantic, classical, and Biedermeier paintings, including works by Caspar David Friedrich and Karl Friedrich Schinkel.

Next head for the **Schinkel Pavilion,** behind the New Wing. This delightful, small summerhouse, built in 1825 like an Italian villa and designed by Schinkel, Berlin's most important architect of the early 19th century, has cozy rooms, each unique and decorated with period arts and crafts. After strolling through Berlin's most beautiful park (laid out in the French style in 1697 and restored to its baroque form after World War II), visit the **Belvedere,** a former teahouse that now contains 18th- and 19th-century Berlin porcelain. On the park's west side is the **Mausoleum** with the tombs of Frederick William III, Queen Louise, and others.

✪ **Ägyptisches Museum (Egyptian Museum)**. Schlossstrasse 70. ☎ **030/32 09 11.** Admission 8DM ($4.55) adults, 4DM ($2.30) students/children. Tues–Fri 10am–6pm, Sat–Sun 11am–6pm. U-Bahn: U-2 to Sophie-Charlotte-Platz, then a 10-minute walk. Bus: 109 or 145 to Luisenplatz/Schloss Charlottenburg.

Across from Charlottenburg Palace is this invaluable collection of Egyptian art. Berlin's most famous art object (and probably the world's best-known single piece of Egyptian art) is on the first floor in a dark room reserved just for her: Created more than 3,300 years ago, the Queen Nefertiti bust amazingly never left the sculptor's studio but rather served as a model for all other portraits of the queen and was left on a shelf when the ancient city was deserted. The bust was discovered early in this century by German archaeologists.

In an adjoining room you can see smaller likenesses of Pharaoh Akhenaton (husband of Nefertiti) and the royal family, including Nefertiti's eldest daughter, Princess Meritaton. Look also for Queen Tiy, Akhenaton's mother. There are many other amazing items here, including the Kalabasha Gate, bronzes, vases, burial cult objects, a mummy and sarcophagi, a papyrus collection, and tools used in everyday life.

✪ **Die Sammlung Berggruen: Picasso und Seine Zeit.** Schlossstrasse 1. ☎ **030/830 14 66** or 030/326 958-0. Admission 8DM ($4.55) adults, 4DM ($2.30) students/children. Tues–Fri 10am–6pm, Sat–Sun 11am–6pm. U-Bahn: U-2 to Sophie-Charlotte-Platz, then a 10-minute walk. Bus: 109 or 145 to Luisenplatz/Schloss Charlottenburg.

Across from the Egyptian Museum, this outstanding collection was previously on display in the London National Gallery but was moved here in 1996 after Berlin offered the collection a home of its own, in renovated former barracks built by August Stüler in 1859. Heinz Berggruen, a Berliner who fled from the Nazis in 1936, has in turn promised to keep the collection here at least 10 years. It contains an astonishing 60 works by Picasso, from his teenage years to late in life and covering his major periods, as well as works by such contemporaries as Cézanne, van Gogh, Braque, and Klee. An absolute must for Picasso fans.

✪ **Bröhan Museum.** Schlossstrasse 1a. ☎ **030/321 40 29.** Admission 6DM ($3.40) adults, 3DM ($1.70) students/children. Tues–Sun 10am–6pm. U-Bahn: U-2 to Sophie-Charlotte-Platz, then a 10-minute walk. Bus: 109 or 145 to Luisenplatz/Schloss Charlottenburg.

Berlin

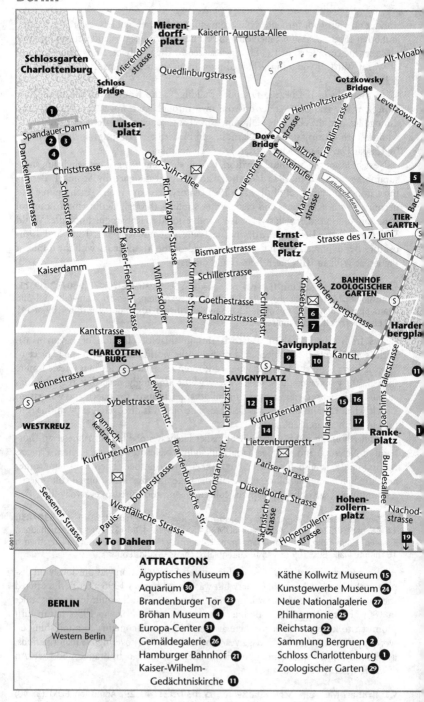

ATTRACTIONS

Ägyptisches Museum ❸
Aquarium ❸⓿
Brandenburger Tor ❷❸
Bröhan Museum ❹
Europa-Center ❸❶
Gemäldegalerie ❷❻
Hamburger Bahnhof ❷❶
Kaiser-Wilhelm-
  Gedächtniskirche ⓫

Käthe Kollwitz Museum ⓯
Kunstgewerbe Museum ❷❹
Neue Nationalgalerie ❷❼
Philharmonie ❷❺
Reichstag ❷❷
Sammlung Bergruen ❷
Schloss Charlottenburg ❶
Zoologischer Garten ❷❾

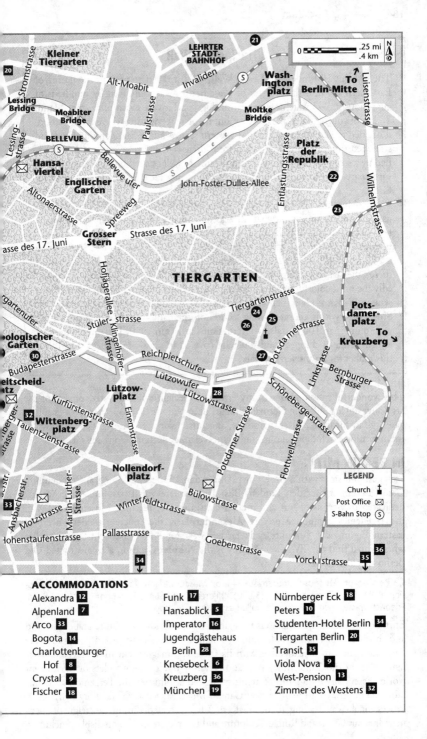

ACCOMMODATIONS

Alexandra 12
Alpenland 7
Arco 33
Bogota 14
Charlottenburger
  Hof 8
Crystal 9
Fischer 18

Funk 17
Hansablick 5
Imperator 16
Jugendgästehaus
  Berlin 28
Knesebeck 6
Kreuzberg 36
München 19

Nürnberger Eck 18
Peters 10
Studenten-Hotel Berlin 34
Tiergarten Berlin 20
Transit 35
Viola Nova 9
West-Pension 13
Zimmer des Westens 32

Tracing the Wall

The hideous 100-mile-long **Berlin Wall,** built in 1961 to prevent the fleeing of East Germans into the sanctity of West Berlin, was reinforced by hundreds of guardhouses, 293 watchtowers, patrol dogs, and a vast swath of no-man's-land. Today, of course, the Wall is history, but if you're wondering where it once stood, it divided the city into eastern and western sectors at the Brandenburg Gate and stretched roughly north and south from there—its location is now best identified by a string of massive construction sites, as well as a red line snaking through some parts of the city, including the Wall's former location beside Brandenburg Gate.

The Museum Haus am Checkpoint Charlie (see below) is the best place to gain an understanding of what life was like during the Cold War. Otherwise, a few sections of the Wall have been left standing, most notably on **Niederkirchnerstrasse** (not far from the museum; S-Bahn/U-Bahn: Potsdamer Platz), where a 250-meter (273-foot) section remains. In Kreuzberg on **Schlesische Strasse** there's the last remaining watchtower (U-Bahn: Schlesisches Tor). But undoubtedly the most colorful remainder of the Wall is in former East Berlin on **Mühlenstrasse** (S-Bahn: Hauptbahnhof; U-Bahn: Warschauer Strasse). Called the **East Side Gallery,** this kilometer-long section on the banks of the Spree was painted with more than 100 murals by international artists in 1990. The murals are now a bit faded and chipped (and some are covered in plastic to protect them), but this makes for an interesting walk.

This wonderful museum, one of my favorites, specializes in decorative objects of the art nouveau (Jugendstil in German) and art deco periods (1889–1939), with exquisite vases, glass, furniture, silver, paintings, and other works of art arranged in drawing-room fashion, including an outstanding porcelain collection. Don't miss it.

IN BERLIN-MITTE

I suggest you start with a stroll down **Unter den Linden** beginning at Brandenburg Gate (S-Bahn: Unter den Linden; Bus: 100), where you'll pass the Neue Wache, dedicated to victims of war and totalitarianism, before reaching Museumsinsel with the excellent Pergamon Museum. **Alexanderplatz,** the concrete modern heart of eastern Berlin, is a 5-minute walk farther west on Karl-Liebknecht-Strasse and is where you'll find the TV tower. Nearby is the **Nikolai Quarter,** a reconstructed Old Berlin neighborhood.

✪ **Pergamon Museum.** Bodestrasse 1–3, on Museum Island. ☎ **030/20 90 50.** Admission 8DM ($4.55) adults, 4DM ($2.30) children. Tues–Sun 10am–6pm. S-Bahn/U-Bahn: Friedrichstrasse, then an 8-minute walk. Bus: 100 to Staatsoper.

Entrance to Berlin's most famous museum is via the bridge on Kupfergraben, behind and to the left of Das Alte Museum. It's named after its most prized possession, the Pergamon Altar, which together with its frieze is a magnificent masterpiece of Hellenistic art of the 2nd century B.C. and certainly one of the wonders of the ancient world. Essentially a museum of architecture and antiquities, the Pergamon also contains the impressive Roman Market Gate of Milet, as well as the dazzling Babylonian Processional Way leading to the Gate of Ishtar, created during the reign of Nebuchadnezzar. Greek and Roman sculpture and Islamic art are also on display, including

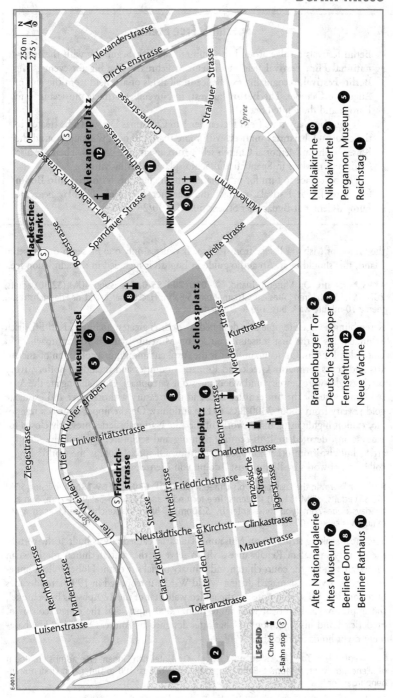

Berlin-Mitte

LEGEND
Church ✝ ■
S-Bahn stop Ⓢ

Alte Nationalgalerie ⑥
Altes Museum ⑦
Berliner Dom ⑧
Berliner Rathaus ⑪

Brandenburger Tor ②
Deutsche Staatsoper ③
Fernsehturm ⑫
Neue Wache ④

Nikolaikirche ⑩
Nikolaiviertel ⑨
Pergamon Museum ⑤
Reichstag ①

Special & Free Events

Berlin festivals revolve around the cultural calendar, beginning with the **International Film Festival** held at the end of February. The biggest event is the **Berlin Festival,** recognizing excellence in all fields of art, held from the end of August to October. The **Berlin Jazzfest,** in November, attracts musicians from Europe and the United States.

If you come any time from December 1 to Christmas Eve, you'll be treated to the colorful **Christmas market,** with more than 150 booths set up around the Kaiser Wilhelm Memorial Church selling ornaments and candies. There are also Christmas markets in Spandau and Schlossplatz in Berlin-Mitte.

The best place to turn for information about all events is **Tourist Info Berlin** (see above). For festivals, contact the **Berliner Festspiele GmbH,** near the Europa-Center at Budapester Strasse 50 (☎ 030/25 48 90).

the facade of Mshatta Palace from Jordan. If you see only one museum on Museum Island, this should be it. An audio guide in English is included in the admission fee.

Altes Museum. On Museum Island. ☎ **030/203 55-0.** Admission 4DM ($2.30) adults, 2DM ($1.15) children. Tues–Sun 10am–6pm. S-Bahn: Hackescher Markt or Friedrichstrasse, then a 10-minute walk. Bus: 100 to Lustgarten.

Resembling a Greek temple and designed by Berlin's greatest architect, Karl Friedrich Schinkel, this is the first museum you see on Museum Island if you approach from Unter den Linden. On its main floor is the Antikensammlung, a collection of ancient arts and crafts, primarily Greek and Roman antiquities and including pottery, ivory carvings, glassware, jewelry, and wood and stone sarcophagi. Outstanding are the Attic red-figure vases of the 5th century B.C. and the treasury with its silver and exquisite gold jewelry from about 2000 B.C. to late antiquity. On the upper floor is a temporary exhibit highlighting major works of the Alte Nationalgalerie (presently closed for renovation), devoted to 19th-century painting and sculpture, primarily by German artists but also from other European countries. Of special note is the world's largest collection of works by Berlin artist Adolph von Menzel.

Berliner Dom. In the Lustgarten, on Museum Island. ☎ **030/202 69-136.** Admission 5DM ($2.85) adults, 3DM ($1.70) students, free for under age 14. Mon–Sat 9am–7pm, Sun and holidays noon–7pm (you must enter by 5:30pm). S-Bahn: Hackescher Markt, then a 10-minute walk. Bus: 100 to Lustgarten.

The most striking structure on Museum Island, the cathedral was built at the turn of the century in Italian Renaissance style to serve as the central church for Prussian Protestants and as the court church and primary burial site of the Hohenzollern imperial family. Severely damaged during World War II, it reopened in 1993 after decades of restoration. Of special note are the gilded wall altar of the 12 Apostles by Schinkel, the impressive Sauer organ with more than 7,000 pipes, and the ornate coffins of Frederick I and his wife, Sophie Charlotte, designed by Andreas Schlüter. The basement crypt holds more coffins.

Brandenburger Tor (Brandenburg Gate). On Unter den Linden. Free admission. Room of Silence, daily 11am–4pm. S-Bahn: Unter den Linden. Bus: 100 to Unter den Linden/Brandenburger Tor.

During the decades of the Wall, the Brandenburger Tor stood in no-man's-land, marking the boundary of East and West Berlin and becoming the symbol of a divided

Germany. After the November 1989 revolution and the fall of the Wall, many Berliners gathered here to rejoice and dance on top of the Wall. The Gate was built from 1788 to 1791 by Carl Gotthard Langhans as the grand western entrance onto Unter den Linden. One of the guardhouses serves as a **Room of Silence,** a place for silence and reflection; the other is home to a **Berlin tourist office,** open daily 9:30am to 6pm. Incidentally, nearby is the **Reichstag,** the German house of parliament built in 1894 in Neo-Renaissance style. After renovation by Sir Norman Foster, including a new glass dome, it will reopen in time for the presidential election on May 23, 1999.

Info Box. Leipziger Platz 21. ☎ **030/22 66 24-0.** Free admission; rooftop observation terrace 2DM ($1.15). Fri–Wed 9am–7pm, Thurs 9am–9pm. S-Bahn/U-Bahn: Potsdamer Platz, then a 1-minute walk. Bus: 142, 248, or 348 to Potsdamer Platz.

Berlin, particularly Berlin-Mitte, boasts what is arguably the world's largest construction site. In place of former Communist-era buildings and the swath of empty land left by the fall of the Wall, a virtual sea of cranes has been erecting office buildings, corporate headquarters, apartment complexes, and federal government buildings. The easy-to-spot red Info Box, in the midst of construction chaos, brings order to Berlin's architectural transformation with maps, models, videos, and computers, with explanations in English. If you wish, you can go to the rooftop observatory for a firsthand look at surrounding new buildings by Sony and Daimler-Benz, with the new Reichstag dome in the distance.

IN KREUZBERG

✪ **Museum Haus am Checkpoint Charlie.** Friedrichstrasse 44. ☎ **030/251 10 31.** Admission 8DM ($4.55) adults, 5DM ($2.85) students/children. Daily 9am–10pm. U-Bahn: Kochstrasse, then a 2-minute walk. Bus: 129 to Kochstrasse.

If this is your first trip to Berlin, this museum is a must-see. Near what was once the most frequently used border crossing into East Berlin, Checkpoint Charlie, this collection documents events that took place around the Berlin Wall, including successful and failed attempts to escape from East Berlin. With displays in English, the museum aptly illustrates these years in Berlin's history with photographs, items used in escape attempts (such as cars with hidden compartments), artwork, and newspaper clippings. The fall of the Wall and the demise of communism in East Germany, Russia, Poland, and Hungary are also documented, and part of the museum is devoted to nonviolent struggles for human rights around the world, including those led by Gandhi, Walesa, and Martin Luther King, Jr.

IN THE TIERGARTEN

✪ **Gemäldegalerie (Picture Gallery).** Matthäiskirchplatz 4. ☎ **030/20 90 55 55.** Admission 8DM ($4.55) adults, 4DM ($2.30) students/children. Tues–Fri 10am–6pm, Sat–Sun 11am–6pm. U-Bahn: Kurfürstenstrasse, then bus no. 148 to Kulturforum. Bus: 129 from the Ku'damm to Potsdamer Brücke, then a 4-minute walk.

Berlin's top art museum, this famous collection offers a comprehensive survey of European painting from the 13th to the 18th centuries. Included among the German, Dutch, Italian, French, English, Flemish, and Spanish works are paintings by Dürer, Cranach, Holbein, Gainsborough, Brueghel, Botticelli, Raphael, Rubens, van Eyck, Vermeer, Murillo, El Greco, Goya, and Velázquez. The top attractions of the Dutch section are 20-some Rembrandts, one of the world's largest collections by this master. Look for his self-portrait and (my favorite) portrayal of Hendrickje Stoffels, his common-law wife—the intimacy of their relationship is captured in her face as she gazes at Rembrandt. The famous *Man with the Golden Helmet,* however, is no longer attributed to Rembrandt.

Another of my favorites is Lucas Cranach's *Fountain of Youth (Der Jungbrunnen)*, which shows old women being led to the fountain, swimming through, and emerging youthful and beautiful. Note that apparently only women need the bath—men regain their youth through relations with younger women! Other highlights of the collection include Cranach's *The Last Judgement*, Botticelli's *Venus*, Dürer's portrait of a Nürnberg patrician, and Hans Holbein's portrait of the merchant Georg Gisze. Of course, these are only a fraction of what the museum offers.

Kunstgewerbe Museum (Museum of Applied Arts). Tiergartenstrasse 6. ☎ **030/266 29 11.** Admission 4DM ($2.30) adults, 2DM ($1.15) students/children. Tues–Fri 10am–6pm, Sat–Sun 11am–6pm. U-Bahn: Kurfürstenstrasse, then bus no. 148 to Kulturforum. Bus: 129 from the Ku'damm to Potsdamer Brücke, then a 5-minute walk.

This museum, housed in a modern red-brick building built expressly for the collection, is devoted to European applied arts from the early Middle Ages to the present, including glassware, porcelain, beer steins, tableware, and measuring instruments. The collection of medieval goldsmiths' works is outstanding, as are the displays of Venetian glass, early Meissen porcelain, and art nouveau (Jugendstil) vases and objects. The bottom floor has changing exhibits of contemporary crafts and product design, from typewriters to teapots or furniture.

Neue Nationalgalerie (New National Gallery). Potsdamer Strasse 50. ☎ **030/266 26 62.** Admission 8DM ($4.55) adults, 4DM ($2.30) students/children; more for special exhibits. Tues–Fri 10am–6pm, Sat–Sun 11am–6pm. U-Bahn: Kurfürstenstrasse, then bus no. 148 to Kulturforum. Bus: 129 from the Ku'damm to Potsdamer Brücke, then a 1-minute walk.

This was one of the first museums to open in the new museum area near the Tiergarten. A starkly modern building designed by Mies van der Rohe and set into a vast square surrounded by a sculpture garden, the Nationalgalerie houses art of the 20th century. The ground floor is devoted to changing exhibits, while the permanent collection in the basement shows works of Munch, Liebermann, Max Slevogt, Emil Nolde, and other members of Die Brücke (The Bridge) group, plus artists like Picasso, Ernst, Kokoschka, Dix, Klee, and Feininger.

Hamburger Bahnhof, Museum für Gegenwart (Museum for Contemporary Art). Invalidenstrasse 50–51. ☎ **030/397 83 40.** Admission 8DM ($4.55) adults, 4DM ($2.30) students/children; more for special exhibits. Tues–Fri 10am–6pm, Sat–Sun 11am–6pm. S-Bahn: Lehrter Stadtbahnhof, then a 3-minute walk.

Separated from the other Tiergarten museums above and located north of the Tiergarten, this 19th-century former train station lends itself perfectly to the massive installations of sculpture, paintings, and other works of contemporary art that grace the spacious halls and upstairs galleries of this new museum. One room is devoted to works by Keith Haring, while another big hall, dominated by Andy Warhol's huge portrait of Mao Tse Tung, features works by Warhol, Rauschenberg, and Lichtenstein. Other artists represented are Nam June Paik, Cy Twombly, Anselm Kiefer, Jeff Koons, Sandro Chia, and Julian Schnabel. The museum's star is conceptual artist Joseph Beuys, with more than 450 drawings from his comprehensive work, *Secret Block for a Secret Person in Ireland;* a number of his installations; and audiovisual archives where you can spend hours watching his films and performance art on interactive computers. A great addition to Berlin's art scene.

IN DAHLEM

You can reach Dahlem by taking U-Bahn U-1 from Wittenbergplatz to the Dahlem-Dorf station; you'll find signs pointing to the museums. The museums for ethnology and East Asian and Indian arts are all under the same roof, with admission to the entire complex only 4DM ($2.30). Look for the sign that says STAATLICHE MUSEEN.

Museum für Vslkerkunde (Ethnological Museum). Lansstrasse 8. ☎ **030/8301 1.** Admission (Dahlem complex combination ticket) 4DM ($2.30) adults, 2DM ($1.15) students/children. Tues–Fri 10am–6pm, Sat–Sun 11am–6pm. U-Bahn: U-1 to Dahlem-Dorf, then a 4-minute walk.

One of the world's largest ethnological museums, it possesses half a million items from around the world, including those from ancient America, Africa, the South Seas, and Asia. Mayan, Incan, and Aztec stone sculpture, Burmese shadow puppets, African masks, and more are on display, but particularly fascinating are the life-size boats and dwellings and facades from various corners of the earth. A good museum for children.

Museum für Indische Kunst (Museum of Indian Art). Lansstrasse 8. ☎ **030/8301 361.** Admission (Dahlem complex combination ticket) 4DM ($2.30) adults, 2DM ($1.15) students/children. Tues–Fri 10am–6pm, Sat–Sun 11am–6pm. U-Bahn: U-1 to Dahlem-Dorf, then a 4-minute walk.

The most significant collection of Indian art in Germany, this museum covers a period of almost 4,000 years with its displays of terra-cotta and stone sculptures, miniatures, bronzes, murals, and frescoes from Turfan. Included are items from throughout India and Nepal, Tibet, Burma, Thailand, Indonesia, and other centers of Buddhism.

Museum für Ostasiatische Kunst (Museum of Far Eastern Art). Lansstrasse 8. ☎ **030/8301 382.** Admission (Dahlem complex combination ticket) 4DM ($2.30) adults, 2DM ($1.15) students/children. Tues–Fri 10am–6pm, Sat–Sun 11am–6pm. U-Bahn: U-1 to Dahlem-Dorf, then a 4-minute walk.

Displayed here are works from China, Korea, and Japan from 3000 B.C. to the present, including woodcuts, paintings, bronzes, ceramics, lacquerware, and sculptures. Chinese and Japanese painting and calligraphy are especially well represented.

Museum für Deutsche Volkskunde (Museum of German Ethnology). Im Winkel 6–8. ☎ **030/839 01 01.** Admission 4DM ($2.30) adults, 2DM ($1.15) students/children. Tues–Fri 10am–6pm, Sat–Sun 11am–6pm. U-Bahn: U-1 to Dahlem-Dorf, then a 5-minute walk (follow the signs).

In Dahlem but not part of the Dahlem complex, this museum is devoted to past generations of middle- and lower-class Germans, like farmers, artisans, and homemakers. It contains a fascinating exhibit of items used in work, leisure time, and religious celebrations, including peasant furniture, clothing, pottery, household items, and utensils for making butter and turning flax into linen. Explanations are in German only, but there's an English pamphlet.

NEAR THE KU'DAMM

Kaiser-Wilhelm Gedächtniskirche (Kaiser Wilhelm Memorial Church). Breitscheidplatz. ☎ **030/24 50 23.** Free admission. Ruined church, Mon–Sat 10am–4pm; new church, daily 9am–7pm; organ concerts in new church, Sat at 6pm. U-Bahn: Zoologischer Garten or Kurfürstendamm.

Completed in 1895 as a memorial to Kaiser Wilhelm I, this church was destroyed by bombs during World War II and was left in ruins as a reminder of the horrors of war. Today it contains a small museum with displays and photographs related to war and destruction. Beside the ruined church is a new church designed by Prof. Egon Eiermann and finished in 1961.

✪ **Käthe-Kollwitz-Museum.** Fasanenstrasse 24 (just off the Ku'damm). ☎ **030/882 52 10.** Admission 8DM ($4.55) adults, 4DM ($2.30) students/children. Wed–Mon 11am–6pm. U-Bahn: Uhlandstrasse.

This small but significant museum shows the powerful drawings, sketches, and sculptures of Käthe Kollwitz (1867–1945), a Berliner who managed to capture human emotions both tender and disturbing in her subjects, mostly the working class. War, poverty, death, hunger, love, and happiness are all deftly rendered with just a few strokes. Who can forget Kollwitz's portrayal of horror on the face of a mother whose child has just been run over, or the wonderment expressed by a young mother and her infant gazing into each other's eyes? If you wish to know more about Kollwitz, rent the 3.50DM ($2) audiotape for a 1-hour self-guided tour.

✪ **Zoologischer Garten (Berlin Zoo).** Budapester Strasse 32 and Hardenbergplatz 8. ☎ **030/25 40 10.** Combination ticket for zoo and aquarium, 19DM ($11) adults, 16DM ($9) students, 9.50DM ($5) children; zoo only, 12DM ($7) adults, 10DM ($6) students, 6DM ($3.40) children. Summer daily 9am–6:30pm (to 5pm in winter). S-Bahn/U-Bahn: Zoologischer Garten.

Founded in 1844, the Berlin Zoo is one of Europe's best—and one of my favorites. A short walk from the Ku'damm or Bahnhof Zoo, it's home to more than 11,000 animals of almost 2,000 species and is a beautiful oasis in the middle of the city. The aquarium contains more than 6,000 fish, reptiles, and amphibians.

ORGANIZED TOURS

BY BUS   Sightseeing tours of Berlin and Potsdam are offered by a number of companies, with buses departing from the Ku'damm area. The oldest and largest is **Severin + Kuhn,** Kurfürstendamm 216 (☎ **030/880 41 90**), open daily 9am to 6pm. Most convenient is its 30DM ($17) Berlin City Tour, which provides commentary but also allows you to disembark at 12 stops throughout the city and then reboard the next bus at your convenience. Buses run every hour, with stops at KaDeWe department store, Potsdamer Platz and the Info Box, Berliner Dom and Museumsinsel, the Nikolai Quarter, the Brandenburg Gate, and Charlottenburg Palace. You can remain on the bus for the entire 2-hour circuit.

BY BOAT   If you're in Berlin from April to the end of October, you can climb aboard one of the many pleasure boats plying the Spree River and Havel and Wannsee lakes. **Stern und Kreis** (☎ **030/53 63 60-0**) offers 3½-hour trips along the Spree, with departures at Jannowitzbrücke in Berlin-Mitte (S-Bahn/U-Bahn: Jannowitzbrücke) and Schlossbrücke near Charlottenburg Palace (Bus: 109 to Schlossbrücke), costing 23DM ($13) round-trip. One-hour trips through Berlin-Mitte, departing from the Nikolai Quarter, cost 13.50DM ($8), while 1-hour trips from Wannsee to the Cecilienhof Palace in Potsdam are 10DM ($6). Contact Stern und Kreis or look for its pamphlet at the tourist information office for an updated schedule and more information. Another company, **Reederei Bruno Winkler,** also offers 3-hour boat tours through Berlin-Mitte, with departures from Schlossbrücke near Charlottenburg Palace at 10am and 2:20pm daily and costing 20DM ($11).

BY BIKE   **Fahrradstation/Berlin by Bike** offers 4-hour guided bicycle tours in English daily in warm weather, with a choice of mountain or city bike and costing 25DM ($14). Call ☎ **28 38 48 48** for more information.

6 Shopping

If it exists, you can buy it in Berlin. A look inside **KaDeWe,** the largest department store on the Continent, made a believer out of me. Start your shopping in KaDeWe, on Wittenbergplatz—with an inventory of 250,000 items, it may be as far as you get.

But that would mean you'd miss the **Ku'damm,** around the corner, the showcase of western Berlin's fashionable and elegant boutiques and art galleries. They may be beyond our budget, but window-shopping and people-watching are free. Another street is the pedestrians-only **Wilmersdorfer Strasse,** where you'll find the Karstadt and Hertie department stores in addition to many smaller boutiques and restaurants. **Friedrichstrasse,** in Berlin-Mitte, now rivals the Ku'damm with its expensive boutiques and shops, including the Galeries Lafayette department store.

Typical souvenirs are stuffed toy bears (the city mascot), porcelain freedom bells (fashioned after the Freedom Bell in the Schöneberg Rathaus), fragments of the Wall, toy Trabants (a former East German car, fast disappearing), and the Brandenburg Gate pictured on ashtrays and bowls. Most department stores have a souvenir section, as do the tourist information offices in the Europa-Center and Brandenburg Gate. If kitsch doesn't appeal to you, Germany is known for kitchen gadgets and cutlery, linens, those luxuriously fluffy Federbetten (feather beds), binoculars and telescopes, cameras, and toys (model trains, tin soldiers, building blocks). If you like porcelain, brands to look for are Rosenthal, antique Meissen, and Berlin's own Königliche Porzellan-Manufaktur (better known as KPM)—assuming, of course, you have a Swiss bank account.

RECOVERING VAT

If you purchase more than 60DM ($34) worth of goods from any one store and are taking your purchases out of the country, you're entitled to partial recovery of the **value-added tax (VAT),** which is 16% in Germany. Most stores will issue a Tax Refund Cheque at the time of the purchase. Fill in the reverse side and attach it to the cash receipt. Upon leaving the *last* EU country you visit before heading home, present to Customs the Tax Refund Cheque, the receipt from the store, and the purchased articles. Airports in Berlin, Frankfurt, and other large cities will refund your money immediately. If you're leaving Germany for a non-EU country, ask the Customs official who comes into your train compartment to stamp your check, or if traveling by car, stop at the border Customs office. You can then mail your Tax Refund Cheque back to the country of purchase in a Tax-Free Envelope provided by the store.

MARKETS

Berlin's best buys are found at the many antiques and flea markets. Some are indoors and are held almost daily; others are open just 1 or 2 days a week.

Under the arches of the elevated track, the indoor **Berliner Antikmarkt,** on Georgenstrasse between the Friedrichstrasse S-Bahn station and the Pergamon Museum (☎ **030/208 26 55**), features vendors of antiques and curios, including jewelry, porcelain, glassware, dolls, silver, books, lamps, and odds and ends. Prices are relatively high, but you may find a bargain. If you get thirsty, drop by Zur Nolle, a pub/restaurant decorated 1920s style with outdoor seating. The market is open Wednesday to Monday 11am to 6pm.

A minute's walk east of the Tiergarten S-Bahn station is Berlin's best-known and biggest outdoor market, the **Grosser/Berliner Trödelmarkt und Kunstmarkt (Art and Junk Market),** on Strasse des 17 Juni (☎ **030/322 81 99**). A staggering selection of books, silverware, china, glass, original artwork, jewelry, clothing, and junk is sold at this market divided into two parts, one with arts and crafts, the other with antiques and junk. The market is open Saturday and Sunday 10am to 4pm.

Kreuzberg is home to most of the city's Turkish population, so here you'll find Berlin's most colorful produce market, the **Turkish Market.** Spread along the bank of the Maybachufer Canal, it offers a taste of the exotic, with German and Turkish vendors selling vegetables, sheep's-milk cheese, pita bread, beans, rice, spices, and odds and ends. The market is open Tuesday and Friday noon to 6:30pm; Friday's markets are livelier, with more vendors. Take the U-Bahn to Kottbusser Tor; then it's about a 5-minute walk.

From December 1 to Christmas Eve, a Christmas market called the **Weihnachtsmarkt,** Breitscheidplatz and from Nürnberger Strasse to Joachimstaler Strasse, is held in the inner city radiating from the Gedächtniskirche onto side streets. Christmas decorations, candles, cookies, sausages, and other goodies are sold from colorful booths. (Other Christmas markets are held in Spandau and on Schlossplatz in Berlin-Mitte.) The market is open daily 11am to 9pm. Take the U-Bahn to Kurfürstendamm, Zoologischer Garten, or Wittenbergplatz.

Winterfeldplatz, in Schöneberg, is Berlin's largest weekly market of fruits, vegetables, meat, flowers, clothing, and accessories; it's a 5-minute walk south of the Nollendorfplatz U-Bahn station. The market is open Wednesday and Saturday dawn to 1pm.

7 Berlin After Dark

Berlin never sleeps. There are no mandatory closing hours for nightclubs, dance clubs, and bars, so you can stay out all night if you want. In fact, a native Berliner once told me, "The reason everyone comes to Berlin is its nightlife"—and he was serious.

Nightlife in Berlin means everything from far-out bars and dance clubs to world-renowned opera and theater. To find out what's going on in the performing arts, pick up a copy of *Berlin Programm.* The performance arts are also covered in *Berlin* (a quarterly published in German and English).

THE PERFORMING ARTS

If you don't mind taking a chance on what's available, the best bargain for last-minute tickets is **Hekticket,** with outlets at Hardenbergstrasse 29a, in the Zoo-Palast building between Bahnhof Zoo and the Kaiser Wilhelm Memorial Church (☎ **030/230 99 30**) and at Rathausstrasse 1 on Alexanderplatz (☎ **030/24 31 24 31**). Unsold tickets for that evening's performances are available for more than 100 venues, including the Staatsoper Unter den Linden, Komische Oper, classical concerts, pop concerts, and cabaret, most at up to 50% off. The Hekticket at Alexanderplatz is open daily 4 to 8pm, while the one near Bahnhof Zoo is open Monday to Friday 9am to 10pm, Saturday 10am to 8pm, and Sunday 4 to 8pm. If you wish to know whether tickets for a performance are available, call first or book through the Internet at **www. BerlinOnline.de/HEKTICKET.**

If you have your heart set on a specific performance and don't mind paying a commission, you can find convenient ticket box offices at **Centrum,** Meinekestrasse 25 (☎ **030/882 76 11**), and at **Showtime Konzert und Theaterkassen,** in the KaDeWe department store on Wittenbergplatz (☎ **030/217 77 55**).

Tickets for theater and opera, sometimes with student discounts, are also available during box-office hours and about an hour before the performance starts at the venue itself.

Finally, if you don't mind the risk, you can wait until the day of a performance for the Deutsche Oper Berlin and the Komische Oper, when unsold tickets are available for about 50% off the regular price.

OPERA   The **Deutsche Oper Berlin,** Bismarckstrasse 35, Charlottenburg (☎ **030/343 84-01** for information, or 030/341 02 49 for tickets; U-Bahn: Deutsche Oper), has performances of opera virtually every evening, usually at 7 or 8pm, except when there's ballet. Tickets run 17DM to 142DM ($10 to $81), with a 50% reduction for students and for last-minute tickets; unsold tickets are available on the day of a performance. The box office is open Monday to Saturday 11am to the start of the performance and Sunday 10am to 2pm.

The **Staatsoper Unter den Linden,** Unter den Linden 7, Berlin-Mitte (☎ **030/208 28 61** for information, or 030/20 35 45 55 for tickets; U-Bahn: Friedrichstrasse or Französische Strasse; Bus: 100), has long been one of Berlin's famous opera houses, featuring opera, ballet, and concerts. Tickets go for 12DM to 115DM ($7 to $65), with a 50% reduction for students for tickets bought in advance. The box office is open Monday to Friday 10am to 6pm and Saturday and Sunday 2 to 6pm; performances are usually at 7pm.

The **Komische Oper (Comic Opera),** Behrenstrasse 55–57, Berlin-Mitte (☎ **030/202 60-360;** S-Bahn: Unter den Linden; U-Bahn: Französische Strasse; Bus: 100), an innovative opera company in eastern Berlin, serves as an alternative to the grander, more mainstream productions of the two other opera houses, presenting a varied program of opera, operetta, symphony concerts, ballet, and even modern dance. Tickets cost 15DM to 108DM ($9 to $62), with unsold tickets for that evening's performance available from 11am for 50% off. The box office, at Unter den Linden 41, is open Monday to Saturday 11am to 7pm and Sunday 1pm to 90 minutes before the performance begins (usually at 7 or 7:30pm).

THEATER   Popular productions, musicals, and spirited revues are presented in the turn-of-the-century **Theater des Westens,** Kantstrasse 12 (near the Ku'damm), Charlottenburg (☎ **030/882 28 88;** S-Bahn/U-Bahn: Zoologischer Garten). Tickets cost 19DM to 59DM ($11 to $34) Friday and Saturday and 17DM to 54DM ($10 to $31) Tuesday to Thursday and Sunday. The box office is open Tuesday to Saturday noon to 7pm and Sunday 2 to 5pm; performances are at 8pm.

International musicals like *West Side Story* are presented at the **Schiller Theater,** Bismarckstrasse 110, Charlottenburg (☎ **030/31 11 31 11;** U-Bahn: Ernst-Reuter-Platz), with the cost of tickets varying with productions. The box office is open daily from 10am.

CLASSICAL & CHURCH MUSIC   Performances of the world-renowned Berliner Philharmoniker (Berlin Philharmonic Orchestra), founded in 1882 and now under the direction of Claudio Abbado, and the Berlin Symphonic Orchestra, founded in 1952 in the former East Germany, take place at the **Philharmonie** in the Kulturforum, Matthaikirchstrasse 1 (☎ **030/254 88-0**). Tickets begin at 15DM ($9), but tickets for the Berlin Philharmonic usually sell out months in advance. The box office is open Monday to Friday 3:30 to 6pm and Saturday, Sunday, and holidays 11am to 2pm. Performances are usually at 8pm, with a matinee on Sunday. You can get to the hall on bus no. 142 or 148.

One of the least expensive places to hear music is a church. The **Berliner Dom** on Museum Island in Berlin-Mitte features organ, choir, and instrumental classical music concerts most weekends, usually on Saturday at 6pm. Prices for these range from 6DM to 16DM ($3.40 to $9). Call ☎ **030/202 69 136** for more information.

The **Kaiser-Wilhelm Gedächtniskirche** on Breitscheidplatz, off the Ku'damm, stages free organ concerts and cantatas in its new addition most Saturdays at 6pm, as well as choirs, soloists, and other performances throughout the month. Pick up the brochure listing the month's performances at the church or call ☎ **030/218 50 23.** You can pick up another brochure here called *Musik in Evangelischen Kirchen* listing concerts in Evangelical churches throughout Berlin, including organ concerts, choirs, cantatas, and classical music, much of it free.

LIVE-MUSIC HOUSES A-Trane, Bleibtreustrasse 1 (on the corner of Bleibtreustrasse and Pestalozzistrasse), Charlottenburg (☎ **030/313 25 50;** S-Bahn: Savignyplatz), is a small but classy venue with local and international jazz nightly beginning at 10pm, with doors opening at 9pm. Cover is usually 10DM to 20DM ($6 to $11) Wednesday to Saturday; students get a 5DM ($2.85) reduction. On Sunday to Tuesday there are free jam sessions; in addition, there are free jam sessions Friday and Saturday after the concerts, usually around 12:30am.

Ewige Lampe, Niebuhrstrasse 11a (entrance on Leibnizstrasse), Charlottenburg (☎ **030/324 39 18;** S-Bahn: Savignyplatz), is a casual jazz bar with bands primarily from the United States, Germany, and Holland, and it can get crowded. Either buy your ticket in advance or get there early. It's open Wednesday to Sunday 8pm to 2am, with live music from 9pm. The cover is usually 10DM ($6), sometimes up to 20DM ($11) for big names.

In the historic Opernpalais just a stone's throw from the Staatsoper, Unter den Linden, and Museum Island, **Opernschänke,** Unter den Linden 5 (☎ **030/20 26 83;** Bus: 100 to Staatsoper), is a remake of a 1920s Berlin saloon with live music Wednesday to Saturday (Friday and Saturday in winter) 6pm to 1am, featuring jazz, swing dance, oldies, pop, and mixed music. It's popular with an older crowd and there's no cover. On Sunday, there's a brunch with live jazz from 11am to 2pm, costing 39DM ($22) and including a glass of champagne.

Dwarfed by the large Theater des Westens next to it, **Quasimodo,** Kantstrasse 12a, Charlottenburg (☎ **030/312 80 86;** U-Bahn: Zoologischer Garten), features top-notch contemporary jazz and rock groups in an intimate setting. It's open daily from 9pm, and concerts usually begin around 10pm. Cover is 10DM to 25DM ($6 to $14), depending on the band.

PUBS & BARS

AROUND THE KU'DAMM & SAVIGNYPLATZ Aschinger, Kurfürstendamm 26 (☎ **030/882 55 58;** U-Bahn: Kurfürstendamm), is one of the most civilized places to go for a beer on the Ku'damm. A basement place with vaulted cellar rooms and subdued lighting, it's actually a brewery, featuring everything from its dark and heavy "bock bier" to a lighter and more thirst-quenching pilsner. German food is also available, either from its buffet or a menu. It's open daily 11am to 1am.

Joe's Bierhaus, Hardenbergstrasse 29, between the Gedächtniskirche and Bahnhof Zoo (☎ **030/262 10 20;** U-Bahn: Zoologischer Garten or Kurfürstendamm), draws an international crowd of visitors with its various venues and convenient location. Best is the outdoor beer garden in summer, but even the interior is ingeniously constructed to resemble a beer garden. Thursday is karaoke night, for which there's a 10DM ($6) cover. There's also a 10DM cover Friday and Saturday, when there's live music and dancing beginning at 9pm. Hearty platters of German food are served for 10DM to 20DM ($6 to $11). It's open Sunday to Wednesday 10am to 2am and Thursday to Sunday 10am to 5am; closed Monday and Tuesday in February.

Named for the antiques and curio market that was once here, **Zillemarkt,** Bleibtreustrasse 48a (☎ **030/881 70 40;** S-Bahn: Savignyplatz), dates from the turn of the century and features a brick floor and fancy grillwork, but best is the backyard patio in summer. A good place for an evening drink, as well as breakfast or Sunday brunch, it's open daily 10am to midnight. **Zwiebelfisch,** Savignyplatz 7–8 (☎ **030/31 73 63; S-Bahn: Savignyplatz**), is a neighborhood bar that's been around for more than 25 years and still enjoys great popularity, in large part because of its fiercely loyal crowd. It's open daily noon to 6am, and because it stays open later than other bars in the area, it's where everyone ends up and can be packed at 4am.

IN KREUZBERG   Kreuzberg has long been the center of Berlin's avant-garde and alternative scene (though in recent years Oranienburger Strasse in Berlin-Mitte has stolen the spotlight). **Madonna,** Wiener Strasse 22 (☎ **030/611 69 43;** U-Bahn: Görlitzer Bahnhof; Bus: 129), is one of Kreuzberg's best-known and longest-running bars, and it seems that anyone familiar with Berlin's bar scene has either been here or heard of it. Though the singer Madonna may first come to mind, its namesake is the other one, present in a ceiling fresco (in which God is a she) and several religious and sacrilegious statues. If you want to dress like everyone else, wear denim or leather. It's open Sunday to Thursday 1pm to 3am and Friday and Saturday noon to 4am.

Morena, Wiener Strasse 60 (☎ **030/611 47 16;** U-Bahn: Görlitzer Bahnhof; Bus: 129), seems to be the watering hole for the hippest avant-garde, where hairstyles range from dreadlocks to bleached long hair to no hair, and nose studs are so common they're almost passé. Across from Madonna (see above), this place is crowded even during the day, especially in nice weather, when you can sit outside. It's open daily 9am to 5am. There are several other bars on Wiener Strasse, including the more radical **Wiener Blut** and the more upscale **Advena** and **Hannibal.**

IN BERLIN-MITTE   Though the trip to the top (8DM/$4.55 adults, 4DM/$2.30 children) is expensive, the **Fernsehturm** on Alexanderplatz is my pick for both the best bird's-eye view of Berlin and a romantic early evening drink. Get there just before the sun goes down, strolling around the observation platform and viewing with amazement the sea of cranes throughout Berlin-Mitte before heading up the stairs to the revolving **Telecafe** (☎ **030/242 33 33**), 650 feet high. Its 30 minutes for a complete spin is a bit dizzying, but what a great view as the city lights begin to twinkle. It's open daily 10am to midnight.

Not far from Alexanderplatz, on the banks of the Spree in the heart of the Nikolai Quarter, **Georg Bräu,** Spreeufer 4 (☎ **030/242 42 44;** S-Bahn/U-Bahn: Alexanderplatz), has spacious indoor seating and outdoor tables. As with most microbreweries, beer is served only in small fifth-of-a-liter glasses to keep it fresh. If that's too much of a bother, for 28.20DM ($16) you can order the 1-meter-long "Georg-Pils," a board with 12 small glasses. German food is served, like boulette, cabbage rolls, kasslerbraten, and schnitzel. It's open Monday to Friday noon to midnight and Saturday and Sunday 10am to midnight. Nearby is **Zum Nussbaum,** Am Nussbaum 3 (☎ **030/242 30 95**), my favorite bar in the Nikolai Quarter—small, cozy, and comfortable, modeled after a bar built in 1507 but destroyed in World War II. There are a few tables outside, where you have a view of the Nikolai Church, and the limited German menu offers würste, boulette, Berliner eisbein, and other local favorites at reasonable prices. It's open daily noon to 2am.

Tacheles, Oranienburger Strasse 53–54 (☎ **030/282 61 85;** S-Bahn: Oranienburger Strasse), has such an alternative identity that for several years it didn't have a phone or a sign outside and didn't seem likely to make it through. No wonder: The building is a bombed-out department store, famous for its extreme state of disrepair and taken over in 1990 by squatting artists who've transformed it into studio/gallery/living space. On the ground floor is **Zapata,** a cafe where characters from *Star Wars* would feel right at home, open daily 10am to about 4am or later (from noon in winter). In summer, you can sit on the patio out back. There are numerous other bars on Oranienburger Strasse, but this place is a good start.

Not far from Oranienburger Strasse, in the direction of Alexanderplatz, is a new complex called **Die Hackeschen Höfe,** a series of courtyards constructed to resemble turn-of-the-century Berlin tenements (the rich lived in the first building facing the street; poorer families were relegated to inner-courtyard flats). In addition to galleries, a cinema, boutiques, and cafes, there's **Oxymoron,** in the first courtyard of the Die Hackeschen Höfe, Rosenthaler Strasse 40 (☎ 030/283 91 88-5; S-Bahn: Hackescher Markt). With a drawing-room ambiance reminiscent of Old Berlin, it's open daily 11am to at least 2am; an adjoining club stages various happenings and events, from "gangster" nights to dancing and jazz.

GAY & LESBIAN BARS

The well-known gay bar **Andreas Kneipe,** Ansbacher Strasse 29 (☎ 030/218 32 57; U-Bahn: Wittenbergplatz), has been in Berlin for more than a quarter of a century. It's popular for both its location off Wittenbergplatz and its laid-back atmosphere. Almost anyone—including women and straight couples—can feel comfortable among the mostly gay crowd. It's open daily 11am to 4am. Andreas Kneipe makes a great starting place for gays.

Motzstrasse seems to be the center of many gay and lesbian bars. The **Knast Bar,** Fuggerstrasse 34 (☎ 030/218 10 26; U-Bahn: Wittenbergplatz), is Berlin's leading leather bar. There's no cover, and it's open daily 9pm to dawn. The **Begine Kulturzentrum für Frauen,** Potsdamerstrasse 139 (☎ 030/215 43 25; U-Bahn: Bülowstrasse; Bus: 19 or 48), is Berlin's most visible headquarters for feminists and a great launching pad for lesbians. It's open daily 6pm to 1am.

DANCE CLUBS & DANCE HALLS

Big Eden, Kurfürstendamm 202, Charlottenburg (☎ 030/882 61 20; U-Bahn: Uhlandstrasse), has been here for more than 35 years and has a strict front-door policy that won't admit anyone who even looks as if he or she is drunk. It attracts young people of every nationality with a large dance floor, pool tables, and video and pinball games and is open Sunday to Thursday 9pm to 4am, Friday 8pm to 5am, and Saturday 8pm to 6am. There's no cover Sunday to Thursday or Friday and Saturday 8 to 9pm, though there's a 5DM ($2.85) drink minimum. Otherwise, from 9pm Friday and Saturday there's a cover of 12DM ($7), 2DM ($1.15) of which goes toward the first drink.

About a 15-minute walk from the Ku'damm, **Cafe Keese Ball Paradox,** Bismarckstrasse 108 (near the Schiller Theater), Charlottenburg (☎ 030/312 91 11; U-Bahn: Ernst-Reuter-Platz), is a large dance hall popular with those over 35, but with a difference—here it's always the women who ask the men to dance (except for the hourly "Men's Choice," when the green light goes on). There are phones on each table to make the asking easier, and house rules state that while men aren't allowed to refuse a dance, women may, unless they're presented with a rose. A live band plays most evenings; Sunday and Monday feature music of the 1960s and 1970s, Tuesday is disco night, Wednesday is Astro Ball (in which dancers are paired according to their zodiac sign), Thursday is singles night, and Friday and Saturday feature hits of today. No jeans or tennis shoes are allowed; most men are in coat and tie, and women are dressed up. It's open Sunday and Monday 3pm to 1am, Tuesday to Thursday 8pm to 3am, and Friday and Saturday 8pm to 4am. Admission is free, but on Friday and Saturday there's a two-drink minimum.

Catering to a slightly more sophisticated crowd than Big Eden (see above), **Far Out,** Kurfürstendamm 156 (☎ **030/320 00 717;** U-Bahn: Adenauerplatz), is modern, spacious, and laid-back, featuring rock from the 1970s to the 1990s. It features a no-smoking night on Tuesday, and Wednesday's "Forever Young" event attracts an over-30 crowd, who get in free. If you want to see it at its roaring best, don't even think about showing up before midnight. It's toward the western end of the Ku'damm, on the side street between the Ciao Ciao restaurant and the Schaubühne am Lehniner Platz theater, open Tuesday to Thursday and Sunday 10pm to 4am and Friday and Saturday 10pm to 6am. Cover is 6DM ($3.40) Tuesday and Wednesday (free for those 30 and older on Wednesday), 8DM ($4.55) Thursday and Sunday, and 10DM ($6) Friday and Saturday.

Metropol, Nollendorfplatz 5 (☎ **030/217 36 80;** U-Bahn: Nollendorfplatz), is hard to miss—a colossal building converted from a former theater. Very popular, on weekends it features a giant-size disco with all kinds of technical gags, including a laser show. There are also live concerts through the week. It's open for dancing Friday, Saturday, and nights before holidays 9pm to 6am. Cover is 20DM ($11).

8 Side Trips: Potsdam & the Spreewald

POTSDAM

If you take only one excursion outside Berlin, it should be to **Potsdam,** only 15 miles southwest. Potsdam was once Germany's most important Baroque town, serving as both a garrison and as a residence of Prussia's kings and royal families from the 17th to 20th centuries. Its most famous resident was Frederick the Great, who succeeded in uniting Germany under his rule and who built himself the delightful rococo palace Schloss Sanssouci ("without care"), which he used as a place for quiet meditation, away from the rigors of war and government. His palace still stands, surrounded by a 750-acre estate, Park Sanssouci, with several other magnificent structures, including the Neues Palais.

ARRIVING   To reach Potsdam, take **S-Bahn 7** directly from Berlin to the Potsdam-Stadt station; the trip takes about 30 minutes and costs 3.90DM ($2.20). From Potsdam-Stadt station, you can then board **bus no. 695** directly for Schloss Sanssouci or Neues Palais. Otherwise, for the most dramatic approach to the palace, take **tram no. 96 or 98** from Potsdam-Stadt station to Luisenplatz, from which it's a 10-minute walk through Sanssouci Park. Or if you'd like to see some of the city, you can **walk** to Sanssouci from the Potsdam-Stadt station in about an hour, passing through the historic town center along the way, centered on Brandenburger Strasse.

VISITOR INFORMATION   Stop by **Potsdam Information,** on Friedrich-Ebert-Strasse 5, about a 5-minute walk from Potsdam-Stadt station (☎ **0331/275 58-0**), open Monday to Friday 10am to 6pm and Saturday and Sunday 10am to 2pm. Information on Schloss Sanssouci and Sanssouci Park can be obtained from the **Sanssouci Visitor Center,** located near Schloss Sanssouci on An der Orangerie across from the windmill (☎ **0331/96 94 202**). It's open daily: March to October 8:30am to 5pm and November to February 9am to 4pm.

SEEING THE SIGHTS   Potsdam's most famous attraction is ✪ **Schloss Sanssouci,** Zur Historischen Mühle (☎ **0331/96 94-202** or 0331/96 94-190). Built in the 1740s by Georg von Knobbelsdorff, it served as Frederick the Great's summer residence for almost 40 years (he died here and is buried on the grounds). With only a dozen rooms, the one-story palace is exceedingly modest compared to most royal palaces, yet its rooms are a delight, filled with paintings, marble, and gold leaf, with playful motifs of grapes, wine, and images of Bacchus. Don't miss the most dramatic view of the palace—from its park side, it sits atop six grassy terraces, cut into the side of a hill like steps in a pyramid, created for Frederick the Great's vineyards.

Schloss Sanssouci can be visited only by joining a 40-minute guided tour, conducted only in German and departing every 20 minutes. The cost of the tour is 10DM ($6) adults and 5DM ($2.85) students/children. Schloss Sanssouci is open Tuesday to Sunday: April to October 9am to 5pm and November to March 9am to 4pm.

At the other end of Sanssouci Park, about a 25-minute walk away, is the estate's largest building, the **Neues Palais** (☎ **0331/96 94-255**), built 20 years after Schloss Sanssouci as a show of Prussian strength following the devastation of the Seven Years' War. Also serving as a summer residence for the royal Hohenzollern family, it's much more ostentatious than Schloss Sanssouci and in comparison seems grave, solemn, and humorless. Of note is the Grotto Room, its walls and ceiling smothered with shells, mica, minerals, fossils, and semiprecious stones. The Neues Palais is open Saturday to Thursday: April to October 9am to 5pm and November to March 9am to 4pm. From November to March, you can see it only by taking a 1-hour guided tour in German, costing 8DM ($4.55) adults and 4DM ($2.30) students/children. The rest of the year, you can see it on your own, costing 6DM ($3.40) and 3DM ($1.70), respectively.

If there are two of you and you plan to see both Schloss Sanssouci and Neues Palais, buy the 25DM ($14) *Familienkarte,* allowing two adults and their children to visit all of Potsdam's palace on a given day.

DINING   Until the Historische Mühle reopens across from Schloss Sanssouci (perhaps in 1999), the best place for a meal in the vicinity of Sanssouci Park is **Drachenhaus,** Maulbeerallee (☎ **0331/29 15 94;** Bus: 695 to Drachenhaus), about halfway between Schloss Sanssouci and Neues Palais. In the form of a Chinese pagoda and perched on the top of a hill, it was built in 1770 as living quarters of the royal vintner. In summer, tables are spread out under the trees. Its limited menu lists chicken and pork dishes from 10.50DM to 23.50DM ($6 to $13), as well as cakes and tortes. No credit cards are accepted. It's open daily: 11am to 7pm in summer and 11am to 6pm in winter.

In town, there's **Contadino,** Luisenplatz 8 (☎ **0331/95 10 923;** Tram: 96 or 98 to Luisenplatz), across the parking lot from Potsdam's own Brandenburger Tor. It offers a large variety of pasta and pizza, all priced below 12DM ($7). No credit cards are accepted, and it's open daily 11am to 1am.

THE SPREEWALD

The **Spreewald** is one of middle Europe's most unique landscapes, formed where the Spree River spreads out into countless streams and canals, a labyrinth of waterways through woodlands. For centuries, transportation through the bayou has been via narrow barges and punts. Today, the most popular thing to do is take a boat ride through this watery wonderland. **Lübbenau,** in the upper Spreewald, is a convenient starting point for 3-hour boat rides through the region, offered daily in good weather from April to the end of October at 9.50DM ($5) adults and 4.50DM ($2.55) children.

To reach Lübbenau, take the **train** from Berlin-Lichtenberg station. Trains depart approximately hourly and cost 17DM ($10) for the 1-hour trip. From Lübbenau train station, it's about a 20-minute **walk** to the town's boat harbor. For more information, contact the **Lübbenau Spreewald information office** at Ehm-Welk-Strasse 15 (☎ **03542/36 68**), open daily in summer 9am to 6pm and in winter Monday to Friday 9am to 4pm.

Brussels & Bruges 8

by Jeanne Oliver

In many ways, Brussels is the city that best symbolizes Europe's struggle toward integration. After centuries of occupation by a series of empires (Spanish, French, Austrian) whose power struggles tore Europe apart, the city now hosts the bureaucratic empire trying to unite Europe. As headquarters for the European Union, NATO, and scores of other organizations, Brussels has become a bastion of officialdom—a hatchery for the regulations that govern and often annoy the rest of Europe.

The Bruxellois are more than a little ambivalent about the city's transformation into a power center. At first, the waves of Eurocrats seemed to bring a new cosmopolitanism to the slightly provincial city, but as some of the oldest neighborhoods were leveled to make way for office towers, people wondered whether Brussels was losing its soul. After all, Brussels isn't all business. This is the city that inspired surrealism and worships comic strips, prides itself on handmade lace and chocolate, and serves each kind of artisanal beer in its own unique glass.

Fortunately, not all of Brussels's individuality has been lost. Though the urban landscape has suffered badly from wanton overbuilding, the city's spirit survives in its many traditional cafes, bars, bistros, and restaurants. Whether elegantly art nouveau or eccentrically festooned with posters and knickknacks, these centuries-old places provide a convivial ambiance the Flemish call *gezellig*.

The imaginatively decorated interiors also reflect the importance of culinary pleasure. The two populations that make up the city—Dutch-speaking Flemish (20%) and French-speaking Walloons (80%)—may have their differences, but they both value a good meal. From crisp "french fries" and waffles on the street corner to succulent Flemish and Walloon specialties, it's hard to eat badly in Brussels.

REQUIRED DOCUMENTS Americans, Canadians, Australians, and New Zealanders need just a valid passport to enter Belgium. U.K. travelers need only an identity card.

OTHER FROMMER'S TITLES For more on Brussels, see *Frommer's Belgium, Holland & Luxembourg* or *Frommer's Europe*.

1   Brussels Deals & Discounts

SPECIAL DISCOUNTS

FOR EVERYONE   On Friday to Sunday night throughout the year and every day in July and August, many first-class hotels rent their **rooms at discounts** from 30% to 70% in order to fill vacancies. You can book these discounts through Belgium Tourist Reservations (see "Visitor Information" later in this chapter).

If you plan to visit many of Brussels's attractions that charge admission (most museums are free), you might want to buy a **Tourist Passport** for 300BF ($9). It includes a restaurant guide; a 24-hour bus, tram, and subway pass and transit map; and discounts at several top attractions, like the Atomium, Mini-Europe, the Comic Strip Museum, the Horta Museum, and Autoworld.

FOR STUDENTS   Students can get half-price tickets to many cultural events, as well as discounts on train and plane fares and certain tours. **Acotra,** 51 rue de la Madeleine, 1000 Bruxelles (☎ **02/512-86-07**), sells discount student train, plane, boat, and bus tickets and books places in youth hostels and private rooms. It also sells the ISIC (International Student Identity Card). Across a small park from Gare Centrale, toward the Grand' Place, it's open Monday to Friday 10am to 5:30pm.

FOR SENIORS   Select cultural arenas and museums offer discounts. See "Seeing the Sights" for details on museums with reduced senior admission.

WORTH A SPLURGE

Brussels is known for its fine dining and superb array of beer. Try to splurge on an **excellent meal** and an evening in one of the city's atmospheric **beer halls.** The view over the **Grand' Place** is stunning, and you can enjoy it from one of the former guild houses on the periphery that have been transformed into cafes.

2   Essentials

ARRIVING

BY PLANE   The completely renovated **Brussels National Airport** at Zaventem is just under 8 miles from the city center. A convenient 20-minute shuttle-train service connects first with Gare du Nord and then with Gare Centrale every 20 minutes from 5:35am to 11:10pm. Second class is 90BF ($3) and first class is 135BF ($4). Buy your tickets at the window near the entrance to the platforms. A taxi from the airport to the city center costs about 1,200BF ($38).

BY TRAIN   Brussels has three major train stations (as well as several smaller ones), but you should try to arrive at **Gare Centrale (Central Station),** as it's in the best neighborhood. Trains leave from Gare Centrale back to the airport three times per hour starting at 5:39am and ending at 11:14pm.

If you're staying near the Grand' Place, your hotel may be within walking distance of Gare Centrale. To reach the Grand' Place from the station, head toward the tower of the Town Hall, a few blocks away. If you're going elsewhere, you can connect to the Métro. When you arrive at Gare Centrale, climb the stairs to the main hall and look for signs to the Métro (a white M on a blue background).

To catch the Métro from **Gare du Nord (North Station),** go to the area adjacent to the central ticket halls. If you prefer a 20-minute stroll into town, follow the sign reading CENTRE, which leads you through a block-long elevated pedestrian walkway and then points you toward town.

Best Bets

You can enjoy Brussels's greatest masterpiece, the **Grand' Place,** for free, and you can see a wide variety of events there—from the summer Music and Light shows to the Sunday bird market—without ever reaching for your wallet.

The many **markets** are a source of free amusement, as are the **state museums,** like the Musées Royaux des Beaux-Arts and the Musée Instrumental. The city's **cafes** are a true bargain, for they allow you to spend hours lingering over just one drink and enjoying the marvelous art nouveau decor and the company of the Bruxellois. Belgium's excellent beers are moderately priced and widely available. Further, the superb **Belgian** *frites* (which we mistakenly call french fries) sold on the street cost only 50BF to 65BF ($1.55 to $2.05)—try them with mayonnaise as the locals do.

Because one of Brussels's worst neighborhoods surrounds **Gare du Midi (South Station),** it's usually best to arrive at one of the other stations. Yet you may find it useful to get off here to catch a direct Métro to the east side ("upper Brussels"), site of several budget hotels. You catch the Métro from the station exit; ask to make sure you're heading the right way. Part of the station includes the terminal for the Eurostar Chunnel train that connects with London (3½ hours).

VISITOR INFORMATION

TIB (Tourist Information Brussels), on the ground floor of the Hôtel de Ville de Bruxelles (Town Hall), Grand' Place (☎ **02/513-89-40;** fax 02/514-45-38; Métro: Gare Centrale), answers questions, gives out the entertainment guide *What's On,* and sells the *Brussels Guide and Map* for 100BF ($3.10). Its staff can reserve you a room for free or reserve concert/theater tickets for 35BF ($1.10). In addition, you can buy tram, Métro, and bus tickets here. March to September, the office is open daily 9am to 6pm (October and November, Sunday hours are 10am to 2pm; December to February, it's closed Sunday).

The **Tourist Information Office,** 63 rue du Marché-aux-Herbes (☎ **02/504-03-90;** fax 02/504-02-70; Métro: Gare Centrale), stocks a wide variety of brochures and reserves hotel rooms in Brussels as well as in the rest of Belgium without a fee, though it does require a deposit (which varies with the room rates). This is the place to go before planning side trips. A block from the Grand' Place, the office is open as follows: June to September, daily 9am to 7pm; April, May, and October, daily 9am to 6pm; and November to March, Monday to Saturday 9am to 6pm and Sunday 1 to 5pm. It publishes an annual *Hotel Guide* with listings by price range and also provides complete information on hostels in Brussels.

You can also contact **Belgium Tourist Reservations,** 111 bd. Anspach (☎ **02/513-74-84;** fax 02/513-92-77; Métro: Bourse), which reserves hotel rooms throughout Belgium and can often obtain substantial discounts. Hotels with unsold rooms will often sell them through this office well below the advertised prices. You'll find the best deals at the last minute, on weekends and in vacation periods, but the service is worth a try no matter when you come to Belgium.

Finally, the **Hotel Reservation Service** (☎ and fax **02/513-82-52;** Métro: Gare Central), in the Gare Centrale, will reserve rooms in one- to five-star hotels for a flat fee of 75BF ($2.35) per party in Brussels or 150BF ($4.70) in other European countries. Open daily 10am to 9pm, it's a private firm staffed with English-speaking hostesses.

What Things Cost in Brussels	U.S. $
Taxi from the airport to the city center	38.00
Métro from train station to outlying neighborhood	1.50
Local telephone call	.36
Double room at the Hôtel Pacific (budget)	53.10
Lunch for one at Taverne Falstaff (moderate)	10.60
Lunch for one at Swiss Sandwich Bar (budget)	3.65
Dinner for one, without wine, at Chez Léon (moderate)	18.20
Dinner for one, without wine, at Au Trappiste (budget)	11.80
Glass of beer	1.90
Coca-Cola in a cafe	1.60
Cup of coffee in a cafe	1.80
Roll of ASA 100 color film, 36 exposures	5.80
Admission to Museum of Lace	2.50
Movie ticket	7.55
Opera ticket	9.00–96.00

CITY LAYOUT

The city center's small cobblestone streets are clustered around the magnificent **Grand' Place.** Two of the most traveled lanes nearby are the restaurant-lined **rue des Bouchers** and **petite rue des Bouchers.** A block from the Grand' Place is the classical colonnaded **La Bourse** (stock exchange), which is also a nightlife center. A few blocks north is the National Opera on **place de la Monnaie** (named after the mint that once stood there). Brussels's busiest shopping street, **rue Neuve,** starts from this square and runs north for several blocks.

The city's uptown, though to the southeast of the center, is literally atop a hill. Here you'll find the second great square, **place du Grand-Sablon,** as well as the Royal Museums of Fine Arts and the Royal Palace. If you head southwest and cross boulevard de Waterloo, you'll come to **place Louise.** A chic shopping street, **avenue Louise,** extends south from the square and a slightly less chic shopping street, **avenue de la Toison d'Or,** runs northeast. They're surrounded by attractive side streets boasting typical Belgian architecture. East of avenue Louise and south of avenue de la Toison d'Or is **Ixelles.** Near the university, this neighborhood has numerous inexpensive restaurants, bars, and cafes. Northeast of Ixelles is the modern European Union district surrounding **place Schuman.**

To make navigating challenging, maps list street names in both French and Dutch. For consistency and ease, I've used the French names in this chapter, and in mailing addresses I've used the French name of the town itself—Bruxelles.

GETTING AROUND

You'll find no better way to explore the historic core of the town than on foot, especially around the Grand' Place. You'll also enjoy strolling uptown around place du Grand-Sablon.

BY METRO   Brussels's pleasant Métro system consists of three major lines in the center, spruced up with art and music in many stations. There are stops at the three major train stations; other important stations are Bourse, the stock exchange; place de Brouckère, near the Opera House and the start of the rue Neuve pedestrian street; Rogier, at the other end of rue Neuve; and place Louise, near the Palais de Justice and avenue Louise.

Rides cost 50BF ($1.55) and allow transfers onto all modes of transport for 1 hour. You can also buy a 1-day pass for 130BF ($4), a 5-ticket card for 240BF ($8), or a 10-ticket card for 320BF ($10). The Métro runs daily 6am to midnight. Signs showing a white M surrounded by blue indicate the stations. Keep an eye on your wallet or purse.

BY BUS & TRAM   A web of buses and trams services areas where the Métro doesn't go. If the stop says SUR DEMANDE, you must flag down the bus. Fares are the same as on the Métro. Make sure to watch your wallet or purse.

BY BICYCLE   Because of the many hills in Brussels and its aggressive car drivers, few locals get around by bicycle. However, if you want to rent a bike, try **Pro Velo,** 32A rue Ernest–Solvay (☎ 02/502-73-55; Métro: Porte de Namur), open daily 8am to 8pm. Rental is 200BF ($6) per day.

BY TAXI   The fare starts at 95BF ($2.95) during the day and 170BF ($5.30) at night, increasing by 38BF ($1.20) per kilometer inside the city or 76BF ($2.35) per kilometer outside. A typical fare from one point to another in the center costs 200BF to 350BF ($6 to $11).

BY RENTAL CAR   Brussels's proximity to the rest of the country, as well as to France, Germany, and Holland, makes a car an attractive option for continuing on. All the top U.S. firms rent here—including Hertz, Avis, and Budget. Note that car rentals are taxed 21% in Belgium. The smallest car at **ABC Rent a Car,** 133 rue d'Anderlecht (☎ 02/513-19-54), is 1,500BF ($47) per day, unlimited mileage and tax included.

FAST FACTS: Brussels

American Express   The office at 2 place Louise, 1050 Bruxelles (☎ 02/676-27-30; Métro: Place Louise), is open Monday to Friday 9am to 5pm and Saturday 9:30am to noon. There's an ATM outside. You can receive mail here free if you've bought American Express traveler's checks or have an American Express card. Otherwise, a small fee will be imposed.

Baby-sitters   Contact **ULB,** 50 av. Franklin-Roosevelt (☎ 02/650-21-71; Métro: Beaulieu), which charges about 280BF ($8.75) per hour. Some of the sitters speak English.

Banks   There are several banks around the Grand' Place and La Bourse, including **Crédit Générale Bank,** 5 Grand' Place (☎ 02/547-11-29), open Monday to Friday 8:45am to 4:30pm; and **Kreditbank,** 17 Grand' Place (☎ 02/517-41-11), open Monday to Thursday 9am to 4:30pm and Friday 9am to 5:15pm.

Business Hours   Most **stores** are open Monday to Saturday 10am to 6 or 7pm; some larger stores stay open Friday to 8 or 9pm. **Post offices** are open Monday to Friday 9am to 5pm. **Banks** generally are open Monday to Thursday 9am to 4:30pm and Friday 9am to 5pm.

Consulates   Brussels has consulates of a number of countries, including the **United States,** 25 bd. du Régent (☎ 02/513-38-30; Métro: Arts–Loi); **Canada,** 2 av. Tervueren (☎ 02/741-06-11; Métro: Merode); the **United Kingdom,** 85

The Belgian Franc

For American Readers At this writing, $1 = approximately 32BF (or 1BF = 3¢), and this was the rate of exchange used to calculate the dollar values given in this chapter (rounded to the nearest dollar if greater than $5).

For British Readers At this writing, £1 = approximately 57BF (or 1BF = 2p), and this was the rate of exchange used to calculate the pound values in the table below.

Note: Exchange rates fluctuate from time to time and may not be the same when you travel to Belgium.

BF	U.S.$	U.K.£	BF	U.S.$	U.K.£
5	.15	.09	300	9.35	5.26
10	.32	.17	400	12.5	7.01
50	1.55	.87	500	15.60	8.77
75	2.35	1.31	1,000	31.25	17.54
100	3.20	1.75	1,500	46.90	26.31
150	4.70	2.63	2,000	62.50	35.08
200	6.25	3.50	2,500	78.10	43.85
250	7.80	4.38	3,000	93.75	52.63

rue Arlon (☎ **02/287-62-11;** Métro: Maalbeek); **Australia,** 6 rue Guimard (☎ **02/286-05-00;** Métro; Arts–Loi); **New Zealand,** 47 bd. du Régent (☎ **02/512-10-40;** Métro: Arts–Loi); and **Ireland,** 19 rue Luxembourg (☎ **02/513-66-33**; Métro: Trone).

Currency The Belgian currency is the **Belgian franc (BF),** made up of 100 centimes. Coins come in 50 centimes and 1BF, 5BF, 20BF, and 50BF; bills are denominated in 100BF, 500BF, 1,000BF, and 10,000BF.

Currency Exchange Most banks charge a 150BF ($4.70) commission on traveler's checks and none on cash. Currency exchange offices charge a lower commission (or none at all) but give a lower rate per dollar. If you're changing a small amount, you may save at an exchange office, but for several hundred dollars or more you'll do best at a bank. The best exchange rate is available to Cirrus or Plus cardholders.

Emergencies If you need a doctor, dial ☎ **02/513-02-02.** If you need a dentist, dial ☎ **02/426-10-26** or **02/428-58-88** (evenings and weekends only). For the **police,** dial ☎ **100** or **101.** For an **ambulance** or in case of a **fire,** dial ☎ **100.**

Holidays The following are official holidays: New Year's Day (January 1), Easter Monday, Labor Day (May 1), Ascension (sixth Thursday after Easter), Whit Monday (seventh Monday after Easter), National Day (July 21), Feast of the Assumption (August 15), All Saints Day (November 1), Armistice Day (November 11), and Christmas (December 25).

Hospitals If you need a hospital, contact **Cliniques Universitaires St-Luc,** 10 av. Hippocrate (☎ **02/764-11-11;** Métro: Alma).

Laundry & Dry Cleaning The most popular chain is **Ipsomat,** with numerous branches open daily 7am to 10pm. There's a branch at 193 rue Blaes

Country & City Codes

The **country code** for Belgium is **32**. The **city code** for Brussels is **2**; use this code when you're calling from outside Belgium. If you're within Belgium but not in Brussels, use **02**. If you're calling within Brussels, simply leave off the code and dial only the regular phone number.

(☎ **02/512-61-71**; Métro: Louise), but check the phone book for the branch nearest your hotel. The store chain **5 à Sec** offers some of the city's best-priced dry cleaning, with 1-day service. Check for the location nearest your hotel. There's one on rue du Marché-aux-Herbes, off the Grand' Place, open Monday to Friday 7:30am to 6pm.

Mail   A convenient post office is at Gare Centrale, open Monday to Friday 9am to 6pm. Postage for a postcard or letter to the United States, Canada, or Australia is 34BF ($1.05); postcards and letters to Great Britain and the rest of Europe are 17BF (53¢). You can receive mail at American Express (see above).

Police   In an emergency, dial ☎ **100** or **101** to reach the police.

Tax   There's a **value-added tax** (**TVA** in Belgium) of 21% on all goods and services. If you spend over 5,000BF ($156.25) in one shop, you can get a tax refund once you leave Belgium by asking the shopkeeper to give you a tax-free form. At the border or airport, show the Customs officials your purchase and receipt and they'll stamp the form. Then you can mail this form back to the Belgian Tax Bureau (the address is on the form), or if you're leaving via the airport, bring it directly to the "Best Change" office, which charges a small commission but gives you an on-the-spot refund.

Telephone   A **local phone call** costs 12BF (35¢) for 3 minutes. It costs 130BF ($3.95) for a 3-minute **international call** to the United States or 120BF ($3.75) with a **PTT telecard,** available at PTT or Telecom offices. PTT telecards cost 200F, 500F, and 1,000BF ($6.25, $15.60, and $31.25) and can be used in all phone booths in the city. You can also make international calls from the PTT office at the airport. In addition, you can dial an American operator using **AT&T's USA Direct** service, which allows collect and credit-card calls at the local number: ☎ **0800-11-0010.**

Tipping   The prices on restaurant menus already include a service charge of 16%, along with a value-added tax (TVA in Belgium) of 21% (you'll see a little note reading *T.V.A. et service compris*), so it's unnecessary to tip. It's acceptable to round up if you want to. Service is included in your hotel bill as well.

3 Accommodations You Can Afford

Since one out of every two visitors to Brussels is here on business, there is a large number of hotels that command fairly steep prices for rooms that emphasize impersonal efficiency over quirky charm. Still, the wide range of available accommodations means that you shouldn't have too much trouble finding lodgings in your budget, especially if you plan in advance. Many of the city's family hotels in old town houses are small and fill up quickly, but they often feature lots of homespun flavor at a fairly reasonable price.

You'll find a few budget offerings in the Grand' Place area, the most charming part of Brussels, and more in the area around avenue Louise. Some of the best youth

Getting the Best Deal on Accommodations

- Note that the residential neighborhood surrounding avenue Louise as well as the streets around the Grand' Place and the train stations have decent, inexpensive hotels.
- Take advantage of the excellent bargains offered at youth hostels—they have quite a few singles and doubles for those who don't want to sleep in a dorm.
- Be aware that hotel prices go down whenever business travelers leave. Weekends, holidays, and July and August are the best times to get discounted rooms. Don't be afraid to ask for a reduction. You may also want to check with Belgium Tourist Reservations to take advantage of the discounts offered (see "Visitor Information," earlier in this chapter).
- Consider taking a room with the shower or the toilet in the hall. The savings are considerable, and the facilities are usually clean and well maintained.

hostels in Europe are in Brussels, offering another viable option. If you arrive without a reservation, you might want to stop by **Tourist Information Brussels,** the **Tourist Information Office, Belgium Tourist Reservations,** or the **Hotel Reservation Service** (see "Visitor Information," earlier in this chapter).

Note: You can find most of the lodging choices below plotted on the map included in "Seeing the Sights" later in this chapter.

NEAR THE GRAND' PLACE

Auberge de Jeunesse Jean-Nihon. 4 rue de l'Eléphant (a 20-minute walk from the Grand' Place), 1080 Bruxelles. ☎ **02/410-38-58.** Fax 02/410-39-05. 159 beds, all units with bathroom. 660BF ($21) single; 550BF ($17) per person double; 450BF ($14) per person triple/quad; 395BF ($12) dorm bed. Sheets 125BF ($4). EURO, MC, V. Métro: Comte de Flandre.

This is Brussels's newest youth hostel, in a neighborhood of apartment buildings. The new building is surrounded by empty lots, which act as a buffer against the urban atmosphere. The rooms have tile baths, with separate rooms for the toilet and shower. Wooden bunk beds are about all you'll find in your room, but the public areas include a garden and terrace, self-service facilities, and a TV/video room. A shop and laundry are also on the premises.

Centre Vincent van Gogh. 8 rue Traversière, 1210 Bruxelles (10 minutes on foot from Gare du Nord, 15 minutes from the Grand' Place), 1210 Bruxelles. ☎ **02/217-01-58.** Fax 02/219-79-95. 224 beds, 11 units with bathroom. 650BF ($20.30) single; 550BF ($17) per person double; 440BF ($14) per person triple/quad; 300BF–390BF ($9–$12) dorm bed. Rates include breakfast. Sheets 100BF ($3.10). V. Métro: Botanique. Bus: 65 or 66 from Gare Centrale.

In two buildings across from each other, the van Gogh offers very pleasant clean rooms with large windows that open like doors onto the street. Both buildings have little gardens in back, and one has a modest kitchen and a snack bar serving meals for 160BF to 200BF ($5 to $6.25) daily 6:30pm to midnight. The friendly reception gives advice on Brussels's hot spots. A 2am curfew is enforced.

Hôtel George-V. 23 rue t'Kint (a 10-minute walk from the Grand' Place), 1000 Bruxelles. ☎ **02/513-50-93.** Fax 02/513-44-93. 17 units, all with bathroom. 1,980BF ($62) single; 1,980BF–2,500BF ($60–$78) double. Rates include breakfast. EURO, MC, V. Parking 250BF ($7.80). Métro: Bourse.

On a quiet residential street not far from La Bourse, the George-V is an excellent choice for anyone wishing a private bath. Dark wood, polished brass, and marbled accents give it an air of elegance seldom found in such economical lodgings. In the lounge you can have a drink before retiring. The rooms were remodeled a few years ago, and if they're not luxurious, they're certainly comfortable.

Hôtel la Légende. 35 rue du Lombard (a 5-minute walk from the Grand' Place), 1000 Bruxelles. ☎ **02/512-82-90.** Fax 02/512-34-93. 45 units, 21 with bathroom (tub or shower). 2,300BF ($72) single with shower; 1,500BF ($47) double with sink only, 2,500BF ($78) double with shower, 2,950BF ($92) double with tub. Rates include breakfast. AE, DC, EURO, MC, V. Métro: Gare Centrale.

The entrance is at the end of a pleasant enclosed courtyard. The lobby is unimpressive, but the rooms are immaculately maintained with white walls and bright print bedspreads. Be aware that the twin-bedded rooms have extremely narrow beds; the double beds are a more sleepable size. The hotel has an elevator, and most rooms have TVs.

Hôtel la Vieille Lanterne. 29 rue des Grands Carmes (a 10-minute walk from the Grand' Place), 1000 Bruxelles. ☎ **02/512-74-94.** Fax 02/512-13-97. 6 units, all with bathroom. 1,700BF ($53) single; 2,100BF ($66) double. Breakfast 100BF ($3.10). AE, DC, EURO, MC, V. Métro: Bourse.

A tiny inn with two rooms per floor, this find is diagonally across from the *Manneken Pis*. It can be hard to spot—you enter through the side door of a trinket shop selling hundreds of *Manneken Pis* replicas. You'll feel right at home in the rooms with their old-style windows and renovated baths, which have marble counters and tiled walls. It's a good idea to write ahead to reserve a room; if you'll be arriving after 2pm, a deposit is required.

Hôtel Pacific. 57 rue Antoine-Dansaert (a 5-minute walk from the Grand' Place, 2 blocks from La Bourse), 1000 Bruxelles. ☎ **02/511-84-59.** 18 units, 2 with shower only. 1,000BF ($31) single without shower; 1,700BF ($53) double without shower, 2,200BF ($69) double with shower. Rates include breakfast. Showers 100BF ($3.10). No credit cards. Métro: Bourse.

A good value in the lively neighborhood of La Bourse, the Pacific has a soft-spoken friendly owner, Paul Pauwels (alas, he usually enforces a midnight curfew). Most rooms are large, though with plumbing from 80 years ago; the front rooms have small balconies. Breakfast is served in a fin-de-siècle room with a zebra skin, copper pots, a Buddhist prayer wheel, and a Canadian World War II steel helmet. Monks from the Dalai Lama's entourage once stayed here and left mystical symbols in some rooms. Each Friday, guests are invited to attend a free 1-hour slow-motion gymnastic session, half yoga and half tai chi chuan. The Pacific is highly recommended to those who prefer atmosphere over comfort.

SOUTH OF GARE DU NORD

✪ **Auberge de Jeunesse Jacques-Brel.** 30 rue da la Sablonnière (a 10- to 15-minute walk from Gare Centrale), 1000 Bruxelles. ☎ **02/218-01-87.** Fax 02/217-20-05. 139 beds, no units with bathroom. 680BF ($21.25) single; 570BF ($18) per person double; 470BF ($15) per person quad; 415BF ($13) dorm bed. Rates include breakfast. Sheets 135BF ($4.20). MC, V. Bus: 65 or 66 from Gare Centrale to Madou.

This youth hostel was once a hospital—it still has special facilities for the disabled. Public facilities include a bar, washing machines, a TV room, and two small sundecks. The rooms (with 1 to 14 beds) have large windows, allowing in lots of light, and showers. A 1am curfew is enforced, but the reception room is open throughout the day. This hostel is in the elegant "upper Brussels" area.

Hôtel Barry. 25 place Anneessens (halfway between La Bourse and Gare du Midi, a 10-minute walk from the Grand' Place), 1000 Bruxelles. ☎ **02/511-27-95.** Fax 02/514-14-65. 34 units, 14 with shower only, 16 with bathroom. 1,280BF ($40) single without bathroom; 1,880BF ($59) double with shower only, 2,280BF ($71) double with bathroom; 3,280BF ($103) triple with bathroom; 3,780BF ($118) quad with bathroom. Rates include continental breakfast. Half board 500BF ($16); full board 900BF ($28). AE, DC, EURO, MC, V. Métro: Anneessens.

This businessperson's hotel is nothing to get excited about, but the rooms are spacious, clean, and well furnished (most with color TVs). The imposing red-brick building on place Anneessens is a school, and there's a monument dedicated to Mr. Anneessens, one of the merchants who built the beautiful houses on the Grand' Place. Breakfast is served here, but other meals are served in a next-door restaurant. Advance bookings are advisable, as the hotel is often sold out to groups.

Hôtel-Résidence Albert. 27–29 rue Royale-Ste-Marie (a 20-minute walk from the Grand' Place), 1030 Bruxelles. ☎ **02/217-93-91.** Fax 02/219-20-17. 22 units, 12 with shower only, 10 with bathroom; 22 apts. TEL. 1,600BF ($50) single with shower only, 1,750BF ($55) single with bathroom; 1,700BF ($53) double with shower only, 2,200BF ($69) double with bathroom; 2,100BF–2,750BF ($66–$86) apt. No credit cards. Métro: Gare du Nord; then walk 5 minutes uphill on rue Dupont.

Here the rooms are free of decoration and have tiny writing desks; some furnishings are fairly new. The private baths are separated by only a curtain, and the rooms with showers have only a freestanding unit. The apartments are suitable for one or two. For maximum quiet, ask for the rooms in the back away from the busy street. A bar is on the premises.

Hôtel Sabina. 78 rue du Nord (off place des Barricades, a 20-minute walk from the Grand' Place), 1000 Bruxelles. ☎ **02/218-26-37.** Fax 02/219-32-39. 24 units, all with bathroom. TV TEL. 1,900BF ($59) single; 2,400BF ($75) double. Rates include buffet breakfast. AE, DC, EURO, MC, V. Métro: Madou.

Though some of the beds are a bit old, each room comes with a writing desk and TV. Most have baths that are no larger than a closet (though with hair dryers). The breakfast room contains a large fireplace, a wood-beamed ceiling, and a TV. Because this hotel is popular with business travelers, reserve in advance for a weeknight stay. Three rooms have a small kitchen.

Relais la Tasse d'Argent and Hôtel Madou. 48 and 45 rue du Congrès, respectively (a 20-minute walk from the Grand' Place), 1000 Bruxelles. ☎ **02/218-83-75.** Fax 02/217-32-74. 17 units, all with bathroom. 1,500BF ($47) single; 1,900BF ($59) double; 2,500BF ($78) triple. Continental breakfast 150BF ($4.65). MC, V. Métro: Madou.

Built in two old family houses, these small hotels really make you feel as though you're a guest in a friend's home. The rooms feature half-size bathtubs and large windows overlooking the street. The lovely breakfast room at no. 48 has a grandfather clock and chintz seating, helping to make this an excellent choice.

Sleep Well. 23 rue du Damier, 1000 Bruxelles. ☎ **02/218-50-50.** Fax 02/218-13-13. 130 beds, no units with bathroom. 640BF ($20) single; 510BF ($16) per person double; 430BF ($13) per person triple/quad; 380BF ($12) per person in 6-bed dorm. Rates include breakfast. Sheets 100BF ($3.10). V. Métro: Rogier.

Behind the City 2 shopping mall and a block from bustling rue Neuve, Sleep Well enjoys probably the best location of all of Brussels's well-placed hostels. Guests of all ages are welcomed, but a 1am curfew and a 10am to 4pm close-out are maintained. The evening cafe serves 15 types of beer for 45BF to 75BF ($1.40 to $2.35). The hostel also sponsors 2-hour city tours in summer for only 100BF ($3.10).

IN THE AVENUE LOUISE AREA

Hôtel Berckmans. 12 rue Berckmans (a 10-minute walk from place Louise), 1060 Bruxelles. ☎ **02/537-89-48.** Fax 02/538-09-00. 23 units, 15 with shower only, 6 with bathroom. TEL. 850BF ($27) single without shower, 1,200BF ($38) single with shower, 1,700BF ($52) single with bathroom; 1,300BF ($41) double without shower, 1,700BF ($53) double with shower, 1,850BF ($58) double with bathroom. Rates include breakfast. AE, DC, EURO, MC, V. Métro: Place Louise. Bus: 60.

Despite the upscale tone of the avenue Louise district, it's still possible to get an inexpensive room in the area, and the Berckmans is comfortable. The rooms vary in size, and those with private bath have the facilities behind a curtain rather than in a separate room. Some rooms have TVs, which adds to the price.

✪ **Hôtel de Boeck.** 40 rue Veydt (behind the Holiday Inn, a 10-minute walk from place Louise), 1050 Brussels. ☎ **02/537-40-33.** Fax 02/534-40-37. 35 units, all with bathroom. 1,400BF–2,500BF ($44–$78) single; 1,650BF–2,900BF ($52–$91) double. Higher rates are for larger rooms. Rates include buffet breakfast. Extra bed 675BF ($21). AE, DC, EURO, MC, V. Métro: Place Louise.

This hotel offers unusually spacious, quiet, and adequately furnished rooms. The prices depend on whether you arrive on a weekend, make a longer stay, or book a room with color TV and/or direct-dial phone, so call first to find out what the best deal is. Fourteen rooms, ideal for small groups, can be used as quads or even quints. Since 1970, the owner has been friendly Londoner Eric Gibbs. Street parking is possible.

Hôtel les Bluets. 124 rue Berckmans (a 10-minute walk from place Louise), 1060 Bruxelles. ☎ **02/534-39-83.** Fax 02/543-09-70. 10 units, 3 with shower only, 7 with bathroom. 1,450BF ($45) single with shower only, 1,650BF ($52) single with bathroom; 2,450BF ($77) double with bathroom and TV. Rates include breakfast. AE, MC, V. Métro: Hôtel des Monnaies.

If you're searching for classic European charm or are a fan of American B&Bs, you'll enjoy this place. You'll feel as though you're staying with friends when you breakfast in the antique-filled dining room or out in the sunroom. A sweeping stairway (no elevator) leads up to the rooms, several of which have 14-foot ceilings and ornate original moldings. There are antiques in all and TVs in some. If you're planning a longer stay or like the convenience of a kitchenette, an apartment is available at 8,450BF ($262.50) per week.

Hôtel Rembrandt. 42 rue de la Concorde (a 15-minute walk from place Louise), 1050 Bruxelles. ☎ **02/512-71-39.** Fax 02/511-71-36. 13 units, 8 with shower only, 5 with bathroom (shower). TEL. 1,400BF ($44) single with shower only, 1,800BF ($56) single with bathroom; 2,200BF ($69) double with shower only, 2,500–2,700BF ($78–$84) double with bathroom. Rates include continental breakfast. AE, DC, MC, V. Métro: Place Louise.

The high ceilings and oak furniture of the Rembrandt seem a world away from the studied chic of nearby avenue Louise. Though the lobby resembles the cluttered living room of someone's slightly dotty aunt, the rooms are relatively spacious, especially the higher-priced doubles. The decor is endearingly old-fashioned, and some rooms have TVs. The bathrooms are tiny, but the beds are good-sized.

NORTH OF GARE DU MIDI

✪ **Hôtel à la Grande Cloche.** 10–12 place Rouppe (a 15-minute walk from Gare du Midi), 1000 Bruxelles. ☎ **02/512-61-40.** Fax 02/512-65-91. 47 units, 16 with shower only, 20 with bathroom. TEL. 1,850BF ($58) single or double without shower, 2,450BF ($77) single or double with shower only, 2,850BF ($89) single or double with bathroom. Rates include continental breakfast. AE, EURO, MC, V. Métro: Anneessens.

This hotel is on a small traffic circle 10 minutes on foot from Gare du Midi and another 10 minutes from the Grand' Place. It offers clean modern rooms, most with small tiled shower and sink areas; many rooms also have large TVs. The elevator-equipped building even has hair dryers in the halls and in some rooms.

Hôtel van Belle. 39 chaussée de Mons (about a 10-minute walk north of Gare du Midi), 1070 Bruxelles. ☎ **02/521-35-16.** Fax 02/527-00-02. 125 units, 112 with bathroom. 1,300BF ($41) single without bathroooom, 2,200BF–2,500BF ($69–$78) single with bathroom; 1,800BF ($56) double without bathroom, 2,500BF ($78) double with bathroom. AE, DC, EURO, MC, V. Métro: Gare du Midi.

Larger and more formal than most choices in this chapter, the van Belle offers services (photocopying, fax machines) that smaller budget hotels don't provide. The smaller, cheaper rooms without baths in the old wing have a sink and were recently renovated; the larger rooms in the modern wing have two chairs and a small writing table. If you phone this hotel from Gare du Midi upon your arrival, someone may pick you up by car for free. There's a free shuttle to the city center after 5pm.

Hôtel Windsor. 13 place Rouppe (a 15-minute walk from Gare du Midi), 1000 Bruxelles. ☎ **02/511-20-14** or 02/511-14-94. Fax 02/514-09-42. 24 units, 9 with shower only. 1,980BF ($62) single or double without shower, 2,375BF ($74) single or double with shower. Rates include breakfast. EURO, MC, V. Métro: Anneessens.

You pass through a quiet little bistro to get to the rooms at this recently renovated hotel. New furnishings, carpets, and wallpaper give the place a contemporary feel, and though there are no rooms with full bath (toilets are down the hall), those rooms that don't have a shower do have a bidet. Most rooms also have a phone and a clock radio.

WORTH A SPLURGE

✪ **Hôtel Mozart.** 23 rue du Marché aux Fromages, 1000 Bruxelles. ☎ **02/502-66-61.** Fax 02/502-77-58. 37 units, all with bathroom (shower). TV TEL. 2,500BF ($78) single; 3,000BF ($94) double; 4,000BF ($125) triple. Rates include breakfast. AE, DC, MC, V. Métro: Gare Centrale.

One flight up from the street, the music of guess who wafts through the sparkling lobby. The salmon-colored walls, plants, and old paintings create an intimate ambiance that's carried into the rooms. Though the furniture is blandly modern, colorful fabrics and exposed beams lend each room a stylish originality. Several rooms are duplexes with a sitting room beneath the loft-style bedroom, and the top rooms have a great view.

4 Great Deals on Dining

Food is such a passion in Brussels that even the streets are named after produce markets: Rue du Marché aux Fromages, rue du Marché aux Herbes, rue du Marché aux Porcs, and rue du Marché aux Poulets are named after the open-air cheese, herb, pork, and chicken stalls that once lined them. This gastronomic obsession has generated nearly 2,000 restaurants, meaning that you can eat well at a reasonable price even though Brussels isn't among Europe's least expensive cities.

Brussels's best dishes are based on local products, most famously the mussels prepared in countless ingenious variations and served in a sturdy iron pot. When ordering mussels (a kilo, 2.2 lbs., is a typical portion), note that the best time is from September through the winter; mussels served in summer are often imported and not as good.

Belgium is renowned for its 400 brands of beer, produced by hundreds of small breweries around the country. Belgians use beer in their sauces the way French chefs use wine. Beef, chicken, and fish are often bathed in a savory sauce based on the local beers, gueuze and faro.

Getting the Best Deal on Dining

- Take advantage of the plat du jour at lunch and the menu du jour at dinner. You'll get good food at a reasonable price.
- Note that the City 2 shopping mall houses many restaurants where the prices are almost uniformly low. See the "Quick Bites & Dessert" box for more.
- Fill up on inexpensive (and delicious) Belgian *frites*. A friend of mine traveling through Europe in her youth managed to live on frites for the last few penniless days of her tour.

Beer is the perfect accompaniment to the sturdy Flemish dishes you'll find on menus. *Waterzooi* is a stew of fish or chicken with a parsley-and-cream sauce. *Stoemp* is a purée of vegetables and potatoes accompanied by sausages. You might want to try *anguilles au vert* (green eels), *bollekes* (spicy meatballs), or *hochepot* (stew). The Belgians deserve credit for perfecting a mighty culinary quintet of cheese, waffles, fried potatoes, chocolate, and beer—and no visit to Brussels is complete without a generous sampling of each.

ON OR NEAR THE GRAND' PLACE

Armand & KO. 16 rue des Chapeliers (1 block from the Grand' Place). ☎ **02/514-17-63.** Reservations suggested Fri–Sat nights. Meals 355–675BF ($11–$21); plat du jour 295BF ($9). AE, MC, V. Tues–Sun noon–2:30pm and 7–11pm. Métro: Gare Centrale. FRENCH/BELGIAN.

This casual family-style bistro serves up dishes of surprising sophistication. The reasonably priced plat du jour might be Alsatian choucroute (sauerkraut), roast beef stuffed with spinach, or sole meunière. A two-course lunch at 395BF ($12) typically includes a creamy soup or green salad and the plat du jour. The wine list favors the Bordeaux and Loire Valley regions of France and begins at 575BF ($18) for the house wine.

Au Bambou Fleur. 13 rue Jules-van-Praet (3 blocks from the Grand' Place). ☎ **02/502-29-51.** Meals 350BF–520BF ($11–$16); lunch special 220BF ($7). AE, V. Mon–Fri 10am–8pm, Sat 10am–9pm, Sun 5–9pm. Métro: Bourse. VIETNAMESE.

In recent years, there's been a proliferation of Vietnamese restaurants in Brussels. They're almost always the cheapest places around, and their lunch specials are always a good deal. To help you decide, the menu posted in the front window has photos of all the dishes.

✪ **Auberge des Chapeliers.** 1–3 rue des Chapeliers (off the Grand' Place). ☎ **02/513-73-38.** Fax 02/502-21-18. Reservations recommended Fri–Sat. Meals 230BF–750BF ($7–$23). AC, AE, DC, EURO, MC, V. Sun–Thurs noon–3pm and 6–11pm, Fri–Sat 6pm–midnight. Métro: Bourse. BELGIAN.

In a 17th-century building where Brussels's best artisans once designed hats, the Auberge des Chapeliers (Inn of the Hat Makers) preserves a charming feel. Behind a beautiful brick facade, the first two floors are graced with wooden beams and paneling and connected by a narrow wooden staircase. The third floor has windows overlooking the nearby streets. Excellent fries accompany the typical Belgian cuisine. Don't miss this conveniently located and reasonably priced choice.

✪ **Au Suisse.** 73–75 bd. Anspach (a 10-minute walk from the Grand' Place). ☎ **02/512-95-89.** Sandwiches 65BF–120BF ($2–$3.75). No credit cards. Tues 10am–7:30pm, Wed–Mon 10am–8pm. Métro: Bourse. SANDWICHES.

Frites on the Streets

Belgian *frites* are twice-fried, giving them a delectably crunchy crust and flavorful interior. Brussels is dotted with dozens of fast-food stands serving frites wrapped in paper cones. Belgians usually eat them with mayonnaise rather than ketchup; though this method may cause apprehension, after you try it you may be converted. Prices run from 50BF to 65BF ($1.55 to $2.05), depending on the portion and where you buy them; the topping (which you must specifically ask for) is 10BF to 15BF (30¢ to 45¢) extra.

The sandwich is a Belgian institution, and nowhere is it treated more respectfully. Dozens of fillings are displayed in a glass counter. You can try any of half a dozen types of raw or smoked herring, creamy mussel or salmon spread, tuna salad, meat salads, sliced cheeses, flavored cream cheeses, various hams and salamis, and many more delicious and unusual choices. You then get your filling in a big hunk of French bread or a hard roll. There are just a few stools at the counter, so it's best to get your sandwich to go.

Aux Bons Enfants. 49 place du Grand-Sablon (a 10-minute walk from the Grand' Place). ☎ **02/512-40-95.** Main courses 275BF–515BF ($9–$16). No credit cards. Thurs–Tues noon–2:45pm and 6–10:30pm. Métro: Gare Centrale. ITALIAN.

After days of mussels and fries, you might be ready to tuck into a plate of pasta or a savory pizza. The decor is a pleasant but uninspiring mix of exposed beams and modern art, but the food is a surprisingly good value for the busy place du Grand-Sablon. Best of all, the restaurant is open on Sunday, when many others are closed.

Cap de Nuit. 28 place de la Vieille Halle-aux-Blés (right off the Grand' Place). ☎ **02/512-93-42.** Meals 260BF–900BF ($8–$28); plat du jour 380BF ($12). AE, DC, EURO, MC, V. Mon–Thurs 6pm–6:30am, Fri 6pm–7:30am, Sat 6pm–8am, Sun 6pm–7am. Métro: Bourse. ITALIAN/BELGIAN.

Cap de Nuit assures that you'll never go hungry late at night, as it serves up pasta and other dishes all the way to 7 or 8am, the latest of any restaurant in town. The modern decor, late hours, and 28 varieties of beer attract a crowd between ages 20 and 40. The plat du jour, served all night, is the best deal and reliably tasty. There are 200 seats in four connecting rooms.

Den Teepot. 66 rue des Chartreux (a 5-minute walk west from the Bourse Métro stop). ☎ **02/511-94-02.** Plat du jour 285BF ($9); two-course fixed-price menu 400BF ($13). No credit cards. Mon–Sat noon–2pm. Métro: Bourse. VEGETARIAN.

If meat and potatoes aren't your favorite fare and greasy fries leave you cold, Den Teepot may be just the lunch place for you. Rice and beans and veggies, organically grown and macrobiotically prepared, are the staples, but, surprisingly, you can also get a beer with your meal.

La Grande Porte. 9 rue Notre-Seigneur (4 blocks west of place du Grand-Sablon). ☎ **02/512-89-98.** Main courses 395BF–525BF ($12–$16). V. Mon–Fri noon–3pm and 6pm–2am, Sat 6pm–4am. Bus: 20 or 48. BELGIAN.

Paper lanterns, marionettes, old posters, and fashionably "distressed" walls create a comfortable, relaxed space to enjoy several Flemish specialties. As the place is near the working-class Marolles district, the food is simple, plentiful, and hearty. A lunch of ballekes, waterzooi, or stoemp with sausages will set you up for the rest of the day . . . and probably the evening as well.

Quick Bites & Dessert

Numerous fast-food **Greek places** near the Grand' Place (Métro: Gare Centrale) make gyros, falafels, and other items for about 125BF ($3.90). The many inexpensive cafeterias and fast-food restaurants in **City 2** (Métro: Brouckère), a huge American-style shopping mall on rue Neuve, make it one of Brussels's great budget centers. The mall, as well as its restaurants (all on the upper level, reached by escalator), is open Monday to Friday 10am to 7pm and Saturday 10am to 8pm. In addition to snack bars, sandwich bars, a beer/wine bar, a pizza shop, and a steak house, there's a cafeteria that serves up hot meals for about 350BF ($10.95).

And don't forget those luscious frites!

Many connoisseurs consider Belgium the world's greatest chocolate confectioner. For Belgians, the real art comes in not merely producing a quality chocolate bar but in filling that chocolate with goodies, creating the perfect praline.

The **Leonidas** chain sells excellent Belgian pralines for the lowest prices in town, 480BF ($15) per kilo (2.2 lbs.). There are 10 branches, including 46 bd. Anspach, off La Bourse (☎ **02/218-03-63;** Métro: Bourse); 49–51 bd. Adolphe-Max, parallel to rue Neuve (☎ **02/217-95-55;** Métro: Brouckère); and 5 chaussée d'Ixelles, off Porte Namur (☎ **02/511-11-51;** Métro: Porte Namur).

Also throughout the city look for signs that read VIGAUFRA, where you'll find fresh waffles for about 45BF to 55BF ($1.40 to $1.70). Generally thicker than American waffles, they're usually sprinkled with powdered sugar and wrapped in paper to be eaten as a quick street snack.

○ **Taverne Falstaff.** 23–25 rue Henri-Maus (at the Bourse Métro stop). ☎ **02/511-98-77.** Reservations recommended. Main courses 275BF–760BF ($9–$24); complete lunch special 340BF ($10.60); sandwiches 70BF–160BF ($2.20–$5). AE, DC, EURO, MC, V. Daily noon–3am (lunch special noon–3pm). Métro: Bourse. BELGIAN.

An art nouveau masterpiece with carved wooden ceilings, painted glass, and mirrors, the Falstaff attracts a boisterous crowd. The best value is the lunch plat du jour or the dinner menu du jour. The restaurant has two halves, each with a different menu: an art nouveau part from 1903 and a newer section from 1965. Service can be slow and impersonal, but the place still captures that Belgian joie de vivre.

t'Kelderke. 15 Grand' Place. ☎ **02/513-73-44.** Main courses 350BF–650BF ($11–$20); mussels 325BF–745BF ($10–$23). AE, DC, EURO, MC, V. Daily noon–2am. Métro: Bourse. BELGIAN.

The Little Cellar is, as its name implies, a brick-vaulted cellar a few steps down from the square (on the "upper" side). The food is good, and the place features a mix of locals and visitors. The cellar is a striking contrast to the grandiose facade of the Grand' Place but is atmospheric in its own way. The menu focuses on traditional Belgian fare like pricey mussels and economical dishes of potatoes mashed with other vegetables and served with a bit of meat.

SOUTH OF GARE DU NORD

Restaurant Istanbul. 16 chaussée de Haecht (a 10-minute walk from Gare du Nord). ☎ **02/218-72-86.** Reservations recommended Fri–Sat nights. Meals 220BF–430BF ($7–$13); plat du jour 280BF ($9). AE, DC, EURO, MC, V. Daily 11:30am–3pm and 6pm–1am. Métro: Botanique. TURKISH.

A long restaurant with small Turkish carpets and ornaments on the wall, the Istanbul serves tasty grilled fare. Turkish music plays on the radio for most meals, and on Friday and Saturday live Turkish music and belly dancing start at 8pm—at no extra charge. Around the corner from the Centre Vincent van Gogh hostel, Istanbul is one of several low-cost Turkish and Middle Eastern restaurants in the area.

BETWEEN AVENUE LOUISE & CHAUSSEE DE WAVRE

Au Trappiste. 3 av. de la Toison d'Or (a 10-minute walk from place Louise). ☎ **02/511-78-39.** Main courses 230BF–450BF ($7–$14); plat du jour 295BF ($9); specials up to 600BF ($19). AE, DC, EURO, MC, V. Daily 10am–midnight. Métro: Namur. BELGIAN.

It may seem impossible to find an inexpensive place to eat in this pricey area, but Au Trappiste is an exception. It's easy to spot: next to the Namur Métro stop, diagonally across from the Hilton tower. It has 120 seats in a high-beamed–ceilinged room with mirrored walls, two large chandeliers, and brass railings. The best deal is the plat du jour, consisting of vegetable soup and a main course like goulash with steamed potatoes, fried fish, breaded veal cutlet, or pasta.

NEAR LA BOURSE

Friture de la Bourse. 29 rue Auguste-Arts (next to the Bourse Métro stop). ☎ **02/511-99-29.** Fries 75BF ($2.35); plat du jour 185BF ($6); mussels 290BF–510BF ($9–$16). No credit cards. Daily 10am–10pm. Métro: Bourse. BELGIAN.

The building housing this restaurant looks broken down, but the 80-seat dining room is clean, high-ceilinged, and spacious. The best-seller is mussels, though the menu lists many tasty dishes, like green eel with fries, rump steak with fries, choucroute, fried sardines, and half a roast chicken, plus a filling three-course fixed-price menu for 435BF ($13.60). French wines are 80BF ($2.50) per half liter. You get good food at reasonable prices. There's also a takeout counter.

✪ **In't Spinnekopke.** 1 place du Jardin aux Fleurs (a 5-minute walk from the Bourse Métro stop). ☎ **02/511-86-95.** Meals 340BF–710BF ($11–$22); plat du jour 295BF ($9). AE, DC, EURO, MC, V. Mon–Fri noon–3pm and 6–11pm, Sat 6–11pm. Bar, Mon–Fri 11am–11pm, Sat 6–11pm. Closed Aug and holidays. Métro: Bourse. BELGIAN.

My favorite typical local place, this restaurant in a 1762 building serves excellent food. Wood beams and paneling, pink floral wallpaper, pink tablecloths, candles, and roses capture a European charm that makes for a special evening out. A large variety of beers is available, and some dishes even come with beer sauces. The prices are a bit high, but the food's worth it.

ON RUE DES BOUCHERS & PETITE RUE DES BOUCHERS

✪ **Chez Léon.** 18–22 rue des Bouchers (right off the Grand' Place). ☎ **02/511-14-15** or 02/513-08-48. Mussel dinner 385BF–600BF ($12–$19); plat du jour 250BF ($8). AE, DC, EURO, MC, V. Daily 11:30am–11pm. Métro: Bourse. BELGIAN.

Chez Léon has been dishing out mussels since 1893, making it Brussels's true king of mussels. Many visitors frequent this bubbling bistro, where the waiters run to and fro frantically. The three dining rooms feature tables with paper tablecloths and wooden stall seating. The kitchen is to the side as you enter.

NEAR THE UNIVERSITY

Bistro Marilou. 104 av. Adolphe-Buyl (a 15-minute walk from the University). ☎ **02/647-80-99.** Three-course lunch menu 395BF ($12); three-course dinner menu 695BF ($22). AE, DC, MC, V. Mon–Sat noon–3pm and 7pm–midnight. Tram: 93 or 94. Bus: 71. BELGIAN/FRENCH.

The owner of this casual bistro was formerly associated with the ritzy Villa Lorraine. Here the emphasis is on simple well-prepared dishes that use the freshest ingredients. Steak, pasta, ribs, and mussels are menu staples along with daily specials. The rustic front room opens onto a peaceful terrace in back, where students and teachers from the nearby university gather at lunch.

Le Campus. 437 av. de la Couronne (a 15-minute walk from the University). ☎ **050/ 648-53-80.** Three-course lunch menu 350BF ($11); plat du jour 245BF ($8). AE, DC, MC, V. Daily 9am–3am. Bus: 71. INTERNATIONAL.

A neighborhood favorite, this unpretentious restaurant offers a decent meal at a decent price. You can sit at one of the rough wood tables in the front room or in the slightly more formal side rooms and enjoy spaghetti, steak, a hearty plate of Alsatian choucroute, or magret de canard (sliced duck).

PICNICKING

You'll find a huge supermarket with a large cold cut/cheese counter perfect for assembling a picnic lunch in **GB,** in the basement of City 2 on rue Neuve. It's open Monday to Thursday and Saturday 9am to 8pm and Friday 9am to 9pm. There's another GB at the corner of rue du Marché-aux-Poulets and rue des Halles, a block from La Bourse. You'll also find ample gourmet food stores in the streets around the Grand' Place.

The best spot for a picnic is the **Parc de Bruxelles,** which extends in front of the Palais Royale (see "Parks & Gardens," later in this chapter).

WORTH A SPLURGE

La Taverne du Passage. 30 Galerie de la Reine (right off the Grand' Place). ☎ **02/512-37-31.** Main courses 525BF–750BF ($16–$23). AE, DC, MC V. Daily noon– midnight. Métro: Gare Centrale. BELGIAN.

This stylish brasserie is in one of the city's most elegant shopping galleries, and the menu offers a wide variety of fish and mussels. House specialties, waterzooi, and choucroute are also available for takeout, but then you'd miss out on the sleek art deco interior replete with dark wood, mirrors, and ceiling fans. The white-jacketed waiters are friendly and efficient as they scurry up and down the long rows of tables.

5 Seeing the Sights

SIGHTSEEING SUGGESTIONS

IF YOU HAVE 1 DAY Spend your first hours at the magnificent **Grand' Place,** whose elaborate buildings and ornate details are a fairy tale come true. In particular, visit the Gothic **Hôtel de Ville de Bruxelles** and the **Musée de la Ville de Bruxelles.** From the Grand' Place, pay a visit to the defiant *Manneken Pis,* then after lunch head uptown to the impressive **Musées Royaux des Beaux-Arts** to see its collection of old masters and modern artists. After a few hours in the museum, walk over to the attractive **place du Grand-Sablon** and its diminutive neighbor, **place du Petit-Sablon.**

IF YOU HAVE 2 DAYS Spread the above activities at a more relaxed pace over 2 days and stop in at **Notre-Dame du Sablon** while on place du Grand-Sablon. Also visit the **Cathédrale des Sts-Michel-et-Gudule** near Gare Centrale. Then explore **rue Neuve,** Brussels's main pedestrian street, and wander about the nearby streets. If you still have extra time, consider a visit to the **Musée Instrumental.**

IF YOU HAVE 3 DAYS Spend Days 1 and 2 as above, then on Day 3 head out to the museum complex at Parc du Cinquantenaire, where you can admire the varied collection of the **Musées Royaux d'Art et d'Histoire,** the superb **Musée Royal de l'Armée et d'Histoire Militaire,** and the fun **Autoworld.** Also consider the **Musée du Costume et de la Dentelle,** near the Grand' Place, and a stroll on the elegant **avenue Louise.**

IF YOU HAVE 5 DAYS   Spend Days 1 to 3 as above. On your next 2 days, visit the massive **Atomium** from the 1958 Brussels world's fair and stop in at the **Bruparck** amusement park opposite the Atomium. Consider a picnic in one of Brussels's parks. You can visit virtually all of Belgium on a day trip from Brussels, and I suggest you spend at least one of your extra days seeing another part of the country, especially the medieval wonders of **Bruges, Ghent,** or **Antwerp.**

THE TOP ATTRACTIONS

The ✪ **Grand' Place** has been the center of the city's commercial life as well as public celebrations since the 12th century. Some say it's the most beautiful square in the world. Most of it was destroyed in 1695 by the order of France's Louis XIV and then rebuilt over the next few years. Thanks to the town's close monitoring of the reconstruction and later alterations, each building preserves its baroque splendor. Prominent merchants and artisans, as well as important guilds, owned these buildings, and each competed to outdo the others with highly ornate facades of gold leaf and statuary, often with emblems of their guilds.

My favorite is the elaborate **Hôtel de Ville** (Town Hall), with its sculptures of drinking monks, a sleeping Moor and his harem, and St. Michael slaying what appears to be a female devil (see below). You'll also want to admire no. 9, **Le Cygne** (The Swan), headquarters of the butchers' guild; no. 10, **L'Arbre d'Or** (The Golden Tree), headquarters of the brewers' guild; and nos. 13 to 19, the ensemble of seven homes known as the **Maison des Ducs de Brabant** (House of the Dukes of Brabant), adorned with busts of 19 dukes.

✪ **Manneken Pis.** At the intersection of rue de l'Etuve and rue du Chêne (4 blocks from the Grand' Place). Mêtro: Bourse.

A small bronze statue of a urinating child, the *Manneken Pis* has come to symbolize the insouciant, mischievous Bruxellois spirit. No one knows when this child first came into being, but it's clear he dates from quite a few centuries ago—the 8th century, according to one legend. Thieves have made off with the tyke several times in history. One criminal who stole and shattered the statue in 1817 was sentenced to a life of hard labor. (The pieces were used to recast another version.)

The *Manneken Pis* owns a vast wardrobe, which he wears on special occasions (during Christmas season he dons a Santa suit, complete with white beard). You can see part of his collection in the Musée de la Ville de Bruxelles in the Maison du Roi (see below). If you want to read about the many legends of the *Manneken Pis,* you'll find an illustrated book for sale in the Musée de la Ville de Bruxelles. And in many shops you'll find replicas, so you can bring the little guy home with you.

Incidentally, the *Manneken Pis* now has a female counterpart called the ***Jeanneke Pis,*** located on the dead-end impasse de la Fidélité off rue des Bouchers. It was the 1987 brainstorm of a local restaurateur who wanted to attract business; its lack of grace is an embarrassment to many Bruxellois.

✪ **Musées Royaux des Beaux-Arts.** 3 rue de la Régence. ☎ **02/508-32-11.** Admission 150BF ($4.70) adults, 100BF ($3.10) seniors, 50BF ($1.55) children. Tues–Sun 10am–1pm and 2–5pm. Closed Jan 1, May 1, Nov 1 and 11, and Dec 25. Tram: 92, 93, or 94. Bus: 20, 34, 38, 60, 71, 95, or 96.

In a vast museum of several buildings, this complex combines the **Musée d'Art Ancien** (classical art) and the **Musée d'Art Moderne** (modern art) under one roof

---

Getting the Best Deal on Sightseeing

- Note that one of the best panoramic views of Brussels's skyline is from the esplanade in front of the huge Palais de Justice, near the place Louise Métro stop. Though the view from the Atomium is indeed spectacular, the one from the esplanade is free.
- Check out some of Brussels's fun markets—the antiques market at place du Grand-Sablon (Saturday 9am to 6pm and Sunday 9am to 2pm), the Middle Eastern bazaar and flea market at Gare du Midi (Sunday 7am to 2pm), the flea market at place du Jeu de Balle (daily 7am to 2pm), and the bird market at the Grand' Place (Sunday 7am to 2pm April to September).
- After browsing the daily flea market in place du Jeu de Balle, take a look around the surrounding neighborhood, the Marolles. Between the Palais de Justice and Gare du Midi, this is an unpretentious working-class area of cozy cafes, drinking-man's bars, and inexpensive restaurants. The Marolles is proudly old-fashioned, and its denizens even speak their own dialect.
- Stroll the length of the elegant Galeries St-Hubert for great window-shopping and people-watching. Built in 1846, this wide glass-topped arcade was the first of its kind in Europe and now contains some of the city's finest shops and cafes.

(they're connected by an underground passage). The collection shows off works from the 14th to the 20th centuries. It starts with Hans Memling's portraits from the late 15th century, which are marked by sharp lifelike details, as well as works by Hieronymus Bosch and Lucas Cranach's *Adam and Eve.*

I particularly admire the subsequent rooms featuring Pieter Brueghel, including his *Adoration of the Magi.* Don't miss the unusual *Fall of the Rebel Angels,* with its grotesque faces and beasts. But don't fear—many of Brueghel's paintings are of a less fiery nature, like the scenes depicting Flemish village life. Later artists represented in the Musées Royaux des Beaux-Arts include Rubens, van Dyck, Frans Hals, Cranach, Guardi, and Rembrandt.

The modern works are housed in a circular building connected to the main entrance. The overwhelming collection includes works by Matisse, Dalí, Tanguy, Ernst, Chagall, Miró, and Magritte. You may want to purchase a museum plan for 20BF (60¢) to help you navigate your way.

Hôtel de Ville de Bruxelles (Town Hall). On Grand' Place. ☎ **02/279-43-65.** Admission 80BF ($2.50) adults, 50BF ($1.55) children. Tues–Fri 9:30am–12:15pm and 1:45–4pm, Sun 10am–1pm. Call or drop by for exact hours of English-language tours. Closed Jan 1, May 1, Nov 1 and 11, and Dec 25. Métro: Bourse.

One of the few buildings to survive the 1695 bombardment by the French (in reprisal for alleged Dutch and British attacks on French channel ports), the brilliant Town Hall dates from 1402. Its facade shows off Gothic intricacy at its best, complete with dozens of statues and arched windows. A 215-foot tower sprouts from the middle, yet it's not placed directly in the center (10 windows are to the left of the tower, 7½ to the right). Legend has it that when the architect realized his error, he jumped from the summit of the tower.

You may visit the interior on 30- to 40-minute tours, which start in a room full of paintings of the past foreign rulers of Brussels, who have included the Spanish, Austrians, French (under Napoléon), Dutch, and finally the Belgians. In the Council Hall you'll see baroque decoration, and in several chambers—such as the Maximilian

Brussels

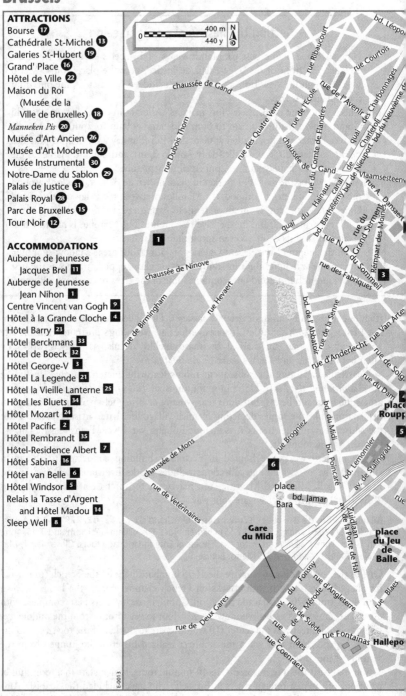

E-0013

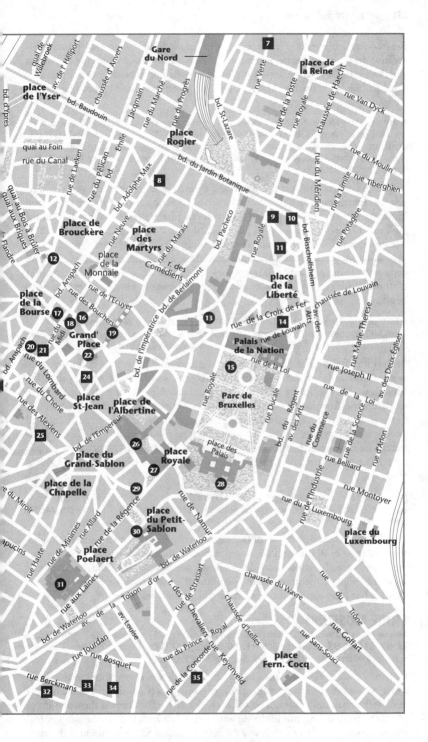

place de l'Yser
quai de Willebroek
av. de l'Héliport
bd. d'Ypres
bd. Baudouin
chaussée d'Anvers
Jacqmain
rue du Marché
rue du Progrès
Gare du Nord

7

place de la Reine
rue Verte
rue de la Poste
rue Royale
chaussée de Haecht
rue Van Dyck

quai au Foin
rue du Canal
rue de Laeken
rue du Pélican
bd. Emile
bd. Adolphe Max
place Rogier
bd. St-Lazare
rue du Moulin
rue du Méridien
rue de la Limite
rue Tiberghien

Quai au Bois à Brûler
quai aux Briques
v. Flandre

8

bd. du Jardin Botanique
bd. Pacheco
rue Royale
bd. Bisschofsheim
rue Potagère

place de Brouckère
rue Neuve
place des Martyrs
rue du Marais
r. des Comédiens

9 **10**

11

chaussée de Louvain
av. des Arts
rue Marie-Thérèse

12

place de la Monnaie

place de la Liberté

place de la Bourse
17
bd. Anspach
rue des Bouchers
rue de l'Ecuyer
bd. de l'Impératrice
bd. de Berlaimont
rue de la Croix de Fer
rue de Louvain

13
14

rue Joseph II
av. des Deux-Églises

18 **16**
Grand' Place
19

20 **21**
bd. Anspach
rue du Midi
rue du Lombard
22

Palais de la Nation
rue de la Loi
15
rue de la Loi
rue de la Science
rue d'Arlon

24

place St-Jean
rue du Chêne
rue des Alexiens

place de l'Albertine
rue Royale
Parc de Bruxelles
bd. du Régent
av. des Arts
rue du Commerce
rue Belliard

25

26
place du Grand-Sablon
27

place Royale
place des Palais
bd. Ducale

28

rue Montoyer
rue de l'Industrie
rue de Luxembourg

place de la Chapelle
rue du Miroir
29
rue de la Régence
place du Petit-Sablon
30
rue Allard
rue des Minimes

place Poelaert
rue de Namur
bd. de Waterloo
place du Luxembourg

capucins
rue Haute
31
rue aux Laines
av. de la Toison d'or
bd. de Waterloo

chaussée du Wavre
rue du Trône
rue Coffart
rue Sans-Souci
place Fern. Cocq

rue Jourdan
rue Bosquet
av. Louise
r. des Chevaliers
rue de Strassart
chaussée d'Ixelles
rue du Prince Royal
rue Keyenveld
rue de la Concorde

35

rue Berckmans
32 **33** **34**

Room—you'll marvel at 17th-century tapestries so detailed they even provide perspective. In the room before the mayor's office is a 19th-century painting of Brussels with a river in the town center—a stream later covered in an attempt to curb malaria. The building is still used as the seat of the civic government, and its wedding room is a popular place to tie the knot.

Musée de la Ville de Bruxelles (Museum of the City of Brussels). In the Maison du Roi, on Grand' Place. ☎ **02/279-43-50.** Admission 80BF ($2.50) adults, 50BF ($1.55) children. Apr–Sept Mon–Thurs 10am–12:30pm and 1:30–5pm, Sat–Sun 10am–1pm; Oct–Mar Mon–Thurs 10am–12:30pm and 1:30–4pm, Sat–Sun 10am–1pm. Closed Jan 1, May 1, Nov 1, and Dec 25. Métro: Bourse.

This 19th-century structure has served as a covered bread market and a prison in its previous incarnations. Today it displays a mixed collection associated with the art and history of Brussels. On the ground floor you can admire detailed tapestries from the 16th and 17th centuries, as well as porcelain, silver, and stone statuary. After climbing a beautiful wooden staircase, you can trace the history of Brussels in old maps, prints, photos, and models. And on the third floor there are dozens of costumes that have been given to the *Manneken Pis* (see above) since 1698, including a hotel receptionist uniform, 18th-century ball costumes, and a Japanese kimono complete with headband.

✪ **Atomium.** Heysel, Laeken. ☎ **02/477-09-91.** Admission 250BF ($8) adults, 200BF ($6) ages 3–12, free for age 2 and under. Apr–Sept daily 9am–8pm; Oct–Mar daily 10am–6pm (Panorama to 9:30pm). Métro: 1A to Heysel, the last stop (a 20-minute trip).

As the Eiffel Tower is the symbol of Paris, the Atomium is the symbol of Brussels, and, as was Paris's landmark, the Atomium was built for a world's fair, specifically the 1958 Brussels world's fair. Rising 335 feet, like a giant plaything of the gods that has fallen to Earth, the Atomium represents an iron crystal molecule magnified 165 billion times. Its metal-clad spheres, representing individual atoms, are connected by enclosed escalators and elevators. Within the Atomium is an exhibit on human life and medical research. However, it's the topmost atom of the molecule that attracts most people: a restaurant/observation deck that provides a sweeping panorama of the metropolitan area.

Mini-Europe. In Bruparck, Heysel. ☎ **02/478-05-50.** Admission 395BF ($12) adults, 295BF ($9) age 12 and under, free for children 40 inches and shorter. Daily 9:30am–6pm. MC, V. Métro: Heysel.

Since Brussels is the new capital of Europe, it's fitting that the city is home to a miniature rendering of all the continent's most notable architectural sights. Even a few natural wonders and technological developments are represented. Built on a scale of 1/25 of the original, the structures of Mini-Europe exhibit remarkable detail. Though children like Mini-Europe the best, adults will certainly find it fun.

MORE MUSEUMS

Musée Instrumental (Instrument Museum). 17 place du Petit-Sablon. ☎ **02/511-35-95.** Admission 80BF ($2.50) adults, 50BF ($1.55) seniors/children. Thurs–Sat 9:30am–4:45pm. Tram: 92, 93, or 94. Bus: 20, 34, 95, or 96.

Only 5% of the museum's immense collection is shown at one time, so the works rotate periodically. In the permanent exhibit you'll see a piano that fits into a book, a viola with a map of Paris inlaid on the back, one of the first lutes in the world (from the 16th century), and two of the earliest models of a keyboard. In the wind instruments section you'll learn that it was a Belgian, Adolphe Sax, who invented the saxophone. On request, small demonstrations are given and the instruments are explained.

Special & Free Events

July and August are especially active in Brussels. On the first Tuesday and Thursday in July, you can watch the **Ommegang** in the Grand' Place, a parade of noble families dressed in historical costumes; July 21, **National Day,** is marked by various celebrations, including fireworks; July 21 to August 20 brings the bustling **Brussels Fair** near Gare du Midi; on August 9, the Bruxellois celebrate the 1213 victory of Brussels over Leuven by planting a **Meiboom** (maytree) at the intersection of rue des Sables and rue du Marais, as bands and other activities commemorate the event.

For the most up-to-date information on this year's special events, contact the **Belgian National Tourist Office,** 780 Third Ave., Suite 1501, New York, NY 10017 (☎ 212/758-8130).

It's only natural that the magnificent Grand' Place should host some of Brussels's most memorable free events. April to September, you can watch a free evening **Music and Light show.** Classical music plays as the square's buildings are dramatically highlighted. Or you can stop by at noon, when the tower of the **Maison du Roi** plays golden carillon chimes reminiscent of an earlier European era. The square still functions as an important **marketplace.** Tuesday to Sunday 8am to 6pm the Grand' Place hosts a flower market, and on Sunday (see "Shopping," later in this chapter) a bird market. During Christmas, a large tree is erected at the center and a crèche is placed at the lower end.

Musée Royal de l'Armée et d'Histoire Militaire. 3 Parc du Cinquantenaire. ☎ **02/733-44-93.** Free admission. Tues–Sun 9am–noon and 1–4:45pm. Closed Jan 1, May 1, Nov 1, and Dec 25. Métro: Merode; it's opposite Autoworld.

This is one of Brussels's often-forgotten museums, where the huge military collection is one of the finest in Europe. It includes an extensive display of armor, uniforms, and weapons from various Belgian campaigns (like the Congo), a massive clutter of World War I artillery pieces, an aircraft hangar of 130 impressive planes, and a World War II collection of Nazi flags that brings the Nürnberg rallies to mind. Anyone interested in military history shouldn't miss this superb, though sometimes cluttered, collection.

Musées Royaux d'Art et d'Histoire. 10 Parc du Cinquantenaire. ☎ **02/741-72-11.** Admission 150BF ($4.70). Daily 10am–5pm. Closed Jan 1, May 1, Nov 1 and 11, and Dec 25. Métro: Merode; it's around the corner from the Military Museum and Autoworld.

A vast museum that opens half its collection one day and the other half the next, this museum shows off antiques, decorative arts (tapestries, porcelain, silver, and sculptures), and archaeology. Highlights are an Assyrian relief from the 9th century B.C., a Greek vase from the 6th century B.C., the A.D. 1145 reliquary of Pope Alexander, some exceptional tapestries, and colossal statues from Easter Island dating from centuries before Christ. This museum is the largest in Belgium.

Autoworld. 11 Parc du Cinquantenaire. ☎ **02/736-41-65.** Admission 200BF ($6) adults, 150BF ($4.70) students. Apr–Sept daily 10am–6pm; Oct–Mar daily 10am–5pm. Métro: Merode; it's across from the Military Museum.

I'm not a car fanatic, but I found this display of an aircraft hangar full of 500 historic cars fascinating. The collection starts with early motorized tricycles of 1899 and moves on to a 1911 Model T Ford, a 1924 Renault, a 1938 Cadillac that was the official White House car for FDR and Truman, a 1956 Cadillac used by Eisenhower and then by Kennedy during his June 1963 visit to Berlin, and more.

Musée du Costume et de la Dentelle (Costume and Lace Museum). 6 rue de la Vio-lette (near the Grand' Place). ☎ **02/512-77-09.** Admission 80BF ($2.50) adults, 50BF ($1.55) children, free for age 5 and under. Apr–Sept Mon–Tues and Thurs–Fri 10am–12:30pm and 1:30–5pm, Sat–Sun 2–4:30pm; Oct–Mar Mon–Tues and Thurs–Fri 10am–12:30pm and 1:30–4pm, Sat–Sun 2–4:30pm. Closed Jan 1, May 1, Nov 1 and 11, and Dec 25. Métro: Bourse.

Honoring the once major industry (some 10,000 Bruxellois made lace in the 18th century) that now operates in a reduced but still prominent fashion, this museum shows off particularly fine lace and costumes from 1599 to the present, with frequent changing exhibitions.

Centre Belge de la Bande Dessinée (Belgian Center for Comic-Strip Art). In the Waucquez Warehouse, 20 rue des Sables. ☎ **02/219-19-80.** Admission 150BF ($4.70) adults, 50BF ($1.55) children. Tues–Sun 10am–6pm. Métro: Rogier or Botanique.

As you'll soon find out, Belgians are crazy for cartoons, and at this unique museum lovers of Tintin and other Belgian comic-book heroes can see their favorite stars. The building was designed by art nouveau architect Victor Horta and is an attraction in itself.

CHURCHES

Cathédrale des Sts-Michel-et-Gudule. Set back off bd. de l'Impératrice near Gare Centrale. ☎ **02/217-83-45.** Cathedral, free; crypt, 40BF ($1.25). Apr–Sept daily 7am–7pm; Oct–Mar daily 7am–6pm. Métro: Gare Centrale.

Dating from 1226, this cathedral is a Gothic masterpiece, highlighted by detailed 16th-century stained-glass windows that are some of the world's finest. The 15th-century facade of the two matching towers appears strangely unfinished, as they end in square tops rather than long points—yet this is exactly how it was designed. In 1983, extensive cleaning and restorations were started; the process uncovered the archaeological remains of a Roman church below the floors. Until the restoration is completed (possibly in 1999), half the interior remains closed.

On Sunday at 10am the Eucharist is celebrated with a Gregorian choir. In July, August, and September, polyphonic masses are sung by local and international choirs at 10am. Chamber music and organ concerts are occasionally performed August to October on weekdays at 8pm. In spring and autumn at 12:30pm, mass is sung accompanied by instrumental soloists and readings by actors (in French only).

Notre-Dame du Sablon. 3B rue de la Régence (off place du Grand-Sablon). ☎ **02/511-57-41.** Free admission. Daily 9am–6pm. Tram: 92, 93, or 94. Bus: 95 or 96.

Between the city park and the Palais de Justice, this Late Gothic 15th- and 16th-century structure is noted for its fourfold gallery with brightly colored stained-glass windows, illuminated from the inside at night, in striking contrast with the gray-white Gothic arches and walls. Also worth seeing are the two baroque chapels decorated with funeral symbols in white marble.

AN AMUSEMENT PARK

Bruparck is Brussels's amusement park. Built on the site of the 1958 Brussels world's fair, it's home to the Atomium and Mini-Europe (see above), the Kinepolis movie complex, Bruparck village, a collection of restaurants and cafes (including a restaurant in a 1930s railway car of the legendary *Orient Express*), Oceade (an indoor/outdoor water-sports pavilion with water slides, pools, and saunas), and a planetarium. Admission to Oceade for 4 hours is 370BF ($12) adults and 290BF ($9) children. Admission to the planetarium is 130BF ($4.05) adults and 100BF ($3.10) age 11 and under.

Both these attractions are open daily in summer and Tuesday to Sunday the rest of the year. Take the Métro to the Heysel stop.

PARKS & GARDENS

The most attractive park in town is the **Parc de Bruxelles,** which extends in front of the Palais Royale. Once the property of the dukes of Brabant, this well-designed park with geometrically divided paths running through it became public in 1776. The many benches make a fine place to stop for a small picnic. It's also historic: Belgium's first battle for independence (in 1830) was fought here. Admission to the park is free. Open daily 6am to 9pm.

A nice park in the center is the **Jardin d'Egmont.** It's often overlooked because it's hidden behind buildings—there are only two small entrance paths. You'll find this sculptured garden between the Palais de Justice and the Palais Royale; enter from rue du Grand-Cerf or a small footpath off boulevard du Waterloo. Free admission. Open daily 6am to 9pm.

Outside the Musée Instrumental you'll see **place du Petit-Sablon,** with a small sculptured garden at the center surrounded by a wrought-metal gate. Forty-eight statues of ancient guilds surround the quaint garden. Admission is free. Open daily 6am to 9pm.

ORGANIZED TOURS

For do-it-yourself **walking tours** of Brussels, refer to the tourist office's *Brussels Guide and Map,* which outlines seven excellent walks throughout the city.

Brussels City-Tours, 8 rue de la Colline, off the Grand' Place (☎ 02/513-77-44; Métro: Gare Centrale), operates a 3-hour tour for 780BF ($24.35) and offers several options for day trips across Belgium, Holland, France, and Luxembourg. At 55 bd. Adolphe-Max, **ARAU Tourville** (☎ 02/219-33-44; fax 02/219-86-75) organizes tours that attempt to help you "discover not only Brussels's countless treasures, but also problems the city faces." It runs specialized architectural tours by coach: "Brussels 1900—Art Nouveau" runs on Saturday at 9:45am and "Brussels 1930—Art Deco" every third Saturday at 10:15am. Coach tours are 500BF ($16).

June 15 to September 15, the **Chatterbus Tour,** 12 rue des Thuyas (☎ 02/673-18-35; fax 02/675-12-67; Métro: Gare Centrale), operates a 3-hour tour daily at 10am from the Galeries St-Hubert, a shopping mall next to 90 rue du Marché-aux-Herbes, a few steps off the Grand' Place. A walking tour covers the historic center, followed by a public transportation ride through areas the average visitor never sees. You'll hear about life in Belgium and get a real feel for the city. The price is 330BF ($10). It's a fascinating experience and no reservation is necessary—just be there by 10am.

6 Shopping

BEST BUYS

Brussels boasts several **outdoor markets,** where half the fun is finding an alluring item and the other half is bargaining down the price. Of course, you'll also enjoy a stroll along the modern shopping promenades, the busiest of which is the pedestrian **rue Neuve,** which starts at place de la Monnaie, the site of the Opera House, and runs north to place Rogier. Here you'll find numerous boutiques as well as department stores, including **City 2,** a huge shopping mall full of stores and inexpensive restaurants (see the box "Quick Bites & Dessert," earlier in this chapter). One of Brussels's largest modern supermarkets, **Delhaize,** is at the corner of rue du Marché-aux-Poulets and boulevard Anspach, diagonally across from La Bourse. Watch for the green sign above the door.

Other interesting shopping malls are the **Anspach Center,** off place de la Monnaie, diagonally across from the Opera House; the **Center Monnaie,** across the street; the **Galeries St-Hubert,** off rue du Marché-aux-Herbes; and **Galerie Agora,** off the Grand' Place.

U.K. travelers, particularly, may wish to shop at **Marks & Spencer,** 21 rue Neuve. At **W. H. Smith,** 75 av. Adolphe-Max (☎ 02/219-27-08; Métro: Rogier), you'll find plenty of English-language newspapers, magazines, and books. For luxury shopping, try the stores on **avenue Louise** and the nearby streets, where you'll find names like Cartier, Burberry, Vuitton, Benetton, and Valentino. You may not find any bargains, but there's lots to look at.

You'll find an interesting street for window-shopping near the Grand' Place, ✪ **rue des Eperonniers,** which hosts many small shops selling antiques, toys, old books, and clothing.

Lace is the overwhelming favorite among visitors to Brussels, followed by **crystal, pewter, jewelry,** and **antiques. Chocolate, beer,** and other foods are a more economical favorite of foreign shoppers. Located in a former guild house, **Maison Antoine,** 26 Grand' Place (☎ 02/512-14-59, Métro: Gare Centrale or Bourse), is one of the best places in Brussels to buy lace. The quality is superb, the service is friendly, and the prices aren't unreasonable.

Belgians view **comic books** quite seriously. Hard covers bind comic books—you're meant to treasure and preserve them. Colorful thin volumes often cost about $12, though you can also find used ones for less. You can buy comics at several stores between nos. 132 and 206 chaussée de Wavre, between rue du Trône and rue Goffart.

OUTDOOR MARKETS

My favorite outdoor market is the **flea market** on place du Jeu-de-Balle, a large cobblestone square a few blocks from Gare du Midi. As at all flea markets, you'll have to sift through lots of junk but can make real finds in the old postcards, comic books, clothes, furniture, African masks, brass fixtures, and other items. The market is held daily 7am to 2pm.

For better-quality goods at decidedly higher prices, check out the **antiques market** on place du Grand-Sablon, open Saturday 9am to 6pm and Sunday 9am to 2pm. You'll also find quite a few **antiques stores,** open throughout the week, on streets in the nearby area (try, for example, rue de Rollebeek). Prices are high, but it's a fun place to look around.

As you near the Grand' Place on Sunday 7am to 2pm, the loud chirping and whistling of birds make it seem as if you're entering a tropical jungle. Yet it's only the ✪ **bird market,** where you can admire thousands of birds—from parakeets to ducks. It's an unusual market in the very center of town and is certainly amusing—and free.

SUNDAY CASBAH   Every Sunday 7am to 2pm, hundreds of merchants assemble their wares along the railroad tracks leading to Gare du Midi, and because many of the merchants are Arabs and southern Europeans, the scene resembles a Middle Eastern casbah. You'll find many excellent food bargains, making it a perfect place to gather provisions for a few days. You can also find household items and many odds and ends at low cost. Hold onto your wallet (busy markets the world over attract pickpockets) and bargain.

The market starts where boulevard du Midi crosses the rail tracks at place de la Constitution and continues on both sides of the tracks for several blocks. Lemonnier is the nearest Métro stop. For a list of other markets, see the *Brussels Guide and Map*, sold at the tourist office.

7 Brussels After Dark

Though Brussels is too conservative and traditional to go really wild at night, it does offer a full array of things to do. The best list of upcoming events is in the weekly English-language *What's On* magazine, available free from the tourist office. It lists dance, opera, live music, film, and TV events for the week, for both Brussels and the rest of Belgium.

Keep in mind that the **tourist office** in the Town Hall on the Grand' Place sells concert and theater tickets.

THE PERFORMING ARTS

OPERA, BALLET & CONCERTS   An opera house in the grand style, the **Théâtre Royal de la Monnaie,** place de la Monnaie (☎ **02/229-12-11;** Métro: Place de Brouckère), is home to the Opéra National, which has been called the best in the French-speaking world. It's also home to the Orchestre Symphonique de la Monnaie, and its resident dance company has performed all over the world. The box office is open Tuesday to Saturday 11am to 6pm. Tickets run 300BF to 3,200BF ($9 to $100); for students 25 and under (available 5 minutes before a show), they're 200BF ($6.25).

As crazy as the Belgians are about cartoons, it should come as no surprise that the most popular venue here is a puppet theater: the **Théâtre Toone VII,** 21 petite rue des Bouchers, at impasse Schuddeveld (☎ **02/511-71-37;** Métro: Bourse). In a tiny room upstairs from a bistro of the same name, such classic tales as *Faust* and *The Three Musketeers* are performed by marionettes. The dialogue is in French, but the plots and characters are so familiar that even if you don't understand a word you'll be able to follow the action. Performances are Tuesday to Saturday at 8:30pm, with tickets at 400BF ($13).

JAZZ   The basic **Preservation Hall,** 4 place de Londres (☎ **02/502-15-97;** Métro: Namur), notwithstanding the name, has only about 50 seats and is always crowded with jazz fanatics. It's undecorated except for wall mirrors. Founded over 30 years ago, it has become one of the "in" places for New Orleans–type jazz and Dixieland lovers, open Tuesday, Thursday, Friday, and Saturday from 9pm. ✪ **Travers,** 11 rue Traversière (☎ **02/217-60-58;** fax 02/223-10-21; Métro: Botanique), is a quintessential smoky jazz club with fewer than a dozen tables lit by candles. Modern art adorns the walls. Two to five concerts are performed per week; call for the schedule. It's open Monday to Saturday 8pm to 2am or later. Concerts start at 8:30pm weeknights and at 10pm Saturday. The cover is 300BF to 400BF ($9 to $13), except for Monday's free jam session.

Sounds, 28 rue de la Tulipe (☎ **02/512-92-50;** Métro: Porte de Namur), is a low-key bar that presents jazz in a relatively large, airy space. Other than a small supplement on the reasonably priced drinks, the music is free. Wednesday is salsa night, and weekend jazz programs include trios and quartets, sometimes with vocalists. It's open Monday to Saturday 11:30am to 4pm and 7pm to 4am.

CAFES & BARS

The city's many cafes and bars run the gamut from art nouveau palaces to convivial watering holes. No visit to Brussels is complete without lingering a few hours in one, preferably savoring one of the incredible variety of beers for which Belgium is famous.

Be aware that Belgian brews are considerably stronger than those in America—the alcohol content can be as high as 12%. You might want to try one of the rich, dark Trappist ales brewed by monks from the monasteries Chimay, Orval, Rochefort, Westmalle, and Westvleteren.

Brussels is also known for its lambic beers, which depend on naturally occurring yeast for fermentation. These are often flavored with fruit and come in bottles with champagne-type corks. Unlike any other beer, they're more akin to a sweet sparkling wine. My favorite is Gueuze, a blend of young and aged lambic beers but one of the least sweet. If you prefer something sweeter, try raspberry-flavored Framboise or cherry-flavored Kriek. Faro is a special low-alcohol beer, sometimes sweetened or lightly spiced.

ON & NEAR THE GRAND' PLACE   It's always satisfying to grab a chair at a sidewalk cafe on the Grand' Place and drink in the beauty of the floodlit golden buildings ringing the square. After you've ordered one drink you can remain for as long as you wish.

A 1911 cafe with columns, neoclassical ornaments and mirrors, and small wooden tables, **A la Mort Subite,** 7 rue Montagne-aux-Herbes-Potagères (☎ 02/513-13-18; Métro: Place de Brouckère), is a good place to enjoy an afternoon coffee or an evening beer. Brussels-born songwriter Jacques Brel is said to have hung out here. It's open daily 10am to 1am. **A l'Imaige Nostre-Dame,** 8 rue du Marché-aux-Herbes 6 (☎ 02/219-42-49; Métro: Bourse), is in a house dating from 1642, just a block from the Grand' Place; here people of all ages enjoy reasonably priced beer amid wooden ceiling beams, old wooden tables, painted windows, and an antique ceramic fireplace. It's open daily noon to midnight.

For those with a mischievous sense of the macabre, **Le Cercueil (The Coffin),** 10–12 rue des Harengs (☎ 02/513-33-61; Métro: Bourse), just off the Grand' Place, provides an atmosphere like no other. The tables are glass panes placed over coffins, and certain drinks are served in ceramic skulls. Purple fluorescent lighting keeps the rooms dim, and ecclesiastical music, especially organ music, plays in the background. Prices are a little high: Half a liter of beer costs 200BF ($6). It's open daily 11am to 3am. On the opposite side of La Bourse from the crowded and smoky Falstaff, **Cirio,** 18 rue de la Bourse (☎ 02/512-13-95; Métro: Bourse), is a quiet cafe popular with older Bruxellois, and there's no better cafe for people-watching. Efficient waiters carrying trays of beer, wine, and coffee with crackers or cookies navigate among the little tables. The art nouveau woodwork, red-and-green-striped banquettes, and polished brass seem to have been perfectly preserved since the late 1800s. It's open daily 11am to 1am.

The oldest cafe here, in a 1690 building (once home to Brussels's bakers), ✪ **Le Roy d'Espagne,** 1 Grand' Place (☎ 02/513-08-07; Métro: Bourse), accommodates patrons in several areas. In addition to the outdoor tables, you can drink in a room that preserves a 17th-century Flemish interior style—a masterpiece of wooden architecture with a wooden walkway and beams above and a fireplace covered by a black metal hood. From the fourth floor, the view of the Grand' Place is spectacular. It's open daily 10am to 1am.

ELSEWHERE   De Ultieme Hallucinatie, 316 rue Royale (☎ 02/217-06-14; Métro: Botanique), was a turn-of-the-century private house that's now an art nouveau restaurant as well as a garden cafe. Rocky walls and plants decorate one side, and a long marble bar occupies the other. There's a more futuristic bar area downstairs with fluorescent lighting and abstract outer-space art, a small outdoor cafe area, and a charming section behind the garden. The place offers a wide selection of beers, as well as wine, coffee, and a few snacks. It's open Monday to Friday 11am to 3am and

Saturday and Sunday 4pm to 3am. A cafe in a 17th-century building, ✪ **Le Fleur en Papier Doré,** 53 rue des Alexiens, off place de la Chapelle (☎ **02/511-16-59;** Métro: Bourse), calls itself a "temple of surrealism" because Magritte allegedly used to relax here. Old prints, plates, horns, porcelain, and other objects cover every inch of the walls. Despite the grandmotherly decor, the cafe attracts a wide assortment of arty types. The three small rooms hold fewer than a dozen tables. On Friday and Saturday from 9 or 10pm, an accordion player pumps out some tunes, and there are occasional poetry readings upstairs. It's open daily 11am to 11pm.

GAY & LESBIAN CLUBS

Rue des Riches-Claires and **rue du Marché-au-Charbon** (not far from La Bourse) host some gay and lesbian bars. **Macho 2,** 108 rue du Marché-au-Charbon (☎ **02/513-56-67**), a block from rue des Riches-Claires, houses a gay men's sauna, pool, steam room, and cafe. It's open Monday to Thursday noon to 2am, Friday and Saturday noon to 4am, and Sunday 2pm to midnight. Admission is 450BF ($14) or 300BF ($9) for men under 25. And **Le Garage** (see below) features a gay night every Sunday 9pm to 3am.

For more information, you can contact **Infor Homo,** 57 av. de Roodebeek (☎02/733-10-24; Métro: Diamant), open Tuesday to Friday 8am to 6pm. Or you can stop by the gay and lesbian community center, **Telsquels,** 81 rue du Marché au Charbon (☎ **02/512-45-87;** Métro: Bourse), open Saturday to Thursday 5pm to 2am and Friday 8am to 4am.

A DANCE CLUB

The first large dance club to open in Brussels (1983), **Le Garage,** 16 rue Duquesnoy (☎ **02/512-66-22;** Métro: Gare Centrale), accommodates a car to the side of the dance floor, plus a video screen. For the most part, the club attracts people 18 to 30. Cover is 100BF ($3.10) on Wednesday, Thursday, and Sunday and 300BF ($9) on Friday and Saturday, which includes three soft drinks or one hard drink. Sunday is gay night.

8 Side Trips: Bruges, Waterloo & More

BRUGES (BRUGGE)

From its 13th-century origins as a cloth manufacturing town to its current incarnation as a tourism mecca, the Flemish town of **Bruges** seems to have changed little. As in a fairy tale, swans glide down the winding canals and the stone houses look as if they're made of gingerbread. Even though glass-fronted stores have taken over the ground floors of ancient buildings and the swans scatter before tour boats chugging along the canals, Bruges has made the transition from medieval to modern with remarkable grace.

ARRIVING   There are **trains** about twice an hour from Gare de Nord, Gare Centrale, and Gare Midi in Brussels. The trip takes 50 minutes, and the train stops at Ghent. Bruges is also well connected to Antwerp and the channel ferry ports of Ostend (Oostende) and Zeebrugge. The Bruges station is on Stationsplein (☎ **050/38-23-82** for rail information), about 1 mile south of town, a 20-minute walk to the town center or a short bus or taxi ride. The bus station adjoins the train station. You can get schedule and fare information by calling ☎ **050/38-23-82.**

If you're **driving** from Brussels, take the E40 but drop your car at one of the parking zones outside the center. It's only a short walk into the heart of the city, where the network of one-way streets makes driving a nightmare.

Boating the Canals

A "must" for everyone is a ✪ **boat trip** on Bruges's canals. The open-top boats operate year-round from several departure points, all marked with an anchor icon on maps available at the tourist office. March to November, the boats operate daily 10am to 6pm; December to February, they operate Saturday, Sunday, school holidays, and public holidays 10am to 6pm (except if the canals are frozen). A half-hour cruise is 170BF ($5) adults and 85BF ($2.65) children over 4. Wear something warm if the weather is cold or windy.

VISITOR INFORMATION The **Tourist Office,** Burg 11, 8000 Bruges (☎ 050/44-86-86; fax 050/44-86-00; www.brugge.be/brugge), is friendly and efficient. It offers brochures outlining walking, coach, canal, and horse-drawn cab tours, as well as detailed information on many attractions. The staff can make reservations in hotels, hostels, and B&Bs for a deposit of 400BF ($13). April to September, it's open Monday to Friday 9:30am to 6:30pm and Saturday and Sunday 10am to noon and 2 to 6:30pm; October to March, hours are Monday to Friday 9:30am to 5pm and Saturday and Sunday 9:30am to 1pm and 2 to 5:30pm.

GETTING AROUND Most city **buses** depart from the Markt or one of the adjacent streets and from the bus station beside the train station, with schedules prominently posted. A single ticket is 40BF ($1.25).

There are **taxi ranks** at the Markt (☎ 050/33-44-44) and outside the train station on Stationsplein (☎ 050/38-46-60).

If you arrive by train, you can rent a **bicycle** (you must present a valid rail ticket) at the Baggage Department (☎ 050/38-58-71) of the rail station for 325BF ($10) per day. Biking is a terrific way to get around or out of town to the nearby village of Damme by way of beautiful canalside roads.

Going around by **tour boat** is also a great way to see Bruges, especially on a fine day, and the view from those open-top boats is unforgettable (see below for details).

SEEING THE SIGHTS Bruges has two hearts in side-by-side monumental squares: the Markt and the Burg. Narrow streets fan out from these, while a network of canals threads its way to every section of the small city. The center is almost encircled by a canal that opens at its southern end to become the Minnewater (Lake of Love), filled with swans and other birds and bordered by the Begijnhof and a fine park. On the outer side of the Minnewater is the rail station. Walking is the best way to see Bruges, but wear good walking shoes—those cobblestones can be hard going.

Begin your tour at the **Markt,** where you'll find the 13th- to 16th-century **Belfry (Belfort)** and **Halls (Hallen),** Markt 7 (☎ 050/38-69-01). Much of the city's commerce was conducted in the Hallen in centuries past. Climb the 366 steps to the Belfry's summit for a panoramic view all the way to the sea. The Belfry and Halls are open daily: April to September 9:30am to 5pm and October to March 9:30am to 12:30pm and 1:30 to 5pm. Admission is 100BF ($3.10) adults and 50BF ($1.55) children.

The **sculpture group** in the center of the Markt depicts two Flemish heroes, butcher Jan Breydel and weaver Pieter de Coninck, who led a 1302 uprising against the wealthy merchants and nobles who dominated the guilds, then went on to an against-all-odds victory over French knights later that same year in the Battle of the Golden Spurs. The large neo-Gothic **Provinciaal Hof** dates from the 1800s and houses the government of West Flanders province.

Bruges

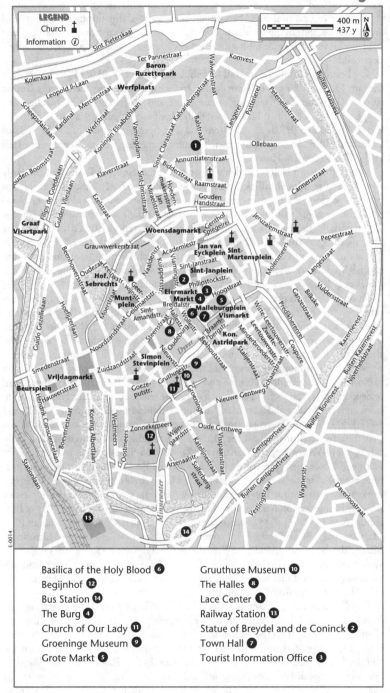

Basilica of the Holy Blood ❻
Begijnhof ⓬
Bus Station ⓮
The Burg ❹
Church of Our Lady ⓫
Groeninge Museum ❾
Grote Markt ❺

Gruuthuse Museum ❿
The Halles ❽
Lace Center ❶
Railway Station ⓭
Statue of Breydel and de Coninck ❷
Town Hall ❼
Tourist Information Office ❸

An array of beautiful buildings, which adds up to a trip through the history of architecture, stands in the **Burg,** a public square just steps away from the Markt, where Baldwin "Iron Arm" once built a fortified castle around which a village (or "burg") developed.

The beautiful Gothic **Town Hall (Stadhuis),** Burg 11 (☎ **050/44-81-10**), is from the late 1300s, making it Belgium's oldest town hall. Don't miss the upstairs **Gothic Room (Gotische Zaal)** with its ornate decor and murals depicting highlights of Bruges's history. The Town Hall is open daily: April to September 9:30am to 5pm and October to March 9:30am to 12:30pm and 2 to 5pm. Admission of 100BF ($3.10) adults and 50BF ($1.55) children includes entry to the neighboring **Renaissance Hall** of the **Old Recorders House.**

Next to the Town Hall is the richly decorated Romanesque ✪ **Basilica of the Holy Blood (Heilige-Bloedbasiliek),** Burg 10 (☎ **050/33-67-92**). Since 1149, this has been a repository of a fragment of cloth impregnated with what's said to be the blood of Christ, brought to Bruges during the Second Crusade by the count of Flanders. The relic is in the basilica museum inside a rock-crystal vial that's itself kept in a magnificent gold-and-silver reliquary. The basilica is open daily: April to September 9:30am to noon and 2 to 6pm and October to March 10am to noon and 2 to 4pm (closed Wednesday afternoon). Admission to the basilica is free; admission to the museum is 40BF ($1.25) adults and 20BF (65¢) children.

Through the centuries, one of the most tranquil spots in Bruges has been the **Begijnhof,** Wijngaardstraat (☎ **050/33-00-11**), and so it remains today. Begijns were religious women, similar to nuns, who accepted vows of chastity and obedience but drew the line at poverty. Today, the begijns are no more, and the Begijnhof is occupied by Benedictine nuns who try to keep the begijns' traditions alive. The beautiful little whitewashed houses surrounding a lawn with trees make a marvelous place of escape. March to November, it's open daily 10am to noon and 1:45 to 5pm (weekends to 5:30pm April to September); December to February, it's open Monday, Tuesday, and Friday 11am to noon and Wednesday and Thursday 2 to 4pm. Admission is 60BF ($1.85) adults and 30BF (95¢) children. The courtyard is permanently open and admission is free.

It took two centuries (the 13th to the 15th) to build the **Church of Our Lady (Onze-Lieve-Vrouwekerk),** Mariastraat (☎ **050/34-53-14**), and you can see its soaring 396-foot-high spire from a wide area around Bruges. Among its many art treasures are the marvelous marble *Madonna and Child* by Michelangelo (one of his few works to be seen outside Italy), a painting by Anthony Van Dyck, and the impressive side-by-side bronze tomb sculptures of Charles the Bold (died 1477) and Mary of Burgundy (died 1482). April to September, the church is open Monday to Saturday 10 to 11:30am and 2:30 to 5pm (to 4pm Saturday) and Sunday 2:30 to 5pm; October to March, the hours are Monday to Saturday 10 to 11:30am and 2:30 to 4:30pm (to 4pm Saturday) and Sunday 2:30 to 4:30pm. Admission to the church and the *Madonna and Child* altar is free; admission to the chapel of Charles and Mary is 60BF ($1.85) adults and 30BF (95¢) children.

The ✪ **Groeninge Museum,** Dijver 12 (☎ **050/33-99-11**), ranks among Belgium's leading traditional museums of fine arts, with a collection that covers the Low Countries' painting from the 15th to the 20th centuries. The Gallery of Flemish Primitives holds some 30 works, which seem far from "primitive," by such painters as Jan Van Eyck (portrait of his wife, Margerita Van Eyck), Rogier van der Weyden, Hieronymus Bosch *(The Last Judgment),* and Hans Memling. Works by Magritte and Delvaux are also on display. April to September, the museum is open daily 9:30am to 5pm; October to March, it's open Wednesday to Monday 9:30am to 12:30pm and 2 to 5pm. Admission is 200BF ($6) adults and 100BF ($3.10) children.

In a courtyard next to the Groeninge Museum is the ornate mansion where Flemish nobleman/herb merchant Louis de Gruuthuse lived in the 1400s. Now the **Gruuthuse Museum,** Dijver 17 (☎ **050/33-99-11**), it features thousands of antiques and antiquities, including paintings, sculptures, tapestries, lace, weapons, glassware, and richly carved furniture. April to September, the museum is open daily 9:30am to 5pm; October to March, it's open Wednesday to Monday 9:30am to 12:30pm and 2 to 5pm. Admission is 130BF ($4.05) adults, 70BF ($2.20) children, and 260BF ($8) families with children under 18.

A popular attraction is the **Lace Center (Kantcentrum),** Peperstraat 3A (☎ **050/33-00-72**). Bruges lace is famous the world over, and there's no lack of shops offering you the opportunity to take some home. This is where the ancient art of lace making is passed on to the next generation, and you get a firsthand look at the artisans who'll be making many of the items for future sale in all the lace shops (handmade lace is the best, though it's more expensive than the machine-made stuff). The center is open Monday to Saturday 10am to noon and 2 to 6pm (to 5pm Saturday). Lace-making demonstrations are in the afternoon. Admission is 60BF ($1.85) adults and 40BF ($1.25) children.

ACCOMMODATIONS   Unlike those in Brussels, Bruges's hotels are geared to visitors, not business travelers. You won't necessarily find discounts on weekends, but hotels are prepared to bargain November to March (except for the Christmas period).

For traditional Flemish charm, you can't beat **Rembrandt-Rubens,** Walplein 38, 8000 Bruges (☎ **050/33-64-39**), on a quiet square near the Begijnhof. This centuries-old mansion has 13 comfortable rooms, 9 with bathroom, costing 1,500BF to 2,300BF ($47 to $72) double, breakfast included. No credit cards are accepted. The **Ensor,** Speelmansrei 10, 8000 Bruges (☎ **050/34-25-89;** fax 050/34-20-18), offers 12 modern rooms, all with bathroom; many overlook the canal. Rates are 2,090BF ($65) for a canal view and 1,860BF ($58) for a rear room. American Express, MasterCard, and Visa are accepted. **Hôtel Lucca,** 30 Naaldensraat (☎ **050/342-067;** fax 050/333-464), has 18 gracious rooms, 13 with shower only and 1 with bathroom, in a 13th-century mansion. The rates are 1,600BF to 1,950BF ($50 to $61) single and 2,500BF ($78) double. American Express, MasterCard, and Visa are accepted.

Passage, Dweersstraat 26, 8000 Bruges (☎ **050/34-02-32;** fax 050/34-01-40), is a hostel with a hotel annex, offering spartan rooms for 1,200BF ($38) and doubles with bathrooms for 1,400BF ($44). American Express, Diners Club, MasterCard, and Visa are accepted. The long oak bar and candlelit wood tables here are welcoming.

DINING   Markt Square is lined with cozy traditional restaurants that offer decent food but few bargains. For real family-style Flemish food, head northwest from Markt to **Bistro d'Eiermarkt,** Eiermarkt 18 (☎ **050/33-03-46**), on lively Eiermarkt Square. Here you'll find specialties like lapin à la flamande (rabbit in beer sauce) for 590BF ($18), waterzooi for 450BF ($14), and a two-course menu for 395BF ($12). If you sit in the tiny downstairs dining room, the family dog may come begging for table scraps. American Express, MasterCard, and Visa are accepted, and the restaurant is open Friday to Wednesday noon to midnight.

A reliable but slightly more expensive choice is **'t Putje,** 't Zand 31 (☎ **050/33-10-78**). This deceptively large place is a triple threat restaurant/brasserie/tearoom. Main meals center on expertly grilled meats and seafood enhanced by classic sauces and served with a dollop of potatoes and vegetables. The two-course lunch menu is a bargain at 295BF ($9), and the three-course dinner is 600BF ($19). À la carte meals are about 800BF to 1,100BF ($25 to $34). You can also enjoy light snacks or a drink on the terrace under red-striped awnings. American Express, Diners Club, MasterCard, and Visa are accepted, and the place is open daily 8:30am to 1am.

Even nonvegetarians will enjoy the delicious daily lunch at **Lotus,** Wapenmakersstraat 5 (☎ 050/33-10-78). For only 285BF ($9), you get a hearty assortment of imaginatively prepared vegetables served in a cheerful Scandinavian-style dining room. The restaurant is open Monday to Saturday 11:45am to 2pm only, and no credit cards are accepted.

BRUGES AFTER DARK   Many of the town's highlights are lit at night, giving the old buildings new luster, and the nightlife can be surprisingly animated for a medieval town. *Exit* magazine is available free at the tourist office and has a "What's On" section (in Flemish but comprehensible) listing the concert and nightlife schedule.

The **Cactus Club,** St. Jakobsstraat 33 (☎ 050/33-20-14), presents an eclectic concert schedule Friday and Saturday nights. Try **De Vuurmolen,** Kraanplein 5 (☎ 050/33-00-79), for a raucous dancing-on-the-tables kind of night; it's open nightly 10pm until the wee hours. **Ma RicaRokk,** 't Zand 8 (☎ 050/33-83-58), is also a bar with dancing; it attracts a young crowd nightly 7pm to 4am (9pm to 6am weekends). For a quieter scene, head to the tavern ✪ **Gran Kaffee de Passage,** Dweersstraat 26, connected to the Passage hostel (see above). It also serves inexpensive meals and is open daily 6pm to 1am. Gays can visit the bar/disco **Ravel,** Karel de Stoutelaan 172 (☎ 050/31-52-74), open Wednesday and Friday to Monday from 10pm.

WATERLOO

On June 18, 1815, the Grand Alliance of British, Dutch, and Prussian forces, along with a smattering of soldiers from the German principalities, defeated the mighty Napoléon Bonaparte and his 74,000 French troops, leaving 40,000 dead. Napoléon himself survived, but his attempt to rebuild his empire was crushed; he was sent to the island of Ste. Helena, where he died 6 years later at age 52.

From Brussels, **bus "W"** leaves for Waterloo on the half hour and on the hour from a small terminal on avenue de Stalingrad, 1 block south of place Rouppe. The 11-mile ride takes 50 minutes and costs 100BF ($3.10). It stops at both the Wellington Museum and the Centre du Visiteur (see below).

You can fill in the details of the Battle of Waterloo at the **Wellington Museum,** 147 chaussée de Bruxelles, in the village of Waterloo (☎ 02/354-78-06), or study a 360° panoramic mural and see a short movie of the battle at the **Centre du Visiteur,** 252 route du Lion (☎ 02/354-78-06). You can survey the actual battlefield from atop the nearby **Lion's Mound,** a pyramid-like hill behind the center. A souvenir shop in the center sells mementos ranging from tin soldiers ($12) to porcelain figurines of Napoléon on a horse ($120) to a replica of Napoléon's cavalry sword ($1,300).

Admission to the Wellington Museum is 90BF ($2.80) adults, 75BF ($2.35) seniors/students, and 40BF ($1.25) ages 6 to 12. It's open daily: April to September 9:30am to 6:30pm and October to March 10:30am to 5pm. The Centre du Visiteur is open daily 9:30am to 6:30pm. Seeing the giant mural and the movie is 300BF ($9) adults, 250BF ($8) seniors/students, and 190BF ($6) children. Entry to the Lion's Mound is 40BF ($1.25) adults/seniors and 20BF (60¢) children.

GHENT, ANTWERP & MORE

For other side-trip options, consider **Ghent,** which rivals Bruges in medieval charm and picturesque canals; modern **Antwerp,** the hometown of 17th-century art master Peter Paul Rubens (you can visit his impressive house), a diamond capital, and a massive port; and **Leuven,** a quaint university town with 22,000 students and architecture dating from hundreds of years ago. Alas, book length constraints prevent me from giving you details about these great destinations—see *Frommer's Belgium, Holland & Luxembourg* for more.

Belgium's excellent **rail network** quickly links you up with these towns: Antwerp is 30 minutes away, Ghent 40 minutes, and Bruges 55 minutes. Note that when arriving by train in Ghent and Bruges, you'll have to take a tram to the city center for 40BF ($1.25).

The national rail company, SNCB, provides several **rail-excursion tickets** to facilitate low-cost trips from Brussels, including "A Day at the Sea or Ardennes," which allows half-price travel to those destinations and weekend passes that offer reductions to a number of Belgian cities on the weekend. You can also buy a railpass that allows 5 days of travel over a 30-day span. Ask for details at the tourist office or any train station.

Budget hotels in Ghent are in short supply, but if you want to spend more than a day, try the **Eden,** Zuidstationstraat 24 (☎ **09/223-51-51;** fax 09/233-34-57), which offers simple but comfortable doubles with bathrooms for 2,400BF to 3,200BF ($75 to $100). It accepts American Express, Diners Club, MasterCard, and Visa. Even cheaper is the **Flandria,** Barrestraat 3 (☎ **09/223-06-26;** fax 09/233-77-89), which has basic but clean rooms (some with bathroom) for 1,400BF to 1,800BF ($44 to $56). It accepts Eurocard, MasterCard, and Visa. To dine at a reasonable price, try 't Galgenhuisje, Groentenmarkt 5 (☎ **09/233-42-51**), which resembles a shadowy medieval tavern and serves Flemish main courses for 450BF to 595BF ($14 to $19). It's open Tuesday to Sunday noon to 1am and accepts American Express, MasterCard, and Visa. Or you might like the 450BF ($14) all-you-can-eat sparerib dinner at **Amadeus,** St. Paulusplaats 20 (☎ **09/225-13-85**), open Monday to Thursday 7pm to midnight, Friday and Saturday 6pm to midnight, and Sunday noon to 3pm and 6pm to midnight. No credit cards are accepted.

In Antwerp, the **Hotel Rubenshof,** Amerikalei 115–117 (☎ **03/237-07-89;** fax 03/248-25-94), has plain but adequate rooms for 1,400BF ($44) without bathroom and 2,400BF ($75) with. American Express, MasterCard, and Visa are accepted. A bit more expensive is the central **Hotel Postiljon,** Blauwmoezelstraat 6 (☎ **03/231-75-75;** fax 03/226-84-50), which offers stylish and immaculate rooms for 2,200BF ($69) without a bathroom and 2,500BF ($78) with. Eurocard and Visa are accepted. For dining, **Pelgrom,** Pelgrimstraat 15 (☎ **03/231-93-35**), has an atmospheric candlelit cellar where you can sit at long wood tables and eat light snacks for 275BF ($9) or hearty Flemish specialties for 495BF ($15). American Express, Diners Club, MasterCard, and Visa are accepted, and it's open daily noon to 11pm. The trendiest place for light meals is the magnificent **Foyer,** Kamedieplaats 18 (☎ **03/233-55-17**), part of the Bourla Theater. Given the neoclassic opulence, the prices are reasonable. Expect to pay about 220BF ($7) for a sandwich and 440BF ($14) for a main meal. At least try to stop in for drinks, if only to bask in the splendor. Eurocard and Visa are accepted, and it's open Monday to Friday noon to midnight, Saturday 11am to midnight, and Sunday 11am to 6pm.

You can even leave Belgium entirely and be back in Brussels for a late supper that same day—albeit a very ambitious outing. On a rapid train, Paris is only 1½ hours away; Amsterdam and Luxembourg just under 3 hours; and London, via the *Eurostar* and the Chunnel, 3½ hours.

9

Budapest & Lake Balaton

by Joseph S. Lieber & Christina Shea

The dramatic political changes of 1989 have irreversibly altered life in Hungary. Budapest, awakened after its long slumber behind the Iron Curtain, is now one of Europe's hottest destinations. Poised between East and West, both geographically and culturally, it's at the center of the region's cultural rebirth.

Budapest came of age in the 19th century, at the start of which the two towns of Buda and Pest were little more than provincial outposts on the Danube. The dawning of a modern Hungarian identity spawned the neoclassical development of the city. The rise of the eclectic style coincided with the great post-1867 boom, creating most of the historic inner city. Indeed, Budapest, notwithstanding its long and tattered history of Roman, Mongol, and Turkish conquest, is very much a fin-de-siècle city, with its characteristic coffeehouse and music hall culture. The decades after World War I and the fall of the Habsburg monarchy were not kind to Hungary's charming capital, and until recently Budapest's glory seemed irretrievably lost. How fitting it is, then, that Budapest's post–Cold War renaissance has come when it has: The city is once again attracting visitors from far and wide as a new century turns.

Budapest retains an exotic feeling seldom experienced in the better-known capitals of Europe. Take a turn off any of the city's main boulevards and you'll quickly find yourself in a quiet residential neighborhood, where the scent of a hearty gulyás wafts from a kitchen window and cigarette smoke fogs the cavelike entry of the corner pub.

REQUIRED DOCUMENTS Citizens of the United States, Canada, the Republic of Ireland, and the United Kingdom need only a valid passport to enter Hungary. Citizens of Australia and New Zealand need a visa as well as a passport; contact the nearest Hungarian embassy for details.

OTHER FROMMER'S TITLES For more on Budapest, see *Frommer's Budapest & the Best of Hungary* or *Frommer's Europe*.

1 Budapest Deals & Discounts

SPECIAL DISCOUNTS

Though some museums offer **student reductions,** very few discount opportunities are available. This shouldn't worry you because prices are already very low, making the city itself a budget best. Even though

Budget Bests

It's hard to know where to begin, so varied are the budget bests in Budapest. Here's a perfect example: This is the place to take in an **opera** or a **classical music performance**—tickets can be as little as $2. And bring the kids to the **Vidám Park,** where entry is free and rides cost between 100FT and 200FT (50¢ and $1). This is an amusement park in the great European tradition, in the middle of the city's most popular park.

Hungary has in the past few years suffered annual inflation rates of about 20%, Western currencies have, in this same period, gained against the Hungarian forint at an even higher rate. The result is more actual **buying power** for Westerners each year. In fact, don't be surprised if your money goes farther here than almost anywhere else in this book. For example, you can eat very well for a fraction of what the same meal would cost in Vienna.

WORTH A SPLURGE

Wine aficionados should drop in at **Le Boutique des Vins,** V. József Attila u. 12, behind the Jaguar dealership (☎ **061/117-5919;** Metro: Deák tér [all lines]). Here you'll find the city's best selection of native wines, with the prices more or less mirroring the variations in quality. Splurge on a Villány red. If you appreciate classy women's clothing, visit the V50 Design Art Studio, V. Váci u. 50 (☎ **061/137-5320;** Metro: Ferenick tere [Blue line]). Designer Valeria Fazekas has an eye that's both subtle and elegant.

2 Essentials

ARRIVING

BY PLANE   Budapest's two airports, **Ferihegy I** (☎ **061/296-6000**) and **Ferihegy II** (☎ **061/296-8000** or 157-7000), are adjacent to each other in the XVIII district in southeastern Pest. Malév and Lufthansa flights land at Ferihegy II; all other flights land at Ferihegy I.

The cheapest way into the city is via **public transportation;** the bus-to-metro trip takes about 1 hour. From either airport, take the red-lettered bus no. 93 to the last stop, Kóbánya-Kispest. From there, the Blue metro line runs to the Inner City of Pest. The cost is two transit tickets (120FT/60¢); you can buy tickets from any newsstand in the airport.

The easiest and most reliable way into the city is the **Airport Minibus** (☎ **061/296-8555**), a public service of the LRI (Budapest Airport Authority). The minibus, which leaves every 10 or 15 minutes throughout the day, takes you directly to any address in the city. The price is 1,200FT ($6) per person.

LRI also runs an **Airport-Centrum** bus, at 500FT ($2.50) per person, which leaves every half hour from both airports. Passengers are dropped off at Pest's Erzsébet tér bus station, just off Deák tér, where all three metro lines converge. Tickets are sold aboard the bus for the 30- to 40-minute trip.

The private **taxi** drivers who hang out at the airport are notoriously overpriced. Our advice is to take only taxis of the recommended fleets.

BY TRAIN   Most international trains pull into bustling **Keleti pályaudvar (Eastern Station),** located in Pest's Baross tér, beyond the Outer Ring on the border of the VII and VIII districts. The Red line of the metro is below the station.

What Things Cost in Budapest	U.S. $
Taxi from Ferihegy Airport to Budapest city center	15.00–20.00
Public transportation within the city	.30
Local telephone call	.10
Double room at the Hilton (very expensive)	208.00–302.00
Double room at the Hotel Astra Vendégház (expensive)	101.00
Double room at Hotel Queen Mary (moderate)	68.00
Double room at Hotel MEDOSZ (inexpensive)	46.00
Bed at Lotus Youth Hostel (budget)	8.00
Lunch for one, without wine, at Le Jardin (moderate)	9.00
Lunch for one, without wine, at Marquis de Salade (budget)	5.00
Dinner for one, without wine, at Kis Buda Gyöngye (expensive)	14.00
Dinner for one, without wine, at Iguana Bar & Grill (moderate)	9.00
Dinner for one, without wine, at Govinda (budget)	4.00
Glass of wine	1.50
Coca-Cola in a street cafe or self-service restaurant	.60
Cup of coffee with milk	1.00
Roll of ASA 100 color film, 36 exposures	5.00
Admission to the National Museum	1.25
Movie ticket	.75–1.75
Ticket at the Hungarian State Opera	2.00–22.50

Some international trains arrive at **Nyugati pályaudvar (Western Station),** on the Outer Ring, at the border of the V, VI, and XIII districts. A station for the Blue line of the metro is beneath Nyugati. Few international trains arrive at **Déli pályaudvar (Southern Station);** the terminus of the Red metro line is beneath the train station.

For domestic train information, call ☎ 061/322-7860; for international train information, call ☎ **061/342-9150.** You can buy tickets at train station offices or from the **Hungarian State Railway (MÁV) Service Office,** VI. Andrássy út 35 (☎ **061/322-9035**).

BY BUS Most buses pull into the **Erzsébet tér bus station** (☎ **061/117-2345** or 061/117-2562), just off Deák tér in central Pest.

BY CAR The border crossings from Austria and Slovakia are generally hassle-free. You may be requested to present your driver's license, vehicle registration, and proof of insurance (the number plate and symbol indicating country of origin are acceptable proof). Hungary doesn't require the International Driver's License. Cars entering Hungary are required to have a decal indicating country of registration, a first-aid kit, and an emergency triangle.

BY HYDROFOIL The Hungarian State Shipping Agency **MAHART** operates hydrofoils on the Danube between Vienna and Budapest in spring and summer. Book your tickets well in advance. In **Vienna,** contact MAHART at Handelskai 265 (☎ **061/729-2161**). The **Budapest** office of MAHART is at the dock where the boats arrive, on the Pest side of the Danube at V. Belgrád rakpart (☎ **061/118-1704** or 061/118-1953), between the Erzsébet Bridge and the Szabadság Bridge).

VISITOR INFORMATION

The city's best information source is **Tourinform** (☎ **061/117-9800** or 061/117-8992), centrally located at V. Sütő u. 2, just off Deák tér (reached by all three metro lines) in Pest, open daily 8am to 8pm. The staff speaks English.

CITY LAYOUT

The city of Budapest came into being in 1873, the result of a union of three separate cities: Buda, Pest, and Óbuda. Budapest, like Hungary itself, is defined by the **river Danube (Duna)**, along which many of the city's historic sites are found. Eight bridges connect the two banks, including five in the city center.

On the right bank of the Danube lies **Pest**, the capital's commercial and administrative center. Central Pest is that part of the city between the Danube and the semi-circular **Outer Ring boulevard (Nagykörút)**, stretches of which are called by the names of former monarchs: Ferenc, József, Erzsébet, Teréz, and Szent István. The Outer Ring begins at the Pest side of the Petőfi Bridge in the south and wraps itself around the center, ending at the Margit Bridge in the north. Several of Pest's busiest squares are found along the Outer Ring, and Pest's major east–west avenues bisect it at these squares.

Central Pest is further defined by the **Inner Ring (Kiskörút)**, which lies within the Outer Ring. It starts at Szabadság híd (Freedom Bridge) in the south and is alternately named Vámház körút, Múzeum körút, Károly körút, Bajcsy-Zsilinszky út, and József Attila utca before ending at the Chain Bridge. Inside this ring is the **Belváros**, the historic Inner City of Pest.

Váci utca is a popular pedestrian shopping street between the Inner Ring and the Danube. It spills into **Vörösmarty tér,** one of the area's best-known squares. The **Dunakorzó (Danube Promenade),** a popular evening strolling place, runs along the river in Pest, between the Chain Bridge and the Erzsébet Bridge. The historic Jewish district of Pest is in the **Erzsébetváros,** between the two ring boulevards.

Margaret Island (Margit-sziget) is in the middle of the Danube. Accessible via the Margaret Bridge or Árpád Bridge, it's a popular park without vehicular traffic.

On the left bank of the Danube is **Buda;** to its north, beyond the city center, lies Óbuda. Buda is as hilly as Pest is flat. **Castle Hill** is widely considered the most beautiful part of Budapest. A number of steep paths, staircases, and small streets go up to Castle Hill, but no major roads do. The easiest access is from Clark Ádám tér (at the head of the Chain Bridge) by funicular or from Várfok utca (near Moszkva tér) by foot or bus. Castle Hill consists of the royal palace itself, home to numerous museums, and the so-called **Castle District,** a lovely neighborhood of small winding streets, centered around the Gothic Matthias Church.

Below Castle Hill, along the Danube, is a long, narrow neighborhood, historically populated by fishermen and other river workers, known as the **Watertown (Víziváros).**

A Note on Addresses

Budapest is divided into 22 districts called **kerülets** (abbreviated ker.). A Roman numeral followed by a period precedes every written address in Budapest, signifying the kerület; for example, XII. Csörsz utca 9 is in the 12th kerület. Because many street names are repeated in different parts of the city, it's very important to know which kerület a certain address is in.

Central Buda is a collection of mostly low-lying neighborhoods below Castle Hill. The main square of central Buda is **Moszkva tér,** just north of Castle Hill. Beyond Central Buda, mainly to the east, are the **Buda Hills.**

Óbuda is on the left bank of the Danube, north of Buda. Though the greater part of Óbuda is modern and drab, it features a beautiful old city center and impressive Roman ruins.

GETTING AROUND

Budapest has an extensive, efficient, and inexpensive public transport system. The system's biggest disadvantage is that, except for 17 well-traveled bus and tram routes, all forms of transport shut down around 11:30pm; certain areas of the city, most notably the Buda Hills, are beyond the reach of the limited night service, so you'll have to take a taxi. Be on the alert for pickpockets on public transportation. Keep your money and other valuables inside your clothing in a money belt.

All forms of public transportation in Budapest require the self-validation of pre-purchased tickets *(vonaljegy);* you can buy them for 60FT (30¢) apiece at metro ticket windows, newspaper kiosks, and the occasional tobacco shop. It's a good idea to stock up: For 540FT ($2.70) you can get a **pack of 10** *(tizes csomag)* and for 1,000FT ($5) a **pack of 20** *(huszos csomag).*

Day passes *(napijegy)* cost 500FT ($2.50) and are valid until midnight of the day of purchase. Buy them from metro ticket windows; the clerk validates the pass at the time of purchase. A **3-day** *turistajegy* costs 1,000FT ($5) and a **weekly pass** 1,230FT ($6).

Inspectors frequently come around checking for valid tickets, particularly in the metro stations. On-the-spot fines (800FT/$4) are assessed to fare-dodgers.

All public transport operates on rough schedules, posted at bus and tram shelters and in metro stations. The Budapest Transport Authority (BKV térkép) produces a more detailed transportation map, available at most metro ticket windows for 200FT ($1).

BY METRO   The metro is clean and efficient, with trains running every 3 to 5 minutes about 4:30am to about 11:30pm. The three lines are universally known by color—Yellow, Red, and Blue. Officially they have numbers as well (1, 2, and 3, respectively), but all signs are color coded. All three lines converge at Deák tér, the only point where any meet.

The **Yellow (1) line** is the oldest metro on the European continent and was fully renovated in 1996. It runs from Vörösmarty tér in the heart of central Pest, out the length of Andrássy út, past the Városliget (City Park), ending at Mexikói út. Tickets for the Yellow line are self-validated on the train itself.

The **Red (2)** and **Blue (3)** lines are modern metros. The Red line runs from eastern Pest, through the center, and across the Danube to Déli Station. The Blue line runs from southeastern Pest, through the center, and out to northern Pest. Tickets should be validated at automatic boxes before you descend the escalator. When changing lines at Deák tér, you're required to validate another ticket at the orange validating machines in the hallways between lines.

Metro tickets are good for 1 hour for any distance along the line you're riding.

BY BUS   Many parts of the city, most notably the Buda Hills, are best accessed by bus *(busz).* Most lines are in service from about 4:30am to about 11:30pm, with less frequent weekend service on some.

Black-numbered local buses constitute the majority of the city's lines. **Red-numbered buses** are express. If the red number on the bus is followed by an "E," the bus runs nonstop between terminals (whereas an "É"—with an accent mark—signifies *észak,* meaning night). A few buses are labeled by something other than a number; one

Budapest Metro

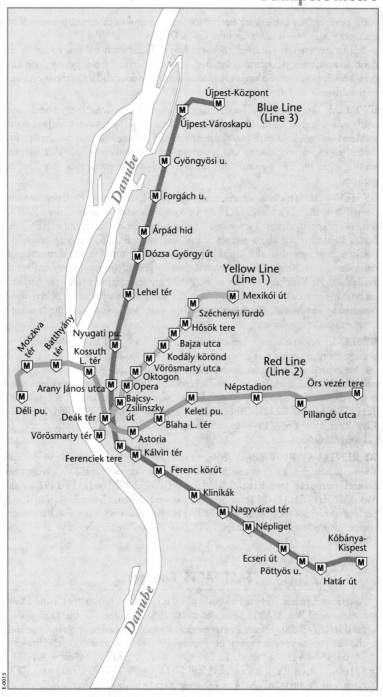

Újpest-Központ

Blue Line
(Line 3)

Újpest-Városkapu

Gyöngyösi u.

Forgách u.

Árpád hid

Dózsa György út

Yellow Line
(Line 1)

Lehel tér

Mexikói út

Széchenyi fürdő

Hősök tere

Nyugati pu.

Bajza utca

Moszkva tér

Batthyány tér

Kossuth L. tér

Kodály körönd

Vörösmarty utca

Oktogon

Red Line
(Line 2)

Arany János utca

Opera

Néstadion

Örs vezér tere

Déli pu.

Bajcsy-Zsilinszky út

Keleti pu.

Pillangő utca

Deák tér

Blaha L. tér

Vörösmarty tér

Astoria

Ferenciek tere

Kálvin tér

Ferenc körút

Klinikák

Nagyvárad tér

Népliget

Kőbánya-Kispest

Ecseri út

Pöttyös u.

Határ út

Danube

E-0015

239

you'll probably use is the Várbusz (Palace Bus), a minibus that runs between Várfok utca, off Buda's Moszkva tér, and the Castle District.

Bus tickets are self-validated on board by the mechanical red box found by each door. You can't buy tickets from the driver. You can board the bus by any door. However, after 8pm you may board only through the front door and must show your ticket to the driver.

BY TRAM   You'll find Budapest's bright yellow trams *(villamos)* very useful, particularly nos. 4 and 6, which travel along the Outer Ring (Nagykörút). Tickets are self-validated on board. As with buses, tickets are valid for one ride, not for the line itself. Trams stop at every station, and all doors open, regardless of whether anyone is waiting to get on. The buttons near the tram doors are for emergency stops, not stop requests.

BY HÉV   The HÉV is a suburban railway network connecting Budapest to various points along the city's outskirts. There are four HÉV lines; only one, the Szentendre line, is of serious interest to visitors. The terminus for the Szentendre HÉV line is Buda's Batthyány tér, also a station of the Red metro line. To reach Óbuda's Fő tér (Main Square), get off at the Árpád híd (Árpád Bridge) stop. The HÉV runs regularly daily 4am to 11:30pm. For trips within the city limits, you need one transit ticket, available at HÉV ticket windows at the Batthyány tér station or from the conductor on board. These tickets are different from the standard transportation tickets and are punched by conductors. If you have a valid day pass you don't need to buy a ticket for trips within the city limits.

BY TAXI   Budapest taxis are unregulated, so fares vary tremendously. Perhaps because there are more taxi drivers than the level of business can support, many drivers are experts at fleecing foreigners. However, if you watch out for yourself, taxis are still a bit cheaper than in the West. Several fleet companies have good reputations, honest drivers, and competitive rates. The most highly recommended company is **Fő Taxi** (☎ **061/222-2222**). Other reliable fleets are **Volántaxi** (☎ **061/166-6666**), **City Taxi** (☎ **061/211-1111**), **Yellow Pages** (☎ **061/155-5000**), and **6×6** (☎ **061/266-6666**).

BY RENTAL CAR   We don't recommend using a car for sightseeing in Budapest. You may, however, want to rent a car for trips outside the capital. We recommend **Denzel Europcar InterRent,** VIII. Üllői út 60–62 (☎ **061/313-1492** or 061/ 313-0207; fax 061/313-1492), where you can find a Suzuki Swift for 4,500FT ($23) per day (insurance included), plus 27FT (14¢) per kilometer. They also have a rental counter at both airports: Ferihegy I (☎ 061/296-6680) and Ferihegy II (☎ 061/ 296-6610).

FAST FACTS: Budapest

American Express   Hungary's main office is between Vörösmarty tér and Deák tér in central Pest, at V. Deák Ferenc u. 10, 1052 Budapest (☎ **061/266-8680;** fax 061/267-2028). There's an express cash Amex ATM on the street in front and also at the airport terminal of Ferihegy I. For lost traveler's checks, call ☎ **00/800-04411** for the U.K. direct operator. Ask to call collect to 44-273-571600, or to dial direct (you pay), call ☎ 00/44-273-571600. For lost AMEX cards, call ☎ **061/267-2024** in Budapest 8am to midnight; after midnight and on Sunday when the office closes early, your call will be automatically transferred to the U.K.

The Hungarian Forint

For American Readers   At this writing $1 = approximately 200FT (or 100FT = 50¢), and this was the rate of exchange used to calculate the dollar values given in this chapter (rounded to the nearest dollar).

For British Readers   At this writing £1 = approximately 320FT (or 100FT = 31p), and this was the rate of exchange used to calculate the pound values in the table below.

Note: Exchange rates fluctuate over time and may not be the same when you travel to Hungary.

FT	U.S.$	U.K.£	FT	U.S.$	U.K.£
100	.50	.31	2,000	10.00	6.20
200	1.00	.62	3,000	15.00	9.30
300	1.50	.93	4,000	20.00	12.40
400	2.00	1.24	5,000	25.00	15.50
500	2.50	1.55	10,000	50.00	31.00
750	3.75	2.33	15,000	75.00	46.50
1,000	5.00	3.10	20,000	100.00	62.00

Baby-sitters   Ficuka Baby Hotel, V. Váci u. 11b, I em. 9 (☎ **061/138-2836;** ask for Judit Zámbo), will send a qualified English-speaking baby-sitter to your hotel for 550FT ($2.75) per hour for one child or 950FT ($4.75) per hour for two children.

Business Hours   Most stores are open Monday to Friday 10am to 6pm and Saturday 9 or 10am to 1 or 2pm. Many shops close for an hour at lunch, and only stores in central tourist areas are open Sunday. Many shops and restaurants close for 2 weeks in August. Banks are usually open Monday to Thursday 8am to 3pm and Friday 8am to 1pm.

Currency   The basic unit of currency is the **forint (FT)**. There are 100 **fillérs** (almost worthless and soon to be taken out of circulation) in a forint. Coins come in denominations of 50 fillérs and 1, 2, 5, 10, 20, 100, and 200FT. Banknotes come in denominations of 100, 500, 1,000, 5,000, and 10,000FT.

Currency Exchange   The best rates for cash and especially for traveler's checks are obtained at banks, not exchange booths. Exchange booths are located throughout the city center, in train stations, and in most hotels. **Inter Change** is one chain of exchange booths to avoid; their rates are up to 20% lower than the prevailing rate. You can also withdraw money in forints from your home bank account by accessing the PLUS or Cirrus networks through any of the ATMs found throughout the city. You're allowed to reexchange into hard currency up to half the amount of forints you originally purchased; make sure you keep all your exchange receipts.

Doctors   IMS, a private outpatient clinic at XIII. Váci út 202 (☎ **061/129-8423**), has English-speaking doctors; it's reached via the Blue metro line (Gyöngyös utca). IMS also operates an emergency service after hours and on weekends at III. Vihar u. 29 (☎ **061/250-1899**). Many luxury hotels also have a staff or private doctor with rented office space. For further options, ask at Tourinform.

Drugstores The Hungarian word is *gyógyszertár* or *patika*. Generally, pharmacies carry only prescription drugs. Hotel "drugstores" are just shops with soap, perfume, aspirin, and other nonprescription items. There are a number of 24-hour pharmacies in the city—every pharmacy posts the address of the nearest one in its window.

Embassies The embassy of **Australia** is at XII. Királyhágo tér 8–9 (☎ 061/201-8899); the embassy of **Canada,** at XII. Budakeszi út 32 (☎ 061/275-1200); the embassy of **Republic of Ireland,** at V. Szabadság tér 7 (☎ 061/302-9600); the embassy of the **United Kingdom,** at V. Harmincad u. 6 (☎ 061/266-2888); and the embassy of the **United States,** at V. Szabadság tér 12 (☎ 061/267-4400). **New Zealand** doesn't have representation in Hungary.

Emergencies Dial ☎ **104** for an ambulance, ☎ **105** for the fire department, or ☎ **107** for the police. To reach the 24-hour English-speaking emergency service, dial ☎ **061/118-8212.**

Hospitals See "Doctors," above.

Laundry & Dry Cleaning Self-service launderettes *(patyolat)* are scarce in Budapest. As far as we know, the city's only centrally located Laundromat is at VII. Rákóczi út 8. It's open Monday to Friday 7am to 5pm and Saturday 7am to 1pm. Perhaps the best bet is to ask at your hotel or pension. Private room hosts are usually happy to make a little extra money doing laundry.

Post Office The **Magyar Posta,** Petőfi Sándor u. 17–19, not far from Deák tér (all metro lines), is the city's main post office, open Monday to Friday 8am to 8pm and Saturday 8am to 3pm. There are 24-hour post offices near Keleti and Nyugati stations.

Safety By Western standards, Budapest is safe—muggings and violent attacks are rare. Nevertheless, visitors are always prime targets. Teams of professional pickpockets plague Budapest. They operate on crowded trams, metros, and buses. Be particularly careful on bus no. 26 (Margaret Island) and tram nos. 4 and 6 or in any other crowded setting. The pickpocket's basic trick is to create a distraction to take your attention away from yourself and your own safety. Avoid being victimized by wearing a money belt under your clothes instead of a fanny pack or a wallet or purse. No valuables should be kept in the outer pockets of a knapsack.

Taxes Taxes are included in all restaurant prices, hotel rates, and shop purchases. Refunds on the 25% **value-added tax (VAT),** which is built into all prices, is available for most consumer goods purchases of more than 25,000FT ($125). The refund process is elaborate. In most shops, the salesperson can provide the necessary VAT reclaim form and will fill it out for you. In addition, make sure you receive a separate receipt indicating the VAT amount. Your name, home address, and passport number should be entered on this receipt. Also save your currency exchange receipts (or credit-card receipts); attach the original sales invoice and the Customs certification to the refund claim form. Use one claim form per sales receipt. Receive certification from Customs by presenting the object of purchase on export (for instance, at the airport), or else submit the claims by mail to **Foreigners' Refund Office** of the APEH Budapest Directorate, XI. Bartók Béla út 156, Budapest (☎ 061/203-0888 or 061/156-9800).

Telephone The Hungarian phone system has been recently privatized, though service still doesn't meet Western standards. For best results, dial slowly and don't be too quick to trust a busy signal—keep trying.

Country & City Codes

The **country code** for Hungary is **36.** The **city code** for Budapest is **1;** use this code when you're calling from outside Hungary. If you're within Hungary but not in Budapest, first dial **06;** when you hear a tone, dial the city code and phone number. If you're calling within Budapest, simply leave off the code and dial only the regular seven-digit phone number.

Warning: Budapest phone numbers are constantly changing as Matáv continues to upgrade its system. All numbers starting with "1" may be subject to change by 2000. In many, but not all, of these cases, the 1 will simply be replaced with 3. If you find that the number you want has changed (you'll hear a recording: *"a hívott szám megváltozott"*), dial ☎ **198** for **local directory assistance.** If the operator speaks no English, try calling CoMo Media, publishers of the English-language phone book, at ☎ **061/266-4916.**

You can access the international operator from most public phones, though older phones are less reliable; a 20FT coin is required to start the call. You can reach the **AT&T** operator at ☎ **00/800-01111,** the **MCI** operator at ☎ **00/800-01411,** and the **Sprint** operator at ☎ **00/800-01877.**

You can also use **direct dial.** Hungarian telephone books list the numbers of all countries that can be directly dialed. If you don't have access to a phone book, 09 is the number for the international operator. Direct dial to the United States and Canada is 00/1, to the U.K. 00/44, to Australia 00/61, and to the Republic of Ireland 00/353.

Public **pay phones** charge varying amounts for local calls depending on the time of day you place your call. You'll get anywhere from 2 to 10 minutes for each 10FT coin. It's cheapest to call late in the evenings and on weekends. Public phones operate with old and new 10FT and 20FT coins or with phonecards (in 50 or 100 units) you can buy at post offices, tobacco shops, and some street vendors.

The **main telecommunications office,** at Petőfi Sándor u. 17 (near Deák tér), is open Monday to Friday 8am to 8pm and Saturday 9am to 3pm. Telephone calls, as well as faxes and telexes, can be made to anywhere in the world. It costs 200FT ($1) per minute to call the United States from this office. Ask at the main desk for a telephone guide information pamphlet in English. You can also purchase a **telephone card** here for making local calls; this would be worth doing only if you are planning to make a lot of local calls. Hotels typically add a surcharge to all calls (although some allow unlimited free local calls), so you're advised to use public telephone booths (often found in hotel lobbies), the telephone office, or the post office.

Tipping   Tipping is generally 10%. Among those who welcome tips are waiters, taxi drivers, hotel employees, barbers, cloakroom attendants, toilet attendants, masseuses, and tour guides.

3 Accommodations You Can Afford

One of the happy developments of the post-1989 boom in Budapest has been the proliferation of new pensions and small hotels. The better choices among these—and the less expensive—are usually outside the city center, but all the places we list can easily be reached by public transportation.

Notwithstanding the arrival of these new places, Budapest retains its reputation as a city without enough guest beds. Indeed, in high season it can be difficult to secure a hotel or pension room or hostel bed, so make reservations and get written confirmation well ahead if possible.

An alternative option is a room in a private apartment. Typically, you share the bathroom with the hosts or with other guests. Breakfast isn't officially included, but the host will often offer continental breakfast for a fee (400FT to 600FT/$2 to $3). You may have limited kitchen privileges (ask in advance). Some hosts will greet you when you arrive, give you a key, and seemingly disappear; others will want to befriend you, show you around, and cook for you. Most rooms are adequate, some even memorable, but any number of reasons may cause you to dislike yours: Noisy neighborhoods, tiny baths, and bad coffee are among the complaints we've heard. The great majority of visitors, though, appear to be satisfied; at the very least, staying in a private room provides a window into everyday Hungarian life you'd otherwise miss.

Most people book private rooms through accommodations agencies. The most established of these are the former state-owned travel agents **Ibusz, Cooptourist, MÁV Tours,** and **Budapest Tourist.** Though newer, private agencies have proliferated, the older ones tend to have the greatest number of rooms. There are agencies in both airports, in all three major train stations, throughout central Pest, and along the main roads into Budapest. The main **Ibusz reservations office** is at Ferenciek tere 10 (☎ **061/118-6866** or 061/118-1120; fax 061/118-4983), reached by the Blue metro line. Prices vary slightly among agencies, but generally a double is 3,000FT to 5,000FT ($15 to $25), plus 3% tax. Most agencies add a 30% surcharge (to the first night only) for stays of less than 4 nights. Arriving at an agency early in the day will afford you the best selection. Make sure you know the exact location of the address on the map before leaving the agency. There's scarcely an address in Budapest that can't be reached by some form of public transport, so regard with skepticism anyone who says you must take a taxi.

In Keleti Station, where most international trains arrive, you're likely to be approached by all sorts of people offering you private rooms. Most are honest folks trying to drum up some business personally. Keep in mind that when the middleman (the agency) is eliminated, the prices tend to be slightly better, so you might consider taking a room from one of these people, especially if you arrive late at night when the agencies are closed or long lines at the agencies drive you to despair. Trust your judgment and don't let anyone pressure you. Feel free to haggle over prices.

Note: You can find most of the lodging choices below plotted on the map in "Seeing the Sights," later in this chapter.

HOTELS
IN CENTRAL PEST
Hotel MEDOSZ. VI. Jókai tér 9, 1061 Budapest. ☎ **061/153-1700** or 061/374-3000. Fax 061/332-4316. 70 units, all with bathroom. TV TEL. 80DM ($46) double. Rates include breakfast. No credit cards. Metro: Oktogon (Yellow line).

The MEDOSZ was formerly a trade-union hotel for agricultural workers. Its location on sleepy Jókai tér, in the heart of Pest's theater district and not far from the Opera House, is as good as it gets off the river. Though the hotel hasn't been renovated since privatization (and the staff has yet to learn to smile), it remains a great value given its location. The rooms are simple but clean, and there's a restaurant and bar in the hotel. Laundry service is available. Next door is one of Budapest's special treats for kids: a puppet theater *(bábszínház)*.

A Note on Rates

Accommodation rates in Budapest remain among the lowest of any European capital. You'll note that many hotels and pensions list their prices in German marks (DM) or U.S. dollars. This is done solely as a hedge against forint inflation; everyone accepts payment in Hungarian forints as well as foreign currencies. For your convenience, we've converted the DM prices into dollars, using an exchange rate of 1.75DM to $1, the rate at press time.

Marco Polo. VII. Nyár u. 6, 1072 Budapest. ☎ **061/342-9586,** 061/342-9587, or 061/342-9588. Fax 061/342-9589. 200 units, 5 dorms, all with bathroom. 4,600FT ($23) per person double; 2,900FT ($15) per person in 12-bed dorm. 10% discount for IYHF members. No credit cards. Metro: Blaha Lujza tér (Red line).

Although this place calls itself a youth hostel, it's really more a budget hotel. On a recent visit, we noticed that most of the guests were well-dressed middle-aged Europeans; this is no backpackers' haunt. Given the central location and clean rooms (opened in 1997), it's a very good deal.

✪ Peregrinus Vendégház. V. Szerb u. 3, 1056 Budapest. ☎ **061/266-4911.** Fax 061/266-4913. 26 units, all with bathroom. MINIBAR TV TEL. 11,500FT ($58) double. Rates include breakfast. No credit cards. Metro: Kálvin tér (Blue line).

This is the guesthouse of Pest's ELTE University, and its location couldn't be better—in the heart of the Inner City, on a small side street just half a block from the quiet southern end of the popular pedestrians-only Váci utca. Reserve at least a week ahead. The building dates from the turn of the century and was renovated in 1994, when the guesthouse was opened. The rooms are simple but comfortable.

IN OUTER PEST

Hotel Délibáb. VI. Délibáb u. 35, 1062 Budapest. ☎ **061/342-9301** or 061/322-8763. Fax 061/342-8153. 34 units, all with bathrooms. TV TEL. 8,500FT ($43) double. Rates include breakfast. No credit cards. Metro: Hősök tere (Yellow line).

The Délibáb enjoys a wonderful location across from Heroes' Square and City Park, in an exclusive neighborhood that's home to most of the city's embassies. It's a 30-minute walk to the center of Pest or a 5-minute ride on the metro. The rooms are surprisingly spacious and have nice wood floors (some have refrigerators); the fixtures are old, but everything works and is clean.

IN CENTRAL BUDA

✪ Charles Apartment House. I. Hegyalja út 23, 1016 Budapest. ☎ **061/201-1796.** Fax 061/212-2584. 26 units, all with bathroom. TV TEL. $40–$45 apt for 1 or 2; $54 apt for 3. MC, V. Bus: 78 from Keleti pu. to Mészáros utca.

Owner Károly Szombati has amassed 22 apartments in a building in a dull but convenient Buda neighborhood (near the large luxury Novotel), as well as four apartments in nearby buildings. All are average Budapest flats. The furnishings are comfortable and clean, and all apartments have full kitchens. Hegyalja út is a very busy street, but only two apartments face out onto it; the rest are in the interior or on the side of the building.

IN THE BUDA HILLS

G. G. Panoráma Panzió. II. Fullánk u. 7, 1026 Budapest. ☎ and fax **061/176-4718.** 4 units, all with bathroom. $45–$69 double. Breakfast $3. No credit cards. Bus: 11 from Batthyány tér to Majális utca or 91 from Nyugati pu.

Getting the Best Deal on Accommodations

- Take advantage of winter discounts—even major hotel operators grant significant price reductions off-season.
- Be aware that rooms in private homes are the cheapest way to go.
- Ask at your hotel if there are rooms without a shower. The staff may assume you want one of the more expensive units with a bathroom.
- If you're willing to stay on the outskirts and spend some time traveling to the city center, you'll usually spend less for a room.

G. G. are the initials of Mrs. Gábor Gubacsi, the friendly English-speaking owner of this guesthouse. All rooms are on the top floor of the home, located on a steep, quiet street in the elegant Rose Hill (Rózsadomb) section of the Buda Hills. Several bus lines converge on the neighborhood, making it fairly convenient. The rooms are small but tastefully furnished; they share a common balcony with a great vista of the hills. There's also a common kitchen and dining area, with full facilities (including minibar), as well as ample garden space. The Gubacsis take good care of their guests.

Hotel Papillon. II. Rózsahegy u. 3/b, 1024 Budapest. ☎ and fax **061/212-4003** or 061/212-4003. 20 units, all with bathroom. TV TEL. 100DM ($57) double. Rates include breakfast. AE, EURO, JCB, MC, V. Bus: 91 from Nyugati pu. to Zivatar utca.

The Papillon is a pleasing Mediterranean-style white building on a quiet Buda side street, in the area where central Buda begins to give way to the Buda Hills (an easy bus ride to the center of the city). An airy feeling pervades the interior and spare pink guest rooms. Seven rooms have terraces; all have refrigerators. There's a small pool on the premises.

✪ **Vadvirág Panzió.** II. Nagybányai út 18, 1025 Budapest. ☎ **061/176-4292** or 061/275-0200. Fax 061/176-4292. 15 units, all with bathroom. TV TEL. 85DM–120DM ($48–$68) double. Rates include breakfast. AE, MC, V. Bus: 5 from Március tér or 15 from Moszkva tér to Pasaréti tér (the last stop).

A 10-minute walk from the bus stop, the Vadvirág is in a gorgeous part of the Buda Hills a few blocks behind the Béla Bartók Memorial House. Sloping gardens and terraces surround it. Inside, the rooms are all different; most are small but tastefully furnished. Half have balconies, and some have refrigerators. Room 2 is the best: It's a small suite with a balcony. There's a sauna (15DM/$9 per hour) and a small restaurant with plenty of outdoor seating.

IN ÓBUDA

✪ **San Marco Guest House.** III. San Marco u. 6, 1034 Budapest. ☎ **061/388-9997** or 061/439-7525. Fax 061/388-9997. 5 units, 2 with shared bathroom. A/C TV. 6,000FT–7,000FT ($30–$35) double. Rates include breakfast. EURO, JCB, MC, V. Tram: 17 from Margit híd (Buda side) to Nagyszombat utca. Bus: 60 from Batthyány tér to Nagyszombat utca.

Paul and Eva Stenczinger run this small pension on the top floor of their house. They speak fluent English and are happy to help with restaurant reservations, theater and train tickets, taxis, and other matters. The San Marco Guest House is comfortable but unassuming—much like the residential Óbuda neighborhood it's located in. Three rooms face the back, where there's a flower-filled garden (breakfast is served here in summer).

IN THE CASTLE DISTRICT

✪ **Hotel Kulturinnov.** I. Szentháromság tér 6, 1014 Budapest. ☎ **061/155-0122** or 061/175-1651. Fax 061/175-1886. 16 units, all with bathroom. TEL. 13,000FT ($65) double. Rates include breakfast. AE, DC, MC, V. Parking: 2,000FT ($10). Bus: "Várbusz" from Moszkva tér or 16 from Deák tér. Funicular: From Clark Ádám tér.

This little place is in the very heart of Buda's Castle District. This is the guesthouse of the Hungarian Culture Foundation, dedicated to forging ties with ethnic Hungarians in neighboring countries. It's open to the public, but few travelers know about it. The rooms are small and simple; nothing is modern, but everything works and the baths are clean. The hotel, though located in the large building directly across from Matthias Church and the Plague Column, can be a bit hard to find; the entrance is unassuming and practically unmarked. Go through the iron grille doorway and pass through an exhibition hall, continuing up the grand red-carpeted staircase to the right.

HOSTELS

International trains arriving in Budapest are usually met by representatives of **Travellers' Youth Way Youth Hostels** (☎ **061/140-8585** or 061/129-8644; fax 061/120-8425) and **Universum Youth Hostels** (☎ and fax **061/275-7046**). Your best bet is to book a bed in advance at a recommended hostel; if you haven't, you can make phone calls on your arrival and try to secure a bed or try your luck with these hawkers. Since they make a commission on every customer, they tend to be pushy and say whatever they think you want to hear about their hostel. Shop around and don't let yourself be pressured. Most hostels that solicit at the station also have a van parked outside. The ride to the hostel is free, but you may have to wait a while until the van is full. There's also a **youth hostel information office** at Keleti station (☎ **06-20/657-988** or 06-20/468-334), off to the side of track 6 near the international waiting room.

The IYHF card is by no means a necessity in Hungary; you will often get a discount by presenting it, but usually not more than 10%.

Lotus Youth Hostel. VI. Teréz krt. 56 (3rd floor), 1066 Budapest. ☎ and fax **061/131-9896.** Fax 061/302-2984. Three 10-bed dorms, two 2- to 4-bed dorms, none with bathroom. 1,400FT ($7) for bed in 10-bed dorm; 1,800FT–2,200FT ($9–$11) for bed in 2- to 4-bed dorm. 10% discount for IYHF members. Rates include breakfast. No credit cards. Metro: Nyugati pu. (Blue line).

This new Central Pest hostel, open year-round, is across from Nyugati train station, on very busy Teréz körút and within walking distance of all central Pest attractions. There's nothing more than a small sign downstairs by the mailbox to let you know you're in the right place. Ring the bell and you'll be buzzed in. You need not repeat this ritual more than once, as all guests are given keys; there's no curfew. The rooms (mixed sex) are clean and spacious, but the baths can get a bit grimy. Each guest gets a locker; locks are provided for a deposit. Guests are expected to be quiet after 10pm. English-language newspapers are provided daily.

WORTH A SPLURGE

Hotel Astra Vendégház. I. Vám u. 6, 1011 Budapest. ☎ **061/214-1906.** Fax 061/214-1907. 12 units, all with bathroom. A/C MINIBAR TV TEL. 178DM ($101) double. Rates include breakfast. AE, DC, MC, V. Metro: Batthyány tér (Red line).

This little gem was opened in 1996 in a renovated 300-year-old building on a quiet side street in Buda's lovely Watertown. The rooms are large, with wood floors and classic Hungarian-style furniture; the overall effect is far more homey and pleasant than most hotel rooms. Indeed, the hotel is tasteful through and through and the staff friendly. Some rooms overlook the inner courtyard, while others face onto the street.

4 Great Deals on Dining

Budapest is awash in new private restaurants, and many of the older, formerly state-owned places have gotten a new lease on life after privatization—together with an aggressive face-lift. Ethnic restaurants have also proliferated in the last few years; you'll find Chinese, Japanese, Korean, Middle Eastern, Turkish, Greek, and Mexican. Of course, most visitors want Hungarian food. In this city, traditional fare runs the gamut from greasy to gourmet. There are few palates that can't find happiness and few budgets that'll be much worse for the wear.

Étterem is the most common Hungarian word for restaurant and is used for everything from cafeteria-style eateries to first-class restaurants. A *vendéglő*, or guesthouse, is a smaller, more intimate restaurant, often with a Hungarian folk motif; a *csárda* is a countryside vendéglő. An *étkezde* is an informal lunchroom open only in the daytime. *Önkiszolgáló* means self-service cafeteria, typically open only for lunch. Stand-up *bufes* are often found in bus stations and near busy transport hubs. A *cukrászda* or *kávéház* is a classic Central European coffeehouse, where lingering has developed into an art form.

There are also a number of types of places that are primarily for drinking but where meals are usually available. A *borozó* is a wine bar; these are often found in cellars (where they're likely to include in their name the word *pince* [cellar] or *barlang* [cave]), and generally feature a house wine. A *söröző* is a beer bar; these places too are often found in cellars. Sandwiches are usually available in borozós and sörözős. Finally, a *kocsma* is a sort of roadside tavern found on side streets in residential neighborhoods; the Buda Hills are filled with them. Most kocsmas serve a full dinner, but the kitchens close early.

The customer initiates the paying ritual by summoning the waiter (or any other restaurant employee). The waiter usually writes out the bill on the spot; occasionally you'll be asked to confirm what you ordered. If you think the bill is wrong, don't be embarrassed to say so; locals will commonly do this. After handing over the bill, in all but the fanciest restaurants, the waiter will stand there waiting patiently for payment. The tip (about 10%) should be included in the amount you give him. State the full amount you're paying (bill plus tip) and the waiter will make change. Never leave a tip on the table.

IN CENTRAL PEST

Chan Chan. V. Váci u. 69. ☎ **061/118-0452.** Reservations recommended. Main courses 1,000FT–4,000FT ($5–$20). DC, DISC, MC, V. Daily 11am–4pm and 6–11pm. Metro: Ferenciek tere (Blue line). THAI.

A welcome new addition to the Budapest restaurant scene, Chan Chan features exotic and original Thai cuisine in an elegant but lively setting. The extensive menu can be overwhelming; either stick to Thai dishes you already know or solicit suggestions from your waiter. We recommend the Mekong catfish soup (a complete meal in itself) or the grilled shark with wild lemongrass and chile sauce. The freshest ingredients are used, and each dish appears lovingly prepared. Service is gracious.

Csarnok Vendéglő. V. Hold u. 11. ☎ **061/269-4906.** Main courses 460FT–800FT ($2.30–$4); menu meals 460FT–480FT ($2.30–$2.40). MC. Mon–Sat 9am–midnight, Sun noon–10pm. Metro: Arany János utca (Blue line). HUNGARIAN.

On the Inner City's quiet Hold utca, the Vendéglő is between Szabadság tér and Bajcsy-Zsilinszky út, not far from the U.S. Embassy. Its name comes from the wonderful turn-of-the-century market hall *(csarnok)* next door. One of the few restaurants

Getting the Best Deal on Dining

- Take advantage of Budapest's low prices and splurge: Meals here cost a third of what they'd be in Austria or Germany.
- Remember that cafeterias are great for simple dining.
- Try Hungarian wine and beer instead of more expensive imports.
- Avoid ordering "specials" unless the price is posted or the waiter tells you the price.

in this part of the Inner City, it's even more notable for its uniformly low prices. The menu features typical Hungarian vendéglő fare, heavy on meat dishes.

✪ **Govinda.** V. Belgrád rakpart 18. No phone. Small menu meal 500FT ($2.50); large menu meal 800FT ($4). Tues–Sun 9am–9pm. Metro: Ferenciek tere (Blue line). INDIAN VEGETARIAN.

This tiny place, owned/operated by Hare Krishnas, features exceptional Indian vegetarian cuisine. There's no proselytizing; just a bit of incense, traditional Indian music, and friendly English-speaking waiters. The chef, trained in India, prepares authentic and exotic offerings for a different menu each day. You choose either a large or small menu meal. It includes soup, bread, a main dish (an assortment of interesting, savory smaller dishes), a drink (such as spicy ginger ale or lemon rosewater), and a dessert. Everything is lovingly prepared. On a hot day, sit upstairs where it's air-conditioned.

IN OUTER PEST

Iguana Bar & Grill. V. Zoltán u. 16. ☎ **061/131-4352.** Reservations recommended. Main courses 900FT–1,800FT ($4.50–$9). AE, DC, MC, V. Sun–Thurs noon–midnight, Fri–Sat noon–2am. Metro: Kossuth Lajos tér (Red line). MEXICAN.

Run by three 30-something American ex-pats, this classy Mexican restaurant opened to immediate success in 1997. It boasts a beautiful spacious interior with a bilevel dining area, but it can be difficult to find a table, especially on the weekend. When you do get seated, crispy homemade tortilla chips and salsa are waiting for you. Though the chef is Hungarian, he trained in the American Southwest, so the flavors are indeed authentic. Fiery souls might start with the jalapeño poppers, breaded jalapeño peppers stuffed with cheese. For an entree, consider one of the daily specials (posted on a chalkboard). Beef burritos or chicken à la Mo (named after a co-owner) also are excellent.

✪ **Kádár Étkezde.** VII. Klauzál tér 9. ☎ **061/321-3622.** Main courses 200FT–500FT ($1–$2.50). No credit cards. Tues–Sat 11:30am–3:30pm. Metro: Astoria (Red line) or Deák tér (all lines). HUNGARIAN.

By 11:45am, Uncle Kádár's, in the heart of the Jewish district, is filled with regulars—from paint-spattered workers to elderly Jewish couples. Uncle Kádár, a neighborhood legend, personally greets them as they file in. From the outside the only sign of the place is a small red sign saying ÉTKEZDE. The place is no more than a lunchroom, but it has a great atmosphere: high ceilings, wood-paneled walls with photos (many autographed) of actors and athletes, and old-fashioned seltzer bottles on every table. The food is simple but hearty and the service friendly. Table sharing is the norm.

✪ **Marquis de Salade.** VI. Hajós u. 43. ☎ **061/302-4086.** Self-serve salad bar 555FT ($2.80); main courses 500FT–1500FT ($2.50–$8); menu meal 520FT–675FT ($2.70–$3.40). V. Daily noon–midnight. Metro: Arany János u. (Blue line). ASIAN/MIDDLE EASTERN/AFRICAN.

This cozy little self-service restaurant turns out an amazing assortment of exceptional salads. On the edge of Pest's theater district, it's a favorite lunch spot of Hungarian actors. The restaurant employs eight cooks from six countries (Russia, Bangladesh, East Africa, Hungary, China, Italy) and the Caucasus Mountains; offerings reflect this diversity. There's additional seating in the upstairs loft, and plans are afoot to expand to the cellar.

Semiramis. V. Alkotmány u. 20. ☎ **061/111-7627.** Main courses 370FT–700FT ($1.85–$3.50). No credit cards. Mon–Sat noon–9pm. Metro: Kossuth Lajos tér (Red line). MIDDLE EASTERN.

A block from Parliament and a few blocks from Nyugati Station, this place serves delicious Middle Eastern cuisine in a small, cozy but poorly ventilated loft decorated with tapestries and colorful straw trivets. The English-speaking waiters are uniformly friendly. Everything is delicious, including the house specialty, chicken breast with spinach *(spenótos csirkemell)*, with far more spinach than chicken. Vegetarians can easily build a meal out of several appetizers; try the yogurt-cucumber salad *(yogurtos saláta)* and the *fül* (a zesty garlic and fava bean dish).

IN THE BUDA HILLS

✪ **Makkhetes Vendéglő.** XII. Németvölgyi út 56. ☎ **061/155-7330.** Main courses 480FT–890FT ($2.40–$4.45). No credit cards. Daily 11am–10pm. Bus: 105 from Deák tér. HUNGARIAN.

In the lower part of the Buda Hills, Makkhetes is a rustic neighborhood eatery. The crude wood paneling and absence of ornamentation give it a distinctly country atmosphere. The regulars start filing in at 11:30am for lunch; the waiters seem to know everyone. The food is good and the portions are large.

Szép Ilona. II. Budakeszi út 1–3. ☎ **061/275-1392.** Main courses 780FT–1,550FT ($3.90–$8). No credit cards. Daily 11:30am–10pm. Bus: 158 from Moszkva tér (departs from Csaba utca, at the top of the stairs, near the stop from which the Várbusz departs for the Castle District). HUNGARIAN.

This cheerful, unassuming restaurant serves a mostly local crowd. There's a good selection of specialties: Try the *borjúpaprikás galuskával* (veal paprika) served with *galuska* (a typical Central European style of dumpling). There's a small sidewalk garden for summer dining. The Szép Ilona is in a pleasant Buda neighborhood; after your meal, have a stroll through the tree-lined streets.

IN ÓBUDA

✪ **Malomtó Étterem.** II. Frankel Leó u. 48. ☎ **061/326-2847.** Reservations recommended for dinner. Main courses 690FT–1,600FT ($3.45–$8). AE, DC, EURO, MC, V. Daily noon–midnight. Tram: 4 or 6 to Margit híd (Buda side), then walk along Frankel Leó utca to the Lukács Baths (Lukács Fürdő). HUNGARIAN.

Across from the Lukács Baths, the Malomtó sits at the base of a hill. There are two outdoor terraces, well shaded from the road, and live guitar music nightly. The menu features a good variety of Hungarian wild game and seafood dishes, in addition to the standards. Since the main-course portions are huge, you may want to bypass soup and salad. The *bélszín kedvesi módra* (beef and goose liver in creamy mushroom sauce) is sumptuous, as is the *sztrapacska oldalassal* (pork ribs with ewe cheese dumplings). Service can be slow.

IN THE CASTLE DISTRICT

✪ **Önkiszolgáló.** I. Hess András tér 4 (in the Fortuna Courtyard). Main courses 120FT–300FT (60¢–$1.50). Mon–Fri 11:30am–2:30pm. Bus: Várbusz from Moszkva tér or 16 from Deák tér to Castle Hill. Funicular: From Clark Ádám tér to Castle Hill. HUNGARIAN.

Coffeehouse Culture

Imperial Budapest, like Vienna, was famous for its coffeehouse culture. Literary movements and political circles alike were identified in large part by which coffeehouse they met in. You can still go to several classic coffeehouses, all of which offer delicious pastries, coffee, and more in an atmosphere of luxurious splendor. Table sharing is common.

Gerbeaud's, V. Vörösmarty tér 7 (☎ **061/118-1311;** Metro: Vörösmarty tér [Yellow line]), is probably the city's most famous coffeehouse. Founded in 1858, it has stood on its current spot since 1870. Whether you sit inside amid the splendor of the turn-of-the-century furnishings or out on one of Pest's liveliest squares, you'll be sure to enjoy the fine pastries that have made the name Gerbeaud famous. It's open daily 9am to 9pm.

Across Andrássy út from the Opera House, ✪ **Művész Kávéház,** VI. Andrássy út 29 (☎ **061/352-1337** or 061/351-3942; Metro: Opera [Yellow line]), boasts a lush interior with marble table tops, crystal chandeliers, and mirrored walls. Despite its grandeur, Művész retains a casual atmosphere. There are tables on the street, but sit inside for the full effect. It's open daily 9am to midnight.

On the ground floor of a spectacular art nouveau palace, **New York Kávéház,** VII. Erzsébet krt. 9–11 (☎ **061/322-3849** or 061/322-1648; Metro: Blaha Lujza tér, [Red line]), has a history as rich as its interior. In the early 20th century it was the city's best-known meeting place for artists, poets, writers, and actors. In spite of the presence of the seemingly permanent scaffolding outside, the interior has been carefully restored. Rather expensive but mediocre meals (main courses 1,800FT to 3,000FT/$9 to $15) are served in a sunken room in the center, but this place is best suited for coffee and pastries. It's open daily 9am to midnight.

✪ **Angelika Cukrászda,** I. Batthyány tér 7 (☎ **061/201-4847** or 061/212-3784; Metro: Batthyány tér [Red line]), is housed in a historic building next to St. Anne's Church on Buda's Batthyány tér. The sunken rooms of this cavernous cafe provide the perfect retreat on a summer afternoon. Stained-glass windows, marble floors, and emerald-green upholstery contribute to the old-world atmosphere. There are excellent pastries and a good selection of teas (a rarity in Budapest, a city of coffee drinkers). It's open daily 10am to 10pm.

More than 100 years old, ✪ **Ruszwurm Cukrászda,** I. Szentháromság u. 7 (☎ **061/175-5284;** Bus: Várbusz from Moszkva tér or 16 from Deák tér to Castle Hill; Funicular: From Clark Ádám tér to Castle Hill), is an utterly charming little place, with tiny tables and chairs and shelves lined with antiques. A particularly tasty pastry is the *dobos torta,* a multilayered cake with a thin caramel crust on top. It's open daily 10am to 7pm.

Across from the Hilton in the Fortuna Courtyard, this is one of only two self-service cafeterias in the Castle District. The food is hearty and cheap. The entrance is marked only by a small sign posting the open hours; it's the second door on the left inside the archway, up one flight. Just follow the stream of Hungarians at lunchtime. Few foreigners find their way here because of the absence of a sign. Bus your own tray when you're done.

IN BUDA'S WATERTOWN

Le Jardin de Paris. I. Fő u. 20. ☎ **061/201-0047.** Reservations recommended. Main courses 1,200FT–1,800FT ($6–$9). AE, DC, MC, V. Daily noon–midnight. Metro: Batthyány tér (Red line). FRENCH.

In the heart of Buda's Watertown, across from the hideous Institut Français, this is a wonderful little bistro. A cozy cellar space, it's decorated with an eclectic collection of graphic arts. A jazz trio entertains diners. The menu contains a variety of nouvelle specialties, and the wine list features French as well as Hungarian vintages. Presentation is impeccable, and the waiters aren't overbearing.

Taverna Ressaikos. I. Apor Péter u. 1. ☎ **061/212-1612.** Reservations recommended. Main courses 650FT–1,090FT ($3.25–$5). AE, EURO, MC. Daily noon–midnight. Bus/tram: Any to Clark Ádám tér, including bus no. 16 from Deák tér. GREEK.

In the heart of Buda's Watertown (Víziváros), next door to the Hotel Alba Budapest, the Ressaikos features generous portions of carefully prepared food at reasonable prices. Try the calamari or the lamb in wine sauce. The menu also features a number of interesting goat dishes. Vegetarians can easily make a meal of the appetizers: stuffed tomatoes, spanikopita, tsatsiki, and the like. The live guitar music in the evenings can get a bit loud, and the service, while attentive, is definitely slow.

WORTH A SPLURGE

Kis Buda Gyöngye. III. Kenyeres u. 34. ☎ **061/368-6402** or 061/368-9246. Reservations highly recommended. Main courses 880FT–3,200FT ($4.40–$16). AE, DC, MC, V. Mon–Sat noon–midnight. Tram: 17 from Margit híd (Buda side). HUNGARIAN.

On a quiet side street in a residential Óbuda neighborhood, Kis Buda Gyöngye ("Little Pearl of Buda") is a favorite of Hungarians and visitors. This cheerful place features an interior garden, which sits in the shade of a wonderful old gnarly tree. Inside, an eccentric violinist entertains diners. Standard Hungarian fare is served. Consider the goose plate, a rich combination platter including roast goose leg, goose cracklings, and goose liver.

Légrádi Testvérek. V. Magyar u. 23. ☎ **061/118-6804.** Reservations highly recommended. Main courses 1,400FT–2,600FT ($7–$13). AE, V. Mon–Sat 6pm–midnight. Metro: Kálvin tér (Blue line). HUNGARIAN.

Very small (nine tables) and inconspicuously marked, on a sleepy side street in the southern part of the Inner City, this is one of the city's most elegant and formal restaurants. The food is served on Herend china, the cutlery is sterling, and an excellent string trio livens the atmosphere. Pass on the initial premenu offer of hors d'oeuvres costing 1,250FT ($6). If you're inclined to try a soup, the cream of asparagus is a fine interpretation of a Hungarian favorite. The chicken paprika served with cheese dumplings seasoned with fresh dill will surpass any you've tried elsewhere, and the veal cavellier, smothered in cauliflower-cheese sauce, is equally delightful.

5 Seeing the Sights

SIGHTSEEING SUGGESTIONS

IF YOU HAVE 1 DAY Spend a few hours in the morning exploring the **Inner City** and **central Pest.** Stroll along the Danube as far as the neo-Gothic **Parliament,** noting along the way the **Chain Bridge.** In the afternoon, visit the major sites of **Castle Hill** and meander the cobblestone streets of the **Castle District.**

IF YOU HAVE 2 DAYS On Day 1, head for Buda's **Gellért Hotel** and take a dip in its spa waters. Then hike up the stairs of **Gellért Hill** for an unparalleled panorama. Devote most of Day 2 to the **Castle District** and the sites of **Castle Hill** and visit some of the smaller museums. Head back to Pest to see **Heroes' Square** and **City Park,** and in the evening stroll the length of grand **Andrássy út** back to the center of Pest.

IF YOU HAVE 3 DAYS OR MORE   On Day 3, take a boat up the Danube to visit **Szentendre,** a charming riverside town. On Days 4 and 5, visit some of the central sites you may have missed, and after lunch cross the Chain Bridge to **Watertown** to explore Buda's historic riverside neighborhood. See **St. Anne's Church,** the **Capuchin Church,** and the **Király Baths.** Check out Pest's indoor **market halls** and visit **Margaret Island.**

THE TOP ATTRACTIONS
IN PEST

Parliament. V. Kossuth Lajos tér. ☎ **061/268-4437.** Guided 30-minute tour in English 700FT ($3.50) Mon–Fri 10am and 2pm and Sat 10am. Ibusz (☎ **061/118-1139**) offers 2,400FT ($12) 2-hour tour in English Wed, Fri, and Sat; starting times vary. No tours when Parliament is in session. Metro: Kossuth Lajos tér (Red line).

Budapest's great Parliament, an eclectic design that mixes the predominant neo-Gothic style with a neo-Renaissance dome, was completed in 1902. Standing proudly on the Danube bank, visible from almost any riverside point, it has from the outset been one of Budapest's symbols, though until 1989 a democratically elected government had convened here only once (just after World War II, before the Communist takeover).

Néprajzi Múzeum (Ethnographical Museum). V. Kossuth Lajos tér 12. ☎ 061/332-6340. Admission 200FT ($1). Tues–Sun 10am–6pm. Metro: Kossuth Lajos tér (Red line).

Directly across from the Parliament building, the vast Ethnographical Museum features an ornate interior equal to that of the Opera House. A ceiling fresco of Justitia, the goddess of justice, by artist Károly Lotz, dominates the lobby. Concentrate on the items from Hungarian ethnography.

✪ **Nemzeti Múzeum (Hungarian National Museum).** VIII. Múzeum krt. 14. ☎ **061/138-2122.** Admission 250FT ($1.25). Tues–Sun 10am–6pm. Metro: Kálvin tér (Blue line).

This enormous neoclassical structure, built in 1837–47, played a major role in the beginning of the Hungarian Revolution of 1848–49; on its wide steps on March 15, 1848, poet Sándor Petőfi and other young radicals are said to have exhorted the people of Pest to revolt against the Habsburgs. The museum's main attraction is the crown of St. Stephen (King Stephen ruled 1000–38), ceremoniously returned by Secretary of State Cyrus Vance to Hungary in 1978 from the United States, where it had been stored since the end of World War II.

IN BUDA

Budapesti Történeti Múzeum (Budapest History Museum). I. In Buda Palace, Wing E, on Castle Hill. ☎ 061/175-7533. Admission 200FT ($1). Guided tours in English 5,000FT ($25) available on advanced request. May 15–Sept 15 Wed–Mon 10am–6pm; Sept 16–May 14 Wed–Mon 10am–5pm. Bus: Várbusz from Moszkva tér or 106 from Deák tér to Castle Hill. Funicular: From Clark Ádám tér to Castle Hill.

This museum, also known as the Castle Museum, is the best place to get a sense of the once-great medieval Buda. It's probably worth splurging for a guided tour; even though the museum's descriptions are written in English, the history of the palace's repeated construction and destruction is so arcane it's difficult to understand what you're really seeing.

✪ **Nemzeti Galéria (Hungarian National Gallery).** I. In Buda Palace, Wings B, C, and D, on Castle Hill. ☎ 061/175-7533. Admission 150FT (75¢). Guided tours in English 1,000FT ($5). Mar–Oct Tues–Sun 10am–6pm; Nov–Feb Tues–Sun 10am–4pm. Bus: Várbusz from Moszkva tér or 106 from Deák tér to Castle Hill. Funicular: From Clark Ádám tér to Castle Hill.

Budapest

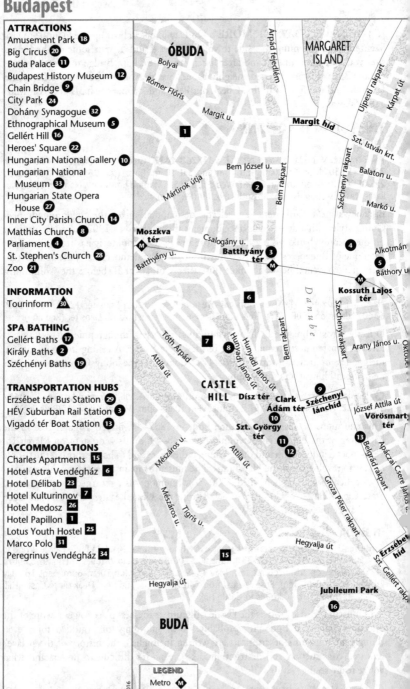

ATTRACTIONS
Amusement Park 18
Big Circus 20
Buda Palace 11
Budapest History Museum 12
Chain Bridge 9
City Park 24
Dohány Synagogue 32
Ethnographical Museum 5
Gellért Hill 16
Heroes' Square 22
Hungarian National Gallery 10
Hungarian National
  Museum 33
Hungarian State Opera
  House 27
Inner City Parish Church 14
Matthias Church 8
Parliament 4
St. Stephen's Church 28
Zoo 21

INFORMATION
Tourinform 30

SPA BATHING
Gellért Baths 17
Király Baths 2
Széchényi Baths 19

TRANSPORTATION HUBS
Erzsébet tér Bus Station 29
HÉV Suburban Rail Station 3
Vigadó tér Boat Station 13

ACCOMMODATIONS
Charles Apartments 15
Hotel Astra Vendégház 6
Hotel Délibab 23
Hotel Kulturinnov 7
Hotel Medosz 26
Hotel Papillon 1
Lotus Youth Hostel 25
Marco Polo 31
Peregrinus Vendégház 34

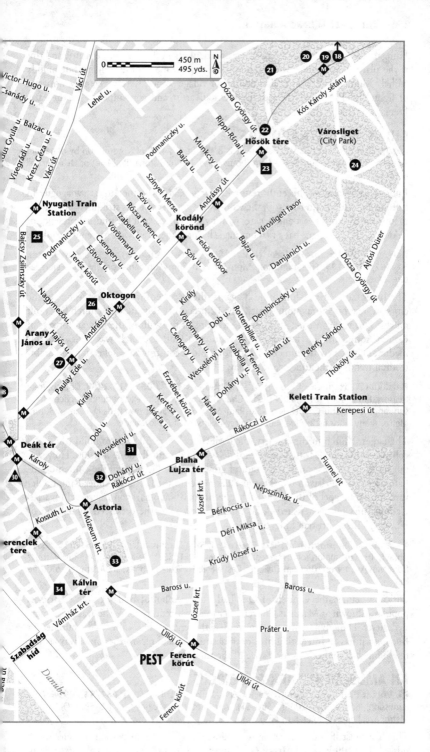

Hungary has produced some fine artists, particularly in the late 19th century, and this is the place to view their work. The giants of the time are the brilliant but moody Mihály Munkácsy; László Paál, a painter of village scenes; Károly Ferenczy, a master of light; and Pál Szinyei Merse, the plein-air artist and contemporary of the early French impressionists.

CHURCHES & SYNAGOGUES

✪ Dohány Synagogue. VII. Dohány u. 2–8. ☎ **061/342-8949.** Admission by donation. Tues–Fri 10am–3pm, Sun 10am–1pm (hours vary). Metro: Astoria (Red line) or Deák tér (all lines).

Built in 1859 and just recently restored, this is said to be the largest synagogue in Europe and the second largest in the world. The architecture has striking Moorish elements; the interior is vast and ornate, with two balconies, and the unusual presence of an organ. The synagogue has a rich but tragic history. There's a Jewish museum next door.

Belvárosi Plébániatemplom (Inner City Parish Church). V. Március 15 tér. ☎ **061/118-3108.** Free admission. Mon–Sat 6am–7pm, Sun 8am–7pm. Metro: Ferenciek tere (Blue line).

The Inner City Parish Church, flush against the Erzsébet Bridge in Pest, is one of the city's great architectural monuments. The 12th-century Romanesque church first built on this spot was constructed inside the remains of the walls of the Roman fortress of Contra-Aquincum. In the early 14th century, a Gothic church was built, and this medieval church, with numerous additions and reconstructions reflecting the architectural trends of the time, stands today.

Bazilika (St. Stephen's Church). V. Szent István tér 33. ☎ **061/117-2859.** Church, free; treasury, 80FT (40¢); tower, 200FT ($1). Church, daily 7am–7pm, except during services; treasury and Szent Jobb Chapel, Mon–Sat 9am–5pm, Sun 1–5pm; tower, daily 10am–4:30pm. Metro: Arany János utca (Blue line) or Bajcsy-Zsilinszky út (Yellow line).

The largest church in the country, the basilica took over 50 years to build (the 1868 collapse of the dome caused significant delay) and was finally done in 1906. However, during this time Pest underwent radical growth; while the front of the church dominates sleepy Szent István tér, the rear faces out onto the far busier Inner Ring boulevard. In the Chapel of the Holy Right (Szent Jobb Kápolna), you can see Hungarian Catholicism's most cherished—and bizarre—holy relic: the preserved right hand of Hungary's first Christian king, Stephen.

✪ Mátyás Templom (Matthias Church). I. Szentháromság tér 2. ☎ **061/115-5657.** Church, free; exhibition rooms beneath the altar, 100FT (50¢). Daily 9am–5pm. Bus: Várbusz from Moszkva tér or 106 from Deák tér Castle Hill. Funicular: From Clark Ádám tér to Castle Hill.

Officially named the Church of Our Lady, this symbol of Buda's Castle District is popularly known as Matthias Church after the 15th-century king who was twice married here. Though it dates to the mid-13th century, like other old churches in Budapest it has an interesting history of destruction and reconstruction, always being refashioned in the architectural style of the time.

AN AMUSEMENT PARK & A CIRCUS

✪ Vidám Park (Amusement Park). XIV. Állatkerti krt. 14–16. ☎ **061/343-0996.** Free admission; rides 100FT–200FT (50¢–$1). Apr–Sept daily 10am–8pm (to 6pm Oct–Mar). Metro: Széchenyi fürdő (Yellow line).

This is a must if you're traveling with kids, but two rides in particular aren't to be missed. The 100-year-old **Merry-Go-Round** *(Körhinta),* constructed almost entirely

Special Events

The **Budapest Spring Festival** is held for 2 weeks in mid- to late March. Performances of everything from opera to ballet, from classical music to drama, are held at all the major halls and theaters. What's more, prices for tickets are so low you can attend virtually every event for what it would cost to attend one musical extravaganza in Salzburg. Tickets are available at the Festival Ticket Service, V. 1081 Rákóczi út 65 (☎ **061/210-2795** or 061/133-2337) and at the individual venues.

of wood, was recently restored to its original grandeur. The riders must actively pump to keep the horses rocking and authentic Wurlitzer music plays. As the carousel spins round and round, it creaks mightily. The **Ferris wheel** *(Óriáskerék)* is also wonderful, though it has little in common with the rambunctious Ferris wheels of the modern age. A gangly bright-yellow structure, it rotates at a liltingly slow pace, gently lifting you high for a remarkable view. The Vidám Park also features Europe's longest wooden roller-coaster.

Nagy Cirkusz (Big Circus). XIV. Állatkerti krt. 7. ☎ **061/343-9630.** Admission 250FT–520FT ($1.25–$2.60), free for under age 4. Performances Wed–Sun (except Sept–Oct), at least 2 or 3 per day. Metro: Hősök tere or Széchenyi fürdő (Yellow line).

It's not the Big Apple Circus or the Cirque de Soleil, but kids love it anyway. Budapest has a long circus tradition, though most Hungarian circus stars opt for the more glamorous and financially rewarding circus life abroad. The box office is open 10am to 7pm.

PARKS & PANORAMAS

Gellért Hegy (Gellért Hill), towering 750 feet above the Danube, offers the city's single best panorama. The hill is named after the Italian Bishop Gellért, who assisted Hungary's first Christian king, Stephen I, in converting the Magyars. Gellért became a martyr when he was rolled in a barrel to his death from the side of the hill on which his enormous statue now stands. On top of Gellért Hill you'll find the Liberation Monument, built in 1947 to commemorate the Red Army's liberation of Budapest from Nazi occupation. Also atop the hill is the **Citadella,** built by the Austrians shortly after they crushed the Hungarian War of Independence of 1848–49. Take bus no. 27 from Móricz Zsigmond körtér.

Margaret Island (Margit-sziget) has been a public park since 1908. The long, narrow island, connected to both Buda and Pest via the Margaret and Árpád bridges, is barred to most vehicular traffic. Facilities on the island include the Palatinus Strand open-air baths (see "Enjoying the Thermal Baths," below), which draw on the famous thermal waters under Margaret Island; the Alfréd Hajós Sport Pool; and the Open Air Theater. Sunbathers line the steep embankments along the river and bicycles are available for rent. Despite all this, Margaret Island is a tranquil place. Take bus no. 26 from Nyugati tér, running the length of the island, or tram no. 4 or 6, stopping at the entrance to the island midway across the Margaret Bridge. (*Warning:* These are popular lines for pickpockets.)

City Park (Városliget) is an equally popular place to spend a summer day. Heroes' Square, at the end of Andrássy út, is the most logical starting point for a walk in City Park. The lake behind the square is used for boating in summer and ice skating in winter. The park's Zoo Boulevard (Állatkerti körút), the favorite street of generations

Enjoying the Thermal Baths

Budapest's baths have a long and proud history, stretching back to Roman times. Under Turkish occupation the culture of the baths flourished, and several still-functioning bathhouses—Király, Rudas, and Rac—are among the architectural relics of this period. In the late 19th and early 20th centuries, Budapest's "golden age," several fabulous bathhouses were built: the extravagant, eclectic Széchenyi Baths in City Park, the splendid art nouveau Gellért Baths, and the neoclassical Lukács Baths. All are still in use.

Because thermal bathing is an activity shaped by ritual and bathhouse employees tend to be unfriendly, many foreigners find a trip to the baths confusing at first. The most baffling step may be the ticket window with its list of prices for different facilities and services, often without English translations: *uszoda*, pool; *termál*, thermal pool; *fürdő*, bath; *gozfürdő*, steam bath, massage, and sauna. Towel rental is *törüközö* or *lepedő*. An entry ticket generally entitles you to a free locker in the locker room *(öltözo)*; you can usually opt to pay extra for a private cabin *(kabin)*.

Budapest's most spectacular bathhouse, the **Gellért Baths,** are in Buda's Hotel Gellért, at XI. Kelenhegyi út 4 (☎ **061/166-6166;** Tram: 47 or 49 from Deák tér to Szent Gellért tér). Enter through the side entrance. The unisex indoor pool is exquisite, with marble columns, majolica tiles, and stone lion heads spouting water. The segregated Turkish-style thermal baths, one off to each side of the pool through badly marked doors, are also glorious though in need of restoration. The outdoor roof pool attracts great attention for 10 minutes every hour on the hour when the artificial wave machine is turned on. Admission to the thermal bath is 400FT ($2); a 15-minute massage is 450FT ($2.25) plus tip. Lockers are free; a cabin is 200FT ($1). Admission to all services costs 1,200FT ($6) adults and 600FT ($3) children. Prices are posted in English. The thermal baths are open all year, daily 6am to 7pm (last entry 6pm).

The **Király Baths,** I. Fő u. 84 (☎ **061/202-3688;** Metro: Batthyány tér [Red line]), are one of Budapest's most important architectural monuments to Turkish rule, a place where Hungarian culture meets the Eastern culture that influenced it. The bath itself, from the late 16th century, is housed under an octagonal domed roof. Sunlight filters through stained-glass windows. In addition to the thermal bath, there are saunas and steam baths. After your treatment, wrap yourself in a cotton sheet and lounge with a cup of tea in the relaxation room. Men can use the baths Monday, Wednesday, and Friday 6:30am to 6pm; reportedly, the men's bath is frequented by a largely gay crowd. Women's days are Tuesday and Thursday 6:30am to 6pm and Saturday 6:30am to noon. It costs 300FT ($1.50) to bathe.

of Hungarian children, is where the zoo, the circus, and the amusement park are all found. Gundel, Budapest's most famous restaurant, is also here, as are the Széchenyi Baths. The Yellow metro line makes stops at Hősök tere (Heroes' Square), at the edge of the park, and Széchenyi Fürdő, in the middle of it.

ORGANIZED TOURS

Ibusz (☎ **061/118-1139** or 061/118-1043) offers 11 boat and bus tours, ranging from basic city tours to special folklore-oriented tours. Bus tours leave from the

Erzsébet tér station, near Deák tér; boat tours leave from the Vigadó tér landing. There's also a free hotel pickup service 30 minutes before departure time.

The Hungarian company **MAHART** operates daily sightseeing cruises on the Danube. The Budapest office of MAHART is at V. Belgrád rakpart (☎ **061/ 118-1704,** 061/118-953, or 061/118-1586). Boats depart from Vigadó tér on weekends and holidays in spring and daily in summer.

Legenda, XI. Fraknó utca 4 (☎ **061/117-2203**), a private company, offers boat tours on the Danube. You can see a majority of the city's grand sights from the river. Tours run mid-April to mid-October; boats leave from the Vigadó tér port, Pier 6 or 7. Tickets are available through most major hotels, at the dock, or through the Legenda office.

6 Shopping

All year long, shoppers fill the pedestrians-only **Váci utca,** from the stately Vörösmarty tér, the center of Pest, across the roaring Kossuth Lajos utca, all the way to Vámház krt. The **Castle District** in Buda, with many folk-art boutiques and galleries, is another popular area for souvenir hunters.

Locals (and budget travelers) might window-shop in these two neighborhoods, but they do their serious shopping elsewhere. One popular street is Pest's **Outer Ring (Nagykörút);** another bustling shopping street is Pest's **Kossuth Lajos utca,** off the Erzsébet Bridge, and its continuation **Rákóczi út,** which extends all the way out to Keleti Station.

The stores of the state-owned Folkart Háziipar should be your main source of Hungary's justly famous folk items. Almost everything is handmade—from tablecloths to miniature dolls, from ceramic dishes to sheepskin vests. The main store, **Folkart Centrum,** is at V. Váci u. 14 (☎ **061/118-5840**). A second store is at VIII. Rákóci út 32 (☎ **061/342-0753**), with similar offerings at similar reasonable prices.

FLEA MARKETS

Budapest's largest and best-known flea market is the **Ecseri Hasznaltcikk Piac,** XIX. Nagykőrösi út 156 (☎ **061/280-8840**). Haggling is standard, and purchases are in cash only. The market runs Monday to Friday 8am to 4pm and Saturday 8am to 3pm. Take bus no. 54 from Boráros tér, about a 7-minute ride. The market is on the left side of the street. Open daily 7am to 6pm, **Józsefvárosi Piac,** VIII. Kőbányai út (☎ **061/314-0833**), has been renamed "Four Tigers" as a result of the influx of Chinese vendors. You'll find bargains aplenty, and all prices are negotiable. Hard currency is welcomed. Dozens of languages are spoken. Take tram no. 28 from Blaha Lujza tér or no. 36 from Baross tér (Keleti Station) and get off at Orczy tér.

7 Budapest After Dark

Budapest is blessed with a rich and varied cultural life. You can still go to the Opera House, one of Europe's finest, for less than $3. Almost all of the city's theaters and halls, with the exception of those hosting internationally touring rock groups, offer tickets for as little as $2 to $4. The opera, ballet, and theater seasons run September to May or June, but most theaters and halls also host performances during the summer festivals. A number of lovely churches and stunning halls offer concerts exclusively in summer. While classical culture has a long and proud tradition in Budapest, jazz, blues, rock, and disco have exploded in the post-Communist era. New clubs and bars have opened everywhere; the parties start late and last until morning.

The most complete schedule of mainstream performing arts is found in the free bimonthly *Koncert Kalendárium,* available at the Central Philharmonic Ticket Office in Vörösmarty tér. The *Budapest Sun,* one of two English-language weeklies, has a comprehensive events calendar; it also lists less-publicized events like modern dance and folk music performances. *Programme in Hungary* and *Budapest Panorama,* the two free monthly tourist booklets, have only partial entertainment listings, featuring what their editors consider the monthly highlights.

The **Central Theater Ticket Office (Színházak Központi Jegyiroda),** VI. Andrássy út 18 (☎ **061/312-0000**), sells tickets to just about everything, from theater and operetta to sports events and rock concerts; it's open Monday to Thursday 9am to 1pm and 1:45 to 6pm (Friday to 5pm). A second branch is at II. Moszkva tér 3 (☎ **061/135-9136**), with similar hours except that it opens at 10am. Of course, you can also buy tickets at the individual venue box offices.

THE PERFORMING ARTS

OPERA & CONCERTS   Completed in 1884, the **Magyar Állami Operaház (Hungarian State Opera House),** VI. Andrássy út 22 (☎ **061/131-2550;** Metro: Opera [Yellow line]), is Budapest's most famous performance hall and an attraction in its own right. Hungarians adore opera, and a large percentage of seats is sold on a subscription basis; buy your tickets a few days ahead if possible. The box office is open Monday to Friday 11am to 5pm.

The Great Hall (Nagyterem) of the **Zeneakadémia (Ferenc Liszt Academy of Music),** VI. Liszt Ferenc tér 8 (☎ **061/341-4788;** Metro: Oktogon [Yellow line]), is Budapest's premier music hall. The academy was built in the art nouveau style of the early 20th century. The acoustics in the Great Hall are said to be the best in the city. Box office hours are 2pm to showtime on the day of performance.

The **Budai Vigadó (Buda Concert Hall),** I. Corvin tér 8 (☎ **061/117-2754;** Metro: Batthyány tér [Red line]), is the home stage of the Hungarian State Folk Ensemble (Állami Népi Együttes Székháza). The ensemble is the oldest in the country and includes 40 dancers, a 20-member Gypsy orchestra, and a folk orchestra. Under the direction of award-winning choreographer Sándor Timár, it performs folk dances from all regions of historic Hungary. The *New York Times* called it "a mix of high art and popular tradition. . . . Every dance crackled with high speed." The box office is open Monday to Saturday 10am to 6pm.

THEATER   Budapest has an extremely lively theater season September to June. For productions in English, try the **Merlin Theater,** V. Gerlóczy u. 4 (☎ **061/117-1337;** Metro: Astoria [Red line]). For musical productions, try the **Madách Theater,** VII. Erzsébet krt. 29–33 (☎ **061/233-2015;** Tram: 4 or 6 to Wesselényi utca). Also staging musical performances is the **Vigszínház (Merry Theater),** XIII. Szent István krt. 14 (☎ **061/269-3920;** Metro: Nyugati pu. [Blue line]), which was recently restored to its original delightfully gaudy neo-Baroque splendor.

LIVE-MUSIC CLUBS

The club scene has found fertile ground since 1989's political changes—so much so, in fact, that clubs come in and out of fashion overnight. Check the *Budapest Sun* for up-to-the-minute club listings.

The popular **Made Inn Mine,** VI. Andrássy út 112 (☎ **061/111-3437;** Metro: Bajza utca [Yellow line]), has a subterranean cavelike atmosphere. Wednesday features a funk dance party and all drinks are half price. For some reason, Thursday is *the* night to be here; you may have to wait in line to enter. It's open daily 8pm to 5am, with the kitchen open to 3am. Cover is 300FT ($1.50) but 500FT ($2.50) Thursday. With a

40-year history, the **Miniatür Espresso,** II. Buday László u. 10, in Buda (no phone; Tram: 4 or 6 to Mechwart liget), is a favorite, offering lace tablecloths, overstuffed chairs, soft lighting, and soothing piano music. Owner Katalin Tálas, who speaks excellent English, is on hand to greet guests. Admission is free, but drinks are costly (beer is 600FT/$3). It's open Monday to Saturday 7pm to 3am.

In the heart of Budapest's theater district, **Piaf,** VI. Nagymező u. 25 (☎ 061/ 312-3823; Metro: Oktogon [Yellow line]), is a sophisticated French-style nightclub with red velvet chairs and a candlelit atmosphere. Upstairs features live piano music, while downstairs is a bar. Drinks are pricey. It's open daily 10pm to 6am. Cover is 350FT ($1.75), from which 250FT goes toward your first drink. The classy multilevel ✪ **Fél 10 Jazz Klub,** VIII. Baross u. 30 (☎ 06-60/318-467 [mobile phone]; Metro: Kálvin tér), is one of the few clubs whose dance floor isn't crammed with teenagers. Live music performances are given nightly. Techno-free dance parties get going in the wee hours. It's open Monday to Friday noon to dawn and Saturday and Sunday 7pm to dawn; cover is 200FT ($1).

BARS

An American-style microbrewery on one of Pest's busiest squares, **Chicago Sörgyár,** VII. Erzsébet krt. 2. (☎ 061/269-6753; Metro: Blaha Lujza tér [Red line]), has a diehard expatriate crowd that comes not just for the fairly good home-brewed beer but for the hamburgers, nachos, and french fries. Happy hour is weekdays 4 to 6pm, with half-price drinks. It's open Monday to Thursday noon to midnight, Friday and Saturday noon to 1am, and Sunday noon to 11pm.

✪ **Tokaji Borbár (Tokaj Wine Bar),** V. Andrássy út 20 (☎ 061/269-3116; Metro: Opera [Yellow line]), is a casual, unpretentious place to sample delicious, fruity whites of the famous Tokaj region. Patrons sit at the bar or stand. It's open Monday to Saturday 1 to 9pm. **Irish Cat Pub,** V. Múzeum krt. 41 (☎ 061/266-4085; Metro: Kálvin tér [Blue line]), is an Irish-style pub with Guinness on tap and a whisky bar. It's a popular meeting place for ex-pats and travelers, serving a full menu, and is open Monday to Thursday and Sunday 11am to 3am and Friday and Saturday 11am to 5am.

GAY & LESBIAN BARS

As with the fickle club scene, "in" bars become "out," or even close down, at a moment's notice. The gay bar scene in Budapest is exclusively male oriented at this point, though this is liable to change. Search out a copy of the English-language **Phone Book** for a more complete listing of gay bars.

Angel Bar & Dance Club, VII. Szövetség u. 33. (☎ 061/351-6490; Metro: Blaha Lujza tér [Red line]), is a basement place with a bar, restaurant, and huge dance floor. It has been around for a while now and is presumably here to stay. The club isn't exclusively gay; many straights attend, especially on Friday. Friday and Sunday, Angel hosts a now-famous transvestite show, starting at 11pm. Cover is 300FT ($1.50), but there are no shows and no cover on Thursday. It's open Thursday to Sunday 10pm to dawn. **Mystery Bar,** V. Nagysándor József u. 3 (no phone; Metro: Arany János utca, Blue line), is a smaller place, with a larger foreign crowd. There are occasional drag shows and live lounge music. Hours vary.

A DANCE CLUB

Bahnhof, VI. Váci út 1, behind the Nyugati train station (☎ 061/20-311-181; Metro: Nyugati pu. [Blue line]), is a huge basement dance club, the hottest thing around for the 20-something crowd. Bahnhof features deejays and live acts and is open Wednesday to Saturday 9pm to 4am, with a 300FT ($1.80) cover.

8   Side Trips: The Danube Bend & Lake Balaton

ALONG THE DANUBE BEND

The delightful towns along the **Danube Bend** are easy day trips. The great natural beauty of the area, where forested hills loom over the river, makes it a welcome departure for the city-weary.

ARRIVING   April to September, **boats** run between Budapest and the towns of the Danube Bend, leaving from the Vigadó tér boat landing. For information, contact **MAHART,** the state shipping company, at the Vigadó tér landing (☎ **061/118-1223**). Ask about discounts for Eurailpass holders and children.

The **HÉV suburban railroad** connects Budapest's Batthyány tér with Szentendre. Trains leave daily, every 20 minutes or so. The one-way fare is 109FT (55¢); subtract 60FT (30¢) if you have a valid Budapest public transport pass. The trip takes 45 minutes. Ten daily trains make the run between Budapest's Nyugati Station and Esztergom. The trip takes about 1¼ hours and tickets cost 266FT ($1.35).

SZENTENDRE   Peopled in medieval times by Serbian settlers, Szentendre (*Sen*-tendreh), 13 miles north of Budapest, counts half a dozen Serbian churches among its historical buildings. Since the turn of the century, Szentendre has been home to an artist's colony and boasts a wealth of museums and galleries. **Tourinform** is at Dumtsa Jenő u. 22 (☎ **26/317-965** or 26/317-966), open Monday to Friday 10am to 4pm. The **Ibusz** office is on the corner of Bogdányi út and Gőzhajó utca (☎ **26/313-597**). April to October, it's open Monday to Friday 9am to 6pm and Saturday and Sunday 10am to 2pm; hours November to March are Monday to Friday 9am to 4pm.

The ✪ **Margit Kovács Museum,** Vastagh György u. 1, is a must-see. The exceptional work of Hungary's best-known ceramic artist is on display. Her sculptures of elderly women and friezes of village life are particularly moving. April to October, the museum is open Tuesday to Sunday 10am to 6pm (November to March to 4pm). Admission is 250FT ($1.25). The **Blagovestenska church** at Fő tér 4 dates from 1752. A rococo iconostasis features paintings of Mihailo Zivkovic. Notice that the eyes of all the icons are on you; the effect is extraordinary. Next door at Fő tér 6 is the **Ferenczy Museum,** dedicated to the art of the prodigious Ferenczy family. The paintings of Károly Ferenczy, one of Hungary's leading impressionists, are featured. April to October, it's open Tuesday to Sunday 10am to 4pm; November to March, hours are Friday to Sunday 10am to 4pm. Admission is 90FT (45¢).

The ✪ **Ámos and Anna Muzeum,** Bogdány u. 10, was the former home of artist couple Imre Ámos and Margit Anna, whose work represents the beginning of expressionist painting in Hungary. Opened after Anna's death in 1991, the collection is Szentendre's best-kept secret. It's open Tuesday to Sunday 10am to 6pm, and admission is 90FT (45¢).

For lunch, we recommend the **Aranysárkány Vendéglő (Golden Dragon Inn),** Alkotmány u. 1/a (☎ **26/311-670**). The food is excellent (like alpine lamb, roast goose, and venison ragout) and the prices are reasonable. It's open daily noon to 10pm and doesn't accept credit cards.

ESZTERGOM   Formerly a Roman settlement, Esztergom (*ess*-tair-gome), 29 miles northwest of Budapest, was the seat of the Hungarian kingdom for 300 years. Hungary's first king, István I (Stephen I), crowned by the Pope in A.D. 1000, converted Hungary to Catholicism, and Esztergom became the country's center of the early church. Though its glory days are far behind it, the quiet town remains the seat of the archbishop-primate—the "Hungarian Rome." **Gran Tours,** centrally located at

Széchenyi tér 25 (☎ **33/413-756**), is the best source of information. It's open Monday to Friday 8am to 4pm and Saturday 8am to noon.

The massive neoclassical **Esztergom Cathedral,** in Szent István tér on Castle Hill, is Esztergom's most popular attraction and one of Hungary's most impressive buildings. The cathedral Treasury (Kincstár) contains a stunning array of ecclesiastical jewels and gold works. Since Cardinal Mindszenty's body was moved to the crypt in 1991 (he died in exile in 1975), it has been a place of pilgrimage for Hungarians. If you brave the ascent of the cupola, you'll be rewarded with unparalleled views of Esztergom and the surrounding Hungarian and Slovak countryside. The cathedral is open daily: 8am to 8pm in summer and 9am to 3pm in winter; the treasury, crypt, and cupola are also open daily: 9am to 5pm in summer and 10am to 3pm in winter. Admission to the cathedral and the crypt are free, but it costs 130FT (65¢) to see the treasury and 50FT (25¢) to see the cupola.

It's definitely worth taking a break from the crowds at the cathedral and strolling through the quiet cobblestone streets of **Víziváros (Watertown).** There you'll find the **Keresztény Múzeum (Christian Museum),** Mindszenty tér 2 (☎ **33/313-880**), in the neoclassical former primate's palace. It houses Hungary's largest collection of religious art and the largest collection of medieval art outside the National Gallery. Hours are Tuesday to Sunday 10am to 5:30pm (closed January to March). Admission is 150FT (75¢).

For lunch, try ✪ **Szalma Csárda,** Nagy-Duna sétány 2 (☎ **33/315-336**). This csárda is absolutely first-rate, with everything made to order and served piping hot. The excellent house soups—fish soup *(halászlé),* goulash *(gulyásleves),* and bean soup*(babgulyás)*—constitute meals in themselves. It's open daily 10am to 10pm and doesn't accept credit cards.

LAKE BALATON

Lake Balaton may not be the Mediterranean, but don't tell that to the Hungarians. Somehow over the years they've managed to create their own central European hybrid of a Mediterranean culture along the shores of their shallow milky-white lake, Europe's largest at 50 miles long and 10 miles wide at its broadest stretch.

The south shore towns are as flat as Pest; walk 10 minutes from the lake and you're in farm country. The air is still and quiet; in summer, the sun hangs heavily in the sky. Teenagers, students, and young travelers tend to congregate in the hedonistic towns of the south shore, where huge 1970s-style beachside hotels are filled to capacity all summer long and disco music pulsates into the early morning hours.

On the more graceful north shore, little villages are neatly tucked away in the rolling countryside, where the grapes of the popular Balaton wines ripen in the strong southern sun. You'll discover the Tihany peninsula, a protected area whose 4¾ square miles jut out into the lake like a knob. Stop for a swim—or the night—in a small town like Szigliget. Moving west along the coast, you can make forays inland into the rolling hills of the Balaton wine country. The city of Keszthély, sitting at the lake's western edge, marks the end of its northern shore.

ARRIVING   From Budapest, **trains** to the various towns along the lake depart from Déli Station. The local trains are interminably slow, so try to get on an express.

ACCOMMODATIONS AROUND THE LAKE   You'll see that anywhere you go on the lake, signs advertising rooms for rent in private homes *(szoba kiadó* or *zimmer frei)* beckon you. Since hotel prices are unusually high in this region and just about every local family rents out a room or two in summer, we especially recommend private rooms. When you take a room without using a tourist agency as the intermediary, prices are generally negotiable. In the height of the season, you shouldn't have to pay more than $40 for a double reasonably near the lake.

THE TIHANY PENINSULA   The Tihany (*Tee*-hine) peninsula is a protected area, and building is heavily restricted. Consequently, it maintains a rustic charm that's unusual in this region. The peninsula also features a lush protected interior, accessible by a trail from Tihany Village, with several little inland lakes as well as a lookout tower offering views over the Balaton.

The rail line circling Lake Balaton doesn't serve the Tihany peninsula. The nearest **rail station** is in Aszófó, about 3 miles from Tihany Village. A local **bus** comes to Tihany from the nearby town of Balatonfüred. You can also go by **ferry** from Szántód or Balatonföldvár or by **boat** from Balatonfüred. Visitor information is available March to October at **Balatontourist,** Kossuth u. 20 (☎ and fax **87/448-519**), open Monday to Friday 8:30am to 4:30pm and Saturday 8:30am to 12:30pm.

The 18th-century baroque ✪ **Abbey Church** is Tihany Village's main attraction. A resident monk carved the exquisite wooden altar and pulpit in the 18th century. The frescoes are by three of Hungary's better-known 19th-century painters: Károly Lotz, Bertalan Székely, and Lajos Deák-Ébner. Next door is the **Tihany Museum** (☎ **87/448-650**), also in an 18th-century baroque structure. The museum features exhibits on the surrounding region's history and culture. You pay a single fee of 150FT (75¢) for both the church and the museum. They're open daily: 9am to 5:30pm in summer and 10am to 3pm off-season.

SZIGLIGET   Halfway between Tihany and Keszthély is the scenic little village of Szigliget (*Sig*-lee-get), with thatched-roof houses, lush vineyards, and a lovely Mediterranean quality. **Natur Tourist,** in the village center, is your best (and only) source of information in Szigliget.

Szigliget is marked by the fantastic ruins of the 13th-century ✪ **Szigliget Castle,** which stands above it on **Várhegy (Castle Hill).** In the days of the Turkish invasions, the Hungarian Balaton fleet, protected by the high castle, called Szigliget its home. You can hike up to the ruins for a splendid view of the lake and countryside; look for the path behind the white 18th-century church at the highest spot in the village. A good place to fortify yourself for the hike is the **Vár Vendéglő** (on the road up to the castle), a casual restaurant with plenty of outdoor seating, serving traditional Hungarian fare. No credit cards are accepted.

The lively **beach** at Szigliget provides a striking contrast to the quiet village. In summer, buses from neighboring towns drop off hordes of beach-goers. The beach area is crowded with fried food and beer stands, ice-cream vendors, a swing set, and a volleyball net. Admission to the beach is 100FT (50¢). Szigliget is also home to the **Eszterházy Wine Cellar,** the largest wine cellar in the region. After a hike in the hills or a day in the sun, a little wine tasting just might be in order.

KESZTHÉLY   At the western edge of Lake Balaton, Keszthély (*Kest*-hay), 117 miles southwest of Budapest, is one of the largest towns on the lake. Though it was largely destroyed during the Turkish wars, the town was rebuilt in the 18th century by the Festetics, an aristocratic family who made Keszthély their home through World War II.

For visitor information, stop at **Tourinform,** Kossuth u. 28 (☎ and fax **83/ 314-144**). Summer hours are Monday to Friday 9am to 6pm and Saturday 9am to 1pm; off-season hours are Monday to Friday 8am to 4pm and Saturday 9am to 1pm. For private-room bookings, try **Zalatours,** Kossuth u. 1 (☎ **83/312-560**), or **Ibusz,** Kossuth u. 27 (☎ **83/314-320**).

The highlight of a visit to Keszthély is the splendid ✪ **Festetics Mansion,** at Szabadsag u. 1 (☎ **83/312-190**), the baroque 18th-century home (with its 19th-century additions) for generations of the Festetics family. Part of the mansion is now open as a museum, the main attraction of which is the ornate library. The museum also features hunting gear and trophies of a bygone era. In summer, it's open daily 9am to 6pm (to 5pm Monday off-season). Admission for foreigners is 550FT ($2.75).

The center of Keszthély's summer scene, just like that of every other place on Lake Balaton, is down by the water on the "strand." Keszthély's **beachfront** is dominated by several large hotels. Even if you're not a guest, you can rent **Windsurfers, boats,** and other **water-related equipment** from these hotels.

INTO THE HILLS   Northeast of the Danube Bend is Hungary's hilliest region, where you can find its highest peak—**Matra Hill** at 3,327 feet. Here you can visit the preserved medieval village of **Hollókő,** one of the most charming spots in Hungary. This UNESCO World Heritage site is a perfectly preserved but still vibrant Palóc village. The rural Palóc people speak an unusual Hungarian dialect and have truly colorful folk customs and costumes. If you're in Hungary at Easter, by all means consider spending the holiday here: Hollókő's traditional celebration features townspeople in traditional dress and masses in the town church.

Hollókő is idyllically set in a quiet, green valley, with hiking trails all around. A recently restored **14th-century castle** is perched on a hilltop over the village. The **Village Museum,** Kossuth Lajos u. 82, contains exhibits detailing everyday Palóc life from the turn of the century. It's open Tuesday to Sunday 10am to 4pm, and admission is 60FT (30¢).

In Hollókő, traditionally furnished **thatch-roofed peasant houses** are available to rent for a night or longer. You can rent a room in a shared house (with shared facilities) or an entire house. The prices vary depending on the size of the room or house and the number of people in your party (2,500FT/$13 for a double room is average). Standard private rooms are also available in Hollókő. All accommodations can be booked in advance through the **Foundation of Hollókő,** at Kossuth Lajos u. 68 (☎ **32/379-266**). You can also make reservations through **Nograd Tourist** in nearby Salgótarján (☎ **32/310-660**).

The easiest way to get to Hollókő is by **bus.** From Budapest's Népstadion bus station (☎ **061/252-4496**), take a bus to Szécseny; there, switch to a local bus to Hollókő. Six daily buses ply the Budapest–Szécseny route. The 2½-hour ride costs 586FT ($2.95). Eight daily buses connect Szécseny with Hollókő. That ride takes about half an hour and costs 113FT (55¢).

10

Copenhagen & Environs

by Nikolaus Lorey

Let's create the perfect city. We'll start with a vast network of streets lined with great stores and cafes. Then we'll add bicycle lanes to span the city, encouraging quiet nonpolluting transport, and generously spread royal palaces and rich museums about. We'll build our city on a pretty yet functional harbor and put an amusement park right in the center, making carnival rides and concerts accessible to all. Finally, we'll govern with a socially minded philosophy that virtually eliminates poverty, crime, and begging. This is no fantasy—it's Copenhagen. And without a doubt this very real city's richest gift is its quality of life.

Copenhageners are a reflection of a kind, gentle lifestyle. They smile easily, laugh a lot, and will often go out of their way to help a stranger. They're known for their terrific sense of humor—poking fun at themselves and others, especially American travelers. The city considers itself Europe's "jazz capital," boasting more than its fair share of exceptional talent. And as every stroller along Strøget will discover, the city attracts some of the world's best street performers.

Even for the value-minded visitor, Copenhagen is a city to love and savor. Getting around is relatively easy—you can walk to almost everything. The hotels and restaurants cater to a variety of budgets and maintain some of the highest standards in Europe. And the bars and clubs serve some of Europe's best brews at a fraction of the prices charged in other Scandinavian cities.

REQUIRED DOCUMENTS Citizens of the United States, Canada, the United Kingdom, New Zealand, and Australia need only a passport to enter Denmark.

OTHER FROMMER'S TITLES For more on Copenhagen, see *Frommer's Scandinavia, Frommer's Gay & Lesbian Europe,* or *Frommer's Europe.*

1 Copenhagen Deals & Discounts

SPECIAL DISCOUNTS

FOR EVERYONE The **Copenhagen Card** entitles you to free museum entry, free public transport, and good discounts on a variety of activities throughout the capital. The card is for 1, 2, or 3 days and costs 140KR ($22), 255KR ($39), or 320KR ($49), respectively. You can buy the card at the DSB ticket office in Central Station, the Copenhagen Tourist Information office (see "Visitor Information," later in this chapter), and many hotels and S-tog stations.

Budget Bests

Tivoli, the city's biggest draw, provides one of Copenhagen's cheapest thrills: Adults can get in for 39KR ($6), kids for half that. You can see one of Copenhagen's most famous sites, *The Little Mermaid,* for free, and the **Carlsberg Brewery tour** is informative, intoxicating, fun, and also free. And if you're looking for a bit of culture, you can see an **opera,** a **ballet,** or a **play** at the Royal Theater for as little as 60KR ($9).

FOR STUDENTS   By flashing an **International Student Identification Card (ISIC),** young people can get discounts at most of the city's museums, at some concert halls, and on planes, trains, and ferries from Denmark. Check the listings throughout this chapter for special student rates.

FOR SENIORS   People over 67 are entitled to half-price tickets at the Royal Theater, reduced admission to some museums, and discounts on ferry trips to Sweden. See the listings for details.

WORTH A SPLURGE

A trip to the nearby **Louisiana Museum of Modern Art in Humlebæk** in North Zealand is definitely worthwhile. For details about this stunning repository of modern art and sculpture, see "Seeing the Sights," later in this chapter. And you should definitely make a side trip to **Elsinore** to see where Hamlet and his dysfunctional family played out their days.

2 Essentials

ARRIVING

BY PLANE   Is it a top-of-the-line department store or an airport? Both. It's **Copenhagen Airport** (☎ 32-31-32-31), 6 miles from the city center and Europe's fanciest place to land. The bank in the arrivals hall is open Monday to Friday 5:30am to 10pm and Saturday and Sunday 7:30am to 10pm; but the exchange rate may be high and there's a charge for each traveler's check you cash. Public phones accept some foreign coins, including American quarters. There's also a bar/cafe, a small market, lockers, car-rental counters (including Avis, Budget, Europcar, Hertz, and Pitzner, a Danish company), an information desk, and courtesy baggage carts.

In the adjacent departure hall, the **Left Luggage Office** (☎ 32-47-47-43), open daily 6am to 10pm, charges 25KR ($3.85) per bag per day (same price as the lockers, which have a 3-day limit), 35KR ($5) for bikes and skis. Opposite the lockers, a post office (enter through the red door) is open Monday to Friday 9am to 5pm.

The **SAS Airport Bus** (☎ 32-32-30-64) departs every 15 minutes and runs between the airport and Copenhagen's Central Station; the trip takes about 25 minutes and costs 40KR ($6); age 11 and under ride free. There are usually several SAS buses parked out front, so be sure you're on the one going downtown, marked HOVEDBANEGÅRD/CITY.

City bus no. 250S also makes the run between the airport and Rådhustorget (Town Hall Square) in the city center, a 5-minute walk from Central Station, where you can connect with other buses and the S-tog trains. The 40-minute trip is about 16.50KR ($2.55). A direct metro line from Central Station and a bridge tunnel are under construction.

A **taxi** into town runs about 120KR ($19). The taxi lane is adjacent to the bus stop.

What Things Cost in Copenhagen	U.S. $
Taxi from Central Station to Kongens Nytorv	18.50
S-tog (subway) from Central Station to an outlying neighborhood	1.70
Local telephone call	.30
Double room at the SAS Royal Hotel (deluxe)	444.00
Double room at the Saga Hotel (moderate)	84.60
Double room at Ms. Tessie Meiling's (budget)	34.60
Lunch for one at Kanal Caféen (moderate)	7.70
Lunch for one at Riz Raz (budget)	6.15
Dinner for one, without wine, at Els (deluxe)	45.40
Dinner for one, without wine, at Café Luna (moderate)	27.55
Dinner for one, without wine, at Københavenercaféen (budget)	17.38
Pint of beer	5.40
Glass of wine	4.60
Cup of coffee in a cafe	3.70
Coca-Cola in a restaurant	2.30
Roll of ASA 100 color film, 36 exposures	6.50
Admission to Tivoli	7.10
Admission to the Ny Carlsberg Glyptotek Museum	2.30
Movie ticket	7.70
Theater ticket (at the Royal Theater)	9.25

BY TRAIN   Copenhagen's **Central Station** is relatively easy to negotiate. Lockers and shops are in the center of the station, while more shops, banks, ticket windows, and platform entrances are around the perimeter. Showers are available for 20KR ($3.10), and you can wash clothes for 10KR ($1.55). Nearby is a **hotel/room reservations service,** in the Copenhagen Tourist Information office at Bernstorffsgade 1 (see "Visitor Information," below).

The **luggage storage office** in the basement is open Monday to Saturday 5:30am to 1am and Sunday 6am to 1am. The daily rates are 25KR ($3.85) per bag or 35KR ($5) per backpack or bicycle. Alternatively, small lockers cost 20KR ($3.10) and big ones are 30KR ($4.60). There are also lockers in a supervised area, and you're given a ticket rather than a key to retrieve your belongings; the cost is 30KR ($4.60) per day for a maximum of 10 days. You can rent a luggage cart for a refundable 10KR ($1.55).

Den Danske Bank **currency exchange office,** on the station's platform side, is open daily 8am to 8pm. Commission rates are 25KR ($3.85) for a cash transaction during banking hours. Exchanging your traveler's checks for Danish currency can be expensive; at this writing, the cost per check is 20KR ($3.10), with a 40KR ($6) minimum—change large denominations at one time. Better yet, use American Express traveler's checks and exchange them at the American Express office for no fee.

From mid-June to mid-September, you can relax and shower for free at the **Intrarail Center,** a popular meeting point for backpackers that's open daily 6:30am to midnight. There's free luggage storage but no lockers. Other station facilities are a supermarket selling groceries and wine and a post office.

The city's **subway (S-tog)** lines converge at Central Station. Go to Platforms 9 to 12 to catch one of these trains.

VISITOR INFORMATION

Copenhagen Tourist Information is near Tivoli's main entrance, Bernstorffsgade 1 (☎ **33-11-13-25;** fax 33-93-49-69). The most useful publication is the free monthly *Copenhagen This Week,* also available in hotels and other spots around town. The staff at the large information desk is patient and helpful and will provide details on everything from hostels and hotels to activities and nightlife to day trips and longer excursions. You can also buy gifts, posters, postcards, and stamps or a brew and burger at Bryg & Burger, next door. The office is open May to September, daily 9am to 9pm; April and October, Monday to Saturday 9am to 5pm; and November to March, Monday to Friday 9am to 5pm and Saturday 9am to noon.

Nearby, **Use-It,** on the second floor of Huset (The House), Rådhusstræde 13 (☎ **33-15-65-18;** fax 33-15-75-18), is an "alternative" information office. Though the office may appear youth oriented, the information is geared toward budget travelers of all ages. Many free publications are distributed here, like *Playtime,* with details on low-cost restaurants, hotels, and sightseeing, plus a city map. The energetic young staff can counsel you on getting a job, renting an apartment, and almost anything else. Use-It also offers a terrific room-finding service. Another handy service is a free locker for a day, with a 50KR ($8) refundable deposit; you can leave belongings for a longer period for 10KR ($1.55) per day. It's open June 15 to September 15, daily 9am to 7pm; the rest of the year, Monday to Friday 10am to 4pm.

CITY LAYOUT

Copenhagen revolves around **Strøget** (pronounced *stro*-yet), a mile-long pedestrian thoroughfare right in the heart of town. Strøget is actually a string of several streets: Østergade, Amagertorv, Vimmelskaftet, Nygade, and Frederiksberggade. And though this strip seems like a centuries-old essential part of city life, it was declared free of automobiles only in 1962.

Strøget's eastern end runs into **Kongens Nytorv** (King's Square), site of the Royal Theater and the Magasin du Nord department store, and the beginning of **Nyhavn—** once Copenhagen's wild sailors' quarter, now a placid pedestrian area. **Købmagergade,** another pedestrian avenue, branches north from the center of Strøget and spawns several smaller pedestrian streets.

The island of **Slotsholmen** lies just a few blocks south of Strøget and is home to Christiansborg Palace, the National Library, and a number of museums.

Strøget's western terminus opens onto **Rådhuspladsen,** Town Hall Square. The wide **Vesterbrogade** continues west past Tivoli Gardens and Central Station (Hovedbanegærden) and into the lovely residential area of **Frederiksberg,** which also has some cafes, museums, parks, and B&Bs.

GETTING AROUND

The compact city center and many pedestrian thoroughfares make walking a breeze. You may be interested in picking up a copy of *Copenhagen on Foot,* a well-written booklet of walking tours distributed free by Use-It (see "Visitor Information," above).

BY SUBWAY (S-TOG) & BUS   Copenhagen is served by an extensive bus and subway network. Regular service begins daily at 5am (6am on Sunday) and continues until 12:30am. At other times a limited night-bus service departs from Town Hall Square.

Fares are based on a zone system, rising the farther you go. Most destinations in central Copenhagen will cost the minimum 11KR ($1.70). Buses and subways use the same tickets, and you can transfer as much as you like for up to 1 hour.

The subway—called the S-tog—works on the honor system. Either pay your fare in the station you're departing from or stamp your own strip ticket in the yellow box on the platform. In Central Station, the S-tog departs from Platforms 9 to 12.

Similarly, when you board a bus, either pay the driver or stamp your ticket in the machine. It's easy to get away without paying, but beware: Fines for fare dodging are stiff. Bus drivers are exceptionally nice and helpful. Most speak some English. If you plan on traveling by train or bus a lot, buy a **10-ticket strip** for 75KR ($12). You can buy tickets on buses and at all rail stations. Children 11 and under ride for half price; those 6 and under ride free.

Dial ☎ **36-45-45-45** for bus information and ☎ **33-14-17-01** for S-tog information.

BY BICYCLE　Wide bike lanes, long, green traffic lights, and beautiful surroundings encourage bike riding for transportation and recreation. About half of all Danes ride regularly, and even high government officials can sometimes be seen pedaling to work. A guide to biking in and around Copenhagen is distributed free by Use-It (see above). You can rent a three-speed at Central Station from **Københavns Cycler,** Reventlowsgade 11 (☎ **33-33-86-13**), for about 50KR ($8) for 1 day, less if you keep the bike longer; there's a 300KR ($46) deposit required. It provides a bike map of the city in English and Danish and is open Monday to Friday 8am to 6pm and Saturday and Sunday 8am to 2pm.

BY TAXI　The basic taxi fare for up to four people is 22KR ($3.40) at the flag drop (make sure your cab has a meter and note that it's a few kroner more at night and on weekends), then 7.70KR ($1.20) per kilometer (0.62 miles) between 4am and 4pm or 9.60KR ($1.50) between 7pm and 7am and on Saturday and Sunday. Payment by credit card is acceptable. An available cab displays the word FRI. To order a taxi in advance, dial ☎ **31-35-35-35.**

BY RENTAL CAR　Unless you're planning an extended trip outside Copenhagen, you'll find that keeping a car here is more trouble than it's worth. Most major U.S. car-rental firms, including Hertz and Avis, have offices in Copenhagen. Compare big-company prices with those charged by local companies, listed in the "Transport" section of *Copenhagen This Week.*

In Denmark, drivers must use their lights at all times, even in daytime, and all occupants of the car, including those in the back seat, must buckle their seat belts.

FAST FACTS: Copenhagen

American Express　The office is in the middle of Strøget, at Amagertorv 18 (☎ **33-11-50-05**), open Monday to Friday 9am to 5pm and Saturday 9am to noon. To report a lost card, call ☎ **80-01-00-21;** lost checks, ☎ **80-01-01-00.**

Baby-sitters　Minerva (☎ **70-20-44-16**) is a multilingual baby-sitter clearinghouse made up of students of all ages, and it charges only 30KR ($4.61) per hour, plus a 25KR ($3.84) fee. The minimum charge during the day is 6 hours; in the evening, 3 hours. Reserve Monday to Thursday 6:30 to 9am and 3 to 6pm, Friday 3 to 6pm only, and Saturday 3 to 5pm only.

Banks　Banks are usually open Monday to Friday 9:30am to 4pm (to 6pm Thursday). The unfortunate news for travelers is that Danish banks charge 20KR

The Danish Krone

For American Readers At this writing $1 = approximately 6.50KR (or 1KR = 15¢), and this was the rate of exchange used to calculate the dollar values given in this chapter (rounded to the nearest dollar if above $5).

For British Readers At this writing £1 = approximately 11KR (or 1KR = 9p), and this was the rate of exchange used to calculate the pound values in the table below.

Note: Exchange rates fluctuate from time to time and may not be the same when you travel to Denmark.

KR	U.S.$	U.K.£	KR	U.S.$	U.K.£
1	.15	.09	10	1.53	.90
2	.30	.18	25	3.84	2.27
3	.46	.27	50	7.69	4.54
4	.61	.36	100	15.38	9.09
5	.77	.45	150	23.07	13.63
6	.92	.54	200	30.76	18.18
7	1.07	.63	300	46.15	27.27
8	1.23	.72	400	61.53	36.36
9	1.38	.81	500	76.92	45.45

($3.10) per traveler's check, with a minimum 40KR ($6) fee. This is daunting, especially if your checks are in small denominations. Exchange cash (only one fee per transaction) or, better, use American Express traveler's checks and exchange them, at *no charge*, at the American Express office on Strøget, or go to Fostex at the train station where the fees are lower.

Another way to avoid the heavy-duty bank fee is to purchase items with traveler's checks (rather than Danish cash) in shops where the rate of exchange is good and there's no fee for the transaction; you keep the change and beat the restricted banking hours, too. For such a transaction, a Frommer's reader suggests **Sven Carlsen Gift and Art Shop,** between Town Hall and Tivoli Gardens, but on the opposite side of the street, at Vesterbrogade 2B (☎ **33-11-73-31**).

Business Hours **Shops** are usually open Monday to Thursday 9:30am to 5:30pm (department stores to 7pm) and Saturday 9am to 2pm (to 5pm the first Saturday of the month); shops in the train station stay open later. **Offices** are open Monday to Friday 9 or 10am to 4 or 5pm.

Currency The Danish currency is the **krone (crown),** or **kroner (KR)** in its plural form, made up of 100 **øre.** Banknotes are issued in 50KR, 100KR, 200KR, 500KR, and 1,000KR. Coins come in 25 and 50 øre, and 1, 2, 5, 10, and 20 kroner; the 1KR, 2KR, and 5KR coins have a hole in the center.

Dentists Emergency care is provided by **Tandlgevagten,** Oslo Plads 14 (☎ **31-38-02-51**). The office, near Østerport Station, is open Monday to Friday 8am to 8pm and Saturday, Sunday, and holidays 10am to noon. Fees are paid in cash.

Doctors To reach a doctor outside normal hours, dial ☎ **33-93-63-00** Monday to Friday 9am to 4pm; other times, call ☎ 38-88-60-41.

Country & City Codes

The **country code** for Denmark is **45.** The **city code** is an integral part of each telephone number. To reach any phone in Denmark, just dial all eight digits of the number.

Embassies   Denmark's capital is home to the embassies of many nations, including those of the **United States,** Dag Hammerskjölds Allé 24 (☎ **31-42-31-44**); **Canada,** Kristen Bernikowsgade 1 (☎ **33-12-22-99**); the **United Kingdom,** Kastelsvej 40 (☎ **35-26-46-00**); **Ireland,** 21 Østbanegade (☎ **31-42-32-33**); and **Australia,** Kristaniagade 21 (☎ **35-26-22-44**). For others, look under "Embassies" in *Copenhagen This Week.*

Emergencies   Dial ☎ **112** for **police, fire,** or **ambulance** service. No coins are needed when dialing from a public phone. **Steno Apotek,** Vesterbrogade 6C (☎ **33-14-82-66**), is a 24-hour pharmacy across from Central Station. However, there's a surcharge for every purchase made from 8pm to 8:30am.

Holidays   Copenhagen celebrates New Year's Day (January 1), Maundy Thursday (Thursday before Easter), Good Friday, Easter Sunday and Monday, Common Prayer Day (late April), Ascension Day, Whitsunday and Monday (mid-May), Constitution Day (June 5), Christmas Eve (December 24), and Christmas Day (December 25).

Hospitals   Even foreigners staying temporarily in Denmark are entitled to free hospital care in the event of a sudden illness. **Rigshospitalet,** Blegdamsvej 9 (☎ **35-45-35-45**), is the most centrally located hospital. For an ambulance, dial ☎ **112.**

Laundry & Dry Cleaning   Look for the word *vask* (wash), such as *møntvask* or *vaskeri*. **Istedgades Møntvask,** fairly near Central Station at Istedgade 45 and Absalomsgade, is open daily 7am to 9pm. For dry cleaning, go to **Zens Vask,** Vester Farimagsgade 3 (☎ **33-12-45-45**), a block from Central Station, open Monday to Friday 9am to 5pm and Saturday 9:30am to 1:30pm.

Mail   Post offices are usually open Monday to Saturday 8am to 6pm. Letters and postcards to North America and Australia cost 5.25KR (81¢), 4KR (61¢) to other countries in Europe.

You can receive mail marked *Poste Restante* most conveniently (in terms of location and hours) at the post office in Central Station, Monday to Friday 8am to 10pm, Saturday 9am to 4pm, and Sunday and holidays 10am to 5pm. Holders of American Express cards or traveler's checks can pick up personal mail at that company's main office (see above), which will hold it for 30 days. American Express doesn't accept parcels.

Police   In an emergency, dial ☎ **112** from any phone—no coins are needed. For other police matters, call **Police Headquarters,** Pilitorvet (☎ **33-14-14-48**).

Tax   Denmark's 25% **value-added tax** is called MOMS (pronounced "mumps") and is usually included in the prices quoted for hotel rates and on restaurant menus. Many stores offer you the opportunity to reclaim sales tax on purchases over 300KR ($46); for details, see "Shopping," later in this chapter.

Telephone   Making a **local telephone call** costs a minimum of 2KR (30¢) for about 2½ minutes; a tone will sound when you have to add more coins. On older phones, deposit coins before dialing; though unused coins aren't returned even if

Networks & Resources

STUDENTS   The **Use-It** office, Rådhusstræde 13 (☎ **33-15-65-18**), is a clearinghouse of information for young people new to Copenhagen (see "Visitor Information," earlier in this chapter).

Danish-language courses are readily available from several sources, among them **K.I.S.S. (Danish Language School),** Nørregade 20 (☎ **33-11-44-77**), where courses last 2½ weeks and cost 255KR ($39.25), including materials. Ask for the *Danish Courses for Foreigners* pamphlet at the Use-It office. **Den Internationale Hojskole** (an international folk high school), Montebello Allé 1, 3000 Helsingør (☎ **49-21-33-61**), has a multilingual staff and offers courses in English and other languages.

Wasteels-Rejser, Skoubogade 6 (☎ and fax **33-14-46-33**), specializes in discount train and plane tickets for travelers age 26 and under. **Kilroy Travels Denmark,** Skindergade 28 (☎ **33-11-00-44**), offers bus, train, plane, and boat discounts to students and those 26 and under. Next door is **Kupeen,** a travel library/bookstore, where you can research your upcoming journeys, check a bulletin board for travel companions, and buy English-language travel books (with an ISIC you get a 10% discount).

The main building of **Copenhagen University,** dating from 1479, is in the heart of the city, next to Copenhagen Cathedral. Alas, like many urban schools, the campus lacks the bustle and energy of student life; students prefer to hang out in nearby cafes.

GAYS & LESBIANS   Since May 1989, gay unions ("registered partnerships," but essentially marriages) and divorces have been legal in Denmark. Gay and lesbian couples have many of the rights of heterosexual married couples, but they can't adopt or gain custody of children or have a church wedding. Open daily noon to 2am, the **Sebastian Bar & Cafe,** Hyskenstræde 10, half a block from Strøget, near Helligaønds Church (☎ **33-32-22-79**), is popular with both men and women and a good place to drop by to learn about Copenhagen's gay scene; ask the bartender or check out the bulletin board.

you reach a busy signal, they're credited toward another call. On newer phones—recognizable by their yellow front plate—wait for the answering party to pick up before inserting money. Reach local **directory assistance** at ☎ **118.** It costs five times as much to make a local call from a hotel room as it does from a pay phone, which you'll usually find in the hotel lobby.

For **international calls** placed through TeleCom, it costs about 20KR ($3.10) per minute to call North America and about 9KR ($1.40) to call Europe. The easiest way to call North America is via **AT&T's USA Direct service.** If you have an AT&T Calling Card, or call collect, you can reach an American operator from any phone by dialing toll-free ☎ **800-10010** or 800-10022.

Tipping   A 15% service charge is automatically added to most restaurant bills. If service has been extraordinary, you might want to round up the bill.

3 Accommodations You Can Afford

By now, Copenhagen has gotten used to its annual invasion of visitors, and you'll find it nice to know that there are enough budget accommodations for everyone. As in most European cities, Copenhagen offers several accommodation alternatives, the most economical of which is probably renting a room in a private home.

The **Accommodation Service (Værelseanvisning),** beside Tivoli's main entrance at Bernstorffsgade 1, specializes in booking private rooms, most 10 to 15 minutes by bus or S-tog from the city center, with rates rarely over 190KR ($29), without breakfast. The service also works with some of the best hotels, selling same-day space that would otherwise remain empty. There's a 17KR ($2.60) per-person booking fee and a deposit required at time of booking. The service desk is open for in-person visits from late May to mid-September, daily 9am to midnight; the last 2 weeks of September, daily 9am to 9pm; in October, Monday to Friday 9am to 5pm and Saturday 9am to 2pm; and the rest of the year, Monday to Friday 9am to 5pm (also Saturday 9am to noon November to March). You can book hotels (not private homes) in advance by contacting **Hotelbooking København,** Gammel Kongvej, 1610 København (☎ **33-25-38-44;** fax 33-12-97-23). The advance-bookings desk is open year-round Monday to Friday 9am to 4:30pm.

Use-It, on the second floor of Huset (an activity center for youth), Rådhusstræde 13 (☎ **33-15-65-18;** fax 33-15-75-18), can provide a full rundown on budget accommodations, including last-minute rooming possibilities posted on its bulletin board. It can also store luggage and hold mail. June 15 to September 15, the office is open daily 9am to 7pm; the rest of the year, Monday to Friday 10am to 4pm.

Note: You can find most of the lodging choices below plotted on the map included in "Seeing the Sights," later in this chapter.

PRIVATE HOMES
IN THE CENTER

Staying in a room in a private home has several advantages: low cost; a more intimate environment than a hotel, but with privacy; and the opportunity to get to know a Danish host. All the hosts below are English-speaking and well traveled. There's a strong network among hosts, and if one is booked he or she will be able to direct you to another. Call ahead to avoid disappointment. Out of courtesy, always let the hosts know when you're to arrive so that you don't tie up their time.

Annette and Rudy Hollender. Wildersgade 19, 1408 Copenhagen K. ☎ **32-95-96-22.** 2 units, none with bathroom. 250KR ($38) single; 300KR ($46) double; 400KR ($62) triple. Breakfast 40KR ($6). No credit cards. Bus: 2 from City Hall, 8 from Central Station, or 9 from airport.

On Christianshavn, an island a 5-minute bus ride from Town Hall Square, this half-timbered house from 1698 is so diminutive it seems like a dollhouse. The three attic rooms have exposed beams; all on the third floor, they share a bath on the second. You eat breakfast in the comfortable kitchen or, on warm days, at a table in the backyard. Annette Hollender checks out local restaurants and attractions so that she can make recommendations.

Margrethe Kaae Christensen. Amaliegade 26 (3rd floor), 1256 København K. ☎ and fax **33-13-68-61.** 2 units, none with bathroom. TV. 260KR ($42) single; 350KR ($56) double. Extra bed 120KR ($19). Rates include self-service breakfast. No credit cards. Bus: 1 or 6 from Central Station to Amalienborg Palace.

This is about as close as you'll be able to get to living at the Amalienborg Palace 50 yards away. You'll be greeted by friendly and lively Ms. Christensen, who offers elegant accommodations. The Blue Room has its own sink and a double bed; the Rose Room, its own entrance and two single beds. Both have cable TV, coffee- and tea-making facilities, and fruit. They share a bath with tub and shower.

Getting the Best Deal on Accommodations

- Try reserving a room in a private home, as it will cost only about half the price of a room in a hotel.
- Seek out the hotels immediately southwest of Central Station, along Colbjørnsensgade and Helgolandsgade (off Istedgade). Though many are above our budget, some offer excellent values. The area may have several pornographic bookstores and video shops, but it's safe.
- Take advantage of accommodations that include breakfast in the price of the room.
- Ask for a room without a private bathroom; you usually get a sink. But be sure the bath is nearby and well maintained.

Solveig Diderichsen. Upsalegade 26, 2100 København O. ☎ **35-43-39-58.** Fax 35-43-22-70. 3 units, none with bathroom. TV. 275KR ($42) single; 350KR ($54) double; 475KR ($73) triple. No credit cards. Take the S-tog or bus no. 9 to Østerport; then walk to Hjalmar Brantings Plads, turn right, take an immediate left, and you're there.

Solveig Diderichsen's seven-room apartment is 100 years old, with high ceilings, pine floors, and large rooms—two doubles and one single—that are clean, comfortable, and equipped with good reading lights and coffee-making facilities. You share a big bath that has a tub and a shower, plus a separate toilet. Ethnic restaurants, a bakery, a grocery store, and a post office are nearby, and the Botanical Garden and some of the city's museums are a 5-minute walk away through a neighborhood park. The apartment, which Ms. Diderichsen shares with her pet husky, is in a quiet part of the city near the American Embassy.

✪ **Tessie Meiling.** Sølvgade 34b, 1307 København. ☎ **33-15-35-76** at home, or 40-68-11-20 mobile phone. 1 unit, without bathroom. TV. 175KR ($27) single per day, 1,000KR ($154) per week; 225KR ($35) double per day, 1,350KR ($208) per week. No credit cards. Bus: 10 from Central Station to Kronprinsessegade, near the Royal Museum of Art.

The kindergarten teacher Tessie Meiling offers one of the city's best values for a stay of a week or more. Her garret apartment, on the third floor (no elevator) of an 1845 house, has a country kitchen with board floors. Wooden cabinets, chests, and tables—and Tessie's artistic hand—are everywhere. Alas, there's only one comfortable room for rent, furnished with two single beds, a color TV, a cassette player, and good reading lamps. You're welcome to use the kitchen, where you'll find the shower (you have privacy when you use it). The building is across from Rosenborg Palace and Garden; the entrance to the apartment is at the back of a narrow walkway.

Turid Aronsen. Brolæggerstræde 13, 1211 København K. ☎ **33-14-31-46.** 3 units, none with bathroom. 220KR ($34) single; 330KR ($51) double; 410KR ($63) triple. No credit cards. Bus: 2 or 6 from Central Station to the canal.

You'll find more upscale lodging in the other private homes here, but none more convenient, only a block from Strøget. The rooms are comfortable, spacious, and stocked with brochures of attractions; two are adjacent to the bath, which is tiled with a shower. Guests enjoy sitting around the kitchen table, though no breakfast is served. Brolægerstræde is only 2 blocks long and around the corner from Huset, the popular activity/information center for young people.

IN FREDERIKSBERG

☉ Betty Wulff. Jyllandsvej 24, 2000 Frederiksberg. ☎ **38-86-29-84.** 3 units, none with bathroom. TV. 260KR ($40) double. No credit cards. Bus: 1 from Central Station (toward Frederiksberg) to P. G. Ramms Allé.

The wood ceilings and walls make the rooms particularly cozy. The beds are fitted with Swedish health mattresses, and two rooms are linked, making them ideal for families. Betty, a scientist with the World Health Organization, serves free coffee and tea throughout the day. You can buy pastries on the corner and munch on them in the front yard; a good Danish restaurant is nearby. You're welcome to store cold food.

Gurli and Viggo Hannibal. Folkets Allé 17, 2000 Frederiksberg. ☎ **38-86-13-10.** 2 units, 1 with bathroom. 300KR ($46) per room. Extra bed 100KR ($15). Continental breakfast for 2 30KR ($4.60). Solo travelers may get a discount Nov–Feb. No credit cards. S-tog: Line C to Peter Bangsvej (toward Ballerup). Bus: 1 from Central Station to P. G. Ramms Allé; then walk 2 blocks.

This helpful couple offers a memorable stay in their modern home. The rooms have blond-wood furniture and lots of closet space. Room 12 features a bathroom and a small anteroom with a hot plate for boiling water, but Room 11 is equally inviting, with a TV and a bathroom downstairs. The bath has a tub and shower, and the pipe-and-cork stairway and framed puzzles in the rooms are particularly unusual. You're welcome to borrow from the small English-language library. If you call ahead, they may pick you up at the S-tog stop. The Hannibals—she's an artist, he's a retired public school math teacher—are smokers, so smokers will feel particularly at home. They've welcomed visitors for 20 years.

Hanne Løye. Ceresvej 1, 1863 Frederiksberg C. ☎ **33-24-30-27.** 3 units, none with bathroom. 310KR ($48) double. Extra bed 155KR ($24). No credit cards. Bus: 1 from Central Station to Frederiksberg City Hall (7th stop; look for the brick tower with clock and copper roof); then walk 4 short blocks.

Old-fashioned furnishings fill the rooms on the second floor of this yellow house with a brown-tile roof, surrounded by a picket fence. The rooms (request the one with the antique mirror at the top of the stairs) are supplied with plates, cups, silverware, and glasses. Ms. Løye, who's an actress, doesn't offer breakfast but does supply hot water for making coffee or tea. Nearby you'll find stores, restaurants, bakeries, and a supermarket. You can luxuriate in the large bath and read one of the books in English that are scattered about. Two self-service laundries and a dry cleaner are within walking distance. Call ahead.

HOTELS
BY NØRREPORT

☉ Hotel KFUM Soldaterhjem. Gothersgade 115, 1123 København K. ☎ **33-15-40-44.** Fax 33-15-44-74. 10 units, none with bathroom. 285KR ($44) single; 430KR ($66) double. No credit cards. S-tog: Nørreport; then walk 1 block to Gothersgade, turn right, and it's a couple of doors down.

Though intended for soldiers, KFUM Soldaterhjem has been taken over by business-people and budget travelers. The rooms (eight singles, two doubles) are devoid of decoration but are spotless; they provide soap and towels. The second-floor reception doubles as a do-it-yourself piano/TV lounge and snack bar (serving short-order meals for less than $5). The rooms are on the fifth floor, a hearty climb. Rosenborg Palace is across from the hotel, and the clean-cut young men of the Royal Guard hang out in the lounge. Reception hours are Monday to Friday 8:30am to 11pm and Saturday, Sunday, and holidays 3 to 11pm; enter the door marked KFUM SOLDATERHJEM. The hotel and cafe are run by the friendly, competent husband and wife Preben Nielsen and Grethe Thomasen. Families are welcome.

✪ **Ibsens Hotel.** Vendersgade 23, 1363 København K. ☎ **33-13-19-13.** Fax 33-13-19-16. 49 units, all with bathroom. TV TEL. 695KR ($107) single; 900KR ($138) double. Rates include breakfast. Lower prices in winter. AC, AE, DC, EURO, MC, V. S-tog: Nørreport.

Managed by Sine Manniche and her two nieces, Ibsens provides old-fashioned ambiance in a renovated 1906 building. Huge antique wooden dressers and decorative cabinets fill the rooms and halls. All rooms have hair dryers and trouser presses and a few have canopied beds. Honeymooners like rooms 256 and 356. The all-you-can-eat breakfast is served in the charming dining room. The reception area is at street level, and there's no elevator (rooms are spread over three floors, and those on the second are the most convenient). Pretty Ørsteds Park and the Botanical Garden are nearby, and Strøget is a 10-minute walk away. A laundry is a block and a half away.

NEAR CENTRAL STATION

✪ **Nebo Missionshotellet.** Istedgade 6 (half a block from Central Station), 1652 København V. ☎ **33-21-12-17.** Fax 33-23-47-74. 96 units, 48 with bathroom. TEL. 310KR–380KR ($48–$58) single without bathroom, 670KR ($103) single with bathroom; 490KR–590KR ($75–$91) double without bathroom, 700KR–880KR ($108–$135) double with bathroom. The higher rates apply in summer. Rates include breakfast. Extra bed 160KR ($24.61). AC, AE, DC, EURO, MC, V. Parking 40KR ($6).

The Nebo offers comfortable rooms (43 singles, 54 doubles) with sinks and phones. This is tops of the three hotels in the area owned by the Church of Denmark and is capably run by a friendly staff. A few rooms are without TVs, but you're free to use the one in the lobby lounge. If you get a courtyard room, you can enjoy the relaxing gurgles of the fountain outside. Breakfast is an all-you-can-eat buffet served in a pretty room adjacent to a garden, where you can eat in summer. Try to stay in late June or July, when rates are lowest.

✪ **Saga Hotel.** Colbjørnsensgade 18–20 (a block from Central Station), 1652 København V. ☎ **33-24-49-44.** Fax 33-24-60-33. 78 units, 24 with bathroom. TEL. 250KR–380KR ($38–$58) single without bathroom, 400KR–580KR ($62–$89) single with bathroom; 350KR–550KR ($54–$85) double without bathroom, 550KR–800KR ($85–$123) double with bathroom; 140KR–185KR ($22–$28) per person triple/quad. Rates include breakfast. AC, AE, DC, EURO, MC, V.

This perennial standby has long welcomed *Frommer's* readers with comfortable rooms (7 singles, 53 doubles, 9 triples, 9 quads), a good breakfast, and a 5% discount off the rates above. Most rooms (with or without bath) have cable TV. The owners/managers, Susanne and Søren Kaas (sister and brother) and Boye Birk, are young and extremely knowledgeable about Copenhagen and ways to save money. The hotel has a pleasant breakfast/dining room where it serves a filling potluck supper, with Danish meatballs, on Tuesday only for 50KR ($8); it also has a cafe and bar and sells souvenirs as well as amber and silver jewelry from Poland. The Saga attracts a congenial group of all ages and nationalities.

IN VESTERBRO

✪ **Hotel Sct. Thomas.** Frederiksberg Allé 7 (a 15-min. walk from Central Station), 1621 København V. ☎ **33-21-64-64.** Fax 33-25-64-60. 23 units, 9 with bathroom (shower). Summer, 395KR ($61) single without bathroom; 495KR ($76) double without bathroom. Winter, 295KR ($45) single without bathroom; 395KR ($61) double without bathroom. Units with bathroom are 20% higher. Rates include buffet breakfast. EURO, MC, V. Bus: 1, 6, 14, 27, or 28 from Central Station (just 2 or 3 stops); then a 1-block walk.

This pretty four-story building (the oldest on this street) is adorned with faux classical columns and is set back slightly from the street. Each room is unique—the doubles are spacious (no. 12 especially so), while the singles are small but adequate; many look onto plant-filled courtyards. In the cozy sitting room, you can avail yourself of a TV, maps, brochures, and free coffee and tea. There's a pleasant restaurant next door and reasonably priced ethnic eateries nearby; a laundry and grocery store are 3 short blocks away. The hotel is 1 block from Vesterbrogade.

IN FREDERIKSBERG

Hotel Cab-Inn. Danasvej 32, Copenhagen, 1910 Frederiksberg C. ☎ **31-21-04-00.** Fax 31-21-74-09. 86 units, all with bathroom. A/C TV TEL. 435KR ($67) single; 575KR ($88) double; 675KR ($104) triple; 775KR ($119) family room for 4. Rates include breakfast. AC, AE, DC, EURO, MC, V. Parking 30KR ($4.60). S-tog: Vesterport; then a 5-minute walk. Bus: 29 to the 2nd stop past the bridge; then walk back half a block.

Small and tidy, the Cab-Inn has tiny high-tech rooms (unlocked by magnetic cards) reminiscent of cabins on trains or ships, with everything built in; some are available for the disabled. The toilet/shower combination is extremely compact. The hotel has a lobby cafe open 24 hours for guests and a service counter selling toiletries and snacks and renting videos. Complimentary coffee- and tea-making facilities are in the rooms. If the hotel is full, it has a sister property nearby. Town Hall Square is a 15-minute walk away.

A GAY HOTEL

Jørgensen's Hotel. Rømersgade 11, 1362 Copenhagen K. ☎ **33-13-81-86.** Fax 33-15-51-05. 17 units, 11 with bathroom; 120 beds in 12 dorms. TV TEL. 350KR–480KR ($54–$74) basic single or double, 450KR–680KR ($69–$105) single or double with bathroom; 105KR ($16) dorm bed. Rates include buffet breakfast. The higher rates apply in high season. MC, V (for room guests only).

This corner house near the Nørreport S-tog station is the city's only gay hotel. Five of the 20 rooms are singles; the 12 dorm rooms have from 5 to 20 double-decker beds each. The reception is a few steps below street level. Jørgensen's is owned by friendly twins, Per and Ole, who are in their 30s.

HOSTELS

Copenhagen's hostels are open to visitors of all ages. Sleeping bags aren't permitted; you must supply your own sheet or rent one for about 25KR ($3.85). You can buy IYHF cards at any hostel for 130KR ($20). In summer, reserve a bed in advance. Throughout Denmark, a 3-day maximum stay is usual in summer.

Bellahøj Vandrerhjem. Herbergvejen 8, 2700 Brønshoj. ☎ **38-28-97-15.** Fax 38-89-02-10. 252 beds in 43 units. 80KR ($12) per person with IYHF card, 105KR ($16) without IYHF card. Breakfast 40KR ($6); dinner 55KR ($8). No credit cards. Closed Jan 15–Mar 1. Bus: 2 from Town Hall Square or 11 from Central Station (20–30 min.); then walk to the corner, turn right, and follow Fuglesangs Allé to the hostel.

In a residential area northwest of the city center and across from a park, the Bellahøj has a pleasant lobby lounge, laundry facilities, a TV room, a table-tennis room, a vending machine, four showers for men and women on each floor, and lockers (no kitchen). The hostel is open 24 hours, but the rooms are off-limits 10am to noon. The rooms (a little on the dingy side) contain 4, 6, or 13 beds each.

Copenhagen Danhostel Amager. Vejlands Allé 200, 2300 København S. ☎ **32-52-29-08.** Fax 32-52-27-08. 529 beds. 80KR ($12) per person with IYHF card, 110KR ($17) without IYHF card. Breakfast 40KR ($6); dinner 58KR ($9). No credit cards. Closed Dec 20–Jan 2. Bus: 37 or 100S from Central Station and change to no. 10 at Mozarts Plads.

This hostel has no curfew, but its location, in the middle of a park 2½ miles south of the city center, can make getting home after midnight tedious. In addition to 60 double and 80 five-bed rooms, there are laundry and cooking facilities, a TV room, a kiosk, and table tennis. Check-in is from 1pm to late evening; try to book in advance.

WORTH A SPLURGE

✪ Selandia Hotel. Helgolandsgade 12 (2 blocks from Central Station), 1653 København V. ☎ **31-31-46-10.** Fax 31-31-46-09. 81 units, 57 with bathroom. TV TEL. 540KR ($83) single without bathroom, 700KR–900KR ($108–$138) single with bathroom; 540KR ($83) double without bathroom, 850KR ($131) double with bathroom. Rates include breakfast. Extra bed 200KR ($31). Ages 4–12 half price. AE, DC, EURO, MC, V.

This inviting small hotel has a pleasant breakfast room and cheerful yellow halls with colorful prints. All the rooms are comfortable and have new windows, cable TV, and a trouser press. They have sinks, and for those without bath, the facilities are nearby and quite clean. The larger **Absalon Hotel** (☎ **33-24-22-11;** fax 33-24-34-11) across the street is under the same ownership but caters more to business travelers and groups; it has 253 rooms (177 with bathroom) and charges 400KR ($62) single without bathroom, 600KR to 775KR ($92 to $119) single with bathroom, 550KR ($851) double without bathroom, and 800KR to 950KR ($123 to $146) double with bathroom. Rates include buffet breakfast. Both hotels are owned/managed by the friendly English-speaking brothers Eric and Mogens Nedergaard.

4 Great Deals on Dining

By all means, sample Danish fare whenever possible. The country is famous for its open-face sandwiches, *smørrebrod*. It literally means "bread and butter," though it's really bread with dozens of toppings—from a single slice of cheese to mounds of sweet shrimp. You can let all the stops out and indulge in a typical Danish buffet, which begins with fish, then moves on to meat, cheese, fruit, and dessert; a new plate is provided for each course.

For a hot meal, a good choice for dinner that is often offered as a special is *frikadeller* (small fried cakes of minced pork, onions, egg, and spices), served with generous portions of potato salad and pickled vegetables. Another popular dish, *biksemad* is meat, potatoes, and onions. *Mørbrad*, or braised pork loin, is served with a cream sauce. *Grov birkes* are tasty nonsweet breakfast rolls, and Danish pastries, whichever ones you select, are rich and wonderful (Napoleon's Hat is exceptional).

No matter what you eat, however, you may wish to follow the Danish custom of drinking a cold Carlsberg or Tuborg beer and an even colder shot of *akvavit*—a 76- to 90-proof potato-based schnapps (the trade name is Aalborg, after the city in Jutland where it's distilled). If coffee's your drink, you'll have to resign yourself to not expecting free refills—that's not the custom here.

Remember that tax and tip are included in the price on the menu, and you're not expected to add anything extra.

A LOCAL BUDGET BEST

You can find smørrebrod almost everywhere. It takes two or three servings to make a meal, and they're eaten with a knife and fork. Most of the places that sell them are open only during the day, so plan accordingly. Here's a favorite:

✪ Kanal Caféen. Fredriksholms Kanal 18 (a 2-min. walk from Christiansborg Palace). ☎ **33-11-57-70.** Reservations recommended at lunch. Meals 40KR–80KR ($6–$12). DC, EURO, V. Mon–Fri 11am–4pm. DANISH.

Getting the Best Deal on Dining

- Look for small, inconspicuous places off the beaten path.
- Try the *dagens ret,* the daily special, a filling meal offered for lunch and/or dinner at a discount price.
- Seek out the eateries in and around Central Station and the nearby Scala Center, both on Vesterbrogade near Tivoli.
- Also try the restaurants around Grabrodretorv, 2 blocks north of the middle of Strøget.
- Take advantage of smörgåsbords and other all-you-can-eat restaurants. Though they're not particularly cheap, they offer terrific values.

Romantic and authentic, this is the place to come for *smørrebrod.* It's always crowded with lots of locals, and the atmosphere is friendly and cozy. Even if you have to wait for a table, it's worth it. The waiter will hand you a list of more than 30 choices—everything from herring to roast beef to ham with fried egg—and you mark off what you want. What you get is substantial. An accompaniment of a large Carlsberg or some cold Aalborg Jubileum schnapps makes a meal here even more memorable. On a canal behind the Parliament Building, the restaurant is in a historic building from the mid-1800s.

IN OR NEAR CENTRAL STATION

Axelborg Bodega. Axeltorv 1. ☎ **33-11-06-38.** Meals 36KR–115KR ($6–$18). AE, DC, EURO, MC, V. Mon–Sat 11am–2am, Sun noon–1am (lunch special 11am–5pm; kitchen closes 9:30pm). DANISH.

The Circus is across the street, so it's appropriate that this fully licensed bodega (Danes use the word to refer to a local bar) is loud, with patrons cheering and joking with each other while downing beers. The menu features open-face sandwiches, tenderloin steak, country ham, cheeses, and omelets for lunch. Beef steak with onions, Wiener schnitzel with sautéed potatoes, roast pork rib with red cabbage, tenderloin with onions, and fried fillet of plaice are offered for dinner. You'll spend about $16 if you order with care.

Bistro. In Central Station. ☎ **33-68-21-21.** Salad and pasta buffet 40KR ($6) at lunch, 60KR ($9) at dinner; daily specials (served all day) 49KR–69KR ($8–$11); main courses (with complimentary salad buffet) 86KR–154KR ($13–$24), half price for age 11 and under who order the same dish as their parents. AC, AE, DC, EURO, MC, V. Daily 11:30am–10pm (serving to 9:30pm). To get to the Bistro, walk through another restaurant, called Spisehjârnet. DANISH.

If you think an outstanding restaurant in a train station is an oxymoron, you're in for a pleasant surprise. At the elegant, airy Bistro, with its columns, arched ceiling, and lights resembling hanging artichokes, choose from several buffets (the restaurant is best known for its cold buffet, above our budget but worth the splurge). You can also order à la carte. Menu offerings include farmer steak, pork chops, schnitzel, and fish dishes. On Sunday a special three-course family dinner is 132KR ($20) per person.

✪ **Mandarin Cafeteria.** Istegade 1 (next to Central Station). ☎ **31-23-67-54.** Special 2-course daily menu 39.50KR ($6). No credit cards. Daily noon–2am. LIGHT FARE/INTERNATIONAL.

This is the cheapest and most central eatery, owned/managed since 1967 by a man from Hong Kong, Cheung-Kau Fung, who serves you in amazing speed from a posted English-language menu, plus over 100 items chalked on three boards. There might be a quarter of a roasted chicken or fish-and-chips for 38.75KR ($6), two hot meatballs with potato salad (frikadeller) for 36KR ($5), a hamburger for 19KR ($2.90), or sweet-and-sour pork for 38KR ($6). Everything is 10% cheaper than posted if you take the food or beverage out and eat or drink it in your hotel or in a park. The two dining rooms with 70 seats (and two TVs) look somewhat run-down, but the food is excellent.

Scala Center. Axeltorv 2 (entrance on Vesterbrogade). ☎ **33-15-12-15.** Meals 20KR–80KR ($3–$12). No credit cards. Daily 9am–5am. INTERNATIONAL.

Across from Tivoli's main entrance, this sparkling center has a variety of fast-food stands adjacent to more expensive cafes and international restaurants. Pizza, pasta, *smørrebrod*, chicken, quiche, hamburgers, and other favorites are available at moderate prices. Scala's ground level features bargain eateries, tops among them **Streckess, Th. Sorensen** for *smørrebrod*, and a popular *gelato* counter, **Bravissimo.** Its third floor is home to more expensive sit-down places. You can shop, catch a movie, play pool, or glide up and down in the glass-bubble elevator. The Mogens Møller sculpture in front symbolizes the sun and the nine planets of the solar system, placed (in small scale) at their equivalent actual distance from the sun.

NEAR THE TOWN HALL

Feinsmækker. Larsbjørnsstræde 7. ☎ **33-32-11-32.** 28KR–36KR ($4.30–$6). No credit cards. Mon–Fri 10:30am–5:30pm, Sat 11am–2:30pm. LIGHT FARE/SNACKS.

Cheese, hummus, roast beef, turkey, chicken, ham, salmon, and tuna are the popular smørrebrod fillings at this cozy cafe with half a dozen tables. All sandwiches are jumbo and served on French bread. There's also fresh-squeezed orange, apple, and carrot juice; carrot cake (in winter); and all kinds of salads. The eatery is 2 short blocks north of Frederiksberggade, near the Town Hall side of Strøget.

✪ **L'Education Nationale.** Larsbjørnsstræde 12 (near the Town Hall side of Strøget, a couple of blocks north of Frederiksberggade). ☎ **33-91-53-60.** Reservations recommended for lunch, required for dinner. Main courses 90KR–155KR ($14–$24). AE, DC, MC, V. Mon–Sat 11am–11pm, Sun 3–11pm. FRENCH.

Eating French in Denmark is a particularly good idea here, where the chef, staff, decor, and food are all français. The charcuterie comes from Lyon, and the pâtés and roulettes are made on the premises. The menu reflects every region of France and changes every few months. Expect generous servings and casual ambiance at this small place, which can get smoky. Check out the big French "breakfast" served 9:30am to 5pm—it includes hearty sandwiches, sausage, and pâté.

Sabines Cafeteria. Teglegaardsstræde 4. ☎ **33-14-09-44.** Meals 34KR–58KR ($5–$9). No credit cards. Mon–Sat 8am–2am, Sun 2pm–2am. LIGHT FARE/SNACKS.

This undecorated place isn't a cafeteria (though it used to be, when Sabine ran it) but a licensed local cafe with a mixed crowd that has included Mick Jagger. The buffet breakfast special features toast, honey, cheese, hard- or soft-boiled egg, yogurt, coffee, and juice or milk for 38KR ($6). Daily specials include smoked salmon, paprika chicken, smoked ham, and more. Copenhageners like to drop in after a movie; that's a good time for coffee and brandy at 30KR ($4.60). Teglegaardsstræde runs perpendicular to Nørre Voldgade, just south of Ørsteds Park.

OFF STRØGET

✪ **Københavnercaféen (Copenhagen Cafe).** Badstuestræde 10. ☎ **33-32-80-81.** Daily special 70KR ($11) with 5 items, 105KR ($16) with 7 items; main courses 54KR–125KR ($8–$19). No credit cards. Daily 11am–midnight (kitchen open 11:30am–10pm). DANISH.

This cafe is half a block from Strøget yet seemingly miles from the hustle and modernity outside. The menu comes with an English translation, and you won't leave hungry. The daily special features herring, fried fillet of fish, roast pork, and bread; the deluxe version adds roast beef, Danish meatballs, chicken, salad, and cheese. Lunch is served until the kitchen closes, dinner from 5pm. The small place fills up fast and can get smoky. There's free piano music on Sunday in winter; otherwise, you're free to play whenever the mood strikes.

Pasta Basta. Valkendorfsgade 22 (near Strøget, behind the Holy Ghost Church). ☎ **33-11-21-31.** Fax 33-13-90-86. Meals 60KR–200KR ($9–$31); Pasta Basta table 69KR ($11). No credit cards. Sun–Thurs 11:30am–3am, Fri–Sat 11:30am–5am. Bus: 9. INTERNATIONAL.

Except for its name, Pasta Basta has everything going for it: a tastefully decorated modern interior, large windows overlooking a romantic cobblestone street, and an all-you-can-eat buffet with good food. You can order the Pasta Basta table as an appetizer. Help yourself to the house wine placed on each table (measuring stripes down the side of the carafe mean you pay for only as much as you drink). The new downstairs bar is inspired by whimsy and deserves a peek.

Restaurant Sporvejen. Grabrødre Torv 17. ☎ **33-13-31-01.** Meals 31KR–69KR ($4.75–$11); coffee 14KR ($2.15), refills 6KR (92¢). No credit cards. Daily 11am–midnight. AMERICAN.

In an authentic old tram car inside a building, complete with poles and straps, the licensed Sporvejen has a "tin-can" interior reminiscent of an American diner. The chef, cooking on a small grill near the door, dishes your dinner right onto the plate in front of you. Specialties include hamburgers and omelets. Check out the photos of the old streetcars, last seen here in 1972.

✪ **Riz Raz.** Kompagnistræde 20 (at Knabrostræde). ☎ **33-15-05-75.** Buffet 40KR ($6) at lunch, 60KR ($9) at dinner, both half price for age 11 and under; main courses (including buffet) 40KR–85KR ($6–$13) at lunch, 60KR–160KR ($9–$25) at dinner. AC, DC, EURO, MC, V. Daily 11:30am–midnight (lunch to 5pm, dinner to midnight; kitchen closes an hour earlier). MEDITERRANEAN.

This well-lit narrow space has low beamed ceilings, one dining niche opening onto the next, and posters and the work of local artists on the walls. The big draw is the reasonably priced buffet. Serve yourself from the counters, starting with cold dishes like broccoli, black-eyed peas, string beans, coleslaw, red cabbage, rice, couscous, and eggplant in yogurt. Then move on to hot dishes like kafta, fava beans, zucchini in tomato sauce, spinach, potatoes, and carrots. Though Greek, Egyptian, and Moroccan dishes are featured, you can always get pasta and can request your food spicier. You won't find a more comfortable or more welcoming place in Copenhagen. The staff is made up of students, most of whom speak several languages. It's fully licensed.

IN & NEAR NYHAVN

Cafe Petersborg. Bredgade 76. ☎ **33-12-50-16.** Open-face sandwiches 31KR–60KR ($4.75–$9); hot meals 58KR–150KR ($9–$23). AC, DC, EURO, MC, V. Mon–Fri noon–3pm and 5–8:30pm. Closed Sat–Sun. DANISH.

This congenial licensed place off the beaten track has good home cooking, a lively local crowd, and an inviting decor—dark paneling and furniture, exposed beams, three dining areas, and tables trimmed with candles and flowers. Come before or after a visit to the nearby *Little Mermaid*. The English menu lists choices like herring, smoked eel or salmon, ham or mushroom omelet, warm fillet of plaice with rémoulade, or frikadeller (Danish meatballs) with white potatoes and red cabbage.

⊙ **KFUM Soldaterhjem Cafe.** Gothersgade 115 (2nd floor). ☎ **33-15-40-44.** Meals 15KR–42KR ($2.30–$7). No credit cards. Mon–Fri 10am–9:30pm for hot food (snacks to 11pm), Sat–Sun 3–11pm. FAST FOOD/DANISH.

This is a real find for low prices and pleasant, if often noisy, surroundings. You can order burgers, chicken, fish, lasagna, salads, and even Danish hot meals. The dining room is casual and Danish in style. The portions are ample, and the crowd is mostly well-scrubbed young men of the Royal Guard.

Nyhavns Færgekro. Nyhavn 5. ☎ **33-15-15-88.** Buffet (with 10 choices of herring) 78KR ($12); dinner main courses 135KR ($21); open-face sandwiches 28KR–53KR ($4.30–$8); desserts 39KR ($6). AC, DC, EURO, MC, V. Daily 11:30am–4pm and 5–11:30pm. DANISH/FRENCH.

This place is unique in Copenhagen because it serves French champagne by the glass. Its desserts—like white-chocolate mousse, profiteroles, petit-fours, and tart of the day—are decadent and delectable. Less indulgent fare for the strong-willed includes 14 open-face sandwiches and traditional Danish meals at lunch (including a daily special), with French fare at dinner. The restaurant has a black-and-white marble floor, a spiral stairway from an old streetcar, and lights that serve as "call buttons" for the friendly servers.

Restaurant Lai Ho. St. Kongensgade 20. ☎ **33-93-93-19.** Reservations suggested. Main courses 20KR–150KR ($3.05–$23). Mon–Thurs 11:30am–11pm, Sat 11:30am–2:30pm, Sun 5pm–midnight. AE, MC, V. CHINESE.

If you're extra hungry and enjoy Chinese food, this is a good choice, 100 yards off Kongens Nytrov. The best-sellers are a deliciously prepared sweet corn soup for 32KR ($4.90) and half a Cantonese duck, complete with all trimmings, for 150KR ($23). This 30-seat place is air-conditioned.

IN THE NORTHWESTERN PART OF TOWN
Bananrepublikken. Nørrebrogade 13. ☎ **35-36-08-30.** Menu items 26KR–89KR ($4–$14). MC, V. Sun–Wed 11am–2am, Thurs 11am–4am. S-tog: Nørrebrogade. LIGHT FARE.

Not to be confused with the trendy safari-clothing store, this is a laid-back cafe with 60 seats and a menu heavy on sandwiches, but you can also get nachos, burgers, and omelets. Live bands perform international music, usually Thursday to Saturday—the cover runs about 40KR ($6)—followed by a deejay and disco music late into the night.

IN THE SOUTHEASTERN PART OF TOWN
⊙ **Cafe Luna.** Skt. Annægade 5, Christianshavn. ☎ **33-54-20-00.** Main courses 65KR–160KR ($10–$25); lunch 45KR–55KR ($7–$9). EURO, MC, V. Daily 9:30am–1am. Bus: 8. CONTINENTAL/DANISH.

The Cafe Luna excels in tasty food, ample portions, and vegetables. Start with tomato soup or an appetizer of warm goat cheese with olives, then move on to a main course of chopped steak, turkey, fish, or something more exotic like roast veal liver and ox sirloin. The sliced turkey breast in wine sauce came with whole-grain bread, broccoli, cauliflower, green beans, cherry tomatoes, red-leaf lettuce, and potatoes. Lunch offerings include sandwiches, cold pasta salad, and several salads, including Greek; you can get a three-item smørrebrod for 30KR ($4.60) or three kinds of herring for 42KR ($6). There's a daily fish dish. The congenial cafe has a dozen tables on two levels and a funky frieze that adds spice to the decor.

PICNICKING
Pick up an assortment of cheeses, pâtés, and charcuterie at **J. Christian Andersen's,** a tantalizing shop off Strøget, at Købmagergade 32 (☎ **33-12-13-45**). It's open

Monday to Thursday 9am to 6pm, Friday 9am to 7pm, and Saturday 9am to 2pm (to 4pm in summer). Look for the Danish cheeses in the center of the store. For a perfect picnic spot, see "Parks & Gardens," later in this chapter.

WORTH A SPLURGE

✪ **Els.** Store Strandstræde 3. ☎ **33-14-13-41.** Reservations recommended. Main courses 152KR ($23); fixed-price lunch 237KR ($36) for 2 courses (main course and choice of appetizer or dessert), 296KR ($46) for 3 courses; 382KR ($59) for 4 courses. AE, DC, EURO, MC, V. Daily noon–3pm and 5:30–10pm. Bus: 1, 6, or 10. NEW DANISH.

Visually and culinarily memorable, Els ("elk") is outstanding for its location (near Kongens Nytorv), atmosphere, and romance. The decor dates from 1853, with six murals of women depicting the four seasons and the twin muses of dance and music. The fixed-price menu changes weekly, ensuring the freshest foods. At dinner, expect to start with lime- and garlic-marinated mussels, duck-liver pâté, or caviar and follow with pheasant, tournedos of veal with morel sauce, or fillet of sole. Be sure to try the homemade five-grain bread and the house apéritif, Pousse Rapière (Armagnac mixed with champagne).

5 Seeing the Sights

SIGHTSEEING SUGGESTIONS

IF YOU HAVE 1 DAY   Start along **Strøget,** the world's longest pedestrian street; then explore **Kongens Nytorv (King's New Square)** and **Nyhavn,** the old sailors' quarter and one of the most charming parts of the city. After lunch (Nyhavn is a terrific area for it), take an imperial tour of **Christiansborg Palace,** visiting the queen's reception rooms and ancient palace foundations. Reserve the rest of the day and the evening for **Tivoli,** where you can enjoy everything from old-time carnival fun to concerts featuring the world's top performers in season.

IF YOU HAVE 2 DAYS   For Day 1, follow the above. Start Day 2 at the mighty **Gefion Fountain** and the nearby *Little Mermaid* (if you're early enough, you might miss the tour buses). Then make your way to the queen's residence, **Amalienborg Palace,** and visit the royal rooms now open. The Changing of the Guard takes place outside at noon. Continue on to fairy-tale **Rosenborg Palace** to see the Crown Jewels. Back in the city center, climb the **Round Tower** for the best view of Copenhagen; if you still have time, visit the **Ny Carlsberg Glyptotek** to see ancient sculptures and French and Danish art of the 19th and early 20th centuries or the impressive **National Museum** to learn about the cultural history of Denmark.

IF YOU HAVE 3 DAYS   Spend Days 1 and 2 as above. On Day 3, consider a trip to the **Carlsberg Brewery** or to the peaceful **Botanical Gardens** and the nearby **Royal Museum of Fine Art** and the **Hirschsprung Collection.**

IF YOU HAVE 5 DAYS   Spend Days 1 to 3 as above. On Day 4, visit the **Louisiana Museum of Modern Art,** the **Karen Blixen Museum,** and **Kronborg Castle** in Helsingør (site of Shakespeare's *Hamlet*), all in North Zealand. (Yes, you can do them all in a day, if you start early.) On Day 5, head west to **Roskilde** and tour its cathedral, final resting place of the Danish monarchy for centuries, and the **Viking Ship Museum.**

TIVOLI & *THE LITTLE MERMAID*

✪ **Tivoli.** Vesterbrogade 3. ☎ **33-15-10-01.** Park, 46KR ($7) adults, 25KR ($3.85) ages 4–12; rides, 20KR ($3.05) each, and an unlimited-ride ticket is available. Park, May to mid-Sept, daily 11am–midnight; Nov 14–Dec 23, limited hours (no rides). Ticket Center, Mon–Sat noon–6pm (also Sun when events are scheduled). Closed mid-Sept to Nov 13 and Dec 24 to mid-Apr.

When Tivoli opened in 1843, the park was well outside the city center. Today it's Copenhagen's centerpiece, attracting over 4 million visitors annually. Tivoli is the city's main showcase for Danish culture, music, and entertainment. Every day brings a full program of open-air concerts, cabaret theater, dancing, pantomime, and other special events. Most are free or fairly priced.

The majority of the performances are staged at night, when the park takes on a truly magical look. Thousands of lights shimmer through the trees, and every Friday and Saturday fireworks light the sky with color. Don't overlook an afternoon visit, though, especially from May to the first half of June, when 100,000 brightly colored tulips organically paint the park. Finally, when you're ready for thrills, hop on the wooden roller coaster, built in 1914. Its incessant creaking gives riders a reason to scream. The Tivoli magic is now part of Copenhagen's Christmas season, when the park hosts a holiday market, a special theatrical production, and ice skating on the lake.

Groften and **Slukefter** are popular spots for a drink. The former, parts of which are open year-round, serves Danish food, and the latter, beside the main entrance to Tivoli, features jazz and blues year-round.

The **Tivolis Billetcenter (Ticket Center),** Vesterbrogade 3 (☎ **33-15-10-12**), sells tickets to concerts and special events in the park. This office also distributes a free daily schedule and is next to the park's main entrance.

✪ **Tivoli Museum.** H. C. Andersens Blvd. 22. ☎ **33-15-10-01.** Admission 20KR ($3.05) adults, 10KR ($1.55) ages 6–14. May to mid-Sept, daily 10am–10pm; mid-Sept to mid-Apr, Tues–Fri 10am–4pm, Sat–Sun 10am–4pm.

This evocative museum opened in 1993 and wonderfully complements the park. If you visit Tivoli, this will tell you about its fascinating history, and if you visit Copenhagen when the famous park is closed, this is the next best thing. You'll learn about the creator of the park, its early days, its legendary performers (including a flea circus that held audiences enthralled for more than 65 years), its pantomime theater (for which the park is well known), its rides, and even its specially made lamps. Start on the ground floor and work your way down, allowing plenty of time because there's lots to see.

Den Lille Havfrue (The Little Mermaid). Langelinie on the harbor. S-tog: Østerport; then walk through the park. Bus: 1, 6, or 9; during summer a shuttle bus operates between Town Hall Square and the statue.

Like famous monuments the world over, this simple green statue on a rock off the shore will seem smaller than you'd imagined, but it'll make you smile all the same. Locals poke fun at the statue's popularity and at times have even vandalized it. Still, this frail bronze figure (actually 1⅓ times human size), created in 1913 by Erik Erikson and inspired by the Hans Christian Andersen fairy tale, remains the most famous monument in Copenhagen. Industrial tanks on the opposite shore create an unsightly background, but adjacent **Kastellet Park,** laid out on the remains of Copenhagen's ramparts, is a beautiful area for strolling and picnicking (open daily 7am to 5:30pm). Don't miss the nearby **Gefion Fountain** or the **bust of Winston Churchill,** adjacent to St. Alban's Church.

THE TOP MUSEUMS

✪ **National Museum.** Ny Vestergade 10. ☎ **33-13-44-11.** Admission 30KR ($4.60) adults, 20KR ($3.05) seniors/students, free for under age 15. Free for everyone Wed. AE, DC, MC, V. Tues–Sun 10am–5pm. Bus: 1, 2, 5, 6, 8, 10, or 41.

Cataloguing life in Denmark from the Stone Age to the present, this vast museum across from Christiansborg Palace includes prehistoric finds, ancient burial chambers, traditional farmers' tools, and centuries-old porcelain, furniture, and housewares.

Copenhagen

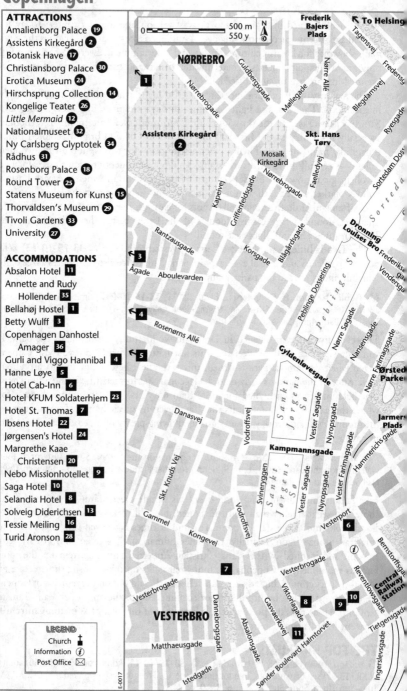

ATTRACTIONS

Amalienborg Palace 19
Assistens Kirkegård 2
Botanisk Have 17
Christiansborg Palace 30
Erotica Museum 24
Hirschsprung Collection 14
Kongelige Teater 26
Little Mermaid 12
Nationalmuseet 32
Ny Carlsberg Glyptotek 34
Rådhus 31
Rosenborg Palace 18
Round Tower 25
Statens Museum for Kunst 15
Thorvaldsen's Museum 29
Tivoli Gardens 33
University 27

ACCOMMODATIONS

Absalon Hotel 11
Annette and Rudy Hollender 35
Bellahøj Hostel 1
Betty Wulff 3
Copenhagen Danhostel Amager 36
Gurli and Viggo Hannibal 4
Hanne Løye 5
Hotel Cab-Inn 6
Hotel KFUM Soldaterhjem 23
Hotel St. Thomas 7
Ibsens Hotel 22
Jørgensen's Hotel 24
Margrethe Kaae Christensen 20
Nebo Missionhotellet 9
Saga Hotel 10
Selandia Hotel 8
Solveig Diderichsen 13
Tessie Meiling 16
Turid Aronson 28

LEGEND
Church †
Information ⓘ
Post Office ✉

E-0017

Getting the Best Deal on Sightseeing

- Note that the best panoramic view of the old city of Copenhagen is from the top of the Round Tower, Købmagersgade 52A, near the Nørreport S-tog station. The tower is 36 yards high, with a 209-yard-long spiral staircase (no steps, just walk-up planks). You can check out the view from noon to 4pm at a cost of 15KR ($2.30) adults or 5KR (80¢) children.
- Be aware that you can check out Copenhagen's most famous monument—*The Little Mermaid*—absolutely for free. Then you can wander over to the adjacent Kastellet Park, a beautiful area for strolling and picnicking.

Interesting, too, are the displays on Greenland's colonization, as well as the Victorian House, with its interior dating from 1890 (tours are available, but make a reservation). The museum has a large atrium entry, a pretty cafe, and a boutique selling replicas of Viking jewelry and other collectibles. Expect to see objects dramatically presented—nothing staid or predictable here. The interactive computer exhibit is fun and educational, and you shouldn't miss the exhibits on the Middle Ages and Renaissance, the Ethnographic Collections, and the Collection of Classical Antiquities. Kids have their own Children's Museum and casual eatery on the ground floor.

✪ **Ny Carlsberg Glyptotek.** Dantes Plads 7 (across from the back entrance to Tivoli). ☎ **33-41-81-41.** Admission 15KR ($2.30) adults, free for children. Free for everyone Wed and Sun. MC, V. Daily 10am–4pm. Closed Jan 1, June 5, and Dec 24–25. S-tog: Hovedbanegård. Bus: 1, 2, 5, 10, 14, 16, 28, 29, 30, 32, 33, 34, or 41; or walk from the city center.

Specializing in ancient art and French and Danish art from the 19th and early 20th centuries, the Glyptotek has impressive Greek statues, Roman portrait busts, and Egyptian and Etruscan art. Founded by brewer/arts patron Carl Jacobsen in 1882, the collection of antiquities has continued to grow and includes Near Eastern, Palmyrene, and Cypriot art, along with extensive works from more recent times. The French sculpture collection features 35 works by Rodin and the complete *ouevre* of Degas. The second-floor modernists are mainly French and include Gauguin (more than 30 works), Corot, Courbet, Manet, Monet, Cézanne, and Renoir; don't miss Gallery 28. The museum is built around a glass-domed conservatory that compels some folks to visit the Glyptotek with little intention of looking at art.

Statens Museum for Kunst (Royal Museum of Fine Arts). Sølvgade 48–50. ☎ **33-91-21-26.** Admission 30KR ($4.60) adults, free for age 15 and under. Museum, Tues and Thurs–Sun 10am–4:30pm, Wed 10am–9pm. Bus: 10, 24, 43, or 184.

The country's largest art museum occupies a monumental building in the Østre Anlæg park, but at press time it was closed for renovations and plans to reopen in late 1998 or early 1999. Danish art is separated from the rest, and though there's an emphasis on late 18th-century works, most are overshadowed by outstanding 19th-century landscapes. The foreign art section is heavy on Dutch and Flemish paintings, but other European modernists, like Matisse and Braque, are also well represented.

✪ **Louisiana Museum of Modern Art.** Gammel Strandvej 13, Humlebæk. ☎ **49-19-07-19.** Fax 49-19-35-05. Admission 55KR ($8) adults, 45KR ($7) seniors/students age 16 and older, 15KR ($2.65) age 15 and under. DC, V. Thurs–Tues 10am–5pm, Wed 10am–10pm. Take the train from Central Station Platform 1 or 2 to Humlebæk, then bus no. 388 from Humlebæk Station (or a 10-minute walk); special round-trip fare is 85KR ($13).

In North Zealand, 45 minutes from Copenhagen's Central Station, this stunning museum boasts a permanent collection that includes works by Warhol, Leichtenstein,

Calder, Moore, and Giacometti, though the world-class special exhibits are the main draw. In recent years, Hopper, Mapplethorpe, Calder, Monet, and Toulouse-Lautrec have been featured. The museum itself, on a spectacular piece of land overlooking the sea, is beautiful. During warmer months you can picnic on the sprawling grounds.

The man who built the original villa on the property had three wives named Louise; thus, the name. It took great courage in 1958 to open a museum 18 miles from Copenhagen, but Louisiana was a success from the beginning. Its Children's Museum opened in 1994.

Den Hirschsprungske Samling (The Hirschsprung Collection). Stockholmsgade 20. ☎ **31-42-03-36.** Admission 25KR ($3.85) adults, 15KR ($2.30) students, free for age 15 and under. Free for everyone Wed. AE, DC, MC, V. Wed 11am–9pm, Thurs–Mon 10am–4pm. S-tog: Østerport or Nørreport. Bus: 10, 14, 40, 42, 43, or 84.

Tobacco manufacturer Heinrich Hirschsprung bequeathed his vast collection of 19th-century Danish art, notably paintings of people and landscapes, to Denmark in 1911. The striking building constructed to house the collection has 16 exhibition areas, a particularly large one devoted to P. S. Kroyer. Works by Anna and Michael Ancher, Viggo Johansen, and Vilhem Hammershoi are prominent. Furniture designed by the artists—chests, chairs, tables—is exhibited along with the art.

THE ROYAL PALACES

Amalienborg Palace & Museum. Slotsplads. ☎ **33-12-21-86** for museum. Grounds, free; museum, 35KR ($5) adults, 25KR ($3.85) students, 5KR (77¢) children. Museum daily 11am–4pm. Closed Jan 1–2 and Dec 19–25. Bus: 1, 6, 9, or 10; or walk from Strøget.

The official residence of Denmark's Margrethe II and her husband, Prince Henrik, is an outstanding example of rococo architecture. Amalienborg is a complex of four mansions dating from 1760 that ring a large cobblestone square. An equestrian statue of Frederik V is at the center, while the Queen's Guards—bearskin hats and all—stand watch around the perimeter. The noontime **Changing of the Guard** is as spirited as any, full of pomp and pageantry, but it's performed only when the queen is in residence (mainly during colder months).

In one of the mansions, the Christian VIII Palais, is the **Amalienborg Museum.** In 1994 Amalienborg Palace opened its interior to the public, revealing regal private and official rooms reconstructed to the period 1863 to 1947. Highlights are **Christian IX's study,** a mix of valuables and Victoriana; **Queen Louise's drawing rooms,** more elegant and less cluttered than her husband's study; **Christian X's study,** with mementos from the Faroe Islands, Greenland, and Iceland, along with an American flag from 1912 and a horseshoe over the door (even kings need luck); and **Frederik VIII's study,** with the original furniture, chandelier, and knickknacks. The museum also houses a costume and jewelry gallery.

Amaliehavens Kiosk, a block from the palace, at Toldbodgade 34 (☎ **33-11-34-40**), where the tour buses stop, sells cards, souvenirs, stamps, sandwiches, and ice cream and has a phone and rest room; friendly owner Jakob Nielsen is a wealth of information. He accepts U.S. traveler's checks.

✪ **Christiansborg Palace.** Christiansborg Slotsplads (on Slotsholmen). ☎ **33-92-64-92.** Admission 33KR ($5) adults, 10KR ($1.50) children. Tours in English daily at 11am and 3pm. Admission with tour is 37KR ($6). May–Sept daily 9:30am–3:30pm; Oct–Apr Tues–Fri and Sun 9:30am–3:30pm. Bus: 1, 2, 6, 8, 9, 10, 28, 29, 31, 37, 42, or 43; or walk from the city center.

Rebuilt early in this century on top of ancient foundations, Christiansborg Palace was home to the royal family until 1794. The ring of water surrounding the tiny island of Slotsholmen resembles a protective moat. Most of the palace's rooms are now used as offices by parliamentary and supreme court officials, though a few of the glamorous reception rooms still serve their original purpose. Admission to the reception rooms is by guided tour only; the tour features 10 rooms, including the **Throne Room,** where the queen regularly receives foreign ambassadors; the **Red Room,** named for the red velvet on the walls; the **Long Hall,** still used for state banquets; and the **queen's library,** with 10,000 books. These and other rooms are resplendent with Murano chandeliers, Flemish tapestries, and other impressive details. The palace entrance is beyond the large courtyard, on the left side of the building. Tours start exactly on time and last 45 minutes.

You can also visit the well-preserved **palace ruins** (the foundations of Bishop Absalon's 1167 castle) for an extra charge of 20KR ($3.10) adults and 5KR (77¢) children.

✪ **Rosenborg Palace.** Øster Voldgade 4a. ☎ **33-15-32-86.** Summer, 40KR ($6.15) adults, 30KR ($4.60) students, 10KR ($1.55) ages 5–15; winter, about 30% lower. AE, MC, V. June–Aug, daily 10am–4pm; May and Sept–Oct 25, daily 11am–3pm; Jan 5–Apr and Oct 26–Dec 19, Tues, Fri, and Sun 11am–2pm. Closed Dec 20–Jan 4. S-tog: Nørreport. Bus: 5, 10, 14, 16, 31, 184, 185, or 350S.

The summer residence of Christian IV (1577–1648) was built during his reign and served as the official royal residence throughout the 17th century. Today you may wander through the opulent **State Apartments** and a **dungeon** containing the kingdom's most valued possessions, including the Crown Jewels, jewel-encrusted swords, dazzling crowns, and priceless necklaces. Be sure to see the display featuring the clothing Christian IV wore on the day he lost an eye and the earrings he had made for his mistress from the bullet fragments. There are no electric lights or heat in the palace, so try to come on a sunny day and allow time to ramble in the sculpted gardens.

OTHER MUSEUMS

Museum Erotica. Købmagergade 24 (half a block north of Strøget). ☎ **33-12-03-11.** Admission 60KR ($9). DC, MC, V. Daily 11am–8pm. Those 16 to 18 must be accompanied by a parent; no one under 16 admitted.

Interested in lust, passion, erotica? Then visit this uninhibited museum, whose founding director, Ole Ege, was a well-known Danish nude photographer in the 1960s. Exhibits focus on erotica through the ages and include wall paintings from the 1st century, a Greek vase from the 6th century, tableaux of Psyche and Amor and *Fanny Hill,* and the sex lives (or lack of them) of the famous, including Josephine Baker and Charlie Chaplin. Sex toys and chastity belts are part of the show. The museum is interesting until you reach the last exhibit, a wall of 12 video monitors showing porno films from 1930 to the present. Since opening in 1992 the museum has stirred great interest, particularly among those from places where erotica is usually kept strictly under wraps.

Thorvaldsen's Museum. Porthusgade 2 (Slotsholmen, adjacent to Christiansborg Palace). ☎ **33-32-15-32.** Free admission. Tues–Sun 10am–5pm; guided tours in English Sun at 3pm July–Aug.

The personal museum of Bertel Thorvaldsen (1770–1844), Denmark's most celebrated sculptor, features his graceful creations as well as other works from his private collection. Notable are his original models of large monuments from around the world. Among the most striking are his portrayals of Hercules, Venus, Jason, Mars, Vulcan, Mercury, and Christ and the Apostles. Don't miss the monumental equestrian statues or the exhibits in the basement: his personal effects, including two silver spoons (the only cutlery he owned), two flintlock pistols, a silver lorgnette, and a gold

Special & Free Events

Most special events are staged during summer. Festivities usually begin at the end of May with the **Copenhagen Carnival,** a raucous Mardi Gras–type party replete with costumes and sambas. **Free park concerts** start in June, including a weekly Saturday rock festival at Femøren and Sunday concerts in Fælledparken. Free concerts are sometimes held in Nikolaj Church. And there's always free entertainment associated with the annual 10-day **Copenhagen Jazz Festival,** which starts the first Friday in July. The **Copenhagen Summer Festival,** emphasizing classical music, runs from late July to mid-August.

Grabrødre Torv (Gray Friar Square), in the center of Copenhagen, comes alive each summer day with street entertainers, outdoor cafes, and occasional live music. Renovated in traditional Danish style, this is a beautiful meeting place for people of all ages.

Nyhavn (New Harbor), off Kongens Nytorv, a picturesque canal lined by historic buildings, is another summer choice. Once the raucous sailors' quarter, Nyhavn has become a favorite strolling area. During summer the cafes lining Nyhavn's pedestrian street appear to specialize in ice cream and beer. Majestic, tall, fully rigged ships are moored all along the canal, and you can also see where Hans Christian Andersen lived during different periods of his life—at nos. 18, 20, and 67. Peek into the courtyards at nos. 18 and 20. Nyhavn's maritime past is still evidenced by a couple of old-time bars and tattoo parlors, such as the one at Nyhavn 17, which has been decorating bodies since 1878 with everything "from wild to mild."

See the tourist board's publication *Copenhagen This Week* for more information on unique and interesting city activities.

snuffbox with his monogram in diamonds (a gift from the city of Turin); his work techniques; and his achievements as a young artist. Audio guides in English are available for a small charge. In the **Copenhagen Cathedral (Church of Our Lady),** for which Bishop Absalon laid the foundations in 1187, you can see splendid works in marble by Thorvaldsen. The cathedral is next to Copenhagen University.

MORE ATTRACTIONS

Christiania. Christianshavn. Free admission. Bus: 8 from Town Hall Sq. to the 3rd stop after the bridge.

Organized squatters took over dozens of disused army buildings on the island of Christianshavn in 1971, creating the Free Town of Christiania. The public, critical of the city's housing situation and curious about this solution, generally supported the group, pressuring the government against taking any action. Today some 900 people live in Christiania. The community, with its piles of garbage, dirt, graffiti, unpaved streets, and sometimes open use of hash and marijuana, looks more like an undeveloped nation than modern Denmark. But these aspects are offset by interesting murals, wonderfully painted houses, and popular nightspots. Visitors are welcome, but you're asked not to take photographs, especially along the main drag, "Pusher Street." A restaurant and a jazz club, **Spiseloppen** and **Loppen,** respectively, are in the building to your right just inside the main entrance; rest rooms and a small gallery are in the same building. There's now also a vegetarian restaurant called **Morgenstedet** (no smoking or alcohol).

Copenhagen Zoo. Roskildevej 32. ☎ **36-30-25-55.** Admission 60KR ($9) adults, 30KR ($4.60) children. Summer, daily 9am–6pm; winter, daily 9am–4pm. S-tog: Valby. Bus: 28, 39, or 550S.

Founded in 1859 and modernized in recent years, this zoo is home to 2,000 animals, from Nordic species to Asiatic red pandas to South American giant anteaters. Gorillas and chimpanzees are in the Tropical Zoo, and 25 species of birds occupy the adjacent Tropical Rain Forest. The children's zoo is terrific, like a farm with cows, llamas, chickens, goats, and other farm animals, as well as a playground, refreshment stand, and Shetland ponies for riding.

Københavns Rådhus (Town Hall). Rådhuspladsen. ☎ **33-66-25-82.** Town Hall, 20KR ($3.10); clock, 10KR ($1.55). Mon–Fri 10am–3pm; guided tours 20KR ($3.10).

Copenhagen's imposing red-brick Town Hall (1905) is one of the city's best-known structures because of its clock tower and its location in the heart of town. There's no need to look inside, unless you're a clock fan. The Town Hall is most famous for Jens Olsen's **World Clock,** a gigantic silver-and-gold timepiece on the ground floor. It began ticking in 1955 and is accurate to within half a second every 300 years. The pillar just east of Town Hall is topped by two men playing lurs, instruments found only in Scandinavia.

PARKS & GARDENS

In addition to the gardens of Tivoli, Copenhagen boasts several greens perfect for picnicking. On the grounds of Rosenborg Palace, the sculptured gardens of **Kongens Have (King's Garden)** attract ducks, swans, gulls, and people. This is the city's oldest park, popular as ever with hand-holders and strollers.

The charming wooded **Botanisk Have (Botanical Garden),** behind the Royal Museum of Fine Arts, is particularly nice on hot summer days. The gates are open daily 8:30am to 6pm April to October (to 4pm the rest of the year).

Like most parks here, the **Park of the Citadel (Kastellet),** behind *The Little Mermaid,* is laid out on Copenhagen's ramparts. Adjacent **Churchill Park,** to the south, is noted for St. Alban's English Church and the impressive Gefion Fountain, depicting the legend of the founding of Denmark. And don't overlook the small but winsomely bulldoggish bust of Sir Winston in the park.

A ribbon of three artificial lakes cuts through Copenhagen (all rectangular and uninspiring); the most appealing, **Lake Peblinge,** is the scene of enthusiastic boating, strolling, sitting, and duck feeding in summer. Nearby, **Ørsteds Park,** with its small lake, pleasant paths, and statues, invites meandering. Cemetery lovers won't be disappointed by the parklike **Assistens Kirkegard,** at Nørrebrogade and Kapelvej, the final resting place of Hans Christian Andersen, Søren Kierkegaard, physicists H. C. Ørsted and Niels Bohr, and tenor sax player Ben Webster (check the directory of famous "residents" at the gate). Nearby, **Fælledparken** is the scene of exuberant outdoor concerts in summer.

Frederiksberg Park, adjacent to the zoo, is one of the city's prettiest green places and also the backdrop for summer concerts. Get there quickly and easily from Central Station via bus no. 28 or 41.

ORGANIZED TOURS

WALKING TOURS   Walking tours of Copenhagen often leave from in front of **Copenhagen Tourist Information** (they're not provided by the office itself) near Tivoli's main entrance, Bernstorffsgade 1 (☎ **32-97-14-40**); drop by or call to get current departure times. At this writing, they depart at 10:30am and 2pm, and the price for a 2-hour tour is 40KR ($6).

Copenhagen on Foot, an excellent brochure distributed free by Use-It (see "Visitor Information," earlier in this chapter), will guide you through the streets at your own pace.

BUS TOURS   Use-It's free *Copenhagen by Bus* brochure takes you through a do-it-yourself tour of all the major sights using city bus no. 6. Those looking for more structure can choose from over a dozen guided bus tours.

HT Sightseeing Tours (☎ 36-45-45-45) offers a do-it-yourself bus tour by providing you with your own map when you buy a ticket. The bus stops at nine selected sites, and you're free to get off, explore, and catch the next bus. Tickets are good for 24 hours and cost 100KR ($15) adults (half price with Copenhagen Card) and 50KR ($8) age 10 and under. Tours depart from Town Hall Square June 15 to August, daily every 20 minutes 10am to 5pm.

HARBOR & CANAL TOURS   Complemented by a vast network of canals running through the old part of the city, boat tours offer both a relaxing cruise and a good education on the city history. Guided tours run May to mid-September only, and a quite reasonable one is offered by **Netto-Bådene** (☎ 31-54-41-02; fax 31-87-21-33), departing daily 10am to 5pm from Holmens Church, opposite the Stock Exchange. The tour lasts 60 minutes and costs 20KR ($3.10) adults and 8KR ($1.25) children.

BREWERY TOURS   The guided tour of the **Carlsberg Brewery,** Ny Carls-bergsvej 140 (☎ 33-27-13-14), shows how barley, hops, yeast, and water are combined to produce the famous beer. The main brewing hall dates from the turn of the century and is dominated by huge copper kettles and a pungent aroma. The hour-long tour, which involves maneuvering lots of stairs, concludes with a visit to the beer museum and free samples. The free tours are usually given Monday and Friday at 11am and 2pm, but call to confirm. To get to the brewery, take bus no. 6 from Town Hall Square; look for the Elephant archway.

6 Shopping

Copenhagen's stores and selections are as wide and varied as any. Everything has its price, however, and here it's usually higher than it is Stateside. Heavy import duties make foreign goods very expensive, which actually is all right because the most unusual objects here are those of Danish design. Be sure to check out the native silver, porcelain, glassware, and antiques.

VAT REFUNDS

Many stores offer non-Scandinavian visitors the opportunity to recover most of the **value-added tax (VAT)** of 25% on purchases over 300KR ($48). Here's how to get the refund (figure on 20% once the handling fee is taken out): After paying, ask the retailer for a Tax-Free Check and leave your purchase sealed until you leave the country. When departing Denmark by train, show both the check and the purchase to an official on board. He or she will validate the check, which must then be returned to the store. If you're flying from Copenhagen, you'll get a cash refund (minus a small commission charge) at the airport's Tax-Free Shopping office. Remember not to check luggage containing the purchase until you've received your refund. Tax refund questions can be answered at ☎ 33-52-55-66.

SHOPPING STREETS

All shopping tours should begin on **Strøget,** the city's mile-long pedestrian thoroughfare and the address of many exclusive stores, such as Royal Copenhagen, Bing & Grondahl, Georg Jensen, Holmegaard, the upscale department store Illum (peek in at the marble atrium with its chandeliers and fountain), and the home furnishings specialty store Illums Bolighus. A pedestrian street called **Strædet** runs parallel to Strøget and has long been known for its antiques stores but is gaining a reputation for its galleries, restaurants, and small upscale shops.

Perpendicular to Strøget, branching north to the Nørreport S-tog station, is **Købmagergade,** also free of cars. Several other city shopping streets are reserved exclusively for walkers and are marked in red on most tourist maps. Besides the upscale shops, Copenhagen has a good number of secondhand stores and small vintage boutiques, especially in and around **Larsbjørnsstræde.** Two favorites are the small shop in **Kvindehuset (Women's House),** Gothersgade 37, and the well-stocked **UFF** at Kultorvet 13 (come here for replacement jeans or Nordic sweaters) or Vesterbrogade 37 at Viktoriagade. Other fertile hunting grounds are the shops along **Vesterbrogade.**

BOOKSTORES
Copenhagen has a wealth of bookstores, called *boghandel,* that carry a good selection of travel books and fiction and nonfiction in English. Tops are **Boghallen,** in the Politiken building, Rådhuspladsen 37, a block from Town Hall, near Strøget (☎ **33-11-85-11**); and **Arnold Busck,** Købmagergade 49 (☎ **33-12-24-53**). Copenhagen's gay and lesbian bookstore is **Pan-Bogcafe,** Teglgårdstræde 13 (☎ **33-69-00-63**).

DENMARK'S LARGEST MALL
In addition to housing myriad cafes and restaurants, the modern **Scala Center,** Axeltorv 2 (☎ **33-15-12-15**), supports a variety of shops, a multiplex cinema, a fitness center, and a dance club. Several stories surround a large atrium where music is sometimes performed, and plenty of well-placed cafe tables encourage you to linger.

A MARKET
The lively **Copenhagen Fleamarket,** on Israels Plads (S-tog: Nørreport), is open every Saturday May to October. The market specializes in antiques (vintage Georg Jensen, if you're lucky) and bric-a-brac and is open 8am to 2pm. Other days it's a fruit-and-vegetable market.

7 Copenhagen After Dark

In Copenhagen, a good night means a late night. On warm weekends, hundreds of rowdy revelers crowd Strøget until sunrise, and merrymaking isn't just for the young: Jazz clubs, traditional beer houses, and wine cellars are routinely packed with people of all ages. The city has a more serious cultural side as well, exemplified by excellent theaters, operas, ballets, and a circus that shouldn't be missed. **Half-price tickets** for some concerts and theater productions are available the day of the performance from the ticket kiosk opposite the Nørreport S-tog station, at Nørrevoldgade and Fiolstræde. It's open Monday to Friday noon to 7pm and Saturday noon to 3pm. On summer evenings there are outdoor concerts in Fælled Park near the entrance, near Frederik V's Vej; inquire about dates and times at the tourist office.

THE PERFORMING ARTS
Copenhagen's cultural scene is dominated by **Det Kongelige Teater (Royal Theater),** at the south end of Kongens Nytorv (☎ **33-69-69-69** from 1 to 7pm; Bus: 1, 6, 7, 9, 10, or 310), home of the famed Royal Danish Ballet, one of the few places in the world regularly staging theater, opera, and ballet under the same roof. Founded in 1748, the theater alternates productions between its two stages. Regular premieres and popular revivals keep the stage lit almost every night of the season (it's dark June and

July). The box office is open Monday to Saturday 1 to 8pm. To get tickets at the box office, pick up a number at the entrance. You may also order tickets by fax: 33-69-69-30. Tickets range from 50KR to 600KR ($8 to $92); they go for half price 1 week prior to the performance for those under 26 and over 67.

LIVE-MUSIC CLUBS

Copenhagen's love affair with jazz and blues is one of Europe's most passionate. Danes wholeheartedly embrace jazz as their own, and even though this capital's clubs aren't as plentiful as those in New Orleans or Chicago, they challenge the American variety in both quality and enthusiasm.

A small but local favorite is ✪ **Ca'feen Funke,** Sankt Hans Torv, at Fælledvej (☎ **31-35-17-32;** Bus: 5, 10, or 16 from Nørreport to Blegdamsvej). Live bands usually perform blues, soul, or funk on Saturday. Otherwise, you might hear American music from the 1960s and 1970s and amuse yourself playing backgammon. Bar food is available. Look for the blue facade and arrive early if you want a seat. It's open Monday to Friday 11am to 2am and Saturday and Sunday noon to 1pm; music usually starts at 9pm.

At the ✪ **Copenhagen Jazz House,** Niels Hemmingsensgade 10 (☎ **33-15-26-00**), expect to hear Danish jazz 80% of the time, foreign jazz the rest. Once the bands pack up and go home, the disco fires up and goes strong until the wee hours. There's a cafe at street level, and the concert hall in the basement seats 300. It's open Wednesday midnight to 4am, Thursday 8:30pm to midnight, and Friday and Saturday 9:30pm to 1am; the disco is open to 5am Thursday to Saturday. Cover ranges from 40KR to 150KR ($6 to $23), depending on the band.

Located 20 yards off Town Hall Square, across from Burger King, **Club Absalon,** Frederiksberggade 38 (☎ **33-11-08-66**), is a bar and dance hall. It can hold up to 750 on three floors. Jazz is performed in the cellar; the other floors offer live bands and recorded music. It's open daily 11pm to 5am and is popular among all age groups. Admission is 30KR ($4.60).

BARS

HOT SPOTS Named after the contemporary Danish author of westerns and murder mysteries, the convivial **Cafe Dan Turrell,** Store Regnegade 3–5 (☎ **33-14-10-47**), attracts students and celebrities who converse over burgers, pasta, and cappuccino. Light fare runs 40KR to 50KR ($6 to $8). It's open Monday to Wednesday 9am to 2am, Thursday 9am to 3am, Friday and Saturday 9am to 4am, and Sunday 10am to 2am.

Trendy **Cafe Victor,** Ny Østergade 8 (☎ **33-13-36-13**), serves crêpes, quiches, and omelets for 45KR to 50KR ($7 to $8) to Copenhagen's young professionals, schmoozing elbow to elbow. Ceiling-to-floor windows look onto the street, and singles and sightseers often drink or enjoy a small cafe-style meal at the bar. The surroundings are elegant and most everyone is dressed up; half the patrons come to eat at the restaurant, half to drink. It's open Sunday to Wednesday 10am to 2am and Thursday to Saturday 10am to 4am. The popular restaurant/bar **Krasnapolsky,** Vestergade 10 (☎ **33-32-88-00**), with minimal decor, can be laid-back or loud. Drinks from the long, well-stocked bar are surprisingly well priced, and it's open Monday to Thursday 10am to 2am, Friday and Saturday 11am to 6am, and Sunday 3pm to midnight.

Both unabashedly upbeat and terminally crowded, the basement bar of **Peder Oxes Vinkælder,** Grabrødretorv 11 (☎ **33-11-11-93**), is one of the best in the city, known for its cocktails and beers from around the world, from Rolling Rock to Foster's. The bulk of the crowd can't afford dinner at the popular and pricey restaurant above (go up and sneak a peak at the room with the violins hanging from the wall). Weekend nights require a strong voice to be heard over the music and the crowd, and it can take 15 minutes to get from one end of the bar to the other. It's open daily noon to 1am.

OLD-TIME BARS **Hviids Vinstue,** Kongens Nytorv 19 (☎ **33-15-10-64**), is Copenhagen's most historic wine cellar, open since 1723. The large crowd of locals and visitors always includes a good share of the audience from the Royal Theater, across the street. It's open Sunday to Thursday 10am to 1am and Friday and Saturday 10am to 1:45am (closed Sunday May to August).

Though sailors have been replaced by landlubbers, the spirit of the city's past as an important port still lingers at **Nyhavn 17,** Nyhavn 17 (☎ **33-12-54-19**). You can enjoy a great view of the harbor as well as live music Thursday to Saturday. There's sailing memorabilia on the walls, and paintings of exotic women overlook the imbibers. The bar, a real neighborhood type of place, is about 120 years old and is open Sunday to Thursday 10am to 2am and Friday and Saturday 10am to 4am.

GAY & LESBIAN BARS

One of the only clubs in Copenhagen primarily for lesbians, **Cafe Babooshka,** Turensensgade 6 (☎ **33-15-05-36; Bus: 1, 14, or 29**), is a cozy, fully licensed place serving hot and cold food. Changing monthly exhibits feature paintings, graphics, and photographs by women, and from time to time there's live music in the evening. It's open Monday to Saturday 4pm to 1am and Sunday 4 to 11pm. **Cosy Bar,** Stud-iestræde 24 (☎ **33-12-74-72**), and **Centralhjsrnet,** Kattesundet 18 (☎ **33-11-85-49**), are two bars primarily for gay men. Both are open daily 8pm to 2am.

A congenial spot, the **Sebastian Bar & Cafe,** Hyskenstræde 10 (☎ **33-32-22-79**), half a block from Strøget near Helligænds Church, is popular with both men and women and a good place to drop by to learn about Copenhagen's gay scene. There's occasional entertainment, from opera to disco, and the cafe food is homemade by the mother and mother-in-law of the owner. Happy hour, called Gay Time, is 5 to 9pm daily. Thursday is billiards night for women. It's open daily noon to 1am (kitchen closes at 10:30pm).

For an update on the scene, call the **Copenhagen Pride Association** at ☎ **33-91-94-95** during normal business hours.

DANCE CLUBS

As in other major cities, dance clubs come and go as fast as hiccups, and once gone, they're just as quickly forgotten. If you're really into this scene, ask at your hotel and check the local glossy giveaways (available in most clubs and record stores). A favorite is the **Copenhagen Jazz House,** Niels Hammingsensgade 10 (☎ **33-15-26-00**). When it's not a popular jazz hall (and a relatively new one, open since 1991), it's an equally popular disco. After the last strains of jazz have died away for the night, the throb of the dance beat takes over and continues until the wee hours. It's open Wednesday midnight to 4am and Thursday to Saturday 6pm to 5am. The cover is 60KR to 90KR ($9 to $14). Free admission Thursday.

8 Side Trips: Helsingør & More

For a leisurely trip through the Danish countryside, your best bet may be the Danish State Railways **"Special Excursion" ticket.** Not every destination is covered, but trips to the Louisiana Museum of Modern Art (see earlier in this chapter), Roskilde, Odense, Legoland, and other highlights are. Call ☎ **33-14-17-01** for details.

HELSINGØR (ELSINORE)

Four hundred years of legal piracy, from the 15th to the 19th centuries, made **Helsingør** rich from tolls assessed on passing ships. Today a walk around this carefully restored old town is proof that this was at one time Denmark's most important parcel. A wonderful architectural legacy and other indelible marks have been made on this seaside village by traders from around the world.

Helsingør is most famous for its 16th-century **Kronborg Castle** (☎ **49-21-05-59**), supposedly the setting for Shakespeare's *Hamlet*. Whether this is true or not true (that is the question), it's inarguable that the castle is nothing less than majestic. The castle tour features the royal apartments (with paintings and tapestries from the 16th and 17th centuries), the ballroom, the chapel, and other ancient areas. The castle is open May to September, daily 10:30am to 5pm; April and October, Tuesday to Sunday 11am to 4pm; and November to March, Tuesday to Sunday 11am to 3pm. Admission is 30KR ($6) adults and 10KR ($1.55) children.

On the Danish coast 28 miles north of Copenhagen, Helsingør can be reached by **train** from Central Station in about an hour; it costs 77KR ($12) round-trip.

RUNGSTEDLUND

You can easily combine a visit to the Karen Blixen Museum in **Rungstedlund** with a trip to Kronborg Castle or the Louisiana Museum of Modern Art. The **Karen Blixen Museum,** at Rungsted Strandvej 111 (☎ **45-57-10-57**), is the 400-year-old memorabilia-filled home of the late author (alias Isak Dinesen, 1885–1962) of *Seven Gothic Tales* and the autobiographical *Out of Africa*. Except for the 17 years she spent in Kenya, Blixen lived here all her life. She was born in the house, originally a wayside inn her parents bought in 1879, and was educated here by tutors. Her books were published to great acclaim in the United States, which she visited only once, for 4 months in 1959. You can visit the house (rent a recorded tour, if you like), where you'll see the small, shiny Corona on which she typed her works, as well as walk to her simple grave under a beech tree on Ewald's Hill. The museum and grounds are open May to September, daily 10am to 5pm; October to April, Wednesday to Friday 1 to 4pm and Saturday and Sunday 11am to 4pm. Admission is 30KR ($4.60) adults and free for age 12 and under; the Copenhagen Card is accepted.

Take the **train** to Rungsted Kyst (half a mile from the museum) or change at Klampenborg for **bus no. 388;** the bus stop is about a block from the museum, which is well marked (walk in the direction the bus is traveling). The train/bus ride costs 76KR ($12) round-trip.

HILLERØD

A not-so-scenic 45-minute train ride to **Hillerød,** 25 miles north of Copenhagen, brings you to **Frederiksborg Palace** (☎ **42-26-04-39**), the Versailles of northern Europe. It was built from 1600 to 1620 in Dutch Renaissance style as a residence for Christian IV, who was king of Denmark and Norway for 60 years. Of particular interest are the immense Neptune Fountain, the elaborate three-dimensional ceiling in the Knights Hall, and the chapel, looking just as it did when Christian IV used it.

The palace is open daily: May to September 10am to 5pm, April and October 10am to 4pm, and November to March 11am to 3pm. Admission is 40KR ($6) adults, 20KR ($3.10) students, and 10KR ($1.55) ages 6 to 14. Audiocassettes are available in English and other languages.

The **train** takes you to Hillerød, where you then take **bus no. 701 or 702** to the palace (or you can walk). The combined train/bus cost is 88KR ($14) round-trip.

ROSKILDE

For centuries in **Roskilde,** 20 miles west of Copenhagen, Danish kings and queens have been laid to rest in the red-brick **cathedral,** most recently Frederik IX in 1985. Today people visit here primarily to see the cathedral and the impressive royal tombs and the **Viking Ship Museum,** on Strandengen. The museum, open daily 9am to 5pm, houses five ships raised from the Roskilde Harbor in 1962. Purposefully sunk as barricades around A.D. 1000, they include two warships, two merchant ships, and a small vessel that was either a ferry or a fishing boat. Films about the excavation of the ships are shown in English, German, French, Italian, and Spanish. Admission is 40KR ($6) adults and 20KR ($3.10) children.

Roskilde's **main square** becomes a fruit, flower, vegetable, and flea market on Wednesday and Saturday mornings. Its **palace,** built in 1733, now houses a collection of paintings and furniture from local merchant families.

In summer, excursion boats ply the **Roskilde Fjord,** and concerts are held throughout the venerable city, as well as in Roskilde Park on Tuesday night. The enormously popular 4-day **Roskilde Festival** (☎ **42-37-05-48**) is held at the end of June every year. While the emphasis is on rock, there's also folk, blues, and jazz, along with film presentations and theatrical performances. The festival is one of the oldest and largest in northern Europe, attracting top performers. Tickets are sold in Danish post offices beginning May 1.

The **tourist office** (☎ **46-35-27-00**) is near the pedestrian street. Trains run frequently between Copenhagen and Roskilde; if you want to explore this area further, take the bus from Roskilde 4¼ miles west to the charming village of **Gammel Lejre.**

A half-hour **train** ride brings you to Roskilde, then you take bus no. 233 to town (or you can walk). The combination train/bus fare is 76KR ($12) round-trip.

DINING   In a 400-year-old wine cellar, **Restaurant Raadhuskælderen,** Fonden bro 1 (☎ **46-36-01-00**), serves good, reasonably priced fare. You'll find everything from hamburgers and large salads to smoked salmon and breast of young rooster with oyster-mushroom sauce. It's open daily 11am to 11pm (Sunday to 9:30pm) and accepts American Express, Diners Club, MasterCard, and Visa.

BORNHOLM ISLAND

Of Denmark's 110 islands, **Bornholm** is the largest and best known. It covers 228 square miles and has 45,000 inhabitants, most of whom live along the 88-mile-long beach. It accommodates more artists and artisans per square mile than any place else in Europe. Set in the Baltic Sea, Bornholm features almost every form of northern European landscape—from beach, waterfalls, forests, and bedrock to animals and plants rare or nonexistent in other parts of Scandinavia.

A 2-day excursion to Bornholm between May and September is great, especially if you travel with children, and can become the highlight of your trip. The **Amusement and Activity Park,** 3740 Svaneke, Hoejevejen 4 (☎ **56-49-60-75**), offers five kinds of water sleds, climbing frames, bowling alleys, minigolf, open-air stage performances, and other outdoor games. It's open May to October, daily 10am to 6pm, and admission is 60KR ($8); free for under age 4.

At the **Rabbit Farm (Small Animals Zoo),** 3720 Askirkeby, Smoerengevejen 22 (☎ **56-97-27-70**), you'll find exhibits of a few hundred domestic rodents, dogs, and cats, which are bred and sold here. Admission is free, and it's open June to October, daily 2 to 6pm. Built around an old farmhouse, the **Botanical Park,** 3700 Rønne, Bolsterbjergvej 26 (☎ **56-99-92-00**), boasts rare old trees, like tulip trees, hiba trees, umbrella trees, and Turkey oaks. Admission is free, and it's open May to October, daily

8am to 5pm. And at the **Museum of Agrarian History,** 3760 Gudhjeim, Melstedvej 25 (☎ **56-48-55-98**), farmers give baking, cooking, weaving, and candlemaking exhibitions, and every second Sunday there's folk dancing. Admission is 25KR ($3.35) adults and 10KR (53¢) children. It's open April to October, daily 10am to 5pm.

The round-trip ferry from Copenhagen, lasting 6 hours, costs 260KR ($40) adults and 160KR ($24) seniors/ages 4 to 14. Cabins cost 50% extra. The ferry departs from Nyhavn—in June and July at 8:30am and 11:30pm and the rest of the year at only 11:30pm. Return trips in June and July are at 3:30 and 11:30pm and the rest of the year at only 11:30pm.

For more information, contact the **Bornholm Tourist Office** at ☎ **56-95-95-00** (fax 56-95-95-68).

ACCOMMODATIONS & DINING   From four-star hotels (double with bathroom 1,000KR/$154, breakfast included) to camping sites and youth hostels (140KR to 180KR/$21 to $27 per person), this amazing island offers lodging for every taste and budget. In **Rønne,** Bornholm's capital (and where the ferry arrives/departs), I recommend the **Hotel-Restaurant Skovly,** Nyker Strandvej 40, 3700 Rønne (☎ **56-95-07-84;** fax 56-95-48-23). On the ground floor of a farmhouse-looking building you'll find 30 units (all with bathroom). In July and August, you can get a single for 380KR ($58) and a double for 760KR ($116), breakfast included. In May, June, and September, the rates are 20% lower. American Express, Diners Club, MasterCard, and Visa are accepted.

Restaurant Perronen, Munch Petersensvej 3, 3700 Rønne (☎ **56-95-84-40**), is in a former train station. Two popular dishes are the Baltic Sea salmon and the smoked herring with chives and an egg yolk in an onion ring; main courses average 70KR ($11). July to September, it's open daily 11am to 9pm; the rest of the year, Wednesday to Monday noon to 9pm. American Express, Diners Club, MasterCard, and Visa are accepted.

11

Dublin & Environs

by Mark Meagher

Dublin lies on the shore of a sheltered crescent bay, bisected by the dark waters of the river Liffey. It's a small city, easily traversed on foot, built on a scale that's comfortable rather than magnificent. The hills and rocky headlands rimming it are lovely in the gentle, unassuming way typical of Ireland's east coast.

Dublin has changed remarkably in the past 20 years. European Union membership has brought capital for countless building projects and a cosmopolitan atmosphere to Dublin's once sleepy streets. With nearly 40% of its population under 25, Dublin has a youthful vigor that comes as a surprise to many, and in some parts of the city you're over the hill if you're past 30. Just what the new Dublin will look like is hard to say: It's already an eclectic mix of visions for the future, like Sam Stephenson's bulky concrete Wood Quay towers and the meticulously planned Temple Bar, the new trendy arts district.

Still, the transformation has been piecemeal, and a stroll across any of the numerous bridges spanning the Liffey will reveal that the prosperity hasn't been shared equally. The south side of the Liffey has seen the bulk of restoration: Layers of soot have been sandblasted from buildings, expensive shops and restaurants abound, and continental cafes vie with traditional pubs. In contrast, many of the neighborhoods in North Dublin, known by its postal code Dublin 1, preserve the language and character that James Joyce recorded, a Dublin of pubs whose pedigree can be measured by the thickness of the creosote left on its walls by generations of heavy smokers.

Dublin is certainly a city of literary ghosts, and for many its streets are peopled with the shades of those long dead and those who live only in the pages of Irish novels. Even if your head isn't full of passages from *Ulysses,* you can't walk far without coming across a plaque or statue commemorating some event from Joyce's great celebration of Dublin and its people. More books of poetry are sold in Ireland than in any other European nation, and this shows in their self-conscious promotion of the city as a place of literary pilgrimage.

REQUIRED DOCUMENTS Citizens of the United States, Canada, Australia, New Zealand, and Britain need only a valid passport to visit Ireland.

OTHER FROMMER'S TITLES For more on Dublin, see *Frommer's Portable Dublin, Frommer's Ireland, Frommer's Ireland from $50 a Day,* or *Frommer's Europe.*

Budget Bests

Dublin's best **accommodations deals** are its rapidly proliferating city-center hostels and B&Bs just outside the city. Most hostels offer private rooms in addition to dorms, and several have expansive common rooms and restaurants. Hostelers tend to be a friendly and outgoing lot, and you're likely to find yourself going out with new friends for a meal or a pint. Since the B&Bs are outside the city, for the most part, they're not the best choice if you plan to be out past the last bus or train, but they do offer one of the best ways to meet the Irish—in their own homes, over a cup of tea and a scone.

Dublin has its share of **free attractions,** like the complex of museums off Marrion Square: The National Museum, National Gallery, National Library, and Natural History Museum are all within a block of each other and all are free of charge.

1 Dublin Deals & Discounts

SPECIAL DISCOUNTS

FOR EVERYONE   You can get **discount passes** for travel on Dublin's extensive network of buses and commuter trains. Here are the most useful passes: the **1-day bus/rail ticket** (IR£4.50/$7) valid for unlimited travel on all city services; the **1-day family pass** (IR£6.50/$10) allowing two adults and up to four children unlimited use of the bus and suburban rail system during off-peak hours; and the **4-day Dublin Explorer Pass** (IR£10/$16) offering unlimited travel on Dublin bus and rail.

Combination tickets are available to several of Dublin's main attractions. The **SuperSaver Card** (available at any Dublin Tourism office) is IR£8 ($13) and provides you with admission to seven popular sites: Malahide Castle, Newbridge House, the James Joyce Museum, the Dublin Writers Museum, the Shaw Birthplace, the Fry Model Railway, and Dublin's Viking Adventure. You'd have to do considerable legwork to get to all these places, as most are outside the city center. Another combination ticket includes the Dublin Experience and the Trinity College Library/ *The Book of Kells* and costs IR£6 ($10) adults, IR£5 ($8) seniors/students, and IR£12 ($19) families.

FOR STUDENTS   Students should consider the **TravelSave stamp,** including a 50% discount on rail travel throughout the country, a 15% discount on most bus fares, and substantially reduced weekly transit passes. You can buy the stamp for IR£8 ($12.80) at the **Union of Students in Ireland/Irish Student Travel Service (USIT),** 19 Aston Quay, Dublin 2 (☎ 01/677-8117); you'll need a valid International Student Identity Card (ISIC). In Dublin, your ISIC and TravelSave stamp will bring big discounts on city bus and rail weekly passes, available at **Dublin Bus,** 59 Upper O'Connell St. (☎ 01/873-4222); the weekly pass is IR£9 ($14) for local and IR£10 ($16) for all-zone travel.

WORTH A SPLURGE

Renting a car for a day or two brings the extraordinary beauty of the Wicklow Hills or the mysterious grandeur of the ancient monuments at Newgrange and Tara within easy reach. Planning ahead can save a lot of money with car rental, and the best rates are reserved for those who rent from their home country: Expect to spend two or three times these rates if you make a last-minute reservation in peak season.

For those who aren't confident of their ability to navigate the Irish roads, **tour buses** leave regularly from Dublin bound for numerous nearby attractions. One-day tours range from IR£10 to IR£30 ($16 to $48).

What Things Cost in Dublin	U.S. $
Taxi from the airport to the city center	21.00
Local telephone call	.32
Double room at the Shelbourne Hotel (deluxe)	284.00
Double room at Ariel House (moderate)	110.00
Double room at Avalon House (budget)	48.00
Continental breakfast at the Kylemore Cafe	3.00
Lunch for one at Juice (moderate)	8.00
Lunch for one at Bewley's Cafe (budget)	6.00
Dinner for one, without wine, at the Commons (deluxe)	56.00
Dinner for one at Roly's Bistro (moderate)	34.00
Dinner for one, without wine, at Chez Jules (budget)	14.00
Pint of Guinness	3.40
Coca-Cola in a cafe	1.30
Cup of coffee	1.30
Roll of ASA 400 color film, 36 exposures	9.60
Admission to see *The Book of Kells* at Trinity College	5.60
Admission to the National Museum	Free
Movie ticket	7.60
Theater ticket	16.00

2 Essentials

ARRIVING

BY PLANE   From **Dublin Airport,** 7 miles north of the city in Collinstown, buses run a regular schedule to the **Busáras Central Bus Station,** Store Street (☎ **01/ 836-6111**). You can take either the express Airlink bus for IR£2.50 ($4), which will get you into town in under 30 minutes, or bus no. 41A, which can take as long as an hour but costs only IR£1.10 ($1.75). A taxi into town will cost IR£12 to IR£14 ($19 to $22).

BY TRAIN & FERRY   Passenger/car ferries from Britain arrive at the **Dublin Ferryport** (☎ 01/874-3293), on the eastern end of the North Docks, and at the **Dun Laoghaire Ferryport.** Call ☎ **01/661-0511** for Irish ferries bookings and information. There's bus and taxi service from both ports.

VISITOR INFORMATION

Dublin Tourism operates five walk-in visitor centers in greater Dublin. Its principal center is in the converted **St. Andrew's Church,** Suffolk Street, Dublin 2 (☎ **01/ 605-7700**), offering all sorts of free information about Dublin and the rest of Ireland. Other services are a currency exchange counter, a car-rental counter, and a hotel reservations desk. The other four centers are at the Arrivals Hall of **Dublin Airport** (no phone); the new ferry terminal, **Dun Laoghaire** (no phone); the **Baggot Street Bridge,** Dublin 2 (☎ 01/602-4229); and **The Square,** Tallaght, Dublin 24 (☎ **01/462-0671**). All centers are open year-round with at least the following hours:

Monday to Friday 9am to 5:30pm and Saturday 9am to 1pm; the offices at the airport and Dun Laoghaire are open daily 9am to 9pm.

In addition, an independent center offers details on concerts, exhibits, and other arts events in the **Temple Bar** section at 18 Eustace St., Temple Bar, Dublin 2 (☎ **01/671-5717**), open year-round Monday to Friday 9am to 5:30pm.

At any of these centers you can pick up the free *Tourism News;* the free *Dublin Event Guide,* a biweekly entertainment guide; or *In Dublin,* a biweekly arts-and-entertainment magazine selling for IR£1.50 ($2.40).

CITY LAYOUT

The **river Liffey** splits Dublin down its center into **North Dublin** and **South Dublin.** The Liffey is the primary means of orientation in this sometimes confounding city of serpentine lanes and streets that change their name with every block.

Most of the regularly visited sites are south of the Liffey, as well as many centers of government and commerce. **Trinity College** is here, its front gate facing the commotion of **College Green,** a peculiar title for this expanse of asphalt and roaring traffic. From College Green, Dame Street sweeps west toward the great monuments of **medieval Dublin:** Christ Church, Dublin Castle, and St. Patrick's Cathedral. Continuing west, the **Liberties** is a somewhat run-down section of the city that has just begun to benefit from urban renewal; here you'll find the Guinness Brewery and the Old Jameson Distillery. Heading south from College Green is Dublin's most fashionable shopping thoroughfare, **Grafton Street,** reserved for pedestrian traffic. At the southern end of Grafton Street is **St. Stephen's Green,** central Dublin's largest park.

Between Dame Street and the Liffey is **Temple Bar,** a region of narrow cobbled streets that was until 10 years ago a sleepy backwater in the bustle of central Dublin. A major renovation has completely transformed the area, and it's now the center of Dublin's arts scene. Temple Bar's few short blocks are home to the Irish Film Centre, the Ark Centre for children, the National Photographic Archive, and numerous galleries, restaurants, and cafes.

O'Connell Street, North Dublin's main thoroughfare, begins at the **O'Connell Street Bridge,** the primary connection between North and South Dublin. Once a fashionable and historic focal point in Dublin, O'Connell Street has lost much of its charm and importance recently and is now lined with fast-food restaurants, movie theaters, and a few great Dublin landmarks like the General Post Office and the Gresham Hotel.

GETTING AROUND

Dublin, though a compact city you can easily explore on foot, is not an easy city to find your way around. Don't hesitate to ask for assistance from passersby: Dubliners will be quick to help, and you'll have an opportunity to discover the unique Irish way with directions.

BY DART   The Dublin Area Rapid Transit (DART) is a light rail line connecting Dublin with the suburbs along the coast north and south of the city. It's the best way to explore the sights in Howth, Sandycove, Dalkey, Killiney, and Bray and tends to be quicker and easier to figure out than the bus system. Admirably punctual, the DART operates Monday to Saturday 7am to midnight and Sunday 9:30am to 11pm. Schedules are available at all stations during operating hours, but, depending on the time of day and the particular station, you can generally expect that the time between trains will be 10 to 20 minutes. Fares vary with the distance you travel, with the minimum single-journey fare 80p ($1.30) and the maximum IR£1.50 ($2.40). For more information, contact **DART,** Pearse Station, Dublin 2 (☎ **01/703-3504**).

BY BUS Dublin Bus operates a fleet of green double-decker buses, high-frequency single-deck buses, and minibuses throughout the city and its suburbs. Because of the traffic congestion in the center of Dublin, public buses can be agonizingly slow, but they're still the best way to reach places that are too far to walk to and not on a DART line. Destinations and bus numbers are posted above the front windows; buses destined for the city center are marked with the Gaelic words *an lar*.

Bus service runs daily throughout the city, starting at 6am (10am on Sunday) and ending with the last bus at 11:30pm, and a Nitelink service from city center to the suburbs extending bus hours to 3am on Thursday, Friday, and Saturday. Frequency ranges from every 10 to 15 minutes for most runs; schedules are posted on revolving notice boards at each stop. Fares depend on the distance you travel and fall between a minimum of 55p (90¢) and a maximum of IR£1.25 ($2). Nitelink fare is a flat IR£2.50 ($4). Buy your tickets from the driver as you enter the bus; exact change is welcomed but not required; notes of IR£5 or higher, however, may not be accepted. For more information, contact **Dublin Bus,** 59 Upper O'Connell St., Dublin 1 (☎ **01/873-4222**).

BY TAXI Taxi rates are fixed in the Dublin metropolitan area. The charge is IR£1.80 ($2.90) for the first mile and 80p ($1.30) per mile after that. Bags are 80p ($1.30) extra, and there's a 80p ($1.30) extra charge for trips at night and on Sunday. If you call ahead to arrange a pickup, there's an extra charge of IR£1.20 ($1.90). There are taxi stands along O'Connell Street and in front of major hotels. Two reliable companies are **Blue Cabs** (☎ **01/676-1111**) and **VIP Taxi Co.** (☎ **01/478-3333**).

BY BICYCLE Riding a bike in Dublin isn't recommended. Traffic is very heavy, the streets are narrow, and pedestrians crowd every corner. If you're determined to take to the streets on wheels, however, you can rent a bicycle for IR£7 ($11) per day or IR£30 ($48) per week at the **Bike Store,** 58 Lower Gardiner St. (☎ **01/872-5399**), around the corner from Isaac's hostel. It's open Monday to Saturday 9:30am to 6pm.

BY RENTAL CAR Renting a car in Dublin isn't advisable because of traffic congestion and parking problems, but when exploring the countryside you may wish to go by car. If you do rent a car in Dublin, be sure you can park it off the street—car theft and break-ins are all too frequent. **Budget,** 151 Lower Drumcondra Rd. (☎ **01/837-9611**) and at the airport (☎ **01/844-5919**), is very reliable and one of the cheapest. Expect to pay between IR£30 and IR£65 ($47 and $101) per day, plus tax and insurance, for its smallest car.

If you can, arrange the rental before you leave home: The rate is likely to be less than half the price of a last-minute rental in Dublin. One of the cheapest and most reliable companies is **Auto-Europe** (☎ **800/223-5555** in the U.S., 0800/89-9893 in the U.K., 1800/12-6409 in Australia).

FAST FACTS: Dublin

American Express The office is opposite Trinity College, just off College Green, at 116 Grafton St., Dublin 2 (☎ **01/677-2874**). It's open Monday to Friday 9am to 5pm and Saturday 9am to noon. Currency exchange is offered Monday to Saturday 9am to 5pm and Sunday 11am to 4pm.

Banks Two convenient banks are the **National Irish Bank,** 66 Upper O'Connell St. (☎ **01/873-1877**), open Monday to Friday 10am to 4pm (to 5pm Thursday), and the **Allied Irish Bank,** 100 Grafton St. (☎ **01/671-3011**), open

The Irish Punt

For American Readers   At this writing $1 = approximately 63p (or IR£1 = $1.60), and this was the rate of exchange used to calculate the dollar values given in this chapter (rounded to the nearest dollar for amounts greater than $5).

For British Readers   At this writing £1 sterling = approximately 83p (Irish) (or IR£1 = £1.20 sterling), and this was the rate of exchange used to calculate the pound values in the table below.

Note: Exchange rates fluctuate from time to time and may not be the same when you travel to the Republic of Ireland.

IR£	U.S.$	U.K.£	IR£	U.S.$	U.K.£
.10	.16	.12	8	12.80	9.60
.25	.40	.30	9	14.40	10.80
.50	.80	.60	10	16.00	12.00
1.00	1.60	1.20	15	24.00	18.00
2.00	3.20	2.40	20	32.00	24.00
3.00	4.80	3.60	25	40.00	30.00
4.00	6.40	4.80	30	48.00	36.00
5.00	8.00	6.00	40	64.00	48.00
6.00	9.60	7.20	50	80.00	60.00
7.00	11.20	8.40	60	96.00	72.00

Monday to Friday 10am to 4pm (to 5pm Thursday). Both have ATMs that accept Cirrus network cards as well as MasterCard and Visa.

Business Hours   Most **business offices** are open Monday to Friday 9am to 5pm. **Stores and shops** are open Monday to Wednesday and Friday and Saturday 9am to 5:30pm and Thursday 9am to 8pm. May to September, many gift and souvenir shops post Sunday hours.

Currency   The basic unit of currency in Ireland is the **punt,** or **Irish pound (IR£),** which is divided into 100 **pence (p).** There are 1p, 2p, 5p, 10p, 20p, 50p, and IR£1 coins and notes of 5, 10, 20, 50, and 100 pounds. You can exchange currency at banks, American Express, the main post office, and the many ATMs located throughout the city.

Embassies   The **American Embassy** is at 42 Elgin Rd., Ballsbridge, Dublin 4 (☎ 01/668-8777); the **Canadian Embassy** is at 65–68 St. Stephen's Green, Dublin 2 (☎ 01/478-1988); the **British Embassy** is at 29 Merrion Rd., Dublin 4 (☎ 01/205-3700); and the **Australian Embassy** is at Fitzwilton House, Wilton Terrace, Dublin 2 (☎ 01/676-1517).

Emergencies   For police, fire, or other emergencies, dial ☎ **999.**

Holidays   Dublin holidays are January 1 (New Year's Day), March 17 (St. Patrick's Day), Good Friday and Easter Monday, May Day (the first Monday in May), the first Monday in June and August (Summer Bank Holidays), the last Monday in October (Autumn Bank Holiday), December 25 (Christmas Day), and December 26 (St. Stephen's Day).

Hospitals   For emergency care, two of the most modern health-care facilities are **St. Vincent's Hospital,** Elm Park, Dublin 4 (☎ 01/269-4533), on the south

Networks & Resources

STUDENTS   The focus of student life is **Trinity College.** On the south side of the Liffey, at the top of Dame Street, the large campus with its many 18th-century buildings is in the heart of Dublin's old city. At the information office just inside the main gate you can find out more about what's going on at the college.

Students and those under 25 should check at the **Union of Students in Ireland/Irish Student Travel Service (USIT),** 19 Aston Quay, Dublin 2 (☎ 01/677-8117), a clearinghouse of information and networking resources.

Before you leave, you can get details on international student/teacher/youth ID cards and fares by calling the national office of **Council Travel** at ☎ 800/2-COUNCIL. Its staff can make your reservations or refer you to the Council Travel office nearest you. Council Travel operates 43 offices in the United States and works through a network of world affiliates. In Canada, CIEE's counterpart is **Travel CUTS,** 187 College St., Toronto, Ontario M5T 1P7 (☎ 416/979-2406; fax 416/979-8167).

GAYS & LESBIANS   For information, contact the **National Lesbian and Gay Federation,** 6 S. William St., Dublin 2 (☎ 01/671-0939). The NLGF publishes the *Gay Community News,* distributed by Books Upstairs, 36 College Green across from Trinity College; Waterstone's, on Dawson Street near Trinity College; The George, South Great George's Street, off Dame Street; and other progressive haunts.

In Dublin, a biweekly sold at newsstands and bookstores (IR£1.50/$2.40) throughout the city, has a page of gay events, current club information, AIDS and health information resources, accommodation options, and helpful organizations.

The following organizations and help lines are staffed by knowledgeable, friendly people: **AIDS Helpline Dublin** (☎ 01/872-4277), Monday to Friday 7 to 9pm and Saturday 3 to 5pm, offering assistance with HIV/AIDS prevention, testing, and treatment; **Gay Switchboard Dublin** (☎ 01/872-1055), Sunday to Friday 8 to 10pm and Saturday 3:30 to 6pm; **Lesbian Line Dublin** (☎ 01/872-9911), Thursday 7 to 9pm; and **LOT (Lesbians Organizing Together),** the central umbrella group of the lesbian community, 5 Capel St. (☎ 01/872-7770; http://qrd.tcp.com/qrd/www/world/europe/ireland/leanow.html).

side, and **Beaumont Hospital,** Beaumont, Dublin 9 (☎ 01/837-7755), on the north.

Laundry   In the city center, try the **Laundry Room,** 8 Lower Kevin St., Dublin 2 (☎ 01/478-1774), or **Suds,** 60 Upper Grand Canal St., Dublin 4 (☎ 01/668-1786). Take your dry cleaning to **Craft Cleaners,** 12 Upper Baggot St., Dublin 4 (☎ 01/668-8198).

Mail   The General Post Office (GPO) is on O'Connell Street, Dublin 1 (☎ 01/705-7000), open Monday to Saturday 8am to 8pm and Sunday and holidays 10:30am to 6:30pm. Branch offices, identified by the sign OIFIG AN POST/POST OFFICE, are open Monday to Saturday 9am to 6pm.

Police   Dial ☎ 999 in an emergency. The metropolitan headquarters for the Dublin Garda Siochana (Police) is in Phoenix Park, Dublin 8 (☎ 01/677-1156).

Country & City Codes

The **country code** for Ireland is **353.** The **city code** for Dublin is **1;** use this code when you're calling from outside Ireland. If you're within Ireland but not in Dublin, use **01.** If you're calling within Dublin, simply leave off the code and dial only the regular phone number.

Tax Ireland's **VAT (value-added tax)** is 17.36% on the price of all goods (except books and children's clothing and footwear). Many stores will refund this amount to foreigners. See "Shopping," later in this chapter.

Telephone Ireland has one of Europe's most sophisticated phone systems, and the quality of international connections is exceptional. Throughout the city you can find pay phones that accept coins, both on the street and in pubs; a **local call** costs 20p (30¢). If you want to use one of the many yellow Callcard phones, almost as common as coin phones, you'll have to buy a **Callcard** (available at post offices, newsstands, and many convenience stores). The Callcard is available in denominations of 10, 20, 50, and 100 units, priced at IR£2.20 ($3.50), IR£3.50 ($5), IR£8 ($13), and IR£16 ($26), respectively.

Tipping In restaurants that don't add a service charge, 10% to 15% is the acceptable amount to tip if the service has been good. Taxi drivers don't expect a tip, but if you wish to give one, 10% is appropriate.

3 Accommodations You Can Afford

The only difficulty you'll encounter with Dublin accommodations is availability, so if you're planning to arrive between June and September be sure to book well in advance. The most appealing city-center locations are always the first to go, and private rooms in the popular hostels can get booked up months in advance, especially for weekends. Also, be aware of the local calendar of events—the biggies are Easter, the Spring Show in May, the Horse Show in August, All-Ireland Finals in September, and international rugby matches.

If you arrive without a reservation, stop by one of the five **Dublin Tourism** locations (see "Visitor Information," above) and make use of its room-finding service.

Note: You can find most of the lodging choices below plotted on the map included in "Seeing the Sights," later in this chapter.

IN THE CITY CENTER—SOUTH OF THE LIFFEY

Ashfield House. 19–20 D'Olier St., Dublin 2. ☎ **01/679-7734.** Fax 01/679-0852. E-mail: ashfield@indigo.ie. 5 units, 16 dorms, all with bathroom. IR£20 ($32) single; IR£36 ($58) double; IR£13 ($21) per person in 4-bed dorm; IR£11.50 ($18) per person in 6-bed dorm; IR£10 ($16) per person in 20-bed dorm. Laundry service £4 ($6). AE, MC, V. Rates include continental breakfast. Bus: Any city-center bus.

Location is the primary appeal of this hostel—it's around the corner from the gates of Trinity College, adjacent to O'Connell Street, and a brief stroll from Temple Bar. There's a lounge in the front hall and a large dining area; the self-catering kitchen is tiny. The rooms are small and clean, but the 20-bed dorm with one shower is definitely to be avoided. Smoking is permitted everywhere but in the rooms. This hostel isn't ideal but does remain one of the few good budget options in the city center.

Avalon House. 55 Aungier St., Dublin 2. ☎ **01/475-0001.** Fax 01/475-0303. E-mail: t.kennedy@avalon.iol.ie. 30 units, 4 with bathroom; 15 dorms, 4 with bathroom. IR£18.50

A Safety Tip

Within the city center, accommodations tend to be cheapest in the area north of the river Liffey, but you should be aware that the crime rate is also higher in this part of town: You should take all necessary precautions.

($30) single; IR£28–IR£30 ($45–$48) double; IR£12–IR£13 ($19–$21) per person in 4-bed dorm; IR£7.50–IR£10.50 ($12–$17) per person in 12-bed dorm. AE, MC, V. Rates include continental breakfast. Bus: 16, 16A, 19, or 22.

This ornate red-sandstone Victorian was erected in 1879 as a medical school, used as commercial offices, and then transformed into a hostel in 1992. Geared for students and budget-conscious travelers, it's less than 2 blocks from St. Stephen's Green. Facilities include a coffee shop, a study/reading room, a bureau de change, a TV lounge, international pay phones, lockers, luggage storage, a self-catering kitchen, and a laundry. The in-house restaurant is open daily 8am to 9pm and serves lunch and dinner for under IR£5 ($8); the food is decent but not much more. Smoking is permitted in the restaurant and all common rooms, but not in the bedrooms. The double rooms have two twin beds.

✪ **Brewery Hostel.** 22–23 Thomas St., Dublin 8. ☎ **01/453-8600.** Fax 01/453-8616. E-mail: breweryh@indigo.ie. 4 units, all with bathroom. 8 dorms, all with bathroom. IR£34 ($54) triple; IR£12 ($19) per person in 4-bed dorm; IR£10 ($16) per person in 8- to 10-bed dorm. MC, V. Secure parking lot. Bus: 1, 2, 3, or 51A.

Down the street from the Guinness Brewery in the historic Liberties district, this hostel is in a stately old town house that's been newly renovated. There's a pleasant outdoor terrace with tables and chairs adjacent to the cramped self-catering kitchen. The four triple rooms are small but bright. Smoking is allowed everywhere except the kitchen and bedrooms. To get there, go west on Dame Street, which changes names several times before you reach the hostel: It becomes Lord Edward before passing Christchurch, then switches to High, Cornmarket, and Thomas.

✪ **Jurys Christchurch Inn.** Christchurch Place, Dublin 8. ☎ **800/843-3311** in the U.S., or 01/454-0000. Fax 01/454-0012. 172 units, all with bathroom. A/C TV TEL. IR£55 ($88) per unit (sleeps up to 3 adults). AE, CB, DC, MC, V. Bus: 21A, 50, 50A, 78, 78A, or 78B.

Smack-dab in the middle of Dublin's most historic area, Jurys offers one of the city's best values for parties of three or four. Each bright room will accommodate up to three adults or two adults and two children, bringing per-person rates down to about IR£18.50 ($30); rooms 419, 501, and 507 are especially spacious. All were refurbished in 1998, and no-smoking rooms are available. Request a fifth-floor room facing west for a memorable view of Christ Church.

✪ **Kinlay House Christchurch.** 2–12 Lord Edward St., Dublin 2. ☎ **01/679-6644.** Fax 01/679-7437. E-mail: kindub@usit.ie. www.iol.ie/usitaccm/. 13 units, 6 with bathroom; 14 dorms, 6 with bathroom. IR£18 ($29) single; IR£28 ($45) double without bathroom, IR£32 ($51) double with bathroom; IR£9.50–IR£13 ($15–$21) per person in dorm. MC, V. Rates include continental breakfast. Bus: 21A, 50, 50A, 78, 78A, or 78B.

Open year-round and run by USIT, Kinlay occupies a beautiful red-brick town house in one of Dublin's oldest neighborhoods, steps from Christ Church Cathedral and on the edge of trendy Temple Bar. There's a large self-catering kitchen and dining room on the ground floor and a smaller kitchen on the third floor. Other common spaces include a TV room and meeting room. The rooms are small but clean. You won't have to worry about a lockout, since there's someone at the front desk 24 hours. Though

---

Getting the Best Deal on Accommodations

- Note that some Dublin guesthouses offer attractive weekend and 3- or 6-day package rates during the low season, with discounts for seniors. Be sure to ask when booking.
- Be aware that if your stay in Dublin is a week or longer, you'll save money by booking one of the many apartments available on a self-catering basis. Minimum rental is usually 1 week, though some are available for 3-day periods. Inquire about credit-card acceptance—many of these operators prefer to work on a cash basis. Check with Dublin Tourism about these apartments.
- June 1 to October 3, take advantage of the on-campus B&B accommodations provided by Trinity College for both individuals and organized groups; the cost is IR£20 to IR£38 ($32 to $61) per person. You have access to laundry and dry cleaning, good parking is provided, and MasterCard and Visa are accepted. Contact the Trinity College Accommodations Office, Dublin 2 (☎ **01/ 608-1177;** fax 01/671-1267).

---

there's supposedly a no-smoking policy, in my experience it isn't respected by staff or guests.

IN THE CITY CENTER—NORTH OF THE LIFFEY

Dublin International Youth Hostel. 61 Mountjoy St., Dublin 7. ☎ **01/830-1766.** Fax 01/830-1600. E-mail: anoige@iol.ie. 5 units, none with bath; 30 dorms, none with bath. IR£25 ($40) double; IR£10.50 ($17) per person in 4- to 6-bed dorm; IR£8–IR£10 ($13–$16) per person in 8- to 28-bed dorm. MC, V. Rates include continental breakfast. Bus: 10.

Comfort, modern convenience, and a beautiful old building are features at An Oige's newest Dublin hostel, 15 minutes by foot from the city center. There's a restaurant in the converted chapel, open June to September on Monday to Saturday 6 to 10pm; it serves basic meals for less than IR£5 ($8). Reception is open 24 hours. A secure car-and-bicycle parking lot is behind the hostel. The self-catering kitchen, TV room, and restaurant are all no-smoking; a separate smoking lounge is available.

Isaac's. 2–4 Frenchman's Lane, Dublin 1. ☎ **01/874-9321.** Fax 01/874-1574. 24 units, none with bath; 40 dorms. IR£18.95 ($30) single; IR£32 ($51) double; IR£7.95–IR£9.25 ($13–$15) dorm. Continental breakfast IR£1.95 ($3.15); full Irish or healthy option breakfast IR£2.95 ($4.70). MC, V. DART: Connelly Station. Bus: 33, 40, or 41.

Around the corner from Busáras Central Bus Station and minutes away from O'Connell Street, this hostel won an award for its restoration of the old wine warehouse it occupies. The dorms and family rooms are comfortably furnished, and there's a well-equipped self-catering kitchen. The on-premises moderately priced restaurant serves all three meals and snacks. Smoking is allowed everywhere but the bedrooms, and the place can get quite smoky. There's a bed lockout from 11am to 5pm.

M. E. C. Hostel (Mount Eccles Court). 42 North Great George's St., Dublin 1. ☎ **01/878-0071.** Fax 01/874-6472. 10 units, 8 with bathroom; 16 dorms, 4 with bathroom. IR£28 ($45) twin or double without bathroom, IR£32 ($51) twin or double with bathroom; IR£60 ($96) family room; IR£12–IR£13 ($19–$21) per person in 4-bed dorm; IR£8.50–IR£11.50 ($14–$18) per person in 6- to 16-bed dorm. MC, V. Rates include continental breakfast. Bus: 1, 40A, 40B, or 40C. One block east of Parnell Sq. East, at the top of O'Connell St.

If you're intrigued by the architecture of Georgian Dublin, you'll love this place. North Great George's Street comprises a short row of beautiful Georgian town houses—the splendid house that's now the James Joyce Centre is adjacent to the hostel. M. E. C. occupies a massive building that was constructed as a convent but renovated over the past few years. The rooms in front have somewhat more appealing views than those in back, which look out on a parking lot. The first floor has a large sitting room with high ceilings, intricate plasterwork, and massive windows. Breakfast is served in a dark but atmospheric basement room with stone walls. Four of the largest, most elegant accommodations are family rooms; each has a loft sleeping area, kitchen, bath, and hide-a-bed couch.

IN THE SUBURBS—SOUTH OF THE LIFFEY
IN DUN LAOGHAIRE

Annesgrove. 28 Rosmeen Gardens, Dun Laoghaire, Co. Dublin. ☎ **01/280-9801.** 4 units, 2 with bathroom. IR£25 ($40) single without bathroom, IR£35 ($56) single with bathroom; IR£36 ($58) double without bathroom, IR£40 ($64) double with bathroom. Children 25% less. Rates include full breakfast. No credit cards. Closed mid-Dec to Jan. DART: Dun Laoghaire. Bus: 7, 7A, or 8 from O'Connell Bridge.

Annesgrove is a pretty two-story home set in a cul-de-sac, close to train and bus transportation and a short walk from the car ferry. Mrs. Anne D'Alton is the gracious hostess, and she'll provide an early breakfast for those with a morning departure. All rooms have sinks, and there's a family room with a double bed and twin beds. There's no smoking in the rooms.

IN RATHFARNHAM

Mrs. Beatrice O'Connor. 15 Butterfield Ave., Rathfarnham, Dublin 14. ☎ **01/494-3660.** 3 units, 2 with bathroom. TV. IR£23 ($37) single without bathroom, IR£25 ($40) single with bathroom; IR£32 ($51) double without bathroom, IR£36 ($58) double with bathroom. Children age 11 and under receive 20% discount. Rates include full breakfast. No credit cards. Private parking lot. Closed Nov–Apr. Bus: 15B to city center, 75 to Dun Laoghaire.

Only 5km (3.1 mls) from the city center, this lovely modern home on a quiet residential street has nicely furnished guest rooms (one on the ground floor) and good bus transportation just outside the door. Mrs. O'Connor is most welcoming and enjoys helping you get the most from your Dublin stay.

Dolores and Tony Murphy. 14 Castle Park, Sandymount, Dublin 4. ☎ **01/269-8413.** 4 units, 1 with bathroom. IR£20 ($32) single; IR£32 ($51) double without bathroom, IR£38 ($61) double with bathroom. Rates include full breakfast. No credit cards. Closed Oct–Apr. DART: Sandymount. Bus: 3.

The Murphys are the delightful hosts at this B&B off Gilford Road. Their modern house is brightly decorated, and you're welcome to enjoy the sun in the small garden out back. The rooms have built-in wardrobes and sinks. The entire family (including Tony and Dolores's daughter, Linda) seems dedicated to making you feel at home, and Dolores will be glad to prepare the evening meal if you give her sufficient notice. No smoking.

IN TEMPLEOGUE

Arus Mhuire. 8 Old Bridge Rd., Templeogue, Dublin 16. ☎ **01/494-4281** or 01/493-7022. 9 units, 7 with bathroom. TV. IR£26 ($42) single without bathroom, IR£28 ($45) single with bathroom; IR£40 ($64) double without bathroom, IR£42 ($67) double with bathroom. Rates include full breakfast. No credit cards. Locked parking lot. Bus: 15B, 49, 65, or 65A.

Mrs. Colette O'Brien's modern home is 4 miles from the city center, but four bus routes are nearby. The rooms are comfortable and attractive, each with a hair dryer and tea/coffeemaker. Mrs. O'Brien offers a laundry service. No smoking.

IN THE SUBURBS—NORTH OF THE LIFFEY
IN CLONTARF

Mrs. Bridget Geary. 69 Hampton Court (off Vernon Ave.), Clontarf, Dublin 3. ☎ **01/833-1199.** 3 units, 1 with bathroom. IR£33 ($53) double without bathroom, IR£38 ($61) double with bathroom. Children 20% less. Rates include full breakfast. No credit cards. Closed Oct–Mar. Bus: 130, 28, 29, or 31.

Mrs. Geary's home is a modern bungalow convenient to the airport, car ferry, and transport into town via either the bus or the train. The rooms are definitely no-frills, with views limited to the yards and roofs of neighboring houses. Clontarf Castle, which serves good moderately priced meals, is a 10-minute walk away. Mrs. Geary's hospitality and graciousness have earned her a loyal following.

Mrs. Eileen Kelly. 17 Seacourt, St. Gabriel's Rd., Clontarf, Dublin 3. ☎ **01/833-2547.** 3 units, 2 with bathroom. IR£40 ($64) double without bathroom, IR£44 ($70) double with bathroom. Rates include full breakfast. No credit cards. Closed Nov–Feb. Bus: 130.

Mrs. Eileen Kelly is an outstanding hostess who welcomes you into the family circle around a cozy open fire in the lounge. Her large rooms are tastefully furnished. Bus transportation to the city center isn't far away. No smoking.

Springvale. 69 Kincora Dr., Clontarf, Dublin 3. ☎ **01/833-3413.** 4 units, all with bathroom. IR£23.50 ($38) single; IR£34 ($54) double. Age 11 and under 20% less. Rates include full breakfast. No credit cards. Parking lot. Closed Dec 25. Bus: 29A, 31, 32, or 130.

According to Frommer's readers, Moira Kavanagh serves "the best breakfast in Ireland." Add to that accolade her attractive home in a quiet residential area off Kincora Grove, featuring nicely appointed rooms complete with tea/coffeemakers, and it's easy to understand her popularity. Nearby are Clontarf Castle, Malahide Castle, the Hill of Howth, golf and tennis facilities, a pool, and a good beach. No smoking.

Wavemount. 264 Clontarf Rd., Clontarf, Dublin 3. ☎ **01/833-1744.** 3 units, 2 with bathroom. IR£34 ($54) double. Children 25% less. Rates include full breakfast. No credit cards. Closed Nov–Jan. Bus: 30.

Wavemount is a pretty two-story home overlooking Dublin Bay. The house itself is spotless and shining, but even more impressive is the warmth with which Maura and Raymond O'Driscoll greet their guests. The breakfasts (with homemade bread) are generous and presented in a bright front room with a bay window looking out to the sea. Mrs. O'Driscoll will also provide dinner if given notice; otherwise, the good Dollymount House Restaurant and Bar is next door. Clontarf Castle is within walking distance, with moderately priced meals and entertainment during summer. The Royal Dublin Golf Club is nearby. No smoking.

IN BELFIELD

Belgrove and Merville. UCD Village, Belfield, Dublin 4. ☎ **01/269-7111.** Fax 01/269-7704. E-mail: ucdvillage@usit.ie. Internet: www.iol.ie/usitaccm/. 1,200 units, all with bathroom. Mid-June to mid-Sept IR£22 ($35) single; IR£66 ($106) apt for up to 3; IR£88 ($141) apt for up to 5. Reduced weekly rates may be available. MC, V. Bus: 10.

Belfield and Merville are two enormous modern student housing projects 3 miles from the city center. During the school year, these three- and four-bedroom apartments serve as dorms for the students of University College Dublin, but in summer they can be rented by the night or the week. The apartments are small, spartan, and low on character, but they do offer an economical alternative to city-center accommodations for families and groups. Each apartment has a small but well-equipped kitchen and a living room/dining room; the bedrooms are tiny, with just enough room for a single bed and a small desk. All linens are supplied; there's electric heating; and the sports complex has tennis courts, squash courts, a gym, and a running track. Shops, a coffee shop, restaurants, and a launderette are in the nearby village, and there's frequent direct bus service to the city.

A GAY & LESBIAN GUESTHOUSE

Frankie's Guest Hotel. 8 Camden Place (off Harcourt St.), Dublin 2. ☎ **01/ 478-3087.** 12 units, 9 with shower only. TV. IR£44–IR£55 ($70–$88) double. Rates include breakfast. AE, EURO, MC, V. Safe back-street parking. Bus: 62.

Frankie has been running this pleasant hotel for 8 years, adding to the lovely walkway and roof garden and keeping the smallish but fresh and simple white rooms to a high standard. Set in a quiet back street, the house has a Mediterranean feel, welcoming mature gay, lesbian, and straight visitors alike. A double room downstairs can accommodate those with disabilities. The hotel is an easy walk to Stephen's Green and Grafton Street, and you can make coffee or tea in your room to renew yourself.

WORTH A SPLURGE

✪ **Ariel House.** 50–52 Lansdowne Rd., Ballsbridge, Dublin 4. ☎ **01/668-5512.** Fax 01/668-5845. 28 units, all with bathroom. TV TEL. IR£50–IR£150 ($80–$240) double. Full Irish breakfast IR£7.50 ($12); continental breakfast IR£4.50 ($7). MC, V. Parking lot. DART: Lansdowne Rd. Bus: 7, 7A, 8, or 45.

Ariel House is a bastion of distinction and quality, opened more than 25 years ago in a 19th-century mansion by Dublin-born and San Francisco–trained hotelier Michael O'Brien. You're welcome to relax in the Victorian-style drawing room with its Waterford chandeliers, open fireplace, and carved cornices. The guest rooms are individually decorated, with period furniture, fine paintings, and crisp Irish linens, as well as hair dryers, garment presses, tea/coffeemakers, and irons/ironing boards. Facilities include a wine bar and a conservatory-style dining room that serves breakfast, morning coffee, and afternoon tea. It's 1 block from the DART station.

4 Great Deals on Dining

The food scene is changing in Ireland, and while Dublin may not always be at the forefront of this change, it certainly is keeping up. You'll find an increasing number of informal restaurants with small menus and big ambitions, serving food based on the best local ingredients. Plates heaped high with limp vegetables and dubious meats are definitely out—you're more likely to find the capital's culinary imagination at work on an Indian curry, a retake on a great continental dish, or a succulent spinach cannelloni.

A LOCAL BUDGET BEST

Bewley's Cafe. 78 Grafton St. (between Nassau St. and St. Stephen's Green). ☎ **01/ 677-6761.** Homemade soup IR£1 ($1.65); main courses IR£3–IR£5 ($4.80–$8); lunch specials from IR£4 ($6). AE, DC, MC, V. Daily 7:30am–10pm (continuous service for breakfast, hot food, and snacks). Bus: Any city-center bus. TRADITIONAL/PASTRIES.

This is Dublin's old reliable, a chain with a 150-year history. The tea and pastries are memorable and the meals dependably filling. The interior is much like other old-time tea shops, with marble-topped tables and lots of mahogany. In addition to lunch or a refreshing tea break, you can purchase teas, coffees, fresh-baked breads, and pastries to take out.

Other locations are at 11 Westmoreland St., Dublin 2; 13 South Great George's St., Dublin 2; 40 Mary St., Dublin 1 (near the ILAC shopping center north of the Liffey); shopping centers in Dundrum, Stillorgan, and Tallaght; and Dublin Airport.

IN THE CITY CENTER—SOUTH OF THE LIFFEY

Café Bell. St. Teresa's Courtyard, Clarendon St., Dublin 2. ☎ **01/677-7645.** All items IR£2–IR£4 ($3.20–$6). No credit cards. Mon–Sat 9am–6pm. DART: Tara St. Bus: 16, 16A, 19, 19A, 22A, 55, or 83. IRISH/SELF-SERVICE.

In the cobbled courtyard of early 19th-century St. Teresa's Church, this serene little place is one of a handful of dining options springing up in historic or ecclesiastical surroundings. With high ceilings and an old-world decor, Café Bell is a welcome contrast to the bustle of Grafton Street a block away and Powerscourt Town House Centre across the street. The menu changes daily but usually includes homemade soups, sandwiches, salads, quiches, lasagna, sausage rolls, hot scones, and other baked goods.

Chez Jules. 16a D'Olier St., Dublin 2 (across from the north wall of Trinity College). ☎ **01/677-0499.** Reservations recommended. Main courses IR£5.75–IR£9.95 ($9–$16); fixed-price 3-course dinner IR£8.90 ($14); fixed-price lunch IR£5 ($8). MC, V. Mon–Fri noon–3pm and 6–11pm, Sat 1–4pm and 6–11pm, Sun 5–10pm. DART: Tara St. Bus: 5, 7A, 8, 15A, 15B, 15C, 46, 55, 62, 63, 83, or 84. FRENCH COUNTRY.

One of Dublin's newest ventures, Chez Jules provides relaxed French dining at pub-grub prices. Except for the checkered tablecloths, this is a dining hall, with long tables, benches, bright lights, and bustle. The staff is especially warm and friendly and the menu modest, augmented by daily chalkboard specials. Some of the dishes, like the au gratin potatoes, are delivered in their skillet. This is solid, tasty country fare, most affordable and satisfying. The vin du pays house wines at IR£7.50 ($12) a bottle are very drinkable and a real bargain.

✪ **Elephant and Castle.** 18 Temple Bar, Dublin 2. ☎ **01/679-3121.** Lunch main courses IR£5.50–IR£8.95 ($8–$14); dinner main courses IR£6.50–IR£12.50 ($10–$20). AE, DC, MC, V. Sun–Thurs 11:30am–11:30pm, Fri–Sat 11:30am–midnight. DART: Tara St. Bus: 21A, 46A, 46B, 51B, 51C, 68, 69, or 86. CALIFORNIAN/INTERNATIONAL.

In the heart of Temple Bar, this favorite with kids is informal and fun, with simple pinewood tables and benches and a decor blending modern art with statues of elephants and cartoon figures. The menu is eclectic, made up of exotic salads and multi-ingredient omelets and such dishes as sesame chicken with spinach and cucumber; fettuccine with shrimp, sun-dried tomatoes, and saffron; linguine with goat cheese, tomato, broccoli, and thyme; and a house-special Elephant Burger with curried sour cream, bacon, scallions, cheddar, and tomatoes.

Fitzers Cafe. 51 Dawson St., Dublin 2. ☎ **01/677-1155.** Reservations recommended. Lunch main courses IR£5.95–IR£9.95 ($10–$16); dinner main courses IR£6.95–IR£12.95 ($11–$21). AE, DC, MC, V. Daily 9am–11:30pm. DART: Pearse. Bus: 10, 11A, 11B, 13, or 20B. INTERNATIONAL.

In the middle of a busy shopping street, this airy Irish-style bistro has a multi-windowed shopfront facade and a modern Irish decor of light woods. The food is excellent and reasonably priced, contemporary and quickly served, with choices ranging from chicken breast with hot chili cream sauce to brochette of lamb tandoori with mild curry sauce to gratin of smoked cod.

Fitzers has three other locations: in the National Gallery, Merrion Square, Dublin 2 (☎ **01/661-4496**); in the Royal Dublin Society (RDS), Ballsbridge, Dublin 4 (☎ **01/667-1302**); and in Temple Bar Square, Dublin 2 (☎ **01/679-0440**).

Getting the Best Deal on Dining

- Save by preparing your own meals in the kitchen of your hostel or self-catering apartment.
- Note that there's an increasing number of hostel restaurants offering decent food at budget prices. See the accommodations section for a few examples: Avalon House, the Dublin International Youth Hostel, and Isaac's.
- Be aware that the Irish have traditionally had their heartiest meal at midday. Despite changes in lifestyle during recent years, the tradition still lingers, and for travelers the lunch menu is often ample and affordable at restaurants where dinner would be out of the question.
- Take advantage of the many restaurants that offer a Tourist Meal, a three-course meal at an inexpensive price. Menu choices are usually the same as for the four- or five-course dinners and savings can run as much as IR£5 ($8).
- Make your evening meal an early one to take advantage of early-bird specials offered by many restaurants between 5:30 and 7pm.
- Note that moderately priced hotel coffee shops will feed you well at prices far below those of more expensive hotel dining rooms.

Gallagher's Boxty House. 20 Temple Bar (between Essex and Fleet sts.). ☎ **01/677-2762.** À la carte dishes IR£6–IR£10 ($10–$16); fixed-price menu (Mon–Fri noon–5pm) IR£5 ($8). DC, MC, V. Daily noon–11:30pm. Bus: Any city-center bus. IRISH.

This traditional Irish restaurant 1 block south of the Liffey grew out of brothers Padraig and Ronan Gallagher's fond memories of the boxty pancakes (traditional potato pancakes served with a variety of fillings) their mother always cooked on Friday when they were growing up. Now, with the menu featuring specialties like bacon and cabbage and bread-and-butter pudding—and boxty, of course—Dubliners flock to Gallagher's. This is definitely a place to bring the entire family.

✪ **Irish Film Centre Cafe Bar.** 6 Eustace St., Temple Bar, Dublin 2. ☎ **01/677-8788** or 01/677-8099. Main courses IR£2–IR£6 ($3.20–$10). MC, V. Daily noon–3pm and 5:30–9pm. Bus: 21A, 78A, or 78B. IRISH/INTERNATIONAL.

One of the most popular drinking spots in Temple Bar, the Cafe Bar features an excellent menu that changes daily. A vegetarian/Middle Eastern menu is available for both lunch and dinner. Weekend entertainments include music and comedy.

Juice. Castle House, 73 South Great George's St., Dublin 2. ☎ **01/475-7856.** Reservations recommended Fri–Sat. Main courses IR£4.95–IR£7.25 ($8–$11); early-bird fixed-price dinner (Mon–Thurs 6:30–7pm) IR£6.95 ($11). Service charge 10%. EURO, MC, V. Sun–Thurs 11am–10pm, Fri–Sat 11am–midnight, Fri–Sat light menu midnight–4am. Bus: 50, 50A, 54, 56, or 77. VEGETARIAN.

Juice tempts carnivorous, vegan, macrobiotic, celiac, and yeast-free diners alike, using organic produce to create delicious dressings and entrees among its largely conventional but well-prepared offerings. The avocado filet of blue cheese and broccoli wrapped in filo was superb, and I recommend highly the spinach-and-ricotta cannelloni. The latter is included in the early-bird dinner—a great deal. Coffees, fresh-squeezed juices, organic wines, and late weekend hours add to the lure of this casual modern place frequented by mature diners who know their food.

Leo Burdock's. 2 Werburgh St., Dublin 8. ☎ **01/454-0306.** Main courses IR£2.50–IR£4.50 ($4–$7). No credit cards. Mon–Fri 12:30–11pm, Sat 2–11pm. Closed holidays. Bus: 21A, 50, 50A, 78, 78A, or 78B. FISH-AND-CHIPS.

For three generations, Brian Burdock's family has been serving up the country's best fish-and-chips. Cabinet ministers, university students, poets, Americans who've had the word passed by locals, and almost every other type in Ireland can be found in the queue, waiting for fish bought fresh that morning and those good Irish potatoes, both cooked in "drippings" (none of that modern cooking oil!). There's great people-watching while you wait, and all that good eating costs a pittance even for ray-and-chips, the priciest choice on the menu (whiting-and-chips are at the bottom of the range). Leo Burdock's is located in the Liberties/Christ Church Cathedral vicinity.

Stag's Head. 1 Dame Court, Dublin 2. ☎ **01/679-3701.** Main courses IR£3–IR£6 ($5–$10). No credit cards. Mon–Fri 12:30–3:30pm and 5:30–7:30pm, Sat 12:30–2:30pm. TRADITIONAL.

Built in 1770, the Stag's Head had its last "modernization" in 1895. Wrought-iron chandeliers, stained-glass skylights, huge mirrors, gleaming wood, and mounted stags' heads set the mood. Choose a light lunch of soup and toasted sandwiches or heaping platters of bacon, beef, or chicken plus two vegetables. The pub is just off Exchequer Street (from Great George's Street)—look for the mosaic depicting a stag's head embedded in the sidewalk of Dame Street in the middle of the second block on the left side coming from College Green, then turn onto the small lane that leads to Dame Court—complicated, but worth the effort.

IN THE CITY CENTER—NORTH OF THE LIFFEY

Beshoff's. 7 Upper O'Connell St., in the International Food Court. ☎ **01/872-4400.** Main courses less than IR£5 ($8). No credit cards. Mon–Thurs 11:30am–midnight, Fri–Sat 11:30am–1am, Sun 12:30pm–midnight. Bus: Any city-center bus. FISH-AND-CHIPS.

This attractive Edwardian-style place 2 blocks north of O'Connell Bridge is a far cry from your everyday fish-and-chips stand: The tables are marble-topped and nicely spaced; there's a cheerful look to the large bustling room; you can order several varieties of fish and various combinations, including chicken; and the place has a wine license.

Beshoff's has another location at 14 Westmoreland St., south of the Liffey (☎ 01/677-8026), with a similar decor and hours.

Kylemore Cafe. 1–2 Upper O'Connell St. ☎ **01/872-2138.** Meals IR£2.50–IR£5 ($3.90–$8); lunch special IR£3.25 ($5). No credit cards. Mon–Sat 7:30am–9pm, Sun 10am–9pm. Bus: Any city-center bus. IRISH.

This large restaurant on busy O'Connell Street is a cafeteria with style; floor-to-ceiling windows flood the large dining room with light. There are plenty of marble-topped tables to seat the throngs of diners who fill the restaurant all day long, so don't be discouraged if it looks full.

Winding Stair. 40 Lower Ormond Quay, Dublin 1. ☎ **01/873-3292.** All items IR£1.50–IR£6 ($2.40–$10). MC, V. Mon–Sat 10am–6pm. Bus: 70 or 80. IRISH/SELF-SERVICE.

Retreat from the bustle of the north side's quays at this cafe/bookshop and browse through some old books while you indulge in a light meal. There are three floors, each full of used books (from novels, plays, and poetry to history, art, music, and sports) and all connected by a winding 18th-century staircase. A cage-style lift serves those who prefer not to climb the stairs. Tall, wide windows provide expansive views of the Ha'penny Bridge and the Liffey. The food is simple and healthy—sandwiches made with additive-free meats or fruits, organic salads, homemade soups, and natural juices. Evening events include poetry readings and recitals.

PICNICKING

One of the best places to buy picnic fixings is **Bewley's Cafe** (see the beginning of this section). With your food, head for St. Stephen's Green, where you'll have your picnic along with half of Dublin's workforce, which flocks to the Green in fine weather and sometimes in weather not so fine. Phoenix Park is another idyllic picnic spot.

WORTH A SPLURGE

✪ **Il Primo.** 16 Montague St., Dublin 2 (off Harcourt St., 50 yards from Stephen's Green). ☎ **01/478-3373.** Reservations required on weekends. Lunch menu IR£3–IR£10 ($4.80–$16); dinner main courses IR£9–IR£16 ($14–$27). AE, MC, V. Mon–Sat noon–3pm and 6–11pm. MODERN ITALIAN.

Word of mouth is what brought me to Il Primo—little else would have, so obscurely is it tucked away off Harcourt Street. From the street all you see are several tables, a bar, wooden stools, and a staircase that happens to lead to some of the most innovative Italian cuisine you'll ever meet up with outside Rome or Tuscany. Awaken your palate with a glass of sparkling Venetian prosecco; open with a plate of Parma ham, avocado, and balsamic vinaigrette; and then go for broke with the ravioli Il Primo, an open handkerchief of pasta over chicken, Parma ham, and mushrooms in light tarragon cream sauce. The proprietor, Dieter Bergman, will assist you in selecting appropriate wines, all of which he personally chooses and imports from Tuscany. Wines are by the milliliter, not the bottle—you pay for only what you drink.

5 Seeing the Sights

SIGHTSEEING SUGGESTIONS

IF YOU HAVE 1 DAY   Start with one of the city bus tours departing from outside **Dublin Bus,** 59 O'Connell St. (☎ **01/873-4222**); these cost IR£6 ($10) and take about 1½ hours. Having gained this overview, walk over the O'Connell Street Bridge to **Trinity College Library,** where *The Book of Kells* is on display. After lunch, walk over to **Christ Church** (don't miss the crypt) and **St. Patrick's** cathedrals. Finish your day at the **Brazen Head,** Dublin's oldest pub. Then get the flavor of Dublin by taking one of the guide-led **pub crawls** (see "Organized Tours," below).

IF YOU HAVE 2 DAYS   Spend Day 1 as above. On Day 2 begin at the **National Museum** to see the Irish antiquities. Pay a brief visit to the nearby **National Gallery** to view the fine collection of old masters and important Irish artists. After lunch, walk up O'Connell Street to Parnell Square and the **Garden of Remembrance,** dedicated to those who've died in the cause of Irish freedom. Across from this memorial are the **Dublin Writers Museum** and the **Hugh Lane Municipal Gallery.** Stroll back over the Liffey to take in **Dublin Castle** and finish the day at the **Guinness Hop Store Gallery.**

IF YOU HAVE 3 DAYS   Spend Days 1 and 2 as above. On Day 3 take a trip to the **Boyne Valley** and the north coast to visit the burial mounds at Newgrange, the site of the Battle of the Boyne, King William's Glen, and other sites. This trip is also worthwhile for the glimpses of Irish countryside it affords.

IF YOU HAVE 5 DAYS   Spend Days 1 to 3 as above. Then schedule a trip to the fabulous Irish countryside. **Glendalough,** a former monastic city, and the **Wicklow Mountains** make an excellent excursion. On the morning of Day 5, go to **Sandycove** to see the James Joyce Museum and the Victorian harbor town of **Dun Laoghaire.** In the afternoon, return to Dublin and take one of the **walking tours** (see "Organized Tours," below).

Trinity College

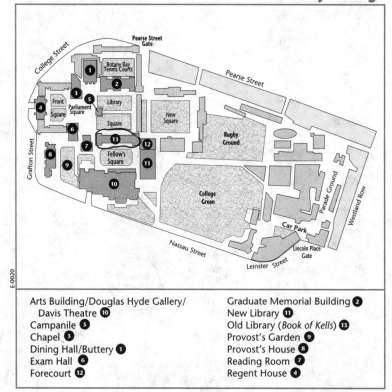

Arts Building/Douglas Hyde Gallery/
Davis Theatre **10**
Campanile **5**
Chapel **3**
Dining Hall/Buttery **1**
Exam Hall **6**
Forecourt **12**

Graduate Memorial Building **2**
New Library **11**
Old Library (*Book of Kells*) **13**
Provost's Garden **9**
Provost's House **8**
Reading Room **7**
Regent House **4**

THE TOP MUSEUMS & GALLERIES

✪ **Trinity College and** *The Book of Kells.* College Green, Dublin 2. ☎ **01/608-2320.** Free admission to college grounds. Old Library/*Book of Kells,* IR£3.50 ($6) adults, IR£3 ($4.80) seniors/students, IR£7 ($11) families, free for under age 12; *Dublin Experience,* IR£3 ($4.80) adults, IR£2.75 ($4.40) seniors/students, free for under age 12. Library, Mon–Sat 9:30am–5pm, Sun noon–4:30pm (opens at 9:30am June–Sept); *Dublin Experience,* May–Sept daily 10am–5pm, closed Oct–Apr. Bus: 5, 7A, 8, 15A, 15B, 15C, 46, 55, 62, 63, 83, or 84.

Trinity College Library (1712–32) is to the right and behind the campanile just inside Trinity College's front gate. Housed in the library's Colonnades exhibition area is *The Book of Kells,* an illustrated and illuminated copy of the gospels created by early 9th-century Irish monks at the monastery of Kells. This exquisitely ornamented volume is the rarest and most important book in Ireland. The exhibition *The Book of Kells: Picturing the Word* provides a vivid insight into the background of this famous national treasure and is open the same hours as the library.

Trinity College is also home to *The Dublin Experience* (☎ 01/608-1177), an excellent multimedia introduction to the history and people of Dublin.

✪ **National Museum of Ireland.** Kildare St. (at Merrion Row), Dublin 2. ☎ **01/677-7444.** Free admission, except for special exhibits; guided tours IR£1 ($1.60). Tues–Sat 10am–5pm, Sun 2–5pm. Bus: 7, 7A, 8, 10, 11, or 13.

This museum holds collections of archaeology, fine arts, and history. The Treasury is the highlight of the archaeological collections. This special exhibition traces the development of Irish art from the Iron Age to the 15th century and includes the Tara

Dublin

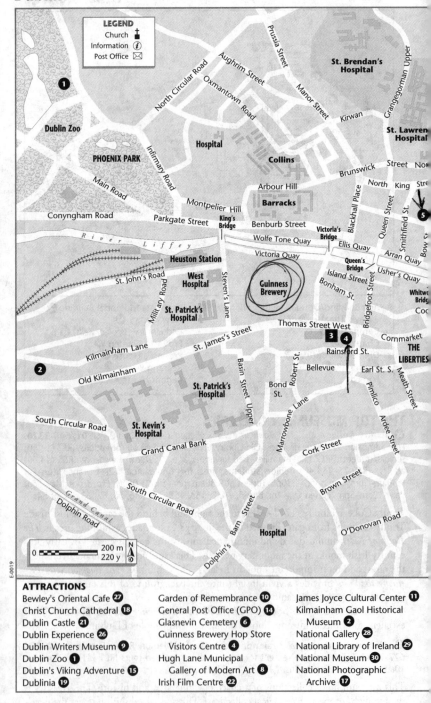

LEGEND
Church ✝
Information ⓘ
Post Office ✉

Dublin Zoo ❶

PHOENIX PARK

North Circular Road

Aughrim Street

Oxmantown Road

Prussia Street

Manor Street

St. Brendan's Hospital

Grangegorman Upper

Kirwan

St. Lawren Hospital

Infirmary Road

Hospital

Arbour Hill

Collins

Brunswick Street Nor

North King Stre

Blackhall Place

Queen Street

Smithfield St.

❺

Main Road

Conyngham Road

Montpelier Hill

Parkgate Street

Barracks

King's Bridge

Benburb Street

Wolfe Tone Quay

Victoria's Bridge

Ellis Quay

Arran Quay

Bow C

River Liffey

Heuston Station

Victoria Quay

Queen's Bridge

Island Street

Usher's Quay

St. John's Road

West Hospital

Steven's Lane

Guinness Brewery

Bonham St.

Bridgefoot Street

Whitw Brid Coc

Military Road

St. Patrick's Hospital

Thomas Street West

❸ ❹

Cornmarket

THE LIBERTIES

Kilmainham Lane

St. James's Street

Basin Street Upper

Rainsford St.

Bellevue

Robert St.

Earl St. S.

Meath Street

❷

Old Kilmainham

St. Patrick's Hospital

Bond St.

Marrowbone Lane

Pimlico

Ardee Street

South Circular Road

St. Kevin's Hospital

Grand Canal Bank

Cork Street

Brown Street

South Circular Road

Barn Street

Dolphin's

Hospital

O'Donovan Road

Grand Canal

Dolphin Road

0 ▭▭▭ 200 m
     220 y

N

E-0019

318

ATTRACTIONS

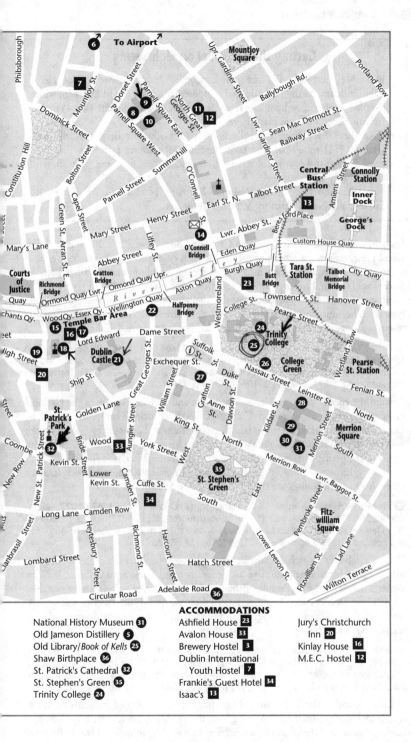

ACCOMMODATIONS

National History Museum 31
Old Jameson Distillery 5
Old Library/*Book of Kells* 25
Shaw Birthplace 36
St. Patrick's Cathedral 32
St. Stephen's Green 35
Trinity College 24

Ashfield House 23
Avalon House 33
Brewery Hostel 3
Dublin International
Youth Hostel 7
Frankie's Guest Hotel 34
Isaac's 13

Jury's Christchurch
Inn 20
Kinlay House 16
M.E.C. Hostel 12

319

Getting the Best Deal on Sightseeing

- Remember that Dublin's compact size makes it ideal to explore on foot. Heritage Trails and Music Trails are well signposted, and you can follow them with detailed explanatory booklets available from Dublin Tourism (see "Visitor Information," earlier in this chapter).
- Take the DART from Connelly Station to Dalkey or Bray. Costing just IR£2.50 ($4) round-trip and taking around 50 minutes each way, this trip gives a delightful journey along the coast and is ideal for those with limited time.
- Note that you can visit the National Museum, National Gallery, National Library, and Natural History Museum all for free.

Brooch, the Ardagh Chalice, and the Cross of Cong, as well as a 20-minute audiovisual presentation. An exhibit of prehistoric Irish gold (the largest display of gold in a European museum) opened in 1991. A second building, entered from Merrion Street, holds natural history exhibits and will be of special interest to youngsters. A third, on Merrion Row (entrance near the Shelbourne Hotel), is devoted to Ireland's geology. The museum's Irish folk life and decorative arts collections were recently moved to a new location at **Collins Barracks,** Benburb Street, Dublin 7.

National Gallery. Merrion Sq. W., Dublin 2. ☎ **01/661-5133.** Fax 01/661-5372. Free admission. Mon–Wed and Fri–Sat 10am–5:30pm, Thurs 10am–8:30pm, Sun 2–5pm. Tours Sat at 3pm and Sun at 2:15, 3, and 4pm. Closed Good Friday and Dec 24–26. DART: Pearse (then 5-minute walk). Bus: 5, 6, 7, 7A, 8, 10, 44, 47, 47B, 48A, or 62.

Around the corner from the National Museum and a block away from the National History Museum, the National Gallery's collections include impressive works by Dutch masters as well as 10 major landscape paintings and portraits by Gainsborough and canvases by Rubens, Rembrandt, El Greco, Monet, Cézanne, and Degas. John Butler Yeats, perhaps Ireland's greatest modern portrait painter, is well represented, as are leading 18th- and 19th-century Irish artists. The gallery has an excellent restaurant where lunch main courses are IR£5 to IR£9 ($8 to $9.60).

✪ **Dublin Writers Museum.** 18–19 Parnell Sq. N., Dublin 1. ☎ **01/872-2077.** Admission IR£2.90 ($4.65) adults, IR£2 ($3.20) seniors/students, IR£1.25 ($2) ages 3–11, IR£7.75 ($12) families (2 adults and up to 4 children). Mon–Sat 10am–5pm (to 7pm June–Aug), Sun and holidays 11:30am–6pm. Bus: 11, 12, 13, 16, 16A, 22, or 22A.

Dublin celebrates its rich literary heritage in two splendid 18th-century Georgian mansions, with permanent displays on George Bernard Shaw, Sean O'Casey, William Butler Yeats, James Joyce, Brendan Behan, and a host of other writers who've enriched the fabric of Dublin's past. The superb bookshop, with mail-order service and specialized book lists, stocks a wide range of Irish titles and provides an out-of-print and antiquarian book search service.

Irish Film Centre. 6 Eustace St., Dublin 2. ☎ **01/677-8788** (box office ☎ 01/679-3477). Institute, free; movie theaters, IR£2–IR£4 ($3.20–$6); *Flashback,* IR£2.50 ($4) adults, IR£2 ($3.20) seniors/students. Institute, daily 10am–11:30pm; theaters, daily 2–11:30pm; *Flashback,* June–Sept Wed–Sun showings at 11am, noon, and 1pm. Bus: 21A, 78A, or 78B.

Dublin's historic Friends Meeting House has been incorporated into this complex, which includes the Irish Film Archive, two movie theaters, a library, a bookshop, a bar/restaurant, and the offices of several film-industry organizations. The audiovisual presentation *Flashback* traces the development of the film industry in Ireland since 1896.

✪ **Guinness Brewery Hop Store Visitor Centre.** James's Gate, Dublin 8. ☎ **01/453-6700,** ext. 5155. Admission IR£3 ($4.80) adults, IR£2 ($3.20) seniors/students, IR£1 ($1.60) under age 12. Apr–Sept Mon–Sat 9:30am–5pm, Sun 10:30am–4:30pm; Oct–Mar Mon–Sat 9:30am–4pm, Sun 12–4pm. Bus: 68A, 78A, or 123.

Founded in 1759, this is one of the world's largest breweries, and today it produces the same dark, creamy, beloved stout for which it has been known since the first day. Although tours of the brewery itself are no longer allowed, you're welcome to explore the adjacent Guinness Hop Store, a converted 19th-century building. It houses the *World of Guinness Exhibition,* an audiovisual showing how the stout is made, plus a museum and a bar where you can sample a glass or two of the famous brew.

THE CASTLE & THE CATHEDRALS

✪ **Dublin Castle.** Dame St., Dublin 2. ☎ **01/677-7129.** Admission IR£2.50 ($4) adults, IR£1.50 ($2.40) seniors/students, IR£1 ($1.60) children. Tours Mon–Fri 10am–5pm, Sat–Sun and bank holidays 2–5pm. The State Apartments are sometimes closed for official functions. Bus: 21A, 50, 50A, 78, 78A, or 78B.

Built between 1208 and 1220, this complex represents some of the oldest surviving architecture in the city, and it was the center of British power in Ireland for more than 7 centuries, until it was taken over by the new Irish government in 1922. Highlights are the 13th-century **Record Tower;** the **State Apartments,** once the residence of English viceroys; and the **Chapel Royal,** a 19th-century Gothic building with particularly fine plaster decoration and carved oak gallery fronts and fittings. The newest developments are the **Undercroft,** an excavated site on the grounds where an early Viking fortress stood, and the **Treasury,** built between 1712 and 1715.

✪ **Christ Church Cathedral and Dublinia.** Christchurch Place (off Lord Edward St.), Dublin 8. ☎ **01/677-8099.** Cathedral, IR£1 ($1.60) adults, 80p ($1.30) students; Dublinia, IR£4 ($6) adults, IR£3 ($4.80) seniors/students/children, IR£10 ($16) families. Daily 10am–5pm. Bus: 21A, 50, 50A, 78, 78A, or 78B.

Christ Church is one of the oldest and most beautiful of Dublin's buildings. Founded by King Sitric in 1038, it was originally a wooden structure but was rebuilt in stone after the 1169 Norman invasion. There are lovely architectural details and stonework in the nave, transepts, choir, and chancel, and the crypt (the oldest section) is said to be one of the best of its kind in Europe. Tours are available on Sunday at 12:15 and 4:30pm.

Cross the elegant bridge from the cathedral to the **Dublinia** exhibit and you walk straight into medieval Dublin as it was between 1170, when the Anglo-Normans arrived, and 1540, when its monasteries were closed. Pick up your personal audio headset and enter the Medieval Maze, where lifelike exhibits depict dramatic, sometimes mystical, episodes from this period. Great for all ages.

✪ **St. Patrick's Cathedral.** Patrick's Close, Dublin 8. ☎ **01/475-4817.** Admission IR£1.50 ($2.40) contribution. Mon–Fri 9am–6pm, Sat 9am–5pm, Sun 10am–4:30pm. Bus: 50, 50A, 54, 54A, or 56A.

This cathedral was built less than 25 years after Christ Church Cathedral (above) in an attempt to outdo that building. Jonathan Swift, author of *Gulliver's Travels,* was dean here from 1713 to 1745, and you can find his tomb in the walls of this impressive Norman cathedral. All services are ecumenical, and all weekday choral services are open to the public. Check with the tourist board for exact days and hours.

Special & Free Events

For free events, nothing in Dublin beats the free **traditional Irish music** that you can hear every night in pubs all over the city. For details, see "Dublin After Dark," later in this chapter. If you're in Dublin during the last 2 weeks of August, check out the **Dublin Summer Music Festival,** a series of free lunchtime band concerts of popular and Irish traditional music in St. Stephen's Green.

For fans of James Joyce, June 16 is the day to be in Dublin. The city celebrates **Bloomsday** in memory of Leopold Bloom, whose wanderings through the city on June 16, 1904, are chronicled in Joyce's *Ulysses.* Contact the James Joyce Cultural Centre at ☎ **01/878-8547** (fax 01/878-8488; E-mail: joycecen@iol.ie).

Many Dublin events cater to lovers of classical music. Lunchtime concerts at the **National Concert Hall,** Earlsfort Terrace, Dublin 2 (☎ **01/671-1533**), are a weekly offering during summer, and most concerts are IR£1 ($1.60). The **AIB Music Festival in Great Irish Houses** is a 10-day festival of classical music performed by leading Irish and international artists in some of the Dublin area's great Georgian buildings and mansions. Contact Crawford Tipping, Blackrock Post Office, Main Street, Blackrock, Co. Dublin (☎ **01/278-1528;** fax 01/278-1529).

The biggest sporting events are the **Dublin Horse Show** in August, the **All-Ireland Hurling and Football Finals** in September, and the **Dublin Marathon** in October.

MORE ATTRACTIONS

✪ **Joyce Tower Museum.** Sandycove, Co. Dublin. ☎ **01/280-9265.** Admission IR£2 ($3.20) adults, IR£1.60 ($2.55) seniors/students/children, IR£6 ($10) families. Apr–Oct Mon–Sat 10am–1pm and 2–5pm, Sunday 2–6pm. DART: Sandycove. Bus: 8.

No James Joyce fan should miss this small museum housed in the Sandycove Martello Tower, where Joyce lived for a while in 1904—it's described in the first chapter of *Ulysses.* The museum contains exhibits on Joyce and Dublin at the time *Ulysses* was written. If you pick up a copy of the "*Ulysses* Map of Dublin" you can make this the starting point of a Joyce tour of the city. Robert Nicholson, the museum's director, is a great source of information on all topics relating to Joyce and has published the best guide to *Ulysses* sites in Dublin, titled simply *The Ulysses Guide.* It's available here, at the James Joyce Cultural Centre, and at some bookstores around Dublin.

✪ **Kilmainham Gaol Historical Museum.** Kilmainham. ☎ **01/453-5984.** Admission IR£2 ($3.20) adults, IR£1.50 ($2.40) seniors, IR£1 ($1.60) children, IR£5 ($8) families. Apr–Sept daily 9:30am–4:45pm; Oct–Mar Mon–Fri 9:30am–4pm, Sun 10am–5pm. Bus: 21, 78, 78A, 78B, or 79 at O'Connell Bridge.

Within these walls political prisoners were incarcerated, tortured, and killed from 1796 to 1924, when the late Pres. Eamon de Valera left as its final prisoner. Its rolls held such names as Robert Emmet, Charles Parnell, and James Connolly. To walk along these corridors, through the exercise yard, or into the Main Compound is a moving experience that lingers hauntingly in the memory.

LITERARY LANDMARKS

The **James Joyce Cultural Centre,** 35 N. Great George's St. (☎ **01/878-8547;** fax 01/878-8488; E-mail: joycecen@iol.ie), is devoted to imparting an increased understanding of the life and works of Joyce through exhibits, audiovisual presentations, an archive, and a reference library. It's housed in a restored 1784 Georgian town house, once the home of Denis J. Maginni, a dancing instructor who appears briefly in *Ulysses*. Guided walking tours are offered through the neighboring streets of "Joyce Country" in Dublin's northern inner city. Admission is IR£2.75 ($4.40) adults, IR£2 ($3.20) students, 70p ($1.10) children, and IR£6 ($10) families; admission and a walking tour is IR£6 ($10) adults and IR£5 ($8) students. The center is open Monday to Saturday 9:30am to 5pm and Sunday 12:30 to 5pm. Take the DART to Connolly Station or bus no. 1, 40A, 40B, or 40C.

Across the river on the south side of town, literary fans pay homage at the **Shaw Birthplace,** 33 Synge St. (☎ **01/475-0854**). Off South Circular Road, this simple two-story terraced house (1838) is the home where George Bernard Shaw was born in 1856. Recently restored, it has been furnished in Victorian style to re-create the atmosphere of Shaw's early days. Admission is IR£2.40 ($3.85) adults, IR£1.15 ($1.85) ages 3 to 11, and IR£7 ($11) families (a combination ticket with the Dublin Writers Museum is available at a reduced rate). It's open May to October, Monday to Saturday 10am to 1pm and 2 to 6pm and Sunday 11:30am to 1pm and 2 to 6pm. Take bus no. 16, 16A, 19, 19A, 22, 22A, or 155.

Glasnevin Cemetery (☎ **01/830-1133**) is the Irish National Cemetery, founded in 1832 and covering over 124 acres. Literary figures buried here include Gerard Manley Hopkins, Christy Brown, and Brendan Behan. James Joyce's parents' grave is here, across the lane from the boulder of Wicklow granite marking Parnell's grave site. Also here are political heroes Michael Collins, Daniel O'Connell, and Roger Casement. A heritage map, on sale in most bookshops, serves as a guide to who's buried where, or you can take one of the guided tours offered by members of the National Graves Association June to August on Sunday at 11:50am; for more information, call ☎ **01/832-1312** or 01/842-3787. The cemetery is open daily 8am to 4pm. You can get there on bus 19, 19A, 40, 40A, 40B, or 40C.

PARKS & GARDENS

Phoenix Park, in western Dublin, is one of the world's largest urban parks. In such a densely developed city, this vast expanse of green is a welcome change. Here you'll find the Dublin Zoo, as well as the residences of the president of Ireland and the U.S. ambassador. Rolling hills, ponds where ducks and swans beg for handouts, and a herd of free-roaming deer all make this an excellent place for a picnic. Take bus no. 10 from O'Connell Street or no. 25 or 26 from Middle Abbey Street.

The **National Botanic Gardens** (☎ **01/837-4388**) are in the northern suburb of Glasnevin, and you can get there by bus no. 13 or 19 from O'Connell Street or no. 34 or 34A from Middle Abbey Street. Spread over 50 acres of an estate that once was the home of poet Thomas Tickell, the gardens are a delight. The vast tropical greenhouses are truly magical, as is the small and fascinating orchid room. The Botanic Gardens are open in summer Monday to Saturday 9am to 6pm and Sunday 11am to 6pm; winter hours are Monday to Saturday 10am to 4:30pm and Sunday 11am to 4:30pm. Admission is free.

ORGANIZED TOURS

WALKING TOURS   You can set out on your own with a map, but the best way to avoid any hassles or missed sights is following one of the four signposted and themed **"tourist trails":** Old City Trail for historic sights; Georgian Trail for the landmark buildings, streets, squares, terraces, and parks; Cultural Trail for a circuit of the top literary sites, museums, galleries, theaters, and churches; and the Rock 'n' Stroll Trail for a tour of contemporary music enclaves, pubs, breweries, nightspots, and more. Each trail is mapped out in a handy booklet, available for IR£2 ($3.20) from the Dublin Tourism office, 14 Upper O'Connell St. (☎ **01/605-7797**).

Several firms offer tours led by knowledgeable local guides. Tour times and charges vary, but most last about 2 hours and cost between IR£4 and IR£6 ($6 and $10). **Discover Dublin Tours** (☎ **01/478-0191**) offers a musical pub crawl led by two professional musicians. The **Dublin Literary Pub Crawl** (☎ **01/454-0228**) departs evenings from the Duke Pub, Duke Street; your guides will recount the stories connecting these pubs with Dublin's literary greats. **Historical Walking Tours of Dublin** (☎ **01/845-0241**) depart from the front gate of Trinity College. All guides are history graduates of Trinity College, and participants are encouraged to ask questions.

BUS TOURS For the standard see-it-all-in-under-3-hours tour, climb aboard the **Dublin Bus** open-deck sightseeing coach. Tours leave from the Dublin Bus office at 59 Upper O'Connell St. (☎ **01/873-4222**). You can purchase your ticket at the office or on the bus: IR£9 ($14) adults and IR£4.50 ($7) children. This tour takes in most of the important sights but doesn't stop at any.

For more flexible touring, there's the **Dublin City Tour,** a continuous guided bus service connecting 10 major points, like museums, art galleries, churches and cathedrals, libraries, and historic sites. For IR£5 ($8) adults, IR£2 ($3.20) under age 16, and IR£12 ($19) families of four, you can ride the bus for a full day, getting off and on as often as you wish. It operates mid-April to September, daily 9:30am to 4:30pm.

6 Shopping

Grafton Street, a pedestrians-only zone near Trinity College, is a chic shopping district where trendy boutiques, department stores, and specialty shops proliferate. **Powerscourt Townhouse Centre** and **St. Stephen's Green Centre** are this area's newest focal points and prime examples of Dublin's ongoing renovation and gentrification. In the **Temple Bar area** are unusual shops selling Asian and Latin American imports, secondhand clothes, and hard-to-find records. North of the Liffey, shopping is best on **O'Connell Street** and **Henry Street.**

RECOVERING VAT

Obtaining a **VAT (value-added tax) refund** is easy in Ireland. Whenever you make a purchase, ask for a **Cashback voucher.** Be aware that there's a handling charge: IR£3.35 ($5) if you spend IR£150 ($240) or less, IR£4.35 ($7) for IR£150 to IR£300 ($240 to $480), and IR£5.35 ($9) for more than IR£300 ($480). You can claim refunds at the airport Cashback windows before you leave the country or by mail after you return home. If you're leaving by ferry, you must mail the Cashback voucher for a refund. Remember that you may have to show your purchases to Customs before leaving the country in order to get the refund, so don't bury them in your luggage. Look for the CASHBACK TAX-FREE SHOPPING sign in shop windows and read the instructions carefully.

If you don't want to carry your purchases while you're traveling, take advantage of the mailing service offered by most shops for an extra charge.

MARKETS

The most interesting city-center market is **Mother Red Caps Market,** Back Lane (☎ **01/454-4655**), in an old shoe factory in the heart of the Liberties, one of Dublin's oldest sections. More than 100 dealers exhibit here, with a good selection of arts and crafts, antiques, used books, and locally produced farm cheeses. It's open Friday and Saturday 10am to 5:30pm.

Of the city's open-air food markets, the **Moore Street Market** is legendary. Just off Henry Street beside the ILAC Shopping Centre, it's supposed to be the market from which Molly Malone wheeled her wheelbarrow through streets broad and narrow. Today vendors shout for attention to sell fruits, vegetables, flowers, and fish Monday to Saturday 9am to 6pm . . . or until supplies run out.

WOOLENS SHOPS

Irish woolens are world renowned, and you'll delight at the range of wool merchandise available. Machine-knit scarves, hats, and sweaters can be reasonably priced, with higher prices reserved for tweeds and hand-knit sweaters. Try **Blarney Woolen Mills,** 21–23 Nassau St., Dublin 2 (☎ **01/671-0068**); **Dublin Woolen Mills,** 41 Lower Ormond Quay, Dublin 1 (☎ **01/677-5014** or 01/677-0301); or **Cleo,** 18 Kildare St., Dublin 2 (☎ **01/676-1421**).

BOOKSTORES

This city of literary legends has quite a few fine bookstores. For new books, try **Fred Hanna,** 27–29 Nassau St., Dublin 2 (☎ **01/677-1255** or 01/677-1936); **Waterstones Bookshop,** 7 Dawson St., Dublin 2 (☎ **01/679-1415**); or **Cathach Books,** 10 Duke St., Dublin 2 (☎ **01/671-8676;** fax 01/671-5120; http://indigo.ie/ ~cathach). For used books, visit **Greene's Bookshop,** 16 Clare St., Dublin 2 (☎ **01/676-2554;** fax 01/678-9091); or **The Winding Stair,** 40 Lower Ormond Quay, Dublin 1 (☎ **01/873-3292**).

7 Dublin After Dark

From singing pubs to buskers to Broadway-style theater, Dublin offers a wealth of after-dark activities. To find out what's going on, pick up the biweekly *In Dublin* magazine for IR£1.50 ($2.40). Here you'll find listings for music performances, stage productions, movie theaters, museum and gallery exhibits. The magazine can also be found online at **www.indublin.ie/**.

THE PERFORMING ARTS

Dublin has been known as a theater center since the **Abbey Theatre,** Lower Abbey Street (☎ **01/878-7222;** E-mail: abbey@indigo.ie; www.abbey_theatre.ie), opened in 1904 with William Butler Yeats as its first director. The current theater was built in 1966, 15 years after the original burned down. The box office is open Monday to Saturday 10:30am to 7pm, and tickets cost IR£8 to IR£15 ($12 to $24), with reductions for students Monday to Thursday. In the same building, the **Peacock** (☎ **01/878-7222**) is a 150-seat theater featuring contemporary plays and experimental works, including plays in Gaelic.

The recently restored 370-seat **Gate Theatre,** Cavendish Row (☎ **01/874-4368**), just north of O'Connell Street off Parnell Square, was founded in 1928. Today its program includes a blend of modern works and classics. Though less well known by visitors, the Gate is easily as distinguished as the Abbey. The box office is open Monday to Saturday 10am to 7pm, and tickets cost IR£10 to IR£12 ($16 to $19) or IR£7.50 ($12) for previews.

Dublin's main venue for classical music, the **National Concert Hall,** Earlsfort Terrace, Dublin 2 (☎ **01/671-1533**), was originally part of University College, Dublin. The hall stays busy with performances several nights a week for much of the year and is home to the National Symphony Orchestra. The box office is open Monday to Saturday 11am to 7pm, with tickets costing IR£6 to IR£20 ($10 to $32).

With its Victorian jewel-box facade and garish red lobby, the **Olympia Theatre,** 72 Dame St., Dublin 2 (☎ **01/677-7744**), looks as if it should be home to high-stepping cancan girls. However, it's one of Dublin's busier old theaters, hosting everything from contemporary Irish plays to rock concerts. The box office is open Monday to Saturday 10am to 6:30pm, and tickets are IR£7.50 to IR£15 ($12 to $24).

With a seating capacity of 3,000, **The Point,** East Link Bridge, North Wall Quay (☎ **01/836-3633**), is Ireland's newest large theater/concert venue, attracting top Broadway-caliber shows and international stars. The box office is open Monday to Saturday 10am to 6pm, and tickets are IR£10 to IR£50 ($16 to $80).

LIVE-MUSIC CLUBS & PUBS

Dozens of clubs and pubs all over town feature rock, folk, jazz, and traditional Irish music. Check *In Dublin* magazine for club schedules. Two of the most popular rock clubs are the **Baggot Inn,** Baggot Street (☎ **01/676-1430**), and **Whelan's,** 25 Wexford St. (☎ **01/478-0766**). Both are open daily, with live music most nights. Admission is IR£2 to IR£6 ($3.20 to $10).

The center of Irish social life, the pub is the place where Dubliners gather for conversation, music, and foaming pints of local brews. Day and night, the pub is for Dubliners an extension of the household, both dining room and parlor. Though pub meals are rarely exciting, they're always filling and offer budgeters an inexpensive alternative to the city's restaurants.

Many pubs host live music at night, usually beginning around 9pm and continuing to 11pm. This is as likely to be country western as the traditional Irish music most visitors prefer to hear, so ask around or walk the streets listening for the sound of the fiddle or uilleann pipes—you're sure to find what you're seeking. Pub hours are daily 10:30am to 11:30pm in summer, to 11pm in winter.

Brazen Head, 20 Lower Bridge St., Dublin 8 (☎ **01/679-5186**), is a couple of long blocks past Christ Church Cathedral and down by the Liffey. At Dublin's oldest pub there are several rooms, each with a slightly different atmosphere. You can have a quiet pint or a meal in one room and join in the music in another.

Davy Byrne's, 21 Duke St., Dublin 2 (☎ **01/677-5217**), figured prominently in Joyce's *Ulysses* and has been famous ever since. However, don't drop by expecting a turn-of-the-century atmosphere: In this upscale neighborhood, Davy Byrne's has had to go with the flow and remodel in pastels and potted plants.

For fans of traditional Irish music, **O'Donoghue's,** 15 Merrion Row, Dublin 2 (☎ **01/660-7194**), is a must. The Dubliners, one of Ireland's favorite traditional bands, got their start here, and impromptu music sessions are held almost every night.

Though Capel Street is looking a bit down at the heels these days, **Slatterys,** 129 Capel St. (☎ **01/872-7971**), continues to be popular for live music of all types, offered in either the upstairs or the downstairs lounge. Traditional Irish music is still the most popular. There's a small cover charge for the music in the upstairs lounge.

GAY & LESBIAN BARS

A great pub to check out is **The George,** 89 S. Great George's St., Dublin 2 (☎ **01/478-2983**). Upstairs at The George is a club called **The Block** (☎ **01/478-2983**), open Wednesday to Saturday 11pm to 2am, with a cover charge of IR£3 ($4.80); it's a comfortable mixed-age venue with something for everyone. And in the Ormond Hotel, Ormond Quay, is **The Playground at Temple of Sound** (☎ **01/872-1811**), a mainly male club currently open only on Sunday starting at 10:30pm; the cover is IR£5 ($8). **Stonewallz,** The Barracks, Griffith College, South Circular Road, Dublin 8 (no phone), is a women-only club currently open only on Saturday 9pm to 2am; the cover is IR£3 ($4.80).

DANCE CLUBS

Here are the most established cutting-edge clubs (with correspondingly strict door policies): **The Kitchen,** in the Clarence Hotel, 6–8 Wellington Quay, Dublin 2 (☎ **01/677-6178**), open Wednesday to Sunday 11pm to 2am; **POD** ("Place of Dance"), Harcourt Street, Dublin 2 (☎ **01/478-0225**), open Wednesday to Sunday 11pm to 3am or later; and **Lillie's Bordello,** 45 Nassau St., Dublin 2 (☎ **01/ 679-9204**), open daily 11pm to 2am.

There are also a few kinder, gentler clubs with less strict door policies and a mixed-age crowd: **Club M,** in Blooms Hotel, Anglesea Street, Dublin 2 (☎ **01/671-5622**), open Tuesday to Sunday 10pm to 2am; **Ri-Ra,** 1 Exchequer St., Dublin 2 (☎ **01/677-4835**), open daily 11:30pm until late; and **Annabel's,** in the Burlington Hotel, Leeson Street Upper, Dublin 4 (☎ **01/660-5222**), open Tuesday to Saturday 10pm to 2am.

Admission charges for these clubs range from IR£4 to IR£8 ($6 to $13).

8 Side Trips: The Countryside Around Dublin

Bus Eireann, in the Busáras Central Bus Station, Store Street (☎ **01/836-6111**), offers about 20 half- and full-day excursions from Dublin, including a Glendalough and Wicklow Gap tour and a Boyne Valley and North Coast tour that passes through gorgeous countryside and visits Newgrange. The Glendalough tour and the Boyne Valley tour are IR£14 ($22) each.

DALKEY

The attractive seaside town of **Dalkey,** 7 miles south of Dublin, is a great place to spend a day exploring and is easily accessible by DART (IR£2.10/$3.40 round-trip from Connelly Station). You can spend the morning climbing to the tower atop **Dalkey Hill,** with its splendid views of Dublin Bay and the Wicklow Hills, and row out to **Dalkey Island** in the afternoon. To rent a rowboat or arrange a ferry trip to this small island graced with an assortment of ruins and a herd of wild goats, make a visit to **The Ferryman,** Coliemore Road, adjacent to Dalkey Island Hotel (☎ **01/298-2834**), where Aidan Fennel docks his fleet of wooden boats; the ferry is IR£3 ($4.80) adults and IR£2 ($3.20) children, and boat rental is IR£5 ($8) per hour.

DINING   P. D.'s Woodhouse, 1 Coliemore Rd. (☎ **01/284-9399**), is Ireland's first and only oakwood barbecue bistro. The early-bird menu, served 6 to 7pm for IR£9.95 ($16), is modest: burgers, chicken, ribs, and catch of the day, grilled to satisfy discerning budget hunger. The lunch menu is reasonable, with main courses at IR£4.95 to IR£8.95 ($8 to $14). It's open Tuesday to Saturday noon–2:30pm, with two seatings for dinner at 7 and 9:30pm. American Express, MasterCard, and Visa are accepted.

The **Guinea Pig,** 17 Railway Rd. (☎ **01/285-9055**), like its namesake, is small and easily overlooked. With a menu emphasizing whatever is freshest and in season, this is a fine restaurant with a deserved following. It's definitely a splurge, and the only good option for budgeters is the special-value menu, offered Sunday to Friday 6 to 9pm and Saturday 6 to 8pm, priced at IR£12.95 ($21). American Express, Diners Club, MasterCard, and Visa are accepted.

BRAY TO GREYSTONES

Bray in County Wicklow, 14 miles south of Dublin, is a small resort town at the southern end of the DART line. A great day's walking excursion begins with the beautiful ride to Bray on the DART (IR£1.30/$2.10 one-way from Connelly Station). From Bray, walk south, following the footpath that continues along the coast to the seaward side of **Bray Head,** a rocky promontory. This path continues for about 3 miles along the rugged coastline, eventually reaching **Greystones,** the next town. Here you can catch the regional rail train north to Dublin; be sure to check the schedule before departing, as it runs much less frequently than the DART.

DINING   Escape, 1 Albert Walk, Bray (☎ **01/286-6755**), offers innovative vegetarian meals at a price you can afford. Lunch specials are IR£2 to IR£5 ($3.20 to $8), and though the options are somewhat ordinary (jacket potatoes, quiches), they're prepared with a flair for spicing, assuring that each is a delightful and unpredictable experience. Dinner main courses are IR£7 ($11) and may include a Sicilian crêpe filled with an assortment of cheese and roasted vegetables or vegetable lasagna; the menu changes daily, and the evening's offerings are usually posted at 6pm. It's open Tuesday to Saturday noon to 10:30pm and Sunday noon to 8:45pm. No credit cards are accepted.

A short walk from either the bus or the train, **Poppies Country Cooking,** Trafalgar Road, Greystones (☎ **01/287-4228**), is a great place to refresh yourself after a day of exploring. Its menu outsizes the modest 10-table place, which overflows into a lovely flowered tea garden out back when the sun appears. From fist-sized whole-grain scones to vegetarian nut roast, the portions are generous and savory; all items are IR£1.50 to IR£4.95 ($2.40 to $8). It's open Monday to Saturday 10am to 6pm and Sunday 11:30am to 7pm. No credit cards are accepted.

GLENDALOUGH

A large area of County Wicklow, 35 miles south of Dublin, has been designated a national park and enjoys protection from further development. The core of the park is centered around **Glendalough,** an ancient monastic settlement along the shores of two exquisite mountain lakes. The **park information center** (☎ **0404/45425**) at the base of Upper Lake provides details on hiking and touring in the Glendalough Valley and surrounding hills, including maps and route descriptions; April to August it's open daily 10am to 6:30pm, and September it's open only Saturday and Sunday 10am to 6:30pm. Admission to the park and monastic grounds is free, and both are open year-round. If you drive, note that the Glendalough visitor center car park is free, while at the Upper Lake car park there's a charge of IR£1.50 ($2.40) per car.

ACCOMMODATIONS   The Glendalough Youth Hostel, Glendalough, Co. Wicklow (☎ **0404/45342**), has a fabulous location between Upper Lake and Lower Lake, with direct access to the many gorgeous walks in the Glendalough Valley. The house, open year-round, is surrounded by fields and has the feel of an old-style farmhouse. There are two private rooms, a men's dorm, and a women's dorm; the private rooms are IR£10 ($16) and the dorms IR£8 ($13). No credit cards are accepted.

Derrybawn House, Glendalough (☎ **0404/45134;** fax 0404/45109), is a comfortable fieldstone manor in an idyllic parkland setting. The house is also convenient for hikers, with the Wicklow Way (a long-distance hiking path) passing through the property and several trails connecting guests to the Glendalough monastic site and the imposing Derrybawn Ridge. The six double rooms are spacious, bright, and tastefully furnished; a single is IR£32.50 to IR£37.50 ($52 to $60) and a double IR£50 to IR£60 ($80 to $96). Rates include breakfast. No credit cards are accepted.

DINING   **A 200-year-old former schoolhouse serves as the setting for **Mitchell's, Laragh, Glendalough (☎ **0404/45302**), a small restaurant in a garden in sight of the mountains. The menu changes daily but often includes rack of Wicklow lamb with honey-and-rosemary sauce or smoked salmon with spiced saffron-scented sauce. Lunch main courses are IR£4.50 to IR£7.50 ($7 to $12); the fixed-price dinner is IR£16.50 to IR£18.50 ($26 to $30); and afternoon tea is IR£3.75 ($6). Easter to

September, it's open daily 12:30 to 3pm and 7:30 to 9pm for meals; the premises are open daily 9am to 9pm. American Express, MasterCard, and Visa are accepted.

The nearby **Avoca Handweavers Tea Shop,** Avoca (☎ **0402/35105**), is worth a visit for lunch, even if you're not interested in woolens. They prepare wholesome meals that are often surprisingly imaginative for cafeteria fare. Offerings may include mint soup prepared with vegetable stock, accompanied by a deliciously hearty spinach tart, sesame-glazed chicken, or locally smoked Wicklow trout; the menu changes often, and the chefs give free reign to their whimsical fancy. All items are IR£2 to IR£5 ($3.20 to $8), and the shop is open March to October, daily 9:30am to 5pm. American Express, Diners Club, MasterCard, and Visa are accepted.

NEWGRANGE

Just 35 miles north of Dublin is **Newgrange,** the most prominent of a group of ancient tombs in the Boyne River Valley in County Meath. Known in Irish as *Brú na Bóinne* (Palace of the Boyne), Newgrange is Ireland's best-known prehistoric monument and one of the archaeological wonders of Western Europe. Built as a burial mound over 5,000 years ago—long before the Great Pyramids and Stonehenge—it sits atop a hill near the Boyne, massive and impressive. All visits to Newgrange begin at the **Brú na Bóinne Visitor Centre** (☎ **041/24488**) in Slane, County Meath, across the river from Newgrange; admission to the center is IR£5 ($8) adults, IR£3.50 ($6) seniors, IR£2.25 ($3.60) students/children, and IR£12.50 ($20) families and includes a bus ride to Newgrange (it's no longer possible to drive directly to the tomb). The center is open daily: March and April 10am to 5pm, May and September 9am to 6:30pm, June to August 9am to 7pm, October 9:30am to 5:30pm, and November to February 9:30am to 5pm.

ACCOMMODATIONS **Lennoxbrook Farm House,** Kells, Co. Meath (☎ **046/45902**), is on a rambling beef-and-sheep farm 20 miles west of Newgrange. It has been the Mullan family home for five generations, and there's an inviting, homey air about the place. Lennoxbrook is an ideal "home away from home" when touring this historic area. The three doubles without bathroom are IR£36 ($58) and the two doubles with bathroom IR£40 ($64). Visa is accepted.

DINING On the premises of a working farm, the **Newgrange Farm Coffee Shop,** Slane (☎ **041/24119**), is housed in a converted cow house, now whitewashed and skylit. The menu ranges from homemade soups and hot scones or biscuits to sandwiches, with tempting desserts like apple tart and cream, carrot cake, and fruit pies. Food can also be enjoyed in an outdoor picnic area, and there's often live traditional music in summer. All items are IR£2 to IR£5.50 ($3.20 to $9). April to June and September, it's open Sunday to Friday 10am to 5:30pm; July and August, it's open daily 10am to 5:30pm. No credit cards are accepted.

Hudson's Bistro, 30 Railway St., Navan (☎ **046/29231**), decked out in sunny colors and bright pottery, is a treat for travelers through the Navan area. Try the tender Greek lamb kebabs with saffron rice, ratatouille chutney, or the authentic and delicious spicy Thai curry with vegetables. Daily soup and entree specials are offered. The staff is friendly and the chefs gladly accommodate vegetarian requests and food allergies. Lunch main courses are IR£4 to IR£6 ($6 to $10); dinner main courses run IR£8 to IR£12.50 ($13 to $20); and the fixed-price dinner is IR£10 ($16). There's a 10% service charge. The bistro is open Monday to Friday noon to 2:30pm and Tuesday to Sunday 6:30 to 11pm. American Express, MasterCard, and Visa are accepted.

12

Edinburgh & Environs

by Richard Jones

Edinburgh has a long and stormy past. You'll be reminded of it every time you gaze up at Edinburgh Castle, one of Europe's most arresting sights. You'll recall it when you follow in the footsteps of Mary Queen of Scots and Lord Darnley through the Palace of Holyroodhouse. In the Old Town, you'll step from the 20th century back to medieval days when wandering through the web of steep alleys (closes) that look down over rooftops or up to soaring spires and castle battlements. It's this uniqueness that has led Edinburgh to be dubbed the "Athens of the north." In striking contrast to the Old Town's twisted closes are the wide streets and spacious squares and crescents of the Georgian New Town. The Old Town and New Town, joined by the sloping lawns and ancient trees of Princes Street Gardens, make Edinburgh one of Europe's most historically fascinating cities.

Though the citizens of Edinburgh take care to preserve their city's history, they don't ignore their contemporary cultural life. The popular Edinburgh International Festival is held every summer. And during the rest of the year, the theaters, concert halls, live-music clubs, galleries, and museums cater to the Scots' cultural appetite. Every block seems to have its own pub, where you can often hear traditional Scottish music while sipping your pint of ale. Elegant and expensive shops line Princes Street in the New Town, while antiques shops, boutiques, and unusual import stores fill the Old Town.

In 1997, a referendum endorsed a Scottish Parliament, so responsibility for domestic issues and affairs will devolve from Westminster to Edinburgh. Elections will be held in May 1999, and a Parliament building, next to Holyroodhouse, will be completed in 2000 for occupation by a Scottish assembly in 2001. This will make Edinburgh an even more vibrant place to visit.

REQUIRED DOCUMENTS Citizens of the United States, Canada, Australia, and New Zealand need only a valid passport for travel to Edinburgh.

OTHER FROMMER'S TITLES For more on Edinburgh, see *Frommer's Scotland, Frommer's Europe,* or *Frommer's Complete Hostel Vacation Guide to England, Wales & Scotland.*

1 Edinburgh Deals & Discounts

SPECIAL DISCOUNTS

If you plan to use the public buses, be sure to buy a **Daysaver Ticket,** which costs only £2.20 ($3.60) adults and £1.50 ($2.40) children; it's good for 1 day and allows you to use the LRT buses as often as you wish. If you plan to be around for a week, you can get a **City Ridacard** good for unlimited travel at £10 ($16) adults and £6 ($10) children. A Ridacard good for 2 weeks costs £20 ($33) adults and £12 ($20) children.

WORTH A SPLURGE

In Edinburgh, the budget hotels are quite good, the attractions admission fees are low, and you won't improve the quality of the food by paying more. The only things you'll have to splurge on are a good bottle of **single-malt whisky** and an occasional **taxi ride.**

2 Essentials

ARRIVING

BY PLANE   The **Edinburgh Airport** is 8 miles northwest of the city. You may wish to stop by the **Edinburgh Tourist Information Desk** (☎ **0131/333-2167** or 0131/344-3125) here before heading into the city. White double-decker Airlink buses regularly make the 25-minute trip into the city at £3.20 ($5) one-way or £5 ($8) round-trip. Waverley Bridge, the last stop, is centrally located between the Old Town and the New Town.

Airport **taxis** will take you into the city center for about £15 to £18 ($24 to $29). If you can get one of the standard black taxis to give you a ride, you'll save a little money, but these aren't supposed to pick up fares at the airport.

BY TRAIN   The cheapest available ticket is the Super Apex at £35 ($57) round-trip. You can book this from 8 to 2 weeks before you intend to travel: Call ☎ **0044/191-227-5959** or 0345/225-225 from England. From London, the Intercity 225 service takes 4½ hours to reach **Waverley Station,** conveniently located in downtown Edinburgh. Following the exit signs up the auto ramp, you'll find yourself on Waverley Bridge. Princes Street and the New Town will be to your right and the Old Town to your left.

VISITOR INFORMATION

The main **Edinburgh and Scotland Tourist Information Centre,** 3 Princes St. (☎ **0131/557-1700**), is at the corner of Princes Street and Waverley Bridge, above the modern underground Waverley Market shopping center. It's open May, June, and September, Monday to Saturday 9am to 7pm and Sunday 10am to 7pm; July and August, Monday to Saturday 9am to 8pm and Sunday 10am to 8pm; April and October, Monday to Saturday 9am to 6pm and Sunday 10am to 6pm; and November to March, Monday to Saturday 9am to 6pm and Sunday 11am to 6pm. Note that there's also an information desk at the airport (see above).

For information on events while you're in town, pick up a free copy of the monthly *Day-by-Day* at the Tourist Information Centre. It lists events, exhibits, theater, and music. For more detailed listings, buy the biweekly *The List,* available at newsstands for £1.80 ($2.95).

Budget Bests

The best values in Edinburgh are the many **free museums and galleries.** These include the two Royal Museums, the Scottish National Gallery, and the Museum of Childhood. Other budget bests are **free live music** in pubs and clubs and **great lunches** in almost any pub.

Students who want to find out more about the university scene should head over to the **Edinburgh University Student Centre** (☎ **0131/650-2656**), on Bristo Square, where a large notice board lists events of interest. If you're looking for an apartment for a few months or longer, you'll find ads for roommates there.

CITY LAYOUT
It's very easy to find your way around Edinburgh. The city is divided into the **Old Town** atop the rocky Mound and the **New Town.** They're separated by Princes Street Gardens. Dominating the Edinburgh skyline is **Edinburgh Castle,** standing high on a crag at the western end of the Old Town. At the opposite end of the Old Town and connected to the castle by the **Royal Mile,** a single street bearing four names along its length, is the **Palace of Holyroodhouse,** the Scottish residence of Elizabeth II and many past kings and queens.

Princes Street, New Town's main thoroughfare, is bordered on the north side by department stores and some of Edinburgh's most elegant clothing stores. Running the length of Princes Street on the south side is **Princes Street Gardens,** a beautiful park filling the valley between the two city sections.

GETTING AROUND
Edinburgh, especially the narrow lanes and closes of the Old Town, is best explored on foot. Almost everything you'll want to see is either along or just a few blocks from the Royal Mile, along Princes Street, or on the nearby streets of the New Town.

BY BUS   Burgundy-and-white **Lothian Region Transport** (☎ **0131/555-6363**) double-deckers run frequently to all parts of the city and its suburbs. Fares vary according to the number of stops you travel, from 50p to £1.50 (81¢ to $2.45). You're expected to have the correct fare when boarding. Deposit your coins in the slot beside the driver and take your ticket. Be sure to hang on to this ticket in case an inspector asks to see it.

You probably won't know how many stops you'll be traveling and thus won't know how much to pay. With plenty of change in hand, ask the driver how much the fare is to your destination. Or you can purchase a **Daysaver Ticket** at £2.20 ($3.60) adults and £1.50 ($2.45) children; it's good for 1 day and allows you to use the LRT buses as frequently as you wish. You can buy Daysavers from the driver or from LRT Travelshops. If you're staying for a week, you can purchase a **City Ridacard** good for unlimited travel at £10 ($16) adults and £6 ($10) children; a Ridacard good for 2 weeks is £20 ($33) adults and £12 (S20) children.

From Sunday to Thursday, the buses stop running a little after 11pm, but on Friday and Saturday some buses run all night. The night fare is £1.50 ($2.40).

BY TAXI   Taxi stands are along Princes Street and at Waverley Station. Fares start at £1.70 ($2.80) and cost £1.70 ($2.80) for the first mile and 20p (32¢) per mile thereafter. From 6pm to 6am there's an extra charge of 60p ($1). You can also call ☎ **0131/229-2468** for a cab.

What Things Cost in Edinburgh	U.S. $
Taxi from the airport to the city center	24.45
Local telephone call	.15
Double room at the Balmoral (deluxe)	317.00
Double room at the Terrace (moderate)	101.06
Double room at the Castle Guest House (budget)	75.00
Lunch for one at Tiles Bistro (moderate)	11.40
Lunch for one at the Baked Potato Shop (budget)	5.30
Dinner for one, without wine, at the Pompadour Room (deluxe)	57.05
Dinner for one, without wine, at Chez Jules (moderate)	25.45
Dinner for one, without wine, at the Queen St. Oyster Bar (budget)	13.05
Pint of beer	2.85
Coca-Cola	1.65
Cup of coffee	1.50
Roll of ASA 100 color film, 36 exposures	7.00–8.00
Admission to Edinburgh Castle	9.80
Movie ticket	6.70
Cheapest ticket at the King's Theatre	8.15

BY BICYCLE   Because Edinburgh is built on a series of hills and ridges, biking around the city is hard in places but fun, and exploring the surrounding countryside by bike is pleasant. **Bike Trax,** 13 Lochrin Place (☎ **0131/228-6333**), rents bicycles for £10 to £15 ($16 to $39). Its staff will also help you pick out a route for a day's cycling. It's open 10am to 5:30pm: daily in summer and Monday and Wednesday to Saturday in winter. You can reach the shop by bus nos. 11, 15, 16, or 17 from Princes Street; get off by the Cameo Cinema.

BY RENTAL CAR   For excursions farther afield, you might want to rent a car. In addition to the major international car-rental agencies, all of which have representatives in Edinburgh, you can try **Condor Self Drive,** 45 Lochrin Place (☎ **0131/229-6333**), which offers its smallest cars for about £19.95 ($33) per day with unlimited mileage. **Melville's,** 9 Clifton Terrace, Haymarket (☎ **0131/337-5333**), offers a rate of £23 ($37) per day.

FAST FACTS: Edinburgh

American Express   The office is at 139 Princes St. (☎ **0131/225-7881**), open Monday to Friday 9am to 5:30pm and Saturday 9am to 4pm.

Baby-sitters   Your best bet is **Guardians Baby-sitting,** 13 Eton Terrace (☎ **0131/343-3870**).

Banks   There are several banks along Princes Street that'll change money, offering the best exchange rate and charging a small commission. The **Royal Bank of Scotland,** 142–144 Princes St. (☎ **0131/226-2555**), is open Monday, Tuesday, Thursday, and Friday 9:15am to 4:45pm; Wednesday 10am to 4:45pm; and Saturday 10am to 1pm.

Country & City Codes

The **country code** for the United Kingdom is **44.** The **city code** for Edinburgh is **131;** use this code when you're calling from outside the United Kingdom. If you're within the United Kingdom but not in Edinburgh, use **0131.** If you're calling within Edinburgh, simply leave off the code and dial only the regular phone number.

Business Hours Most **shops** are open Monday to Saturday 10am to 5:30 or 6pm (to 7:30pm Thursday) and Sunday 11am to 5:30pm. Some smaller shops may close for lunch. **Offices** are open Monday to Friday 9am to 5pm.

Consulates The consulate of the **United States** is at 3 Regent Terrace (☎ 0131/556-8315), which is an extension of Princes Street beyond Nelson's Monument. The consulate of **Canada** is at Standard Life House, 30 Lothian Rd. (☎ 0131/220-4333). Visitors from New Zealand should contact their High Commission in London (see "Fast Facts: London," in chapter 17).

Currency Exchange There are currency exchange counters at the Tourist Information Centre in Waverley Market, at Waverley Station, and at many banks on Princes Street and the Royal Mile. The banks charge a lower fee. For a currency exchange chart, see "Fast Facts: London," in chapter 17.

Emergencies If you need a doctor or dentist, check the Yellow Pages or ask at your hotel. For **police** assistance or an **ambulance,** dial ☎ **999.** There are no 24-hour pharmacies in Edinburgh. **Boots,** 48 Shandwick Place (☎ **0131/ 225-6757**), is open Monday to Saturday 8am to 9pm and Sunday 10am to 5pm.

Holidays Edinburgh celebrates New Year's Day (January 1), January 2, the first Monday in May, May 8 (Victoria Day), Christmas Day (December 25), and Boxing Day (December 26), and the spring and autumn bank holidays, in mid-April and mid-September, respectively.

Hospital The **Royal Infirmary,** 1 Lauriston Place (☎ 0131/536-1000), is one of the most convenient hospitals.

Laundry & Dry Cleaning In the Dalkeith Road area is **Capital Launderette and Drycleaners,** 208 Dalkeith Rd. (☎ 0131/667-0825), open Monday to Friday 8:30am to 5pm and Saturday 8:30am to 4pm. For dry cleaning, try **Johnston's,** 23 Frederick St. (☎ 0131/225-8095), open Monday to Friday 8am to 5:30pm and Saturday 8:30am to 4pm.

Mail The **Central Post Office** is at 2–4 Waterloo Place, at the north end of North Bridge. It's open Monday to Friday 9am to 5:30pm and Saturday 9am to 12:30pm.

Taxes For details on VAT refunds, see "Shopping," later in this chapter.

Telephone **Public phones** cost 10p (16¢) for the first 3 minutes and accept coins of various denominations. You can also purchase a phonecard, for use in special phones at post offices and newsstands. A 3-minute phone call to the United States will cost about £4.50 ($7). Alternatively, you can reach an AT&T operator, and receive U.S. rates for collect or credit-card calls, by dialing toll-free ☎ **0800/89-0011.**

Tipping In most restaurants, tax and service charge are included, so it's unnecessary to leave a tip. If a service charge hasn't been included in the bill, the standard tip is 10%. Taxi drivers also expect a 10% tip.

3 Accommodations You Can Afford

Despite the city's relatively small size and great popularity with visitors, there are surprisingly few budget hotels in the center. Indeed, Edinburgh's best accommodation deals are 15 to 20 minutes by foot from Waverley Station.

The cheapest accommodations in Edinburgh, aside from hostels, are home stays. People with an extra bedroom or two in their home will take in paying guests for about £22 ($35) per person per night. Home stays are generally available only in summer but occasionally in other months as well. The **Edinburgh and Scotland Tourist Information Centre,** 3 Princes St. (☎ **0131/557-1700**), has a list of hundreds of home stays, and its staff will also make reservations for you for £3 ($4.80).

Note: You can find most of the lodging choices below plotted on the map included in "Seeing the Sights," later in this chapter.

IN THE CITY CENTER

Castle Guest House. 38 Castle St., Edinburgh EH2 3BN. ☎ **0131/225-1975.** 8 units, none with bathroom. TV. £21–£23 ($34–$37) single; £42–£46 ($68–$75) double. Minimum stay 2 nights July–Aug. Rates include full breakfast. No credit cards. Bus: All buses.

Mr. and Mrs. J. C. Ovens have been accepting guests into their 200-year-old home for more than 40 years. The rooms are all quite cozy and have tea-making facilities and central heating. You can choose from among five breakfasts. The Castle Guest House is less than 2 blocks from Princes Street and about 10 minutes on foot from Waverley Station. The street affords an excellent view of the castle.

Elder York Guest House. 38 Elder St., Edinburgh EH1 3DX. ☎ **0131/556-1926.** 13 units, 4 with bathroom. TV. £25–£27 ($40–$44) single without bathroom; £40–£44 ($65–$72) double without bathroom, £54 ($88) double with bathroom. Rates include full breakfast. MC, V. Bus: All buses.

It's a steep climb up to this guesthouse occupying the top floors of an old five-story town house. The rooms are small but adequately furnished, with comfortable chairs, new wallpaper, and tea- and coffee-making facilities. The breakfast room is pleasant but the staff somewhat weary. The hotel is only a couple of blocks from Waverley Station and right beside the intercity bus terminal.

Princes Street East Backpackers. 5 W. Register St., Edinburgh EH2 2AA. ☎ **0131/556-6894.** 110 beds, no units with bathroom. £24 ($39) double; £9.50 ($15) dorm bed, discounted to £7 ($11) per night for stays of 2 weeks. MC, V. From Waverley Station, turn left onto Princes St., right onto Andrew St., then right onto W. Register St.

Opened in 1994 by a young German-American, this hostel occupies several floors of a small building a block behind Edinburgh's main shopping street. It can accommodate about 250 people in either single or twin rooms or in dorms sleeping 4 to 10. Kitchen and laundry facilities are available, as is a TV/video lounge with a large video library. Sunday dinners are free.

Another hostel operated by the same management is **Princes Street West,** 3–4 Queensferry St., Edinburgh EH2 4PA (☎ **0131/226-2939**). Its dorm beds are £10 ($16) and doubles £13 ($21) per person.

16 Lynedoch Place. 16 Lynedoch Place, Edinburgh EH3 7PY. ☎ **0131/225-5507.** Fax 0131/332-0224. 4 units, all with bathroom. TV. £35–£40 ($57–$65) per person per night. MC, V. Bus: All buses.

A short walk from the west end of Princes Street, this 1821 home retains all its original architectural elements: sash windows, shutters, pine doors, moldings, cornices, and marble fireplaces. You'll be treated to modern comforts like central heating, hair

---

Getting the Best Deal on Accommodations

- Be aware that home stays, usually available only in summer, are generally cheaper than hotel rooms—check the tourist office for availability.
- Take advantage of accommodations about a 10- to 15-minute bus ride out of the city center—they tend to be cheaper than those in town.
- Try the guesthouses along Dalkeith Road, near the university residence halls.

---

dryers, and tea- and coffee-making facilities in the rooms, which are attractively furnished with antique armoires and chests. The warm hosts, Andrew and Susie Hamilton, really make you feel at home. A hearty breakfast—fruit, cereals, bacon, eggs, tomatoes, mushrooms, and sausages—is served in the light-filled dining room. The gardens at front and back are a special bonus.

✪ **Terrace Hotel.** 37 Royal Terrace, Edinburgh EH7 5AH. ☎ **0131/556-3423** or 0131/556-1026. Fax 0131/556-2520. 14 units, 11 with bathroom. TV. £25–£27.50 ($41–$45) single without bathroom, £34.50–£37.50 ($56–$61) single with bathroom; £44.00–£48.50 ($72–$79) double without bathroom, £56–£72.50 ($91–$118) double with bathroom. The higher prices apply July–Sept; the lower rates, Jan–Feb. Rates include full breakfast. MC, V. Bus: All buses.

This landmark Georgian, on an elegant and usually pricey street, offers great value. The owner, Annie Mann, is constantly improving her exceedingly clean hotel. The spacious lounge and breakfast room feature beautiful fireplaces, and the sweeping staircase is illuminated by a huge oval skylight. The guest rooms range from roomy to spacious, and most have 14-foot ceilings that make them seem positively immense. The smallest are on the top floor. The hotel is centrally heated, but each room also has an individual heater—a plus on really cold winter days.

SOUTH OF THE CITY CENTER

Crion Guest House. 33 Minto St., Edinburgh EH9 2BT. ☎ **0131/667-2708.** Fax 0131/662-1946. 7 units, 4 with bathroom. TV. £18–£25 ($29–$41) per person single/double without bathroom; £20–£31 ($33–$51) per person double with bathroom. Rates include full breakfast. V. Bus: 3, 7, 8, 30, 31, 63, 69, 80, or 89.

Minto Street is one of Edinburgh's budget guesthouse districts, and the Crion is one of the best on the street. The proprietress, Mrs. Cheape, is friendly and has done much to make her small house as homey as possible. Floral-print draperies with matching valances and bedspreads give the guest rooms a country flavor, while in the breakfast room you'll find classic Edinburgh plasterwork wainscoting and an elegant fireplace. The first-floor rooms make this a good choice for those who have problems with stairs.

✪ **Gifford House.** 103 Dalkeith Rd., Edinburgh EH16 5AJ. ☎ **0131/667-4688.** 7 units, all with bathroom. TV. £25–£45 ($41–$73) single; £48–£68 ($78–$111) double; £63–£120 ($103–$196) triple/quad. Rates include full breakfast. No credit cards. Free parking. Bus: 14, 21, 33, or 82 to Royal Commonwealth Pool.

This old stone home boasts a beautiful stairwell topped by a huge skylight. Mrs. Margaret Dow, the friendly manager, offers large rooms with high ceilings, central heating, tea-making facilities, clock radios, and hair dryers; most have been redecorated recently and contain attractive matching duvets. The rooms in back offer a view of Arthur's Seat and Salisbury Crags. A variety of dishes is available at breakfast, and special diets are catered to.

✪ **Kariba Guest House.** 10 Granville Terrace, Edinburgh EH10 4PQ. ☎ **0131/229-3773.** 9 units, 6 with bathroom. TV. £42 ($68) double without bathroom, £52 ($85) double with bathroom. Rates include full breakfast. No credit cards. Bus: 10 or 27 to Gilmore Place.

This small guesthouse has a warm atmosphere thanks to the owner, Agnes Holligan, who's full of information. A lot of time and energy were put into restoring this Victorian home to its former glory, and the plasterwork cornices and ceilings are particularly attractive. The rooms are furnished in a plain, modern fashion and equipped with tea- and coffee-making facilities. Breakfast is served in the large dining room.

Pollock Halls. St. Leonard's Hall, 18 Holyrood Park Rd., Edinburgh EH16 5AY. ☎ **0131/667-1971** or 0131/667-0662. Fax 0131/662 9479. 1,500 rms. £25–£45 ($41–$73) per person. Rates include full breakfast and showers. Open Mar–Apr and June–Sept. Bus: 14, 21, or 33 to Royal Commonwealth Pool.

For most of the year these are dorms for Edinburgh University, but from March to April and June to the end of September the 1,000 single and twin rooms, plus the close to 500 rooms with private bath, are available to the public. There are plenty of facilities, including a self-service laundry, TV rooms, lounges, and bars. Many rooms have excellent views of the Salisbury Crags and Arthur's Seat. The entrance gate is beyond the Royal Commonwealth Pool complex. Once through the gates, follow the signs to St. Leonard's Hall.

NORTH OF THE CITY CENTER

Ardenlee Guest House. 9 Eyre Place, Edinburgh EH3 5ES. ☎ **0131/556-2838.** 8 units, 6 with bathroom. TV. £22–£30 ($37–$50) single without bathroom; £30 ($49) one person in double with bathroom; £48–£60 ($78–$98) two people in double with bathroom. The lower rates apply to low season. Rates include full breakfast. MC, V. Bus: 23 or 27 to Dundas St.

Next door to the Dene (see below) is this comfortable three-floor guesthouse run by David and Judy Dinse. You'll find attractively decorated large rooms with tea-making facilities. Potted plants are a nice touch. You have your choice of how you'd like your eggs fixed each morning, and they cater to vegetarians and others on special diets.

Blairhaven Guest House. 5 Eyre Place, Edinburgh EH3 5ES. ☎ **0131/556-3025.** 9 units, none with bathroom. TV. £20–£25 ($32–$40) single; £36–£44 ($58–$70) double. Rates include full breakfast. No credit cards. Bus: 23, 27, or 37 to Dundas St.

Though the orange-and-white interior of this basic B&B is austere, this house is relatively well located on a quiet street, and the back rooms overlook an attractive garden. Blairhaven, about a 15-minute walk from the city center, is especially recommendable during the busy summer festival season.

Dene Guest House. 7 Eyre Place (off Dundas St.), Edinburgh EH3 5ES. ☎ **0131/556-2700.** Fax 0131/557-9876. 10 units, 5 with bathroom. TV. £20–£26.50 ($33–$43) single without bathroom; £39–£55 ($64–$90) double without bathroom, £45–£65 ($73–$106) double with bathroom. Rates include full breakfast. MC, V. Bus: 23 or 27 to Dundas St.

Five minutes north of Waverley Station by bus is the Dene, operated by Hamish McDougall and Simone McLauchlan, who've embarked on upgrading and modernizing this Georgian town house and restoring and enhancing its original features. The guest rooms are simply decorated and cozy, and the three four-bed family rooms now have showers. All rooms have tea- and coffee-making facilities and clock radios; hair dryers and ironing facilities are available on request.

Ravensdown Bed and Breakfast. 248 Ferry Rd., Edinburgh EH5 3AN. ☎ **0131/552-5438.** Fax 0131/552-7559. 7 units, all with bathroom. TV. £30 ($49) single; £44–£56 ($72–$91) double; £66–£84 ($108–$137) triple. Rates include full breakfast. No credit cards. Bus: 23 to Clark Rd. or 27 to Golden Acre.

The friendly and helpful proprietors, Mr. and Mrs. Leonardo Welch, operate a pleasant guesthouse offering large, clean rooms. All come with tea-making facilities and comfortable chairs for relaxing. Try to get one of the south-facing rooms—the view of the Edinburgh skyline is magnificent.

WEST OF THE CITY CENTER

Ashdene House. 23 Fountainhall Rd., Edinburgh EH9 2LN. ☎ **0131/667-6026.** 5 units, all with bathroom. TV TEL. £23–£30 ($37–$49) per person. Age 16 and under discounted in parents' room. Rates include full breakfast. No credit cards. Bus: 42 to Mayfield Church.

A comfortable two-story brick Edwardian house, Ashdene is a totally no-smoking B&B on a quiet leafy street about 10 minutes from the city center. The house is exceptionally well kept and regularly renovated—a new dining room and lounge area are the latest improvements. All rooms are equipped with hair dryers and tea-making facilities.

Belford Youth Hostel. 6–8 Douglas Gardens, Edinburgh EH4 3DA. ☎ **0131/225-6209.** Fax 0131/539-8695. 21 units, 110 dorm beds. £30–£35 ($49–$57) double; £9.50–£11 ($15–$18) dorm bed. Breakfast £2 ($3.25). MC, V. Bus: Free shuttle bus to/from downtown in summer only.

In a large renovated stone church complete with stained-glass windows and cathedral ceilings, this is one of the most unusual hostels around. It's also one of the least private, since none of the walls reach to the top of the lofty building, creating dozens of sleeping "cubicles." The doubles are a great value, though. Otherwise, there are 4 to 10 beds per room. A recreation room with a pool table and TV, a bar, a kitchen, and a laundry are available for guests' use.

Beresford Hotel. 32 Coates Gardens, Edinburgh EH12 5LE. ☎ **0131/337-0850.** Fax 0131/538-7123. 10 units, 8 with bathroom. TV. £17.50–£25 ($29–$41) per person without bathroom, £20–£30 ($33–$48.90) per person with bathroom. AE, MC, V.

The proprietors, Donald and Agnes Mackintosh, run the best of the half dozen or so B&Bs on this short block, a stone's throw from the Haymarket BritRail station. Every room in this simple but thoroughly adequate home has a firm bed, a color TV, and tea- and coffee-making facilities. A lounge is available for guests.

Eglinton Youth Hostel. 18 Eglinton Crescent, Edinburgh EH12 5DD. ☎ **0131/337-1120.** 160 beds. £11.50–£12.50 ($19–$20) per night age 18 and older, £9.95–£10.95 ($16–$18) per night age 17 and under. Rates include continental breakfast. MC, V. Closed Dec. Bus: 3, 4, 12, 13, 31, or 44 to Palmerston Place.

This is the larger of the two official hostels in town, about 400 yards from the Haymarket train station and the same distance from the Gallery of Modern Art. There are 180 beds on three centrally heated floors, with accommodations in dorms of 4 to 8 beds each, plus a self-catering kitchen, a TV lounge, a common room, a self-service laundry, and a small grocery. Facilities also include a restaurant/cafeteria with filling though basic fare. Eglinton Crescent is the second left off Palmerston Place.

WORTH A SPLURGE

Greenside Hotel. 9 Royal Terrace, Edinburgh EH7 5AB. ☎ **0131/557-0022.** 15 units, all with bathroom. TV TEL. £30–£40 ($49–$65) single; £50–£80 ($82–$130) double; £25–£40 ($41–$65) per person in family room. Rates include full breakfast. AE, DC, MC, V. Bus: 44.

Royal Terrace is as elegant as its name implies, and at the Greenside you can experience a bit of this at reasonable rates. The guest rooms vary quite a bit from floor to floor, but all have their advantages. In the basement is a suitelike room that extends under the front walk and has an arched ceiling. One back room is absolutely huge and has a comparably large bath. All have hair dryers and coffeemakers. Taffeta wallpaper enlivens the basement breakfast room, where you can choose either a full Scottish breakfast, complete with oat cakes, or a continental breakfast that includes ham and cheese. The neatly landscaped back garden is made for relaxing on summer afternoons.

4 Great Deals on Dining

Edinburgh is basically a meat-and-potatoes town. Most restaurants and pubs serve the same foods you'd find in London. The local specialty is *haggis,* a concoction of the heart, liver, and lungs of a sheep, minced and cooked in the sheep's stomach with oatmeal, onions, and seasonings. Scots love it.

LOCAL BUDGET BESTS

PUB GRUB   Pubs along the Royal Mile and Rose Street, running parallel to Princes Street, offer plenty of local atmosphere and good prices.

The ✪ **Café Royal Bistro,** 17 W. Register St. (☎ **0131/557-4792**), is popular with young workers and students. Behind the Burger King across from Waverley Market, this cafe is above the elegant and much more expensive Café Royal Oyster Bar. Its rooms have an old lived-in feel, and the high ceilings make it feel airy. Excellent prices on such dishes as shrimp scampi, chicken Kiev, gammon steak, and poached salmon make this one of my favorites. A variety of burgers, sandwiches, and baked potatoes is available, and a good breakfast is served from 11am. In the evenings, Trivia Quizzes and other events are staged, including a Friday disco night. MasterCard and Visa are accepted, and it's open daily 10am to 6pm.

In the **Royal Mile,** 127 High St. (☎ **0131/556-8274**), you'll find great traditional Scottish fare, and the location, midway between the castle and the palace, makes it an ideal lunch spot. The daily special includes soup, a main course, vegetables, and a dessert. You can also try *neeps* (turnips) and *tatties* (potatoes). Other items are roast beef, cauliflower with cheese, and pots of mussels with Provençal sauce. MasterCard and Visa are accepted, and it's open daily 12:30 to 2:30pm and 6 to 9:30pm.

AFTERNOON TEA   A day spent exploring the Royal Mile can add up to several miles of walking, so if you find your stamina flagging, duck into **Clarinda's Tea Room,** 69 Canongate (☎ **0131/557-1888**), for the very British experience of afternoon tea (you can have it in the morning, too). This tiny cubbyhole of a tearoom is only steps from Holyroodhouse and is decorated in the manner you'd expect—lace tablecloths, bone china, and antique Wedgwood plates on the walls. There are plenty of teas from which to choose, plus a long list of tempting sweets. Homemade soup, lasagna, baked potato with cheese, salads, and similar dishes are also offered. No credit cards are accepted, and it's open Monday to Saturday 9am to 4:45pm and Sunday 10am to 4:45pm.

CAFETERIAS   All the major department stores along Princes Street have cafeterias serving economical meals. In addition, many of the smaller stores have small cafes with equally good prices.

Bewley's, 4 S. Charlotte St. (☎ **0131/220-1969**), is part of a chain, a stylish place with dark wood and polished brass. It offers some fine cafe fare: baked potatoes with fillings like chili, plus the traditional sausage-and-chips and chicken of the day. These are accompanied by a good selection of vegetables that haven't been overcooked. MasterCard and Visa are accepted, and it's open Monday to Saturday 8am to 6:30pm and Sunday 9:30am to 6:30pm.

Jenner's, 48 Princes St. (☎ **0131/225-2442**), has four restaurants. There are menus posted at the Princes Street doors so that you can decide which one appeals to

Getting the Best Deal on Dining

- Try to have an early evening meal—many of the restaurants listed here close at 5:30 or 6pm.
- Take advantage of the department stores along pricey Princes Street—they're surprisingly inexpensive places to eat.
- Eat pub grub or fast food on Sunday—finding a place to eat on Sunday can be a real problem in Edinburgh.

you. The first-floor **Rose Street restaurant** offers breakfast, salads, and hot dishes like beef bourguignonne and lemon-and-herb chicken breast. The **Princes Street restaurant** offers a roast of the day and several high teas as well as an afternoon cream tea. The **fifth-floor restaurant** serves breakfast, salads, and hot dishes, while the **Precinct** offers such items as lasagna, haddock and french fries, and grilled salmon with lemon-and-dill butter. Access, American Express, Diners Club, and Visa are accepted. It's open Monday, Wednesday, Friday, and Saturday 9am to 5:30pm; Tuesday 9:30am to 5:30pm; and Thursday 9am to 7:30pm.

The **Netherbow Cafe,** 43 High St., Royal Mile (☎ **0131/556-9579**), is a pleasant spot in summer, when you can sit out on the terrace. The chalkboard menu behind the counter proffers good soups, light quiches, and assorted light fare like burgers, baked potatoes, and heroes. Breakfast items and afternoon cream teas are also available. American Express, MasterCard, and Visa are accepted. It's open Monday to Saturday 9:30am to 4:30pm (to 7:30pm in summer, depending on the theater schedule).

IN THE CITY CENTER

Baked Potato Shop. 56 Cockburn St. ☎ **0131/225-7572.** Potatoes £2.35–£3.20 ($3.85–$5). No credit cards. Daily 9am–9pm. Bus: All buses. STUFFED POTATOES.

Little bigger than a closet, with seating for only four, the Baked Potato Shop is primarily a takeout place. The potatoes are huge and stuffed with hot and cold vegetarian fillings (such as curry or cauliflower and cheese) or with chili. However, try the vegetarian haggis—it tastes just like the real thing.

Café Byzantium. 9 Victoria St. ☎ **0131/220-2241.** Sandwiches £1.75–£2.50 ($2.85–$4.05); buffet lunch £3.75 ($6); lunch main courses £3–£3.75 ($4.90–$6). No credit cards. Mon–Sat 10am–5:30pm. Bus: All buses. INDIAN/ENGLISH.

On the top floor of an antiques/kitsch market in the middle of trendy Victoria Street, this popular Indian-owned buffet-style restaurant is a terrific choice. Under a Victorian-era vaulted ceiling are about two dozen tables usually filled with young trendies and older Edinburghers. Meals range from croissants and toasted sandwiches to heartier fare like Indian curries, macaroni and cheese, and fish-and-chips. The portions are large, and few meals top £5 ($8).

Chez Jules. 29 Cockburn St. ☎ **0131/225-7007.** Main courses £5.50–£8.00 ($9–$13). MC, V. Daily 6–11pm. Bus: All buses. FRENCH.

This restaurant is an offshoot of the Pierre Victoire chain, moderately priced French restaurants with imaginative menus. What Chez Jules lacks in elbow room it more than makes up for in food. You can get a big pot of mussels for £3.40 ($4.80). It's all very French, with candles, red-and-white-checked tablecloths, and Gallic accents, making for a pleasant dining experience. There's another Chez Jules at 61 Frederick St. (☎ **0131/225-7983**).

Cornerstone Café. In St. John's Church, Princes St. at Lothian Rd., West End. ☎ **0131/229-0212.** Main courses £1.75–£4.25 ($2.80–$7). No credit cards. Summer, Mon–Fri 11am–9pm, Sat noon–9pm; winter, Mon–Sat 9:30am–3:45pm. Bus: All buses. VEGETARIAN.

A church crypt is the unlikely location of this quality cafe serving well-priced home-made soups, salads, quiches, baked potatoes, and sandwiches. A quiet oasis in the busiest part of town, the Cornerstone is an excellent alternative to department-store fare, and there's outdoor seating during warm weather.

✪ **Helios Fountain.** 7 Grassmarket. ☎ **0131/229-7884.** Meals £2–£3.50 ($3.25–$6). MC, V. Mon–Sat 10am–6pm, Sun noon–4pm (to 8pm during the Festival). Bus: All buses. VEGETARIAN.

Beyond the New Age store selling books, toys, and other gifts you'll find a comfortable cafe where you can select from several vegetarian dishes and salads made fresh daily. Among the dishes you might find anything from baked potato with cheese and tofu pie to a specialty called red dragon pie (a warming blend of adiki beans, vegetables, and wheatberry in tomato sauce topped with mashed potato). Great desserts and cakes, too.

✪ **Henderson's Salad Table and Wine Bar.** 94 Hanover St. ☎ **0131/225-2131.** Meals £3.35–£5.50 ($5–$9). AE, MC, V. Mon–Sat 8am–10:45pm, Sun noon–6pm. Bus: All buses. VEGETARIAN.

This is an excellent change from the meat-and-potatoes diet. A delicious assortment of salads (served by the scoop) and hot meals is available all day in this large basement restaurant. Batik and stained-glass room partitions, nightly live jazz or similar music, and colorful wall hangings create a relaxing atmosphere. Tempting cakes and pies and a large variety of herbal teas are ideal for afternoon tea or dessert. About a dozen wines are served by the glass.

Jekyll and Hyde. Brodie's Close, 304 Lawnmarket, High St. No phone. Meals £3.25–£6 ($5–$10). No credit cards. July–Aug daily 10am–7pm; Sept–June Mon–Sat 10am–4pm. Bus: All buses. INTERNATIONAL.

If you know your Edinburgh history, you'll recognize the name attached to this narrow close—Deacon Brodie was the stealthy criminal who inspired Robert Louis Stevenson's *The Strange Case of Dr. Jekyll and Mr. Hyde*. The kitchen of this spartan cafe is more than 700 years old, while the dining room dates back only 400 years. Imaginative sandwiches and simple lunches are the mainstays. Try the smoked salmon pâté or herring sandwich with sour cream or stop by for a cappuccino and a pastry.

✪ **Maxies Bistro.** 32B W. Nicolson St. ☎ **0131/667-0845.** Lunch £3.95 ($6) for 2 courses, £4.95 ($8) for 3 courses; dinner £5.95–£11.95 ($10–$19). MC, V. Mon–Sat 11am–midnight. Bus: All buses. CONTINENTAL.

Near the George Square University buildings, Maxies is a popular student lunch and evening spot. It's downstairs, making for a cozy cellarlike atmosphere. There's a selection of about 28 wines by the glass, plus good food. The chalkboard menu changes daily, but you'll find hearty soups and dishes like cauliflower with cheese, beef bourguignonne, stir-fried beef, prawns, and pheasant, pigeon, and other game in season—all decently prepared and a good value.

✪ **Queen Street Oyster Bar.** 16A Queen St. (at Hanover). ☎ **0131/226-2530.** Main courses £3.50–£4.00 ($6–$7). MC, V. Mon–Sat noon–1am, Sun 6:30pm–1am. Bus: All buses. INTERNATIONAL.

Without a recommendation from a knowledgeable local, you could easily overlook this seven-table basement bar, where dark woods and delicious aromas combine to create one of the most appealing budget finds in town. Winning appetizers are smoked mussels with horseradish, raw local oysters, and venison pâté. Fish, meat, and vegetarian specials change daily. Spicy chili (made with fresh oysters), ratatouille niçoise (mixed vegetables in tomato sauce), and smoked trout salad (the whole trout) are always available, as are Guinness Stout and a variety of ales.

Tiles Bistro. 1 St. Andrew Sq. (1 block north of Princes St.). ☎ **0131/558-1507.** Main courses £5–£7 ($8–$11). MC, V. Mon–Thurs 11am–11pm, Fri–Sat 11am–midnight, Sun (summer only) noon–6pm. Bus: All buses. SCOTTISH/CONTINENTAL.

This stunning bar/brasserie features beautiful tiled columns and arches, stained glass, an ornate ceiling, and a polished wooden bar with half a dozen "real ales." Both bright and lively, Tiles is particularly busy at lunch, when businesspeople and others dine on appetizers like mussels in herbed cream, smoked salmon, and deep-fried Brie. Main courses include chicken-and-ham pie, roast lamb in rosemary sauce, zucchini-and-mushroom bake, kebabs, lamb chops, and lasagna.

✪ **Whigham's Wine Cellars.** 13 Hope St., Charlotte Sq. ☎ **0131/225-8674.** Meals £5.50–£8 ($9–$13). AE, MC, V. Mon–Thurs noon–midnight, Fri–Sat noon–1am (Sun in summer). Bus: All buses. SCOTTISH/SEAFOOD.

This is an appealing spot at the west end of Princes Street. At night, the tables in the cellar alcoves are lit with candles, making for romance. There's a good selection of wines and fine dishes that range from sweet honey-roasted ham to beef Stroganoff and pasta with garlic and mushrooms in a cream, tomato, and chive sauce. Try the smoked trout, oysters, or crab pâté to start.

PICNICKING

In the basement of **Marks & Spencer,** 54 Princes St. (☎ 0131/225-2301), stands cooler after cooler of freshly made sandwiches, salads, pasta salads, cakes, cookies, fruits, vegetables, and anything else you might want. Best of all, the prices are extremely low. No credit cards are accepted. It's open Monday and Tuesday 9:30am to 7pm, Wednesday and Friday 9am to 7pm, Thursday 9am to 8pm, and Saturday 8:30am to 6pm. Enjoy your picnic fixings in the **Princes Street Gardens,** across the street. If you feel like taking a walk before eating, head up to the top of Salisbury Crags or Arthur's Seat.

WORTH A SPLURGE

Witchery by the Castle. Castlehill, Royal Mile. ☎ **0131/225-5613.** Main courses £14–£21.50 ($23–$35). AE, DC, MC, V. Daily 6–11:30pm. Bus: 1 or 6. SCOTTISH.

Boasting a long association with witchcraft and once a favored haunt of the legendary Hell Fire Club, this atmospheric candlelit restaurant has much to offer, including a resident ghost. The creative menu changes almost monthly and can include delicious Angus steak, Skye prawns, Tay salmon, scallops, and monkfish. The downstairs Secret Garden restaurant is notable for its stunning hand-painted ceiling depicting the story of the Tarot.

5 Seeing the Sights

Be aware that many museums usually closed on Sunday are open on Sunday during the Edinburgh Festival and some museums open only in summer also are open on public holidays.

Getting the Best Deal on Sightseeing

- Remember to ask about public transport discount cards.
- Take advantage of the Edinburgh for Less Card, which provides discount vouchers for a variety of sights (like the Camera Obscura) and some restaurants, shops, and theaters. It costs £3.95 ($6.43), is valid for two people for 4 days, and is available at the tourist office.
- Note that the Old Town's narrow lanes (wynds) and closes are fascinating and well worth the effort to explore on foot.
- Combine visits to Edinburgh's free attractions listed below with the climb through Holyrood Park to Arthur's Seat, which at 823 feet offers a truly breathtaking view.

SIGHTSEEING SUGGESTIONS

IF YOU HAVE 1 DAY   Even if you have only 1 day, you can see the two most important sights and maybe a few less important ones. Start at **Edinburgh Castle,** approaching through the Princes Street Gardens, which have a gate opening onto the castle parking lot. This will give you the best feel for the loftiness of Castle Hill. After spending a couple of hours at the castle, head down the **Royal Mile,** stopping at the Royal Mile pub for lunch. Then tour the **Palace of Holyroodhouse,** once the throne of Mary Queen of Scots.

IF YOU HAVE 2 DAYS   With 2 days you can split the **Royal Mile** into two royal half miles, covering one on Day 1 and one on Day 2. This gives you more time to explore the **medieval closes** and stop at the small museums along the way. I recommend **Lady Stair's House, Huntly House, John Knox House, St. Giles's Cathedral,** and (if you have time) a visit to the **Brass Rubbing Centre** to make your own rubbing. On one of your 2 days you should also try to visit the **National Gallery of Scotland** and climb the **Scott Monument,** both in the New Town along Princes Street Gardens.

IF YOU HAVE 3 DAYS   Spend Days 1 and 2 in the Old Town visiting the sights above. On Day 3, take a trip outside the city to see the **Scottish highlands** and a loch or two, preferably **Loch Ness,** for a chance to glimpse Nessie, the elusive creature rumored to live in the depths of those waters.

IF YOU HAVE 5 DAYS   Follow the above, but add to these a day in the New Town visiting the **Georgian House, Royal Museum of Scotland and National Portrait Gallery,** and **Royal Botanic Gardens.** If one of your 5 days happens to be sunny, change your plans and take a picnic lunch up on **Salisbury Crags**—you can't beat the view from up there. The rest of the day, you might visit the **Scottish Gallery of Modern Art** or a few more sights along the Royal Mile.

THE CASTLE & THE PALACE

✪ **Edinburgh Castle.** Castle Hill. ☎ **0131/225-9846.** Admission £6 ($10) adults, £4.50 ($7) seniors, £1.50 ($2.45) children. Apr–Sept daily 9:30am–6pm; Oct–Mar daily 9:30am–5pm. Closed Jan 1–2 and Dec 25–26. Bus: Lawnmarket no. 1 or 6.

Perched on a hill overlooking Edinburgh, the castle constantly draws the eye. Whether it's catching the first rays of the sun, enshrouded in fog, or brightly illuminated at night, Edinburgh Castle is the city's most striking sight. The earliest documented use of this natural redoubt as a fortification dates from the late 11th century, though the

Edinburgh

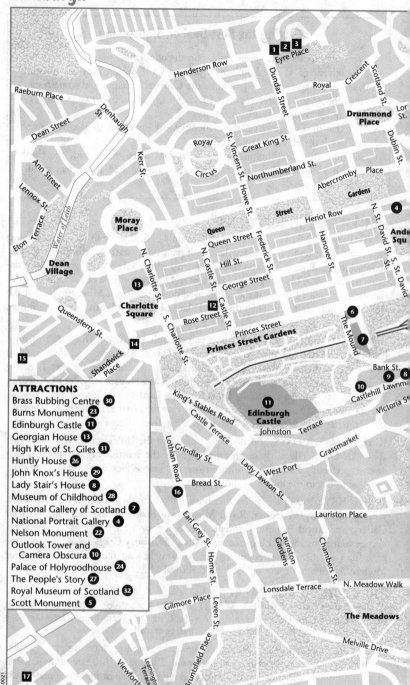

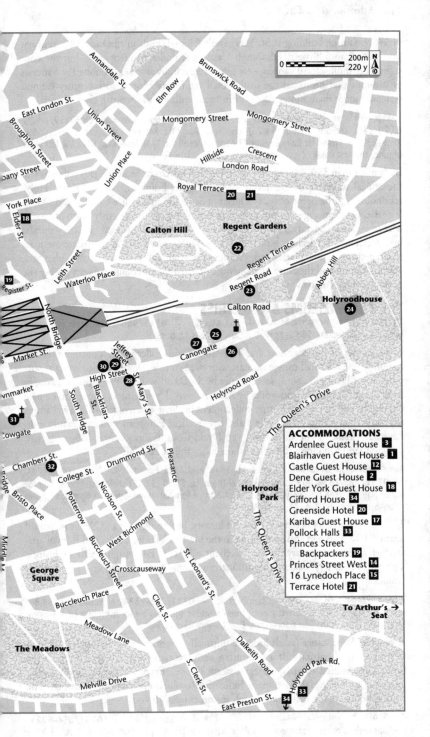

ACCOMMODATIONS

Ardenlee Guest House **3**
Blairhaven Guest House **1**
Castle Guest House **12**
Dene Guest House **2**
Elder York Guest House **18**
Gifford House **34**
Greenside Hotel **20**
Kariba Guest House **17**
Pollock Halls **33**
Princes Street
 Backpackers **19**
Princes Street West **14**
16 Lynedoch Place **15**
Terrace Hotel **21**

To Arthur's →
Seat

345

oldest remaining building is **St. Margaret's Chapel,** built in the early 12th century. For more than 500 years Edinburgh Castle was under frequent siege, but the constantly expanding fortifications were never successfully stormed. Among the batteries of cannons that protected the castle you'll see **Mons Meg,** a 15th-century cannon weighing more than 5 tons. Also within these walls are the Scottish crown jewels.

Palace of Holyroodhouse. Canongate. ☎ **0131/556-1096.** Admission £5.30 ($9) adults, £3.70 ($6) seniors, £2.60 ($4.25) children. Apr–Oct Mon–Sat 9:30am–5:15pm, Sun 9am–4:30pm; Nov–Mar daily 9:30am–3:45pm. Closed Jan 1–3, 2 weeks in May, the last week of June, the first week of July, and Dec 25–26. Bus: 1 or 6.

Built more than 300 years ago for the kings and queens of Scotland, this palace is still the official residence of the queen when she visits Edinburgh each summer. Holyroodhouse was the home of Mary Queen of Scots, Bonnie Prince Charlie, and Queen Victoria. Uniformed guides will delight in describing to you the grisly death of Queen Mary's personal secretary, David Rizzio, who in 1566 was murdered (56 stab wounds) by associates of her jealous husband, Lord Darnley. Elsewhere in the palace are massive tapestries, ornate plasterwork ceilings, a portrait gallery of the Stuart rulers, the Throne Room, and the State Apartments, still used for entertaining guests during the queen's summer residency.

THE TOP MUSEUMS & GALLERIES

✪ **National Gallery of Scotland.** The Mound. ☎ **0131/556-8921.** Free admission. Mon–Sat 10am–5pm, Sun 2–5pm. Bus: Any Princes St. bus.

At the corner of Princes Street and The Mound, this gallery has an outstanding collection for such a small museum. Start with the Scottish galleries, which contain portraits by Sir Henry Raeburn, social scenes by Sir David Wilkies, magnificent seascapes by William McTaggart, and works by Allan Ramsay. If you're lucky enough to be here in January, you can see the Turner collection of brilliant watercolors—displayed annually in that month only. The gallery also has excellent European works by Rembrandt, Raphael, Titian, El Greco, Rubens, van Dyck, Goya, Gainsborough, Monet, Degas, Gauguin, and van Gogh. There's a whole room full of Poussins.

Royal Museum of Scotland and Scottish National Portrait Gallery. 1 Queen St. ☎ **0131/225-7534.** Admission £3 ($4.90) adults, £1.50 ($2.45) seniors/students, free for under age 16. Free for everyone Tues after 5pm. Mon–Sat 10am–5pm (to 8pm Tues), Sun noon–5pm. Bus: 2/12, 4, 4A, 9, or 9A.

The exhibits here all pertain to Scottish history, beginning with the Neolithic period nearly 6,000 years ago and continuing to the present. Viking, Celtic, and Roman artifacts tell a fascinating story that's an excellent adjunct to Edinburgh's medieval history. The portrait gallery contains traditional and some not-so-traditional paintings of famous Scots.

Royal Museum of Scotland. Chambers St. ☎ **0131/225-7534.** Admission £3 ($4.80) adults, £1.50 ($2.45) seniors/students, free for under age 16. Free for everyone Tues 5–8pm. Mon–Sat 10am–5pm, Sun noon–5pm. Bus: Lawnmarket or Tron.

A Venetian Renaissance facade hides an unusually bright and airy Victorian interior at this museum of natural history, industry, and decorative arts 2 blocks south of the Royal Mile. Stuffed animals, minerals, steam engines, Egyptian artifacts, and working models of the engines that made the Industrial Revolution possible are on display. The soaring beauty of the main hall is itself reason enough to visit.

✪ **Scottish National Gallery of Modern Art.** Belford Rd. ☎ **0131/556-8921.** Free admission, except for special exhibits. Mon–Sat 10am–5pm, Sun 2–5pm. Bus: 13 from George St.

Housed in an 1820s neoclassical building, this is Scotland's finest collection of 20th-century art. Its greatest strength is in its holdings of German expressionism, surrealism, and French art, with such masterpieces as Otto Dix's *Nude Girl on a Fur,* Giacometti's *Woman with Her Throat Cut,* and Magritte's *The Black Flag.* The collection also includes works by Picasso, Matisse, Miró, Hockney, Moore, and Lichtenstein. The cafe/dining room is excellent.

Georgian House. 7 Charlotte Sq. ☎ **0131/225-2160.** Admission £4.20 ($7) adults, £2.80 ($4.55) students/children. Easter–Oct Mon–Sat 10am–5pm, Sun 2–5pm. Closed Nov–Apr. Bus: 19, 80, or 81, or walk 2 blocks over from the west end of Princes St.

Edinburgh's New Town is a model of 18th-century urban planning. In contrast to the chaos of the Old City, symmetry reigns in the grand boulevards, parks, squares, and elegant row houses on this side of Princes Street Gardens. Furnished in original Georgian style, this house shows what life was like in the New Town 200 years ago, when this area was indeed new. The furnishings include Chippendale, Hepplewhite, and Sheraton styles, as well as porcelain by Derby and Wedgwood.

MONUMENTS

Scott Monument. E. Princes Street Gardens. ☎ **0131/529-4068.** Admission £1.50 ($2.40). Apr–Sept Mon–Sat 9am–6pm; Oct–Mar Mon–Sat 9am–3pm. Bus: 2/12, 3, 4, 4A, 10, 11, 15, 15A, 16, 43, 44, 80, or 80A.

Looking more like a church spire than a monument to a writer, this Gothic structure dominates East Princes Street Gardens. In the center of the spire is a large seated statue of Sir Walter Scott and his dog, Maida. The monument rises to a height of more than 200 feet. You're treated to a spectacular view of the city from an observation area at the top of 287 steps.

Nelson Monument and the National Monument. Calton Hill. ☎ **0131/556-2716.** Nelson Monument, £2 ($3.20); National Monument, free. Apr–Sept Mon 1–6pm, Tues–Sat 10am–6pm; Oct–Mar Mon–Sat 10am–3pm. Bus: 26, 85, or 86.

Erected in memory of Admiral Horatio Lord Nelson, victor at the Battle of Trafalgar, this 106-foot tower atop Calton Hill was built to resemble a telescope, and it offers superb views over the city. The "Greek" ruins beside the monument are all that was built of a monument to commemorate Scottish soldiers and sailors who died in the Napoleonic Wars. Lack of funds prevented its completion, and now it's one of the most eye-catching structures in the city, going by the name of Edinburgh's Disgrace.

MORE ATTRACTIONS

Between Edinburgh Castle and the Palace of Holyroodhouse, along the **Royal Mile,** are dozens of interesting shops, old pubs, fascinating little museums, and Edinburgh's oldest cathedral. You'll find many of the sights here down the narrow **closes** (alleys) that lead off the Royal Mile. Regardless of whether they have a specific attraction to offer, all the closes are worth exploring simply for their medieval atmosphere.

High Kirk of St. Giles (St. Giles's Cathedral). High St. ☎ **0131/225-9442.** Free admission. May–Sept daily 9am–7pm; Oct–Apr daily 9am–5pm. Bus: 1, 6, 34, 35, 40, or 42.

This is the spiritual heart of the Church of Scotland. A church has existed on this site since the 9th century, and parts of this one date from 1120. Since then, many alterations have changed the building immensely. Scottish religious reformer John Knox, who established the Protestant religion in Scotland, became the minister here in 1560. The unusual main spire is in the form of a thistle, one of the symbols of Scotland. The **Thistle Chapel of the Ancient and Noble Order of the Thistle** was designed by Sir Robert Lorimer in 1910 and features beautifully crafted stone, wood, and glass.

Special & Free Events

For 3 weeks in late August and early September, Edinburgh goes on a cultural binge. The city's most famous event, the ✪ **Edinburgh International Festival,** 21 Market St., Edinburgh EH1 1BW (☎ **0131/473 2000,** or seasonally 0131/ 225-5756; fax 0131/473 2003), encompasses music, dance, opera, performance art, and theater. Tickets are £5 to £50 ($8 to $82) per show, though money-saving series tickets are available. Contact the box office by mail, phone, or fax beginning in April. The dates for the 1999 festival are August 15 to September 4.

Other major events are also held during August:

The **Edinburgh Festival Fringe,** 180 High St., Edinburgh EH1 1QS (☎ **0131/226-5257**), is world famous. Among the 13,000-plus performances are found more offbeat and experimental theatrical performances along with musicals, comedy, kids' shows, cabaret, contemporary music, and more. Tickets cost £3 to £15 ($4.90 to $24), with close to 200 free performances. The **Edinburgh Military Tattoo,** 32 Market St., Edinburgh EH1 1QB (☎ **0131/225-1188;** fax 0131/225-8627), is a military musical extravaganza held on the esplanade in front of the castle just before dusk. The word *tattoo* is derived from the Dutch "taptoe," which means "turn off the taps," a sign that was transmitted by drum beat each evening indicating that the soldiers should return to their barracks and the beer taps should be turned off. Tickets cost £9 to £21 ($14 to $34).

The **Edinburgh International Jazz Festival,** 29 St. Stephen's St., Edinburgh EH3 8DD (☎ **0131/557-1642;** fax 0131/225-3321), features international stars and unknowns at various locales. Tickets are £5 to £25 ($8 to $32). The **Edinburgh International Film Festival,** 88 Lothian Rd., Edinburgh EH3 9BZ (☎ **0131/228-4051**), screens world premieres of films along with an eclectic program. Tickets are £4 to £8 ($6 to $13).

Dubbed the "Cannes for the literary glitterati," the **Edinburgh Book Festival,** 137 Dundee St., Edinburgh EH11 1BG (☎ **0131/228-5444;** fax 0131/228-4333), held in a tented village in Charlotte Square Gardens, was originally held every 2 years but has proved so successful that it's now held every August. Thousands of books are displayed, and more than 250 authors participate in a variety of events. Tickets to most events at the 1998 festival were under £5 ($8), and many of the events were free.

John Knox House. 43 High St. ☎ **0131/556-9579.** Admission £1.75 ($2.80) adults, £1.25 ($2) seniors, 75p ($1.20) children. Mon–Sat 10am–4:30pm. Bus: 1 or 6.

Tradition has it that John Knox, the leader of Scotland's Protestant Reformation, lived here between 1561 and 1572. Built in 1490 and a museum since 1853, this may be the oldest house in Edinburgh. The wooden gallery surrounding the upper floors is the last of its kind in the city. Inside are paintings and lithographs of Knox, along with his letters, sermons, and early tracts.

Huntly House Museum. 142 Canongate. ☎ **0131/529-4143.** Free admission. Mon–Sat 10am–5pm. Bus: 1 or 6.

To learn more about the history of Scotland, and Edinburgh in particular, head for this small museum on Canongate (the lower section of the Royal Mile). In this restored 16th-century town house you'll find collections of silver, glass, and pottery; local archaeology exhibits; and several period rooms.

Writers' Museum. Lady Stair's Close, Lawnmarket. ☎ **0131/529-4901.** Free admission. Mon–Sat 10am–5pm. Bus: Lawnmarket no. 1 or 6.

In Lady Stair's Close off the Lawnmarket, less than 100 yards from the George IV Bridge, this museum is a must for fans of Scottish literature. Robert Burns, Sir Walter Scott, and Robert Louis Stevenson are commemorated with collections of their works, personal effects, and portraits. The house was built in 1622 for a prominent merchant and takes its name from Elizabeth, dowager-countess of Stair, who owned the house in the early 18th century.

Museum of Childhood. 42 High St. ☎ **0131/529-4142.** Free admission. Mon–Sat 10am–5pm. Bus: 1 or 6.

With its displays of antique teddy bears, amazingly detailed dollhouses, riding and pulling toys, board games, and porcelain dolls, this museum is more for adults than for children. However, there are also some video presentations and an activity area that should amuse the kids.

People's Story. 163 Canongate. ☎ **0131/529-4057.** Free admission. Mon–Sat 10am–5pm. Bus: 1 or 6.

Most museums focus on the lives of historical figures and artifacts of the wealthy. This, however, is a people's museum that tells the story of the common folk of Edinburgh from the Middle Ages to the present. Sights, sounds, and even smells are reproduced to surround you with the people's story.

Outlook Tower and Camera Obscura. Castle Hill. ☎ **0131/226-3709.** Admission £3.85 ($6) adults, £3.10 ($5) students, £2.40 ($3.90) seniors, £1.95 ($3.15) children. Apr–Oct Mon–Fri 9:30am–6pm, Sat–Sun 10am–6pm; Nov–Mar daily 10am–5pm. Bus: 1 or 6.

The camera obscura, a device that produces an upside-down image on the wall of a black room, was installed in 1850 and has been a popular attraction ever since. It's like walking inside a huge camera. Also here are exhibits on pinhole photography and holography.

Brass Rubbing Centre. Chalmer's Close, High St. ☎ **0131/556-4364.** Admission 90p–£15 ($1.45–$24) for brass rubbing, depending on brass size. Mon–Sat 10am–5pm. Bus: 1 or 6.

The center provides instruction and replicas of medieval church brasses and Neolithic Scottish stone carvings in all sizes for you to make your own rubbings. There are also ready-made rubbings for sale; rubbings vary in price. The center is housed in an old church and has a number of rubbings and old brasses on display.

Edinburgh Zoo. 134 Corstorphine Rd. ☎ **0131/334-9171.** Admission £6 ($10) adults, £3.80 ($6) seniors, £3.20 ($5) ages 3–14. Apr–Sept Mon–Sat 9am–6pm, Sun 9:30am–6pm; Mar and Oct Mon–Sat 9am–5pm, Sun 9:30am–5pm; Nov–Feb Mon–Sat 9am–4:30pm, Sun 9:30am–4:30pm. Bus: 2, 26, 31, 36, 69, 85, or 86.

The Edinburgh Zoo covers 80 acres of parkland and houses nearly 1,500 animals. The main attraction is the penguin parade, which takes place daily at 2pm April to September. With more than 100 penguins, this is the world's largest self-supporting captive colony, and they're an unforgettable sight when they go for their afternoon stroll. The newest attraction is the 642-yard-long Darwin Maze, shaped like a giant turtle and containing 1,600 yew trees. Information boards tell the story of evolution along the way.

PARKS & GARDENS

Edinburgh is filled with parks and gardens. The largest is **Holyrood Park,** which begins behind the Palace of Holyroodhouse. With rocky crags, a loch, sweeping meadows, and the ruins of a chapel, it's a wee bit of the Scottish countryside in Edinburgh. **Arthur's Seat,** at 823 feet, and the **Salisbury Crags** offer unbeatable views over Edinburgh to the Firth of Forth. This is a great place for a picnic.

The tranquil **Princes Street Gardens** separate the Old Town from the New Town. Old trees and brilliant green lawns fill the valley between the two sections of the city. Along the paved footpaths of the gardens are dozens of wooden benches given by the people of Edinburgh in memory of loved ones. These benches are excellent places to enjoy a picnic lunch or to relax while savoring the views of the city. The gardens are open daily dawn to dusk. Take one of the Princes Street buses.

Edinburgh's 70-acre **Royal Botanic Garden,** Inverleith Row (☎ **0131/552-7171**), is known for its extensive collection of rhododendrons that flower profusely every spring. With a large arboretum, research facilities, and wild areas providing a sharp contrast to the neatly manicured gardens, this is one of Europe's finest botanical gardens. It's also the second oldest botanical garden in Britain, established as a physic garden in 1670 by two physicians. Admission is free. The botanic garden is open daily: April to August 9:30am to 7pm, September 9:30am to 6pm, October 9:30am to 5pm, November to January 9:30am to 4pm, February 9:30am to 5pm, and March 9:30am to 6pm. Take bus no. 8, 19, 23, 27, or 37.

ORGANIZED TOURS

WALKING TOURS Robin's **Edinburgh Tours,** 66 Willowbrae Rd. (☎ **0131/661-0125**), offers four walking tours focusing on different aspects of Edinburgh history. The "Grand City Tour" and "The Royal Mile: Old Town" present a standard historical overview, while the "Ghosts and Witches" and "Dr. Jekyll's Ghosts" tours present a darker side of Edinburgh's history. One tour goes into some underground vaults off the Royal Mile. Tickets are £5 ($8) adults, £4 ($7) students, and £3 ($4.90) children. These tours start in front of the Waverley Market Tourist Information Centre.

Grisly, ghostly tours are an Edinburgh specialty, and among the best is the **Witchery Tour** (☎ **0131/225-6745**), led by highwayman Adam Lyal (deceased). This tour of haunted Edinburgh lasts 1¼ hours, costs £7 ($11) (includes a book), and leaves from in front of the Witchery Restaurant, outside the gate to Edinburgh Castle. Reservations are required. You can expect strange things to happen on this tour of darkest Edinburgh.

BUS TOURS **Scotline Tours,** 87 High St. (☎ **0131/557-0162**), offers a 4-hour tour that covers all the city's most important sights and includes stops at both the castle and Holyroodhouse. Tickets are £9 ($15) adults and £4.50 ($7) children. A less expensive option is to choose Lothian Region's **Edinburgh Classic Tour,** which is a day pass for an open-topped double-decker bus that makes a regular circuit past all the major attractions in both Old and New Town. You can get on and off the bus to visit an attraction and then catch a later bus. Tickets cost £5.50 ($9) adults, £4.50 ($7) students, and £1.50 ($2.45) children and are available on the bus. If you purchase the tour, you'll also be entitled to some discounts on entry fees to attractions and at cafes/restaurants. For information, contact **Lothian Region Transport,** 27 Hanover St., Edinburgh EH2 2DL (☎ **0131/554-4494**).

6 Shopping

Princes Street in the New Town is Edinburgh's main shopping area, with several large department stores and dozens of shops selling designer clothes and other equally expensive items. Also try the Mill Shop store here for bargains in woolens and knitwear. **George Street,** running parallel to Princes Street, has such luxury stores as Austin Reed. **Victoria Street** and **Grassmarket** in the Old Town both have some unusual shops.

Cadenheads Whisky Shop, 172 Canongate, Royal Mile (☎ 0131/556-5864), sells hundreds of whiskys, including a good selection of rare single malts. For Scottish woolens and cashmere, try **Scotch House,** 39–41 Princes St. (☎ 0131/556 1252), or **Designs on Cashmere,** 28 High St. (☎ 0131/556 6394). Edinburgh's largest bookstore is **Waterstone's,** 128 Princes St. (☎ 0131/226 2666).

In shops all over Edinburgh you'll see signs saying TAX-FREE SHOPPING. These signs refer to the process by which you as a visitor can recover the **value-added tax (VAT)** that amounts to about 11% of everything you buy. Usually shops will require a minimum purchase of £30 to £50 ($48 to $80). Once you've filled out the forms, present them to Customs before leaving the country, along with the purchases themselves. After the forms have been stamped by Customs, mail them back to the store with the envelope provided by the store. Within a few weeks your refund will be mailed to your home address in the form you've requested (such as a check in U.S. dollars or a credit on your credit card).

7 Edinburgh After Dark

For a city of its size, Edinburgh offers an array of after-dark activities. Whether your interest is theater, dance, or folk, classical, or rock music, Edinburgh will entertain you for next to nothing. On any given night you might see a play for £5.50 ($9), stop by a pub for a bit of free traditional music, and then head to a dance club (get there before 11pm to get in for £3/$4.90 or less) for some dancing—a jam-packed night out for only £8.50 ($14), not including drinks.

Pick up a free copy of *Day-by-Day* at the Tourist Information Centre at Waverley Market. This pamphlet comes out every month and lists exhibits, theater, music, films, and other information. The best source of listings information is the biweekly *The List,* available at newsstands for £1.80 ($2.95).

THE PERFORMING ARTS

You'll find most of the city's performance venues clustered on or near Lothian Road at the west end of Princes Street. Edinburgh, too, has a West End theater district.

THEATER   This is a fine theater town, with good performances at low prices. The culmination of the theater year is the annual summer **Edinburgh International Festival.** Tickets start as low as £5.50 ($9) at many theaters, and even the most expensive theaters have tickets for under £8 ($13). And it's sometimes possible to catch a free preview. Check *The List* (see above) to find the best deals while you're in town.

The **Festival Theatre,** 13–29 Nicolson St. (☎ 0131/529-6000), is the brand-new glass-fronted showcase for opera, dance, drama, and other entertainment. Guided tours are given, but you'll need to reserve ahead. Tickets are £5.50 to £45 ($9 to $73)—the higher price for opera. The box office is open Monday to Saturday 11am to 6pm (to 8pm on performance nights).

The Victorian **King's Theatre,** 2 Leven St. (☎ 0131/220-4349), has about 1,300 seats and features a wide variety of performances by repertory companies. Ballet, opera, light opera, pantomime, musicals, and drama all showcase here. Tickets are £5.50 to £22.50 ($9 to $37). The box office is open Monday to Saturday 10am to 8pm.

Next to the John Knox House, the **Netherbow Arts Centre,** 43 High St. (☎ 0131/556-9579), is a stage for experimental productions and the best of new Scottish theater. There are occasional lunchtime performances. Tickets cost £3 to £6 ($7 to $10). The box office is open Monday to Saturday 10am to 4:30pm.

Edinburgh's main playhouse, the **Royal Lyceum Theatre,** Grindlay Street off Lothian Road (☎ 0131/229-9697), seats 658 and features contemporary and classical dramas and comedies performed by the resident company. Concessionary tickets of £1 ($1.65) are available on a very limited basis. Otherwise expect to pay £5 to £15 ($8 to $24), with student seats at £5 ($8) Tuesday to Thursday. The box office is open Monday to Saturday 10am to 7pm (to 6pm on nonperformance nights).

You can catch new experimental productions by English and Scottish playwrights, plus dance and comedy, at the contemporary **Traverse Theatre,** Cambridge Street, off Lothian Road (☎ 0131/228-1404). It's one of Britain's best theaters, and its bar and cafe are popular. Tickets cost £5 to £8 ($8 to $13). The box office is open Monday 10am to 6pm, Tuesday to Saturday 10am to 8pm, and Sunday 4 to 8pm.

CLASSICAL MUSIC　There are two major halls: **Usher Hall,** on Lothian Road (☎ 0131/228-8616), where the Royal Scottish Orchestra performs; and the **Queen's Hall,** Clerk Street (☎ 0131/668-2019), an 850-seat concert hall that's the home of the Scottish Chamber Orchestra and also features jazz, folk, rock, and dance. It showcases other groups as well. Check *Day-by-Day* or *The List* for schedules and programs. Tickets at either hall range from £4.50 to £25 ($7 to $41).

LIVE-MUSIC CLUBS

Fans of folk, rock, and jazz can have a field day in Edinburgh, where most clubs offer free live music every night. At most you might have to pay £3 to £7 ($4.90 to $11) on Friday or Saturday for the top local bands. Music usually starts around 11pm. For the greatest concentration of clubs and pubs featuring live music at least 1 night a week, head for **Victoria Street** and **Grassmarket** in Old Town.

For fine traditional music, try **Fiddlers Arms,** 11–13 Grassmarket (☎ 0131/229-2665), 1 block west of the end of Victoria Street. On Monday, local musicians get together to play old favorites in a corner of the pub's front room. Admission is free, and it's open Monday to Thursday 11am to 11pm, Friday and Saturday 11am to 1am, and Sunday 12:30pm to midnight. Located in an old church that has been converted into a commercial building, **Finnegans Wake,** 9A Victoria St. (☎ 0131/226-3816), is one of Edinburgh's most popular spots for Scottish and Irish traditional folk music. Admission is free, and it's open daily 5pm to 1am.

Among live-music rock/pop venues are **La Belle Angèle,** 11 Hasties Close, 231 Cowgate (☎ 0131/225-2774), and **The Venue,** Calton Road (☎ 0131/557-3073). The first is where Oasis made its debut in Scotland. It offers a broad range of sounds—house, Latin, jazz—and all kinds of live bands, including cabaret-style artists like Holly Cole.

PUBS & BARS

There's a pub on nearly every block, and many have live music at least 1 night a week. In all of them, either a pint of ale or a shot of scotch whisky will cost £1.75 to £2.25 ($2.85 to $4.10). Most pubs also serve lunch from noon to 2:30pm. If you want to experience the scene's diversity, stroll along Rose Street (parallel to Princes Street), lined with pubs from Milnes at the east end to Scotts at the West.

The ornate Victorian **Guildford Arms,** 1 W. Register St. (☎ **0131/556-4312**), is popular with an older and more upscale crowd. A glorious plasterwork ceiling and etched-glass windows contribute to the sumptuous decor. The bar features 12 real ales and is open Monday to Wednesday 11am to 11pm, Thursday to Saturday 11am to midnight, and Sunday 12:30 to 11pm. On the same tiny block as the Guildford Arms, the ever-popular **Café Royal,** 17 W. Register St. (☎ **0131/556-1884**), known for its circular bar, appeals to a casual crowd. Stained-glass windows and unusual painted tiles of famous inventors make this a particularly interesting spot. Upstairs in the Café Royal Bistro Bar there's music spun by a deejay every Friday and other occasional entertainment. It's open Monday to Wednesday 10am to 11pm, Thursday to Saturday 10am to midnight, and Sunday 10am to 11pm.

The atmospheric **Green Tree,** 184 Cowgate (☎ **0131/225-1294**), with low ceilings and dark brick walls, is directly under South Bridge, literally in the foundation of the bridge. There's live traditional music on Tuesday at 9:30pm. It's popular with students from the nearby university and is open daily 11am to 12:30am. The small, dark **Malt Shovel,** 13 Cockburn St. (☎ **0131/225-6843**), is an Edinburgh legend that has spawned at least two companion pubs in the area. Besides the free live jazz and traditional music on Tuesday, it has one of the best selections of single-malt whiskys in town. It's open Sunday to Thursday 11am to 12:30am and Friday and Saturday 11am to 1am.

Other notable pubs are the historic **Deacon Brodie's,** 435 Lawnmarket (☎ **0131/225-6531**), and **Greyfriars Bobby,** 34 Candlemaker Row (☎ **0131/225-8328**), named after the famous dog, a Skye terrier who kept a 14-year vigil at his master's grave. And for piano entertainment, head for the sophisticated yet comfortable **Fingers Piano Bar,** 61 Frederick St. (☎ **0131/225-3026**). All three are open daily 11am to 12:30am.

GAY & LESBIAN BARS

The heart of the gay community is centered on **Broughton Street** around the Playhouse Theatre. **Casekudas,** 22 Greenside Place (☎ **0131/558-1270**), is Edinburgh's best-known gay bar. As one local wag put it, "Casekudas answers that eternal question of what's under the kilt." There's a cafe downstairs and a weekend disco upstairs. At 36 Broughton St., the **Blue Moon Cafe** (☎ **0131/556-2788**) is primarily a dining spot where you can linger over a coffee or enjoy a burger, focaccia sandwich, or salad along with a mixed crowd. Nachos, chili, and other snacks are also offered.

Up the street is **C. C. Blooms,** 23–24 Greenside Place (☎ **0131/556-9331**), a popular bar with a dance floor downstairs and karaoke 1 night a week. A few doors down is **Route 66,** 6 Baxters Place (☎ **0131/524-0061**)), a gay pub. There's no dancing here, just quiet conversation depending on the hour (the later it is, the louder it gets).

DANCE CLUBS

Dance clubs in Edinburgh generally open around 10pm and stay open until 3 or 4am. Drinks average £2 ($3.25) for beer or hard liquor, and many offer special drink prices on certain nights or early in the evening.

Club Mercado, 36–39 Market St. (☎ **0131/226-4224**), is popular with under-25s and features mainstream Top 40 dance music. Admission is free Friday to 10:30pm; otherwise it's £5 to £10 ($8 to $16). It's open Friday to Sunday 10:30pm to 3:30am. **Century 2000,** 31 Lothian Rd. (☎ **0131/229-7670**), is Edinburgh's largest disco and one of the most popular. Admission is £3 to £6 ($4.90 to $10), and it's open Wednesday to Sunday 10:30pm to 3am.

8 Side Trips: Burghs & Villages

Lothian Region Transport, 27 Hanover St. (☎ **0131/554-4494**), offers more than 20 excursions from Edinburgh. Among the best is the tour to **Loch Ness** and the **Grampian Mountains,** available only early April to early November and costing £26 ($42) adults and £18 ($29) children. Along the way toward the home of the fabled Loch Ness monster, the coach travels through beautiful mountains, forests, fields, and farmland.

For a less expensive all-day excursion, try the trip to beautiful **Loch Lomond.** In summer, the tour is combined with a visit to either the Argyllshire or the Trossachs mountains. In winter the tour travels through the Argyllshire mountains. The cost is £15.50 ($25) adults and £10.50 ($17) children.

You can also book your tour at the **Ticket Centre** on Waverley Bridge (☎ **0131/555-6363**).

LINLITHGOW

Mary Queen of Scots was born in the royal burgh of **Linlithgow,** a county town in West Lothian, 18 miles west of Edinburgh. Direct **trains** (☎ **0345/484-950**) depart every 15 minutes, and the journey takes about 20 minutes; avoid traveling on the hour since the journey takes longer and involves a change. The round-trip fare is £4.70 ($8) adults and £2.35 ($4) children. **Buses** depart Edinburgh from the station in St. Andrew's Square (☎ **01324/613-777**) every 20 minutes and take around an hour. The round-trip fare is £4.15 ($7) adults and £2.10 ($3.45) children. If you have a **car,** take A902 to Corstorphine and then A8 to M9, exiting at junction 3 to Linlithgow.

You can still explore the roofless ✪ **Linlithgow Palace** (☎ **01506/842-896**), birthplace of Mary Queen of Scots in 1542, even if it's but a shell of its former self. The queen's suite was in the north quarter but was rebuilt for the homecoming of James VI (James I of England) in 1620. The palace burned to the ground in 1746. The Great Hall is on the first floor, and a small display shows some of the more interesting architectural relics. The ruined palace is half a mile from Linlithgow Station (you can walk or take a taxi). Admission is £2.30 ($3.75) adults, £1.75 ($2.85) seniors, and £1 ($1.65) children. It's open April to September, Monday to Saturday 9:30am to 6:30pm and Sunday 2 to 6pm; October to March, Monday to Saturday 9:30am to 4:30pm and Sunday 2 to 4pm.

Just south of the palace stands the medieval *kirk* (church), **St. Michael's Parish Church** (☎ **01506/842-188**), open daily 10am to 4:30pm. It has been where many a Scottish monarch has worshiped since its consecration in 1242. Despite being ravaged by the disciples of John Knox and transformed into a stable by Cromwell, it's one of Scotland's best examples of a parish church.

NORTH BERWICK

The royal burgh of **North Berwick,** created in the 14th century, was once an important Scottish port. In East Lothian, 24 miles east of Edinburgh, it's today a holiday resort popular with the Scots. Visitors are drawn to its golf courses, beaches, and harbor life on the Firth of Forth. You can climb the rocky shoreline or enjoy the outdoor pool in July and August.

Trains (☎ **0345/484-950**) depart from Edinburgh at 37 minutes past the hour for the 30-minute trip. The round-trip fare is £5.50 ($9) adults and £2.75 ($4.50) children. **Buses** to North Berwick (☎ **0131/663-9233**) depart from Edinburgh's Charlotte Square at 3 and 33 minutes past the hour from 8:03am to 5:33pm and take 1¼ hours. The round-trip fare is £2.75 ($4.50) adults and £1.40 ($2.30) children. If you have a **car,** take A198 from Edinburgh straight to North Berwick.

At the **information centre,** Quality Street (☎ **01620/892-197**), you can pick up information on boat trips to the offshore islands, including **Bass Rock,** a volcanic island that's a breeding ground for about 10,000 gannets.

Some 2 miles east of North Berwick (25 miles east of Edinburgh on A198) stand the ruins of the 14th-century diked and rose-colored **Tantallon Castle** (☎ **01620/892-727**). (**Buses** leave from outside the tourist office in North Berwick Monday to Saturday at 9 and 11am and 1 and 3pm and Sunday at 1pm only. The one-way fare is 75p/$1.20.) This castle was the ancient stronghold of the Douglases until its defeat by Cromwell's forces in 1650. Overlooking the Firth of Forth, the castle ruins still are formidable, with a five-story square central tower and a dovecote, plus the shell of its east tower, a D-shaped structure with a wall from the central tower. It's open April to September, Monday to Saturday 9:30am to 6pm and Sunday 2:30 to 6pm; October to March, Monday to Wednesday and Saturday 9:30am to 4pm, Thursday 9:30am to noon, and Sunday 2 to 4pm. Admission is £2.30 ($3.75) adults, £1.75 ($2.85) seniors, and £1.00 ($1.65) children.

DIRLETON

The little town of **Dirleton,** a preservation village 19 miles east of Edinburgh and 5 miles west of North Berwick, vies for the title of "prettiest village in Scotland." The town plan, drafted in the early 16th century, is essentially unchanged today. It has two greens shaped like triangles, with a pub opposite **Dirleton Castle,** placed at right angles to a group of cottages.

Buses (☎ **0131/663-9233**) leave Edinburgh's St. Andrew's Square station at 10 past and 20 to the hour and take 1 hour. The last bus leaves at 5:10pm. The one-way fare is £1.50 ($2.45) adults and 75p ($1.20) children. If you have a **car,** take A198 from Edinburgh straight to Dirleton.

A rose-tinted 13th-century castle with surrounding gardens, once the seat of the wealthy Anglo-Norman de Vaux family, **Dirleton Castle** (☎ **01620/850-330**) looks like a fairy-tale fortification, with its towers, arched entries, and oak ramp. You can see ruins of the Great Hall and kitchen, as well as what's left of the lord's chamber where the de Vaux family lived. The 16th-century main gate has a hole through which boiling tar or water could be poured to discourage unwanted visitors. The castle's country garden and bowling green are still in use. Admission is £2.30 ($3.75) adults, £1.75 ($2.85) seniors, and £1.00 ($1.65) children. It's open April to September, daily 9:30am to 6pm; October to March, Monday to Saturday 9:30am to 4pm and Sunday 2 to 4pm.

13

Florence & Tuscany

by Patricia Schultz

Five hundred years ago, Florence was the nerve center of European culture and life. It was here in the 14th, 15th, and 16th centuries that many of the most important developments in art, science, literature, and architecture took root and flourished. During the Renaissance, Florence was one of the world's richest and most aesthetically beautiful cities. And much of that city remains to be experienced today.

Florence is no longer the axis around which the world revolves, but the taste, elegance, and sensibilities that marked the Renaissance are alive and well. The city boasts Europe's richest concentration of artistic wealth, much of which you can see or sense without even entering its world-class museums. Young Florentines hurry down the narrow cobblestone streets, across the stone-paved piazzas, and past the august palazzi with the same confidence and pride as their forebears. A little of the Medici remains in each of them.

Europe's cultural revolution was financed in large part by the Medicis, Florence's powerful ruling family throughout much of the Renaissance. They came to power as shrewd bankers and used their acumen and wealth to foster artistic and intellectual genius. The city is filled with this heritage: Half a dozen major museums, as well as myriad churches and palazzi, house major paintings and sculpture of that period when Florence was, as D. H. Lawrence said, "Man's perfect center of the Universe."

However, not only the sights and the history make Florence special. The nuts and bolts of where you stay and what you eat will make this city special in- and off-season. Many of the hotels I've listed are in imposing palazzi from the time of the Medicis and Michelangelo. You may find yourself sleeping beneath a ceiling decorated with frescoes whose origins reach back into the centuries or sampling a glass of chianti in the *cantina* of a palazzo built before Verrazano set eyes on New York Harbor. The rustic though delicious cuisine of this region, *cucina toscana,* from the heart of the nation's wine- and olive-producing farmland, is one of Italy's—and the world's—finest.

REQUIRED DOCUMENTS See chapter 23 on Rome.

OTHER FROMMER'S TITLES For more on Florence, see *Frommer's Tuscany & Umbria; Frommer's Italy; Frommer's Italy from $50 a Day; Frommer's Gay & Lesbian Europe; Frommer's Europe;* or *Frommer's Food Lover's Companion to Italy.*

1   Florence Deals & Discounts

SPECIAL DISCOUNTS

Surprisingly, Florence—noble tourist mecca even before the glory days of the Renaissance—isn't a city that has ever felt inclined to offer enticing discounts. Because its centuries-old university and dozens of year-round programs for foreign students increase the need for student-oriented discounts, most students and those under 26 head straight for the local branch of the national **C.T.S. (Centro Turistico Studentesco Giovanile),** via dei Ginori, half a block north of the Church of San Lorenzo (☎ **055/28-97-21** or 055/28-93-70; fax 055/29-21-50), open Monday to Saturday 9am to noon. The crowds and lines will test your patience, but some of the discounts (particularly those on intra-European air travel) can be worth it.

WORTH A SPLURGE

Florence is one of the great culinary centers of Italy. Under "Great Deals on Dining," later in this chapter, you'll find a number of restaurants that are particularly worth a splurge. Nonvegetarians should set aside at least one evening to splurge on Tuscany's specialty, *bistecca alla fiorentina*—expensive but worth it.

Florence also has an outstanding selection of **charming one-of-a-kind hotels.** If you can afford to spend a little bit more on accommodations, you'll inevitably be treated to an extraordinary and memorable stay.

Since the Renaissance, Florence has been known for the impeccable artisanship of its goldsmiths. Invest in a family heirloom and take home a little **Italian gold**—18 karats of beautifully crafted jewelry not easy to come by in the States.

Finally, don't miss the *gelato* **(ice cream).** At about 3,000L ($1.70) per serving, this light, delicious delicacy is worth every lira and calorie. You'll walk it off in a minute (or two).

2   Essentials

ARRIVING

BY PLANE   Alitalia, British Air, Lufthansa, and many other European airlines service Florence's newly expanded **Amerigo Vespucci Airport** (☎ **055/37-34-98**), also called **Peretola** after the zone in which it's located. However, to date there are no direct flights to/from the United States (but there are easy connections through London, Paris, Amsterdam, Frankfort, and so on). The regularly scheduled city **bus no. 62** connects the airport with piazza della Stazione in downtown, making the journey in about 30 minutes; it costs 1,500L (85¢) each way. Slightly more expensive but without the local stops is the hourly **SITA bus** to/from downtown's bus station at via Santa Caterina 15r (☎ **055/48-36-51**), behind the train station; it costs 6,000L ($3.40). Metered **taxis** line up outside the airport's arrival terminal and charge about 25,000L ($14) to most hotels in the city center.

An even larger number of U.S. flights connect in major European cities for Pisa's **Galileo Galilei Airport** (☎ **050/50-07-07**). Frequent 1-hour **train** service to Florence's Stazione Santa Maria Novella costs 9,500L ($5). If your flight leaves from Pisa airport and you'll be going there by train from Florence, you can check in your baggage for all flights and receive your boarding pass at the **Air Terminal** on Track 5 in Florence's S.M.N. train station; show up 30 minutes before train departure.

BY TRAIN   Most Florence-bound trains roll into the **Stazione Santa Maria Novella** (☎ **055/2351**), which you'll often see abbreviated as S.M.N. The station is

---

Budget Bests

You're likely to find bargains on almost everything in this shopper's paradise. The famous **San Lorenzo market** stretches for half a dozen blocks, with hundreds of stalls. Wool mufflers (about $15), sweaters (about $30), and leather jackets (beginning at $200) are the best buys, but budget shoppers will be able to find just about anything here at reasonable prices.

You can always save money on food and drink by consuming them **standing up** at one of the city's ubiquitous bars. Prices double—at least—if you sit down. Florence's abundance of **take-away sandwich spots** and **piazzas with stone seats** make this an easy town to indulge in cheap lunches so that dinners can enjoy more attention.

---

on the western edge of the city's compact historic center, a 10-minute walk from the Duomo and a 15-minute walk from piazza della Signoria and the Uffizi. The city's best budget hotels are immediately east of here.

With your back to the tracks, you'll find an **I.T.A. hotel booking service** office toward the station's left exit next to a 24-hour pharmacy. They'll make hotel reservations for a 3,000L to 10,000L ($1.70 to $6) fee (depending on the hotel's category). It's open Monday to Saturday: April to October 9am to 9pm (to 8pm November to March). The **train information office** is near the opposite exit to your right. Walk straight through the large glass doors into the outer hall for tickets at the *biglietteria* and a bank that changes money Monday to Saturday 8:20am to 7:20pm. Adjacent to Track 16 is an **Albergo Diurno,** or day hotel, where you can wash up or take a shower after a long train ride. At the head of Track 16 is a 24-hour luggage depot where you can drop your bags while you search for a hotel. It charges 2,000L ($1.10) per piece— they won't be accepted if they're not properly closed (no open shopping bags).

Some trains stop at the outlying **Stazione Campo di Marte** or **Stazione Rifredi,** which are worth avoiding. Though there's 24-hour bus service between these satellite stations and the S.M.N. station, bus departures aren't always frequent and taxi service is erratic and expensive.

BY CAR   Driving to Florence is easy; the problems begin once you arrive. Almost all autos are banned from the historic center—only those with special permits are allowed in. You'll likely be stopped at some point by the traffic police, who'll assume from your rental plates that you're a visitor heading to your hotel. Have the name and address of your hotel ready (even better is a written or faxed confirmation), and they'll wave you through. You can drop off baggage at your hotel (they'll give you a sign for your car advising traffic police you're unloading), then you must relocate to a parking lot. Ask your hotel which is most convenient: Special rates are available through many of the hotels I suggest or at some lots. Standard rates are 2,000L to 3,000L ($1.10 to $1.70) per hour; some lots offer a 24-hour rate of 25,000L to 30,000L ($14 to 17). Don't park your car on the street; towing and ticketing are the likely result and they'll set you back substantially—the bureaucracy and headaches are beyond description.

VISITOR INFORMATION

The main train station's **Ufficio Informazioni Turistiche** (☎ 055/28-28-93) distributes fairly good free maps, hotel lists, and so on and is just outside the station. With your back to the tracks, take the left exit, cross onto the concrete median, and turn right; it's about 100 feet ahead. Ask for a copy of *Avvenimenti,* a helpful monthly publication. The office is usually open summer daily 8am to 7:30pm and winter Monday to Saturday 8:15am to 1:45pm.

What Things Cost in Florence	U.S. $
Taxi from the train station to piazza della Signoria	7.80
Public bus from any point within the city to any other point	.80
Local telephone call	.11
Double room at the Excelsior (deluxe)	525.00
Double room at the Torre Guelfa (splurge)	140.45
Double room at the Locanda Orchidea (budget)	46.05
Continental breakfast (cappuccino and croissant standing at a cafe)	2.25
Continental breakfast (cappuccino and croissant at most hotels)	3.95
Lunch for one at Trattoria del Pennello (moderate)	14.05
Lunch for one at Caffè Italiano (budget)	9.00
Lunch for one, standing, at the average bar/cafe	5.00
Dinner for one, without wine, at Sabatini (deluxe)	46.00
Dinner for one, without wine, at Trattoria Antellesi (moderate/splurge)	18.00
Dinner for one, without wine, at Ristorante Acqua al Due (budget)	12.00
Pint of beer (at Fiddler's Elbow)	4.20
Glass of wine (at Chiodo Fisso)	3.40
Coca-Cola to take out (at any cafe in town)	1.40
Cup of cappuccino, standing (at any cafe in town)	1.10
Roll of ASA 100 color film, 36 exposures	5.60
Admission to the Uffizi Galleries	6.75
Movie ticket (at the Astro Cinema)	5.05
Cheapest theater ticket (at the Teatro Communale)	8.45

The city's largest **A.P.T. tourist office** is at via Cavour 1r (☎ **055/29-08-32;** fax 055/29-08-33), about 3 blocks north of the Duomo. This office, less harried than the station offices, offers lots of literature, including up-to-the-minute details on current (sometimes extended) museum hours and concert schedules. It's open Monday to Saturday: summer 8am to 7pm and winter 8am to 2pm. Ignore publications carrying the address of the information office just off piazza della Signoria at chiasso Baroncelli 17r; it relocated in 1998 to an obscure side street just south of piazza Santa Croce, Borgo Santa Croce 29r (☎ **055/23-40-444**). It's open Monday to Saturday 8:15am to 7:15pm. Sunday hours hadn't been decided at press time.

The bilingual *Concierge Information* magazine, free from the concierge desks of top hotels, contains a monthly calendar of events, as well as details on museums, sights, and attractions. *Firenze Spettacolo,* a 3,000L ($1.70) Italian-language monthly sold at most newsstands, is the most detailed and up-to-date listing of nightlife, arts, and entertainment.

CITY LAYOUT

Florence is a compact city that's best negotiated on foot. No two sights are more than a 20- or 25-minute walk apart, and all the hotels and restaurants in this chapter are in the *centro storico* (see below).

The city's relatively small and beautiful *centro storico* (**historic center**) is loosely bounded by the S.M.N. train station to the northwest, piazza della SS. Annunziata to the northeast, piazza Santa Croce to the east, and the **Arno River** to the south. South of the river is the **Oltrarno** ("on the other side of the Arno"), considered an adjunct to the *centro storico*. The following are all found within:

Piazza del Duomo, dominated by Florence's magnificent tricolored cathedral, bell tower, and ancillary baptistery, is at the geographic center of the visitor's city. You'll inevitably walk along many of the streets radiating from this imposing square, the geographic, religious, and commercial nucleus of the city. **Borgo San Lorenzo,** a narrow street running north from the baptistery, is best known for the excellent outdoor market at its far end: Selling everything from marbleized paper-wrapped pencils and boxes to leather bags and jackets, it borders the train station neighborhood, home to a cluster of the city's cheapest hotels.

Via dei Calzaiuoli, Florence's most popular pedestrian thoroughfare and shopping street, runs south from the Duomo, connecting the church with the statue-filled **piazza della Signoria.** West and parallel to this is **via Roma,** which becomes **via Por Santa Maria** on its way to the ponte Vecchio. Midway between the two is **piazza della Repubblica,** a busy shop- and cafe-ringed square surrounded by expensive shopping streets and the central Post Office. Farther west is **via dei Tornabuoni,** the designer-lined Madison Avenue of Florence and its elegant offshoot, **via della Vigna Nuova.**

Exit piazza della Signoria by via Vaccereccia, then turn left for 2 blocks to the pedestrian **ponte Vecchio (Old Bridge),** the Arno's oldest and most famous span. Topped with dozens of tiny goldsmiths' and jewelers' shops, the bridge crosses over to the **Oltrarno,** a neighborhood of artisans and shopkeepers that's best known for the Pitti Palace, just a few blocks past the bridge, and the Boboli Gardens behind it, and lovely piazza Santo Spirito west of that.

Confused? Climb the 414 steps to the top of Giotto's *campanile* (bell tower) that flanks the Duomo and you'll be rewarded with a beautiful eagle's-nest view of Florence; it should help you navigate. For a sunset memory that'll stay with you, view Florence from afar at the hilltop piazzale Michelangiolo or the other high-altitude vantage point of Fiesole.

STREET NUMBERING   Unlike in other Italian cities, there are two systems of street numbering: black *(nero)* and red *(rosso).* Black numbers are used for residential and office buildings, including hotels, while red numbers are used to identify commercial enterprises, including restaurants and stores. In this chapter, red-numbered addresses are indicated by an "r" following the number. Florence is scheduled to eliminate all red numbers, renumber the black, and inevitably create the major confusion that they've resisted for decades. Resistance guarantees that it'll be years before this is put into effect. It's not unusual to find that via Roma 10r, is adjacent to via Roma 157. The addresses used in this chapter don't reflect any future change.

GETTING AROUND

Florence—with almost all of its *centro storico* closed to commercial traffic—is one of the most delightful cities in Europe to explore on foot. A leisurely walk will take you from one end of the tourist area to the other (from the train station to piazza Santa Croce) in about 40 minutes—or 5 hours if you window-shop. The free map given out by the tourist office lacks a street index but may be all you need. The best **full city map** is the yellow-jacketed map by Studio F.M.B. Bologna, available at most newsstands for 7,000L ($3.95).

BY BUS   You'll rarely need to take advantage of Florence's efficient A.T.A.F. bus system, since the city is so wonderfully compact. Bus tickets cost 1,500L (85¢), and you must buy them before boarding. A four-pack *(biglietto multiplo)* runs 5,800L

($3.25) and a **24-hour pass** is 6,500L ($3.65). Tickets are sold at the **A.T.A.F. booth** at the head of Track 14 in the train station (☎ 055/56-50-222) and at tobacco shops *(tabacchi),* bars, and most newsstands. Once on board, validate your ticket in the box near the rear door or you stand to be fined 75,000L ($42) during spot checks, no excuses accepted.

If you intend to use the bus system, the first thing you should do is pick up a bus map at any of the tourist offices. Since most of the historic center is *zona blu* and limited as to traffic, buses make runs on principal streets only, leaving the rest a more enjoyable area in which to stroll. This means, however, that you may be better off just getting around by foot.

BY TAXI   You can't hail a cab but can find one at taxi ranks in or near major piazzas or call one to your restaurant or hotel by dialing ☎ **4242,** 4798, or 4390. Taxis charge 1,500L (85¢) per kilometer, but there's a minimum fare of 6,500L ($3.65) and most hops average about 10,000L to 15,000L ($6 to 8); don't forget to include a 10% tip. Union negotiations were expected to raise rates by the time you get here.

BY BICYCLE   Despite the relatively traffic-free historic center, the alternative of biking found in other European cities has never really caught on. Permanent shops such as **Alinari,** via Guelfa 85r (☎ **055/28-05-00**), rent bikes by the hour (4,000L/$2.25) and day (20,000L/$11), while the city sets up temporary sites about town during summer (look in front of the Biblioteca Nazionale south of piazza Santa Croce on the Arno). Alinari also rents out Vespas to more serious Honda motorpeds by the hour (respectively 9,000L to 40,000L/$5 to $23) or the day (45,000L to 150,000L/$25 to $85).

BY RENTAL CAR   Auto-rental agencies in Florence are centered around the Europa Garage on borgo Ognissanti. **Avis** is at no. 128r (☎ **055/21-36-29**) and **Italy by Car** is nearby at no. 134r (☎ **055/28-71-61**); **Eurodollar** has offices at via il Prato 80r (☎ **055/238-24-80**). Italy by Car has the lowest daily rates, with stick-shift models starting at a steep 100,000L ($56) per day with unlimited mileage, tax not included; all offer special weekend and weekly rates. Most car-rental services have representatives at the Florence and Pisa airports, though you'll probably pay more to pick up a car at the airport and drop it off in town. It's almost always less expensive to book before you leave home.

Florence's historic center, where most hotels are, is off-limits to all vehicular traffic, except that of local residents. **Parking** near the center will cost about 25,000L to 30,000L ($14 to $17) per day. Ask your hotel about the lot most convenient to the hotel; many of the lots offer to pick up and drop off and have a special arrangement with most hotels.

FAST FACTS: Florence

American Express   A new office is east of piazza della Repubblica at via Dante Alighieri 22r (☎ **055/5-09-81**); the smaller original office on via Guicciardini will be closed by the time you arrive. Traveler's checks will be changed without a fee. It's open Monday to Friday 9am to 5:30pm and Saturday 9am to 12:30pm.

Banks   Standard bank hours are Monday to Friday 8:20am to 1:20pm and 2:45 to 3:45pm. The ATM *(bancomat* in Italian) craze has finally hit Italy; call your bank to make sure your card and the number of digits in your PIN are compatible with the Italian system and to get a list of ATMs in Florence. There's an ATM at the train station. Look for privately owned change *(cambio)* offices around town; their rates are often good, but the fine print confesses they usually charge a 3% to 6% and even up to 10% commission according to the size of the transaction. The state rail will change money at any hour at Window 19.

Business Hours   In summer, most **businesses and shops** are open Monday to Friday 9am to 1pm and 3:30 to 7:30pm and Saturday morning only. Mid-September to mid-June, most shops are open Tuesday to Saturday 9am to 1pm and 3:30 to 7:30pm and Monday afternoon only. More and more stores are opting to follow an *orario continuato* ("no-stop" schedule). The exceptions are *alimentari* (small grocery stores), which are open Monday to Saturday but in low season are closed Wednesday afternoon and in high season are closed Saturday afternoon. In Florence, as throughout Italy, just about everything is closed on Sunday, except touristy shops with special permits. **Restaurants** are required to close at least 1 day per week (their *giorno di riposo*), though the day varies. Many serve lunch on Sunday but close for dinner; plan Sunday dinner in advance or you may spend unwanted time looking for an alternative. You may be surprised in late July or August to find that most of them close *per ferie* from 2 to 4 weeks.

Consulates   The consulate of the **United States** is at lungarno Amerigo Vespucci 38 (☎ **055/239-82-76**), near its intersection with via Palestro; it's open Monday to Friday 9am to noon and 2 to 4pm. The consulate of the **United Kingdom** is at lungarno Corsini 2 (☎ **055/28-41-33**), near piazza Santa Trinita; it's open Monday to Friday 9:30am to 12:30pm and 2:30 to 4:30pm. Citizens of **Australia, New Zealand,** and **Canada** should consult their missions in Rome (see "Fast Facts: Rome" in chapter 23). There has been some talk of closing these consulates since 1997, but it will most likely be years before anything is put into effect.

Crime   Petty thefts are performed deftly and swiftly by Florence's Gypsy *(zingari)* population, despite the efforts of plainclothes police. They show up in small groups at the most touristed spots and will jostle or distract you while their cohorts (sometimes no more than 10 years old) relieve you of your valuables. Gypsy and non-Gypsy incidents alike are known to happen at the crowded markets or on public buses.

Currency   See "Fast Facts: Rome" in chapter 23.

Dentists & Doctors   For a list of English-speaking dentists or doctors, ask at the American or British consulate or at the American Express office. Visitors in need of emergency medical care can call **Volunteer Hospital Interpreters** at ☎ **055/234-45-67;** the interpreters are always on call and offer their services free of charge.

Drugstores   Two addresses offering English-speaking service and 24-hour schedules are the **Farmacia Communale,** at the head of Track 16 in the train station (☎ **055/21-67-61**), and **Molteni,** at via dei Calzaiuoli 7r, just north of piazza della Signoria (☎ **055/21-54-72**).

Emergencies   In Florence, as throughout Italy, dial ☎ **113** for the **police.** Some Italians recommend the military-trained **Carabinieri** (call ☎ **112**), whom they consider a better police force. To report a **fire,** dial ☎ **115.** For an **ambulance,** dial ☎ **118.**

Holidays   See "Fast Facts: Rome" in chapter 23. Florence's patron saint, San Giovanni (John the Baptist), is honored on June 24.

Country & City Codes

The **country code** for Italy is **39**. The **city code** for Florence is **055;** use this code when you're calling from outside Italy, within Florence, and within Italy.

Laundry & Dry Cleaning   Florence has a particularly bad track record with self-service Laundromats that shut down as soon as they open. Ask at your hotel where the closest location of the week is located and expect to spend about 12,000L ($7) for one load, wash and dry. They are generally open daily 8am to 8pm.

Mail   Florence's **main post office** is on via Pellicceria, off the southwest corner of piazza della Repubblica. Purchase stamps *(francobolli)* at Windows 21 and 22 (stamps are also sold in almost all *tabacchi*/bars). Letters sent "Fermo Posta" (Italian for General Delivery or *Poste Restante*) can be picked up at Windows 23 and 24 by showing a passport. The post office is open Monday to Friday 8:15am to 7pm and Saturday 8:15am to 12:30pm.

All packages heavier than 1 kilo (2¼ lb.) must be properly wrapped and brought around to the **parcel office** at the back of the building (enter at via dei Sassetti 4, also known as piazza Davanzati). If you're uncertain about the complex parcel-post standards, take your shipment to **Olica,** borgo SS. Apostoli 27r (☎ **055/23-96-917**), off via Por Santa Maria and south of the post office, where they'll box and wrap your shipment for 4,500L to 15,000L ($2.50 to $8) according to size (they follow regular store hours).

Police   Throughout Italy, dial ☎ **113** for the police. Some Italians recommend the Carabinieri (call ☎ **112**), a division of the Italian army, whom they consider a better-trained police force.

Rest Rooms   There are public toilets at the train station, on the ground floor of the Palazzo Vecchio, and in all museums. The cost of a coffee or mineral water will give you access to any bar's facilities, which are reserved for the use of patrons only.

Tax   See "Fast Facts: Rome" in chapter 23.

Telephone   Public **pay phones** accept either coins (100L, 200L, or 500L coins) or a phonecard (sometimes only one or the other). The latter, a *carta telefonica* (or *scheda telefonica*), is available at *tabacchi* and bars in 5,000L ($2.80), 10,000L ($5.60), and 15,000L ($8.50) denominations and can be used for local or international calls. Break off the perforated corner of the card before using it. **Local phone calls** cost 200L (11¢), enough to put you in contact with AT&T, MCI, or Sprint's direct dialing international operators—see Fast Facts: Rome in chapter 23. To make a call, lift the receiver, insert a coin or card, and dial. You may find old pay phones that still accept special tokens, *gettoni,* which you'll sometimes receive in bars in exchange for change, though by now the system is rather extinct.

You can place **long-distance and international phone calls** at the Telecom office north of the Duomo at via Cavour 21r (open daily 8am to 9:45pm). Several countries also have direct operator service, allowing callers to use AT&T or MCI calling cards or call collect (reverse charges) from almost any phone. Consult "Fast Facts: Rome" in chapter 23.

Tipping   See "Fast Facts: Rome" in chapter 23.

3 Accommodations You Can Afford

Many budget hotels are concentrated in the area surrounding the train station. You'll find most of the hotels in this convenient and relatively safe, if charmless, area on noisy via Nazionale and its first two side streets, via Fiume and via Faenza; an adjunct is the area surrounding the Mercato San Lorenzo. The area between the Duomo and piazza della Signoria, particularly along and near via dei Calzaiuoli, is a good though invariably more expensive place to look.

During summer, it's important to arrive early, as many hotels fill up for the next night even before all their guests from the previous day have checked out. If you have trouble with or are intimidated by the language barrier, try the **room-finding office** in the train station, near Track 16 (see "Essentials," earlier in this chapter). Peak season is mid-March to mid-July, September to early November, and December 23 to January 6.

A continental breakfast in an Italian hotel can be one of the great disappointments of budget travel. The usual cost of an unremarkable roll, butter, jam, and coffee is 7,000L ($3.95); you can get coffee and a croissant for about half that (standing) at any cafe. The hotel breakfast is generally not worth the price but in many cases is locked into the rates—and can even be a bargain on occasion.

Note: You can find the lodging choices below plotted on the map included in "Seeing the Sights," later in this chapter.

NEAR THE TRAIN STATION & THE MERCATO SAN LORENZO

Being within easy striking distance of the train station explains the proliferation of cheap to moderately priced hotels in this area; some buildings house as many as six pensione-like (one- and two-star) hotels. This is also the area of the sprawling Mercato San Lorenzo and the Medici Chapels and is generally safe. You're never more than a few blocks from the Duomo.

Albergo Azzi. Via Faenza 56 (1st floor), 50123 Firenze. ☎ **055/21-38-06.** Fax 055/21-38-06. 12 units, 3 with bathroom. 52,000L ($29) single without bathroom; 80,000L ($45) double without bathroom, 100,000L ($56) double with bathroom; 105,000L ($59) triple without bathroom, 118,000L ($66) triple with bathroom; 120,000L ($67) quad without bathroom. Breakfast 6,000L ($3.40). Off-season rates about 20% less. AE, CB, DC, MC, V.

Sandro and Valentino, the new young owners of this ex-pensione also known as the Locanda degli Artisti (Artists' Inn), are musicians and are slowly creating a home-away-from-home for traveling artists, artists manqués, and students. Not for the fastidious or fussy, this venerable place exudes a relaxed bohemian feel—not all the doors hang straight and not all the bedspreads match, though visible strides are being made. In the meantime, the lovely open terrace with a view where breakfast is served in warm weather will disappoint no one. The **Albergo Anna** (8 units, 4 with bathroom) is in the same building—same management, same phone, and similar rates.

✪ **Albergo Centrale.** Via dei Conti 3 (2nd floor; off via Cerretani), 50123 Firenze. ☎ **055/21-57-61.** Fax 055/21-52-16. 18 units, 15 with bathroom. TV TEL. *For Frommer's readers:* 130,000L ($73) single with bathroom; 150,000L ($84) double without bathroom, 180,000L ($101) double with bathroom; 190,000L ($107) triple without bathroom, 230,000L ($129) triple with bathroom. Rates include continental buffet breakfast. Rates discounted Jan 10–Mar 10 and Aug. AE, DC, MC, V.

You'll greatly appreciate the Centrale's bright spacious rooms with matching antique armoires and headboards. Throughout you'll note the careful housekeeping and attentive touches like lace doilies or dried flower arrangements. The presence of

A Note on Special Rates

In this chapter, several hotels, like the Centrale, offer special rates "for Frommer's readers"—look for these words in the rates listings. To avoid any confusion with the hotels, please make it clear on booking or arrival (or both) that you're a Frommer's reader and are requesting the special rates. Note that a hotel's rates may have increased by the time you plan your trip, but it will still offer our readers a discount.

Normandy-born manager Mariethérèse Blot is everywhere in this comfortable pensione in a 14th-century patrician residence called the Palazzo Malaspina, many of whose rooms overlook the Medici Chapels. This is perfect for families; off-season guests who stay for 4 nights minimum pay for only 3. And here you get the most ample buffet breakfast in town at this price.

Albergo Merlini. Via Faenza 56 (3rd floor), 50123 Firenze. ☎ **055/21-28-48.** Fax 055/28-39-39. 10 units, 2 with bathroom. 60,000L ($34) single without bathroom; 80,000L ($45) double without bathroom, 100,000L ($56) double with bathroom; 110,000L ($62) triple without bathroom, 130,000L ($73) triple with bathroom. Breakfast 9,000L ($5). Off-season rates about 15% less. MC, V.

Family-run (with the English-speaking Signora Mary at the helm for more than 40 years), this cozy walk-up is proudly appointed with wooden-carved antique headboards and furnishings setting it apart. The optional breakfast is served on a sunny glassed-in terrace decorated in the 1950s with frescoes by talented American art students. Enjoy your cappuccino with a view of the Medici Chapel's cupola, Florence's many bell towers, and the city's terra-cotta roofscape. This is a notch above the average one-star place.

Albergo Mia Cara. Via Faenza 58 (2nd floor), 50123 Firenze. ☎ **055/21-60-53.** Fax 055/230-26-01. 22 units, 9 with bathroom. For Frommer's readers: Single with/without bathroom (call for rates); 70,000L ($39) double without bathroom, 80,000L ($45) double with bathroom; 94,500L ($53) triple without bathroom, 108,000L ($61) triple with bathroom; 119,000L ($67) quad without bathroom, 136,000L ($76) quad with bathroom. Breakfast 7,000L ($3.95). Ask about off-season discounts. No credit cards.

The only way you'll pay less than at this one-star hotel is at the Noto family's **Archi Rossi Hostel** on the ground floor. You'll find new marble pavements and windows, spacious no-frills rooms, renovated plumbing, and attractive iron headboards—now if they'd only up the wattage of the light fixtures. But who cares when you get lower-than-low prices and good housekeeping? Angela, the English-speaking daughter running both operations, can be reached at the above numbers or ☎ **055/29-08-04** for information regarding the downstairs hostel, where units without bathrooms (22,000L/$12 per person) and with bathrooms (24,000L/$14) sleep four to six.

Albergo Monica. Via Faenza 66B (1st floor; at via Cennini), 50123 Firenze. ☎ **055/28-38-04.** Fax 055/28-17-006. 15 units, 1 with shower only, 10 with bathroom. A/C TV TEL. 80,000L ($45) single without bathroom, 100,000L ($56) single with bathroom; 120,000L ($67) double without bathroom, 180,000L ($101) double with bathroom; 190,000L ($107) triple with shower only, 230,000L ($129) triple with bathroom; 250,000L ($140) quad with bathroom. Rates include buffet continental breakfast. For Frommer's readers: Rates are discounted 5% in high season. Rates are discounted another 40% off-season, which includes Frommer's discount. AE, DC, MC, V.

Gracious co-owners Giovanna Rocchini and her sister and the hotel's polylingual manager, Rhuna Cecchini, have recently supervised the face-lift of their already fine hotel, resulting in a bright airy ambiance and newly redone baths. Their prices have

> ## Getting the Best Deal on Accommodations
>
> - Try one of the budget hotels in the area west of the train station centered around via Faenza and via Fiume.
> - Book early to secure the hotel and price category you want; or once you arrive in town, take advantage of the room-finding office in the train station, near Track 16.
> - Enjoy an inexpensive stand-up breakfast at one of Florence's cafes rather than at your hotel (unless it's obligatory). You have a better chance of avoiding it during off-season, when hotel owners are more flexible.
> - Ask how many rooms share each hallway bath: One or two is minimum traffic but three or four might mean problems with housekeeping. With an ideal one-to-one ratio, the option of a room without a private bath should become a real consideration, as you'll be the only one using it.

increased but so have the amenities, and it's only their train station location that keeps the prices subdued compared to those of competitors nearer the Duomo. Highlights are the terra-cotta floors, the occasional exposed-brick archway, and the wonderful terrazza where breakfast is served the minute the weather turns warm. Most rooms are in the back of the building over the terrace, ensuring a quiet stay and pleasant rooftop views.

Albergo Serena. Via Fiume 20 (2nd floor), 50123 Firenze. ☎ **055/21-36-43.** Fax 055/28-04-47. 7 units, 3 with bathroom. TEL. 85,000L ($48) double without bathroom, 110,000L ($62) double with bathroom; 115,000L ($65) triple without bathroom, 150,000L ($84) triple with bathroom. Continental breakfast 10,000L ($6). Ask about off-season discounts. MC, V.

Run with pride by the Bigazzi family, this unpretentious but dignified one-star place offers pleasant surprises: some brand-new nicely tiled baths, molded ceilings, and turn-of-the-century stained-glass French doors. The rooms are airy and bright and kept clean as a whistle by the owner's wife. If this place is full, try the smaller and less expensive **Otello Tourist House** upstairs (☎ and fax **055/239-61-59**). It has just four simple but lovely units, two with bathroom, and is run by English-speaking Anna and her husband, Otello.

✪ **Hotel Bellettini.** Via dei Conti 7 (off via dei Cerretani), 50123 Firenze. ☎ **055/21-35-61.** Fax 055/28-35-51. A/C TEL. 27 units, 23 with bathroom. 110,000L ($62) single without bathroom, 130,000L ($73) single with bathroom; 150,000L ($84) double without bathroom, 180,000L ($101) double with bathroom; 243,000L ($137) triple with bathroom; 306,000L ($171) quad with bathroom. Rates include buffet breakfast. AE, DC, MC, V.

A huge stone plaque proudly hangs in the wooden-beamed breakfast salon, proof that a hotel has existed in this Renaissance palazzo since the 1600s. Young Gina and Marzia, sisters who are third-generation hoteliers, arrived in 1993 to take over this gem. Terra-cotta tiles and wrought-iron beds decorate most rooms, while the mix of handsome antiques found throughout the two-floor hotel as well as the architectural elements (stained-glass windows, hand-painted wood coffered ceilings) guarantee a distinctive air. Room no. 44 even offers a tiny balcony that, when blooming with jasmine and geraniums by late spring, makes it second best only to room no. 45 with its view of the Medici Chapels and the Duomo's cupola. Breakfast is big, with fresh fruit, sliced ham, homemade breads, sweets, baked goods, and more. Amenities like dry cleaning, laundry service, and baby-sitting are another reason to make this a hotel to remember.

Beware the *Zanzare*

One- and two-star hotels rarely offer air-conditioning, and open windows mean Florentine mosquitoes *(zanzare)*, a local problem that can prove most annoying. Most hotels carry incense-like spirals whose scent seems to keep them at bay.

✪ **Hotel Casci.** Via Cavour 13 (between via de' Gori and via Guelfa), 50129 Firenze. ☎ **055/21-16-86.** Fax 055/239-64-61. E-mail: CASCI@pn.itnet.it. www.traveleurope.it/ h4.htm. 25 units, all with bathroom. TV TEL. 120,000L ($67) single; 170,000L ($96) double; 225,000L ($126) triple; 280,000L ($157) quad. Rates include continental breakfast. Off-season rates 30%–40% less. AE, DC, MC, V.

The arrival of the gracious Lombardi family has transformed this former pensione from a student crash pad into an attractive hotel that aims to please an older, more discerning guest. The firm mattresses are draped in spreads of paisley or floral designs, with coordinated wooden headboards matching the armoires. Signora Lombardi is a stickler for cleanliness—most baths are new and literally gleam. An ambitious crew, the family offers amenities like hair dryers, laundry service, and tour-booking services. The central location means some rooms (with double-paned windows) overlook busy via Cavour, so ask for a room overlooking the inner courtyard's magnolia tree. An ample breakfast buffet is served in a frescoed room, one of the many throwbacks to the past century, when Gioacchino Rossini lived in this palazzo from 1851 to 1855.

Hotel Fiorita. Via Fiume 20 (3rd floor), 50123 Firenze. ☎ **055/28-31-89.** Fax 055/28-36-93. E-mail: htlfior@tin.it. 13 units, 6 with bathroom. A/C TEL. 91,000L ($51) single without bathroom; 119,000L ($67) double without bathroom, 161,000L ($91) double with bathroom; 169,000L ($95) triple without bathroom, 227,000L ($128) triple with bathroom; 281,000L ($158) quad with bathroom. Rates include continental breakfast (not mandatory—deduct 7,000L/$3.95 from rates). Off-season rates about 25% less. Air-conditioning 20,000L ($11) per day. AE, MC, V.

The Maselli family has recently gussied up their one-star place to meet two-star standards, but despite the addition of welcomed amenities (the air-conditioning is a summer blessing), things are still a bit old around the edges. The rooms are unimaginatively decorated, but you'll find a venerable charm in the original stained-glass doors and windows that hint of the palazzo's late 19th-century origins and in the sunny breakfast room. A TV and a minibar are in each room with bath.

✪ **Hotel Nuova Italia.** Via Faenza 26 (off via Nazionale; around the corner from the San Lorenzo Market), 50123 Firenze. ☎ **055/26-84-30** or 055/28-75-08. Fax 055/21-09-41. 20 units, all with bathroom. A/C TEL. *For Frommer's readers:* 120,000L ($67) single; 170,000L ($96) double; 230,000L ($129) triple; 280,000L ($135) quad. Rates include breakfast. Ask about off-season discounts. AE, MC, V.

This top-notch hotel is carefully watched over by the affable English-speaking Luciano and American-born Eileen Viti and their daughter, Daniela. Eileen met Luciano more than 30 years ago, when she stayed at his family's hotel on the recommendation of Arthur Frommer's original *Europe on $5 a Day.* Today the couple is especially welcoming to our readers. The improvement of their hotel is a work in progress and a labor of love: One season triple-paned soundproof windows and ultra-rare mosquito screens were installed; the next, baths were retiled, air-conditioning was installed, and new carpeting was laid. Dry cleaning and laundry service are available, and they'll even arrange for baby-sitting. The family's love of art is manifested in all the framed posters and paintings, and Eileen is a great source about local exhibits. The recent arrival of Daniela's daughter, Rebecca, has secured the fourth generation of Viti hoteliers.

✪ **Pensione Burchianti.** Via del Giglio 6 (off via Panzani), 50123 Firenze. ☎ and fax **055/21-27-96.** 11 units, 5 with shower only, 6 with bathroom. 50,000L ($28) single with shower only, 70,000L ($39) single with bathroom; 100,000L ($56) double with shower only, 120,000L ($67) double with bathroom; 120,000L ($67) triple with shower only, 160,000L ($90) triple with bathroom. Rates include continental breakfast (not mandatory—deduct 5,000L/$3.10 per person from rates). Ask about discounts for groups of 3 students or more, seniors, and off-season. No credit cards.

Opened in the late 19th century by the Burchianti sisters (the last of whom died in 1973) in the noble 16th-century Salimbeni palazzo, this once renowned pensione gets a star for sheer theatricality. It has hosted royals and VIPs (you might get Benito Mussolini's room), and much of that grandeur, now faded around the edges, is intact. Leaded and stained-glass windows and doors, beautifully frescoed walls and ceilings, hand-painted wooden coffered ceilings, and remnants of antique furniture fill the high-ceilinged guest rooms and public areas (steer clear of the two rooms as painstakingly plain as the others are theatrical). If you love nostalgic threadbare romance, you'll be in heaven, but not everyone loves this place. Imaginative plumbing results in the eyesore addition of prefabricated shower stalls stuck in corners and sinks bolted onto precious 19th-century frescoed walls with the toilet down the hall. Yet the pretty sun-filled salon and handsome breakfast room seem right out of a Merchant/Ivory film.

BETWEEN THE DUOMO & THE ARNO

✪ **Hotel Firenze.** Piazza Donati 4 (on via del Corso, off via dei Calzaiuoli), 50122 Firenze. ☎ **055/26-83-01** or 055/21-42-03. Fax 055/21-23-70. 61 units, all with bathroom. TV TEL. 80,000L ($45) single; 120,000L ($67) double; 165,000L ($93) triple; 200,000L ($112) quad. Rates include continental breakfast. No credit cards.

A recent renovation has transformed this former student hangout into a shining two-star hotel with little impact on its consistently low rates—some of the most attractive in town for value. Sitting on its own quiet little piazza amid the *centro storico*'s pedestrian zone of shops and landmark buildings, the hotel is two adjoining palazzi now boasting brightly tiled sunlit rooms that are simply decorated, with the best baths I've seen in this price range. This is a relatively large operation without any of the warmth or ambiance of a smaller family-run hotel, and the concierge and management are efficient but generally uninvolved.

✪ **Locanda Orchidea.** Borgo degli Albizi 11 (1st floor; between the Duomo and the Bargello Museum), 50122 Firenze. ☎ and fax **055/248-03-46.** 7 units, none with bathroom. 55,000L ($31) single; 82,000L ($46) double; 120,000L ($67) triple. No credit cards. Closed Dec 24–26 and 1 or 2 weeks in Aug.

The elegant and friendly English-speaking proprietor, Maria Rosa Cook, will tirelessly recount for you the history of this 13th-century palazzo where Dante's wife, Gemma Donati, was born (Dante's home and the Casa di Dante Museum aren't far away). One of its floors houses an old-fashioned **locanda** (inn) with large rooms thoughtfully decorated with floral bedspreads and white lace touches. You're meant to feel like a guest in her home; women traveling alone feel particularly comfortable. The rooms overlooking a lovely garden and a magnificent wisteria vine are the best, with large windows that let in lots of light; those on the cobblestone Borgo degli Albizi are prone to noise. Signora Cook and Miranda, her take-charge daughter, run a serious operation and discourage partyers.

Pensione Alessandra. Borgo SS. Apostoli 17 (between via dei Tornabuoni and via Por Santa Maria), 50123 Firenze. ☎ **055/28-34-38.** Fax 055/21-06-19. E-mail: htlalessandra@ mclink.it. 25 units, 17 with bathroom. TV TEL. 90,000L ($51) single without bathroom, 120,000L ($67) single with bathroom; 140,000L ($79) double without bathroom, 180,000L

($101) double with bathroom; 190,000L ($107) triple without bathroom, 240,000L ($135) triple with bathroom; 230,000L ($129) quad without bathroom, 300,000L ($169) quad with bathroom. Rates include continental breakfast. AE, MC, V.

The street-level etched-glass doors hint of the architectural significance of the Alessandra's *palazzo nobile*, designed in 1507 by Baccio d'Angnolo, a pupil of Michelangelo. This is a good spot to opt for a room without a bath, since only seven rooms share four nearby communal baths, all large and newly redone. The attentive housekeeping and the spacious high-ceilinged rooms are most welcome, as is the free air-conditioning (request it on reserving; most but not all rooms are equipped). There's a 12:30am curfew, though an all-night concierge can buzz you in after that. Signora Anna and her family run a smooth, lovely operation.

Pensione Maria Luisa de' Medici. Via del Corso 1 (2nd floor; between via dei Calzaiuoli and via del Proconsolo), 50122 Firenze. ☎ and fax **055/28-00-48.** 9 units, 2 with bathroom. 99,000L ($56) double without bathroom, 125,000L ($70) double with bathroom; 137,000L ($77) triple without bathroom, 172,000L ($97) triple with bathroom; 175,000L ($98) quad without bathroom, 220,000L ($124) quad with bathroom. Rates include breakfast. No credit cards.

Named after the last Medici princess, this pensione around the corner from Dante's house is one of Florence's more eclectic and unusual places. The rooms are named after members of the Medici clan, whose recent portraits grace their walls. The owner, Dr. Angelo Sordi (physician, collector, history and design buff), has furnished the rooms with 1960s avant-garde Italian furniture—an unexpected collection contrasting with the museum-quality baroque paintings and sculpture in the large foyer. With enormous rooms sleeping up to five, the Maria Luisa is good for families, who'll also relish the ample breakfast served in the room by Dr. Angelo or his Welsh partner, Evelyn Morris; sustained by eggs, cereal, yogurt, and juice, you shouldn't mind the three-story climb up or down.

Soggiorno Brunori. Via del Proconsolo 5 (2nd floor; south of piazza del Duomo), 50122 Firenze. ☎ **055/28-96-48.** 9 units, 1 with bathroom. 80,000L ($45) double without bathroom, 102,000L ($57) double with bathroom; 108,000L ($61) triple without bathroom, 138,000L ($78) triple with bathroom; 136,000L ($76) quad without bathroom, 174,000L ($98) quad with bathroom. Optional breakfast 9,000L ($5). No credit cards. Closed 1–2 months between Jan and Feb.

The rooms are clean but a bit tired from the wear and tear of countless backpackers, but the prices are among the lowest around. Things are brightened up considerably by the young English-speaking owners, Leonardo and Giovanni, who are friendly, with a wealth of hints they're anxious to share. Their unusually spacious rooms make this a fine selection for backpacking groups. This is a casual place to kick back, with barebone amenities that may not appeal to the après-college crowd: For example, each of the two communal baths is shared by four rooms. You may want to ask for one of the two rooms away from the noisy street, one of the last in this pedestrian zone still open to traffic. There's a 12:30am curfew.

IN THE OLTRARNO
✪ **Pensione la Scaletta.** Via Guicciardini 13 (2nd floor; near piazza de Pitti), 50125 Firenze. ☎ **055/28-30-28** or 055/21-42-55. Fax 055/28-95-62. 12 units, 11 with bathroom. TEL. 75,000L ($42) single without bathroom, 110,000L ($62) single with bathroom; 125,000L ($70) double without bathroom, 160,000L ($90) double with bathroom; 200,000L ($112) triple with bathroom; 230,000L ($129) quad with bathroom. Rates include continental breakfast. Ask about off-season discounts. *For Frommer's readers:* There's a 10%–15% discount if you pay cash (ask on arrival). MC, V.

Order an iced tea and head for the umbrella-shaded rooftop terrace at sunset—then marvel at the stunning 360° panorama. Overlooking the Pitti Palace and housed in one of only two historic palazzi on this street to survive World War II, this comfortable top-floor pensione is efficiently run by Barbara Barbieri and her enthusiastic son, Manfredo. The rooms are clean and spacious but vary greatly in decor and unthreatening mixes of patterns and colors. Those that front busy via Giucciardini have double-paned windows, while the quieter ones in back overlook the Boboli Gardens for 20,000L ($11) per room above the rates above. Manfredo whips up a fixed-price dinner for 20,000L ($11) on request; afterward, you can repair to the terrace for your *vin santo* and sensational views—the real reason for staying here.

Pensione Sorelle Bandini. Piazza S. Spirito 9, 50125 Firenze. ☎ **055/21-53-08.** Fax 055/28-27-61. 14 units, 5 with bathroom. TV TEL. 145,000L ($81) double without bathroom, 175,000L ($98) double with bathroom; 190,000L ($107) triple without bathroom, 230,000L ($129) triple with bathroom. Ask about single/quad rates. Rates include continental breakfast. No credit cards (personal checks from U.S. banks accepted).

This is your chance to live like the noble families of yore. In rooms with 15-foot ceilings, the 10-foot windows and oversize antique furniture are proportionately appropriate. But on closer inspection, you'll see that the resident cats have left their mark on common-area sofas and everything seems a bit ramshackle, musty, and uneven. But that seems to be the point—or so the loyal return guests will have you believe, judging from the students, professors on sabbatical, and families who love the huge lofty-ceilinged rooms (Room 9 sleeps five and offers a view of the Duomo from its bathroom window). Magnificent in its day, this aristocratic 15th-century palazzo's highlight is the pensione's monumental roofed veranda where Mimmo, the English-speaking manager, oversees breakfast and encourages brown-bag lunches and the chance to relax and drink in the marvelous views. But this place isn't for everyone.

A HOSTEL

Ostello Santa Monaca. Via Santa Monaca 6, 50124 Firenze. ☎ **055/26-83-38** or 055/239-67-04. Fax 055/28-01-85. E-mail: s.monaca.hostel@dada.it. 13 units with 8–10 bunk beds; males and females separate. 23,000L ($13) per person, sheets and hot shower included. No credit cards. Bus: 11, 36, or 37 from the S.M.N. train station; get off at the 2nd stop after the bridge. From the train station walk around to piazza Santa Maria Novella; go along via dei Fossi, which begins at the far left corner of the piazza, until it ends at the Arno; cross ponte alla Carraia (bridge) to the Oltrarno and walk along via de' Serragli; via Santa Monaca will be the 3rd right (about a 15-minute walk).

Much more convenient than the remote though beautiful IYHF hostel (**Ostello Villa Camerata,** viale Augusto Righi 2/4, 50137 Firenze; ☎ **055/60-14-51**), this privately run hostel is a lively gathering spot, as well as a great place to trade budget tips and meet travel companions. The rooms are closed 9:30am to 2pm, and the building is locked up 1 to 2pm. You can register 8am to 1pm. There's an airtight 12:30am curfew, and the doors aren't reopened until 6:30am. Breakfast isn't available; the hostel has arrangements at a nearby trattoria for fixed-price meals. Reservations are accepted by fax, e-mail, or letter with a mandatory confirmation 2 days before arrival. Big news at press time was the new self-service laundry room—not cheap at 13,000L ($7) a load, but great for those times when convenience knows no price tag.

WORTH A SPLURGE

Hotel Mario. Via Faenza 89 (1st floor; near via Cennini), 50123 Firenze. ☎ **055/21-68-01.** Fax 055/21-20-39. 16 units, all with bathroom. A/C TV TEL. 200,000L ($112) single; 240,000L ($135) double; 300,000L ($169) triple. Rates include continental breakfast. Off-season rates about 35% less. AE, CB, DC, DISC, MC, V.

In a traditional Old Florence atmosphere, owner Mario Noce and his family run a first-rate ship that has long been a favorite with Frommer's readers. Your room may have a wrought-iron headboard and massive reproduction antique armoire and look out onto a peaceful garden; the rare amenities include hair dryers, fresh flowers, fruit, and an enthusiastic staff. The characterful beamed ceilings in the common areas date from the 17th century, though the building became a hotel only in 1872. I'd award Mario's a star if not for its location—it's a bit far from the Duomo nerve center, something many readers prefer.

✪ **Hotel Torre Guelfa.** Borgo SS. Apostoli 8 (between via dei Tornabuoni and via Por Santa Maria), 50123 Firenze. ☎ **055/239-63-38.** Fax 055/239-85-77. 11 units, all with bathroom. A/C MINIBAR TV TEL. 170,000L ($96) single; 250,000L ($140) double; 300,000L ($169) triple; 330,000L ($185) quad. Rates include continental breakfast. Ask about off-season discounts. AE, MC, V.

To experience the breathtaking 360° view from this new hotel's 13th-century tower justifies these budget-testing prices. This is the tallest privately owned tower in Florence's *centro storico*, and its view is only one reason to stay in this landmark hotel before it applies for three-star status and raises its rates even more. Though you're just two steps from the ponte Vecchio (and equidistant from the Duomo), you'll want to put sightseeing on hold and linger in your canopied iron bed, your room made even more inviting by warm-colored walls and paisley carpeting (for a view similar to the medieval tower's, ask for Room 15 with a huge private terrace). But follow the wafting strains of classical music to the salon, whose vaulted ceilings and lofty proportions hark back to the palazzo's 14th-century origins.

The Torre Guelfa's young owners have created the **Relais Uffizi** (call number above), a sibling hotel a few cobbled lanes away in an evocative alley opening onto the Uffizi Gallery and piazza Signora. Similar in spirit, decor, price, and size (11 rooms), it isn't blessed with a tower, but it does have a lounge area with an unmatched view of the piazza, all housed in a handsome 14th-century refurbished palazzo.

4 Great Deals on Dining

For details on dining in Italy, see the introduction to "Great Deals on Dining" in chapter 23 on Rome.

Judging from the innate elegance of the Florentines and the tony stores that supply their wardrobes, you'd never think the local cuisine would be so unabashedly rustic and simple. In true Tuscan style, when they tell you that theirs is the best and most genuine, you'd best believe them.

Almost all the places below specialize in *cucina povera* or *cucina rustica,* based on the region's agricultural role in history. Slabs of crusty bread are used for *crostini,* spread with chicken-liver pâté as the favorite Florentine antipasto. Hearty Tuscan peasant soups often take the place of pasta, especially *ribollita* (a rich soup of twice-boiled cabbage, beans, and bread) or *pappa al pomodoro* (a similarly thick soup made from tomatoes and drizzled with olive oil). Look for *pasta fatta in casa* (the homemade pasta of the day) or the typically Tuscan *pappardelle,* thick flat noodles often covered with a simple tomato sauce. Your *contorno* (side dish) of vegetables will likely be the classic *fagioli all'uccelletto,* humble pinto beans smothered in a sauce of tomatoes and rosemary or sage, sometimes served plain, simply dressed with virgin olive oil and accompanied by fresh tuna. Tuscans have come down in history known as the "bean eaters" because of their great and timeless love for such a simple dish.

Getting the Best Deal on Dining

- Choose a casual eatery where you'll feel comfortable ordering just one course (easier done at lunch)—though whether a modest pasta dish will satisfy your appetite may be another matter. You won't get the heaping portions common-place in many American restaurants serving Italian food. A *primo* in Italy is meant to be just that: the first of many courses.
- If the weather is nice, grab a *panino* to go, choose a different piazza every day for lunch and a lesson on neighborhood life, and leave more lire for an evening's trattoria experience.
- Order the *menu turistico,* a potential bargain, but first ask about what's included—the selection is often limited and one of the "courses" or *piatti* is probably a vegetable side dish.
- Try the local *vino della casa* (table wine) instead of a finer bottled wine. Better yet, make do with *acqua minerale* and indulge in a leisurely after-dinner drink at a cafe or wine bar.
- Round off your dinner with dessert elsewhere: Order an ice cream to go at a neighborhood *gelateria* and stroll the city's deserted side streets.

Rustic grilled meats are a specialty, the jewel being *bistecca alla fiorentina,* an inch-thick charcoal-broiled steak on the bone: It's usually the most expensive item but is often meant to be shared by two (if you're not a sharer, tell the waiter it's "per una per-sona sola"). Florentines also sing the praises of *trippa alla fiorentina,* but calf's intestines, cut into strips and served with onions and tomatoes, aren't for everyone. Tuscany's most famous red wines are from the designated area known as Chianti between Florence and Siena. You might be pleasantly surprised with the far less expensive *vino della casa* (house wine). A full bottle is brought to the table—you'll be charged *al consumo,* according to the amount consumed. Though you won't swoon over the unfussy and limited desserts, the pudding-like *tiramisù* made with whipped mascarpone cheese is almost always great, if not typically Florentine. But after dinner, walk through the city's quiet streets until you find a *gelateria* (or see the box "Get Thee to a *Gelateria,*" below) and round off your meal with a scoop of one of their myriad flavors, like *riso* (rice) and whisky or a refreshingly unique fruit flavor you'd never find at home, like *cocomero* (watermelon) or *ficchi* (fig).

Keep in mind that in the listings, prices are for a pasta or soup and second course only. Don't forget to add in charges for bread and cover, service, and vegetable side dishes when calculating what you'd expect to pay. Also note that *primi* means pasta and soup courses and *secondi* means main courses. The menu's listing of *contorni* are vegetable side dishes that accompany your entree, which otherwise will appear alone.

LUNCH FOR LESS

Lunch in Florence is your big chance to eat informally, well, and for little, saving your appetite and lire for a special dinner. The traditional cheap lunch will be *panini* sand-wiches—fresh, crusty, and delicious. In Italy, every morsel is edible art and you'll swear you've never had such a delicious $5 lunch. Maybe it's the glass of chianti classico to wash it down.

Alimentari Orizi. Via Parione 19r (off via dei Tornabuoni). ☎ **055/21-40-67.** Sandwiches 4,500L–5,000L ($2.50–$2.80). No credit cards. Mon–Fri 9am–3pm and 5–8pm, Sat 9am–3pm. SANDWICH BAR.

A Note on Restaurant Hours

Almost all restaurants (and stores and offices) close *per ferie* (for vacation) at some point in July or August for 2 to 6 weeks. Which weeks (and how many) may vary from year to year, so call ahead: Your hotel will always know a reliable neighborhood choice if one of my suggestions is closed. Many restaurants also close at some point over the Christmas and New Year's holidays. *Giorno di riposo* is the day each week when the restaurant is permitted to close. A good majority of restaurants serve Sunday lunch but close for Sunday dinner and all day Monday: These meals may need a little advance planning.

Surprisingly few spots will make sandwiches to your specifications and fewer yet will offer the chance to pull up a seat and enjoy it with a glass of wine on the premises at no extra cost. Search out this small *alimentari* (grocery store) just off elegant via dei Tornabuoni, where a choice of crusty rolls and breads and a variety of quality meats and cheeses are sliced and arranged according to your whim. Signor Orizi is now armed with ketchup, mayonnaise, and mustard to accommodate American tastes. There's a bar and half a dozen stools, but if the sun is shining you might ask for your creation *da portare via* ("to take away") and find a nearby piazza bench with a view. The arrival of a new coffee machine and fresh pastries make this a good breakfast option as well.

✪ **Cantinetta del Verrazzano.** Via dei Tavolini 18/20r (off via dei Calzaiuoli). ☎ **055/26-85-90.** Focaccia sandwiches 4,000L ($2.25); wine 2,000L–5,000L ($1.10–$2.80). AE, DC, MC, V. Mon–Sat 8am–9pm. WINE BAR.

Though it looks like it's been here forever, this wood-paneled *cantinetta* (with a full-service bar/*pasticceria* and seating area) helped spawn a revival of stylish wine bars as convenient spots for fast-food breaks Tuscan style. This handsome prototype is owned by the Castello di Verrazzano, one of Chianti's best-known wine-producing estates. It promises a delicious self-service lunch or snack of focaccia, plain or studded with peas, rosemary, onions, or olives, and fresh from the wood-burning oven; buy it hot by the slice or *farcite* (sandwiches "filled" with prosciutto, arugula, cheese, or tuna). Try a glass of any of their full-bodied chianti to make this the perfect respite. For 10,000L ($6) an *assaggio* (tasting or sampling) of Chianti-area salames or wines often makes a delicious appearance. Food selections are always as abundant if you come back for an informal dinner.

NEAR THE TRAIN STATION & THE MERCANTO SAN LORENZO

Nerbone. In the Mercato Centrale, entrance on via dell'Ariento, stand no. 292 (ground floor). ☎ **055/21-99-49.** Sandwiches 4,000L ($2.25); pasta and soup 6,000L ($3.40); meat courses 7,000L ($3.95). No credit cards. Mon–Sat 7am–2pm. ITALIAN.

Every time I stop by, Signor Stagi is proud to remind me that nothing changes at Nerbone—sometimes not even the prices, year after year. One of the city's best basic eateries, this red-and-green food stand inside Florence's covered meat-and-produce marketplace is best described as a hole-in-the-wall minus the wall. Packed with market-goers and vendors and local working-class types, Nerbone offers four small tables next to a meat counter. Daily specials include a limited choice of pastas, soups, huge plates of cooked vegetables, and fresh sandwiches. Service is swift, and wine and beer are sold by the glass. If at first you can't find Nerbone, just ask: It's worth the hunt and promises lots of local color and good eats.

Palle d'Oro. Via Sant'Antonio 43–45r (in the Mercato San Lorenzo area). ☎ **055/28-83-83.** Pastas and soups 7,000L–8,000L ($3.95–$4.50); meat courses 8,000L–19,000L ($4.50–$11). AE, DC, MC, V. Mon–Sat noon–2:30pm and 6:30–9:30pm. ITALIAN.

Everyone seems to prefer the front bar area of this trattoria, usually packed with the market's vendors and shoppers enjoying a quick lunch of pasta, soup, and vegetable side dishes. The prices aren't much higher than those above for table service in the less-crowded back room, but the front area's advantage is that you're not expected to order a full meal. Wherever you wind up, make sure you look for the house specialty, *penne della casa,* pasta made with porcini, prosciutto, and veal. For a cholesterol boost with a kick, try the homemade *gnocchi alla gorgonzola.*

Trattoria il Contadino. Via Palazzuolo 69r (between via de'Canacci and via dell'Albero). ☎ **055/238-26-73.** *Menu turistico* 15,000L ($8) at lunch, 16,000L ($9) at dinner. No credit cards. Mon–Sat noon–2:30pm and 6–9:30pm. ITALIAN.

The *menu turistico* is the only game at this simple trattoria (and one of the cheapest offerings in town). Consisting of a pasta, a main course, a side dish of a fresh vegetable, mineral water, and wine, it seems to meet with everyone's approval, judging by the two-room turnout at this simple place with red-and-white-checkered tablecloths. Unless you come early, expect to wait.

Trattoria Zà-Zà. Piazza Mercato Centrale 26r. ☎ **055/21-54-11.** Primi 7,000L–11,000L ($3.95–$6); meat courses 13,000L–20,000L ($7–$11); *menu turistico* 20,000L ($11). AE, DC, MC, V. Mon–Sat noon–3pm and 7–11pm. ITALIAN.

The walls are lined with chianti bottles and photos of old movie stars and not-so-famous patrons, the long wooden tables crowded with an eclectic mix of visitors and locals. Convenient to the San Lorenzo Market, this place serves Tuscan favorites at reasonable prices amid a cheerful clatter. This is a reliably good spot to try the fabled *bistecca fiorentina* without losing your shirt (the menu usually quotes prices per *etto* or 100 grams), so consult your waiter: The average steak is about 25,000L to 30,000L ($14 to $17) per person. Things don't change much here, except for the tables that have been set up on an unremarkable piazza and a new wine bar under the same management next door at no. 27r: John Torta offers a wide range of Tuscan wines by the glass, from the humble and good to limited-selection and sublime (daily 7pm to 2am). Zà-Zà has a serious competitor in **Mario,** around the corner at via Rosina 2 (also closed Sunday); it's open for lunch only and admirably absorbs the overflow.

BETWEEN THE DUOMO & THE ARNO

Caffè Caruso. Via Lambertesca 16r (off via Por Santa Maria). ☎ **055/28-19-40.** Pasta 6,000L–8,000L ($3.40–$4.50); meat courses 6,000L–8,000L ($3.40–$4.50). No credit cards. Mon–Sat 8am–8pm. ITALIAN.

On a quiet side street in the heart of town (the first right off via Por Santa Maria when coming from the ponte Vecchio), this family-run "caffè(tteria)" offers a surprisingly varied selection of inexpensive hot dishes in an airy setting with lots of seating. It's busy with locals during lunch, but the continuous hours promise less commotion if your appetite is flexible. Choose from the display of four or five pastas and over a dozen vegetable side dishes, making this a recommended destination for light (or not) eaters and vegetarians. Self-service keeps prices rock bottom for this area. Keep it in mind for an inexpensive breakfast or coffee break or an afternoon beer that promises a quiet table for postcard scribbling.

Caffè Italiano. Via Condotta 56r (off via dei Calzaiuoli). ☎ **055/29-10-82.** Primi 6,000L ($3.40); secondi 10,000L ($6). No credit cards. Daily 12:30–3pm. (Bar daily: winter 7:30am–1am, summer to 8pm.) ITALIAN.

Get Thee to a *Gelateria*

There are innumerable *gelato* sources around town. The following are not only the best but also have the largest selections. Ask for a cone *(cono)* or cup *(coppa)* (Vivoli offers cups only, eschewing the concession of America's love of cones) from 2,000L to 7,000L ($1.10 to $3.95)—point and ask for as many flavors as can be squeezed in (you can have a field day with the 7,000L size).

Of all the centrally located gelaterie in Florence, **Festival del Gelato,** via del Corso 75r, just off via dei Calzaiuoli (☎ **055/239-43-86**), has been the only serious contender to the premier Vivoli (below), offering about 50 flavors along with pounding pop music and colorful neon. It's open Tuesday to Sunday: summer 8am to 1am and winter 11am to 1am.

Vivoli, via Isole delle Stinche 7r, a block west of piazza Santa Croce (☎ **055/239-23-34**), is world famous, but recent taste tests have detractors wondering if it's now relying a bit too heavily on its reputation. Exactly how renowned is this brightly lit *gelateria?* Taped to the wall is a postcard bearing only "Vivoli, Europa" for the address, yet it was successfully delivered to this world capital of ice cream. It's open Tuesday to Sunday 9am to 1am (closed August and January to early February).

One of the major advantages of the always crowded **Gelateria delle Carrozze,** piazza del Pesce 3–5r (☎ **055/23-96-810**), is its location at the foot of the ponte Vecchio (Old Bridge)—if you're coming off the ponte Vecchio and about to head straight on to the Duomo, this gelateria is immediately off to your right on a small alley that forks off the main street. Look for the Canadian-born co-owner, Silvia, who's often found dishing out the delicious flavors of the day: She's helpful with Frommer's readers in need of directions or insider's tips. There are tables inside for those who prefer to sit and maybe even make a lunch of it, with fresh sandwiches made daily on home-baked bread (9000L/$5). In summer it's open daily 11am to 1am; in winter, hours are Thursday to Tuesday 11am to 8pm.

Umberto Montano, the young owner of this handsome *caffè* (his other stylish restaurants—see below—are two of the city's best), has created an inviting turn-of-the-century ambience near piazza della Signoria and offers a simple and delicious lunch at reasonable rates to standing-room-only crowds (come early). Delicate but full-flavored soups and an unusual variety of mousselike soufflés of parmesan or broccoli might be the choice of *primi*. Stop by in the afternoon for dessert: Made on the premises by a talented pastry chef, the choices go perfectly with the bar's exclusive blend of coffee from Africa. Coffee connoisseurs drop in regularly for the latter alone.

For a wonderful splurge, try Montano's new **Osteria del Caffè Italiano,** via Isola delle Stinche 11–13r (☎ **055/28-93-68**). And if you're looking for a super splurge, you can't beat his **Alle Murate,** via Ghibellina 52r (☎ **055/24-06-18**).

Trattoria del Pennello. Via Dante Alighieri 4r (between via dei Calzaiuoli and via del Proconsolo). ☎ **055/29-48-48.** Pasta courses 10,000L ($6); second courses 12,000L–22,000L ($7–$12); *menu turistico* 30,000L ($17). No credit cards. Tues–Sat noon–3pm and 7–10pm, Sun noon–3pm. Closed Aug. ITALIAN.

This is one of Florence's oldest restaurants, housed since the 1500s in a palazzo said to have been owned by the Alighieri family, hence the restaurant's second name of "da Dante" (Dante's; the Dante Museum is around the corner). It's popular and attractive, and one of its many specialties is the antipasti—the front-room table groans under the day's changing array of two dozen delicious types. Prices vary with the quantity and the dish, but expect to spend 10,000L to 16,000L ($6 to $9) for a healthy sampling. Continue by ordering the *tris di primi a piacere*, your choice of any three pastas for a minimum of two people (14,000L/$8 per person). Lesser appetites might be as happy with a simple pasta and perfectly prepared grilled chop for about the same cost. It's easier to find now that the new American Express Office opened just a few buildings west.

Trattoria le Mossacce. Via del Proconsolo 55r (a block south of the Duomo). ☎ **055/29-43-61.** Pasta courses 7,500L–8,500L ($4.20–$4.75); meat courses 9,000L–12,000L ($5–$7). AE, MC, V. Mon–Fri noon–2:30pm and 7–9:30pm. ITALIAN.

This is a much-loved straightforward place for *cucina toscana*, deftly prepared and served in a lively and pleasant atmosphere. Favorites on the menu are the thick *ribollita* ("twice-boiled") soup or any of the daily changing pastas. If the thought of a thick slab of steak is your idea of heaven, indulge in the regional specialty here, the *bistecca alla fiorentina*, a splurge worth 22,000L ($12).

EAST OF VIA PRECONSOLO

Running north-south from the east side of piazza del Duomo past the Bargello Museum, this main street changes name before eventually finishing at the Arno. To its east is the piazza Santa Croce neighborhood and the Mercato Sant'Ambrogio.

✪ **Il Pizzaiolo.** Via de' Macci 113r (at corner of Via Pietrapiana near the Mercato Sant'Ambrogio). ☎ **055/24-11-71.** Reservations required for dinner: two seatings only, 8 and 9:30pm. Pizza 8,000L–13,000L ($4.50–$7); primi 10,000L–12,000L ($6–$7); secondi 12,000L–15,000L ($7–$8). No credit cards. Mon–Sat 12:30–3pm and 8pm–midnight. PIZZERIA/TRATTORIA.

The ever-present crowd milling about on the sidewalk (and they have reservations!) is confirmation that this new place serves the best pizza in town. Italy remains proudly and adamantly regionalistic about its food: Southerns contend that they're the best pizza makers on the peninsula. And so Florence was elated to welcome Carmine, who headed north after 30 years in Naples, bringing with him his family, his expertise, and integral ingredients like garlic and oregano. The simple *pizza margherita* (fresh tomatoes, mozzarella, and oregano) is perfection, as is the more endowed *pizza pazza*, a "crazy pizza" with fresh tomatoes, artichokes, olives, mushrooms, and oregano.

Pizzeria I Ghibellini. Piazza San Pier Maggiore 8–10r (at the end of borgo degli Albizi east from via del Proconsolo). ☎ **055/21-44-24.** Pizza 6,000L–12,000L ($3.40–$7); pasta courses 6,000L–8,000L ($3.40–$4.50); meat courses 8,000L–20,000L ($4.50–$11). AE, DC, MC, V. Thurs–Tues noon–4pm and 7pm–12:30am. ITALIAN.

With its exposed brick walls and ceilings and curved archways inside and its white umbrella-shaded tables in this picturesque piazzetta, I Ghibellini is a good bet year-round. Pizza is the draw, and there's a long list to make your choice difficult: Try the house specialty, *pizza alla Ghibellini* (prosciutto, mascarpone, and pork sausage). The many pastas include *penne alla boccalona*, whose tomato sauce with garlic and a pinch of hot pepper is just spicy enough.

✪ **Ristorante Acqua al Due.** Via della Vigna Vecchia 40r (at via dell'Acqua, east of the Bargello). ☎ **055/28-41-70.** Reservations required. Pasta courses 8,000L–10,000L ($4.50–$6); meat courses 10,000L–20,000L ($6–$11); assaggio 13,000L ($7) for pasta, 6,000L ($3.40) for dessert. AE, MC, V. Daily 7:30pm–1am. ITALIAN.

This is the perfect place to sample as much as you can at one sitting without breaking the bank or bursting your seams. The specialty is the *assaggio di primi*, a sampling of five types of pasta in various sauces. These aren't five full-size portions, but don't expect to have room for an entree after. There are also *assaggi* of salads *(insalate)* and sweets *(dolci)*, but good pasta is the draw. If you don't have a reservation, come back when you do. Low prices and late hours make this comfortable place popular with a young international crowd. Too bad it doesn't do lunch.

Trattoria Cibreo. Via Andrea del Verrocchio 4r (near via Pietrapiana and the Mercato Sant'Ambrogio). ☎ **055/234-11-00.** Primi 7,000L ($3.90); main courses 15,000L ($8). AE, DC, MC, V. Tues–Sat 1–2:30pm and 7:30–11pm. ITALIAN.

This is the casual, lesser-priced trattoria of the celebrated team of chef/owner Fabio Picchi and his wife, Benedetta; its limited menu comes from the same creative kitchen that put their premier (and by now world famous) 50-seat *ristorante* next door on the map. Picchi takes his inspiration from traditional Tuscan recipes, and the first thing you'll note is the absence of pasta. After you taste the velvety *passata di peperoni gialli* (a cream-free yellow bell-pepper soup), you won't care much. The stuffed roast duck demands the same admiration. Desserts, like the bitter-chocolate tart, are made to perfection by Benedetta. To complete the experience, enjoy your after-dinner espresso at the handsome Caffè Cibreo across the way.

IN THE OLTRARNO

Head south over the ponte Vecchio for the "Left Bank" of Florence. Rents and prices are catching up with the north, Duomo side of the river, but the atmosphere is still one of artisan shops and casual eateries with a more palpable bohemian feel.

Bar Ricchi. Piazza Santo Spirito 9r. ☎ **055/21-58-64.** Primi 6,000L ($3.40); secondi 8,000L ($4.50). AE, V. Mon–Sat noon–2:30pm. (Bar, winter, Mon–Sat 7am–8:30pm; summer, Mon–Sat 7am–1am.) ITALIAN.

Don't miss this bar when spring arrives and tables appear on one of Florence's great piazzas; its great inexpensive lunch menu is available year-round—if only they'd repeat the performance for dinner. Four or five pastas are made up on order and, as an alternative to the usual entrees, peruse the "super salads" (8,000L/$4.50). A shady piazza table is ringside, but take a look inside at the 350 framed designs from a 1980 contest to design the unfinished facade of Brunelleschi's Church of Santo Spirito.

Borgo Antico. Piazza Santo Spirito 6r. ☎ **055/21-04-37.** Pizza 10,000L ($6); primi 10,000L ($6); secondi 18,000L ($10). AE, MC, V. Daily 12:45–2:30pm and 7:45pm–midnight. ITALIAN.

In the spirit of the Oltrarno's "Left Bank" atmosphere and Santo Spirito, its favorite piazza, the Borgo Antico is a relaxed spot where you can order as little or as much as you want and enjoy it among a mix of visitors and Florentines. The scene inside is always buzzing, but from April to September tables are set out where the million-dollar view of Brunelleschi's church is free. There are a dozen great pizzas and a number of combination "super salads." Specialties of the day get equally creative (expensive). This is one of the few places that stays open Sunday for dinner. It's almost always hectic, and if you get the hint they'd like your table, you'd do well not to linger.

Il Cantinone. Via Santo Spirito 6r (off piazza Santa Trinita). ☎ **055/21-88-98.** Crostini 6,000L–7,000L ($3.75–$4.40); primi 10,000L–12,000L ($6–$7); secondi 20,000L–30,000L ($11–$17). AE, MC, V. Tues–Sun 12:30–2:30pm and 7:30–10:30pm. WINE BAR.

In the brick-vaulted wine cellar of a 16th-century palazzo, this is a well-known candlelit wine bar that can seem more jovial than romantic on nights when the wine gets flowing—and you'll find a fine selection of Chianti's best. Five or six reds are available by the glass, but don't overlook a liter of the good house wine, a bargain at 13,000L ($9). Order a number of appetizers and first courses and you'll understand why they call Tuscany's peasant food the food of kings. *Crostini* are large slabs of home-baked bread covered with prosciutto, *funghi* (mushrooms), tomatoes, mozzarella or *salsiccia* (sausage). *Primi* courses might be a hearty *pappa al pomodoro* or *ribollita* soup, with a pasta of the day. Ordering a full meal (expected at dinner, though never enforced) makes this a more costly choice. This is a strictly Tuscan experience, in the most positive sense of the word.

Osteria del Cinghiale Bianco. Borgo San Jacopo 43r (off piazza Santa Trinita). ☎ **055/21-57-06.** Primi 6,000L–9,000L ($3.40–$5); secondi 15,000L–20,000L ($8–$11). No credit cards. Thurs–Mon noon–3pm and 7–10:30pm. ITALIAN.

Housed in an 11th-century medieval tower, this characteristic trattoria is dedicated to the *cinghiale,* the wild boar that roams the Tuscan hills. Its presence is felt strongly during the autumn game season, but year-round dishes like pasta with cinghiale sauce or wild-boar sausage *(salsiccia)* antipasto will satisfy your curiosity if not your palate. Much of the menu is cinghiale-free, like the delicious *strozzapreti* ("priest stranglers"— don't ask), a baked pasta filled with spinach and ricotta in a light butter sauce.

Trattoria Casalinga. Via Michelozzi 9r (between via Maggio and piazza Santo Spirito). ☎ **055/21-86-24.** Primi 5,500L–6,500L ($3.10–$3.65); secondi 7,500L–15,000L ($4.20–$8). Mon–Sat noon–2:30pm and 7–10pm. AE, DC, MC, V. ITALIAN.

Casalinga refers to the home cooking that keeps this recently expanded unpretentious place always full. Along with the larger seating capacity came the frayed nerves of the help and a sometimes erratic performance from the kitchen—or so I've heard. I've never experienced anything but a smile and a good meal in this family place. So maybe they won't win any culinary awards, but the menu is reliable, straightforward Tuscan: Try the hearty *ribollita* or the *ravioli al sugo di coniglio* in rabbit-flavored sauce. Save dessert or an after-dinner *caffè* for one of the outdoor cafes in nearby piazza Santo Spirito.

PICNICKING

Shopping for food in Italy is always a wonderful cultural experience, though not necessarily a fast and easy one in Florence's *centro storico* since there are few supermarkets. Cold cuts are sold at a *salumeria.* They also sell cheese, though for a wide selection or yogurt you'll have to find a *latteria.* Vegetables and fruit can be found at a produce stand and store called *orto e verdura* and often at a small *alimentari,* the closest thing to a neighborhood grocery store. For bread to put all that between, visit a *forno,* which, with a *pasticceria,* will supply you with dessert. And for a bottle of wine, search out a shop selling *vino e olio.* **Via dei Neri,** which begins at via de' Benci near piazza Santa Croce and stretches over toward piazza della Signoria, is lined with small specialty food shops and is a good area for purchasing food for an outing.

   If you prefer to find all you need under one roof, visit the colorful **Mercato Centrale,** a block-long two-story marketplace that is a must-see and not just for food shoppers. Open Monday to Friday 7am to 2pm and Saturday 7am to 2pm and 4 to 8pm, it's at via dell'Ariento 12, looming in the midst of the open-air San Lorenzo Market, on the block between via San Antonino and via Panicale.

   If you're just as happy to have someone else make up your sandwiches, seek out **Forno Sartoni,** via dei Cerchi 34r, behind the Coin department store on via dei Calzaiuoli and around the corner from the new American Express Office. This is something of an institution, with fresh rolls and breads in front; the crowd in back is waiting for pizza bubbling from the oven, sold by the slice and weighed by the ounce—the average slice is 2,500L ($1.40). It also makes up a limited but delicious selection of fresh sandwiches (with prosciutto, mozzarella, and arugula, for example, at about 3,500L/$1.95) on freshly baked focaccia. Sartoni is predominantly a baker, so for a greater variety of quality cold cuts stop by **Alimentari Orizi** (above) and have the combination panino of your choice made up as you wait.

The **Boboli Gardens,** on the opposite side of the Arno (see "Seeing the Sights," later in this chapter) behind the Palazzo Pitti, is without a doubt the best green picnic spot in town (though with a 4,000L/$2.25 admission). A grand amphitheater behind the palazzo provides historic seating, but it's worth the hike to the top where the grounds join with those of the Fortezza Belvedere for the breathtaking view and green grass. If you'd just as soon pull up a park bench in the *centro storico,* a number of the city's most beautiful piazzas have stone benches and open spaces: **Piazza Santa Croce** comes to mind as much for its church's three-toned marble facade as for its proximity to Vivoli's for a postlunch *gelato.* **Piazza Santa Maria Novella** offers stone benches and the only plots of grass in any of the city's squares. And if summer has set in, there are just two shady piazzas with benches: **piazza Massimo d'Azeglio** east of the Accademia near the Synagogue and lovely **piazza Santo Spirito** in the Oltrarno near the Palazzo Pitti.

WORTH A SPLURGE

Il Latini. Via Palchetti 6r (off via della Vigna Nuova). ☎ **055/21-09-16.** Reservations suggested. Primi 8,000L–10,000L ($4.50–$6); meat courses 15,000L–20,000L ($8–$11); fixed-price meal 50,000L ($28). AE, MC, V. Tues–Sun 12:30–2:30pm and 7:30–10:30pm. Closed July 20–Aug 10. ITALIAN.

Octogenarian Narcisio Latini and his sons, Giovanni and Torello, operate one of the busiest tavernlike trattorias in town. There's always a line waiting for a cramped seat at one of the long wooden tables (this is an even longer affair if you haven't reserved). But the raucous, delicious Tuscan adventure is worth the wait, with most of the wines and much of the menu's selection coming from the Latini's estate in Chianti. There's a written menu, but you probably won't see it: One of the brothers will explain the selection in a working version of English. Gargantuan eaters can indulge in the *menu completo*—a hearty, meaty fixed-price feast for 50,000L ($31), plus all the wine and mineral water you can drink. More restrained appetites and wallets should just order à la carte. Foreign visitors to Florence love this place, but so do the Florentines and everyone becomes fast and famous friends.

✪ **Trattoria Antellesi.** Via Faenza 9r (near the Medici Chapels and the Mercato San Lorenzo). ☎ **055/21-69-90.** Primi 8,000L–12,000L ($4.50–$7); secondi 15,000L–24,000L ($8–$14). AE, DC, MC, V. Mon–Sat noon–2:30pm and 7–10:30pm. ITALIAN.

At their trattoria in a converted Renaissance palazzo, the Florentine chef, Enrico, and his wife, the Arizona-born manager/sommelier Janice Verrecchia, guarantee a lovely Tuscan experience of authentic dishes and a well-thought-out wine list. Knowledgeable and never without a smile, Janice will talk you through a memorable dinner that should start with their signature antipasto of pecorino cheese and pears. Follow that with light crêpes stuffed with ricotta and spinach and then baked *(crespelle alla fiorentina)* or *spaghetti alla chiantigiana* with chianti-marinated beef cooked in tomato sauce. This is the spot to try the Tuscan cuisine's crown jewel—*bistecca alla fiorentina*—and, while you're at it, some of the cantina's excellent moderately priced red wines for 21,000L to 24,000L ($12 to $14).

5 Seeing the Sights

SIGHTSEEING SUGGESTIONS

IF YOU HAVE 1 DAY   There's so much to see in Florence, each attraction as historically significant and aesthetically captivating as the next, that the best approach is to look through the entries below (especially the starred ones), choose the sites according to your interests, and check their hours.

Except in the dead of winter (and I've begun to see that even this is no exception) there are always lines at the **Uffizi.** Regardless, begin your day here, as this is Italy's most significant picture gallery and the most important art museum in Europe after the Louvre in Paris. You'd have to race at breakneck speed through the 45 rooms to see everything, so I suggest you choose a particular period or painter after picking up a color-coded floor plan upon entry and bypass rooms of less interest if you want to make it out in 1 day, with your wits still about you.

Next, try to visit the **Accademia** (more lines!), where there are several sculptures by Michelangelo, whose legendary *David*—one of the great sculptures of all time—outshines them all. Lunch on piazza della Signoria in the shadow of the Palazzo Vecchio and its many statues is expensive (try instead the nearby **Cantinetta dei Verrazzano** or **Caffè Italiano,** both fun and inexpensive), but for a memorable break splurge on an outdoor iced tea at the piazza's historic **Caffè Rivoire** (or if it's winter, indoors with a cup of their famously sinful hot chocolate with fresh whipped cream). Find time after lunch to visit the **Duomo** and **Baptistery,** which remain open until late afternoon.

For a quick shot at shopping—but as much for the color and experience—head north from the Duomo to the sprawling open-air **Mercato San Lorenzo** (see "Markets," later in this chapter, for hours); take advantage of the bargains on leather goods and wool sweaters—gloves and scarves in particular and a growing number of T-shirts with interesting graphics that make great gifts that pack well. Finally, try not to miss an opportunity to make dinner a memorable Tuscan experience at one of the restaurants I've recommended.

IF YOU HAVE 2 DAYS   The above schedule is quite busy: Spread its wealth over 2 days while incorporating some of the following. Divide the wonders of the **Uffizi** into the East and West galleries, spending part of each of your 2 days there at a more leisurely pace. There's so much to see and savor you could return a dozen times. And if it's still early and you're anxious to continue your exploration of Renaissance art (but this time with sculpture), remember that the nearby **Bargello** is one of the many museums closing at 2pm.

Many museums are housed in the **Pitti Palace** across the ponte Vecchio in the Oltrarno neighborhood, but foremost is its **Galleria Palatina** and collection of masterworks by Raphael. A picnic lunch is preferable, but even a stroll through the **Boboli Gardens** behind the Pitti Palace is a lovely way to recharge your batteries while taking in the captivating views. If it's not too late, return to the **Duomo** and consider a Stairmaster workout to the gods, climbing to the top of Brunelleschi's dome or making the only slightly less strenuous hike to the top of Giotto's freestanding bell tower for an eagle's-nest view of the city and surrounding hills.

After that, you deserve a marvelous dinner highlighted by the Tuscan menu's *bistecca alla fiorentina* and an outdoor drink at any of the bars in the lively piazza Santo Spirito.

IF YOU HAVE 3 DAYS   Approach the above suggestions at an even more leisurely and human pace, interspersed with a casual stroll through the *centro storico*'s storelined pedestrian streets and a look at the goods sold at the covered **Mercato Nuovo,** a miniature version of the larger Mercato San Lorenzo but a weak competitor with a far more limited selection. While you're in the neighborhood, visit the **Palazzo Vecchio** in piazza della Signoria, whose upstairs salons merit a stop. Then window-shop along the **ponte Vecchio** and the dazzling wares of its dozens of small gold and jewelry stores. If you think you've seen the full splendor and magnitude of the Renaissance, visit the **Medici Chapels** (behind the Church of San Lorenzo)—Michelangelo's homage to the Medici rulers and his lifelong patrons—and you'll swoon all over again.

A Note About Museum Hours

Remember that stores close for long lunch breaks and many of the museums close for the day at 2pm or earlier (the last entrance is at least 30 minutes before closing), and many are closed Monday. The first thing you should do is stop by the tourist office for an up-to-date listing of museum hours and possible extended hours. Churches and the markets are good alternatives for spending your afternoons, since they usually remain open to 7pm.

The treasures of Florence's half-dozen important churches can easily consume Day 3 (because of their size and number, lines aren't a problem): Fra Angelico's frescoes at **San Marco;** the Giotto frescoes and the tombs of Michelangelo, Galileo, and a host of others at **Santa Croce;** the Brunelleschi fresco cycle and the Spanish Chapel at **Santa Maria Novella;** the revolutionary early Renaissance frescoes of the Brancacci Chapel in **Santa Maria del Carmine;** and the Gothic **Orsanmichele** will easily combine for a splendid full day. You'll never see them all, so map out your preferences and remember that almost all churches close during lunch and discourage visits Sunday morning during mass hours. Don't forget that Santa Croce is but two steps from the legendary Vivoli *gelateria.*

IF YOU HAVE 5 DAYS Some visitors have fallen so deeply in love with Florence that on Day 5 they've been seen sitting at a cafe searching the classified ads of *Il Pulce* looking for a job and an apartment. If you have 5 full days, I suggest you stretch out the hectic itineraries above. On Day 4, despite Florence's unique pleasures and charms, get out of town. **Siena, Lucca, San Gimignano,** and nearby **Fiesole** are all lovely towns you can easily reach on a day trip (see "Side Trips," at the end of this chapter). Or consider a 1-day **hiking or biking trip** into the surrounding hills (see "Organized Tours," below). You'll never run out of things to do in 5 days. A week's stay would be better. A lifetime would be nice.

THE DUOMO, BAPTISTERY & CAMPANILE

✪ **Duomo (Cathedral of Santa Maria del Fiore).** Piazza del Duomo. ☎ **055/230-28-85.** Cathedral, free; cupola ascent, 10,000L ($6); excavations, 3,000L ($1.70). Summer Mon–Fri 8:30am–6pm, Sat 8:30am–5pm, Sun 1–5pm (open Sun morning for services only; cupola and excavations closed Sun); winter Mon–Sat 10am–5pm, Sun 1–5pm (open Sun morning for services only; cupola and excavations closed Sun). Last entrance to ascend the cupola 40 minutes before closing.

The red-tiled dome of Florence's magnificent Duomo dominates the skyline as we approach the 21st century just as it did when it was built more than 5 centuries ago. At the time it was completed in 1434 it was the world's largest unsupported dome, meant to dwarf the structures of ancient Greece and Rome. In Renaissance style, it's a major architectural feat and was the high point of architect Filippo Brunelleschi's illustrious career; it took 14 years to complete. The cathedral's exterior of white-, red-, and green-patterned marble (the colors of the Italian flag) is from Tuscan quarries. The "modern" facade (replacing the original) was added in the late 19th century when Florence became the capital of the united Italy; its painstaking multiple-year cleaning and renovation was completed in 1996. The tricolored mosaic is an interesting contrast to the sienna-colored medieval fortresslike palazzi throughout the city.

Though much of the interior decoration has been moved to the Museo dell'Opera del Duomo (below), the cathedral still boasts three stained-glass windows on the entrance wall by Lorenzo Ghiberti (sculptor of the bronze reliefs of the baptistery doors) next to Paolo Uccello's giant clock using the heads of four prophets. In late

Florence

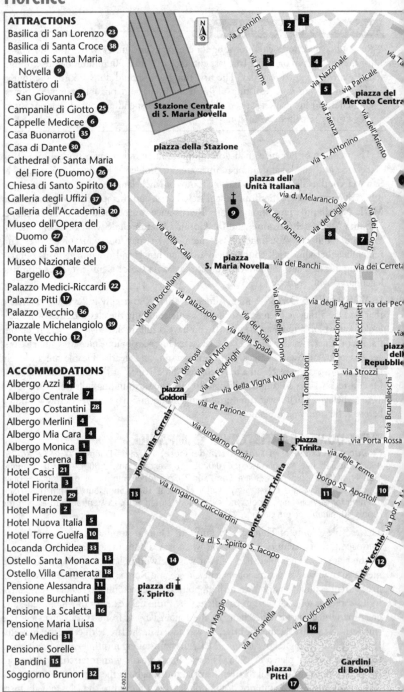

ATTRACTIONS
Basilica di San Lorenzo ㉓
Basilica di Santa Croce ㊳
Basilica di Santa Maria
  Novella ⑨
Battistero di
  San Giovanni ㉔
Campanile di Giotto ㉕
Cappelle Medicee ⑥
Casa Buonarroti ㉟
Casa di Dante ㉚
Cathedral of Santa Maria
  del Fiore (Duomo) ㉖
Chiesa di Santo Spirito ⑭
Galleria degli Uffizi ㊲
Galleria dell'Accademia ⑳
Museo dell'Opera del
  Duomo ㉗
Museo di San Marco ⑲
Museo Nazionale del
  Bargello ㉞
Palazzo Medici-Riccardi ㉒
Palazzo Pitti ⑰
Palazzo Vecchio ㊱
Piazzale Michelangiolo ㊳
Ponte Vecchio ⑫

ACCOMMODATIONS
Albergo Azzi ④
Albergo Centrale ⑦
Albergo Costantini ㉘
Albergo Merlini ④
Albergo Mia Cara ④
Albergo Monica ①
Albergo Serena ③
Hotel Casci ㉑
Hotel Fiorita ③
Hotel Firenze ㉙
Hotel Mario ②
Hotel Nuova Italia ⑤
Hotel Torre Guelfa ⑩
Locanda Orchidea ㉝
Ostello Santa Monaca ⑬
Ostello Villa Camerata ⑱
Pensione Alessandra ⑪
Pensione Burchianti ⑧
Pensione La Scaletta ⑯
Pensione Maria Luisa
  de' Medici ㉛
Pensione Sorelle
  Bandini ⑮
Soggiorno Brunori ㉜

E-0022

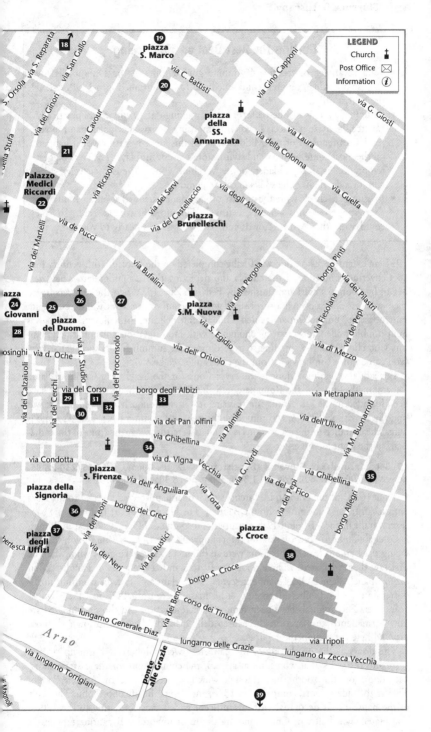

Getting the Best Deal on Sightseeing

- Take advantage of the free 40-minute guided tours of the Duomo, led by English-speaking volunteers and scheduled to be continued into 1999. Ask at the tourist office.
- Note that Florence is the perfect city for walking—its *centro storico* practically car-free, its maze of streets lined with imposing Renaissance palazzi and tower residences redolent of the Middle Ages. In this ancient setting you'll happen on the most contemporary and stylish store-window displays. The city's biggest temptation is the gold-laden ponte Vecchio, whose dozens of jewelry store windows dazzle like the souks of oil-rich emirates.
- In summer, check with the tourist office about extended evening hours for alternating museums—these are usually Florence's best-kept secret, so you could avoid the daytime crowds and get the museums nearly to yourself.

1995, an extensive restoration was finally completed on the colorful 16th-century frescoes covering the inside of the cupola and depicting the Last Judgment. They were begun by Giorgio Vasari and finished by Federico Zuccari. When the restorers began their work, they discovered a surprise: A good portion of the work was executed not in "true fresco" but in tempera, which is much more delicate. Brunelleschi's cupola was built double-walled and is strong enough to withstand the thousands of athletic visitors who climb the 463 spiraling steps leading to the summit for its spectacular view (you can enjoy a similar view from the campanile; see below).

Beneath the Duomo's floor is the crypt (look for the Scavi della Cripta di Santa Reparata), the ruins of the Romanesque Santa Reparata Cathedral, believed to have been founded in the 5th century on this site; it was continuously enlarged until it was done away with in 1296 to accommodate the present structure. Brunelleschi's tomb is here. The entrance to the excavations is through a stairway near the front of the cathedral, to the right as you enter.

✪ **Battistero di San Giovanni (Baptistery).** Piazza del Duomo. ☎ **055/230-28-85.** Admission 5,000L ($2.80). Mon–Sat 1:30–6:30pm, Sun 8:30am–1:30pm.

In front (west) of the Duomo is Florence's octagonal baptistery, dedicated to the city's patron saint, San Giovanni (John the Baptist). The highlight of the Romanesque baptistery, built in the 11th and 12th centuries and so one of Florence's oldest buildings, is Lorenzo Ghiberti's bronze exterior doors known as the *Gates of Paradise,* on the side facing the Duomo (east). The doors were so dubbed by Michelangelo, who, when he first saw them, declared, "These doors are fit to stand at the gates of Paradise." Ten bronze panels depict Old Testament scenes, like Adam and Eve, in stunning three-dimensional relief. Ghiberti labored over his masterpiece from 1425 to 1452, dying 3 years later. The originals have been removed for restoration and those completed are now permanently displayed in the Museo dell'Opera del Duomo (below); all those exposed here are convincing replicas.

The doors at the north side of the baptistery were Ghiberti's "warm-up" to the gates and the work that won him, at age 23, the commission for the eastern doors. The doors on the south side, through which you enter, are by Andrea Pisano. They're the oldest doors, completed in 1336, and depict the life of St. John. The vault of the baptistery is decorated with magnificent gilded mosaics dating to the 1200s, dominated by a figure of Christ, and are the most important Byzantine mosaics in Florence.

✪ **Campanile di Giotto (Giotto's Bell Tower).** Piazza del Duomo. ☎ **055/230-28-85.**
Admission 10,000L ($6). Apr–Oct daily 9am–7pm; Nov–Mar daily 9am–5pm; last entrance 40
minutes before closing.

Giotto spent his last 3 years designing the Duomo's "Tuscanized Gothic" *campanile*
(bell tower), and so it's often referred to simply as Giotto's Tower. Clad in the same
three colors as the cathedral, it's 20 feet shorter than the dome. The bas-reliefs on its
slender exterior are copies of works by Andrea Pisano, Francesco Talenti, Luca della
Robbia, and Arnoldi (the originals are in the Museo dell'Opera del Duomo). The view
from the top of Giotto's Tower is about equal to that from the Duomo; there are, however, a mere 414 steps here (as opposed to the Duomo's 463). There are fewer crowds
on this rooftop, but you won't get the chance to get up-close and personal with
Brunelleschi's architectural masterpiece.

THE TOP MUSEUMS
✪ **Galleria degli Uffizi (Uffizi Galleries).** Piazzale degli Uffizi 6 (south of the Palazzo Vecchio and piazza della Signoria). ☎ **055/2-38-85.** Admission 12,000L ($7). Tues–Sat
8:30am–6:50pm, Sun 8:30am–1:50pm; ticket office closes 45 minutes before museum.

The Uffizi is one of the world's most important art museums and should be the first
stop in Florence for anyone interested in the rich heritage of the Renaissance. Six centuries of artistic development are housed in this impressive Renaissance palazzo, commissioned by Duke Cosimo de' Medici in 1560 and initiated by Giorgio Vasari to
house the Duchy of Tuscany's administrative offices (*uffizi* means "offices"). The collection, whose strong point is Florentine Renaissance art but includes major works by
Flemish and Venetian masters, was amassed by the Medici and bequeathed to Florence
in 1737 by Anna Maria Ludovica, the last of the Medici line.

The gallery consists of 45 rooms where paintings are grouped into schools in
chronological order, from the 13th to the 18th centuries—but as you wander, don't
overlook the building's rich details, including frescoed ceilings, inlaid marble floors,
and tapestried corridors. Vasari's monumental staircase leads up to the superb collection that begins in Room 2 in the east wing, with Giotto's early 14th-century
Madonna, thought by most scholars to be the first painting to make the transition
from the Byzantine to the Renaissance style. Look for the differences between Giotto's
work and his teacher Cimabue's *Madonna in Maestà* (Madonna Enthroned) on the
opposite wall. Some of the best-known rooms are dedicated to 15th-century Florentine painting. In Room 7 are major works by Paolo Uccello, Masaccio, Fra Angelico,
and Piero della Francesca. As you proceed, look for the elegant Madonnas of Filippo
Lippi and Pollaiolo's delightful little panels.

For many, the Botticelli rooms (10 to 14) are the undisputed highlight. The most
stunning are the recently restored *Primavera* (Allegory of Springtime), whose three
graces form the principal focus, and *The Birth of Venus* ("Venus on the Half-Shell").
Botticelli's *Adorazione dei Magi* (Adoration of the Magi) is interesting for the portraits
of his Medici sponsors incorporated into the scene, as well as a self-portrait of the artist
on the far right.

Other notable works are Leonardo da Vinci's unfinished *Adorazione dei Magi* (Ado-
ration of the Wise Men) and his famous *Annunciation* in Room 15, Lukas Cranach's
Adame e Eva in Room 20, Michelangelo's circular *Doni Tondo* or *Sacra Famiglia* (Holy
Family) in Room 25 (his only oil painting), Raphael's *Madonna with the Goldfinch* in
Room 26, Titian's *Flora* and *La Venere di Urbino* (Venus of Urbino) in Room 28, Tin-
toretto's *Leda* in Room 35, Caravaggio's *Medusa* and *Bacco* in Room 43, Rembrandt's
Autoritratti (two self-portraits) in Room 44, and Canaletto's *Veduta del Palazzo Ducale
di Venezia* (View of the Ducal Palace in Venice) in Room 45.

Getting Tickets to the Uffizi

As tourism to Italy increases, so do the lines to get into the major museums. Much of the problem behind the Uffizi's often alarming wait is the security policy regulating the number of visitors inside at any one time. Now you can buy tickets in advance for a designated time and day, eliminating an often 3-hour wait in peak season. You can stand (and stand) in line at the museum or try the following:

- Call ☎ 055/47-19-60 Monday to Friday 8am to 6:30pm. You'll receive information (there's always an English speaker on hand) on how to send an international bank draft (this is the expensive and complicated option for non-credit-card holders), or you'll be given the fax number to authorize payment by credit card (MasterCard or Visa only). They permit groups of 40 reserved ticket holders to enter every 15 minutes: In high season be flexible with alternative days you want to request; requests must be made a minimum of 5 days in advance (some exceptions will be made). Cost is the usual museum admission of 12,000L ($7) plus a 2,400L ($1.35) fee. It'll be the best 2,400L you ever spend.

- On arrival in Florence, you must pick up the tickets at the tourist office at the train station (see "Visitor Information"); at the I.T.A. office, viale Gramsci 9/a (not a terribly convenient address); or at the Uffizi's ticket-sales booth on the designated day and time your visit has been approved. Show up 5 minutes early and walk directly past the hours-long line of those who don't read this book.

Since the May 1993 bombing that damaged 200 works (37 seriously), the museum has staged an amazing recovery. Only four of those damaged were superior examples from the Italian Renaissance; two were destroyed beyond repair. Restorators, many of whom had recently spent decades working to undo the devastating effects of the 1966 floods, have again been working around the clock to repair damage to this day. The **Vasari Corridor** is also once again open, but by appointment only (☎ 055/238-86-51 or 055/238-81). The 12,000L ($7) admission is also good for the museum.

✪ **Galleria dell'Accademia (The Accademia).** Via Ricasoli 60 (between piazza del Duomo and piazza San Marco). ☎ 055/238-86-09. Admission 12,000L ($7). Tues–Sat 8:30am–6:50pm, Sun 8:30am–1:50pm; last entrance 30 minutes before closing.

Nowhere in Europe do so many wait in line for so long to see so little. The Accademia is home to Michelangelo's *David,* his (and perhaps the world's) greatest work. Michelangelo was just 29 and only recently recognized for his promising talents following the creation of the *Pietà,* completed when he was 26, now in St. Peter's Basilica in Rome. Sculpted from a 17-foot column of white Carrara marble that had been quarried for another sculptor's commission, worked on, then deemed inferior and left abandoned and unwanted, *David* looms in stark perfection beneath the rotunda of the main room built exclusively for its display in 1873, when it was moved here from piazza della Signoria (a life-size copy stands in its place; a second copy lords it over piazzale Michelangiolo). From its beginning nicknamed "Il Gigante" (The Giant), the colossal statue is now protected by a high transparent Plexiglas shield after a 1991 attack that damaged its left foot (it was undetectably repaired).

The museum houses several other Michelangelos, including four never-finished *Prisoners* or *Slaves* struggling to free themselves, commissioned though never completed

A Tip on Seeing *David*

The wait to get in to see *David* can be up to an hour. Try getting there before the museum opens in the morning or an hour or two before closing time.

for the tomb of Julius II; Michelangelo believed he could sense their very presence captured within the stone and worked to release their forms from within. They offer a fascinating insight of how he approached each block of marble that would yield his many masterpieces. The *Palestrina Pietà* is also here (Florence possesses another *Pietà*, displayed in the Museo dell'Opera del Duomo). A number of 15th- and 16th-century Florentine artists are here; search out the *Madonna del Mare* (Madonna of the Sea) attributed to Botticelli.

✪ **Museo Nazionale del Bargello (Bargello Museum).** Via del Proconsolo 4 (at via Ghibellina, near the Uffizi). ☎ **055/238-86-06.** Admission 8,000L ($4.50). Tues–Sat, the 2nd and 4th Sun of each month, and the 1st, 3rd, and 5th Mon of each month 8:30am–1:50pm.

If a visit to the Accademia has whetted your appetite for more fine Renaissance sculpture, then set aside time to see this national museum's outstanding collection. This stark 13th-century building originated as the city's Town Hall and served as the city's jail in Renaissance times. In the middle of the majestic courtyard is a tank where prisoners used to be tortured and executed; some hangings took place out the windows facing via del Proconsolo for public viewing. Today Il Bargello, named for the police chief or constable *(bargello)* who ruled from here, houses three stories of treasures by Florentine Renaissance sculptors and a collection of Mannerist bronzes.

On the ground floor, begin with Michelangelo's room, including another *David* (originally called *Apollo* and sculpted 30 years after the original), *Brutus,* and the *Pitti Tondo,* depicting the Madonna teaching Jesus and San Giovanni to read. Take a look at his *Bacchus* (1497): It was done at age 22 and was the artist's first major work, effortlessly capturing the Roman god's drunken posture. Among the other important sculptures are Ammanati's *Leda and the Swan,* Giambologna's significant *Winged Mercury,* and several Donatellos, including *St. George, St. John the Baptist,* and *David,* the first nude statue to be done by an Italian artist since classical times. In another room are the two bronze plaques by Brunelleschi and Ghiberti made for the competition to decide who'd sculpt the baptistery's second set of doors—Ghiberti's won.

✪ **Palazzo Pitti (Pitti Palace).** Piazza Pitti (south of the ponte Vecchio in the Oltrarno, at the end of via Giucciardini). ☎ **055/21-34-40.** Galleria Palatina and Monumental Apartments, 12,000L ($7); Museo degli Argenti (Silver Museum), 4,000L ($2.25); Galleria d'Arte Moderna (Modern Art Gallery), combined ticket with Galleria del Costume (Costume Institute), 8,000L ($4.50). Palatina and Monumental Apartments, Tues–Sat 8:30am–6:50pm, Sat 8:30am–1:50; all others, Tues–Sun 8:30am–1:50pm; last entrance 45 minutes before closing. Call to confirm hours.

The Pitti was begun in 1458 for wealthy textile merchant/banker Luca Pitti in an attempt to keep up with the Medici, and it's ironic that it was Medici descendants who bought this rugged golden palazzo in 1549 (in what was a rural area) as the official residence of Florence's rulers when they were still residing in the Palazzo Vecchio. They tripled its size, elaborately embellishing and gracing it with the Boboli Gardens that still fan up the hill behind it, once the quarry from which the palazzo's *pietra dura* was taken. Today it's home to seven museums.

The first-floor **Galleria Palatina** is the star attraction, home to one of the nation's finest collections of Italian Renaissance and baroque masters after the Uffizi's, and by far the most visited of the palazzo's museums. In addition to the outstanding Raphaels, including his prized and much beloved *Madonna of the Chair, Angelo and Maddalena Doni,* and veiled *La Fornarina* (his baker's daughter and Raphael's mistress), the museum's treasures include a large collection of works by Andrea del Sarto; Fra Bartolomeo's beautiful *Descent from the Cross* and *San Marco;* some superb works by Rubens, including *The Four Philosophers* and *Isabella Clara Eugenia;* canvases by Tintoretto and Veronese; and some stunning Titian portraits, including *Pope Julius II, The Man with the Gray Eyes,* and *The Music Concert.*

The restored **Appartamenti Monumentali (Royal or Monumental Apartments)** are ornate, gilded, and chandeliered, with portraits of the Medicis and tapestries and furnishings from the days of the Medici and later the dukes of Lorraine. Upstairs, the **Galleria d'Arte Moderna** (☎ 055/238-86-16) houses an interesting array of 19th-century Italian impressionists (the *machaioli* school from the words "to spot") said to have inspired the French, and early 20th-century art. Visit the **Museo degli Argenti (Silver Museum),** on the ground floor, for a look at 16 rooms filled with the priceless private treasure of the Medici—and not just silverware. Other small museums that open and close without notice are the **Museo della Porecellana** (Porcelain), the **Coach and Carriage Museum,** and the **Galleria del Costume.**

Museo di San Marco. Piazza San Marco 3 (north of the Duomo on via Cavour). ☎ **055/238-86-08.** Admission 8,000L ($4.50). Tues–Sat, the 2nd and 4th Sun of each month, and the 1st, 3rd, and 5th Mon of each month 8:30am–1:50pm; the ticket office closes 30 minutes before the museum.

Built in the 13th century, then enlarged and rebuilt by Michelozzo as a Dominican monastery in 1437, this small museum is a monument to the devotional work of the Florence-born friar/painter Fra Angelico. Directly to your right upon entering is a room containing the largest collection of his movable paintings in Florence. The chapter room nearby is home to Fra Angelico's large and impressive *Crucifixion* fresco. On the ground floor, visit the Refectory, dedicated to the work of Ghirlandaio (under whom Michelangelo apprenticed), particularly his *Cenacolo* (Last Supper), one of the most important of Florence's nine such Last Suppers found in ancient refectories (the tourist office has a listing of the others and their hours). At the top of the stairs leading to the monks' cells on the second floor is his stunning and beautiful masterpiece, *The Annunciation,* said to have moved Fra Angelico to tears. Each of the cells is decorated with a fresco from *The Life of Christ* painted by Fra Angelico or one of his assistants under the master's direction and intended to aid in contemplation and prayer.

At the end of the corridor is Savonarola's cell, which includes a stark portrait of the monastery's former prior by his convert and student, Fra Bartolomeo, as well as his sleeping chamber, his notebook, his rosary, and remnants of the clothes worn at his execution. A religious fundamentalist who inspired the people to participate in bonfires of their vanities (including the burning of priceless artwork and precious hand-illuminated books), Savonarola was burnt at the stake in piazza della Signoria for heresy in 1498; a bronze plaque marks the spot.

Museo dell'Opera del Duomo (Museum of the Duomo). Piazza del Duomo 9. ☎ **055/230-28-85.** Admission 8,000L ($6). Apr–Oct Mon–Sat 9am–7:30pm; Nov–Mar Mon–Sat 9am–7pm; last entrance is 60 minutes before closing.

Opened in 1891 and ever since overlooked, this quiet, airy museum behind the cathedral contains much of the art and furnishings that once embellished the Duomo. A bust of Brunelleschi at the entrance is a nod to the architect who gave us the Duomo's magnificent cupola, and over the door hang two glazed della Robbia terra-cottas. In the second inner room to your left are sculptures from the old Gothic facade (destroyed in 1587), including work by the original architect, Arnolfo di Cambio

Special & Free Events

The **Maggio Musicale** ("Musical May") is Italy's oldest and most important music festival and one of Europe's most prestigious. Events take place at various indoor and outdoor locations, including the courtyard of the Pitti Palace and the final night's grand concert in piazza della Signoria. Following in the revered footsteps of creative director Riccardo Muti, Maestro Zubin Mehta has been the honorary director since 1985, often conducting Florence's Maggio Musicale Orchestra. World-class guest conductors and orchestras appear during the festival, which, despite its moniker, runs late April to June (but never later than the first few days of July). For schedules and ticket information, inquire at one of the tourist offices (see Teatro Comunale in "Florence After Dark").

From June to August, the Roman amphitheater in nearby Fiesole comes alive with dance, music, and theater for the **Estate Fiesolana** ("Summer in Fiesole"). A.T.A.F. bus no. 7 travels to Fiesole from the train station and piazza del Duomo. July sees the annual **Florence Dance Festival** held in the beautiful amphitheater in the Cascine Park. A wide range of dance is performed, varying from classic to modern, with an emphasis on the latter. Again, check with the tourist office for details.

The highlight of June 24, the feast day of Florence's patron saint, San Giovanni (St. John the Baptist), is the **Calcio Storico,** a no-holds-barred cross between rugby, soccer, and wrestling played with a ball and few (if any) rules. Color teams (the Greens, the Blues, and so on) representing Florence's four original parishes, clad in 16th-century costume, square off against each other in playoff games in the dirt-covered piazza Santa Croce, competing vigorously for that year's bragging rights and final prize: a cow. The final *partita* is most worth seeing, often falling on or around June 24. Fireworks light the night sky of June 24, best viewed from along the north banks of the Arno east of the ponte Vecchio. See the tourist office for ticket information for numbered seats in the bleachers lining the piazza. No tickets are needed to view the equally dazzling procession in full historical regalia that wends its way through the cobblestone streets and piazzas prior to each match.

(1245–1302). Also here are a number of statues, the most noteworthy being a weather-worn but noble *St. John* by Donatello and Nanni di Banco's intriguing *San Luca*.

The highlight of the center room upstairs is the enchanting twin white marble choirs *(cantorie)* dating to the 1430s by Donatello and Luca della Robbia that face each other, as well as two statues by Donatello: his celebrated *Magdalene* (originally in the baptistery) and *Zuccone* (from Giotto's bell tower). In the next room, the *Sala delle Formelle* (Room of the Panels), are the original bas-reliefs that decorated the first two stories of the exterior of Giotto's campanile. One of the most important displays is four of the original bronze panels from Ghiberti's *Gates of Paradise* door of the baptistery (the other six will soon appear after restoration). A major attraction is Michelangelo's last (unfinished) *Pietà,* one of two in Florence (the other is in the Accademia; his most famous and earliest is in St. Peter's Basilica in Rome). The artist intended this for his own tomb and sculpted it when he was 80 and partially blind—it's said that Nicodemus, holding Christ, is a self-portrait. A priceless 14th- to 15th-century silver-gilt altarpiece with scenes from the life of St. John can be found in the last room on the second floor.

Catching the Sunset from Piazzale Michelangiolo

If you've ever wondered where to go to see the view plastered across those jillions of postcards showing orange-and-pink sunsets over Florence, **piazzale Michelangiolo** is it. The Technicolor palette may be subdued by reality, but the same breathtaking perspective of the Arno and the trellis of bridges crossing it, Florence's terra-cotta rooftops punctuated by slender bell towers and cupolas, and the hill town of Fiesole beyond is the same and has been for centuries. In the daytime, caravans of tour buses overwhelm the parking lot—often obliterating the bronze copy of Michelangelo's *David* that gives the piazzale ("wide piazza") its name (but note the spelling difference).

Hop on the no. 13 bus at the ponte alla Grazie (the first bridge east of the ponte Vecchio) for a 15-minute ride up in time for sunset. If you come a bit earlier, it's an easy walk to the nearby **Church of San Miniato al Monte,** south of the piazzale on via del Monte alle Croci 34. Dating to the 11th century, it's one of Florence's most beloved churches—a favorite wedding site, and at approximately 4:30pm daily, when the remaining Benedictine monks sing vespers in Gregorian chant, a magical place. Crown your afternoon with a gelato back at the piazzale, at the **Gelateria Michelangiolo** (☎ 055/234-27-05), open daily 10am to 1am.

Museo della Casa Buonarroti. Via Ghibellina 70 (5 blocks east of the Bargello). ☎ **055/24-17-52.** Admission 10,000L ($6). Wed–Mon 9:30am–1:30pm. From piazza Santa Croce, you'll find Casa Buonarroti at the top of via delle Pinzochere, 2 blocks north.

This graceful house, which Michelangelo bought late in life for his nephew, was turned into a museum by his heirs. Today it houses two of the master's most important early works: *Madonna alla Scala* (Madonna on the Stairs) and *Battaglia dei Centauri* (Battle of the Centaurs), both sculpted in his teenage years, when he was still working in relief. The museum also houses a sizable collection of his drawings and scale models and is used for temporary exhibits.

PALAZZI

Palazzo Vecchio and Loggia dei Lanzi. Piazza della Signoria. ☎ **055/276-84-65.** Palazzo Vecchio (Appartamenti Monumentali), 10,000L ($6). Palazzo, Mon–Wed and Fri–Sat 9am–7pm, Sun 8am–1pm; Loggia dei Lanzi, daily 24 hours.

In Italy, all roads lead to Rome, but in Florence all roads lead to the elegant piazza della Signoria—the cultural, political, and social heart of the city since the 14th century. The square is dominated by an imposing rough-hewn fortress, the late 13th-century **Palazzo Vecchio (Old Palace).** Its severe Gothic style, with crenellations and battlements, is highlighted by a campanile that was a supreme feat of engineering in its day. It served as Florence's city hall for many years (a role it fulfills again today) and then home to Duke Cosimo de' Medici (that's Giambologna's bronze statue of him on horseback anchoring the middle of the piazza). He lived here for 10 years beginning in 1540 before moving to new accommodations in the Palazzo Pitti, hence its name as the Old Palace. You'll enter through the stunning main courtyard, with intricately carved columns and extraordinarily colorful 16th-century frescos by Vasari; the central focus is the Putto Fountain, a copy of Verrocchio's original (displayed upstairs).

The highlight is the massive first-floor **Salone dei Cinquecento (Hall of the Five Hundred),** whose rich frescoes by Vassari depict Florence's history; formerly the city's council chambers, it's still used for government and civic functions. *The Genius* *of Victory* statue is by Michelangelo. Upstairs, the richly decorated and frescoed salons, such as the private quarters of Cosimo's wife, Eleanora de Toledo, offer an intriguing glimpse into how the ruling class of Renaissance Florence lived.

A small disk in the ground in front of the piazza's enormous **Neptune fountain** (Ammanati, 1576) marks the spot where religious fundamentalist Savonarola was hanged then burned at the stake for heresy in 1498—a few years after inciting the original bonfires of the vanities while ruling the city during the Medici's temporary exile from Florence (even Botticelli got caught up in the fervor and is said to have tossed a painting to fuel the flames). Flanking the life-size copy of Michelangelo's *David* (the original is in the Accademia) are copies of Donatello's *Judith and Holofernes* and the *Marzocco,* the heraldic lion of Florence. On the south side of piazza della Signoria is the 14th-century **Loggia dei Lanzi,** Florence's captivating outdoor sculpture gallery. It has finally been freed of its scaffolding, but entrance to the loggia is now blocked by an excavation of medieval and earlier foundations at the foot of its stepped entrance.

Palazzo Medici-Riccardi. Via Cavour 1 (north of piazza del Duomo). ☎ **055/276-03-40.** Palazzo, free; Cappella dei Magi, 6,000L ($3.40). Mon–Tues and Thurs–Sat 9am–1pm and 3–6pm, Sun 9am–1pm.

Built for Cosimo the Elder, one of the early rulers of the Medici dynasty, by Brunelleschi's student Michelozzo, this austere palazzo became the Palazzo Medici from 1460 to 1540 (before Cosimo I moved to the Palazzo Vecchio, then the Palazzo Pitti) and became the prototype for subsequent residences of the nobility. Only two rooms are open to the public, but they make your trip worthwhile: The tiny **Cappella dei Magi (Chapel of the Magi)** takes its name from the magnificent frescoes by Benozzo Gozzoli, who worked several members of the Medici family, his master Fra Angelico, and himself (look for a child on the far left with a red hat inscribed *Opus Benotii*) into his beautiful depictions of the Wise Men's journey through the Tuscan countryside. It's held by many to be Florence's single most beautiful fresco. Across the courtyard and upstairs is an elaborate 17th-century **baroque gallery** commissioned by the subsequent owners, the Riccardi; amid the gilt and stucco are Luca Giordano's frescoes masterfully illustrating the apotheosis of the Medici dynasty. The palazzo now houses government offices, though parts are frequently used for temporary and traveling exhibits.

CHURCHES

✪ **Basilica di San Lorenzo and the Cappelle Medicee (Medici Chapels).** Piazza Madonna (at the end of borgo San Lorenzo, north of the Duomo). ☎ **055/238-86-02.** San Lorenzo and Biblioteca Medicea-Laurenziana, free; Medici Chapels, 10,000L ($6). Basilica, daily 8am–noon and 3:30–5:30pm; Biblioteca Medicea-Laurenziana, Mon–Sat 9am–1pm; Medici Chapels, Tues–Sat, the 1st and 3rd Sun of each month, and the 2nd and 4th Mon of each month 8:30am–1:50pm.

The San Lorenzo Basilica (whose facade was never finished) was the Medici's parish church as well as the resting place for most of the clan. The key feature of the main part of the church is the **Biblioteca Medicea-Laurenziana,** a stunning bit of architecture by Michelangelo containing one of the world's largest and most valuable collections of manuscripts and codices, most not on display. An elaborate Michelangelo stone staircase leads to it from the quiet cloister, the one real reason to peak in here after a visit to the church next door.

San Lorenzo is best known, however, for **Le Cappelle Medicee** (the Medici Chapels) that you can't reach from or through the church: You enter by going around through the open-air Mercato San Lorenzo to the back of the church. Upon entering, you pass through the **Cappella dei Principi (Chapel of the Princes),** added on in 1604 but not finished until 1962. The goal of your visit is the **New Sacristy,** which contains the Michelangelo-designed tombs for the powerful Lorenzo de' Medici (with statues of female *Dawn* and male *Dusk*) and Giuliano de' Medici (with statues of female *Night* and male *Day*), some of his greatest work. The **Old Sacristy,** designed by Brunelleschi and decorated by Donatello, contains several important works, including a sarcophagus by Verrocchio. A large number of charcoal sketches confirmed to be Michelangelo's were discovered by chance in the 1980s in a room beneath the sacristy now open to the public.

Basilica di Santa Croce and the Cappella Pazzi. Piazza Santa Croce. ☎ **055/24-46-19.** Basilica, free; Pazzi Chapel, 4,000L ($2.25). Basilica, winter Mon–Sat 8am–12:30pm and 3–6:30pm, Sun 3–6pm; summer Mon–Sat 8am–6:30pm, Sun 3–6pm. Pazzi Chapel, Mar–Oct Thurs–Tues 10am–12:30pm and 2:30–6:30pm; Nov–Feb Thurs–Tues 10am–12:30pm and 3–5:30pm.

Begun in 1294 by Arnolfo di Cambio, the original architect of the Duomo, the cavernous Church of Santa Croce is the largest Franciscan church in the world. The humble presence of St. Francis is best felt in the two chapels to the right of the main altar: Covered with faded early 14th-century frescoes by Giotto and his gifted student, Taddeo Gaddi, they depict the life of the saint. To the left of the main altar is a wooden *Crucifix* by Donatello, whose portrayal of Christ was thought too provincial by early 15th-century standards.

Santa Croce is the final resting place for many of the most renowned figures of the Renaissance. Michelangelo's tomb, designed by Vassari, is the first on the right as you enter; the three allegorical figures represent *Painting, Architecture,* and *Sculpture.* Dante's empty tomb is right next to him (he was exiled from Florence in 1302 for political reasons and died and was buried in Ravenna in 1321; there's a statue dedicated to the Florentine-born poet on the left side of the steps leading into the church), while Machiavelli rests in the fourth. Galileo and Rossini, among others, were also laid to rest here.

The entrance to the tranquil **Cappella Pazzi** or **Pazzi Chapel** (marked MUSEO DELL'OPERA DI SANTA CROCE) is to the left as you leave the church. Commissioned in 1443 by Andrea de' Pazzi, a key rival of the Medici family, and designed by Filippo Brunelleschi, the chapel is a significant example of early Renaissance architecture. Serving as the church's museum, it houses many works from the 13th to the 17th centuries, highlighted by one of Cimabue's finest works, the *Crucifixion,* which suffered serious damage in a 1966 flood (it's now displayed on an electric cable that'll lift it out of the reaches of future floods).

Basilica di Santa Maria Novella. Piazza Santa Maria Novella (just south of the train station). ☎ **055/28-21-87.** Basilica, free; Cappella degli Spagnoli (Spanish Chapel), 5,000L ($2.80). Basilica, Mon–Sat 7am–12:15pm and 3–6pm, Sun 3–6pm; Cappella degli Spagnoli (Spanish Chapel), Mon–Thurs and Sat 9am–2pm, Sun 8am–1pm.

Begun in 1246 and completed in 1360 (with a green-and-white marble facade added in the 15th century), this cavernous Gothic church was built to accommodate the masses who'd come to hear the Word of God as preached by the Dominicans. To educate the illiterate, they filled it with cycles of frescoes that are some of the most important in Florence—a claim not to be taken lightly. In the **Cappella Maggiore (Main Chapel)** directly behind the main altar, Ghirlandaio created a fresco cycle supposedly depicting the lives of the Virgin and St. John the Baptist, when in fact what we see is a dazzling illustration of life in the days of Renaissance Florence. To the right of this in the Cappella Filippo Strozzi are frescoes by Filippino Lippi, while to the left of the Cappella Maggiore is a 15th-century crucifix by Brunelleschi, his only work in wood.

In the left aisle near the main entrance is an early 15th-century painting of the Trinity with the Virgin and St. John the Evangelist by Masaccio, revolutionary for its early Renaissance perspective.

If you're not yet frescoed out, exit the church and turn right to visit the **Chiostro Verde (Green Cloister)** and its **Cappellone degli Spagnoli (Spanish Chapel),** whose important and captivating series of early Renaissance frescoes (recently restored) by Andrea de Bonaiuto illustrate the history of the Dominican church. The chapel got its name from the nostalgic Eleanora de Toledo, wife of Cosimo de' Medici, who permitted her fellow Spaniards to be buried here. The Green Cloister took its name from the prevalent green tinge of Paolo Uccello's 15th-century fresco cycle, heavily damaged in the 1966 floods.

Church of Santa Maria del Carmine and the Cappella Brancacci. Piazza Santa Maria del Carmine (west of piazza Santo Spirito and the Palazzo Pitti in the Oltrarno). ☎ **055/238-21-95.** Church, free; Cappella Brancacci, 5,000L ($3.40). Mon and Wed–Sat 10am–5pm, Sun 1–5pm.

This baroque church dates from the 18th century, when a fire ravaged the 13th-century structure built for the Carmelite nuns; the smoke damage was major, but the fire left the Brancacci Chapel miraculously intact. This was a miracle indeed, as the frescoes begun by Masolino in 1425 and continued by his brilliant student Masaccio (who quickly outshone his maestro) are crucially seminal to the painters of the encroaching Renaissance. They've recently been painstakingly restored (1990), showing more clearly than ever the painters' unprecedented use of perspective, emotion, and chiaroscuro. The *Expulsion of Adam and Eve* (extreme upper-left corner) best illustrates anguish and shame, while *The Tribute Money* is a study in unprecedented perspective. The bulk of the frescoes depict the life of St. Peter (who appears in a golden orange mantel). The lower panels were finished by Filippino Lippi (son of the great Filippo Lippi) in 1480, 50 years after the premature death of the Tuscan-born Masaccio at 27.

PARKS & GARDENS

The expansive **Giardini Boboli** begins behind the Pitti Palace and fans upward to the star-shaped Fortezza Belvedere crowning the hill. Enter the gardens via the rear exit of the Pitti Palace if you're visiting the museum or the entrance to the left facing the palace if you're bypassing the museum. The green gardens, particularly beautiful in spring, were laid out in the 16th century by the great landscape artist Tribolo. They're filled with an amphitheater, graveled walks, grottoes, and antique and Renaissance statuary and are the best spot in Florence for a picnic lunch. The view from the fortress is stunning, but there's not much to see inside unless there's a special exhibit; ask at the tourist office or look for posters around town.

The Boboli Gardens are open daily 9am to dusk (closed the first and last Monday of the month); fortress hours vary with exhibits. Admission to the gardens is 4,000L ($2.25); admission to fortress grounds is free, but exhibit admission varies.

ORGANIZED TOURS

Florence's historic center is conveniently compact (though chockablock with sites) and now that it's almost entirely closed to traffic, walking along its palazzo- and store-lined streets is a true pleasure. A bus tour isn't the most enjoyable way to see this wonderful city, unless you're not accustomed to wandering about solo.

American Express offers two half-day bus tours, including visits to the Uffizi, the Medici Chapels, and the breathtaking piazzale Michelangiolo. Each tour costs 50,000L ($28). American Express is also the place to inquire about organized tours to the Chianti region and other cities and small towns in Tuscany. You can book the same tours through most other travel agencies throughout town. Recently introduced is a daily walking tour called **Enjoy Florence** (☎ toll free from anywhere in Italy **167/274-819**). It departs at 10am, with a second tour on Monday, Wednesday, and Friday at 5pm from the Thomas Cook exchange office just west of the ponte Vecchio on the Duomo side of the river; it costs 30,000L ($17) for those over 26 and 25,000L ($14) for those under 26.

By calling ☎ **055/234-23-71** you can contact **I Bike Italy** (E-mail: i_bike_italy@compuserve.com; www.ibikeitaly.com) to sign up for 1-day rides in the surrounding countryside March to November, or you can book **Country Walks in Tuscany** year-round at the same number. Guided walks are 75,000L ($42) and guided bike rides (21-speed bikes supplied) 95,000L ($53); a shuttle to the outskirts of town and an enjoyable lunch in a local trattoria are included in both. Extended 2- and 3-day biking and hiking tours were being firmed up at press time. It might stretch your budget, but you should get out of this tourist-trodden stone city and get a glimpse of the incomparable Tuscan countryside. To see some of Tuscany on your own, see "Side Trips," at the end of this chapter.

6 Shopping

In terms of good-value shopping, Florence is heaven. Good value usually means high prices, though moderate in comparison to what you may pay back home for similar made-in-Italy products. This one-time capitalist capital, where modern banking and commerce first flourished, has something for every taste and price range—whether it's a bargain-price wool sweater at the open-air market or a butter-soft leather jacket that'll burst your budget. Florentine merchants aren't the born negotiators of the south and few will encourage bartering. A polite suggestion that you're looking for the best price will open (or shut) the door to bargaining. Buy a lot in the off-season and pay with cash and you might get lucky.

BEST BUYS

Alta moda fashion in Florence is alive and well and living on **via dei Tornabuoni** and its elegant offshoot, **via della Vigna Nuova,** where some of the high priests of Italian and international design and fashion share space with the occasional bank, which you may have to rob in order to afford any of their goods. But it makes for great window-shopping.

Perpendicular to the top (north) end of via Tornabuoni and of a different caliber is the main drag of **via dei Cerretani** that changes into **via dei Panzani** as it heads from the Duomo west to the train station. Some of the clothing and accessories stores can be rather tasteful, but mostly it's mediocre casual wear thrown together with that inborn Florentine flare.

Between the Duomo and the river are the pedestrians-only **via Roma** (which becomes **via Por Santa Maria** after passing piazza della Repubblica and the new La Rinascente department store before reaching the ponte Vecchio) and the parallel **via dei Calzaiuoli;** lined with fashionable jewelry and clothing stores (and the city's second largest department store, Coin), they're the city's main shopping streets. Stores here are only slightly less high fashion and less high priced than those on via dei Tornabuoni. A *gelato* stop is a guaranteed spirit-lifter. **Via del Corso** and (to a lesser degree) its extension east of via del Proconsolo, **borgo degli Albizi,** are also recommended, boasting historic palazzi as well as more approachable boutiques.

Leather is perhaps what Florence is most famous for. Many travelers are happily (albeit mistakenly) convinced they can buy a leather jacket for a song. For quality and selection, no European city can hold a candle to Florentine quality, but prices are higher than all those rumors you've heard. Expect to spend $200 to $300 for a leather jacket with moderate workmanship, detail, and skin quality. The area around **piazza Santa Croce** is the best place to shop for leather, but the pushcarts at the San Lorenzo Market aren't a bad destination for unfussy shoppers. Leather apparel may be beyond your budget, but consider the possibilities of small leather goods, from wallets, belts, and eyeglass cases to fashion accessories, all of which you'll find at the San Lorenzo Market or in myriad *pelletterie,* leather-goods shops.

Florence has been known for its gold for centuries, and jewelry shops of all sizes and levels still abound. Dozens of exclusive gold stores have lined both sides of the pedestrian **ponte Vecchio** since the days of the Medici. Gold is almost always 18 karat (ask them to point out the teensy obligatory stamp), beautifully machine crafted (hand made is something of generations past), and (though not a bargain) moderately priced—think instant heirlooms. There are also a number of stores specializing in high-quality costume jewelry *(bigiotteria)* where only the price tells you it's not the real thing.

MARKETS

There's nothing in Italy, and perhaps nothing in Europe, to compare with Florence's sprawling open-air **Mercato San Lorenzo** north of the Duomo (to get there head down the street called **borgo San Lorenzo**). Hundreds of awninged pushcarts crowd along the streets around the San Lorenzo Church and the Mercato Centrale, offering countless varieties of hand-knit and machine-made wool and mohair sweaters, leather jackets, handbags, wallets, and gloves—not to mention the standard array of souvenir T-shirts and sweatshirts, wool and silk scarves, and Florentine writing paper and endless other souvenirs.

The market stretches for blocks between piazza San Lorenzo and past the Medici Chapel to via Nazionale, along via Canto de' Nelli and via dell'Ariento, with stalls spilling over onto side streets. The days of bargaining have passed. Getting a pushcart salesperson (many of whom aren't even Florentine or Italian) to knock 10% off the original price is a major accomplishment—and one that might happen in the off-season and usually when you're buying more than one item, a costly one, and paying in cash. The market operates daily 9am to 7pm mid-March to October; November to late March it's closed Sunday and Monday and closing hours depend on weather and what kind of day it has been in terms of customer turnout. Many vendors accept credit cards, but there goes the discount.

Much smaller is the outdoor **Mercato del Porcellino,** once known as the Straw Market and today more commonly known as the **Mercato Nuovo (New Market),** where a couple of dozen pushcarts crowd beneath an arcade 2 blocks south of piazza della Repubblica. Vendors offer mostly handbags, scarves, embroidered linen tablecloths, and souvenirs. The market is named for the bronze boar *(porcellino)* on the arcade's river (south) side—his snout has been worn smooth by the countless Florentines and visitors who have touched it for good luck. The market is open 9am to 6pm: daily mid-March to November 3 and Tuesday to Saturday the rest of the year.

DEPARTMENT STORES

Standa, via dei Panzani 31r (☎ 055/239-89-63), is a well-located mid- to low-end department store where you can come up with some surprising finds in accessories, household goods, and miscellaneous items. **La Rinascente,** piazza della Repubblica 1r (☎ 055/21-69-24), and **Coin,** via dei Calzaiuoli 56r (☎ 055/28-05-31), are as close to Bloomingdale's and Macy's as you'll get here, filled with made-in-Italy apparel and accessories. Check out the sales in January and July.

7 Florence After Dark

The best source for entertainment happenings is the Italian-language monthly *Firenze Spettacolo* (2,700L/$1.50), offering comprehensive listings on dance, theater, and music events. The magazine is available at most newsstands. *Avvenimenti* is available from any of the tourist offices.

THE PERFORMING ARTS

The two principal performing arts festivals in Florence are the **Maggio Musicale** and the **Estate Fiesolana.** For more on both, see the "Special & Free Events" box, earlier in this chapter. Stop by the tourist office for a list of the season's concerts that take place in the city's churches and theaters.

One of Italy's busiest stages, Florence's contemporary **Teatro Comunale,** corso Italia 16 (☎ 055/21-08-04 or 055/21-11-58; fax 055/277-94-10), offers everything from symphonies to ballet to plays, opera, and concerts. The large main theater seats 2,000, with orchestra rows topped by horseshoe-shaped first and second galleries. The smaller Piccolo Teatro seating 500 is rectangular, offering good sight lines from most any seat. Tickets are 15,000L to 45,000L ($9 to $25), with prices escalating to 200,000L ($112) for special or opening-night performances. The Teatro Comunale is the seat of the annual Maggio Musicale.

The excellent, centrally located, and recently renovated **Teatro Verdi,** via Ghibellina 101 (☎ 055/21-23-20), schedules regular dance and classical music events, often top foreign performers, troupes, and orchestras and the occasional European pop star. Tickets vary greatly—expect to pay 10,000L to 35,000L ($6 to $20).

BARS, CLUBS & DISCOS

Nightlife isn't Florence's strongest suit, but it has improved considerably over the last few years.

A self-proclaimed "guitar club," the intimate **Chiodo Fisso,** via Dante Alighieri 16r (☎ 055/238-12-90), between via dei Calzaiuoli and via del Proconsolo, east of the new American Express building, is one of the few places to listen to live acoustic and Italian folk music. There's no admission, but drink prices are relatively steep. A bottle of chianti will set you back 25,000L ($14); a minicarafe (basically two glasses) is 6,000L ($3.40). It's open daily 9pm to 3am. The forever busy Irish pub **Fiddler's Elbow,** piazza Santa Maria Novella 7r (☎ 055/21-50-56), about 3 blocks from the train station, is always abuzz with young international travelers, Italian military on leave, and assorted locals. One of the few places where you can get an authentic pint or half pint of Guinness on tap, it's open daily 3pm to 1:30am.

In the city center near Santa Croce Church, **Full-Up,** via della Vigna Vecchia 25r (☎ 055/29-30-06), is a long-enduring upscale disco/piano bar that's one of the top (and more restrained) dance spaces in Florence for the postcollegiate set in a somewhat dated atmosphere. There are plenty of theme evenings (revival, samba, punk), so call to find out what's on. It's open Wednesday to Monday 9pm to 3am. Cover (including one drink) runs 15,000L to 25,000L ($8 to $14). There's no dancing for the professional habitués at the upscale **Il Barretto,** via del Parione 50, off via dei Tornabuoni (☎ 055/239-41-22), just the lovely and intimate ambiance of a small piano bar that now offers a limited but good traditional Tuscan menu as well. It's open daily 6pm to 2am, and the piano bar begins at 10pm. Forever known as Yab Yum and recently reincarnated with a new attitude is **Yab,** via Sassetti 5r (☎ 055/21-51-60), just behind the main Post Office in piazza Repubblica; this dance club for 20-somethings is a perennial favorite, a relic of a 1980s disco that's open Monday and Wednesday to Saturday 9pm to 3am.

A balanced combination of visitors and Italians—teenagers, students, and an under-30 crowd—fill the two-floor **Space Electronic Disco,** via Palazzuolo 37 (☎ **055/29-30-82**). On the first floor is a video karaoke bar, a pub, an American-style bar, and a conversation area. Head upstairs for the dance floor with laser lights and a flying space capsule hovering above. It's open daily 10pm to 3am (closed Monday off-season). Cover is 25,000L ($14), which includes the first drink; you'll get a 10,000L ($6) discount if you say Frommer's sent you.

Another dance club with a young American/Florentine crowd in this same area bordering the Cascine Park is **Meccanò,** piazzale delle Cascine (☎ **055/331-33-71**), where you can spend summer nights on the indoor/outdoor dance floor with a wide range of music. Upstairs at the new **La Piccionaia** restaurant (9:30pm to midnight), dancing on the table is encouraged (Tuesday to Saturday 11:30pm to 4am). Admission is 30,000L ($17).

CAFFÈS

These caffès are more enjoyable and less ear-taxing than the bars above, and you can while away a nocturnal hour or two. For more conventional caffès, check out the historic bars lining piazza della Repubblica, particularly **Gilli's,** or the turn-of-the-century **Caffè Rivoire** in piazza della Signoria, both with indoor/outdoor seating.

Piazza Santo Spirito, hiding behind a tangle of back streets just blocks from the Pitti Palace, is the locals' most loved piazza. Once a haven for drug users, the square has cleaned up its act but still claims enough edginess to be an authentic hangout for the "alternative" crowd. At the of-the-moment **Cabiria Café,** piazza Santo Spirito 4r (☎ **055/21-57-32**), there's some seating inside, but the outdoor tables overlook the dramatic Santo Spirito Church. There's a variety of reasonably priced fresh dishes (about 5,000L/$2.80), but this place bustles with young trendies who come to hang out before and after dinner. It's open Monday and Wednesday to Saturday 8am to 1:30am.

The **Caffè degli Artisti/Art Bar,** via del Moro 4r (☎ **055/28-76-61**), also known as Caffè del Moro because of its street location (north of the ponte alla Carraia), is a longtime favorite worth searching out. An interesting crowd comes to mingle and talk (though music can get loud) and sample the long list of "cocktails" and mixed drinks that are uncommon to this wine-imbibing society. The atmosphere is upscale, and a downstairs room with wooden tables attracts groups of friends who come and linger for hours. It's open Monday to Saturday 7pm to 1am.

From the clever Florentine Midas who gave Florence the internationally famous restaurant and trattoria Cibreo, the handsome **Caffè Cibreo,** via Andrea del Verrochio 5r (☎ **055/234-58-53**), across the street (near the Mercato Sant'Ambrogio), first became known for its informal and inexpensive lunch and dinner menus, many of whose dishes came from the acclaimed kitchen across the way (dinner 7:30pm to midnight). But this is also a lovely spot for an attractive older crowd who take their hot chocolate, tea blends, or coffee roasts seriously or want to people-watch before or after dining.

GAY & LESBIAN BARS

Florence is one of the largest gay communities in Italy, with a tradition of gay tolerance that goes back to the early days of the Renaissance and some of the Medici's homosexual proclivities. The Florentine fondness for *buon gusto* and inherent discretion remain all important, however—except for the remarkable *travestiti* and *transsessuali* who populate the Cascine Park in the dark hours.

Tabasco, piazza Santa Cecilia 3 (☎ **055/21-30-00**), is Florence's (and Italy's) oldest gay dance club, a stone's throw from piazza della Signoria and Michelangelo's *David,* god of anatomical perfection. The crowd is mostly men in their 20s and 30s. The dance floor is downstairs, while a small video room and piano bar are up top. There are occasional cabaret shows and karaoke. Open 9pm to 3am, on Monday, Wednesday, and Thursday it's a bar only; on Tuesday, Friday, Saturday, and Sunday it's a disco. Cover is 15,000L ($8) Sunday to Thursday, 20,000L ($11) Friday, and 25,000L ($14) Saturday. It's hard to find, at the end of a dead-end alley just off via Vaccchereccia and next to the well-known Bar Rivoire.

Florence's leading gay bar, **Crisco,** via S. Egidio 43r (☎ **055/248-05-80**), east of the Duomo, is for men only. Its 18th-century building contains a bar and a dance floor open Sunday, Monday, Wednesday, and Thursday 10:30pm to 3:30am and Friday and Saturday 10:30pm to 5 or 6am. The cover is 12,000L to 16,000L ($7 to $9), depending on the night. In summer at **Santanassa Bar,** via del Pandolfini 26 (☎ **055/24-33-56**), near piazza Santa Croce, the crowd is international. On the street level is a crowded bar, sometimes with a live piano player. On Friday and Saturday the cellar becomes a disco. It's open Sunday to Thursday 10pm to 4am and Friday and Saturday 10pm to 6am. The bar is open year-round; the disco, only September to June. Cover, including the first drink, is 12,000L ($7) Sunday to Thursday and 15,000L to 20,000L ($8 to $11) Friday and Saturday.

ArciGay/Lesbica (also called Azione Gay e Lesbica), Italy's largest and oldest gay organization, has a center in Florence north of the Mercato San Lorenzo on via San Zanobi 54r (☎ and fax **055/47-65-57;** www.agora.stm.it/gaylesbica.fi).

8 Side Trips: Fiesole & the Tuscan Countryside

FIESOLE

Fiesole sits on a hill rising above Florence 5 miles north of town and a half-hour bus ride on the no. 7 leaving from piazza San Marco. For centuries, families of means have fled the city's summer heat, plagues, and ennui and taken to the cool cypress-studded environs of Fiesole; consequently, it came to be known for its magnificent hillside villas and million-dollar views. Many of the villas are now associated with American university programs, such as that of the famous art critic Bernard Berenson, who left his Villa I Tatti to Harvard University, or the Rockefeller Villa bequeathed to Georgetown University.

The pre-Roman Etruscans had set up camp here in Faesulae centuries before the Romans established a riverside trading base down below, circa 59 B.C. Their presence is still felt at the important **archaeological site (Zona Archeologica),** a vast area of 2,000-year-old Etruscan and Roman ruins (☎ **055/59-477**). Its highlight is the large 3,000-seat amphitheater used for the Estate Fiesolana music, dance, and theater festival June to August. Admission is 10,000L ($6). It's open daily 9am to dusk (closed first Tuesday of every month). Next to it is the **Museo Civico (Museo Faesulanum),** whose finds prove the importance of Fiesole over Florence in their nascent days (admission on joint ticket with the Zona Archeologica). The town center surrounds a large square dedicated to sculptor Mino da Fiesole (ca. 1430–84). Fronting the square is a Romanesque **cathedral** (heavily altered in a 19th-century renovation), the 17th-century **Bishop's Palace,** and the **St. Maria Primerana Church.**

But Fiesole is all about its lofty views over the Arno Valley, and no one leaves without a look at the splendid panorama of Florence and the countryside. For a heart-stopping view (in every sense of the word) you'll have to hike up the very steep pedestrian-only via di San Francesco west (left) out of the main square—not for the weak of heart. There's a church and museum that follow temperamental hours, but the trek leads to a ✪ **terrace belvedere** and a view that never ends.

You'll have worked up an appetite by now, but Fiesole's abundant restaurants, bars, and cafes principally work as tourist traps. Sip a Campari or order a *gelato* while waiting for the bus back to reality, but don't plan on eating here.

THE TUSCAN COUNTRYSIDE

Tuscany is thought by many to be the most beautiful of Italy's 19 regions. Most of its towns and hill towns are serviced by two **bus lines:** SITA, via Santa Caterina da Siena 15r (☎ **055/48-36-51**), and LAZZI, piazza Stazione 4–6 (☎ **055/23-98-840**), whose depots are on either side of Florence's train station.

Pisa is easily reached by frequent train departures, but **Lucca** has a local-only train service that's best avoided. **San Gimignano** can be reached only by bus, and **Siena,** though serviced by train, is far more commonly and easily reached by bus. The same agencies offering city tours offer half- and full-day tours of the Chianti area (April to October), Pisa, and San Gimignano/Siena (see "Organized Tours," earlier in this chapter). Unless you're an organized tour person, these are destinations best seen on your own (with the exception of Pisa, they're compact, car-free, and imminently strollable).

SAN GIMIGNANO

You may have seen, heard, or dreamed about **San Gimignano delle Belle Torri** ("San Gimignano of the Beautiful Towers"). Of the 70-some extant in the Middle Ages, only 13 towers are left—enough to give it its distinctive hill-town profile and sobriquet of the Medieval Manhattan. It's one of Florence's favorite day trips, and in the high season will appear overrun and void of magic unless you arrive early or stay late. If the crowds dampen your spirits, take to the cool, quiet back streets that promise glimpses of the stunning Tuscan countryside.

ARRIVING   Since this town is 34 miles southwest of Florence and 23 miles from Siena, plan on a full day and check out the **bus** schedules first (about 10,000L/$6 from Florence to San Gimignano with a mandatory but easy change in Poggibonsi, about 8,500L/$4.80 from San Gimignano to Siena).

SEEING THE SIGHTS   The heart of town is the ancient **piazza della Cisterna,** whose adjacent **piazza Duomo,** of herringbone bricks, is the location of both the 12th-century **Duomo,** famous for its frescoes by Ghirlandaio of the local Santa Fina (open daily 9:30am to 12:30pm and 3 to 5:30pm, with free admission), and the **Museo Civico,** whose *Madonna Maestà* by Lippo Mimmi (1317) is the town's masterpiece (☎ **0577/94-03-40;** open Wednesday to Sunday 9:30am to 7:30pm in summer and 9:30am to 6pm in winter; admission to Museo and Torre each 8,000L/$4.50). Climb up the museum's **Torre Grossa,** finished in 1311, the town's highest—it's like sitting on top of a flagpole with a view that'll make your heart skip a beat.

ACCOMMODATIONS   The nicest place in town is **La Cisterna Hotel,** piazza della Cisterna 24, 53037 San Gimignano (☎ **0577/94-03-28;** fax 0577/94-20-80). Many of the doubles have views that remind you that, while Tuscany's hill towns are beautiful to view from a distance, they're even more wonderful for the vantage points they offer. All 50 units have bathrooms, each costing 146,000L ($82) without a view. Expect to pay an extra 20,000L ($11) for a view and an additional 20,000L ($11) for a balcony, money well spent. Rates include breakfast. The hotel is closed January 7 to March 8 and accepts American Express, Diners Club, MasterCard, and Visa. The hotel's **Restaurant le Terrazze** gets crowded at lunch and is more relaxed and romantic at dinner. It's open Thursday to Tuesday 12:30 to 2:30pm and 7 to 10:30pm.

Also see the **Bel Soggiorno** below.

DINING For an unpretentious and inexpensive lunch, try the daily changing specialty at the tiny **Trattoria Chiribiri,** piazza della Madonna, off via San Giovanni near Porta San Giovanni (☎ **0577/94-19-48**). It's owned by a group of talented young people, and their home cooking makes the prices even more interesting. Pastas cost about 10,000L ($6) and entrees about 12,000L ($7). It's open Thursday to Tuesday noon to 10pm (off-season hours may vary) and accepts no credit cards.

The ✪ **Ristorante Bel Soggiorno,** via San Giovanni 41 (☎ **0577/94-31-49**), is the place for the best the region has to offer. Much of the ingredients come from the family's farm and wine-producing estate, and it shows in the freshness and quality of everything from the thick-crusted bread to the hazy green olive oil drizzled on everything except dessert. The respected wine cellar draws a crowd of bigwigs from the Chianti wine industry. Most soups or pastas cost 13,000L ($7) or less; perfectly grilled meats are the specialty, at about 20,000L ($11). It's open Tuesday to Sunday 12:30 to 2:30pm and 7 to 10:30pm and accepts American Express and Visa. The Bel Soggiorno is also one of the town's better hotels (☎ and fax **0577/94-03-75**), offering 21 units with bathroom; doubles are 120,000L ($67). American Express and Visa are accepted.

SIENA

There's train service to **Siena,** 21 miles south of Florence in the southern confines of the Chianti area, but buses are more frequent and convenient, since they'll drop you off closer to the center rather than at the remote train station.

ARRIVING For those choosing to forgo San Gimignano and head straight for Siena, **SITA buses** leave Florence direct for Siena about every 30 minutes from the station at via Santa Caterina da Siena 15r (☎ **055/48-36-51**). The bus journey follows a lovely route for the most part, takes about 75 minutes, and costs 10,000L ($6) each way. Make sure you get on the *rapido* and not the local.

SEEING THE SIGHTS The "musts" to see are the stunning **Duomo** and its adjacent museum and the unique shell-shaped central square, **il Campo.** Siena's 12th-century black-and-white-striped marble Duomo sits atop its highest hill. It's one of Italy's most beautiful and ambitious medieval churches. In 1339, plans were launched to expand the extant cathedral to create Christendom's largest church outside Rome. The 1348 bubonic plague arrived, money ran dry, and the unfinished structure to the right of the Duomo still stands. Called the **Facciatone (Big Facade),** it's incorporated into the church's **Museo dell'Opera** (☎ **0577/28-11-61**), where original masterworks from the Duomo have been brought over the centuries. Mid-March to October, the museum is open daily 9am to 7:30pm (to 1:30pm the rest of the year); admission is 6,000L ($3.40). Your entry into the Duomo will be dazzling: The zebra-striped theme continues, with a priceless 14th- to 16th-century polychrome marble pavement of more than 50 panels only partially on view in the interests of conservation. The octagonal pulpit carved by Nicola Pisano in the 13th century found in the left transept is one of the many masterpieces.

The important **Pinacoteca Nazionale (Picture Gallery)** is at via San Pietro 29 (☎ **0577/28-11-61**). It's impossible to appreciate or understand the breadth and importance of the Sienese school of painting and its local history-makers (like Guido da Siena, Duccio, Simone Martini, and Beccafumi) without wandering through more than 40 rooms of masterworks from the 12th to the 17th centuries (concentrating on the 14th and 15th centuries). April to October, it's open Monday 8:30am to 1:30pm,

Tuesday to Saturday 9am to 7pm, and Sunday 8am to 1pm; November to March, hours are Monday to Saturday 8:30am to 1:30pm and Sunday 8am to 1pm. Admission is 8,000L ($4.50).

Your most insightful meandering will be throughout the hilly side streets of Siena's large traffic-free *centro storico*. All roads seem to slide into the central square, il Campo. Instead, head up to the 16th-century **Fortezza Medicea** on viale Maccari. The fort with a view has been transformed into the **Enoteca Italica** (☎ 0577/28-84-97), the area's most evocative spot for a wine tasting of Chianti's (and Italy's) best labels. The cost is 3,000L to 6,000L ($1.70 to $3.40) per glass, and it's open daily noon to 12:30am.

If it's late afternoon and the hour of the *passeggiata*, you'll be swept up in the flow of well-dressed humanity, window-shopping and cruising the store-lined via di Città, banchi di Sotto, and banchi di Sopra. Break away while there's still light: A sprint up the 505 steps of the ✪ **Torre del Mangia** in il Campo's Palazzo Comunale are worth the workout for the unparalleled view. Or opt to just sit for a moment or an hour in any of the campo's cafes and commit to memory one of Europe's most beautiful old piazzas and the heart of Siena.

ACCOMMODATIONS   The ✪ **Hotel Piccola Etruria,** via delle Donzelle 3, off banchi di Sotto, 53100 Siena (☎ **0577/28-80-88;** fax 0577/28-84-61), is one of my favorite hotels in Tuscany, because the Fattorini family runs it with such pride. Their recent renovation spared no cost, and they continue to ask extremely modest rates. The 13 doubles with bathroom are 103,000L ($58). Breakfast is 7,000L ($3.95). American Express, Diners Club, MasterCard, and Visa are accepted.

For a splurge, try the **Palazzo Antellesi Apartments,** via Sallustio Bandini 35 (☎ **055/24-44-56** or 212/932-3480 in New York; fax 055/234-55-52 or 212/932-9039 in New York; e-mail: antellesi@mail.dada.it; http://idt.net/~manpico/). The Piccolomini family is one of Siena's oldest and most respected: You might've strolled past their Palazzo Piccolomini on banchi di Sotto or marveled at the Piccolomini Library in the Duomo. The family has opened one of its lesser ancestral palazzi, renting four lovely and fully furnished apartments by the week. Rates are discounted for multiple-week or monthly stays. The central one-bedroom penthouse apartments sleeping two to three begin at $920 per week (10% off January 15 to March 15). No credit cards are accepted, though personal checks are.

DINING   The pizza is too good and the prices are too reasonable to expect **Pizzeria da Carlo e Franca,** via di Pantaneto 138 (☎ 0577/22-04-85), to ever be anything less than crowded. Of the more than 30 varieties, the *pizza alla boscaiola* with tomatoes, sausage, mushrooms, mozzarella, and garlic is the favorite. Full pizzas average 6,000L ($3.40). It's open Thursday to Tuesday noon to 3pm and 5pm to midnight and accepts no credit cards.

A Tuscan theme prevails at the popular ✪ **Antica Trattoria Papei,** piazza del Mercato 6 (☎ **0577/28-08-94**), run by three generations of the Papei family. This "Old Trattoria" has been around a mere 50 years, but its convivial atmosphere, time-tested family specialties (with the local specialty of game), and outdoor tables in one of the city's oldest piazzas guarantee its future. Primi cost 10,000L ($6) and entrees 15,000L ($8). It's open Tuesday to Sunday noon to 2:20pm and 7 to 10:30pm and accepts MasterCard and Visa.

LUCCA

A quintessential Tuscan hill town minus the hill (this area of the otherwise rolling *lucchesia,* the picturesque olive-producing corner of Tuscany, is uncustomarily flat),

Lucca has somehow been overlooked by bus tourism that whizzes by en route to Pisa, a city I feel holds much less whimsy and appeal. That sits just fine with Lucca, a wealthy little city contained within its spectacular Renaissance walls.

ARRIVING   Quasi-hourly **LAZZI buses** leave Florence for Lucca Monday to Saturday (buses are less frequent on Sunday), costing about 9,000L ($5) each way for the 70-minute ride. Pisa is just 14 miles southwest (47 miles west of Florence) and is connected by frequent bus service from Lucca, costing 4,000L ($4.25) each way. To visit Pisa directly from Florence, it's easiest to make the 1-hour trip by **trains** that leave every 30 to 60 minutes for about 9,500L ($5) each way.

SEEING THE SIGHTS   An unhurried small-town atmosphere prevails within Lucca's protective swath of walls. Rent bikes from the local tourist office, **A.P.T.,** Vecchia Porta San Donato, piazzale Verdi (☎ **583/41-96-89**), for about 3,000L ($1.70) for the first hour (and less after) to experience the tree-lined 2½-mile promenade (and a great jogging path) atop the walls. The 16th-century brick walls were Lucca's third and final set of ramparts and are Europe's best Renaissance defense walls. This makes Lucca Italy's most perfectly preserved walled city, a mélange of architecture from Roman to medieval to baroque (with neoclassical and art deco or "Liberty" thrown in). Its straight, level streets follow the grid of ancient Roman roads in a town whose origins go back to the Etruscan days of 600 or 700 B.C. The store-lined **via Fillungo** is the principal venue for the day's ritual *passaggiata*.

A sophisticated silk and textile trade made this town famous throughout medieval Europe, evident today in the 60-some churches that once numbered far more (many are closed). The two standouts are the **Duomo** and **San Michele in Foro,** both exquisite examples of Pisan-Lucchese architecture. The center of town is **piazza Napoleone,** named for the French ruler who conquered the city and made his sister, Elisa, duchess in 1805 (he eventually gave her and her Italian husband the entire Duchy of Tuscany). From here it's equidistant to these two churches, north to San Michele in Foro (St. Michael in the Forum) and east to the Duomo.

The **Duomo,** piazza San Martino, was begun in the 11th century and is known for its symmetrical facade of multiple loggias with carved columns. Competing for historical importance inside is the revered *Volto Santo* (Holy Visage of Christ), said to be carved by Nicodemus, a contemporary of Christ (art historians attribute it to a much later date). It arrived in Lucca in 782, attracting pilgrims from all over Europe, and was believed to have had miraculous powers. One of Lucca's most celebrated monuments is the far more recent marble tomb of Ilaria del Carretto by Jacopo della Querica (1408), in the sacristy. A beloved figure in local history, Ilaria was the young wife of an affluent lord of Lucca who hired the day's finest sculptor to immortalize her. The Duomo is open daily 9am to 6pm.

San Michele in Foro is the social, if not religious, center of town and the original site of the Roman Forum (hence its name). Begun in 1143, it's dedicated to the winged Archangel Michael, who crowns its facade. The exquisite Romanesque facade is composed of four tiers of patterned pillars of which no two are alike. Things are less exuberant inside, where the only works of interest are a painting of Filippino Lippi in the left transept and a glazed terra-cotta bas relief by Andrea della Robbia. The church is open daily 8am to 12:30pm and 3 to 6pm. A big **outdoor market** is held here daily the last 2 weeks of September, but even when empty the piazza is a lively crossroads.

All Lucca was a stage for Giacomo Puccini, born here in 1858, in the shadow of San Michele in Foro. The **Opera Theater of Lucca,** an Italian-American collaboration that organizes concerts mid-June to mid-July (the 1999 season is its fourth), is held in his honor, though not all productions are by the Lucchese maestro. The feast day of the town's patron saint, Paolino, falls on July 12. Contact Alan Yaffe, General Manager at the University of Cincinnati, Ohio, at ☎ **513/556-5662** (fax 513/556-0202; e-mail: OperaLucca@uc.edu).

ACCOMMODATIONS   The ✪ **Piccolo Hotel Puccini,** via di Poggio 9, 55100 Lucca (☎ **0583/554-21;** fax 0583/534-87; e-mail: hotelpucciniLU@onenet.it; www.onenet.it/LU/Hotel_Puccini/), is lovely even minus any real competition. Lucca is the hometown of Puccini, and this charming three-star hotel sits in front of the building where the composer was born and a block from San Michele in Foro. Enthusiastic young owners have brightened up the place, giving it the charm so sorely needed. All 14 units have bathrooms, phones, and TVs, with singles at 92,000L ($52) and doubles at 128,000L ($72). The optional breakfast is 12,000L ($7), and American Express, MasterCard, and Visa are accepted.

Hotel Diana, via del Molinetto 9, 55100 Lucca (☎ **0583/49-22-02;** fax 0583/47-495; e-mail: aldiana@tin.it), is a good money saver with an excellent location in a 16th-century palazzo a block from the Duomo. The absence of a breakfast room means the optional *piccola colazione* will be served in your room (5000L/$2.80). With TVs and phones, the two singles without bathroom are 50,000L ($28) and the seven doubles with bathroom are 98,000L ($55). American Express, Diners Club, MasterCard, and Visa are accepted.

DINING   ✪ **Da Giulio,** via delle Conce 47, north of piazza San Donato (☎ **0583/55-948**), is the kind of ultra-Tuscan locale that draws urbane Florentines for a memorable lunch *alla toscana.* Save your appetite and lire for the rustic specialties, from the thick *zuppa di farro* (8,000L/$4.50) made with elmer (a kind of barley) to any of the roasted or grilled meats (15,000L/$8). Giulio's stays open for Sunday lunch the third Sunday of each month, when an important Antiques Fair rolls into town. It's open Tuesday to Saturday 12:30 to 2:30pm and 7 to 11pm and accepts American Express, Diners Club, MasterCard, and Visa.

Da Guido, via C. Battisti 28, near piazza Sant'Agostino (☎ **0583/47-219**), is a no-frills family-run place that in some ways is even more authentic than the polished Giulio's. With the TV locked into the sports channel and amiable proprietor Guido running a smooth operation, you can count on *primi* (with a homemade pasta or two usually making an appearance) costing less than 6,000L ($3.40) and entrees under 8,000L ($4.50). It's open Monday to Saturday 12:30 to 2:30pm and 7 to 11pm and accepts American Express.

PISA

The truth about **Pisa** is that unless you're determined to see for yourself if that certain tower really leans (it does) and have your photo taken as you pretend to hold it up, you may be disappointed with what is not a quaint little town but a large impersonal city—one blessed, however, with a magnificent **campo dei Miracoli (Field of Miracles).** The tower, possibly the most recognized human-built structure anywhere in the Western world, has been closed to the public since 1990, but visitors from all over the world are drawn to see it.

ARRIVING   See "Lucca," above.

SEEING THE SIGHTS   Medieval Pisa was a powerful port (before its waters receded) and, together with Genoa, Venice, and Amalfi, was one of Italy's (and Europe's) four great maritime powers in the Mediterranean and beyond. At home, it turned much of its revenue and attention to the flourishing of the arts and architecture. Its greatest legacy remains in the spacious green Campo dei Miracoli, the city's only real claim to fame.

The eight-story white-marble campanile known as the ✪ **Leaning Tower of Pisa** was begun in 1174 as the freestanding bell tower to the adjacent **Duomo** (begun in 1063), whose **Battistero** (begun in 1153) is the largest of its kind in Italy; it completes the trio of remarkable structures in the emerald-green piazza (itself a rarity for Italy's urban squares). They set the style for Pisa Romanesque architecture in Italy, more simply known as Pisan, with its roots in the great Moorish architecture of Spain's Andalusia (Pisa had strong trade connections with Spain and Africa). The 12th-century was Pisa's golden age, and this triad is its timeless landmark.

Many legends persist about the tower, which, if it were to stand upright, would measure about 180 feet tall. It currently leans at least 14 feet from the perpendicular (and appearing twice that from some angles). Various manners of ingenious engineering have been employed in the interests of arresting the continuing listing (about 1 millimeter a year), like shoring up its foundation of water-soaked clay. Contrary to hearsay, it wasn't built leaning to prove the inordinate (and assuredly peculiar) talents of the architect, but rather it started to list at some time after the completion of the first three stories when it was discovered, too late, that the foundation wasn't rock solid. Construction was suspended for a century and then resumed, with completion in the late 14th century.

At press time, the latest brainstorm to stop its possible collapse was to secure it with industrial-strength cables attached to the closest structure, rather than blocking off the entire visitor-clogged area should it topple without notice (this is one of the world's most closely watched buildings, but 1997 earthquakes in neighboring Umbria have put all Tuscany on the alert). Try to see it from all angles: It definitely appears more exaggerated from certain angles.

DINING   The blocks around the campo dei Miracoli are filled with sandwich bars and pizza places. One of the best medium-priced restaurants is **Antica Trattoria "da Bruno,"** via Luigi Bianchi 12 (☎ **50/56-08-11**), specializing in Pisan cuisine, like *pasta e ceci* (a tomato-based soup made with chick peas) and *baccala con porri* (codfish simmered with leeks). Fresh fish makes up a good part of the changing menu but hikes the price considerably. It's open Wednesday to Sunday 12:30 to 2:30pm and 7:30 to 10:30pm and accepts Visa only.

Geneva & Bern 14

by Nikolaus Lorey

Geneva is the quintessential international city. Ever since it hosted its first conference in the 8th century, it has been a privileged site for summit meetings and a favored headquarters of international organizations. The Red Cross and League of Nations were founded here, and the city is home to the World Health Organization (WHO), Centre Européen de Recherches Nucléaires (CERN), and countless other acronyms.

Despite these ties, few places are as conscious as Geneva of its essential quality—being first and foremost its own city. Surrounded almost totally by France, Geneva didn't join the Swiss Confederacy until 1815 and still displays its official name with pride: Republic and Canton of Geneva. On the Ile Rousseau, the statue of Jean-Jacques Rousseau bears an inscription describing him simply as a citizen of Geneva—citoyen de Genève. Other citizens have included Voltaire, Byron, Lenin, Richard Burton, Alain Delon, Audrey Hepburn, and Romania's exiled King Michael.

Argentine writer Jorge Luís Borges lived here as a child during World War I and returned in his 80s, just before his death; he proclaimed Geneva the one place "most propitious for happiness." When you see the deep-blue lake, with the snowcapped Alps in the distance and the jet d'eau arcing gracefully above the very proper skyline, you may feel the same.

REQUIRED DOCUMENTS Citizens of the United States, Canada, the United Kingdom, Australia, and New Zealand need only a valid passport. Remember to carry it if you visit Chamonix or the Salève in France or take a boat excursion that stops at the French villages on Lake Geneva's south shore.

OTHER FROMMER'S TITLES For more on Geneva, see *Frommer's Switzerland* or *Frommer's Europe*.

1 Geneva Deals & Discounts

SPECIAL DISCOUNTS

If you plan to visit far-flung sections of the city by bus or tram, you'll save money by purchasing a 1-, 2-, or 3-day **transit pass** valid on buses and trams and good for unlimited rides within the city and the outskirts. And for only 2.50SF ($1.80) you can have an inexpensive boat ride across Lake Geneva from one bank to the other.

Budget Bests

Geneva's best bargains are undoubtedly its **museums**—most are free. An exception is the must-see International Red Cross Museum, which charges 10SF ($7).

In this chapter you'll find a number of **inexpensive hotels** with doubles for 90SF ($64), and this includes a continental breakfast. With your remaining francs, you should be able to get lunch and dinner and stay within your budget.

In summer, head to the parks and quays along the banks of the lake for another bargain—**free music.** Classical, jazz, and pop music make a wonderful accompaniment to a picnic dinner. In addition, free concerts are offered from June to September on Saturday at 6pm at the Cathédrale St-Pierre and on Sunday and Monday evenings at the Eglise St-Germain.

And don't pass up the opportunity to have Geneva's delicious **cheese fondue.** This meal is not only filling and entertaining but also one of the city's best food bargains.

WORTH A SPLURGE

The four-star **Hôtel Excelsior** will offer reasonable rates to *Frommer's* readers who show them this book (see "Accommodations You Can Afford," later in this chapter).

2 Essentials

ARRIVING

BY PLANE OR TRAIN   With only 175,000 residents, Geneva is a small city. The **Geneva–Cointrin Airport,** though busy with all the comings and goings of employees and visitors to the city's numerous international organizations, is compact and easily negotiated. It's 3 miles from Geneva.

Getting into the city from the airport is a breeze. In the air terminal's basement is a station with trains leaving about every 10 to 15 minutes for the 6-minute trip to the city's **Gare de Cornavin (Cornavin Station),** place Cornavin (☎ 022/157-22-22). If you happen to be heading for another Swiss city, you may be able to depart directly from the airport station without having to change trains at Cornavin. The train from the airport into the city costs 4.80SF ($3.40) one-way and runs daily 5:30am to 12:36am. Whether you arrive by air or train, you'll find yourself at Cornavin Station, on the right bank. For rail info, call ☎ 022/157-22-22 (fax 022/715-25-30).

Taking a **taxi** into town is highly inadvisable. A taxi takes much longer than the train and, costing 50SF ($36), is much more expensive.

VISITOR INFORMATION

The **main tourist office,** at 3 rue du Mont-Blanc (☎ 022/738-52-00), is open July to September, daily 8am to 8pm, and October to June, Monday to Saturday 9am to 6pm. The staff will make hotel reservations in the city for 5SF ($3.60) and elsewhere in Switzerland for 10SF ($7). Here you can pick up a free copy of *What's On in Geneva,* a useful publication with details on sightseeing, the performing arts, and special events. A **branch of the tourist office** is at 4 place du Molard (☎ 022/311-98-27), with shorter open hours.

From June 15 to September 15, the **Centre d'Accueil et de Renseignements (CAR)** (☎ 022/731-46-47) provides information from a van parked on rue du Mont-Blanc in front of the train station. It's open daily 8:30am to 11pm.

Infor Jeunes, 13 rue Verdaine (☎ 022/311-44-22), near place Bourg-de-Four in the Old City, is an information center for young travelers. The staff can answer all

What Things Cost in Geneva	U.S. $
Taxi from the airport to city center	35.00
Public transportation for an average trip within the city	1.55
Local telephone call	.50
Double room at Le Richemond (deluxe)	514.00
Double room at the Hôtel Excelsior (moderate)	128.00
Double room at the Hôtel de la Cloche (budget)	57.00
Lunch for one, without wine, at Café des Antiquaires (moderate)	14.00
Lunch for one, without wine, at Restaurant Manora (budget)	13.00
Dinner for one, without wine, at La Perle du Lac (deluxe)	63.00
Dinner for one, without wine, at Les Armures (moderate)	25.00
Dinner for one, without wine, at La Cave Valaisanne (budget)	16.00
Glass of wine	2.85
Coca-Cola	2.00
Cup of coffee	1.80
Roll of ASA 100 color film, 36 exposures	5.00
Admission to the Red Cross Museum	7.00
Movie ticket	11.00
Theater ticket	26.00

sorts of questions about Geneva Monday to Friday 10am to 10pm and Saturday and Sunday 2 to 10pm.

CITY LAYOUT

Geneva is at the western end of **Lake Geneva,** known in French as Lac Léman, site of the impressive jet d'eau. The blue-green waters of the lake meet the **Rhône River,** which divides the city into a left and a right bank. On the **Rive Gauche (Left Bank)** are the Old City, some major shopping streets, the famous flower clock, the university, and several important museums. On the **Rive Droite (Right Bank)** are the train station, the major international organizations, and many attractive parks.

GETTING AROUND

Unless you want to see both the Old City on the left bank and the international organizations on the right bank in 1 day, you can easily explore Geneva on foot.

BY BUS & TRAM   Geneva isn't very big, so you'll be able to walk almost everywhere. For longer distances, the **Transports Publics Genevois (TPG)** (☎ **022/ 308-34-34**) offers a fine network of buses and trolleys, as well as two trams (nos. 12 and 13). If you're going three stops or less, the fare is 1.50SF ($1.10); for more than three stops the ticket costs 2.20SF ($1.60) and is good for 1 hour with no limits on transfers. Tickets are dispensed from coin-operated machines at every stop.

There's also a series of *cartes journalières* (day passes). A 1-day pass is 8.50SF ($6), a 2-day pass 15SF ($9), and a 3-day pass 19SF ($14). *Cartes multiparcours* are 12 three-stop tickets for 15SF ($11) or 6 one-hour tickets for 12SF ($9). Those staying for longer periods should consider the monthly passes. The *carte orange* is 70SF ($50), the *carte vermeil* (for seniors and the disabled) 40SF ($29), and the *carte azure* (for those 25 and under) 35SF ($25).

BY TAXI Taxicabs are easy to find but not cheap. The meter starts at 6SF ($4.30) and rises 3.10SF ($2.20) per kilometer. From 8pm to 6am, the per-kilometer rate is 3.50SF ($2.50). You can hail taxis on the street or at stands at Cornavin Station and Plainpalais. If you want one to come pick you up, call ☎ **331-41-33.**

BY BICYCLE A bike is an excellent way to visit the countryside, but it's not practical for sightseeing in the city, where the Old City streets are steep and made of cobblestones. For cycling in the countryside, pick up a map of the canton of Geneva from the tourist office and head out through farmland and vineyards to the many picturesque villages.

At **Cornavin Station,** you can rent multispeed bicycles for 17SF ($12) per half day or 21SF ($15) per full day. Mountain bikes are 29SF ($24). It accepts most credit cards and is open daily 6:45am to 7pm.

Horizon Motos, 22 rue de Pâquis (☎ **022/738-36-96;** fax 022/738-02-82), rents mountain bikes, mopeds, and motorcycles Monday to Friday 8am to noon and 1:30 to 7pm and Saturday 8am to 5pm. The mountain bikes and mopeds are 44SF ($31) per day and 259SF ($185) per week. Unless you pay with a credit card, you must leave a 500SF ($357) refundable deposit. Motorcycles start at 77SF ($55) per day, including insurance; you need a valid motorcycle license.

BY BOAT Shuttling back and forth between the right and left banks in summer are small boats known as *mouettes genevoises.* These water buses are the cheapest way to take a cruise on the lake. For as little as 2.50SF ($1.80) you can cross from one side of the lake to the other, or for 12SF ($9) you can get a round-trip ticket that allows you to get off at any of the five stops and get back on a later boat.

BY RENTAL CAR Rent a car only for excursions from the city. Most of the major international agencies have offices in Geneva. For budget rentals, try **Léman,** 6 rue Amat (☎ **022/732-01-43;** fax 022/732-02-04), where you can rent a Peugeot 106 for 100SF ($71) per day, with unlimited mileage. It's open Monday to Saturday 8am to 7pm and Sunday 9am to 5pm.

FAST FACTS: Geneva

American Express The office is at 7 rue du Mont-Blanc (☎ **022/731-76-00;** fax 022/732-72-11), open Monday to Friday 8:30am to 5:30pm and Saturday 9am to noon.

Baby-sitters The tourist office lists several agencies, including **Service de Placement de l'Université,** 4 rue de Candolle (☎ **022/329-39-70** or 022/705-77-02), which you must call between 8:30am and 1pm and 2 and 4:30pm for service that evening. **Le Chaperon Rouge,** 4 rue Rodo (☎ **022/781-06-66**), accepts calls daily 8:30am to 1pm—it's organized by the local Red Cross.

Business Hours Hours for most **shops** are Monday to Saturday 8:30am to 6:30pm. **Offices** are open Monday to Friday 8am to noon and 2 to 6pm.

Consulates Geneva's consulates include **Australia,** 56 rue Moillebeau (☎ 022/918-29-00); the **United Kingdom,** 37–39 rue Vermont (☎ 022/734-38-00); **Canada,** 11 chemin du Pré-de-la-Bichette (☎ 022/733-90-00); **New Zealand,** 28 chemin du Petit-Saconnex (☎ 022/734-95-30); and the **United States,** 29 rte. Pré-Bois, near Geneva–Cointrin Airport (☎ 022/798-16-15).

Currency The basic unit of currency is the **Swiss franc (SF),** which is divided into 100 **centimes.** There are coins of 5, 10, and 20 centimes and ½, 1, 2, and

The Swiss Franc

For American Readers   At this writing, $1 = approximately 1.40SF (or 1SF = 71¢), and this was the rate of exchange used to calculate the dollar values given in this chapter (rounded to the nearest dollar).

For British Readers   At this writing, £1 = approximately 2.30SF (or 1SF = 43p), and this was the rate of exchange used to calculate the pound values in the table below.

Note: Exchange rates fluctuate from time to time and may not be the same when you travel to Switzerland.

SF	U.S.$	U.K.£	SF	U.S.$	U.K.£
1	.71	.43	10	7.14	4.35
2	1.43	.87	15	10.71	6.52
3	2.14	1.30	20	14.29	8.70
4	2.86	1.74	30	21.43	13.04
5	3.57	2.17	40	28.57	17.39
6	4.28	2.60	50	35.71	21.74
7	5.00	3.04	75	53.57	32.61
8	5.71	3.48	100	71.43	43.48
9	6.43	3.91	125	89.29	54.35

5 francs, and banknotes of 10SF, 20SF, 50SF, 100SF, 500SF, and 1,000SF. Banks all over Geneva have currency exchange windows and offer good rates.

Emergencies   Dial ☎ **117** for the police and ☎ **118** for the fire department. In medical emergencies, dial ☎ **372-81-00** or go to the Hôpital Cantonal, 24 rue Micheli-du-Crest (☎ 022/382-33-11). If you need a dentist, go to one of the cliniques dentaires at 5 chemin Malombré (☎ 022/346-64-44) and 60 av. Wendt (☎ 022/733-98-00); both are open daily 7:30am to 8pm.

The free weekly *Geneva Agenda* contains addresses and phone numbers of pharmacies open to 9 or 11pm each week; in emergencies, dial ☎ **111** for urgent pharmaceutical needs or ☎ **144** for an ambulance.

Holidays   Public holidays in Geneva include New Year's Day (January 1), Good Friday, Easter Monday, Ascencion Day (early March), Whitmonday (late May), Swiss National Holiday (August 1), Geneva Day (September 11), and Christmas Day (December 25).

Laundry   The **Salon Lavoir,** 4 rue de Montbrillant, on the first street behind Cornavin Station, will do your laundry for 17SF ($12) Monday to Friday 7:30am to 12:30pm and 1:30 to 6:30pm (Thursday to noon) and Saturday 8am to noon.

Mail   The main post office is at 18 rue du Mont-Blanc, 2 blocks from Gare de Cornavin. It's open Monday to Friday 7:30am to 6pm and Saturday 8 to 11am.

Police   In an emergency, dial ☎ **117.**

Tax   The **value-added tax (VAT)** of 6.5%, levied on purchases above 500SF ($357), is refundable; simply ask the store for a VAT form and present it to the Customs official when leaving the country.

Country & City Codes

The **country code** for Switzerland is **41.** The **city code** for Geneva is **22;** use this code when you're calling from outside Switzerland. If you're within Switzerland but not in Geneva, use **022.** If you're calling within Geneva, simply leave off the code and dial the regular phone number.

Telephone   A large **long-distance phone center** is at the Gare de Cornavin, open daily 7am to 10:30pm. You can also make long-distance calls at the main post office on rue du Mont-Blanc, 2 blocks from the station. **Local calls** start at 70 centimes (50¢); phones accept coins in various denominations.

Tipping   A service charge is usually added to restaurant bills and taxicab fares in Geneva, so it's unnecessary to leave a tip beyond the few centimes you might receive back when you break a franc. However, if a special service is performed by a waiter or cab driver, a larger tip would be appropriate.

3 Accommodations You Can Afford

Despite its reputation as one of the world's more expensive cities, Geneva has a few inexpensive hotels. The choices are even better in summer, when many student dorms open to visitors. These are often the best deals, with attached bathrooms for less than you'd spend for a room without a bathroom in a regular hotel.

It's a good idea to reserve in advance. If you have trouble finding a room when you arrive, remember that the **tourist office** will make hotel reservations for 5SF ($3.60)—see "Visitor Information," earlier in this chapter.

Note: You can find the lodging choices below plotted on the map included in "Seeing the Sights," later in this chapter.

ON THE RIGHT BANK

Auberge de Jeunesse. 28 rue Rothschild, 1202 Genève. ☎ **022/732-62-60.** 350 beds. 70SF ($50) double with bathroom for IYHF members, 75SF ($53) for nonmembers; 80SF ($57) quad with bathroom for IYHF members, 110SF ($79) for nonmembers; 28SF ($20) dorm bed for IYHF members, 33SF ($24) for nonmembers. Youth hostel membership 25SF ($18). MC, V. Bus: 1 to Wilson; or turn left from Gare de Cornavin and walk 6 blocks up rue de Lausanne.

Geneva's official youth hostel has an excellent location less than a 15-minute walk from Gare de Cornavin and 2 blocks from the lake. It's housed in a former hospital and a modern building designed specifically as a hostel. The dorms have 6, 8, or 10 beds. Outstanding features include a large glass-walled/glass-ceilinged lobby, a TV lounge, a no-smoking library and quiet room, a self-catering kitchen, rooms for the disabled, and a self-service restaurant featuring plats du jour for only 12.50SF ($9). There's a midnight curfew, and the hostel is also closed 10am to 4pm.

✪ **Hôtel de la Cloche.** 6 rue de la Cloche, 1201 Genève. ☎ **022/732-94-81.** Fax 022/738-16-22. 8 units, none with bathroom. 50SF ($36) single; 80SF ($57) double; 95SF ($68) triple; 125SF ($89) quad. Continental breakfast 2.50SF ($1.80). Showers 2SF ($1.40) for 1-night stay, free for longer stays. AE, DC, MC, V. Bus: 1. From Gare de Cornavin, walk down rue du Mont-Blanc, turn left at quai du Mont-Blanc and left at rue de la Cloche; the hotel is across from the Noga Hilton.

Built in the 1880s, this small hotel was once the apartment of the director of the Grand Casino. Many luxurious features remain, like the beautiful blue-and-white

---

Getting the Best Deal on Accommodations

- Take advantage of the super bargains offered by student dormitories, available for visitors during summer.
- Note that if you arrive without a reservation, the tourist office will make one for you for a small fee.
- Be aware that you can get a small reduction at most hotels if you pay in cash instead of with a credit card.
- Skip the breakfast offered by your hotel (unless it's included in the rates, of course) and save money by having tea or coffee and a brioche in a coffee shop.

---

porcelain sink in the bathroom near the entrance (some guests have offered to buy it, according to the managers, M. and Mme Chabbey). The rooms are spacious, with solid antique furniture.

✪ **Hôtel des Tourelles.** 2 bd. James-Fazy, 1201 Genève. ☎ **022/732-44-23.** Fax 022/732-76-20. 23 units, 15 with bathroom. TV. 70SF ($50) single without bathroom, 90SF ($64) single with bathroom; 120SF ($86) double with bathroom. Rates include buffet breakfast. Extra bed 20SF ($14). AE, DC, EURO, MC, V. Tram: 13. Turn right when you come out of Gare de Cornavin, staying to the right of the large church on bd. James-Fazy; the Tourelles is on the left side just before the bridge over the river.

Named after the turrets on the corner of the building, this is one of Geneva's best budget hotels. The turret rooms are huge, with seating alcoves and views of the river and the Old City. Some rooms have bay windows and antiques; all have color TVs with 30 channels. The hotel is clean and the management is friendly.

Hôtel Rio. 1 place Isaac-Mercier, 2201 Genève. ☎ **022/732-32-64.** Fax 022/732-82-64. 25 units, 9 with bathroom (shower). TV TEL. 68SF ($49) single without bathroom, 90SF ($64) single with bathroom; 88SF ($63) double without bathroom, 120SF ($86) double with bathroom; 98SF ($70) triple without bathroom, 130SF ($93) triple with bathroom; 110SF ($79) quad without bathroom, 157SF ($112) quad with bathroom and kitchenette. Free showers. Rates include continental breakfast. AE, MC, V. From Cornavin Station, turn right, walk straight ahead, and you'll see the hotel after 3 minutes.

The Rio is managed by the friendly English-speaking Denise Ray (who also manages the Beau Site—see below), and the reception is on the second floor, reached by an elevator. At this ideal choice for families or small groups, the clean rooms are comfortably furnished and have soundproofed windows; six of the rooms are quads. You're offered free coffee or tea daily 10am to 10pm.

✪ **Hôtel St-Gervais.** 20 rue des Corps-Saints, 1201 Genève. ☎ and fax **022/732-45-72.** 26 units, 24 with sink only, 1 with shower only, 1 with bathroom. 62SF ($44) single without bathroom; 78SF ($56) double without bathroom, 98SF ($70) double with shower only, 105SF ($75) double with bathroom. Rates include continental breakfast. AE, DC, EURO, MC, V. Bus: 10 or 44 to Coudance. Turn right as you exit Cornavin Station and walk down rue Cornavin to rue des Corps-Saints, which veers off from it where rue Cornavin turns toward the river.

On seven floors of a building with an elevator, the St-Gervais features recently remodeled rooms, most small and geometrically creative; a few are square. The carpets are pretty, the furniture is modern, and everything is spotless. The English-speaking management is friendly.

Hôtel Tor. 3 rue Lévrier, 1201 Genève. ☎ **022/909-88-20.** Fax 022/909-88-21. 22 units, all with bathroom. TV TEL. 75SF–100SF ($53.55–$71.40) single; 90SF–130SF ($64–$93) double; 150SF ($107) triple; 170SF ($121) quad. Rates include continental breakfast. AE,

EURO, MC, V. Bus: 10 to Coudance. From Gare de Cornavin, walk down rue du Mont-Blanc and turn left onto rue Lévrier.

On the third floor of an elevator building close to the bus terminal, the Tor offers rooms that are spacious and well furnished; some have kitchenettes. The management is pleasant and speaks excellent English.

ON THE LEFT BANK

Cité Universitaire de Genève. 46 av. Miremont, 1206 Genève. ☎ **022/839-22-22.** Fax 022/839-22-23. 520 units, none with bathroom. 36SF ($26) single; 52SF ($37) double; 65SF ($46) studio. Rates apply to students with official ID; nonstudents pay 20% more. Refundable key deposit 5SF ($3.60). No credit cards. Three-night minimum stay, shorter periods if space is available. Closed Oct–June. Bus: 3 from place des 22 Cantons, near the Notre-Dame Church (off Cornavin Station), to Crêtes de Champel (last stop).

The Cité Universitaire de Genève is the largest and best hostel, open to visitors from July to the end of September. Each room has its own sink, single bed, and desk with chair, and most have fantastic views of the Salève. Studios come with small kitchens. Breakfast, lunch, and dinner are available in the ground-floor cafeteria, open Monday to Friday 7am to 10pm and Saturday and Sunday 8am to 10pm. Breakfast is 5.80SF ($4.15); lunch, 9.50SF ($7); a plat du jour, 8.50SF ($6); and dinner, 11.50SF ($8).

Hôtel Beau Site. 3–4 place du Cirque, 1204 Genève. ☎ **022/328-10-08.** Fax 022/329-23-64. 25 units, 10 with shower only, 1 with bathroom. 57SF ($41) single without bathroom, 63SF ($45) single with shower only; 79SF ($56) double without bathroom, 83SF ($59) double with shower only, 102SF ($73) double with bathroom; 94SF ($67) triple without bathroom, 98SF ($70) triple with shower only; 104SF ($77) quad without bathroom, 110SF ($79) quad with shower only. Rates include buffet breakfast. AE, EURO, MC, V. Bus: 1, 4, or 13 to place du Cirque.

This is a funky old place popular with young travelers. Large high-ceilinged rooms with parquet floors, doors painted red and gray, an antique sewing machine, and a TV lounge with a large overstuffed couch all contribute to the atmosphere. If English-speaking manager Denise Ray isn't around (she also manages the Rio—see above), someone at the desk who speaks enough English will check you in.

Hôtel Central. 2 rue de la Rôtisserie, 1204 Genève. ☎ **022/818-81-00.** Fax 022/818-81-01. 30 units, all with bathroom. TV TEL. 70SF–140SF ($50–$100) single or double; 130SF–160SF ($93–$114) triple; 160SF–190SF ($114–$136) quad. Rates include continental breakfast. AE, DC, MC, V. Bus: 5 or 44 to Bel-Air.

On the edge of the Old City, a block from rue du Marché—one of Geneva's two main shopping streets—the businesslike Central is convenient for touring and shopping. The rooms may be small but are spotless and have new carpets and modern furnishings. The hotel is on the upper floors of an elevator building with a shopping arcade on the ground floor.

Hôtel de l'Etoile. 17 rue des Vieux-Grenadiers, 1205 Genève. ☎ **022/328-72-08.** Fax 022/321-16-24. 30 units, all with bathroom. TV TEL. 80SF ($57) single; 120SF ($86) double; 160SF ($114) triple. Continental breakfast 6SF ($4.30). AE, MC, V. Bus: 1, 7, or 44 to Ecole-de-Médecine.

In the Plainpalais area, this hotel is much nicer than the street it's on. Refurbished not long ago, the guest rooms are pleasant, with standard modern furniture and cozy beds. The owners, M. and Mme Dousse, speak English.

Hôtel du Lac. 15 rue des Eaux-Vives, 1207 Genève. ☎ and fax **022/735-45-80.** 12 units, none with bathroom. 55SF ($39) single; 80SF ($57) double; 110SF ($79) triple. Continental breakfast 6SF ($4.30). No credit cards. Bus: 15 to place des Eaux-Vives.

This immaculate and well-maintained hotel occupies the sixth and seventh floors of a modern apartment building (with elevator). The owner, Mme Elsa Salvadori, takes great pride in keeping her hotel in top shape, doing much of the work herself. All the sixth-floor rooms have balconies, and many rooms have connecting doors, so families or two couples can share.

✪ Hôtel Kaufmann. 48 bd. des Tranchées, 1206 Genève. ☎ **022/346-29-33.** Fax 022/346-22-11. 23 units, 10 with bathroom. MINIBAR TV. 50SF–70SF ($36–$50) single without bathroom, 105SF ($75) single with bathroom; 80SF–90SF ($57–$64) double without bathroom, 105SF–130SF ($75–$93) double with bathroom. Rates include continental breakfast. AE, DC, EURO, MC, V. Bus: 8 to Musées.

Next door to the Museum of Natural History, a 5-minute walk from the Old City, this cozy hotel is owned/managed since 1995 by Jane Grolleau, a former Swissair flight attendant who speaks perfect English. All age groups will feel at home. The breakfast room, with open-ended serving hours on weekends, features a fireplace. The rooms are spacious, and the area is quiet. The Kaufmann is slightly off the beaten track, but it's one of the best finds for visitors who want to save money.

Hôtel le Grenil. 7 av. de Ste-Clothilde, 1205 Genève. ☎ **022/328-30-55.** Fax 022/321-60-10. 48 units, 35 with bathroom. 100SF ($71) single without bathroom, 130SF ($93) single with bathroom; 120SF ($86) double without bathroom, 150SF ($107) double with bathroom; 170SF ($121) triple with bathroom; 190SF ($136) quad with bathroom. Rates include buffet breakfast. AE, DC, EURO, MC, V. Bus: 1 or 4 to place du Cirque; then walk down bd. St-Georges to av. de St-Clothilde.

The rooms here are amazingly similar to those you might find in any modern hotel in North America; even more surprising is that Le Grenil is sponsored by the YMCA and YWCA of Geneva. Besides standard rooms (most with TV, radio, and phone), the hotel has rooms for the disabled. Other amenities are a TV lounge, a dining room serving lunch and dinner (half board available), an art gallery off the large lobby, and a theater in the basement.

✪ Hôtel le Prince. 16 rue des Voisins, 1205 Genève. ☎ **022/807-05-00.** Fax 022/807-05-29. 24 units, all with bathroom. TV TEL. 80SF ($57) single; 100SF ($71) double; 115SF ($82) triple. Rates include continental breakfast. AE, MC, V. Bus: 1 to pont d'Arve; then walk across rue de Carouge and turn left at the next intersection.

Near the university in the Plainpalais district, this hotel is an excellent deal. The management is wonderfully friendly, and many rooms have lots of light and minibars—most have just been remodeled and the rest will soon follow.

Hôtel Pax. 68 rue du 31-Décembre, 1207 Genève. ☎ **022/787-50-70.** Fax 022/787-50-80. 32 units, 12 with bathroom. MINIBAR TV TEL. 78SF ($56) single without bathroom, 113SF ($81) single with bathroom; 99SF ($71) double without bathroom, 131SF ($94) double with bathroom; 121SF ($86) triple without bathroom, 161SF ($115) triple with bathroom. Rates include breakfast. AE, DC, EURO, MC, V. Bus: 9 to rue du 31-Décembre.

Not as close to the city center as some of the hotels listed here, the Pax is certainly acceptable and moderately priced. Many of the rooms are quite spacious and have large windows. Color TVs are in every room.

WORTH A SPLURGE

✪ Hôtel Excelsior. 34 rue Rousseau, 1211 Genève. ☎ **022/732-09-45.** Fax 022/738-43-69. 60 units, all with bathroom (shower or tub). TV. 115SF ($82) single with shower, 145SF ($104) single with tub; 180SF ($129) double with shower, 190SF ($136) double with tub. May also have 1 rm with kitchen. Rates include continental breakfast. *Frommer's readers receive 10% discount by showing this book.* Extra bed (up to 3) 25SF ($21). AE, DC, MC, V. Bus: 44 to Coudance.

This four-star hotel (with elevator), a 3-minute walk from Cornavin Station, has rustic-style rooms with color TVs (20 channels). A street-level restaurant called La Brocherie serves meals with beverage for 32SF ($23) and plats du jour for 14SF ($10). It's the best deal in Geneva. Ask for M. Böhlmann, who'll treat you like a VIP.

4 Great Deals on Dining

Situated in the middle of Europe and containing a bit of the cultures of France and Italy—and many other nations—Geneva offers a large variety in the way of food. However, many typical Swiss meals can be exceptional bargains.

Most popular is fondue in its three varieties: cheese, in which bread is dipped; beef, in which beef is cooked in a pot of hot oil; and Chinese, in which meat and vegetables are cooked in a broth. One thing you won't find is chocolate fondue. Though they have wonderful chocolate and love fondue, the Swiss leave the combining of the two to chocoholic Americans. Other Swiss specialties are *raclette,* another cheese dish that features melted cheese over potatoes, and *rösti,* a sort of hash-browned potatoes with onions.

ON THE RIGHT BANK

Migros. 18 rue de Lausanne. ☎ **022/738-68-80.** Meals 9.60SF–15SF ($7–$11). No credit cards. Mon 9am–7pm, Tues–Wed and Fri 8am–7pm, Thurs 7:30am–8pm, Sat 8am–6pm. SWISS.

Sixteen Migros restaurants are scattered all over Geneva. The largest (130 seats) and most centrally located is diagonally across from Cornavin Station, to your left at the corner of rue Lausanne and rue des Alpes. It's two escalators down from street level in the Le Cygne shopping center. Plats du jour start at 9.60SF ($7), and each weekday the restaurant serves at least six inexpensive specials, such as paella, boeuf bourguignonne with rice pilaf, and spaghetti bolognese.

Restaurant la Véranda. 20 rue des Alpes. ☎ **022/732-80-95.** Meals 20SF–30SF ($14–$21). AE, DC, MC, V. Daily noon–2pm and 6:45–10pm. INTERNATIONAL.

You'll find this popular place diagonally across the street when leaving the main exit of Cornavin Station, in the basement of Hôtel International-Terminus. Pasta dishes range from a 12.50SF ($9) spaghetti bolognese to a 18SF ($13) tagliatelle with salmon sauce; coq au vin is 19SF ($14), a vegetable menu (very filling) 25.90SF ($19), and pizza 9.50SF ($7). Spaghetti and a green salad *à discrétion* (all you can eat) is 23SF ($16). It gets crowded at lunch, so come early to get a seat.

✪ **Restaurant Manora.** 4 rue Cornavin. ☎ **022/731-31-46.** Meals 4.90SF–17.90SF ($3.50–$13). No credit cards. Mon–Sat 7am–9:30pm, Sun 9am–9pm. Bus: 44 to Coudance. SWISS.

One of Geneva's best bargains, the Manora is a large self-service restaurant that's packed day and night. Plats du jour start at an incredible 7.90SF ($6) for risotto or pasta and a vegetable. A filling medium-size plate from the outstanding salad bar costs only 6.90SF ($4.95), and even a large plate of entrecôte with fries and a vegetable is 17.90SF ($13). The wide selection of cakes and desserts will tempt you. A large section is reserved for nonsmokers.

ON THE LEFT BANK

Au Carnivore. 30 place du Bourg-de-Four. ☎ **022/311-87-58.** Meals 15SF–40SF ($11–$29). AE, EURO, MC, V. Daily 11:30am–2:30pm and 6:30–11pm. Bus: 26 to Molard. SWISS.

The bilevel place du Bourg-de-Four is one of the most beautiful squares in the Old City as well as a great dining spot popular with students, businesspeople, and visitors.

Getting the Best Deal on Dining

- Try typical Swiss meals that are exceptional bargains: fondue, raclette, and rösti.
- Take advantage of the ubiquitous *plat du jour,* or, if you're very hungry, the *menu complet,* which consists of the plat du jour with a soup or appetizer and a dessert. Plats du jour are often available only at lunch, so to save money you might want to eat a large meal at noon and something light in the evening.
- Note that if you eat standing at a counter rather than sitting at a table you can save at least 10%.

As its name implies, Au Carnivore specializes in meats, and only Argentine and U.S. beef are served. Though many menu items are beyond our budget, a few lower-priced items make excellent deals.

Café des Antiquaires. 35 Grand-Rue. ☎ **022/311-24-16.** Meals 15SF–38SF ($11–$27). No credit cards. Mon–Fri 8:30am–7pm, Sat 8:30am–10pm. Bus: 4 or 5 to place Neuve. SWISS.

Close to the Hôtel de Ville (City Hall) is this small dark cafe popular with locals, who get their own large reserved table just inside the front door (don't sit down at the table with the black wrought-iron ashtray). The house specialty is cheese fondue for a reasonable 18SF ($13), and the plats du jour go for about 14SF ($10). Try a glass of kirsch after your meal to help digest all that cheese—the Swiss wouldn't dream of having fondue without this sweet apéritif. In fact, they often have their kirsch in the middle of the meal, calling it *coup du milieu.*

Café du Molard. 4 place du Molard. ☎ **022/310-35-53.** Meals 14.50SF–32SF ($10–$23). AE, DC, EURO, V. Daily 7am–midnight. Bus: 26 to Molard. ITALIAN.

If you're craving good old-fashioned Italian cooking, try this restaurant, which features homemade pasta dishes as well as 18 types of pizza. This place is very popular with young Genevans, who often start a night out on the town here. There are 80 seats inside on two levels and 200 outside in summer.

La Cave Valaisanne. Place du Cirque. ☎ **022/328-12-36.** Meals 13SF–25SF ($9–$18). AE, CB, DC, EURO, MC, V. Daily 11am–1am. Tram: 15 to Cirque. SWISS.

La Cave Valaisanne has four dining rooms, one of which is Chalet Suisse, a popular Swiss restaurant where the specialty is fondue. It offers numerous varieties of this cook-it-yourself meal, though the basic cheese fondue is the house favorite. Raclette is also available. The *lunch-affaire*—egg salad or soup, an entree, and ice cream—for 22SF ($16) is a great deal.

Dent de Lion. 14 rue des Eaux-Vives. ☎ **022/700-27-14.** Meals 14SF–23SF ($10–$16). Mon–Sat noon–10pm. Tram: 12 to Eaux-Vives. VEGETARIAN.

This small restaurant (26 seats) is always packed at lunch with businesspeople who wedge themselves into the tiny tables. The plat du jour is 15SF ($11) and the menu complet, which features the same main dish but with soup and dessert included, 25SF ($18). The plat du jour might be tofu Stroganoff served on a large mound of brown rice with a vegetable on the side. Takeout is available.

Grand Passage. 50 rue du Rhône. ☎ **022/310-66-11.** Meals 7SF–21SF ($5–$15). AE, DC, EURO, V. Mon–Fri 8:30am–6:30pm, Sat 8am–5pm. Bus: 10 to Molard. SWISS.

This department store cafeteria is the place for an inexpensive lunch in the heart of the shopping district. Here you can get tasty plats du jour for about 14SF ($10). At the store's place du Molard entrance are booths selling Middle Eastern fast food for about 7.50SF ($5).

La Zofage. 6 rue des Voisins. ☎ **022/329-51-13.** Fax 022/320-14-40. Meals 8SF–15SF ($6–$11). MC, V. Daily 7am–10:30pm. Bus: 15 to Plainpalais. SWISS.

One of the city's least expensive restaurants, simply furnished La Zofage is down a few steps from street level and is frequented mostly by students. The plat du jour is about 11.50SF ($8) and might be chicken Cordon Bleu with vegetables or potatoes or cannelloni au gratin with a salad.

Restaurant les Tropiques. 11 rue Sautter. ☎ **022/346-89-44.** Meals 12SF–35SF ($9–$25). MC, V. Mon–Fri 7:30am–midnight, Sat 8am–midnight. Bus: 5 to last stop. INTERNATIONAL.

Off the beaten track near the City Hospital, this bilevel restaurant offers a large choice of food, from pizza *à emporter* (to take away) to *entrecôte flambée au whisky* served with Créole rice. Plats du jour are served Monday to Friday for 14SF to 17SF ($10 to $12), and menus for children, from spaghetti Napoli to hamburger steak, are 5SF to 11SF ($3.60 to $8). You'll find no tourists here but will always find one of the 200 seats vacant.

✪ **Taverne de la Madeleine.** 20 rue Toutes-Ames. ☎ **022/310-60-70.** Meals 11SF–20SF ($8–$14). No credit cards. Mon–Fri 7am–6pm, Sat 9am–3am. Bus: 10 to Molard. SWISS.

The simple, cozy restaurant is Geneva's oldest, tucked into a small terrace below the Cathédrale St-Pierre and across from the much smaller Madeleine Church. Though it doesn't serve alcohol, it's popular, especially at lunch. The restaurant offers several daily specials, including two vegetarian meals. Try the succulent little fillets of Lake Geneva perch, with salad and a huge pile of fries, for 20SF ($14). Large salads with ham, bacon, eggs, and cheese are 14SF to 16SF ($10 to $11), while the vegetarian plats du jour average 15SF to 17SF ($11 to $12).

PICNICKING

Picnics are your best budget dining bet—with plenty of beautiful parks around the city, try to enjoy at least one picnic while you're here. Moreover, shopping for supplies can be one of the highlights of your trip if you go to the Left Bank's **Halle de Rive** on place du Rive. This marketplace extending through the whole block is filled with all kinds of delicacies. Stroll through the aisles before making your choices. On Wednesday and Saturday, place du Rive fills with stalls as farmers display and sell the most beautiful produce. You'll find dozens of stalls selling fresh breads, cheese, hams, and sausages by the 100 grams or even by the slice. Pick up some delicious fresh fruit and a bottle of wine and you're all set.

WORTH A SPLURGE

✪ **Les Armures.** 1 rue du Puits-St-Pierre. ☎ **022/310-34-42.** Fax 022/818-71-13. Meals 17SF–35SF ($12–$25). AE, CB, DC, EURO, MC, V. Daily 11:45am–3pm and 6pm–midnight. Minibus: 17 to rue de l'Hôtel-de-Ville. SWISS.

In the heart of the Old City, beside the arsenal, is a favorite of Genevans. This trilevel restaurant is decorated with suits of armor, swords, shields, and lances, like a real armory. Though there's a wide assortment of pizza at 12SF to 15SF ($9 to $11), Swiss dishes are the specialty: fondue, raclette, and *viande séchée* (air-dried beef) for 18SF to 24SF ($13 to $17). Also popular is *choucroute garni*, sauerkraut with several types of ham and sausage, for 28SF ($20).

5 Seeing the Sights

SIGHTSEEING SUGGESTIONS

IF YOU HAVE 1 DAY   For an overview of Geneva, head first to the **Old City.** Strolling the narrow cobblestone lanes and climbing the stairways of this once forti-fied city on a hill provides a glimpse into the city's medieval history. In the afternoon, head over to the Right Bank for a visit to the **Palais des Nations** or the **International Red Cross Museum,** institutions representative of Geneva's international spirit. Save time to stroll through the **lakeside parks** and view the **jet d'eau** and the **flower clock,** both of which are the symbols of Geneva.

IF YOU HAVE 2 DAYS   For Day 1, follow the above. In the morning on Day 2, visit another of Geneva's fine museums, such as the **Watch and Clock Museum** or the **Museum of Art and History,** and view the **Reformation Monument** below the walls of the Old City. In the afternoon, take a **lake cruise** to see the beautiful surroundings of Geneva.

IF YOU HAVE 3 DAYS   For Days 1 and 2, follow the above. On Day 3, take a trip to the **Alps** for some stunning vistas or maybe even some skiing. **Mont Blanc,** the Continent's rooftop, is possible in a long day, or try the **Salève,** which you can reach more easily. Both are in France, so be sure to take your passport.

IF YOU HAVE 5 DAYS   For Days 1 to 3, follow the above. On Days 4 and 5, you may be enticed by Geneva's lesser-known museums, like the **Collections Baur** and the **Voltaire Institute and Museum.** And then there are the parks, such as the **Jardin Botanique.** Also try to visit the suburb of **Carouge,** an unusual old enclave within the modern city. Another possibility is an all-day excursion to the **Jura Mountains** and the Genevan countryside or to **Lausanne** or **Montreux,** two beautiful cities on Lake Geneva.

IN OR NEAR THE OLD CITY

With its narrow cobblestone streets and tiny stairways, the Old City is a great place for a stroll. Pretty fountains dot the streets, and colorful Swiss and Genevan flags wave between the buildings. You'll find art galleries and inviting bistros, and bibliophiles will appreciate the shops selling rare books. Geneva was for many centuries a walled city, and you can see part of the walls by walking along **rue de la Croix-Rouge.**

Wandering is the best strategy for knowing the Old City, but there are several sites you may want to visit: Calvin's church, the 12th-century **Cathédrale St-Pierre** (see below); the 16th-century **Hôtel de Ville (City Hall),** where the Red Cross was founded; **place du Bourg-de-Four,** which was probably the ancient Roman forum and today is filled with sidewalk cafes; the **Maison Tavel,** Geneva's oldest house and now a museum (see below); and the old **City Arsenal,** with its covered patio, wall mosaics, and cannons.

Maison Tavel. 6 rue du Puits-St-Pierre. ☎ **022/310-29-00.** Free admission. Tues–Sun 10am–5pm. Tram or bus: 3, 5, 12, or 15 to place Bel-Air.

This museum occupies Geneva's oldest house. One of its most interesting exhibits is a large model of the city in about 1850. Made of copper and nickel, the model was built by an architect as a hobby. There's also an unusual display of ornately carved doors from several old houses.

Cathédrale St-Pierre. Cour St-Pierre. ☎ **022/310-29-29.** Free admission. June–Sept daily 9am–7pm; Oct–May Mon–Sat 10am–noon and 2–5pm, Sun 11am–5pm. Tram: 12 to place Neuve. Bus: 3 or 5 to place Neuve or 17 to rue de l'Hôtel-de-Ville.

Getting the Best Deal on Sightseeing

- Take advantage of the fact that, as throughout Switzerland, many of Geneva's museums are free—like the Maison Tavel, the Watch and Clock Museum, the Voltaire Institute and Museum, and the Museum of Art and History.
- Note that Geneva has no tower or high-rise from which you can get panoramic views. However, 15 minutes away by tram is Salève Hill, which offers a breathtaking view of the city, Lake Geneva, and the surrounding Alps. Remember to take your passport along—it's in French territory.
- Be aware that the best way to familiarize yourself with the unique character of Geneva is by strolling along the 4 miles of lake promenades, in full view of Mont Blanc and the clear waters of Lake Geneva, as well as the jet d'eau and many ducks and swans.

Built 750 years ago, the cathedral is a fantastic demonstration of how a simple chapel grew into this Old City landmark. It incorporates Romanesque and Gothic styles, with Greco-Roman pillars imitating those of Rome's Pantheon. The highlights are the archaeological site (see below), the 4th-century baptistery, 5th-century mosaics, and Calvin's original chair.

Site Archéologique St-Pierre. At the Cathédrale St-Pierre, cour St-Pierre. ☎ **022/738-56-50.** Admission 6SF ($4.30) adults, 3.50SF ($2.50) children. Tues–Sun 10am–1pm and 2–6pm. Tram: 12 to place Neuve. Bus: 3 or 5 to place Neuve or 17 to rue de l'Hôtel-de-Ville.

In the center of Geneva's Old City you'll find one of Europe's largest archaeological sites. The cathedral dates only from 1160, but during renovation evidence was unearthed of a church on this site as long ago as the 5th century. You can now walk through the ages beneath the cathedral and an adjacent chapel and street. Layer on layer of history has been exposed and left as if the archaeologists were still digging. Old wells and a large mosaic floor are evidence of Roman occupation. Beneath the cathedral, the archaeological site has its own entrance, to the right side of the cathedral's main steps.

Musée d'Art et d'Histoire. 2 rue Charles-Galland (3 blocks from place du Bourg-de-Four in the Old City). ☎ **022/418-26-00.** Free admission. Tues–Sun 10am–5pm. Bus: 5, 6, 8, or 17 to Athénée.

Geneva's largest museum houses a wide variety of art and antiquities. Exhibits range from Egyptian mummies to entire rooms from Swiss châteaux, complete with paneling, antique heating systems, furniture, and the art that was in the rooms when the museum acquired them. Wandering from one lavish room to the next provides an excellent glimpse of the château lifestyle. Another large hall contains all manner of arms and armor, including one of the folding ladders used by the Savoyards to scale the walls of the city when they attacked Geneva in 1602. Upstairs in the galleries, several rooms are devoted to turn-of-the-20th-century Swiss artist Ferdinand Hodler. His Alpine landscapes in shades of lavender and blue are especially beautiful.

Collections Baur. 8 rue Munier-Romilly. ☎ **022/346-17-29.** Admission 5SF ($3.55) adults, 4SF ($2.85) students. Tues–Sun 2–6pm. Bus: 8 to Florissant.

In a former private home near the Museum of Art and History you'll find this excellent collection of Asian art and ceramics. Displayed are more than 1,000 years of Chinese ceramics as well as beautiful antique jade pieces. Watch for the large jade vase with its high-relief images. Japanese swords, lacquer boxes, netsuke, and objects for tea ceremonies are also here.

Eglise Russe (Russian Church). 9 rue Rodolphe-Toepffer. ☎ **022/346-47-09.** Admission 1SF (70¢). Daily 9am–noon and 2–5pm. Bus: 3 to Athénée.

Built in 1866, this little jewel-box church, with its gold domes and spires, seems oddly out of place in Geneva. It's especially beautiful at night, when lights illuminate the gold domes.

Musée Historique de la Réformation et Musée Jean-Jacques Rousseau. In the University Library, promenade des Bastions. ☎ **022/418-28-00.** Admission 5SF ($3.60). Mon–Fri 9am–noon and 2–5pm, Sat 9am–noon. Tram no. 12 or bus no. 3 or 5 to place Neuve; the museum is inside the park on the right and across from the Reformation Museum.

If you're interested in the philosopher Rousseau and can read French, you'll find this two-room museum interesting. Documents pertaining to the Reformation, portraits of important figures, and a case filled with Rousseau busts are among the items here. In an adjoining room you'll also see a folio from a 2nd-century manuscript of Homer's *Iliad.* The museum is on the ground floor of the library, straight ahead as you enter. If the doors are locked during normal hours, ask at the desk to be let in.

OUTSIDE THE OLD CITY

For years, Geneva and watches have been synonymous, so it's fitting that one of the sights most associated with this city is the **flower clock** in the **Jardin Anglais (English Garden).** All year this clock ticks away with as many as 6,300 flowers filling the area within its 50-foot circumference. The Jardin Anglais is on the left bank at the foot of pont du Mont-Blanc. From this spot you can walk through one park after another for more than a mile along the left bank of Lake Geneva.

No other sight is more representative of Geneva than the ✪ *jet d'eau,* a huge fountain of water that rises 390 feet into the air on quai des Eaux-Vives. Visible from all over the city, the jet d'eau rises from the Eaux-Vives Jetty on the Left Bank but is best seen from the Right Bank with the Alps and the Old City as a backdrop. The fountain pumps 132 gallons of water per second into the air, and at any given moment 7 tons of water is suspended above the surface of Lake Geneva. The water jet operates from the beginning of March until the first Sunday of October but may be turned off when the weather is bad.

Musée de l'Horlogerie et de l'Emaillerie (Watch and Clock Museum). 15 rte. de Malagnou. ☎ **022/418-64-70.** Free admission. Wed–Mon 10am–5pm. Bus: 1 or 8 to Tranchées.

A visit to Geneva wouldn't be complete without seeing this extensive collection of clocks, watches, enamel watch cases, and musical snuff boxes. Exquisite clocks and watches that are works of art rather than mere timepieces are displayed on two floors of an old château surrounded by a park. The ticking of timepieces immediately greets you upon entering, and as you wander through the rooms you'll find yourself rushing from one clock to the next as they each mark the hours, half hours, and quarter hours with sonorous chimes and dancing figures.

✪ **Palais des Nations.** Av. de la Paix. ☎ **022/907-45-39.** Fax 022/907-00-32. Admission 8.50SF ($6) adults, 6.50SF ($4.65) students, 4SF ($2.85) age 6 and over, free for age 5 and under. Jan–Dec 14 daily 10am–noon and 2–4pm; July–Aug daily 9am–6pm. Closed Dec 15–31. Bus: 8 or F to Appia.

This massive art deco building was constructed between 1929 and 1936 as the headquarters of the League of Nations, the predecessor of the United Nations, and today it's the U.N.'s European headquarters. Inside are huge conference halls and assembly rooms. An organized tour of the palace is available in several languages, which will give you an idea of the large role Geneva plays in international peacekeeping. Though this

Geneva

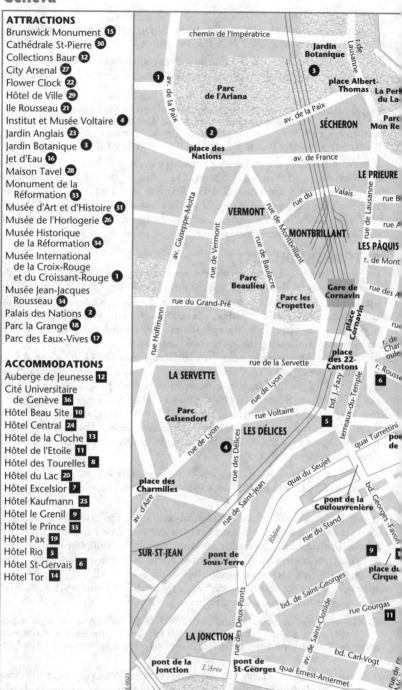

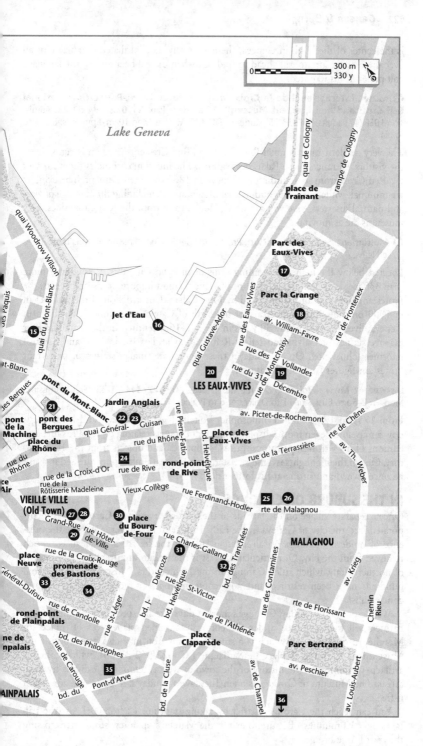

Lake Geneva

place de
Trainant

quai de Cologny

rampe de Cologny

Parc des
Eaux-Vives

17

rte de Frontenex

Parc la Grange

18

av. William-Favre

quai Gustave-Ador

rue des Eaux-Vives

Jet d'Eau **16**

quai du Mont-Blanc

quai Woodrow Wilson

les Pâquis

15

t-Blanc

rue des Montchoisy

rue des Vollandes

rue du 31e Décembre

19

20

LES EAUX-VIVES

av. Pictet-de-Rochemont

rte de Chêne

av. Th. Weber

les Bergues

pont du Mont-Blanc

Jardin Anglais

21

pont
de la
Machine

pont des
Bergues

place du
Rhône

quai Général-Guisan

22 **23**

rue du Rhône

rue Pierre-Fatio

bd. Helvétique

place des
Eaux-Vives

rue de la Terrassière

rue du
Rhône

ce
Air

rue de la Croix-d'Or

rue de la
Rôtisserie

Madeleine

rue de Rive

24

**rond-point
de Rive**

Vieux-Collège

rue Ferdinand-Hodler

rte de Malagnou

25 **26**

MALAGNOU

**VIEILLE
VILLE
(Old Town)** **27** **28**

Grand-Rue

rue Hôtel-
de-Ville

29

30 place
du Bourg-
de-Four

rue Charles-Galland

31

bd. des Tranchées

rue des Contamines

av. Krieg

place
Neuve

rue de la Croix-Rouge

**promenade
des Bastions**

énéral-Dufour

33

34

rue de Candolle

Dalcroze

bd. Helvétique

rue
St-Victor

32

rte de Florissant

Chemin
Rieu

rond-point
de Plainpalais

ne de
npalais

rue St-Léger

bd. des Philosophes

rue de Carouge

35

Pont-d'Arve

bd. du

rue de l'Athénée

place
Claparède

bd. de la Cluse

av. de Champel

Parc Bertrand

av. Peschier

av. Louis-Aubert

36

AINPALAIS

is the center of the U.N. in Geneva, there are many more affiliated organizations all over the city. Be sure to call ahead to find out when there'll be a tour in the language you prefer. ID is required.

✪ **Musée International de la Croix-Rouge et du Croissant-Rouge (International Red Cross and Red Crescent Museum).** 17 av. de la Paix. ☎ **022/734-57-23.** Admission 10SF ($7) adults, 5SF ($3.55) students. DC, MC, V. Wed–Mon 10am–5pm. Bus: 8 or F to Appia.

The very modern International Red Cross and Red Crescent Museum is across from the visitors' entrance to the Palais des Nations. The museum chronicles the history of the Red Cross from its founding in Geneva in 1863 by Henri Dunant. The exhibits are minimal, while numerous audiovisual presentations, including film footage of wars and natural disasters, give you a dramatic look at the work the Red Cross does. Few museums are as moving.

✪ **Monument de la Réformation.** Promenade des Bastions. Free admission. Tram: 12 to place Neuve.

Located below the highest remaining walls of the Old City, this massive wall more than 330 feet long commemorates one of Geneva's most important historic events: the Protestant Reformation, as preached by John Calvin. Construction of the wall began in 1909 on the 400th anniversary of the birth of Calvin, who, though not born in Geneva, lived here for nearly 30 years in the mid-16th century. In the center are four massive statues of Calvin and fellow Reformation leaders Farel, Beza, and Scottish reformer John Knox. On each side of these figures are smaller statues of important Protestant figures from other nations.

Institut et Musée Voltaire. 25 rue des Délices. ☎ **022/344-71-33.** Free admission. Mon–Fri 2–5pm. Bus: 7 or 11 to Délices or 6 to Prairie.

From 1755 to 1765, French philosopher Voltaire lived in Geneva, and his home is now a museum. Seven rooms display original documents relating to Voltaire's life, first editions of his writings, paintings, prints, sculptures, and objects from the 18th century. One of the highlights is a life-size statue of the great philosopher, dressed in a suit he once owned and sitting at his former desk.

IN THE SUBURB OF CAROUGE

Once a separate village on the far side of the narrow Arve River, **Carouge** was incorporated into the city of Geneva in the early 19th century. However, despite the presence of modern buildings on all sides, it still has the feel of a small village much removed from the city. Of particular interest is the **Italian architecture,** reminiscent of northern Italy, which ruled Carouge in the 18th century. Most of the village's old buildings have been restored and now contain shops, boutiques, restaurants, and dance clubs.

Wednesday and Saturday, Carouge's **market days,** are an especially fun time to visit. Farmers sell their produce under the curiously trimmed plane trees on **place du Marché,** in the center of which is a small fountain. You may also want to visit the **Museum of Carouge,** 2 place de Sardaigne (☎ 022/342-33-83), which contains artifacts pertaining to the history of the town as well as temporary exhibits by local artists. The Museum of Carouge is open Tuesday to Sunday 2 to 6pm, and admission is free.

You can reach the Carouge district by taking tram no. 12 from Bel Air (the trip takes only 12 minutes). Be sure to exit at the Marché stop, a few stops after crossing the river l'Arve bridge.

Special & Free Events

Despite its reputation as one of Europe's most expensive cities, Geneva offers a wealth of **free concerts and other events,** especially in summer. Along the quays lining the lake and in the parks extending back from the quays are regular concerts in bandshells and on lawns. On Saturday nights **concerts and organ recitals** are held at the Cathédrale St-Pierre in the center of the Old City, and at the smaller Eglise St-Germain, a block away on the Grand-Rue, there are **concerts** on Sunday and Monday at 6pm in summer. For a listing of events, check the weekly *Geneva Agenda,* distributed free at tourist offices and newsstands, or *What's On in Geneva,* published twice a month and handed out free by the tourist office and hotels; this lists free events for English-speaking people.

Geneva also hosts numerous festivals, the most popular of which are the **Fêtes de Genève** during the first week of August and **L'Escalade** in mid-December. The former celebration is marked by revelry and numerous free concerts all over the city. L'Escalade celebrates Geneva's defeat of invading forces in 1602. The festival features hundreds of people in period costumes marching through the streets by torchlight, children in Halloween-like costumes, special meals, and candles. Both events are rather a departure for staid Geneva.

PARKS & GARDENS

Geneva's founders are to be congratulated for their forethought in preserving the banks of Lake Geneva. Stretching along both banks are several miles of promenades connected to several parks. Many of these parks have been created from the grounds of ancient châteaux, while others surround the modern buildings of the international organizations headquartered here.

Formerly the grounds of a château, the **Parc de l'Ariana** surrounds the Palais des Nations on the Right Bank. When the last owner of the château died without an heir, he donated the grounds to the city to be used as a park, on the condition that it be open to the public forever. You can stroll beneath centuries-old cypresses and cedars and enjoy the peace and quiet surrounding the U.N.'s European headquarters. Adjacent to this park is the **Jardin Botanique,** where thousands of trees, shrubs, and flowers from all over the world are displayed.

On the Left Bank, you can walk along quai Gustave-Ador past the jet d'eau and on to the **Parc la Grange** and the adjacent **Parc des Eaux-Vives.** Here you'll find a large rose garden and a beautiful 18th-century château that's now a popular expensive restaurant. If it's a warm day and your stroll through the parks has you longing for a dip in cool water, continue another 100 yards or so beyond the Parc des Eaux-Vives to **Genève-Plage,** Geneva's favorite beach.

ORGANIZED TOURS

WALKING TOURS   Geneva is divided into two sections—the old and the new. The Old City preserves Geneva's medieval history with its narrow streets and houses dating from the 13th century. Because buses aren't allowed in the Old City, it's necessary to get out and walk.

The **tourist office,** 3 rue du Mont-Blanc, offers an audiocassette tour that allows you to hear the history of the Old City as you explore at your own pace. (Tourist offices tours are offered in English, French, German, Italian, and Japanese.) In about 2½ hours the tour covers 2,000 years of Genevan history and provides details on 26 points of interest. For 10SF ($7) you'll be provided with the tape and a map of the Old City. If you don't have your own tape player, you can use one of the tourist office's, but you'll have to present your passport and leave a 50SF ($36) refundable deposit.

An alternative is the 2-hour guided tour offered by the tourist office from June to September on Monday, Wednesday, and Friday at 5pm. The cost is 10SF ($7) adults, 7SF ($5) students, and 4SF ($2.85) age 11 and under. In addition to visiting the major sites in the Old City, the tour includes a visit to a private collection of 18th-century furniture and Chinese cloisonné and ends with a sampling of Genevan wines. It starts in front of the Town Hall at 2 rue de l'Hôtel-de-Ville.

In addition, there are specialized walking tours of the Old City focusing on different periods of history. Contact the Geneva Tourist Office Information Desk in Cornavin Station at 3 rue du Mont-Blanc for details.

BUS TOURS On the right bank, **Keytours,** 7 rue des Alpes (☎ **022/731-41-40**), offers a 2-hour bus tour pointing out the highlights of both the Left Bank and the Right Bank from May to October daily at 10am and 2pm; November to April, the tour runs only at 2pm. It quickly shows you the highlights of Geneva and includes a tramway tour through the Old City. You'll see the shores of the lake and its parks, the flower clock, the jet d'eau (March to October), the modern buildings of the international organizations, monuments, and commercial centers. The cost is 32SF ($23) adults and 16SF ($11) children.

6 Shopping

Watches, knives, cheese, and chocolate are among Geneva's best buys. These are the products for which Switzerland is famous, and you'll find them in abundance. Check prices carefully, though: Unfortunately, many Swiss watches are currently cheaper in the United States than in Switzerland. Swiss army knives are still a good deal, and as for chocolate—Swiss chocolate is incomparable and just isn't the same when you buy it in another country, so indulge.

The **Chocolatier du Rhône,** 3 rue de la Confédération (☎ **022/781-36-39**), with its own tiny cafe, sells what many consider the best chocolate in the world. A pound of this delectable product costs around 55SF ($39), but you don't have to buy such a large quantity. Pick and choose a few of your favorites. Make sure you try the prize-winning mocha glacé. A small assortment will cost less than 20SF ($14).

Geneva's Left Bank shopping area is along the exclusive **rue du Rhône** and adjacent streets. Here you'll find shop after shop of designer fashions and expensive watches. Along the winding streets of the **Old City** you'll find antiques stores and galleries.

For Swiss army knives and watches, stroll along the pedestrians-only **rue du Mont-Blanc** on the Right Bank. You'll find an endless assortment of watches, knives, and other souvenirs, all at comparable prices.

Note: Before you head out for a day of shopping, remember that shops in Geneva don't open until 1pm on Monday and many of the smaller shops close for lunch between noon and 2pm.

MARKETS

A rare experience is a visit to a Swiss **street market** offering the most perfect produce you'll ever see. You'll find these bustling and beautiful markets near the Cours de Rive on Wednesday and Saturday and in Carouge on place du Marché on Saturday.

Wednesday and Saturday are the days for Geneva's large and busy **flea market,** on place de Plainpalais. In summer a **book market** is held on place de la Madeleine, at the edge of the Old City below Cathédrale St-Pierre. In winter you're likely to find crafts from all over the world on this square. If you're looking for **local crafts,** you'll find them for sale on rue du Rhône near place du Molard on Thursday.

7 Geneva After Dark

Geneva isn't known for its nightlife. Few plays are performed in English, and there's little in the way of live popular music. There are, however, regular ballet, opera, and classical music performances, as you'd expect from such a sophisticated city. The tourist office's monthly "List of Events" has thorough listings.

THE PERFORMING ARTS

From September to July, operas and ballets are performed at the **Grand-Théâtre de Genève,** place Neuve (☎ **022/418-30-00**). The building, which opened in 1879, was modeled on Paris's rococo Opéra Garnier. Destroyed by fire in 1951, it was rebuilt in the same style with a modernized interior. Tickets for opera are 37SF to 127SF ($26 to $91) and those for ballet 19SF to 87SF ($14 to $62).

Victoria Hall, 14 rue du Général-Dufour (☎ **022/328-35-73**), is Geneva's main venue for classical music performances. Tickets are 20SF to 75SF ($14 to $54). Tram no. 13 leads there.

LIVE-MUSIC CLUBS

For free live jazz, try **Halles de l'Ile,** place de l'Ile (☎ **022/311-52-21**), a sophisticated restaurant on an island in the middle of the Rhône River. The building, formerly a marketplace, features large windows opening onto the rushing blue-green river. It's open Monday to Saturday 8pm to midnight.

Au Chat Noir, 13 rue Vautier in the suburb of Carouges (☎ **022/343-49-93**), offering hot jazz, rock, soul, and blues nightly, is the "in" place to be. It's open daily 9pm to 4am. You can reach it by tram no. 12 from place Bel-Air in 12 minutes (exit at the first stop after crossing the river l'Arve). The bar is about 100 yards off place du Marché. Reservations are recommended on weekends.

BARS & DANCE CLUBS

Your best option for bars and dance clubs is the suburb of **Carouge** (take tram no. 12). On **rue Vautier** just off place du Marché you'll find half a dozen or more bars and dance clubs that feature live or recorded rock. Admission is generally free or only a few francs. Drink prices vary, generally 5.20SF to 18SF ($3.70 to $13).

One very popular club is **Le Moulin à Danses,** 20 bis rue du Stand (☎ **022/329-85-87;** Bus: 10 to Stand). In an old factory building, it's open Wednesday 10pm to 2am (couples preferred and rock, tango, and cha cha are played), Thursday 10pm to 3am (everyone welcome, and "zonk music"—tropical melodies like samba—is played), and Friday and Saturday 11pm to 4am (everyone welcome and disco is played). Admission is free when a deejay plays recorded music and 15SF ($11) when there's live music. On the first Thursday of every month the club hosts a dance contest (first prize is a bottle of champagne).

GAY & LESBIAN BARS

There are only a few in Geneva, and the two easist to find are the **Tube Bar** (for men), 3 rue de l'Université (☎ **022/329-82-98**), open Monday to Friday 9:30pm to 2am and Saturday and Sunday 5pm to 2am; and **Bar la Breteille** (for lesbians), 17 rue des Etuves (☎ **022/732-75-96**), open daily 5pm to 2am.

8 Side Trips: Bern, the Alps & Lake Geneva

Geneva is surrounded by water and mountains, and if you're visiting for more than a day, try to make an excursion to the Alps or cruise around Lake Geneva on one of the excursion boats that ply its blue-green waters every summer. If you're in town for 3 days or more, try a mountain trip and a lake trip.

BERN

One of Europe's loveliest cities and Switzerland's capital, **Bern** traces its origins to the 12th century. Since much of its medieval architecture has remained untouched, the United Nations declared it a world landmark in 1983. Market days are Tuesday and Saturday. If you're fortunate enough to arrive on the fourth Monday of November, you'll see the centuries-old **Zwiebelmarkt (Onion Market),** the last big event before the onset of winter, as residents traditionally stock up on onions. Bern is a convenient center for exploring the lakes and peaks of the **Berner Oberland,** an important center for winter sports.

ARRIVING   The **Bern–Belp Airport** (☎ **031/960-21-11**) is 6 miles south of the city. International flights arrive from London, Paris, and Nice, but transatlantic jets aren't able to land. Fortunately, it's a short hop to Bern from the international airports in Zurich and Geneva. **Taxis** are about 40SF ($28) to the city center, so it's better to take the shuttle bus that runs between the airport and the Bahnhof for 17SF ($12) one-way.

Bern has direct connections to the continental **rail network.** Bern also lies on major Swiss rail links, particularly those connecting Geneva and Zurich; each city is only 90 minutes away. The **Bahnhof,** on Bahnhofplatz, is in the center of town. If your luggage is light, you can walk to your hotel; otherwise, take one of the taxis waiting outside.

For **information** about tickets and train schedules for the Swiss Federal Railways, call ☎ 157-22-22 (no area code).

VISITOR INFORMATION   The **Bern Tourist Office,** in the Bahnhof, on Bahnhofplatz (☎ **031/311-66-11**), is open June to September, daily 9am to 8:30pm; October to May, Monday to Saturday 9am to 6:30pm and Sunday 10am to 5pm. If you need help finding a hotel, the tourist office can make a reservation for you.

GETTING AROUND   The public transport system, the **Stadtische Verkehrsbetriebe (SVB),** is a 48-mile network of buses and trams. Buy a ticket from the self-service automatic machines at each stop (conductors don't sell tickets). If you're caught traveling without one, you'll be fined. A short-range ticket (six stations) costs 1.50SF ($1.05); a regular ticket, valid for 45 minutes one-way only, is 2.40SF ($1.70). Or you can purchase a **1-day ticket** for 7.50SF ($5), entitling you to unlimited travel on the SVB network. Just get the ticket stamped at the automatic machine before you begin your first trip. One-day tickets are available at the ticket offices at Bubenbergplatz 5 (☎ **031/321-86-31**) and in the underpass of the Bahnhof (☎ **031/321-86-41**).

You can catch a **taxi** at the public cab ranks or call a dispatcher. Call **Nova Taxi** at ☎ **031/301-11-11** or **Bären Taxi** at ☎ **031/371-11-11.**

SEEING THE SIGHTS   The **Zutgloggeturm (Clock Tower),** on Kramgasse, was built in the 12th century and restored in the 16th. Four minutes before every hour, crowds gather for the world's oldest (since 1530) and biggest horological puppet show. Mechanical bears, jesters, and emperors put on an animated performance. The tower marked the west gate of Bern until 1250.

The ✪ **Bärengraben (Bear Pits),** on the opposite side of the river, is a deep moon-shaped den where the bears, Bern's mascots, have been kept since 1480. According to legend, when the duke of Zähringen established the town in 1191, he sent his hunters into the encircling woods, which were full of wild game. The duke promised to name the city after the first animal slain, which was the Bär (bear). Since then the town has been known as Bärn or Bern. Today, the bears are beloved, pampered, and fed by residents and visitors (carrots are most appreciated). Below the Bear Pits, you can visit the **Rosengarten (Rose Gardens),** from which there's a much-photographed view of the medieval sector and the river.

The ✪ **Cathedral of St. Vincent,** on Münsterplatz (☎ 031/311-05-72; Bus: 12), is one of Switzerland's newer Gothic churches, dating from 1421; the belfry, however, was completed in 1893. The most exceptional feature of this three-aisle pillared basilica is the tympanum over the main portal, depicting the Last Judgment with more than 200 figures, some painted. Mammoth 15th-century stained-glass windows are in the chancel. The choir stalls from 1523 brought the Renaissance to Bern. In the Matter Chapel is a remarkable stained-glass window, the *Dance of Death,* created in the last year of World War I but based on a much older design. The 300-foot-tall belfry offers a panoramic sweep of the Berner Alps; to get to the viewing platform, you must climb 270 steps. Admission to the cathedral is free, but the viewing platform costs 3SF ($2) adults and 1SF (65¢) children. Easter Sunday to October, it's open Tuesday to Saturday 10am to 5pm and Sunday 11am to 5pm; off-season hours are Tuesday to Friday 10am to noon and 2 to 4pm, Saturday 10am to noon and 2 to 5pm, and Sunday 11am to 2pm.

The ✪ **Kunstmuseum (Fine Arts Museum),** Hodlerstrasse 12 (☎ 031/311-09-44; Bus: 20), features the world's largest collection of works by Paul Klee. He was born in Switzerland in 1879, the same year that the building housing the collection was constructed. The Klee collection includes 40 oils and 2,000 drawings, gouaches, and watercolors. The museum's other works emphasize the 19th and 20th centuries. The important 20th-century collection has works by Kandinsky, Modigliani, Matisse, Soutine, and Picasso. There's also a collection of Italian 14th-century primitives, notably Fra Angelico's *Virgin and Child.* Admission to the permanent collection is 6SF ($3.95); special exhibits cost 10SF to 18SF ($7 to $12) extra. It's open Tuesday 10am to 9pm and Wednesday to Sunday 10am to 5pm.

The most panoramic attraction in the immediate vicinity is the ✪ **belvedere atop Mont Gurten.** There's also a children's fairyland and a walking area. The belvedere is connected to Bern by the Gurtenbahn cable train, one of the fastest in Europe. It departs from a station beside the Monbijoustrasse, about 1½ miles from Bern's center. A round-trip is 7.50SF ($4.95), and it operates year-round, daily 7:30am to sunset. For details, contact **Gurtenbahn Bern,** Eigerplatz 3 (☎ 031/961-23-23). To reach the departure point, take tram no. 9 (2.50SF/$1.65 each way) to the Gurtenbahn station. If you're driving, follow the road signs to Thun; there's a parking lot in the hamlet of Wabern, a short walk from the cable train station.

ACCOMMODATIONS & DINING   You might want to stay at the **Hôtel Gold-ener Schlüssel,** Rathausgasse 72 (☎ 031/311-02-16; Tram: 9; Bus: 12), offering 29 rooms, 20 with bathroom. A double with bathroom is 135SF ($96), breakfast included. MasterCard and Visa are accepted. For dining, **Gfeller am Bärenplatz,** Bärenplatz 21 (☎ 031/311-69-44; Tram: 3, 5, 9, or 12), is four restaurants in one. You can get Swiss-style meals in the tearoom, choose from an all-you-can-eat Chinese buffet, or order a pizza to share. The least expensive choice is the self-service cafeteria, Schnipo. The tearoom is open Monday to Friday 6:30am to 10pm, Saturday 6:30am to 6pm, and Sunday 8:30am to 6pm; the pizzeria and Chinese restaurant are open daily 11am to 2:30pm and 5 to 11:30pm; and Schnipo is open Monday to Saturday 10am to midnight and Sunday 11am to 11pm. American Express, MasterCard, and Visa are accepted.

Both places are in the historic city center, a 10-minute walk from the Central Station.

THE SALÈVE

Standing on Geneva's Right Bank gazing across at the Old City, you can't help but be awed by the massive wall of rock towering at the city's back. This is the **Salève,** rising nearly 4,500 feet and commanding a spectacular view of Geneva, the lake, the Rhône River, and miles of French and Swiss countryside. To the south is the panorama of the Alps, with Mont Blanc rising above the surrounding peaks, and to the north are the Juras. You can reach the peak of the Salève by cable car from the mountain base in 3 minutes. At the top is a modern observatory, a restaurant, and walking and cross-country ski trails. Because the Salève is across the French border, you'll need your passport. However, it's not necessary to change money: Swiss francs are accepted at the cable-car ticket window. The round-trip fare is 20SF ($14) adults and 12SF ($9) seniors/children.

To reach the Salève, take bus no. 8 from Geneva to the last stop at the town of Veyrier, still on the Swiss side of the border. When you get off the bus, you'll see the border station. Walk through and then follow the signs marked TÉLÉPHÉRIQUE. It's less than a 10-minute walk.

CHAMONIX & MONT BLANC

If the Salève whets your appetite for more mountains, a trip into the heart of the French Alps may be just the thing you need. The ski resort of **Chamonix,** at 3,370 feet, sits at the foot of the **Mont Blanc** massif, which rises to 15,625 feet. Surrounding Chamonix are dozens of lesser peaks and glaciers. Though most popular in winter, when skiers flock to the many slopes, this area is beautiful year-round. In summer, flowers fill the green meadows and tiny Alpine lakes sparkle in the sun. But whenever you go, pick a sunny day, for it's under clear skies that you can most fully appreciate the views of the surrounding peaks.

Trains from Geneva to Chamonix, 62 miles south, leave not from Cornavin Station but from the Eaux-Vives Station on the Left Bank. Tram no. 12 stops in front of this station, but to take this tram you must be on the Left Bank, since it doesn't cross the river. There's no direct train to Chamonix from Geneva; it's necessary to change trains twice. Your best trains to take for a day in the mountains leave Geneva at 7:07 and 8:26am and 2:36 and 5:35pm. The entire journey takes about 2½ hours; the round-trip fare is 48SF ($34) second class and 72SF ($51) first class.

From Chamonix, there are three possible ascents out of the valley, all presenting unsurpassed views of peaks and glaciers. The longest and most expensive is the ascent by cable car to **L'Aiguille du Midi** at 12,500 feet. The trip is in two stages and costs 190F ($35) round-trip, or you can choose to stop at the halfway point, **Plan de l'Aiguille** (7,500 feet), for a round-trip fare of only 80F ($15). The last ascent out is to the resort of **Montenvers** overlooking the Mer de Glâce glacier, which is nearly 4½ miles long and averages 3,900 feet in width. This is done by electric rack railway. By far the best view and value is from **Le Brevent,** with its stunning panorama of Mont Blanc, Chamonix nestled in the valley below, and the fingerlike glaciers that reach down from the peaks.

Expensive all-day tours to Chamonix are offered from Geneva by **Keytours,** 7 rue des Alpes (☎ **022/731-41-40**), with the cost depending on which ascent you make.

The excursion for 143F ($102), lunch included, offers a trip to Le Brevent or La Mer de Glâce. For 166F ($119), lunch included, you'll climb to L'Aiguille du Midi, and for 189F ($135) you'll continue past L'Aiguille du Midi, again by cable car, to Helbronner Point on the French-Italian border. This is an additional 3¼-mile trip across snow-fields and glaciers. Whether you go by train or escorted motorcoach, don't forget your passport—Chamonix is in France.

ACCOMMODATIONS & DINING   If you want to stay in Chamonix, try the **Hôtel Chamonix,** 58 place de l'Eglise (☎ **04-50-53-11-07** in France). A single or double with bathroom is 280F to 380F ($51 to $69); breakfast is 35F ($6). American Express, Diners Club, MasterCard, and Visa are accepted. This Alpine town at the foot of Mont Blanc has numerous **restaurants and self-service eateries.** The average price for a meal, with wine, is 120F ($22). One good choice is **Restaurant Alpina,** 79 av. du Mont-Blanc (☎ **04-50-53-47-77**), on the seventh floor of the Alpina Hotel, boasting a fantastic view of Mont Blanc. The two-course menu is 150F ($27) and the three-course menu 220F ($40). It's open daily noon to 2pm and 7 to 10pm and accepts American Express, Diners Club, MasterCard, and Visa.

LAKE CRUISES

Lake Geneva is a 45-mile-long crescent-shaped body of water, the entire north shore and either end of which are in Switzerland, while the south shore is in France. Along the shores are small villages, châteaux, fields, farms, and vineyards, and framing it all are the ever-present mountains, both the **Alps** and the **Juras.**

There are numerous tours of the lake, ranging from a short 40-minute trip in a little *mouette* (water bus) to all-day cruises of the entire lake on sleek yachts. The 40-minute trip leaves from the dock near the flower clock on the Left Bank and costs 9.50SF ($7). The castle of Baron M. de Rothschild, the villa of the Empress Joséphine, and Diodati Villa, where Lord Byron stayed in 1816, are some of the sights pointed out. A 2-hour cruise at 24.50SF ($18) passes more beautiful villas and châteaux and travels as far as the start of the French portion of the lake's south shore. These cruises leave from quai du Mont-Blanc on the Right Bank at 10:15am and 3pm March to November. The all-day cruise costs 57SF ($41) and leaves from quai du Mont-Blanc at 9:15am and returns at 10:50pm. This cruise is available daily late May to late September.

ACCOMMODATIONS & DINING   You might want to stay on the lake in Lausanne or Montreux, in good hotels not more than a 15-minute walk from the train station. In **Lausanne,** try the **Hôtel du Port,** 5 place du Port (☎ **021/616-49-30;** fax 021/616-83-68), a small hotel with only 17 rooms (14 with bathroom). Singles are 51SF to 100SF ($36 to $71) and doubles 98SF to 125SF ($70 to $89), breakfast included. An à la carte meal is 23SF ($16). American Express, Discover, and Visa are accepted. The **Restaurant Mirabeau,** 31 av. de la Gare (☎ **021/320-62-31**), offers filling meals for 20.50SF to 27.50SF ($15 to $20). It's open daily 11:30am to 2pm and 6:30 to 9:45pm and accepts American Express, Diners Club, Discover, and Visa.

In **Montreux,** on the lake shore 52 miles east of Geneva, the **Hôtel Elite,** 25 av. du Casino (☎ **021/966-03-03;** fax 021/966-03-10), has 35 rooms (all with bathroom). Singles are 60SF ($43) and doubles 100SF to 130SF ($71 to $93). American Express, Diners Club, Discover, and Visa are accepted. The **Buffet de la Gare,** 22 rue de la Gare (☎ **021/963-12-31**), is a large restaurant in the train station, serving excellent meals for 15SF to 25SF ($11 to $18). It's open Monday to Friday 6am to 10:30pm and Saturday and Sunday 8am to 10:30pm and accepts American Express, Diners Club, Discover, and Visa.

15 Innsbruck & Environs

by Beth Reiber

One of the joys of being in Innsbruck is its mountains—no matter where you are, you can see majestic peaks towering above the rooftops. This Alpine town of 120,000 offers bracing fresh air, narrow cobblestone streets, a beautifully preserved medieval Old City, and mountains on all sides. Little wonder the Winter Olympics were held here in 1964 and 1976—it's a skier's mecca year-round, due to the Stubai Glacier 10 miles south. Even when much of the Alps is suffering from lack of snow, Innsbruck will have business as usual. In summer, it also offers excellent hiking programs. On the other hand, many people come simply for the scenery.

First mentioned in documents in the 12th century, Innsbruck gained international stature under Maximilian I, who became the German emperor in 1507 and constructed the town's two most important buildings: the Goldenes Dachl and the Kaiserliche Hofburg. For much of its history, Innsbruck, capital of Tyrol, was a major crossroads of the Holy Roman Empire, and still today nearly everyone traveling from Munich to Rome or from Zurich to Vienna by car or train passes through it, making it a convenient stopover. If you're tired of big cities, come to Innsbruck to unwind.

REQUIRED DOCUMENTS   See chapter 28 on Vienna.

OTHER FROMMER'S TITLES   For more on Innsbruck, see *Frommer's Austria* or *Frommer's Europe*.

1 Innsbruck Deals & Discounts

SPECIAL DISCOUNTS

Students and children under 15 pay **reduced admission** (usually 20% to 50% off) to museums, cable cars, and the zoo. Anyone under 26 can obtain considerable savings by buying airline and train tickets at **Ökista** (Student Travel Office), Andreas-Hofer-Strasse 16 (☎ 58-89-97), in the city center, a 10-minute walk from the train station. The office is open Monday to Friday 9:30am to 5:30pm.

Anyone spending at least 1 night in one of Innsbruck's pensions or hotels can become a member of **Club Innsbruck** free of charge. This entitles you to free transportation on ski buses and discounts for ski passes, cable cars, certain museums, several sports facilities, and guided hikes and events sponsored by the club. Another way to save money is by purchasing an **Innsbruck Card,** allowing unlimited travel on

Budget Bests

If you're willing to stand up to eat and drink, you can save money by eating at an *imbiss* (food stand), where you'll pay less than 35S ($2.80) for a sausage and roll. In a restaurant, order from the **posted daily menu** *(Tagesgericht),* usually cheaper than ordering from the standard menu. Relaxing over a coffee and Sachertorte in one of Innsbruck's open-air coffee shops, such as the Hofgartencafe in the middle of a beautiful public garden (open in summer daily noon to 1am), is a delightful and inexpensive experience not to be missed.

For bargains on entertainment, check with the **Innsbruck Information Office,** Burggraben 3 (☎ **0512/5356**), to see whether any **free cultural performances** are scheduled. You may discover a free concert in a park or a church, music hall, or theater. Mid-June to the end of August, for example, there's the free Tyrolean Folk Art Evening held out in front of the Goldenes Dachl every Thursday at 8:30pm, featuring Tyrolean music and folk dances. Mid-May to the end of September, brass bands play at various squares in the city center every Saturday at 11am and from the balcony of the Goldenes Dachl every Sunday at 11:30am.

Innsbruck also offers an excellent program of **free hikes** led by expert guides. Contact the tourist office for details.

---

public transport in Innsbruck and Igls as well as on several lifts; it also includes admission to most attractions and museums, like the Tyrolean Folk Art Museum, Ambras Castle, the Alpine Zoo, and the Kaiserliche Hofburg. A 24-hour Innsbruck Card is 230S ($18). Contact the **Innsbruck Information Office** (☎ **0512/5356**) for details.

WORTH A SPLURGE

If you're here to ski, take advantage of the 1-day **"Stubai Package,"** which includes ski rental, lift tickets, and transportation to and from Stubai Glacier. Offered by the Innsbruck Information Office, it costs 599S ($48) in summer and 540S ($43) in winter.

Even if you don't ski, you can still visit the Stubai Glacier with a **discounted ticket** offered by the Innsbruck Information Office. The nonskier pass, including transportation to and from the glacier and a round-trip lift ticket, is 285S ($23).

2 Essentials

ARRIVING

BY PLANE   Small **Innsbruck Airport,** Fürstenweg 180 (☎ **0512/22525**), 2 miles west of downtown, is used only for commuter flights to and from Vienna, Zurich, and Frankfurt (the closest major airport is Munich). A **taxi** from Innsbruck's airport to either the train station or downtown is 130S ($10). Much cheaper is **public bus F,** which costs 21S ($1.70) and travels to Maria-Theresien-Strasse in the center of town.

If you're coming from the Munich airport, there's a bus transfer service called **Four Seasons Travel,** located in Innsbruck at Andreas-Hofer-Strasse 9 (☎ **0512/584 157**). Otherwise, those with railpasses will probably want to take the train (see chapter 19 for specifics on Munich's train station).

BY TRAIN   Innsbruck's train station, the **Hauptbahnhof (Central Station),** is conveniently located in the city center. From here, you can catch a streetcar or tram, bus, or taxi to your destination. For train information and schedules, call ☎ **1717.**

What Things Cost in Innsbruck	U.S. $
Taxi from the airport to the train station	10.40
Public transportation (bus, tram)	1.70
Local telephone call (per minute)	.16
Double room, with continental breakfast, at Goldener Adler (deluxe)	128.00
Double room, with continental breakfast, at Weisses Rössl (moderate)	97.60
Double room, with continental breakfast, at Pension Paula (budget)	43.20
Lunch for one, without wine, at Al Dente (moderate)	9.60
Lunch for one, without wine, at Zach (budget)	5.00
Dinner for one, without wine, at Ottoburg (deluxe)	16.00
Dinner for one, without wine, at Gasthaus Weisses Rössl (moderate)	11.00
Dinner for one, without wine, at Schnitzelparadies (budget)	8.00
Glass of wine	2.30
Coca-Cola in a restaurant	2.15
Cup of coffee with milk (in a restaurant or coffeehouse with table service)	2.10
Roll of ASA 100 color film, 36 exposures	4.80
Admission to the Tyrolean Folk Art Museum	3.20
Movie ticket (depending on the seat)	5.60–8.00
Theater ticket (standing room)	3.20

VISITOR INFORMATION

If you're arriving in Innsbruck by train, your first stop should be the **Innsbruck Information Office** (☎ **0512/58 37 66**), to the left as you exit the station (look for the HOTEL INFORMATION sign). It's open in summer daily 8am to 10pm and in winter Monday to Saturday 9am to 9:15pm and Sunday 10am to 9:15pm. Here you can pick up maps of the city and information on tours, excursions, and nightlife. The staff will also reserve accommodations for you for a 40S ($3.20) fee and a 15% deposit.

Once you're in the city, there's a larger, conveniently located **Innsbruck Information Office** at Burggraben 3 (☎ **0512/5356**), just off Maria-Theresien-Strasse near the Old City. At this well-organized and helpful main office, you can also pick up maps and brochures and make hotel reservations. Be sure to pick up their monthly brochure *Veranstaltungen* ("Events"). Computers impart information on destinations and attractions throughout the region of Tyrol, and on-site cameras show skiing conditions. You can also purchase bus tickets here and exchange money daily at the same rates as at banks. This office is open Monday to Saturday 8am to 7pm and Sunday and holidays 9am to 6pm. You can visit Innsbruck's home page at **www.tiscover.com/innsbruck;** the e-mail address is **info@innsbruck.tvb.co.at.**

If you plan on traveling, hiking, or mountain climbing in the surrounding province of Tyrol, contact **Tirol Werbung,** Maria-Theresien-Strasse 55 (☎ **0512/5320-0**), for brochures and maps. It's open Monday to Friday 8am to 6pm.

CITY LAYOUT

The **Inn River** divides the city into right and left banks; Innsbruck's name, in fact, translates as "Inn Bridge." On the right bank is the **Alstadt (Old City),** which contains most of Innsbruck's attractions, including the Hofkirche, Kaiserliche Hofburg, Goldenes Dachl, and the Tyrolean Folk Art Museum. Also on the right bank is the main train station, less than a 10-minute walk southeast of the Old City. Running south from the Old City is the city's main street, **Maria-Theresien-Strasse.** From there, **Burggraben** runs into **Marktgraben,** which goes down to the river and the **Alte Innbrücke (Old Inn Bridge).** This bridge and the **Universitätsbrücke** are the two most important river crossings; the other six are on the outskirts.

You'll undoubtedly spend most of your time in the neighborhood of the Altstadt. It's easily navigable on foot—indeed, much of it now is made up of pedestrians-only cobblestone streets. The heart of the city is along **Herzog-Friedrich-Strasse** and **Hofgasse,** Innsbruck's most picturesque streets.

GETTING AROUND

Most of Innsbruck's major sights are clustered in or around the Altstadt, within easy walking distance of each other. A plus is that many of the downtown streets have been closed to traffic, making for really pleasant walking. You'll want to wear good walking shoes, however, to navigate the cobblestone streets.

BY TRAM & BUS   Trams (streetcars) and buses provide public transportation. A single ticket, which permits transfers, costs 21S ($1.70) and may be purchased from the driver. Other options include a **1-day transportation pass** for 32S ($2.55) or a **group of four tickets** for 58S ($4.65). Keep in mind, however, that if you're traveling to one of the outlying villages, prices for the bus or tram will be higher than those given here.

If you plan on using public transportation a lot (especially if you're staying in accommodations on the outskirts of town) and plan on seeing most of Innsbruck's major sights, you can save money by purchasing an **Innsbruck Card,** which includes unlimited transportation in Innsbruck and Igls; use of the Nordkette, Patscherkofel, and Hungerburg lifts; and admission to most of Innsbruck's sights, including the Tyrolean Folk Art Museum, the Kaiserliche Hofburg, the Hofkirche, the Maximilianeum, Ambras Castle, and the Alpine Zoo. Cards are available for 24 hours for 230S ($18), 48 hours for 300S ($24), or 72 hours for 370S ($30). Children pay half price.

You can purchase all the ticket options from the **Innsbruck Information Office,** where you can also purchase a detailed transportation map for 10S (80¢). For more information on tram and bus tickets or travel routes, contact the **Innsbrucker Verkehrsbetriebe** at ☎ **0512/5307.**

BY TAXI   Innsbruck is so small you probably won't ever need a taxi. But if you do, the meter starts at 52S ($4.15) for the first 1,300 meters (0.8 miles), increasing by 2S (15¢) every 1,100 meters after that. From 10pm to 6am, as well as on Sunday and holidays, the meter starts at 57S ($4.55). Luggage is an extra 10S (80¢) apiece. To or from the airport, expect to pay 130S ($10). The trip from Innsbruck's train station to the village of Igls costs about 150S ($12). To call a taxi, dial ☎ **5311,** 1716, or 1718.

BY BICYCLE   Bikes are available for rent year-round at the main train station near the baggage-storage counter. It costs 90S ($7) for a 1-day rental if you have a Eurailpass or are in possession of a train ticket for that day. Otherwise, a day's rental is 150S ($12). Be sure to pick up a free pamphlet at the Innsbruck Information Office called "Cycling Around Innsbruck-Igls," which shows recommended routes through the neighboring countryside along with the degree of difficulty and number of hours required.

BY RENTAL CAR   It's much cheaper to rent a car in Europe if you make arrangements before you leave home. However, if you need one for travel in Innsbruck, go to **Avis,** next to the casino at Salurner Strasse 15 (☎ **0512/57 17 54**). It's open Monday to Friday 7:30am to 6pm, Saturday 8am to noon, and Sunday 9am to noon. One-day rental of an Opel Corsa or VW Polo with unlimited mileage is 1,032S ($83), including 20% value-added tax.

Hertz, with prices starting at 996S ($80) for a 1-day rental of a Ford Fiesta, including unlimited mileage and tax, is off Brixner Strasse, across from the main train station at Südtirolerplatz 1 (☎ **0512/58 09 01**). It's open Monday to Friday 7:30am to 6pm and Saturday 8am to 1pm.

Since there are often special holiday packages, more favorable weekend rates, and other deals, it pays to shop around.

FAST FACTS: Innsbruck

American Express   The office, where you can exchange money and cash American Express traveler's checks for free, is at Brixner Strasse 3 (☎ **0512/58 24 91**). It's open Monday to Friday 9am to 5:30pm and Saturday 9am to noon.

Baby-sitters   For baby-sitting in Innsbruck, call the **Babysitter Zentrale** (☎ **0512/1799**) Monday to Friday noon to 6pm. Since baby-sitters are students, no service is available during school vacations.

Banks   Banks are open Monday to Thursday 7:45am to 12:30pm and 2:15 to 4pm and Friday 7:45am to 3pm. If you want to exchange money outside these hours, your best bet is the **Innsbruck Information Office,** Burggraben 3 (☎ **0512/5356**), open Monday to Saturday 8am to 7pm and Sunday and holidays 9am to 6pm. You can also go to the money exchange counter at the main train station, open daily 7:30am to 8pm in winter and 7:30am to 9pm in summer, though the commission fee there is fairly steep.

Business Hours   Most shops and businesses are open Monday to Friday 9am to 6pm and Saturday 9am to 5pm. Some shops are also open later on Thursday, until 7:30pm.

Consulates   There are no U.S., Australian, Canadian, or New Zealand consulates in Innsbruck—the nearest are in Munich or Vienna. The **British Consulate** is at Matthias-Schmid-Strasse 12 (☎ **0512/588 320**).

Currency   See "Fast Facts: Vienna" in chapter 28.

Dentists & Doctors   If you're in need of an English-speaking doctor or dentist, contact the Innsbruck Information Office. Otherwise, call the **University Clinic,** Anichstrasse 35 (☎ **504**).

Emergencies   For urgent medical assistance, including an English-speaking doctor or dentist, call the **University Clinic** (☎ **504**). For an **ambulance,** call ☎ **144;** for the **police,** call ☎ **133;** and for the **fire department,** ☎ **122**.

There's a centrally located pharmacy, **St. Anna Apotheke,** at Maria-Theresien-Strasse 4 (☎ **0512/58 58 47**), open Monday to Friday 8am to 6pm and Saturday 8am to noon. A list of pharmacies that are open late or on Sunday is posted on the door of every pharmacy.

Holidays   Bank holidays in Innsbruck are New Year's Day (January 1), Epiphany (January 6), Easter Monday, Labor Day (May 1), Ascension Day, Whitmonday, Corpus Christi, Assumption Day (August 15), Austria Day (October 26), All Saints' Day (November 1), Immaculate Conception (December 8), and Christmas (December 25–26).

Country & City Codes

The **country code** for Austria is **43.** The **city code** for Innsbruck is **0512;** use this code when you're calling from outside Austria. If you're within Austria but not in Innsbruck, use **512.** If you're calling within Innsbruck, simply leave off the code and dial only the regular phone number.

Hospitals   The **General Hospital** (and University Clinic) is located at Anichstrasse 35 (☎ **504**). Another hospital is the **Sanatorium der Barmherzigen Schwestern,** Sennstrasse 1 (☎ **0512/59 3 80**).

Laundry   There's a conveniently located **laundry facility** in central Innsbruck, Münzwäscherei Hell, located at Amraser Strasse 15 (☎ **0512/34 13 67**), a few blocks behind the train station. For 150S ($12) you can have 4 kilos (8.8 lb.) washed and dried. It's open Monday to Friday 8am to 6pm. At many of the pensions on the outskirts, the proprietor will wash and dry your laundry or allow you to do so.

Mail   Innsbruck's **main post office,** open daily 7am to 11pm, is at Maximilian Strasse 2 (☎ **500-0**), 4 blocks from the train station. Poste Restante mail can be picked up here. Additionally, there's another post office located beside the train station (to your left if facing the station) at Brunecker Strasse 1 (☎ **500-7408**), open Monday to Friday 7am to 8pm and Saturday 8am to 6pm. An airmail letter to the United States is 13S ($1.05) for 20 grams, as is an airmail postcard. The city postal code for Innsbruck is 6020.

Telephone   Public telephones are found throughout the city, including in booths on sidewalks and in hotels and coffee shops. For local calls, insert two 1-schilling coins for a 1-minute call (insert more for longer calls—unused coins will be returned). Since hotels usually add a stiff fee to phone calls, make long-distance calls from post offices (the main post office, located at Maximilian Strasse 2, is open daily 7am to 11pm). It costs 31.50S ($2.50) to make a 3-minute call to the United States Monday to Friday 8am to 6pm; after 6pm and on weekends the rate falls to 28S ($2.25) for 3 minutes.

If you need to make a lot of local calls (and don't want to bother with coins) or wish to make long-distance calls from a public telephone, you can purchase a telephone card from any post office in values of 50S ($4), 100S ($8), and 200S ($16). The card can be inserted into slots on specially designated telephones found virtually everywhere.

Tipping   A service charge is included in hotel and restaurant bills, and taxi fares. Still, it's customary to round up to the nearest 10S (80¢) for both restaurant bills and taxi fares costing less than 100S ($8). For higher bills or fares, add 10%.

A Note on Telephone Numbers

Telephone numbers are slowly being changed in Innsbruck. If you need information on a telephone number in the city, dial ☎ **1611.** And incidentally, if you come across a number with a dash (as in 5307-03), the number following the dash is the extension number. Treat it as you would any number and simply dial the whole number.

3 Accommodations You Can Afford

Most of Innsbruck's budget accommodations are on the outskirts of town and in neighboring villages, easily reached in less than 30 minutes by public transportation. The cheapest are pensions (often called a *gasthof* or *gästehaus*), especially those offering rooms without private baths. But if you'd rather stay in the Altstadt (Old City) and feel like pampering yourself a bit, there are some good choices for a splurge.

Though most of the cheaper pensions charge the same rates all year, some of the more expensive hotels and guesthouses charge more during peak season, generally mid-June to September and during the Christmas/New Year holidays. Remember that if the recommendations below are full, the **Innsbruck Information Office** (see "Visitor Information") will reserve accommodations for you. If you contact the Innsbruck Information Office in advance, however, either by calling ☎ **0512/5356-38** or by e-mail at ibk.info@netway.at, no fee or deposit will be charged.

Note: You can find most of the lodging choices below plotted on the map in "Seeing the Sights," later in this chapter.

IN INNSBRUCK

Bistro. Pradler Strasse 2, 6020 Innsbruck. ☎ **0512/34 63 19.** Fax 0512/34 63 19. 9 units, all with bathroom. 460S ($37) single; 720S ($58) double; 930S ($74) triple. AE, DC, MC, V. A 15-minute walk northeast of the station.

All rooms here are large, and some even have panoramic views of the Alps. The pension has a pleasant modern restaurant serving excellent Austrian, Italian, and French food, charging 140S ($11) for fixed-price meals for hotel guests. The only disadvantage is that it's a bit far from the center of town, about a 10-minute walk northeast of the train station, past the overhead tracks and the Sill River.

Delevo. Erler Strasse 6, 6020 Innsbruck. ☎ **0512/58 70 54.** Fax 0512/58 70 54-18. 19 units, 13 with bathroom. 500S ($40) single without bathroom, 600S–700S ($48–$56) single with bathroom; 600S–700S ($48–$56) double without bathroom, 800S–900S ($64–$72) double with bathroom; 900S–1,000S ($72–$80) triple without bathroom, 1,100S–1,200S ($88–$96) triple with bathroom; 1,100S–1,200S ($88–$96) quad without bathroom, 1,400S–1,500S ($112–$120) quad with bathroom. Rates include continental breakfast. AE, MC, V. From Südtiroler Platz north of the train station, walk west on Brixner Strasse to Erler Strasse (a 5-minute walk northwest from the station).

This very simple hotel, without an elevator, offers plain rooms that could use some sprucing up, though rooms with baths do have the extras of phones and TVs. The main advantage to staying here is its convenient location, about halfway between the train station and the Altstadt. There's also a ground-floor restaurant. The highest prices in each category above are charged in peak season.

Innbrücke. Innstrasse 1, 6020 Innsbruck. ☎ **0512/28 19 34.** 27 units, 7 with bathroom; 1 apt. 320S ($25.60) single without bathroom, 400S ($32) single with bathroom; 500S ($40) double without bathroom, 700S ($56) double with bathroom; 720S ($58) triple without bathroom, 975S ($78) triple with bathroom; 1,300S ($104) apt. Rates include continental breakfast. AE, MC, V. Bus: A to Innbrücke; then walk across the bridge.

This guesthouse, managed by the same family for four generations, has a picturesque location right beside the Inn River and less than a 2-minute walk from the Altstadt. It occupies three floors (with elevator) of a building whose foundations date from 1425. Rooms with a view of the river are the same price as quieter, smaller rooms that face toward the back of the hotel. There's also an apartment large enough for a family of four. Facilities include a restaurant and a small bar.

An Accommodations Tip

You may be approached at the train station by people asking whether you need a room for the night; I'd say that most are reputable, but use your common sense. If you've already made reservations at one of the accommodations in this book, it's only fair to honor the reservation by showing up.

✪ **Paula.** Weiherburggasse 15, 6020 Innsbruck. ☎ **0512/29 22 62.** Fax 0512/29 22 62. 14 units, 3 with shower only, 5 with bathroom. 320S ($26) single without bathroom; 540S ($43) double without bathroom, 620S ($50) double with shower only, 660S ($53) double with bathroom. Rates include continental breakfast. No credit cards. Bus: K from the train station to Sankt Nikolaus, then a 5-minute walk.

This country-style chalet, on a hill on the left bank not far from the Alpine Zoo, offers splendid panoramic views of Innsbruck and the surrounding mountainside. Try to get one of the rooms facing the front with a balcony and chairs. The owner of this pension speaks a little English. Highly recommended.

Stoi. Salurner Strasse 7 (enter from Adamgasse), 6020 Innsbruck. ☎ **0512/58 54 34.** Fax 05238/872 82. 18 units, 8 with bathroom. 400S ($32) single without bathroom, 480S ($38) single with bathroom; 600S ($48) double without bathroom, 700S ($56) double with bathroom; 750S ($60) triple without bathroom, 850S ($68) triple with bathroom; 870S ($70) quad without bathroom, 950S ($76) quad with bathroom. No credit cards. *For Frommer's readers:* Ask about the 15% rate reduction. From the station, walk west on Salurner Strasse (3 minutes).

Keep your eyes peeled for this 100-year-old building. It's tucked behind another building a stone's throw from the casino, but otherwise staying here isn't much of a gamble. A very simple pension, without an elevator, it caters primarily to younger travelers, offering clean and perfectly adequate rooms. Ask for one of the four rooms on the south side with a balcony. Since the office closes at 9pm, make sure you check in before then; you'll receive a front door key, enabling you to come and go as you please. No breakfast is served, but a machine dispenses coffee for 10S (80¢).

Tautermann. Stamser Feld 5, Hötting, 6020 Innsbruck. ☎ **0512/28 15 72.** Fax 0512/28 15 72-10. 28 units, all with bathroom. TV TEL. 550S–600S ($44–$48) single; 850S–900S ($68–$72) double; 1,000S–1,100S ($80–$88) triple; 1,200S–1,300S ($96–$104) quad. Rates include buffet breakfast. AE, DC, MC, V. Bus: A from the train station to Höttinger Kirche.

Located across the Inn River, just a 6-minute (uphill) walk from the Altstadt, this simply furnished guesthouse offers rooms spread over three floors of a modern apartment house (no elevator). Half the rooms have minibars and clock radios, and the TVs are hooked up to cable with some programs in English. The higher prices in each category above are for peak season. The owners speak English.

Weisses Kreuz. Herzog-Friedrich-Strasse 31, 6020 Innsbruck. ☎ **0512/59 4 79.** Fax 0512/594 79 90. 39 units, 30 with bathroom. TV TEL. 430S–500S ($34–$40) single without bathroom, 730S–780S ($58–$62) single with bathroom; 1,080S–1,400S ($86–$112) double with bathroom. Rates include buffet breakfast. AE, V. Tram: 3 from the train station to Maria-Theresien-Strasse (2nd stop); or a 10-minute walk from the station.

With one of the most enviable locations in town, in the Altstadt across from the Goldenes Dachl, this inn boasts a 500-year history. Mozart stayed here when he was 13 during a 1769 journey with his father to Italy. Though the inn has been updated with modern conveniences, including an elevator and two smart restaurants serving Tyrolean and Asian-influenced cuisine, it remains true to its historic atmosphere, with white-walled rooms furnished with finished pine furniture, radios, and (in most) cable TVs. The most expensive doubles feature larger rooms and sofa beds.

Getting the Best Deal on Accommodations

- Stay in a pension on the outskirts of Innsbruck or in a neighboring village, where rates are much cheaper than in the city center.
- Try to avoid visiting during Innsbruck's peak season, about mid-June to September and over the Christmas and New Year holidays. If you must come during these times, reserve a room in a hotel or pension that charges the same rates year-round.
- If you like breakfast, stay in accommodations that offer morning buffets, allowing you to eat as much as you wish and perhaps save on lunch.

○ **Weisses Rössl.** Kiebachgasse 8, 6020 Innsbruck. ☎ **0512/58 30 57.** Fax 0512/58 30 57-5. 14 units, all with bathroom. TV TEL. 850S–900S ($68–$72) single; 1,200S–1,400S ($96–$112) double; 1,500S–1,800S ($120–$144) triple; 1,800S–2,000S ($144–$160) quad. Rates include buffet breakfast. AE, MC, V. Tram: 3 from the train station to Maria-Theresien-Strasse (second stop); or a 10-minute walk from the station.

This is a delightful inn, located in the center of the Altstadt. The house, built in 1410 and called the Weisses Rössl ("White Horse") since 1590, was recently renovated to enhance its original rustic splendor. The second floor has its original wood ceiling, and there's even a "light well"—an empty, open shaft that used to provide the only light to the floors below before the advent of electricity. The inn also boasts a fine traditional restaurant, with an outdoor terrace for summer dining. This place is a true find, just a 10-minute walk from the train station.

Zach. Wilhelm-Greil-Strasse 11, 6020 Innsbruck. ☎ **0512/58 96 67.** Fax 0512/58 96 67-7. 24 units, all with bathroom. TV TEL. 750S–850S ($60–$68) single; 1,150S–1,350S ($92–$108) double; 1,500S–1,700S ($120–$136) triple. Rates include buffet breakfast. AE, DC, MC, V. From the station, walk west on Salurner Strasse to Wilhelm-Greil-Strasse (4 minutes).

If you prefer modern lodging over ancient inns, this established hotel, renovated in 1996, is a good choice. With a convenient location between the Altstadt and the train station (less than a 5-minute walk from both), it offers cheerful, colorfully decorated rooms with safes and tiled baths with lots of counter space. The prices above reflect both the seasons and the size of the room, some of which have sofa beds.

OUTSIDE INNSBRUCK

○ **Rimml.** Harterhof Weg 82, Kranebitten, 6020 Innsbruck. ☎ **0512/28 47 26.** Fax 0512/28 47 26. 11 units, 9 with bathroom. 250S ($20) single without bathroom, 350S ($28) single with bathroom; 500S ($40) double without bathroom, 600S ($48) double with shower; 650S ($52) triple without bathroom, 800S ($64) triple with bathroom. Rates include continental breakfast. No credit cards. Bus: LK from Bozner Platz (near the train station) to Klamm-strasse (about 20 minutes).

All the rooms in this rural-style guesthouse are on the ground floor and have their own sinks, and most have baths. There's a peaceful garden for sunning as well as for eating breakfast on warm days. Proprietor Frau Rimml, who speaks fluent English, clearly enjoys her work and is helpful in advising guests what to see and do. More important, Frau Rimml can sometimes pick guests up at the train station. If not, she says that when guests arrive in Innsbruck, they should purchase a 1-day ticket for 32S ($2.55) for the trip to her pension in Kranebitten; she'll then reimburse guests for the ticket, which they can use to return to Innsbruck and for transportation throughout the city for the rest of the day.

⭘ **Steffi.** Dorfplatz 2, 6161 Natters. ☎ **0512/54 67 70.** Fax 0512/54 67 70. 10 units, all with bathroom. 310S ($25) single; 600S ($48) double; 820S ($66) triple; 1,050S ($84) quad. Rates include continental breakfast. No credit cards. Tram: STB from the train station to Natters.

This delightful pension, up in the mountains only 3 miles south of Innsbruck, is beautifully decorated with dried flower arrangements, plants, and antiques. The owners are a charming couple named Brigitte (who wears dirndls in summer) and Edwin Klien-Frech, formerly English teachers. They both speak excellent English, make sure their guests are well cared for, and provide a personal touch that makes staying here a pleasure. The rooms, all with radios, are cozily furnished, and there's a sun terrace and garden with folding chairs, as well as a public lounge with cable TV. If you give advance notice, they'll pick you up at the train station, a 15-minute ride away, but even the tram ride straight up the mountain is a hit with guests. You'll love this place.

WORTH A SPLURGE

⭘ **Goldener Adler.** Herzog-Friedrich-Strasse 6, 6020 Innsbruck. ☎ **0512/57 11 11.** Fax 0512/58 44 09. 35 units, all with bathroom. TV TEL MINIBAR. 1,080S ($87) single; 1,600S–2,100S ($128–$168) double. Rates include buffet breakfast. AE, DC, MC, V. Tram: 3 from the train station to Maria-Theresien-Strasse (second stop); or a 10-minute walk from the station.

You can't go wrong staying here. Everyone who was anyone seems to have passed through this 600-year-old inn, including Mozart, Goethe, Emperor Maximilian, Tyrolean freedom fighter Andreas Hofer, and numerous other kings, queens, and poets. On the Altstadt's most famous pedestrian passage near the Goldenes Dachl, it successfully weds historic charm with modern amenities, offering comfortable rooms named after famous people who've stayed here (the Andreas Hofer room with its canopy bed is the most popular). Four restaurants serve Tyrolean and international cuisine; they range from old-world rustic to elegant. Rates, the same throughout the year, are based on room amenities.

4 Great Deals on Dining

You'll find most of Innsbruck's restaurants clustered in and around the Altstadt. These range from cheap pizzerias catering primarily to students to traditional restaurants serving Austrian and Tyrolean cuisine. Familiar Austrian dishes include Wiener schnitzel, goulash, and *backhendl* (breaded and grilled chicken), but there are some local specialties to look for too—omelets filled with cranberries or *Tiroler knödel with gröstl*, for example. The latter consists of tennis-ball-size dumplings made of white bread, flour, smoked bacon, milk, egg, and salt, served with a stew made of potatoes, beef, and onions. The beverage of choice is beer from the barrel, served either in a small glass called a *seidel* (a third of a liter) or in a medium-size glass or earthenware mug called a *krügerl* (half a liter).

A LOCAL BUDGET BEST

University Mensa. Herzog-Sigmund-Ufer 15. ☎ **58 43 75.** Fixed-price meals 30S–60S ($2.40–$4.80) students, 40S–70S ($3.20–$6) nonstudents. No credit cards. Mon–Thurs 11am–2pm, Fri 11am–1:30pm. Closed Feb, July, and Aug. Tram: 1 to Anichstrasse. AUSTRIAN.

Conveniently located a 5-minute walk southwest of the Altstadt or a 15-minute walk from the train station, this student cafeteria serves absolutely the cheapest meals in Innsbruck and requires no student or other ID. Nonstudents simply pay a bit more (the nonstudent prices are written in parentheses on the chalkboard containing the

---

Getting the Best Deal on Dining

- For a quick, cheap meal, grab a bite at one of Innsbruck's many stand-up food stands (called an *imbiss*), serving everything from wurst to pizza and beer (try the *imbiss* at the Kaufhaus Tyrol department store, Maria-Theresien-Strasse 33, or the evening-only *imbiss* in front of the Goldenes Dachl).
- Try the special menu of the day *(Tagesgericht)*, which is often a complete meal in itself at prices cheaper than ordering à la carte.
- Put together your own meal by purchasing cooked foods at a butcher shop or the grocery section of a department store; eat it in your room or on a bench along the river.

---

daily menu). There are usually three complete meals offered, as well as a few items à la carte. Traditional meals include *germüsesuppe* (vegetable soup) and goulash (beef stew in spicy sauce). The mensa is near Universitätsbrücke (University Bridge), upstairs in the gray building facing the river.

IN OR NEAR THE ALTSTADT

Al Dente. Meraner Strasse 7. ☎ **0512/58 49 47.** Main courses 86S–150S ($7–$12). AE, DC, MC, V. Mon–Sat 7am–11pm, Sun and holidays 11am–11pm. Just off Maria-Theresien-Strasse, about halfway between the Altstadt and the train station (5 minutes from both). PASTA.

This cafe/restaurant is small and pleasant and is a good place for a meal or a cappuccino. As its name suggests, it specializes in pasta, as well as a few other dishes, like risotto and gnocchi and a great variety of salads. There's also a salad bar. If you're craving tagliatelle and a chef's salad, this is the place.

Churrasco. Innrain 2. ☎ **0512/58 63 98.** Pizza and pasta 68S–118S ($5–$9). AE, DC, MC, V. Daily 9am–midnight. A 1-minute walk west of the Altstadt, beside the Innbrücke. PIZZA/PASTA.

The pizza here is merely good rather than fantastic, but what sets this place apart is its great location beside the Inn River. With outdoor seating in summer, it's been a popular student hangout seemingly forever. You'll find it just west of the Altstadt.

Gasthaus Weisses Rössl. Kiebachgasse 8. ☎ **0512/58 30 57.** Meals 80S–170S ($6–$14). MC, V. Mon–Fri 11am–2pm and 5–10pm, Sat 11am–2pm and 6–10pm. AUSTRIAN.

This is a great place for a traditional meal in the heart of the city. Up on the first floor of an old inn, this old-fashioned restaurant has a wooden ceiling and wooden benches and is decorated with antiques, pewter plates, and antlers. Its English menu includes fish, rump steak, schnitzel, beef filet with onions and potatoes, Cordon Bleu, goulash, gröstl, and grilled sausages. There's also a children's plate of pork chops and french fries for 70S ($6) and daily specials not on the English menu, including fixed-price meals and a daily lunch for 90S ($7). Since it's popular, you're best off making a reservation.

Philippine. Templstrasse 2. ☎ **0512/58 91 57.** Main dishes 82S–148S ($7–$12); fixed-price meals 82S–112S ($7–$9). AE, DC, MC, V. Mon–Sat noon–2:30pm and 6–10pm. A 1-minute walk southwest of Maria-Theresien-Strasse, on the corner of Müllerstrasse and Templstrasse. VEGETARIAN.

If you're tired of the hearty and somewhat heavy Austrian cuisine, try this airy vegetarian restaurant. It offers à la carte dishes such as zucchini-tofu gratin with tomatoes, Asian-influenced stir-fries, and vegetarian spaghetti, as well as lunch and dinner

Cafes & Konditoreis

If all you want is a cheap cup of coffee, head for **Eduscho,** a coffee shop that sells both the brew and the beans. Located just south of the Altstadt at Maria-Theresien-Strasse 1 (☎ **0512/56 39 43**), it's open Monday to Friday 8am to 6:30pm and Saturday 8am to 5pm. A cup of coffee consumed at one of its stand-up tables is just 8S (65¢).

At **Cafe Central,** Gilmstrasse 5 (☎ **0512/5920**), conveniently located halfway between the train station and the Altstadt, you can read English-language newspapers while enjoying a cup of excellent coffee or tea. This is Innsbruck's oldest coffeehouse, founded in 1878. It features live piano music on Friday and Sunday 8 to 10pm. You can come here for just a cup of coffee—a *kleiner brauner* (a small cup of strong, black coffee with whipped cream) is 26S ($2.10)—or eat a complete meal of spaghetti or an omelet or maybe just an *apfelstrudel*. It's open daily 7:30am to 11pm.

Cafe Munding, Kiebachgasse and Schlossergasse (☎ **0512/58 41 18**), is one of the nicest coffeehouses in town, with walls that serve as a gallery for local artists. The building itself is in the middle of the Altstadt and dates from the Middle Ages; in the summer you can sit outside. There are various coffees (a large coffee with milk costs 35S/2.80), including Irish coffee and Viennese blends. A specialty is homemade ice cream (more than 20 kinds) and cakes. It's open daily 8am to 10:30pm (to 8pm in winter).

fixed-price meals and a children's menu. There are flowers and candles on every table. On the ground floor of the restaurant is a casual cafe, open Monday to Saturday 10am to 11pm, with the same menu.

Schnitzelparadies. Innrain 25. ☎ **0512/57 29 72.** Meals 80S–130S ($6–$10). AE, DC, MC, V. Mon–Sat 10am–11pm, Sun 9:30am–3pm. Tram: 1 to Anich; or a 4-minute walk southwest of the Altstadt, on the corner of Innrain and Bürgerstrasse. AUSTRIAN.

As its name ("Schnitzel Paradise") implies, this budget-priced restaurant near the university specializes in generous portions of schnitzel, made from veal, turkey, or pork and served in half a dozen ways. There's an English menu, service is quick, and there's always free coffee you can serve yourself. The dining hall itself looks like an American chain clone, but at these prices no one is complaining.

Shere Punjab. Inn Strasse 19. ☎ **0512/28 27 55.** Main dishes 75S–110S ($6–$9). AE, DC, MC. Daily 11am–2pm and 5–11pm. A 2-minute walk west of the Altstadt, across the Innbrücke bridge and the Inn River. INDIAN.

Along the Inn River on the opposite side from the Altstadt, this small family-run place is one of Austria's oldest Indian restaurants, open since 1950. Try the chicken tikka or the lentil soup for an appetizer, followed by one of the many meat, fish, chicken, or vegetable dishes, all served with rice. Strangely enough, there's also pizza and pasta. Daily 11am to 2pm, a special fixed-price lunch menu is available for 65S ($5); it includes a soup, main course, rice, and dessert.

Wienerwald. Maria-Theresien-Strasse 12. ☎ **0512/58 41 65.** Meals 65S–128S ($5–$10). AE, DC, MC, V. Daily 10am–midnight. A 2-minute walk south of the Altstadt. AUSTRIAN.

Wienerwald, a chain of reliable restaurants found throughout German-speaking Europe, made a name for itself with grilled chicken but has since branched out to include a variety of other chicken dishes, such as red pepper chicken, lemon pepper chicken, chicken Cordon Bleu, chicken with chili sauce, and even a chicken burger. One of the least expensive items, however, remains its quarter of a grilled chicken at 40S ($3.20); add a side dish for 30S ($2.40). There's also a salad bar and a menu in English.

Zach. Wilhelm-Greil-Strasse 11. ☎ **0512/58 30 54.** Main dishes 25S–82S ($2–$7). No credit cards. Mon–Thurs 8am–6:30pm, Fri 7:30am–6:30pm, Sat 7:30am–12:15pm. Halfway between the train station and the Altstadt, about a 5-minute walk from both. AUSTRIAN.

This well-known butcher shop sells meats on one side of the store and simple dishes and complete meals from a self-service counter on the other side, including bratwurst, frankfurter with roll, Wiener schnitzel with fries, and salads. There are daily specials for 70S to 75S ($5 to $6) for a complete meal, available Monday to Friday 11am to 2pm. These may range from lasagna or beef goulash to spinach dumplings. Although there are a few seats for sit-down dining, most people stand at one of the chest-high tables. Avoid the busy lunch hour if you want to sit down.

STREET FOOD

There are **food stands** *(Imbisse)* in every city in Austria. During the day, try the *imbiss* at **Kaufhaus Tyrol,** Maria-Theresien-Strasse 33 (☎ **0512/5915-0**), located at the southernmost entrance of this large department store. It offers bratwurst, pizza by the slice, schnitzel burgers, beer, and more, with most prices less than 35S ($2.80). It's open the same hours as the department store: Monday to Friday 9am to 7pm and Saturday 9am to 5pm.

In the evenings when Kaufhaus Tyrol is closed, a wurst stand sets up business outside the store on the sidewalk, selling sausages, fries, beer, and soda. In addition, try the *imbiss* in the Altstadt, right in front of the Goldenes Dachl on Herzog-Friedrich-Strasse, open daily 7pm to 1am and selling the usual sausages and drinks.

PICNICKING

Innsbruck's largest department store, **Kaufhaus Tyrol,** is in the center of town at Maria-Theresien-Strasse 33 (☎ **0512/5915-0**). It has a well-stocked grocery department in its basement, selling takeout food, including salads and meat dishes, as well as the usual fruits, vegetables, cheeses, and sausages. It's open Monday to Friday 9am to 7pm and Saturday 9am to 5pm.

Not far away is **Hörtnagel,** Burggraben 4 (☎ **0512/59 7 29**), near the Innsbruck Information Office. It offers the usual cheeses, wursts, and fruits, as well as a delicatessen. Hours here are Monday to Wednesday 7:45am to 6:30pm, Friday 7:30am to 6:30pm, and Saturday 7:30am to 1pm.

And where to eat your goodies? The best place is along the Inn River, where there are public benches, and in the Hofgarten.

WORTH A SPLURGE

Ottoburg. Herzog-Friedrich-Strasse 1. ☎ **0512/57 46 52.** Main dishes 85S–235S ($7–$19). AE, DC, MC, V. Daily 11am–2:30pm and 5:30–10:30pm. Closed Tues Nov–Jan. In the Altstadt, between the Goldenes Dachl and the Inn River. AUSTRIAN.

There's no better place for a taste of Tyrolean history—and its cuisine—than this atmospheric medieval-era restaurant in the heart of the Altstadt. The Ottoburg was first mentioned in documents in the 11th century, when it was listed as an apartment house (Emperor Maximilian lived here for a year); it was converted to a restaurant 150 years ago. The building is topped with a 1494 Gothic tower and contains four intimate dining rooms with carved wooden ceilings and neo-Gothic decor. Local and house specialties on the English menu include Tyrolean Herrengröstl, goulash, Wiener schnitzel, and "Grandmother's Cooking Pot" (pork mignon in a fine mushroom sauce with tiny dumplings). There are also daily and seasonal specials (such as wild game) listed only on the German menu—ask for a translation. In summer there's outdoor seating on the Altstadt's most famous pedestrian lane.

5 Seeing the Sights

SIGHTSEEING SUGGESTIONS

IF YOU HAVE 1 DAY   If you have only 1 day, spend it in the **Altstadt (Old City),** where you'll find most of Innsbruck's top attractions and historic buildings, including the **Goldenes Dachl, Hofkirche, Tyrolean Folk Art Museum,** and **Kaiserliche Hofburg.** Top off the day with a meal in a traditional Austrian restaurant.

IF YOU HAVE 2 DAYS   Spend Day 1 as above. On Day 2, head to the **Alps,** for which Innsbruck is famous. If you ski, go straight to **Stubai Glacier,** where you can ski every day of the year. If not, join an organized **hiking tour** (offered free in summer) or take the funicular and then the cable car to **Hafelekar,** a 7,700-foot-high peak just north of the city, where you'll have a breathtaking view. If it's a Thursday in summer, see whether the **Tyrolean Folk Art Evening** is taking place in front of the Goldenes Dachl.

IF YOU HAVE 3 DAYS   Spend Days 1 and 2 as above. On Day 3, go to the **Alpine Zoo,** where you'll see animals native to the Alps. In the afternoon, head for **Ambras Castle** (open only in summer), built in the 16th century and housing a collection of arms and armor.

IF YOU HAVE 4 DAYS   Spend Days 1 to 3 as above. On Day 4, take an excursion to **Wattens,** where you can tour the fantastic Swarovski Kristallwelten and then continue onward to the silver mines in **Schwaz.**

THE TOP ATTRACTIONS

Maximilianeum in the Goldenes Dachl. Herzog-Friedrich-Strasse 15. ☎ **0512/528 11 11.** Admission 60S ($4.80) adults, 50S ($4) seniors, 30S ($2.40) students, 20S ($1.80) children. Summer daily 10am–6pm; winter Tues–Sun 10am–12:30pm and 2–5pm. Tram: 1 or 3.

In the heart of the Altstadt is Innsbruck's most famous landmark, the Goldenes Dachl (Golden Roof), easily recognized by its gleaming balcony made of 2,657 gilded copper tiles. Built in the late 15th century by Emperor Maximilian to celebrate his marriage to his second wife, Bianca Maria Sforza, it was used as a royal box for watching civic events in the square below, including tournaments between armored knights, dances, and theatrics. If you look closely at the building's reliefs, you can see images of Maximilian and his two wives (his first wife, Mary of Burgundy, died in a riding accident and was much grieved; his second wife brought him great wealth and went largely ignored). Though you aren't allowed onto the balcony, the building's facade is the most photographed sight in Innsbruck. On Thursday evening in summer, Tyrolean Folk Art Evenings are staged in the square in front of the building.

The best thing to do at the Goldenes Dachl is go inside to the **Maximilianeum,** a museum dedicated to Innsbruck's most influential resident, Emperor Maximilian. The museum itself is quite small—just one room filled with portraits of Maximilian and artifacts of his time—but the 20-minute film in English describing the emperor's life and the history of Innsbruck makes a visit worthwhile.

✪ **Kaiserliche Hofburg (Imperial Court Palace).** Rennweg 1. ☎ **0512/58 71 86.** Admission 55S ($4.40) adults, 35S ($2.80) seniors/students, 10S (80¢) children. Daily 9am–5pm. Tram: 1 or 3. Bus: O, L, K, or N.

Getting the Best Deal on Sightseeing

- Buy the Innsbruck Card—available for 24 hours at 230S ($18), for 48 hours at 300S ($24), and for 72 hours at 370S ($30)—which offers unlimited public transport and free entry to Innsbruck's major sights and museums.
- Buy a combination ticket whenever possible—such as the one for the Hofkirche and Volkskunstmuseum.

On the northeastern edge of the Altstadt, this imperial palace is to Innsbruck what Versailles is to Paris—but on a much smaller scale. Built in 1460 and enlarged by Emperor Maximilian in the 1500s as a residence for his second wife, it was reconstructed in the baroque style by Empress Maria Theresa in the mid-18th century. On view are the private living quarters used by Maria Theresa and her family whenever they visited, including the royal chapel, dining rooms, and bedrooms, all with original furnishings, tapestries, paintings, and portraits. The most fascinating of the 20-some rooms available for viewing is the **Giants' Hall,** lavishly decorated in rococo style with elaborate stucco designs and a painted ceiling. What's striking about the room, however, is the collection of portraits of Maria Theresa's 16 children, including her youngest daughter, Antonia, who went on to become that ill-fated queen of France, Marie Antoinette.

Hofkirche (Court Church). Universitätsstrasse 2. ☎ **0512/58 43 02.** Admission 20S ($1.60) adults, 14S ($1.10) students, 10S (80¢) children. Combination ticket for Hofkirche and Volkskunstmuseum, 50S ($4) adults, 39S ($3.15) students, 25S ($2) children. Mon–Sat 9am–5pm. Tram: 1 or 3. Bus: O, L, K, or N.

A minute's walk east of the Kaiserliche Hofburg is the royal Court Church. Emperor Maximilian conceived of the church as his memorial and place of burial. Inside is his elaborate tomb, decorated with reliefs depicting scenes from the emperor's life, and surrounded by 28 larger-than-life bronze statues representing his ancestors and relatives, including his father, his two wives, his son, and daughter. The tomb, however, is empty—Maximilian died before the church was built and was buried in Wiener Neustadt. Several other important figures are interred here, though, including Tyrolean freedom fighter Andreas Hofer and Archduke Ferdinand II. You'll find Ferdinand's final resting place up the stairs in the **Silberne Kapelle (Silver Chapel);** just outside the chapel's iron gate is the tomb of Ferdinand's wife, Philippine Welser. A commoner, she wasn't allowed to be buried beside her husband, but his undying love for her lives on in Ambras Castle (see below). Note that the Hofkirche is located through the same entryway as the Volkskunstmuseum described below; the combination ticket for both offers a reduction.

✪ **Tiroler Volkskunstmuseum (Tyrolean Folk Art Museum).** Universitätsstrasse 2. ☎ **0512/58 43 02.** Admission 40S ($3.20) adults, 25S ($2) students, 15S ($1.20) children. Combination ticket for Hofkirche and Volkskunstmuseum, 50S ($4) adults, 39S ($3.15) students, 25S ($2) children. Mon–Sat 9am–5pm, Sun and holidays 9am–noon. Tram: 1 or 3. Bus: O, L, K, or N.

Housed in a former monastery adjoining the Court Church, this is my favorite museum in Innsbruck. Certainly it's one of the best folk art museums in the country, with its collection of items used by common folk in Tyrol from the Middle Ages to this century. Included are sleighs; a beautiful collection of painted furniture

Innsbruck

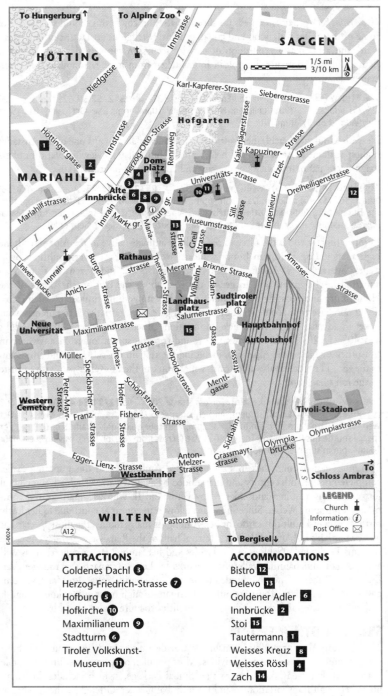

LEGEND
Church ✝
Information ⓘ
Post Office ✉

ATTRACTIONS
Goldenes Dachl ❸
Herzog-Friedrich-Strasse ❼
Hofburg ❺
Hofkirche ❿
Maximilianeum ❾
Stadtturm ❻
Tiroler Volkskunst-
Museum ⓫

ACCOMMODATIONS
Bistro 12
Delevo 13
Goldener Adler 6
Innbrücke 2
Stoi 15
Tautermann 1
Weisses Kreuz 8
Weisses Rössl 4
Zach 14

(Bauernmöbel); ornamental bells for sheep, goats, and cows (you should see the size of some of these); farming tools and cooking utensils; religious artifacts; clothing; glassware; and a fascinating collection of nativity scenes *(Krippe).* It also contains more than a dozen reconstructed Tyrolean rooms taken from inns, farmhouses, and patrician homes.

Stadtturm (City Tower). Herzog-Friedrich-Strasse 21. ☎ **0512/57 59 62.** Admission 22S ($1.75) adults, 11S (90¢) children. Nov–Feb daily 10am–4pm; Mar–Oct daily 10am–5pm (July–Aug to 6pm). Tram: 1 or 3.

Near the Goldenes Dachl, the Stadtturm, at 185 feet tall, remains one of the Altstadt's highest structures. At one time it held a prison, but today its viewing platform offers magnificent panoramic views of the city and Alps. It was built in 1440.

Alpenzoo (Alpine Zoo). Weiherburggasse 37. ☎ **0512/29 23 23.** Admission 70S ($6) adults, 30S ($2.40) children. Daily 9am–6pm. Tram 1 or bus 4, C, D, or E to Talstation, then the Hungerburg funicular to the Mittelstation Alpenzoo; or special shuttle bus from Maria-Theresien-Strasse 45 or in front of the Hofburg Alpenzoo (mid-May to Sept only).

Europe's highest zoo is the place to see all those animals native to the Alps and Alpine region, including European bison, wildcats, wolves, otters, beavers, vultures, owls, eagles, buzzards, elk, Alpine ibex, rabbits, brown bears, and dozens of fish (in an aquarium). The easiest way to get to the zoo, above the city on the slopes of the Hungerburg and boasting a great view, is via the Hungerburg funicular, which is free if you purchase your zoo ticket at the funicular gate. An alternative is to purchase your ticket in advance at the Innsbruck Information Office. This ticket, 80S ($6) adults and 40S ($3.20) children, allows free round-trip transportation from anywhere in Innsbruck or Igls to the Alpenzoo, including the ride on the cable car and admission to the zoo. The ticket is also a postcard, which you can then use after your visit to write to the folks back home.

Schloss Ambras (Ambras Castle). Schloss Strasse 20. ☎ **0512/34 84 46.** Admission 60S ($4.80) adults, 30S ($2.40) students and children; 25S ($2) extra mid-Jan to Mar. Apr–Oct Wed–Mon 10am–5pm; mid-Jan to Mar at 2pm, with tour guide only. Tram: 3 or 6. Bus: K; or special shuttle bus from Maria-Theresien-Strasse (across from McDonald's), leaving every hour 10am–5pm in summer, at 1:45pm in winter.

Two miles east of Innsbruck in a district called Ambras stands this imposing castle, completed in the 16th century and surrounded by a lovely park. Originally a medieval fortress, it was acquired and enlarged by Ferdinand II, who was married to a commoner, Philippine Welser. Since she wasn't allowed to appear at court due to her lowly birth, Ferdinand built this castle for her. Among its many rooms, the most spectacular is the **Spanish Hall,** one of the finest festival halls of the Renaissance. Today the castle contains Ferdinand's Cabinet of Curiosities and his famous armor collection, as well as a portrait and painting gallery with works by Lucas, Cranach the Younger, Van Dyck, and Rubens. One-hour guided tours are offered mid-January to March at 2pm, costing 25S ($2) extra. Tours are only in German, though most guides know English and will translate for foreign visitors. An English brochure is also available.

SKIING & OTHER SPORTS

The Tyrolean Alps surrounding Innsbruck provide a ready-made playground for both summer and winter sports and activities. Most popular, of course, is **skiing,** available year-round. For 1-day skiers, there's the "Stubai Package," which includes ski rental, lift tickets, and transportation to and from Stubai Glacier. Offered by the Innsbruck Information Office, it costs 599S ($48) in summer and 540S ($43) in winter. There

Special & Free Events

The new year in Innsbruck kicks off with an annual **Ski Jump Competition,** held in January (the 1964 Olympic ski jump is right on the edge of town). The **International Dance Festival,** which can feature everything from modern dance and ballet to flamenco, is held at the end of June. If you're a music fan or history buff, you'll want to take advantage of the **Festival of Early Music,** held annually in August, with concerts at Castle Ambras's Spanish Hall and other historic venues. It features everything from baroque operas to concerts with historical instruments. And from the end of November until Christmas, there's the annual **Christmas market** in the Altstadt.

If you're in Innsbruck in summer on a Thursday, be sure to head to Herzog-Friedrich-Strasse in front of the Goldenes Dachl for the **Tyrolean Folk Art Evening.** It begins at 8:30pm on Thursday from June to August and includes free entertainment of Tyrolean music and folk art dancing.

Other free events from mid-May to September include **brass band concerts** in the Altstadt every Saturday at 11am and a **medieval brass band** playing from the Goldenes Dachl's famous balcony on Sunday at 11:30am.

are also ski packages covering wider areas for more days. Other winter activities are **cross-country skiing, snow boarding, day and evening tobogganing,** and **dog-sleigh rides.**

Throughout the year, enthusiasts can partake in rides on a **piloted four-man bob-sled,** and every Thursday evening free **lantern hikes** are offered to an alpine hut, where participants can purchase food and drink. In summer, additional activities include **white-water rafting, hang gliding, mountain biking,** following a fixed-rope climbing route, **golfing,** and **hiking.** Particularly good are the **free mountain walks** led by experienced guides, offered daily June to September at 8:30am, including transportation and use of climbing shoes and rucksack. Hikes last about 3 to 5 hours. No previous experience in mountain hiking is necessary.

For more information on sports activities, contact the **Innsbruck Information Office** at Burggraben 3 (☎ **0512/5356**).

PARKS & GARDENS

The two largest and most famous parks are the **Hofgarten,** in the Altstadt, and the **Amraser Schlosspark,** 2 miles east of town, next to Schloss Ambras. Smaller parks are the **Rapoldipark,** behind the train station, and **Walther Park,** on the left riverbank, near Alte Innbrücke. All feature restaurants and coffee shops and are popular hangouts during the summer months, where you can enjoy a beer or a soft drink and admire the Alpine panorama. Most popular, however, is the Hofgarten, with a cafe packed in summer and live music.

ORGANIZED TOURS

If you have a limited amount of time, take the 2-hour **bus/walking tour** of city highlights, accompanied by an English-speaking guide. It departs from the train station daily at noon, with additional departures at 2pm June to September. Tickets are 160S ($13) adults and 70S ($6) ages 7 to 10. The bus stops at the Olympic ski jump, built for the 1964 Games, and includes a 20-minute walk through the Old City. Tickets are available at the Innsbruck Information Office at Burggraben 3 and the train station.

6 Shopping

Innsbruck isn't a bargain town for Austrian souvenirs and goods—prices are simply too high. However, it's fun to look, and you might find something worth the extra money. The best shopping area is in the Altstadt and along Maria-Theresien-Strasse, where you'll find traditional Tyrolean sweaters and clothing, Gmünder ceramics, petit-point items, and enamel jewelry. One good shop is **Tiroler Heimatwerk,** just off Maria-Theresien-Strasse at Meraner Strasse 2 (☎ **0512/58 23 20**); it sells ceramics, linens, pewter, Tyrolean wood carvings, traditional clothing, and other local products. It's open Monday to Friday 9am to 1pm and 2 to 6pm and Saturday 9am to noon.

If you purchase goods at any one store costing more than 1,000S ($80), you're entitled to a partial refund of the 13% **value-added tax (VAT).** Ask the clerk to give you a Tax-free Shopping Cheque or U-34 Customs form. Upon departing the last European Union country on your way home, have it stamped by Customs, whether you leave by train, car, or plane. Many airports have counters where you can receive your refund immediately; otherwise, mail your form back to the store after it's been stamped by Customs.

7 Innsbruck After Dark

For theater and musical performances, pick up the free monthly *Veranstaltungen* ("Events"), a publication listing theater, concerts, dance, and other cultural programs, available at the Innsbruck Information Office at Burggraben 3. You can also purchase tickets for the theater, concerts, and other events at the Innsbruck Information Office, including tickets for performances in Vienna. You'll pay a 10% commission for Innsbruck tickets, 18% for Vienna.

THE PERFORMING ARTS

For an evening of Tyrolean entertainment, including traditional music, yodeling, and folk dancing, see the **Tiroler Alpenbühne** (☎ **0512/263 263**), held in the Gasthaus Sandwirt am Inn, Reichenauerstrasse 151 (Bus: R or O), or in the Messe-Saal at Ing.-Etzel Strasse 35 (Tram: 1; or a 10-minute walk north of the train station). Held daily at 8:45pm May to September, it costs 220S ($18), which includes one free drink. There's a similar program, **Tiroler Unterhaltungsabend,** held throughout the year on Wednesday at 8:30pm at Hotel Sailer, just a couple minutes' walk west of the train station at Adamgasse 6–10 (☎ **0512/53 63**). It costs 380S ($30), including a snack, drink, and souvenir. For more information, contact the Innsbruck Information Office.

In the heart of the city across from the Kaiserliche Hofburg, the **Tiroler Landestheater,** Rennweg 2 (☎ **0512/52 0 74;** Tram: 1 or 3; Bus: O, L, K, or N), is Innsbruck's most important venue for performances of opera, operetta, and theater, including one-act plays, comedies, and other lighthearted productions. There are two theaters: the Grosses Haus for opera and large productions, and the Kammerspiele for plays. Tickets for opera run from 85S to 460S ($7 to $37), but standing-room tickets cost only 50S ($4); for theater, expect to spend 70S to 390S ($6 to 31), with standing room costing 40S ($3.20). Students can purchase unsold tickets on the night of the performance for 90S ($7). The box office is open Monday to Saturday 8:30am to 8:30pm and Sunday and holidays 6:30 to 8:30pm. Performances take place at 7:30 or 8pm.

For live music, including jazz, blues, and folk, the best and most convenient spot is **Treibhaus,** Angerzellgasse 8 (☎ **0512/58 68 74**), hidden away on a side street off

Museum Strasse, just a block east of Burggraben in the heart of the city. It also offers frequent cabaret and other theatrical productions. Since there's a comfortable cafe/bar here (complete with a children's play corner), you might just want to come for a drink or for one of its more than 30 kinds of pizza. The cafe is open Monday to Friday 9am to 1am and Saturday 10am to 1am. On Sunday, 11am to 1pm, there's free jazz. Check *Veranstaltungen* for current performances.

PUBS & BARS

Many of Innsbruck's night locales are located in or around the Altstadt, making it easy to bar-hop—or pub-crawl—from one to the next. In the heart of the Altstadt, right next to the Goldenes Dachl, a very young student crowd congregates at **Elferhaus,** Herzog-Friedrich-Strasse 11 (☎ **0512/58 28 75**), open daily 10:30am to 2am. It's long, narrow, and smoky and can get very crowded. Almost next door, with an entry buried between stores along the covered sidewalk, is the much more sophisticated **Piano,** Herzog-Friedrich-Strasse 5 (☎ **0512/57 10 10**), a trendy bar and the place to be seen for Innsbruck's yuppie crowd. Many business types stop by here for a drink after work. It's open Monday to Saturday 10am to 1am.

Nearby, on a small alley-like street behind the Goldenes Dachl, is **La Copa,** Badgasse 4 (☎ **0512/58 74 95**), popular with a mixed crowd. This cozy place with vaulted ceilings is great for that après-ski drink; the crowds start pouring in after 10pm. For the brave, there's a house specialty called the B-52, a drink with a secret recipe. Beside La Copa and under the same management is **La Cabaña,** which has the extra attraction of free, live Latin American music. La Copa is open Tuesday to Saturday 8pm to 2am; La Cabaña is open daily 7pm to 2am.

South of the Altstadt is a very popular microbrewery, **Theresien-Bräu,** Maria-Theresien-Strasse 51 (☎ **0512/58 75 80**), which attracts people of all ages. Quite large and quite hip for an Austrian brewery (which tend toward the traditional), it offers an Austrian menu and is open daily 10am to 1am. Halfway between the train station and the Altstadt, about a 5-minute walk from each, is **Jimmy's,** Wilhelm-Greil-Strasse 17 (☎ **0512/57 04 73**). This American-style restaurant/bar is decorated like a 1950s diner, with memorabilia of the era, lots of chrome, and a Wurlitzer jukebox. It specializes in American and Tex-Mex food (available evenings only), from tacos and enchiladas to burgers and salads. It's open Monday to Friday 11am to 1am and Saturday and Sunday 6pm to 1am.

Finally, in summer there's no finer place to be—judging by the crowds—than the **Hofgarten Cafe** (☎ **0512/58 88 71**), located in the Hofgarten on the northern edge of the Altstadt. It features both indoor and outdoor seating and live music. Many natives make it a tradition to stop off for a beer after work—and then perhaps another, and another. It's open in summer daily noon to an astonishing 4am; in winter, Tuesday to Thursday 6pm to 2am and Friday and Saturday 6pm to 4am.

DANCE CLUBS

Next to Jimmy's (above), **Blue Chip,** Wilhelm-Greil-Strasse 17 (☎ **0512/56 50 00**), is Innsbruck's most popular disco for the younger crowd. In a basement with a modern decor, it features soul, funk, and many other types of music—everything except pop hits. Admission is free, except during a rare concert. It's open in summer Thursday to Saturday 10pm to 4am and in winter Wednesday to Saturday 9pm to 4am.

Catering to all ages is **Club Filou,** in the Altstadt at Stift Gasse 12 (☎ **0512/58 02 56**). It has a small bar on the ground floor, but the real action is in the basement at its disco. The dance floor is small, but that doesn't stop the crowds from pouring into this place. The action here continues full swing until the wee hours of the morning. In summer there's an outdoor garden. The bar is open daily 6:30pm to 4am, while the disco is open daily 9pm to 4am.

8 Side Trips: The Alps & More

ALPINE PEAKS

The Alps surrounding Innsbruck are famous for skiing, but you can also take cable cars to nearby peaks year-round simply for the magnificent scenery. You can also enjoy a meal or a drink at one of the lift peak restaurants. **Hafelekar,** Innsbruck's "house mountain," 7,400 feet above sea level, is 3 miles north of the city center. Take bus C, D, E, or 4 from the train station or tram 1 from Maria-Theresien-Strasse (make sure it's going north) to the Talstation stop, where you board the **Hungerburg funicular,** built almost a century ago to connect Innsbruck with the surrounding mountain scenery. At Hungerburg Station, you then switch to the **Nordkette cable car,** which takes you to the Hafelekar peak, where the panoramic view of Tyrol's Alps is breathtaking. The round-trip price is 245S ($20) adults, 195S ($16) seniors/high school students, and 123S ($10) children. Ski passes allowing multiple trips cost more.

If you wish to combine a cable-car ride with some easy hiking, I'd recommend **Patscherkofel mountain,** 7,400 feet above sea level and 3 miles southeast of Innsbruck. Take tram no. 6 or bus J from the train station to Igls to board the **Patscherkofelbahn cable car** to the top. The round-trip price of the cable car is 185S ($15) adults, 150S ($12) seniors/high school students, and 90S ($7) children. From the peak, you can take the popular Zirbenweg path that winds along the crest of the mountain to Tulfeinalm, where you can then board the **Glungezer chairlift** for Tulfes and then take a local bus back to Igls. The walk takes about 2 hours and is recommended for all types of walkers, even children.

Contact the Innsbruck Information Office for more details.

WATTENS & SCHWAZ

If you have a day to spare, I suggest an excursion to nearby **Wattens** to visit the fantastic **Swarovski Kristallwelten** and then an onward trip to the **Schwaz Silver Mines.** If you plan to visit both, take a morning bus from the Busbahnhof near the Innsbruck train station. Buses depart for Wattens every 30 or 60 minutes; get off at the Wattens Ost stop, about a 15-minute ride. After touring Kristallwelten (plan on spending about 2 hours), reboard the bus at the Wattens Ost stop for the Silberbergwerk Schwaz stop. There aren't many buses that continue onward to Schwaz—only four or so a day, depending on the day of the week and season. Be sure of the schedule. The last bus from Schwaz back to Innsbruck is at 6pm. Round-trip cost of the bus from Innsbruck is 79S ($6) for Wattens or 107S ($9) for Schwaz. Alternatively, you can take a local train to Wattens and then a taxi; ditto for Schwaz. If you have a car, take the A12 Autobahn.

Even if you know what Swarovski is—the world's leading producer of full-cut crystal—you won't be prepared for its **Kristallwelten (Crystal Worlds),** Kristallweltenstrasse 1 (☎ 05224/51080-0). Instead of the usual dry self-promoting factory tour you might expect, Swarovski Kristallwelten is an experiment in fantasy, with theatrical, three-dimensional displays that give it a Disney-esque quality. The attraction itself is subterranean, hidden from view by a man-made hill. Entry is past a giant head spouting water. Designed by Viennese multimedia artist Andre Heller, the interior consists of magical cavernlike chambers, with displays relating to crystal. You'll see the world's largest cut crystal, weighing 137 pounds, a glass-enclosed wall containing 12 tons of crystal, works by artists ranging from Salvador Dalí to Keith Haring, and costumes, crystal art, and other displays relating to crystal. There's a crystal dome that gives a pretty good idea of what it would be like to be encapsulated inside a crystal, a meditation room, and a three-dimensional show. New-age music, produced by Brian Eno with the use of crystal, adds a dreamlike quality. At the conclusion of your self-guided tour is a cafe and a shop selling Sarovski crystal. Admission is 75S ($6) adults, 65S ($5) students/children (free for age 11 and younger). It's open daily 9am to 6pm.

The **Schwazer Silberbergwerk (Schwaz Silver Mines),** Alte Landstrasse 3 (☎ 05242/72372-0), in the village of Schwaz, were once the largest medieval silver mines in central Europe. In the early 1500s, Schwaz boasted 10,000 miners and was the second largest town in Austria after Vienna, its silver forming the financial basis of the Habsburg Empire. Today, part of the mines' 300-mile network of tunnels has been opened to 2-hour tours, which begin with an impressive 7-minute train ride through a narrow tunnel that took a whole generation of miners 26 years to dig. The tour continues on foot, with displays and explanations of the lives of the miners and problems they faced, from the transportation of ore and dead rock to water seepage and ventilation. Although tours are given only in German, an accompanying booklet with English translations is available.

Participants are given hard hats and waterproof jackets. Good walking shoes are recommended. Tours are given in summer daily 8:30am to 5pm; in winter daily 9:30am to 4pm. Cost of the tour is 150S ($12) adults, 130S ($10) seniors, 75S ($6) ages 5 to 15, and 30S ($2.40) age 4 and younger. For more information, call the mines at ☎ **05242/72372-0,** or inquire at the Innsbruck Information Office, where you can also purchase tickets in advance.

DINING   For a convenient lunch or snack, stop by the **Schenke zum Knappen,** Alte Landstrasse 3A (☎ **05242/782373-13**), next to the Schwaz Silver Mines. It offers steaks, grilled sausage, baked fish, Wiener schnitzel, and Cordon Bleu, with meals costing 65S to 195S ($5 to $16). It's open daily, summer 9am to 10pm and winter 10:30am to 10pm. No credit cards are accepted.

16 Lisbon & Environs

by Herbert Bailey Livesey

Much of Lisbon has the undeniably bedraggled aspect of a Third World seaport, an impression that's particularly sharp if you arrive from one of northern Europe's prosperous cities. But give Lisbon a chance. Withhold judgment until you walk with peacocks on the ramparts of its Moorish fortress, until you join the nightly throngs passing between the marinas and restaurants of the rescued waterfront and watch from many overlooks as the sunset turns the ancient city rose and pink.

Beyond all that, Lisbon has striven mightily to catch up. For years the city spruced itself up for its 1998 Expo, which commemorated the 500th anniversary of Vasco da Gama's epochal voyage to India. Construction was extensive, and it continues. This ambitious undertaking has added an important new subway line, as well as the 130-acre site of Expo itself (much of which is to be converted to permanent uses), and has inspired private interests to give their tattered buildings facelifts and convert long strips of former maritime warehouses into lively districts of clubs, bars, cafes, and marinas.

In overall appearance, the city resembles San Francisco, for Lisbon is at the edge of an ocean, was built on seven hills traversed by antique trams, and has a dramatic red-orange suspension bridge spanning its harbor. It has even been subject to devastating earthquakes. However, that only skims reality, for despite its location on the Atlantic, Lisbon (pop. 1.5 million) has a pronounced Mediterranean mien. Pastel houses with facades layered with abstract and pictographic tiles tumble down its steep slopes, and the mosaic sidewalks are fitted chunks of irregular stones, often arranged in elaborate black-and-white patterns.

It isn't an entirely Latin Mediterranean that Lisbon evokes. The Arabs were here for centuries, and the twisting streets of the Alfama hint of Moroccan souks. They and the Crusaders left a fortress that broods from the crest of the highest hill. In addition, the dissolution of the last of Portugal's African colonies in the 1970s and the resulting return of tens of thousands of overseas citizens ensured that this swiftly became one of Europe's most multiethnic, multiracial capitals.

After the devastating 1755 earthquake, which leveled much of the city and killed 40,000, Lisbon arose under the supervision of the marquês de Pombal, whose enlightened urban planning continues to serve the city well. The downtown Baixa is an orderly grid of shopping streets sloping gently up from the harbor to the broad tree-lined avenida da Liberdade. Sidewalk cafes invite lingering along the way,

Budget Bests

Inexpensive eating places abound, many self-described as *cervejarias* (beer halls) or *adegas* (taverns). Servings are nearly always large, so half portions are often available. In places where you can choose to sit or stand at the counter, standing is usually cheaper.

Most **museums** are free on Sunday morning, and some are free on Wednesday morning.

Because Lisbon's touristic nuclei is so compact, downtown or in outlying Belém you can see most things **on foot** or for the modest price of a **subway or tram** ticket.

---

and parks and gardens and plazas ward off monotony throughout the city. After a recent fire devastated parts of Baixa and adjoining Chiado, the ruins revealed that parts of the present city were built atop older structures. Most of the damage has been repaired and Pombal's vision retained.

The pace has picked up here since Portugal's entry into the European Union. Even though Portugal remains one of the EU's poorer countries, its annual economic growth rate is running at over 5%, and the unemployment rate is one of Europe's lowest. It's expected to be among the first wave of nations to participate in the monetary union scheduled to take place in 1999. In anticipation of this move into greater Europe, Lisbon's shops are becoming increasingly chic, restaurants more sophisticated, and nightlife hours longer.

REQUIRED DOCUMENTS   Citizens of the United States, Canada, Australia, and New Zealand, and British subjects, require only a valid passport.

OTHER FROMMER'S TITLES   For more on Lisbon, see *Frommer's Portugal, Frommer's Gay & Lesbian Europe,* or *Frommer's Europe.*

1 Lisbon Deals & Discounts

SPECIAL DISCOUNTS

FOR EVERYONE   Consider purchasing a **Lisboa Card,** which provides free admission to 25 museums and free, unrestricted access to all forms of public transport. Discounts of 10% to 50% are also given by a variety of other places and services, such as sightseeing companies, the Port Wine Institute, and the National Ballet. The cards are valid for periods of 24, 48, and 72 hours and cost 1,700$ ($10), 2,800$ ($16), and 3,600$ ($21), respectively. When buying the card, keep in mind the free museum admissions on Sunday and the Monday closings.

FOR STUDENTS   Lisbon's youth and student travel agency, **Tagus Turismo Juvenil,** rua Camilo Castelo Branco 20 (☎ **01/352-55-09**), offers special rates on flights, car rentals, and sightseeing tours in Portugal and abroad. It's open Monday to Friday 10am to 1pm and 2:30 to 5:30pm. Some museums offer free admission to students and seniors, so bring along the appropriate ID.

WORTH A SPLURGE

An evening at a **fado club** (with dinner and entertainment) may run 8,000$ ($47) per person, but you really should try to experience this Portuguese song form at least once. A dinner reservation guarantees you a seat, but drop in after midnight just for drinks and pay a minimum, typically 2,000$ to 3,000$ ($12 to $17). The music usually goes on until at least 3am.

What Things Cost in Lisbon	U.S. $
Taxi from the airport to Rossio Square	14.80
Metro fare	.95
Local telephone call	.15
Double room at the Hotel de Lapa (deluxe)	255.80
Double room at the Hotel Metropole (moderate)	99.40
Double room at the Globo (budget)	26.15
Lunch for one, without wine, at Trindade (moderate)	13.35
Lunch for one, without wine, at Andorra (budget)	7.90
Dinner for one, without wine, at Tavares (deluxe)	45.00
Dinner for one, without wine, at Casanostra (moderate)	22.95
Dinner for one, without wine, at Sol Nascente (budget)	11.05
Glass of beer	.70–.95
Coca-Cola in a restaurant	.92–1.15
Small cup of espresso (bica)	.45–.70
Roll of ASA 100 color film, 36 exposures	7.55
Admission to Mosteiro dos Jerónimos	2.30
Rock concert ticket	23.25–29.05
Movie ticket	2.40–3.60
Theater ticket	18.45–24.20

2 Essentials

ARRIVING

BY PLANE   From **Portela Airport** to the heart of town is only about 6 miles. Expect to pay about 2,000$ to 2,800$ ($12 to $16) for a **taxi,** depending on traffic and destination. The **AERO-BUS** costs 430$ ($2.50), though TAP passengers get one trip free. It runs from the airport to the Cais do Sodré rail station every 20 minutes 7am to 9pm. It makes 10 intermediate stops, including praça dos Restauradores and the Rossio.

BY TRAIN   From Madrid or Paris, arrivals are at **Estação Santa Apolónia,** Lisbon's major terminal, by the river near the Alfama. In addition to Santa Apolónia, which also serves the northern environs, there are three other stations: **Rossio** (with trains to Sintra), **Cais do Sodré** (with trains to the Estoril Coast), and **Sul e Sueste** (with trains to the Algarve).

VISITOR INFORMATION

The national **Portuguese Tourist Office,** at Palácio Foz, praça dos Restauradores (☎ **01/346-33-14** or 01/342-52-31), is the best info source. It has very few free brochures, but several attendants can answer most questions in English. It's open Monday to Saturday 9am to 8pm and Sunday 10am to 6pm. A branch office is near the airport's arrivals area, open 6am to 2am.

Not far away is the **Lisboa Turismo,** rua do Jardim do Reqedor 50 (☎ **01/343-36-72**), a municipal tourist office selling the Lisboa Card. It has English-speaking attendants eager to assist and is open daily 9am to 6pm.

For a listing of useful information, addresses, phone numbers, and events, pick up **What's On in Lisbon** or **Your Companion in Portugal** at the tourist office or any major hotel. The best sources for up-to-the-minute details on entertainment around town are the weekly magazine **Sete,** the free monthly guides **LISBOAem** and **Agenda Cultural,** and the newspaper **Diário de Noticias.**

CITY LAYOUT

The heart of the city extends some 2 miles from **praça do Comércio** to **praça do Marquês de Pombal** (named after the prime minister who rebuilt the city after the 1755 earthquake). Between praça do Comércio and **praça Dom Pedro IV** (known as the Rossio, pronounced "row-*see*-yo") is the **Baixa,** a grid of small shopping streets. Connecting the Rossio to praça do Marquês de Pombal is **avenida da Liberdade,** Lisbon's somewhat tattered rendition of the Champs-Elysées.

If you look at Lisbon from the waterfront, up to your right is the **Alfama,** crowned by the Castelo São Jorge (St. George's Castle). Rising to the left is the **Bairro Alto,** the old business district that still houses many antiques shops, fado clubs, and budget eating places, plus increasing numbers of chic restaurants and clubs.

NEIGHBORHOODS The **Baixa** ("Lower Town," pronounced "*bye*-shah") stretches from the river to the Rossio, once the site of the Inquisition's auto-da-fés. Such streets as rua do Ouro (Street of Gold) and rua da Prata (Street of Silver) have now diversified their consumer offerings. Rua Augusta and rua de Santa Justa are pedestrian streets lined with boutiques and shops selling leather goods, real and faux jewelry, handcrafts, and more.

The shopping continues along rua do Carmo, rua Garrett, and largo do Chiado, which link the Baixa with the **Bairro Alto** ("Upper Town"). Many years ago its steep, claustrophobic streets harbored often unsavory characters, but today the Bairro Alto has been pacified (to a large degree) by ongoing gentrification.

To the north of both the Baixa and the Bairro Alto extends the broad **avenida da Liberdade,** where banks, airline offices, and tour operators rub elbows with cheesy souvenir shops, first-run cinemas, and occasional sidewalk cafes, some of which have space on the central pedestrian promenade.

Rising steep and narrow to the walls of St. George's Castle is the **Alfama,** the ancient Arab quarter. Since it miraculously escaped the 1755 earthquake, its medieval aspect remains intact. Except for the castle, a handful of churches and museums, and a smattering of shops and restaurants, this is a colorful but largely residential working-class neighborhood.

Four miles from praça do Comércio is **Belém (Bethlehem),** a Lisbon district that has a separate urban identity. The focal point of Portugal's 16th-century maritime activities, Belém offers several museums and monuments as well as commemorations of the achievements of Portugal's colonial glories. Here too is the eastern end of Europe's longest single-span suspension bridge, the ponte 25 de Abril.

GETTING AROUND

A 4-day **tourist pass (passe turístico)** valid for all city buses, trams, subways, the Santa Justa Elevator, and the funiculars costs 1,640$ ($10); the 7-day version is 2,320$ ($14). They're sold at the Santa Justa Elevator (see below) daily 8am to 8pm.

Most of Lisbon's tourist areas are compact enough to be comfortably covered on foot—but remember that steep hills can make parts of a sightseeing or shopping trip fairly strenuous. Only the sights in the area of Parque Eduardo VII and the Belém district require public transportation or a car.

A Taxi Warning

Drivers are known to take advantage of visitors by using roundabout routes to destinations from the airport and exploiting confusion over currency by shortchanging. Beware especially of the men who intercept travelers on the way from trains to the taxi rank: Counting on your ignorance of the currency, they offer to drive you to your destination for up to *10 times* the actual cost by metered taxi.

BY SUBWAY   The Metro (subway) is shaped like a bent paper clip and has a new extension down to riverside. A *bilhete* (**ticket**) for a single ride costs 80$ (45¢), but a **1-day unlimited-use ticket** is only 200$ ($1.15). For still bigger savings, purchase the **7-day unlimited-use ticket** for 620$ ($3.60). The system operates daily 6:30am to 1am.

BY BUS & TRAM   Far more extensive are the bus *(autocarro)* and tram *(eléctrico)* networks. A ticket bought on board (from the driver on the old trams and buses, from a change-providing machine on the new trams serving Belém) is 160$ (95¢) and an advance-purchase ticket good for two trips is 155$ (90¢). Multiuse tickets good for 1 day are 430$ ($2.50) and for 3 days 1,000$ ($6). Booths are in most of the major squares (such as Rossio and Figueira) and at the base of the Santa Justa Elevator. Route maps are usually available there as well. Buses run daily 6am to midnight and trams 6:30am to midnight.

BY ELEVATOR & FUNICULAR   Near the Rossio, the **Santa Justa Elevator** links rua do Ouro in Baixa with praça do Carmo I in Bairro Alto. The fare is 160$ (95¢), and hours are Monday to Saturday 7am to 11pm and Sunday 9am to 11pm. The bridge from the top to the Largo do Carmo was closed during construction of new Metro lines but should have reopened by now.

Lisbon's three funiculars are the **Gloria,** from praça dos Restauradores to rua de São Pedro Alcântara; the **Lavra,** from the east side of avenida da Liberdade to campo Martires da Pátria; and the **Bica,** from calçada do Combro to rua da Boavista. Fares and operating hours are essentially the same as those for the Santa Justa Elevator.

BY TAXI   You can hail cabs—the newer ones in beige, the older versions in green and black—in the street or in ranks in major plazas. If the green roof light is on, the taxi is occupied. The initial cost is 250$ ($1.45) and each extra 170 meters (138 meters 10pm to 6am) costs 10$ (6¢). Surcharges are applied for summoning a taxi by phone (150$/85¢) and for luggage that has to be carried in the trunk or on the roof (300$/$1.75). Fares increase 10pm to 6am.

BY RENTAL CAR   Due to maddening traffic and the daredevil tactics of native drivers, I strongly recommend that you use a car only for excursions out of the city. Most international car-rental companies have offices at the airport. Two in-town local firms are **Rupauto,** rua da Beneficiência 99 (☎ 01/793-32-58), and **Viata,** rua Filipe da Mata 26A (☎ 01/793-31-48). Expect to pay a minimum of around 4,500$ ($26) per day, plus extras and tax. Shopping for the best rates is rewarded.

FAST FACTS: Lisbon

Addresses   Lisbon addresses consist of a street name, a building number, and the story, denoted by a numeral and the symbol °. "Rua Rosa Araújo 2–6°" means the sixth floor at no. 2 on that street. In Europe the ground floor isn't counted as the first floor, so 6° actually means seven stories up.

The Portuguese Escudo

For American Readers   The rate of exchange used to calculate the dollar values given in this chapter (rounded to the nearest dollar) is $1 U.S. = 172$ (or 1$ = 0.0058¢ U.S.).

For British Readers   The rate of exchange used to calculate the pound values in the table below is £1 = 290$ (or 1$ = 0.0035p).

Note: Because of substantial fluctuations in exchange rates, those indicated above represent approximate midpoints established over the last 3 years.

Esc	U.S.$	U.K.£	Esc	U.S.$	U.K.£
100	.58	.34	1,000	5.81	3.45
200	1.16	.69	1,250	7.27	4.31
300	1.74	1.03	1,500	8.72	5.17
400	2.33	1.38	2,000	11.63	6.90
500	2.91	1.72	2,500	14.53	8.62
600	3.49	2.07	5,000	29.07	17.24
700	4.07	2.41	7,500	43.60	25.86
800	4.65	2.76	10,000	58.14	34.48
900	5.23	3.10	12,500	83.33	50.00

American Express   The office is at av. Duque de Loulé 108 (☎ 01/315-58-77; Metro: Rotunda I), open Monday to Friday 9:30am to 1pm and 2:30 to 6:30pm.

Banks   Banks are open Monday to Friday 8:30am to 3pm; some offer a foreign exchange service Monday to Saturday 6 to 11pm. The bank at the airport is always open. You can change money on Saturday and Sunday 8:30am to 8:30pm at the bank at the Santa Apolónia train station.

ATMs are widely available, so you can obtain cash with major credit cards as well as Cirrus and Plus network cards. One ATM is near the arrivals gate at the airport, so you can easily obtain escudos to cover transportation into the city and tips at the hotel. There are also different machines that can exchange bills in French, German, British, and U.S. denominations for Portuguese *escudos.* One is at the Caixa Geral de Depositos, catercorner from the Estação Rossio (rail station).

Business Hours   Typically, **shops** are open Monday to Friday 9am to 1pm and 3 to 7pm (some now stay open through lunch) and Saturday 9am to 1pm. Some are also open Saturday afternoon. **Restaurants** are usually open noon to 3pm and 7 to 11pm or midnight. **Offices** are generally open Monday to Friday 9am to 1pm and 3 to 5:30pm or 6pm.

Currency   The Portuguese currency unit is the **escudo,** written 1$00. Hundredths of an escudo **(centavos)** follow the "$"; for example, 100 escudos is written "100$00." (However, in this chapter I've omitted the final "00.") Coins are minted in 50 centavos, and 1, 5, 10, 20, 50, 100, and 200 escudos. Notes are printed in 500, 1,000, 2,000, 5,000, and 10,000 escudos.

Doctors   English-speaking doctors can be found at the **British Hospital,** rua Saraiva de Carvalho 49 (☎ 01/395-50-67). Embassies and hotel concierges can also recommend doctors.

Embassies   As a capital, Lisbon is home to the embassies of many countries, including the **United States,** avenida das Forças Armadas (☎ **01/726-66-00**); the **United Kingdom,** rua São Domingos à Lapa 37 (☎ **01/396-11-91**); **Canada,** av. da Liberdade 144–56, 3° (☎ **01/347-48-92;** Metro: Avenida); and **Australia,** av. da Liberdade 244–4° (☎ **01/353-25-55;** Metro: Avenida). They're open Monday to Friday, usually 9 or 9:30am to 12:30 or 1pm and 2 or 2:30 to 5 or 5:30pm, but call ahead before making the trip.

Emergencies   Call ☎ **115** for an ambulance, the fire department, or the police. Look in any newspaper or dial 16 for 24-hour pharmacies. Closed pharmacies post notices indicating the nearest open one.

Holidays   Holidays are New Year's Day (January 1), Freedom Day (April 25), Worker's Day (May 1), Camões and Portugal Day (June 10), St. Anthony's Day (June 13), Assumption Day (August 15), Day of the Republic (October 5), All Saints' Day (November 1), Feast of the Immaculate Conception (December 8), and Christmas (December 25). Other public holidays with shifting dates are Good Friday, Shrove Tuesday, and Corpus Christi. When holidays land on Tuesday or Thursday, the intervening Monday or Friday is often declared a day off, making for many 4-day weekends throughout the year. Halloween recently has become an important holiday, with many workers receiving the next day off.

Hospitals   See "Doctors," above.

Laundry   Two self-service launderettes are **Lava Neve,** rua de Alegria 37 (Metro: Avenida), and **Lavatax,** rua Francisco Sanches 65A (☎ **01/812-33-92**). *Tinturaria* is the Portuguese word for dry cleaning. Hotel laundry and dry-cleaning services are much more expensive.

Mail   The convenient **post office** *(correios)* at praça dos Restauradores 58 (Metro: Restauradores), is open Monday to Friday 8am to 10pm and Saturday and Sunday 9am to 6pm. The airport post office is open 24 hours.

Police   Call ☎ **115** for the police.

Tax   The **value-added tax (IVA in Portugal)** varies from 8% to 17%. For refund information, see "Shopping," later in this chapter.

Telephone   There's a **central phone office** on praça dos Restauradores, near the Rossio and diagonally across from the National Theater, open daily 8am to 11pm. **Local calls** cost 15¢.

To make **international calls,** dial "00" and then the country code ("1" for the U.S.), the area code, and the number. Some phones are equipped for credit-card calls (Visa and MasterCard, but not phone company cards). If you're calling direct from a hotel, however, there may be steep surcharges.

To make a **collect call,** or at more economical U.S. calling-card rates, use **AT&T's USA Direct** by dialing ☎ **05017-1-288** or **MCI's Call USA** by dialing ☎ **05017-1-234.** Collect calls, or those at U.S. calling-card rates, can be made through an **international operator** by dialing ☎ **098.**

Country & City Codes

The **country code** for Portugal is 351. The **city code** for Lisbon is 1; use this code when you're calling from outside Portugal. If you're within Portugal but not in Lisbon, use **01.** If you're calling within Lisbon, simply leave off the code and dial only the regular phone number.

For **long-distance calls** within the country, dial "0" (zero) before the city code and then the number. The dial tone for long-distance calls may be unusual, but make sure there's a tone before beginning to dial and that the tone then stops. Dial steadily, without long pauses; the connection can take up to a minute, during which some unfamiliar tones may be heard. A persistent tone means that the call has failed. To confuse things further, the country is in the later stages of changing from six-digit numbers to seven-digit numbers.

In post offices and at scattered CrediFone locations, special phones take **pre-paid cards** in 50- and 120-unit denominations (750$/$4.40 and 1,750$/$10) sold at post offices; 120 units buys about 3 minutes to the United States at standard rates and over 3½ minutes during discount periods. International calls can also be made at the Central Post Office, praça dos Restauradores, daily 8am to 10pm.

Tipping   Though restaurant prices usually include a service charge, it's appropriate to tip an extra 5% to 10%. Taxi drivers get about 10% for long rides and 15% to 20% on short rides. Give 150$ to 200$ (85¢ to $1.15) to porters and bellhops for each bag, depending on their weight and the distance carried. It's customary to leave a similar amount for the chambermaid for each night of a hotel stay.

3 Accommodations You Can Afford

Budget accommodations abound throughout the city, but the most convenient areas to stay are off avenida da Liberdade, near Rossio Square, in Baixa, and in the Bairro Alto. The customary admonition that lodgings shouldn't be judged solely by the often grimy or otherwise unpromising state of their exteriors, lobbies, and staircases goes double in Lisbon. Go in and ask to see some rooms before deciding. A laudatory by-product of Expo '98 was the incentive it gave managers of hotels and *pensãos* to undertake needed renovations. Breakfast is no longer routinely included in room rates, so when it is, that can be considered a bonus saving.

High season is from Easter until the end of October, when most of the cheaper places jack up their prices by as much as 30%. During that period, some can be almost as expensive as the larger hotels. Most room rates include VAT, but ask to be sure.

Note: Most of the lodging choices below are plotted on the map included in "Seeing the Sights," later in this chapter.

OFF AVENIDA DA LIBERDADE

Alegria. Praça da Alegria 12, 1200 Lisboa. ☎ **01/347-55-22.** Fax 01/347-80-70. 28 units, 20 with bathroom. TEL. 2,500$ ($15) single/double without bathroom, 3,500$–4,500$ ($20–$26) single/double with bathroom. No credit cards. Metro: Avenida.

This few-frills pension on the parklike praça da Alegria ("Happy Square") is ideal for budgeters and backpackers. The adjacent police station makes the area less intimidating at night. The small reception area is off the ground-floor lobby, and while the staircase is in the usual appalling condition, the good-size rooms on three floors have a variety of interesting furnishings, and many overlook the square. Some rooms have TVs; all have shower or tub, but not all have toilets. The prices are by no means firm, especially off-season, so bargaining is in order.

Astória. Braamcamp 10, 1200 Lisboa. ☎ **01/386-13-17.** Fax 01/386-04-91. 82 units, all with bathroom. A/C TEL. 7,500$–12,500$ ($44–$15) single; 9,500$–15,000$ ($55–$87) double. Rates include breakfast. AE, DC, MC, V. Metro: Rotunda.

Getting the Best Deal on Accommodations

- Note that *pensãos* and *residências* often offer discounts of at least 10% to guests staying more than a week.
- Try your hand at bargaining—hoteliers won't be offended—especially off-season and weekends.
- Rooms with shower stalls are nearly always cheaper, often substantially so, than those with full tubs with showerheads. Ask about this when booking.

Just off the Rotunda, with its monument to Pombal, the Astória has squeaky clean small rooms furnished in light wood. The sculptured ceilings interject a note of old-world charm in this otherwise contemporary place. More than half the rooms have TVs. The owner speaks English, as do some of his assistants. Guests have the use of a lounge with a bar.

Casal Ribeiro. Braamcamp 10-R/C. Dto. (west of the Rotunda), 1200 Lisboa. ☎ **01/386-15-44.** Fax 01/386-00-67. 30 units, all with bathroom. TV TEL. 7,000$ ($41) single; 8,000$ ($47) double; 9,000$ ($52) triple. Rates include breakfast. DC, MC, V. Metro: Rotunda.

This pension's cream exterior with green trim is promising, and most of the pleasant, if compact, rooms off well-lighted halls don't disappoint. They're equipped beyond expectations in this category, each with a TV, radio, and bath. Guests can meet in the agreeable lounge by the reception desk. English is spoken.

✪ **Nacional.** Castilho 34, 1200 Lisboa. ☎ **01/355-44-33.** Fax 01/356-11-22. 59 units, all with bathroom. A/C TV TEL. 11,000$ ($64) single; 12,900$ ($75) double; 14,800$ ($86) triple. Rates include breakfast and parking. AE, DC, MC, V. Metro: Rotunda.

The clamorous character of the Baixa and Barrio Alto aren't for everyone. For them, this modern three-star mid-rise in a quieter and definitely cleaner neighborhood of office and apartment buildings might be the ticket. The uniformed staff is attentive to guests' needs, and many of them speak English. The crisply furnished rooms have safes, hair dryers, and American-style showers. Minibars are available on request.

IN BAIXA

Duas Nações. Victoria 41, 1100 Lisboa. ☎ **01/346-07-10.** Fax 01/347-02-06. 66 units, 33 with bathroom. TEL. 3,500$ ($20) single without bathroom, 4,500$–6,000$ ($26–$35) single with bathroom; 4,500$ ($26) double without bathroom, 5,500$–7,500$ ($32–$44) double with bathroom; 9,000$ ($52) triple with bathroom. Rates include breakfast. AE, DC, MC, V. Metro: Rossio.

A few strides east of the pedestrian rua Augusta, this economical place is a happy surprise. The high-ceilinged commodious doubles contain personal safes, and those with baths have tubs long enough to float an NBA point guard. Breakfast is served in a large dining room with blue-and-white scenic tile murals. Renovation work is ongoing, so see your room before accepting. English is spoken.

Insulana. Assunção 52, 1100 Lisboa. ☎ **01/342-31-31.** Fax 01/342-89-24. 32 units, all with bathroom. A/C TV TEL. 7,000$ ($41) single; 8,000$ ($47) double. Rates include breakfast. AE, DC, MC, V. Metro: Rossio.

Still a little musty and in need of a spruce-up, this three-floor hotel (with elevator) compensates with a location in the heart of Baixa and such extras as TV and radio not usually found at this price. The larger rooms have carved bedsteads, desks, and leather chairs. Take breakfast in either the bar or your room.

NEAR THE ROSSIO

✪ **Florescente.** Portas de São Antão 99 (next to the Grand Teatro Politeama), 1100 Lisboa. ☎ **01/342-66-09.** Fax 01/342-77-33. 64 units, 15 with sink and toilet only, 49 with bathroom. TEL. 3,500$ ($27) single with sink and toilet only, 4,000$ ($23) double with sink and toilet only, 5,000$–7,000$ ($29–$40) single/double with bathroom; 8,000$ ($47) triple with bathroom. MC, V. Metro: Restauradores.

One block off praça dos Restauradores, this place offers small, clean rooms off narrow tile-lined corridors on four floors (no elevator). The street-level reception is attractive, and the new staff members, some multilingual, are more welcoming than those they replaced. They buzz in visitors after deciding they pose no danger, though the neighborhood isn't threatening. Some rooms are significantly larger than others, and half come with TV and/or air-conditioning. Breakfast isn't served, but many coffee shops and budget restaurants are nearby.

✪ **Gerês.** Calçada do Garcia 6, 1100 Lisboa. ☎ **01/881-04-97.** Fax 01/888-20-06. 20 units, 14 with bathroom. TEL. 4,000$ ($23) single without bathroom, 5,000$–5,500$ ($29–$32) single with bathroom; 6,000$–7,000$ ($35–$41) double without bathroom, 7,500$–8,500$ ($44–$49) double with bathroom. Rates include breakfast. AE, MC, V. Metro: Rossio.

Quite possibly the best value in town, this homey place combines hyperclean rooms with a fairly quiet but handy location only a little over a block from the Rossio. Its repainted rooms occupy two floors; those with bath have satellite TV. The English-speaking owner/manager has installed video surveillance of the lobby. Her rates as noted above are somewhat higher in summer but may be subject to negotiation during all but peak periods.

Internacional. Betesga 3, 1100 Lisboa. ☎ **01/346-64-01.** Fax 01/347-86-35. 53 units, all with bathroom. A/C TV TEL. 8,000$ ($47) single; 9,500$ ($55) double. Rates include breakfast. AE, DC, MC, V. Metro: Rossio.

In this popular hotel near the southeast corner of the Rossio, the room dimensions (including ceiling height) vary substantially. Most rooms have an easy chair or two and a desk, and safes are a welcome bonus. Guests can get together in the TV salon next to the bar. The creaky floors testify to the building's age. The rates above are likely to be about 15% higher in summer.

Nova Goa. Arco Marquês do Alegrete 13, 1100 Lisboa. ☎ **01/888-11-37.** Fax 01/886-78-11. 43 units, all with bathroom. TV TEL. 9,000$ ($52) single; 12,000$–13,000$ ($70–$76) double; 14,000$–16,000$ ($81–$93) triple. Rates include breakfast and IVA. MC, V. Metro: Rossio.

A few steps away from the Portugal (below), this centrally located *pensão* occupies five floors of a corner building. An elevator carries guests from the ground-level reception desk, manned by a manager who has some English. The rooms have linoleum floors, desks, and various combinations of double and twin beds; some have views of Castelo São Jorge. Tram 12 passes the front door.

✪ **Portugal.** João das Regras 4, 1100 Lisboa. ☎ **01/887-75-81.** Fax 01/886-73-43. 59 units, all with bathroom. A/C TV TEL. 7,500$ ($44) single; 10,000$ ($58) double. Rates include breakfast. AE, DC, MC, V. Metro: Rossio.

This is a largely unnoticed frugal find, a rejuvenated but appealingly old-fashioned hotel with large rooms, high ceilings, marble baths, and blissful quiet despite a location barely 1 block off praça da Figuera. And it doesn't have the oppressively smoky air found in too many Lisbon hotels. You can meet friends in the quirky bar/lounge next to the spacious lobby.

IN THE BAIRRO ALTO

Casa de S. Mamede. Escola Politécnica 159, 1200 Lisboa. ☎ **01/396-31-66.** Fax 01/395-18-96. 28 units, all with bathroom. TV TEL. 8,500$–10,000$ ($49–$58) single; 13,000$–14,000 ($76–$81) double. Rates include breakfast. No credit cards. Metro: Rato.

A freestanding former private residence west of the Jardim Botânico, this *pensão* (without elevator) has three floors of rooms. They vary substantially in size, but some are quite large, with pine furniture, carpeting, sofas, and glass chandeliers. The obvious value is enhanced by the amiable staff, tile-lined breakfast salon, and recent installation of TVs in the rooms. Higher rates noted above apply in summer.

Globo. Teixeira 37, 1200 Lisboa. ☎ **01/346-22-79.** 13 units, 5 with sink only, 8 with bathroom. 2,000$–2,500$ ($12–$15) single with sink only, 3,000$ ($17) single with bathroom; 3,500$ ($20) double with sink only, 4,500$ ($26) double with bathroom. No credit cards. Tram: 24. Bus: 100.

The Globo is bracketed by two good restaurants on a quiet Bairro Alto street 1 block west of rua de São Pedro Alcântara. Showers and toilets have been added to rooms that didn't have them a couple of years ago. That cuts into the already skimpy floor space, but the rooms are still pleasant, often with armoires squeezed in. Most have double beds, a few with an added single. The cheapest singles don't have windows. This good budget choice has gotten better. Some English is spoken by the young manager.

NEAR PARQUE EDUARDO VIII

América. Tomáz Ribeiro 47, 1050 Lisboa. ☎ **01/352-11-77.** Fax 01/353-14-76. 22 units, all with bathroom. A/C TV TEL. 6,000$ ($35) single; 7,000$ ($41) double; 8,000$ ($47) triple. Rates include breakfast. AE, DC, MC, V. Metro: Picoas.

Don't make this a first choice, but the neighborhood is good enough for the Sheraton, across the street, and an adequate room here goes for a fifth of one in the big guy. The mattresses are due for replacement, though. Security is enhanced by the streetside lobby, which discourages surreptitious entry. On the seventh floor are the recently renovated bar and breakfast room, with views. Metro and bus stops are only steps away.

Lisbonense. Pinheiro Chagas 1, 1000 Lisboa. ☎ **01/54-46-28.** 30 units, all with bathroom. A/C TEL. 4,500$ ($26) single; 7,000$ ($41) double. Rates include breakfast. No credit cards. Metro: Saldanha.

Ensconced in a once-stylish building up the hill from the Lisboa Sheraton, the well-maintained Lisbonense (with elevator) occupies four floors. The reception is on the third floor, and there's usually someone on hand who speaks English. The smallish rooms, freshly painted, are clean and neat, with warm wood furnishings. All baths are being updated, and air-conditioning has been added. Seven rooms have TVs, but everyone has access to the petite TV lounge, which doubles as the breakfast room.

✪ **Miraparque.** Av. Sidónio Pais 12, 1050 Lisboa. ☎ **01/352-42-86.** Fax 01/357-89-20. 100 units, all with bathroom. A/C MINIBAR TV TEL. 9,200$ ($54) single; 10,200$ ($59) double; 13,100$ ($76) triple. Rates include breakfast. AE, DC, MC, V. Metro: Parque.

This low-key contemporary hotel justifies every escudo. Identified by its terra-cotta–hued exterior, it does "look at the park," the one named for Eduardo VII. They repaint the interior every year or so, and housekeeping standards are high. The rooms are spacious and uncluttered, with safes, desks, and an easy chair or two. The buffet breakfast is laid out in the full-service restaurant, which otherwise offers a traditional menu. The metro stop is around the corner and the ornate sports pavilion is across the street. English is spoken.

ON THE OUTSKIRTS

Pousada da Juventude de Catalazete. Estrada Marginal, 2780 Oeiras. ☎ and fax **01/443-06-38.** 102 beds. June–Sept, 1,700$ ($10) per person; lower the rest of the year. Rates include breakfast. No credit cards.

This hostel looks over the beach in Oeiras, less than half an hour by train from Lisbon's Cais do Sodré station and 15 minutes from Estoril. You must be a member of the International Youth Hostel Federation. The hostel is open daily 8am to midnight, with lights out from then until 7am. Smoking, eating, and drinking alcoholic beverages are prohibited. There are some rooms with bath for families; all other rooms have four or six beds. You must use your own sleeping bag or sheets when utilizing the hostel's blankets. All three meals are served.

WORTH A SPLURGE

Reservations at the following two hotels can be made through **Marketing Ahead,** 433 Fifth Ave., New York, NY 10016 (☎ **212/686-9213**).

Metrople. Rossio 30, 1100 Lisboa. ☎ **01/346-91-64.** Fax 01/346-91-66. 36 units, all with bathroom. A/C TV TEL. 15,300$ ($89) single; 17,100$ ($99) double. Rates include breakfast. AE, DC, MC, V. Metro: Rossio.

Even in high season, this three-star hotel just scratches the high end of the budget chart, and it slips into downright affordability in winter. The turn-of-the-century building, on the west side of the Rossio, is as central as can be, and the entire building has been renovated in recent years without altering the deco tone of the public rooms. The second-floor lounge is especially pleasant, with a TV salon at one end, a bar at the other, and tables set up for breakfast. Rooms in back are the quietest. A simple breakfast buffet is included.

✪ **Senhora do Monte.** Calçada do Monte 39, 1100 Lisboa. ☎ **01/886-60-02.** Fax 01/887-77-83. 328 units, all with bathroom. A/C TV TEL. 14,000$–17,000$ ($61–$99) single; 17,500$–19,000$ ($102–$110) double, 25,000$–27,000$ ($145–$157) double with terrace; 25,000$ ($145) triple. Rates include breakfast. AE, DC, MC, V. Tram: 28. Bus: 12, 17, 26, or 35.

Only five rooms lack a view in this panoramically perched hotel overlooking all Lisbon. The top-floor cafe/bar, in particular, offers stunning sunset views over the Tejo, the castle-crowned Alfama, Baixa, and Bairro Alto. Every room has a tiled bath, 11 have balconies, and 4 have terraces; most have air-conditioning. Since the hotel is on a small street in the Graça area, it's wise to take a cab here the first time; after that, it's a 3-block walk downhill to the tram that goes into the heart of town.

4 Great Deals on Dining

By far the best areas for seeking out budget restaurants are the blocks west of rua da Misericórdia and rua de São Pedro Alcântara in the Bairro Alto, as well as rua das Portas de Santo Antão, east of praça dos Restauradores. Rua dos Correiros, in Baixa, has over a dozen charging less than 1,700$ ($10) for a fixed-price three-course meal, with wine.

Lisbon's meals are still relatively cheap and built around a number of hearty dishes. One is *caldo verde,* a soup with mashed potatoes, shredded kale, and peppery sausage cooked in beef broth. Then there's the ubiquitous *bacalhau* (cod), available in over 300 recipes. *Frango* (chicken), often spit-roasted and fragrant with generous showers of garlic, is highly popular. *Carne de porco a alentejana* is pork stewed with clams in a sauce spiced with herbs. *Barrigas de freira* ("nuns' tummies") is a popular egg dish, and *cozido a portuguesa* is a flavorful Portuguese version of the New England boiled dinner.

Dining Notes

The practice of charging a *couvert* (cover) is common. It's a charge for bread, butter, and the little tins of pâté typically set on each table, and most places add it to the bill whether or not you consume those items. Some restaurants, however, will skip the charge if the extras remain untouched. In many *cafetarias,* customers are expected to prepay for snacks or beverages to be taken at the bar. Look for the sign PRÉ-PAGAMENTO near the cashier. Tell her what you want, pay, and take the receipt to the bar.

Another common savory dish is grilled sardines—large ones, not like those found in cans—with a fresh salad. *Açorda* is one of those dishes every native had as a child and loves as an adult. Newcomers may find it less adorable. Essentially, it's a porridge of bread, eggs, and parsley or cilantro, tossed with shrimp or fish, and whipped enthusiastically into a fragrant mush. Additional possibilities are *lulas recheadas* (stuffed squid), *leitão* (roast suckling pig), and *ensopada de enguias* (eels stewed with bread).

Main courses are often served with two starches, typically fried potatoes and rice. Portuguese cooks, be forewarned, aren't fastidious about the removal of bones, shells, or skin. And unlike their Spanish cousins, they have a taste for spicy seasonings, a result of influences from their former colonies in Africa, Asia, and South America. *Piri-piri* is a favorite hot sauce that often shows up, unannounced, in chicken and pork dishes or in a bowl on the table.

For dessert, try *pudim Molotov,* a cross between a sponge cake and a pudding served with caramel sauce. Any of a dozen types of cheese are also eaten for dessert. A special one is *serra da estrêla,* a creamy smoked sheep cheese. Breakfast usually consists of coffee and a croissant.

As for wine, it's hard to go wrong ordering the unlabeled house version—*vinho da casa. Vinho verde* is a distinctive young country white with a slight spritz. Coffee comes in varying forms, the most popular being *bica* (black espresso), *carioca* (espresso with a dash of milk), *garoto* (espresso with more milk), and *galão* (a large glass of coffee with milk).

IN CHIADO

A Brasileira. Garrett 120–122. ☎ **01/346-95-41.** Meals 250$–390$ ($1.45–$2.25). No credit cards. Daily 8am–2am. Tram: 28. SANDWICHES/SNACKS.

The city's oldest coffee shop, a block from praça de Camões in the Chiado district, serves a strong aromatic Brazilian espresso for 155$ (90¢). The outside tables are enjoyable for coffee or quick lunches. Inside is a fin-de-siècle coffeehouse where conversations swirl, cards and chess are played, and service is offhand at best. Modern paintings occupy the spaces above the large mirrors. There's a dining room downstairs.

Bernardí. Garrett 104–106. ☎ **01/347-31-33.** Main courses 1,500$–2,500$ ($9–$15). AE, MC, V. Mon–Sat 8am–2am. Metro: Rossio. Tram: 28. PORTUGUESE.

This antiquarian cafe near A Brasileira (above) is great for a breakfast of coffee and pastries or fresh croissants. A standard version costs 210$ ($1.20) at the bar or 600$ ($3.50) at a table. Lunch or dinner possibilities include grilled salmon for 2,200$ ($13) and rice with duck for 1,500$ ($9). Keep it in mind for afternoon or late-night hot chocolate or snacks. To imbibe at the bar, prepay at the cashier on the right and obtain a voucher.

Getting the Best Deal on Dining

- Ask about the *ementa turística* (tourist menu), which usually includes an appetizer or soup, a main course, a dessert, bread, and a beverage for a price often lower than an à la carte main course alone. Some restaurants that offer it tend to conceal that fact, so make a request to see it.
- In places where the *ementa turística* is unappealing or unavailable, consider ordering only a main course. The portions are usually large, so skipping appetizers, desserts, or both is a cost-paring possibility.
- Try *cervejarias,* restaurants where the featured beverage is draft beer. They're large, informal places featuring hearty portions at sensible prices.
- Note that a quick, light meal at a snack bar or *pastelaria* will help you keep to your budget.
- Take advantage of *adegas* and *tascas*—economical, often family-style restaurants with good food at budget prices.
- Be aware that eating and drinking at the bar usually costs less than doing so at a table.
- Enjoy a picnic, for scenic relaxing spots are plentiful in Lisbon.

✪ **Trindade.** Nova da Trindade 20. ☎ **01/360-21-20.** Main courses 1,200$–2,700$ ($7–$16); *ementa turística* 2,300$ ($13). AE, DC, MC, V. Daily 9am–2am. Tram: 24. PORTUGUESE.

In business since 1836, this cavernous *cervejaria* occupies the site of the former 13th-century Convento dos Frades Tinos, which was leveled by the 1755 earthquake. Several rooms with arched ceilings and fine blue-and-white tile murals remind of those origins. The kitchen does a better job with seafood than with meat, and beware of the pricier items, which include spiny lobsters and huge tiger shrimp. Snacks are available at the stand-up bar in the second room. When it's full, head to the larger rooms in back, where the high ceilings help to dissipate the clouds of tobacco smoke.

IN THE BAIRRO ALTO

Adega do Teixeira. Teixeira 39 (1 block west of rua de São Pedro Alcântara). ☎ **01/342-83-20.** Main courses 1,500$–1,950$ ($9–$11); *ementa turística* 2,500$ ($15). AE, MC, V. Mon–Fri noon–3pm and 7:30pm–midnight, Sat 7:30pm–midnight. Tram: 24. PORTUGUESE.

Worth seeking out behind the Instituto do Vinho do Porto (see "Lisbon After Dark," later in this chapter), this little-known restaurant has outdoor tables under an awning. The owner, ever anxious to please, comes forward quickly when potential patrons appear. Given the slightest encouragement, he steers them into the kitchen to peer into the bubbling pots. An array of breads, cheese, olives, sausage slices, and fish nuggets arrives even before you've ordered. Because it's on a quiet side street, it's less likely than most Bairro Alto spots to be packed on weekends. The fish is extremely fresh.

Bota Alta. Travessa da Queimada 37 (at the corner of rua da Atalaia). ☎ **01/392-79-59.** Main courses 1,400$–2,300$ ($8–$13); *ementa turística* 2,550$ ($15). AE, DC, MC, V. Mon–Fri noon–2:30pm and 7–10:30pm, Sat 7–10:30pm. Tram: 24. PORTUGUESE.

At night, songs bounce off the walls of the labyrinthine streets of the Bairro Alto, for this section is at the heart of Lisbon's fado district. "High Boot" is one of the most popular bistros, attested by the framed photos and testimonials from celebrities like actor John Hurt. Its two rooms are crowded with as many tables as will fit, with old tile dadoes and mismatched drawings and paintings as the decor. Nutty-tasting brown rice comes with many main courses. Fish is the best bet.

✪ Casanostra. Rosa 84–90 (3 short blocks east of rua de São Pedro Alcântara). ☎ **01/342-59-31.** Reservations suggested. Main courses 1,600$–2,600$ ($9–$15); *ementa turística* 3,950$ ($23). MC, V. Tues–Sun noon–midnight, Sat 7pm–midnight. Tram: 24. ITALIAN.

That's Casanostra as in "Our House," not the Mafiosa "Our Thing," as the logo makes clear. They've made a little more room between the once-jammed tables, making it more comfortable for the knowing locals and sophisticated foreigners who crowd in to choose from the bounty of pastas with fresh sauces that precede such dishes as whole boned trout stuffed with cured ham, cheese, and mushrooms. The decor is contemporary trattoria—with industrial lighting, creamy walls, and lime-green chairs. The place is popular with the young club set, so reserve or go early.

Mama Rosa. Grémio Lusitano 14 (a short walk west of rua de São Pedro Alcântara). ☎ **01/346-53-50.** Pizzas, pastas, and main courses 1,200$–2,600$ ($7–$15); *ementa turística* 2,400$ ($14). MC, V. Mon–Fri 12:30–4pm and 7:30pm–1am, Sat 7:30pm–1am, Sun 7:30pm–midnight. Tram: 24. PIZZA/ITALIAN.

This snug, loud, and sometimes smoke-filled trattoria features the conventional red-checked tablecloths of the breed and some of the best pizza in town. To serve the largely under-30 customers it attracts, the kitchen fills orders past midnight. Good desserts too.

✪ Patô Baton. Travessa Fiéis de Deus 28 (at the corner of rua das Gáveas). ☎ **01/362-63-72.** Main courses 1,750$–2,400$ ($10–$14); *ementa turística* 3,300$ ($19). AE, DC, MC, V. Tues–Sun 8pm–1am. Closed Sun in summer. Tram: 24. ECLECTIC.

The name ("Duck Stick") means nothing. The owner just liked the sound of it, illustrative of the frisky character of his upscale bistro and its Frenchified menu. A Miró replica near the door is an introduction to a collection of abstract paintings hanging on the stippled pink walls. The filling dishes include such daily specials as *bife a portuguesa*—beef tenderloin beneath a fried egg ringed with sliced roast potatoes, carrots, tomatoes, and pickles. In summer they put tables on the steps outside, the only ones in the Bairro Alto. Most patrons don't start showing up until 11pm.

Pedro-das-Arábis. Rua da Atalaia 70. ☎ **01/346-84-94.** Main courses 900$–1,300$ ($5–$8); *ementa turística* 2,900$ ($17). MC, V. Daily 7:30pm–1am. Tram: 24. MOROCCAN.

"Pete of Arabia?" Not much of a ring to that, but the young owner knows what makes an adventure on the plate. He took over a defunct Spanish restaurant, painted it, and hung a few Moroccan ornaments. His chef concentrates on couscous, several kinds prepared to order. An appetizer isn't really necessary while you wait, because Pedro brings bowls of spicy olives, a ratatouille, cold cumin-flavored meatballs, and a plate of square flat bread. He speaks fluent English, by the way.

✪ Tasca do Manel. Barroca 24. ☎ **01/346-38-13.** Main courses 980$–1,800$ ($6–$10); *ementa turística* 2,500$ ($15). MC, V. Mon–Fri noon–4pm, Sat–Sun 7pm–midnight. Tram: 24. Walk along Queimada, 4 blocks west of rua de São Pedro Alcântara, then turn left. PORTUGUESE.

Almost every item on the menu merits consideration at this eat-in tavern frequented by Bairro Alto professionals, and the close quarters don't deter the nighttime throngs on weekends. The fish is only hours from the depths and the grilled meats are prime choices. *Arroz de marisco* (rice with shellfish) is a specialty. The traditional boiled dinner known as *cozido* is available, with a half portion for under $7. In fall and winter look for game, especially partridge and hare.

ON OR NEAR THE ROSSIO

Andorra. Portas de Santo Antão 82 (1 block east of praça dos Restauradores). ☎ **01/342-60-47.** Main courses 1,200$–1,800$ ($7–$10); *ementa turística* 1,360$ and 2,100$ ($8 and $12). MC, V. Mon–Sat 12:30–3pm and 6–11pm. Metro: Restauradores. PORTUGUESE.

Temptations are great along this pedestrian street, the city's best-known restaurant row. This place has a leg up on most of its competitors, with a tiled tavern look inside and a rank of tables thrusting into the street. Two tantalizing choices among many are *arroz de cherne* (rice with mixed fish) and *frango à piri-piri*, which comes with two pieces of spicy chicken, three vegetables, fries, and rice. This is a place to sample any of a long roster of Portuguese seafood dishes, but beware that the giant shrimp and lobster go for up to 9,000S ($52).

Bonjardim. Travessa de Santo Antão 8–10. ☎ **01/342-74-24.** Main courses 990$–1,800$ ($6–$10); *ementa turística* 2,250$ ($13). DC, MC, V. Daily noon–11:30pm. Metro: Restauradores. PORTUGUESE.

This self-styled "Rei da Brasa" (loosely, "King of the Grill") specializes in spit-roasted chicken. Dining downstairs is preferable to the room upstairs, which is less attractive and can get loud and smoky. Students, merchants, couples, and families all come for the unfussy, unadorned food. For 1,200$ ($7), get a *whole* chicken, cooked to tender perfection, and for another 250$ ($1.45) a 10-inch platter of fries. Ask for a bowl of *piri-piri*, and brush the fiery sauce over the meat (carefully—it isn't for wimps). Fish and other meats are available, but chicken's the reason you come here. It's even sold at a streetside takeout window.

Across the way is another **Bonjardim** (Rei dos Frangos), Travessa de Santo Antão 10 (☎ **01/342-43-89**), with similar fare, prices, and hours, but a little less space. Both have outdoor tables in good weather.

Pastelaria Suiça. Praça Dom Pedro IV 105. ☎ **01/342-80-92.** Main courses 600$–1,100$ ($4–$7). No credit cards. Daily 7am–10pm. Metro: Rossio. PORTUGUESE.

The pronounced Portuguese sweet tooth is serviced by scores of *pastelarias,* many of which go well beyond tarts and cakes to soups, sandwiches, and even full meals. This always-busy cafe is one of the largest and best known in Lisbon. It goes through an entire block, with tables on the east side of the Rossio and their mirror image on the west side of praça da Figueira. It covers most bases with pastry and ice-cream counters, tearooms, and bars. Omelets and salads are available, as are breakfasts of juice, croissant, bacon, eggs, and coffee for 900$ ($5). Lunch patrons may be asked to move inside from the desirable sidewalk tables unless they've ordered a meal, not just a beverage. The whole place was stripped and rebuilt for Expo, which isn't likely to harm its popularity.

Sol Dourado. Jardim do Regedor 19–25 (half a block east of praça dos Restauradores). ☎ **01/347-25-70.** Main courses 1,650$–2,400$ ($10–$14); *ementa turística* 2,900$ ($17). AE, DC, MC, V. Daily noon–midnight. Metro: Restauradores. PORTUGUESE.

There's no dearth of economical eateries in this neighborhood, but this is better than most. Sol Dourado specializes in pork with baby clams, one of the humble glories of the Portuguese kitchen. *Arroz de marisco,* a kind of simple paella, is another option. Attentive service and outdoor tables are two pluses. The same owners operate **Lagosta Real** at rua Portas de São Antão 37 and the **Marisqueria da Baixa** on the same street at no. 41.

ON THE RIBEIRINHA

✪ **Espalha Brasas.** Doca de Santo Amaro, Armazem 12 ☎ **01/396-20-59.** Main courses 1,500$–2,200$ ($9–$13). MC, V. Mon–Sat 12:30pm–4am. Bus: 12 or 20. PORTUGUESE.

A few blocks of two-story marine warehouses along the western waterfront (the Ribeirinha) have been converted to restaurants and clubs. This is among the liveliest. The barbecue in the open kitchen turns out tempting plates like grilled marlin for 1,800$ ($10) and skewered turbot and shrimp (with salad and a baked potato) for 2,200$ ($13). While you can put together a standard dinner from the menu, this is mainly a grazing place. But order only a side of fried squid and you still get bread, flavored butters, a round of cheese, and four jars of pâtés. The place is much in demand on weekends, and the walk-up reservation list can mean a wait of an hour or more. Many of the staff speak English. Take a taxi.

IN BELÉM

Rosa dos Mares. Belém 10. ☎ **01/364-92-75.** Main courses 760$–2,400$ ($4.40–$14); *ementa turística* 2,100$ ($12). MC, V. Daily noon–11pm. Closed 2–3 weeks in Feb. Tram: 15 or 17. PORTUGUESE.

Some Belém restaurants close on Sunday, which is short-sighted, since the major attractions are open then but closed Monday. Places like this, across from the east end of the Jerónimos Monastery, get the extra business. Stop in for a full meal or just a sandwich. When the tables inside and out are full, you can be served at the bar. A representative fixed-price meal: vegetable soup; a platter-size main course of roast goat (tastes like rabbit) with rice, roast potatoes, baked tomato, and puréed spinach; flan or fruit salad; and wine, water, or beer and coffee.

Skip dessert and walk a few doors down to the **Antiga Confeitaria de Belém** (☎ 01/363-74-23). A landmark bar/tearoom since 1837, it serves the beloved *pastéis de Belém,* a delectable cream-filled tart served with a shake of powdered sugar. Port or a *bica* go well with one, two, or three.

IN THE ALFAMA

Senhor Leilao de Arco da Coneicão. Bacalhoeiros 4 (near avenida Infante D. Henrique). ☎ **01/886-98-60.** Main courses 950$–2,200$ ($6–$13); *ementa turística* 2,350$ ($14). AE, DC, MC, V. Mon–Sat noon–4pm and 7–10:30pm. Tram: 12. PORTUGUESE.

Everyone comes here for the roast suckling pig, and the supply can run out before a meal service is over. So go early—it's worth it. The flesh drops off the bone; the crackled skin is the texture of crisp butter. If you aren't comfortable eating a creature only allowed to live a few weeks on mother's milk, you might try *arroz de pato,* the traditional duck-and-rice casserole. Service is often slow and forgetful, at least when there's only one waitress (often the case). These are pleasant rooms hung with clocks, plates, and old engravings.

Sol Nascente. São Tomé 86 (not far down the Alfama hill from Castelo São Jorge). ☎ **01/887-72-13.** Main courses 950$–1,700$ ($6–$10); *ementa turística* 1,900$ ($11). AE, DC, MC, V. Tues–Sun 8am–2am. Tram: 28. PORTUGUESE.

Don't let the stratospheric 9,000$ ($52) item on the menu deter you: That's for lobster, always an exception to Lisbon's usually reasonable prices. The size of main dishes is substantial enough so that you can skip appetizers or order half portions *(doces)* for 950$ to 1,700$ ($6 to $10). A plate of five fat grilled sardines, with boiled potatoes, steamed kale, and shaved carrots, is only 1,300$ ($8). Choices for dining space include the immaculate large dining room and the tables on the plaza shared with the Fundação Ricardo Espírito Santo, the decorative arts museum.

THE CHAINS

The Portuguese pizza-and-burger joints, **Abracadabra,** are similar to the American imports, though service tends to be slower. Two branches are at Centro Comercial Imaviz, next to the Sheraton Hotel, and on praça Dom Pedro IV.

PICNICKING

Celeiro, rua 1 de Dezembro 81 (☎ 01/342-74-95; Metro: Rossio), is a well-stocked supermarket near Rossio Square that offers ready-cooked fare like roast chicken at 1,025$ ($6) per kilo (2.2 lb.). Of the many *charcutarias* downtown, you might seek out **Tábuas,** rua Barros Queiroz 45 (☎ 01/342-61-69; Metro: Rossio), off the northeast corner of the Rossio. It carries prepared salads, wines, breads, fruits, and a large selection of cheese, sausages, and cured hams. Enjoy your picnic in any of the city's numerous parks. Favorites are the grounds of the **Castelo São Jorge** atop the Alfama, the belvedere of **rua de São Pedro de Alcântara** in the Bairro Alto, and **Parque Eduardo VII,** which has picnic tables.

WORTH A SPLURGE

Cais da Ribeira. Armazém A (on the waterfront behind the Cais do Sodre rail station). ☎ 01/342-36-11. Reservations required. Main courses 1,700$–6,750$ ($10–$39); *ementa turística* 5,200$ ($30). DC, MC, V. Mon–Fri noon–3pm and 7:30–11pm, Sat 7:30–11pm. Metro: Cais do Sodré. PORTUGUESE.

This former warehouse for the fishing fleet has been converted into an immensely popular seafood restaurant. The wide windows provide views of ferries and wheeling gulls while patrons tuck into the signature fish stew *caldeirada à Fragateira* or any of a dozen specimens from the day's catch, preferably charcoal-grilled. Main courses come with vegetables, so by skipping extras and avoiding the costlier crustaceans you can stay within your budget and have what may be the most memorable meal of your Lisbon stay. The immediate neighborhood gets a little dicey at night, so it might be better to save this for lunch.

5 Seeing the Sights

SIGHTSEEING SUGGESTIONS

IF YOU HAVE 1 DAY After breakfast, take a map and head for the maze of streets lacing the hillside **Alfama** district. From Rossio Square, head past the boutiques of rua Augusta and turn left onto rua da Conceição. Follow the signs to the **Sé,** a 12th-century cathedral that has undergone various face-lifts. Continue left beyond the Sé and, a bit farther along on the right, stop for the view from the **belvedere** of Santa Luzia. Follow largo do Contador Mor (opposite) to the end and turn left onto chão da Feira to enter the grounds of the **Castelo São Jorge.** You can see all of Lisbon and the broad river Tejo from its ramparts. (This is a steep uphill route, so you may prefer to take a taxi to the castle and follow the directions in reverse downhill.)

Wind your way down through the Alfama to praça do Comércio and catch the new no. 15 tram to **Belém** to visit the **Mosteiro dos Jerónimos.** Down by the river is the **Torre de Belém** and the **Monument of the Discoveries.** After lunch in the **Bairro Alto,** head for the **Museu da Fundação Calouste Gulbenkian,** whose select collection of exquisite art is superbly displayed in a custom-built setting.

IF YOU HAVE 2 DAYS Spend the morning of Day 1 as above, but have lunch in **Belém** and then visit the **Mosteiro dos Jerónimos,** the **Museu da Marinha** at its western end, and the nearby **Museu dos Coches.**

On Day 2, spend the morning at the **Museu da Fundação Calouste Gulbenkian.** After lunch in the **Bairro Alto,** head for the **Jardim Botânico** and stroll back toward the river along rua Dom Pedro V, which passes the attractive praça do Príncipe Real. Continue on the same street, which changes to rua de São Pedro de Alcântara, until you reach a **belvedere** with an encompassing view of downtown Lisbon. Next visit the 16th-century **Igreja de São Roque,** with a dazzling chapel dedicated to St. John the Baptist, constructed in Rome in 1742 of lapis lazuli, alabaster, and amethyst. Continue along the same street, now called rua da Misericórdia, to praça de Camões and turn left through largo do Chiado to rua Garrett, where reconstruction is still under way in the wake of the 1988 fire. At the end of rua Garrett, turn left onto rua do Carmo. Both streets are lined with intermittently appealing shops. At rua de Santa Justa, off to the right is the **Elevador de Santa Justa,** built by Raul Mesnier de Ponsard, a Portuguese engineer, not by Gustave Eiffel as is often claimed. Follow rua do Carmo into **Rossio Square,** stopping for a leisurely coffee at one of its cafes.

IF YOU HAVE 3 DAYS   Spend Day 1 strolling the **Alfama** and seeing the **Castelo São Jorge** and the nearby **Fundação Ricardo Espírito Santo,** with its collection of 17th- and 18th-century Portuguese and colonial furnishings and art objects. In the castle's vicinity are several restaurants for lunch.

The **Museu da Fundação Calouste Gulbenkian** can easily fill the morning of Day 2. Head to **Belém** for lunch and then visit the **Mosteiro dos Jerónimos, Museu da Marinha, Torre de Belém, Monument of the Discoveries, Museu dos Coches,** and **Museu Nacional de Arte Antiga.**

Spend the morning of Day 3 in the **Bairro Alto** as in "If You Have 2 Days" and the afternoon exploring the shops of the **Baixa** area between Rossio Square and praça do Comércio. Catch tram no. 28 (Graça) on rua da Madalena to the **Igreja da Graça** and have a sunset drink at the bar of the **Albergaria da Senhora do Monte,** calçada do Monte 39.

IF YOU HAVE 5 DAYS   Spend Days 1 to 3 as above, reserving Tuesday or Saturday for a morning visit to the **Feira da Ladra flea market.** On the afternoon of Day 4, visit the **Igreja da Madre de Deus,** beautifully restored inside with tile murals and carved wood, and the nearby **Museu do Azulejo.** On Day 5, go to **Sintra,** the magical mountain retreat with the fairy-tale Pena Palace and Paço Real.

THE CASTLE & THE MONASTERY

✪ **Castelo São Jorge (St. George's Castle).** Alfama District. Free admission. Daily 9am–sunset. Tram: 28. Bus: 37.

Over 2,000 years ago, this strategic hill was the site of important Roman and Moorish fortifications, later amplified by the Christian kings. Today it's a place for relaxation in gardens and playgrounds and beside ponds and waterways. The trees are filled with birdsong and aviarian chatter. Free-roaming peacocks shriek and preen, caged roosters crow, and ducks, geese, and mute swans compete for territory. There are keeps and battlements to wander and many stone benches and tables at which to rest. Take a camera, for there are many photo ops, not just of the city below but also of the play of light over the trees and ancient walls. A moderately expensive restaurant, **Casa do Leão,** occupies part of a ruined wall, and in front of the entrance is a small **outdoor cafe.** The views are spectacular. It's a steep uphill walk from the nearest bus and tram stops, so you might want to take a taxi all the way to the castle entrance and walk back down.

✪ **Mosteiro dos Jerónimos (Jerónimos Monastery).** Praça do Império, Belém. ☎ **01/362-00-34.** Church, free; cloister, 400$ ($2.35) adults, 200$ ($1.15) seniors/ages 14–25, free for age 13 and under. Tues–Sun 10am–1pm and 2–5pm (to 6:30pm in summer). Closed holidays. Tram: 15 or 17. Bus: 27, 28, 29, 43, or 49.

The Alfama

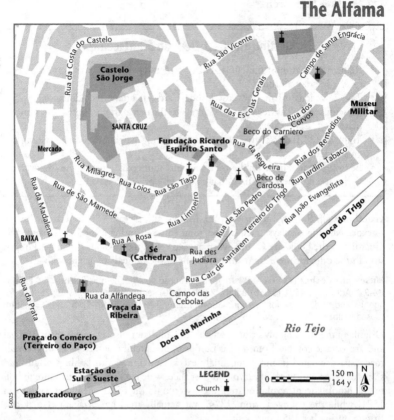

An extravagant expression of gratitude for the discoveries of Vasco da Gama—who's buried here—and other Portuguese navigators, this monastery is unmistakable, gleaming white in the sun. It contains the Gothic-Renaissance **Church of Santa Maria,** famed for its deeply carved stonework. Formerly on the bank of the river, which has since shifted direction, the church evolved from a chapel built by Prince Henry the Navigator to its current soaring majesty, replete with decorative allusions to the sea and the fruits of the empire it spawned. Three Portuguese kings, their sarcophagi decorated with elephants, are also buried here. Since admission to the church is free and the entrance fee admits you to only the adjacent cloister, you might wish to save the 400$ for one of the other Belém museums.

THE TOP MUSEUMS

✪ **Museu da Fundação Calouste Gulbenkian (Gulbenkian Foundation Museum).**
Av. de Berna 45. ☎ **01/795-02-36.** Admission 500$ ($2.90) adults, free for seniors/students. Free for everyone Sun. Tues–Sun 10am–5pm. Closed holidays. Metro: Palhavã. Tram: 24. Bus: 16, 26, or 30 to praça de Espanha.

A magnificent art treasury, this museum houses one of the largest privately amassed collections of paintings, furniture, ceramics, sculptures, tapestries, and coins on the Continent. The gift of an Armenian multimillionaire, the made-to-order building contains objects and artworks from 5,000 years of history, with Egyptian artifacts from the 3rd millennium B.C., 14th-century Chinese porcelain, 17th-century Japanese prints, Greek gold coins from 500 B.C., stone cylinder seals of Mesopotamia (3000 B.C.), silk carpets from Armenia, and paintings by Rubens, Rembrandt,

---

Getting the Best Deal on Sightseeing

- Remember that most museums are free on Sunday morning and some are free on Wednesday morning.
- Take advantage of the low-cost Lisboa Card—it offers free admission to 25 museums as well as free unlimited access to the metro, trams, buses, and funiculars for 1, 2, or 3 days.
- Tram no. 28 traverses the city's most intriguing neighborhoods, providing a great orientation.
- Be aware that 2-hour public tram and bus tours pass most of the important sights at a far lower cost than that charged by private companies.

Gainsborough, Renoir, Turner, Watteau, Monet, and Degas. Keep an eye out for the unexpected little displays, such as the room of enchanting Venetian cityscapes by Guardi and the book-size Gothic ivory miniatures of the Passion. If you get hungry, stop in the cafe, for there aren't many options in the immediate neighborhood.

Museu dos Coches (Coach Museum). Praça Afonso de Albuquerque, Belém. ☎ **01/363-80-22.** Admission 450$ ($2.60) adults, 225$ ($1.30) seniors/teachers/ages 14–25, free for age 13 and under. Free for everyone Sun morning. Tues–Sun 10am–1pm and 2:30–5pm. Closed holidays. Tram: 15. Bus: 14, 27, 43, or 49.

Originally the royal family's riding school, this museum displays more than 70 royal and aristocratic coaches from several European monarchies. Some are as long as railroad cars, decorated in mind-bogglingly excessive manner with lashings of gilt and swags of velvet and swirls of carving. If ever there were emblems of wealth sure to boil the blood of nascent revolutionaries, these would do the trick. The oldest dates from 1581, while the youngest, from 1824, was actually used by Elizabeth II of Great Britain during her 1958 state visit.

Fundação Ricardo Espírito Santo (Museum of Decorative Arts). Largo das Portas do Sol 2. ☎ **01/886-21-83.** Admission 500$ ($2.90) adults, 250$ ($1.45) seniors/age 11 and under. Wed–Mon 10am–5pm. Closed holidays. Tram: 28 to Graça. Bus: 37.

In a 17th-century palace halfway up the Alfama hill, this museum displays Portuguese decorative pieces and furniture from the 17th and 18th centuries, most in the Indo-Portuguese style derived from Portugal's Far Eastern colonial experience. On the premises is a school of decorative arts, since the work of the foundation includes restoration and reproduction. The artisans are masters of wood carving, cabinetry, inlay, painting, lacquerwork, and gilding, and they've done restorations for Versailles and Fontainebleau as well as the Rockefellers.

Museu de Arte Antiga (Museum of Ancient Art). Janelas Verdes 9, Lapa. ☎ **01/396-41-51.** Admission 500$ ($3.35). Free Sun morning. Tues 2–6pm, Wed–Sun 10am–6pm. Bus: 49.

A refurbished palace is the setting for 8 centuries of art (12th to 19th), including ceramics, silver, and tapestries, as well as one of the two most important collections of

---

An Attractions Tip

It's always a good idea to call ahead about openings, since the Portuguese notion of holidays is elastic, even taking in such occasions as Halloween and Fat Tuesday, the last day before Lent.

Lisbon

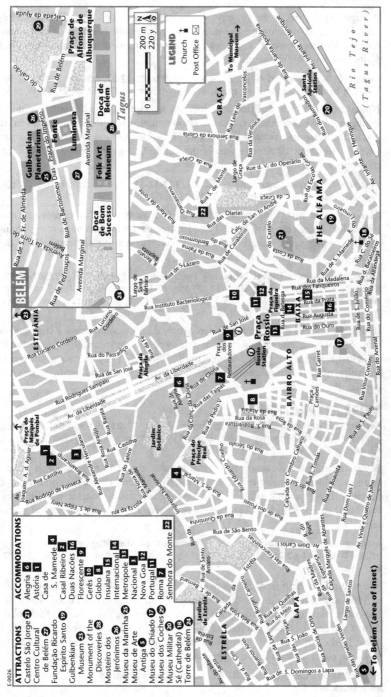

LEGEND
Church ✝
Post Office ⊠

N
0 — 200 m
0 — 220 y

Rio Tejo (Tagus River)

BELÉM (area of inset)

ATTRACTIONS
Castelo São Jorge 21
Centro Cultural de Belém 27
Fundação Ricardo Espírito Santo 19
Gulbenkian Museum 23
Monument of the Discoveries 28
Mosteiro dos Jerónimos 25
Museu da Marinha 26
Museu de Arte Antiga 5
Museu do Chiado 17
Museu dos Coches 29
Museu Militar 18
Sé (Cathedral) 20
Torre de Belém 24

ACCOMMODATIONS
Alegria 6
Astória 1
Casa de S. Mamede 4
Casal Ribeiro 2
Duas Nações 16
Florescente 9
Gerês 10
Globo 8
Insulana 15
Internacional 14
Metropole 13
Nacional 3
Nova Goa 12
Portugal 11
Roma 7
Senhora do Monte 22

473

E-0026

Portuguese paintings in the country. Works by Cranach, Velázquez, Brueghel, Holbein, Dürer, and Murillo are on view, as is the unforgettable Hieronymus Bosch masterpiece *The Temptations of St. Anthony.* Don't miss the enormous 17th-century silver platter weighing 2,000 pounds.

Museu de Arte Popular. Av. Brasília, Belém. ☎ **01/301-12-82.** Admission 400$ ($2.30). Tues–Sun 10am–12:30pm and 2–5pm. Closed holidays. Tram: 15. Bus: 27, 28, 29, 43, 49, or 51.

Not far from the Torre de Belém, this folkloric museum displays not only traditional Portuguese naïve art but also costumes, kitchen implements, tools, furniture, leather goods, and ceramics. It's on the water side of the highway and railroad line, so you have to walk about 10 minutes west of the Centro Cultural to cross over the pedestrian bridge.

Museu do Chiado. Serpa Pinto 6. ☎ **01/347-32-11.** Free admission. Tues 2–6pm, Wed–Sun 10am–6pm. Closed holidays. Tram: 28. Bus: 15.

This new facility, replacing the old Museum of Contemporary Art, houses a permanent collection of post-1850 art and frequent temporary exhibits of painting, sculpture, photography, and mixed-media works. Portuguese artists are featured, but the building itself is at least as interesting.

Museu da Marinha (Naval Museum). Praça do Império, Belém. ☎ **01/362-00-10.** Admission 400$ ($2.35) adults, 200$ ($1.15) ages 10–18, free for seniors/ages 9 and under. Free for everyone Sun morning. Tues–Sun 10am–5pm (to 6pm summer). Closed holidays. Tram: 15. Bus: 27, 28, 29, 43, 49, or 51.

In the west wing of the Mosteiro dos Jerónimos, this museum contains a large collection of maps, maritime paraphernalia, and finely detailed models of ships old and new, including Egyptian and Greek warships from 3000 B.C. In an annex across the way is an exhibit of life-size royal barges, galleons, and sailing ships, and nearby is the Gulbenkian Planetarium.

MORE ATTRACTIONS

Centro Cultural de Belém. Praça do Império, Belém. ☎ **01/301-96-06.** Center, free; admission varies for temporary exhibits. Daily 11am–8pm. Tram: 15 or 17. Bus: 27, 28, 29, 43, or 49.

A vast contemporary structure that seems to take inspiration from Moorish palaces and gleams like the nearby Jeróminos Monastery, this center spreads a cornucopia of activities. These typically include a large traveling art exhibit, concerts, and film festivals, but that's the short list. On the premises are several shops and galleries and a cafeteria.

Monumento dos Descobrimentos (Monument of the Discoveries). Av. Brasília, Belém. ☎ **01/301-62-28.** Admission 275$ ($1.60). Tues–Sun 9:30am–7pm. Tram: 15 or 17. Bus: 43 or 49.

Several hundred yards from the Torre de Belém, this imposing monument was built in 1960 to commemorate the 500th anniversary of the death of Prince Henry the Navigator, who founded Portugal's first observatory and the Sagres Nautical School. It depicts the prince leading a throng of sailors, captains, priests, and poets to imperial glory. In the pavement is a map chronicling Portuguese discoveries from 1427 to 1541. An elevator can take you to the top.

Sé (Cathedral). Castelo, Alfama. ☎ **01/86-67-52.** Free admission. Daily 9am–5pm. Tram: 28 to Graça. Bus: 37.

Special & Free Events

All Portugal hoped that **Expo '98** would be the transforming event its boosters had promised for years. Natives and visitors tolerated the disruptions of construction for that long, as new metro lines, bridges, and the exposition ground itself appeared. Billed as the last World's Fair of the 20th century (a title the 1992 event in Seville had claimed), it was held from late May to October 1998 in a satellite city on the east bank of the Tejo. Reached by the new Vasco da Gama Bridge, the Expo site contains an oceanarium and the usual futuristic architecture and technological extravaganzas, the future uses of which are still uncertain. Contact the **Portuguese National Tourist Office,** 590 Fifth Ave., New York, NY 10036 (☎ 212/354-4403), for details on post-Expo attractions.

On June 12 and 13, Lisbon celebrates the **Feast Day of St. Anthony** with *marchas* (strolling groups of singers and musicians). On the evening of June 12 revelers parade in costume along avenida da Liberdade. Festivities include dances, bonfires, and general merriment in the taverns until dawn, especially in the Alfama. Festivities on June 24 and 29 in the Alfama honor Lisbon's other popular saints—**John, Peter,** and **Paul.**

In July, Sintra holds its annual **music festival.** In August, Estoril does likewise. In the fall, Cascais holds an annual **jazz festival.** Check local newspapers for details.

Built in the 12th century as a fortress-church by Portugal's first Christian king, Afonso Henriques, this is Lisbon's oldest surviving church. Its original Romanesque facade and towers were left largely undamaged by two violent earthquakes, though much of the rest of the exterior and interior has been repeatedly renovated (not always to good effect).

Torre de Belém (Tower of Belém). Off av. Brasília, Belém. ☎ **01/301-68-92.** Admission June–Sept 400$ ($2.30); Oct–May 250$ ($1.45) adults, 200$ ($1.15) students. Tues–Sun 10am–1pm and 2:30–5pm. Tram: 15 or 17. Bus: 43 or 49.

Blending elements of the Gothic and Renaissance in a style known as Manueline, with seafaring motifs and allusions to the purloined fruits of the colonies, this 16th-century watchtower was built as protection against pirates but now contains a small museum of arms and armor. Its upper platform delivers a panoramic view of the Tejo, but since there isn't much else to the interior you might simply wish to appreciate the tower from the outside, without paying admission.

PARKS & GARDENS

The most important botanical gardens are the **Jardim Botânico** and **Jardim da Estrêla** and the largest parks are the **Parque de Monsanto** and underutilized **Parque Eduardo VII,** which contains the ornate Sports Pavilion and a small lake with ducks, geese, and a pair of peacocks. The following small parks and terraces offer views of the city: **Alto de Santa Catarina,** on rua da Santa Catarina; **Castelo São Jorge,** at the top of the Alfama district; **Luenta dos Quarteis, Moinho dos Mochos, Alto da Serafina,** and **Montes Claros** in Parque de Monsanto; **Ponte,** viaduto Duarte Pacheco; belvedere of **Santa Luzia** in Bairro Alto; **Zimborio da Basilica da Estrêla** on largo da Estrêla; and **rua de São Pedro de Alcântara.**

ORGANIZED TOURS

BY TRAM   Along its entire route, **tram no. 28** passes through Lisbon's most picturesque neighborhoods—the Bairro Alto, Alfama, and Graça—and is almost as much fun as an amusement park ride.

Since 1901, trams have negotiated the intimate alleys and tight corners of Lisbon's old quarters. Rather than being put out to pasture, Lisbon's trams are still going strong. **Carris** (☎ **01/363-93-43**), the city's public transport company, offers 2-hour tram tours, including an enlightening circuit through the Old City and trendier quarters. Tours depart from praça do Comércio. Starting times are 1:30 and 3:30pm and tickets (sold on board) are 2,800$ ($16) adults and 1,500$ ($9) ages 4 to 10; those 3 and under ride free.

BY BUS   **Carris** (see above) also offers a bus tour, allowing you to get on and off at any of 10 stops from Parque Eduardo VII to Belém. Tickets, 2,000$ ($12), are good for a full day, and you can buy them on board. The buses leave praça do Comércio at 11am, noon, and 1, 2, 3, 4, and 5pm. Other tours are available through **RN Tours** at ☎ **01/57-75-23** and **Cityrama Tours** at ☎ **01/355-85-67.**

6 Shopping

RECOVERING VAT

The **value-added tax (IVA in Portugal)** varies according to the item or service sold—in most cases from 8% to 17%. Visitors from non–European Union countries are entitled to a refund of the tax if purchases in a single duty-free store total at least 12,180$ ($71), exclusive of IVA. (Participating stores display a TAX-FREE FOR TOURISTS sign.) To obtain the refund, have the shop fill in the front of the Tax-Free Check, then fill in the back. When leaving Portugal, carry your purchases, Tax-Free Checks, and passport in your hand luggage for presentation to Customs. Redeem the stamped checks at the Tax Refund counter for cash or credit on a credit card. There are Tax Refund counters at the Lisbon airport and the Lisbon harbor. For information, call ☎ **01/418-87-03.** If you're traveling from Portugal to another EU country (Spain, for example) and are returning from there to a non-EU home country, then you need to show your purchases and tax-free forms to Customs agents there.

BEST BUYS

Words to remember are *saldos* (sales) and *descontos* (discounts), most often seen after Christmas and in late summer.

Except for several minimalls (such as **Imaviz,** next to the Sheraton) and one megamall (**Amoreiras,** with over 350 shops), small shops are the norm. The best buys are ceramics, porcelain, pottery, and embroidered and leather goods, but bargains are no longer as common as they once were. One of the better shops at which to view some of what's available is the **Centro de Turismo e Artesanato,** rua Castilho 61B (☎ **01/386-38-30**). The stock is extensive, and the personable manager speaks fluent English and will arrange for packing and shipping anywhere. Late-night shoppers might want to seek out **Francesinha Handicraft Shop** at rua da Barroca 96 (☎ **01/347-46-87**) in Bairro Alto, open daily 3pm to midnight.

The smartest shops are on **rua Garrett** and the surrounding streets, in an area known as the **Chiado. Rua da Escola Politécnica** is the upper end of a long street with several names (rua do Alecrim, rua da Misericórdia, rua de São Pedro de Alcântara, rua Dom Pedro V, rua da Escola Politécnica). Scattered all along it are antiques shops.

A flashy new **Virgin Megastore** (☎ 01/346-01-48) on the west side of praça dos Restauradores has numerous listening posts at which to sample its extensive stock of CDs; it also sells videos and computer software. While the selection isn't too wide, **Livaria Europa-América,** av. Marquês Tomar 1 (☎ 01/356-37-91), stocks books and magazines in several languages, including English. A better bet is **Livaria Británica,** rua Luís Fernamdes 14 (☎ 01/342-84-72), which carries only English-language works, with a British emphasis.

MARKETS
On Tuesday and Saturday the **Fiera da Ladra** ("Thieves" or Flea Market) goes from 9am to 6pm in campo de Santa Clara behind the Igreja São Vicente. Take bus no. 12 from the Santa Apolónia Station.

7 Lisbon After Dark

Lisbon's nightlife has exploded. Only a few years ago, most clubs and discos locked up by 2am. Now, following the lead of their Spanish neighbors, many of them rock until dawn. A few don't bother opening until 6am, thumping on until noon! For information on performances and productions, contact the **tourist office** or the **Agência de Bilhetes para Espectáculos Públicos,** praça dos Restauradores (☎ 01/347-58-23; Metro: Restauradores), open daily 9am to 10pm. The latter sells tickets to all cinemas and theaters except the National Theater of São Carlos, as well as for the frequent concerts by name rock bands stopping in Lisbon on their world tours.

The *Diário de Noticias* has the latest listings (in Portuguese), as does the weekly magazine *Sete.*

THE PERFORMING ARTS
The season for opera, theater, ballet, and concerts is October to May, with additional performances throughout the year. The main venues are the **Teatro Nacional de Dona Maria II,** in Rossio Square (☎ 01/342-22-10; Metro: Rossio); the **Teatro Nacional de São Carlos,** at rua Serpa Pinto 9 (☎ 01/346-59-14; Tram: 12); the **Fundação Calouste Gulbenkian,** av. de Berna 45 (☎ 01/793-51-31; Tram: 24); the **Teatro Municipal São Luís,** rua António Maria Cardoso 40 (☎ 01/347-12-79; Tram: 28); the **Teatro Trindade,** largo da Trinidade 7-A (☎ 01/342-32-00; Tram: 24); and the new **Centro Cultural de Belém,** praça do Império (☎ 01/361-24-00; Tram: 15 or 17).

Opera tickets run 400$ to 3,000$ ($2.30 to $17); theater tickets, 1,000$ to 2,500$ ($6 to $15). Ballet and concert tickets vary greatly depending on the performance but are usually in the same range as theatrical performances.

LIVE-MUSIC CLUBS
Fado is to Lisbon what jazz is to New Orleans and flamenco is to Seville—a native art that relies on emotion and spontaneity. Don't leave Lisbon without experiencing it. Fado clubs *(adegas típicas* or *restaurantes típicos)* serve dinner before and during the entertainment, which usually starts about 10pm. You can dine elsewhere and arrive around 11pm to enjoy the show for a lesser cover charge. Ask how much this is before entering—it's typically about 2,500$ to 4,000$ ($15 to $23), which covers admission and two or three drinks.

Contrary to what other sources insist, the well-known fado club **Lisboa à Noite,** rua das Gáveas 69 (☎ 01/346-85-57; Metro: Restauradores; Tram: 24), isn't unusually expensive, though the minimum (which covers a couple of highballs, a small carafe of wine, and an appetizer/snack) may kick to a higher level when the famous owner/diva, Fernanda Maria, is in residence and performing. The interior is more restrained than in others of the breed, as are the routine pitches to buy cassettes and souvenirs. It's open daily 8:30pm to 3am. No cover, but there's a 2,900$ ($17) minimum.

Not far from Lisboa à Noite (above), **Machado,** rua do Norte 91 (☎ **01/346-00-95;** Metro: Restauradores), has a colorful folkloric setting of bad paintings and signed photos of semicelebrated guests. Every 20 minutes or so, three guitarists take their places at the back of the small stage. The singer stands in front, shawl pulled tightly around her, head thrown back, eyes closed, crying out the ritual of despair and lost love. It's often electrifying, especially when the headliner comes on. Plates of food run from 2,200$ to 4,200$ ($13 to $24). The club is open Tuesday to Sunday 8pm to 3am. There's a 2,500$ ($15) minimum. One of the less expensive quality fado clubs, **Parreirinha da Alfama,** beco do Espírito Santo 1 (☎ **01/886-82-09;** Bus: 37), is cozy, and patrons often join in the singing. Sets are every 20 minutes 10pm to 3am. Main courses run 1,000$ to 3,200$ ($6 to $19). Go later just for music and drinks. It's open Monday to Saturday 8pm to 3am.

As riveting as fado can be, an evening of it goes a long way. Alternative entertainments are available. Jazz, rock, and Afro-Brazilian pop are popular, and a number of clubs present live groups several nights a week. An entirely new nighttime scene has sprung up along the waterfront running west of the city center to the 25 de Abril Bridge, a linear district known as the **Ribeirinha.**

Go to **Hot Clube de Portugal,** praça da Alegria 39 (☎ **01/346-73-69;** Metro: Avenida), for the sounds of mainstream and fusion jazz in a traditional subterranean environment, usually blue with cigarette smoke. It's open Tuesday to Saturday 10pm to 2am, with live performances at 11pm and 12:30am Thursday to Saturday. Cover runs from 500$ to 1,250$ ($2.90 to $7) when there's live music, which begins about 11:30pm.

BARS

A burgeoning crop of nightbirds is keeping Lisbon bars and clubs open later and later. Many of the popular spots don't even bother to open until 10pm or later.

Across from one of the most appealing parks and belvederes in the city, **Harry's Bar,** rua de São Pedro de Alcântara 57 (☎ **01/346-07-60;** Tram: 24 or Elevador da Glória), is a long-lived cocktail lounge (with a picture of Marilyn Monroe on one wall) drawing a mixed crowd of couples, gays and lesbians, tourists, artists, and journalists. Recorded songs by Portuguese pop singers alternate with the likes of Johnny Cash. It's open Monday to Saturday 10pm to 6am.

Save the **Instituto do Vinho do Porto,** rua de São Pedro de Alcântara 45 (☎ **01/347-57-07;** Tram: 24 or Elevador da Glória), for after dinner. Behind massive wood doors near Harry's Bar is a multiroom lounge featuring Portugal's trademark postprandial tipple. Decorated in dated Eisenhower style, the nonetheless comfortable retreat is a library of every variety and price level of port wine, some white and dry, most red and semidry or sweet. It may take two or three selections from the big menu to get to a bottle they have open and in stock, but it's a marvelous way to sample one of the nation's proudest products. Glasses of wine cost as little as 150$ (85¢) to as much as 9,000$ ($52) for a rare vintage. It's open Monday to Friday 10am to 11:45pm and Saturday 11am to 10:45pm.

The unusual **Pavilhão Chines Bar,** rua Dom Pedro V 89 (☎ **01/342-47-29;** Tram: 24), goes on for several rooms packed with an eclectic and often kitschy collection of toys, collectibles, and oddities, especially from the Far East. The main bar has a lovely marquetry top, a touch of class amid the rows of souvenir plates, bronze Cupids, cartoons of the Great War antagonists, gobs and gaggles of Victoriana, cases of Toby jugs, ceramics of Buddha, Hussars . . . and Popeye. Martini olives are skewered with hand-carved toothpicks. There are two billiard tables and another bar in a rear room. It's open Monday to Friday 2pm to 2am, Saturday 6pm to 2am, and Sunday midnight to 2am.

GAY & LESBIAN BARS

Harry's Bar (above) attracts a mixed straight and gay crowd. Near the Bairro Alto, **Memorial,** rua Gustavo de Matos Sequeira 42 (☎ **01/396-88-91;** Bus: 6, 27, 49, or 58), is an important meet-and-greet spot for Lisbon's gay community. It caters mostly to gay men, but lesbians are welcome. On Thursday the club has live entertainment. It's open Tuesday to Sunday 10pm to 4am. Cover is 1,200$ ($7) Tuesday, Wednesday, Friday, and Sunday and 1,500$ ($9) Thursday.

Trumps, rua da Imprensa Nacionale 104B (☎ **01/397-10-59;** Bus: 6, 49, or 58), is Lisbon's largest gay dance club, near the Bairro Alto. It caters to a mixed crowd, but most of its clientele is gay men. Trumps has a spacious dance floor, a long bar, and a staff that speaks French and Spanish. It's open Tuesday to Sunday 11am to 4am. Cover (credited toward drinks) is 1,200$ ($7).

DANCE CLUBS

Lisbon's classier nightspots are permitted to charge an outrageous cover to keep out the riffraff, but well-dressed respectable-looking types are usually admitted free. A moderate cover may be charged if the place is full, however.

Salsa Latina, estação Marítima de Alcântrara (☎ **01/395-05-50;** Bus: 12 or 20), revels in its voluptuous tropical tone, throbbing with Latin rhythms—the tango, mambo, and their musical kin. The marble dance floor is full of energetic dancers who cool off on the terrace between sets. Usually open Tuesday to Saturday 10pm to 4pm, but frequent changes are the rule, so call ahead. Opened in 1982, **Fragil,** rua da Atalaia 128 (☎ **01/346-95-78;** Tram: 24), remains one of the hottest clubs in town, popular with the film, fashion, and design crowd. The decor changes whenever the owner gets bored, roughly every 2 or 3 months. It's open Monday to Saturday 11pm or midnight to 6am or later. Cover varies (some people are charged admission, some aren't).

Often the last stop on the nocturnal circuit, **Kremlin,** escadinhas da Praia 5 (☎ **01/395-7101;** Tram: 15, 16, 17, 18, 29, or 30; Bus: 14, 28, 32, 40, or 43), is an examplar of pounding, frenetic dance clubs that doesn't open until 2am and holds a party every 3 or 4 months when it changes decor. The crowd is mixed, but those in their 20s and early 30s predominate. It's open Monday to Thursday 2 to 6am and Friday and Saturday 2 to 10am or later.

Next door to Kremlin (above), **Plateau,** escadinhas da Praia 7 (☎ **01/396-51-16;** Tram: 15, 16, 17, 18, 29, or 30; Bus: 14, 28, 32, 40, or 43), is smaller, with an end-of-civilization decor, but the crowd, mood, and music are much the same. The difference is that getting past the rope depends on the whim of the no-neck guarding the gate. Try to be rich and famous. It's open Tuesday to Saturday midnight to 4:30am.

8 Side Trips: Palaces & Picturesque Towns

THE ESTORIL COAST

This stretch of Atlantic shore west of the capital was long favored by aristocratic expatriates and continues to harbor representatives of Europe's dwindling nobility. Alas, unrestricted development has taken its toll. Almost 60 **trains** leave the Cais do Sodré Station in Lisbon daily 5:30am to 2:30am. Estoril is a 30-minute ride and Cascais 40 minutes. The round-trip fare to Cascais is 360$ ($2.10).

Estoril is some 15 miles from Lisbon and has a **casino/nightclub** (☎ 01/468-45-21), open daily, except Christmas Eve, 3pm to 3am. Dinner starts at 8:30pm and the floor show, which includes topless showgirls, is at 11pm. International headliners sometimes appear. Figure on spending at least $60 per person for dinner and the show. Bring your passport for entrance. The casino is a rather grave affair, the only whoops and groans coming from the craps table, surrounded by Americans accustomed to a more boisterous form of losing. My advice, after a look around, is to press on to the next, more hospitable town.

That's **Cascais,** a few miles farther, once a drowsy village that has followed the familiar progression from fishing port to artists' colony to here-comes-everybody. Working boats still find berths among the pleasure craft, and tamarisk and hibiscus struggle for space between boîtes and boutiques. You'll find a pretty beach, umbrella-covered sidewalk cafes, and a lively nightlife that attracts a mostly younger crowd.

After Cascais, the coast starts to bend north and you'll need a car to continue. The temper of the sea changes, raked directly now by the intimidating Atlantic. Wave action has bored gaping cavities into the sheer cliffs at **Boca do Inferno,** a popular photo op. Farther along, the land flattens, the vegetation thins, and fine white sand streams in gusts across the road. Eventually, the land lifts again toward the headlands, pocketing the beaches. Breakers belly into milk-green curls before collapsing in an unending thunderous boil. This is prime windsurfing territory, but both surfers and swimmers must be careful of the powerful undertow.

ACCOMMODATIONS & DINING   For an overnight stay in Cascais, try the unpretentious **Hotel Baía,** avenida Marginal, 2750 Lisboa (☎ 01/483-10-33). Its front rooms have small balconies with unobstructed views of the beach and bay, and on its roof is a covered pool. Even in summer, the rates aren't bad—16,500$ ($96) single and 19,500$ ($113) double, including breakfast—but the rest of the year they drop. Spring for an ocean view. American Express, Diners Club, MasterCard, and Visa are accepted.

At mealtime, check out the seafood restaurants on the streets bordering the nearby fish market. Veer past the very good but very pricey O Pescador on rua das Flores and find instead **O Batel,** Travessa das Flores 4 (☎ 01/483-02-15), facing the market. The *ementa turística* is 2,550$ ($15), but if you aren't too hungry, consider one of the cheaper main courses alone, like *arroz do mariscos.* The portions are substantial. It accepts MasterCard and Visa and is open Thursday to Tuesday noon to 3pm and 7 to 10:30pm.

SINTRA

An hour in **Sintra,** a place of myth and magic, has everyone agreeing with Lord Byron, who called this hill town a "glorious Eden." At every turn of the road is another battlement, spire, or watchtower. About 18 miles from Lisbon, the town swells regularly with day-trippers from the capital. Botanists thrill to some 90 species of unusual plants thriving in the Sintra hills. Romantics revel in Sintra's two marvelous palaces.

Three or four **trains** an hour make the run to Sintra from Lisbon's Estação Rossio. The unscenic trip takes 45 minutes and costs 185$ ($1.05) one-way. Despite its hilly situation, the walk from the station to the center of the town is fairly level and takes only about 15 minutes. A **taxi** costs 500$ ($2.90). The local **tourist office,** at praça da República 23 (☎ 01/923-11-57), is open daily 9am to 7pm (to 8pm in summer).

The **main square,** bordered by pastel shops and houses, is dominated by the huge conical twin chimneys of the **Paço Real** (☎ 01/923-00-85). The palace is open Thursday to Tuesday 10am to 1pm and 2 to 5pm. What survives today dates mainly from the 14th to the 16th centuries, with fragments from a Moorish fortress that was once on the site. It's largely baroque, with Gothic, Manueline, and Islamic flourishes. Most impressive are the decorative tilework, tapestries, gilded ceilings, and royal kitchen, positioned, logically enough, at the base of those two giant chimneys. Look too for the Sala das Pegas: Its ceiling is covered with depictions of chattering magpies, a king's sour take on the gossiping ladies of the court.

An uphill lane leading to **Seteais** becomes a narrow channel between walls with mottled skins of moss and lichen. Bars of sunlight pierce the canopy of oak and eucalyptus from time to time, and high iron gates permit glimpses of the villas they protect. Byron walked the halls of the **Palácio dos Seteais,** now a luxury hotel. From there, he could see the ocean and, looking still farther up, the golden cupolas of the **Palácio da Pena** (☎ 01/923-02-27), perched on a 1,300-foot mountaintop. It's an extraordinary piece of romantic architecture from 1839, when it was ordered built as a royal residence. Purists are offended by the palace's agglomeration of styles, not to mention its pink-and-yellow exterior. But Pena has nothing to do with aesthetics and everything to do with fantasy. A fanciful pastiche of Moorish, Gothic, and Manueline conceits, it also incorporates a cloister and chapel from the ruins of a 16th-century monastery. It's open Tuesday to Sunday 10am to 1pm and 2 to 5pm, with last entrance at 4:30pm.

Admission to both Sintra palaces is 200$ ($1.15) October to May and 600$ ($3.50) June to September.

ACCOMMODATIONS   If any place in Portugal deserves a splurge, it's Sintra, and I have just the place: The **Quinta das Sequoias,** Estrada de Monserrate, 2710 Sintra (☎ 01/924-38-21), is a country manor converted to a guesthouse of exceptional style. Surrounded by its own 40-acre forest preserve, it has a pool in the courtyard, a lounge with a billiard table, an honor bar, a TV, a VCR, and a selection of videos. Breakfast is served at a long table in a dining room with a massive fireplace. The six units, all with bathrooms, are decorated with considerable flair, including generous deployment of antique furnishings and objects. They're most affordable in winter at 16,000$ ($93), but aren't too steep in summer at 22,000$ ($128). American Express, Diners Club, MasterCard, and Visa are accepted. Rates include breakfast and views of Pena Palace from almost every window. The infinitely gracious manager is fluent in English. Get the directions from Sintra when reserving (well in advance).

DINING   At the corner of praça and rua das Padarias is an unusual wedge-shaped wine shop that serves light meals of cheese, grilled sausages, crusty bread, and half bottles of the local pressings. **Lojo do Vinho** (no phone) is open daily 9am to 9pm in winter and to midnight in summer. The set menu is a little steep at 1,850$ ($11), but smaller snacks and sandwiches cost as little as 250$ ($1.45). No credit cards are accepted.

If you want a full meal, walk up rua das Padarias to **Alcobaca** (☎ 01/923-16-51). Since there's barely room for 12 tables, conversation with your fellow diners is all but inevitable. The *ementa turística* is 1,500$ ($9), and *arroz do mariscos* for two, a soupy rice concoction with baby clams and bits of crab, is only 3,000$ ($17). Half a roast chicken is 850$ ($4.95). The owner speaks English and takes a motherly interest in your well-being. It's open daily noon to 4pm and 7 to 10:30pm and accepts MasterCard and Visa.

For similar food, admittedly more expensive but in a more atmospheric setting, head up the nearby cross street to **O Chico,** Arcos do Teixeira 8 (☎ 01/923-15-26). At ground floor, massive black casks serve as both bar and concealment for the tiny kitchen. The beams are hung with water jugs and *cataplanas,* a traditional cooking vessel. Outside is a row of resin tables and upstairs a dining room. The *ementa turística* is 3,200$ ($19), and main courses go from 1,500$ to 2,400$ ($9 to $14). It's open daily noon to 4:30pm and 7:30 to 10:30pm and accepts American Express, Master-Card, and Visa.

QUELUZ

Just 9 miles from Lisbon, the frosted-pink **Queluz Palace** (☎ 01/435-00-39) is Portugal's rococo rendition of Versailles. The Sun King would've loved it. Built in 1747, it had been a hunting lodge for 200 years before being transformed into a royal residence. Most notable are the Throne Room, Queen's Dressing Room, Don Quixote Chamber, and Music Salon. They're fitted with splendid examples of Arraiolo carpets from the Alentejo region, Italian glassware and marble, Dutch tiles, Austrian porcelain, and Chinese screens. One wing serves as a guesthouse for state visitors, who've included Elizabeth II and former President Reagan. The manicured gardens are a fragrant as well as visual delight. The palace is open Wednesday to Monday 10am to 1pm and 2 to 5pm. Admission from October to May is 200$ ($1.15); from June to September, 470$ ($2.75); free Sunday morning and for age 11 and under.

Trains from Estação Rossio stop at Queluz–Belas on the Lisboa–Sintra route, so it's possible to do both Sintra and Queluz in a long day trip. There are three or four departures an hour during the day; the one-way fare is 155$ (90¢). The walk to the palace takes about 20 minutes, following signs after turning left from the station. Taxis are available.

DINING   A stunning restaurant, **Cozinha Velha** (☎ 01/435-02-32), has been installed in the palace's royal kitchen, with its mammoth fireplace and beamed ceiling. Its cuisine and service are equal to the setting. Sadly, as a meal for two easily breeches 14,000$ ($81), it can't be described as a budget choice. But you may want to splurge after seeing all that grandeur. It's open daily noon to 3pm and 7:30 to 10pm and accepts American Express, Diners Club, MasterCard, and Visa.

London, Bath & Environs

by Richard Jones

London is swinging once again, attracting more visitors than any other European city. Here you'll find world-class museums, great shopping, historic pageantry, unparalleled theater, cutting-edge fashion, and super nightlife. *The* place to be, London is bursting with energy and vitality in every area—from Britpop to Brit film.

Many people who come hoping to see some vestiges of London's history are disappointed when they see this modern city, where often the only things marking the past are little blue plaques commemorating former residences. Don't despair: The past is alive and well here—you just have to know how to look for it. With some notable exceptions, history is more evident in London's institutions than in its buildings. Though less pronounced than it once was, the British class system stubbornly endures. The scandal-ridden royals aren't just a tourist attraction—they head a very real aristocracy that continues to wield wealth and power. And despite its declining relevance in today's world, Royal London's pomp and pageantry survive with daily ceremonies like the Changing of the Guard at Buckingham Palace and the Ceremony of the Keys at the Tower of London.

So check out all the top sights, explore the narrow alleys of The City, enjoy lunch in a local pub, attend a free concert in a church, and party the night away in a hot club. And be sure to strike up a conversation or two with the locals.

REQUIRED DOCUMENTS   Citizens of the United States, Canada, Australia, and New Zealand need only a valid passport to enter the United Kingdom.

OTHER FROMMER'S TITLES   For more on London, see *Frommer's London; Frommer's London from $70 a Day; Frommer's Irreverent Guide to London; Frommer's Memorable Walks in London; Frommer's England; Frommer's England from $60 a Day; Frommer's Gay & Lesbian Europe; Frommer's Complete Hostel Vacation Guide to England, Wales & Scotland;* or *Frommer's Europe.*

1 London Deals & Discounts

SPECIAL DISCOUNTS

FOR STUDENTS   Students in England enjoy discounts on travel, on theater and museum tickets, and at some nightspots. The **International**

Budget Bests

Not only does London offer many of the world's "bests," but most of these attractions are either free or cost less than comparable sights elsewhere. Most of London's **museums** are free, as are the main sections of major attractions like **Westminster Abbey** and the **Houses of Parliament.** The **Changing of the Guard** at Buckingham Palace is also free, along with the often-acerbic diatribes delivered at **Speakers' Corner** every Sunday in Hyde Park. **Theater tickets** here are still cheaper than those to comparable New York City productions, and **cheap seats** are regularly available at the opera, ballet, and symphony.

Student Identity Card (ISIC) is the most readily accepted proof of status. You should buy this card before you leave home, but if you've arrived without one and are a good enough talker (or are carrying a registrar-stamped and -signed copy of your current school transcript), you can obtain one for about £5 ($8) at **S. T. A. Travel,** 86 Old Brompton Rd., SW7 (☎ **0171/361-6262;** Tube: South Kensington). The office is open Monday to Thursday 9:30am to 6pm, Friday 10am to 6pm, and Saturday 10am to 4pm. S. T. A. has several other offices in London and offers many special travel discounts, including airfares.

Another organization offering cheap intra-European flights is **Campus Travel,** 52 Grosvenor Gardens, SW1 (☎ **0171/730-3402;** fax 0171/730-6893).

FOR SENIORS　　In Britain, senior citizen usually means a woman at least 60 or a man at least 65. Seniors often receive the same discounts as students. Unfortunately for visitors, some discounts are available only to seniors who are also British subjects. More often, however, your passport or other proof of age will also be your passport to cutting costs.

2　Essentials

ARRIVING

BY PLANE　　London is served by three major airports: Heathrow, Gatwick, and Stansted. All have good **public transport links to central London.** For rail information, call ☎ **0171/222-1234.**

Heathrow: The cheapest route from Heathrow is by **Underground** or subway ("the tube"), the 15-mile journey taking about 45 minutes and costing £3.30 ($5) to any downtown station (for discounts, see "Getting Around," below). Service is convenient, as the Underground platforms are directly below the airport terminals. But Heathrow is big, and even those with light luggage are advised to use one of the free baggage carts for the long walk to the train. Trains operate from 6am to midnight, departing every 5 minutes at peak times and every 9 minutes at off-peak hours and weekends. A speedier though more expensive link is provided by the **Heathrow Express** (☎ **0845/600-1515**), taking 15 minutes from the airport to Paddington Station and costing £5 ($8). A **shuttle bus** operates to central hotels, charging £10 ($16).

Gatwick: Convenient nonstop **trains** make the 25-mile trek from Gatwick to Victoria Station in about 30 minutes, costing £9.50 ($15). The station is just below the airport, and trains depart every 15 minutes 6am to 10pm (hourly, on the hour, at other times). A **shuttle bus** operates to central London, charging £16 ($26).

Stansted: The **Stansted Skytrain** makes the 40-minute journey from the airport, 30 miles northeast of London, to Liverpool Street Station for £10.40 ($17). Trains

What Things Cost in London	U.S. $
Taxi from Heathrow Airport to central London	73.35
Underground from Heathrow Airport to central London	5.35
Local telephone call	.15
Double room at the Dorchester Hotel (deluxe)	410.00
Double room at Tophams Ebury Court (moderate)	184.00
Double room at the Oakley Hotel (budget)	67.20
Lunch for one at Pollo (moderate)	14.00
Lunch for one at most pubs (budget)	8.55
Dinner for one, without wine, at the English House (deluxe)	52.65
Dinner for one, without wine, at Bahn Thai (moderate)	25.00
Dinner for one, without wine, at Khan's (budget)	12.80
Pint of beer	3.20
Coca-Cola in a restaurant	1.65
Cup of coffee	1.20
Roll of ASA 100 film, 36 exposures	8.00
Admission to the British Museum	Free
Movie ticket	7.20–12.80
Cheapest West End theater ticket	11.20

depart Monday to Friday every half hour 5:30am to 11pm, Saturday 6:30am to 11pm, and Sunday 7am to 11pm.

BY TRAIN Trains from Paris arrive at **Waterloo Station** and **Victoria Station,** visitors from Amsterdam are deposited at **Liverpool Street Station,** and arrivals from Edinburgh pull into **King's Cross Station.** All four are well connected to the city's extensive bus and Underground network. The stations contain London Transport Information Centres, luggage lockers, phones, restaurants, and pubs.

VISITOR INFORMATION

The **London Tourist Board (LTB)** maintains several Information Centres. Its staff distributes city maps, answers questions, and, in a pinch, can help you find accommodations. When entering England via Heathrow, visit the LTB in the arrivals terminal before making your journey into the city; it's open daily 9am to 6pm. Those arriving via Gatwick or by train from Paris can visit the well-staffed office in Victoria Station's forecourt. The office is open Easter to October, daily 9am to 8pm; the rest of the year, Monday to Saturday 9am to 7pm and Sunday 9am to 5pm.

Other LTB Information Centres are in Harrods and Selfridges department stores, both open year-round during store hours, and at the Tower of London, open Easter to October, daily 10am to 6pm. **Visitorcall** (☎ **0839/123-456**) is a recorded service from LTB with 30 lines providing daily information on various topics, including "What's On This Week," "Changing of the Guard," and "Museums." Though cheaper after 6pm, this service is charged at premium rates and you're much better off purchasing a listings magazine like *Time Out* or *What's On and Where to Go in London* or even phoning the attraction directly.

The **Britain Visitor Centre,** 1 Regent St., W1, just steps from Piccadilly Circus, provides information on all of Britain. It's open Monday to Friday 9am to 6:30pm, Saturday 9am to 5pm, and Sunday 10am to 4pm. Hours are usually slightly reduced in winter.

For information on Scotland, dial ☎ **0171/930-8661;** for Wales, dial ☎ **0171/409-0969;** for all of Ireland, dial ☎ **0171/839-8417.**

For information about travel by bus, tube, or British Rail, visit a **London Transport Information Centre,** located in the major train stations, or call the London Regional Transport Travel Information Service at ☎ **0171/222-1234,** open 24 hours.

NEIGHBORHOOD NOTES

London is often referred to as a "city of villages" that sprang up around the square mile of the original walled Roman city. Most of the walls have long since disappeared, but the political autonomy of **The City** of London still separates it from the surrounding areas. The City has always been London's financial center, and it's crammed with tiny streets and a sense of history befitting its ancient beginnings. The **West End** is the general name of a large, imprecise area west of The City, to Hyde Park. The West End encompasses the Houses of Parliament, Buckingham Palace, and the nation's densest cluster of shops, restaurants, and theaters. You'll get to know this area well.

Beyond the West End, south of Hyde Park, are the fashionable residential areas of **South Kensington** and **Chelsea.** Take a close look at these neighborhoods—you've probably never seen so many beautiful city buildings you'd like to own. Hugging The City's eastern side is one of London's poorest areas. Traditionally, the **East End** was undesirable because both the prevailing winds and the flow of the Thames move from west to east. In the plague-ridden days before sewers, life on the "wrong" side of The City was dangerous indeed. Today the East End is still home to poorer immigrants (mostly from the Indian subcontinent) but is seeing a gentrification as well.

The borough of **Southwark,** across the river from The City on the south bank of the Thames, became famous as London's entertainment quarter during Elizabethan times, when theaters and brothels were banned from The City. Today the area is home to the reconstruction of Shakespeare's Globe Theatre and the Tate Galleries modern art collection. A pedestrian footbridge will soon connect Southwark with The City of London.

Note: Throughout this chapter street addresses are followed by designations like SW1 and EC1. These are the **postal areas.** The original post office was at St. Martin-le-Grand, in The City, so the postal districts are related to where they lie geographically from there. For example, Victoria is SW1 since it's the first area southwest of St. Martin-le-Grand; Covent Garden is west (west central) and so its postal area is WC1 or WC2; Liverpool Street is east of there and so its postal area is EC1.

GETTING AROUND

London can be a difficult city to negotiate. It seems as though no two streets run parallel, and even locals regularly consult maps, but in the winding streets of The City and in the tourist area of the West End there's no better way to go than on foot. Be warned that cars have the right-of-way over pedestrians; take care even when the light seems to be in your favor.

BY UNDERGROUND & BUS   Commuters constantly complain about it, but visitors find London's public transport network fast and efficient. Underground stations are abundant, and above ground you can catch one of the famous red double-decker buses. Both the Underground and the buses are operated by **London Transport** (☎ **0171/222-1234**), which sets fares based on a zone system—you pay for each zone

A Map Note

See the inside front cover of this guide for a London Underground map.

you cross. For most tube trips, you'll travel in the same zone and the fare will be £1.30 ($2.10) adults or 60p (97¢) children.

To save time at ticket windows or machines, you can buy a carnet (booklet) of 10 tickets for use anywhere in Zone 1, costing £10 ($16) adults or £5 ($8) ages 5 to 15. A **1-day Travelcard** is good for unlimited transport in two zones on the bus and tube after 9:30am Monday to Friday and anytime weekends and public holidays; it costs £3.50 ($6) adults and £1.80 ($2.95) ages 5 to 15. **Weekly Travelcards** valid in Zone 1 are £13 ($21) adults and £5.20 ($8) ages 5 to 15, and £16.60 ($27) and £5.50 ($9), respectively, for both Zones 1 and 2. Children 4 and under always ride free. You'll need to present a photo to buy the weekly ticket; photo booths are in tube stations—four passport-size photographs cost about £2.50 ($4.10).

The tube runs every few minutes Monday to Saturday about 5:30am to midnight (7:30am to 11pm Sunday). You can buy tickets from the station ticket window or an adjacent coin-operated machine. Hold on to your ticket throughout your ride; you'll need it to exit. Pick up a handy tube map, distributed free at station ticket windows. To calculate your journey time, allow 3 minutes for each station passed en route.

Scheduled for completion in late 1999 or early 2000, the Jubilee Underground line will be extended south of the river as well as into the East End, thus providing much-needed fast access from central London to both Greenwich and Docklands.

Though it looked as if the red double-deckers were going to be retired, they aren't, so you can still enjoy the view from the top of the bus. Take a seat, either upstairs or down, and wait for the conductor to collect your fare. On the newer type of bus, pay the driver as you enter and exit through the rear doors. The bus fare in central London's Zone 1 is 90p ($1.45) adults or 40p (65¢) children. **One-day bus passes** are available for £2 ($3.25) adults or £1 ($1.65) children; **weekly passes** are £6.60 ($11) adults or £4 ($7) children for one zone and £8.80 ($14) adults or £5.20 ($8) children for three zones. The first you can use before 9:30am, but it's not valid on N-prefixed night buses; the second grants unlimited use day or night.

Many visitors shy away from buses because their routes can be confusing. Get a free bus map from the tourist office or just ask any conductor about the route and then take advantage of a "top deck" sightseeing adventure. Like the tube, regular bus service also stops after midnight, sometimes making it difficult to get back to your hotel. At night, buses have different routes and different numbers from their daytime counterparts. Service is not frequent either; if you've just missed your night bus, expect a long wait for the next one or hunt down a minicab (see below). The central London night-bus terminus is Trafalgar Square.

BY TAXI For three or four people traveling a short distance, cabs can make economic sense. The fare begins at £1.40 ($2.30), then climbs at a fast clip. There's an extra charge of 40p (65¢) per person, 10p (15¢) per large piece of luggage, and 40p (65¢) on weekends and after midnight. But the thrill of viewing London's famous monuments from the roomy back seat of a taxi is almost enough to get your eye off the meter. If you know in advance you'll be needing a cab, you can order one by calling ☎ 0171/286-0286, but you'll pay more for it.

Minicabs are meterless cars driven by entrepreneurs with licenses. Technically, these taxis aren't allowed to cruise for fares but must operate from sidewalk offices—many of which are centered around Leicester Square. Minicabs are handy at night after the

Networks & Resources

STUDENTS The **University of London,** just north and east of Bloomsbury's Russell Square, is the city's largest school. It has a majority of commuter students and doesn't really have a campus. Bloomsbury unfortunately lacks the verve and bustle of a college community, but the area pubs and inexpensive restaurants serve as frequent student hangouts.

The **University of London Student Union (ULU),** Malet Street, WC1 (☎ 0171/580-9551; Tube: Goodge St.), caters to over 55,000 students and may be the largest of its kind. In addition to a gym and fitness center, the building has several shops, two restaurants, two banks, a ticket-booking agency, and an S. T. A. travel office. Concerts and dances are regularly scheduled here. Stop by or phone for information on university activities.

GAYS & LESBIANS There's a large gay community here, supported by a plethora of publications, shops, pubs, nightclubs, cafes, and special services. *Capital Gay* is the premier "alternative" paper. Written by and for both men and women, this free weekly features previews, reviews, news, and events listings. *The Pink Paper* is nationally distributed and also free. Both are available at gay bars, bookstores, and cafes. At least two monthlies are regularly available around town: *Gay Times* is oriented toward men and is known for both news and features; *HIM* supplements its high-quality reporting with glossy photos. The popular listings magazine *Time Out* also provides excellent coverage.

The **Lesbian and Gay Switchboard** (☎ 0171/837-7324) offers information, advice, counseling, and a free accommodations agency. The line is open 24 hours and always busy. The **Lesbian Line** (☎ 0171/251-6911) offers similar services to women only. Call Tuesday to Thursday 7 to 10pm and Monday and Friday 2 to 10pm. If you're looking for books and such, head to **Gay's the Word Bookshop** (see "Shopping," later in this chapter).

tube stops running and cabs suddenly become scarce. Always negotiate the fare beforehand. If you're approached by a lone driver on the street, a firm but polite "No, thank you" is called for. Only black cabs are allowed to pick up fares on the streets, and to get into any other vehicle that purports to be a taxi is dangerous.

BY BICYCLE Bike lanes are becoming more common here as the cycling lobby grows more vociferous. Cycling can be a quick and convenient way to get around London's increasingly congested roads, though take care of unyielding motorists. If you want to rent a bike, try **On Your Bike,** 52–54 Tooley St., SE1 (☎ 0171/378-6669; Tube: London Bridge). Bikes rent from £12 to £15 ($20 to $24) per day, and you'll have to pay a deposit equal to the value of the bike. Weekly rental prices are negotiable. The shop is open Monday to Friday 9am to 6pm and Saturday 9:30am to 5:30pm (in summer, also Sunday 11am to 4pm). **Bikepark,** 14½ Stukeley St., WC2 (☎ 0171/430-0083; Tube: Covent Garden), is more centrally located and rents a variety of bikes for £10 to £15 ($16 to $24) per day. It requires a £200 ($320) deposit and is open Monday to Friday 7:30am to 7:30pm, Saturday 10am to 6pm, and Sunday 10:30am to 4pm (summer only). It's also at 250 King's Rd., SW3 (☎ 0171/565-0777; Tube: Sloane Square).

BY RENTAL CAR It's not smart to keep a car here, and security measures have closed many streets in The City. However, if you're planning excursions, a rental is worth looking into. To secure the lowest rates, you should reserve and pay before you leave home (see chapter 2). A tiny Peugeot with manual transmission will cost about $193 per week. If you leave it until you arrive in England, expect to pay £26 to £45 ($42 to $73) per day, depending on the season. The least expensive rentals I've found are from **Practical Rental,** 111 Bartholomew Rd., NW5 (☎ **0171/284-0199**). **Avis** (☎ **0181/848-8733**) and **Budget** (☎ **0800/626-063**) have several branches throughout the city. Gasoline (petrol) costs about £3 ($4.80) per Imperial gallon (about $4 per U.S. gallon).

FAST FACTS: London

American Express   There are several offices, including 6 Haymarket, SW1 (☎ 0171/930-4411; Tube: Charing Cross), near Trafalgar Square. It's open Monday to Friday 9am to 5:30pm and Saturday 9am to noon.

Baby-sitters   If your request for a recommendation from a member of your hotel staff is answered with a blank stare, phone **Childminders** (☎ 0171/935-3000).

Banks   Most banks are open Monday to Friday 9:30am to 3:30pm, but many stay open to 5pm and some are open Saturday 9:30am to noon. Banks generally offer the best exchange rates, but American Express and Thomas Cook are competitive and don't charge a commission for cashing traveler's checks, no matter the brand. A convenient **Thomas Cook** office is at 1 Woburn Place, Russell Square, WC1 (☎ 0171/837-5275; Tube: Russell Square), open Monday to Friday 8am to 5pm and Saturday 9am to noon. Places with the longest hours (sometimes open all night) offer the worst rates. Beware of Chequepoint and other high-commission bureaux de change.

Business Hours   Stores are usually open Monday to Saturday 10am to 6pm and Sunday noon to 6pm. Most also stay open at least an extra hour 1 night during the week. Knightsbridge shops usually remain open to 7pm on Wednesday, while West End stores are traditionally open late on Thursday. Some shops around Covent Garden stay open to 7 or 8pm nightly. Though major stores open on Sunday, many smaller stores still close on Sunday.

Currency   The basic unit of currency is the **pound sterling (£),** divided into 100 **pence (p).** There are 1p, 2p, 10p, 20p, 50p, £1, and £2 coins; banknotes are issued in £5, £10, £20, and £50.

Drugstores   Boots, 75 Queensway, W2 (☎ 0171/229-1183; Tube: Bayswater), is open Monday to Saturday 9am to 10pm and Sunday noon to 5pm.

Embassies & High Commissions   The Embassy of the **United States,** 24 Grosvenor Sq., W1 (☎ 0171/499-9000; Tube: Bond St.), doesn't accept visitors—all inquiries must be made by mail or phone. The High Commission of **Canada,** Macdonald House, 1 Grosvenor Sq., W1 (☎ 0171/258-6600; Tube: Bond St.), is open Monday to Friday 8 to 11am. The High Commission of **Australia** is in Australia House, on the Strand, WC2 (☎ 0171/379-4334; Tube: Charing Cross or Temple), open Monday to Friday 9am to 1pm. The High Commission of **New Zealand** is in New Zealand House, 80 Haymarket, SW1 (☎ 0171/930-8422; fax 0171/839-4580; Tube: Piccadilly), open Monday to Friday 9am to 5pm.

The British Pound

At this writing, $1 = 61p (or £1 = $1.63), and this was the rate of exchange used to calculate the dollar values given in this chapter (rounded to the nearest dollar if more than $5).

Note: Exchange rates fluctuate from time to time and may not be the same when you travel to Britain.

£	U.S.$	£	U.S.$	£	U.S.$
.01	.02	2	3.30	10	17.00
.02	.03	3	4.90	15	24.50
.10	.16	4	6.60	20	32.60
.20	.32	5	8.00	25	40.80
.25	.40	6	9.80	30	48.90
.50	.80	7	11.50	40	66.00
.75	1.20	8	13.10	50	81.50
1.00	1.60	9	14.70	60	97.80

Emergencies   **Police, fire,** and **ambulance** services can be reached by dialing ☎ **999.** No money is required.

Holidays   Most businesses are closed New Year's Day, Good Friday, Easter Monday, the first Monday in May, and December 25 and 26. In addition, many stores close on bank holidays, which are scattered throughout the year. There's no uniform policy for museums, restaurants, and attractions with regard to holidays. To avoid disappointment, always phone before setting out.

Mail   Post offices are plentiful and normally open Monday to Friday 9am to 5pm and Saturday 9am to noon. The **Main Post Office,** 24 William IV St., Trafalgar Square, WC2 (☎ **0171/930-9580;** Tube: Charing Cross), is open Monday to Saturday 8am to 8pm.

Police   In an emergency, dial ☎ **999** from any phone; no money is needed. At other times, dial the operator at ☎ **100** and ask to be connected with the police.

Tax   Unlike in the United States, where tax is tacked on at the register, in England a 17.5% **value-added tax (VAT)** is figured into the price of most items. Foreign visitors can reclaim the VAT for major purchases. See "Shopping," later in this chapter, or ask at stores for details.

Telephone   There are two kinds of **pay phone.** The first accepts coins and the other operates with a phonecard, available from newsstands in £1, £2, £4, £10, and £20 denominations. The minimum cost of a **local call** is 10p (16¢) for the first 2 minutes (peak hours). You can deposit up to four coins at a time, but

Country & City Codes

The **country code** for the United Kingdom is **44.** There are two London **city codes: 171** and **181;** use these codes when you're calling from outside the United Kingdom. If you're within the United Kingdom but not in London, use **0171** or **0181.** If you're calling within London, simply leave off the code and dial only the seven-digit number.

phones don't make change, so unless you're calling long distance, use 10p coins only. **Phonecard** phones automatically deduct the price of your call from the card, and these cards are especially handy if you want to call abroad. Some large hotels and touristy street corners also have phones that accept major credit cards. Lift the handle and follow the instructions on the screen.

To reach the **local operator,** dial ☎ **100.** London **information** ("directory enquiries") can be reached by dialing ☎ **192,** and there's a charge from some phones.

To make an **international call,** dial ☎ **155** to reach the international operator. To dial direct, dial **00,** then your country code (Australia, 61; New Zealand, 64; South Africa, 27; United States, 1), then the local number. You can phone home by dialing a local toll-free number in London and paying with your calling card. To phone Australia, dial ☎ 0800/89-0061; for New Zealand, ☎ 0800/89-0064; for South Africa, ☎ 0800/89-0027; and for the United States, ☎ 0800/89-0011 (AT&T), 0800/89-0222 (MCI), or 0800/89-0877 (Sprint).

Tipping   Most (but not all) restaurants automatically add a discretionary service charge. The restaurant's policy will be written on the menu. Where a service charge isn't included, a 10% to 15% tip is customary. Taxi drivers also expect 10% to 15% of the fare. Note that tipping is rare in pubs.

3 Accommodations You Can Afford

The bed-and-breakfast is one of England's greatest traditions. Morning menus differ but usually include cereal, eggs, bacon or sausage, toast, and all the coffee or tea you can drink. The bad news is that, in general, London's budget hotels aren't as nice or as cheap as those on the Continent. The rooms are uniformly small and wear is often evident. However, you'll find many affordable rooms provided in family homes. The advantage is affordability; the disadvantage is that you'll be 20 or so minutes outside central London. If you're interested, try **At Home in London,** 70 Black Lion Lane, W6 9BE (☎ **0181/748-1943;** fax 0181/748-2701; E-mail: athomeinlondon@ compuserve.com), or **London Homestead Services,** Coombe Wood Road, Kingston-upon-Thames, KT2 7JY (☎ **0181/949-4455;** fax 0181/549-5492). Prices are £18 to £35 ($29 to $57) for a double with a bath, including breakfast. Both accept Master-Card and Visa. Contact them about a month before you leave.

From early July to late September (and sometimes during Christmas and Easter), dozens of dorms open their doors to visitors. The rooms are almost all uniformly spartan, and some residence halls offer only singles, but they're inexpensive and centrally located. Try to reserve a space months in advance. The **King's Campus Vacation Bureau** (☎ **0171/928-3777;** fax 0171/928-5777; E-mail: vac.bureau@ kcl.ac.uk), handles bookings for several University of London residence halls.

Note: You can find most of the lodging choices below plotted on the map included in "Seeing the Sights," later in this chapter.

Accommodations Tips

Here are a few things to keep in mind when renting a room in London: Though beds are made up daily, sheets aren't usually changed during a stay of less than a week. If you need new bedding, request it. And remember that even local phone calls made from your room can be deathly expensive—inquire about the rate before dialing.

IN BAYSWATER & PADDINGTON

Bayswater runs along Hyde Park's northern edge and encompasses Paddington Station. It's a densely packed residential community, populated by a large number of Indians and Pakistanis. It's also jammed with budget hotels. Bayswater's proximity to the park, good restaurants (especially along Queensway and Westbourne Grove), and transport links to the West End make it a desirable place to locate. The Central and District Underground lines run to Bayswater and Paddington stations, while bus nos. 12, 88, and 289 travel the length of Bayswater Road.

✪ **Dean Court Hotel.** 57 Inverness Terrace (1 block from Queensway), London W2. ☎ **0171/229-2961** or 0171/229-9982. Fax 0171/727-1190. 30 units, none with bathroom; 40 beds in multishare rms, none with bathroom. £42 ($68) double; £45 ($73) twin; £60 ($98) triple; £14 ($23) per person in multishare per night, £75–£79 ($122–$129) per week. Rates include English breakfast. MC, V. Tube: Bayswater or Queensway.

Brightly decorated rooms (some with antique armoires), big breakfasts, a capable management, and an exceptionally kind budget philosophy are all hallmarks of this top hotel. Most rooms have high ceilings and single beds and are equipped with hair dryers. Multishare rooms rarely have more than four people sharing. The hotel is on a quiet Bayswater street.

Dolphin Hotel. 34 Norfolk Sq., London W2. ☎ **0171/402-4943.** 30 units, 10 with bathroom. TV. £35 ($57) single without bathroom; £46 ($75) double without bathroom, £58 ($95) double with bathroom; £63 ($103) triple with bathroom. Rates include continental breakfast. English breakfast £3 ($4.90). AE, DC, MC, V. Tube: Paddington.

Norfolk Square is a budget hotel–packed horseshoe around a park just steps south of Paddington Station. There are too many hotels with too few distinguishing marks to mention them all, but the Dolphin is one of the better choices. In-room refrigerators, coffeemakers, and (sometimes) phones help it stand out. Its recently redecorated rooms are typical of the square and a good bet. Breakfast—whether continental or English—is served in your room.

Hyde Park House. 48 St. Petersburgh Place, London W2. ☎ **0171/229-1687.** 12 units, 1 with bathroom. TV. £27 ($44) single; £40 ($65) double without bathroom; £65 ($106) triple with bathroom. Rates include continental breakfast. No credit cards. Tube: Bayswater; then turn left onto Moscow Rd. and left again at the church.

Announced by an awning in the middle of a block of row houses, this family-run B&B has quilts on the beds and a refrigerator and tea-/coffeemaker in each room. The baths come with hair dryers, and the small rooms are in good condition. The rates include free use of the kitchen and unlimited attention from the family's friendly dogs.

Lords Hotel. 20–22 Leinster Sq., London W2. ☎ **0171/229-8877.** Fax 0171/229-8377. E-mail: lords@netcomuk.co.uk. 60 units, all with bathroom. A/C TV TEL. £42 ($68) single; £56 ($91) double; £68 ($111) triple. Rates include continental breakfast. AE, DC, MC, V. Tube: Bayswater; then turn left onto Moscow Rd. and right at the Russian Orthodox church (Ilchester Gardens); Lords is 2 blocks up on your left.

This well-run place offers basic rooms that are both clean and neat. Some are equipped with TVs and radios, and a few have balconies—all at no extra charge. The hotel caters to people of all ages, but the basement bar, which stays open late, attracts a lively young crowd.

IN VICTORIA

Victoria Station dominates the area, separating pricey Belgravia on its northwest from more accessible Pimlico to the southeast. If you're shopping around, note that

Getting the Best Deal on Accommodations

- Take advantage of off-season rates. Prices tumble—sometimes by as much as 30%—and often there's room for further negotiation.
- Note that many hotels offer discounts if you stay a week or more.
- Remember to ask if the hotel has anything cheaper. Never accept a room until you're sure you've secured the lowest price.
- Request to see a room before renting it. Hoteliers are more likely to offer their nicest rooms to travelers who look before they buy.
- If booking in advance, insist on written confirmation of your booking, since there have been instances of travelers arriving to find their booking hasn't been honored.
- Be aware that the London Tourist Board operates a credit-card booking line (MasterCard and Visa) at ☎ **0171/932-2020** (fax 0171/932-2021). A £5 ($8) fee is charged.

although there are hundreds of hotels here, the majority aren't up to standard. Victoria is known not for its sights, shopping, or entertainment but for its proximity to busy Victoria Station.

Ivy House Hotel. 18 Hugh St., London SW1. ☎ **0171/834-9663.** Fax 0171/828-9823. 9 units, none with bathroom. TV. £25 ($41) single; £36 ($59) double; £50 ($82) triple; £65 ($106) quad. Rates include continental breakfast. AE, MC, V. Tube: Victoria.

Kishan and Joanne Shah, the young husband and wife who run the small Ivy House, began their careers as hoteliers in 1994 and live on the premises with their children. The three floors of modest rooms are freshly wallpapered and feature new curtains and bedspreads. Besides tea kettles and intercoms, the rooms feature few amenities.

Luna and Simone Hotels. 47–49 Belgrave Rd., London SW1. ☎ **0171/834-5897.** Fax 0171/828-2474. 35 units, 27 with bathroom. TV TEL. £30 ($49) single without bathroom; £44 ($72) double without bathroom, £60 ($98) double with bathroom. Rates include English breakfast. MC, V. Tube: Victoria.

This excellent family-run hotel is now better than ever. Well-decorated clean rooms and a hearty breakfast in a smoke-free dining room make this a fine value. All rooms have hair dryers and some have small balconies.

✪ **Melbourne House.** 79 Belgrave Rd., London SW1. ☎ **0171/828-3516.** Fax 0171/828-7120. 15 units, 13 with bathroom; 1 2-room family suite. TV TEL. *For Frommer's readers:* £30 ($49) single without bathroom, £50 ($82) single with bathroom; £70 ($114) double with bathroom; £95 ($155) triple with bathroom; £105 ($171) suite. Rates include English breakfast. No credit cards (except to hold room). Tube: Victoria.

Melbourne House, another of the rare breed of recommendable budget hotels on Belgrave Road, is run by the friendly John and Manuela. The couple totally renovated the hotel in 1997 and offer spacious, spotless rooms with tea- and coffee-making facilities and modern baths equipped with hair dryers.

✪ **Oak House.** 29 Hugh St., London SW1. ☎ **0171/834-7151.** 6 units, none with bathroom. TV. £35 ($57) double. No credit cards. Tube: Victoria.

One of my favorite hotels in this area is also one of the closest to Victoria Station, between Eccleston and Elizabeth bridges. Like the hotel, the sign outside stands out from those of the other B&Bs on the block. If their delightful accents don't convince you that the proprietors, the Symingtons, are Scottish, the tartan carpeting throughout will. All the rooms are doubles and very small. The conscientious owners have fitted all with orthopedic mattresses, hair dryers, electric shaver outlets, tea- and coffee-making facilities, a cutting board, a knife, and even a bottle opener. No reservations are accepted, so when you get to the station just cross your fingers and call.

Oxford House Hotel. 92–94 Cambridge St. (south of Belgrave Rd. near Gloucester St.), London SW1. ☎ **0171/834-6467.** 17 units, none with bathroom. £34–£36 ($55–$59) single; £44–£48 ($72–$78) double; £57–£61 ($93–$99) triple; £78–£84 ($127–$137) quad. Rates include English breakfast. Prices increase by £2 ($3.25) per person if you stay only 1 night. (Add 5% if you pay by credit card.) MC, V. Tube: Victoria.

This hotel is owned by interior designer Yanus Kader; his wife, Terri; and their two sons. The rooms are comfortable and pretty, featuring floral motifs and coordinated curtains. The beautiful dining area with an open kitchen will remind you of home.

IN CHELSEA & SOUTH KENSINGTON

The expensive residential areas of Chelsea and South Kensington offer little in the way of accommodations for budgeters. With a few exceptions, the cost of lodging here reflects location rather than quality. A room in adjacent South Kensington is only steps away from more than half a dozen top museums and the ritzy boutiques of Knightsbridge.

More House. 53 Cromwell Rd., London SW7. ☎ **0171/584-2040.** Fax 0171/581-5748. 55 units, none with bathroom. £25 ($40) single; £40 ($64) double; £46 ($74) triple. Rates include English breakfast. 10% discount for stays of 1 week or more. No credit cards. Closed Sept–June. Tube: Gloucester Rd.; then turn right and walk 5 short blocks along Cromwell Rd.

This Catholic-run dorm with an institutional feel is home to foreign students during the school year, but singles and doubles are rented to visitors of all faiths from June to August. The house is well located across from the Science Museum and is extremely functional. There's a refrigerator on every floor, plus microwaves, laundry facilities, and a licensed bar.

✪ **Oakley Hotel.** 73 Oakley St., London SW3. ☎ **0171/352-5599.** Fax 0171/727-1190. 13 units, 2 with bathroom. £32 ($52) single without bathroom; £44 ($73) double without bathroom; £56 ($91) double with bathroom; £63 ($103) triple without bathroom, £75 ($122) triple with bathroom; £14 ($23) per person multishare quad. Rates include English breakfast. AE, MC, V. Tube: Sloane Square; then take a long walk or the no. 11 or 22 bus down King's Rd. to Oakley St.

Well-decorated rooms and a fun atmosphere make this economical hotel a welcome oasis in tab-happy Chelsea. The local council of this chic neighborhood forbids a "hotel" sign, but a knock on the green door will be answered by a friendly Australian. Aside from singles and doubles, the hotel has several multishare rooms at great rates. You have free use of the kitchen. All rooms have hair dryers.

IN EARL'S COURT

Just west of exclusive Chelsea and Knightsbridge, Earl's Court has dozens of hotels; many are hostel types where the quality is often suspect. But the many superbudget accommodations means that cheap restaurants, pubs, and services are also nearby. The Earl's Court tube station is in the middle of Earl's Court Road, which, along with Old Brompton Road to the south, is the area's chief shopping strip.

Aaron House. 17 Courtfield Gardens, London SW5. ☎ **0171/370-3991.** Fax 0171/373-2303. 23 units, 13 with bathroom. TV. £35 ($57) single without bathroom, £45 ($73) single with bathroom; £48 ($78) double without bathroom, £58 ($95) double with bathroom; £72 ($117) triple with bathroom. Rates include continental breakfast. MC, V. Tube: Earl's Court; then walk about 3 blocks east, on the west side of Courtfield Gardens.

Aaron House is perhaps the nicest budget hotel in Earl's Court, which isn't saying much given the low quality of the competition. The front rooms, all with bath, are particularly large and overlook a peaceful Victorian square. Every room has tea- and coffee-making facilities.

Hotel Boka. 33–35 Eardley Crescent, London SW5. ☎ **0171/370-1388.** 52 units, 10 with shower only. £24 ($39) single without shower, £29 ($47) single with shower only; £33 ($54) double without shower, £41 ($67) double with shower only; £14 ($23) per person multishare rm. Rates include English breakfast. Discount for stays longer than 1 night. AE, MC, V. Tube: Earl's Court; take the Warwick Rd. exit, cross the street, and turn left onto Eardley Crescent (look for the bright blue tiled columns).

The best thing about the Boka is its great location, at the center of an architecturally handsome Victorian crescent. The accommodations here are standard white-walled rooms, where TVs can be rented for £1 ($1.60) per night.

Manor Hotel. 23 Nevern Place, London SW5. ☎ **0171/370-6018.** Fax 0171/370-6018. 27 units, 11 with bathroom. TV TEL. £30 ($49) single without bathroom, £40 ($65) single with bathroom; £45 ($73) double without bathroom, £60 ($98) double with bathroom; £58 ($95) triple without bathroom, £80 ($130) triple with bathroom. Rates include continental breakfast. Discount for stays of 1 week or more. MC, V. Tube: Earl's Court.

The owners of the Manor Hotel have replaced the threadbare carpets so that they now coordinate with the new wallpaper. The manor is still no palace, but it's thoroughly recommendable and only 2 minutes from the Earl's Court Underground station.

Mowbray Court Hotel. 28–32 Penywern Rd., London SW5. ☎ **0171/373-8285.** Fax 0171/370-5693. 82 units, 60 with bathroom. TV TEL. £45 ($73) single without bathroom, £50 ($82) single with bathroom; £55 ($90) double without bathroom, £60 ($98) double with bathroom; £64 ($104) triple without bathroom, £72 ($117) triple with bathroom; £76 ($124) quad without bathroom, £85 ($139) quad with bathroom. Rates include continental breakfast. AE, DC, MC, V. Tube: Earl's Court.

A few minutes' walk from the Earl's Court Underground station on a reasonably quiet side street, this hotel offers comfortable rooms outfitted with safes and even trouser presses. Dry-cleaning service is available.

IN BLOOMSBURY

Bloomsbury's proximity to the West End in general, and to Soho in particular, has long made it desirable for visitors. The area derives energy from its two most important institutions: the University of London and the British Museum. Gower Street's budget hotels are some of the city's most popular. Most of the B&Bs lining this street are so similar to each other that only their addresses distinguish them. The stairs are steep, the rooms basic (almost none with bath), and the prices fairly uniform. Special touches and extra-friendly management set a few apart.

✪ **Arran House Hotel.** 77 Gower St., London WC1. ☎ **0171/636-2186.** Fax 0171/436-5328. 28 units, 4 with shower only, 9 with bathroom. TV TEL. £35 ($57) single without bathroom, £46 ($75) single with bathroom; £47 ($77) double without bathroom, £55 ($90) double with shower only, £65 ($106) double with bathroom. Rates include English breakfast. MC, V. Tube: Goodge St.

The Arran House stands out on the block because of its exceptionally hospitable owner, John Richards, who has ensured that even guests in the front rooms get a quiet night's sleep (he soundproofed the windows). In addition to laundry and tea- and coffee-making facilities, the hotel offers light meals.

Garth Hotel. 69 Gower St., London WC1. ☎ **0171/636-5761.** Fax 0171/637-4854. 17 units, 11 with shower only, 1 with bathroom. TV. £35 ($57) single without bathroom, £40 ($65) single with bathroom; £48 ($78) double without bathroom, £55 ($90) double with shower only. Rates include English or Japanese breakfast. AE, MC, V. Tube: Euston Square or Goodge St.

The Japanese-run Garth is an unlikely phenomenon on Gower Street, a strip whose hotels have come to epitomize the classic English-style B&B. The Garth suffers from the limitations that afflict other B&Bs on the block: small rooms, street noise, and steep stairs; however, this place is cleaner. You can choose from an English-style breakfast or a traditional Japanese morning meal, including rice, seaweed, and a raw egg.

Hotel Cavendish. 75 Gower St., London WC1. ☎ **0171/636-9079.** Fax 0171/580-3609. 20 units, none with bathroom. £28–£32 ($45–$51) single; £36–£48 ($59–$72) double. Rates include English breakfast. AE, MC, V. Tube: Euston Square or Goodge St.

This is a nicely furnished, clean, and cozy home run by Mrs. Phillips. The cheaper doubles are slightly smaller than the more expensive ones. The rooms have tea-making facilities. You have use of a TV lounge, and best of all, there's a shady walled garden for those sunny summer days.

Jesmond Hotel. 63 Gower St., London WC1. ☎ **0171/636-3199.** Fax 0171/636-3199. 16 units, 3 with bathroom. TV. £31 ($51) single without bathroom; £45 ($73) double without bathroom, £55 ($90) double with bathroom; £57 ($93) triple without bathroom, £67 ($109) triple with bathroom. Rates include English breakfast. MC, V. Tube: Euston Square or Goodge St.

The proprietors, Mr. and Mrs. Beynon, have been to the United States many times and are acutely aware of American habits and desires. All rooms have coffee- and tea-making facilities and hair dryers in the shared baths. The front rooms have double-glazed windows, minimizing any noise.

✪ **Ridgemont Hotel.** 65–67 Gower St., London WC1. ☎ **0171/636-1141.** Fax 0171/636-2558. 34 units, 8 with bathroom. TV. £30 ($48) single without bathroom, £40 ($65) single with bathroom; £44 ($72) double without bathroom, £55 ($90) double with bathroom; £57 ($93) triple without bathroom, £72 ($117) triple with bathroom; £68 ($111) quad without bathroom, £78 ($127) quad with bathroom. Rates include English breakfast. No credit cards. Tube: Goodge St.

Although it's priced just above our budget, the Ridgemont has a friendly atmosphere and warm-hearted Welsh proprietors, Royden and Gwen Rees, making it another good choice along the strip. The Reeses offer complimentary coffee and tea in their lounge.

A GAY & LESBIAN HOTEL

Philbeach Hotel. 30–31 Philbeach Gardens, London SW5. ☎ **0171/373-1244.** Fax 0171/244-0149. 40 units, 15 with bathroom. TV TEL. £45 ($72) single without bathroom, £50 ($80) single with bathroom; £55 ($88) double without bathroom, £70 ($104) double with bathroom. Rates include continental breakfast. AE, DC, MC, V. Tube: Earl's Court.

One of Europe's largest gay hotels, the Philbeach has standard budget-hotel rooms, a real garden, and a decent restaurant and bar. Located in a pretty Victorian town house, the hotel is open to both men and women.

IYHF HOSTELS

The **International Youth Hostel Federation (IYHF)** runs four hostels in central London (three are listed below). You have to have a membership card to stay at one, available for about £9.30 ($15) at any hostel. You can save about £1 ($1.60) per night by supplying your own sheets. For full coverage of hostels in the London area as well as throughout Great Britain, see *Frommer's Complete Hostel Vacation Guide to England, Wales & Scotland.*

✪ City of London Youth Hostel. 36 Carter Lane, London EC4. ☎ **0171/236-4965.** Fax 0171/236-7681. 199 beds. £20.50 ($33) per person under 18 in dorm with 1 or 2 beds, £24.50 ($33) per person over 18 in dorm with 1 or 2 beds; £19 ($31) per person under 18 in dorm with 3 or 4 beds, £22.50 ($37) per person over 18 in dorm with 3 or 4 beds; £17.90 ($29) per person under 18 in dorm with 5 to 8 beds, £21.30 ($35) per person over 18 in dorm with 5 to 8 beds; £17 ($28) per person under 18 in dorm with 15 beds, £19 ($31) per person over 18 in dorm with 15 beds. MC, V. Tube: Blackfriars (take exit 1 out of the station, walk along Queen Victoria St., taking second left onto St. Andrew's Hill, then right onto Carter Lane, hostel is immediately on left) or St. Paul's (take the Cathedral exit, go left, then turn right, make your way toward the front steps of the cathedral, and follow Dean's Court, a small street, to the corner of Carter Lane).

This top pick, in a wonderfully restored building that was once a school for choirboys, boasts a good number of singles, and most of the multishares have no more than four beds each. The hostel is in the heart of The City on a back street near St. Paul's Cathedral—a location good for sightseeing but poor for dining and nightlife, though the hostel's Chorister's restaurant is open to 8pm (see "Dining" for a review). Otherwise, most City places close when the bankers go home. Some rooms have TVs.

Earl's Court Youth Hostel. 38 Bolton Gardens, London SW5. ☎ **0171/373-7083.** Fax 0171/835-2034. 154 beds. £16.45 ($27) per person IYHF members under 18, £18.70 ($30) per person IYHF members over 18. Add £1.70 ($2.80) nonmembers. Rates include sheets and breakfast. MC, V. Tube: Earl's Court; then turn right and Bolton Gardens is the fifth street on your left.

In well-located but slightly seedy Earl's Court, this hostel is lively, and you won't find school groups here. Stores in the area tend to stay open late. Most accommodations are in 10-bed single-sex dorms. Laundry and kitchen facilities are available.

Holland House. Holland Walk, Holland Park, London W87QU. ☎ **0171/937-0748.** Fax 0171/376-0667. 201 beds. £16.45 ($27) per person under 18, £18.70 ($30) per person over 18. Rates include English breakfast. MC, V. Tube: High St. Kensington or Holland Park.

This hostel enjoys the most beautiful setting of all London's IYHF hostels, right in the middle of Kensington's Holland Park. The bunk-bedded rooms accommodate 12 people each. You'll find a kitchen, a TV room, a quiet room, and laundry facilities. Reasonably priced meals are also available.

WORTH A SPLURGE

✪ Aster House Hotel. 3 Sumner Place, London SW7. ☎ **0171/581-5888.** Fax 0171/584-4925. E-mail: asterhouse@btinternet.com. 12 units, all with bathroom. TV TEL. £70–£100 ($114–$163) single; £115–£145 ($187–$236) double. Rates include breakfast. MC, V. Tube: South Kensington; then walk 3 blocks down Old Brompton Rd. to Sumner Place on your left.

The Aster House is the most beautiful of a number of small B&Bs on this quiet South Kensington street. The pride with which the owners run the place is evident the moment you step into the plushly carpeted interior. All the rooms—with baths featuring amenities usually found in more expensive hotels—are decorated prettily in floral fabrics and comfortable eclectic furnishings. Some of the beds are even finished off with tent treatments. Take special note of the award-winning rear garden. The enormous breakfast buffet includes the usual eggs and sausages, as well as health-oriented fresh fruits, cold meats, cheeses, yogurt, and muesli. The meal is served in L'Orangerie, the beautiful glass-covered pièce de résistance of this special hotel.

Harlingford Hotel. 61–63 Cartwright Gardens, London WC1. ☎ **0171/387-1551.** Fax 0171/387-4616. 44 units, all with bathroom. TV TEL. £60 ($98) single; £75 ($122) double;

£85 ($139) triple; £95 ($155) quad. Rates include English breakfast. AE, MC, V. Tube: Russell Square; then walk 3 blocks north.

The Harlingford is the nicest hotel on Bloomsbury's best-located Georgian crescent. You'll be particularly pleased by the bright ground-floor dining room, where a hearty breakfast is served. The rooms are equipped with tea- and coffee-making facilities, but let the well-furnished cozy communal lounge entice you away from the TV in your room. A coffee machine on the landing sits next to a free ice dispenser for chilling your bubbly.

4 Great Deals on Dining

The quality of English food has improved immensely in recent years, and even budget fare is now quite palatable, except for the still often overcooked vegetables and the ubiquitous canned peas. Note that in England appetizers are often called starters, while desserts are referred to as sweets or pudding.

London's ethnic restaurants represent the city's best budget values and add spice to the foodscape. Top Indian chefs and good-quality ingredients keep the standards high even in the cheapest of curry houses. And don't forget the three quintessential British experiences: fish-and-chips, pub grub like bangers and mash, and afternoon tea with tiny sandwiches.

LOCAL BUDGET BESTS

FISH-&-CHIPS Fast-food restaurants have taken their toll in London, but "chippies" are still to be found. Nowadays, fish-and-chips are usually offered by Middle Eastern places too, but the most authentic joints won't have a kebab in sight. Several kinds of fish are used, but when thickly battered and deep-fried they taste similar; cod is the cheapest. Sitting down will up the price of the meal considerably, so do as most locals do and get it to take away—wrapped in a paper cone, doused with vinegar, and sprinkled with salt. The bill should never top £7 ($11).

Two of the most popular chippies are **Rock & Sole Plaice,** 47 Endell St., at Shorts Gardens, near Covent Garden Market (☎ 0171/836-3785; Tube: Covent Garden), open daily 11:30am to 11pm for takeout; and the **North Sea Fish Bar,** 8 Leigh St., WC1 (☎ 0171/387-5892; Tube: St. Pancras), just southeast of Cartwright Gardens at Sandwich Street in Bloomsbury, open Monday to Saturday noon to 2:30pm and 5:30 to 10:30pm.

PUB GRUB Pub food can vary from snacks at the bar to a complete restaurant meal, but it's usually cheap, good, and filling. Most pubs offer food, and there are so many pubs that if you don't like what you see in one, you can move on to the next. Most pubs display their dishes so that you can select by sight. Popular items are bangers and mash (sausages and mashed potatoes), meat or vegetable pies (including cottage pie, made with ground beef and a whipped potato topping), pasties (meat-filled pastries), and ploughman's lunch (a plate of crusty French bread with several cheeses, salad, and chutney). Wash it all down with a beer.

Behind the bar, food and drink are kept apart as vigilantly as an Orthodox rabbi keeps milk from meat. Order and pay for each separately. A good pub lunch will seldom top £7 ($11), and careful ordering can cut that amount.

Many popular pubs are listed under "London After Dark," later in this chapter. These pubs are known especially for their food: the **Cittie of Yorke,** 22 High Holborn, WC1 (☎ 0171/242-7670; Tube: Chancery Lane); the **Coal Hole,** 91 The Strand, WC2 (☎ 0171/836-7503; Tube: Temple or Covent Garden); the **Australian,**

29 Milner St., Chelsea, SW3 (☎ **0171/589-6027;** Tube: Sloane Square), which has won numerous awards for its excellent food; the **Kings Head and Eight Bells,** 50 Cheyney Walk, SW3 (☎ **0171/352-1820;** Tube: Sloane Square); the **Silver Cross,** Whitehall, WC2 (☎ **0171/930-8350;** Tube: Westminster or Charing Cross); the **Hung Drawn and Quartered,** 27 Great Tower St., EC3 (☎ **0171/626-6123;** Tube: Tower Hill).

AFTERNOON TEA   As much as the tea itself, it's tradition that makes afternoon tea a pleasant and civilized activity. The pot is usually served with a spread of sandwiches and cakes and pastries that more than make a meal. Accordingly, an authentic tea is expensive and usually served in top hotels, where a jacket and tie are required for men.

Brown's Hotel, Albemarle and Dover streets, W1 (☎ **0171/493-6020;** Tube: Green Park), serves the best fixed-price tea in London. For £17.95 ($29), you can sit in one of three wood-paneled, stained-glass lounges and feel like a millionaire. Tailcoated waiters will make sure you don't leave hungry, as they fill your table with tomato, cucumber, and meat sandwiches, as well as scones and pastries. Choose from a variety of teas. Tea is served daily 3 to 6pm.

The **Ritz Hotel,** Piccadilly, W1 (☎ **0171/493-8181;** Tube: Green Park), is probably the most famous spot for afternoon tea in the world, and even at £23.50 ($38) per person you have to book at least a week in advance. It's served daily 2 to 6pm.

IN & AROUND SOHO—PICCADILLY & TRAFALGAR SQUARE

Bar Italia. 22 Frith St., W1. ☎ **0171/437-4520.** Sandwiches £2.50–£5 ($4.10–$8). No credit cards. Daily 24 hours. Tube: Tottenham Court Rd. LIGHT FARE.

This place is lively and fun. You can stand up and munch on a Parma ham-and-cheese sandwich accompanied by good frothy cappuccino or sit at one of the few tables.

Cafe in the Crypt. In the Church of St. Martin-in-the-Fields, Trafalgar Sq., WC2. ☎ **0171/839-4342.** Rolls and sandwiches £1.75–£2.20 ($2.85–$3.60); main courses £5.50–£6.10 ($9–$10). No credit cards. Mon–Sat 10am–8pm, Sun noon–8pm. Tube: Charing Cross. ENGLISH.

This very atmospheric cafeteria-style restaurant is set in the crypt of the church. Coffee and croissants are available mid-morning, and fresh salads, soups, sandwiches, and hot and cold dishes, both meat and vegetarian, are served at lunch. For example, you might find salmon with lemon-lime and spinach-and-nut roulade.

Chuen Cheng Ku. 17 Wardour St., W1. ☎ **0171/437-1398.** Meals £4.95–£8.50 ($8–$13). AE, DC, MC, V. Daily 11am–11:45pm (dumplings served to 5:45pm). Tube: Leicester Square. CHINESE.

At lunch, this huge restaurant serves 21 kinds of steamed, fried, or boiled dumplings wheeled to tables on trolleys. Favorites are steamed pork buns and shrimp dumplings, each about £1.75 ($2.85). Adventurers can choose duck's tongue in a sauce of black beans and chili and other exotics. It takes a few servings to satisfy the appetite, which can be done for about £6.95 ($11).

Gaby's Continental Bar. 30 Charing Cross Rd. (just off Leicester Sq.), WC2. ☎ **0171/836-4233.** Meals £5–£8 ($8–$13). No credit cards. Mon–Sat 9am–midnight, Sun 11am–10pm. Tube: Leicester Square. CONTINENTAL.

This sandwich bar/cafe offers home-cooked specialties like stuffed eggplant and cabbage rolls, which are displayed in the window. Hungarian goulash and lamb curry are

---

Getting the Best Deal on Dining

- Seek out the budget restaurants on the side streets around Covent Garden and Soho—the festive atmosphere of these areas makes finding them fun.
- Look for places with a number of taxis parked outside—you can be sure that the food is good and the prices are low.
- Remember to take advantage of British standbys like affordable and delicious pub grub and fish-and-chips.
- Note any restaurants that don't have signs welcoming tourists; they usually care about making you a repeat customer.

---

also usually served, and like most main courses they cost less than £6 ($10), with salad or rice. Everything is made fresh daily according to the chef's mood, and there's always a wide selection of good-tasting well-priced meals. The restaurant is known for its sandwiches, especially salt beef (England's approximation of corned beef), cheapest when you buy it to take out for about £3.50 ($6). There's also a broad selection of vegetarian dishes. Gaby's is fully licensed.

New Piccadilly Restaurant. 8 Denman St. (just off the bottom of Shaftesbury Ave., a few feet from Piccadilly Circus), W1. ☎ **0171/437-8530.** Meals £3.50–£6.75 ($6–$11). No credit cards. Daily 11am–9:30pm. Tube: Piccadilly Circus. ENGLISH/CONTINENTAL.

Appealing decor and a straightforward English cafe menu make this central restaurant a safe budget mainstay. The long dining room is lined with Formica-topped tables on either side, and you can choose from a large number of specialties, like fish-and-chips, chicken with mushroom sauce, and steak risotto for about £4.50 ($7). For a pound less, try one of their many pizzas or a pasta dish. Add £1.25 ($2.05) for soup, plus £1.50 ($2.45) for apple pie or ice cream, and you'll have eaten a satisfying three-course meal for about £7.25 ($12). The place has no liquor license; you're encouraged to bring your own alcohol.

New World. 1 Gerrard Place, W1. ☎ **0171/734-0396.** Meals £7–£10 ($11–$16); fixed-price meals from £7.20 ($12). AE, DC, MC, V. Mon–Thurs 11am–11:45pm, Fri–Sat 11am–midnight, Sun 10:45am–10:45pm. Tube: Leicester Square or Piccadilly Circus. CHINESE.

Reminiscent of Hong Kong's massive catering halls, this giant Cantonese palace seating 700-plus is one of Chinatown's largest restaurants. The immense menu matches the dining rooms in size and reads like a veritable summary of pan Chinese cookery. The usual poultry, beef, pork, and vegetable stir-fry dishes are represented, and at lunch dim sum is served in the traditional manner, via trolley.

Pierre Victoire. 6 Panton St., SW1. ☎ **0171/930-6463.** Fixed-price lunch £4.90 ($8); pretheater dinner £7.90 ($13); main courses £6–£9 ($10–$15). MC, V. Daily noon–4pm and 5:30–11pm. Tube: Piccadilly Circus. FRENCH.

With a comfortable candlelit dining room, okay food, and unbeatable prices, this franchised French restaurant has all the hallmarks of permanence. The bistro food includes roast pork with spinach and garlic, as well as chicken in white wine and cream sauce. Vegetables are served on separate side plates, and fresh bread is included with every meal. There are too many other branches to name—check the phone book for the one nearest you.

✪ **Pollo.** 20 Old Compton St. (near Frith St., a few doors down from the Prince Edward Theater), W1. ☎ **0171/734-5917.** Main courses £3.30–£7 ($5–$11). No credit cards. Mon–Sat 11:30am–11:30pm. Tube: Leicester Square. ITALIAN.

An extremely popular Italian/English restaurant in the heart of the hustle, Pollo offers good food and embarrassingly low prices that keep the crowds coming. There must be 150 menu items, with few topping £5 ($8). Pastas in a myriad of shapes and sizes are served with a choice of over a dozen red and white sauces, plus pizzas and a good selection of vegetarian dishes. The list of Italian desserts is impressive too. The atmosphere is lively, but if you don't like crowds, Pollo isn't for you. Expect to be rushed and jostled.

Wong Kei. 41–43 Wardour St., W1. ☎ **0171/437-6833** or 0171/437-3071. Meals £5.80 ($9). No credit cards. Daily noon–11:30pm. Tube: Leicester Square or Piccadilly Circus. CHINESE.

There are many good, cheap Chinese restaurants in Soho, most serving Cantonese fare. Sitting at the end of Chinatown's Gerrard Street and Lisle Street, Wong Kei is one of the cheapest in the area, with an extensive menu and very abrupt staff. At least a dozen popular dishes, including chicken with garlic sauce and beef with vegetables, cost under £4 ($7). As is the rule at most Chinese restaurants in London, if you want rice you have to order it separately, for 90p ($1.45). Tea is free, and hearty eaters can take advantage of the fixed-price meal of three dishes plus rice for only £5.80 ($9) per person (two people minimum).

The Wren at St. James's. 35 Jermyn St., SW1. ☎ **0171/437-9419.** Soups, sandwiches, and pies £2.50–£3.50 ($4–$6). No credit cards. Mon–Sat 8.30am–5pm, Sun 10am–4pm. Tube: Piccadilly Circus. VEGETARIAN.

Inside a popular parish church near Piccadilly Circus, the Wren serves simple continental breakfasts and imaginative vegetarian lunches that may include a variety of sandwiches and vegetable pies, plus a host of tossed green salads. Interesting and tasty soups, like cream of parsnip or apple, carrot, and cashew, are made fresh daily along with a hearty casserole dish. Smoking isn't allowed in the dining room. In warm weather, the courtyard is a pleasant alternative. Expect lines because the quality of the food is high and the portions are generous.

IN THE CITY

Almost everyone in the square mile of The City of London goes home by 6pm, and restaurant workers are no exception. Below are some good lunch selections.

Al's Cafe. 11–13 Exmouth Market, EC1. ☎ **0171/837-4821.** Meals £4.50–£6 ($7–$10). AE, V. Mon–Fri 7am–11pm, Sat–Sun 10am–8pm. Tube: Angel or Farringdon. ENGLISH.

One of London's funkiest cafes is best known for lunch, when it's packed with office types chowing on half-pound bacon cheeseburgers, spicy sausages with grilled onions, and delicious homemade soups like carrot and bean. Most everything comes with thick-cut chips, and a long list of salads and sandwiches is also available. Al's gets high marks for top ingredients that include Italian focaccia and service with a smile. Good, filling all-day breakfasts are served too.

Chorister's. In the City of London Youth Hostel, 36 Carter Lane, EC4. ☎ **0171/236-4965.** Meals £3–£4.95 ($4.90–$8). No credit cards. Daily noon–2pm and 5–8pm. Tube: Blackfriars or St. Paul's. ENGLISH/CONTINENTAL.

A stone's throw from St. Paul's Cathedral, Chorister's is inside the City of London Youth Hostel. The decor is basic though clean, and the crowd tends to be largely teenage hostelers, but the food is filling and varied. You can choose from a selection of baked potatoes with numerous fillings or even a three-course lunch or dinner for £4.95 ($8).

Ferrari's. 8 W. Smithfield, EC1. ☎ **0171/236-7545.** Meals £2.50–£6 ($4.10–$10). No credit cards. Mon–Fri 5:15am–3pm. Tube: St. Paul's. ENGLISH.

For a little nicer meal in the same area as Piccolo (below), turn left at the Museum of London and then right onto Little Britain Street until you reach the Smithfield Market, London's wholesale meat center (about 6 blocks from the St. Paul's Underground station). The restaurant is just across the square. Small and plain, Ferrari's is famous for its sandwich menu, which includes Norwegian prawn and farmhouse pâté. The cakes are irresistible.

Japanese Canteen. 394 St. John St., EC1. ☎ **0171/833-3222.** Meals £5–£13 ($8–$21). No credit cards. Daily noon–2:30pm and 6–10:30pm. Tube: Angel. JAPANESE/PUB.

Lenin and Trotsky supposedly used to drink in this funky pub cum Japanese noodle shop, typically dark brown on the outside. The dining rooms are painted white and fitted with blond-wood tables and benches. Rock music plays in the background. In addition to sushi, the menu includes ramen soup (with fresh noodles), vegetarian tempura, and small bento box combos with teriyaki, tempura, and breaded pork cutlets. Don't expect authentic Japanese food, though. There's another branch at 5 Thayer St., W1 (☎ **0171/487-5505;** Tube: Bond St. or Marble Arch).

Piccolo. 7 Gresham St. (off Martin's Le Grand St.), EC2. No phone. Meals £2–£3 ($3.30–$5). No credit cards. Mon–Fri 6am–7:30pm, Sat 6am–4pm. Tube: St. Paul's. ENGLISH.

This sandwich bar, with fewer than a dozen stools all facing the street, is perfect for a quick bite after visiting St. Paul's Cathedral and offers the widest range of sandwiches you're ever likely to come across. Bacon and turkey, roast chicken, and all the standards are priced below £3 ($4.90). The shop is between St. Paul's Underground station and the Museum of London.

AROUND COVENT GARDEN

Food for Thought. 31 Neal St. (across from the Covent Garden Underground station), WC2. ☎ **0171/836-9072.** Main courses £3–£5 ($4.90–$8). No credit cards. Mon–Sat 9:30am–9pm, Sun noon–4pm. Tube: Covent Garden. VEGETARIAN.

This unusual restaurant makes vegetarian food that appeals to all palates and wallets. Delicious dishes, like cauliflower quiche and South Indian curry made with eggplant, carrots, peppers, cauliflower, and spinach, are usually priced around £3 ($4.90) and served downstairs in a small pine dining room with a terra-cotta tile floor (no smoking). Evening specials like cannelloni filled with a julienne of eggplant, sun-dried tomatoes, and mozzarella are only £5 ($8). Really tasty soups and salads are also available, plus a good selection of healthful desserts.

Neal's Yard Beach Cafe. 13 Neal's Yard, WC2. ☎ **0171/240-1168.** Sandwiches £3.95–£5 ($6–$8). No credit cards. Mon–Sat 9:30am–8pm, Sun 9:30am–7:30pm. Tube: Covent Garden. LIGHT FARE.

This place is brilliantly Mediterranean in both decor and cuisine. Enjoy large focaccia sandwiches made with mozzarella, spinach, tomato, and avocado and a whole range of vegetable and fruit juices. The emphasis is on fresh and healthy, except for the fine ice creams (though they also serve soy ice cream).

Wagamama. 4 Streatham St., WC1. ☎ **0171/323-9223.** Meals £8–£10 ($13–$16). MC, V. Mon–Sat noon–11pm, Sun 12:30–10pm. Tube: Tottenham Court Rd. JAPANESE.

This Japanese noodle bar is one of London's hippest and most popular restaurants. There's always a line to get into the minimalist dining room, which is infused with a health-oriented Zen-like philosophy. The kitchen's offerings are limited to a variety of vegetarian stir-fries and several kinds of steaming noodle soups. Enjoy an ice-cold lager or fresh-squeezed juice while you wait for a table. There's another branch at 10A Lexington St., W1 (☎ **0171/292-0990;** Tube: Piccadilly Circus or Oxford Circus).

IN BAYSWATER & PADDINGTON

The Cafe. 106 Westbourne Grove (close to Chepstow Rd.), W2. ☎ **0171/229-0777.** Meals £3.30–£5 ($5–$8). No credit cards. Mon–Sat 7.30am–7:15pm, Sun 8:30am–6pm. Tube: Bayswater. ENGLISH.

The Cafe looks like an American diner. Sit in a booth and open the menu to find sandwiches for about £1.20 ($1.95), meat pies for about the same, and ice cream for 60p ($1). The only things missing are the jukebox selectors mounted above each table.

✪ **Khan's.** 13–15 Westbourne Grove, W2. ☎ **0171/727-5420.** Meals £4.50–£8 ($7–$13). AE, DC, MC, V. Daily noon–3pm and 6–11:45pm. Tube: Bayswater; then turn left onto Westbourne Grove from Queensway. INDIAN.

Khan's is said to have the best Indian food in Bayswater, so it attracts crowds—don't expect a leisurely quiet meal (it'll be rushed and noisy). The menu, which includes all the staples, guarantees that only halal meat is used, conforming to the Muslim dietary code. Curry dishes cost about £3 ($4.90), with a whole tandoori chicken, enough for two, under £7 ($11).

IN BLOOMSBURY

Anwar's. 64 Grafton Way, W1. ☎ **0171/387-6664.** Meals £3.30–£5 ($5–$8). No credit cards. Daily noon–11pm. Tube: Warren St. INDIAN.

Anwar's not only maintains a high standard of quality but also is one of the cheapest Indian restaurants in London. Few dishes top £4 ($7), and most cost just £3.50 ($6). There's a wide choice of meat and vegetable curries and other Indian specialties, including thalis and tandoori chicken for £3 ($6). Anwar's is cafeteria style; help yourself and bring your meal to a Formica-covered table. Despite this "canteen" approach, the food is top-notch.

Greenhouse Basement. 16 Chenies St., WC1. ☎ **0171/637-8038.** Main courses £3.95 ($6). No credit cards. Mon–Sat 10am–8:30pm, Sun noon–4:30pm. Tube: Goodge St. VEGETARIAN.

Below the sidewalk, this dining room has an appealing candlelit atmosphere. The fare is fresh and healthful. Several salads are offered daily, along with such dishes as lasagna and mixed vegetable masala and other Eastern/Middle Eastern–inspired dishes.

IN THE EAST END

The East End, an amorphous area hugging The City's eastern edge, has always been one of London's poorest areas. The residents have traditionally been newly arrived immigrants. At the turn of the century, the East End was one of Europe's largest Jewish ghettos. Today it's primarily Indian and Bangladeshi, and ethnic restaurants from the subcontinent abound.

Brick Lane Beigel Bakery. 159 Brick Lane, E1. ☎ **0171/729-0616.** Bagels and cakes 30p–£1.50 (50¢–$2.40). No credit cards. Daily 24 hours. Tube: Aldgate East. SANDWICHES.

There's always a line for these tiny bagels (here pronounced *bi*-guls), which are premade into sandwiches filled with cream cheese, salt beef, chopped herring, or smoked salmon. It's especially busy after midnight, when most other places are shut and a line of taxi drivers forms curbside by the door. There are two adjacent bagel shops on Brick Lane—this one is the better. Ironically, both are near the corner of Bacon Street.

The Spice. 8 Brick Lane, E1. ☎ **0171/375-2709.** Meals £4.95–£7.95 ($8–$13). AE, MC, V. Sun–Thurs noon–3pm and 6pm–12:30am, Fri–Sat noon–3pm and 6pm–1am. Tube: Aldgate East. INDIAN.

Brick Lane and the surrounding streets are lined with over 50 curry houses and restaurants. It's where Londoners go to enjoy some of the best Indian food at the keenest prices. The Spice is relatively new to the Lane but already establishing itself as a popular venue. The service is friendly and attentive and the varied menu includes a range of birianes (complete meals in themselves) for around £6 ($10). For those not used to spicy Indian food, I recommend an onion bhajee starter at £1.45 ($2.40) followed by chicken tikka masala at £5.95 ($10), with pilau rice at £1.60 ($2.60).

THE CHAINS

✪ **Cranks.** 8 Adelaide St. (where The Strand meets Trafalgar Sq.), WC2. ☎ **0171/836-0660.** Meals £3–£8 ($4.90–$13). No credit cards. Mon–Sat 9:30am–8pm, Sun 10am–7pm. Tube: Charing Cross. VEGETARIAN.

When Cranks opened its first health-oriented vegetarian restaurant in the early 1960s, the British public laughed. Today more than half a dozen branches continue to "crank out" decent cuisine at reasonable prices, though the quality has diminished with the chain's turn to express takeout. Lasagna, lentil-and-spinach quiche, stir-fried vegetables, a weekly casserole, and other tasty dishes are prepackaged for takeout. Sandwiches are available for £1.20 to £2.90 ($1.95 to $4.70). There are a few tables so that you can eat here, but the price will be increased by about 40p to 50p (65¢ to 81¢).

Other Cranks branches are 1 The Market, Covent Garden, WC2 (☎ **0171/379-6508;** Tube: Covent Garden); 9–11 Tottenham St. (off Tottenham Court Rd.), W1 (☎ **0171/631-3912;** Tube: Goodge St.); 23 Barret St., W1 (☎ **0171/495-1340;** Tube: Bond St.); and 8 Marshall St., W1 (☎ **0171/437-9431;** Tube: Piccadilly Circus or Oxford Circus), 3 blocks east of Regent Street in the heart of Soho.

Pizza Express. 30 Coptic St., WC1. ☎ **0171/636-3232.** Pizza £3.40–£5.75 ($6–$9). AE, MC, V. Daily noon–midnight. Tube: Holborn. PIZZA.

Come here for terrific pizza that ranges from an ordinary margherita to all kinds of imaginative combinations like sultanas, olives, capers, and pine nuts and onions. Each of the outlets is sleekly decked out with tile and marble, even if it's only faux.

Prêt à Manger. 77 St. Martin's Lane, WC2. ☎ **0171/379-5335.** Sandwiches £1–£5 ($1.65–$8). No credit cards. Mon–Thurs 8am–10pm, Fri–Sat 8am–11pm, Sun 10am–8pm. Tube: Leicester Square. SANDWICHES.

The majority of upscale ready-to-eat foods found at Prêt à Manger are gourmet sandwiches made with inventive ingredients like poached salmon, goat's cheese, chicken and avocado, tarragon chicken, and hearty herb-laced breads. There's a small selection of salads and sushi, hot croissants, and a huge assortment of cakes. You line up cafeteria style, then take your meal to stylish matte-black tables.

There are about 50 locations in London. Among them are 12 Kingsgate, Victoria Street, SW1 (☎ **0171/828-1559;** Tube: Victoria); 17 Eldon St., EC2 (☎ **0171/628-9011;** Tube: Moorgate or Liverpool St.); 28 Fleet St., EC4 (☎ **0171/353-2332;** Tube: Aldwych); and 298 Regent St., W1 (☎ **0171/637-3836;** Tube: Oxford Circus).

✪ **The Stockpot.** 18 Old Compton St., Soho. ☎ **0171/287-1066.** Soups 95p ($1.45); main courses £3–£5.50 ($4.90–$9). No credit cards. Mon–Sat 11am–11:30pm, Sun noon–11pm (sometimes varies by location). Tube: Leicester Square. ENGLISH.

Members of the Stockpot chain feature contemporary styling and subscribe to a generous budget-minded philosophy. Menus change daily but regularly include two homemade soups; a dozen main courses like chicken à la king, gammon steak and pineapple, beef Stroganoff, omelets, chili, and fish-and-chips; and an excellent selection of desserts for under £1.70 ($2.70).

Other central London locations are 273 King's Rd., SW3 (☎ **0171/823-3175;** Tube: Sloane Square), in Chelsea, a few blocks past the fire station; 6 Basil St., SW3 (☎ **0171/589-8627;** Tube: Knightsbridge), in Knightsbridge, between Harrods and Sloane Street; and 40 Panton St., SW1 (☎ **0171/839-5142;** Tube: Piccadilly Circus), just off Haymarket.

PICNICKING

There are plenty of supermarkets around offering run-of-the-mill staples. Cold cuts and cheeses from the deli counter are usually cheaper than the prewrapped stuff that hangs in the cooler.

For unusual picnic goodies, try the large and fascinating **Loon Fung Supermarket,** 42–44 Gerrard St., W1 (☎ **0171/437-7332;** Tube: Leicester Square), in the center of Soho's Chinatown. The most adventurous will try the black-jelly fungus or steamed, congealed chicken's blood. The rest will enjoy dried cuttlefish, a traditional snack that goes well with beer. Loon Fung is open daily 10am to 7pm.

For the top picnic spots, see "Parks & Gardens," later in this chapter.

WORTH A SPLURGE

Bahn Thai. 21A Frith St. (just south of Soho Sq.), W1. ☎ **0171/437-8504.** Meals £8–£17 ($13–$28); fixed-price pretheater menu £12.50 ($20). AE, DC, MC, V. Mon–Sat noon–2:45pm and 6–11:15pm, Sun 12:30–2:30pm and 6:30–10:30pm. Tube: Tottenham Court Rd. THAI.

In the middle of Soho is one of London's best Southeast Asian restaurants. Two floors of wooden tables, plants, and decorative wall hangings give the place an authentic feel. But it's the food you've come for, and on a good day you won't be disappointed. Excellent, unusual soups, seafood, and rice dishes punctuate a huge creative menu. The two-course pretheater menu is a good value and includes tea.

✪ English House. 3 Milner St., SW3. ☎ **0171/584-3002.** Main courses £13.50–£17.25 ($22–$28); 3-course fixed-price Sun supper £20.75 ($33); 3-course lunch £15.75 ($25). AE, DC, MC, V. Mon–Sat 12:30–2:30pm and 7:30–11:30pm, Sun 12:30–2pm and 7:30–10pm. Tube: South Kensington or Sloane Square. ENGLISH.

Set on a beautiful Chelsea back street, the English House looks like an ideal country home. As a fire roars in the cozy dining room, you're treated to well-prepared dishes served by an expertly trained staff. Though the tables are too close together, dining here is romantic. Start with the casserole of wild mushrooms and pearl barley or grilled scallops with roasted kumquats. Among the main courses may be roast chump (a chop) of lamb with bubble and squeak (fried greens and potatoes), grilled salmon with sesame vegetables and coriander jus, or filet of beef.

5 Seeing the Sights

If you enjoy museums and intend to visit as many as you can, you might want to consider purchasing the **London White Card.** The card costs £15 ($24) for 3 days or £25 ($40) for 7 days and grants access to 15 major museums, including Apsley House, the Courtauld Gallery, the Museum of London, the Museum of the Moving Image, the National Maritime Museum at Greenwich, the Natural History Museum, the Science Museum, and the Victoria & Albert. The total admissions to these museums alone, which you'd most likely want to visit anyway, add up to £36 ($58). You can purchase the pass at BTA offices, at participating museums and galleries, and at the Tourist Information Centres at Victoria Station and at any of the London Transport Information Centres.

SIGHTSEEING SUGGESTIONS

When you've traveled a long way and have only a few days, moving fast makes some sense. If soaking up local culture in a Chelsea cafe is more your cup of tea, you'll have to make modifications to my suggestions below.

IF YOU HAVE 1 DAY   Most hotels start serving breakfast at 7:30am, so try to rise early. Then take the tube to Charing Cross or Embankment (within 1 block of each other) and cross into **Trafalgar Square,** the city's unofficial hub. Here the commercial West End meets **Whitehall,** the main street of government, and the **Mall,** the regal road that leads to Buckingham Palace. In the center of the square is Nelson's Column, erected in 1843 to commemorate Nelson's defeat of Napoléon at the 1805 Battle of Trafalgar. The **National Gallery** is on the northern side of the square, while the northeast side is dominated by the **Church of St. Martin-in-the-Fields.**

Turn down Whitehall and go inside **Banqueting House** to view the magnificent ceiling painted by Rubens. Across from Banqueting House, visit the home of the Queen's Life Guards to see the **Changing of the Guard** Monday to Saturday at 11am and Sunday at 10am and 4pm (not to be confused with the larger affair at Buckingham Palace). From here, take a leisurely stroll across St. James's Park, being sure to stop on the bridge that crosses the picturesque lake for a stunning view of Buckingham Palace. Make your way to **Buckingham Palace,** timing your arrival for 11:30am to view the Ceremony of the Changing of the Guard, before backtracking to Whitehall and continuing on to pass the **Cenotaph,** dedicated to those "Glorious Dead" who gave their lives in two world wars, and just opposite it, behind tall iron gates, is **10 Downing St.,** home of the prime minister. At the foot of Whitehall lies Parliament Square, site of **Big Ben** and the spectacular **Houses of Parliament. Westminster Abbey** is across Parliament Square. After lunch, take the tube into The City to visit **St. Paul's Cathedral,** then take the tube to the **Tower of London.**

IF YOU HAVE 2 DAYS   Follow the itinerary above but at a more leisurely pace. Or reverse your Whitehall walk, starting in **Parliament Square** (Westminster tube) and ending at **National Gallery** in Trafalgar Square. Continue north along Charing Cross Road, turn right on Long Acre, and visit trendy **Covent Garden.** Walk down to The Strand and go left toward The City. On arrival at **Temple Bar,** an unmistakable midroad monument, go through any of the gates on your right and stroll through the 18th-century courtyards of **Middle and Inner Temples,** two of London's Inns of Court (home to the bewigged and robed Lawyers). Return to **Fleet Street** and lunch at any of its many pubs. In the afternoon, visit **St. Paul's Cathedral** and then stroll the streets of The City. On Day 2, take a **morning cruise** on the Thames from Charing Cross Pier to the **Tower of London** and then rejoin the boat to visit **Greenwich,** where you can lunch. In the afternoon, tour Greenwich, being sure to visit the **Royal Naval College** to view the "Painted Hall." Either take the boat back to Charing Cross Pier or walk under the river, via the foot tunnel, and take the Dockland's Light railway through Dockland's to **Tower Pier.**

IF YOU HAVE 3 DAYS   Spend Days 1 and 2 as above. On Day 3, visit more of the major attractions listed below. Attend a **lunchtime recital** at one of London's churches (see "London After Dark"). In the afternoon, line up to visit the **Houses of Parliament** or attend one of the court cases at either the **Old Bailey** (criminal) or the **Royal Courts of Justice** (civil). In the evening, tour the historic pubs of London.

IF YOU HAVE 5 DAYS   Spend Days 1 to 3 as above. On Days 4 and 5, explore London's historic neighborhoods (notably **Chelsea** and **South Kensington**) or participate in the active cultural scene. If you like museums, make a pilgrimage to South Kensington: In addition to the **Victoria & Albert,** there are no fewer than six museums here, including the **Natural History Museum,** the **Science Museum,** the **Geological Museum,** and the **Museum of Instruments.** Also worth a stop is **Kensington Palace,** in Kensington Gardens, once home to Diana, Princess of Wales. It's still home to several members of the royal family, including Princess Margaret, and contains State Apartments. If you've planned ahead, at 9:30pm you can attend the free **Ceremony of the Keys** at the Tower of London (see the listing below for details).

THE TOP ATTRACTIONS

✪ **British Museum.** Great Russell St., WC1. ☎ **0171/323-8599** or 0171/636-1555, or 0171/580-1788 for recorded information. Main galleries free but £1 ($1.63) donation requested; special exhibits vary but can be as much as £4.50 ($7) adults, £3 ($4.90) seniors/students/age 16 and under. Museum tours, £6 ($10) adults, £3 ($4.80) ages 10–16, free for age 9 and under. Mon–Sat 10am–5pm, Sun 2:30–6pm; 90-minute tours Mon–Sat at 10:30am and 1:30pm, Sun at 3 and 3:30pm. Tube: Holborn, Russell Square, or Tottenham Court Rd.

Britain's largest and oldest national museum houses an unmatched collection of antiquities—many the spoils of the Empire Where the Sun Never Set. Important finds from Egypt, Greece, Rome, and Cyprus share this warehouse of history with spectacular collections from Asia and the Middle East. The Rosetta Stone, at the entrance to the **Egyptian Sculpture Gallery** (Room 25), is interesting as an artifact yet even more fascinating for the way it changed our understanding of hieroglyphics, which had been a mystery for 1,400 years. The sculptures from the Parthenon, known as the **Elgin Marbles** (Room 8), are the most famous of the museum's extensive collection of Greek antiquities. They're named for Lord Elgin, who took these treasures from Athens; today the Greek government seeks their return.

To the right of the entrance on the ground floor are the **British Library Galleries.** Rotating thematic displays are drawn from the library's collection of over 8 million books. Included in the permanent exhibit are two copies of the Magna Carta (1215), Shakespeare's First Folio (1623), and the Gutenberg Bible (ca. 1453), the first book printed using movable (hence, reusable) type.

Buckingham Palace. The Mall, SW1. ☎ **0171/839-1377** or 0171/839-1377, ext. 3387 for reservations for the disabled. State Apartments, £9 ($15) adults, £6.50 ($11) seniors, £5 ($8) ages 5–17; Queen's Gallery, £3.50 ($6) adults, £2.50 ($4.10) seniors, £2 ($3.25) children; Royal Mews, £3.70 ($6) adults, £2.60 ($4.25) seniors, £2.10 ($3.40) ages 5–17; Gallery and Mews combination ticket, £6.20 ($10) adults, £4.20 ($7) seniors, £3.20 ($5) children. State Apartments, Aug–Sept daily 9:30am–4:30pm. Queen's Gallery, daily 9:30am–4pm. Royal Mews, Apr–Sept Tues–Thurs noon–4pm; Oct–Mar Wed noon–4pm. Opening times subject to change on short notice. Tube: Victoria, St. James's Park, or Green Park.

As the home of one of the world's few remaining monarchs, Buckingham Palace has strong symbolic interest and is one of the city's biggest draws. Built in 1703 for the duke of Buckingham, the palace became the sovereign's official residence in 1837, when Queen Victoria decided to live here (when the queen is at home, the Royal Standard is flown from the flagstaff on the building's roof).

Buckingham Palace opens its doors to visitors in August and September, when the royal family is away on vacation. Eighteen rooms are on view, including the Throne Room, the State Dining Room, three drawing rooms, and the Music Room. Tickets to see these State Apartments go on sale from 9am at the ticket office on Constitution Hill, on the south side of Green Park. Hours-long waits should be anticipated. Physically disabled visitors can jump the line by reserving tickets directly from the palace.

Getting the Best Deal on Sightseeing

- Note that many of the best London museums are free—like the British Museum and the National Gallery.
- Consider purchasing the London White Card (see the beginning of this section) if you're a museum/gallery enthusiast.
- Walking is the best way to get around and see the city, but if you use public transport take advantage of discounts like the Travelcard (see "Getting Around," earlier in this chapter).
- Enjoy the varied free pastimes London offers—like touring outdoor markets, catching the entertainment at Covent Garden, attending a concert in a church, checking out the proceedings at the Old Bailey and the Royal Courts of Justice, and window-shopping along Oxford and Regent streets and King's Road.
- Set aside a morning and ride the no. 188 bus from Euston to Greenwich (see "Side Trips: Bath, Stonehenge & More" at the end of this chapter, for information on Greenwich).

The **Changing of the Guard,** outside the palace's front gates, takes place daily just before 11:30am from mid-April to July and on alternate days the rest of the year. (It's canceled during bad weather and during major state events, so call ☎ **0839/123-411** before setting out.) The Queen's Foot Guards, with their scarlet coats and bearskin hats, march accompanied by barked orders and foot stomping in a half-hour ceremony that replaces the sentries who stand guard in front of the palace.

The **Queen's Gallery,** the palace's small art museum, has since 1962 been displaying rotating exhibits taken from the royal family's collections. The **Royal Mews** is the queen's working stables, displaying ornately gilded carriages and live horses in stalls with their names above.

✪ **Houses of Parliament.** Parliament Sq., SW1. ☎ **0171/219-4272.** Free admission. House of Commons, public admitted Mon–Tues and Thurs from 2:30pm, Wed and Fri from 9:30am; House of Lords, public admission is dependent on debating schedule, so call ☎ 0171/219-3107. Line up at St. Stephen's Entrance, just past the statue of Oliver Cromwell; debates often run into the night and lines shrink after 6pm. Tube: Westminster.

To most people, the Houses of Parliament, with their trademark clocktower, are the ultimate London symbol. Officially known as the Palace of Westminster, the spectacular 19th-century Gothic Revival building has over 1,000 rooms and 2 miles of corridors. The clocktower, at the eastern end, houses the world's most famous timepiece. **Big Ben** refers not to the clocktower, as many people assume, but to the largest bell in the chime, a 13½-tonner named for the first commissioner of works. Listen to the familiar chime, which has inspired ostentatious doorbells around the world. At night, a light shines in the tower when Parliament is sitting. You may watch parliamentary debates from the Stranger's Galleries of Parliament's two houses.

Rebuilt in 1950 after extensive damage caused by a German air raid in 1941, the **House of Commons** remains small. Only 437 of its 651 members can sit at one time, while the rest crowd around the door and the Speaker's Chair. The ruling party and the opposition sit facing each other, two sword lengths apart. Debates in the **House of Lords** aren't usually as interesting or lively as those in the more important Commons, but the line to get in is usually shorter and a visit here will give you an appreciation for the pageantry of Parliament.

The British Museum

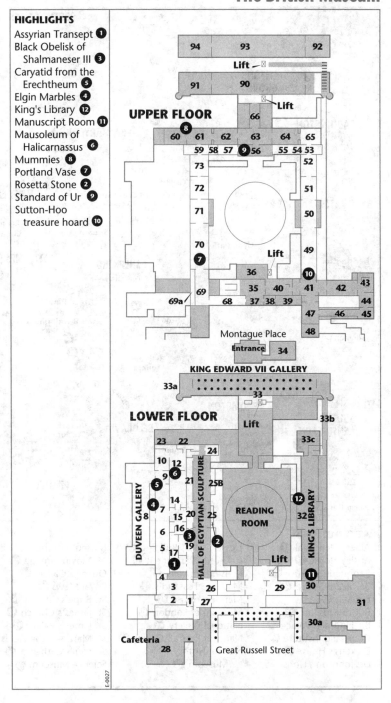

HIGHLIGHTS

Assyrian Transept ①
Black Obelisk of
  Shalmaneser III ③
Caryatid from the
  Erechtheum ⑤
Elgin Marbles ④
King's Library ⑫
Manuscript Room ⑪
Mausoleum of
  Halicarnassus ⑥
Mummies ⑧
Portland Vase ⑦
Rosetta Stone ②
Standard of Ur ⑨
Sutton-Hoo
  treasure hoard ⑩

UPPER FLOOR

94 93 92

Lift

91 90

66

60 ⑧ 61 62 63 64 65
59 58 57 ⑨ 56 55 54 53

Lift

73   52

72   51

71   50

70   49

⑦

Lift

36   ⑩

35 40   41 42 43
69a 69 68 37 38 39   44

47 46 45

48

Montague Place

Entrance 34

KING EDWARD VII GALLERY

33a
        33
                          33b

LOWER FLOOR

Lift

                          33c

23 22
        24
10 12
⑨ ⑥
⑤   25B   ⑫
        21   32
④ 7 14
8   15 20 25   **READING**
  6 16 ⑧   **ROOM**
  5   19
    17 ②
④
  4
  3
  2 1 27   26   29   30

                          31

Cafeteria
28   **Great Russell Street**   30a

E-0027

509

Inner London

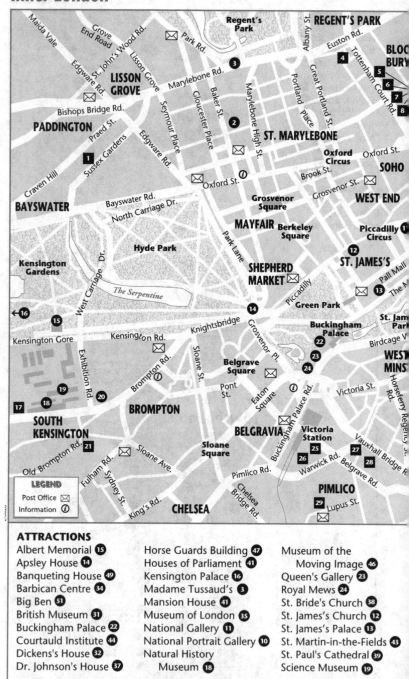

ATTRACTIONS

Albert Memorial **15**	Horse Guards Building **47**	Museum of the
Apsley House **14**	Houses of Parliament **41**	Moving Image **46**
Banqueting House **49**	Kensington Palace **16**	Queen's Gallery **23**
Barbican Centre **34**	Madame Tussaud's **3**	Royal Mews **24**
Big Ben **51**	Mansion House **41**	St. Bride's Church **38**
British Museum **31**	Museum of London **35**	St. James's Church **12**
Buckingham Palace **22**	National Gallery **11**	St. James's Palace **13**
Courtauld Institute **44**	National Portrait Gallery **10**	St. Martin-in-the-Fields **43**
Dickens's House **32**	Natural History	St. Paul's Cathedral **39**
Dr. Johnson's House **37**	Museum **18**	Science Museum **19**

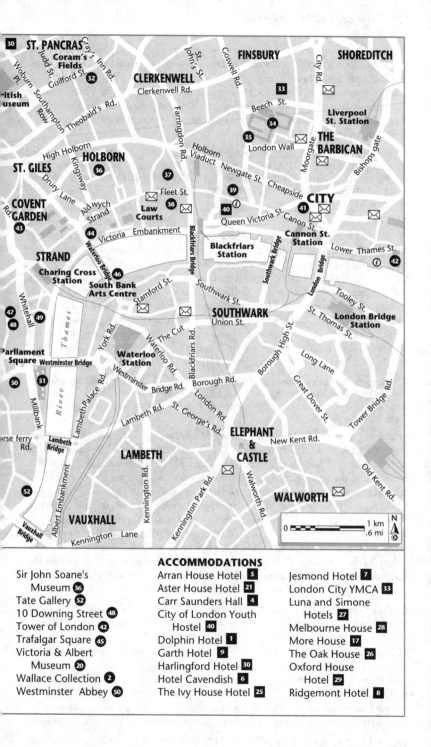

30 ST. PANCRAS
Coram's Fields
Gray's Inn Rd.
Judd St.
Guilford St. **32**
Woburn Pl.
Southampton Row
Theobald's Rd.
·itish useum

St. John's St.
Goswell Rd.
FINSBURY
CLERKENWELL
Clerkenwell Rd.
Beech St. **33**
City Rd.
SHOREDITCH
Liverpool St. Station
34
London Wall **35**
Farringdon Rd.
Holborn Viaduct
Newgate St. Cheapside
Moorgate
Bishops gate
THE BARBICAN

High Holborn
HOLBORN **36**
ST. GILES
Kingsway
Drury Lane
Aldwych
Strand
Fleet St. **37**
Law Courts **38**
39
40 ⓘ
41 CITY
Queen Victoria St. Canon St.

COVENT GARDEN **43**
Rd.
44 Victoria Embankment
Blackfriars Bridge
Blackfriars Station
Cannon St. Station
Lower Thames St.
London Bridge
42 ⓘ

STRAND
Charing Cross Station
South Bank Arts Centre **46**
Waterloo Bridge
Stamford St.
Southwark Bridge
Southwark St.
SOUTHWARK
Union St.
St. Thomas St.
Tooley St.
London Bridge Station

47
48
49
Whitehall
Thames
York Rd.
The Cut
Waterloo Rd.
Waterloo Station
Blackfriars Rd.
Borough High St.
Long Lane
Great Dover St.
Tower Bridge Rd.

Parliament Square
Westminster Bridge
50 **51**
River
Millbank
Westminster Bridge Rd.
Borough Rd.
London Rd.
St. George's Rd.
ELEPHANT & CASTLE
New Kent Rd.
Old Kent Rd.

·rse ferry Rd.
Lambeth Bridge
Lambeth Palace Rd.
Lambeth Rd.
LAMBETH
Kennington Rd.
Kennington Park Rd.
Walworth Rd.
WALWORTH

52
Albert Embankment
Vauxhall Bridge
VAUXHALL
Kennington Lane
Kennington Park Rd.

0 1 km
.6 mi
N

ACCOMMODATIONS

Sir John Soane's Museum **36**
Tate Gallery **52**
10 Downing Street **48**
Tower of London **42**
Trafalgar Square **45**
Victoria & Albert Museum **20**
Wallace Collection **2**
Westminster Abbey **50**

Arran House Hotel **5**
Aster House Hotel **21**
Carr Saunders Hall **4**
City of London Youth Hostel **40**
Dolphin Hotel **1**
Garth Hotel **9**
Harlingford Hotel **30**
Hotel Cavendish **6**
The Ivy House Hotel **25**

Jesmond Hotel **7**
London City YMCA **33**
Luna and Simone Hotels **27**
Melbourne House **28**
More House **17**
The Oak House **26**
Oxford House Hotel **29**
Ridgemont Hotel **8**

Note: The Commons sits from mid-October to the end of July, with breaks after Christmas, Easter, and Whitsunday. The Lords is open only when Parliament is in session, but they don't always sit regularly.

On the west side of the Houses of Parliament is a pleasant park, **Victoria Tower Gardens.** A little way inside the gardens you'll find a cast of Auguste Rodin's *The Burghers of Calais,* commemorating the heroism of the six burghers at the surrender of their town to Edward III in 1347.

✪ **St. Paul's Cathedral.** St. Paul's Churchyard, EC4. ☎ **0171/236-4128.** Cathedral and crypt, £4 ($7) adults, £3.50 ($6) seniors/students, £2 ($3.25) age 16 and under; galleries, £3 ($4.90) adults, £2.50 ($4.10) seniors/students, £1.50 ($2.45) age 15 and under. Mon–Sat 8:30am–4pm, Sun for services only. Tube: St. Paul's.

St. Paul's, dedicated to the patron saint of The City of London, is the architect Sir Christopher Wren's masterpiece. Capped by one of the largest domes in Christendom, the great edifice is one of the few cathedrals ever to be designed by a single architect and completed during his lifetime. Wren is buried in the cathedral's crypt; his epitaph, on the floor below the dome, reads LECTOR, SI MONUMENTUM REQUIRIS, CIRCUMSPICE (Reader, if you seek his monument, look around you). You can climb the 259 steps to the **Whispering Gallery,** just below the dome. Acoustics here are such that even whispers can be heard on the other side of the dome. Another steep climb to the **Golden Gallery** presents you with an unrivaled view of London. The cathedral has been the setting for many important ceremonies, including the funerals of Admiral Lord Nelson (1806) and Sir Winston Churchill (1965) and the wedding of Prince Charles and Lady Diana Spencer (1981).

✪ **Victoria & Albert Museum.** Cromwell Rd., SW7. ☎ **0171/938-8500,** or 0171/ 938-8441 for a recording. Admission £5 ($8) adults, £3 ($4.90) seniors, free for students and under age 18. Free for everyone 4:30–5:50pm. Mon noon–5:50pm, Tues–Sun 10am–5:50pm. Tube: South Kensington.

In a city of fantastic museums, the Victoria & Albert is tops. The V&A is the world's greatest repository of the decorative arts: If it's aesthetic and useful—and has been crafted within the last 15 centuries—you'll find it here. Comprehensive collections from around the world stretch for 7 miles and include room upon room of porcelain figurines, costume jewelry, hunting tapestries, enamel washing bowls, carved end tables, silver forks and spoons, musical instruments, gilded mirrors, ceramic bowls and plates, ivory letter openers, wax molds, stained-glass lamps, lace doilies—you name it. The famous Dress Collection covers fashion from the 16th century to the present. A magnificent new **Glass Gallery** opened in 1995 on Level C. Also don't miss the refurbished **Raphael Gallery** displaying the seven tapestry cartoons by Raphael and the sumptuous new **Silver Galleries.** The **Twentieth-Century Primary Galleries** feature temporary exhibits of furniture, sculpture, and modern design.

✪ **Tate Gallery.** Millbank, SW1. ☎ **0171/887-8000.** Permanent collection, free; temporary exhibits, £4–£7 ($7–$11) adults, £3.50 ($6) seniors/students/children. Mon–Sat 10am–5:50pm, Sun 2–5:50pm. Closed Dec 24–26. Tube: Pimlico.

This is London's museum of modern art and the primary gallery for British painting (don't miss the Blakes and Turners). Large and airy, the gallery also holds an especially good cubist collection; many major works by Dalí, Hockney, and Miró; and plenty of new contemporary paintings. The architecturally postmodern **Clore Gallery** houses an extensive collection of Turner's oils and drawings and is known for its cutting-edge exhibits. If you like your art to push the limits, attend the free daily 1-hour lecture at 1pm.

National Gallery. Trafalgar Sq., WC2. ☎ **0171/747-2885** or 0171/839-3321. Main galleries, free; temporary exhibits, varies. Mon–Sat 10am–6pm (to 8pm Wed June–Aug), Sun noon–6pm. Closed Jan 1, Good Friday, and Dec 24–26. Tube: Charing Cross or Leicester Square.

The collection is divided chronologically in four wings. The **Sainsbury Wing** houses the gallery's most precious early Renaissance works by Giotto, Masaccio, Raphael, and Piero della Francesca. The **West Wing** carries the story of art forward into the 16th century with works by Correggio, Holbein, Titian, and Brueghel. Rembrandt, Rubens, Ruisdael, and other Spanish and Dutch artists' works are displayed in the **North Wing.** The **East Wing** focuses on paintings from 1700 to 1920, exhibiting works by Hogarth, Gainsborough, Turner, and Constable as well as Monet and Cézanne. A new state-of-the-art **Micro Gallery** lets you examine any painting in the museum's vast holdings at the touch of a button. There's a great gift shop. Phone for details on current shows.

✪ **Tower of London.** Tower Hill, EC3. ☎ **0171/709-0765.** Admission £8.50 ($14) adults, £6.40 ($11) seniors/students, £5.50 ($9) ages 5–15; free for age 4 and under. Mar–Oct Mon–Sat 9am–6pm, Sun 10am–6pm; Nov–Feb Tues–Sat 9am–6pm, Sun–Mon 10am–6pm. Last tickets sold 1 hour before closing, though you really need 2½ hours to see the whole place. Free guided tours given every half hour from 9:30am. Tube: Tower Hill.

Begun by William I (the Conqueror) soon after the Norman Conquest in 1066, this complex has served as a fortress, a royal palace, a treasury, an armory, and a menagerie, but it's best remembered as a prison. The two young sons of Edward IV are thought to have been murdered here in 1485, and Henry VIII's second wife, Anne Boleyn, was executed nearby. Today the closest the Tower comes to torture is the suffocating feeling you get on weekends, when it seems as though everyone in London is there.

The Tower is home to the Crown Jewels, displayed in a fortified **Jewel House** built with moving walkways to help the crowds along. The Imperial State Crown, worn by the monarch at major state occasions, is encrusted with more than 2,800 diamonds and is the world's priciest hat. Other valuables are the exquisite Koh-i-noor diamond, in the crown of the Queen Mother; and the Star of Africa, the largest cut diamond in the world, set in the cross of the Queen Mother's Orb and Scepter. Make a point to see Henry VIII's anatomically exaggerated armor (you'll know it when you see it) in the **White Tower.**

A visit to the Tower isn't cheap—but it's worth every pound. Upon entering, wait by the first gate for the excellent guided free tour.

Tower Bridge. E1. ☎ **0171/378-1928** or 0171/407-0922, or 0171/378-7700 for information about scheduled bridge openings. Admission £5.70 ($9) adults, £3.90 ($6) seniors/ages 5–15, free for age 4 and under. Apr–Oct daily 10am–6:30pm; Nov–Mar daily 9:30am–6pm. Last entry 1¼ hours before closing. Closed Jan 1, Jan 28, and Dec 24–26. Tube: Tower Hill or London Bridge.

Here's a lyrical London landmark you should try not to miss. Inside the towers is an exhibition telling the 100-year story of the bridge, which includes some Animatronic characters plus interactive and other displays explaining the way the hydraulic system

---

A Tower Tip

If you've planned ahead, at 9:30pm you can attend the free **Ceremony of the Keys,** during which the Tower is secured for the night and attendees find themselves locked in this imposing fortress. (Don't worry too much: The Tower has long since ceased to be a prison and you're politely ushered out through a small side door.) You must book tickets at least 6 weeks in advance by writing to Ceremony of the Keys, HM Tower of London, London EC3N 4AB.

operates. Unless you're passionate about Victorian engineering, save your money and enjoy the free panoramic views from the walkways above. The bridge opens about 500 times a year. If you want to see the bridge open, call for information about scheduled openings for the following week.

✪ **Westminster Abbey.** Broad Sanctuary, SW1. ☎ **0171/222-5152** or 0171/222-7110. Abbey (nave and cloisters), free; Royal Chapels, £4 ($7) adults, £2 ($3.25) seniors/students, £1 ($1.65) age 15 and under. Abbey, Mon–Tues and Thurs–Sat 8am–6pm, Wed 8am–7:45pm (the only time photography is permitted is Wed 6–7:45pm); Royal Chapels, Mon–Fri 9:20am–3:45pm, Sat 9am–1:45pm and 3:45–4:45pm. Tube: Westminster or St. James's Park.

The Benedictine abbey, which housed a community of monks as early as A.D. 750, was called Westminster (West Monastery) because of its location west of The City. In 1050, Edward the Confessor enhanced the site and moved his palace next door, making Westminster the primary site of England's church and state. All of England's monarchs have been crowned here since William the Conqueror's coronation on Christmas Day in 1066. Many are buried here too, among a clutter of tombs of statesmen, poets, and benefactors. And, of course, in September 1997 Westminster Abbey was the site of the funeral service for the adored Diana, Princess of Wales.

When not in use, the Coronation Chair (built 1300) sits behind the High Altar. Incorporated into the chair is the Stone of Scone, which has been associated with Scottish royalty since the 9th century. Captured by Edward I in 1297, the Stone has been stolen back by Scottish nationalists several times (most recently in the 1950s) but always recovered. The abbey's **Henry VII Chapel,** added in 1503, is one of the most beautiful places you may ever see—its exuberant architectural extravagances and exquisite intricate carvings will take your breath away. Comprehensive "Super Tours" condense the abbey's 900-year history into 1½ hours for £7 ($11) per person.

Kensington Palace. The Broad Walk, Kensington Gardens, W8. ☎ **0171/937-9561.** Admission £7.50 ($12) adults, £5.70 ($9) seniors/students, £5.30 ($9) children. May–Oct 5, daily 10am–6pm by guided tour; last tour leaves at 4:45pm. Closed Oct 6–Apr for ongoing restoration. Tube: Queensway or Bayswater on north side of gardens; High St. Kensington on south side.

Once the residence of British monarchs, Kensington Palace hasn't been the official home of reigning kings since George II. It was acquired in 1689 by William and Mary as an escape from the damp royal rooms along the Thames. Since the end of the 18th century, the palace has been home to various members of the royal family, and the State Apartments are open for tours.

It was here in 1837 that a young Victoria was roused from her sleep with the news that her uncle, William IV, had died and that she was now queen of England. You can view a nostalgic collection of Victoriana, including some of her memorabilia. In the

---

For Diana Fans

Princess Diana is buried on a picturesque island on the Oval Lake at **Althorp**, the Spencer family estate in Northamptonshire. The grounds will be open for a limited time each year (in 1998, July 1 to August 30). You won't have access to the grave site or island and can view the island only across the lake. Admission is £9.50 ($15) adults, £7 ($11) seniors, and £5 ($8) children.

Of course, you must book tickets long in advance by calling ☎ **01604/592-020** or writing Althorp Admissions, c/o Wayhead, The Hollows, St. James's Street, Nottingham, NG1 6FJ. A special train and bus service will be operated by Virgin Trains; since details weren't set at press time, call ☎ **0345/484-950.**

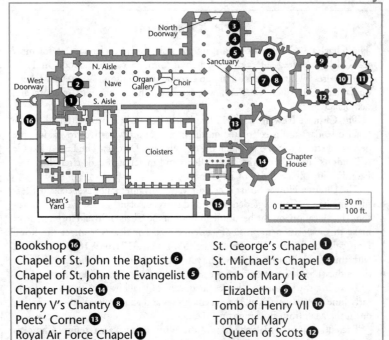

Bookshop **16**
Chapel of St. John the Baptist **6**
Chapel of St. John the Evangelist **5**
Chapter House **14**
Henry V's Chantry **8**
Poets' Corner **13**
Royal Air Force Chapel **11**
St. Andrew's Chapel **3**
St. Edward's Chapel
(Coronation Chair) **7**

St. George's Chapel **1**
St. Michael's Chapel **4**
Tomb of Mary I &
Elizabeth I **9**
Tomb of Henry VII **10**
Tomb of Mary
Queen of Scots **12**
Tomb of the Unknown Warrior/
Memorial to Churchill **2**
Undercroft Museum **15**

apartments of Queen Mary II, wife of William III, is a striking 17th-century writing cabinet inlaid with tortoiseshell. Paintings from the Royal Collection line the walls of the apartments. A rare 1750 ladies court dress and splendid examples of male court dress from the 18th century are on display in rooms adjacent to the State Apartments.

Kensington Palace is now the London home of Princess Margaret as well as the Duke and Duchess of Kent. Of course, it was once the home of Diana, Princess of Wales, and her two sons (Harry and William now live with their father at St. James's Palace, where Diana's body lay in the Chapel Royal during the week prior to her funeral). The palace is probably best known for the millions and millions of flowers that were placed in front of it during the days following Diana's death. In fact, there's been talk of building some sort of monument or garden here dedicated to Diana, but local residents have objected and the project's fate is uncertain at press time.

Kensington Gardens are open daily to sunset (they are open even when the palace is closed) to the public for leisurely strolls through the manicured grounds and around the Round Pond. One of the most famous sights here is the controversial Albert Memorial, a lasting tribute not only to Victoria's consort but also to the questionable artistic taste of the Victorian era.

MORE ATTRACTIONS

✪ **Museum of the Moving Image (MOMI).** South Bank, SE1. ☎ **0171/401-2636.** Admission £5.95 ($10) adults, £4.85 ($8) seniors/students, £4 ($6.40) age 14 and under. Daily 10am–6pm (last admission 5pm). Tube: Waterloo is closer, but the short walk over Hungerford Bridge from the Embankment Underground station is more scenic.

Special & Free Events

The **Charles I Commemoration,** on the last Sunday in January, is solemnly marked by hundreds of cavaliers marching through central London in 17th-century dress. Prayers are said at the Banqueting House in Whitehall, where, on January 30, 1649, Charles I was executed "in the name of freedom and democracy."

The **Chinese New Year** falls in late January or early February (based on the lunar calendar) and is celebrated on the nearest Sunday. Festive crowds line the decorated streets of Soho to watch the famous Lion Dancers. The **Easter Parade** is London's largest. Brightly colored floats and marching bands circle Battersea Park, kicking off a full day of activities.

The **Chelsea Flower Show** is held in May. This international spectacular features the best of British gardening, with displays of plants and flowers of all seasons. The location, on the beautiful grounds of the Chelsea Royal Hospital, helps make this exposition the rose of garden shows. For tickets, contact the Royal Horticultural Society, Vincent Square, SW1 (☎ **0171/649-1885**), or check with the British Tourist Authority in your home country (see the Appendix for the address) for the name of the overseas booking agent handling ticket sales.

Trooping the Colour celebrates the queen's official birthday on a Saturday in early June. You can catch all the queen's horses and all the queen's men parading down the Mall from Buckingham Palace.

The end of June signals the start of the **Wimbledon Lawn Tennis Championships,** tennis's most prestigious event. Grounds admission tickets are available at the gate for early rounds of play at about £9 ($15) or £4.50 ($7) after 5pm. Advance Center Court and Court 1 seats for later rounds are sold by lottery; some same-day Center Court seats are available on the first 9 days of the tournament; same-day Court 1 seats are available throughout the tournament, but lines are long and often form the night before. Apply September through December of the previous year to the All England Lawn Tennis and Croquet Club, P.O. Box 98, Church Road, Wimbledon, SW19 5AE (☎ **0181/946-2244**).

The **Notting Hill Carnival,** in late August, is one of Europe's largest annual street festivals. This African-Caribbean street fair in the community of Notting Hill attracts over half a million people during its 2 days. Live reggae and soul music combine with great Caribbean food to ensure that a great time is had by all.

You have another chance to see the royals during the **State Opening of Parliament** in late October or early November. Though the ceremony itself isn't open to the public, crowds pack the parade route to see the procession. Early November is also the season for **Guy Fawkes Day,** commemorating the anniversary of the Gunpowder Plot, an attempt to blow up James I and his parliament. Huge organized bonfires are lit throughout the city, and Guy Fawkes, the plot's most famous conspirator, is burned in effigy.

In mid-November, the **Lord Mayor's Show** takes to the streets with an elaborate parade celebrating the inauguration of the new chief of The City of London. Colorful floats, military bands, and the lord mayor's 1756 gold State Coach are all part of the event.

This lively hands-on celebration of film and TV is one of the city's most engaging museums. The chronologically arranged exhibits are staffed by costumed actors who never step out of character. The museum itself is as entertaining as a good movie. Displays strike the perfect balance between technology and the culture it produced. You can watch Russian movies on an agitprop train, create your own animated strips for a zoetrope, read the news from a TelePrompTer and then watch yourself on a monitor, and "fly" over London using chromakey technology. The emphasis here is on things British, but MOMI's extraordinarily popular slant owes much to Hollywood.

National Portrait Gallery. 2 St. Martin's Place (around the corner from the National Gallery), WC2. ☎ **0171/306-0055.** Free admission. Mon–Sat 10am–6pm, Sun noon–6pm. Closed Jan 1, Good Friday, May 1, and Dec 24–26. Tube: Charing Cross or Leicester Square.

A walk through this gallery, founded in 1856, takes you back through centuries of British social history. It's home to the only known portrait of William Shakespeare, as well as the best-known painting of the late Diana, Princess of Wales. The newest gallery exhibits 20th-century portraiture and photography.

✪ **Saatchi Collection.** 98A Boundary Rd., NW8. ☎ **0171/624-8299.** Admission £4 ($7) adults, £2 ($3.25) seniors/students, free for under age 12. Thurs–Sun noon–6pm. Tube: St. John's Wood.

Charles Saatchi is as controversial in the art world as he is in the advertising world. Britain's largest private collector of modern art built this personal museum specifically to house his large and brilliant collections. Each year the Saatchi holds an exhibition focusing on the freshest talent, making this collector one of the most influential movers on the contemporary art scene.

Courtauld Institute Galleries. Somerset House, The Strand, WC2. ☎ **0171/873-2526.** Admission £4 ($7) adults, £2 ($3.25) seniors/students/ages 5–15, free for age 4 and under. Mon–Sat 10am–6pm, Sun 2–6pm. Tube: Temple or Covent Garden.

The glories here are the impressionist and postimpressionist works: Manet's *Bar at the Folies Bergère,* Monet's *Banks of the Seine at Argenteuil,* and a number of Cézannes, including *The Card Players.* The collection also includes other remarkable works—a whole gallery of Rubens as well as some fine Renaissance paintings and works by Brueghel, Cranach, and others. Note that the gallery may be closed for refurbishment when you get there—call first.

Museum of London. 150 London Wall, EC2. ☎ **0171/600-0807.** Admission £4 ($7) adults, £2 ($3.25) children. Tues–Sat 10am–5:50pm, Sun noon–5:50pm. Tube: St. Paul's or Barbican.

This museum provides a perfect introduction to London, enabling you to trace the city's history from its Roman days to the 20th century. Highlights are an audiovisual presentation of the Great Fire as recounted by Samuel Pepys, Elizabethan jewelry, 18th-century prison cells, and the lord mayor's coach. Each era in the city's history is presented in a stimulating and interesting manner complete with evocative background music.

Highgate Cemetery. Swain's Lane, Hampstead. ☎ **0181/340-1834.** East side, £1 ($1.65); west side, £4 ($7) donation for tour. Times vary; phone for information. Only small cameras allowed, at the discretion of cemetery wardens. Tube: Archway.

Swain's Lane divides London's Highgate Cemetery in two. The old overgrown "Egyptian" west side filled up years ago and is now accessible only by guided tour. The most famous resident of the east side is Karl Marx, whose grave is topped by a huge bust—the Chinese government helps pay for its upkeep. Highgate is still an active burial ground and its keepers have asked that visitors make advance arrangements to visit. Tours are usually scheduled daily, year-round; call ahead before heading out to Highgate.

Freud Museum. 20 Maresfield Gardens, Hampstead, NW3. ☎ **0171/435-2002.** Admission £3 ($4.90) adults, £1.50 ($2.45) students, free for age 11 and under. Wed–Sun noon–5pm. Tube: Finchley Rd.

This was the home of Sigmund Freud, founder of psychoanalysis, who lived, worked, and died in this rather plain house after he and his family left Nazi-occupied Vienna as refugees in 1938. On view are rooms containing original furniture, paintings, photographs, letters, and the personal effects of Freud and his daughter, Anna. Of particular interest is Freud's study and library with his famous couch and large collection of Egyptian, Roman, and Asian antiquities. Exhibits and archive film programs are also on view.

Madame Tussaud's. Marylebone Rd., NW1. ☎ **0171/935-6861.** Admission £9.25 ($15) adults, £6.95 ($11) seniors, £6.10 ($10) ages 5–15, free for age 4 and under. July–Aug daily 9am–5:50pm; Sept–June Mon–Fri 10am–5:30pm, Sat–Sun 9:30am–5:30pm. Closed Dec 25. Tube: Baker St.

Eerily lifelike figures have made this century-old waxworks world famous. The original moldings of members of the French court, to whom Mme Tussaud had direct access, are fascinating. But the modern superstars and the Chamber of Horrors, to which this "museum" donates the lion's share of space, are the stuff tourist traps are made of. Madame Tussaud's is expensive and overrated. If you must go, go early to beat the crowds; better still, reserve tickets 1 day in advance, then go straight to the head of the line.

Apsley House. The Wellington Museum. 149 Piccadilly, Hyde Park Corner, W1. ☎ **0171/499-5676.** Admission £4 ($7) adults, £2.50 ($4.10) children. Tues–Sun 11am–5pm. Closed Jan 1, May 1, and Dec 24–26. Tube: Hyde Park Corner.

The original home of the first duke of Wellington contains handsome Adam and Wyatt interiors, a superb collection of paintings (including masterpieces by Velázquez, Goya, and Rubens), sculpture, furniture, porcelain, and silver. It was to this house that the duke returned after his great victory over Napoléon at Waterloo.

Sir John Soane's Museum. 13 Lincoln's Inn Fields, WC2. ☎ **0171/430-0175.** Free admission. Tues–Sat 10am–5pm (the first Tues of each month also 6–9pm). Tube: Holborn.

A fantastic array of archaeological antiquities, architectural drawings, and important works by Hogarth, Turner, and Watteau are housed in the former home of the

---

A Little Tussaud Trivia

1. Cybill Shepherd was added to the museum's collection in 1997, making her the first American TV star to be displayed.
2. Darlene Conley, star of the daytime soap *The Bold and the Beautiful,* was added to the collection later in 1997, making her the first American TV soap star to be displayed. Her figure is now in the Amsterdam branch; though it was supposed to move eventually to the London branch, those plans seem to have been put on hold.
3. The royal family are the only exhibits you can't stand alongside for photos. When it was announced that the Prince and Princess of Wales were separating, their mannequins were moved slightly apart. When they were divorced, Diana was moved to the end of the royal line. However, since her death she has ben brought down from the royal enclosure so that people can get closer to her.

Literary London

London boasts an extremely long and rich literary tradition. **Geoffrey Chaucer** lived above Aldgate, in the easternmost part of The City until 1386, and playwright **Joe Orton** lived on Noel Road in Islington until his 1967 murder. **Marguerite Radclyffe Hall,** author of the first lesbian novel *The Well of Loneliness,* lived in Chelsea and is buried in Highgate cemetery. **Oscar Wilde, Dylan Thomas, Virginia Woolf, Fanny Burney, George Orwell, D. H. Lawrence, George Bernard Shaw, Rudyard Kipling, George Eliot, Dorothy L. Sayers, William Blake**—the list of authors who made London their home goes on and on. Alas, a little blue plaque is usually all that's left to mark the past, but there are some exceptions.

The wonderful Georgian town house where lexicographer Samuel Johnson lived and worked, compiling the world's first English dictionary, is now a shrine called **Dr. Johnson's House,** 17 Gough Sq., Fleet Street, EC4 (☎ **0171/ 353-3745;** Tube: Blackfriars, Temple, or Holborn). His original dictionary, which is on display, includes the definition "Dull: to make dictionaries is dull work." There's not much here in the way of furnishings, but the long upstairs room in which he worked has plenty of ambiance. Admission is £3 ($4.90) adults, £2 ($3.25) seniors/students, and £1 ($1.65) age 15 and under. It's open May to September, Monday to Saturday 11am to 5:30pm; October to April, Monday to Saturday 11am to 5pm.

Thomas Carlyle's House, 24 Cheyne Row, SW3 (☎ **0171/352-7087;** Tube: Sloane Square), is an 18th-century Queen Anne on a beautiful Chelsea backstreet. The Scottish historian/philosopher lived here 47 years, until his death in 1881. His house remains virtually unaltered, to the extent that some of the rooms are without electric light. In this eerie atmosphere you can imagine yourself sitting in one of the writer's original Victorian chairs or playing the same piano that Chopin himself played. Admission is £3 ($4.80) adults and £1.50 ($2.40) age 16 and under. It's open April to October, Wednesday to Sunday 11am to 5pm.

Dickens's House, 48 Doughty St., WC1 (☎ **0171/405-2127;** Tube: Russell Square), was home to one of London's most famous novelists for a short but prolific period. It was here that he worked on *The Pickwick Papers, Nicholas Nickleby,* and *Oliver Twist.* His letters, desk and chair, and first editions are on display, along with some memorabilia of his wife, Catherine. On Wednesday evening in summer a one-man play is presented. Admission is £3.50 ($6) adults, £2.50 ($4.10) seniors/students, £1.50 ($2.45) children, and £7 ($11) families (two adults, three children). It's open Monday to Saturday 10am to 5pm.

architect of the first Bank of England. The house is packed with objects, seemingly displayed in a haphazard manner. But enter the small room where Hogarth's *The Rake's Progress* is displayed and ask the guard to show you the room's secret. You'll be convinced that there's a method to the madness.

Wallace Collection. Hertford House, Manchester Sq. (steps from Oxford St.), W1. ☎ **0171/935-0687.** Free admission (donation requested). Mon–Sat 10am–5pm, Sun 2–5pm (from 11am in summer). Tube: Bond St.

It's hard to know which is more impressive, the art and antiques or the house in which they're displayed. The collection includes masterpieces by Rembrandt, Rubens,

Murillo, and van Dyck, plus superb examples of 18th-century furniture, Sèvres porcelain, clocks, objets d'art, and, quite unexpectedly, an impressive array of European and Asian arms and armor.

PARKS & GARDENS

Hyde Park is the park most often associated with London, and it's one of the city's most popular with its Serpentine Lake and Rotten Row bridle path. As in other Royal Parks, wood-and-canvas deck chairs are scattered about so that you too can sit in an English garden waiting for the sun. Note, though, that fee collectors will stop by and demand 60p ($1) for the privilege of using these seats; the benches and grass are free. The park is especially lively on Sunday, when artists hang their wares along the Bayswater Road fence and the northeast corner, near Marble Arch, becomes Speakers' Corner, where anyone can stand on a soapbox and pontificate on any subject. Though this tradition is often touted as an example of Britain's tolerance of free speech, few people realize that this ritual began several hundred years ago when condemned prisoners were allowed some final words before they were hanged on Tyburn gallows, which stood on the same spot. Take the tube to Hyde Park Corner.

A huge irregular circle north of central London, **Regent's Park** is the city's playground, famous for its zoo, concerts, and open-air theater in summer. A band plays free beside the lake twice daily May to August. Get there by tube to Regent's Park or Baker Street, or Camden Town for the zoo.

✪ **St. James's Park,** opposite Buckingham Palace, is perhaps the most beautiful of London's parks. Swans, geese, and other waterfowl, including a family of pelicans, make their home here (feedings daily at 3pm). A central location, a beautiful lake, and plentiful benches make this park perfect for picnicking. Take the tube to St. James's Park. Adjacent **Green Park** is so named because it lacks flowers (except briefly in spring), offering instead large shade trees under which to picnic on hot summer days.

The **Chelsea Physic Garden,** 66 Royal Hospital Rd., SW3 (☎ **0171/352-5646**), founded in 1673, is England's second-oldest botanical garden. Set behind high brick walls, it consists of a rare collection of old and exotic plants, shrubs, and trees, including Asian herbs and a 19th-century fruiting olive tree. It was founded by the Society of Apothecaries to teach their apprentices how to identify medicinal plants and has expanded to include rare species from the New World. Admission is £3.50 ($6) adults and £1.80 ($2.95) students and children. The garden is open April to October, Wednesday noon to 5pm and Sunday 2 to 6pm. Take the tube to Sloane Square or bus no. 11, 19, 22, or 319.

An important research facility, the ✪ **Royal Botanic Gardens,** better known as **Kew Gardens** (☎ **0181/940-1171** or 0181/332-5622), also happens to be London's most beautiful indoor/outdoor garden. The architectural brilliance of the iron-and-glass greenhouses and Chinese-style pagoda combine with chrysanthemums, rhododendrons, peonies, and one of the world's largest orchid collections to make a visit to Kew unforgettable. The gardens are open daily: April to October 9:30am to 6:30pm and November to March 9:30am to 4pm. Admission is £4.50 ($7) adults, £3 ($4.90) seniors/students, and £2.50 ($4.10) ages 5 to 15. Kew can be reached by tube in about 30 minutes. April to October, you can reach the gardens by boat from Westminster Pier, near the Westminster Underground station. The trip upstream takes about 90 minutes, costing £6 ($10) one-way or £10 round-trip ($16) adults and £3 ($4.90) one-way or £5 ($8) round-trip ages 4 to 14; free for age 3 and under. For information, call ☎ **0171/930-2062.**

ORGANIZED TOURS

WALKING TOURS   London's most interesting streets are best explored on foot. If you want to stroll on your own, my *Frommer's Memorable Walks in London* details 11 great walks both on and off the beaten path.

If you want to join a tour, several high-quality companies will help you find your way inexpensively. Excellent walks are offered by **The Original London Walks,** P.O. Box 1708, London NW6 (☎ **0171/624-3978**), which has some experts on its team and constantly updates its program to cover such topics as London's Haunted Pubs and Jane Austen's London; and **Discovery Walks,** 67 Chancery Lane, WC2 (☎ **0181/530-8443**), whose themes include Ghosts and Jack the Ripper. They operate regularly scheduled theme-based city tours on a daily basis; write or phone for a free brochure or consult the "Around Town" section of *Time Out.* Tours generally cost £4 to £5 ($7 to $8) and represent one of the best bargains in London.

BUS TOURS   At £12 ($20) per person, the panoramic tours offered by **London Transport** (☎ **0171/222-1234**) are cheapest. Buses depart frequently from outside the Piccadilly Circus Underground station (Haymarket), Victoria Station (opposite the Palace Theatre), Marble Arch (Speakers' Corner), and the Baker Street Underground station. May to mid-September, tours run daily 9am to as late as 7pm; the rest of the year, tours are given daily 9am to 5pm.

Do-it-yourselfers should purchase a **Travelcard** (see "Getting Around," earlier in this chapter) and take the front seat on the upper deck of a public double-decker. Two of the more scenic bus routes are **no. 11,** which passes King's Road, Victoria Station, Westminster Abbey, Whitehall, Horse Guards, Trafalgar Square, the National Gallery, The Strand, the Law Courts, Fleet Street, and St. Paul's Cathedral; and **no. 53,** which passes the Regent's Park Zoo, Oxford Circus, Regent Street, Piccadilly Circus, the National Gallery, Trafalgar Square, Horse Guards, Whitehall, and Westminster Square.

6 Shopping

Even the most jaded capitalists are awed by the sheer quantity of shops in London. The range and variety of goods are so staggering that a quick stop into a store can easily turn into an all-day shopping spree.

RECOVERING VAT

The British government encourages visitors to part with their pounds by offering to refund the 17.5% **value-added tax (VAT).** Not all retailers participate in this program, and those that do require a minimum purchase, usually £50 ($80). The procedure is cumbersome: Show the sales clerk your passport and fill out a special form at each shop you visit. Then present the forms and the goods to a Customs officer upon departing Great Britain. After the official validates your VAT forms, mail them back to the stores where you made your purchases. Several months later you'll receive your refund—in pounds sterling minus a small commission. You can avoid the bank charges usually encountered when cashing foreign-currency checks by using your credit cards for the purchases and requesting that your VAT refund be credited to your account.

SHOPPING AREAS

The **West End** is the heart of London shopping, and mile-long **Oxford Street** is its main artery. Its sidewalks are terminally congested—with good reason. A solid row of shops stretches as far as the eye can see, so if you have only 1 day to shop, spend it here. At its midsection, Oxford Street is bisected by **Regent Street,** a more elegant thoroughfare, lined with boutiques, fine china shops, and jewelers. At **Piccadilly Circus,** Regent Street meets Piccadilly, which, along with St. James's Street, Jermyn Street, the Burlington Arcade, and Old and New Bond streets, make up one of the world's swankiest shopping areas. Street fashions galore can be found around Covent Garden Market and on Longacre, Shorts Gardens, and Neal Street as well as at the famous youth-oriented Camden Markets.

The best shops in **Chelsea** are along **King's Road,** a mile-long street straddling the fashion fence between trend and tradition. In the late 1970s and early 1980s, this was the center of punk fashion. Things have quieted down somewhat since, but the chain-store boutiques are still mixed with a healthy dose of the avant-garde.

Kensington is another trendy area for urban designs. The best young fashion flourishes on **Kensington High Street** in general, and in **Hype DF,** 48–52 Kensington High St. (☎ **0171/938-4343**), in particular.

TRADITIONAL SALES

January sales are a British tradition, when prices can be reduced by as much as 30%. All the big department stores start their sales just after Christmas, and the smaller shops usually follow suit. Several department stores (chiefly Harrods and Selfridges) compete for all-night lines by offering one or two particularly remarkable specials. Be aware that some goods, shipped in especially for the sales, aren't as high quality as those offered the rest of the year.

DEPARTMENT STORES & BOOKSTORES

Department stores are the city's most famous shopping institutions, and a handful stand out as top attractions as well. All the following accept American Express, Diners Club, MasterCard, and Visa.

By many estimates, ✪ **Harrods,** 87–135 Brompton Rd., SW1 (☎ **0171/730-1234;** Tube: Knightsbridge), is the world's largest department store, selling everything from pins to pianos. The store claims that you can buy anything here—and it may be true. Even if you're not in a shopping mood, the incredible ground-floor food halls are worth a visit. Admire the stained-glass ceiling and the unbelievable fresh-fish fountain in the seafood hall. It's closed Sunday. **Selfridges,** 400 Oxford St., W1 (☎ **0171/629-1234;** Tube: Marble Arch or Bond St.), seems almost as big and more crowded than its chief rival. Opened in 1909 by Harry Gordon Selfridge, a salesman from Chicago, this store revolutionized retailing with its varied merchandise and dynamic displays.

Liberty, 210–220 Regent St., W1 (☎ **0171/734-1234;** Tube: Oxford Circus), has a worldwide reputation for selling fine textiles in unique surroundings. The pretty old-world store has an incomparable Asian department. If you're British, **Marks & Spencer,** 458 Oxford St., W1 (☎ **0171/935-7954;** Tube: Oxford Circus), is where you buy your quality underwear. M&S is known for well-priced, quality family clothes—but don't expect the latest fashion trends. And fans of *Ab Fab*'s Edina and Patsy may want to stop by **Harvey Nichols (Harvey Nicks),** 109–125 Knightsbridge, SW1 (☎ **0171/235-5000;** Tube: Knightsbridge), to check out its top-brand designer labels.

Foyle's, 113–119 Charing Cross Rd., WC2 (☎ **0171/437-5660;** Tube: Tottenham Court Rd.), London's leading bookstore, offering books on every subject imaginable, is spread over several massive floors. In addition to stocking London's largest selection of gay and lesbian books, **Gay's the Word Bookshop,** 66 Marchmont St., WC1 (☎ **0171/278-7654;** Tube: Russell Square), holds regular readings and sells calendars, kitsch clothing, jewelry, and associated paraphernalia.

MARKETS

Outdoor markets are where bargain hunters shop for food, clothing, furniture, books, antiques, crafts, and junk. Dozens of markets cater to different communities, and for shopping or browsing they offer a unique and exciting time. Few stalls officially open before sunrise. Still, flashlight-wielding professionals appear early, snapping up gems before they reach the display table. During wet weather stalls may close early.

Brixton is the heart of African-Caribbean London and the **Brixton Market,** Electric Avenue, SW9 (Tube: Brixton), is its soul. Electric Avenue (immortalized by Jamaican singer Eddie Grant) is lined mostly with exotic fruit and vegetable stalls. But continue to the end, turn right, and you'll see a good selection of the cheapest secondhand clothes in London. Take a detour off the avenue through the enclosed Granville Arcade for African fabrics, traditional West African teeth-cleaning sticks, reggae records, and newspapers oriented to the African-British community. It's open Monday, Tuesday, Thursday, and Saturday 8am to 6pm, Wednesday 8am to 1pm, and Friday 8am to 7pm.

The **Camden Markets,** along Camden High Street, NW1 (Tube: Camden Town), are a trendy collection of stalls, in parking lots and empty spaces extending all the way to Chalk Farm Road and specializing in original fashions by young designers and junk from people of all ages. Cafes and pubs (some offering live music) line the route, making for an enjoyable day. When you've had enough of shopping, turn north and walk along the peaceful and pretty Regent's Canal. It's open Saturday and Sunday 8am to 6pm.

The market where you're most likely to spot a bargain is the **Bermondsey Market,** aka the New Caledonian Market, at the corner of Long Lane and Bermondsey Street, SE1 (Tube: London Bridge). It's held Friday only, opening at 7am. Though opinions vary about when it closes (anywhere from noon to 3pm), it's vital to arrive early. The **Camden Passage Market,** off Upper Street, N1 (☎ **0171/359-0190;** Tube: Angel), is smaller than Portobello (below) and usually cheaper too. It's open Wednesday 7am to 2pm and Saturday 9am to 5pm. The stores are also open regular hours here, Tuesday to Saturday.

The **Portobello Market,** located along Portobello Road, W11 (Tube: Notting Hill Gate; you can ask anyone for directions from there), is the granddaddy of them all, famous for its overflow of antiques and bric-a-brac along a road that never seems to end. As at all antiques markets, bargaining is in order. Saturday 8am to 4pm is the best time to go, as the market consists mainly of fruit and vegetable stalls during the week.

7 London After Dark

As the sun sets and a hush descends on the rest of the land, the capital's theaters, clubs, and pubs swing into action. **TicketMaster** (☎ **0171/344-4444**) makes credit-card bookings for theaters, opera, ballet, and pop-music concerts. Its hot line is open 24 hours. TicketMaster locations include the London Tourist Board Information Centre, Victoria Station forecourt (open Monday to Saturday 9am to 7pm and Sunday 9am to 5pm), and Harrods department store, Knightsbridge (open Monday, Tuesday, and Thursday to Saturday 9am to 6pm and Wednesday 9am to 8pm).

Attending a play in London is almost a required experience, one that'll most likely deliver great pleasure. More theatrical entertainment is offered here than in any other city, at prices far below New York's. *Time Out* offers a comprehensive roundup of the week's events (on the Internet at **www.timeout.co.uk**).

Lunchtime Church Concerts

Lunchtime concerts are regularly scheduled in various churches. These concerts, usually by young performers, are all free, though it's customary to leave a small donation. A list of churches offering concerts is available from the London Tourist Board. I've included my favorites here.

St. Bride's Church, Fleet Street, EC4 (☎ 0171/353-1301; Tube: Black-friars), was completed by Christopher Wren in 1703, and its tall tiered spire is said to have become the model for wedding cakes when it was copied by a baker. Concerts begin at 1:15pm and feature professional musicians or top students on Tuesday and Friday, while Wednesday is devoted to organ recitals. You'll want to arrive early to explore the ancient crypt of this handsome church. When Christopher Wren designed **St. James's Church,** 197 Piccadilly, W1 (☎ 0171/381-0441; Tube: Piccadilly Circus), he said that it best embodied his idea of what a parish church should be. In addition to regular free recitals Wednesday to Friday at 1:10pm, there are inexpensive evening concerts Thursday to Saturday.

St. Martin-in-the-Fields, Trafalgar Square, WC2 (☎ 0171/839-8362; Tube: Leicester Square or Charing Cross), was once really "in the fields." Its wide tower-topped portico was the model for many colonial churches in America. It's famous for its music program. There are chamber-music recitals Monday, Tuesday, Wednesday, and Friday at 1:05pm, plus concerts by candlelight Thursday to Saturday and many other special performances of oratorios. On Sunday it's worth attending the sublime evensong. Tickets for concerts range from £6 to £16 ($10 to $26).

THE PERFORMING ARTS

THEATER   The term *West End,* when applied to theater, refers to the commercial theaters around Shaftesbury Avenue and Covent Garden. Currently, there are more than 40 such houses where comedies, musicals, and dramas are regularly staged. Tickets cost £10 to £32.50 ($16 to $53), plus a 12½% booking fee, and are usually most expensive for musicals, as demand is highest. But discounts are available. The Society of West End Theatre operates a **discount ticket booth** in Leicester Square, where tickets for many shows are half price, plus a £2 ($3.25) service charge. They're sold only on the day of performance, and there's a limit of four per person. No credit cards are accepted. The booth is open Monday to Saturday from noon on matinee days (which vary with individual theaters) and 1 to 6:30pm for evening performances. All West End theaters are closed Sunday.

Blockbuster shows can be sold out months in advance, but if you just *have* to see the most popular show, one of the many high-commission **ticket agencies** can help you. Always check with the box office first for last-minute returns. Free West End theater guides listing all the current productions are distributed by tourist offices, hotels, and ticket agencies.

If you have an International Student ID Card (ISIC), you can purchase tickets to top shows at drastically reduced prices. Not all theaters participate in this program, so call first for availability. Those that participate offer their **student-priced seats** on a standby basis half an hour before the performance.

You can see Shakespeare's plays and other classical and contemporary theater at the **Royal National Theatre,** South Bank, SE1 (☎ 0171/928-2252 for the box office, 0171/633-0880 for information and backstage tours; Tube: Waterloo), and at the new

Globe Theatre, Bankside, SE1 (☎ 0171/902-1500; Tube: London Bridge), an out-door playhouse built from oak and thatch and based on what little we know of the design for the 1599 theater. There's no heat or light inside and no sound system. The benches seat 1,000; up to 500 "groundlings" can stand, and just as in Shakespeare's day their commentary on the action is encouraged.

Dozens of **fringe theaters** devoted to "alternative" plays, revivals, contemporary dramas, and even musicals are often more exciting than established West End productions and are lower in price. Expect to pay around £7 to £21 ($11 to $34). Among them the ✪ **Almeida Theatre,** Almeida Street, N1 (☎ 0171/359-4404; Tube: Angel), is outstanding, a small theater where you're likely to catch such great talents as Diana Rigg and Ralph Fiennes performing in classics like *Who's Afraid of Virginia Woolf?* and *Ivanov* or Jonathan Miller directing Shakespeare. Check *Time Out* for show times.

OPERA & DANCE   Not until the 1946 premiere of Benjamin Britten's *Peter Grimes* did British opera gain serious attention. But since then great composers have lifted British opera onto the world stage. The best thing about dance in London (and true to a lesser extent for opera) is that the major houses offer inexpensive standby seats sold on the day of performance only while the prices at fringe theaters rarely top £7 ($11). Check *Time Out* for major programs and current fringe offerings.

The 2,350-seat **London Coliseum,** St. Martin's Lane, WC2 (☎ 0171/632-8300 for the box office; Tube: Leicester Square or Charing Cross), is home to the English National Opera (ENO), an innovative company that continues to thrill enthusiasts and traditionalists. Operas are always sung in English, and many productions have been transported to Germany, France, and the United States. The ENO season runs September to July; visiting companies, often dance, perform during summer. The box office is open Monday to Saturday 10am to 8pm. Tickets run £6.50 to £55 ($11 to $90).

Home to the Royal Opera and the Royal Ballet, the **Royal Opera House,** Bow Street, Covent Garden, WC2, is rich in history, having first hosted an opera in 1817. The theater will be closed until December 1999 for a major expansion. Meanwhile, the Royal Ballet and Royal Opera perform at various venues in London, regionally, and overseas. For details, call ☎ 0171/240-1200 or fax 0171/212-9502.

Sadly, the old Sadler's Wells Theatre on Rosebery Avenue, EC1, has been demolished. Visiting opera and dance companies will be appearing at the **Peacock Theatre,** Portugal Street, off Kingsway, WC2 (☎ 0171/314-8800; Tube: Aldwych or Holborn), until the new theater is built in a couple of years. Tickets are £7.50 to £40 ($12 to $65). The box office is open Monday 10am to 6pm and Tuesday to Saturday noon to 8pm.

CLASSICAL MUSIC   The sprawling mazelike **Barbican Centre,** Silk Street, EC2 (☎ 0171/638-8891; Tube: Barbican or Moorgate), has an excellent concert hall that the London Symphony Orchestra calls home. Even if you're not attending a performance, pop down before a show for a free concert in the foyer. Concerts and times vary. The box office is open daily 9am to 8pm, and tickets are £6 to £30 ($10 to $49).

The **Royal Albert Hall,** Kensington Gore, SW7 (☎ 0171/589-8212; Tube: South Kensington), attracts top symphonies (when there's no rock concert or boxing match), despite its infamous echo. The box office is open daily 9am to 9pm. Tickets run £5 to £47 ($8 to $77), with standing room for as little as £3 ($4.80).

The **Royal Festival Hall and Hayward Gallery,** South Bank, SE1 (☎ 0171/960-4242; Tube: Waterloo or Embankment), contains three well-designed modern concert halls. Concerts are staged nightly and encompass an eclectic range of styles. The Royal Festival Hall is the usual site for major orchestra performances. The smaller Queen Elizabeth Hall is known for its chamber-music concerts and contemporary dance performances, while the intimate Purcell Room usually hosts smaller chamber ensembles and young solo performers. In addition, there are free concerts in the lobby of the Royal Festival Hall (Wednesday to Sunday 12:30 to 2pm, and jazz Friday 5:15 to 6:45pm). The box office is open daily 10am to 9pm. Tickets are £5 to £50 ($8 to $82).

Perhaps the best auditorium for both intimacy and acoustics, **Wigmore Hall,** 36 Wigmore St., W1 (☎ 0171/935-2141; Tube: Bond St. or Oxford Circus), presents instrumental and song recitals, chamber music, and early-music and baroque concerts. The Sunday Morning Coffee Concerts, with tickets at £8 or £9 ($13 or $15), are great values. Buy the cheapest seats, as it doesn't matter where you sit. The box office is open Monday to Saturday 10am to 8:30pm, with tickets at £6 to £45 ($10 to $73).

Britain's clearinghouse and resource center for "serious" music, the **British Music Information Centre,** 10 Stratford Place, W1 (☎ 0171/499-8567; Tube: Bond St.), provides free phone and walk-in information on current and upcoming events. Recitals for as little as £2 or £3 ($3.25 or $4.90) are usually offered weekly, often Tuesday and Thursday at 7:30pm; call for exact times.

LIVE-MUSIC CLUBS

ROCK   Since the 1960s British rock explosion, London hasn't let up on the number of clubs featuring homegrown talent, and the tradition continues with the current demand for Britpop groups. The West End in general, Soho in particular, has a number of intimate places featuring every kind of music. Archaic drinking laws require most late-opening clubs to charge admission, which unfortunately often gets pricey. As usual, check *Time Out* for up-to-the-minute details.

Rock Garden, 6–7 Covent Garden Piazza, WC2 (☎ 0171/836-4052; Tube: Covent Garden), is far from fashion conscious. Because this small basement club is near touristy Covent Garden Market, most of the 250 or so revelers are usually foreigners. The quality of music varies, as the club's policy is to give new talent a stage. But Dire Straits, The Police, and many others played here before fame visited them, and triple and quadruple bills ensure a good variety. It's open Monday to Thursday 5pm to 3am, Friday 5pm to 5am, Saturday 4 to 10pm, and Sunday 7:30 to 11:30pm. Admission is free Monday to Friday to 8pm; after 8 cover is £5 to £8 ($8 to $13). At 10pm Saturday it becomes Gardens nightclub, for which admission is £12 ($20).

Popular with locals, the split-level **Wag,** 35 Wardour St., W1 (☎ 0171/437-5534; Tube: Leicester Square or Piccadilly Circus), is a good hangout despite its attitude-heavy management. The downstairs stage usually attracts newly signed cutting-edge bands, while dance disks spin up top. The door policy can be selective, but if it's your kind of music, you probably already dress for the part. It's open Wednesday to Thursday 10pm to 3am, Friday 10pm to 4am, and Saturday 10pm to 5am. Cover is £4 to £10 ($7 to $16), depending on the day. On Saturday before 11pm you'll save £2 ($3.25).

Many of London's best noise polluters are in Camden Town and adjacent Kentish Town, just east of Regent's Park. Smaller, cheaper, and often better than its competitors, the **Bull & Gate,** 389 Kentish Town Rd., NW5 (☎ 0171/485-5358; Tube: Kentish Town), is the unofficial headquarters of London's pub rock scene. Independent and unknown bands are often presented back-to-back by the half dozen. Music is Monday to Saturday 9 to 11:30pm, with £3.50 to £5 ($6 to $8) cover. **Camden**

Palace, 1A Camden High St., NW1 (☎ **0171/387-0428;** Tube: Mornington Crescent or Camden Town), features a variety of music from punk to funk. When the bands stop, records spin and feet keep moving to the beat. It's open Tuesday 10pm to 2am and Friday and Saturday 10pm to 6am. Cover is £5 to £20 ($8 to $33).

JAZZ, FUNK & SOUL   You can get information on jazz concerts and events from **Jazz Services** (☎ 0171/405-0737) and from *Time Out.*

In addition to those listed below, the major jazz venues to check out are **Vortex N16,** 139 Stoke Newington Church St. (☎ **0171/254-6516;** BritRail: Stoke Newington); **Jazz Cafe,** 5 Parkway, NW1 (☎ **0171/344-0044;** Tube: Camden Town); **Pizza Express Jazz Club,** 10 Dean St., W1 (☎ **0171/439-8722;** Tube: Tottenham Court Rd.); and the **606 Club,** 90 Lots Rd., SW10 (☎ **0171/352-5953;** Tube: Earls Court or Fulham Broadway).

The small **Bluenote Club,** 1 Hoxton Sq., N1 (☎ **0171/729-8440;** Tube: Old St.), puts on a whole range of sounds from Asian, African, and Latin to jazz, fusion, bebop, and soul. It's open Monday to Wednesday 9pm to 1:30am, Thursday 10pm to 3am, Friday and Saturday 10pm to 5am, and Sunday 1pm to midnight. Cover is £3 to £8 ($4.90 to $13).

The austere underground **100 Club,** 100 Oxford St., W1 (☎ **0171/636-0933;** Tube: Tottenham Court Rd.), usually hosts jazz on Wednesday, Friday, and Saturday nights, with a free jazz session at lunchtime on Friday. The stage is in the center of a smoky basement, looking just the way a jazz club is supposed to look. Sunday evening is usually given over to rhythm and blues, Monday brings a jitterbug session, while Tuesday and Thursday lean more toward popular sounds. It's open Monday and Wednesday 7:30pm to midnight, Tuesday and Saturday 7:30pm to 1am, Thursday 8pm to 1am, and Friday 8:30pm to 3am. Cover is £5 to £8 ($8 to $13); a student discount is available. **Ronnie Scotts,** 47 Frith St., W1 (☎ **0171/439-0747;** Tube: Leicester Square), is the capital's best-known jazz room. Top names from around the world regularly grace this Soho stage, but fans be forewarned: This place is pricey. Call for events and show times. It's open Monday to Saturday 8:30pm to 2am and Sunday 7:30 to 11pm. Cover is £15 ($24).

BARS & PUBS

BARS   Spanish in atmosphere, **Bar Solona,** 13 Old Compton St., W1 (☎ **0171/287-9932;** Tube: Leicester Square or Tottenham Court Rd.), offers lots of hidden vaulted nooks, hanging hams, and Flamenco guitarists on weekends. Fresh tapas are displayed behind a glass counter, at which you can also order jugs of sangría. Unfortunately, the compact subterranean bar, beneath Café Boheme, can become quite smoky. It's open daily 11am to 3am. Cover is £4 ($7) on Friday and Saturday after 9pm.

Named after a kitschy musical revue in San Francisco and known to locals as BBB, **Beach Blanket Babylon,** 45 Ledbury Rd., W11 (☎ **0171/229-2907;** Tube: Bayswater or Westbourne Park), looks like a phantasmagorical film set with plaster-sculpted fireplaces, tall towers, purple velvet benches, and a kaleidoscopic window. A gangplank connects the spirited bar to a trendy eclectic restaurant that's always full with a see-and-be-seen crowd. It's open daily noon to midnight, with no cover.

PUBS   There's nothing more British than a pub. The public house is exactly that: the British public's place to meet, exchange stories, tell jokes, and drink. Americans tend to think of pubs as evening entertainment, but to the British these institutions are all-day affairs. There's no taboo about spending an afternoon in a pub, and on Sunday afternoon the whole family might go. (Note that children under 14 aren't allowed in pubs at all, and no one under 18 may legally drink alcohol.)

Beer is the main drink sold here; don't even try to order a martini in most places. Sold in Imperial half pints and pints (20% larger than U.S. measures), the choice is usually between lager and bitter. Expect to pay between £1.75 and £2.50 ($2.85 and $4.10) for a pint. Many pubs serve particularly good "real" ales, distinguishable at the bar by hand pumps that are "pulled" by the barkeep. Real ales are natural "live" beers, allowed to ferment in the cask. Unlike lagers, English ales are served at room temperature and may take some getting used to. For an unusual and tasty alternative to barley pop, try cider, a flavorful fermented apple juice that's so good you'll hardly notice the alcohol—until later.

Generally, there's no table service in pubs, and drinks (and food) are ordered at the bar. Tipping is unusual and should be reserved for exemplary service. Most pubs are open Monday to Saturday 11am to 11pm and Sunday noon to 3pm and 7 to 10:30pm. A few close daily 3 to 7pm.

Carpeted floors, etched glass, and carved-wood bars are the hallmarks of most pubs. But each one looks unique, and each has its particular flavor and crowd. Greater London's 7,000-plus pubs ensure that you'll never have to walk more than a couple of blocks to find one, and part of the enjoyment of pubbing is discovering a special one on your own. But I've listed a few tried-and-true pubs to help you on your way.

On the south bank of the Thames offering a stunning vista of St. Paul's and the London skyline opposite, the **Anchor Tavern,** Bank End, Bankside, SE1 (☎ 0171/407-3003; Tube: Mansion House or London Bridge), was built in 1777 and drips with atmosphere. Alas, the service can be very slow and unenthusiastic, which does tend to let the ambiance of the place down slightly. London's only Arts and Crafts pub, the ✪ **Blackfriar,** 174 Queen Victoria St., EC4 (☎ 0171/407-3003; Tube: Blackfriars), is remarkable for its stunning exterior and interior design. Marble, beaten copper, brass fittings, and gas lamps adorn both. In the grotto bar, drinkers are watched over by mischievous demons, their legs swinging nonchalantly from delicate marble ledges, while copper reliefs of jovial monks enjoy frothing tankards of beer or sing in rustic choirs around the walls. Note that the pub isn't open on weekends.

Chelsea's ✪ **Ferret and Firkin,** 114 Lots Rd., SW10 (☎ 0171/352-6645; Tube: Fulham Broadway or Sloane Square, then bus no. 11 or 22 down King's Rd.), offers the best pub night out in London. The beer served is brewed in the basement and really packs a punch. But the best thing is the Friday- and Saturday-night musical entertainment that often turns the place into a raucous sing-along. You don't have to be under 30 to crowd in here, but only the younger revelers will know all the words. Nine other Firkin pubs are just as fun and flavorful, but most are difficult to reach.

The **Lamb & Flag,** 33 Rose St., WC2 (☎ 0171/497-9504; Tube: Covent Garden or Leicester Square), is an old timber-framed pub in a short cul-de-sac off Garrick Street in Covent Garden. It was once nicknamed the "Bucket of Blood" because of the bare-knuckle fistfights held here in the 18th century. Today it's a basic though atmospheric pub, famed for its amazing selection of cheeses. Better known as the French House, **Maison Berlemont,** 49 Dean St., W1 (☎ 0171/437-2799; Tube: Piccadilly Circus or Tottenham Court Rd.), is an exceptional reminder of Soho's ethnic past, still run by a Berlemont. It was the unofficial headquarters of the French Resistance in exile during World War II and continues to attract a loyal French-speaking crowd.

In the upstairs dining room of the popular **Sherlock Holmes,** 10 Northumberland St., off Trafalgar Square, WC2 (☎ 0171/930-2644; Tube: Charing Cross), you'll find a re-creation of Holmes's living room at 221B Baker St., while the head of the hound of the Baskervilles and other relevant "relics" decorate the downstairs bar. On the edge of Hampstead Heath, the 17th-century **Spaniards Inn,** Spaniards Lane, NW3 (☎ **0181/731-6571;** Tube: Hampstead), was once a favored haunt of Charles Dickens, John Keats, and a host of other literary and artistic greats, as well as highwayman Dick Turpin, whose ghost still returns.

The 1667 **Ye Olde Cheshire Cheese,** Wine Office Court, 145 Fleet St., EC4 (☎ **0171/353-6170;** Tube: Blackfriars or St. Paul's), is where Dr. Johnson took his tipple, and it's an attraction in its own right. Ducking through the low doors will transport you back in time, as the cracked black varnish, wooden benches, and narrow courtyard entrance give it authentic period charm. Meals here are delicious and filling but expensive. It's understandable why ✪ **Ye Olde Mitre,** 1 Ely Court, Ely Place off Hatton Garden, EC1 (☎ **0171/405-4751;** Tube: Chancery Lane or Farringdon), is often referred to as London's best-kept secret. This pub is so well tucked down a dingy alley that first-time visitors often turn back halfway along the passage fearing they've gone the wrong way. The delightful Elizabethan interior has long been a favorite haunt of journalists. I suggest that you order one of the justifiably famous toasted ham-and-cheese sandwiches.

The **Cittie of Yorke,** 22 High Holborn, WC1 (☎ **0171/242-7670;** Tube: Chancery Lane), is a vast atmospheric place with reputedly the longest bar in England. It's a favorite gathering place for lawyers and judges, who appreciate the private cubicles. Across the river, ✪ **The George,** off the Borough High Street in Southwark, SE1 (☎ **0171/407-2056;** Tube: London Bridge), is London's only surviving galleried 17th-century coaching inn, once a haunt of Charles Dickens.

GAY & LESBIAN CLUBS

A well-established bar with pub hours, **Comptons of Soho,** 53 Old Compton St., W1 (☎ **0171/479-7961;** Tube: Leicester Square or Tottenham Court Rd.), is a great pre-club stop, as patrons always know what's going on later and club fliers are available from the barman. You'll find lots of shaved heads and leather bomber jackets. It's open Monday to Saturday 11am to 11pm and Sunday noon to 10:30pm. **Freedom,** 60–66 Wardour St., W1 (☎ **0171/734-0071;** Tube: Piccadilly Circus), is a cafe/restaurant/bar/club that attracts a hip artsy crowd. Breakfast and lunch are pretty leisurely, and you can hang out all day if you like, eating the soups, salads, and sandwiches or just nursing a coffee. The scene heats up in the evening and late night. The downstairs bar/club is open Wednesday to Saturday 9:30pm to 3am; cover is £5 ($8.15) after 10pm.

The Box, 32–34 Monmouth St., WC2 (☎ **0171/240-5828;** Tube: Covent Garden or Leicester Square), is a gay cafe/bar with a downstairs dance bar. Sunday is women's night. It's open Monday to Saturday 11am to 11pm and Sunday noon to 10:30pm. The place for lipstick lesbians is the **Glass Bar,** West Lodge, Euston Square Gardens, 190 Euston Rd., NW1 (☎ **0171/387-6184;** Tube: Euston), where you'll find comfortable couches and candlelight. It's open Tuesday to Friday from 6pm and Saturday from 7pm, with a cover of £1 ($1.65); you can't get in after 11:30pm and the club closes when the management gets tired, if you can believe it. It's also open Sunday noon to 6pm.

Ku-Bar, 75 Charing Cross Rd., W1 (☎ **0171/437-4303;** Tube: Leicester Square), has an upstairs candlelit bar and attracts a stylish young crowd. It's open daily from 4pm but isn't a late-night scene. **The Yard,** 57 Rupert St., W1 (☎ **0171/437-2652;** Tube: Piccadilly Circus), is a pleasant place to while away an afternoon or early evening. There are two bars: The upstairs room is cozy, while the downstairs bar can be cruisey at night. The outdoor courtyard is a welcome summer retreat. The food's pretty good too. Wednesday night is reserved for stand-up comedy. The yard is open daily 11am to 11pm.

Gay or straight, no trip through clubland would be complete without a visit to ✪ **Heaven,** Under the Arches, Craven Street, WC2 (☎ **0171/930-2020;** Tube: Embankment or Charing Cross), a colossal danceteria with two dance floors, three bars, and a stage where live bands sometimes perform. The crowd varies, but the sound system is always great. Wednesday features The Fruit Machine, a mixed gay night. It's open Tuesday, Wednesday, Friday, and Saturday 10pm to 4am. Cover is £4 to £8 ($7 to $13), depending on the day of the week, the time, and whether you have a flier. The other "big" scene is the **Fridge,** Town Hall Parade, Brixton Hill, SW2 (☎ **0171/326-5100;** www.fridge.co.uk; Tube: Brixton), which sizzles on Thursday, Friday, and Saturday until 4am. Thursday is currently Breakbeat night. A small cafe/bar is attached. After 11pm, cover is £8 ($13) to £12 (20), depending on the event.

DANCE CLUBS

The hippest Londoners go to "One-Nighters," weekly dance events held at established clubs. The very nature of this scene demands frequent fresh faces, outdating recommendations before ink can dry on a page. *Time Out* is the clubber's bible (on the Internet at **www.timeout.co.uk**). Discount flyers to dance clubs are distributed throughout the West End and can be found most easily at Tower Records on Piccadilly Circus, the Virgin Megastore, and other similar stores. Otherwise, expect to part with some money to get in. Once inside, beware: £5 ($8) cocktails aren't uncommon. The lowest prices below are usually for Monday and other weeknights, while the highest are for Friday and Saturday. Some places discount prices if you arrive before, say, 10pm. Call ahead and ask if this applies.

The popular **Hippodrome,** at the corner of Cranbourn Street and Charing Cross Road, near Leicester Square, WC2 (☎ **0171/437-4311;** Tube: Leicester Square), is London's big daddy of discos, with a great sound system and lights to match. Very touristy, very fun, and packed on weekends. It's open Monday to Saturday 9pm to 3am, with a £5 to £12 ($8 to $20) cover. The **Limelight,** 136 Shaftesbury Ave., WC2 (☎ **0171/434-0572;** Tube: Leicester Square or Piccadilly Circus), is the London outpost of a small worldwide chain of churches cum dance clubs. The cavernous club features several dance floors and attracts a good-looking crowd. The music is usually mainstream, but phone for special events before heading out. It's open Monday to Friday 10pm to 3am and Saturday 9pm to 3:30am. Cover is £2 to £13 ($3.25 to $21).

The best regular weekend raver in England, ✪ **Ministry of Sound,** 103 Gaunt St., SE1 (☎ **0171/378-6528;** Tube: Elephant & Castle), has worked hard to keep its underground atmosphere and warehouse style. The vast main floor is frenetic and debauched. No alcohol is served, but for the all-night dancing multitudes booze isn't the drug of choice. It's open Friday and Saturday 10:30pm to 6:30am, with a £10 to £15 ($16 to $24) cover.

At **Smithfield's,** 340 Farringdon St., EC1 (☎ **0171/236-8112;** Tube: Farringdon), you can create your own eclectic evening, moving from small room to small room and from sound to sound at this maze of rooms originally built for the meat vendors at the meat market. There are four dance floors and several bars. On weekends it's open 9pm to 3am, charging £5 ($8) before 10pm and £8 ($13) after.

8 Side Trips: Bath, Stonehenge & More

Just a few miles from Trafalgar Square, you'll be confronted with an England that's strikingly different from the inner city. The air is cleaner, the people are friendlier, and everything is cheaper.

The **Britain Visitor Centre,** 1 Regent St., W1 (no phone), just south of Piccadilly Circus, offers free leaflets and advice and can book trains, buses, and tours. For train journeys under 50 miles, the cheapest ticket is a Cheap Day Return. Try to avoid day trips on Friday, when fares increase to catch the mass exodus of city-dwellers.

HAMPTON COURT PALACE

Hampton Court Palace (☎ **0181/781-9500**) was built in 1514 by Cardinal Thomas Wolsey, who was forced to give it to Henry VIII. Five of the king's six wives lived here. The State Apartments, added by William and Mary in the 1690s, were designed by Sir Christopher Wren. Some were badly damaged by fire in 1986 but have been painstakingly restored. When the weather cooperates, a visit to this mammoth Tudor structure on 50 landscaped acres is one of the most satisfying day trips from London. Highlights are the huge 16th-century kitchens, the Astronomer's Clock, the Tudor tennis court, and a run through the famous garden maze.

Entrance to the palace, courtyard, and cloister is £9.25 ($15) adults, £7 ($11) seniors, and £6.10 ($10) age 15 and under. Guided tours are given March to September, daily at 11:15am and 2:15pm, and are free with admission. The palace is open mid-March to mid-October, Monday 10:15am to 6pm and Tuesday to Sunday 9:30am to 6pm; mid-October to mid-March, Monday 10:15am to 4:30pm and Tuesday to Sunday 9:30am to 4:30pm. Closed January 1 and December 24 to 26.

Hampton Court is about 15 miles from central London, and you can reach it by **train** in 30 minutes from Waterloo Station; round-trip fares are £4.10 ($7) adults and £2.05 ($3.35) children. April to October, you can reach Hampton Court by **boat** from Westminster Pier, near the Westminster Underground station. The trip upstream takes about 3½ hours and costs £8 ($13) one-way or £12 ($19) round-trip adults and £4 ($6) one-way or £7 ($11) round-trip ages 4 to 14 (age 3 and under ride free). For information, call ☎ **0171/930-2062.**

GREENWICH

Greenwich is only a few miles from Piccadilly Circus, but it feels as though it's eons away. This famous Thames-side town is the traditional docking site of ocean ships that for centuries have traveled up the river to dock here. It's also the place where Greenwich mean time is fixed—you can take a picture of yourself straddling the **meridian** by the Old Royal Observatory.

The **Royal Naval College** (☎ **0181/858-2154**), commissioned by Charles II and constructed by Sir Christopher Wren, is one of the most magnificent classical complexes in Britain. Admission is free and it's open daily 2:30 to 5pm.

The *Cutty Sark,* King William Walk, SE10 (☎ **0181/858-3445**), now permanently in dry dock, is open as a museum. This most famous of 19th-century clipper ships made regular tea runs to China covering almost 400 miles of ocean per day. You can roam the beautifully restored decks and examine the masts and rigging. It's open April to September, Monday to Saturday 10am to 6pm and Sunday noon to 6pm; October to March, it closes an hour earlier. Admission is £3.50 ($6) adults and £2.50 ($4.10) age 14 and under.

You can reach Greenwich by **Docklands Light Railway** in 15 minutes from the Tower Hill Underground station. You take the train to Island gardens and walk through the river tunnel. You can also make the trip by **boat** from Charing Cross Pier, opposite the Embankment Underground station. Boats depart every 45 minutes 10:30am to 3pm. The last return trip is 4:10pm. The trip downstream takes about 45 minutes and costs £7.25 ($12) round-trip adults and £3.95 ($6) round-trip age 15 and under. For boat information, call ☎ **0171/839-3572.** For more information, contact the **Greenwich Tourist Information Centre,** 46 Greenwich Church St., SE10 (☎ **0181/858-6376**).

BATH

In 1702, Queen Anne made the trek from London 115 miles west to the mineral springs of **Bath,** thereby launching a fad that was to make the city England's most celebrated spa. The most famous personage connected with its popularity was the 18th-century dandy Beau Nash. In all the plumage of a bird of paradise, he was carted around in a sedan chair, dispensing (at a price) trinkets to courtiers and aspirant gentlemen.

ARRIVING   At least one **train** per hour leaves London's Paddington Station bound for Bath during the day; the trip takes 70 to 90 minutes and costs £27 ($44) adults and £13.50 ($22) children. For schedules and information, call ☎ **0345/484-950.** One **National Express coach** leaves London's Victoria Coach Station every 2 hours during the day for the 2½-hour trip, costing £18 ($29) adults and £9 ($15) children. For schedules and information, call ☎ **0990/808-080.**

VISITOR INFORMATION   The **Bath Tourist Information Centre,** at Abbey Chambers, Abbey Church Yard (☎ **01225/477-101**), is open May to September, Monday to Saturday 9:30am to 6pm and Sunday 10am to 4pm; off-season, Monday to Saturday 9:30am to 5pm and Sunday 10am to 4pm.

SEEING THE SIGHTS   The 18th-century architects John Wood the Elder and his son provided a proper backdrop for Nash's activities. They designed a city of honey-colored stone from the nearby hills, a feat so substantial and lasting that Bath is England's most harmoniously laid-out city. It attracted a following among leading political and literary figures, such as Dickens, Thackeray, Nelson, and Pitt, and most important, Jane Austen. Canadians may know that General Wolfe lived on Trim Street, and Australians may want to visit the house at 19 Bennett St., where their founding father, Admiral Phillip, lived.

Bath has had two lives. Long before its Georgian and Victorian popularity, it was known to the Romans as Aquae Sulis. The foreign legions founded their baths here (which you can visit today) to ease their rheumatism in the curative mineral springs. Remarkable restoration and planning have ensured that Bath retains its handsome look. It has somewhat of a museum appearance, with the attendant gift shops. Prices—because of the massive tourist invasion—tend to be high. But Bath remains one of the high points of the West Country.

Built on the site of a much larger Norman cathedral, **Bath Abbey,** Orange Grove (☎ **01225/422-462**), is a fine example of the late Perpendicular style. When Elizabeth I came to Bath in 1574, she ordered a national fund to be set up to restore the abbey. When you go inside and see its many windows, you'll understand why the abbey is called the "Lantern of the West." Note the superb fan vaulting, with its scalloped effect. Beau Nash was buried in the nave and is honored by a simple monument totally out of keeping with his flamboyant character. Admission to the abbey is free, but a £2 ($3.25) donation is requested. The abbey is open April to October, Monday to Saturday 9am to 6pm; November to March, Monday to Saturday 9am to 4:30pm; year-round, Sunday 1 to 2:30pm and 4:30 to 5:30pm.

Founded in A.D. 75, the **Roman Baths,** Abbey Church Yard (☎ **01225/477-785**), were dedicated to the goddess Sulis Minerva. They're among the finest Roman remains in the country and are still fed by Britain's most famous hot-spring water. After centuries of decay, the original baths were rediscovered during Queen Victoria's reign. The site of the Temple of Sulis Minerva has been excavated and is now open to view. The

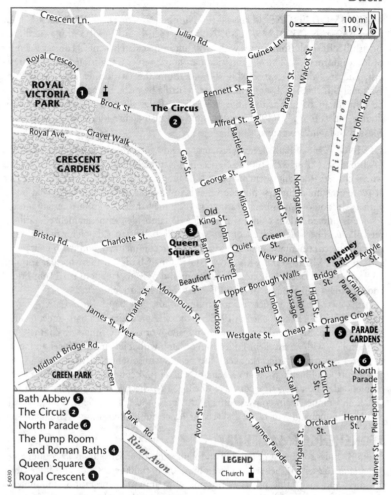

Crescent Ln.

Julian Rd.

Guinea Ln.

Walcot St.

Royal Crescent

**ROYAL
VICTORIA
PARK** **1**

Brock St.

Bennett St.

Lansdown Rd.

Paragon St.

River Avon

St. John's Rd.

The Circus

2

Alfred St.

Royal Ave.

Gravel Walk

Bartlett St.

**CRESCENT
GARDENS**

Gay St.

George St.

Milsom St.

Broad St.

Northgate St.

Bristol Rd.

Charlotte St.

Old
King St.

3

**Queen
Square**

Barton St.

John St.

Quiet

Green
St.

New Bond St.

**Pulteney
Bridge**

Argyle St.

Queen

Beaufort
St.

Trim

Upper Borough Walls

Bridge
St.

Grand
Parade

James St. West

Charles St.

Monmouth St.

Sawclose

Union St.

Union
Passage

High St.

Orange Grove

5

**PARADE
GARDENS**

Midland Bridge Rd.

Westgate St.

Cheap St.

Midland Bridge Rd.

Green

GREEN PARK

4

Bath St.

York St.

Church
St.

6

**North
Parade**

Stall St.

Pierrepont St.

Park Rd.

Avon St.

St. James Parade

Southgate St.

Orchard
St.

Henry
St.

Manvers St.

River Avon

Bath Abbey	**5**
The Circus	**2**
North Parade	**6**
The Pump Room
and Roman Baths	**4**
Queen Square	**3**
Royal Crescent	**1**

0 — 100 m
0 — 110 y

N

LEGEND
Church ✝

E-0030

museum displays many interesting objects from Victorian and recent digs (look for the head of Minerva). You can enjoy coffee, lunch, and tea in the 18th-century **Pump Room,** overlooking the hot springs. There's also a drinking fountain with hot mineral water that tastes horrible but is supposedly beneficial. Admission is £6.30 ($10) adults, £5.60 ($9) seniors, and £3.80 ($6) children. The baths are open April to September, daily 9am to 6pm (August also 8 to 10pm); October to March, Monday to Saturday 9:30am to 5pm and Sunday 10:30am to 5pm.

You'll also want to visit some of Bath's buildings, crescents, and squares. The **North Parade** (where Oliver Goldsmith lived) and the **South Parade** (where English novelist/diarist Frances Burney once resided) represent harmony and are the work of John Wood the Elder. The younger Wood designed the elegant half-moon row of town houses called the **Royal Crescent.** On **Queen Square** (by Wood the Elder) both Jane Austen and Wordsworth once lived. Also of interest is **The Circus,** built in 1754, as well as the shop-lined **Pulteney Bridge,** designed by Robert Adam and often compared to Florence's ponte Vecchio.

ACCOMMODATIONS   The well-run **Number Ninety Three,** 93 Wells Rd., Bath, Avon BA2 3AN (☎ **01225/317-977;** Bus: 3, 13, 14, 17, 23, or 33), is a traditional British B&B: small (four rooms with TVs) but immaculately kept. Its owner is a mine of local information. The elegant Victorian house serves a traditional English breakfast, and it's within easy walking distance from the city center and the rail and National Bus stations. Evening meals are available by prior arrangement. Parking can be difficult in Bath, but the hotel will advise. Rates are £38 to £55 ($63 to $91) double and £60 to £75 ($99 to $124) triple and include breakfast. American Express, MasterCard, and Visa are accepted.

DINING   One of Bath's leading restaurants and wine bars, the **Moon and Sixpence,** 6A Broad St. (☎ **01225/460-962**), occupies a stone building east of Queen Square, with a conservatory and sheltered patio. The food may not be the equal of that served at more acclaimed choices, but the value is unbeatable. At lunch a large cold buffet with a selection of hot dishes is featured in the wine bar. In the upstairs restaurant, full service is offered. Main courses might include lamb filet with caramelized garlic or medaillons of beef filet with bacon, red wine, and shallot sauce. Look for the daily specials on the continental menu. Reservations are recommended, and main courses are £11 to £13 ($18 to $21), with a two-course lunch buffet in the wine bar running £5.95 ($10). It's open daily noon to 2:30pm and 5:30 to 10:30pm (to 11pm Friday and Saturday) and accepts American Express, MasterCard, and Visa.

Bath's best-known French bistro is **Beaujolais,** 5 Chapel Row, Queen Square (☎ **01225/423-417**). Opened in 1973, it's the oldest restaurant in Bath under its original ownership. Begin with a salad of warm scallops or rabbit terrine with chutney. You might follow with an excellent grilled loin of lamb with a julienne of ginger and leeks. One area is reserved for nonsmokers, and people with disabilities (wheelchair access), children (special helpings), and vegetarians will all find comfort. Reservations are recommended. The two-course lunch is £7.50 ($12), the two-course dinner is £13.50 ($22), and dinner main courses run £10.90 to £14.50 ($18 to $24). It's open daily noon to 2:30pm and 7 to 11pm and accepts American Express, MasterCard, and Visa.

STONEHENGE & SALISBURY

About 82 miles southwest of London and 9 miles north of Salisbury is ✪ **Stonehenge** (☎ **01980/624-715**), believed to be from 3,500 to 5,000 years old. This huge circle of lintels and megalithic pillars is Britain's most important prehistoric monument. Despite its familiarity through photographs, you can't help but be impressed when you first see Stonehenge, an astonishing engineering feat—the boulders, the bluestones in particular, were moved many miles, possibly from as far away as southern Wales, to this site.

ARRIVING   A **Network Express train** departs hourly from Waterloo Station in London bound for Salisbury; the trip takes 2 hours. **Buses** also depart four or five times per day from London's Victoria Station, heading for Salisbury; the trip takes 2½ hours. From Salisbury, take a **Wilts & Dorset bus** (☎ **01722/336-855** for schedules) to Stonehenge; the trip takes 30 minutes, and a round-trip costs £4.40 ($7). Use Salisbury as a refueling stop, as the visitor center, including the toilets, is rather squalid at Stonehenge, though improvements are promised.

SEEING THE SIGHTS   The widely held view of the 18th- and 19th-century romantics that **Stonehenge** was the work of the Druids is without foundation. The boulders, many weighing several tons, are believed to have predated the arrival here of the Celtic Druidic cult. Recent excavations continue to bring new evidence to bear on the origin and purpose of the prehistoric circle.

The site is now surrounded by a fence to protect it from vandals and souvenir hunters. Your ticket permits you to go inside the fence, all the way up to a short rope barrier about 50 feet from the stones. A modular walkway has been introduced to cross the archaeologically important area that runs between the Heel Stone and the main circle of stones. This lets you complete a full circuit of the stones, an excellent addition to the well-received audio tour. Admission is £3.90 ($6) adults, £2.90 ($4.70) students, and £2 ($3.25) children. It's open daily: June to August 9am to 7pm; March 16 to May and September to October 15, 9:30am to 6pm; and October 16 to March 15, 9:30am to 4pm.

While in **Salisbury,** be sure to visit England's finest example of the Early English, or pointed, style: ✪ **Salisbury Cathedral,** at The Close (☎ **01722/328-726**). Construction was begun as early as 1220 and took 38 years to complete; this was rather fast in those days since it was customary for a cathedral building to require at least 3 centuries. The soaring spire was completed at the end of the 13th century. Despite an ill-conceived attempt at renovation in the 18th century, the architectural integrity of the cathedral has been retained.

The 13th-century octagonal Chapter House (note the fine sculpture) possesses one of the four surviving original texts of the Magna Carta, along with treasures from the diocese of Salisbury. The cloisters enhance the beauty of the cathedral, and the exceptionally large close, with at least 75 buildings in its compound (some from the early 18th century and others predating that), sets off the cathedral most effectively. The cathedral is open daily: May to August 8:30am to 8:30pm and September to April 8am to 6:30pm. Visiting the cathedral costs £2.50 ($4), plus 30p (50¢) to see the Chapter House.

About 2½ miles west of Salisbury in the town of Wilton on A30 is **Wilton House** (☎ **01722/746-729**), one of England's great country estates and home of the earls of Pembroke. It dates from the 16th century but has undergone numerous alterations, most recently in Victoria's day, and is noted for its 17th-century state rooms by celebrated architect Inigo Jones. It's believed that Shakespeare's troupe may have entertained here. Preparations for the D-day landings at Normandy were laid out here by Eisenhower and his advisers, with only the silent Van Dyck paintings in the Double Cube room as witnesses.

The house displays paintings by Van Dyck, Rubens, Brueghel, and Reynolds. A dynamic film introduced and narrated by Anna Massey brings to life the history of the family since 1544, the year it was granted the land by Henry VIII. You then visit a reconstructed Tudor kitchen and Victorian laundry, plus "The Wareham Bears," a unique collection of some 200 miniature dressed teddy bears. Growing on the 21-acre estate are giant Cedars of Lebanon, the oldest of which were planted in 1630. The Palladian Bridge was built in 1737 by the ninth earl of Pembroke and Roger Morris. There are rose and water gardens, riverside and woodland walks, and a huge adventure playground for children.

Admission is £7 ($12) adults and £4.50 ($7) ages 5 to 15; free for under age 5. To enter the grounds costs £4 ($7) adults and £2.75 ($5) children. Wilton House is open April to October, daily 11am to 6pm (last admission at 5pm).

DINING   In the heart of Salisbury, the 1320 creaky-timbered **Salisbury Haunch of Venison,** 1 Minster St. (☎ **01722/322-024**), serves excellent dishes, especially English roasts and grills. Perhaps begin with grilled venison sausages in Dijon mustard sauce, then try roast haunch of venison with gin and juniper berries. Or there's a medley of fish and shellfish and grilled Barnsley lamb chops with "bubble and squeak" (cabbage and potatoes). Main courses run £6.95 to £11.95 ($11 to $19), and it's open daily noon to 3pm and Monday to Saturday 7 to 9:30pm (the pub, with less expensive fare, is open Monday to Saturday 11am to 11pm and Sunday noon to 3pm and 7 to 11pm). American Express, Diners Club, MasterCard, and Visa are accepted.

WINDSOR CASTLE

Windsor Castle is the largest inhabited castle in the world, on a site that's been a home to monarchs for more than 900 years. On a bend in the Thames about 20 miles west of London, the castle sits on 4,800 acres of lawn, woodlands, and lakes. You can view the **State Apartments,** formal rooms used for official occasions, furnished with antiques and paintings, including masterpieces by Holbein, Rembrandt, and Van Dyck. The **Gallery** displays a rotating selection of the royal family's collection, including paintings by Dalí, Constable, and Chagall. Queen Mary's Dollhouse is a miniature masterpiece created in 1923 by Sir Edward Lutyens on a 1-to-12 scale. It took 3 years to build. Within the castle precincts, **St. George's Chapel,** dedicated to the Most Noble Order of the Garter, is one of the finest examples of late medieval architecture in the country.

Admission is £9.50 ($15) adults, £7 ($11) seniors/students, and £5 ($8) age 16 and under. Prices are reduced if sections of the castle are closed. The castle is open daily from 10am, closing at 3pm in January and February, at 4pm in March, and at 5pm in April to October. For more information, call ☎ **01753/831-118.**

Trains to Windsor depart from London's Waterloo Station (☎ **0345/484-950**) Monday to Saturday every 30 minutes and Sunday every hour. Trains from Paddington Station make the journey to Windsor in 50 minutes, but involve changing at Slough Station. The fares are £5.70 ($9) adults and £2.85 ($5) children.

The exclusive **Eton College** is across a cast-iron footbridge in the village of Eton and is usually combined with a visit to the palace. The school's students are famous for attending classes in high collars and tails. If you're feeling peckish, note that Eton High Street has many excellent (though not necessarily budget) restaurants.

Madrid & Environs 18

by Herbert Bailey Livesey

Spain's landlocked capital spreads over a high windswept plateau like wine spilled on aged linen. To the north and west are mountains tall enough to carry snow on their peaks until spring, and rivers rise among them to curl around the city to the west and south. But the plateau, the Meseta, is a parched tan emptiness right up to the edges of the city. This may seem an odd place for a national capital until you recognize that Spain has always been a fractious country, with the centrifugal forces of linguistic and ideological regionalism yanking at the fabric of unity. The 16th- and 17th-century monarchs chose this location, where only a crude settlement had previously stood, because it was at the center of the Iberian peninsula and might counteract separatist compulsions. Climate, access to seaways, mineral deposits, or defendable elevations had nothing to do with the selection.

Most of Madrid's citizens have come from every other region of Spain, making it a melting pot of the nation's highly diverse strengths, sensibilities, customs, and cultures. It is of, and for, Spain—not Catalunya or Galicia or the País Vasco or Andalucía, the old kingdoms and ministates on the periphery that like to think of themselves as autonomous nations.

Since Franco's death in 1975, Madrid has broken free of the dictator's authoritarian shroud to make a breathless sprint from economic isolation and social stagnation to the dynamic promise of the 21st century. A result is that Europe's highest capital (in altitude) is now also one of its most progressive. Stretched along the expansive Paseo de la Castellana are the headquarters of the nation's vigorous national and international enterprises. Nowadays the word mañana signals progress, not procrastination.

Many first-time visitors are surprised by Madrid's energy and sophistication. Yet scratch the high-tech surface and you'll see that the core of tradition runs deep and strong. Tapas, zarzuela, flamenco, and the paseo continue to be enduring passions among a populace that manages to enjoy the best of both the new order and the Old World.

REQUIRED DOCUMENTS Citizens of the United States, Canada, and New Zealand need only a valid passport for stays of up to 3 months. A British subject entering from Britain needs only an identity card but will need a passport if entering from a third country. Australian citizens need a passport and a visa.

Budget Bests

Most restaurants and cafeterias post a changing *menú del día* (available at lunch and sometimes at dinner) that offers soup or salad, a main course, and dessert, plus bread and a glass of wine or other beverage, for between 900P and 2,000P ($6 and $14). Make this the main meal and in the evening embark on a round of *mesón* and *taberna* hopping to sample the tasty and filling snacks called *tapas*. Or stick to sandwiches or pizzas, which are at least as Spanish as they are American.

For shoppers, the best time to visit Madrid is during the *rebajas* (**sales**) that take place in January, February, and July; all the stores participate, offering discounts that typically increase as the month goes on.

OTHER FROMMER'S TITLES For more on Madrid, see *Frommer's Barcelona, Madrid & Seville; Frommer's Spain; Frommer's Gay & Lesbian Europe;* or *Frommer's Europe.*

1 Madrid Deals & Discounts

SPECIAL DISCOUNTS

FOR EVERYONE Ask about the frequent promotions offered by **Iberia** (☎ **800/772-4642**).

When you're planning to do a lot of traveling on Madrid's public transit system, purchase a *bono* for the bus or Metro (see "Getting Around," later in this chapter).

Many of Madrid's more luxurious hotels offer special **weekend packages** at significantly reduced rates. One of the better offerings is at the Hotel Villa Real, and the first-class Carlton, near Atocha Station, has even more attractive weekend deals. For information and reservations, contact **Marketing Ahead, Inc.,** 433 Fifth Ave., New York, NY 10016 (☎ **800/223-1356** or 212/686-9213; fax 212/686-0271), which also represents some of the hotels below.

FOR STUDENTS Students should have an **International Student Identity Card (ISIC)** to benefit from discounts on travel, lodging, and admissions. Those who arrive without an ISIC can obtain one at the **Instituto de la Juventud,** José Ortega y Gasset 71 (☎ **91/347-77-00;** Metro: Lista), open Monday to Friday 9am to 2pm and 4 to 6pm. The office also issues hostel and student travel cards and provides information on youth discounts.

A student travel agency called **TIVE,** Fernando el Católico 88 (☎ **91/543-02-08;** Metro: Moncloa), also issues hostel cards and can provide discounts on all forms of public transportation to visitors under 26 (under 30 if they're university students). It's open Monday to Friday 9am to 2pm.

FOR SENIORS Seniors 65 or over can obtain **half-price train tickets** on all rail travel from the city. Pick up a copy of *Guía del Ocio* (available at most newsstands) for information about discounts on such events as concerts staged in Madrid's parks.

WORTH A SPLURGE

To really get a feel for the spirit of Spain, spend the money you've saved from a diet of tapas on a **flamenco show,** a *zarzuela* **(folkloric light opera),** or a lavish production at the newly reopened **Teatro Real.**

What Things Cost in Madrid	U.S. $
Taxi from the airport to the Puerta del Sol	20.00
Public transportation within the city	.90
Local telephone call	.10
Double room at the Palace Hotel (deluxe)	314.00
Double room at the Hotel Suecia (moderate)	120.70
Double room at the Hotel Riesco (budget)	32.45
Lunch for one, without wine, at Champagnería Gala (moderate)	12.05
Lunch for one, without wine, at Artemisa (budget)	8.25
Dinner for one, without wine, at El Olivo (deluxe)	28.55
Dinner for one, without wine, at Palacio de Anglona (moderate)	16.55
Dinner for one, without wine, at Carmencita (budget)	8.95
Glass of beer (*una caña*) in a bar	.90
in a club	2.75
Small glass of wine (*una copa*) in a bar	.65
Coca-Cola	1.25
Cup of coffee	.85
Roll of ASA 100 color film, 36 exposures	3.90
One-hour development of one roll, 36 exposures	11.35
Admission to the Prado Museum	2.75
Movie ticket	3.60
Cheap theater ticket	6.90

2 Essentials

ARRIVING

BY PLANE   Madrid's **Barajas Airport** (☎ 91/305-83-43) is about 9 miles east of the city center. The yellow airport bus runs from 4:45am to 1:30am (with departures every 15 minutes) between the airport and Plaza de Colón in the center. The fare is 350P ($2.40). A taxi costs about 2,800P ($19), depending on traffic, and the journey takes roughly 30 minutes, though during rush hours it can take up to an hour.

BY TRAIN   Trains from Lisbon, France, and points in the northeast arrive at Chamartín station. The south of Spain is served by the **Chamartín** and **Atocha** stations and the west by the **Príncipe Pío** (also called Norte) station. All these are on the Metro (see "Getting Around," below) for easy access to anywhere in the city. For information from **RENFE** (Spanish Railways), including the high-speed AVE train between Madrid and Seville, call ☎ 91/328-90-20 (daily 7am to 11pm). Non-Spanish speakers, however, may prefer to have a travel agent make reservations and obtain tickets. You can also book trips, in English, on the Internet at **www.renfe.com,** which provides much useful information about fares and routes.

VISITOR INFORMATION

Barajas Airport has an **Oficina de Información Turistica** (☎ 91/305-83-44), open Monday to Friday 8am to 8pm and Saturday 8am to 1pm. Tourism offices operated by the regional government in the city are at Duque de Medinaceli 2 (☎ **91/429-49-51;** Metro: Banco de España) and in the Torre de Madrid, Plaza de España (☎ **91/541-23-25;** Metro: España); both are open Monday to Friday 9am to 7pm and Saturday 9am to 1pm.

The **Oficina Municipal de Turismo** is at Plaza Mayor 3 (☎ **91/366-48-74;** Metro: Sol). Open Monday to Friday 10am to 8pm and Sunday 10am to 2pm, the bureau is only marginally useful, since it's primarily a distribution center for brochures and maps and the attendants aren't much help with other information.

From July to September in the vicinity of Plaza de España, Puerta del Sol, Plaza Mayor, and the Prado Museum, you'll find young people dressed in a distinctive blue-and-yellow uniform whose job is helping visitors. They each speak at least two languages other than Spanish and can offer advice on museums, hotels, restaurants, and special interests.

Even without much Spanish you should be able to decipher the weekly *Guía del Ocio,* available at newsstands for 125P (85¢). It includes details on entertainment, concerts, art exhibits, sports, fairs, and processions. Undubbed movies are designated *V.O.,* and most foreign-language films are from the United States or Great Britain. Thursday's edition of the daily newspaper *El País* has a "Guía" to the week's events, as does Friday's edition of *Diario 16.*

CITY LAYOUT

Madrid is divided into two distinct parts: old and new. In the old section, whose historic and geographic center is the **Puerta del Sol,** the streets randomly curve and twist; in the newer area to the north and east, the streets are laid out in a grid.

Most of the recommended lodgings in this chapter are around the Puerta del Sol. These streets will quickly become familiar: to the north, **Calle de Alcalá, Gran Vía** (with many theaters, cinemas, and stores), and **Plaza de España;** to the south, **Calle Mayor** (off which is Plaza Mayor), **Calle de Atocha,** and **Carrera de San Jerónimo.** (By the way, *calle* is pronounced "*cahl*-yay.")

Paseo de la Castellana is the main north-south thoroughfare bisecting the city. South of Plaza de Colón it turns into **Paseo de Recoletos,** and after crossing Alcalá it becomes **Paseo del Prado,** named for the Prado Museum, which stands on the southeast corner of Plaza de Canovas del Castillo, identified by its Neptune fountain.

Moncloa, the university area, lies in the northwest of the city, and **Calle de Serrano,** with its smart shops, is east of Castellana between Plaza de la Independencia and Plaza República de Argentina.

GETTING AROUND

The tourist office provides a map of Madrid that includes a schematic of the public transit system. The bus and subway networks are efficient and extensive. Buses travel in their own lanes on often-congested streets. For general information on public transport, call the **Consorcio de Transportes** at ☎ **91/580-19-80.** Taxis are plentiful and not too expensive compared to those in other capital cities (see below).

Since traffic is nearly always bad, from early morning to late evening, plan to cover distances of under 10 blocks by walking.

BY METRO (SUBWAY)   Consulting a map of the Metro system, identify the number of the line on which you wish to travel and the name of the station at the end of the line. All the Metro stations have a large map at the entrance. A single ticket costs 130P (90¢), and a *bono* of 10 tickets is a more economical 670P ($4.60). The subway runs daily 6am to 1:30am.

Madrid Metro

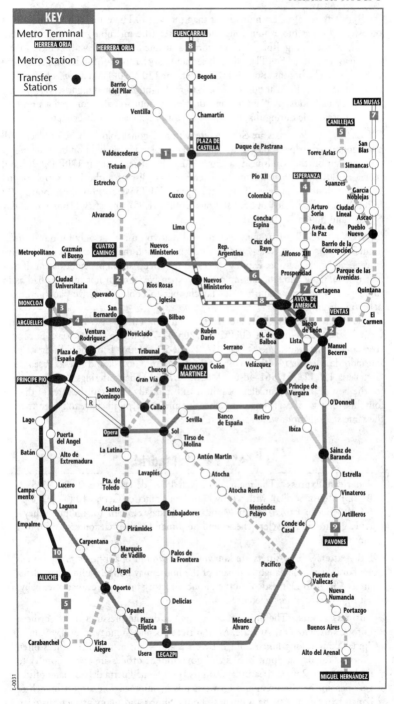

KEY

Metro Terminal
HERRERA ORIA

Metro Station ○

Transfer Stations ●

FUENCARRAL 8

HERRERA ORIA 9

Begoña

Barrio del Pilar

Ventilla

Chamartín

PLAZA DE CASTILLA

Valdeacederas 1

Duque de Pastrana

Torre Arias

LAS MUSAS 7

CANILLEJAS 5

San Blas

Simancas

Tetuán

Pio XII

ESPERANZA 4

Suanzes

García Noblejas

Estrecho

Colombia

Arturo Soria

Ciudad Lineal

Ascao

Cuzco

Alvarado

Lima

Concha Espina

Avda. de la Paz

Pueblo Nuevo

Cruz del Rayo

Alfonso XIII

Barrio de la Concepción

Metropolitano

Guzmán el Bueno

CUATRO CAMINOS

Nuevos Ministerios

Rep. Argentina

Prosperidad

Parque de las Avenidas

Cartagena

Quintana

Ciudad Universitaria

2

Ríos Rosas

Nuevos Ministerios

6

8

AVDA. DE AMERICA

VENTAS

El Carmen

MONCLOA 3

Quevedo

Iglesia

Diego de León

2

ARGUELLES 4

San Bernardo

Bilbao

Rubén Darío

N. de Balboa

Lista

Manuel Becerra

Ventura Rodriguez

Noviciado

Serrano

Goya

Plaza de España

Tribunal

Chueca

ALONSO MARTINEZ

Colón

Velázquez

Príncipe de Vergara

PRINCIPE PIO

Santo Domingo

Gran Vía

R

Callao

Sevilla

Banco de España

Retiro

O'Donnell

Lago

Opera

Sol

Tirso de Molina

Ibiza

Puerta del Angel

La Latina

Antón Martin

Sáinz de Baranda

Batán

Alto de Extremadura

Lavapiés

Atocha

Estrella

Campamento

Lucero

Pta. de Toledo

Atocha Renfe

Vinateros

Laguna

Acacias

Embajadores

Menéndez Pelayo

Artilleros

Empalme

Pirámides

Conde de Casal

9

PAVONES

Carpentana

Marqués de Vadillo

Palos de la Frontera

10

Urgel

Pacífico

Puente de Vallecas

ALUCHE

Oporto

Delicias

Nueva Numancia

5

Opañel

Portazgo

Carabanchel

Vista Alegre

Plaza Elíptica

3

Méndez Alvaro

Buenos Aires

Usera

LEGAZPI

Alto del Arenal

1

MIGUEL HERNÁNDEZ

E-0031

541

BY BUS   Buses often are more direct than the Metro. There are both red and yellow buses, the former more numerous and the latter (the microbus) more comfortable, with air-conditioning. Route information is available from the E.M.T. kiosks in Plaza de Callao, Puerta del Sol, Plaza de Cibeles, and Atocha (open Monday to Friday 8am to 8:15pm). The booths also sell single tickets for 130P (90¢) and a *bono* of 10 tickets for 670P ($4.60). Regular buses run 6am to midnight. A limited night service *(buhos)* runs every half hour 12:30am to 2am, then every hour to 6am. For obvious reasons, taxis are preferable during that period (see "Fast Facts," later in this chapter).

BY TAXI   Metered taxis are either white with a diagonal colored band or black with a horizontal red stripe. If they're available, they display a green light on the roof and/or a green sign on the windshield saying LIBRE. The meter starts at 170P ($1.20) and increases 80P (55¢) per kilometer. There's a long list of authorized supplemental charges, including one for each piece of luggage, 50P (35¢); to/from the airport, 350P ($2.40); to/from the bus and rail stations, 150P ($1.05); and after 11pm and all day Sunday and holidays, 150P ($1.05).

BY RENTAL CAR   I strongly recommend that you use a car only for out-of-town excursions. City traffic is heavy at nearly all hours, and the kamikaze habits of native drivers can be hair-raising. Parking spaces on the streets are all but nonexistent. If that isn't discouraging enough, renting a car is expensive, though not quite as bad as in some other European countries. It's far cheaper to book a fly/drive package before departing from home.

The major car-rental firms are **Hertz,** Gran Vía 60 (☎ **91/541-99-24;** Metro: Gran Vía); **Avis,** Gran Vía 60 (☎ **91/205-42-73;** Metro: Gran Vía); **Europcar (National),** General Yague 6 (☎ **91/721-12-22;** Metro: Estrecho); **Budget,** Juan Hurtado de Mendoza 7 (☎ **91/457-59-68;** Metro: Cuzco); and **Atesa,** Paseo de la Castellana 130 (☎ **91/561-48-00;** Metro: Serrano). Their offerings change, so shop for the best deal. Many smaller local firms substantially undercut the rates of the big four, but their services are less comprehensive and cars typically have to be returned to the same stations from which they were rented.

FAST FACTS: Madrid

American Express   The main office is at Plaza de las Cortes 2 (☎ **91/572-03-03;** Metro: Sevilla), with a busy branch at Francisco Gervás 10 (☎ **91/572-03-20;** Metro: Cuzco), open Monday to Friday 8:30am to 4:30pm. They'll replace cards and traveler's checks and hold mail for their customers for up to 1 month free.

Baby-sitters   Baby-sitters are known as *canguros* in Spanish. As many hostals are family-run, the daughter or son of the house may oblige. Failing that, check under "Servicio Doméstico" in the phone directory for agencies that offer baby-sitting. Always ask for references.

Business Hours   The Spanish siesta survives despite pressures from northern Europe and across the Atlantic. Most **offices** operate Monday to Friday 9am to 7pm, taking a long lunch hour between 2 and 4pm; in summer, offices often close for the day at 3pm. **Banks** and **government offices** are open Monday to Friday 9am to 2pm and Saturday 9am to 1pm. Some Puerta del Sol bank offices are open in the afternoon and on weekends in summer. The airport branch of Banco Exterior de España is open 24 hours. **Shops and many attractions** open at 10am, close for lunch 1:30 to 5pm, and then reopen to 8pm. (Exceptions are branches of the department stores El Corte Inglés and FNAC.) One consequence of these working hours is 4 rush hours per day instead of the usual 2.

Consulates The consulate of the **United States** is in the embassy at Calle Serrano 75 (☎ **91/577-40-00**), open Monday to Friday 9am to noon and 3 to 5pm. The consulate of the **United Kingdom** is at Marqués de la Enseñada 16, 2nd floor (☎ **91/308-52-01**), open Monday to Friday 8am to 2:30pm; the consulate of **Canada** is in the embassy at Núñez de Balboa 35 (☎ **91/431-43-00**), open Monday to Friday 9am to 12:30pm; and the consulate of **Australia** is at Paseo de la Castellana 143 (☎ **91/579-04-28**), open Monday to Thursday 8:30am to 1:30pm and 2:30 to 4:45pm and Friday 8:30am to 2:15pm.

Crime See "Fast Facts: Barcelona" in chapter 6.

Currency The unit of currency is the Spanish **peseta (P),** with coins of 1, 5, 10, 25, 50, 100, 200, and 500 pesetas. Be aware that the 500P coin is easily confused with the 100P coin, and that the old 25P coin has been replaced with a smaller brass coin with a hole in the center. Notes are issued in 1,000P, 2,000P, 5,000P, and 10,000P denominations.

Currency Exchange You can change money at any **bank** advertising *cambio.* A standard commission is charged, which makes cashing traveler's checks in small denominations expensive. A number of U.S. banks have representation in Madrid, Citibank being one of the most visible. In an emergency, the Chequepoint offices found in such heavily touristed locations as the Puerta del Sol are open off-hours and weekends. They don't charge a commission, but their exchange rate is much lower than those prevailing at banks.

ATMs are located throughout the city, especially in tourist and commercial areas. Most machines provide directions in four or five languages, including English. Some Stateside banks charge excessive fees for this service, so address that issue before leaving for Spain, but as a rule, cash obtained through ATMs is dispensed at a more favorable rate, with lower fees, than for traveler's checks.

Dentists & Doctors For bilingual dental and medical attention, call ☎ **061** or check with the appropriate consulate for its list of approved dentists and doctors.

Emergencies For the municipal **police,** dial ☎ **092;** the **fire** brigade, ☎ **080;** an **ambulance,** ☎ **522-22-22.** For a **24-hour pharmacy,** phone ☎ **098.** If the nearest pharmacy is closed, it'll post a notice giving the address of the nearest open one.

Holidays The majority of Catholic Spain's holidays are religious. Each town celebrates its own saint's day, and in Madrid this is the fiesta of San Isidro, in May, when many businesses close at 2pm all week to enjoy the concerts, plays, art shows, neighborhood fairs, and most important bullfights of the year.

Madrid's holidays are New Year's Day (January 1), Epiphany (January 6), San José (March 19), Maundy Thursday, Good Friday, Easter Sunday, Labor Day (May 1), San Isidro (May 15), Corpus Christi (May or June), Santiago Apóstol (July 25), Feast of the Assumption (August 15), Fiesta Hispanidad (October 21), All Saints' Day (November 1), Our Lady of Almudena (November 9), Spanish Constitution Day (December 6), Immaculate Conception (December 8), and Christmas Day (December 25).

August is the traditional time when Spaniards flee to the beach or mountains. Consequently, many of the smaller shops, restaurants, and businesses close for the month.

The Spanish Peseta

For American Readers   The rate of exchange used to calculate dollar values given in this chapter (rounded to the nearest dollar) is $1 = 145P.

For British Readers   The rate of exchange used to calculate the pound values in the table below is £1 = 240P.

Note: Because of substantial fluctuations in exchange rates, those indicated above represent approximate midpoints established over the last 3 years. Currency exchange rates are published daily in most major newspapers.

P	U.S.$	U.K.£	P	U.S.$	U.K.£
10	.07	.04	2,000	13.79	8.33
25	.17	.10	3,000	20.69	12.50
50	.34	.21	4,000	27.59	16.67
100	.69	.42	5,000	34.48	20.83
200	1.38	.83	6,000	41.38	25.00
300	2.07	1.25	7,000	48.28	29.17
400	2.76	1.67	8,000	55.17	33.33
500	3.45	2.08	9,000	62.07	37.50
1,000	6.90	4.17	10,000	68.97	41.67

Hospitals   Options are the **Hospital La Paz,** Castellana 261 (☎ **91/734-26-00;** Metro: Begoña), on the north side of town, or the **Hospital 12 de Octubre,** Carretera de Andalucía, km 5.4 (☎ **91/390-80-00**), on the south side.

Laundry   The **Lavomatique,** Mesón de Paredes 83 (☎ **91/527-21-02;** Metro: Embajadores), will wash and fold your clothes for about one-third the amount charged by a hotel. Ironing is extra. It's open Monday to Friday 9am to 1:30pm and 4:30 to 8pm and Saturday 9am to 1:30pm. If that one isn't convenient, ask your concierge for the lavandería nearest your hotel.

Mail   The main post office, **Correos,** is the grand Palacio de Comunicaciones on Plaza de las Cibeles (☎ **91/536-01-11;** Metro: Banco de España). It's open for stamps Monday to Friday 8am to 9pm and Sunday and holidays 10am to 1pm at Window H. Stamps are also sold at tobacconists (*estancos*). An airmail letter or postcard to the United States is 95P (65¢).

Tax   The government sales tax, known as **IVA (value-added tax),** is currently 7%. It's often, but not always, included in the price of products and services.

Taxis   To call a taxi, try **Radio Taxi** at ☎ **91/447-32-32, Radioteléfono Taxi** at ☎ **91/547-82-00,** or **Teletaxi** at ☎ **91/455-90-08.**

Telephone   The minimum charge for **local telephone calls** is 15P (10¢). Many hotels and hostels tack on a hefty surcharge for long-distance calls. Most public phones have clear instructions in English. Place at least 25P worth of coins in the rack at the top and let them roll in as required. Some new high-tech public phones provide on-screen instructions in four languages and accept the **Tarjeta Telefónica,** available in 1,000P ($7) and 2,000P ($14) denominations at *estancos* (tobacconists), post offices, and the *locutorios telefónicas* (central phone offices) in Plaza Colón and at Gran Vía 30 (both of which have one USA Direct phone).

Country & City Codes

The **country code** for Spain is **34.** The **city code** for Madrid is **1;** use this code when you're calling from outside Spain. If you're within Spain but not in Madrid, use **91.** If you're calling within Madrid, simply leave off the code and dial only the regular phone number.

The locutorios are open Monday to Friday 9am to midnight and Saturday, Sunday, and holidays noon to midnight.

To **make collect or calling-card calls** at more economical rates, dial ☎ **900/99-00-11** to access **AT&T's USA Direct** (to do so from a public phone might require coins or a phonecard) or ☎ **900/99-00-14** to access **MCI's Call USA.** When calling from a hotel, check first to make sure there's no service charge or surcharge, or at least how much it is.

To make **international calls** to the United States and Canada, dial 07, wait for another tone, then dial 1, followed by the area code and number. The average cost of a 3-minute call to the United States is 1,800P ($12).

Tipping The custom is widespread, though the amounts expected are often less than those in other countries. In bars, round out the change and leave at least 10P (7¢), even after a cup of coffee. In hotels, a service charge is included in the bill, but give the porter about 100P (70¢) per bag; the maid, about 100P (70¢) for each night stayed; the doorman, 50P (35¢), or 100P (70¢) if he goes to some trouble to get a taxi. In restaurants, if the service charge isn't included, leave a 10% to 15% tip, about 5% if it is. Give taxi drivers between 5% and 10%, tour guides 10%, and ushers (theater or bullfight) 50P (35¢).

Water Tap water is entirely safe but doesn't taste very good. Bottled water is widely available, either fizzy *(con gas)* or still *(sin gas).*

3 Accommodations You Can Afford

There are hundreds of *hostals* in Madrid, all graded and loosely overseen by the tourism authorities. Note that these aren't youth hostels in the conventional sense, though they're popular with young travelers. While they don't have all the conveniences of a conventional hotel, they're usually family-run and more personal.

Most of the places below are in the old part of the city around the Puerta del Sol and Gran Vía or the neighborhood of the three major art museums that form a "Golden Triangle" along or near Paseo del Prado. Sometimes two or more hostals are in the same building, so if one recommended here is booked up, check out one on another floor. Ask to see the room and bath before accepting. Many of the hostals are in houses from the late 19th or early 20th century, with high ceilings, elaborate moldings, and some ornate or antique furnishings. Don't be put off by entrances, which can be scruffy. They're often in sharp contrast to the scrupulously clean rooms.

Spanish hotels and hostals typically use twin beds in their rooms; the queen- and king-size beds routinely found in roadside motels in North America are still rare. Taller guests and couples will want to know that a double bed is a *cama matrimonio.* In addition, rooms intended for single occupancy are invariably tiny. People willing to spend a little extra for more space can ask for a double for individual use—*doble para uso individual.* The price will be more than for a single but less than for the full double.

A Hostal Tip

As a rule, Madrid's hostals occupy one or two floors of mixed-use buildings, and they're rarely on the ground floor. To gain entrance, it's often necessary to press a button and then respond to a shouted "Sí?" or "Dígame!" on the intercom. Keep your answer simple—your last name or 'Frommer's!" will nearly always get you buzzed in.

Air-conditioning is far from universal. But since Madrid summers can be torrid, you may want to take notice of the accommodations below that have this facility. Rooms advertising "shower only" may have only a small tub with a shower and washbasin, sometimes only curtained off from the rest of the room. Be aware that the rates below don't include IVA (VAT) unless so indicated.

Note: You can find the lodging choices below plotted on the map included in "Seeing the Sights," later in this chapter.

NEAR THE PRADO & THYSSEN MUSEUMS

✪ **Coruña.** Paseo del Prado 12 (3rd floor), 28014 Madrid. ☎ **91/429-25-43.** 6 units, none with bathroom. TV. 2,200P ($15) single; 4,200P ($29) double; 5,800P ($40) triple. No credit cards. Metro: Atocha.

They don't come any cleaner or sprightlier than this hostal (with elevator). The only drawback is the lack of private baths, but since there are only six rooms, sharing the common bath isn't likely to be a problem. All the rooms are freshly painted, with bare polished floors and crisp coverlets on the double or twin beds, plus basins. Even the front rooms, facing the busy Paseo del Prado, are quiet. The Prado Museum is across the way.

✪ **Mora.** Paseo del Prado 32, 28014 Madrid. ☎ **91/420-15-69.** Fax 91/420-05-64. 62 units, all with bathroom. A/C TV TEL. 6,300P ($43) single; 8,500P ($59) double. AE, DC, MC, V. Metro: Atocha.

This is one of the top budget choices, even with recent jumps in prices, and its equals aren't evident. A spacious lobby with glinting chandeliers sets the tone. The adjacent restaurant, Bango (under separate management), attracts a polished crowd for meals of similarly low cost (see "Great Deals on Dining," later in this chapter). The narrow but bright halls lead to rooms of substantially varied configuration but crisply furnished in muted tones, with carpeting. Admittedly, some are too small to contain second thoughts, so inspect first. English is spoken at the front desk. The Prado is across the street and the Centro de Arte Reina Sofía is a short walk away.

Prim. Prim 15 (2nd floor), 28004 Madrid. ☎ **91/521-54-95.** Fax 91/523-58-48. 12 units, 8 with shower only or bathroom. 2,300P ($16) single with sink only, 3,000P ($21) single with shower only, 3,500P ($24) single with bathroom; 3,300P ($23) double with sink only, 5,000P ($35) double with bathroom. Rates include IVA. No credit cards. Metro: Colón or Banco de España.

On a safe, pleasant street a block west of Paseo de Recoletos, this hostal is being thoroughly refurbished, including combining smaller rooms to make larger units. Ask for one of the redone units. One of my recommended restaurants, Spaghetti & Bollicine (see "Great Deals on Dining," below), is on the ground floor. The owner speaks some English. There's an elevator, but the hostal is only one floor up.

Sud Americana. Paseo del Prado 12 (6th floor), 28014 Madrid. ☎ **91/429-25-64.** 8 units, none with bathroom. 2,500P ($17) single; 4,800P ($33) double. Showers 250P ($1.70). No credit cards. Metro: Atocha.

Getting the Best Deal on Accommodations

- Be aware that some hotels give discounts if you pay in cash instead of with a credit card.
- Take advantage of the steep weekend discounts offered by some four-star hotels.
- Inquire at the TIVE office at Calle José Ortega y Gasset 71 about which hostals offer discounts to people carrying an International Student Identity Card (ISIC).
- Ask if service and taxes are included in the quoted room rate, for they can add as much as 20% to the bill.
- Check if breakfast is included in the rates. Most places don't include breakfast, so those that do can represent significant savings.

Ask for one of the larger front rooms for the light and the view of the Prado. The traffic noise is relatively muted. Señor Pedro Alonso Garrido has been welcoming Frommer's readers for more than 30 years to his well-run, nicely decorated hostal with sinks in every room. It's in the same excellently maintained building as the Coruña (above), with an elevator.

ON OR NEAR THE GRAN VÍA

California. Gran Vía 38 (2nd floor), 28013 Madrid. ☎ and fax **91/522-47-02** or 91/531-61-01. 26 units, all with bathroom. A/C TV TEL. 7,200P ($50) single; 9,500P ($66) double; 12,750P ($88) triple. AE, DC, MC, V. Metro: Callao or Gran Vía.

Easily found on the busiest stretch of the Gran Vía, among cinemas and popular restaurants, this three-star place shares the second floor with the haughtier and more expensive Atlántico. Though humbler in style and furnishings than its neighbor, the California has a more amicable tone and a pleasant bar/breakfast room.

Continental. Gran Vía 44 (3rd floor), 28013 Madrid. ☎ **91/521-46-40**. 29 units, all with bathroom. TEL. 3,600P ($25) single; 5,000P–5,600P ($35–$39) double. MC, V. Metro: Gran Vía.

The Continental is one of several hostals in this centrally located building. This one stands out because the management continues to make improvements, which compensate for the often glum reception. A small TV lounge, where light refreshments are available, adjoins the breakfast room. On the fifth floor is the slightly more expensive **Valencia** (☎ 91/522-11-15), offering 30 units, all with bathroom.

Greco. Infantas 3 (3rd floor), 28004 Madrid. ☎ **91/522-46-32** or 91/522-46-31. 18 units, all with bathroom. TV TEL. 3,400P ($23) single; 5,500P ($38) double; 7,500P ($52) triple. MC, V. Metro: Banco de España or Gran Vía.

A grandfather clock thunks away in the vestibule off the snug TV salon with its large black-and-white ceramic guard dog. The rooms have quirky blond modern furniture, filling relatively large spaces. The quarters in front have balconies above the quiet street, only 1 block north of the Gran Vía. Most rooms have strongboxes. Beer and soft drinks are available in the lounge.

✪ Italia. Gonzalo Jiménez Quesada 2, 28004 Madrid. ☎ **91/522-47-90**. Fax 91/521-28-91. 28 units, all with bathroom. A/C TV TEL. 5,000–5,700P ($35–$39) single; 6,000–7,200P ($41–$50) double; 7,500P–9,700P ($52–67) triple. AE, DC, MC, V. Metro: Callao.

This is one of the most desirable hostals on the Gran Vía. The windows in the front rooms are triple-glazed, giving relief from the traffic noise. The rooms, with parquet floors and velvet side chairs, have safes in the closets. All the baths were done in marble and tile a few years back. A full-service dining room serves all meals, including a 1,400P ($10) *menú del día*, combination plates, and sandwiches.

María Cristina. Fuencarral 20 (2 blocks north of the Gran Vía, 2nd floor), 28004 Madrid. ☎ **91/531-63-00** or 91/531-63-09. 18 units, all with bathroom. TV TEL. 3,800P ($26) single; 5,000P ($35) double; 7,500P ($52) triple. MC, V. Metro: Gran Vía.

There's no elevator, but a freshly painted staircase leads up to the tidy reception area with its aquarium. Beyond that is a TV lounge/sitting room with wood paneling and an Oriental rug. The rooms upstairs are furnished with pine beds and tables, and the baths are small but adequately appointed. Light refreshments are available. The operators still need to brush up on their people skills, however.

Sonsoles. Fuencarral 18 (2 blocks north of the Gran Vía, 2nd floor), 28004 Madrid. ☎ **91/532-75-23** or 91/532-75-22. Fax 91/310-04-78. 27 rms, all with bathroom. TV TEL. 2,900P ($20) single; 3,900P ($27) double; 4,900P ($34) triple. MC, V. Metro: Gran Vía.

The dimly lit entrance gives way to an attractive lobby and TV lounge with stairs leading to the second floor. A third sitting room features a tank of tropical fish. Double-glazed windows in the rooms facing Fuencarral muffle street noises. Coke and coffee machines occupy space near the reception desk. There are some semipermanent residents, since prices are negotiable for longer stays. Sonsoles has a family atmosphere, and the husband speaks some English. And since they've held prices steady, it continues to be a budget favorite.

Triana. Salud 13 (2nd floor), 28013 Madrid. ☎ **91/532-68-12** or 91/532-30-99. Fax 91/522-92-29. 29 units, all with bathroom. TV TEL. 3,350P ($23) single; 5,450P ($38) double. Rates include IVA. MC, V. Metro: Gran Vía, Callao, or Sol.

Just south of the Gran Vía, overlooking Plaza del Carmen, this is a convenient and ingratiating hostal. Double glass doors open onto a bright lobby with easy chairs, and there's a TV lounge. Some of the decor, including floral fabrics and lots of white paint and wood, is unusual for Madrid. Ask for one of the larger rooms overlooking the plaza, for they get extra light and are more fetchingly decorated, with small balconies. Some English is spoken.

FROM PUERTA DEL SOL TO PLAZA MAYOR

Francisco I. Calle del Arenal 15, 28013 Madrid. ☎ **91/548-02-02.** Fax 91/542-28-99. 58 units, all with bathroom. A/C TV TEL. 6,900P ($48) single; 9,700P ($67) double; 11,250P ($78) triple. Rates include breakfast and IVA. Half- and full-board rates available. AE, DC, MC, V. Metro: Opera or Sol.

Under the same ownership as the París, at the other end of the Puerta del Sol, this hotel is run by an amiable manager and his staff. The lobby with wood paneling and marble sets the tone. Near the TV lounge's leather chairs is a well-stocked bar. The sixth-floor dining room is more than adequate for its price range, and the guest rooms are of sensible size and newly renovated, all with safes. The rates above are for high season; bargaining should be productive at other times.

La Perla Asturiana. Plaza Santa Cruz 3 (2nd floor), 28012 Madrid. ☎ **91/366-46-00.** Fax 91/366-46-08. 33 units, 28 with bathroom. TV TEL. 2,800P ($19) single without bathroom, 3,600P ($25) single with bathroom; 5,000P ($35) double with bathroom; 7,200P ($50) triple with bathroom. AE, MC, V. Metro: Sol.

This hostal is next to the southeast portal to Plaza Mayor, on Plaza Santa Cruz, which is used mostly as a parking lot and bus stop. The front rooms are large, but ask for one on the south side, since the buses stop at the east. Besides a comfortable TV lounge, there's a small dining room for breakfast and refreshments. If a bathtub is important to you, check first, because some of these are barely large enough to wet your ankles.

✪ **Plaza Mayor.** Atocha 2, 28012 Madrid. ☎ **91/360-06-06** or 91/360-08-28. Fax 91/360-06-10. 20 units, all with bathroom (shower or tub). A/C TV TEL. 5,800P ($40) single; 7,000P–8,000P ($48–$55) double. Rates include breakfast. AE, MC, V. Metro: Sol.

A sparkling new hotel inside the shell of a 19th-century convent, this represents a welcome addition to Madrid's often dreary budget housing stock. Despite the name, the brick-red structure wedges into Plaza Santa Cruz, slightly east of Plaza Mayor. Double-thick windows seal off the grumble of the buses that congregate in the square. The rooms are of sufficient size and the mattresses firm (four rooms have double beds), and the corner rooms are desirable for their light. English is spoken.

Riesco. Correo 2 (3rd floor), 28012 Madrid. ☎ **91/522-26-92** or 91/532-90-88. 26 units, all with bathroom (shower or tub). TEL. 3,200P ($22) single with shower, 3,600P ($25) single with tub; 4,300P ($30) double with shower, 5,000P ($35) double with tub; 6,000P ($41) triple with tub. Rates include IVA. No credit cards. Metro: Sol.

The Riesco enjoys a superb location, next to the Comunidad de Madrid building on the Puerta del Sol and a 5-minute walk from Plaza Mayor. Pass through the marble lobby and up to the third floor to discover a hostal featuring a lounge with deep leather sofas around an electric fireplace and a large TV. The rooms have desks and chairs (doubles have phones), and some have views of the Puerta del Sol. Fifteen of them are air-conditioned.

Rifer. Calle Mayor 5 (4th floor), 28013 Madrid. ☎ **91/532-31-97.** 12 units, all with bathroom (shower or tub). 3,500P ($24) single; 4,400P ($30) double with shower only, 5,000P ($35) double with bathroom. Rates include IVA. No credit cards. Metro: Sol.

The building's scrubbed entrance has an elevator to carry you up to this small hostal, a longtime favorite with readers and minutes from the Puerta del Sol and Plaza Mayor. The friendly greeting switches from Spanish to English if the lady of the house is on duty. The rooms are newly painted and simply furnished, with marble floors and pressed bed linen.

If the Rifer is full, the **Riosol** (☎ 91/532-31-42), two floors down, is an adequate alternative, at even lower prices. A stand at the entrance sells newspapers and magazines in English.

Victoria I. Calle Carretas 7 (just off the Puerta del Sol, 2nd floor), 28013 Madrid. ☎ **91/522-99-82.** 18 units, 16 with bathroom. TV TEL. 3,800P ($26) single without bathroom; 5,500P ($38) double with bathroom; 7,000P ($48) triple with bathroom. Rates include IVA. AE, MC, V. Metro: Sol.

This small hostal has recently been renovated, down to the matching curtains and bed linen. Señora María Teresa is outgoing, attentive, and proud of her superclean place. Most rooms are compact, some downright claustrophobic, so check first. This is the original of three hostals owned by the same family, with top honors going to the Victoria III (below). However, this one is popular year-round, so book ahead. Students on strict budgets may want to consider **Victoria II,** in the same building, with bare-bones doubles for 3,300P ($23).

✪ **Victoria III.** Carrera de San Jerónimo 30 (4th floor), 28014 Madrid. ☎ **91/420-23-57.** 12 units, all with bathroom. A/C MINIBAR TV TEL. For Frommer's readers: 3,800P ($26) single; 5,500P ($38) double; 7,000P ($48) triple. Rates include IVA. AE, DC, MC, V. Metro: Sevilla.

This is the best of a trio of budget choices in the Puerta del Sol area owned/operated by the same conscientious management (see the previous entry). The furnishings are new, the mattresses are firm, and all reasonable comforts are available, including a common bar/lounge. The room dimensions are tight, however. The TV carries CNN and even comes with remote control. Also rare in this category are the minibars, stocked with beer and soft drinks. The reception is pleasant, though English isn't spoken. The only sign out front is next to the buzzer at the door. Show this book to get the prices listed above.

AROUND PLAZA SANTA ANA

Inglés. Echegaray 8, 28014 Madrid. ☎ **91/429-65-51.** Fax 91/420-24-23. 51 units, all with bathroom. TV TEL. 7,700P ($53) single; 10,800P ($75) double. AE, DC, MC, V. Metro: Sol.

A large ship model in the front window welcomes guests into the brightly lit lobby and comfortable TV lounge, with deep sofas and armchairs. Just beyond is the bar/cafeteria where breakfast is served. All rooms have radios and many have sitting areas. Safe-deposit boxes are available. The renovated facade helps to brighten a dimly lit, albeit lively, street. Nearby Plaza Santa Ana and Calle de las Huertas jump with tapas and music bars.

Lisboa. Ventura de la Vega 17, 28014 Madrid. ☎ **91/429-46-76.** Fax 91/420-98-94. 22 units, all with bathroom. TEL. 4,000P ($28) single; 6,000P ($41) double; 8,000P ($55) triple. Rates include IVA. AE, DC, MC, V. Metro: Antón Martín or Sol.

Amid one of Madrid's heaviest concentrations of tapas bars, the Lisboa (with elevator) offers rooms spread over four floors. Some have double beds with bronze bedsteads. The small lounge has a TV and VCR. While there's no restaurant or bar on the premises, scores of eating places are within a few minutes' walk. A sign in English in the lobby advises guests not to leave the building with handbags.

Santander. Echegaray 1 (at the corner of Carrera de San Jerónimo), 28014 Madrid. ☎ **91/429-95-51** or 91/429-66-44. 40 rms, all with bathroom. TEL. 5,600P ($39) single; 7,000P ($48) double; 11,000P ($76) triple. Rates include IVA. No credit cards. Metro: Sol.

Nothing seems to change here, including, these past 3 years at least, the room rates. That makes it a better deal than ever. The shiny glass-and-brass doorway on Echegaray leads into a foyer with marble walls and a carved-wood reception desk. The rooms (some with TV) are generally of good size, with parquet floors, a dressing table, and a wardrobe; some have giant tubs. There's a TV lounge, cafeteria, and bar.

WORTH A SPLURGE

Many four-star hotels have deeply discounted weekend rates, allowing for a taste of near-luxury in the middle of a 2-week visit. The delightful Hotel Villa Real, for example, up a short hill from the Prado, has a rack rate of 33,000P ($228) for a double during the week that's sharply reduced to 19,500P ($135) Friday to Sunday. To make reservations in the United States for the Villa Real and the two hotels below, contact **Marketing Ahead, Inc.,** 433 Fifth Ave., New York, NY 10015 (☎ **800/223-1356** or 212/686-9213; fax 212/686-0271).

Carlos V. Maestro Vitoria 5, 28013 Madrid. ☎ **91/531-41-00.** 67 units, all with bathroom. A/C MINIBAR TV TEL. 11,020P ($76) single; 13,870P ($96) double; 18,720 ($129) triple. AE, DC, MC, V. Metro: Sol.

Two years of top-to-bottom renovations were worth the wait, as everything here is fresh and new. Superbly situated in the pedestrian shopping district north of the Puerta del Sol and owned/operated by three generations of the same family, the Carlos V gives good value at rates only slightly higher than those quoted previously in this section. In addition to the expected comforts, each room has a safe, hair dryer, and satellite TV with English channels. A new bar and breakfast/snack area adjoin the tastefully appointed second-floor lounge, and there's a computer to surf the Internet. Some fifth-floor rooms have balconies. English is spoken.

✪ **Gaudí.** Gran Vía 9, 28013 Madrid. ☎ **91/531-22-22.** Fax 91/531-54-69. 88 units, all with bathroom. A/C MINIBAR TV TEL. 17,900P ($123) single; 21,900P ($151) double. AE, DC, MC, V. Metro: Gran Vía.

A majestic turn-of-the-century building at the "good" end of the Gran Vía was gutted and transformed into this near-luxury hotel with three-star prices. Plaza Mayor and the Prado and Thyssen museums are all within walking distance, and retreating at siesta time to these quiet teak-lined quarters is restorative. An above-par restaurant and stylish bar are added benefits. The weekend rates include the extensive breakfast buffet, which otherwise costs 1,500P ($10).

4 Great Deals on Dining

It's possible to eat fairly well for relatively low cost. In the old part of the city, around the Puerta del Sol and Plaza Mayor, the selection of *cafeterías* and *cerveserías* offering decent food is enormous. A little to the east, in the area bounded by Carrera de San Jerónimo, and calles Huertas, León, Echegaray, and Ventura de la Vega, are dozens of lively tapas bars.

A Spanish *tortilla* is a thick omelet of eggs, potatoes, and onions, generally served at room temperature when eaten as a tapa. *Gazpacho* is a cold tomato-based soup made with garlic, vinegar, bread, and olive oil, garnished with onions, green peppers, and egg. *Paella*, a specialty of Valencia, has many variations but is most familiar as rice cooked in saffron with chunks of chicken with fish and shellfish. *Cocido madrileño* is a boiled dinner served in courses as soup, then vegetables, then meats and sausage. A popular first course is *judías*, a simple bean stew. *Perdiz* (partridge) and *codorniz* (quail) appear on menus regularly, along with *cochinillo asado* (roast suckling pig) and *cordero asado* (roast lamb).

An increasing number of foreign restaurants have opened—Moroccan, French, German, Chinese, Greek, Japanese, American, you name it. Spaniards are slow to accept other cuisines, however, partly because their own is so varied and extensive. And apart from a few of their tapas, they don't like spicy-hot dishes. That puts a crimp in the efforts of chefs trying for authenticity in Szechuan, Hunan, Tex-Mex, Indian, and Mexican dishes. Of the various foreign cuisines, the one best reproduced is Italian. Pastas and pizzas are nearly as common in Madrid as in Chicago or New York, and most Spanish cooks have learned the meaning of *al dente*. That's why the relatively few foreign restaurants below are mostly Italian.

Some restaurants package meals *para llevar*—to take out. The Tele-Pizza chain delivers to homes and hotels on scooters. When adapting to Spanish dining hours proves difficult—lunch at 2:30pm and dinner at 10:30pm—look for *cafeterías* and *cervecerías*. Their primary distinction is that they stay open longer, not infrequently from 7am to midnight. They're especially good alternatives on Sunday, when the relatively few restaurants that choose to stay open are packed in the afternoon, with waits of an hour or more.

NEAR THE PRADO & THYSSEN MUSEUMS

Bango. Paseo del Prado 32 (opposite the Botanical Garden). ☎ **91/420-07-90.** Main courses 900P–1,800P ($6–$12); *menús del día* 1,100P and 1,500P ($8 and $10). MC, V. Daily 7am–midnight. Metro: Atocha. SPANISH.

A paragon of the *cafetería* type of place, Bango attracts a surprisingly glossy sort of patron, both local and foreign. It sets out an enticing variety of tapas, as well as freshly

---

Getting the Best Deal on Dining

- Take advantage of the *menú del día* at lunch (sometimes at dinner)—it usually comprises a first course of soup or salad, a main course of meat or fish, bread, often dessert, and wine or another beverage.
- Eat tapas instead of ordering full meals, and remember that they're often cheaper if you eat at the bar *(barra)* rather than sit at a table *(mesa)*.
- Try the inexpensive *platos combinados* served in *cafeterías, cervecerías,* and some bars—they're one-dish meals of meat or fish, rice or fries, and maybe a vegetable and bread and beverage on the side.

---

squeezed juice at breakfast, full lunches and dinners, and sandwiches and desserts. Bango is one to remember on Sunday, when most restaurants close, or when regular Spanish dining hours seem too late.

✪ **Champagnería Gala.** Moratín 22 (west of Paseo del Prado). ☎ **91/429-25-62.** *Menú del día* 1,750P ($12). No credit cards. Sun–Thurs 1:30–4:30pm and 9pm–2am, Fri–Sat 1:30–4:30pm. Metro: Atocha. SPANISH.

That something different is going on here is announced by the blood-orange walls with painted vines in the front room and the glassed-over courtyard with real and artificial plants in back. This fun place is filled nightly with a frisky crowd that keeps track of what's hot, making the prices all the more remarkable. *Paellas* and *fideuàs* (a similar dish using thin noodles instead of rice) with 13 choices of components come with do-it-yourself *pa amb tomaquet* (Catalan bread rubbed with tomato pulp and drizzled with oil), a seasonal salad, wine, aïoli and romesco sauces, dessert, coffee, and fruit liqueur—all for only 1,750P ($12). Even for one person, the paella pan is 12 inches across. Food isn't served Friday and Saturday nights, when the whole place is given over to drinking and dancing. Avoid Sunday afternoon, when it's impossibly crowded. The hostess with the flame-red hair is owner Esperanza Fernandez Aranda.

NORTH OF THE GRAN VÍA

✪ **Bocaito.** Libertad 4–6 (2 blocks north of the Gran Vía). ☎ **91/532-12-19.** Main courses 750P–1,500P ($5–$10). AE, MC, V. Mon–Sat 1–4pm and 8:30pm–midnight. Metro: Chueca or Gran Vía.

Many aficionados believe this to be Madrid's top tapas bar. Most items are sliced, cooked, and/or assembled to order by the several men behind the horseshoe-shaped bar. They aren't doctrinaire—some salads have kiwi fruit, a relatively recent import. In back are a couple of attractive dining rooms. While a few dishes get steep—eggs scrambled with baby eels, a delicacy, costs 2,500P ($17)—most main courses are under 1,500P ($10). For a special treat, take a companion and share the plate of *fritura malagueña*—lightly fried fish and shellfish—for 3,300P ($23) for two.

✪ **Carmencita.** Libertad 16 (1 block north of Calle de Las Infantas). ☎ **91/531-66-12.** Main courses 900P–3,500P ($6–$24); *menú del día* 1,300P ($9). AE, DC, MC, V. Mon–Fri 1–4pm and 9pm–midnight, Sat 9pm–midnight. Metro: Chueca. SPANISH.

This atmospheric tavern, founded in 1850, retains extensive tile dadoes and lace curtains behind its maroon shutters. A bust of Juan Carlos I stands in the vestibule in recognition of a past *plato de oro* award. A typical *menú del día* (Monday to Friday at lunch only) consists of lentils with sausage followed by deep-fried fish and dessert, with wine. The classic stew *cocido madrileño* is often available though not always on the menu.

A Dining Tip

In Spain, a *cafetería* is an informal, inexpensive sit-down restaurant with table service. What Americans call a cafeteria is an *autoservicio* or *buffet*. A *cervesería* is usually a cross between a bar and a *cafetería*, with beer on draft the featured beverage and food choices ranging from tapas and sandwiches to *platos combinados* and sometimes full meals.

✪ **Nabucco.** Hortaleza 108 (near Plaza Santa Barbara). ☎ **91/310-06-11.** Pastas and pizzas 690P–950P ($4.75–$7); main courses 990P–1,450P ($7–$10). AE, DC, MC, V. Sun–Thurs 1:30–4pm and 8:45pm–12:15am (Fri–Sat to 1am). Metro: Alonso Martínez. ITALIAN.

Uncommonly spacious, with high ceilings, terrazzo floors, sienna walls with cream trim, and urns and statuary in niches, Nabucco presents a believable echo of an upscale Roman trattoria. It brings in businesspeople at lunch, couples and families at dinner. The 12 pizzas come with the paper-thin crusts in favor in Madrid, and one of them paired with the house salad provides ample sustenance for lunch or dinner. On the other hand, even usually pricey osso bucco is only 1,450P ($10). Just about everything is available for takeout. Some English is spoken.

✪ **Spaghetti & Bollicine.** Prim 15 (off Paseo de Recoletos). ☎ **91/521-45-14.** Main courses 1,100P–1,700P ($8–$12); *menú del día* 1,300P ($9). AE, MC, V. Mon–Thurs 2–4pm and 9pm–midnight (to 1am Fri), Sat 9pm–1am. Metro: Colón or Banco de España. ITALIAN.

On afternoons, visitors and young executives fill this trattoria. At night, everyone in the attractive crowd looks to have been born after 1965. The prices are moderate yet fleshed out with little lagniappes. Your waitress brings a complimentary glass of sparkling wine and tomato bruschetta and lights a candle. *Primi piatti* (first courses) are mostly risottos and pastas. A meal-in-itself salad of fresh greens and vegetables is dressed with fruity olive oil and balsamic vinegar. Some of the soups and properly al dente pastas (puttanesca, for example) are given more of a spicy kick than the Spanish norm.

AROUND & NEAR PLAZA SANTA ANA

Artemisa. Ventura de la Vega 4 (near Carrera de San Jerónimo). ☎ **91/429-50-92.** Main courses 925P–1,195P ($6–$8); *menú del día* 1,200P ($8). AE, DC, MC, V. Mon–Sat 1:30–4pm and 8:30pm–midnight, Sun 1:30–4pm. Metro: Sol or Sevilla. VEGETARIAN.

Lines of avid eaters are frequently encountered at the door of this restaurant, especially at lunch. Very fresh ingredients are used in compiling the mostly vegetarian dishes. Two of the better choices are vegetable lasagna at 975P ($7) and *paella* at 875P ($6). Meat eaters can choose the main course of sausage with kidney beans for 875P ($6). Another branch is at Tres Cruces 4 (☎ **91/521-87-21**), near Plaza del Carmen.

D'A Queimada. Echegaray 17 (near Carrera de San Jerónimo). ☎ **91/429-32-63.** Main courses 260P–2,900P ($1.80–$20); *menú del día* 975P ($7); paella or cocido 1,300P ($9). MC, V. Daily 11:30am–5pm and 8pm–midnight. Metro: Sol. SPANISH.

They've toned down the garish signs screaming their offerings, but not by much. The interior is just as gaudy, and the huge pan of *paella* near the front door reaches out and grabs at appetites. The staff is amiable, and most of the dishes the kitchen turns out are from Galicia, in the northwestern corner of the country. Seafood prevails.

La Biotika. Amor de Dios 3 (1 block south of Calle de las Huertas). ☎ **91/429-07-80.** Main courses 600P–900P ($4.15–$6); *menú del día* 1,000P ($7). No credit cards. Mon–Fri 1–4pm and 8–11:30pm, Sat–Sun and holidays 1:30–4pm and 8–11:30pm. Metro: Antón Martín. VEGETARIAN.

A True Taste of Spain: Tapas

Now gaining fame around the world, tapas are small portions of food served in most Madrid bars. While they often precede lunch or dinner, you can make a complete meal of tapas alone—a good way to control portions and cost.

Popular tapas are *boquerones* (anchovy-size fish fried or marinated in oil), *croquetas* (fritters of cod or other ingredients), *empañadillas* (pastries filled with tuna or chicken), *setas* (large mushrooms usually fried with garlic), *morcilla* (blood sausage with rice and onions), *pimientos fritos* (fried sweet peppers), *pimientos de Padrón* (grilled jalapeño-size peppers, most of which are mild, but a few of which are little firecrackers), *patatas bravas* (roast potatoes with piquant sauce), steamed *mejillones* (mussels), *chipirones in su tinta* (baby squid in their ink), stuffed or deep-fried *calamares* (squid), *chorizo* and *salchichón* (sausages), and *queso manchego* (cheese from La Mancha). *Warning:* Delectable *jamón de Serrano* (air-cured ham) is widely available and should be sampled but is very expensive—a 4-ounce portion can cost $20 or more.

Areas to begin exploration of this delectable Spanish invention are the streets on and around **Plaza Santa** and **Calle Victoria,** which leads to it, and down **Calle San Miguel,** which borders Plaza Mayor on the west. Trolling through these concentrations of bars, *mesónes,* and *tascas* will lead to many delicious discoveries and not a few tales to carry home.

Step into the health-food/produce shop in front and the enticing aromas will draw you into the dim bare cafe in back. Offered are salads and rice- and grain-based dishes at minimal prices. The menu changes twice a year to take advantage of seasonal produce. Typical, however, are chilled gazpacho, plates of scrambled eggs with mushrooms, or hummus with tahini and cabbage salad, topped by a fruit tart. Have tea, alcohol-free beer, or a "biological" drink (a blenderized health drink) to wash them down. The owner speaks a little English.

La Trucha. Núñez de Arce 6 (near Plaza Santa Ana). ☎ **91/532-08-82.** Main courses 900P–2,400P ($6–$17); *menú de la casa* 2,800P ($19). AE, V. Mon–Sat 12:30–4pm and 7:30pm–midnight. Closed July. Metro: Sol. SPANISH/TAPAS.

Trout *(trucha)* is the signature dish of this popular tavern. One version is *trucha a La Trucha,* in the style of the province of Navarre. The whole fish is split open, filled with chopped ham and garlic, and then sautéed. Another is the smoked fillets of trout included in the platter of fish and roe called a *verbena.* This is a popular stop on the tapas circuit, partly because most of the dishes are cooked to order and the men behind the counter make new patrons feel like old friends. There's a larger but similar branch at Calle Manuel Fernández y González 3 (☎ **91/429-58-33**).

Shao-lin. Calle de las Huertas 64. ☎ **91/429-37-33.** *Menús del día* 725P and 895P ($5 and $6). V. Daily 11:30am–4pm and 7:30pm–midnight. Metro: Sol. CHINESE.

Near the bottom of Calle de las Huertas down from Plaza del Angel, on a street known more for its nightlife than its food, this unobtrusive place has been around for years. Recent renovations tossed out the usual trappings of gilded dragons in favor of restrained beiges. Delicacy and care in preparation characterize the food as well. There are a few mildly piquant dishes from the Hunan and Szechuan genres, but they don't scare off the gastronomically conservative Madrileños.

Toscana. Manuel Fernández y González 17. ☎ **91/429-69-50.** Main courses 500P–2,300P ($3.45–$16); *menú del día* 2,000P ($14). No credit cards. Mon–Sat 1–4pm and 8pm–midnight. Closed Aug. Metro: Sevilla. SPANISH.

Toscana was overhauled a few years ago to compete with the several good tapas bars on this and adjacent blocks. Now it has rough white plaster walls and dark heavy beams that show their adz marks. The place is jammed most nights, but the squat little tables and stools clear quickly. A man stands behind the bar ladling out portions of the nightly special, which might be a hearty half portion of veal stew spooned over fries for 700P ($4.80) or grilled cod with tomatoes for 1,300P ($9).

AROUND PUERTA DEL SOL & PLAZA MAYOR

El Cuchi. Cuchilleros 3. ☎ **91/266-31-08.** Main courses 1,200P–2,900P ($8–$20); *menú del día* 1,600P ($11). AE, DC, MC, V. Daily 1–4pm and 8pm–midnight. Metro: Sol. MEXICAN/INTERNATIONAL.

This giddily colorful restaurant is at the foot of the stairs leading down through the Arco de Cuchilleros from the southwest corner of Plaza Mayor. A sign above the door reads: WE DON'T SPEAK ENGLISH, BUT WE WON'T LAUGH AT YOUR SPANISH. The message is repeated in French and German, a fair indication of the lighthearted attitude of this branch of an Anglo-Mexican chain. Bread loaves are found in baskets above each table. It's as Mexican as McDonald's is American, meaning that they don't let authenticity get in the way of a peseta. Many items are expensive, but careful choices (like barbecued chicken and mixed salad) can come to less than 2,000P ($14).

Madrid I. Carrera de San Jerónimo 16 (east of Puerta del Sol). ☎ **91/521-90-31.** *Platos combinados* 550P–800P ($3.80–$5); *menús del día* 975P and 1,275P ($7 and $9). MC, V. Daily 8:30am–12:30am. Metro: Sol. SPANISH.

Most of the dining bases are covered at this unpretentious place. In front is a tapas bar; in back, a dining room for *platos combinados;* and upstairs, a room with an open buffet Monday to Friday. Pictures of turn-of-the-century Madrid comprise most of the decor. Apart from breakfasts, lunches, and dinners, they offer pizzas for 675P to 775P ($4.65 to $5), *paella* for 575P ($4), and sandwiches and burgers for 250P to 675P ($1.70 to $4.65).

Mi Pueblo. Costanilla de Santiago 2 (1 block north of Calle Mayor). ☎ **91/948-20-73.** Main courses 975P–1,925P ($7–$13); *menú del día* 1,850P ($13). MC, V. Tues–Sat 1:30–4pm and 8:30–11:30pm, Sun 1:30–4pm. Closed the first 3 weeks in Aug. Metro: Sol. SPANISH.

Earthenware shades on the hanging lamps, ladderback chairs around the closely spaced tables, and ceramics and craftworks on the walls set the folkloric tone. *Pueblo* means "people" or "town," and this *casera* (homestyle) cooking borrows recipes from every region. These include *brocheta catalana,* a shish kebab of steak and vegetable chunks, and *relleños madrileños,* five whole vegetables stuffed with ground meat and delivered to your table in a bubbling casserole. Music on the stereo is retro-pop and jazz. Pipe and cigar smoking are forbidden. Now if only the taciturn staff could lighten up and the coffee could be improved.

Museo de Jamón. Victoria 1/Carrera de San Jerónimo 6 (1 block east of Puerta del Sol). ☎ **91/521-03-46.** *Platos combinados* 450P–725P ($3.10–$5); *menús del día* 950P–1,600P ($7–$11). MC, V. Daily 9am–midnight. Metro: Sol. SPANISH/TAPAS.

A "museum of ham," indeed. This big shiny tapas bar/restaurant specializes in the most popular edible flesh in Spain. Hams are cured by a variety of methods, and they hang by their hooves like rows of bowling pins high on the walls and above the bar.

The street-level room has a bar and a takeout counter. Portions range in price from reasonable to stunning—$20 and more for 3 ounces at the high end—so the best way to sample this delicacy is in a sandwich, at 95P *(una chaquita)* to 260P (65¢ to $1.80). Combo plates are less intimidating, such as grilled loin of pork with eggs for 500P ($3.45). *Paella* for two is only 1,600P ($11) in the upstairs dining room, where there's a guitarist some nights. The Museo de Jamón at the corner of Calle Mayor and Calle San Cristóbal is a virtual mirror image.

Pozo Real. Pozo 6. ☎ **91/521-79-51.** Main courses 375P–1,250P ($2.60–$8.60); *menús del día* 775P, 1,000P, and 2,100P ($5, $7, and $15). No credit cards. Daily noon–4pm and 8pm–midnight. Metro: Sol. SPANISH.

Though it's just steps off heavily traveled Calle Victoria, this is a folksy neighborhood place that sees few tourists, so expect heads to turn when you walk in (the regulars quickly go back to their conversations). Meals, served in the two tiny rooms in back, are simple and straightforward. A sample first course is *pastel de verduras*, mixed vegetables drizzled with oil and vinegar. Most main courses (broiled fish or chicken, usually) come with fried potatoes or, less often, salad or a vegetable. Flan or fruit can follow. Keep this place in mind for Sunday, when most other restaurants are closed.

Rodríguez. Calle San Cristóbal 15 (near Plaza Santa Cruz). ☎ **91/531-11-36.** Main courses 450P–1,500P ($3.10–$10); *menús del día* 950P, 1,000P, and 1,400P ($6, $7, and $10). No credit cards. Fri–Wed 1–4pm and 8–11:30pm. Metro: Sol. SPANISH.

This brightly lit family-run restaurant is known for its hearty *potajes* and *cocidos*, classic Castilian stews. A particular fave is *fabes con almejas*, a soup of white beans, onions, wine, and clams. Only a block off Plaza Mayor and much cheaper than the restaurants on that square, this is a significant value. A "super" *menú del día* employs fancier ingredients for only 2,000P ($14).

Santa Cruz. Atocha 2 (on Plaza Santa Cruz). ☎ **91/360-06-06.** Main courses 1,500P–2,200P ($10–15); *menú del día* 1,000P ($7) at lunch, 1,500P ($10) at dinner. Daily 1:30–4pm and 8:30–11:30pm. AE, DC, MC, V. Metro: Sol. SPANISH.

Above a tapas bar that stays busy most of the day and evening, this small triangular room with only a dozen tables is a find, open less than 2 years. While the food hews to established Castilian recipes, it's executed with admirable care, avoiding the overcooking and greasiness that characterize too many places. Here eggs scrambled with green beans and veal loin with fries taste new. It can get smoky, but there are big windows to crack open by most of the tables.

Viuda de Vacas. Cava Alta 23. ☎ **91/366-58-47.** *Menú del día* 1,750P ($12). AE, MC, V. Mon–Wed and Fri–Sat 1:30–4:30pm and 9pm–midnight, Sun 1:30–4:30pm. Metro: Lavapiés. SPANISH.

Looking as if it were around when Cervantes walked these streets, this is a customary Sunday afternoon stop for shoppers at the nearby Rastro street market. Worn quarry tiles are underfoot, and the two rooms are ringed by high dadoes of cracked *azulejos*. The waiters, who are brothers, do most of the smoking, standing at the old zinc-topped service bar. They bring big bowls of thick pea soup and hunks of meat or fish, heavy on the oil and garlic, fries on the side.

NEAR THE ROYAL PALACE

La Bola. Bola 5 (2 blocks north of the Teatro Real). ☎ **91/547-69-30.** Main courses 1,350P–2,200P ($9–$15); *menú del día* 2,125P ($15). Mon–Sat 1:30–4pm and 9pm–12:30am. No credit cards. Metro: Santo Domingo. SPANISH.

Easily spotted by its crimson exterior, this place has been on stage since 1870, so of course Hemingway and Ava Gardner made it a regular stop, as attested by photos on the walls. Ask about that history and they hand you a leaflet. The big menu item at 1,975P ($14) is *cocido madrileño,* the traditional Sunday boiled dinner of Castilian families. Several kinds of meat and vegetables are slow-cooked together for hours. The rich broth is strained off and tiny noodles dropped in at the last moment as a first course. That's followed with the vegetables (potatoes, chickpeas, cabbage) and the meats (usually chicken, *chorizo,* beef, pork), mostly cheap cuts with only a couple of bites each. That's what makes it manageable. Fish dishes are well suited to smaller appetites. A lagniappe of liquid sorbet follows.

La Pampa. Bola 8 (2 blocks north of the Teatro Real). ☎ **91/542-44-12.** Main courses 325P–3,205P ($2.25–$22); *menú de la casa* 1,450P ($10). AE, DC, MC, V. Daily 1–4:30pm and 8:30pm–12:30am. Metro: Santo Domingo. ARGENTINE.

When the Spanish enthusiasm for exotic seafood starts to pall, head here. Grilled meat is the centerpiece: fist-thick slabs, charcoal-crusted outside, fragrant juices spilling at the touch of a knife. The only certain way to get a vegetable is to order the house salad at the outset (they don't want to clutter up the wooden carving boards with broccoli). The assortment of steaks, chops, sausages, and organ meats meant for two at 3,675P ($25) will serve at least three. The kitchen grills to order, but if unspecified, the meats show up on the pink side of medium. Live music is usually offered on Thursday.

Palacio de Anglona. Segovia 13 (about 2 blocks west of Plaza Puerta Cerrada). ☎ **91/366-37-53.** Reservations recommended on weekends. Pizzas 785P–855P ($5–$6); main courses 1,135P–1,600P ($8–$11). AE, MC, V. Daily 8:30pm–3am. Metro: La Latina. ITALIAN.

These several rooms deploy tiny Milanese tensor lamps hanging low over tables set along walls built out in neoclassical forms with sponged terra-cotta paint. Pizzas are prominent on the card, with unusual ingredients on 10-inch crusts that have the thinness and texture of French crêpes. If they or the substantial main courses don't seem enough, consider starting with the plate of roasted vegetables—flavorful mushrooms, asparagus, zucchini, broccoli, and eggplant.

CAFES

Madrid's cafes hold a special place in the lives of its citizens, serving a function somewhere between tapas bars and full-service restaurants. Food, though always available, is secondary, pushed aside by every Spaniard's favorite occupation—talk. Many of the older cafes, dating to pre–World War I days and even farther, nurture reputations as hotbeds of intellectualism or ideology. Others are favored primarily as meeting places, where a cup of coffee or a beer is the sole price of admission to a table you can hold for hours.

The authentic **Café Comercial,** Glorieta de Bilbao 7 (☎ **91/521-56-55;** Metro: Bilbao), began life in the last century. Artists and intellectuals have been challenging each other at regular *tertulias* (get-togethers) ever since, reflected in big mirrors hung beneath a towering ceiling. Though this place's reputation is decidedly left-wing radical, no ideological litmus test is set and most of the patrons seem involved in less cosmic interests. Go for coffee or drinks and the surroundings, not to eat. But tapas and sandwiches begin at 250P ($1.70). It's open daily 9am to midnight.

Hemingway made the **Café Gijón,** Paseo de Recoletos 21 (☎ **91/521-54-25;** Metro: Banco de España), famous among Americans, and it's been a home to the Spanish tradition of the *tertulia* since 1888. That's a more-or-less formal occasion when friends and colleagues get together for discussions of philosophy, the arts, politics, . . . or soccer. Outside in summer or inside in cooler weather, this is a relaxing place to sip a coffee or beer or read a newspaper. Be prepared for thick clouds of cigarette smoke. Tapas run 360P to 1,000P ($2.50 to $7), while the *menú del día* is 1,500P ($10). No credit cards are accepted, and it's open daily 9:30am to midnight.

A near-legendary priest opened the **Café de Oriente,** Plaza de Oriente 2 (☎ **91/541-15-64;** Metro: Opera), to steer troubled young men and ex-convicts on a better path. It sits at the edge of its namesake plaza, facing the Royal Palace, which appears especially imposing at night when it's illuminated. Outdoors in warm months, there are tables. Indoors, the look is belle époque, with much gilt, brass, and velvet. The dining room in the brick cellar is attractive, though far too expensive for these pages. Tapas and snacks begin at 550P ($3.80); pizzas are 800P to 1,050P ($5 to $7). Major credit cards are accepted, and it's open daily 8:30am to 1:30am.

Not only a cafe but also a cultural center with galleries and performance spaces upstairs, the **Circulo de Bellas Artes,** Alcalá 42 (☎ **91/531-77-00** or 91/531-77-06; Metro: Banco de España), is often packed, usually with professors, students, and others of an intellectual bent. They're drawn by a full schedule of art exhibits, music recitals, lectures, films, workshops, and similar events, some of which may be of interest despite the language difference. There's a 100P (70¢) entrance charge to the center. In the cafe, the limited-choice *menú del día*—at 1,000P ($7)—struggles to stay on par with that of lower-order college cafeterias. Go instead for culture and conversation. No credit cards are accepted, and it's open daily 9am to midnight.

THE CHAINS

Spanish fast-food chains proliferate. One local favorite, **Vips,** offers sit-down eating from abbreviated menus along with sales of books, magazines, records, tapes, videos, beer, wine, cookies, and meats. Popular from breakfast to late-night munch attacks, it's open daily 9am to 3am. Menu items run 250P to 1,275P ($1.70 to $9). Branches are at Gran Vía 43, Princesa 5, Velázquez 84 and 136, Paseo de la Castellana 85, Orense 16 and 79, Paseo de la Habana 17, Julian Romea 4, and Alberto Aguitera 56.

Foster's Hollywood, on the scene for decades, deals in burgers and fries, barbecued spareribs, and the like at fair prices. Dinners run 995P to 1,775P ($7 to $12). Locations include Velázquez 80, Guzmán el Bueno 100, Magallanes 1, Avenida de Brasil 14–16, and on Plaza de Isabel II, behind the Teatro Real. Most are open daily 1pm to 1am.

Nebraska is another home-grown cafeteria chain offering a *menú del día* for 1,075P ($7) in the bar area. Burgers cost 780P to 1,195P ($5 to $8) and *platos* 1,075P to 1,470P ($7 to $10). Menus are available in English. Locations include Alcalá 18, Gran Vía 32 and 55, Calle Mayor 1, and Goya 39. They're open daily 9am to midnight.

A Barcelona chain, **Pans & Company,** has set up shop in the capital. It features hot and cold sandwiches on freshly baked baguettes, often accompanied by salads or fries. Prices start at 195P ($1.35) and top out at 695P ($4.80). The more convenient locations are Princesa 3, Plaza Callao 3, Goya 5, Gran Vía 30, Serrano 41, and Orense 8. A similar but fancier operation is the chainlet **Bocata y Olé,** so far with locations at General Martinez Campos 2, Goya 45, Fernando VI 2, and Glorieta Cuatro Caminos 1. Splashes of pictographic tiles distinguish them from burger joints, and their good sandwiches and salads stay mostly between 390P and 525P ($2.70 and $3.60).

PICNICKING

For one-stop shopping, go to the supermarket at **El Corte Inglés** (see "Shopping," later in this chapter) or the covered **Mercado de San Miguel** on Plaza San Miguel near the northwest corner of Plaza Mayor. Everything at the old market is as fresh as the morning, from sausages and cheeses to dewy produce. Many bakeshops and gourmet shops sell salads and sandwiches that are perfect for picnics. One possibility is **Rodilla,** on Plaza Callao; another is **Ferpal,** at Calle del Arenal 7, near the Puerta del Sol.

Take the chosen fixings to **El Retiro park,** the **Parque del Oeste** (northwest of the Royal Palace), or the **Casa de Campo.**

WORTH A SPLURGE

✪ **El Mentidero de la Villa.** Santo Tomé 6 (near the Palacio de Justicia). ☎ **91/308-12-85.** Reservations recommended. Main courses 1,950P–2,400P ($13–$17); *menú del día* 2,400P ($17). AE, DC, MC, V. Mon–Fri 1:30–4pm and 8:30pm–midnight, Sat 8:30pm–midnight. Closed 2 weeks in Aug. Metro: Colón. ECLECTIC.

The recent introduction of a *menú del día* bestows the opportunity to experience innovative marriages of techniques and ingredients too rarely seen in this otherwise sophisticated but gastronomically hidebound city. The shyly gracious multilingual owner restlessly tinkers with his menu, and his kitchen does wondrous things with rarely seen aquatic creatures and such unexpected items as cock's comb. All this is served with panache in an out-of-the-way bistro sufficiently romantic to inspire frequent assignations between people who aren't married . . . to each other. Just beware of the à la carte card or risk blowing the day's budget. And write down the address, since most cabdrivers don't know the street.

5 Seeing the Sights

SIGHTSEEING SUGGESTIONS

As a capital city for more than 4 centuries, Madrid is the principal repository of the nation's patrimony, its history and culture enshrined in at least 60 museums. The glimpses they provide into prehistory, the Roman and Arab epochs, and the Golden Age of Spain intrigue and delight. Since Madrid reveals itself slowly, the more days you have available, the better. However, if time is limited, the following suggestions will help you spend it wisely.

IF YOU HAVE 1 DAY   Everyone's first stop should be the **Museo del Prado.** Justifiably world famous, this early 19th-century building houses a superlative collection of paintings from the Gothic period through the High Renaissance, notably by the Spanish masters Murillo, El Greco, Goya, and Velázquez.

From the Prado, walk west along uphill Carrera de San Jerónimo to the **Puerta del Sol.** Though it means "Gate of the Sun," Puerta del Sol is a plaza shaped like a half moon. The spiritual heart of Madrid, it's ground zero for the roads radiating into every corner of the country. On the north side is a statue of a bear nibbling at the berries of a *madroño* tree, a vignette serving as the emblem of Madrid.

Continue west down Calle Mayor a few blocks and you'll see a ramp on the left leading through an archway into **Plaza Mayor.** Cafe tables spread out into the pedestrians-only plaza in all but the coldest months. They're irresistible for taking in the shifting scene of buskers, caricaturists, lovers, and poets. (Nurse the drinks and eat elsewhere, for prices are exorbitantly high in the plaza.) Felípe III, who sits astride his horse in the center, ordered the plaza's construction. Since the 17th century it has been the site of various dramas, from inventive executions during the Spanish Inquisition to fiestas and bullfights. It now sees many other kinds of celebrations, including opera, rock concerts, and fireworks displays.

Next should be the **Palacio Real.** Return to the Puerta del Sol and walk west downhill on Calle del Arenal, eventually passing the south side of the just-reopened Teatro Real, to the renovated **Plaza de Oriente.** The palace faces the plaza from the other side of Calle de Bailén, and this assemblage of greenery, statuary, and aristocratic architecture is one of the city's finest public spaces. The palace has over 2,000 rooms, only 50 or so open to the public. Guided tours are conducted in several languages.

IF YOU HAVE 2 DAYS   Spend Day 1 as above, but on Day 2 leave Madrid early for a visit to **Toledo,** an hour away. See "Side Trips" at the end of this chapter.

IF YOU HAVE 3 DAYS   Three days in Madrid will allow you time to return to the **Prado,** which you can't absorb in one visit. The Prado ticket includes entrance to the **Cason del Buen Retiro,** an annex 3 blocks east up Calle de Felípe IV that contains lesser works of the vast Prado collection. Nearby, to the north, is the **Museo de Ejército.** Step across Calle de Alfonso XII, which passes in front of the Cason del Buen Retiro, and into the **Parque del Retiro,** delightful at any time but particularly from midday on Sunday when Madrileños are out for the *paseo;* the main pathways grow crowded with mimes, musicians, and jugglers.

On Day 2 visit **Toledo** as suggested above, and on Day 3 spend more time exploring the vicinity of **Plaza Mayor,** visit the nearby covered market of **San Miguel,** and wander down Calle Mayor to see **Plaza de la Villa,** a cluster of some of Madrid's oldest buildings. The **Convento de las Descalzas Reales,** founded by Juana of Austria, is sumptuously decorated and deserves a visit. The wealth of art at this still-functioning convent is the bequest of its aristocratic former residents.

IF YOU HAVE 5 DAYS   Spend Days 1 to 3 as above. On Day 4 choose from a number of fascinating museums, depending on your interests. Among the possibilities are the **Museo de Artes Decorativas,** which highlights Spanish trends in the decorative arts through the centuries, and the **Museo Lázaro Galdiano,** displaying the eponymous collector's idiosyncratic choices in painting, sculpture, silverware, enamels, and ivories. For archaeology enthusiasts, the recently revamped collections of the **Museo Arqueológico Nacional** are excellent, especially the Iberian and classical antiquities.

On Day 5, take another trip out of Madrid to Felípe II's **Monasterio de San Lorenzo de El Escorial** (see "Side Trips," at the end of this chapter). In the foothills of the Guadarrama Mountains, this somber granite pantheon to the Spanish kings broods over the plains below.

THE TOP MUSEUMS

Most museums have a day or at least a few hours when admission is free, usually Saturday morning or Wednesday, and reduced fees are common for students and seniors. Most museums are closed on Monday, so save for that day the Palacio Real and the Centro de Arte Reine Sofía, which are open.

Most museums are also closed January 1, Good Friday, May 1, and December 26, but many, including the Prado, now stay open through the afternoon siesta, when most stores are closed.

✪ **Museo del Prado.** Paseo del Prado. ☎ **91/420-28-36.** Admission 500P ($3.45) adults, 250P ($1.70) students. Free for everyone Sat to 2:30pm. Free for seniors/under age 12 on Sun. Admission includes entrance to Cason del Buen Retiro, an annex 3 blocks east up Calle de Felípe IV. Tues–Sat 9am–7pm. Metro: Atocha or Banco de España. Bus: 10, 14, 27, 34, 37, 45, or M6.

Madrid's most famous museum contains Spanish paintings from the 12th to the 18th centuries as well as Italian masters and painters from the Venetian and Flemish schools. Only a tenth of its nearly 20,000 works can be displayed at any given time, a fact that has prompted a frustrating search for additional space and rising complaints

The Prado

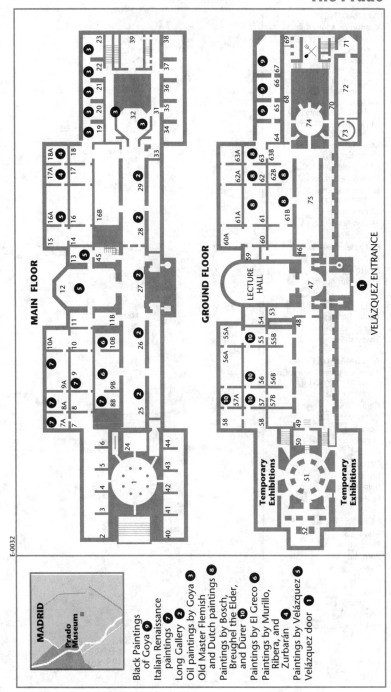

MAIN FLOOR

GROUND FLOOR

VELÁZQUEZ ENTRANCE

MADRID
Prado Museum

Black Paintings of Goya ⑨
Italian Renaissance paintings ⑦
Long Gallery ②
Oil paintings by Goya ③
Old Master Flemish and Dutch paintings ⑧
Paintings by Bosch, Breughel the Elder, and Dürer ⑩
Paintings by El Greco ⑥
Paintings by Murillo, Ribera, and Zurbarán ④
Paintings by Velázquez ⑤
Velázquez door ①

E-0032

561

Madrid

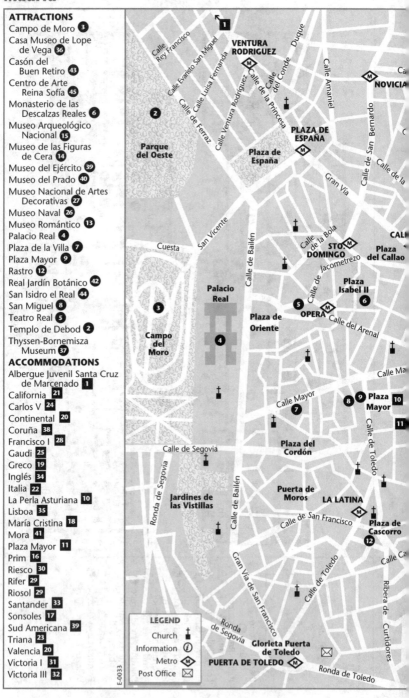

E-0033

Calle de Genova

14

SERRANO
Calle de Goya

0 ——— 300 m
——— 330 y
N

Calle de la Palma

Calle de Fuencarral

13

Calle Fernando VI

Plaza de la Villa

Plaza de Colón
COLÓN

Jardines del Descubrimiento

15

Calle de El Escorial

Corredera Baja de San Pablo

Calle Bárbara de Braganza

Calle de Serrano

del Pez

Calle de Valverde

Hortaleza

Calle de Gravina

CHUECA

Calle de Augusto Figueroa

Calle del Almirante

Paseo Recoletos

16

Calle de Prim

Plaza de la Independencia

17

Calle de Fuencarral

18

19

Calle de Barquillo

GRAN VÍA

21   **22**

Red. de San Luis

Gran Vía

23

Calle Montera

25

Plaza de la Cibeles   Calle de Alcalá

BANCO DE ESPAÑA

27

26

SEVILLA

Calle de Montalbán

Calle de Alcalá

Carrera de San Jerónimo

Calle A. Maura

Plaza de la Lealtad

Paseo del Prado

SOL

30

31

32

33

34

35

Calle de la Cruz

Calle del Prado

Plaza de las Cortes

37

Plaza C. del Castillo

39

Calle de Alfonso XII

Parque del Retiro

Plaza Jacinto Benavente

Calle de Cervantes

38

40

Museo del Prado

36

Calle de las Huertas

Calle Atocha

Calle de Espalter

TIRSO DE MOLINA

Calle de la Magdalena

ANTÓN MARTÍN

44

Calle de la Cabeza

Calle de Gobernador

41

42

43

Baja

Calle Jesús y María

Calle del Amparo

Calle de Levapiés

Calle Atocha

Real Jardín Botánico

Calle de Alfonso XII

Calle de Santa Isabel

ATOCHA

Paseo de la Infanta Isabel

Calle Mesón de Paredes

Calle Miguel Servet

Plaza Lavapiés

45

LAVAPIES

Estación de Atocha

Calle de Embajadores

Ronda de Atocha

Sta. María de la Cabeza

563

A Museum Tip

Always check museum hours before setting out, particularly at the smaller ones, for they're prone to sudden changes.

about mismanagement, complicated by charges of corruption and political interference. Massive ongoing repairs have lately focused on the roof, a planned 2-year project that might still be unfinished.

Whatever the behind-the-scenes problems, this is one of Europe's great repositories. If you have limited time to enjoy this awe-inspiring collection, give priority to the works of Goya, Velázquez, and El Greco, whose *Adoration of the Shepherds* enthralls with its emotion. In the Velázquez rooms, see his portrait of Don Baltasar Carlos, the expressions on the faces of *Los Borrachos* (The Drunkards), and from the last years of his life, the classic *Las Meninas*. Velázquez and Goya were court painters, hence the multitude of their paintings here. Goya's cartoons are especially popular, though his brutally candid portraits of the royal family and powerful and somber series of "Black Paintings" also have their admirers.

Other important canvases are those of the Spaniards Ribera, Zurbarán, and Murillo, as well as masterpieces by Hieronymus Bosch (especially the nightmarish *Garden of Earthly Delights*), Dürer, Titian, Tintoretto, Rubens, and van Dyck. Too often ignored among these riches are the startling Gothic diptychs and triptychs on the main floor, all in gilded frames carved in the detail accorded facades of cathedrals. A good plan is to focus on two or three specific sections, returning for visits of an hour or so on separate occasions. You can't absorb the whole at one lunge.

✪ **Museo Thyssen-Bornemisza.** Paseo del Prado 8. ☎ **91/369-01-51.** Admission to the permanent collection 700P ($4.80) adults, 400P ($2.75) seniors/students; for the permanent collection and temporary exhibits 900P ($6) adults, 500P ($3.45) seniors/students; free for under age 12. Tues–Sun 10am–7pm. Metro: Atocha or Banco de España. Bus: 1, 2, 5, 9, 10, 14, 15, 20, 27, 34, 37, 45, 51, 52, 53, 74, 146, or 150.

The artworks on display in the late 18th-century Palacio de Villa Hermosa were collected by two generations of the Thyssen-Bornemisza family. It stands on the northwest corner of Plaza de Canovas del Castillo, opposite the Prado. The Prado's directors had hoped to have the palace as an annex in order to get some of their long-unseen works out of storage, but the renovated building was one of the inducements used to obtain the Thyssen-Bornemisza holdings, one of the world's greatest private collections. The facade remains intact, while the interior has been adapted to show off the masterpieces it contains.

Those works, paintings for the most part, range from the late 13th century to the present. The authorities were especially eager to obtain the part of the collection covering the last 100 years, which are scantily represented in the capital's museums. To see the artworks in historical order, cross the central court and take the central staircase or elevator to the second floor. The gallery numbering indicates the suggested itinerary, which proceeds counterclockwise. In the first galleries are Italian primitives of the last centuries before the Renaissance and their successors, including Tintoretto and Bernini. Also represented are Dutch, Spanish, Flemish, German, and French artists. Of particular note, because they're rarely seen in Spain, are the rooms containing works by such 19th-century American artists as the landscapist Albert Bierstadt and the portraitist John Singer Sargent and the French impressionists and postimpressionists Manet, Monet, Renoir, and Degas. They're followed by examples of the modernist schools of cubism, constructivism, surrealism, and abstract

Getting the Best Deal on Sightseeing

- Take advantage of the free admission to most museums on either Sunday or Wednesday, and in several cases until 2pm on Saturday.
- Over-65 seniors *(jubilados)* are usually accorded half-price admission, as are students. The effective age limit for discounts for young people varies from 12 to 18.
- People-watching from a table at the cafes that thrust out into Plaza Mayor is a treat, but nurse your drinks or snacks. Even if you linger over a soft drink for an hour, no one will suggest that you move on.
- Catch the Madrid Vision Bus, which makes a circuit of the major sites and plazas, allowing you to debark and reboard as often as you wish for 1 or 2 days.

expressionism, exemplified by Picasso and Hopper, Dalí and de Kooning, Mondrian and Cornell.

Monasterio de las Descalzas Reales. Plaza de las Descalzas 3. ☎ **91/542-00-59.** Admission 650P ($4.50) adults, 250P ($1.70) seniors/students/age 11 and under. Tues–Wed and Fri–Sat 10:30am–12:45pm and 4–5:45pm, Thurs 10:30am–12:45pm, Sun and holidays 11am–1:45pm. Metro: Sol or Callao.

In the heart of old Madrid, near the Puerta del Sol, this richly endowed royal convent was founded in the mid–16th century in the palace where Juana of Austria, Felípe II's sister, was born. She used it as a retreat and brought the Poor Clare nuns here. For many years the convent sheltered only royal women, typically the daughters of aristocrats who sequestered the girls until they were old enough for arranged marriages. They didn't live a spartan existence, judging from the wealth of religious artwork that surrounded them, including tapestries, sculptures, and paintings by Rubens, Brueghel the Elder, and Titian. The main staircase features trompe-l'oeil paintings and frescoes, and you can view 16 of the 32 lavishly decorated chapels. Compulsory tours for groups of 25 or fewer are conducted in Spanish by guides who hasten them from canvas to tapestry to chapel. Try to slow their pace, for there's much to savor.

✪ **Museo Arqueológico Nacional.** Serrano 13 (facing Calle Serrano). ☎ **91/577-79-15.** Admission 500P ($3.45) adults, 200P ($1.35) seniors/students/age 11 and under. Free for everyone Sat 9:30am–2:30pm. Tues–Sat 9:30am–8:30pm, Sun and holidays 9:30am–2:30pm. Metro: Serrano or Retiro. Bus: 1, 9, 19, 51, 74, or M2.

In the same vast building as the National Library (with a separate entrance on Paseo de Recoletos), the Archaeological Museum houses an agglomeration of antiquities from prehistory to the Middle Ages. Arranged chronologically on three floors, the displays are clearly labeled. Most of the artifacts are related specifically to the development of the Iberian peninsula, though there are some Egyptian and Greek objects. Most illuminating are the rooms devoted to the Iberian period, before the waves of sequential conquerors arrived, and those containing relics of the Visigoths, who left relatively little behind, rendering these objects of even greater interest.

A particular treasure is the *Dama de Elche,* a resplendent example of 4th-century B.C. Iberian sculpture, easily equal to the better-known works being produced in Greece at the time. The Visigothic era, roughly from the 5th to the early 8th centuries A.D., is represented by bronzes and funerary offerings from Mérida and some intricate votive crowns and jewelry. Galleries farther on contain Roman mosaics, Etruscan pottery, Greek vases, Gothic sculpture and architectural fragments, and Mudéjar woodwork. Inside the front gate, to the left after you enter, is a reproduction of the Caves

Special & Free Events

Every year Madrid launches itself into fiesta after fiesta, with parades, dancing in the streets, fireworks, craft fairs, daily bullfights, and concerts. Check the weekly *Guía del Ocio* for full details, but the following are the highlights:

Around Christmas and New Year's the city is alive with excitement that culminates in a great gathering beneath the Puerta del Sol's big clock on **New Year's Eve.** Take 12 grapes and pop one in your mouth for each strike of the clock at midnight. Those who are up to the challenge will have good luck all year.

On January 5, the **Los Reyes (Three Kings)** arrive (by helicopter, nowadays) for an exuberant parade on horseback through the streets, during which excited children lining the route are showered with candy.

In March, the **Madrid Theater Festival** attracts a galaxy of international companies. On the Saturday before Lent begins, hundreds of gaily decorated floats parade down Paseo de la Castellana in a **Carnaval** procession. **Semana Santa (Holy Week)** is celebrated with due solemnity, and processions of the penitents take place all over Madrid, including around the Puerta del Sol. Around **Easter** there's a gathering of horses and their riders from Seville, who step through the streets attired in colorful traditional style, beginning and ending in El Retiro.

The most important festival celebrates Madrid's patron saint, **San Isidro,** in mid-May, with a protracted program of activities and the best bullfights of the year. **Veranos de la Villa** provides summer entertainment for the long, warm evenings, including open-air movies at the Cine del Retiro and flamenco shows in another corner of the park. Fall brings Madrid's acclaimed **jazz festival** and the **Feriarte,** Spain's major antiques fair.

The **Fundación Juan March,** Castelló 77 (☎ **91/435-42-40**), offers free concerts from fall to spring, on Monday and Saturday at noon and Wednesday at 7:30pm, changing the theme monthly.

Religious festivals are celebrated with parades and pageantry, particularly the Procession of the Three Kings on January 5, Carnaval before Lent, and the solemn processions of the penitents during Holy Week.

of Altamira. Since access to the real thing, in northwestern Spain, is restricted, these simulations of the 15,000-year-old paintings approximate the experience.

THE ROYAL PALACE

✪ **Palacio Real.** Bailén s/n. ☎ **91/542-00-59.** Admission 850P ($5.85) adults, 250P ($1.70) seniors/students/age 11 and under; 100P (70¢) extra for guided tours. Mon–Sat 9:30am–5:30pm, Sun and holidays 9am–2pm. Metro: Opera. Bus: 3, 25, 33, 39, or M4.

This opulent palace was built for Felípe V on the site of the medieval Alcázar, a fortified castle that burned in the mid–18th century. It was designed by Giovanni Battista Sacchetti in a mix of baroque and neoclassical styles. Of note are the Italian architect Sabatini's majestic staircase, the many dazzling chandeliers, Gasparini's rococo drawing room, the Throne Room with its Tiepolo ceiling, and the superb tapestries.

King Juan Carlos and Queen Sofía don't live here, but the palace is still used for state functions. Some lucky visitors get to see the **State Dining Room** set for a banquet. The table, which can seat almost 150, stretches off into the distance, gleaming with silver, gold, and cut glass and illuminated by 15 giant chandeliers. Next door is the **Clock Room,** where over 60 clocks, mostly French, strike the hour together.

As well as the palace apartments, the tour takes in the **library, coin and music museums, Royal Pharmacy, Carriage Museum,** and **Royal Armory,** easily one of the highlights with its imposing displays of weaponry and armor, some designed for battle dogs and the royal toddlers.

Guided tours are no longer mandatory, but during peak periods visitors are assembled by common language groups. At slower times, there are multilingual guides.

MORE MUSEUMS

Casa Museo de Lope de Vega. Cervantes 11. ☎ **91/429-92-16.** Admission 200P ($1.35). Tues–Fri 9:30am–2pm, Sat 10am–1:30pm. Metro: Antón Martín or Sevilla. Bus: 6, 26, 32, 57, or M9.

An extraordinarily prolific 17th-century playwright, Lope de Vega is credited with over 1,800 works. He lived in this house on a street now named for a contemporary he bitterly resented, Miguel de Cervantes, author of *Don Quijote de La Mancha*. The house, relatively modest considering his substantial popular success, has been carefully reconstructed and declared a national monument. Inside are his study, bedroom, and kitchen and out back his garden.

Centro de Arte Reina Sofía. Santa Isabel 52 (at the corner of Atocha). ☎ **91/467-50-62.** Admission 500P ($3.45) adults, 250P ($1.70) students/under age 12. Free for everyone Sat 10am–2:30pm; free for seniors and children Sun. Mon and Wed–Sat 10am–9pm, Sun 10am–2:30pm. Metro: Atocha. Bus: 6, 14, 26, 27, 32, 45, 57, or C.

This museum was intended to serve as a repository of 20th-century art, yet its collection is still somewhat sparse and unbalanced, even with the recent acquisition of the holdings of the closed Museo de Arte Contemporáneo. Its direction has been controversial from the outset, with some government members contending that it should concentrate on Spanish artists and its directors insisting that its mission should focus on currents in international thought. To date, its successes have usually been with temporary exhibits rather than with highlights from its permanent collection. One triumph was the wresting of Picasso's fabled mural, *Guernica,* from the Prado, which had held it since its return from New York's Museum of Modern Art after Franco's death. It's now the centerpiece of the Reina Sofía. Largely second-rank work by mostly Spanish artists like Dalí, Miró, Gris, and Solana supplements the Picasso masterwork. For the moment, the center's most interesting element may be the former 18th-century hospital itself, renovated inside and with new see-through elevator shafts on the exterior.

Museo de América. Av. de los Reyes Católicos 6. ☎ **91/549-26-41.** Admission 500P ($3.45) adults, 200P ($1.35) students/age 11 and under. Free for everyone Sun and holidays. Tues–Sat 10am–3pm, Sun 10am–2:30pm. Metro: Montcloa. Bus: 46, 62, 82, 83, A, D, or G.

This museum in the University City/Moncloa section received a $15-million renovation and reopened after 13 years. Its expanded galleries are devoted to ethnological and archaeological collections from Spain's former colonies in the Americas. Of note are those rooms dealing with the social organization and daily lives of the various Native American tribes and nations and the wealth of artifacts related to the observance of their religions. Pre-Colombian jewelry, statuary, and other artifacts are illustrative.

Museo de Cera (Wax Museum). Paseo de Recoletos 41. ☎ **91/308-08-25.** Admission 900P ($6) adults, 600P ($4.15) seniors/under age 12. Daily 10:30am–2:30pm and 4:30–8:30pm. Metro: Colón. Bus: 5, 14, 27, 45, 53, M6, or M7.

More than 450 wax figures should satisfy those who enjoy this sort of place, but Madame Tussaud's this isn't. Prominently featured are scenes from *Don Quijote,* famous bullfighters, and a host of famous and not-so-famous historical and contemporary personages. The museum's principal virtue may be that it's open when most others are closed. Squeamish adults and parents bringing their children are forewarned that the requisite chamber of horrors graphically depicts grisly tortures employed during the Inquisition. These are, of course, precisely the displays the little ones will want to see.

Museo de Artes Decorativas. Montalban 12 (off Plaza de las Cibeles). ☎ **91/522-17-40.** Admission 400P ($2.75) adults, 200P ($1.35) students/age 11 and under. Free for seniors/under age 12 on Sun. Tues–Fri 9am–3pm, Sat–Sun 10am–2pm. Metro: Banco de España. Bus: 14, 27, 34, 37, 45, or M6.

This museum is crammed with furniture, leatherwork, wall hangings, ceramics, rugs, porcelain, glass, jewelry, toys, dollhouses, clothes, and lace. After the first floor, the museum progresses in chronological order, tracing the development of Spanish interior decoration from the 15th to the 19th centuries. By the fifth floor, the amplitude may have become numbing to any but scholars and practitioners, but the immense variety of objects still has the capacity to intrigue.

Museo Lázaro Galdiano. Serrano 122. ☎ **91/561-60-84.** Admission 300P ($2.05) adults, 150P ($1.05) students, free for seniors/under age 12. Free for everyone Sun. Tues–Sun 10am–2pm. Closed holidays and Aug. Metro: Argentina or Nuñez de Balboa. Bus: 9, 16, 19, 51, or 89.

Madrid was the beneficiary of the financier/author José Lázaro Galdiano's largess. When he died, he left the city his 30-room turn-of-the-century mansion and substantial private collection. There are paintings from Spain's Golden Age, including works by Spaniards El Greco, Ribera, Zurbarán, Murillo, and Goya. Among Renaissance Italians represented are Tiepolo and Leonardo da Vinci, and canvases by Englishmen Gainsborough and Constable are on view. However, the museum is most admired for its array of enamels, ivories, and works in gold and silver, most created during the Middle Ages. Admittedly, the collection isn't always as carefully arranged as it deserves and the sometimes sullen staff doesn't enhance the experience.

Museo Sorolla. General Martínez Campos 37. ☎ **91/310-15-84.** Admission 400P ($2.75) adults, 200P ($1.35) students/age 11 and under. Free for everyone Sun. Tues–Sat 10am–3pm, Sun 10am–2pm. Metro: Iglesia. Bus: 5, 7, 16, 61, 40, or M3.

The museum of painter Joaquín Sorolla has a down-to-earth quality after the conspicuous grandeur of many of Madrid's other museums. Sorolla (1863–1923) was born and reared on the coast of Valencia, and his later works were influenced by the French impressionists. Many are seascapes, and he had a knack for painting water so that it appears wet on the canvas. The museum is in the house and studio where he lived and worked the last 11 years of his life—it has been kept (on the ground floor at least) as it was when he died. He was an avid collector, as is evidenced by the large quantity of Spanish ceramics he owned.

Real Fábrica de Tapices (Royal Tapestry Factory). Fuenterrabia 2. ☎ **91/551-34-00.** Admission 50P (35¢). Mon–Fri 9am–12:30pm. Closed holidays and Aug. Metro: Menéndez Pelayo. Bus: 10, 14, 26, 32, 37, C, or M9.

Tapestries are still being made in this 1889 factory as they were when its predecessor opened in the 18th century. Many of the tapestries in the Palacio Real and at El Escorial were made here, with some of the earliest designs by artists as prominent as Goya. The guided tour first enters a room where enormous custom-made carpets are created, then moves on to where antique tapestries are painstakingly restored and new tapestries are made on vast wooden looms. The tour is in Spanish, but just to observe is illuminating.

Museo del Ejército (Army Museum). Méndez Núñez 1. ☎ **91/522-89-77.** Admission 100P (70¢). Tues–Sun 10am–2pm. Metro: Retiro. Bus: 15, 19, 27, 34, 37, or 45.

One of the two remaining buildings of the palace that used to stand in what is now El Retiro park houses this museum. It was founded by Manuel Godoy, who made his spectacular climb from obscurity into the arms of Carlos IV's wife, María Luisa of Parma. Weaponry of every kind—from the surprisingly dainty sword of the semimythical El Cid to firearms from the 1936–39 Civil War—is displayed alongside armor, uniforms, flags, dioramas, miniatures, and thousands of other bits of memorabilia.

Museo Municipal. Fuencarral 78. ☎ **91/588-86-72.** Admission 300P ($2.05) adults, 150P ($1.05) seniors/students/age 17 and under. Tues–Fri 9:30am–8pm, Sat–Sun 10am–2pm. Metro: Tribunal.

Here the history of Madrid is explained through paintings and prints, documents, scale models, carriages, and costumes. In the basement are two large Roman mosaic floors and other artifacts. Easily as interesting is the eye-popping rococo entrance, crowded with cherubim and warriors, designed by Pedro de Ribera to grace what was formerly an 18th-century hospice for the city's poor.

Museo Romántico. San Mateo 13. ☎ **91/448-10-45.** Admission 400P ($2.75) adults, 200P ($1.35) students, free for seniors/age 11 and under. Free for everyone Sun. Tues–Sat 9am–3pm, Sun and holidays 10am–2pm. Closed Aug. Metro: Tribunal. Bus: 37, 40, or M10.

This collection of furniture, paintings, and objets d'art from the Romantic period of the early 19th century was assembled by the philanthropic marquis of La Vega–Inclán. Housed in an 18th-century baroque mansion, it juxtaposes dollhouses and Goyas with antic flair.

Real Academia de Bellas Artes de San Fernando (Royal Academy of Fine Arts of San Fernando). Alcalá 13. ☎ **91/522-14-91.** Admission 300P ($2.05) adults, 150P ($1.05) students, free for seniors/under age 18. Free for everyone Sat–Sun. Tues–Fri 9am–7pm, Sat–Mon 9am–2pm. Metro: Sol or Sevilla. Bus: 3, 5, 15, 20, 51, 52, or M12.

This center, in a recently restored building east of the Puerta del Sol, offers a wide variety of works by artists like El Greco, Zurbarán, Sorolla, Ribera, Murillo, Rubens, and Fragonard, plus one room filled with Goyas, produced in his mature years. After a showy display of these heavyweights, the rooms in back contain a diversity of Chinese terra-cottas, Egyptian bronzes, and small sculptures.

OTHER ATTRACTIONS

Panteón de Goya. San António de la Florida 5. ☎ **91/547-79-21.** Admission 200P ($1.35) adults, 100P (70¢) seniors/age 17 and under. Tues–Fri 10am–2pm and 4–7pm, Sat–Sun 10am–2pm. Metro: Norte. Bus: 41, 46, 75, or C.

Carlos IV commissioned Francisco de Goya to decorate the ceiling in the dome of the chapel in this 1797 hermitage. His frescoes, depicting the story of St. Anthony of Padua, are populated with plump cherubs and voluptuous angels modeled after members of the Spanish court and Madrid society. Some of the women portrayed were rumored to have unsavory professions. Goya is buried here, but somehow his head got lost in transit from Bordeaux, where he was first interred.

Parque de Atracciones. Casa de Campo. ☎ **91/463-29-00.** Park, 475P ($3.25); park and all rides, 1,800P ($12) adults, 1,000P ($7) age 7 and under. Feb–May Tues–Fri 3–9pm or

11pm, Sat–Sun 10am–8pm; June–Nov Mon–Fri 10am–8pm, Sat–Sun 10am–midnight. Call to verify times, which are subject to frequent change. Metro: Batán. Bus: 33 (from Plaza Isabel II) or 65, and Sun also from Ventas, Puente de Vallecas, and Estrecho.

Not merely an amusement park, the Parque de Atracciones, in the spacious Casa de Campo west of the Royal Palace, has an auditorium that stages shows in summer (free with admission). Restaurants, electronic games, and a cinema round out the entertainment. To make a special excursion of the trip, take the cable car from the Paseo del Pintor Rosales, at the western edge of the city, high above the trees of the Casa del Campo. After a ride of a little over 10 minutes, it deposits you within a 10-minute walk of the amusement park. Fares are 360P ($2.50) one-way and 515P ($3.55) round-trip.

Zoo Aquarium. Casa de Campo. ☎ **91/711-99-50.** Admission 1,560P ($10.75) adults, 1,255P ($8.65) seniors/ages 4–7, free for age 3 and under. Daily 10am–sunset (ticket office closes half an hour earlier). Metro: Batán. Bus: 33 from Plaza Isabel II, and on Sun and holidays also from Ventas, Puente de Vallecas, and Estrecho.

Madrid's zoo is Spain's best, though it doesn't really compare to the superior facilities of San Diego, New York, or Berlin. Most animals are housed in open pens rather than cages, separated from the public by ditches. Over 3,000 mammals, birds, and reptiles are grouped according to their continent of origin. Highlights are the two pandas, Chang-Chang and his offspring, Chu-Lin, the first panda in Europe to be born in captivity. The aquarium and dolphin show (1 and 5pm) also deserve attention. It's a 15-minute walk from the park's cable-car station (see Parque de Atracciones above).

PARKS & GARDENS

Along with the Casón del Buen Retiro and the building that houses the Army Museum, the 321-acre **Parque del Retiro** is what's left of a 17th-century palace and grounds ordered built by Felípe IV. Now the tree-lined walks, formal rose garden, Crystal Palace, boating lake, monuments, and grottoes offer a popular but tranquil retreat. Madrileños like to see and be seen, and on weekends entire three- and four-generation families dress up for the *paseo* through this park.

To the south of the Prado Museum is the **Jardín Botánico,** laid out in the 18th century, where a wide range of exotic flora can be enjoyed. The garden is at its most appealing in spring and summer, of course, but serious gardeners will find plantings of interest even in winter. North and west of the Royal Palace, respectively, are the **Jardines de Sabatini** and **Campo del Moro.** Just to the north of these is the **Parque de la Montaña,** which contains the Templo de Debod, a 4th-century B.C. Egyptian temple given to Spain in appreciation of its assistance with the building of the Aswan High Dam. The temple and the elevation on which it stands are at the lower end of the larger **Parque del Oeste (West Park),** adjoining **La Rosaleda (Rose Garden).**

Bordering these on Paseo Pintor Rosales are several open-air bars, and the eastern terminus of the *teleférico* (cable car) that swings out over the Manzanares River and deep into **Casa del Campo.** This semiwild preserve, west of the Royal Palace and the city, is an enormous playground for all Madrileños. Here are the zoo, the Parque de Atracciones, an exhibition center, a boating lake, a sports center, restaurants, and plenty of space to get away from it all.

ORGANIZED TOURS

The best deal is the distinctive **Madrid Vision Bus,** which makes 14 stops at major museums, plazas, and avenues all year. For the full 1,800P ($12) ticket, you can get off and reboard as many times in 1 day as you wish; the cost is 2,200P ($15) for 2 days. Or take the 1½-hour tour, boarding at any point but without the on/off option, for 1,500P ($10). The air-conditioned buses carry multilingual guides who provide information over earphones. Departures are Tuesday to Sunday 10am to 6:15pm. Convenient places to pick up the bus are at the Prado, the Puerta del Sol, or El Corte Inglés department store. For details and departure times, which vary by day and season, call **Trapsatur,** San Bernardo 23 (☎ **91/541-63-20**).

Trapsatur offers a variety of other tours, from half-day circuits of Madrid to day-long excursions to nearby cities like Toledo, El Escorial, and Segovia. Day and night tours of Madrid cost as little as 2,750P to 4,950P ($19 to $34), and a full-day tour to Toledo is 8,500P ($59). Similar possibilities and prices are supplied by **Juliá Tours,** Gran Vía 68 (☎ **91/559-96-05**), and **Pullmantur,** Plaza de Oriente 8 (☎ **91/556-11-14**).

6 Shopping

Madrid's shopping selection is enormous and the service, particularly in smaller stores, friendly. You'll find everything expected of a modern European capital—from modish clothing boutiques to cigar shops along the two pedestrian walkways, **Calle Preciados** and **Calle del Carmen,** north of the Puerta del Sol. Should you desire a splurge or a bit of upscale window-shopping, head for the **Salamanca** district, between calles Serrano and Velázquez, Goya, and Juan Bravo, where the tony designer stores compete. The **AZCA area,** between Paseo de la Castellana and Orense, Raimundo Fernández Villaverde, and Avenida General Perón, is also worth a visit (Metro: Nuevos Ministerios) for its range of stores, El Corte Inglés department store, and the new high-fashion mall, **La Moda.** A North American–style mall known as **Madrid-2** is at La Vaguada (Metro: Barrio del Pilar), with over 350 stores, including an excellent food market.

Across from the Prado in the lower floors of the Palace Hotel is **La Galeria del Prado,** where gleaming marble, brass, glass, and plants set the stage for some of Madrid's most elegant stores. The major department store is **El Corte Inglés,** with bargain basements *(oportunidades)* in some of their stores. Branches include Preciados 3, Goya 76, Princesa 42, and Raimundo Fernández Villaverde 79. All branches have some English-speaking salespeople, as well as those tending the information desks. Competition has arrived just up the street from the Preciados location in the form of **FNAC,** which concentrates on photo and audio equipment, video games, TVs, computers, and books. El Corte Inglés has opened a mirror-image operation right next door.

Madrid Rock, Gran Vía 25, carries a substantial stock of CDs in most musical persuasions and sells tickets to upcoming pop concerts. Nearby, a large and convenient bookstore with a sizable English-language section is **La Casa del Libro,** Gran Vía 29 (☎ **91/521-21-13**). The **Librería El Galeón,** Calle Sagasta 4 (☎ **91/445-57-38**), is a gay bookstore open Monday to Friday 9:30am to 1:30pm.

Bargains can no longer be found in profusion at the famed **El Rastro flea market,** and you can forget about plucking an unsigned Goya drawing or a Roman coin out

Shopping Tips

El Corte Inglés, FNAC, and the larger shopping centers are open 10am to 9 or 9:30pm; however, almost everything else closes for lunch at 1:30 or 2pm and doesn't reopen until 5pm. In July and August, many stores close on Saturday afternoon, and smaller ones may even close completely for their month's vacation.

January, February, and July are the times for the big sales *(rebajas),* when virtually every store in Madrid offers discounts that increase as the month proceeds.

of the heaps on display. Still, it's fun to browse—but always keep control over purses and personal belongings. The market takes place in the streets of the triangle formed by San Isidro Cathedral, Puerta de Toledo, and Glorieta de Embajadores. Ribera de Curtidores is its main street. On Sunday mornings, thousands of Madrileños throng these streets to purchase everything from songbirds to audiotapes to picture frames. Saturday morning is quieter for browsing through the antiques shops and secondhand stalls. Bargaining is expected.

7 Madrid After Dark

No city revels in the night as does Madrid. With dinner often ending past midnight and clubs and discos staying open until 6am—and even later—the question is not what to do but when to sleep. For details, check the weekly *Guía del Ocio* or the daily entertainment section in *El País,* which publishes a booklet of listings and reviews in its Friday editions. The listings are in Spanish but aren't difficult to decipher.

THE PERFORMING ARTS

The big cultural news is the late 1997 reopening of the 1,750-seat ✪ **Teatro Real (Royal Opera House)** after almost a decade of false starts and the agonizingly slow construction costing $157 million. It hadn't experienced an operatic performance for over 70 years, opening and closing irregularly over that time to serve as an orchestral concert hall. Guided tours of the long-awaited grand renovation are available Saturday, Sunday, and holidays, every 30 minutes 10:30am to 1:30pm.

All Madrid's performing arts are enjoying a renaissance, with the high visibility of Spanish tenors Plácido Domingo and José Carreras and touring organizations like the National Ballet of Spain gathering critical bouquets on five continents. At any time of year, there's a diverse cultural calendar ranging from theater to dance to opera. And there's the *zarzuela,* a popular native form of operetta. Theater tickets range from as little as 200P ($1.35) to as much as 2,800P ($19) or more. On certain days (usually Wednesday or Sunday's first performance) discounts of up to 50% are available. Most performances are at 10:30pm, but some start at 8 or 9pm.

English-language theatrical productions do stop in Madrid from time to time, but they don't stay long. Visitors who don't understand Spanish are hardly deprived, not with the availability of classical and modern dance, symphonies and chamber music recitals, concerts by touring pop and rock stars, and opera and *zarzuela,* in which knowledge of the language isn't critical.

It's best to buy tickets at the theater since agencies charge a considerable markup. If the preferred performance is sold out, it may be possible to get tickets at the **Localidades Galicia,** Plaza del Carmen 1 (☎ **91/531-27-32;** Metro: Sol), to the left of the Madrid Multicine, open Tuesday to Sunday 10am to 1pm and 4:30 to 7:30pm (closed holidays). It also sells bullfight and soccer tickets.

THEATER, OPERA & ZARZUELA The first season at the **Teatro Real,** Plaza de Oriente s/n (☎ **91/558-87-87;** Metro: Opera), included productions of *Turnadot, La Vida Breve, La Nozze di Figaro,* and *Porgy & Bess,* as well as solo recitals and five ballets. The privately run **Neuvo Apolo,** Plaza de Tirso de Molina 1 (☎ **91/429-52-38;** Metro: Tirso de Molina), shows mainly imported musicals like *West Side Story,* plus ballet, occasional *zarzuelas,* and other folkloric singing festivals.

The **Teatro de la Comedia,** Príncipe 14 (☎ **91/521-49-31;** Metro: Sevilla), shows classic Spanish plays by authors like García Lorca and Valle Inclán. Run by City Hall, the smallish **Centro Cultural de la Villa de Madrid,** under Plaza de Colón, Jardines del Descubrimiento (☎ **91/575-60-80;** Metro: Colón), puts on plays, recitals, dance events, and concerts of all kinds and is the scene of much activity during the Fall Festival (Festival del Otoño).

The **Teatro de la Zarzuela,** Jovellanos 4 (☎ **91/524-54-00;** Metro: Banco de España or Sevilla), can now focus on the musical form for which it's named, now that the Teatro Real has finally reopened.

CLASSICAL MUSIC The National Orchestra of Spain performs in new quarters, the **Auditorio Nacional de Música (National Auditorium of Music),** Príncipe de Vergara 146 (☎ **91/337-01-00;** Metro: Cruz del Rayo), where 2,000 music lovers can enjoy the best of Spanish and international classical music in a modern setting of wood and marble with fantastic acoustics. There's also a smaller concert hall, seating 600. Recitals and chamber music groups are often heard, frequently for free, at **Fundación Juan March,** Castelló 77 (☎ **91/435-42-40;** Metro: Núñez Balboa), and **Círculo de Bellas Artes,** Marqués de Casa Riera 2 (☎ **91/531-77-00;** Metro: Banco de España).

FLAMENCO The clubs in which full-bore flamenco is performed are called *tablaos.* Though not the birthplace of the Andalucian meld of music and dance, Madrid boasts *tablaos* that are fairly authentic, if expensive. For the best value, try **Torres Bermejas,** Mesonero Romanos 11 (☎ **91/532-33-22;** Metro: Callao); **Corral de la Morería,** Morería 17 (☎ **91/365-84-46;** Metro: Opera); or **Café de Chinitas,** Torija 7 (☎ **91/559-51-35;** Metro: Santo Domingo). Doors usually open at 9 or 9:30pm, and the show starts at about 10:45pm and ends at 12:30am or even later. To save money, go after dinner, when the still-hefty admission at least includes a drink. The later performances are usually better anyway, after the tour groups leave and the performers are warmed up. These stages feature large troupes with several dancers, two or three guitarists, and one or two singers, all in costume.

For a more intimate, grittier experience, try **La Soleá,** Cava Baja 34 (☎ **91/965-33-08;** Metro: Tirso de Molina). It has moved down the street to slightly larger, fancier quarters, but the smoke-filled space observes the same musical format: one or two guitarists and two or three singers who try to outdo each other at the hoarse, plaintive *cante hondo* (deep song) far into the night. Dancing is discouraged, but that doesn't stop the occasional customer who gets caught up in the passionate music. No admission. Closing days are unpredictable.

JAZZ BARS

Café Central, Plaza del Angel 10 (☎ **91/369-41-43;** Metro: Sol or Antón Martín), is the place for live jazz and is usually packed with students, visitors, and Madrid's night beauties. Black bench seating, marble-topped tables, and glistening brass set the scene. Performances are at 11pm and 12:30am. While jazz is the main course, the cafe frequently hosts folkies, blues belters, and performers of related music. Calle de las Huertas runs through this plaza, so the cafe can be the start or end of an extended pub crawl. It's open daily 1pm to 2 or 3am. Cover is usually about 900P ($6) Monday to Thursday and 1,100P ($8) Friday to Sunday.

Not far from the Café Central, the **Café Jazz Populart,** Calle de las Huertas 22 (☎ **91/429-84-07;** Metro: Antón Martín), is a showcase for American blues, Latin salsa, and Caribbean reggae as well as the many shadings of jazz. The large room allows a little individual elbow room, and the tone is laid-back at the marble-topped bar or the tables ringing the stage. One sour note is the caricature of a blackface minstrel the club uses as a logo. Sometimes there's a cover. In any event, an hour or two here is nearly always cheaper than at the better-known Café Central. It's open daily 6pm to 2 or 3am, with shows at 11pm and 12:30am.

BARS & PUBS

AROUND PLAZA DE SANTA ANA   *The* destination for a grand *tapeo*, Plaza de Santa Ana and the streets adjoining it are hip-to-hip with beer pubs and ancient taverns. While sherry *(fino)* is the classic tipple with tapas, red and white wines and beer are more evident, and no one sneers at an order for mineral water or Coca-Cola. Ask for a *copa de tinto* or *blanco* for a small tumbler of the wine or for a *caña* to get a short glass of about 6 ounces of draft beer.

As its name suggests, the **Cervecería Alemaña,** Plaza de Santa Ana 6 (☎ 91/429-70-33; Metro: Sol or Antón Martín), was once a popular haunt of German residents; Hemingway liked it, too. It has been in business since 1904, and the bullfighting prints on wood-paneled walls, the marble-topped tables, and the beamed ceiling provide a vintage atmosphere. It's open Sunday to Thursday 10:30am to 12:30am and Friday and Saturday 10:30am to 2am. Two doors up from the Alemaña is the no-seat **Cervecería Santa Ana,** Plaza de Santa Ana 6 (☎ 91/429-43-56; Metro: Sol), where a congenial crowd hangs out. Many of the customers are students, not least because the beer is relatively cheap. The place also serves good tapas and is open Thursday to Tuesday 10am to midnight.

La Fontana de Oro, Victoria 2 (☎ 91/531-04-20; Metro: Sol), is a fairly persuasive replica of a Dublin pub, one of at least 20 recently opened. Small groups do Irish songs from the stage, at times in Spanish, at others in English. Guinness Stout and hard cider are on tap, but not cheap. Open daily from 9am to 5am, it's about midway between the Puerta del Sol and Plaza de Santa Ana, with plenty of better places to eat all around. Students and 20-something singles have made **Viva Madrid,** Manuel Fernández González 7 (☎ 91/310-55-35; Metro: Sol or Antón Martín), a trendy meeting place. Both the facade and the interior of this 1890 tavern are resplendent with intricately patterned tiles, and mythical creatures hold up carved ceilings. Light meals and *tapas* are served in the room behind the bar. It's open daily 5:30pm to 2:30am.

ALONG CALLE DE LAS HUERTAS   For maxed-out bar-hopping, Calle de las Huertas, parallel Calle de Santa María, and adjoining streets can't be exhausted in a month of Saturdays. It starts a bit east of Plaza Mayor but doesn't shift into high gear until Plaza del Angel, south of Plaza de Santa Ana, when it runs downhill toward Paseo del Prado.

Over 380 years ago, Cervantes lived over **Casa Alberto,** Calle de las Huertas 18 (☎ 91/429-93-56; Metro: Sol or Antón Martín), and this narrow bar has been in business for almost half that time. With a stone bar and an elaborately carved wood ceiling, Alberto is popular with a mixed crowd that drops in for its *ambiente* and tapas Tuesday to Saturday noon to 4pm and 9pm to midnight and Sunday and Monday 9pm to midnight. Full meals are served in back. Just a saunter away, **Múñiz,** Calle de las Huertas 29 (no phone; Metro: Antón Martín), hasn't an ounce of Casa Alberto's charm, but its huge selection of well-prepared snacks and *raciones* more than compensates. It's open Monday to Saturday 10am to 1am.

Both cocktail lounge and disco/bar, **Cher's,** Calle de las Huertas 50 (☎ 91/429-83-32; Metro: Antón Martín), is named for whom you think. The crowd gets younger as the night wears toward dawn and they crank up the karaoke machine. It's open daily 7pm to 5:30am. With rock and Latino music roaring out of every other door, **La Fidula,** Calle de las Huertas 57 (☎ 91/429-29-47; Metro: Antón Martín), makes its statement with recitals by performers of classical music, art song, and poetry Friday and Saturday from about midnight. The room is cozy even without music, and the Irish coffees don't diminish the mood. It's open Sunday to Thursday 7pm to 3am and Friday and Saturday 7pm to 4am.

ALONG THE GRAN VÍA They call the **Museo Chicote,** Gran Vía 12 (☎ **91/532-67-37;** Metro: Gran Vía), a "museum" because it's been around since 1931 and is reputed to have been the city's first cocktail lounge. Hemingway was a regular, and he met many of his glamorous chums here. Check out the photos of celebrity drinkers to either side of the entrance—Coop, Ava, Tyrone, Sophia, Sinatra, and Dalí among them. The art deco details are original, and the bartenders can mix up anything you can imagine. It's open daily 1pm to 2am.

PLAZA DE SANTA BÁRBARA & SOUTH Consensus points to **Bocaito,** Libertad 6 (☎ **91/532-12-19;** Metro: Banco or Chueca), as the best tapas bar in town, and that opinion has considerable merit (see "Great Deals on Dining," earlier in this chapter). The strongest beer in the country is allegedly served at **Cervecería Internacional,** Regueros 8 (☎ **91/319-48-68;** Metro: Chueca), and there's unquestionably a selection from all over the world. There's a beer shop too, plus a restaurant; it's open daily noon to 2am.

The exceptionally long bar at the **Cervecería Santa Bárbara,** Plaza de Santa Bárbara 8 (☎ **91/319-04-49;** Metro: Alonso Martínez), props up the elbows of a diverse crowd of Madrileños. A marble floor, crimson walls with wrought-iron screens, and friendly waiters add to the agreeable atmosphere. The place is also known for its seafood, invariably expensive. Stick to the beer. It's open daily 11:30am to 11:30pm. Around the corner is its cousin, the **Santa Bárbara Pub,** Fernando VI 3 (☎ **91/319-08-44;** Metro: Alonso Martínez or Chueca), billed as Madrid's first English pub. You won't find warm beer, but there are authentic touches of Blighty in the central bar and low, round tables. It's open Sunday to Thursday noon to 2am and Friday and Saturday noon to 3am.

This is the Malasaña district, with gritty but chummy bars thumping out indie, techno, reggae, and mainstream rock, occasionally live. The neighborhood is fine for just hanging, listening, and maybe dancing until breakfast. **La Vaca Austera,** La Palma 20 (☎ **91/523-14-87;** Metro: Tribunal), appeals to traditionalists. This place is for gut-bucket rock, served by a deejay who slips in a little funk and fusion as the hours click by. There's a pool table. Open nightly. Down the street is **Louie Louie,** La Palma 43 (no phone; Metro: Tribunal), full of Spanish Gen-Xers in jeans once it gets past midnight. It's scruffy and dark, with a pool table and music cranked high. The front door is locked, but just ring the bell high on the left door frame. You'll be buzzed in.

GAY & LESBIAN BARS

In the Chueca area (between Calles Hortaleza and Barquillo), several places for gays and a smaller number for lesbians have sprung up in recent years. The **Librería El Galeón** is a gay bookstore (see "Shopping," earlier in this chapter) in the area.

Café Figueroa, Augusto Figueroa 17 (☎ **91/521-16-73;** Metro: Chueca), is a stylish older spot with loudspeakers inside 1930s radio cabinets. Carnaval in February is a big event, when the celebrants get up in costume and the TV stations send camera crews. **Café Aquarella,** Calle Gravina (☎ **91/570-69-07;** Metro: Chueca), has elevated gay table-hopping to a fine art. And a couple of blocks away at Libertad 34 is the **Black & White** disco (☎ **91/31-11-41;** Metro: Chueca). Women patronize **Truco,** a *bar de copas* at Gravina 10 (☎ **91/532-89-21;** Metro: Chueca).

DANCE CLUBS

Madrid's most popular dance clubs operate with a selective entrance policy, so dress stylishly and try to look as young, gorgeous, celebrated, and/or rich as possible. Admission, usually including a drink, can exceed 2,000P ($14), and even a soft drink can cost over 1,000P ($7). They're usually open daily to 4 or 5am, and nothing much happens before 2am. Conversely (or perversely) it's easier to get past the unsmiling gents at the door when arriving before then. Some have a "matinee" period, usually 7 to 9 or 10pm, attended primarily by teenagers. After closing for an hour or two, they reopen to older patrons.

Years ago, a palatial 1930s movie house was transformed into the popular **Joy Eslava,** Arenal 11 (☎ **91/366-37-33;** Metro: Sol or Opera). They tore out the orchestra seats to make room for three bars and a dance floor, but kept the box seats and stage. Laser shows, videos, and a variety of energetic performers keep things moving. The best nights are Friday and Saturday, and because this place is in its post-chic phase, it isn't difficult to get past the velvet ropes. Matinees are held on Friday and Saturday. It's open Monday to Friday 11:30pm to 5am and Friday to Sunday 7pm to 6am. Cover is 1,500P ($10).

A vintage mansion near the Puerta del Sol, the **Palacio de Gaviria,** Calle del Arenal 9 (☎ **91/526-60-69;** Metro: Sol), has been converted into a multispacio with several salons, each serving up expensive drinks and live or recorded music for dancing, from salsa to disco. Wednesday is tango night, with a buffet. It's open Monday to Wednesday 10:30pm to 3am, Thursday 10:30pm to 4am, Friday and Saturday 11pm to 5am, and Sunday 8pm to 2am. Cover is 1,000P ($7). Those who keep abreast of design trends should be impressed that **Teatriz,** Hermosilla 15 (☎ **91/577-53-79;** Metro: Serrano), a restaurant/cocktail lounge/dance club, was put together by France's Philippe Starck. It's designed within an inch of its life—even the books on the shelves are bolted into seemingly casual position. Save this for a splurge, since a drink or two here would pay for a three-course meal at most of my recommended restaurants. Cover is 2,000P ($14).

After a night of serious clubbing, don't miss **La Chocolatería de San Ginés,** Pasadizo de San Ginés 5 (no phone; Metro: Sol), in business since 1894. Drop in for hot chocolate and churros (deep-fried dough dusted with sugar) for an early breakfast; it's squeezed between the Joy Eslava disco and the Iglesia de San Ginés. Day laborers and night people mingle in the line that forms at the door before dawn. It's open Tuesday to Thursday 7 to 10pm and 1 to 7am and Friday and Sunday 7pm to 7am.

8 Side Trips: Palaces & Picturesque Towns

ARANJUEZ

On the banks of the Río Tajo (Tagus), **Aranjuez** is 29 miles south of Madrid. The principal reason to make the excursion is the baroque **Royal Palace.**

ARRIVING   Those who wish to avoid the expense and bother of a **rental car** will find that there are **trains** about every 30 minutes from Madrid's Atocha Station that take 45 minutes to Aranjuez and cost 345P ($2.35) one-way. **Buses** from the Sur Bus Station, Canarias 17 (☎ **91/468-42-00**), cost 825P ($6).

SEEING THE PALACE   Expanded from a much smaller 14th-century edifice, the palace was a summer retreat of the Bourbons in the late 18th century, and the leisurely lifestyle shows in the formal gardens, parklands with stands of majestic elms, and the palace itself. Damaged frequently over the centuries by war and natural disaster, the rambling residence was repeatedly restored, and the existing structure dates primarily from 1752. While it isn't up to the standards of its glory years, there's still much of interest. Of special note is the Porcelain Room or *Cabinet,* its walls and ceilings covered in meticulously painted porcelain made in the factory of Buen Retiro.

Out on the grounds, past numerous ornamental fountains, is the royal hideaway, the **Casa del Labrador (Laborer's House)**, erected in 1805 at the behest of Carlos IV. No humble cottage, it's intended to echo the Petit Trianon at Versailles, as lavishly furnished in silks, marble, fine woods, statuary, and porcelains as the main palace. It's open Tuesday to Sunday: April to September 10am to 6:30pm (October to March to 5:30pm). Admission is 600P ($4.15) adults and 300P ($2.05) seniors/students/children.

DINING   Aranjuez itself doesn't reward lingering. Though the surrounding farms are noted for their prized strawberries and asparagus, no local restaurant does them justice. If you're traveling by car, eating might best be held off for **Chinchón,** a short detour off NIV to and from Madrid. Two Gothic castles and one of Spain's most distinctive main plazas are reason enough to stop. The houses enclosing the roughly circular plaza have two and three floors of balconies from which citizens have watched bullfights and other celebrations for centuries. Dining choices include tapas at any of the taverns around the plaza or at the restaurant of the nearby *parador,* one of a commendable state-owned chain of inns. A favorite, with enough atmosphere to satisfy the deepest romantic, is the **Mesón Cuevas del Vino,** Benito Hortelano 13 (☎ **91/894-02-06**). Housed in a former olive oil mill and wine cellar, it turns out traditional regional meals of roast pork and lamb. For a *digestif,* try the anís liqueur made in the town and named after it. No credit cards are accepted, and it's open Wednesday to Monday 1 to 4:30pm and 7 to 11pm.

TOLEDO

Toledo, 43 miles southwest of Madrid, was once the capital of Visigothic Spain, and it bristles with steeples and towers spread over the pate of an unlikely hill moated by the Río Tajo. Those familiar with the painting of the city by El Greco, who lived most of his creative life here, will be struck by how closely his 16th-century *View of Toledo* conforms to the present, in overall impression if not in detail. Toledo is clogged with tour buses and their cargoes every day. If possible, stay overnight to get a less trammeled picture of the city when it's briefly returned to its permanent residents. Otherwise, try to leave Madrid early to avoid the worst of the crush and wear comfortable shoes to tackle the steep cobblestone streets and alleys. The city's craggy foundation dips and rises over several hills.

ARRIVING   Reach Toledo by **train** from Madrid's Atocha Station or by **bus** from the Calle Canarias Sur station. The one-way trip is a little under 2 hours by train but as little as 1 hour by bus, proving that nearly all trips in Spain of under 100 miles are best taken by bus. For more information, call the **Toledo Tourist Office** (☎ **25/22-08-43**), open Monday to Friday 9am to 2pm and 4 to 6pm, Saturday 9am to 7pm, and Sunday 9am to 3pm. The round-trip train fare is 1,950P ($13), while the bus costs 1,190P ($8).

SEEING THE SIGHTS   The logical first stop is the **cathedral.** One of the most glorious examples of Spanish Gothic architecture, it was built in large part between the 13th and 15th centuries. Like many Spanish cathedrals, it's nearly enclosed by the town, the surrounding houses snuggling up to and around the bases of its flying

A Telephone Warning

Note that Toledo's phone numbers will be switching to seven digits during the lifetime of this guide.

buttresses. Surmounted by a 300-foot tower, the cathedral has five naves and dozens of side chapels. Highlights are the choir and the richly carved altarpiece. In the Sacristy are paintings by El Greco, Rubens, and Titian, a collection extraordinary not only for its artistry but also for the fact that it hasn't been spirited away to a museum. The cathedral is open Monday to Saturday 10:30am to 1pm and 3:30 to 6pm and Sunday 10:30am to 1:30pm and 4 to 7pm (to 6pm in winter); the last tour is at 12:30pm. Tickets for the cathedral treasury are 350P ($2.40).

The next stop is the **Iglesia Santo Tomé (Church of St. Thomas)** to see El Greco's famous *The Burial of the Count Orgaz;* tickets are 130P (90¢). Afterward, go on to the **Casa y Museo del Greco** (☎ 925/22-40-46), an intriguing example of a 16th-century Toledan house containing a small collection of the artist's paintings, including a view of the city. Queen Isabel had a hand in the building that houses the **Museo Santa Cruz** (☎ 925/22-10-36), which has an impressive Plateresque facade. The paintings within are mostly of the 16th and 17th centuries, with yet another by El Greco. It's open Monday 10am to 2pm and 4:30 to 6:20pm, Tuesday to Saturday 10am to 6:30pm, and Sunday 10am to 2pm. Tickets are 250P ($1.70).

The **Alcázar** (same hours as Museo Santa Cruz) occupies the highest elevation of the city. Damaged frequently over its centuries as a fortress and royal residence, it was leveled during a Civil War siege. The existing structure is essentially a replica but is built over the old cellars and foundations. Tickets for the Alcázar are 150P ($1.05), and it's open Tuesday to Saturday 9:30am to 1:30pm and 4 to 6:30pm (to 5:30pm in winter).

Closer to its original 14th-century state is the **Synagoga del Trásito,** one of Toledo's two surviving synagogues. Past the unassuming exterior are some fine examples of Mudéjar craftsmanship (note the *artesando* ceiling) and a small but compelling museum of Jewish relics and artifacts.

ACCOMMODATIONS & DINING It's no surprise that a destination as heavily touristed as Toledo is short on truly appealing budget hotels. Characteristic is the lackluster **Maravilla,** Plaza de Barrio Rey 7, 45001 Toledo (☎ 925/22-33-00), whose only virtues are price (6,350P/$44 double) and a central location. In its favor, all the units have bathrooms. American Express, MasterCard, and Visa are accepted.

If you can afford to treat yourself, reserve ahead at **El Cardenal,** Paseo de Recaredo 24, 45003 Toledo (☎ 925/22-49-00). Owned by the same people who run Madrid's Botín restaurant, this 18th-century mansion offers a hotel as well as the city's top restaurant. The furnishings are traditional, and all 27 units have bathrooms, TVs, phones, and air-conditioning. Doubles are 8,625P to 11,500P ($60 to $79), the higher rates for summer. American Express, Diners Club, MasterCard, and Visa are accepted. The restaurant, open to all, serves traditional Castellano dishes, like lamb and pork roasts. Full meals are about 3,000P ($21). You'll find El Cardenal near the Puerta de Bisagra, the only remaining Moorish gate in the city's wall.

With time and transportation, a worthwhile outing carries you across the Río Tajo to the *parador* standing on a promontory opposite the city at Cerro del Emperador s/n (☎ 925/22-18-50). From its terrace, an unobstructed view of Toledo recalls El Greco's memorable rendition. While meals in the first-class dining room here are above our budget, they justify a splurge. Alternatively, you can get a sandwich and a beer in the bar.

If you want to go all the way and spend the night, you'll have to reserve *months* in advance. One of the 74 spacious doubles (with bath) goes for about 18,000P ($124). American Express, Diners Club, MasterCard, and Visa are accepted.

EL ESCORIAL

Felípe II commissioned Juan Bautista de Toledo and his assistant, Juan de Herrera, to build **El Escorial,** a gloomy Xanadu, on this hillside in the Sierra de Guadarrama 34 miles northwest of Madrid. Its purported intent was to commemorate an important victory over the French in Flanders, but the likely real reason was that the ascetic Felípe was increasingly unnerved by the stress of overseeing an empire that bridged four continents. This retreat insulated him from the pressures and intrigues of the Madrid Court. He ruled the troubled empire from his largely unadorned cells here for the last 14 years of his life.

ARRIVING **Trains** for El Escorial leave frequently from Madrid's Atocha, Chamartín, Recoletos, and Nuevos Ministerios stations. They take under 1 hour and cost 775P ($5) round-trip. **Buses** leave from Empresa Herranz, Isaac Peral 10, Moncloa (☎ **91/543-36-45**), and cost 750P ($5) round-trip; buses drop off closer to Felipe's royal monastery.

SEEING THE PALACE The squared-off monastery/palace is praised for its massive, brooding simplicity. That impression is allayed inside, where you can appreciate its considerable size and wealth of accoutrements. The extraordinary library reflects the scholarly king's all-embracing intellectual interests, with tens of thousands of volumes and rare manuscripts in many languages and representative of the three primary religions that had existed in Spain. Also in the building is a sizable church with a large frescoed dome, beneath which is a royal pantheon with sarcophagi containing the remains of most of Spain's monarchs since Carlos V. Museums and royal apartments contain canvases by El Greco, Titian, Ribera, Tintoretto, Rubens, and Velázquez, among many.

An all-inclusive ticket is 850P ($6). The monastery is open Tuesday to Sunday and holidays 10am to 6pm (to 5pm in winter). The **tourist office** at El Escorial can be reached at ☎ **91/890-59-05.**

A pleasant town has grown up around the monastery/palace. Its full name is San Lorenzo de El Escorial and it's not nearly as touristy as you might expect, given its proximity to Madrid. Avoiding weekends is a good idea, however.

DINING There are a number of appealing bars and cafes, some with outside tables, at which to have a snack or sandwich. For a complete meal, a popular inn is the 18th-century **La Cueva,** Calle San Antón 4 (☎ **91/890-15-16**). With care in selection, you can keep the cost at near-budget level. No credit cards are accepted, and the inn is open Tuesday to Sunday 1 to 4:30pm and 8:30 to 11pm.

SEGOVIA

If you have time for a 2-day, 1-night adventure out of Madrid, spend the first day exploring **El Escorial** and continue on to **Segovia.**

ARRIVING As is true throughout Spain, **buses** are preferable to **trains** for almost all trips under 100 miles, for price, convenience, and time consumed. Between Segovia and Madrid, the bus takes 90 minutes but the train 2 hours, and the bus leaves you at the terminal at Paseo de Ezequile González 10, much closer than the rail station on Paseo Obispo Quesada. There are up to 15 buses daily from Madrid; a one-way fare is 810P ($6).

SEEING THE SIGHTS In Segovia you'll find what may be the most recognizable structure in Spain: the ✪ **Acueducto Romano.** A spectacular engineering feat even if it were contemplated today, the double-tiered aqueduct cuts across the city to the snow-fed waters of the nearby mountains. Almost 2,400 feet long and nearly 95 feet at its highest point at the east end of town, it boasts over 160 arches fashioned of stone so precisely cut that no mortar was used. Probably completed in the 2nd century A.D. (though some sources date it as many as 3 centuries earlier), it has survived war and partial dismantling by the Moors. Amazingly, it carried water until only a few years ago.

The layout of Segovia routinely evokes comparison with a ship. Using that image, the aqueduct marks the stern. The land rises from there, accommodating several Romanesque churches and a Flamboyant Gothic **cathedral** begun and completed in the 16th century. Its spires are the ship's "riggings." Constructed at the command of Carlos V to replace one destroyed during the Communero Revolt against his policies, it deserves at least a brief tour. More interesting, if only for historic reasons, is the attached 15th-century **cloister.** After the earlier cathedral was razed by rebels, its cloister was moved stone by stone and reassembled here. It contains a small museum. Admission to the cathedral is free, but the cloister and museum cost 250P ($1.70) adults and 50P (35¢) children. They're open daily: June to September 10am to 6pm and October to May 10am to 1pm and 3:30 to 6pm.

The cathedral abuts Plaza Mayor; at no. 10, opposite, is the **tourist information office** (☎ 921/46-03-34). It hands out good maps and can help with lodging and bus and train schedules. Continuing west, the "prow" of the raised old town rears above the confluence of the rivers Clamores and Eresma and that dramatic position is held by the **Alcázar,** almost as familiar a symbol of Castilla (Castile) as the aqueduct. Satisfying though it is as fulfillment of "castles in Spain" fantasies (at least from the outside), the Alcázar is really a late-19th-century replica of the medieval fortress that stood here before a devastating 1868 fire. Admission is 375P ($2.60) adults and 175P ($1.20) ages 8 to 14, and it's open April to September daily 10am to 7pm (to 6pm the rest of the year). But since the interior is of only modest interest, my suggestion is to take your photos of the exterior and save the admission fee for dinner.

The town is truly walkable, so take your time on the way back to Plaza de Azoguejo and the aqueduct. These narrow medieval streets suffer less from the ravages of mass tourism (except on weekends and holidays) than other destinations in Madrid's orbit and reveal much about what life must've been like here 500 years ago. To many eyes, the several Romanesque churches of the 12th and 13th centuries are more visually appealing than the later Gothic temples. Seek out **San Esteban** (on the plaza of that name), **La Trinidad** (on the street of that name), and **San Juan de los Caballeros** (on nearby San Agustin).

ACCOMMODATIONS & DINING   If you want to stay the night, one of the best hotels in town, regardless of price, is **Los Linajes,** Dr. Velasco 9, 40003 Segovia (☎ 921/46-04-75). Behind its 11th-century facade lies a thoroughly modern facility, with a bar and lounge and terraces bestowing fine views. Its 55 units have TVs and bathrooms. Doubles are 10,500P ($72), perhaps a little lower off-season with negotiation. American Express, Diners Club, MasterCard, and Visa are accepted.

Gastronomically, Segovia is celebrated as the locus of the "zone of roasts," meaning suckling pig *(cochinillo asado)* and young lamb *(cordero)* so tender the flesh falls apart at the touch of a tine. The traditional place to sample these is **Mesón de Candido,** Plaza del Azoguejo 5 (☎ 921/42-59-11). Layers of authentic atmosphere and views of the aqueduct add to the experience, and the *menú del día* is a not-bad 2,700P ($19). It's open daily 12:30 to 4:30pm and 8 to 11:30pm. Less expensive, with similar food but at no great markdown in quality, is **Casa Duque,** Cervantes 12 (☎ 921/43-05-37). The *menú del día* is 1,900P ($13), and it's been on the scene for over 100 years. Casa Duque is open daily 12:30 to 5pm and 8 to 11:30pm. Both restaurants accept American Express, Diners Club, MasterCard, and Visa.

Munich & Environs

by Beth Reiber

Named after the Münichen monks who settled more than 1,200 years ago on the banks of the Isar River, Munich is the capital of the state (or Land) of Bavaria and a sprawling city of 1.3 million. Home of industrial giants like BMW and Siemens, it's Germany's important cultural capital, with 4 symphony orchestras, 2 opera houses, dozens of world-class museums, more than 20 theaters, and one of Germany's largest universities. The diverse student population and the foreign residents who make up more than 20% of the population ensure an active avant-garde cultural scene and a liberal attitude in an otherwise conservative region.

Munich is a striking city, largely the product of the exuberant imagination and aspirations of past Bavarian kings and rulers. Royal residences, majestic museums, steepled churches, and ornate monuments celebrate architectural styles from baroque and Gothic to neoclassical and postmodern. Add wide boulevards, spacious parks, thriving nightlife, and at least six breweries and you have what amounts to one of Germany's most interesting, exciting, and festive cities.

REQUIRED DOCUMENTS See chapter 7 on Berlin.

OTHER FROMMER'S TITLES For more on Munich, see *Frommer's Munich & the Bavarian Alps, Frommer's Germany, Frommer's Europe,* or *Frommer's Europe's Greatest Driving Tours.*

1 Munich Deals & Discounts

SPECIAL DISCOUNTS

FOR EVERYONE If you plan on doing a lot of traveling back and forth on Munich's excellent subways, buses, and trams, you can save by purchasing a **1-day transportation pass** for 8DM ($4.55) or the **Munich Welcome Card** for 11DM ($6), allowing unlimited travel on public transportation and up to 50% discounts on admission to museums and sights around Munich. Information on both is given in more detail below.

FOR STUDENTS If you're a student, your ticket to lower prices is the **International Student Identity Card (ISIC).** With it you can realize substantial savings on museum admission fees, with 50% or more off the regular price. In addition, both the opera and the theater offer student discounts for unsold seats on the night of performance—show up about an hour before the performance to see what's available.

Budget Bests

You can save money by standing up in Munich, whether it's eating or visiting the theater. Eat lunch at an *imbiss,* a food stall or tiny store selling everything from German sausages and grilled chicken to pizza. Concentrated primarily in Old Town, most of these places even sell beer to wash it all down. If you'd rather sit for a meal, you can often save money by ordering from the *Tageskarte* (changing daily menu), which includes both the main course and side dishes. Even better, pack a meal and take it to one of Munich's many **beer gardens,** where all you'll have to buy is beer—some even offer free concerts.

Standing up is also the cheapest way to see performances of the **Staatstheater,** with tickets costing less than 11DM ($6).

If you've arrived in Europe without an ISIC and can show proof of current student status, you can obtain one at the **Studiosus Urlaubscenter,** Oberanger 6 (☎ **089/235 05 20**), a travel agency that deals with student/youth travel and can also assist with securing reduced-price train or plane tickets. It's open Monday to Friday 9am to 7pm and Saturday 10am to 4pm. Take the S-Bahn or U-Bahn to Marienplatz.

FOR SENIORS   If you're a senior citizen (at least 65), you're entitled to a **50% discount** at most museums in Munich.

WORTH A SPLURGE

Though prices can add up, it's worth spending the extra time and money to see Munich's famous museums, particularly the **Alte Pinakothek, Neue Pinakothek, Deutsches Museum, Staatsgalerie Moderner Kunst,** and **Städtische Galerie im Lenbachhaus.** To keep costs down, buy a combination ticket whenever possible or the Munich Welcome Card.

2 Essentials

ARRIVING

BY PLANE   Germany's own Lufthansa provides the largest number of flights to Munich's **Franz Josef Strauss Airport** (☎ **089/97 52 13 13**), 17 miles northeast of Munich in Erding. After stopping by the information counter (in the Zentralbereich, or Central Area, open Monday to Friday 10am to 8pm and Saturday, Sunday, and holidays noon to 8pm) to pick up a map and brochures, proceed to the Flughafen München **S-Bahn station,** where you can board the S-8 bound for Marienplatz (the city center) or the Hauptbahnhof (main train station). Trains leave every 20 minutes, and the trip to the Hauptbahnhof takes about 40 minutes.

The cost of an ordinary ticket is 13.60DM ($8), though if you have a validated Eurailpass you can ride the S-Bahn free. If you don't have a Eurailpass, you can save with a *Streifenkarte* (strip ticket), allowing 11 short journeys or 5 longer ones and a short one for 15DM ($9). Note that the trip from the airport is such a long one that it takes up eight strips on the ticket (fold the ticket to the number 8 slot and insert it into the machine at the station entrance). In any case, the trip into town using the Streifenkarte is 10.90DM ($6), a savings compared to the 13.60DM ($8) charged for the ordinary one-way ticket above.

Alternatively, you can purchase a **1-day transportation pass** for greater Munich for 16DM ($9), advisable if you plan on using public transportation at least twice the

What Things Cost in Munich	U.S. $
Taxi from the airport to Munich's main train station	60.00
U-Bahn from the main train station to Schwabing	1.95
Local telephone call (for 90 seconds)	.10
Double room at the Kempinski Vier Jahreszeiten (deluxe)	317.00
Double room at the Uhland (moderate)	82.65
Double room at the Am Kaiserplatz (budget)	45.00
Lunch for one at Nürnberg Bratwurst Glöckl (moderate)	12.00
Lunch for one at Donisl (budget)	6.85
Dinner for one, without wine, at Aubergine (deluxe)	100.00
Dinner for one, without wine, at Hundskugel (moderate)	25.00
Dinner for one, without wine, at Bella Italia Am Stachus (budget)	8.55
Liter of beer	5.95
Glass of wine	2.50
Coca-Cola in a restaurant	1.85
Cup of coffee	2.35
Roll of ASA 100 color film, 36 exposures	4.55
Admission to the Deutsches Museum	5.70
Movie ticket	7.00
Ticket to the Staatstheater am Gärtnerplatz (standing room)	4.55

remainder of the day. If you have any questions regarding transportation to the city center, stop by the MVV counter next to the information counter in the Zentralbereich; you can also purchase tickets here.

Though more expensive, the **Lufthansa City/Airport Bus** departs every 20 minutes from both terminals and the Zentralbereich and costs 15DM ($9) for the 40-minute trip to the Hauptbahnhof. A **taxi** is prohibitive, costing as much as 100DM ($60) one-way.

BY TRAIN If you come by train, you'll arrive at the **Hauptbahnhof,** Munich's main train station, in the center of town; it serves as a nucleus for the many tram, U-Bahn (underground subway), and S-Bahn (metropolitan railway) lines. In the train station there's an information office and a post office. Beside Track 11 is **EurAide,** a special service for English-speaking travelers providing free train and sightseeing info and selling various rail tickets. In summer it's open daily 7:30am to noon and 1 to 6pm and in winter Monday to Friday 7:45am to noon and 1 to 4pm and Saturday 7:45am to noon.

VISITOR INFORMATION

You'll find a branch of Munich's **Tourismus Information** (☎ **089/233 30256**) just outside the Hauptbahnhof's main exit at Bahnhofplatz 2. Open Monday to Saturday 10am to 8pm and Sunday 10am to 6pm, it distributes city maps for 50 pfennig (30¢) and brochures. For a 10% to 15% deposit that goes toward the cost of your hotel room, the tourist office here and at the airport will find you a hotel room, a valuable service if the places in this book are full. Also at the Hauptbahnhof is EurAide (see above).

In the city center, there's another convenient tourist office in the **Rathaus (Town Hall)** on Marienplatz (☎ **089/233 30272**), open Monday to Friday 10am to 8pm and Saturday 10am to 4pm. You can book concert tickets here.

You can obtain information on the Internet at **www.muenchen-tourist.de**.

If you want to know what's going on in Munich, pick up a copy of the *Monatsprogramm* at the tourist office. Costing 2.50DM ($1.40), it tells what's being performed when in the theaters and opera houses and how to get tickets. It also lists concerts (modern and classical), museum hours, and special exhibits. Though much of the information in this pocket-size booklet is in German only, those who don't understand German will also find it useful.

Another good source is *Munich Found,* an English-language magazine published 10 times a year and available at newsstands for 4DM ($2.30). In addition to articles of local interest, including special exhibits and events, it contains a calendar for classical music, opera, ballet, theater, rock concerts, and other nightlife activities. The only problem is finding a copy of this valuable magazine—it sells out fast.

CITY LAYOUT

The heart of Munich, **Old Town (Altstadt),** lies directly east of the Hauptbahnhof. Its very center is **Marienplatz,** a cobblestone plaza only a 15-minute walk from the train station and connected to the rest of the city by an extensive subway network. Over the centuries it served as a market square, a stage for knightly tournaments, and the site of public executions. Today it's no less important, bordered on one side by the impressive Rathaus Town Hall, famous for its chimes and mechanized figures.

Much of Old Town is a **pedestrian zone** where you'll find the smartest boutiques, most traditional restaurants, and oldest churches, plus the Viktualienmarkt outdoor market. Most of Munich's museums are within an easy walk or short subway ride from the center.

Schwabing, north of the city center and easily reached by U-Bahn, is home to Munich's university and nightlife. Its bohemian heyday was at the turn of the century, when it served as a mecca for Germany's most talented young artists and writers, including Kandinsky, Klee, Mann, and Rilke. Today Schwabing is known for its sidewalk cafes, fashionable bars, and dance clubs, most on Leopoldstrasse and Occamstrasse. Though brochures like to call Schwabing the "Greenwich Village of Munich," most of the people milling about here are visitors, including lots of young people from outlying villages in for a night on the town.

As for other areas worth exploring, the **Englischer Garten** with its wide green expanses and beer gardens stretches northeast from the city center. Oktoberfest is held at **Theresienwiese,** just south of the Hauptbahnhof, while the **Olympiapark,** home of the 1972 Olympic Games, is on the northern edge of town. **Schloss Nymphenburg,** the royal family's summer residence, is northwest of town, accessible by streetcar from the train station.

GETTING AROUND

A by-product of the 1972 Olympics is the extensive **pedestrian zone,** making Munich a perfect city to explore on foot. In fact, many of its museums can be reached on foot from the city center, Marienplatz. All you need is the map issued by the tourist office to set you off in the right direction.

BY SUBWAY Munich's wonderful underground network, created in conjunction with the Olympics, is the ultimate in German efficiency. I've seldom waited more than a few minutes for a train. What's more, Munich's subway stations have something I

Munich U-Bahn & S-Bahn

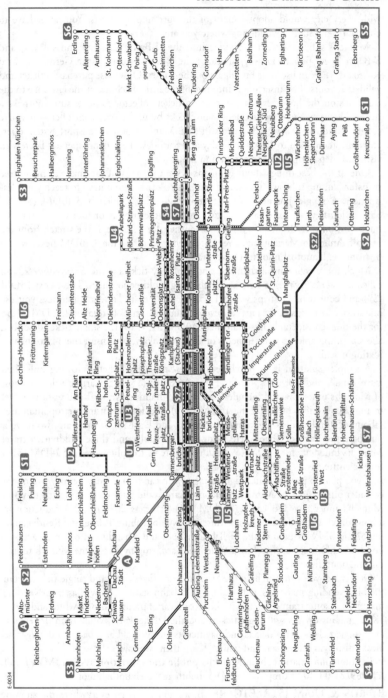

wish every city would adopt—maps of the surrounding streets. You never have to emerge from a station wondering where you are.

Munich's subway system is divided into the **U-Bahn** (underground subway) and **S-Bahn** (metropolitan railway). Because the S-Bahn is part of the German Federal Railroads, you can use your Eurailpass on these lines. Otherwise purchase a ticket and validate it yourself by inserting it into one of the little machines at the entrance to the track. It's on the honor system—there's no ticket collector to make sure you have a ticket. However, there are frequent spot checks by undercover controllers—if you're caught without a ticket you'll pay a stiff fine. Munich's public transport system operates daily about 5am to 1am. On Friday and Saturday, the S-Bahn operates later, with last trains departing Marienplatz around 2:30am.

One of the best things about Munich's system is that you can make as many **free transfers** among subways, buses, and trams (streetcars) as you need to reach your destination. A **single journey** to most destinations in Munich is 3.40DM ($1.95). Shorter journeys—trips of at most two stops on the subway or four on the tram or bus—cost only 1.70DM (95¢). A short journey, for example, is the stretch from the Hauptbahnhof to Marienplatz; a regular journey requiring the 3.40DM ticket would be from the Hauptbahnhof to Universität.

Much more economical than the single-journey tickets is the *Streifenkarte* (also called a *Mehrfahrtkarte*), a strip ticket allowing multiple journeys. These cost 15DM ($9) and consist of 11 strips worth 1.35DM (75¢) each. For short journeys you use one strip. Most trips in the city, however, require two strips (a total of 2.70DM/$1.55 for the ride, considerably less than the 3.40DM/$1.95 for the single ticket described above). Simply fold up two segments of the Streifenkarte and insert them into the validating machine.

A simpler solution is to purchase a *Tageskarte* (day ticket), allowing unlimited travel on all modes of transport for 1 day. An 8DM ($5) Tageskarte is valid for most of Munich's inner city and includes the entire U-Bahn network. If you want to travel to the far outskirts, purchase the 16DM ($10) card for the entire metropolitan area (about a 50-mile radius, including the airport and Dachau). If there are two of you, purchase the **Partner Tageskarte,** allowing two adults and three children to travel Munich's inner city for 12DM ($7) and the entire metropolitan area for 24DM ($14) for the entire day.

If you plan to pack as much sightseeing as you can into a 1-day period, you might consider purchasing the **Munich Welcome Card,** valid for 1 day's unlimited travel in Munich's inner city and costing 11DM ($6). It offers 20% to 50% reduction in admission costs for the Deutsches Museum, Nymphenburg Palace, the Residenzmuseum, the BMW Museum, the Hellabrunn Zoo, and a handful of other attractions. For more information or to buy a Welcome Card, stop by one of the Munich tourist information offices.

Otherwise, you can purchase the Streifenkarte, Tageskarte, and single tickets from the blue vending machines at U-Bahn and S-Bahn stations, as well as from vending machines at some tram stops and in the second car of trams bearing a white-and-green "K" sign. Bus drivers sell single tickets and the Streifenkarte, while tram drivers sell only single tickets. Strip tickets and day tickets are also sold at tobacco and magazine kiosks displaying the green-and-white "K" in their window.

For more information about Munich's **public transportation system (MVV),** call ☎ **089/21 03 30** or drop by the MVV booth at the Hauptbahnhof.

BY BUS & TRAM (STREETCAR) Buses and trams go everywhere the subway doesn't. As mentioned above, one ticket allows for as many transfers as necessary to reach your destination. The free map provided by the tourist office indicates bus and tram routes for the inner city. For night owls, six bus and four tram lines run nightly approximately 1:30 to 5am, designated by an "N" in front of their number. Contact MVV for more information, including a brochure listing the night lines along with their stops and time schedules.

BY TAXI   Munich's public transport system is so efficient that you should never have to fork over money for a taxi. If you do take a taxi, you'll pay 5DM ($2.85) as soon as you step inside, plus 2.20DM ($1.25) per kilometer. If you need to call a taxi, phone ☎ **089/2161-0** or 089/194-10. Taxis ordered by phone bring a 2DM ($1.15) surcharge; luggage is an extra 1DM (55¢) per bag.

BY BICYCLE   One of the most convenient places to rent bikes is **Radius Touristik,** inside the Hauptbahnhof across from Track 30 (☎ **089/59 61 13**). April to October, it's open daily 10am to 6pm and charges 25DM ($14) for 1 day's rental of a three- to six-gear bike and 35DM ($20) for a mountain bike; 10% discounts are available for students and readers of this book, and weekly rates are also available.

In addition, bicycles are for rent at several **train and S-Bahn stations** in Munich. Pick up the pamphlet *Bahn und Bike* at the Hauptbahnhof.

BY RENTAL CAR   You'll find counters for all the major car-rental companies at the Franz Josef Strauss Airport. In addition, you'll find counters for **Hertz** (☎ **089/550 22 56**), **Avis** (☎ **089/550 22 51**), and **Budget Sixt** (☎ **089/550 24 47**) at the Hauptbahnhof (main train station). Other car-rental agencies can be found in the phone book under "Autovermeitung."

Prices vary, but expect to pay about 119DM ($68) for a 1-day rental of a VW Polo or Ford Fiesta with unlimited mileage and tax. It pays to shop around, since car-rental prices vary widely depending on the time of year, the day of the week, and the type of car. Weekend rates, for example, are always lower.

FAST FACTS: Munich

American Express   There's a convenient office in the Old City near Marienplatz at Kaufingerstrasse 24 (☎ **089/22 80 13 87;** U-Bahn: Marienplatz), open Monday to Friday 9am to 5:30pm (closed 1 to 2pm in winter) and Saturday 10am to 1pm. Another office is at Promenadeplatz 6 (☎ **089/29 09 00;** U-Bahn: Karlsplatz or Marienplatz), open Monday to Friday 9am to 5:30pm and Saturday 9:30am to 12:30pm. No fee is charged to cash American Express traveler's checks.

Banks   Banks are open Monday to Friday 8:30am to 12:30pm and 1:30 to 3:30pm (to 5:30pm Thursday). You can also exchange money at post offices. If you need to exchange money outside bank hours, your best bet is the **Reise Bank currency exchange office** (☎ **089/551 08 37**) at the main exit of the Hauptbahnhof, open daily 6am to 11pm. It has a 24-hour ATM for obtaining cash from American Express, Diners Club, MasterCard, and Visa. There's a 24-hour ATM for MasterCard and Visa across from the Hauptbahnhof at the Bayerische Vereinsbank on the corner of Bayerstrasse and Schillerstrasse.

Business Hours   Since the law changed in 1996, stores can stay open to 8pm Monday to Friday and to 4pm Saturday. Some of the smaller stores, however, continue to close at 6pm; some smaller neighborhood shops still close for lunch about 12:30 to 2 or 2:30pm. Department stores are open weekdays 9:30am to 8pm and Saturday 9am to 4pm.

Consulates   Different departments may have different hours, so it's always best to call. The consulate of the **United States,** Königinstrasse 5 (☎ **089/288 80;** Bus: 53), is open Monday to Friday 8am to 11am. The consulate of the **United Kingdom,** Bürkleinstrasse 10 (☎ **089/21 10 90;** U-Bahn: Lehel), is open Monday to Friday 8:45 to 11:30am and 1 to 3:15pm. The consulate of **Canada,** Tal Strasse 29 (☎ **089/219 95 70;** S-Bahn: Isartor), is open Monday to Thursday 9am to noon and 2 to 5pm and Friday 9am to noon and 2 to 3:30pm. The consulate of **Ireland,** Mauerkircherstrasse 1a (☎ **089/98 57 23;** Tram: 20; Bus: 54 or 87), is open Monday to Friday 9am to noon and 1 to 4pm.

Currency   See chapter 7 on Berlin.

Dentists & Doctors   If you need an English-speaking doctor or dentist in Munich, your best bet is to contact the American or British consulate. If it's a weekend or evening dental or medical emergency, contact the **Notfallpraxis,** Elisenstrasse 3 (☎ **089/55 17 71;** S-Bahn/U-Bahn: Hauptbahnhof; Tram: 17, 19, 20, or 21 to Hauptbahnhof), where doctors of various specialties are on hand. It's open Monday, Tuesday, and Thursday 7pm to midnight, Wednesday and Friday 2pm to midnight, and weekends and holidays 8am to midnight. For evening dental emergencies, you can also go to the **Zahnärztliche Klinik,** Lindwurm Strasse 2a (☎ **089/51 60 0** or 089/51 60 29; U-Bahn: Sendliner Tor).

Emergencies   Important numbers include ☎ **110** for the **police** and ☎ **112** for the **fire** department and **ambulance.** For medical emergencies on weekends or evenings, call the **Notfallpraxis** (see "Dentists & Doctors," above).

A convenient pharmacy, the **Internationale Ludwigs-Apotheke,** Neuhauser Strasse 11 (☎ **089/260 30 21**), on Munich's famous pedestrian lane, is open Monday to Friday 9am to 8pm and Saturday 9am to 4pm. It's one of the best places to fill international prescriptions; it'll also recommend English-speaking doctors. Pharmacies take turns offering night and weekend services; those offering such services are always posted outside every pharmacy door. Otherwise, for information regarding the nearest open pharmacy, call ☎ **089/59 44 75.**

Holidays   Because of its large Catholic population, Munich has more holidays than much of the rest of the country. While many museums and restaurants remain open, shops and businesses close. Holidays in Bavaria are New Year's Day (January 1); Epiphany (January 6); Good Friday, Easter Sunday and Monday; Ascension Day, Whitsunday, Whitmonday, and Corpus Christi (all in April or May); Assumption Day (August 15); Labor Day (May 1); German Reunification Day (October 3); All Saints' Day (November 1); and Christmas (December 25 and 26).

Though it's not an official holiday, note that many museums and shops are also closed for the parade on Faschings Dienstag, the Tuesday before Ash Wednesday.

Hospitals   If you need to go to a hospital, contact your consulate for advice on which one is best for your ailment. Otherwise, call for an ambulance or the medical emergency service (see "Emergencies," above).

Laundry & Dry Cleaning   A *reinigung* is a dry cleaner; a *wäscherei* or *waschsalon* is a laundry. Most laundries close at 6pm. Ask the staff at your hotel or pension for the location of the closest waschsalon; otherwise, there's one a few minutes' walk south of the train station at Paul-Heyse-Strasse. A wash load including detergent costs 7DM ($4), while a dryer costs 1DM (55¢) per 10 minutes.

Country & City Codes

The **country code** for Germany is **49.** The **city code** for Munich is **89;** use this code when you're calling from outside Germany. If you're within Germany but not in Munich, use **089.** If you're calling within Munich, simply leave off the code and dial only the regular phone number.

Mail Munich's main post office across from the Hauptbahnhof is closed for renovation. Inside the Hauptbahnhof is a small post office up on the first floor across from Track 20, where you can mail letters and make international phone calls but can't mail packages or exchange money. It's open Monday to Friday 7am to 8pm, Saturday 8am to 4pm, and Sunday and holidays 9am to 3pm. If you need to mail a package, go to the Postfiliale 2, north of the Hauptbahnhof at Arnulfstrasse 32, 80335 Munich (☎ **089/54 54-2336**), open Monday to Friday 8am to 8pm, where you can also have your mail sent *Poste Restante.* You'll find another post office at Residenzstrasse 2, near Marienplatz, open Monday to Friday 8am to 6pm and Saturday 8am to 1pm. Mailboxes are yellow.

Airmail letters to North America cost 3DM ($1.70) for the first 20 grams, while postcards cost 2DM ($1.15). If you want to mail a package back home (it can't weigh more than 20kg/44 lb. if sent to the United States), you can buy a box that comes with tape and string at the post office. Boxes come in five sizes and range from 2.90DM to 5.50DM ($1.65 to $3.15).

Police The emergency number for the police is ☎ **110.**

Tax Germany's 16% federal tax is already included in most hotel and restaurant bills, including all the locales listed in this book. Tax is likewise included in the price of goods, which you can partially recover on items taken out of the country. For information on how you can recover the **value-added tax (VAT),** refer to "Shopping," later in this chapter.

Telephone Telephone booths in Munich are yellow or silver and pink. A **local telephone call** is 20 pfennig (11¢) for the first 90 seconds; put more coins in to be sure you're not cut off (unused coins will be returned). Phones in some restaurants require 50 pfennig (28¢). Otherwise, you might wish to purchase a **telephone card,** available in values of 12DM ($7) and 50DM ($29). Telephone cards are becoming so popular in Germany that many public phones accept only cards. You can purchase them at any post office.

Incidentally, if you come across a phone number with a dash, the numbers after the dash are the extension number. Simply dial the entire number as you would any phone number. For **information** on local numbers, call ☎ **11833.**

For **long-distance calls,** use a telephone card or go to the post office instead of calling from your hotel, since hotels usually add a stiff surcharge—even a local call made from your hotel room is likely to cost at least 50 pfennig (28¢). Due to recent deregulation of Germany's telephone industry and Telecom's loss of monopoly over domestic phone service, competition among phone companies is expected to lower long-distance rates, especially for private lines. As of press time, it costs 7.20DM ($4.10) to make a 3-minute long-distance call to the United States from a post office, but note that since the post office charges a 2DM ($1.15) fee to use one of its booth phones, you may be better off buying a telephone card. As an alternative, you can use a credit card to phone or send a fax from a machine in the Reise Bank at the Hauptbahnhof.

Tipping Gratuities are included in hotel and restaurant bills. However, it's customary to round restaurant bills up to the nearest mark; if a meal costs more than 20DM, most Germans will give a 10% tip. Don't leave a tip on the table—include it in the amount you give your waiter. For taxi drivers, round up to the nearest mark. Porters charge 5DM ($1.20) for two bags.

3 Accommodations You Can Afford

Most of Munich's accommodations are clustered around the main train station, the Hauptbahnhof, particularly its south side. While this area may not be the city's most charming, what it lacks in atmosphere it certainly makes up for in convenience. The farther you walk from the station, the quainter and quieter the neighborhoods become.

Though a *pension,* the German equivalent of a B&B, is generally less expensive than a hotel, there's often only a fine line between the two. In any case, the cheaper the room, the greater the likelihood you'll be sharing a bath down the hall. Pensions in Munich often charge a small fee for use of the shower—unless, of course, you have a shower in your room. All rooms in pensions and hotels, however, have their own sink, and most include a continental breakfast in their rates. Single rooms, alas, are expensive in Munich; you can save a lot of money by sharing a room.

Remember that if the accommodations below are full, try the tourist office, whose staff will find a room for you for a 10% to 15% deposit of your total room rate. All prices here include tax and service charge. When indicated, the higher prices are generally those charged April to October, including Oktoberfest, and during major conventions (called *messe* in German).

Note: You can find most of the lodging choices below plotted on the map included in "Seeing the Sights," later in this chapter.

PRIVATE HOMES & APARTMENTS

Renting a room in a private home can be a bargain for budget travelers, while private apartments with kitchens can help save on meals. Note that these listings prefer guests who stay at least 2 or 3 nights.

Frau Anita Gross. Thalkirchner Strasse 72 (about a 20-minute walk from Marienplatz), 80337 München. ☎ **089/52 16 81.** 2 units, both with bathroom. TV TEL. 105DM ($60) smaller apt for 2; 120DM ($68) larger apt for 2, 140DM ($80) for 3, 160DM ($91) for 4. No credit cards. Bus: 58 from the Hauptbahnhof to Kapuziner Strasse.

These two apartments are perfect for those who like being on their own and having all the comforts of home. They're owned by personable Frau Anita Gross, who lives elsewhere but will pick you up at the train station if given notice; she speaks perfect English and provides maps and information. Each cheerful, modern apartment boasts a radio, an ironing board/iron, and a kitchenette with a refrigerator, toaster, hot plate, coffeemaker, pots and pans, and tableware. Even coffee, tea, and sugar are provided. Bikes are available for 15DM ($9) per day. The larger apartment has a balcony, replete with table and chairs in fine weather. Be sure to call or write in advance for a reservation.

Frau Audrey Bauchinger. Zeppelinstrasse 37 (across the Isar River from the Deutsches Museum), 81669 München. ☎ **089/48 84 44.** Fax 089/48 91 787. Internet: http://munich-online.com/ab-rooms. 6 units, 2 with shower only, 3 with bathroom; 2 apts. 45DM ($26) single with shower only; 75DM ($43) double without bathroom, 85DM–105DM ($48–$60) double with shower only, 125DM ($71) double with bathroom; 35DM ($20) per person triple

Getting the Best Deal on Accommodations

- A room without a private shower is usually cheaper than one with—however, you may be charged extra for each shower you take down the hall. If the charge for a shower is high and there are more than two of you, you might save by taking a room with a private shower.
- Accommodations that offer cooking facilities help you save on dining bills.
- Ask if breakfast is included in the room rate—if it's buffet style, you can eat as much as you wish.
- Before placing a call, inquire about the surcharge on local and long-distance phone calls.
- Note how far the accommodation is from the town center. You might find an inexpensive room on the outskirts, but what you'll end up spending for transportation into the city may negate the savings.
- Avoid coming to Munich during a major convention—rooms may be scarce and many hotels and pensions raise their rates.

without bathroom; 130DM–160DM ($74–$91) apt for 2, plus 40DM ($23) per extra person. Rates include 1 shower per night; extra showers 5DM ($2.85). AE, MC, V. S-Bahn: Marienplatz, then bus no. 52 to Schweigerstrasse (first stop after the river).

In a typical Munich apartment block on the banks of the scenic Isar, the rooms and apartments here are owned/managed by a former teacher from Virginia who married an Austrian antiques dealer. The rooms are clean and quiet and spread on several floors (no elevator), with different options available. There's only one single, which has a shower; others are doubles, some with shower only or with a private bath across the hall. The simple triple, ideal for students and backpackers, is in the Bauchinger apartment and shares the family bath. Those looking for greater luxury should consider one of the apartments; those who wish to use the attached kitchen stocked with tea and coffee pay 160DM ($91), while those who don't pay 30DM ($17) less. New arrivals receive a sheet on what to see in Munich. Frau Bauchinger prefers cash; if you pay by credit card, she'll add a 5% surcharge.

Fremdenheim Weigl. Pettenkoferstrasse 32 (just off Georg-Hirth-Platz, about a 10-minute walk south of the train station), 80336 München. ☎ **089/53 24 53.** 3 units, none with bathroom. 35DM ($20) single; 70DM ($40) double. Rates include showers. No credit cards. U-Bahn: Theresienwiese. Bus: 58 to Georg-Hirth-Platz. If you want to walk from the Hauptbahnhof's south exit, head down Goethestrasse to Pettenkoferstrasse, then turn right.

The three rooms on the second floor of this building serviced by elevator are owned/managed by Daniela Busetti, who speaks excellent English and is the granddaughter of the original owner. Though she lives in the same building, her apartment is separate, affording you more privacy than most basic private accommodations. The cheerful, clean rooms consist of one single without a sink and two doubles with washbasins.

NEAR THE HAUPTBAHNHOF

Unless otherwise noted, these pensions have the same rates year-round.

Armin. Augustenstrasse 5, 80333 München. ☎ **089/59 31 97.** Fax 089/59 52 52. 20 units, none with bathroom. 50DM–60DM ($29–$34) single; 80DM–90DM ($46–$51) double; 120DM–140DM ($68–$80) triple. Rates include continental breakfast and showers. No credit cards. Parking 15DM ($9). Closed the Fri before Christmas to Jan 7. Walk 1 block north from the Hauptbahnhof on Dachauerstrasse and turn right onto Augustenstrasse (about a 6-minute walk).

Popular with student groups, backpackers, and families, this reasonably priced pension offers plain, uncluttered rooms with dark wooden furniture. Iranian-born owner Armin Georgi speaks English and is happy to dispense information on his adopted hometown as well as book sightseeing tours. A washer/dryer is available for 11DM ($6) per load, and there's a communal room with a TV and a pleasant lobby with drinks available. The rates given above are for readers who book directly with the hotel; the higher price in each room category is for during Oktoberfest and major conventions.

Augsburg. Schillerstrasse 18, 80336 München. ☎ **089/59 76 73.** Fax 089/550 38 23. 26 units, 12 with shower only. 46DM–48DM ($26–$27) single without bathroom, 55DM ($31) single with shower only; 70DM–75DM ($40–$43) double without bathroom, 86DM–90DM ($49–$51) double with shower only; 105DM ($60) triple without bathroom, 120DM–125DM ($68–$71) triple with shower only. Rates 4DM ($2.30) per person higher during Oktoberfest. Breakfast 6DM ($3.40); showers 3.50DM ($2). No credit cards. Closed Dec 23–Jan 8. From the main exit of the station onto Bahnhofplatz, turn right and walk 2 minutes.

One of many hotels and pensions on Schillerstrasse, the Augsburg is probably the most economical and the best for its price. Its reception is on the third floor (no elevator), and though the rooms are rather bare, no one can complain at these prices. The rooms are carpeted and clean, and there's hot water all the time. It's owned/managed by Anna and Heinz Paintner.

Flora. Karlstrasse 49, 80333 München. ☎ **089/59 70 67** or 089/59 41 35. Fax 089/59 41 35. 45 units, 25 with bathroom; 1 apt. 50DM–70DM ($29–$40) single without bathroom, 80DM–120DM ($46–$68) single with bathroom; 75DM–95DM ($43–$54) double without bathroom, 110DM–140DM ($63–$80) double with bathroom; 110DM–135DM ($63–$77) triple without bathroom, 145DM–160DM ($83–$91) triple with bathroom; 130DM–150DM ($74–$86) quad without bathroom, 160DM–200DM ($91–$114) quad with bathroom; 360DM ($205) apt. Rates include buffet breakfast and showers. No credit cards. Walk 6 minutes from the north exit of the Hauptbahnhof; it's near the corner of Dachauerstrasse and Karlstrasse.

A family-owned operation since 1956, the first-floor Flora is now run by the original owner's son, Adolf, and granddaughters, Judith and Angy. Great for the price, it features small but clean rooms with wall-to-wall carpeting. A couple of rooms facing away from the street have small balconies. The apartment with three bedrooms and two baths sleeping seven to nine is perfect for families. Breakfast is served in a cheerful dining room with a stucco ceiling. The higher prices above are those charged during Oktoberfest and major conventions.

✪ **Helvetia.** Schillerstrasse 6 (a few minutes' walk from the Hauptbahnhof's south exit), 80336 München. ☎ **089/55 47 45.** Fax 089/550 23 81. 46 units, 3 with shower only. TEL. 53DM–68DM ($30–39) single without bathroom; 78DM–99DM ($44–$56) double without bathroom, 99DM–115DM ($56–$66) double with shower only; 99DM–126DM ($56–$72) triple without bathroom, 140DM–168DM ($80–$105) quad without bathroom; 175DM–210DM ($100–$120) quint without bathroom. Rates include continental breakfast and showers. Dorm bed 19DM–24DM ($11–$14) per person, plus 7DM ($4) for breakfast and sheets. AE, MC, V. From the main exit of the station onto Bahnhofplatz, turn right and walk 2 minutes.

A good choice on Schillerstrasse, this pension is owned by Mr. Kahrazi, an outgoing young Iranian who has lived in Germany much of his life and speaks fluent English. He offers clean and fairly large rooms decorated with pine furniture. Most of the doubles and triples have two sinks, and several rooms comfortably sleeping up to five even have three sinks. Most rooms face away from the street, assuring a quiet night's rest, but those facing the front have soundproof windows. For budget travelers, there's a dorm with 10 beds. Laundry service is available for 8.50DM ($4.85). The highest prices above are those charged during summer, Oktoberfest, and major conventions.

Hungaria. Brienner Strasse 42, 80333 München. ☎ 089/52 15 58. 12 units, none with bathroom. 48DM–55DM ($27–$31) single; 75DM–85DM ($43–$48) double; 95DM–105DM ($54–$60) triple; 120DM ($68) quad. Rates include continental breakfast. Showers 3DM ($1.70). No credit cards. U-Bahn: U-2 to Königsplatz (1 stop); or less than a 10-minute walk north of the Hauptbahnhof, reached by walking north on Dachauerstrasse and turning right onto Augustenstrasse.

Charming English-speaking Dr. Erika Wolff has owned/managed this delightful small pension since 1957. The reception area is on the second floor, to which there's unfortunately no elevator. The rooms are bright and cheerful, and its location is convenient to the Lenbachhaus, Glyptothek, and Antikensammlungen.

✪ **Jedermann.** Bayerstrasse 95, 80335 München. ☎ **089/53 32 67** or 089/53 36 17. Fax 089/53 65 06. E-mail: hotel-jedermann@cube.net. Internet: www.hotel-jedermann.de. 55 units, 3 with shower only, 34 with bathroom. 65DM–85DM ($37–$48) single without bathroom, 95DM–150DM ($54–$86) single with bathroom; 95DM–140DM ($54–$80) double without bathroom, 110–150DM ($63–$86) double with shower only, 130DM–220DM ($74–$125) double with bathroom; 110DM–170DM ($63–$97) triple without bathroom, 165DM–260DM ($94–$148) triple with bathroom. Rates include buffet breakfast and showers. Crib available. MC, V. Parking 10DM ($6). From the south exit of the train station, turn right onto Bayerstrasse and walk 8 minutes.

This delightful place has been owned by the English-speaking Jenke family since 1962. Its lobby and rooms were recently renovated, and the breakfast room is a pleasant place to start the day with an all-you-can-eat buffet. There are nice touches of flowers, antiques, and traditional Bavarian furniture throughout, and each room with a bath has the extras of a radio, an alarm clock, a satellite TV with CNN, a hair dryer, and modem hookups. Most rooms have safes and some have bidets. Chocolates left on pillows are a thoughtful touch. The higher rates above are those charged during major conventions and trade fairs. In the lobby is a computer you can use to play games, surf the Internet, and send e-mail, free of charge.

✪ **Süzer.** Mittererstrasse 1 (150 yards from the south side of the train station), 80336 München. ☎ **089/53 35 21** or 089/53 66 42. Fax 089/53 60 80. E-mail: Erol-Suezer@t-online.de. 11 units, 4 with bathroom. TV TEL. *For Frommer's readers:* 85DM ($48) double without bathroom, 105DM ($60) double with bathroom; 120DM ($68) triple without bathroom; 150DM ($86) quad without bathroom. Rates include continental breakfast and showers. AE, DC, MC, V. From the train station, take a right out of the south exit onto Bayerstrasse and then a left at Mittererstrasse.

This tiny pension is on the third floor (take the elevator to the left or you'll end up at a doctor's office). It's owned by Herr Erol Süzer, an outgoing Turk who speaks excellent English, is always looking for ways to improve his pension, and is eager to answer questions (alas, some of the people working for him don't speak English or German). All the rooms are decorated with Scandinavian-style wooden furniture and wainscoting and come with radio alarm clocks; five have refrigerators (with ice cubes!). Among the various services provided at this modest pension are a tiny reception/breakfast area with a cable TV, a fax machine, and a computer hooked up to the Internet that you can use to send e-mail for a nominal fee. You can also buy beer or coffee for 2DM ($1.15), though unlimited tea or coffee is served with breakfast. One load of laundry washed and dried is 10DM ($6). A new phone allows direct international dialing through MCI, Sprint, or AT&T. You can even sign up here for city tours. The rates are special for bearers of this book (not photocopies), which you should show on arrival—but only if you reserve directly with the pension.

NEAR THERESIENWIESE

Schubert. Schubertstrasse 1, 80336 München. ☎ **089/53 50 87.** 7 units, 2 with shower only. 50DM ($29) single without bathroom; 85DM ($48) double without bathroom, 95DM ($54) double with shower only. Rates include continental breakfast. Showers 3DM ($1.70). No credit cards. U-Bahn: U-3 or U-6 from Marienplatz to Goetheplatz (2 stops).

In an unadorned building on a tree-lined street, this small pension is a true find. It's owned by outgoing Frau Käthe Fürholzer, who speaks some English, and its walls are decorated with Bavarian mementos and pictures, including a collection of beer-stein tin tops (designed to keep the flies out and the beer fresh in former days). The rooms are clean and orderly in good German fashion.

✪ **Westfalia.** Mozartstrasse 23, 80336 München. ☎ **089/53 03 77** or 089/53 03 78. Fax 089/543 91 20. 19 units, 11 with bathroom. TEL. 60DM–65DM ($34–$37) single without bathroom, 85DM–95DM ($48–$54) single with bathroom; 85DM–95DM ($48–$54) double without bathroom, 115DM–135DM ($66–$77) double with bathroom; 115DM–125DM ($66–$71) triple without bathroom, 140DM–150DM ($80–$86) triple with bathroom. Rates include buffet breakfast. Showers 3DM ($1.70). AE, V. U-Bahn: U-3 or U-6 from Marienplatz to Goetheplatz. Bus: 58 from the Hauptbahnhof to Goetheplatz.

A century old, this imposing and elaborate building is across from the Oktoberfest meadow. The lobby is on the top floor, reached by elevator, where you'll be met by the owner Peter Deiritz and his family. Since buying the pension in 1990, the Deiritzes have been renovating slowly, making it brighter and adding Bavarian pine furniture and TVs to rooms. The pension itself is cozy, clean, and comfortable, and the breakfast room and corridor feature 19th-century paintings by Munich artists. This is the kind of place many visitors to Bavaria are looking for.

IN OLD TOWN

✪ **Am Markt.** Heiliggeistrasse 6, 80331 München. ☎ **089/22 50 14.** Fax 089/22 40 17. 31 units, 12 with bathroom. TEL. 65DM–70DM ($37–$40) single without bathroom, 110DM–116DM ($63–$66) single with bathroom; 112DM–120DM ($64–$68) double without bathroom, 160DM–165DM ($91–$94) double with bathroom; 170DM ($97) triple without bathroom, 210DM ($120) triple with bathroom. Rates include continental breakfast and showers. No credit cards. Parking 12DM ($7). S-Bahn: From the Hauptbahnhof, take any S-Bahn to Marienplatz (2 stops).

Next to Munich's colorful outdoor market, the Viktualienmarkt, this hotel has a nostalgic flair. The rooms are a bit plain and small, but the breakfast room and entryway are tastefully decorated and display photos of some celebrities who've stayed here— and most who haven't. At any rate, the hotel looks more expensive than it is, and you can't beat its location. It has many repeat guests, so book early.

Pension Lindner. Dultstrasse 1, 80331 München. ☎ **089/26 34 13.** Fax 089/26 87 60. 9 units, 1 with shower only, 1 with bathroom. 60DM ($24) single without bathroom; 100DM ($57) double without bathroom, 125DM ($71) double with shower only, 140 ($80) double with bathroom. Prices 20%–30% higher during Oktoberfest. Rates include continental buffet breakfast and showers. No credit cards. S-Bahn: From the Hauptbahnhof, take any S-Bahn to Marienplatz (2 stops).

With a great location just a stone's throw from the Münchner Stadtmuseum and a 3-minute walk from Marienplatz, this 30-year-old pension with elevator offers simple and pleasant rooms at rates that make it the best bargain in the Old City. Double rooms come with TV and radio. The owner, Frau Sinzinger, prefers initial inquiries by phone so that she can answer any questions immediately (be mindful of the time difference) and will then reconfirm via mail or fax.

IN SCHWABING

✪ **Am Kaiserplatz.** Kaiserplatz 12, 80803 München. ☎ **089/34 91 90** or 089/39 52 31. 10 units, 6 with shower only. 45DM–59DM ($26–$34) single without bathroom; 79DM–85DM ($45–$48) double without bathroom, 89DM–95DM ($51–$54) double with shower only; 105DM ($60) triple without bathroom or with shower only; 130DM–140DM ($74–$80) quad without bathroom or with shower only; 150DM–160DM ($86–$91) quint without bathroom or with shower only; 180DM ($103) 6-bed room without bathroom or with shower only. Rates include continental breakfast and 1 shower per overnight stay. No credit cards. Take any S-Bahn in the direction of Marienplatz, changing there to U-Bahn U-3 or U-6 for Münchener Freiheit.

If you like touches of the Old World, you can't do better than this place for its price. On the ground floor of a Jugendstil building almost a century old (several architects have offices here—always a good sign), this pension features spacious rooms, each in a different style: for example, the English Room, the Farmer's Room, and the Baroque Room. Extravagantly furnished with chandeliers, sitting areas, lace curtains, or washbasins shaped like seashells, they're highly recommended. Friendly Frau Jacobi, who has run the place for 25 years and is now assisted by her English-speaking son Thomas, is a native of Munich. Breakfast is served in your room.

BETWEEN THE CITY CENTER & THE ISAR RIVER

Beck. Thierschstrasse 36, 80538 München. ☎ **089/22 07 08** or 089/22 57 68. Fax 089/22 09 25. E-mail: pension.beck@bst-online.de. 44 units, 8 with bathroom. TV TEL. 50DM–56DM ($29–$32) single without bathroom, 68DM–78DM ($39–$44) single with bathroom; 78DM–90DM ($44–$51) double without bathroom, 95DM–120DM ($54–$68) double with bathroom; 40DM–42DM ($23–$24) per person triple, quad, or quint without bathroom, 45DM–50DM ($26–$29) per person triple, quad, or quint with bathroom. Rates include continental breakfast and showers. Crib available. No credit cards. Parking 5DM ($2.85); licenses for street parking free. S-Bahn: S-8 from the airport or any S-Bahn from the Hauptbahnhof in the direction of Ostbahnhof to Isartorplatz, then a 3-minute walk. U-Bahn: Lehel, then a 5-minute walk. Tram: 17 from the Hauptbahnhof to Isartorplatz.

It's hard to believe that Frau Beck is over 75, so energetically does she run this astonishingly cheap pension (no elevator). The owner since 1950, she speaks very good English, is talkative, and makes sure guests know what to see in her beloved Munich. The building is more than 100 years old, with rooms spread over four floors in two buildings. One of the best things about this place is that there are small kitchens and refrigerators you can use for free, saving money on meals (ask the reception for plates, pots, pans, and utensils). Frau Beck welcomes families, with four rooms large enough for five. The rooms, though old, are large, clean, and perfectly adequate, with modern wooden furniture and carpeting; a few have balconies. This pension, near the Deutsches Museum and a 10-minute walk from the city center and Englischer Garten, is directly connected to the airport and train station via S-Bahn.

A YOUTH HOTEL

To sleep in a youth hostel *(jugendherberge)* in Bavaria, you can't be older than 26 and must have a youth hostel card. If you don't have a card, you can still stay at a hostel by paying 6DM ($3.40) extra per night for a guest membership; after 6 nights, your guest membership automatically becomes a regular youth hostel card, good around the world for 1 year.

✪ **4 You München.** Hirtenstrasse 18, 80335 München. ☎ **089/55 21 66-0.** Fax 089/55 21 66-66. E-mail: info@the4you.de. Internet: www.the4you.de. 10 units and 148 beds in hostel, none with bathroom; 29 units in hotel, all with bathroom. Hostel, 54DM ($31) single; 76DM ($43) double; 24DM–29DM ($14–$16) dorm room. Hotel, 89DM–139DM ($51–$79) single; 119DM–179DM ($68–$102) double. Rates include showers. Buffet breakfast 7.50DM ($4.25); sheets 5DM ($2.85) for hostel only. AE, DC, V. Walk 2 minutes north from the Hauptbahnhof.

Opened in 1996 after the renovation of an older building, this environment-friendly, handicapped-accessible hotel is a great addition to Munich's youth accommodations with a fantastic location steps from the train station. Utilizing solar energy and recycled rainwater, it consists of two sections: a youth hostel with dorms sleeping 4 to 10, plus simple singles and doubles without bath; and a hotel on the top two floors offering baths, phones, radios, and hair dryers (some rooms have TVs). This ecologically minded place has even placed in each room waste bins divided for recycling. The hostel, which does *not* require a youth hostel card, is open to those 26 and younger (space permitting, those older than 26 can stay by paying a 16% VAT supplement), families, and disabled persons of any age; the hotel is open to anyone. In fact, families find this a great place, since there's a day-care facility with hourly rates, cribs, changing tables, and toys. Extras include nightly events, a bar, and a self-service restaurant. There's no curfew. I wish all European cities had accommodations like this!

WORTH A SPLURGE

Europäischer Hof. Bayerstrasse 31 (across from the Hauptbahnhof's south side), 80335 München. ☎ **089/55 15 10.** Fax 089/55 15 12 22. E-mail: heh_munich@compuserve.com. 151 units, 134 with bathroom. TV TEL. 88DM–118DM ($50–$67) single without bathroom, 138DM–238DM ($79–$1356) single with bathroom; 108DM–158DM ($62–$90) double without bathroom, 168DM–260DM ($96–$148) double with bathroom; 185DM–295DM ($105–$168) triple with bathroom. Rates include buffet breakfast and showers. Discounts available July–Aug to bearers of this book. AE, DC, MC, V. Parking 16DM ($9).

You can't get any closer to the train station than this modern hotel with a sleek marble lobby and a courteous staff. All rooms have cable TVs, but there are various types of rooms available, from bathless rooms with sinks to luxurious doubles with minibars and trouser pressers. No-smoking rooms are available. Rates are also determined by the season, with more charged in September and October, including Oktoberfest and major conventions. There's a restaurant, and in its elegant breakfast room you can eat as much as you want. Free coffee is available from a machine; ask the front desk for a token. From its appearance, you'd expect this place to be more expensive.

✪ **Uhland.** Uhlandstrasse 1 (near the Oktoberfest meadow, about a 10-minute walk from the train station), 80336 München. ☎ **089/54 33 5-0.** Fax 089/54 33 52 50. E-mail: Hotel_Uhland@compuserve.com. Internet: www.munich-online.de/uhland. 30 units, all with bathroom. MINIBAR TV TEL. 110DM–200DM ($63–$119) single; 145DM–280DM ($83–$160) double; 180DM–320DM ($103–$182) triple; 190DM–350DM ($108–$200) quad. Rates include buffet breakfast. Crib available. AE, MC, V. Free parking. U-Bahn: U-4 or U-5 to Theresienwiese, then a 3-minute walk. Bus: 58 from the Hauptbahnhof to Georg-Hirth-Platz (3rd stop).

The facade of this 100-year-old building is striking—ornate baroque with flower boxes of geraniums at all windows. In former days, each floor was its own grand apartment. It was converted into a hotel more than 40 years ago by the Hauzenberger/Effinger family and has kept up with the times, offering connections for laptop computers in every room, a computer in the small communal living room (you can use it for free but must pay to send e-mail), and a coffee machine in the living room that freshly grinds and brews each cup. Each room is slightly different; a few even have balconies. There's a "children's room," with bunk beds and a stereo. The higher prices are charged during Oktoberfest and major conventions.

4 Great Deals on Dining

Typical Bavarian restaurants are boisterous, frequently with wooden tables and chairs, beamed ceilings, and half-paneled walls bearing simple hooks on which you can hang your jacket or hat. You sit wherever there's an empty chair (no one will seat you), making it easy to strike up a conversation with others at your table, especially after a few rounds of beer. Since this is Bavaria, which tends toward excess, the meals are hearty and huge. You don't have to spend a fortune for atmosphere or the food.

Most of Munich's restaurants are in the city center, around the train station and Marienplatz and in nightlife districts like Schwabing. Since the menu is almost always posted outside the door, you'll never be in the dark about prices. Many restaurants offer a *Tageskarte* (daily menu) with special complete meals of the day. In fact, most entrees in Munich's German restaurants are complete meals, including a main course and a couple of side dishes (often potatoes and sauerkraut). The prices below are for complete meals.

Note that the beer halls under "Munich After Dark," later in this chapter, also serve food.

FAVORITE MEALS   With its six breweries, dozens of beer gardens, and the world's largest beer festival, Munich is probably best known for beer, which is almost a complete meal in itself. Bavarians even drink it for breakfast. The freshest is draft beer, *vom fass. Weissbier* is made from wheat instead of barley and full of nutritious (that's one way to look at it) sediment. In summer, a refreshing drink is a *radler,* half beer and half lemon soda.

To accompany your beer you might want to order food. For breakfast try *weisswurst* (white sausage), a delicate blend of veal, salt, pepper, lemon, and parsley. Don't eat the skin unless you want to astound those around you—it would be like eating the wrapper around a hamburger. Another popular dish is *leberkäse* (also *leberkäs*), which translates as liver cheese but is neither one. It's a kind of German meat loaf of beef and bacon that looks like a thick slab of bologna, often served with a fried egg on top— it's great with a roll, mustard, and sauerkraut.

Other Bavarian specialties are *leberknödl* (liver dumplings, often served in a soup or with sauerkraut), *kalbshaxe* (grilled veal knuckle), *schweinshaxe* (grilled pork knuckle), *schweinsbraten* (pot-roasted pork), *sauerbraten* (marinated beef in a thick sauce), and *spanferkel* (suckling pig).

NEAR THE HAUPTBAHNHOF

Dinea. In the Kaufhof department store (6th floor), Karlsplatz 21. ☎ **089/512 51 20.** Meals 10DM–15DM ($6–$9). No credit cards. Mon–Fri 9am–7:45pm, Sat 8:30am–3:45pm. S-Bahn: Karlsplatz/Stachus. GERMAN/VARIED.

This self-service cafeteria is your best bet for a meal with a panoramic view over the city rooftops. The fixed-price meals for 10DM to 14DM ($6 to $8) change daily; the soups and salad bar are cheaper. If you want to splurge, try one of the delicious desserts. In the morning it serves breakfast.

Thessaloniki. In the Elisenhof (1st floor), Prielmayerstrasse 1 (catercorner from the train station's main exit). ☎ **089/59 82 49.** Meals 10DM–24DM ($6–$14). AE, V. Daily 10am–midnight. S-Bahn/U-Bahn: Hauptbahnhof. GREEK.

In a small Elisenhof shopping center, this reasonably priced restaurant with comfortable booth seating, subdued lighting, murals of Greek landscapes, and the ubiquitous Greek music offers all the specialties, from gyros and souvlaki to moussaka, grilled

---

Getting the Best Deal on Dining

- Try dining at an *imbiss,* an inexpensive food stall or tiny hole-in-the-wall serving *wurst,* french fries, beer, and soda. The food is served over the counter and you eat standing up.
- Take advantage of the special menu of the day, *Tageskarte,* usually a complete meal in itself.
- Note that butcher shops and food departments of department stores offer takeout foods like *leberkäs,* grilled chicken, and salads.
- For breakfast or an afternoon coffee, go to the coffee-shop chains Tschibo and Eduscho, which sell both the beans and the brew. You can bring your own pastry and drink a cup of coffee standing up for about 3DM ($1.70).
- Ask whether there's an extra charge for bread (restaurants in Bavaria charge for each piece of bread consumed) and whether the entree comes with vegetables or side dishes.
- Remember to inquire whether there's a daily special not listed on the menu.

---

beef, lamb, and seafood, as well as pizza for less than 11DM ($6). You can eat well for less than 20DM ($11), making it a good choice in the vicinity of the train station.

Wienerwald. Bayerstrasse 35 (across from the train station's south side). ☎ **089/54 82 97 13.** Meals 15DM–20DM ($9–$11). AE, DC, MC, V. Daily 8am–midnight. S-Bahn/U-Bahn: Hauptbahnhof. GERMAN.

The Wienerwald chain is one of the great successes of postwar Germany, with more than 20 locations in Munich and hundreds more throughout Germany and Austria. Legend has it that the founder came to the Oktoberfest, saw the mass consumption of grilled chicken, and decided to open his own restaurant serving only that at a great price. A quarter of a grilled chicken and a side dish is less than 11DM ($6). Other menu items are various chicken dishes, schnitzel, soups, salads (including a salad bar), and fish. Takeout food is available, with an entrance to the left of the main door.

Another branch is near the Deutsches Museum at Steinsdorfstrasse 21, on the corner of Zweibrückenstrasse (☎ **089/29 15 86;** S-Bahn: Isartor), open daily 9am to midnight.

IN OLD TOWN

Bella Italia Am Stachus. Herzog-Wilhelm-Strasse 8 (just south of Karlsplatz). ☎ **089/59 32 59.** Meals 6DM–17DM ($3.40–$10). No credit cards. Daily 11:30am–midnight. S-Bahn: Karlsplatz/Stachus. ITALIAN.

This popular chain of Italian-staffed restaurants is the best place in town for inexpensive pizza or pasta, including lasagna, tortelloni, cannelloni, and spaghetti, all between 6DM and 13DM ($3.40 and $7). The daily specials are less than 12DM ($7). This restaurant offers indoor seating as well as tables under trees. The pizza Bella Italia (with ham, mushrooms, olives, peppers, artichoke, and salami) is especially good.

Buxs. Frauenstrasse 9 (just off the Viktualienmarkt). ☎ **089/29 19 55-0.** Meals 12DM–16DM ($7–$9). No credit cards. Mon–Fri 11am–8pm, Sat 11am–3pm. S-Bahn/U-Bahn: Marienplatz, then a 5-minute walk over the Viktualienmarkt. VEGETARIAN.

This pleasant self-service restaurant is modern, bright, and spotless, with outdoor seating in summer overlooking the Viktualienmarkt. It offers more than 40 salads, vegetables, warm dishes, and desserts, which change daily according to what's fresh. About 90% of the ingredients are organically grown. You can select as much or as little of each salad or dish as you wish, making it a great place to try a variety of foods—prices are determined by weighing each plate, with each 100 grams at 2.95DM ($1.70). Expect to spend 12DM to 16DM ($7 to $9) for a satisfying meal.

Donisl. Weinstrasse 1 (off Marienplatz). ☎ **089/29 62 64.** Meals 8DM–12DM ($4.55–$7). AE, DC, MC, V. Daily 9am–11pm. S-Bahn/U-Bahn: Marienplatz. GERMAN.

The Donisl is popular with visitors because of its convenient location, typical Bavarian decor, local specialties, and prices. Its cheapest dish is *weisswurst* for 8DM ($4.55), so if you're on a tight budget come for breakfast or lunch. Even its main dishes are affordable—the Donisl prides itself that no meal costs more than 12DM ($7). Try the *leberkäse, schweinsbraten, schweinshaxe, Wiener schnitzel,* or *mastente* (duck), each served with a side dish and best washed down with the freshly tapped beer. If all you want is a quick snack, at the entrance is a small *imbiss* with even lower prices.

Marché Mövenpick. Neuhauser Strasse 19 (between Karlsplatz and Marienplatz). ☎ **089/260 60 61.** Meals 12DM–20DM ($7–$11). AE, MC, V. Daily 8am–11pm. S-Bahn/U-Bahn: Marienplatz. GERMAN/INTERNATIONAL.

A hugely successful chain of cafeterias belonging to the Swiss-owned Mövenpick group, the Marché is based on a marketplace theme, with counters selling various kinds of food. On entering, you'll be given a card that's stamped for each item you order. There are two floors, with most of the low-priced dishes on the lower level. Simply pick up a tray and wander through, stopping at counters that tempt you. In addition to a salad and a vegetable bar, there are counters selling pasta, main dishes that may range from grilled chicken to pork chops, soups, desserts, fruit juices, and other drinks. A complete meal will be between 12DM and 20DM ($7 and $11). Even better, come after 8pm, when you can eat all you want on the ground-floor level for 19DM ($11).

✪ Nürnberger Bratwurst Glöckl am Dom. Frauenplatz 9. ☎ **089/29 52 64.** Meals 14DM–29DM ($8–$17). No credit cards. Daily 9:30am–midnight. S-Bahn/U-Bahn: Marienplatz. GERMAN.

Though you could easily spend 30DM ($17) for Bavarian specialties like pork filet and *schweinshaxe,* to experience this great place all you have to order is its famous *schweinwürstl* (six small sausages with sauerkraut) or one of its other sausage plates for less than 15DM ($9). This is Bavaria at its finest: a rough wooden floor, wooden tables, hooks for clothing, beer steins and tin plates lining a wall shelf, Bavarian specialties grilled over an open wood fire, and beer from wooden barrels. Upstairs is the Albrecht Dürer Room, quiet and intimate, but I prefer the ground floor's liveliness. An evening here could possibly be your most memorable in Munich.

Prinz Myshkin. Hackenstrasse 2 (off Sendlinger Strasse, a few minutes' walk from Marienplatz). ☎ **089/26 55 96.** Pizza 16.50DM–19DM ($9–$11); main courses 18DM–25DM ($10–$14). AE, MC, V. Mon–Sat 11:30am–11pm, Sun 10am–11pm. S-Bahn/U-Bahn: Marienplatz. VEGETARIAN.

If you want to splurge on something other than German cuisine, this trendy restaurant serves vegetarian dishes in a refined, relaxed setting. Boasting a high vaulted ceiling, artwork, candles, and background music that's likely to be soft jazz, it serves a variety of changing salads, soups, and appetizers; these may include vegetarian quiche, Japanese miso soup, or a wild-rice salad. In addition to pizza, it offers innovative main dishes inspired by the cuisines of Asia, Italy, Greece, and Mexico, with past dishes ranging from various ravioli to a Thai-inspired dish of paprika, mushrooms, onions, pineapple, and bananas in coconut-curry sauce. Monday to Friday 11:30am to 2pm it offers a fixed-price business lunch for less than 15DM ($9).

Munich's Beer Gardens

The city's beer gardens are as fickle as the weather—if the weather's bad, the beer gardens don't open. By the same token, if suddenly in the middle of February the weather turns gloriously warm, the beer gardens start turning on the taps.

Generally speaking, however, beer gardens are open on sunny days from May to September or October, usually 10 or 11am to 11pm. Ranging from tiny neighborhood gardens that accommodate a few hundred to those that seat several thousand, beer gardens number about 35 in and around Munich, making it the beer garden capital of the world. Many of the larger ones boast traditional Bavarian bands on weekends. The smallest beer available is usually a liter—after all, you're here to drink beer—which costs about 10.40DM ($6).

Caution: Many of the beer gardens are in the middle of huge parks, making them a bit difficult to find. Take note of how you got there; it's even harder to find your way out of the park after you've had a few liters of beer.

These four beer gardens allow you to bring your own food: **Augustiner Keller,** Arnulfstrasse 52 (☎ **089/321 83 257**), about a 10-minute walk northwest of the Hauptbahnhof; **Viktualienmarkt,** in the city center near Marienplatz (☎ **089/29 75 45**), closed Sunday and holidays (see "Picnicking"); **Chinesischer Turm,** in the Englischer Garten (☎ **089/39 50 28**), reached by taking U-Bahn U-3 or U-6 to Giselastrasse; and **Hirschgarten,** Hirschgartenstrasse 1 (☎ **089/17 25 91**), near Nymphenburg Palace (take the S-Bahn to Laim).

Ratskeller. Under the Town Hall, on Marienplatz. ☎ **089/21 99 89-0.** Meals 14DM–30DM ($8–$17). AE, MC, V. Daily 10am–11:30pm. S-Bahn/U-Bahn: Marienplatz. GERMAN/CONTINENTAL.

Many town halls contain a cellar restaurant. Munich's is cavernous, with low vaulted ceilings, white tablecloths, and flowers on the tables. Popular with businesspeople and middle-aged shoppers, this dignified restaurant with an English menu doesn't have a dress code, but shorts aren't appropriate. Besides such Bavarian and Franconian specialties as roast suckling pig, roast pork, wurst, and *leberkäs,* it has a few vegetarian dishes, as well as changing specials. This is a good choice for *weisswurst* in the morning (7.60DM/$4.35 a pair), an afternoon coffee and dessert, or a glass of Franconian wine in the adjoining wine cellar, open daily from 3pm and featuring live music nightly.

Weisses Bräuhaus. Tal 7. ☎ **089/29 98 75.** Meals 12DM–25DM ($7–$14). No credit cards. Daily 8:30am–11pm. S-Bahn/U-Bahn: Marienplatz. GERMAN.

This boisterous place is famous for its beer (*bräuhaus* means "brewery"), and the kind to order is wheat beer, either *weizenbier* or *weissbier.* A simple white interior with a wooden floor and long wooden tables, this typical Bavarian restaurant has an English menu whose cheapest and most famous meal is *weisswurst* (7.20DM/$4.10, available only until noon). If you're hungry, order the Bavarian Farmer's Feast—roast and smoked pork, pork sausage, liver dumplings, mashed potatoes, and sauerkraut. Other choices are *leberkäs* (liver cheese on the English menu), suckling pig, *schweinsbraten,* potato pancakes, and breaded calf's head.

IN SCHWABING

Gaststätte Leopold. Leopoldstrasse 50. ☎ **089/38 38 680.** Meals 13.50DM–32DM ($8–$18). AE, DC, MC, V. Daily 10:30am–midnight. U-Bahn: U-3 or U-6 to Giselastrasse. AUSTRIAN.

Popular with those over 40, this large, open restaurant with antiques, wainscoting, a hand-painted ceiling, and an atmosphere reminiscent of decades past can be a haven from the Schwabing throngs, though later it can get crowded. In summer, tables and chairs are set outside, where you can watch the passing crowds on busy Leopoldstrasse, the center stage of nightlife in Schwabing. It serves Austrian cuisine, including baked chicken, Wiener schnitzel, roast beef, wurst, and duck, but oxen dishes are its specialty.

Mama's Kebap Haus. Feilitzsch-strasse 7. ☎ **089/39 26 42.** Meals 5DM–13DM ($2.85–$7). No credit cards. Daily 11am–1am. U-Bahn: U-3 or U-6 to Münchener Freiheit. TURKISH.

This simple self-service restaurant in the heart of Schwabing's nightlife district is always crowded with young diners, who stop for an inexpensive meal before or after hitting the nightspots. You can eat the Turkish or Italian pizza by the slice, kebabs, and daily specials at one of the half-dozen tables or get takeout.

Mensa Universität. Leopoldstrasse 13. ☎ **089/38 19 60.** Meals 3.30DM–5.50DM ($1.90–$3.15). No credit cards. Mon–Thurs 11am–2pm, Fri 11am–1:45pm. Closed Jan 1, Easter, and Dec 25. U-Bahn: U-3 or U-6 to Giselastrasse. GERMAN.

Technically for students (including those with international IDs), this cafeteria is so big and busy that if you look anything like a student you won't have trouble getting a meal. The Mensa is back from Leopoldstrasse, behind the multistory pink building, in a plain concrete-and-glass two-story structure. Your only problem may be figuring out the system. The daily menus are posted on TV screens, as well as on bulletin boards. There are usually four meals at four prices—each with its own colored chip you buy at one of the ground-floor booths. You then head up to the cafeteria that's dishing out the meal you've selected and hand in the chip when you've picked up your tray. A meal for 3.30DM ($1.90), for example, may consist of beef stew, potatoes, salad, and a roll; a meal for 5.50DM ($3.15) offers a main course and a choice of three side dishes. If in doubt about what's being offered and which cafeteria to go to, just ask one of the students.

The **Mensa Technische Universität,** Arcisstrasse 17 (☎ **089/28 66 39 10**), is convenient for lunch if you're visiting the Alte and Neue Pinakothek, open the same hours.

Munich's First Diner (MFD). Feilitzsch-strasse and Leopoldstrasse (behind the Hertie department store). ☎ **089/33 59 15.** Meals 13DM–26DM ($7–$15). AE, MC, V. Mon–Thurs 9am–1am, Fri 9am–3am, Sat 7:30am–3am, Sun 7:30am–1am. U-Bahn: U-3 or U-6 to Münchener Freiheit. AMERICAN.

If you prefer a burger and fries over sausages and sauerkraut, head to MFD, decorated with the requisite chrome and red vinyl stools and benches. Catering to the youth that make Schwabing their own, it offers a full cocktail bar, loud music, breakfast anytime (including an American breakfast), and an English menu of salads (meals in themselves), sandwiches, pizza, and pasta, with meals delivered by a fleet of in-line skating staff.

PICNICKING

Department stores (such as Hertie across from the train station or Kaufhof on Marienplatz) have basement food departments. These sell fruits and vegetables, cheeses, sausages, breads, drinks, and cakes, as well as ready-made salads, *leberkäs,* grilled chicken, and more.

Another great place for inexpensive picnic food is a **butcher shop,** since these often sell *leberkäse,* grilled chicken, and other dishes. Two of the most convenient are Räucheronkel, Orlandostrasse 3 near the Hofbräuhaus, and the chain Vinzenz Mur, with a convenient branch at Rosenstrasse 7, just off Marienplatz. With about the same hours as regular shops, both stores offer prepared meats, salads, and more, along with chest-high tables where you can stand to eat your purchases.

If you want more traditional surroundings, the **Viktualienmarkt** can't be beat. Munich's most famous outdoor market, from the early 1800s, is a colorful affair with permanent little shops and booths and stalls set up under umbrellas. Wurst, bread, cakes, honey, cheese, wine, fruits, vegetables, flowers, and meats are sold, and in the middle of the market there's even a beer garden, where you're welcome to sit at one of the outer tables (only at those without a tablecloth) and eat your purchase. There are also a lot of stand-up fast-food counters offering sausages, sandwiches, and other dishes. The market is open Monday to Friday 8am to 6pm and Saturday 8am to 2pm.

Another good place to search for picnic ingredients is **Schmankerlgasse,** an underground passage leading from the Hertie department store near the Hauptbahnhof to Karlsplatz. It's lined with food stalls, each specializing in something different, like sandwiches, pizza, fish, vegetarian dishes, Chinese food, Greek specialties, pasta, desserts, croissants, fruit juices, cheeses, and vegetables. You can stand and eat it here, sit at one of the tables, or take it with you. Schmankerlgasse is open Monday to Friday 9:30am to 8pm and Saturday 9am to 4pm.

And where can you go to eat your goodies? Try along the **Isar River** or somewhere in the huge expanse of the **Englischer Garten.** Better yet, take your food to one of the **beer gardens** (see the box above), where all you have to buy is one of those famous mugs of foaming beer.

WORTH A SPLURGE

✪ **Hundskugel.** Hotterstrasse 18 (a 4-minute walk from Marienplatz). ☎ **089/26 42 72.** Meals 16DM–40DM ($9–$23). No credit cards. Daily 11am–11pm. S-Bahn/U-Bahn: Marienplatz. GERMAN.

In operation since 1440, this may be Munich's oldest restaurant. Its facade, brightly lit and decorated with flower boxes, hints at what's waiting inside: intimate rooms with low-beamed ceilings, little changed over the centuries. It serves Bavarian and German traditional food, including *spanferkel* with dumplings and *kraut* salad, *tellerfleisch* (beef cooked in meat stock and cut into slices), and the Hundskugel Spezial (broiled pork tenderloin with potatoes, mushrooms, and vegetables, baked with cheese), an experience you won't forget. A three-course daily special for less than 20DM ($11) is available until it runs out.

5 Seeing the Sights

SIGHTSEEING SUGGESTIONS

IF YOU HAVE 1 DAY Begin with a breakfast of Munich's famous weisswurst at a traditional Bavarian restaurant. To get a feel for the atmosphere of the capital, stroll through **Old Town,** starting at **Stachus (Karlsplatz)** and walking down the pedestrian lane of **Neuhauser Strasse** with its many shops and boutiques, stopping at the venerable **Frauenkirche,** Munich's largest church and most celebrated landmark. Continue to **Marienplatz,** the heart of the city, where you'll find the **Neues Rathaus (New Town Hall).** You can take an elevator up to the Rathaus tower for a view over the city; at 11am and noon daily you can watch the Rathaus's famous glockenspiel (chimes) with figures of dancers and jousting knights.

From Marienplatz, head for **St. Peter's Church,** affectionately called Alte Peter (Old Peter). Then visit the **Viktualienmarkt,** the colorful open-air market, where you might want to eat lunch at one of its many stand-up food stalls or at the beer garden in its center. In the afternoon, head toward the **Deutsches Museum,** the world's largest technological museum, or the **Alte Pinakothek,** with works by the old masters. Spend the evening at one of Munich's famous **beer halls.**

IF YOU HAVE 2 DAYS   Spend your first morning as above, but in the afternoon devote yourself to the **Alte Pinakothek** and the **Neue Pinakothek** across the street, with its collection of late 18th- and 19th-century works. On Day 2, spend the morning at the **Deutsches Museum.** In the early afternoon visit **Nymphenburg Palace,** summer residence of the Wittelsbach Electors of Bavaria and Germany's largest baroque palace.

IF YOU HAVE 3 DAYS   Spend Day 1 entirely in **Old Town** as suggested above, but include in your walk visits to the **Residenz,** the official residence of the Wittelsbach family, and its **Treasure House.** You should also visit the **Stadtmuseum,** the Municipal Museum, with displays relating to the history and development of Munich. End the day with beer at one of Munich's famous **beer halls.**

Spend Day 2 at the **Deutsches Museum** and **Nymphenburg Palace.** On Day 3 visit the **Alte Pinakothek** and **Neue Pinakothek;** the **Antikensammlungen,** with its collection of antiquities; the **Glyptothek,** with one of Europe's finest collections of Greek and Roman sculpture; and the **Lenbachhaus,** devoted to Munich's artists. End the day with a stroll through the **Englischer Garten,** stopping off for a liter at its Chinesischer Turm **beer garden.**

IF YOU HAVE 5 DAYS   Spend Days 1 to 3 as above. On Day 4, head for the **Haus der Kunst,** repository for art since the beginning of the 20th century. Nearby is the **Bavarian Museum,** relating to the history of Bavaria with an outstanding collection of nativity scenes. Spend the afternoon shopping or visiting the **BMW Museum** and the **Olympic Village.** Or go to **Dachau,** a former concentration camp that's been set up as a memorial to those who died under Hitler's regime. On Day 5, take an excursion to **Neuschwanstein,** Germany's most famous castle, in the foothills of the Bavarian Alps.

THE TOP MUSEUMS & PALACES

✪ **Alte Pinakothek.** Barer Strasse 27. ☎ **089/238 05-0.** Admission 7DM ($4) adults, 4DM ($2.30) seniors/students/children. Combination ticket for Alte and Neue Pinakothek, 12DM ($7) adults, 6DM ($3.40) seniors/students/children. Tues–Sun 10am–5pm. U-Bahn: U-2 to Theresienstrasse, then a 7-minute walk. Tram: 27 to Pinakothek. Bus: 53 to Schellingstrasse.

Begun as the collection of the Wittelsbach family in the early 1500s, this museum contains virtually all European schools of painting from the Middle Ages to the early 19th century. It has one of the world's largest collections of Rubens, plus galleries filled with German, Dutch, Flemish, Italian, Spanish, and French masterpieces. Represented are Dürer, Cranach, Brueghel, Rembrandt, Raphael, Leonardo, Titian, Tiepolo, El Greco, Velázquez, Murillo, Poussin, and Lorrain. You'll also find galleries of religious allegorical paintings, portraits of peasants and patricians, Romantic landscapes, still lifes, and scenes of war and hunting. They're housed in an imposing structure built by Leo von Klenze between 1826 and 1836 and modeled on Venetian Renaissance palazzi.

Though it's difficult to pick the collection's stars, Dürer is well represented with *Four Apostles, The Baumgartner Altar, Lamentation for the Dead Christ,* and, my favorite, his famous *Self-Portrait.* Watch for Titian's *Crowning with Thorns,* Rembrandt's *Birth of Christ* with his remarkable use of light and shadows, Rubens's *Self-Portrait with His Wife in the Arbor* and *Last Judgment,* and Brueghel's *Land of Cockaigne.*

Munich

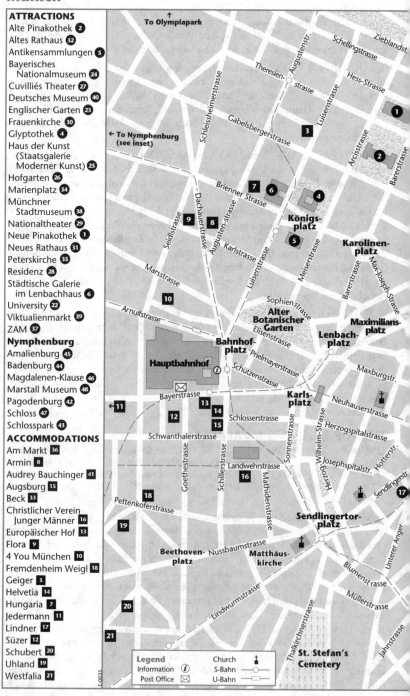

To Olympiapark

← **To Nymphenburg**
(see inset)

Zieblandst

Schellingstrasse

Hess-Strasse

Theresien- strasse

Augustenstr.

Luisenstrasse

Arcisstrasse

Barerstrasse

Schleissheimerstrasse

Gabelsbergerstrasse

Brienner Strasse

Dachauerstrasse

Augusten-strasse

Karlstrasse

Luisenstrasse

Meiserstrasse

Barerstrasse

Max-Joseph-Strasse

Königs-platz

Karolinen-platz

Seidlstrasse

Marsstrasse

Arnulfstrasse

Sophienstrasse

Alter Botanischer Garten

Elisenstrasse

Maximilians-platz

Lenbach-platz

Bahnhof-platz

Hauptbahnhof

Prielmayerstrasse

Schützenstrasse

Maxburgstr.

Bayerstrasse

Karls-platz

Neuhauserstrasse

Schlosserstrasse

Herzogspitalstrasse

Schwanthalerstrasse

Sonnenstrasse

Wilhelm-Strasse

Hotterstr.

Goethestrasse

Schillerstrasse

Landwehrstrasse

Mathildenstrasse

Herzog

Josephspitalstr.

Sendlingerstr.

Sendlingertor-platz

Pettenkoferstrasse

Beethoven-platz

Nussbaumstrasse

Matthäus-kirche

Unter Anger

Lindwurmstrasse

Blumenstrasse

Müllerstrasse

Jahnstrasse

Thalkirchnerstrasse

St. Stefan's Cemetery

Legend
Information ⓘ
Post Office ✉

Church ✝
S-Bahn ○
U-Bahn ▭

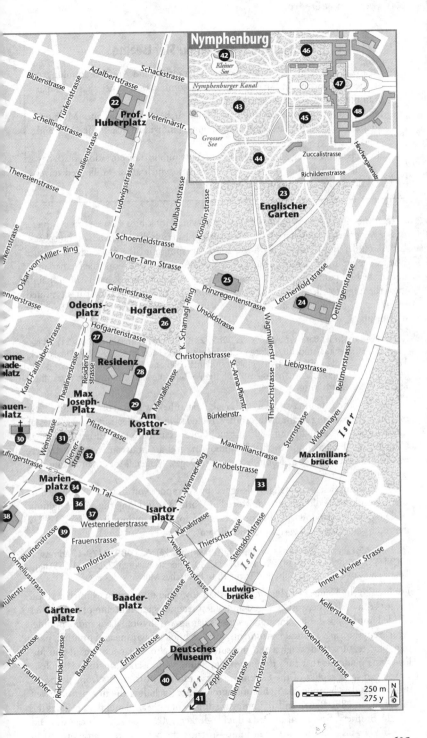

Nymphenburg

Blütenstraße
Adalbertstraße
Schackstraße
Türkenstraße
Schellingstraße
Amalienstraße
22
Prof.-
Huberplatz
Veterinärstr.
Theresienstraße
Ludwigstraße
Kaulbachstraße
Königinstraße

42
Kleiner
See
46
Nymphenburger Kanal
47
43
45
48
Grosser
See
44
Zuccalistrasse
Richildenstrasse
Hirschgartenstr.

23
Englischer
Garten

Schoenfeldstrasse
Von-der-Tann Strasse
Turkenstrasse
Oskar-von-Miller- Ring
ennerstrasse
Galeriestrasse
Odeons-
platz
Hofgarten
Hofgartenstrasse
26
Prinzregentenstrasse
25
Lerchenfold strasse
24
Oettingenstrasse
Unsöldstrasse
K. Scharnagl- Ring
Wagmüllerstr.

ome-
ade-
latz
Kard.-Faulhaber-Strasse
Theatinerstrasse
Residenz-
strasse
27
Residenz
28
Christophstrasse
St.-Anna-Pfarrstr.
Liebigstrasse
Reitmorstrasse

auen-
latz
30
31
Weinstrasse
Diener-
strasse
Max
Joseph-
Platz
Pfisterstrasse
29
Am
Kosttor-
Platz
Marstallstrasse
Bürkleinstr.
Maximilianstrasse
Sternstrasse
Widenmayer
Isar

ufingerstrasse
32
Knöbelstrasse
Maximilians-
brücke
Marien-
platz **34**
35
Im Tal
36
37
Isartor-
platz
Th.-Wimmer-Ring
33
38
Westenriederstrasse
39
Frauenstrasse
Rumfordstr.
Kanalstrasse
Thierschtstrasse
Zweibrückenstrasse
Steinsdorfstrasse
Isar
Innere Weiner Strasse
Corneliusstrasse
Blumenstrasse
Kellerstrasse

üllerstr.
Gärtner-
platz
Baader-
platz
Baaderstrasse
Morassistrasse
Erhardtstrasse
Ludwigs-
brücke
Rosenheimerstrasse
Klenzestrasse
Fraunhofer
Reichenbachstrasse
Deutsches
Museum
40
Zeppelinstrasse
Lillenstrasse
Hochstrasse
Isar
41

0 ——— 250 m
275 y
N

Getting the Best Deal on Sightseeing

- Be aware that some museums, like the Glyptothek and Antikensammlungen or the Alte and Neue Pinakothek, offer a combination ticket that's cheaper than buying a separate ticket for each.
- Note that some museums and attractions, such as the Deutsches Museum, offer a family ticket that's cheaper than buying individual tickets for adults and children.
- If you plan on doing a lot of sightseeing using public transportation in a 1-day period, purchase the Munich Welcome Card, which allows unlimited travel and discounts of up to 50% on selected sights.

In Albrecht Altdorfer's *Battle of Alexander*, which took him 12 years to complete, notice the painstaking detail of the thousands of lances and all the men on horseback. Yet Alexander the Great on his horse is easy to spot amid the chaos, as he pursues Darius fleeing in his chariot. Another favorite is Adriaen Brouwer of the Netherlands, one of the best painters of the peasant genre. The Alte Pinakothek has 17 of his paintings, the largest collection in the world. *Cabinet 10*, in which Brouwer has captured the life of his subjects as they drink at an inn, play cards, or engage in a brawl, is delightful.

Neue Pinakothek. Barer Strasse 29. ☎ **089/238 05-195.** Admission 7DM ($4) adults, 4DM ($2.30) seniors/students/children. Combination ticket for Alte and Neue Pinakothek, 12DM ($7) adults, 6DM ($3.40) seniors/students/children. Tues 10am–8pm, Wed–Sun 10am–5pm. U-Bahn: U-2 to Theresienstrasse, then a 7-minute walk. Tram: 27 to Pinakothek. Bus: 53 to Schellingstrasse.

Across from the Alte Pinakothek is the Neue Pinakothek, with its comprehensive view of European painting in the 19th century. Included in the collection are examples of international art from around 1800 (David, Goya, Gainsborough, Turner), as well as German and French impressionism, symbolism, and art nouveau. Corinth, Liebermann, Cézanne, Gaughin, Rodin, van Gogh, Degas, Manet, Monet, and Renoir all have canvases here.

The building itself is a delight, designed by Alexander von Branca and opened in 1981 to replace the old museum destroyed in World War II. Using the natural lighting of skylights and windows, it's the perfect setting for the paintings it displays. Follow the rooms chronologically, starting with Room 1.

✪ **Deutsches Museum.** Museumsinsel 1 (Ludwigsbrücke). ☎ **089/2179-1.** Admission 10DM ($5.70) adults, 7DM ($4) seniors, 4DM ($2.30) students/children, 22DM ($12.55) families. Daily 9am–5pm. S-Bahn: Isartor. Tram: 18 to Deutsches Museum.

I've been to the Deutsches Museum more than any other museum in Munich and still haven't seen it all. The world's largest and oldest technological museum of its kind, it's divided into 53 exhibits, including those relating to physics, navigation, mining, vehicle engineering, musical instruments, glass technology, writing and printing, photography, textiles, and weights and measures. There's also a planetarium. If you followed the guideline that runs through the museum, you'd walk more than 10 miles.

You can see a replica of the Gutenberg press, musical instruments from electronic drums to a glass harmonica, 50 historic automobiles (including the first petrol-driven motorcar, an 1886 Benz), and an impressive display of early airplanes that includes the Wright brothers' first serial plane (a double-decker 1909 Type A). You can descend into the bowels of a coal and a salt mine—it takes the better part of an hour just to walk through. Would you like to watch the developing of a black-and-white photograph? How about pondering the meaning behind the prehistoric drawings of the Altamira Cave? What makes the museum fascinating for adults and children alike is that there are buttons to push, gears to crank, and levers to pull. Don't miss it.

✪ **Nymphenburg Palace and Marstallmuseum, Amalienburg, and the Royal Pavilions.** Schloss Nymphenburg 1. ☎ **089/179 08-0.** Combination ticket to everything in summer (6 attractions), 8DM ($4.55) adults, 5DM ($2.85) seniors/students/children; combination ticket in winter (3 attractions), 6DM ($3.40) adults, 4DM ($2.30) seniors/students/children. Nymphenburg Palace only, 4DM ($2.30) adults, 3DM ($1.70) seniors/students/children. Nymphenburg Palace and Amalienburg, summer Tues–Sun 9am–12:30pm and 1:30–5pm; winter Tues–Sun 10am–12:30pm and 1:30–4pm. Marstallmuseum, summer Tues–Sun 9am–noon and 1–5pm; winter Tues–Sun 10am–noon and 1–4pm. Badenburg, Pagodenburg, and Magdalenenklause, summer Tues–Sun 10am–12:30pm and 1:30–5pm; closed Oct–Mar. Tram: 17 to Schloss Nymphenburg.

The former summer residence of the Wittelsbach family who ruled over Bavaria, Nymphenburg is Germany's largest baroque palace. Construction began in 1664 but took more than a century to complete; then the palace stretched 625 yards long and looked out over a park of some 500 acres. You could spend a whole day in just the sculptured garden, with its statues, lakes, botanical gardens, and waterfalls, and in its park pavilions (each a miniature palace in itself). But first visit the main palace and nearby Marstallmuseum for its outstanding collection of carriages.

There are no guided tours of Nymphenburg—you wander on your own in the two wings open to the public. On entering, the first room you'll see is the glorious Steinerne Saal (Stone Hall), two stories high and richly decorated in late rococo style with stucco work and frescoes, used for parties and concerts. But probably the most interesting room in gossip circles is Ludwig I's Gallery of Beauties. The 36 portraits, commissioned by Ludwig, represent the most beautiful women in Munich in his time, from all walks of life. Among them are Queen Marie of Bavaria (mother of Ludwig II), Helene Sedlmayr (daughter of a shoemaker), and Lola Montez, a dancer whose scandalous relations with Ludwig prompted an 1848 revolt by a disgruntled people who forced Ludwig's abdication. (Lola was banished and moved to California, where she made a name for herself during the Gold Rush days.)

Outside the main palace (to the left as you face the ticket booth) is the **Marstallmuseum,** with a splendid collection of state coaches, carriages, and sleds used for weddings, coronations, and special events. Housed in what used to be the royal stables, the museum culminates in the fantastic fairy-tale carriages of Ludwig II, which are no less extravagant than his castles. On the first floor above the Marstallmuseum is a fine collection of Nymphenburger porcelain, with delicate figurines, tea services, plates, and bowls from the mid–18th century to the 1920s.

Now head for the park. To your left is **Amalienburg,** a delightful, small pink hunting lodge unlike anything you've ever seen. One of the world's great masterpieces of rococo art, this lodge was built by François de Cuvilliés for Maria Amalia, Charles Albert's wife. Legend has it that she used to station herself on a platform on the roof to shoot game that were driven past her. The first couple of rooms in this lodge are simple enough (note the small dog kennels in the first room), with drawings in the spirit of the hunt, but then the rooms take off in a flight of fantasy, with an amazing amount of decorative silver covering the walls with vines, grapes, and cherubs. Its Hall of Mirrors is as splendid a room as you're likely to find anywhere, far surpassing anything in the main palace.

In the park are three pavilions: the **Magdalenenklause,** designed as a meditation retreat for Max Emanuel, complete with artificial cracks in the walls to make it look

---

Special & Free Events

Munich's most famous event is the **Oktoberfest,** held from mid-September to the first Sunday in October. The celebration began in 1810 to honor Ludwig I's marriage, when the main event was a horse race in a field called Theresienwiese. Everyone had so much fun that the celebration was held again the following year, and then again and again. Today the Oktoberfest is among the largest fairs in the world.

Every year the festivities get under way with a parade on the first Oktoberfest Sunday, with almost 7,000 participants marching through the streets in folk costumes. Most activities, however, are at the Theresienwiese, where huge beer tents sponsored by local Munich breweries dispense both beer and merriment, complete with Bavarian bands and singing. Each tent holds up to 6,000, which gives you some idea of how rowdy things can get. During the 16-day period of the Oktoberfest, an estimated 6 million visitors guzzle over a million gallons of beer and eat 700,000 broiled chickens—pure gluttony, and a lot of fun! In addition to the beer tents, there are carnival attractions and amusement rides. Entry to the fairgrounds is free, though rides cost extra.

During the last 2 weeks in April, a smaller **Frühlingsfest (Spring Festival)** is held at Theresienwiese; it gives a taste of the Oktoberfest without the crowds and tourists.

Munich's other major event is **Fasching (Carnival),** which culminates Shrove Tuesday in a parade through town and a festive atmosphere of food and drink at the Viktualienmarkt. From the end of November until Christmas, an outdoor **Christmas Market** brings color and cheer to the Old City.

---

like a ruin; the **Pagodenburg,** an elegant two-story tea pavilion, with Dutch tiles on the ground floor and Chinese black-and-red-lacquered chambers upstairs; and **Badenburg,** Max Emanuel's bathhouse with its Chinese wallpaper and two-story pool faced with Dutch tiles (this qualifies as Europe's first heated indoor pool). Afterward, stop for a coffee and cake at the **Schlosscafe** in the Palmenhaus, a greenhouse built in 1820 with outdoor seating.

The Residenz, Residenzmuseum, and Schatzkammer. Max-Joseph-Platz 3. ☎ **089/29 06 71.** Combination ticket for the Residenzmuseum and Schatzkammer, 10DM ($6) adults, 6DM ($3.40) seniors/students, free for age 15 and under. Ticket for either the Residenzmuseum or the Schatzkammer, 6DM ($3.40) adults, 4DM ($2.30) seniors/students. Tues–Sun 10am–4:30pm (you must enter by 4pm). S-Bahn: Marienplatz. U-Bahn: U-3, U-4, U-5, or U-6 to Odeonsplatz. Tram: 19 to Nationaltheater.

While Nymphenburg Palace was the Wittelsbach summer home, the Residenz was the family's official in-town residence for 4 centuries until 1918. The **Residenzmuseum,** a small part of the residence, is open to the public. Though it's a mere fraction of the total palace, it's so large that I wonder how its inhabitants ever managed to find their way around. In fact, it's so large that only half the museum's 160 rooms are open to the public in the morning; the other half is open in the afternoon. No matter when you come, you'll see court rooms, apartments, bedchambers, and arcades in everything from Renaissance and baroque to rococo and neoclassical. The Antiquarium is the largest Renaissance room north of the Alps; in the Silver Chamber is the complete table silver of the House of Wittelsbach—some 3,500 pieces. The Ancestors Hall contains the portraits of 121 members of the Wittelsbach family—eerie because of the

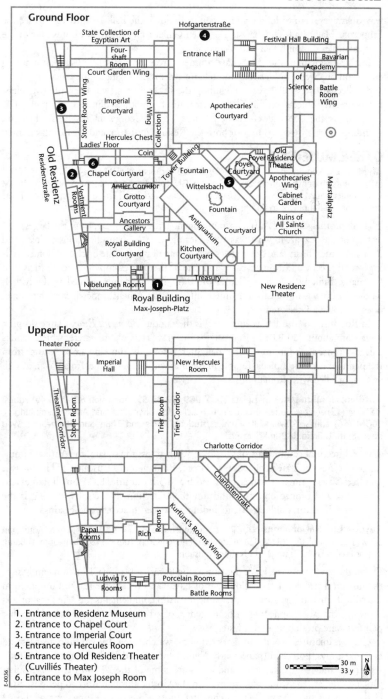

The Residenz

Ground Floor

Hofgartenstraße

4

State Collection of Egyptian Art

Four-shaft Room

Entrance Hall

Festival Hall Building

Bavarian Academy

Court Garden Wing

of

Science

Battle Room Wing

Stone Room Wing

Imperial Courtyard

Trier Wing

Apothecaries' Courtyard

3

Hercules Chest

Collection

Ladies' Floor

Coin

Tower Building

Fountain

Old Residenz Theater

Foyer

Foyer Courtyard

6

Chapel Courtyard

2

Wittelsbach

5

Apothecaries' Wing

Old Residenz

Residenzstraße

Antler Corridor

Fountain

Cabinet Garden

Vestment Rooms

Grotto Courtyard

Antiquarium

Courtyard

Ruins of All Saints Church

Marstallplatz

Ancestors Gallery

Royal Building Courtyard

Kitchen Courtyard

Treasury

New Residenz Theater

Nibelungen Rooms

1

Royal Building
Max-Joseph-Platz

Upper Floor

Theater Floor

Theatiner Corridor

Imperial Hall

New Hercules Room

Stone Room

Trier Room

Trier Corridor

Charlotte Corridor

Charlottentrakt

Kurfürst's Rooms Wing

Rooms

Papal Rooms

Rich

Ludwig I's Rooms

Porcelain Rooms

Battle Rooms

1. Entrance to Residenz Museum
2. Entrance to Chapel Court
3. Entrance to Imperial Court
4. Entrance to Hercules Room
5. Entrance to Old Residenz Theater (Cuvilliés Theater)
6. Entrance to Max Joseph Room

0   30 m
   33 y

N

E-0036

way their eyes seem to follow you as you walk down the hall. Be sure, too, to see the Emperor's Hall, the Rich Chapel, the Green Gallery, and the Rich Rooms, one of the best examples of South German rococo.

In the Residenz is also the Schatzkammer (Treasure House), housing an amazing collection of jewelry, gold, silver, and religious items belonging to the Bavarian royalty and collected over 1,000 years, including the royal crown, swords, scepters, goblets, bowls, toiletry objects, serving platters, treasures from other countries, and more. The highlight is the 1586 jewel-studded Statue of St. George on his horse. Plan on spending at least 1½ hours to tour both the Residenzmuseum and the Schatzkammer.

OTHER MUSEUMS

Glyptothek. Königsplatz 3. ☎ **089/28 61 00.** Admission 6DM ($3.40) adults, 3.50DM ($2) seniors/students; combination ticket for Glyptothek and Antikensammlungen, 10DM ($6) adults, 5DM ($2.85) seniors/students. Tues–Wed and Fri–Sun 10am–5pm, Thurs noon–8pm. U-Bahn: U-2 to Königsplatz.

The Glyptothek and the Antikensammlungen, across the square, form the largest collection of classical art in what was West Germany. The Glyptothek houses Greek and Roman statues, busts, and grave steles in a setting of plain white brick and domed ceilings, reminiscent of a Roman bath, and one of the best examples of neoclassicism in Germany. Built by Leo von Klenze, the building was commissioned by Ludwig I, whose dream was to transform Munich into another Athens. Indeed, the Glyptothek does resemble a Greek temple.

In Room II (to your left as you enter) is the famous *Barberini Faun,* a large sleeping satyr from about 220 B.C. In Room IV is the grave stele of Mnesarete, which depicts a dead mother seated in front of her daughter. Also in the museum are sculptures from the pediments of the Aphaia Temple in Aegina, with scenes of the Trojan War, as well as a room filled with Roman busts.

Antikensammlungen. Königsplatz 1. ☎ **089/59 83 59.** Admission 6DM ($3.40) adults, 3.50DM ($2) seniors/students; combination ticket for Glyptothek and Antikensammlungen, 10DM ($6) adults, 5DM ($2.85) seniors/students. Tues and Thurs–Sun 10am–5pm, Wed noon–8pm. U-Bahn: U-2 to Königsplatz.

The architectural counterpart of the Glyptothek across the square, the Antikensammlungen houses the state's collection of Greek, Roman, and Etruscan art. The focus is on Greek vases (primarily Attic from the 6th and 5th centuries B.C.). Small statues and terra-cotta and bronze objects round out the collection. Particularly striking is the Greek and Etruscan gold jewelry, including necklaces, bracelets, and earrings.

Bayerisches Nationalmuseum. Prinzregentenstrasse 3. ☎ **089/211 24-1.** Admission 3DM ($1.70) adults, 2DM ($1.15) seniors/students/children. Tues–Sun 9:30am–5pm. U-Bahn: U-4 or U-5 to Lehel. Tram: 17 to Nationalmuseum.

Down the street from the Haus der Kunst, the Bavarian National Museum emphasizes the historical and cultural development of Bavaria, as well as the rest of Europe, from the Middle Ages to the 19th century. The museum complements the Alte Pinakothek, showing what was happening in other genres of art and crafts at the same time that painters were producing their masterpieces.

Glass, miniatures, wood and ivory carvings, watches, jewelry, clothing, textiles and tapestries, toys, porcelain (particularly Nymphenburg and Meissen), medieval armor, sculpture, and religious artifacts and altars are some of the 20,000 items on display. Outstanding are the wood sculptures from the Gothic through Rococo periods, especially carvings by Tilman Riemenschneider (notice the facial expressions of the 12 Apostles in Room 12), as well as works by Erasmus Grasser, Michael Pacher, Johann Baptist Staub, and Ignaz Günther, to name only a few.

One delightful thing about this museum is that the architecture complements the objects. The Late Gothic Church Art Room (Room 15), for example, is modeled after a church in Augsburg, providing a perfect background for the religious art it displays. Similarly, Room 9 is the Augsburg Weavers Room, while Room 10 is the interior of a cozy inn from Gothic times in Passau.

My favorite floor is the basement. Part of it is devoted to folk art, including furniture and complete rooms showing how people lived long ago. Notice the wooden floors and low ceiling (to save heat). The other half of the museum houses an incredible collection of nativity scenes *(Krippe)* from around Europe. Some of the displays are made of paper, while others are amazingly lifelike. Both the vastness and the quality of this collection are impressive.

Note: Because of renovations, parts of the museum will be closed until 2000. If you're interested in a specific collection, call ahead to make sure it's open at the time of your visit.

Staatsgalerie Moderner Kunst (State Gallery of Modern Art). In the Haus der Kunst, Prinzregentenstrasse 1. ☎ **089/21 12 71 37.** Admission 6DM ($3.40) adults, 3.50DM ($2) seniors/students/children. Tues–Wed and Fri–Sun 10am–5pm, Thurs 10am–8pm. U-Bahn: U-3 or U-6 to Odeonsplatz, then a 10-minute walk; or U-4 or U-5 to Lehel, then an 8-minute walk). Bus: 53 to Königinstrasse.

The State Gallery of Modern Art is in the west end of the massive columned Haus der Kunst (1937). The building is a product of Hitler's regime and now displays much of the modern art he tried to suppress. Devoted to art of the 20th century, it has a large collection of German works, particularly Klee, Marc, Ernst, Kirchner, and Beckmann. Other highlights are cubism, American abstract expressionism, surrealism, and art of the 1920s and 1930s, with works by Braque, Corinth, Dalí, Kandinsky, Kokoschka, Matisse, Mondrian, Picasso, and Warhol. The east wing features changing exhibits, for which there's a separate entrance fee.

Städtische Galerie im Lenbachhaus. In the Lenbach House, Luisenstrasse 33 (off Königsplatz, not far from the Glyptothek). ☎ **089/233-0320.** Admission 8DM ($4.55) adults, 4DM ($2.30) seniors/students; more for special exhibits. Tues–Sun 10am–6pm. U-Bahn: U-2 to Königsplatz.

The City Gallery is the showcase for Munich's artists from the Gothic period to the present, in a setting that couldn't be more perfect. The museum is the former Italianate villa of the artist Franz von Lenbach, built at the end of the last century. Some rooms have been kept as they were then.

Though landscape paintings from the 15th to the 19th centuries, as well as examples of German Jugendstil (art nouveau), are part of the collection, the great treasure is the Blaue Reiter (Blue Rider) group of artists. Wassily Kandinsky, one of the great innovators of abstract art, was a key member of this Munich-based group, and the Lenbach House has an outstanding collection of works of his early period, from shortly after the turn of the century to the outbreak of World War I. Other Blue Rider artists represented are Klee, Marc, Macke, and Münter.

ZAM—Zentrum für Aussergewöhnliche Museum (Center for Out-of-the-Ordinary Museums). Westenriederstrasse 41. ☎ **089/290 41 21.** Admission 8DM ($4.55) adults, 5DM ($2.85) students/age 4 and over. Daily 10am–6pm. S-Bahn: Isartor; or a 5-minute walk from Marienplatz.

This is actually six small museums in one, each unique. Where else, for example, can you find a museum devoted to the chamber pot? Other collections are devoted to pedal cars (the largest collection in the world, according to the *Guinness Book of World Records*), the life of Kaiserin Elisabeth of Austria, padlocks (used for locking everything from torture devices to chastity belts), perfume bottles, and the Easter rabbit! Each collection has its own room, and you can view the entire complex in about an hour. Explanations are only in German, but there's an English pamphlet.

BMW Museum. Petuelring 130. ☎ **089/3822-33 07.** Admission 5.50DM ($3.15) adults, 4DM ($2.30) students/seniors/children, 12DM ($6.85) families. Daily 9am–5pm (you must enter by 4pm). U-Bahn: U-3 to Olympiazentrum, then a 2-minute walk.

Anyone interested in cars, motorcycles, and the history of the automobile should stop here. Housed in a modern building resembling a giant silver bowl (or is it a wheel?), it features videos (including one describing how the future was imagined by people in the past—essentially, technology as a threat), slide shows, and displays of motors and cars from the days of the "oldies" to the age of the robot and beyond. A computer allows you to custom design your own BMW. Several displays explain in-car navigation systems and how they'll revolutionize personal transport.

Münchner Stadtmuseum. St. Jakobsplatz 1. ☎ **089/233-223 70.** Admission 5DM ($2.85) adults, 2.50DM ($1.40) seniors/students, 7.50DM ($4.25) families, free for age 5 and under; more for special exhibits. Tues and Thurs–Sun 10am–5pm, Wed 10am–8:30pm. S-Bahn/U-Bahn: Marienplatz.

The Munich City Museum relates the history of the city—but that's not all. The Puppet Theater Collection is outstanding, with puppets and theater stages from around the world, while the Musical Instrument Collection (open only in the afternoon) displays European instruments from the 16th to the 20th centuries and primitive instruments from around the world. There are also sections devoted to medieval weaponry, the history of photography, and life in Munich in the 17th, 18th, and 19th centuries, including parlors, dining rooms, kitchens, and bedrooms. But the most valuable pieces are the 10 Morris Dancers carved by Erasmus Grasser, completed in 1480 for display in Munich's old town hall. The morris (or morrice) dance, popular in the 15th century, was a rustic ambulatory dance performed by companies of actors at festivals.

A ZOO

Münchener Tierpark Hellabrunn (Munich Zoo). Tierparkstrasse Siebenbrunner Strasse 6. ☎ **089/62 50 80.** Admission 10DM ($5.70) adults, 7DM ($4) seniors/students, 5DM ($2.85) ages 4–14, free for age 3 and under. Summer daily 8am–6pm; winter daily 9am–5pm. U-Bahn: U-3 to Thalkirchen. Bus: 52.

Munich's zoo is home to 5,000 animals and includes the Elephant House (built in 1913); an aviary; a high-tech "Jungle World" with tropical plants, bats, and birds; an aquarium; and all the usual inhabitants like penguins, rhinos, and lions, in environments that mimic native habitats. It also has a petting zoo, playgrounds, and camel and pony rides.

PARKS & GARDENS

The **Englischer Garten** is one of the largest city parks in Europe. Despite its name, it owes its existence to an American rather than an Englishman. Benjamin Thompson, who fled America during the Revolution because of his British sympathies, was instrumental in the park's creation and landscaping. Stretching 3 miles along the Isar River in the heart of the city, it offers beer gardens, sunbathing (including nude sunbathing, a surprise to quite a few unsuspecting visitors), and recreation.

Much more formal are the 500 acres of **Nymphenburg Park** (see above). On the north end of Nymphenburg Park is the **New Botanical Garden,** but the most conveniently located garden is the **Hofgarten,** right off Odeonsplatz and laid out in the Italian Renaissance style.

ORGANIZED TOURS

For those who like to be guided, **Panorama Tours** of the Gray Line (☎ **089/59 15 04**) offers sightseeing trips of Munich lasting 1 to 2½ hours. The 1-hour trip is adequate for an overview, with buses departing from in front of the Hertie department store, across from the Hauptbahnhof, daily at 10am and 2:30pm (also at 11:30am May to October). The fare is 17DM ($10) for adults and 9DM ($5) for children. Daylong excursions are also offered, including one to Neuschwanstein and Linderhof costing 75DM ($43) adults and 38DM ($22) children; entrance fees are extra.

If you like cycling, a unique tour is offered by **Mike's Bike Tours of Munich** (☎ **089/651 42 75**); it passes sights like the Deutsches Museum, the Residenz, and the Hofbräuhaus as it follows bike paths along the Isar and through the Englischer Garten and Schwabing, with stops along the way for historical explanations and picture taking. Conducted in English and German, these leisurely 4-mile, 4-hour tours are 29DM ($17) and depart from underneath the Old Rathaus tower at the east end of Marienplatz daily at 11:30am and 4pm April to Oktoberfest and at 12:30pm in March and during Oktoberfest. No reservations are required. For more serious cycling, there's a 10-mile, 6-hour tour that includes the above but then goes farther afield to the Olympic Park and Nymphenburg Palace and includes two stops at beer gardens. It departs at 12:30pm and costs 39DM ($22); call to reserve a spot in this tour.

6 Shopping

As Germany's fashion center, Munich has upscale boutiques, department stores, and designer names, primarily in the pedestrian-zoned Old Town. If you're looking for souvenirs (beer mugs, Bavaria's simple blue-and-white pottery, porcelain, nutcrackers), your best bet in terms of price is the department stores, including **Hertie** (across from the Hauptbahnhof), **Karstadt** (on Karlstor, right off Stachus/Karlsplatz, and at Neuhauser Strasse 44), and **Kaufhof** (Karlsplatz 21–24 and on Marienplatz). For beer mugs and cuckoo clocks, try **Max Krug**, Neuhauser Strasse 2 (☎ **089/22 45 01**), in business since 1926.

Another good place to hunt for Bavarian and German souvenirs and gifts is along **Orlandostrasse,** about a 5-minute walk from Marienplatz near the Hofbräuhaus. This small pedestrian lane has several shops selling T-shirts, beer steins, dolls in Bavarian costume, pipes, postcards, Christmas tree ornaments, and nutcrackers.

RECOVERING VAT

If you purchase more than 60DM ($34) worth of goods from any one store and are taking your purchases out of the country, you can recover part of the **value-added tax (VAT),** 16% in Germany. Many shops, including those above, will issue a Tax Cheque at the time of purchase. Fill in the reverse side, and upon leaving the last European Union country you visit, present the articles to Customs. Airports in Berlin, Frankfurt, Munich, and other large cities have counters that will refund your money immediately.

MARKETS

Munich's most famous market is the **Viktualienmarkt,** from the early 1800s. Here you can buy bread, cheese, honey, cakes, fruit, wine, vegetables, and much more. It's a wonderful place to obtain picnic supplies. The market is open year-round, Monday to Friday 8am to 6pm and Saturday 8am to 2pm.

In summer, students set up shop on the east side of Leopoldstrasse, between Münchener Freiheit and Siegestor, to sell their artwork at the **Schwabinger Art Market,** held nightly from 6:30pm May to October.

If you're here in December, enjoy the **Christkindlmarkt** on Marienplatz, a colorful hodgepodge of stalls offering everything from Bavarian foods to Christmas decorations. It's held from the beginning of December to Christmas Eve.

Even better is the **Auer Dult,** a flea market lasting 8 days and held in April, July, and October. It has been a tradition for more than 600 years, currently held on Mariahilfplatz (take bus no. 52 from Marienplatz). Everything from spices, leather goods, jewelry, and sweaters to antiques, kitchen gadgets, and ceramics is sold, and there are rides and amusements for children. For more information, contact the tourist office.

7 Munich After Dark

Since commercial ticket agencies sell opera and theater tickets at a higher price to make a profit, it makes sense to buy your tickets directly from the theater or opera. To find out where you can buy tickets in advance, get a copy of the *Monatsprogramm,* issued monthly for 2.50DM ($1.40). It lists all major theaters and what's being played when. *Munich Found,* an English-language magazine costing 4DM ($2.30), lists operas, plays, classical concerts, rock and jazz concerts, movies, and more. Some venues, such as the Staatstheater am Gärtnerplatz, offers standing-room tickets you can buy in advance; others allow student discounts.

THE PERFORMING ARTS

THEATER & OPERA   Also known as the Altes Residenztheater, the **Cuvilliés Theater,** Residenzstrasse 1 (☎ 089/2185-1940; S-Bahn: Marienplatz; U-Bahn: Odeonsplatz or Marienplatz), is a small but sumptuous 18th-century work of art and Germany's finest rococo tier-boxed theater. Seating 400, it features mainly classical plays and chamber music. The box office, at Max-Joseph-Platz 1, is open Monday to Friday 10am to 6pm and Saturday 10am to 1pm. Tickets are 10DM to 53DM ($6 to $30).

Contemporary plays from German playwrights like Brecht, Böll, and Handke are presented at the **Münchner Kammerspiele—Schauspielhaus,** Maximilianstrasse 26 (☎ 089/237 213 28; Tram: 19 to Maximilianstrasse). You'll also find German productions of international plays, from Shakespeare to Albee. Its box office is open Monday to Friday 10am to 6pm and Saturday 10am to 1pm. Tickets are 10.50DM to 47.50DM ($6 to $27).

The **Nationaltheater (Bayerische Staatsoper)** is on Max-Joseph-Platz (☎ 089/2185-1920; S-Bahn/U-Bahn: Marienplatz, then a 3-minute walk). With opera performed in its original language, the Nationaltheater's Bavarian State Opera House is famous for its progressive versions of the classics. It also stages ballet. The box office, at Maximilianstrasse 11, is open Monday to Friday 10am to 6pm and Saturday 10am to 1pm. Tickets are 11DM to 20DM ($6 to $11) for most opera and 8DM to 10DM ($4.55 or $6) for ballet. Students can purchase standing-room tickets in advance for 6DM ($3.40). Students may also obtain unsold seats on the night of the performance for 12DM ($6), but only with presentation of a valid ID from their home university (an international student ID isn't enough).

At the **Residenztheater,** Max-Joseph-Platz 1 (☎ 089/2185-1940; S-Bahn/ U-Bahn: Marienplatz), the Bayerisches Staatsschauspiel performs classics in German, including Schiller, Goethe, Shakespeare, and Pirandello. Tickets, available in advance at the box office at Max-Joseph-Platz 1, Monday to Friday 10am to 6pm and Saturday 10am to 1pm, cost 20DM to 65DM ($11 to $37). And at the **Staatstheater am Gärtnerplatz,** Gärtnerplatz 3 (☎ 089/201 67 67; U-Bahn: Frauenhoferstrasse; Bus: 52 or 56 to Gärtnerplatz), you can see light operas, operettas, ballets, and musicals

A Note on Advance Tickets

Tickets you buy in advance for the Bayerische Staatsoper, Staatstheater am Gärtnerplatz, and several other venues are valid for use on Munich's public transport system at least 3 hours before the beginning of the performance until the end of services the same day. When buying your ticket, ask whether it's valid on the system.

beautifully performed, usually in German. Tickets are 25DM to 30DM ($14 to $17); in addition, standing-room tickets are available for 8DM to 13M ($4.55 to $7). For students, unsold seats are available for 12DM ($7) on the performance night.

CLASSICAL MUSIC The **Gasteig,** Rosenheimer Strasse 5 (☎ 089/480 98-0; S-Bahn: Rosenheimer Platz; Tram: 18 to Gasteig), serves as the stage for major concerts. Its largest concert hall, the Philharmonie, seats 2,400 and features performances of the Munich Philharmonic Orchestra (with James Levine as chief conductor), the Munich Bach Orchestra and Chorus, the Bavarian Radio Symphony Orchestra, and guest orchestras and ensembles. The Kleiner Konzertsaal (Small Concert Hall) features a wide range of musical talent, from flamenco guitar to concerts of Renaissance and baroque music. Tickets for the Munich Philharmonic Orchestra are 40DM to 200DM ($23 to $114).

At the **Prinzregententheater,** Prinzregentenplatz 12 (☎ **089/29 16 14 14;** U-Bahn: U-4 to Prinzregentenstrasse), built in 1901 with stunning art nouveau frescoes that Hitler considered decadent and ordered covered, you can see performances of the Bayerischen Staatsorchester (Bavarian State Orchestra), the Munich Philharmonic, and the Bavarian Radio Symphony Orchestra, as well as piano recitals, operas, and ballets. Here you'll also find the New Academy Theater, an experimental theater used by the Bavarian Academy of Performing Arts. Ticket prices vary.

LIVE-MUSIC CLUBS The intimate **Schwabinger Podium,** Wagnerstrasse 1, at the corner of Siegestrasse (☎ **089/39 94 82;** U-Bahn: U-3 or U-6 to Münchener Freiheit), is a great place in Schwabing to sit back and listen to rock, blues, oldies, and other popular music. It's open Sunday to Thursday 8pm to 1am and Friday and Saturday 8pm to 3am. Cover is 6DM ($3.40).

Mr. B's, Herzog-Heinrich-Strasse 38 (☎ **089/53 49 01;** U-Bahn: Goetheplatz), is one of the smallest places you'll find for jazz, blues, and rhythm—only three tables and a bar, with room for about 20 lucky people. Get there when it opens at 8pm Tuesday to Sunday; live music starts at about 9 or 9:30pm. Cover is usually 8DM ($4.55), but occasionally 12DM ($7) for big names.

BEER HALLS

About 10% cheaper than its sibling Augustiner Restaurant, next door, the **Augustiner Bierhalle,** Neuhauser Strasse 16, on the main pedestrian lane in Old Town (☎ **089/23 18 32 57;** S-Bahn/U-Bahn: Stachus/Karlsplatz or Marienplatz), is much smaller than the Hofbräuhaus, with correspondingly lower prices. It still, however, has typical Bavarian decor, with dark wood–paneled walls, wooden tables, and simple hooks for hats and coats. An English menu lists specialties like weisswurst, Munich-style sauerbraten, and handmade goulash with potatoes. It's open Monday to Saturday 9am to midnight and Sunday 10am to midnight. There's free live Dixieland music Sunday noon to 3pm.

Without a doubt, the **Hofbräuhaus,** Platzl 9 (☎ **089/22 16 76;** S-Bahn/U-Bahn: Marienplatz), which celebrates its 410th birthday in 1999, is the world's most famous beer hall. Everyone who has ever been to Munich has probably spent at least one evening here. There are several floors in this huge place, but the main hall is the ground-floor Schwemme. It features your typical Bavarian brass band, waitresses in dirndls, and tables full of friendly Germans who often break into song and link arms as they sway. If you've never been to the Oktoberfest, this place will give you an idea of what it's like. German food is available (there's also a first-floor restaurant), including various sausages, *leberkäs,* boiled pork knuckle with sauerkraut and potatoes, and roast chicken. It's open daily 9am to 11:30pm.

BARS

Once the center of everything bohemian, Schwabing today is more likely to be filled with out-of-towners than with natives. Still, it's definitely worth a stroll through Munich's most famous night district, and the crowds are still huge in summer. The busiest streets are the main boulevard, **Leopoldstrasse,** scene of a nightly art market in summer, and the smaller side streets, **Feilitzschstrasse** and **Occamstrasse,** near the Münchener Freiheit U-Bahn station. Here are a few places to whet your thirst:

The **Alt-Schwabinger Wirtshaus,** Occamstrasse 8 (☎ **089/33 48 46;** U-Bahn: U-3 or U-6 to Münchener Freiheit), under various names and ownership, has been a part of the Schwabing nightlife scene for almost 20 years, attracts a slightly older crowd than some of the other bars, and is simply decorated with the usual wooden floor, large bar area, and wooden tables. Thursday features a free live band playing oldies beginning at 9pm; Sunday there's free jazz 4 to 8pm. It's open Monday to Thursday 6pm to 1am, Friday and Saturday 3pm to 3am, and Sunday 3pm to 1am.

Dingsbums, Occamstrasse 5 (☎ **089/34 99 01;** U-Bahn: U-3 or U-6 to Münchener Freiheit), is a tiny place, complete with a disc jockey who plays oldies and top hits; it really packs 'em in, and in case you're interested, there seem to be many more men than women. The specialty is the *ein meter Pils oder Alt,* a 1-meter (1-yd.) wooden board with 15 small beers on it. For a half liter of beer you'll pay 5.80DM ($3.30); for *ein meter Pils oder Alt,* 43DM ($25). It opens daily at 8pm, closing at 1am weekdays and 3am Friday and Saturday.

The 111 kinds of beer from 25 countries are the claim to fame of **Haus der 111 Biere,** Franzstrasse 3 (☎ **089/33 12 48;** U-Bahn: U-3 or U-6 to Münchener Freiheit), open Monday to Thursday 4pm to 1am, Friday 4pm to 3am, Saturday 3pm to 3am, and Sunday and holidays 3pm to 1am. Its two floors are often packed with people from around the world, and it's easy to strike up a conversation. Much newer and trendier than the bars above is **Roxy,** 48 Leopoldstrasse (☎ **089/34 92 92;** U-Bahn: U-3 or U-6 to Giselastrasse). Its glass facade overlooks the action on Leopoldstrasse; in summer you can sit at its sidewalk cafe. It offers breakfast all day, sandwiches, pasta, and burgers and is open daily 8am to 3am.

GAY & LESBIAN BARS

Much of Munich's gay and lesbian scene takes place south of Old Town, particularly on **Müllerstrasse** and **Hans-Sachs-Strasse.**

At Munich's premier gay disco, **New York,** Sonnenstrasse 25 (☎ **089/59 10 56;** U-Bahn: U-1, U-2, U-3, or U-6 to Sendlingertorplatz), the strident rhythms and electronic sounds might've been imported from New York, Los Angeles, or Paris. The sound system is accompanied by laser light shows. The crowd ranges from 20 to 35 and often wears jeans. It's open daily 11pm to 4am. There's no cover Monday to Thursday but a 10DM ($6) cover on Friday and Saturday, including the first drink.

The **Teddy Bar,** Hans-Sachs-Strasse 1 (☎ **089/260 33 59;** U-Bahn: U-1, U-2, U-3, or U-6 to Sendlingertorplatz; Tram: 17), is a cozy gay bar that draws a congenial crowd, both foreign and domestic. There's no cover. From October to April, Sunday brunch is 11am to 3pm. The bar's open Sunday to Thursday 6pm to 1am and Friday and Saturday 6pm to 3am. Across the street is **Nil,** Hans-Sachs-Strasse 2 (☎ **089/26 55 45;** U-Bahn: U-1, U-2, U-3, or U-6 to Sendlingertorplatz; Tram: 17), an unpretentious gay bar that's fairly quiet during the day but packed at night. It's open daily 3pm to 4am.

Just around the corner, at Ickstattstrasse 2a, is **Mylord** (☎ **089/260 44 98;** U-Bahn: U-1, U-2, U-3, or U-6 to Sendlingertorplatz; Tram: 17), opened more than 30 years ago and once a popular lesbian hangout. Today the artsy crowd that may include dancers, musicians, artists, and actors ranges from mixed to homosexual, transvestite to transsexual, drawn by the comfortable living-room atmosphere cultivated by the friendly proprietress, Marietta. It's open Sunday to Thursday 6pm to 1am and Friday and Saturday 6pm to 3am.

DANCE CLUBS

Dance clubs in Munich are suffering from elitism. Most have doors with one-way mirrors that can be opened only from the inside—so the doorman can look over potential customers and decide whether they're the right material. In winter, coats must be checked (for a small fee).

People come to **Far Out,** Am Kosttor 2, near the Hofbräuhaus (☎ **089/22 66 62** or 089/22 66 61; S-Bahn/U-Bahn: Marienplatz, then a 7-minute walk northeast), primarily to dance; there's a conspicuous lack of seating. It gets so crowded on weekends that the doorman lets in only regular patrons. On Wednesday the music tends to be mellower, drawing an older crowd. There are more than 70 cocktails on its menu, and sandwiches and ice cream are available. It's open Wednesday to Friday and Sunday 10pm to 4am and Saturday 11pm to 6am. The cover is 5DM ($2.85) Sunday and Wednesday and 10DM ($6) Thursday, Friday, and Saturday.

If you're in your early 20s, head to **Kunstpark Ost,** Grafingerstrasse 6 (☎ **089/49 00 35 17;** S-Bahn/U-Bahn: Ostbahnhof), one of Europe's largest youth entertainment complexes, with clubs, bars, cinemas, galleries, and even a weekend flea market. A disco is open Friday and Saturday from 10pm, with admission 10DM to 15DM ($6 to $9). Concerts ranging from jazz to rock are staged at three venues, Babylon, Incognito, and Colosseum, as well as at bars like the huge Kalibar and Milchundbar, both open Sunday to Thursday 9pm to 3am.

Sunset, Leopoldstrasse 69 (☎ **089/39 03 03;** U-Bahn: U-3 or U-6 to Münchener Freiheit), is a small basement place that's more democratic than most, allowing as many as will fit through its doors. Because of its location in Schwabing, it attracts both Germans and foreigners, most in their 20s. Admission is free except on Friday and Saturday, when it's 5DM ($2.85). Sunset is open Sunday and Tuesday to Thursday 10pm to 4am and Friday and Saturday 9pm to 5am.

8 Side Trips: Neuschwanstein & Dachau

If you don't have a Eurailpass, there are a couple of other options for train travel in Bavaria worth considering if there are at least two of you. Though offers may change through 1999, examples of special tickets available at press time include the **Schönes Wochenende (Weekend Ticket),** costing 35DM ($20) and allowing two adults and up to three children to travel on local trains on Saturday or Sunday, and the **Bayern Ticket,** available for 35DM ($20) for two adults and up to four children and valid for 1 day Monday to Friday 9am to 4pm as well as 6pm to 2am the following day. Inquire at EurAide at the Hauptbahnhof for more information on these and other bargain tickets.

NEUSCHWANSTEIN

Of the dozens of castles dotting the Bavarian countryside, none is as famous as ✪ **Neuschwanstein** (☎ **08362/81035**), created by the extravagant Bavarian king Ludwig II. No doubt you've seen pictures of this fairy-tale castle, perched on a cliff above the town of Hohenschwangau, but even if you haven't it'll seem familiar, for this is the castle that served as the model for Walt Disney's castle at Disneyland.

Construction on Ludwig II's most famous castle began in 1869, but only a third of the original plans had been completed at the time of his mysterious death in 1886 (his body, as well as the body of his doctor, was found floating in a lake, but no one has ever proven whether he was murdered or committed suicide). Neuschwanstein, one of several overly ornate castles Ludwig left to the world, is a lesson in extravagance and fantasy, with almost every inch covered in gilt, stucco, wood carvings, and marble mosaics. Swans are used as a motif throughout, and Ludwig's admiration of Richard Wagner is expressed in operatic themes virtually everywhere, including murals illustrating *Tristan and Isolde* in his bedroom, the most opulent room in the palace—it took 14 artisans more than 4 years to produce the elaborate wood carvings.

You can see the castle by joining a 35-minute guided tour, available in English (avoid weekends in summer, when the wait to get in can be as long as 2 hours). The tour is 11DM ($6) adults and 8DM ($4.55) seniors/students; age 14 and under are free. It's open daily: April to September 9am to 5:30pm and October to March 10am to 4pm; it's closed January 1, Shrove Tuesday, November 1, and December 24, 25, and 31. Incidentally, the guided tour requires climbing 165 stairs and descending 181 stairs. In addition, it takes about 30 minutes to walk up the hill from the Hohenschwangau bus stop to Neuschwanstein. An alternative is to take one of the horse-drawn carriages for 8DM ($4.55) per person that will take you two-thirds of the way, but it's still a 10-minute climb from the carriage stop to the castle.

Although overshadowed by Neuschwanstein and not quite as fanciful, there's another worthwhile castle here: **Hohenschwangau Castle** (☎ **08362/821127**), built in the 1830s by Ludwig II's father, Maximilian II. Young Ludwig spent much of his childhood here, where he was greatly influenced by the castle's many murals depicting the saga of the Swan Knight Lohengrin, immortalized in an opera by Wagner. Charging 11DM ($6) adults and 8DM ($4.55) seniors/students/children (free for under age 6) for 35-minute guided tours, it's open daily: mid-March to mid-October 8:30am to 5:30pm and late October to early March 9:30am to 4pm.

To reach Neuschwanstein, take the **train** from Munich's Hauptbahnhof to Füssen, a 2-hour trip costing 34DM ($19) one way. From in front of Füssen station, take the **bus** from platform 2 (2.40DM/$1.35) to Hohenschwangau. For more information on the castles or Hohenschwangau, contact the **Hohenschwangau tourist information office** (☎ **08362/81 98 40**), in front of the bus stop and open daily in summer 9am to 6pm and in winter 9:30am to 4pm (closed November to mid-December).

DINING **Müller,** Alpseestrasse (☎ **08362/81991**), is on Hohenschwangau's main road in the middle of the village, between the two castles. Hohenschwangau's largest restaurant, with an outdoor beer garden, it has an English menu offering traditional Bavarian and international food, including trout, sausage, Wiener schnitzel, spaghetti, and pork chops, with platters costing 9.50DM to 23DM ($5 to $13). American Express, Diners Club, MasterCard, and Visa are accepted, and it's open daily 8am to 11pm.

More picturesque is the **Hotel-Schlossrestaurant** (☎ **08362/81110**), about two-thirds of the way up the hill to Neuschwanstein (at the carriage drop-off). Try to get a seat outside. Its English menu, with platters costing 9.50DM to 18.90DM ($5 to

$11), lists pork with horseradish, bacon and french fries, pancakes filled with boiled ham or apples and cranberries, chicken, perch fillet, sausage, chicken, and more. It's open daily: 9am to 6pm in summer and 10am to 5pm in winter. No credit cards are accepted.

DACHAU

About 12 miles from Munich is **Dachau,** site of Germany's first concentration camp under the Hitler regime and now a memorial to those who died under the Nazis. Some 200,000 prisoners—primarily political and religious dissidents, Jews, Gypsies, and other "undesirables"—passed through Dachau's gates between 1933 and 1945, of whom 32,000 lost their lives, mostly from disease, starvation, torture, execution, and medical experiments.

At the **KZ-Gedenkstätte Dachau (Concentration Camp Memorial),** Alte Römerstrasse 75 (☎ **08131/17 41**), a few of the camp's original buildings have been preserved or reconstructed, including a couple barracks with rows of bunkers, guard towers, morgue, and crematorium, in a landscaping that even today is bleak and desolate. But what really makes a visit here a sobering experience is the museum, with photograph after photograph illustrating the horrors of the Holocaust. They show the expressionless faces of children with the eyes of the old, bodies piled high on top of each other, and prisoners so malnourished they can't walk. Since most explanations are only in German, be sure to see the 25-minute English documentary, shown at 11:30am and 2 and 3:30pm. In addition, free 2-hour guided tours in English are offered at 12:30pm: Tuesday to Sunday June to August and Saturday, Sunday, and holidays September to May. Note that the memorial isn't recommended for children under 12.

Visiting the Dachau concentration camp isn't pleasant, but perhaps it's necessary: A plaque near the museum exit reminds us that those who forget the past are destined to repeat it. If you need something a bit uplifting after visiting the camp, walk through the older medieval city in the center of Dachau, which has a history stretching back 1,200 years and was once known for its artists' colony.

Admission to the Dachau memorial is free, and it's open Tuesday to Sunday 9am to 5pm. To get there, take **S-Bahn S-2** going in the direction of Petershausen to Dachau (about a 20-minute ride). A one-way ticket costs 6.80DM ($3.90), or use four strips on the Streifenkarte; otherwise, buy a Tageskarte for the entire metropolitan area for 16DM ($9). In Dachau, transfer to **bus no. 726** to the KZ-Gedenkstätte stop or **bus no. 724** to the K-Z Gedenkstätte-Parkplatz.

20 Nice & the Côte d'Azur

by Jeanne Oliver

The Côte d'Azur is a name that exerts an almost hypnotic pull on the imagination. The mountains of Provence meet the sea to form one of the world's most dramatic coastlines, studded with harbors and bays, hamlets and beach resorts. Bathed in sun and breezes, the fertile region is carpeted with olive trees, pines, and fragrant flowers.

Painters Paul Signac and Henri Matisse were the first to fall under the spell of the Côte d'Azur (Azure Coast), followed by English aristocrats looking to escape foggy London winters. Pablo Picasso, Marc Chagall, Fernand Léger, and Coco Chanel gravitated to the coast in the first half of the 20th century, transforming fishing villages into flourishing artist colonies.

The transition from artist colonies to megaresorts began with the first Cannes Film Festival in 1946, which added a potent dose of tinsel-town glamor to the region's natural allure. Ten years later, a bikini-clad Brigitte Bardot cavorted on a St-Tropez beach in the 1956 film *And God Created Woman* and set off a stampede of visitors in search of sun, sea, and sex. That same year, Grace Kelly married Prince Rainier in Monaco and it seemed that on this rocky coast of fairy-tale beauty dreams really could come true.

Many people now complain that this region has been "ruined" by an influx of visitors and rampant overdevelopment. While not exactly a Paradise Lost, it has become a paradise somewhat obscured by horrendous traffic jams, bland apartment blocks, and tacky souvenir shops. Still, this sun-drenched coast offers something for everyone. Whether your passion is browsing art museums, local markets, or chic shops, whether you're a beach stroller or a high roller or simply want to enjoy the dazzling scenery, you'll find your own paradise on the Côte d'Azur.

Nice, among the least expensive of France's resorts, is a good base for exploring the region. At the center of the Côte d'Azur, it's very much a Mediterranean city. Life is lived out on cafe terraces, in parks and gardens, and on the promenade des Anglais curving around the sparkling bay. In Vieux Nice, the medieval part of the city, narrow streets wind through pastel-colored houses and open onto intimate squares.

REQUIRED DOCUMENTS   See chapter 21 on Paris.

OTHER FROMMER'S TITLES   For more on Nice and the Côte d'Azur, see *Frommer's Provence & the Riviera, Frommer's France,*

Budget Bests

Most of the **beach** is free in Nice, though it's a beach of pebbles rather than one of comfy sand. Strolling the **promenade des Anglais** along the azure sea is free, and there's no charge for wandering the back streets of **Vieux Nice.**

The fine Mediterranean climate and lush parks make **picnicking** a delight that can cut costs considerably. Try the *pan bagnat,* a small round bread loaf stuffed with salade niçoise–type goodies and moistened with olive oil. Look for it in streetside kiosks, *boulangeries* (bakeries), and *charcuteries* (France's delicatessens). Expect to pay 15F to 20F ($2.50 to $3.30).

Frommer's Gay & Lesbian Europe, Frommer's Europe, or *Frommer's Europe's Greatest Driving Tours.*

1 Nice Deals & Discounts

SPECIAL DISCOUNTS

FOR EVERYONE Nice doesn't offer many special discounts. However, you should know that buying tickets on a city bus costs far more than buying them beforehand at a kiosk, newsstand, bookstore, or shop. One ticket costs 8F ($1.30), but if you by a *carnet* (**book**) of 10 tickets the price drops to 6.80F ($1.10) each. Another way to save money on transport is to buy a *billet touristique* (**tourist ticket**), allowing you to board any bus and travel as much as you like during 1 full day for 22F ($3.65).

The *cartes touristiques* are bus passes good for several days of unlimited travel on the TN (Transports Urbains de Nice); the 5-day pass is 85F ($14) and the 7-day pass 110F ($18). For more information, ask at the tourist office or any shop or newsstand selling bus tickets; or you can drop in at the **Centre d'Information TN,** 10 av. Félix-Faure, at the corner of rue Gubernatis (☎ **04-93-16-52-10**), open Monday to Friday 7:15am to 7pm and Saturday 7:15am to 6pm.

Also note that there's a **special museum pass (passe musées)** that costs 40F ($7) and offers free admission to all Nice museums for a week. You can buy one in any museum or tourist office.

FOR STUDENTS Students can save money at some museums by showing the **International Student Identity Card (ISIC).** As for the buses, students are entitled to **discount tickets** (bought in books of 10), but first you must apply for a special student identity card, costing 60F ($10) at the ticket kiosk in the central bus station, 10 av. Félix-Faure, or at Bus Masséna, Galerie Marchande du Parc Autos, place Masséna.

Nice has a major university and a large student population. For information on low youth and student fares, inexpensive tours and charter flights, and other deals, head for **Usit Voyages,** at 10 rue Belgique (☎ **04-93-87-34-96**)—it's the Council Travel representative—or the **Office du Tourisme Universitaire,** 80 bd. E.-Herriot (☎ **04-93-37-43-30**).

WORTH A SPLURGE

Scrimp on everything else but budget enough money to **rent a car** for a day and enjoy the incomparable scenic drives that surround Nice. The Grande Corniche road running from Nice to Menton offers spectacular views over the coast and on the Route Napoléon that twists north through the Alps to Sisteron (and beyond) you'll pass lakes, lavender fields, and remote mountain villages. Another superb drive is

What Things Cost in Nice	U.S. $
Taxi from the airport to the city center	16.00
Public transportation for an average trip within the city limits	1.60
Local telephone call	.20
Double room at the Hôtel Négresco (deluxe)	470.00
Double room at the Hôtel Ibis (moderate)	74.00
Double room at the Hôtel Notre-Dame (budget)	33.00
Lunch for one, without wine, at Lou Balico (moderate)	15.00
Lunch for one, without wine, at Saetone (budget)	11.00
Dinner for one, without wine, at Chantecler (deluxe)	100.00
Dinner for one, without wine, at La Taverne de l'Opéra (moderate)	20.00
Dinner for one, without wine, at Au Soleil (budget)	10.00
Glass of wine	2.40
Coca-Cola	1.60
Cup of coffee	3.00
Roll of ASA 100 color film, 36 exposures	5.00
Admission to Musée Masséna	4.00
Movie ticket	6.50
Train ticket (one-way) to Monaco	3.15

route D2210 running through the dramatic gorges of the Loup Valley on the edge of Vence.

2 Essentials

ARRIVING

BY PLANE   The **Aéroport Nice–Côte d'Azur** ranks just after Paris's airports in terms of activity. It's at the western edge of town, on the coast only 5 miles from downtown, and has two terminals. Terminal 1 receives international flights and Terminal 2 is for domestic flights. Public **bus no. 23** runs the route between the airport and the central train station. The bus will take you to the train station Monday to Friday about every 20 minutes and Saturday and Sunday about every 30 minutes 6am to 10:30pm, charging 8F ($1.30) for the 30-minute trip.

Even more convenient is the airport **Express bus,** which runs from Terminals 1 and 2 along the promenade des Anglais to the bus station (Gare Routière) about every 20 minutes. The 20-minute trip is 21F ($3.50). For information, call ☎ **04-93-56-35-40.**

A **taxi,** by contrast, will cost about 100F ($17) for the trip from the airport into town, depending on your final destination and traffic conditions.

BY TRAIN   If you're traveling to Nice from Paris, you can save on accommodations by taking the overnight train. But you may prefer to experience France's state-of-the-art TGV, which will get you to Nice in 7 hours. There are at least three daily Paris–Nice TGVs (more in summer); otherwise you may have to change in Marseille or Toulon. The price is 567F ($95) one-way, but there are reductions for students, seniors, and weekend stays. Seat reservations are required and can be made at any travel agency in Paris or at a train station.

Nice has two train stations, of which the largest and most convenient is the **Gare Nice-Ville,** avenue Thiers (☎ 08-36-35-35-35), normally called the Gare SNCF (the Société Nationale des Chemins de Fer is France's national rail company). The station has luggage lockers as well as showers, sinks, and toilets kept moderately clean. The city's helpful tourist office is right next to the station (out the doors and to the left), and numerous good hotels and restaurants are nearby. Outside the station are also several bureaux de change, where you can change money.

To go straight to place Masséna in the town center, take **bus no. 15** from the station or turn left and walk to avenue Jean-Médecin and take any bus heading south.

BY BUS   If you arrive by bus, you'll pull into Nice's **Gare Routière** (☎ 04-93-85-61-81), between Vieux Nice and place Masséna.

BY CAR   You'll approach on Autoroute A8, La Provençal, which skirts the city on its northern boundary. Follow the signs for Centre-Ville (downtown) and place Masséna.

VISITOR INFORMATION

The **Office de Tourisme** is right outside the train station on avenue Thiers (☎ 04-93-87-07-07; fax 04-93-16-85-16; www.nice-coteazur.org). It's open daily: June to September 7:30am to 8pm and October to May 8am to 7pm.

CITY LAYOUT

Downtown Nice is fairly compact. You should find almost everything there—hotels, restaurants, the train and bus stations, the beach—easy to reach on foot. City buses are useful for going to some outlying museums. Many of the most interesting sights are outside Nice, but you can easily reach them by train or bus.

Imagine downtown Nice as a triangle pointed north. At its apex, the northern point, is the **Gare Nice-Ville** (central train station). Near the station are numerous hotels and restaurants as well as the tourist office. The base of the triangle lies along the waterfront. The eastern point is **Vieux Nice,** the old city, and **Le Château,** a hill on which a castle once stood; the western point is at **Pont Magnan,** to the west of the deluxe Hôtel Négresco and the Musée Masséna.

Near the center of the triangle's base, closer to Vieux Nice than to Pont Magnan, is **place Masséna,** the main square, bordered by the Jardins Albert-1er. Nearby is a pedestrian mall covering several blocks of rue Masséna, rue de France, rue Halévy, and rue Paradis; People come here to stroll, window-shop, and eat at the numerous restaurants.

Avenue Jean-Médecin is the main north-south street, beginning at place Masséna and heading north through the heart of the shopping district, then passing just to the east of the train station. Along the waterfront, the wide **promenade des Anglais** is the name of the shore road from the center of town westward; the **quai des Etats-Unis** is its name eastward through Vieux Nice to Le Château.

GETTING AROUND

Nice is a good town for walking, with the occasional bus ride thrown in. (For details on Nice's **buses,** see "Nice Deals & Discounts," earlier in this chapter.) There's a route map posted at each major bus stop and also a sign indicating the *point de vente le plus proche,* the nearest place where booklets of bus tickets are sold. Free maps of the bus network are handed out at the tourist offices, in hotels, and at the TN bus information office at 10 av. Félix-Faure.

For your first sightseeing excursion, consider the **Trains Touristiques de Nice,** rubber-tired tourist "trolleys" that travel a ring route passing Nice's downtown attractions. See "Seeing the Sights," later in this chapter.

BY TAXI   Taxis are rather expensive; the average fare within the city limits is 80F ($13). If you're traveling in a group of three, the price per person isn't so bad. Call ☎ **04-93-13-78-78.**

BY TRAIN   Perhaps the best way to move along the Côte d'Azur is by train. Trains run about every hour or two, sometimes much more frequently, depending on the destination. Some of the stations connected by the rail line are (from west to east) St-Raphaël Valescure, Cannes, Juan-les-Pins, Antibes, Biot, Cagnes-sur-Mer, Nice-Ville, Beaulieu-sur-Mer, Eze-sur-Mer, Monaco–Monte Carlo, Menton, and Vintimille (Ventimiglia) on the Italian border.

BY RENTAL CAR   Car rentals are expensive and are accelerated by a 28% value-added tax (called TVA in France). The cheapest rates are for standard shifts. If you drive only an automatic shift, it's probably better to make arrangements from home since they're substantially more expensive to rent and not always available. Expect to pay about 500F ($83) per day for a subcompact including the first 250 kilometers (156 miles), tax, and insurance. A week's rental with unlimited mileage runs about 2,400F ($400). Auto fuel costs about $4 per American gallon in France.

In Nice, **Hertz** has an office in each of the two terminals at the airport, in Aérogare 1 (☎ **04-93-21-36-72**) and Aérogare 2 (☎ **04-93-21-42-72**). **Avis** has three offices: at the train station (☎ **04-93-87-90-11**), at the airport (☎ **04-93-21-36-33**), and downtown off place Masséna at 2 av. des Phocéens (☎ **04-93-80-63-52**). **Europcar** (National, Tilden) has an office at 6 av. de Suéde (☎ **04-92-14-44-50**), 2 short blocks west of place Masséna, and near the train station at 14 av. Thiers (☎ **04-93-82-17-34**).

If you find a place to park in Nice, you'll probably have to pay. Find a parking ticket machine, insert 10F ($1.65) for each 60 minutes you want, push the button to get your ticket, and place the ticket on your dashboard, where it'll be visible from outside. When your time is up, move the car or buy another ticket. Fines for parking illegally are breathtakingly high. Even parked legally, you may return to find your car trapped by cars behind and ahead, which have been parked bumper-to-bumper with yours. Car break-ins are routine in Nice. Don't leave luggage or valuables in your car.

BY BICYCLE   The oldest rental agency in Nice is **Arnaud,** 4 place Grimaldi (☎ **04-93-87-88-55**), at the corner of rue de la Liberté and rue Grimaldi. Daily rental for a regular bike is 100F ($17), and the same for a mountain version. There's a hefty deposit of 2,000F ($333) for a bike, which can be put on your credit card. The deposit is refunded when you return the vehicle. It's open Monday to Saturday 9am to 7:30pm. Rental motorbikes and mopeds aren't available.

FAST FACTS: Nice

American Express   The office is at 11 promenade des Anglais (☎ **04-93-16-53-53** for exchange, 04-93-16-53-47 for tours), at the corner of rue du Congrès. May to September, hours are Monday to Friday 9am to 6pm and Saturday 9am to noon; October to April, it's open Monday to Friday 9am to noon and 2 to 6pm and Saturday 9am to noon. Cardholders can use the Express Cash machine on the rue du Congrès side of the building. For 24-hour traveler's check refunds, call toll-free ☎ **0800-90-86-00.**

Baby-sitters Call ☎ **04-93-21-62-01** for the Association Niçoise de Services. Rates are 50F ($8) an hour.

Business Hours **Banks** are normally open Monday to Friday 9am to noon and 1 or 1:30 to 4:30pm. Some are open Saturday morning, and some currency exchange booths have long hours (see "Currency Exchange," below). Most **museums, shops, and offices** open around 9am, close for lunch at noon, and reopen about 2pm, staying open to 7pm in summer or 5 or 6pm in winter. Most shops are open Saturday, but are closed Sunday and sometimes Monday as well. **Post offices** are normally open Monday to Friday 8am to 7pm and Saturday 8am to noon.

Currency See "Fast Facts: Paris" in chapter 21.

Currency Exchange When changing money, ask if there's a fee or commission charged—a large one can wipe out the advantage of a good exchange rate. Banks and *bureaux de change* (exchange offices) usually offer better exchange rates than hotels, restaurants, and shops. At the intersection of rue de France and rue Halévy is the **Change Bureau,** 1 rue Halévy, open daily 8am to 7pm. A block to the west on rue de France at rue Massenet is another exchange office. Check to see which offers more francs for your dollar. As of this writing, neither exacts a commission or fee for the transaction.

Doctors Call **S.O.S. Médecins** at ☎ **04-93-85-01-01,** open 24 hours.

Emergencies The emergency number for the **police** is ☎ **17;** in other cases, call ☎ **04-92-17-20-31.** To report a **fire,** dial ☎ **18.** For **medical emergencies,** call ☎ **04-93-92-55-55.** For a **doctor,** call S.O.S. Médecins at ☎ **04-93-85-01-01,** open 24 hours. **Hôpital St-Roch,** 5 rue Pierre-Dévoluy (☎ **04-92-03-33-33**), has an emergency room open 24 hours. The **pharmacy** at 7 rue Masséna (☎ **04-93-87-78-94**) is open daily 7:30pm to 8:30am.

Holidays See "Fast Facts: Paris" in chapter 21.

Laundry Nice has many convenient laundries. Most are open daily 7am to 9pm. They charge around 19F ($3.15) to wash 5 kilos (11 lb.) of clothing and 3F (50¢) for 5 minutes of drying for up to 7 kilos (15½ lb.). There's a laundry in the east wing of the central bus station. Near the train station, look for the **Laverie du Mono,** 8 rue Belgique, between rue Paganini and rue d'Angleterre.

Mail Post offices are open Monday to Friday 8am to 7pm and Saturday 8am to noon. The city's **main post office** is at 23 av. Thiers (☎ **04-93-88-55-41**), across from the train station. *Poste Restante* is held at the post office on place Wilson (☎ **04-93-85-94-20**), 4 blocks east of avenue Jean-Médecin along rue de l'Hôtel des Postes. Airmail letters within Western Europe cost 3F (60¢), to the United States 4.40F (90¢), and to Australia 5.20F (85¢).

Tax France's **TVA (value-added tax)** should already be included in the cost of items you buy, and prices quoted to you should be TTC (*Toutes Taxes Compris,*

Country & City Codes

The **country code** for France is **33.** The **city code** for Nice is **4;** use this code when you're calling from outside France. If you're within France but not in Nice, use **04.** If you're calling within Nice, simply leave off the code and dial only the regular phone number.

all taxes included). The rate of tax varies depending on the item or service being purchased. For how to get a tax refund on large purchases, see "Paris Deals & Discounts" in chapter 21.

Telephone   See "Fast Facts: Paris" in chapter 21 for more details. Avoid making phone calls from your hotel; many hotels charge at least 2F (40¢) for a local call. A 1-minute call within Western Europe costs about 4.50F (90¢), to the United States 8F ($1.30), and to Australia 13F ($2.15).

Tipping   See "Fast Facts: Paris" in chapter 21.

3 Accommodations You Can Afford

Hotels in Nice are scattered throughout town, and distance from the waterfront lowers the price somewhat. As elsewhere in Europe, each hotel room is different. In the same little hotel you might find rooms you think are wonderful and rooms you can't bear to stay in. Ask to see the room before checking in, and if you don't like it, ask to see another.

In the 19th century, Nice developed as a fashionable winter resort, but since the end of World War II most of its visitors have come in summer. Prices given here are for the high summer season, when you may be required to eat breakfast at your hotel. Off-season, many hotels sometimes lower their prices, so always inquire about possible discounts.

The **Office de Tourisme** at the train station (see "Visitor Information") will help you find a room for a fee. In summer there may be quite a wait, so get in line early. The tourism agents won't start calling until 10am, because that's when most hotels know whether they'll have vacant rooms. When they find you a room, you'll pay a fee at the tourism office of 10F ($1.65) for a room in a one-star hotel and 20F ($3.30) for a two-, three-, or four-star hotel. However, when you check in at the hotel, you'll be entitled to a discount on your first night's stay: one star 5F (80¢), two stars 10F ($1.65), three and four stars 20F ($3.30). Thus, the actual fee you pay for the service is only 5F (85¢) for one star, 10F ($1.65) for two stars, and nothing for three and four stars.

Note: You can find the lodging choices below plotted on the map included in "Seeing the Sights," later in this chapter.

SOUTH OF THE TRAIN STATION

The district south of the train station and avenue Thiers is fairly quiet. Hotels cluster on nearly every street, and the sea is a 15-minute walk away. To get there, walk out the station door, turn left, and take the *passage souterrain* (underground walkway); you'll emerge at avenue Durante and rue de Belgique.

Hôtel Baccarat. 39 rue d'Angleterre, 06000 Nice. ☎ **04-93-88-35-73.** Fax 04-93-16-14-25. 33 units, all with bathroom (tub or shower). TV TEL. 163F ($27) single; 216F ($36) double; 83F ($14) per bed in five-bed room. Breakfast 20F ($3.30). Half board and full board can be arranged. MC, V.

The Baccarat, managed by the friendly English-speaking Mme Christine Delacourt, is less than a 5-minute walk from the main train station. The rooms, spread over five floors (with elevator), are large and extremely well maintained. Mme Delacourt has worked wonders with fabrics, covering the beds and chairs with pretty floral or pastel prints. Six rooms are in a "romantic" style, with small fabric canopies framing the beds. Mme Delacourt keeps several rooms for nonsmokers, and some rooms hold up

A Note on Hotels

In June, July, August, and early September, you might have a problem finding a room. Many of the city's cheaper places are booked up by French vacationers. If you haven't reserved a room, plan to arrive early in the day to look for one and/or check with the tourist office. If you can't find exactly the room you want, take one that'll do for a night, then spend a little time the next day reserving another for the rest of your stay.

to five beds—a good choice for small groups. If you take half or full board, the hot meals are served in the nearby Restaurant de Paris.

Hôtel Clair Meublé. 6 rue d'Italie (at rue d'Angleterre), 06000 Nice. ☎ **04-93-87-87-61.** Fax 04-93-16-85-28. 14 units, all with bathroom (tub or shower). 140F ($23) single; 210F ($35) double; 270F ($45) triple; 320F ($53) quad. Extra bed 50F ($8). No credit cards.

The Clair Meublé is 3 blocks from the train station and 100 yards off avenue Jean-Médecin. Ring a buzzer to enter and go up one flight to the reception. Gleaming white-tile floors and blue wallpaper give a sleek modern look to this excellent hotel. The large sunny rooms come with kitchenettes, and many have balconies. The freshly tiled baths are small but perfectly adequate. Room no. 5 is ideal for a family, with one large and one small bed and two bunk beds. The couple who owns the hotel is friendly and helpful. And if you arrive by plane, they'll pick you up at the airport.

✪ **Hôtel Durante.** 16 av. Durante, 06000 Nice. ☎ **04-93-88-84-40.** Fax 04-93-87-77-76. 26 units, all with bathroom (tub). TV TEL. 390F–480F ($55–$80) single/double. Continental breakfast 45F ($8). Buffet breakfast 60F ($10). MC, V. Free parking.

The two-star Durante is a beautifully decorated place, with a superb location on a quiet dead-end street. Everything here has a touch of elegance. The rooms have French windows opening onto a verdant courtyard with flowers, plus kitchenettes with a refrigerator, a two-burner hot plate, dishes, and utensils. The management is cordial and distinguished, and in fall and winter (except for Christmas and Carnival) it offers a 1-night discount to guests staying for a week.

Hôtel les Orangers. 10 bis av. Durante (half a block south of av. Thiers), 06000 Nice. ☎ **04-93-87-51-41.** Fax 04-93-82-57-82. 12 units, 8 with shower only, 4 with bathroom (shower). TEL. 95F–150F ($16–$25) single with shower only; 200F ($33) double with shower only; 220F ($37) double with bathroom; 285F ($48) triple with shower only, 300F ($50) triple with bathroom; 350F ($58) quad with bathroom; 85F ($14) dorm bed. Continental breakfast 20F ($3.30). MC, V.

Over the years, Liliane and Marc Servole, the charming English-speaking couple who owns and operates this hotel, have played host to scores of *Frommer's* readers. The white-tile floors give a fresh, light look to bright rooms (some with balconies) outfitted with a refrigerator, a hot plate, pots, pans, and cutlery. There's a grocery store 1½ blocks away on rue d'Italie, so you can make your own breakfasts, snacks, and light suppers. The Orangers is in demand—reserve ahead if you can.

Hôtel Lyonnais. 20 rue de Russie (at rue d'Italie, near Notre-Dame), 06000 Nice. ☎ **04-93-88-70-74.** Fax 04-93-16-25-56. 31 units, 4 with shower only, 4 with bathroom (shower). TEL. 110F–145F ($18–$24) single without bathroom, 160F–190F ($27–$32) single with shower only, 202F ($34) single with bathroom; 160F–190F ($27–$32) double without bathroom, 160F–210F ($27–$35) double with shower only, 225F ($38) double with bathroom; 165F–210F ($28–$35) triple without bathroom, 195F–290F ($33–$48) triple with shower only. Continental breakfast 20F ($3.30). Showers 15F ($2.50). AE, EURO, MC, V.

Getting the Best Deal on Accommodations

- Seek out hotels away from the waterfront—distance from the sea lowers the price.
- Take advantage of low-season discounts.
- Consider staying in a room with a sink or shower only—prices often vary greatly according to how much plumbing a room contains.
- Be sure to make reservations during high season, as many of Nice's cheaper rooms are booked in advance.
- Try to book a room with a kitchenette, which allows you to save money on meals. In addition, rooms with kitchenettes tend to be larger.

The diminutive lobby is one flight up, and then there's an elevator to take you to the rooms. Though somewhat small and showing their age, they're clean and tidily furnished and have large windows letting in lots of light. Rooms without baths have a tiny *cabinet de toilette* with a sink and bidet. There are several rooms suitable for four people at a charge of 75F ($13) per person. Friendly owner Serge Goullet also manages 13 large rooms in a nearby building, with kitchenettes, bathrooms (shower), and private terraces with panoramic views. At 250F ($42) double and 480F ($80) quad, they're an excellent value.

✪ **Hôtel Normandie.** 18 rue Paganini (at rue d'Alsace-Lorraine), 06000 Nice. ☎ **04-93-88-48-83.** Fax 04-93-16-04-33. 44 units, all with bathroom (tub or shower). A/C TV TEL. 250F ($42) single; 320F ($53) double; 390F ($55) triple; 460F ($77) quad. Breakfast 25F ($4.15). Ask about low-season discounts. AE, DC, MC, V.

The rooms at the Hôtel Normandie are extremely comfortable and cheerfully decorated in red, white, and blue. The building has five floors and an elevator; eight rooms are singles and four are triples. It has been owned for the past decade by the cordial Anquetil family, and the English-speaking desk manager, Roger, comes from Argentina. The Normandie is located 2 blocks from the train station and 1 block east of avenue Durante.

Hôtel Notre-Dame. 22 rue de Russie (3 blocks from the train station), Nice 06000. ☎ **04-93-88-70-44.** Fax 04-93-82-20-38. 17 units, all with bathroom (shower). 180F ($27) single; 200F ($33) double; 300F ($50) triple; 350F ($58) quad. Continental breakfast 20F ($3.30). AE, EURO, MC, V.

The Yung family that manages this hotel works closely with the Clair Meublé (above) and has the same obsession with cleanliness and tip-top maintenance. If one hotel is full, they'll try to book you into the other. The freshly tiled floors and baths are sparkling white and contrast nicely with the blue wallpaper. If you're traveling in a group of four, try to book room no. 3, 9, 16, or 20, each with bunk beds. The hotel is on four floors and has an elevator.

NORTH OF THE TRAIN STATION

Hôtel Monsigny. 17 av. Malausséna, 06000 Nice. ☎ **04-93-88-27-35.** Fax 04-93-82-09-13. 48 units, all with bathroom (tub or shower). A/C TV TEL. 300F ($50) single; 360F ($50) double; 450F ($75) triple; 500F ($83) quad. Rates include breakfast. AE, DC, MC, V.

The three-star Monsigny (with elevator) offers beautifully furnished large rooms on five floors. If you're a family, try to book room no. 28—it's a beauty with four beds. To find the hotel, walk through the railway underpassage 2 blocks east from central station; 2 blocks up the street you'll see the hotel to your left.

NEAR AVENUE JEAN-MEDECIN

Directly across avenue Jean-Médecin from the Notre-Dame church is a quiet residential area with several excellent budget hotels. The area is a short walk from the train station, and buses along avenue Jean-Médecin make access to the waterfront easy.

Hôtel Astor. 33 rue Pastorelli, 06000 Nice. ☎ **04-93-62-18-82.** Fax 04-93-92-19-12. 30 units, all with bathroom (tub or shower). TV. 150F ($25) single; 250F ($42) double. Continental breakfast 30F ($5). AE, DC, MC, V. Bus: 15 from train station to Victor Hugo, then a 2-minute walk.

This cozy hotel, 100 yards from the central place Masséna, has newly furnished rooms with large windows spread over six floors connected by an elevator. Some of the top-floor rooms have a balcony. The friendly manager is English-speaking Mr. Vandesteene, who comes from Belgium and goes the extra mile for Frommer's readers.

Hôtel du Petit Louvre. 10 rue Emma-Tiranty (near Marks & Spencer), 06000 Nice. ☎ **04-93-80-15-54.** Fax 04-93-62-45-08. 34 units, all with bathroom (shower). TEL. 170F ($28) single; 200F ($33) double. Continental breakfast 25F ($4.15). EURO, V. Closed Nov–Jan.

M. and Mme Vila (she speaks English) run this neat and attractive place and will welcome you enthusiastically. Though the location is superb and the facilities are a cut above the budget range, the prices are delightfully reasonable. To find the hotel, go to the Notre-Dame church on avenue Jean-Médecin and look for rue Emma-Tiranty on the east side a bit to the south.

Hôtel Pastoral. 27 rue Assalit (a block east of the intersection of av. Jean-Médecin and av. Thiers), 06000 Nice. ☎ **04-93-85-17-22.** 15 units, some with shower only. TEL. 105F ($18) single without bathroom; 120F–150F ($20–$25) double without bathroom, 150F–170F ($25–$28) double with shower only. Continental breakfast 20F ($3.30). Showers 10F ($1.65). Use of kitchenette 16F ($2.65) per person per day. No credit cards.

Up one flight from the street, the Pastoral offers a familial atmosphere and a floor of large old-fashioned but well-tended rooms. The communal showers and toilets are in good condition, and you can opt for a kind of portable kitchenette (with a refrigerator, two hot plates, and cutlery) to be moved into your room. Three back rooms open onto an interior courtyard filled with potted plants, creating a "pastoral" look, and are likely to be quieter on busy summer nights.

Sibill's Hotel. 25 rue Assalit (at St-Siagre), 06000 Nice. ☎ **04-93-62-03-07.** 56 units, all with bathroom (tub or shower). A/C TV TEL. 325F ($54) single; 430F ($72) double; 480F ($80) triple; 510F ($85) quad. Rates include continental breakfast. AE, MC, V.

This three-star hotel offers surprising comfort at a moderate price. The glistening lobby sets the tone for the faultlessly maintained carpeted rooms. About half the rooms have recently been refurbished in cool pastels, but all are a good size. Double-glazed windows and thick curtains keep out sound and light for a good night's sleep. Some rooms have phone jacks to plug in portable computers. The train station is a 5-minute walk away, as is the busy shopping district on avenue Jean-Médecin.

NEAR THE SEA

If you're longing to be near the Mediterranean, don't despair. Several hotels just steps from the water rent attractive rooms at affordable prices. In summer, though, these rooms become even more enticing, so reserve early. A good place to look is the pedestrian mall formed by rue de France and rue Masséna between rue du Congrès and avenue Jean-Médecin.

Hôtel Canada. 8 rue Halévy, 06000 Nice. ☎ **04-93-87-98-94.** Fax 04-93-87-17-12. 18 units, all with bathroom (tub). TV TEL. 220F–340F ($37–$57) single/double without kitchenette, 290F–390F ($48–$55) single/double with kitchenette. Extra bed 70F ($12). Continental breakfast 30F ($5). AE, DC, MC, V. Bus: 12 from train station to Grimaldi.

In the midst of Nice's pedestrian zone is the shiny doorway to the Canada, and up a flight of 22 marble stairs between mirrored walls is the bright modern lobby. The rooms have tiny tiled baths and TVs, and each has its own touch: a special piece of artwork here, a brass headboard there. They're all very nice and very much in demand in summer, so reserve ahead.

✪ **Hôtel Félix.** 41 rue Masséna, 06000 Nice. ☎ **04-93-88-67-73.** Fax 04-93-16-15-78. 14 units, all with bathroom (tub or shower). A/C TV TEL. 210F–240F ($35–$40) single; 240F–340F ($40–$57) double. Continental breakfast 30F ($5). AE, DC, MC, V. Bus: 5, 12, or 22 from train station to place Masséna, then a 5-minute walk.

The Félix is in a quiet pedestrian zone yet convenient to the beach and the waterfront's nightlife. The two charming sisters who own/manage the hotel will welcome you in English, French, or Italian and show you to a clean and comfortable room on one of the three floors. Most rooms have a balcony adorned with flower-filled window boxes. Other extras include double-glazed windows, a hair dryer in the bath, fluffy towels, and a firm bed. The only inconvenience: There's no elevator—it's a 19th-century house where installment of an elevator is too difficult.

Hôtel Harvey. 18 av. de Suède (just off promenade des Anglais), 06000 Nice. ☎ **04-93-88-73-73.** Fax 04-93-82-53-55. 64 units, all with bathroom (tub or shower). A/C TV TEL. 300F ($50) single; 400F ($57) double; 480F ($80) triple; 540F ($90) quad. Continental breakfast 30F ($5). AE, EURO, MC, V. Bus: 12 from train station to Grimaldi.

All of the rooms in this renovated six-floor hotel (with elevator) have been modernized with basic conveniences. There's a cozy lobby and breakfast room. Try to book either room no. 104 or 109—each is really a suite with a bath (including tub and bidet) that's as large as the bedroom. No outside visitors are allowed in the rooms at night. The Hôtel Harvey is a typical hotel for families looking for a quiet atmosphere. Avenue de Suède is part of a pedestrian zone; no cars are allowed in the street facing the hotel. Mme. Passeri, the owner since 1967, keeps in personal contact with her guests.

✪ **Hôtel Meublé Célimène.** 63 rue de France, 06000 Nice. ☎ **04-93-88-61-51.** 10 units, all with bathroom (shower). TV. 200F–240F ($33–$40) studio for 1 or 2; 280F ($47) studio for 3. No credit cards. Bus: 12 from train station to Rivoli.

Many of Nice's hotels feature kitchenettes in the rooms, making the accommodations really efficiency apartments; a *hôtel meublé* is precisely that. The Célimène is wonderful, with a quiet location next to the Musée Masséna and cheery second-floor rooms. Not only is it charming but it's cheap—so it's usually booked up by guests staying a week or longer. The office, one flight up, is open only 10:30am to 12:30pm. M. Beringer is the owner, and he and his son speak English fluently. If you can plan your stay well in advance, try to make this your residence.

Hôtel Solara. 7 rue de France, 06000 Nice. ☎ **04-93-88-09-96.** Fax 04-93-88-36-86. 14 units, all with bathroom (shower). A/C MINIBAR TV TEL. 210F–290F ($35–$48) single; 270F–350F ($45–$58) double; 330F–410F ($55–$58) triple. Continental breakfast 30F ($5). EURO, MC, V. Bus: 5 from train station to place Masséna or 12 from train station to Grimaldi.

The Solara is aptly named. This marvelous hotel occupies the top two floors of a coolly quiet building—ring the bell and take the elevator up. The rooms are modern and luminous, with beige walls and handsome lamps. Some have balconies and Mediterranean views, even if you can't actually see the water. The rooms on the fifth floor are the nicest.

IN PONT MAGNAN

A 20-minute stroll from avenue Masséna west along promenade des Anglais brings you to Pont Magnan, an upscale residential district with white and pastel apartment blocks facing the Mediterranean. It's not near the center of town, but bus transportation is fast and frequent. Take bus no. 24 from the train station; bus no. 3, 10, 12, or 22 from downtown; or bus no. 8 or 11 along promenade des Anglais and get off at Magnan.

✪ **Hôtel Villa Eden.** 99 bis promenade des Anglais (near square Général-Ferrié), 06000 Nice. ☎ **04-93-86-53-70.** Fax 04-93-97-67-97. 15 units, all with bathroom (tub). A/C TV TEL. 200F–390F ($33–$65) single/double; higher rates are for rooms with sea view. Extra bed 90F ($15). Continental breakfast 30F ($5). AE, DC, EURO, MC, V. Free parking. Bus: 12, 23, or 24 from train station to Magnan.

Believe it or not, it's possible to stay in a beautiful renovated villa on promenade des Anglais across from the beach and still be within our budget. The homey quarters in high-ceilinged rooms with period furnishings and color TVs, some with a terrace facing the Mediterranean, are a perfect setting for a pleasant stay. You can take breakfast in a small garden with oleander and lemon trees or walk to the beach to swim. The entrance to this Shangri-La is through a narrow corridor lined with flowers, plants, and trees. An affordable dream. The manager is M. Tafti.

IN CIMIEZ

Relais International de la Jeunesse "Clairvallon." 26 av. Scuderi, Cimiez, 06100 Nice. ☎ **04-93-81-27-63.** Fax 04-93-53-35-88. 150 beds. 75F ($13) dorm bed. Rates include showers. Half board *(demi-pension)* 135F ($23); full board *(pension complète)* 165F ($28). No credit cards. Bus: 15 from train station to Scuderi, then see directions below.

This private hostel operated by young people is in the northern reaches of Cimiez, one of Nice's finest residential districts. Surrounded by aristocratic villas, the hostel, with a pool, tennis courts, and pretty grounds, was itself once a villa. You don't have to have a hostel card or be a certain age to stay here. Registration is after 5pm, and curfew is 11pm. There are four- to eight-bed rooms with showers.

It's about 3 miles north of place Masséna, but the bus runs every 10 minutes on weekdays and every 15 or 20 minutes on weekends. When you get off the bus, turn left onto winding avenue Scuderi, walk about 500 yards past imposing villas and palm trees, and you'll see the hostel on the right, near some cypress trees.

WORTH A SPLURGE

Hôtel Busby. 36–38 rue du Maréchal-Joffre, 06000 Nice. ☎ **04-93-88-19-41.** Fax 04-93-87-73-53. 80 units, all with bathroom (tub or shower). A/C TV TEL. 500F–700F ($83–$117) double. AE, DC, MC, V. Closed Nov 15–Dec 20. Bus: 9, 10, 12, or 22.

This place should please you if you want an elegant central hotel that has all the modern amenities. Totally renovated and air-conditioned, the hotel has kept its old Niçois facade, with balconies and shutters at the tall windows. The rooms are dignified yet colorful, and some contain pairs of mahogany twin beds and two white-and-gold wardrobes. The bar is cozy, and the long dining room has marble columns, mirrors, and ladderback chairs. The restaurant is open December 20 to May.

✪ **Hôtel Ibis.** 14 av. Thiers, 06000 Nice. ☎ **04-93-88-85-55.** Fax 04-93-88-58-00. 200 units, all with bathroom (tub). TV. 395F ($66) single; 447F ($75) double; 490F ($82) triple. Self-service buffet breakfast 35F ($6). AE, DC, MC, V.

This hotel is practically next to the central station; when leaving the station, turn right and you can't miss seeing the huge brown building. Opened in 1993, it immediately became a success story because of its ideal central position and its top service, which includes free use of a pool in the courtyard. All rooms are equipped with color TVs (14 channels, including CNN), and there are three elevators for the hotel's 10 floors. The restaurant serves three types of menus—Solo (one course) 55F ($9), Duo (two courses) 75F ($13), and Trio (three courses) 95F ($16)—plus a children's menu (*IBIS enfant*).

4 Great Deals on Dining

The cuisine along the Côte d'Azur is a refreshing alternative to classical French cooking. Making liberal use of local products like olive oil, garlic, tomatoes, and fresh herbs, the whole approach to dining is more casual, spontaneous, and often cheaper than in Paris.

For restaurant dining, the best value is usually a menu du jour (fixed-price meal), offering two or three courses, sometimes with wine (look for *vin compris*) at a better price than you'd get by ordering à la carte. An alternative to a multicourse meal is a *plat du jour*, a main-course platter garnished with vegetables and little extras that easily constitutes a filling meal. Service charge and tax are included in prices.

Happily for budget travelers, inexpensive Italian-style food is popular. You'll find pasta prepared in dozens of imaginative ways and more pizza shops than there are pebbles on the beach. For lighter fare, you can't do better than *salade niçoise,* usually made with lettuce, tomatoes, onions, anchovies, hard-boiled eggs, olives, and tuna. Hearty and strongly flavored soups are a staple of the local diet. *Soup au pistou* is a vegetable soup, perked up with garlic and basil pesto (*pistou*). *Soupe au poisson* is a deep red savory liquid made from fish, tomatoes, and garlic and served with cheese, croutons, and *aïoli* (Provençal garlic mayonnaise). The most famous Mediterranean soup is *bouillabaisse,* featuring an assortment of local seafood such as *rascasse* (rock cod), *congre* (eel), and *dorade* (snapper). Though bouillabaisse can be expensive, try to splurge once on this savory stew.

A particular restaurant may close any day (or part of a day), so be sure to check the hours before heading out to eat. For more dining details, see the introduction to the dining section in chapter 21 on Paris.

SOUTH OF THE TRAIN STATION

Palais de Chine. 41 rue d'Angleterre (almost at the corner of av. Thiers). ☎ **04-93-82-22-98.** Meals 55F–100F ($9–$17). MC, V. Fri–Wed noon–2:30pm and 7–11pm. CHINESE/THAI.

Chinese restaurants aren't as widespread in France as they are in North America, so this fine one is a welcome surprise. The cordial proprietors offer two four-course menus du jour, for 68F and 92F ($11 and $15), including wine. You could begin with eggrolls and then try the fillet of fresh fish with lemon sauce. There's also a more elaborate menu with more choices for 115F ($19). Soups cost 22F to 40F ($3.65 to $7). They also prepare delicious Thai dishes for 32F to 85F ($5 to $14).

✪ Restaurant au Soleil. 7 bis rue d'Italie (at rue d'Italie). ☎ **04-93-88-77-74.** Three-course menus 60F and 75F ($10 and $13). AE, EURO, MC, V. Sun–Fri 8am–10pm. Closed Dec–Feb. FRENCH.

Big display windows let lots of light into this large familial eatery named after the sun. Owners Roger and Gaëtane Germain have been serving *Frommer's* readers for 39 years with obvious pleasure. The salade niçoise appetizer on the fixed-price menu includes chunks of tuna, and the breaded veal cutlet is a popular choice for a main course. On

Street Eats

Street-corner vendors bake trays of *pissaladière*—onion tart garnished with anchovies—and sell cut portions for about 10F ($1.65). Look for vendors offering *socca,* a kind of baked pancake made from chickpea flour that's often eaten for breakfast, also costing 10F ($1.65). For the best *socca* in Nice, visit **Thérése** the socca seller in front of 5 Cours Saleya. She'll cut the pancake in front of you, sprinkle it with pepper, and hand it to you wrapped in paper.

You could live on healthy and delicious *pan bagnat* (a small, round bread loaf stuffed with salade niçoise–type goodies and moistened with olive oil) for the duration of your visit and barely put a dent in your wallet.

---

the higher-priced menu, try the calamars armoricaine (squid in tomato sauce). Finish with a freshly prepared chocolate mousse. If you're staying in the neighborhood, drop by for the 33F ($6) breakfast, with an omelet, juice, bread, and coffee.

Restaurant de Paris. 28 rue d'Angleterre (south of av. Thiers). ☎ **04-93-88-99-88.** Meals 35F–65F ($6–$11). MC, V. Daily 11:30am–3pm and 6:30–10:30pm. FRENCH.

The three menus du jour here offer five or six choices for each course, and the prices are great: 38F to 60F ($6 to $10). Or you can order a *plat du jour* like beef bourguignonne for only 30F ($5). The specialty here is meat; the fondue bourguignonne is a hearty meal for 60F ($10). The place is brightly lit and modern, with ceiling fans and sidewalk tables.

✪ **Restaurant la Petite Biche.** 9 rue d'Alsace-Lorraine (between rue Paganini and rue d'Angleterre, next to the Hôtel Normandie). ☎ **04-93-87-30-70.** Three-course menus 64F–82F ($11–$14). V. Daily 11:30am–2:30pm and 6:30–10:30pm. FRENCH/NIÇOISE.

The "Little Doe" is a brightly decorated place with deer heads on the wall, rough chandeliers, stone pillars, burnished copper vessels, big oil paintings, and mirrors. The fixed-price dinner allows you to choose from among 21 appetizers, 10 main courses with vegetables, and 7 desserts. *Aïoli de cabillaud* (cod with Provençal mayonnaise) is a good local dish, or you can sample the *soupe du pêcheur* (fisherman's soup). For dessert, try a slice of apricot tart.

Restaurant le Saetone. 8 rue d'Alsace-Lorraine (between rue Paganini and rue d'Angleterre). ☎ **04-93-87-17-95.** Three-course menu 68F ($11); pizza 36F–49F ($6–$8). MC, V. Thurs–Tues 11:30am–2pm and 6–10pm. FRENCH.

Le Saetone pleases with a homey decor and good food at unbeatable prices. It offers several three-course menus du jour, but the top sellers are the 12 varieties of pizza, especially the Pizza Provençale, topped with tomatoes, herbs of Provence, garlic, olives, and cheese. Its convenient location (only a few minutes' walk from the train station) also helps draw the crowds. The tables often fill at mealtimes, so get here early.

✪ **Via Veneto.** 37 bis rue d'Angleterre. ☎ **04-93-82-02-10.** Reservations suggested for dinner. Meals 40F–92F ($7–$15); menu du jour 60F and 92F ($10 and $15); plat du jour 35F–48F ($6–$8). AE, DC, EURO, MC, V. Mon–Sat 11:30am–2:30pm and 6:30–11pm. FRENCH/ITALIAN.

Managed by a Frenchman of Italian descent, this beautifully furnished place serves a popular three-course menu du jour with 18 choices of first and second courses (like tagliatelle or lasagna al forno, entrecôte or grilled steak with vegetables, followed by cheese or tiramisu). Ask for the English menu. The specialty is pâtés fraîches or pasta fatta in casa (all kinds of homemade noodles, from spaghetti to macaroni and ravioli filled with meat or ricotta). While the best deal is the *menu,* you'll see most of the customers ordering a pasta dish, spiced with tomatoes, meat, cheese, carbonara, or seafood sauce. Rigatoni alla carretera is a special treat for vegetarians—the rigatoni is topped with tomatoes, parsley, garlic, basil, and olive oil.

NEAR AVENUE JEAN-MEDECIN

La Nissarda. 17 rue Gubernatis. ☎ **04-93-62-17-82.** Three-course menu 90F ($15) and 150F ($25). MC, V. Mon–Sat 11:30am–2pm and 6:45–10pm. NIÇOISE.

About a 10-minute walk from place Masséna, this restaurant is owned by the Normandy-born Pruniers, who work hard to maintain Nice's culinary traditions. The rectangular space is decorated with paintings of Provençal scenes, but fortunately the food is a lot better than the art. The petits farcis niçois on the fixed-price menus is a good introduction to the stuffed vegetables that are a specialty of Nice, and the daube à la Provençale (beef stew) is very well prepared. Best of all is the rouget (red mullet) marinated in lime and olive oil, served with salad.

Le Coquet. 18 rue Pertinax (at rue Miron). ☎ **04-93-62-17-82.** Three-course menu 60F ($10), with wine. No credit cards. Mon–Fri 11:30am–3pm and 6:30–11pm. FRENCH/NIÇOISE.

Le Coquet is a simple place frequented mainly by shopkeepers and store clerks—and the occasional visitor. There's not much in the way of decor, but the food is very tasty. This is a good place to try local specialties like tripes niçoise for 40F ($7) or pastasciutta with tomato sauce. You might also try choucroute garnie—a hearty Alsatian dish of sauerkraut topped with pork cuts.

NEAR THE SEA

Georgie's Restaurant. 12 rue Halévy (100 yards off promenade des Anglais). ☎ **04-93-87-80-60.** Three-course menus 89F ($15) and 130F ($22); *plat du jour* 45F ($8). AE, DC, MC, V. Daily noon–3pm and 6–11pm. FRENCH/SEAFOOD.

This is a good place to try bouillabaisse (enough for two or three) for 110F ($18) or an equally large seafood platter (scallops, scampi, mussels, grilled fish) served with fries for 120F ($20). The three-course 130F ($22) menu starts with a choice of fish terrines and continues with bouillabaisse plus a mixed salad, and ends with ice cream (you have at least 10 choices). Smaller nonfish dishes include plain omelets, spaghetti bolognese, and frogs' legs. If you sit in the correct chair on the sidewalk terrace, you can glimpse the Mediterranean.

✪ **La Pizza.** 34 rue Masséna. ☎ **04-93-87-70-29.** À la carte meals 24F–66F ($4–$11); pizza 41F–57F ($7–$10); *plat du jour* 55F ($9). AE, MC, V. Daily 11:30am–2am. ITALIAN.

Crowded every afternoon and evening, both winter and summer, La Pizza has found the formula: fresh, delicious pizzas and fast service at good prices. Salads, omelets, and a *plat du jour,* plus wine and beer, are served as well. You might have a short wait for a table, as crowds of young and old press into this place.

IN VIEUX NICE

Restaurant Acchiardo. 38 rue Droite (near the corner of rue du Château). ☎ **04-93-85-51-16.** Three-course menus 60F–100F ($10–$17). No credit cards. Mon–Fri noon–1:30pm and 7–9:30pm, Sat noon–1:30pm. Follow the signs to the Palais Lascaris, on rue Droite, and walk past the palace and the church to the Acchiardo. FRENCH.

Corn cobs and other farm souvenirs decorate the ceiling beams and walls of this tiny place near the St-Jacob church, presaging good eating. The feeling is certainly French provincial, though the smiling staff can get by in English. The seafood is particularly good, including hake (steamed whitefish in garlic sauce); with potatoes, carrots, and

---

Getting the Best Deal on Dining

- Take advantage of the street snack stands selling socca, pizza, and sandwiches.
- Note that standing at the counter at a cafe rather than sitting at a table with waiter service can save you 30%.
- Try the menu du jour (fixed-price meal), often the most economical and tastiest choice. And there's always the plat du jour, cheaper though less filling.
- Ordering bottled water can increase the cost of your meal by a third. Ask for *une carafe d'eau*—tap water.

---

celery, this would make a typical big *plat du jour*. Ask for the English menu and don't forget to peek into the catacomb-like wine cellar, built during the reign of Louis XIV.

PICNICKING

Buying food in markets is a pleasure in Nice, and there's a wealth of great picnic spots. After you stroll through the flower portion of the market at the **Cours Saleya** (Tuesday to Sunday 7am to 1pm), head to the eastern side to find stands of luscious fruit, pungent cheese, *charcuterie* (smoked sausages), and freshly baked breads. Try *fougasse*—bread stuffed with olives, anchovies, ham, or local cheese. For the best *socca* in Nice, visit **Thérèse** the socca seller in front of 5 Cours Saleya. You can take your feast to the **promenade des Anglais,** grab a chair, and gaze at the sea while you eat. You're also only steps away from the stairs leading to the park around the hilltop **Château** with magnificent views over the bay.

If you're staying around the train station, you can assemble your picnic from the **Liberation market** that surrounds avenue Malaussena. Open Tuesday to Sunday 7am to 1pm, this market also offers numerous stands selling local products, and is less touristy.

There's no reason to fast on Monday, when the markets are closed. Head for the **Prisunic department store,** on avenue Jean-Médecin between rue Biscarra and avenue Maréchal-Foch. You'll find huge chunks of cheese, *charcuterie,* pâté, and various salads and side dishes at a few francs for a 200-gram portion. Generally the prices are lower than at the markets, but the quality isn't quite as high. When you're done in the grocery section, head for the doors at the corner of Jean-Médecin and avenue Maréchal-Foch, where the bakery is. You can consume your picnic on **place Masséna,** the **Jardins Albert-1er,** or head to the **promenade des Anglais** or the **beach.**

WORTH A SPLURGE

La Taverne de l'Opéra. 10 rue St-François-de-Paule. ☎ **04-93-85-72-68.** Three-course menu 120F ($20). AE, DC, MC, V. Mon–Sat noon–2:30pm and 7–10:30pm. Closed Dec. FRENCH/NIÇOISE.

Down by the waterfront in Vieux Nice, only a carnation's throw from the flower market and even closer to the opera house, is this grand old tavern heavy with charm and atmosphere. La Taverne de l'Opéra is a great place to try some of the specialties of Nice's cuisine—the seafood is simply splendid. A bargain here is the choice of 12 kinds of pizza averaging 40F ($7).

✪ **Lou Balico.** 20 av. St-Jean-Baptiste. ☎ **04-93-85-93-71.** Reservations suggested. Two-course lunch with coffee 75F ($13); six-course *menu de dégustation* 153F ($26). AE, MC, V. Mon–Fri 11:30am–2:30pm and 6:30–10:30pm, Sat 11:30am–2:30pm. NIÇOISE.

I advise you to save Lou Balico for the end of your stay; otherwise the range of deliciously prepared Niçois specialties will spoil any other dining in Nice. The 75F menu is a good value that includes a lightly fried beignet or crudités as a starter followed by the plat du jour, but the menu de dégustation gives you a chance to try a fine pissaladière, eggplant beignets, roast lamb with fresh pasta, mesclun salad with bacon bits and croutons, and goat cheese with herbs of Provence and olive oil. For dessert, try the *tourte de blette,* a pie stuffed with a local spinachlike vegetable, sugared up, and sprinkled with pine nuts.

5 Seeing the Sights

A spectacular natural setting is Nice's greatest asset. The **promenade des Anglais,** running nearly the full length of the Baie des Anges (Bay of Angels), opens the city to sea and sky. Flowers and plants flourish in the mild climate, filling parks and cascading down from window sills. The play of light and color has inspired many fine painters, whose works you can discover in the city's excellent museums.

SIGHTSEEING SUGGESTIONS

IF YOU HAVE 1 DAY   You'll of course head to the **promenade des Anglais** for a look at the sweep of sea and hillside that forms the Baie des Anges (Bay of Angels). A promenade along the promenade is imperative. After, you can divide your time among the **beach,** the **Musée Matisse,** and the **Musée Chagall** in beautiful Cimiez or around **Vieux Nice,** the labyrinthine old part of town.

IF YOU HAVE 2 DAYS   With 2 days you can see the chief sights of **Nice** and make an excursion to at least two other places along the Riviera. Consider **Monaco** and **Cannes.** With the fast and frequent train service, you can easily travel both east and west of Nice on the same day.

IF YOU HAVE 3 DAYS OR MORE   With 3 days at your disposal, you can spend Day 1 in **Nice,** Day 2 east of Nice (in **Monaco** and visiting the beautiful Villa Kérylos in **Beaulieu-sur-Mer**), and Day 3 to the west (in **St-Paul-de-Vence** and at the Matisse Chapel in **Vence**). Add the Musée Picasso at the Château Grimaldi in **Antibes** and spend a few hours in **Juan-les-Pins** or **St-Tropez** as well.

IN CIMIEZ

Founded by the Romans, who called it Cemenelum, Cimiez, a hilltop suburb of Nice, was the capital of the Maritime Alps province. All around the **Villa des Arènes** (which contains the Matisse Museum) are the ruins of **Roman Cemenelum,** including baths and a theater still used for performances. In the 19th century, Queen Victoria and her court made Cimiez their winter home. Even without the museums, Cimiez merits a visit.

✪ **Musée Matisse.** 164 av. des Arènes de Cimiez. ☎ **04-93-81-08-08.** Admission 25F ($4.15). Tues–Sun 10am–6pm. Bus: 15, 17, 20, or 22 from place Masséna to Arènes or Monastère.

The works of Henri Matisse (1869–1954) are displayed in the 17th-century Villa des Arènes. It's fascinating to view the artist's works—paintings, drawings, sculptures, and studies for the chapel at Vence—in this setting in which he actually worked. Here you'll find a unique Riviera atmosphere, filled with trees, vistas, and even furniture you may recognize in his paintings. The museum has several permanent collections, including pieces like *Nude in an Armchair with a Green Plant* (1937), *Nymph in the Forest* (1935/1942), and a chronologically arranged series of paintings from 1890 to 1919. The most famous of these is *Portrait of Madame Matisse* (1905), usually displayed near another portrait of the artist's wife, by Marquet, painted in 1900.

A Museum Tip

The beaches are open every day, but the museums aren't. Some museums are closed on Monday, others on Tuesday, and many for a month every year, often in rainy November. Check the hours to be sure before heading out. For a complete list of museums and hours, get the free brochure *Les Musées de Nice* at the tourist office.

As a special treat, the city offers free admission to its museums on February 1 and 11, March 1, April 5 and 15, May 3, June 7 and 10, July 5, August 2, September 6, October 4, November 1, and December 6.

Musée d'Archéologie. 160 av. des Arènes de Cimiez. ☎ **04-93-81-59-57.** Admission 25F ($4.15). Apr–Sept Tues–Sun 10am–noon and 2–6pm; Oct–Mar Tues–Sun 10am–1am and 2–5pm. Bus: 15, 17, 20, or 22 from place Masséna to Arènes or Monastère.

Nice's archaeological museum was opened in 1989. Roman Cemenelum was the capital of the province of the Maritime Alps, an important passageway to Gallia and Hispania. Many artifacts found at local excavations are displayed here. There are also Greek and Etruscan pieces. Enter the museum through the archaeological site on avenue Montecroce.

Musée National Message Biblique Marc-Chagall. Av. du Docteur-Ménard at bd. de Cimiez. ☎ **04-93-53-87-20.** Admission 30F ($5) adults, 28F ($4.65) ages 18–26 and over 60, free for age 17 and under; more for special exhibits. July–Sept Wed–Mon 10am–7pm; Oct–June 10am–12:30pm and 2–5:20pm. Bus: 15 from place Masséna to Musée Chagall.

The Chagall family donated 450 of the painter's finer works on biblical subjects to France, his adopted homeland, and they've been put on permanent exhibition in this squat modern building of white stone built at French government expense and set in its own park. It's pleasantly light and airy inside, which is just the right mood for Chagall's lyrical works: three large stained-glass windows in the concert hall, a room of stunning paintings illustrating the Song of Songs, and several rooms of grand-scale canvases portraying Moses and the burning bush, Isaac's sacrifice, and similar themes.

Eglise et Monastère de Cimiez/Musée Franciscain. Place du Monastère. ☎ **04-93-81-00-04.** Free admission. Mon–Sat 10am–noon and 3–6pm. Bus: 15, 17, 20, or 22 to Cimiez Archéologie or Monastère.

Not far from the Musée Matisse is this medieval monastery that now houses a museum dedicated to the art and history of the Franciscan order. The church contains a few very fine paintings by the Niçois primitives and a school that flourished here in the 15th and 16th centuries. Writer Roger Martin du Gard and artist Raoul Dufy are buried in the cemetery, and so is Matisse, near an olive grove.

IN NICE

The wide **promenade des Anglais** fronts the bay. Split by "islands" of palms and flowers, it stretches for about 4 miles. Fronting the beach are rows of grand cafes, the Musée Masséna, villas, hotels, and chic boutiques.

Crossing this boulevard in the briefest of bikinis or thongs are some of the world's most attractive people. They're heading for the **beach**—"on the rocks," as it's called here. Tough on tender feet, the beach is smooth, round pebbles, one of the least attractive (and least publicized) aspects of the cosmopolitan resort. Many bathhouses provide mattresses for about 65F ($11) a day.

✪ **Musée Masséna.** 35 promenade des Anglais, next to the Hôtel Négresco (entrance in the back at 65 rue de France). ☎ **04-93-88-11-34.** Admission 25F ($4.15) adults, 15F ($2.50)

Getting the Best Deal on Sightseeing

- Half of the 2-mile-long pebbled beach is free, so take advantage of this stretch and sunbathe, swim, people-watch, or just daydream.
- Take advantage of the special museum pass (passe musées) that costs 40F ($7) and offers free admission to all Nice museums for a week. You can get one in any museum or tourist office.
- Head to Le Château, the only hill facing the sea (at the eastern end of the waterfront), for the best panoramic view of Nice and the beach. You can either walk up 157 easy steps or take an elevator for only 5F (80¢) round-trip.
- Stroll along the lovely promenade des Anglais, a pedestrian zone that's as wide as a boulevard. Take a seat in one of the hundred blue wooden chairs (no rental charge) and just gaze out to sea when you feel like a break. However, beware of the in-line skaters who use the promenade as a racetrack.

---

seniors/students. Daily 10am–noon and 2–6pm. Bus: 3, 7, 8, 9, 10, 12, 14, or 22 to Rivoli; or an easy walk 4 blocks west from rue Halévy along rue de France.

In a sumptuous villa, the Musée Masséna holds collections of paintings, artifacts, photographs, and other art and memorabilia pertaining to Nice and its region. Primitive paintings, ceramics, jewelry, armor, and memorabilia of Napoléon and Maréchal Masséna fill the grand halls, but the greatest attraction is perhaps the halls themselves. The front garden is now a little public park with palm trees, shrubs, and benches.

When leaving the museum, wander next door to the **Hôtel Négresco,** 37 promenade des Anglais, a Nice landmark and one of the world's great hotels. Opened in 1913 by Henri Négresco, a native Romanian, the sumptuous guest rooms and grand public spaces of this belle époque palace were converted into a hospital at the beginning of World War I, a year later. By 1918, Négresco was ruined and his hotel was left a shambles. The hotel's rebirth came in 1957, when it was bought by a Belgian company and put in the charge of M. and Mme Augier, who've worked to restore its former glories. In 1974, the French government granted the Négresco the status of Perpetual National Monument. The deluxe double rooms are about $450 per night, so look elsewhere for accommodations. Be sure to check out the uniforms (really costumes) of the staff.

✪ **Le Château.** Above Vieux Nice.

This hill at the eastern end of the quai des Etats-Unis is named after the fortress that once stood here. There are beautiful groves of evergreens and plantings of cacti, with a path to take you around the hilltop. Several viewpoints afford breathtaking vistas of the town and sea. An **elevator** at the end of the quai des Etats-Unis, near the Hôtel Suisse, will transport you uphill for 5F (80¢) round-trip; it operates daily 10am to 5:50pm. Also here is the **Tour Bellanda,** an old tower where Berlioz lived for some time, which now houses a small naval museum. On the northwest side of the hill is the **old cemetery** of Nice, the largest one in France. In addition to magnificent views of the surrounding mountains, the cemetery offers a fascinating display of funeral statuary over the tombs. My favorite is the Gastaud family plot, which shows a hand trying to raise the top of the tomb.

Musée des Beaux-Arts. 33 av. des Baumettes. ☎ **04-92-15-28-28.** Admission 25F ($4.15) adults, 15F ($2.50) seniors/children. Tues–Sun 10am–noon and 2–6pm. Closed Jan 1, Easter Sun, May 1, and Dec 25. Bus: 38 to Chéret or 3, 7, 12, 18, or 22 to Grosso.

Nice

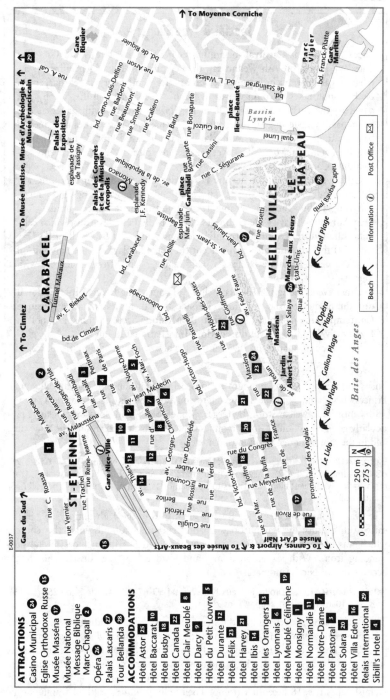

ATTRACTIONS
Casino Municipal ⓐ
Eglise Orthodoxe Russe ⑮
Musée Masséna ⑰
Musée National
  Message Biblique
  Marc-Chagall ②
Opéra ㉖
Palais Lascaris ㉗
Tour Bellanda ㉘

ACCOMMODATIONS
Hôtel Astor ㉕
Hôtel Baccarat ⑩
Hôtel Busby ⑱
Hôtel Canada ㉒
Hôtel Clair Meublé ⑧
Hôtel Darcy ⑨
Hôtel du Petit Louvre ⑤
Hôtel Durante ⑫
Hôtel Félix ㉓
Hôtel Harvey ㉑
Hôtel Ibis ⑭
Hôtel les Orangers ⑬
Hôtel Lyonnais ⑥
Hôtel Meublé Célimène ⑲
Hôtel Monsigny ①
Hôtel Normandie ⑪
Hôtel Notre-Dame ⑦
Hôtel Pastoral ③
Hôtel Solara ⑳
Hôtel Villa Eden ⑯
Relais International ㉙
Sibill's Hotel ④

Special & Free Events

Nice's big event is **Carnival,** beginning 2 or 3 weeks before Mardi Gras (Fat Tuesday), just before Ash Wednesday, the beginning of Lent. Depending on the religious calendar, Nice's Carnival season can begin in January or February; most of the action takes place on weekends. Festive decorations fill the city: by day, parades—the corsi and batailles de fleurs (flower battles)—with marchers and floats pass by reviewing stands in place Masséna; by night, parties and masked balls continue until all hours. On Mardi Gras, the last day of Carnival, the city puts on a grand fireworks show over the Mediterranean. Many of the events surrounding Carnival are also free.

Other yearly celebrations are the **Festin des Cougourdons** in April, held at the Jardins des Arènes in Cimiez. This is a popular fête with songs and dances, and you can buy the cougourdons (carved and decorated dried gourds). And every Sunday in May at the Jardin des Arènes is the **Fête des Mais,** which celebrates the return of spring with folkloric shows and picnics. On **Bastille Day** (July 14) the city puts on a magnificent fireworks display over the bay, and on the **Fête de la Musique** (June 21) parks, squares, and street corners fill with musicians.

Other events along the Riviera include, of course, the **Festival International du Film** held every May in Cannes. In Nice itself, there's a **Festival de Musique Contemporaine** in January, a **Festival de Musique Sacrée** in June, and both a **Jazz Festival** and a **Festival du Folklore International** in July.

For more information on the events listed above, contact the tourist office.

Nice's municipal fine-arts museum is housed in a mansion built for the Ukrainian Princess Kotschoubey in the 1870s. Here you can see paintings from the 17th and 18th centuries as well as works by Degas, Monet, Sisley, and Bonnard. There's a particularly good collection of works by Jules Chéret, who painted around the same time and in the same manner as Toulouse-Lautrec.

Eglise Orthodoxe Russe (Russian Orthodox Church). Av. Nicholas-II. ☎ **04-93-96-88-02.** Admission 12F ($2). Daily 9am–noon and 2:30–6pm (shorter hours in winter). From main station, walk west along av. Thiers to bd. Gambetta, then north on av. Nicholas-II (a 5-minute walk).

Nice was a fashionable resort for Russian aristocrats in the 19th century, and in the early 20th century the tsar Nicholas II and his mother commissioned this church, which was inaugurated in 1912. Its richly decorated interior includes several outstanding icons. With six onion domes and vivid colors, the Russian church has become one of Nice's landmarks.

Palais Lascaris. 15 rue Droite, in Vieux Nice. ☎ **04-93-62-05-54.** Admission 25F ($4.15). Tues–Sun 10am–noon and 2–6pm. Closed Nov.

The Palais Lascaris, deep within the maze of Vieux Nice's winding streets, was the grand home of a prominent Niçois family, the Lascaris-Ventimiglias. This sumptuous palace was built around 1648 and passed through a succession of owners until it was acquired by the city of Nice in 1922 and completely restored. The most stunning interior feature is the monumental staircase that leads to the second floor. You'll also find Flemish tapestries, 18th-century trompe-l'oeil ceilings, and a wealth of antique furniture. As you enter, pick up a sheet (in English, for free) that describes the palace in detail.

ORGANIZED TOURS

BUS TOURS   Even if you're allergic to bus tours, you might find that an organized trip makes it easier to see the sights around Nice. **Santa Azur,** 11 av. Jean-Médecin (☎ **04-93-85-46-81**), offers a day trip to St-Tropez for 130F ($22) and a half-day trip to St-Paul-de-Vence for 100F ($17), among other excursions. They even have a whirlwind day tour of the Côte d'Azur that includes Cannes, St-Paul, Eze, Monaco, and Monte Carlo for 350F ($58).

A good introduction to the city is aboard the **Trains Touristiques de Nice,** train-like vehicles that depart from a signboard on the waterfront in front of the Hotel Meridian every 20 minutes 10am to 7pm in summer. The "trains" make a 40-minute tour of the city's high points, including Le Château. The purchase of one ticket at 30F ($5) allows you to reboard anywhere along the route throughout the day. For information and reservations, call ☎ **04-93-71-44-77.**

WALKING TOURS   Walking tours of Vieux Nice, called *visites commentées,* are sponsored by **Caidem,** 4 rue Blacas (☎ **04-93-62-18-12**), and begin from the Palais Lascaris at 3pm on Tuesday and Sunday throughout the year. Lasting 1½ hours, they're in French with a few words of English explanation and emphasize the Nice baroque. The cost is 45F ($8).

6 Shopping

Shopping in Nice runs the gamut from chic designer boutiques to bustling flea and flower markets. The most upscale shopping streets are **rue Paradis** and **avenue de Verdun.** Only a small notch down are the department stores on **avenue Jean-Médecin,** which include **Galeries Lafayette** on place Masséna. Don't expect any bargains, however, unless you hit the sales in January and June.

Rue Masséna is lined with moderately priced shops and the surrounding side streets are where to pick up usual souvenirs. The best deals in Nice are in shops offering local products. Candied fruit is a specialty, and you'll find the best selection at **Auer,** 7 rue St-François-de-Paule (☎ **04-93-85-77-98**), just outside the Cours Saleya. The shop dates back to 1802 and offers exotic jams and jellies as well. The secret to Provençal cooking is rich, fruity olive oil, and the place to buy it is **Moulin à Huile Alziari,** 14 rue St-François-de-Paule (☎ **04-93-85-76-92**). The tiny shop is cluttered with attractively labeled bottles and cans of fine olive oil pressed in its own mill (moulin). You might also opt for a bottle of "flower water" containing essence of rose, orange, or witch hazel. For more subtle odors, head to **Aux Parfums de Grasse,** 10 rue St-Gaétan (☎ **04-93-85-60-77**), selling 80 scents in flasks and bottles costing 15F ($2.50) for a lipstick-size container to 75F ($13) for 1 liter. The owner will help you combine various brands to create your personal fragrance.

Then there are the markets. The famous **Marché aux Fleurs (Flower Market)** is held Tuesday to Sunday 6am to 5:30pm (except Sunday afternoon) in Vieux Nice at the Cours Saleya. The faded elegance of this 19th-century promenade provides a perfect setting for a market teeming with flowers, fruits, and vegetables. (Take note that the food portion closes at 1pm.) When the plant life disappears on Monday, some of the restaurants that cluster along the marketplace close, but a flea market moves in (8am to 5pm). Tuesday to Saturday 10am to 6pm, there's another flea market on **place Robilante,** next to the Port.

In the general vicinity of Vieux Nice, on **rue Antoine-Gauthier, rue Catherine-Ségurane,** and **rue Emmanuel-Philibert,** behind Le Château, is the **Marché d'Art des Antiquaires,** featuring antiques Monday to Saturday 10am to noon and 3 to 6:30pm.

Forgot your beach novel? Need a *Newsweek?* Nice has several bookstores that carry books in English. Try **The Cat's Whiskers,** 26 rue Lamartine (☎ **04-93-80-02-66**), a block east of Notre-Dame, just off avenue Jean-Médecin, which is owned and run by an Englishwoman. **Maison de la Presse,** 1 place Masséna (☎ **04-93-87-79-42**), has a variety of international newspapers and magazines and a section devoted to English-language books.

7 Nice After Dark

Nice has an active nightlife, from jazz to opera, from movies to cafe life. Cultural offerings are outlined in *L'Info,* a quarterly booklet distributed for free at the tourist office and at hotels, and in *La Semaine des Spectacles,* which catalogs the week's entertainment possibilities for all the towns of the Côte d'Azur.

OPERA, CONCERTS & BALLET

The **Opéra de Nice,** 4 rue St-François-de-Paule (☎ **04-93-53-01-14**), has an active winter season. Performances can include anything from the classics done by European masters to Duke Ellington's *Sophisticated Ladies* by New York's Opera Ensemble. The concerts and recitals performed at the Opéra are equally varied. Ballets are often new works or modern interpretations of classical pieces. The box office is open Tuesday to Saturday 11am to 7pm, and tickets run 50F to 300F ($8 to $50).

Nice also sponsors a series of concerts in local churches Sunday at 3pm. For details, contact the **Orchestra d'Harmonie de la Ville de Nice,** 34 bd. Jean-Jaurès (☎ **04-93-80-08-50**).

THEATER

One of the city's main theatrical venues is the **Théâtre de Nice,** Promenade des Arts (☎ **04-93-80-52-60**), which presents a mix of classical and contemporary works and occasional dance and musical programs. Tickets run 40F to 170F ($7 to $28) and are on sale Tuesday to Saturday 1 to 6pm. The **Théâtre de la Cité,** 3 rue Paganini (☎ **04-93-16-82-69**), is a cultural center presenting both classical and contemporary works. Tickets are about 80F ($13), and the box office is open Tuesday to Saturday 1 to 6pm. All productions are in French, of course.

JAZZ & ROCK

One of Nice's prime locations for officially sponsored jazz is **CEDAC de Cimiez,** 49 av. de la Marne (☎ **04-93-53-85-95**), a cultural center presenting jazz concerts October to June. Tickets run 80F to 100F ($13 to $17). Contact them for current programs. During July, the Grande Parade de Jazz brings famous musicians to the **Parc et Arènes de Cimiez** (☎ **04-93-21-22-01**) for outdoor concerts that last long into the night.

BARS

The most active nightlife centers in **Vieux Nice.** As soon as darkness falls, swarms of young Niçois fill the narrow streets, piling into cramped bars and socializing on the cafe terraces lining the squares. The colorful Cours Saleya that sells flowers and food by day is transformed into a giant outdoor party at night when one bar after another opens its doors.

By far the most popular hangout in Vieux Nice is **Chez Wayne,** 15 rue de la Préfecture (☎ **04-93-13-46-99**), which draws a huge crowd of British and American visitors as well as locals. Though the amusingly decorated bar opens at 3pm, the action doesn't really start until 9 or 9:30pm when the band tunes up. You'll be lucky to squeeze in the door much less elbow your way to the bar. Rock bands play nightly except Monday, when the bar is open but quieter. There's no cover charge.

Smaller but just as rowdy, **Hole in the Wall,** 3 rue de l'Abbaye (☎ 04-93-80-40-16), also presents rock bands every night except Monday, when it's closed. This English pub-style place offers beer at 55F ($9) and a fat, juicy hamburger for 47F ($8). There's no cover charge.

Le Bar des Oiseaux, 5 rue St-Vincent (☎ 04-93-80-27-33), is also in Vieux Nice but has a different idea. Open Monday to Saturday 7pm to 2am, it offers a changing program that may include a poetry reading, a philosophy night, or concerts presenting jazz, African music, or Italian songs. There's a 20F ($3.35) music charge for the concerts.

GAY & LESBIAN BARS

A favorite hangout for lesbians is **Cabaret le Retro,** 227 bd. de la Madeleine (☎ 04-93-44-86-58), in the western part of Nice. It's open daily 11pm to 5am. Near the Négresco and promenade des Anglais, **Le Blue Boy,** 9 rue Spinetta (☎ 04-93-44-68-24), is the Riviera's oldest gay disco. With two bars and two floors, it's a vital nocturnal stop for passengers of the dozens of all-gay cruises that make regular stops at Nice and such nearby ports as Villefranche. Cover is 50F ($8) Saturday and 30F ($5) other days. It's open daily 11pm to 6 or 7am.

DANCE CLUBS

Whether in jeans, spangles, or a suit, you'll feel comfortable at **Le Mississippi,** 5 promenade des Anglais (☎ 04-93-82-06-61). There's a piano bar downstairs and dancing upstairs with a live band that plays a variety of danceable music. The disco attracts all ages and is open nightly 10pm to 4am. Men pay 90F ($15) admission, but women pay only on weekends.

Two other popular clubs are **Le Studio,** 29 rue Alphonse-Karr, off rue Masséna (☎ 04-93-82-37-66; open Tuesday to Sunday 10pm to 4am; admission 110F/$18, including two drinks), and **L'Accordéon,** 36 rue de France, just off promenade des Anglais (☎ 04-93-87-25-42; open daily 11pm to 5am; admission 50F/$8, but free for women). L'Accordéon usually attracts students and a younger crowd.

8 Side Trips: The Côte d'Azur

You'll soon find that the sights in Nice are only half the story—many great attractions are within an hour's train or bus ride. Trains to points east and west of Nice are cheap and fast. Ask for a train schedule *(fiche horaire)* for St-Raphaël–Vintimille at the station; it lists the hours for trains along the coast from St-Raphaël to the Italian border, via Cannes, Antibes, Nice, and Monaco.

Buses are particularly useful for trips to Vence and St-Paul-de-Vence, sites of the splendid Matisse Chapel and the Fondation Maeght. Buses to both destinations depart from Nice's Gare Routière, the central bus station.

BEAULIEU-SUR-MER

The name of this town means "beautiful place by the sea," and it's fitting for the site of one of the most beautiful villas on the Riviera.

The masterpiece ✪ **Villa Kérylos,** rue Gustave-Eiffel (☎ 04-93-01-01-44), was created by the archaeologist Théodore Reinach. Fascinated with ancient Greece, he had this amazing classical villa built on a rocky peninsula. His design is purely

Hellenic down to its furniture and mosaics, with minimal concessions to the 20th century. But where does neoclassicism end and art deco begin? The courtyard, the library, the gardens, and even the baths—everything is lovingly created. Admission is 45F ($8) adults and half price for children, with a guided tour included. July and August, it's open Tuesday to Sunday 2:30 to 6:30pm; September, October, and December to June, hours are Tuesday to Sunday 2 to 6pm. Take the **train** to Beaulieu from Nice, for 11F ($1.85) one-way, second class, with 15 daily connections. You can also take a **bus** for 19F ($3.15) round-trip.

ACCOMMODATIONS The **Hôtel Résidence Frisia,** 2 bd. Eugène-Gauthier, 06310 Beaulieu-sur-Mer (☎ 04-93-01-01-04; fax 04-93-01-31-92), is very central, facing the harbor and beach. It offers 32 units, all with air-conditioning, hair dryers, bathrooms (tub or shower), TVs, and phones. Mid-July to mid-September, a single or double is 690F ($115) and a quad (with a mountain view only) 720F ($120); off-season rates are 15% lower. The continental breakfast is 48F ($8), and American Express, MasterCard, and Visa are accepted. Parking is free.

Three minutes from the train station and the beach, the **Hôtel Le Havre Bleu,** 29 bd. du Maréchal-Joffre, 06310 Beaulieu-sur-Mer (☎ 04-93-01-01-40; fax 04-93-01-29-92), has 22 units, all with bathrooms, TVs, and phones. Singles or doubles are 290F ($48), and the continental breakfast is 30F ($5). American Express, MasterCard, and Visa are accepted. There's plenty of parking space.

DINING Le **Chevalier Blanc,** 3 bd. Maréchal-Joffre (☎ 04-93-01-31-27), serves à la carte dishes only, including bouillabaisse for 90F ($15) and spaghetti bolognese for 32F ($5). The cuisine is typical Provençal, and it's open daily 6:30am to 1am. MasterCard and Visa are accepted.

Centrally located in the harbor area, **Restaurant African Queen,** Port de Plaisance (☎ 04-93-01-10-85), is very popular with locals, whose favorite order is a three-course menu for 80F ($13). It serves mainly French and Italian dishes, like mussels in white-wine sauce, tagliatelle with tomato sauce, grilled chicken al diavolo, and tiramisu. There are 120 seats inside and out. It's open daily noon to midnight, and Visa is accepted.

ST-JEAN-CAP-FERRAT

Facing Beaulieu-sur-Mer and the Villa Kérylos across the water is another idyllic spot, with another exceptional villa.

The Mediterranean-style **Musée Ile de France,** St-Jean-Cap-Ferrat (☎ 04-93-01-33-09), set in lovely gardens, was once the home of the baroness Ephrussi de Rothschild, who gave it to the Institut de France in the 1930s. The sumptuous house is filled with her collected treasures: Renaissance tapestries, furniture (including pieces that belonged to Marie Antoinette), porcelain and art objects from Asia, and masterpieces by European painters. Admission to the villa and garden is 46F ($8) adults and 35F ($6) ages 18 to 24. The museum is open daily 10am to 6pm and the gardens Tuesday to Sunday 9am to noon; both are closed in November. Take the **train** to Beaulieu-sur-Mer and then the **bus** to St-Jean-Cap-Ferrat; or take the **bus** from Nice's Gare Routière to St-Jean-Cap-Ferrat. The round-trip bus fare is 9F ($1.50).

EZE & LA TURBIE

The Côte d'Azur is sprinkled with picturesque Mediterranean mountain villages built high on the craggy rocks, well defended by battlements and the occasional tumble-down fort. Pirate raids made these inaccessible spots popular places to live in the Middle Ages. Today they're popular again because of their antique charm and

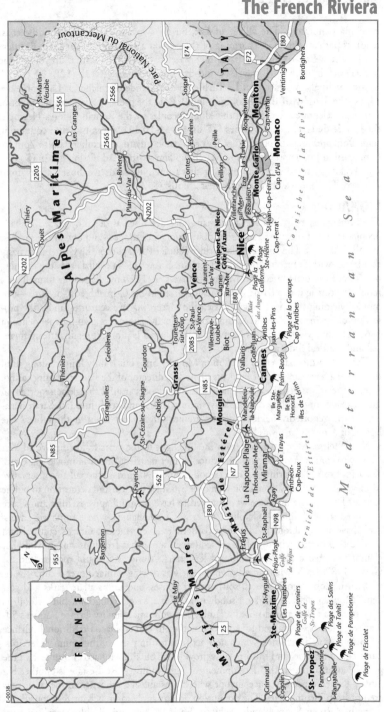

sweeping panoramas. The village of **Eze,** on the Moyenne Corniche (middle coast road), is perhaps the most charming of these. Hop a **bus** from Nice's Gare Routière and get off at Eze to climb up its narrow mazelike streets. The farther up you go, the farther back in time you'll travel. Round-trip bus fare to Eze is 12F ($2).

You might also want to visit **La Turbie** on the Grande Corniche for **La Trofée des Alpes (the Trophy of the Alps),** built in 6 B.C. at the order of Augustus, emperor of Rome, to celebrate the defeat of the Alpine peoples by the Roman legions. Nearby is the **Musée de la Trofée des Alpes** (☎ **04-93-41-10-11**), a minimuseum containing finds from area archaeological digs. It's open daily: July to September 9am to 7pm (to 6pm April to June) and October to March 9:30am to 5pm. Admission is 22F ($3.65). On weekdays, there are four **buses** a day from Nice and five **buses** a day from Monaco. The one-way fare from Nice is 23.50F ($3.90).

MONACO

The principality that Somerset Maugham once described as "a sunny place for shady people" is one of the most glamorous destinations in Europe—and one of the smallest at only 370 acres. The current ruler, Prince Rainier III, is part of the Grimaldi dynasty that began with François Grimaldi, a Genoan. Known as "la Malizia" or "the cunning one," François penetrated the Monaco fortress in 1297 by disguising himself as a monk, capturing it in a battle that's memorialized in the Grimaldi coat-of-arms—two monks wielding swords. Monaco passed the succeeding five centuries under the protection of Spain, France, and Sardinia before finally gaining its own independence in 1861. Though Monaco has its own seat at the United Nations, it retains strong financial and political links to France.

The first casino was set up in 1856 in Monte Carlo, but it only limped along until the arrival a few years later of François Blanc, the director of the Bad Homburg casino. A public relations genius, Blanc made sure newspapers around the globe reported on the escapades of dissolute dukes, showy industrialists, and celebrities like Sarah Bernhardt, who reportedly made a suicide attempt after a bad night at the tables. The legend of Monte Carlo was born.

Nevertheless, Monaco faded from the limelight in the years following World War II, only to come roaring back when Prince Rainier married American movie star Grace Kelly in 1956. The princess's Hollywood connection initially appalled conservative Monégasques, but they were soon won over by Grace's charm and dedication to public service. Though the marriage was rumored to have been unhappy, Rainier and Grace produced three children—Caroline, Albert, and Stephanie—whose romantic adventures have been tabloid fodder for two decades. Nevertheless, Grace's cultural and charitable projects helped polish the country's somewhat frivolous image while her glamor attracted a new generation of jet-setters. Monégasques still mourn Princess Grace's 1982 death, when an automobile she was driving plunged over a cliff.

With its cobblestone streets, softly tinted houses, and immaculate parks and gardens, Monaco may seem like a subdivision of the Magic Kingdom, but behind its fairy-tale facade lies a hard-nosed scramble for economic viability. Prince Rainier's 50-year reign has been marked by a determination to end Monaco's traditional reliance on income from its casinos, which now account for only 4% of the country's receipts. Banking, commerce, and tourism now provide the bulk of Monaco's revenue, and the prince has encouraged the development of light industry. Real estate is another big money-earner, especially since anyone who can establish a residence in the country is exempt from income taxes. The exemption doesn't apply to French citizens, but Europeans like Ringo Starr, Claudia Schiffer, Boris Becker, and Plácido Domingo have found it advantageous to become Monaco residents.

ARRIVING   Monaco can be reached by **train** or **bus** from Nice in less than 30 minutes. Round-trip fare for the train is 38F ($6) and for the bus 17F ($2.85). French francs are accepted in Monaco, and you don't need a passport to enter (unless you're planning to visit the Casino at Monte Carlo).

Do note, however, that Monaco is no longer part of France's telephone system. The new **country code** for Monaco is **377.** The **city code** for all points in Monaco is built into every phone number in the principality. If you're within Monaco, use the complete eight-digit number. If you're calling Monaco from France, dial 00 first, then 377.

THE PRINCIPALITY'S DISTRICTS   Monaco squeezes several districts into its territory. The train station is near **Moneghetti,** site of the Jardin Exotique, prehistoric caves, and an anthropological museum. **Monaco-Ville (The Rock)** is the oldest part of Monaco on a rocky hillside graced by the Palais du Prince, the Oceanographic Museum, lush gardens, narrow streets, and the cathedral where Princess Grace is entombed under a marble slab reading GRATIA. **La Condamine,** the harbor district at the foot of the Rocher, is where most of the Monégasques live; and **Monte Carlo,** famous and infamous, is just uphill from La Condamine. You can walk around virtually all of Monaco in a few hours. Avoid visiting the principality during the **Grand-Prix** (May 13–17, 1999) since many streets are closed to everything but whizzing racecars.

SEEING THE SIGHTS   If you arrive by train from Nice, your first stop should be the **Jardin Exotique** (☎ **93-15-29-80**), open daily 9am to 7pm. It encloses the world's largest open-air cacti and succulents plantation, over 6,000 species, most of Mexican and African origin, and affords spectacular views over the principality. Admission is 39F ($7) adults and 18F ($3) children, students, and seniors. The price includes admission to the **Grotte de l'Observatoire,** prehistoric caves of stalactites and stalagmites, and the **Musée d'Anthropologie Préhistorique,** tracing Paleolithic, Neolithic, and Bronze Age societies. You'll be surprised to find that elephants once roamed the Riviera.

From the Jardin Exotique, you can walk or take bus no. 2 to **Monaco-Ville.** The bus deposits you at place de la Visitation, and you can continue straight ahead through the old streets to place du Palais, dominated by the stately **Palais du Prince** (☎ **93-25-18-31**). The oldest part of the palace, from the 13th century, is the north side. If you get to the old city of Monaco in the morning and if the royal family isn't in residence, you can tour some of the Italianate apartments with their paintings and tapestries, then witness the changing of the guard just before noon. A palace wing is occupied by the **Musée Napoléonien et des Archives du Palais,** an outstanding collection of objects linked to Bonaparte, whose family, incidentally, was related to the princely Grimaldis. The second floor is devoted to exhibits on the history of Monaco. Admission to the palace is 30F ($5); admission to the museum is 20F ($3.30); admission to both is 40F ($7). The palace is open June to September only, daily 9:30am to 6:30pm. December to May, the museum is open Tuesday to Sunday 10:30am to 12:30pm and 2 to 5pm; June to September, it's open daily 9:30am to 6:30pm; and October it's open daily 10am to 5pm.

When you leave place du Palais, take the road on the right, Col. Bellando de Castro, which leads down to the **Cathédrale de Monaco,** where Princess Grace and other members of the royal family are buried. Built in 1875 from white stone mined in La Turbie, the cathedral is notable for an elaborate altarpiece dedicated to St. Nicolas. It's open daily 9:30am to 7pm.

Across the street is an entrance to the **Jardins St-Martin,** a lush collection of exotic tropical plants with splendid views over the Mediterranean. The gardens were created by Prince Albert I, whose statue you can see here gazing at the sea, and they are always open.

The gardens end at the **Musée de l'Océanographie,** avenue St-Martin (☎ 93-15-36-00). This fine aquarium was founded by Prince Albert I, a naturalist and scientist, and the museum contains his collection of specimens, acquired during 30 years of expeditions aboard his oceanographic boats. For many years, the late explorer Jacques Cousteau directed the museum; the yellow contraption outside is one of Commandant Cousteau's early submersible vessels. Don't miss the magnificent view from the second-floor terrace. Admission is 60F ($10). It's open daily: October and March 9:30am to 7pm; November to February 10am to 6pm; April, May, June, and September 9am to 7pm; and July and August 9am to 8pm.

From Monaco-Ville, you can walk through **La Condamine** to **Monte Carlo** or take bus no. 1 and follow the signs to place du Casino.

The oldest part of the famous **Casino de Monte Carlo** was built in 1878 by Charles Garnier, architect of the Paris Opéra. Wander into its posh turn-of-the-century gaming rooms, but don't expect anything as exciting as Mata Hari shooting a Russian spy, which happened here once upon a time. The casino opens at noon and remains receptive, as it were, late into the night. Games played are roulette and blackjack; admission is 50F ($8) and a minimum token is 20F ($3.30). Also on place du Casino is the opulent **Hôtel de Paris,** built in 1864. The doormen can be snooty, but try to take a peek at the lobby that has often served as a movie set. It helps to say that you want to pick up a brochure from reception.

Back down at sea level, follow avenue de la Princesse-Grace to the **Musée National** (☎ 93-30-91-26), housed in a villa designed by Charles Garnier. This is a great place to bring the kids since the museum contains one of the world's greatest collections of dolls and mechanical toys. It's open daily: October to Easter 10am to 12:15pm and 2:30 to 6:30pm and the day after Easter to September 10am to 6pm. Admission is 26F ($4.30) adults and 15F ($2.50) children.

Near the museum is Monaco's most popular beach, **Plage de Larvotto** (☎ 93-15-28-76). There's no charge for bathing on this strip of beach, whose sands are frequently replenished with sand hauled in by barge. The beach is open to public access at all hours.

If you're looking for a pool, try the stupendous **Stade Nautique Rainier-III** (☎ 93-15-28-75), overlooking the yacht-clogged harbor on quai Albert-1er at La Condamine. This gift from Prince Rainier to his subjects is open daily: July and August 9am to midnight and March to June and September to November 9am to 6pm. Admission is 22F ($3.65).

ACCOMMODATIONS   Only a few minutes' walk from the train station, the **Hôtel Cosmopolite,** 4 rue de la Turbie, MC 98000 Monaco (☎ 93-30-16-95; fax 93-30-23-05), is a good backpackers' hotel. It offers 24 clean but very basic units, 4 with a shower and toilet in a partitioned corner of the room and 20 with sink only. The friendly atmosphere is thanks to owner Mme Lydie. Singles run 190F to 260F ($32 to $43), doubles 250F to 370F ($42 to $62), and triples 300F to 400F ($50 to $67); the continental breakfast is 36F ($6). No credit cards are accepted.

Next door is the **Hôtel de France,** 6 rue de la Turbie, MC 98000 Monaco (☎ 93-30-24-64; fax 92-16-13-34), managed by the friendly M. Louis Pauleau. The units are small but neatly outfitted with tiny bathrooms such as you'd find on a ship, TVs, and phones. Singles are 310F ($52), doubles 380F ($63), and triples 450F ($75); the continental breakfast (not obligatory) is 40F ($7). Nearby parking is 40F ($7) per day. MasterCard and Visa are accepted.

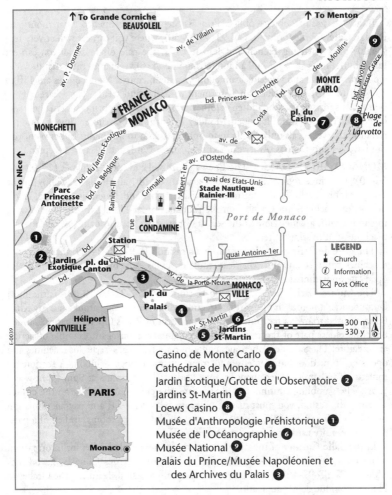

Monaco

↑ To Grande Corniche
BEAUSEOIL

↑ To Menton

av. de Villaini

des Moulins

MONTE CARLO

bd. Princesse- Charlotte bd.

la Costa

pl. du Casino ⑦

⑨

⑧ Plage de Larvotto

FRANCE MONACO

MONEGHETTI

av. P. Doumer

bd. du Jardin-Exotique

bd. de Belgique

Rainier-III

av. de

To Nice ↑

Parc Princesse Antoinette

Grimaldi

av. d'Ostende

bd. Albert-1er

quai des Etats-Unis
Stade Nautique
Rainier-III

Port de Monaco

LA CONDAMINE

rue

Station
Charles-III

Jardin Exotique

bd.

pl. du Canton

bd.

③

av. de la Porte-Neuve

quai Antoine-1er

MONACO-VILLE

①

②

pl. du Palais

④

av. St-Martin

⑥

Jardins St-Martin

⑤

Héliport
FONTVIEILLE

E-0039

LEGEND
✝ Church
ⓘ Information
✉ Post Office

0 ————— 300 m
0 ————— 330 y
N

PARIS

★

Monaco ◉

Casino de Monte Carlo ⑦
Cathédrale de Monaco ④
Jardin Exotique/Grotte de l'Observatoire ②
Jardins St-Martin ⑤
Loews Casino ⑧
Musée d'Anthropologie Préhistorique ①
Musée de l'Océanographie ⑥
Musée National ⑨
Palais du Prince/Musée Napoléonien et
    des Archives du Palais ③

DINING At the **Restaurant and Café de Paris,** place du Casino (☎ 92-16-20-20), you pay for the unique location, in front of the Hôtel de Paris and the casino, but you don't have to eat; sipping coffee or a Coke and watching the world pass by is an affordable experience. It's open daily 9am to 3am, and American Express, Diners Club, MasterCard, and Visa are accepted.

Restaurant le Bistroquet, Galérie Charles-III (☎ 93-50-65-03), is around the downhill corner from the Café de Paris; it doesn't have the same view (from the terrace you get a glimpse of the casino's roof only), but the prices are lower. You can get a plate of pasta for 65F ($11) and a salade niçoise for 75F ($13). It's open daily noon to 2am (or later). American Express, Diners Club, MasterCard, and Visa are accepted.

Restaurant le Biarritz, 3 rue de la Turbie (☎ 93-30-26-17), 100 yards from the train station, serves a tasty three-course meal for 65F ($13); it might be spaghetti, steak haché, or mussels, then ice cream, mousse au chocolat, or fresh fruit. Other items served are pizza, ham omelet, pork chops, and sole meunière. Visa is accepted, and it's open daily 10am to midnight.

In a true case of noblesse oblige, Princess Stephanie has opened a cafe/boutique, **Replay Café,** 57 rue Grimaldi (☎ **93-30-02-30**), where you can eat well at very reasonable prices. Mixing French and Italian styles, the cafe offers an all-you-can-eat lunch buffet for 75F ($15) and an interesting 95F ($16) vegetarian meal that includes a polenta pancake and vegetable cannelloni as a main course. Main courses are 45F to 75F ($8 to $13) and include an assortment of pastas and salads. The adjacent boutique sells sportswear and children's clothes. I'm told that the princess actually works here from time to time. It's open Monday to Saturday 9am to midnight, but the restaurant serves meals only 11:30am to 3pm and 7pm to midnight. In between, you can have tea and pastries. American Express, MasterCard, and Visa are accepted.

MONACO AFTER DARK   The **Loews Casino,** 12 av. des Spélugues (☎ **93-50-65-00**), is a huge room filled with one-armed bandits, adjoining the lobby in the Loews Monte-Carlo. It also features blackjack, craps, and American roulette. Additional slot machines are available on the roof starting at 11am—for those who want to gamble with a wider view of the sea. It's open daily 4pm to 4am (to 5am for slot machines). Admission is free.

The **Café de Paris,** place du Casino, has a casino (☎ **92-16-24-29**) that offers slot machines from 10am, and American roulette, craps, and blackjack from 5pm. It's open late and admission is free.

The **Monte Carlo Casino,** place du Casino (☎ **377-92-16-20-00**), is the most famous and glamorous in the world, attracting Mata Hari, King Farouk, and Aly Khan (Onassis used to own a part interest). The architect of Paris's Opéra, Charles Garnier, built the oldest part of the casino, and it remains an extravagant example of period architecture. The Salle des Amériques contains only Las Vegas–style slot machines and opens at 2pm; doors for roulette and trente-quarante open at noon. A section for roulette and chemin-de-fer opens at 3pm, and blackjack begins at 9pm (5pm weekends). The gambling continues until very late, the closing depending on the crowd. To enter the casino, you must carry a passport, be at least 21, and pay an admission of 50F to 100F ($8 to $17) if you want to enter the private rooms. In lieu of a passport, an identity card or driver's license will suffice.

In the **Salle Garnier** of the casino, concerts are held periodically; for information, contact the tourist office—the Direction du Tourisme et des Congrès, 2a bd. des Moulin (☎ **33-92-166-166**). The music is usually classical, featuring the Orchestre Philharmonique de Monte Carlo.

The casino also contains the **Opéra de Monte-Carlo.** This world-famous house, opened in 1879 by Sarah Bernhardt, presents a winter and spring repertoire that traditionally includes Puccini, Mozart, and Verdi. The famed Ballets Russes de Monte-Carlo, starring Nijinsky and Karsavina, was created in 1918 by Sergei Diaghilev. The national orchestra and ballet company of Monaco appear here. Tickets may be hard to come by, but you can make inquiries at the **Atrium du Casino** (☎ **92-16-22-99**), open Tuesday to Sunday 10am to 12:30pm and 2 to 5pm. Standard tickets are 100F to 580F ($17 to $97).

ROQUEBRUNE

Roquebrune, like Eze, is a picturesque fortified village, but this one has a fairy-tale castle, the **Château de Roquebrune** (☎ **04-93-35-62-87**), dating from the 10th century but extensively rebuilt in the 13th. A museum in the castle details the area's colorful history. Admission is 20F ($3.30) adults, 15F ($2.50) seniors, and 10F ($1.65) children; the château is open Thursday to Tuesday 10am to noon and 2 to 6pm.

The village and castle are on the Grande Corniche, accessible by bus. The round-trip **bus** fare from Nice to Roquebrune is 20.50F ($3.40). Not far east of Roquebrune lies the Italian border: **Portofino** and other beautiful towns on the Italian Riviera are also easy day trips from Nice.

ST-PAUL-DE-VENCE & VENCE

St-Paul-de-Vence is a picture-perfect medieval village perched on a hill with one of the Riviera's finest art collections, the Fondation Maeght, nearby. Vence, a few miles farther, is the site of Henri Matisse's masterful chapel. You can visit the Fondation Maeght and Matisse's chapel with time left over to explore the narrow streets of these towns, but you need to plan carefully since the chapel has limited hours and the Fondation Maeght closes for lunch most of the year.

The town of **St-Paul** is a beautifully preserved example of a fortified hilltop village. In the 1920s, artists Paul Signac, Modigliani, Pierre Bonnard, and Chaim Soutine "discovered" St-Paul, gathering at the restaurant Colombe d'Or, which now contains an impressive art collection. Other artists, writers, and personalities followed, including actor Yves Montand, who made St-Paul his home in later life. At the farthest tip of the village is a cemetery with the tomb of Marc Chagall, another regular visitor. The village contains a number of art galleries (usually closed noon to 2pm) and many souvenir shops. The best time to visit is in the afternoon, when the tour buses leave.

Outside the walled village is the ✪ **Fondation Maeght,** St-Paul-de-Vence (☎ **04-93-32-81-63**), the best museum in the south of France. Designed by the Spanish architect José Luís Sert, the museum and its park are one, an organic whole that's itself a work of art. Sculpture graces the lawns, placed expertly among the fountains, pools, trees, and shrubs. In the collection is a large number of works by Giacometti, Arp, Braque, Chagall, Bonnard, Kandinsky, Hepworth, Léger, Miró, Calder, Tàpies, and others. Changing exhibits are mounted frequently. There's a library, a bookshop, and a cafeteria. Admission is 45F ($8). The museum is open daily: July to September 10am to 7pm and October to June 10am to 12:30pm and 2:30 to 6pm.

The easiest way to reach St-Paul is by **bus** from Nice's Gare Routière. The trip takes about 40 minutes, and the bus leaves you in front of the entrance to the village before continuing on to Vence. To find the Fondation Maeght, go down the hill in the direction of the bus and turn right at the parking lot to follow the road leading up another hill. One-way bus fare from Nice is 22F ($3.65).

North of St-Paul, you can visit the sleepy old town of **Vence,** with its Vieille Ville (Old Town). If you're wearing the right kind of shoes, the narrow, steep streets are worth exploring. The cathedral on place Godeau is unremarkable except for some 15th-century choir stalls. But if it's a Tuesday or Thursday, most visitors quickly pass through the narrow gates of this once-fortified walled town to where the sun shines more brightly.

It was a golden autumn along the Côte d'Azur. The great Henri Matisse was 77, and after a turbulent time of introspection he set out to create his masterpiece, the ✪ **Chapelle du Rosaire**—in his own words, "the culmination of a whole life dedicated to the search for truth." You might pass right by the chapel of the Dominican nuns of Monteils, on avenue Henri-Matisse just outside Vence (☎ **04-93-58-03-26**), finding it unremarkable—until you spot a 40-foot crescent-adorned cross rising from a blue-tile roof.

The light inside picks up the subtle coloring in the simply rendered leaf forms and abstract patterns—sapphire blue, aquamarine, and lemon yellow. In black-and-white ceramics, St. Dominic is depicted in a few lines. The Stations of the Cross are also black-and-white tile, with Matisse's self-styled "tormented and passionate" figures. The bishop of Nice himself came to bless the chapel in late spring 1951 when the artist's work was completed. Matisse died 3 years later. December 13 to October, the chapel is open Tuesday and Thursday 10 to 11:30am and 2:30 to 5:30pm. Admission is 10F ($1.65); donations are welcome.

BIOT

Though roses and carnations are grown here, the village of Biot has been noted through the centuries for its potters and, more recently, for its glass blowers. Come for the Musée Léger, but plan to spend an hour or so exploring the town. Take the **train** to Antibes for 24F ($4) one-way, then the **bus** to Biot.

Fernand Léger (1881–1955) was one of the creators of cubism, but he started as an impressionist. The more than 340 paintings in the ✪ **Musée National Fernand-Léger,** chemin du Val-de-Pome (☎ 04-92-91-50-30), reflect his evolution as a painter. Fascinated by the transformations of modern society, he developed an "aesthetics of the machine," painting even the human figure as a system of tubes and mechanical parts. This led to his being called a "tubist." His brash conception earned much criticism, but his work speaks for itself. Admission is 30F ($5) adults and 20F ($3.30) ages 18 to 24 and over 60. It's open Wednesday to Monday 10am to noon and 2 to 6pm (to 5pm in winter).

ANTIBES & JUAN-LES-PINS

Greek settlers from Marseille founded **Antibes** in the 4th century B.C. and called it Antipolis ("the opposite city"), a reference to its location across the Baie des Anges from Nice. **Juan-les-Pins** is part of Antibes but with a separate beach. There are 12 daily **train** connections from Nice; the 24-minute trip costs 24F ($4).

The 14th-century granite **Château Grimaldi** was built on the ruins of a Roman camp. Picasso came here in 1946 and spent the fall painting and potting. Many of the works you'll see at the ✪ **Musée Picasso,** in the Château Grimaldi, place Mariéjol (☎ 04-92-90-54-20), were created in that one season. Picasso's works are displayed along with those of several contemporaries. Admission is 30F ($5) adults and 18F ($3) ages 17 to 24 and over 60. Summer hours are Tuesday to Sunday 10am to noon and 2 to 6pm (Tuesday to Monday in winter).

The **Musée Archéologique,** on the bastion St-André (☎ 04-92-90-54-35), depicts the town's Greek and Roman history through artifacts—there are some very beautiful amphoras—found in the excavations and coastal waters. Admission is 10F ($1.65) adults and 5F (80¢) ages 15 to 24 and over 60. It's open daily 10am to noon and 2 to 6pm (closed November).

ACCOMMODATIONS   The **Hôtel Royal,** 16 bd. du Maréchal-Leclerc, 06600 Antibes (☎ 04-93-34-03-09; fax 04-93-34-23-31), offers 27 units (all with bathroom, TV, and phone), plus a three-star restaurant. The hotel faces the beach, which has an admission of 40F ($7), including mattress and shower. Singles are 580F ($97) and doubles/triples 740F ($123). These rates are for July and August; they're considerably lower off-season. Garage parking is 35F ($6) per day. American Express, Diners Club, MasterCard, and Visa are accepted.

Thirty yards from the beach is the **Hôtel Savoy,** 144 bd. Wilson, 06160 Juan-les-Pins (☎ 04-93-61-13-82; fax 04-93-67-29-72), offering 25 units, all with bathroom, TV, and phone. Singles cost 310F ($52) and doubles 420F ($70). The continental breakfast is 35F ($6). American Express, Diners Club, MasterCard, and Visa are accepted.

DINING   Facing the beach, the **Restaurant Chez Olive,** 2 bd. du Maréchal-Leclerc (☎ 04-93-34-42-32), offers 60 seats inside and 60 more on a terrace. Serving Provençal fare, it features menus du jour for 86F, 126F, and 154F ($14, $21, $26) and is open Tuesday to Sunday 11am to midnight. American Express, Diners Club, MasterCard, and Visa are accepted. The **Restaurant du Midi,** 93 bd. Poincaré (☎ **04-93-61-35-16**), serves an excellent menu for 85F ($14). American Express, Diners Club, and MasterCard are accepted. It's open Tuesday to Saturday 10am to midnight.

CANNES

Cannes is a much more glamorous resort than Nice, and the prices reflect that difference, especially during the famous **International Film Festival.** When the festival is on, the town is at its most frenzied, with mobs of paparazzi on the seafront boulevards and mobs of stars and wannabes posing everywhere. It was on the sandy beaches of this chic resort in the 1920s that Coco Chanel soaked up some sun and startled Paris by returning with a tan, a fashion that quickly caught on and became popular worldwide. There are **train** connections about every half hour from Nice, with the 40-minute trip costing 32F ($5).

Wander down the **promenade de la Croisette,** the elegant waterfront promenade lined with designer boutiques, and have a look at the home of the film festival, the **Palais des Festivals.** The esplanade running along La Croisette is a peaceful oasis of flowers and trees and a great place for a picnic. Above the harbor, the old town of Cannes sits on **Suquet Hill,** where you'll see a 14th-century tower, which the English dubbed the Lord's Tower.

Nearby is the **Musée de la Castre,** in the Château de la Castre, Le Suquet (☎ **04-93-38-55-26**), containing fine arts, with a section on ethnography. The latter includes relics and objects from everywhere from the Pacific islands to Southeast Asia, including both Peruvian and Mayan pottery. There's also a gallery devoted to relics of ancient Mediterranean civilizations. Five rooms are devoted to 19th-century paintings. The museum is open Wednesday to Monday: April to June 10am to noon and 2 to 6pm, July to September 10am to noon and 3 to 7pm, and October to March 10am to noon and 2 to 5pm. Admission is 10F ($1.65) adults, free for children.

Another museum of note, the **Musée de la Mer,** Fort Royal (☎ **04-93-38-55-26**), displays artifacts from Ligurian, Roman, and Arab civilizations, including paintings, mosaics, and ceramics. You can also see the jail where the "Man in the Iron Mask" was incarcerated. Temporary exhibits of photography are also shown. June to September, it's open daily 10am to noon and 2 to 6pm. Admission is 10F ($1.65).

Cannes's sandy **beaches** extend over 3 miles—half free (or public), half owned by hotels charging 100F to 160F ($17 to $27) for a mattress, towel, and cabin. The choice public beach is **Plage du Midi,** west of the old harborfront, with the best sun in the afternoon. **Plage Gazagnaire,** another good beach, is east of the new port, ideal in the morning.

ACCOMMODATIONS Cannes has moderately priced hotels, but if you're thinking of coming during the Film Festival (May 12 to 23, 1999), be aware that prices skyrocket and most hotels are booked a year in advance.

Ideally located between the train station and La Croisette, the **Hôtel Splendid,** 4–6 rue Félix-Faure, 06400 Cannes (☎ **04-93-99-53-11;** fax 04-93-99-55-02), whose facade looks from the waterfront like a sugar wedding cake topped with flags, is the best deal in the three-star category. It offers 62 units, all with air-conditioning, bathrooms (tub or shower), TVs, and phones; 42 have fully equipped kitchenettes. Singles with a sea view (there are 47) run 690F to 900F ($115 to $150) and doubles or twins 740F to 980F ($123 to $163). Singles with a view of rue Félix-Faure are 590F to 690F ($98 to $115) and doubles or twins 650F to 740F ($108 to $123). These rates are for April to October and are reduced 20% to 30% in other months. Rates include a continental breakfast. American Express, Diners Club, MasterCard, and Visa are accepted.

When leaving the Cannes train station, you'll directly face the **Hôtel Atlas,** 5 place de la Gare, 06400 Cannes (☎ **04-93-39-01-17;** fax 04-93-39-29-57). There are 52 units, 42 with bathrooms (tub or shower), TVs, and phones. The rooms are carpeted and air-conditioned and have double-glazed windows to ensure a good night's sleep. Though not lavish, everything looks new and fresh, and there's an elevator. Singles cost 250F to 390F ($42 to $65) and doubles or twins 300F to 440F ($50 to $73). The continental breakfast is 38F ($6). The lower rates apply except in July and August and during the Film Festival. American Express, Diners Club, MasterCard, and Visa are accepted. Yves Tarniquet is the friendly manager.

The **Hôtel Les Charmettes,** 47 rue de Grasse, 06400 Cannes (☎ **04-93-39-17-13;** fax 04-93-68-08-41), is a modern, somewhat boxy three-story hotel near the center of Cannes, with a laissez-faire attitude. It welcomes a large number of gays. Each room is soundproof, air-conditioned, and individually decorated in a pleasing style. Breakfast is the only meal served, though you can get drinks in the lobby. Doubles range from 260F to 350F ($43 to $58). American Express, Diners Club, MasterCard, and Visa are accepted.

The best budget find in Cannes, the **Hôtel National,** 8 rue du Maréchal-Joffre, 06400 Cannes (☎ **04-93-39-91-92;** fax 04-92-98-44-06), is halfway between the train station and the beach. It's owned by an English/French couple, the Potters—he originates from London and is very friendly and helpful. There are 16 units on three floors (no elevator), 11 with bathroom (shower). Singles are 140F to 190F ($23 to $32), doubles 165F to 275F ($28 to $46), and triples 275F to 330F ($46 to $55). The continental breakfast is 25F ($4.15). Rates are slightly higher in July and August and during the Film Festival. American Express and MasterCard are accepted.

Le Chalit Youth Hostel, 27 av. du Maréchal-Galliéni, 06400 Cannes (☎ **04-93-99-22-11;** fax 04-93-39-00-28), is clean and the atmosphere is easygoing, thanks to owner/manager Annik. You have free use of hot plates for do-it-yourself breakfasts and dinners 7 to 9am and 6:30 to 9pm. There are 16 beds with 3 to 7 double-decker cots per room. The rate is 85F ($14) per person per night, but rises to 120F ($20) during the Film Festival. No credit cards are accepted. No curfew. From the train station, turn right uphill to boulevard Carnot and follow the sign on the corner of rue Montaigne.

DINING   Restaurants are expensive in Cannes, but it's easy to supplement restaurant meals with picnics. **Rue Meynadier,** parallel to rue Félix-Faure, has stores selling regional products, and there's a morning food market at **Marché Forville** (Tuesday to Sunday 7am to 1pm) where you can pick up fruits, vegetables, and cheese. The **Esplanade G.-Pompidou,** next to the Festival Palace, is a tranquil spot to enjoy your goodies.

For excellent dining on a budget, the best address is ✪ **Au Bec Fin,** 12 rue du 24 Aout (☎ **04-93-38-35-86**), just steps from the train station. The menu offers a wide selection of bistro dishes with an emphasis on Provençal cuisine. The pastas are made on the premises and include an excellent spaghetti with seafood sauce for 90F ($15). The hearty choucroute is a bargain at 65F ($11), and lamb with curry sauce is another specialty. There's a three-course menu for 75F ($13), but the higher-price 94F ($16) menu often includes a wonderful bourride—fish fillets in a stew spiced with saffron and garlic and served with boiled potatoes. The bistro attracts a well-heeled crowd of locals who could obviously afford to spend a great deal more on food but prefer to feast here in a convivial ambiance. The bistro is open Monday to Saturday 11:30am to 2:30pm and 6:30 to 10pm (except Saturday evening) and accepts American Express, MasterCard, and Visa.

Located 150 yards off the beach, **Le Palais du Dragon,** 9 rue du Bivouac-Napoléon (☎ **04-93-38-68-11**), is a small Chinese restaurant, the only large item being a papier-mâché dragon next to the entrance. Chicken with coconut sauce is 38F ($6), curry chicken 45F ($8), crunchy pork 55F ($9), a scallops platter 75F ($13), and Peking duck 55F ($9). The three-course menu is 59F ($10) at lunch and 95F ($16) at dinner. It's open daily noon to 2pm and 7 to 10pm but always crowded. American Express and Visa are accepted.

A family-run restaurant facing La Croisette and the Music Pavilion, **Le Rendez-Vous,** 35 rue Félix-Faure (☎ **04-93-68-55-10**), is one of the smallest in a long row of eateries but probably the best for quality, quantity, and service. Spaghetti bolognese, fruits de mer, and seafood pizza are all good, and the bouillabaisse at 195F ($33) is enough for three. The three-course menu du jour is 89F ($15). The inside room has a beautiful stucco ceiling. Try to sit on the veranda—it's like watching TV. The restaurant is open daily noon to 2:15pm and 6:45 to 10pm and accepts American Express, Diners Club, MasterCard, and Visa.

Cannes's largest cafeteria, 50 yards from La Croisette and the Film Festival Palace, the **Grand Café,** 2 rue Félix-Faure, at the corner of Allées de la Liberté (☎ **04-93-99-93-08**), offers 230 seats inside and out. Pizzas (10 choices) run 25F to 45F ($4.15 to $8), a generous portion of steamed mussels is 55F ($9), steak tartare goes for 69F ($12), and a cheese omelet is 40F ($7). Four kinds of lunch and dinner menus are served Monday to Friday, ranging from 40F ($7) (spaghetti bolognese with salad) to 60F ($10) (minestrone soup, Wiener schnitzel, crème caramel). It's open daily 9am to midnight, and American Express, Diners Club, MasterCard, and Visa are accepted.

CANNES AFTER DARK   **Jane's,** in the cellar of the Gray d'Albion hotel, 38 rue des Serbes (☎ **04-92-99-79-79**), is a stylish and appealing nightclub with an undercurrent of coy permissiveness. The crowd is well dressed (the men often wearing jackets and ties) and covers a wide gamut of age groups. The cover is 50F to 100F ($8 to $17), depending on business, and on some slow nights women enter for free. It's open Wednesday to Sunday 11pm to 5am.

ST-TROPEZ

Sun-kissed lasciviousness is rampant in this carnival town, 47 miles southwest of Cannes, but the true Tropezian resents the fact that the port has such a bad reputation. "We can be classy, too," one native has insisted. Creative people in the lively arts along with ordinary folk create a volatile mixture. One observer has said that St-Tropez "has replaced Naples for those who accept the principle of dying after seeing it. It is a unique fate for a place to have made its reputation on the certainty of happiness."

Colette lived here for many years. Even the late diarist Anaïs Nin, confidante of Henry Miller, posed for a little cheesecake on the beach in 1939 in a Dorothy Lamour bathing suit. Earlier, St-Tropez was known to Guy de Maupassant, Matisse, and Bonnard.

Artists, composers, novelists, and the film colony are attracted to St-Tropez in summer. Trailing them is a line of humanity unmatched anywhere else on the Riviera for sheer flamboyance.

The nearest **rail station** is in St-Raphaël, a neighboring resort; at the Vieux Port, four or five boats per day leave the **Gare Maritime de St-Raphaël,** rue Pierre-Auble (☎ **04-94-95-17-46**), for St-Tropez (trip time: 50 min.), costing 100F ($17) round-trip. Some 15 **Sodetrav buses** per day, leaving from the Gare Routière in St-Raphael (☎ **04-94-95-24-82**), go to St-Tropez, taking 1½ to 2¼ hours, depending on the bus. A one-way ticket is 48.50F ($8). Buses run directly to St-Tropez from Toulon and Hyères.

Near the harbor is the **Musée l'Annonciade (Musée de St-Tropez)** at place Georges-Grammont (☎ **04-94-97-04-01**), installed in the former chapel of the Annonciade. As a legacy from the artists who loved St-Tropez, the museum shelters one of the finest modern art collections on the Riviera. Many of the artists, including Paul Signac, depicted the port of St-Tropez. The collection includes such works as Van Dongen's yellow-faced *Women of the Balustrade* and paintings and sculpture by Bonnard, Matisse, Braque, Utrillo, Seurat, Derain, and Maillol. The museum is open Wednesday to Monday: June to September 10am to noon and 3 to 7pm and December to May and October 10am to noon and 2 to 6pm. Admission is 30F ($5) adults and 15F ($2.50) children.

Two miles from St-Tropez, **Port Grimaud** makes an interesting outing. If you approach the village at dusk, when it's softly bathed in Riviera pastels, it'll look like some old hamlet, perhaps from the 16th century. But this is a mirage. Port Grimaud is the dream fulfillment of its promoter, François Spoerry, who carved it out of marshland and dug canals. Flanking these canals, fingers of land extend from the main square to the sea. The homes are Provençal style, many with Italianate window arches. Boat owners can anchor right at their doorsteps. One newspaper called the port "the most magnificent fake since Disneyland."

The hottest Riviera **beaches** are at St-Tropez. The best for families are those closest to the center, including the amusingly named **Plage de la Bouillabaisse** and **Plage des Graniers.** The more daring are the 6-mile sandy crescents at **Plage des Salins** and **Plage de Pampellone,** beginning some 2 miles from the town center and best reached by bike if you're not driving. "Notoriously decadent," **Plage de Tahiti** occupies the north end of Pampellone; it's a strip of golden sand that has long been favored by exhibitionists wearing next to nothing and cruising each other shamelessly. If you ever wanted to go topless or wear a daring bikini, this is the place.

ST-TROPEZ AFTER DARK **Le Papagayo,** in the Résidence du Nouveau Port (☎ **04-94-97-07-56**), is one of the largest nightclubs in St-Tropez, with two floors, three bars, and lots of attractive women and men from throughout the Mediterranean eager to pursue their bait. The decor was inspired by the psychedelic 1960s in an urban setting like New York. The cover is 100F ($17) and includes the first drink. April to October, it's open nightly 11:30pm to around 6am.

Le Pigeonnier, 13 rue de la Ponche (☎ **04-94-97-36-85**), rocks, rolls, and welcomes a clientele that's 80% to 85% gay, male, and ages 20 to 50. Most of the socializing revolves around the long, narrow bar, where men folk from all over Europe seem to enjoy chitchatting. There's also a dance floor. The cover is 70F ($12) and includes your first drink. Other than a reopening for a brief sojourn at Christmas and New Year's, the place is open only April to October, daily 11:45pm to sometime between 6 and 8am, depending on the energy of the crowd.

Paris & the Ile de France

by Jeanne Oliver

The treasures of Paris are legendary and inexhaustible. The Musée du Louvre, the Tour Eiffel, the Musée d'Orsay, the Cathédrale Notre-Dame, the Arc de Triomphe, and dozens of other monuments and museums reflect the grandeur of a city whose influence has spread throughout the world. Yet visiting the highlights merely scratches the surface. Wander the Marais or the Latin Quarter, for example, and you'll find medieval streets, hidden squares, and funky shops that perfectly balance the majestic proportions of the Champs-Elysées or the *grands boulevards* lined with stately 19th-century residences.

But Paris has never been content to rest on the past's artistic and architectural accomplishments. Monuments like the Latin Quarter's Institut Arabe, the Beaubourg's Centre Pompidou, the Bastille's Opéra, and southeast Paris's Bibliothèque National have transformed old neighborhoods. The skyscrapers of La Défense have created a futuristic office world in the west of Paris, and the La Villette complex is a futuristic science world in the city's northeast corner. The boldness and imagination of these hugely expensive projects reflects the determination of the French to keep their capital in the forefront.

Despite the grandiose projects, Parisians have come to accept that their city no longer dominates the world's cultural scene. You may be surprised by the number of Hollywood blockbusters playing in French cinemas or American best-sellers sold in Parisian bookstores. The days are long gone when French people "refused" to speak English. Now you'll find Parisians eager to practice whatever English they've acquired.

Even as Paris becomes a modern international city, the traditional art of living that Parisians have honed to perfection continues to exert its magic. And you don't need to spend a fortune to appreciate it. Spend a lazy afternoon people-watching from a cafe terrace. Bring a crusty baguette and some wine to a neatly manicured park and watch a game of *boules*. Catch the briny aroma of fresh mussels or the pungency of roasting chicken at an outdoor market. The lusciously arranged shop windows, the flowers that pour over iron balconies, and the meandering streets of individually crafted houses compose an urban landscape of exquisite beauty and grace. *Ça, c'est Paris!*

REQUIRED DOCUMENTS For visits of less than 3 months, all U.S., Canadian, and New Zealand citizens need is a valid passport. Australian travelers need a visa in addition. U.K. travelers need only a National Identity Card.

Budget Bests

No other city offers such a wealth of free and low-cost sightseeing. Head to the top of **Sacré-Coeur** or the department store **Samaritaine** for unbeatable views over Paris. Picnic in one of the city's flowery parks—the **Jardin du Luxembourg** and **Jardin des Tuileries,** for example—and then admire the museum-quality sculpture for free. Browse St-Germain's **art galleries** and the **antiques shops** in Le Louvre des Antiquaires for another visual treat. The outdoor **food markets** where Parisians shop for groceries provide a colorful tour of French gastronomy.

Paris is a great town for **walking,** but at some point you'll need to have a meal, a coffee, or rest your feet. Since some neighborhoods are more expensive than others, try to avoid running out of steam in a **touristy area** where your only choices are likely to be overpriced tourist traps. The Champs-Elysées and the Eiffel Tower are must-sees, but if you can avoid being hungry or footsore in those neighborhoods you'll save a lot of money. Stay away from famous **literary cafes** and **big places** on well-traveled avenues. Seek out **local watering holes** on side streets and ask for *un café* (an espresso) or *un deca* (decaffeinated coffee). You'll pay less standing up at the bar, and having coffee at an inside table is often cheaper than having it outside.

OTHER FROMMER'S TITLES   For more on Paris, see *Frommer's Paris, Frommer's Paris from $70 a Day, Frommer's Irreverent Guide to Paris, Frommer's France, Frommer's Gay & Lesbian Europe, Frommer's Europe, Frommer's Memorable Walks in Paris,* or *Frommer's Food Lover's Companion to France.*

1 Paris Deals & Discounts

SPECIAL DISCOUNTS

FOR EVERYONE   A **Carte Orange** is a weekly or monthly pass for all of Paris's subway or bus lines in zones 1 and 2. (Don't rush to pay supplemental charges for passes that'll carry you beyond zone 2. The Métro lines end at the outer edge of zone 2, and most of the interesting monuments lie within these zones.) Even if you want to go to Versailles or Fontainebleau (zone 4) for the day, it's cheaper to buy Métro tickets on an individual basis. Don't even consider buying a supplement for up to zone 6.

The price of a Carte Orange for zones 1 and 2 is 75F ($13) for 1 week *(coupon hebdomadaire)* or 255F ($43) for a month *(coupon mensuel).* If you take more than seven trains in a day, a 30F ($5) 1-day pass, the **Mobilis,** will be your best bet since it offers unlimited travel in zones 1 and 2. Know in advance that to obtain your pass you'll need to provide a passport-size photo of yourself, the cost of which will increase the overall expense by a few francs.

Barring the purchase of any of the above passes, an individual Métro ticket at 8F ($1.30) is a good deal, considering the distance and speed at which you'll travel. Even better is a **carnet,** a packet of 10 individual Métro tickets at an unbeatable 48F ($8).

La Carte Musées et Monuments (Museum and Monuments Pass) is sold at any of the museums that honor it, at any branch of the Paris tourist office, or in Métro and RER stations. It offers free entrance to the permanent collections of 65 monuments and museums in Paris and the Ile de France. The cost of a 1-day pass is 70F ($12), a 3-day pass 140F ($23), and a 5-day pass 200F ($33). In addition to the substantial savings offered, the pass allows you to bypass long waiting lines to get into the Louvre.

What Things Cost in Paris	U.S. $
Taxi from Charles de Gaulle Airport to the city center	37.00
Taxi from Orly Airport to the city center	28.00
Public transportation for an average trip within the city (from a Métro *carnet* of 10)	.80
Local telephone call	.30
Double room at the Ritz (deluxe)	680.00
Double room at the Hôtel Abbatial St-Germain (moderate)	111.00
Double room at the Hôtel du Globe (inexpensive)	65.00
Lunch for one, including wine, at Bofinger (moderate)	29.00
Lunch for one, without wine, at Le Café du Commerce (inexpensive)	14.00
Dinner for one, without wine, at Jules Verne (deluxe)	150.00
Dinner for one, without wine, at Aux Charpentiers (moderate)	26.00
Dinner for one, without wine, at La Petite Hostellerie (budget)	10.00
Glass of wine	2.50
Coca-Cola	2.50
Cup of coffee (espresso)	2.25
Roll of ASA 100 color film, 36 exposures	7.00
Admission to the Louvre	7.50
Movie ticket	8.00
Theater ticket (at the Comédie-Française)	14.00

Another money-saver involves the **VAT (TVA in French)** refund. France imposes a value-added tax of up to 20.6% on most goods, but if you're not a European resident you can get a refund. You must spend more than 1,200F ($200) in one store and show the clerk your passport to prove your eligibility. You'll then be given an export sales document in triplicate (two pink sheets and a green one), which you must sign, as well as an envelope addressed to the store. Travelers departing Paris from Charles de Gaulle Airport may visit the Europe Tax-Free Shopping (ETS) refund point to receive an immediate refund in cash. Otherwise, when you leave Paris, arrive at the airport early to avoid lines at the *détaxe* (refund) booth at French customs. If you're traveling by train, go to the *détaxe* area in the station before boarding—you can't get your refund documents processed on the train. Your reimbursement will either be mailed by check (in French francs) or credited to your credit-card account. In some cases, you may get your refund immediately, paid at an airport bank window. Some large department stores or stores advertising "Duty-Free Shopping" may discount the VAT at the time of purchase.

FOR CHILDREN & YOUTH   Anyone 17 and under is **admitted free** to France's national museums, including the Louvre, the Musée d'Orsay, and the Musée Picasso. Those 18 to 25 receive a **50% discount.** If you plan to travel by train, the SNCF offers a full menu of discounts. If you have a child 15 or under, check out the **Carte Kiwi 4 X 4,** offering a 50% reduction for the child and up to four adults traveling along. It costs 291F ($49) and is good for a month, but only a limited number of seats are available and the discounts aren't offered for periods of peak travel or on holidays. Reserve in advance. There's also a **12–25 card,** costing 270F ($45) and valid for

1 year; it offers 25% to 50% discounts to ages 12 to 25. Even without the card, the 12-to-25 set can get 25% off on trains, except during peak travel periods or holidays. For more information, ask at any rail ticket office in France or call the **SNCF** at ☎ **01-53-90-20-20.**

FOR STUDENTS & UNDER-25s   Many reductions are offered to holders of a valid **International Student Identity Card (ISIC).** Before leaving home, you can obtain one for $20 from the **Council on International Educational Exchange (CIEE),** 205 E. 42nd St., New York, NY 10017 (☎ **800/GET-AN-ID** or 212/822-2600). In Paris, the ISIC is sold for 60F ($10) at **Council Travel,** 1 place de l'Odéon, 6e (☎ **01-44-41-89-89;** Métro: Odéon), provided you show proof of student registration and bring a passport-size photo. You can gain admission to national museums at half price and reductions on train, bus, plane, and even cinema and theater tickets. Flash your ISIC whenever you pay for something—even if no reduction is advertised. You'll be astounded at the discounts granted.

If you're not a student but are between 18 and 24, you may be entitled to many of the same reductions on all sorts of sights and transportation tickets. Ask whenever you're going to pay for something—your passport should serve as proof of your age.

FOR SENIORS   France's consideration for seniors is apparent in the availability of a **Carte Vermeil,** valid for 1 year. With this card, travelers over 60 receive reductions of between 20% and 50% on certain train trips whose calendar is more or less equivalent to the one described above for the Carte Kiwi. Unlike the Carte Kiwi, the Carte Vermeil also allows some discounts on entrance to museums and sites of historic interest. A Carte Vermeil valid for four train rides of any length in France goes for 146F ($24). An equivalent card for an unlimited number of train rides, valid for a full year, is 285F ($48). Be prepared to show an ID or a passport as proof of your age when you buy the card.

WORTH A SPLURGE

The **restaurants** of Paris are world renowned and justifiably so. More than the simple consumption of food, dining is an art kept alive by inventive chefs and demanding Parisian gourmets. By all means, set aside some money in your budget to experience a meal in one of the city's fine restaurants.

2 Essentials

ARRIVING

BY PLANE   Paris has two airports handling international traffic. The largest, busiest, and most modern of the two is **Aéroport Charles-de-Gaulle** or CDG (☎ 01-48-62-22-80), sometimes called Roissy–Charles-de-Gaulle, 14½ miles north of town. Terminal 1 (Aérogare 1) is used by foreign airlines; Terminal 2 (Aérogare 2) is reserved for Air France, its affiliate Air Inter, and some foreign airlines, including Air Canada. A shuttle bus *(navette)* connects the two terminals.

There are several ways of getting to and from the airport. The cheapest is the **Roissybus,** leaving every 15 minutes for place de l'Opéra; it takes 45 to 50 minutes and costs 40F ($7). The **RER suburban train** stops at Terminal 2 (look for the Aéroport Charles-de-Gaulle 2 stop). A **shuttle bus** connects Terminal 1 to the RER train station named Aéroport Charles-de-Gaulle 1. From the station, RER Line B3 trains depart about every 15 minutes on the half-hour trip into town, stopping at the Gare du Nord, the mammoth Châtelet–Les Halles Métro interchange, and the RER stations of St-Michel, Luxembourg, Port-Royal, and Denfert-Rochereau, before heading

Useful Phone Numbers

Info RATP for Orly bus, Roissybus, and Orlyval: ☎ **08-36-68-77-14.** Info Cars Air France: ☎ **01-41-56-89-00.** Info SNCF for RER service information: ☎ **01-53-90-20-20.**

south out of the city again. A ticket into town on the RER is 47F ($8) second class or 69F ($12) first (not worth it).

Air France runs **shuttle buses** from both terminals to the Porte-Maillot Métro station, next to Paris's huge convention center on the western end of the city, and to place Charles-de-Gaulle–Etoile and the Arc de Triomphe, near some of the budget hotels below. There are several buses per hour charging 55F ($9) for the 40-minute trip.

A **taxi** into town from Charles de Gaulle takes 40 to 50 minutes and costs about 220F ($37) 7am to 8pm, about 40% more at other times. Taxis are required to turn the meter on and charge the price indicated (plus a supplement for baggage—see "Getting Around"). Check the meter before you pay since rip-offs of arriving tourists are not uncommon.

Orly Charter flights and some international airlines arrive at **Aéroport d'Orly** (☎ **01-49-75-15-15**), 8½ miles south of the city. The airport has two terminals: French domestic flights land at Orly Ouest and intra-European and intercontinental flights at Orly Sud. Shuttle buses connect these terminals and other shuttles connect them to Charles de Gaulle every 30 minutes or so.

Air France operates **coaches** from Exit E on the arrival level at Orly Ouest and Exit F Platform 5 at Orly Sud into the downtown terminal at Invalides. The trip takes 30 minutes and leaves every 12 to 15 minutes, costing 40F ($7) one-way and 65F ($11) round-trip. You can request that the bus stop at Montparnasse-Duroc.

An airport **shuttle bus** leaves every 15 minutes for the RER Pont de Rungis Aéroport d'Orly, where you board a Line C2 train that stops at several downtown stations, including St-Michel, Invalides, and Gare d'Austerlitz (35 min). This airport shuttle leaves from Exit F on the arrival level at Orly Ouest and from Exit H Platform 1 at Orly Sud. The cost is 30F ($5) second class or 46F ($8) first.

You can also take the **Orlyval service** using RER Line B. This departs from Exit F near the baggage-claim area at Orly Sud and Exit W Hall 2 on the departure level at Orly Ouest. You'll connect at the Antony station—total trip time to Châtelet is about 30 minutes for 57F ($10).

The **Orly bus** operates from Exit E arrival level at Orly Ouest and from Exit H Platform 4 at Orly Sud to Denfert-Rochereau for 30F ($5). And a **taxi** from Orly into the city costs about 170F ($28) and takes 40 to 50 minutes.

BY TRAIN Paris has six major train stations. For information, call the **Société Nationale des Chemins de Fer (SNCF)** (☎ **08-36-35-35-35**) and ask for someone who speaks English or go to a travel agent or the station information booths.

Coming from northern Germany and Belgium, you'll probably arrive at the **Gare du Nord** (Eurostar trains from London arrive here as well). Some trains from Normandy come into the **Gare St-Lazare,** in northwest Paris. Trains from the west (Brittany, Chartres, Versailles) head to the **Gare de Montparnasse;** those from the southwest (the Loire Valley, Bordeaux, the Pyrénées, Spain) to the **Gare d'Austerlitz;** those from the south and southeast (the Riviera, Lyon, Italy, Geneva) to the **Gare de Lyon.** From Alsace and eastern France, Luxembourg, southern Germany, and Zurich, the arrival station is the **Gare de l'Est.** All train stations are next to a Métro station bearing the same name.

BY BUS International buses pull into the **Gare Routière Internationale du Paris-Gallieni (International Bus Terminal),** 28 av. du Général-de-Gaulle, Bagnolet (☎ 01-49-72-51-51). The Métro station here is at Gallieni.

VISITOR INFORMATION

FOR EVERYONE At the airports are small info offices where for a fee their staff will help you make a hotel reservation. But the prime source of travel information is the **Office de Tourisme de Paris,** 127 av. des Champs-Elysées, 8e (☎ **01-49-52-53-54;** fax 01-49-52-53-00; www.paris-promotion.fr; Métro: Charles-de-Gaulle–Etoile or George-V), open daily 9am to 8pm (Sunday 11am to 6pm November to April). For a fee, the staff will make an accommodations reservation for you on the same day you want a room: 8F ($1.30) for hostels and *foyers* (homes), 20F ($3) for one-star hotels, 25F ($4) for two-star hotels, and 40F ($6) for three-star hotels. In slow periods, hotels with unsold rooms often sell them at a huge discount through the Office de Tourisme, providing you with a good way to stay in a three-star hotel at a two-star price. The office is often very busy in summer, so you'll probably have to wait in line.

The Office de Tourisme has three **auxiliary offices:** at the Gare du Nord (Monday to Saturday 8am to 9pm), Gare de Lyon (Monday to Saturday 8am to 9pm), and the Eiffel Tower (May to September only, daily 11am to 6pm). You can also reserve concert, theater, or cabaret tickets without an extra fee.

FOR STUDENTS Paris, with its huge student population and an emphasis on scholastics stretching back to the Middle Ages, has all sorts of organizations designed to provide information on student travel and discounts.

One of the most influential of these organizations is **Accueil des Jeunes en France (AJF),** 4 rue Dunkerque, 75010 Paris (☎ **01-42-85-86-19;** Métro: Gare du Nord). Its large bureaucracy is helpful in working out curriculum issues at the city's universities and passing out information about networks and organizations for students and young people trying to navigate through the labyrinth of French bureaucracies.

Though AJF maintains some facilities for travel arrangements in-house, for issues involving overnight lodgings and travel, it works closely with **O.T.U. Voyages,** 119 rue St-Martin, 75004 Paris (☎ **01-40-29-12-12;** Métro: Châtelet). Its staff will assist you in finding inexpensive lodgings in hostels, economical hotels, or (usually in midsummer) converted dorms belonging to the University of Paris. It will also negotiate discounted rail, bus, and plane tickets; issue student IDs; and provide details about activities that are either exclusive to young people or of special interest to them.

Many budget travelers have found lodgings through the **Union des Centres de Rencontres Internationales de France (UCRIF-Etapes Jeunes),** 27 rue de Turbigo, 2e (☎ **01-40-26-57-64;** fax 01-40-26-58-20; E-mail: ucrif@ad.com; Métro: Etienne-Marcel). The UCRIF is the centerpiece and communications headquarters for more than 60 cost-conscious hostels, many with different owners and management philosophies, throughout France. Fourteen of the hostels are in Paris and the Ile de France. About 75% of all bookings have in the past derived from school groups or private clubs within France, the remaining 25% coming from travelers, many from outside France. The UCRIF won't make individual bookings but will advise anyone who calls of the availability and location of its member hostels, a service it provides for free. Singles usually cost 120F to 280F ($20 to $47) and doubles 240F to 440F ($40 to $73). Even better, anyone who simply shows up at one of the hostels without a reservation receives a discount of about 10%.

CITY LAYOUT

The river Seine divides Paris into the **Right Bank (Rive Droite)** and the **Left Bank (Rive Gauche).** In the middle of the river are two islands, **Ile de la Cité** and **Ile St-Louis.** The heart of Paris and the place from which all distances in France are measured is Notre-Dame on Ile de la Cité. Directly north across the river the sprawling palace of the Louvre is the starting point for the city's system of *arrondissements* (districts). They're numbered from 1 to 20 progressing in a clockwise spiral from the Louvre's courtyard. The key to finding any address in Paris is looking for the number of the arrondissement, rendered either as a number followed by "e" or "er" (1er, 2e, and so on) or, more formally, as part of the postal code (the last two digits indicate the arrondissement—75007 indicates the 7th arrondissement, 75017 the 17th).

The courtyard of the **Louvre** is also the tip of the promenade leading west through the **Jardin des Tuileries** up the **Champs-Elysées** to the **Arc de Triomphe** and beyond to the **Grand Arche de La Défense.** The surrounding **1er** and **8e** contain the city's most expensive hotels, restaurants, shops, and cafes. Here's where you'll find the designer stores along **avenue de Montaigne** and **rue du faubourg St-Honoré,** the ritzy **place Vendôme,** and the **Palais Royal.** North of the Louvre on the Right Bank is Charles Garnier's ornate 19th-century **Opéra (9e)** surrounded by major department stores like Galeries Lafayette and Printemps, and still further north is **Montmartre (18e)** topped by the **Sacré-Coeur.** East of the Louvre on the right bank is the **Marais (3e and 4e)** home of 17th-century royal mansions, the historic Jewish quarter, and the city's gay scene. Across pont Marie is **Ile St-Louis,** a beautifully preserved enclave of 17th-century town houses and mansions. East of the Marais is the **Bastille (11e),** site of the new Opéra and lively nightlife. Northeast of the Bastille is the **Père-Lachaise cemetery (20e)** and the **Ménilmontant** neighborhood where recent immigrants from North Africa live.

On the Left Bank, the **Latin Quarter (5e)** is home to the **Sorbonne** and the **Panthéon.** The cobblestone streets that once drew medieval scholars are still filled with inexpensive shops and cafes catering to students. The **St-Germain-des-Prés area (6e)** centers around the **St-Germain-des-Prés church** and stretches from the Seine to **boulevard du Montparnasse.** Within its boundaries, you'll find the shady **Jardin du Luxembourg,** arts and antiques stores along rue Bonaparte and rue de Seine, and the famous literary cafes where Sartre and Hemingway came to write. South of St-Germain-des-Prés is **Montparnasse (14e),** also associated with the literary life of the 1920s and 1930s. East of St-Germain, the **Tour Eiffel,** the **Musée d'Orsay,** and the **Hôtel des Invalides** are in the **faubourg St-Germain (7e)** amidst 18th-century mansions that have become embassies, government buildings, or ultraexpensive residences. Beyond the arrondissements stretch the vast *banlieue* (suburbs) of Greater Paris, where the majority of Parisians live.

GETTING AROUND

BY METRO (SUBWAY)   The Métro is fast, clean, safe for the most part, and easy to navigate. The first Métro line was opened in 1900. It's operated by the Régie Autonome des Transports Parisiens (RATP), just like the city buses.

The Métro has 13 lines and more than 360 stations (there's bound to be one near your destination), and it's connected to the RER (Réseau Express Régional), which has four lines that stop at only a few stations, crisscrossing the city in minutes and connecting downtown Paris with its airports. The trains run 5:30am to past midnight, finishing their final runs before 1am. Both the Métro and the RER operate on a zone system, at a different fare per zone, but it's unlikely you'll be traveling any farther than zone 1.

A Map Note

See the inside back cover of this guide for a Paris Métro map.

A single ticket *(un billet)* costs 8F ($1.30), but if you ask for *un carnet* (a booklet) you'll get 10 (loose) tickets for 48F ($8). If you're going to be here for more than a few days, it may be a better idea to get a weekly or monthly unlimited-ride Carte Orange (see "Paris Deals & Discounts," earlier in this chapter).

Be sure to keep your ticket until exiting the train platform and passing the *limite de validité des billets.* An inspector may ask to see it at any time before that.

The older Métro stations are marked by curvaceous art nouveau gateways reading MÉTROPOLITAIN; others are marked by "M" signs. Every Métro stop has maps of the system, and these are also available at ticket booths. Once you decide which line you need, make sure you're going in the right direction: On Métro Line 1, "Direction: Esplanade de La Défense" means a westbound train and "Direction: Château de Vincennes" is the opposite. To change train lines, look for the orange CORRESPONDANCE signs; blue signs reading SORTIE mark the exits.

Near the exits is always a *plan du quartier,* a detailed map of the streets and buildings surrounding each Métro station, with all exits marked. It's often a good idea to consult this before you climb the stairs, especially at large stations; you may want to use a different exit stairway so as to be on the other side of a busy street or closer to where you're going.

For more information on the city's public transportation, stop in at either of the two offices of the **Services Touristiques de la RATP,** at 53 bis quai des Grands-Augustins, 6e (☎ **01-40-46-42-17;** Métro: St-Michel), or place de la Madeleine, 1er (☎ **01-40-06-71-45;** Métro: Madeleine); or call ☎ **08-36-68-77-14.**

BY BUS   Though generally slower than the Métro, buses allow you to see the sights as you ride. They take the same tickets as the Métro and also operate on a zone system, shown on charts in each bus.

BY TAXI   Taxis are fairly expensive and also scarce because there are only 15,000 on the streets. Look for them at specially marked taxi ranks at key locations. The meter begins at 13F ($2) and rises 3.45F (50¢) during the day and 5.70F ($1) at night for every kilometer thereafter. Additional charges, 6F to 10F ($1 to $2), are imposed for luggage weighing more than 5 kilograms (11 lbs.), a fourth adult in the cab, or for cabs leaving from the train stations and marked taxi stops. Tip 10%. For radio cabs, call ☎ **01-45-85-85-85,** 01-42-70-41-41, or 01-42-70-00-42, though you'll be charged from the point where the taxi begins the drive to pick you up. Taxi drivers are required by law to transport customers with disabilities and to help with wheelchairs and luggage.

BY RENTAL CAR   Because of Paris's narrow streets, difficult and/or expensive parking, and sometimes unpredictable drivers, I strongly advise against driving in the city. Even for out-of-town excursions, the best means of transit is usually the extensive network of trains and buses. Rental cars and fuel are expensive, and traffic fines are staggering. If you rent a car from a Paris-based chain like **Autorent,** 18 rue de la Convention, 15e (☎ **01-45-54-22-45;** Métro: Boucicaut), it'll usually cost a minimum of 1,500F ($250) per week, with the first 1,000 kilometers (620 mi.) included free, for use of their smallest cars, either a Fiat 500 or a Fiat Panda. A second, smaller branch of Autorent is at 36 rue Fabert, 7e (☎ **01-45-55-12-54;** Métro: Invalides). Insurance adequate for most drivers is included in the company's rates for week-long rentals.

A Pickpocket Warning

Most of the time the Métro is safe. However, precautions are in order in the northern parts of the city and in deserted stations or in the long corridors between stations late at night.

As a visitor, you're a special mark. You may feel safer riding in the first train car, where the engineer is. Watch out for pickpockets, especially on the Métro. These include bands of ragamuffins who'll surround you, distract you by waving something in your face, pick your pockets clean, and disappear, all within seconds. Don't let them near you. Be rude if you have to. Another trick is to crowd behind you as you're passing through the turnstile, taking advantage of your momentary discomfort to pick your pocket or handbag. Women should ensure that handbags close firmly, preferably with a zipper.

North American travelers, however, usually find that it's less expensive to rent from the French branch of U.S.-based car-rental companies, like **Avis** (☎ **800-331-2112**), **Budget** (☎ **800/572-0700**), and **Hertz** (☎ **800/654-3001**), but only if they reserve their vehicle several days before departing from home. Rates of between $201 and $275 per week, with unlimited mileage, are usually quoted for any of those firms' smallest vehicles, in most cases a flotilla of cramped but peppy Renault Clios, Opel Corsas, or Fiats. Collision-damage waivers cost an extra $15 to $18 per day. Each of the outfits above maintains branches at the airports as well as outlets throughout Greater Paris. Before you rent, remember that government taxes are calculated at a whopping 20.6% of the total rental contract, gasoline is horrendously expensive, and picking up any car at either of the city's airports entails a 54F ($9) surcharge.

FAST FACTS: Paris

American Express   With a grand Paris office, American Express, 11 rue Scribe, 9e (☎ **01-47-77-79-50**; Métro: Opéra, Chaussée-d'Antin, or Havre-Caumartin; RER: Auber), is extremely busy with customers buying and cashing traveler's checks (not the best rates for transactions), picking up mail, and solving travel problems. It's open Monday to Friday 9am to 6:30pm; the bank is also open Saturday to 5:30pm, but the mail-pickup window is closed.

Business Hours   Normally, **banks** are open Monday to Friday 9am to noon and 1 or 1:30 to 4:30pm. Some have long hours on Saturday morning. Some currency exchange booths are open very long hours (see "Currency Exchange," below).

The *grands magasins* (**department stores**) are generally open Monday to Saturday 9:30am to 6:30pm; **smaller shops** close for lunch and reopen around 2pm, but this has become rarer than it used to be. Many stores stay open to 7pm in summer; others are closed Monday, especially in the morning. Large offices remain open all day, but some also close for lunch.

Currency   The French **franc (F)** is divided into 100 **centimes.** There are coins of 5, 10, and 20 centimes and ½, 1, 2, 5, 10, and 20 francs. Sometimes you'll find two types of coin for one denomination (new commemorative coins were minted for the 1989 bicentennial of the Revolution). Bills come in denominations of 20, 50, 100, and 500 francs.

The French Franc

For American Readers At this writing, $1 = approximately 6F (or 1F = 16¢), and this was the rate of exchange used to calculate the dollar values given throughout this chapter (rounded to the nearest dollar).

For British Readers At this writing, £1 = approximately 10F (or 1F = 12p), and this was the rate of exchange used to calculate the pound values in the table below.

Note: Exchange rates fluctuate and may not be the same when you travel to France.

F	U.S.$	U.K.£	F	U.S.$	U.K.£
1	.16	.10	10	1.60	1.00
2	.32	.20	25	4.16	2.50
3	.48	.30	50	8.33	5.00
4	.64	.40	75	12.50	7.50
5	.80	.50	100	16.66	10.00
6	.96	.60	200	33.33	20.00
7	1.12	.70	300	50.00	30.00
8	1.20	.80	400	66.66	40.00
9	1.44	.90	500	83.33	50.00

Currency Exchange Call a bank or look in the financial pages of your newspaper to find the current rate of exchange. You'll get slightly less than this when you exchange money. Always ask if there's a fee or commission charged on the transaction. A big fee or commission can wipe out the advantage of a favorable exchange rate.

Banks and bureaux de change (exchange offices) almost always offer better exchange rates than hotels, restaurants, and shops, which you should use only in emergencies. I've always found good rates, no fees or commissions, and quick service at the **Comptoir de Change Opéra,** 9 rue Scribe, 9e (☎ **01-47-42-20-96;** Métro: Opéra; RER: Auber), open Monday to Friday 9am to 6pm and Saturday 9:30am to 4pm. The bureaux de change at train stations (except Gare de Montparnasse) are open daily. Those at 63 av. des Champs-Elysées, 8e (Métro: F.-D.-Roosevelt); 140 av. des Champs-Elysées, 8e (Métro: George-V); 200 rue de Rivoli, 1er (Métro: Tuileries); and 9 rue Berger, 1er (Métro: Les Halles), keep long hours. Also see "American Express," above.

A common trick of exchange offices is to advertise the selling rate *(vente)* of the U.S. dollar, always substantially higher than the purchase rate *(achat)* that interests most visitors. Remember that the exchange office is *buying* currency from you; check the rates under *achat.*

Many forms of ATMs operate in Paris and the rest of France, and many of them accept the cards of North American issuers like Cirrus, Plus, and Visa. Citibank, one of the largest financial entities in the world, maintains a toll-free **ATM Locator Service** number (☎ **800/248-4286**), listing the location of ATM machines throughout the world. When you withdraw currency from an ATM you get the most favorable rate of exchange, but there is usually a service fee of about $3 for the transaction.

Networks & Resources

FOR STUDENTS   The nationally funded organization engineered to respond to the needs of full-time students in Paris is **CROUS (Centre Régional des Oeuvres Universitaires).** Its self-stated mission is to improve the living and working conditions of French and foreign students.

Most of the efforts of CROUS are for persons studying within the French university system for at least a semester, so if that's you, consider contacting them at 39 av. Georges-Bernanos, 5e (☎ **01-40-51-36-00;** Métro: Port-Royal). Receptionists are on hand at a welcome center Monday to Friday 9am to noon and 2 to 5pm. CROUS is a sprawling multifaceted bureaucracy that's among the most decentralized in Paris, so you might need to navigate through the red tape. If you hit it just right, however, they can arrange everything from discounted meals in student restaurants to medium- to long-term lodgings in university dormitories. An affiliated organization with a slightly different acronym is **CNOUS (Centre National des Oeuvres Universitaires et Scolaires),** 69 quai d'Orsay, 7e (☎ **01-44-18-53-00;** Métro: Invalides).

FOR GAYS & LESBIANS   "Gay Paree," with one of the world's largest homosexual populations, has many clubs, restaurants, organizations, and services. Other than publications (see below), one of the best information sources on gay and lesbian activities is the **Centre Gay et Lesbien,** 3 rue Keller, 11e (☎ **01-43-57-21-47;** Métro: Bastille). Well equipped to dispense information and coordinate the activities and meetings of gay people from virtually everywhere, it's open daily 2 to 8pm. On Sunday it presents *Le Café Positif,* featuring music, cabaret, and information about AIDS and the prevention of sexually transmitted diseases.

Gay magazines that focus mainly on cultural events include *Illico* (free in gay bars but around 12F/$2 at newsstands) and *e.m@le* (available free at bars and bookstores). Women might like to pick up a copy of *Lesbia,* to check the ads if for no other reason. These publications and others are available at Paris's largest and best-stocked gay bookstore, **Les Mots à la Bouche,** 6 rue Ste-Croix-la-Bretonnerie, 4e (☎ **01-42-78-88-30;** Métro: Hôtel-de-Ville). It's open Monday to Saturday 11am to 11pm and Sunday 3 to 8pm. French- and English-language publications are inventoried.

Most post office branches now have ATMs or you can check out the branch offices of BNP (Banque Nationale de Paris), Societé Generale, and Crédit Lyonnais. Note that ATMs in Paris require a four-digit PIN.

Dentists   You can call your consulate and ask the duty officer to recommend a dentist. For dental emergencies, call SOS Dentaire at ☎ **01-43-37-51-00** daily 9am to midnight.

Doctors   Call your consulate and ask the duty officer to recommend a doctor. Otherwise, call the 24-hour SOS Médicins at ☎ **01-47-07-77-77.**

Embassies & Consulates   If you have a passport, immigration, legal, or other problem, contact your consulate. Call before you go, as they often keep strange hours and observe both French and home-country holidays. The embassy of the **United States,** at 2 av. Gabriel, 8e (☎ **01-43-12-22-22;** Métro: Concorde), is open Monday to Friday 9am to 6pm. Passports are issued at its consulate at 2 rue St-Florentin (☎ 01-43-12-22-22; Métro: Concorde). To get a passport replaced

Country & City Codes

The **country code** for France is **33.** The **city code** for Paris is **1;** use this code if you're calling from outside France. If you're calling Paris from within Paris or from anywhere else in France, use **01,** which is now built into all phone numbers, making them 10 digits long.

costs $55. The embassy of **Canada** is at 35 av. Montaigne, 8e (☎ **01-44-43-29-00;** Métro: F.-D.-Roosevelt or Alma-Marceau), open Monday to Friday 9am to noon and 2 to 5pm. The Canadian consulate is at the embassy. The embassy of the **United Kingdom** is at 35 rue du Faubourg St-Honoré, 8e (☎ **01-44-51-31-00;** Métro: Concorde or Madeleine), open Monday to Friday 9:30am to 1pm and 2:30 to 6pm. The consulate is at 16 rue d'Anjou, 8e (☎ 01-44-51-31-00), open Monday to Friday 9:30am to 12:30pm and 2:30 to 5pm. The embassy of **Australia** is at 4 rue Jean-Rey, 15e (☎ **01-40-59-33-00;** Métro: Bir-Hakeim), open Monday to Friday 9am to 1pm and 2:30 to 5:30pm.

Emergencies   For the police, call ☎ **17.** To report a fire, dial ☎ **18.** For an ambulance, call the fire department at ☎ **01-45-78-74-52;** a fire vehicle rushes patients to the nearest emergency room. S.A.M.U., ☎ **15,** is an independently operated, privately owned ambulance company. You can reach the police at 9 bd. du Palais, 4e (☎ **01-53-71-53-71** or 01-53-73-53-73; Métro: Cité). Paris has a number of all-night pharmacies, including the **Pharmacie Dhéry,** 84 av. des Champs-Elysées, 8e (☎ **01-45-62-02-41;** Métro: George-V), in the Galerie des Champs-Elysées shopping center.

Holidays   France has lots of national holidays, most tied to the church calendar. On these days, shops, businesses, government offices, and most restaurants close. They include New Year's Day (January 1); Easter Monday (late March or early April); Labor Day (May 1); Ascension Thursday (May or June, 40 days after Easter); Whitmonday, also called Pentecost Monday (51st day after Easter, June or July); Bastille Day (July 14); Assumption Day (August 15); All Saints' Day (November 1); Armistice Day (November 11); and Christmas Day (December 25).

In addition, schedules may be disrupted on Shrove Tuesday (the Tuesday before Ash Wednesday, January or February) and Good Friday (late March or early April).

Hospitals   One hospital with an English-speaking staff is the **British Hospital of Paris,** 3 rue Barbès Levallois-Perret (☎ **01-46-39-22-22;** Métro: Anatole-France), north of Neuilly, over the city line northwest of Paris.

Laundry & Dry Cleaning   To find a laundry near you, ask at your hotel or consult the Yellow Pages under *Laveries Automatiques.* Take as many 10F, 2F, and 1F pieces as you can. Dry cleaning is *nettoyage à sec;* look for shop signs with the word *pressing.* Washing and drying 6 kilos (13¼ lbs.) of stuff usually costs about 35F ($6).

Mail   Large post offices (PTT) are normally open Monday to Friday 8am to 7pm and Saturday 8am to noon; small post offices may have shorter hours. There are many post offices around the city; ask anybody for the nearest one. Airmail letters within Europe cost 3F (60¢); to the United States, 4.40F (90¢).

The city's **main post office** is at 52 rue du Louvre, 75001 Paris (☎ **01-40-28-20-00;** Métro: Louvre), open 24 hours for urgent mailings, telegrams, and telephone calls. This is where you should go to pick up *Poste Restante* (general delivery) mail; be prepared to show your passport and pay a small fee for each letter you receive.

Police   Dial ☎ **17** in emergencies.

Telephone   Public phone booths are in cafes, restaurants, Métro stations, post offices, airports, train stations, and sometimes on the streets. Finding a coin-operated phone in France may be an arduous task. Simpler and more widely accepted is the **télécarte,** a prepaid calling card. These debit cards are priced at 40F ($7) and 96F ($16) for 50 and 120 unités, respectively. Télécartes are available at most post offices and Métro stations.

If possible, avoid making calls from your hotel, which might double or triple the charges. Also note that numbers beginning with 08 carry a special surcharge that runs about 50¢ a minute.

To make **international calls,** dial ☎ **00** (double zero) to access international lines. For information, dial ☎ **12.**

Tipping   Service is supposedly included at your hotel, but it's still customary to tip the bellhop about 6F ($1) per bag. You might use 5% of the daily room rate as a guideline; if you have lots of luggage, tip a bit more. Though your *addition* (restaurant bill) or *fiche* (cafe check) will bear the words *service compris* (service charge included), it's customary to leave a tip. In a fancy restaurant 10% will do; in a cheap place or a café 5% is fine. Remember, service has supposedly already been paid for.

Taxi drivers appreciate 10% of the fare as a tip. At the theater and cinema, tip the usher who shows you to your seat 2F (40¢). In public toilets, there's often a posted fee for using the facilities. If not, the maintenance person will expect a tip of about 2F (40¢). Put it in the basket or on the plate at the entrance. Porters and cloakroom attendants are usually governed by set prices that are displayed. If not, give a porter 5F to 8F ($1 to $1.50) per suitcase and a cloakroom attendant 2F to 4F (30¢ to 70¢) per coat.

3 Accommodations You Can Afford

In general, you'll find that budget-priced French accommodations are reliably clean and comfortable. If you're used to the amenities offered for the same money in North American motels, however, you may be disappointed. The rooms tend to be smaller, even in expensive hotels (unless you opt for a modern chain), and vary greatly in size and furnishings. Ask to see a room before checking in, and if you don't like it, ask to see another. If you're reserving by phone and room size is important, you'd do better to reserve a triple in a modest hotel than a double in a higher-priced place. Most hotels sell their largest rooms as triples, and they're generally much larger than doubles at a comparable price. Also, if you're looking for a double room, keep in mind that a double bed is cheaper than two twin beds, but the two twin beds are likely to be in a larger room.

If you're a light sleeper, ask for a room in the rear or make sure the windows are double glazed—garbage is picked up early and loudly every morning in most places. Also, acoustics in old hotels can be unpredictable; your neighbors' noise may be as annoying as street noise. I'm a big believer in earplugs and wouldn't take a vacation without them.

A Note on Bathrooms

You'll often find a variety of plumbing arrangements, from units with "EC" (*eau courante*, or running water, meaning a sink) to those with private bathrooms that include either a shower and toilet or a tub/shower combination and toilet. Sometimes the tub/shower arrangement doesn't have a shower curtain. Some rooms have a "shower only," with the toilet in the hall. Bathless rooms can be a real bargain, but many hotels charge for the use of the shower, which should be factored into the cost. The trend these days is to renovate small hotels and put a shower, toilet, and sink in each room, so those marvelously cheap bathless rooms are dwindling.

If you want to find the most attractive room at the best price, plan ahead. During the busiest times—late spring/early summer and early fall—rooms at the best budget hotels are reserved several months in advance. The dead of winter and August are lighter months. Nevertheless, coming to Paris at any time without a reservation could mean paying a lot more than you expected. In order to make a reservation from abroad at a hotel that doesn't accept credit cards, you may be required to send a bank check or traveler's check in French francs, which can add to the overall cost of the room.

If you do come to town without a reservation, try to arrive early in the day and head to one of the tourist offices in the airports, train stations, or on the Champs-Elysées. For a small fee, they'll book a room for you (see "Visitor Information," earlier in this chapter). It's also worth knowing that three-star hotels with unsold rooms often sell them through the tourist office at a steep discount. These can be great last-minute deals, but availability varies from day to day, so it's wise not to count on booking a room this way.

It's important to be flexible about what part of the city you stay in. Paris is relatively small and very well connected by public transport. Even on the fringes you won't be more than a half hour from the center of town, where hotel rates are highest. The areas around the city's major train stations, especially the Gare du Nord, Gare de Lyon, and Gare de l'Est, have a large supply of reasonably priced accommodations even if the neighborhoods are a bit bland. Less frequented residential quarters like the 9e, 11e, 13e, and 15e arrondissements also have many small budget hotels.

Note: You can find most of the lodging choices below plotted on the map included in "Seeing the Sights" later in this chapter.

IN & AROUND THE LATIN QUARTER

The Latin Quarter—with its narrow streets, bookstores, and bohemian cafes—lives deep in the imagination of many visitors. Besides the university, the outdoor market on rue Mouffetard, and the busy intersections of boulevards St-Michel and St-Germain, you'll find the Panthéon and (only 15 minutes away on foot) Notre-Dame. Hotels in this area cater to students and budgeters, offering rock-bottom digs or very comfortable lodgings, as you wish. You can also eat cheaply in this neighborhood.

Delhy's Hôtel. 22 rue de l'Hirondelle, 75006 Paris. ☎ **01-43-26-58-25.** Fax 01-43-26-51-06. 21 units, 7 with shower only. TV TEL. 203F ($34) single with sink; 296F ($49) double with sink; 386F ($64) double with shower. Shower 25F ($4). Continental breakfast 30F ($5). AE, MC, V. Métro: St-Michel.

If you can do without a toilet in the room, this no-frills hotel on a narrow pedestrian street offers a good deal. The tidy rooms are small but pleasantly decorated in subdued pastels. The narrow halls, winding staircase, and cozy breakfast room are well maintained, and the location is great. If you don't take a room with a shower, however, you'll have to trudge down to the ground-floor shower.

Getting the Best Deal on Accommodations

- Be aware that making reservations is your best bet, especially in summer, when budget rooms may be occupied and the room reservation service at the tourist office may be very busy.
- Note that a room without a bath can be marvelously cheap—if you don't mind the slight inconvenience.
- Look for a room that doesn't require you to take breakfast. Even for a stay of only a day or two, this can be a big savings.
- Try to negotiate the price downward in winter, when there's less demand for budget rooms. You can best do this in the evening.
- Ask for a discount if you stay more than 3 nights or for a seniors' discount if you're over 60.

Hôtel de la Faculté. 1 rue Racine, 75006 Paris. ☎ **01-43-26-87-13.** Fax 01-46-34-73-88. 19 units, all with bathroom (shower). TEL. 365F–430F ($61–$72) single/double; 475F ($79) triple. Breakfast 29F ($5). MC, V. Métro: Odéon, St-Michel, or Cluny–La Sorbonne. RER: St-Michel.

In a prime Latin Quarter location, steps off busy boulevard St-Michel, this modest hotel offers you a chance to stay in the heart of literary and artistic Paris, near the former haunts of Picasso, Sartre, and Hemingway. Though built in the 1920s, the Hôtel de la Faculté was last renovated in 1994. The tiny lobby leads to a minuscule elevator and a winding staircase, and down the narrow halls are rooms with new rustic furnishings. Everything may seem a bit squeezed in, but the prices won't squeeze your budget.

Hôtel Gerson. 14 rue de la Sorbonne, 75005 Paris. ☎ **01-43-54-28-40.** Fax 01-44-07-13-90. 24 units, 16 with bathroom (shower). 213F ($36) single without bathroom, 283F ($44) single with bathroom; 256F ($43) double without bathroom, 360F ($60) double with bathroom; 409F ($68) triple with bathroom. Showers 25F ($4). Continental breakfast 25F ($4). MC, V. Métro: Cluny–La Sorbonne. RER: Luxembourg.

The one-star Gerson is in the heart of the Latin Quarter, just a few steps down the hill from place de la Sorbonne. It's the quintessential low-budget hotel, with soft beds and many nicks in the woodwork, but it has clean rooms, some with private baths that are newish and presentable.

Résidence les Gobelins. 9 rue des Gobelins, 75013 Paris. ☎ **01-47-07-26-90.** Fax 01-43-31-44-05. 32 units, all with bathroom (shower or tub). TV TEL. 315F ($53) single; 365F–445F ($61–$74) double. Breakfast 38F ($6). AE, MC, V. Métro: Gobelins.

A short walk from the Latin Quarter, this hotel offers good value at a reasonable price. The lobby and reception area are attractive and the rooms are furnished in a light summery style with an accent on pastels and wicker furniture. Rooms facing the street tend to be smaller and less expensive. The inner courtyard has been turned into a delightful garden with a trellis, climbing vines, flowers, and potted plants.

✪ **Hôtel le Home Latin.** 15–17 rue du Sommerard, 75005 Paris. ☎ **01-43-26-25-21.** Fax 01-43-29-87-04. 55 units, all with bathroom (shower or tub). TV TEL. 385F ($64) single; 450F ($75) double. Breakfast 39F ($7). AE, V. Métro: St-Michel or Maubert-Mutualité.

Since the 1970s this has been a mecca for clean and uncomplicated lodgings. The hotel consists of two side-by-side buildings the management unified in the 1970s, retaining the two entrances. The guest rooms are functional, some with small balconies overlooking the street. Those facing the courtyard are quieter than the ones opening onto the street. The elevator doesn't go past the fifth floor, but guests in the sixth-floor *chambres mansardées* tend to appreciate their romantic position under the eaves, plus the great views over the rooftops.

Hôtel Marignan. 13 rue du Sommerard, 75005 Paris. ☎ **01-43-54-63-81.** 30 units, 24 with toilet only, 6 with bathroom (shower or tub). 220F ($37) single with sink; 330F ($55) double with toilet only, 440F ($73) double with bathroom; 430–540F ($72–$90) triple with bathroom; 500–660F ($83–$110) quad with bathroom. Rates include continental breakfast and showers. No credit cards. Métro: Maubert-Mutualité (2-min. walk) or St-Michel (6-minute walk).

Owners Paul and Linda Keniger have invested much time and energy in renovating their hotel. In the process, they've retained much of the architectural detailing, like the stucco ceiling moldings. The rooms have tiled baths, wood dressers, and new carpets and beds. The Kenigers (Paul is French and Linda is American) welcome families, and you'll have a washer/dryer and iron at your disposal. They also don't mind if you bring your own food into the dining room; the kitchen is available during low season.

Hôtel St-Jacques. 35 rue des Ecoles (at the corner of rue des Carmes), 75005 Paris. ☎ **01-44-07-45-45.** Fax 01-43-25-65-50. 35 units, 32 with bathroom (shower or tub). TV TEL. 210F–320F ($35–$53) single without bathroom, 370F–400F ($62–$67) single with bathroom; 440F–500F ($73–$83) double with bathroom; 550F–590F ($92–$98) triple with bathroom. Breakfast 25F–35F ($4–$6). AE, MC, V. Métro: Maubert-Mutualité.

In a 19th-century building, with an interior that has been blandly modernized but is bigger than you might expect, this is a serviceable and improving hotel where the rates are more or less affordable. The hotel was remodeled in 1996, and the rooms have been spruced up, with antique or antique-style furniture often added. The hotel is better than it's been in years, and it has one winning asset: location. You're only a few steps from Notre-Dame and the Sorbonne and only 10 minutes from the Louvre.

✪ **Port-Royal Hotel.** 8 bd. Port-Royal, 75005 Paris. ☎ **01-43-31-70-06.** Fax 01-43-31-33-67. 46 units, 21 with bathroom (shower or tub). TEL. 205F ($34) single with sink only; 218F ($36) double with sink only, 325F ($54) double with bathroom. Continental breakfast 27F ($4.50). No credit cards. Métro: Gobelins.

When you enter the spacious air-conditioned lobby you'll wonder if you booked yourself into a three-star hotel by mistake. Rest assured: The Port-Royal has the rates of a superbudget hotel but the polished style of a much pricier place. The halls are freshly painted and the rooms recently decorated with flowery pastel wallpaper. The front rooms have double-glazed windows, and many rooms have (nonworking) fireplaces. The rooms are of different sizes, of course, but tend to be larger than you'd expect for the price. The hotel has recently added an elevator.

IN & AROUND ST-GERMAIN-DES-PRES

In an area fast moving upscale, there are still some good budget hotels. You'll be near the Jardin du Luxembourg as well as the art galeries, cinemas, bookstores, and jazz clubs that have made this the neighborhood of choice for politicians and intellectuals. Dining tends to be expensive, but you're a stone's throw from the cheaper Latin Quarter.

Hôtel des Académies. 15 rue de la Grande-Chaumière, 75006 Paris. ☎ **01-43-26-66-44.** Fax 01-43-26-03-72. 21 units, 5 with shower only, 12 with bathroom (shower). TEL. 220F ($37) single with sink and toilet; 300F ($50) single/double with shower only; 345F–360F ($58–$60) single/double with bathroom. Continental breakfast 36F ($6). MC, V. Métro: Vavin.

This building dates to 1710, and it has been a hotel for more than 90 years. Few other buildings in the district give as potent a sense of Old Montparnasse, with its location on a quiet side street and ambiance that's either charmingly retro or dowdy, depending on your viewpoint. As there's no elevator, upper-floor rooms cost a few francs less. Breakfast is served in your room whenever you want it. There's an absolute rule against disturbing the peace after 10pm, and anyone who does is asked to leave the next morning. Some aspects of the decor are just too kitschy, but many cost-conscious travelers find this hotel suitable.

Hôtel des Bains. 33 rue Delambre, 75014 Paris. ☎ **01-43-20-85-27.** Fax 01-42-79-82-78. 41 units, all with bathroom (shower). TV TEL. 393F–405F ($66–$68) single/double; 560F ($93) suite for 2, 620F ($103) suite for 3, 655F ($109) suite for 4. Breakfast 45F ($8). No credit cards. Parking 66F ($11). Métro: Vavin or Edgar-Quinet.

In a residential neighborhood near Montparnasse's most important crossroads, this bland yet clean and comfortable hotel (last renovated in 1995) occupies the premises of what used to be public baths. There's an elevator to carry you and your bags up from the street-level reception area. The rooms contain either carpeted or frequently waxed wooden floors, small desks with reading lights, and cheerful bedspreads and draperies. All have safes and hair dryers. Breakfast is a self-service buffet.

Hôtel du Globe. 15 rue des Quatre-Vents, 75006 Paris. ☎ **01-46-33-62-69.** 15 units, all with bathroom (shower or tub). 390–495F ($65–$83) single/double. Continental breakfast 45F ($8). V. Métro: St-Sulpice.

On a historically evocative street, this building was a town house in the 17th century and was converted into a hotel in the early 1970s. Inside, you'll find most of the original stonework and dozens of timbers and beams that a team of craftspeople labored to expose. Each room is decorated with individual flair in a nostalgic or old-fashioned style. The rooms with tubs are almost twice as large as those with showers, so for the extra expense you'll usually get a lot more than just a plumbing improvement. There's no elevator (you'll have to lug your luggage up narrow antique stairs) and no breakfast area (breakfast trays are brought to your room). The largest and most desirable rooms are nos. 1, 12 (with a baldachin-style bed), 14, 15, and 16.

Hôtel Henri IV. 25 place Dauphine, 75001 Paris. ☎ **01-43-54-44-53.** 21 units, 2 with shower only. 125F–145F ($21–$24) single without shower; 180F–200F ($30–$33) double without shower, 230F–260F ($38–$43) double with shower. Rates include breakfast. No credit cards. Métro: Pont-Neuf.

One of Europe's most famous and most consistently crowded budget hotels sits at this dramatic location on the northernmost tip of Ile de la Cité, across the river from the St-Germain neighborhood and beside a formal park. The guests are mostly bargain-conscious academicians, journalists, and francophiles (as well as U.S. backpackers), many of whom reserve rooms 2 months in advance. The low-ceilinged lobby, a flight above street level, is cramped and bleak, the creaky stairway very narrow. The rooms, past their prime, are thought romantically threadbare by many, rundown by others. Each has a sink, but not even the two rooms with shower have a toilet.

IN & AROUND THE MARAIS

With its trendy boutiques, bustling nightlife, and two excellent museums—the Musée Picasso and Musée Carnavalet—you'll never run out of things to do in this neighborhood. There's a wide variety of restaurants and cafes at every price level.

Castex Hôtel. 5 rue Castex, 75004 Paris. ☎ **01-42-72-31-52.** Fax 01-42-72-57-91. 27 units, 8 with shower only, 19 with bathroom (shower). 290F ($48) single with bathroom; 320F ($53) double with shower only, 340F ($57) double with bathroom. Continental breakfast 25F ($4). EURO, MC, V. Métro: Bastille or Sully–Morland.

Owned by the Bouchand family for almost 70 years, the Castex is a great value. The rooms are large and exceptionally well kept, each with a writing table or a desk and chair; some have views over the courtyard. The staff is friendly and accommodating, and the son, who's carrying on the family tradition of hotel management, speaks English very well. Reserve well in advance.

Hôtel de Nevers. 53 rue de Malte, 75011 Paris. ☎ **01-47-00-56-18.** Fax 01-43-57-77-39. 34 units, 7 with shower only, 11 with bathroom (shower). TV TEL. 170F ($28) single with sink; 220F ($37) single/double with shower only, 245F ($41) single/double with bathroom; 310F ($52) triple with bathroom; 380F ($63) quad with bathroom. Shower 20F ($3). Breakfast 25F ($4). MC, V. Métro: République.

The plant-filled lobby patrolled by two cats sets a friendly tone for a hotel offering excellent value. You can take the elevator, but be sure to note the original gleaming brass railing along the staircase. The corridors are painted in light pastels that make them seem wider than they are. Though the rooms aren't large, they're immaculate, and the owners have worked wonders with bright wallpaper and curtains. The spacious sixth-floor triples have skylights, sloping ceilings, and views over the rooftops.

Hôtel Pratic. 9 rue d'Ormesson, 75004 Paris. ☎ **01-48-87-80-47.** Fax 01-48-87-40-04. 23 units, 10 with bathroom (shower or tub). TV TEL. 180F ($30) single without bathroom, 250F ($42) single with bathroom; 245F ($41) double without bathroom, 340F ($57) double with bathroom. Continental breakfast 25F ($4). AE, DC, V. Métro: St-Paul.

Near the pretty place du Marché Ste-Catherine, this hotel was recently renovated with a new breakfast room and freshly decorated halls, but most rooms are extremely small. A particular curiosity is the oval-shaped bath between the first and second floors. The best, and priciest, rooms overlook the square and have baths and double-glazed windows.

NEAR THE EIFFEL TOWER

This neighborhood is in the 7e arrondissement, a proper district of leafy streets and fine residences, including the art nouveau creations of the architect Jules Lavirotte on avenue Rapp (no. 29 is his masterpiece). There are many restaurants and food shops on avenue Bosquet, rue de Grenelle, and rue St-Dominique, but this is primarily a quiet residential area.

Hôtel Eiffel Rive Gauche. 6 rue du Gros Caillou, 75007 Paris. ☎ **01-45-51-24-56.** Fax 01-45-51-11-77. 30 rms, all with bathroom (tub or shower). TV TEL. 370F–420F ($62–$70) single/double. Buffet breakfast 40F ($7). AE, MC, V. Métro: Ecole-Militaire. RER: Pont de l'Alma.

This family-run hotel is so famous among the budget-travel crowd that after years of appearing in this and many other guidebooks around the world, it has practically achieved cult status. It's more crowded on weekdays (because of business travelers) than weekends. The rooms are well maintained and clean. Touches of Parisian charm are the iron balustrades above the streetside windows and the potted geraniums in the window boxes. Beware of the surcharges added to long-distance calls you make from your room.

Hôtel Rapp. 8 av. Rapp, 75007 Paris. ☎ **01-45-51-42-28.** Fax 01-43-59-50-70. 16 units, all with bathroom (shower). TEL. 270F ($45) single; 350F–370F ($58–$62) double. Breakfast 25F ($4). MC, V. Métro: Alma-Marceau. RER: Pont de l'Alma.

This hotel is in a sedate residential neighborhood, close to the Seine and the Eiffel Tower. It has four floors (no elevator), with cream-colored rooms containing old-fashioned but dignified furnishings you may think charming. The overall impression is restrained, discreet, and comfortably bourgeois.

NEAR THE ARC DE TRIOMPHE

Place Charles-de-Gaulle–Etoile boasts the tremendous Arc de Triomphe. Baron Haussmann's 12 grand avenues, including the Champs-Elysées, radiate from the vast square like the rays of a star (*étoile* means "star"). The respectable neighborhoods north of here shelter offices, showrooms, restaurants, and hotels.

When you arrive at the enormous Charles-de-Gaulle Métro station, check the *plan du quartier* for your hotel's location and take the exit closest to the street you're seeking. This will prevent you from circling the vast square aboveground and save you a good 15 minutes.

✪ **Hôtel Niel.** 11 rue Saussier-Leroy, 75017 Paris. ☎ **01-42-27-99-29.** Fax 01-42-27-16-96. 36 units, 12 with shower only, 12 with bathroom (shower). TEL. 215F ($36) single with sink only, 275F ($46) single with shower only; 270F ($45) double with sink only, 330F ($55) double with shower only, 375F ($63) double with bathroom. Breakfast 25F ($4). AE, MC, V. Métro: Charles-de-Gaulle–Etoile or Ternes.

Named after the grand boulevard nearby, in a neighborhood studded with Haussmann-style buildings, this hotel is simple but clean, the kind of place embodying the most favorable aspects of the French bourgeoisie. Don't expect raucous behavior or late-night noise. Mme Foucreau, the on-site owner, is too strict for that, a fact that many loyal early-to-bed guests appreciate. The rooms are on six floors (with elevator) and usually outfitted with only a writing table, lamp, comfortable bed, and built-in closet.

BETWEEN PLACE DE L'OPERA & PLACE PIGALLE

✪ **Hôtel Navarin et d'Angleterre.** 8 rue Navarin, 75009 Paris. ☎ **01-48-78-31-80.** Fax 01-48-74-14-09. 26 units, 24 with bathroom (shower or tub). TV TEL. 245F ($41) single with toilet only, 315F ($53) single with bathroom; 250F ($42) double with toilet only, 340–380F ($57–$63) double with bathroom. Breakfast 30F ($5). MC, V. Métro: St-Georges or Notre-Dame-de-Lorette.

This four-story walkup has been managed by the charming Maylin family for more than a quarter of a century. You'll seldom find more warmth and charm in a hotel, and each room is unique. In summer, breakfast is served (7:30 to 9:30am) in a small garden with an acacia tree and fountain. If you book a room facing this garden, you'll be awakened by singing birds—unusual in a big city like Paris. The rooms were modernized in 1995, but the old-fashioned sitting room and antique furniture in the lounge still radiate a fin-de-siècle atmosphere.

NEAR THE GARE DU NORD & GARE DE L'EST

Though this isn't the most glamorous neighborhood, you'll be near Métro stations with a lot of lines that can whisk you all over Paris. The neighborhood is full of fast-food outlets, cafes, and grocery stores. Try to avoid returning to the Gare de l'Est at night, as the station becomes rather seedy.

Hôtel des Voyageurs. 9 rue du 8-Mai-1945, 75010 Paris. ☎ **01-40-34-54-34.** Fax 01-40-34-00-84. 43 units, 23 with bathroom (tub or shower). TV TEL. 203F ($34) single without bathroom, 253F ($42) single with bathroom; 296F–306F ($49–$50) double with bathroom. Breakfast 25F ($4). AE, DC, MC, V. Métro: Gare de l'Est.

Across from the Gare de l'Est, this hotel was built late in the 19th century but simplified later. The rooms are compact and have modest but clean modern furniture. You'll find a friendly but no-nonsense staff, many German-speaking guests, and absolutely no pretensions. Its Reims-born owners state that the occupancy rate is often as much as 80%, but if you arrive without reservations and there are no rooms, they'll direct you to the under-the-same-management **Albouy,** 4 rue Lucien-Sampaix, where the 34 units (all with bathroom) have almost identical rates. The Albouy is a 3-minute walk away, near place de la République.

✪ **Hôtel Little Regina.** 89 bd. de Strasbourg, 75010 Paris. ☎ **01-40-37-72-30.** Fax 01-40-36-34-14. 33 units, 23 with bathroom (shower). TV TEL. 200F ($33) single without bathroom; 320F ($53) single/double with bathroom. Breakfast 25F ($4). AE, V. Métro: Gare de l'Est.

Facing the Gare de l'Est, this six-floor hotel with elevator was built in the 19th century. It adopted an English-sounding name to reassure its hordes of British visitors descending on Paris for world fairs. The Little Regina has been under the same family management, with many of the same kindly staff, since the 1960s and has become the well-deserved leader of the budget hotels in this working-class neighborhood. The rooms are relatively large, with ample wardrobe space, comfortable beds, and (in most cases) modern pine furniture. One of the more interesting rooms is no. 17, featuring a full panorama over the busy rail station.

Little Hôtel. 3 rue Pierre-Chausson, 75010 Paris. ☎ **01-42-08-21-57.** Fax 01-42-08-33-80. 33 units, all with bathroom (shower or tub). TV TEL. 310F ($52) single; 350F ($58) double; 460F ($77) triple. AE, DC, MC, V. Métro: Jacques-Bonsergent.

This pleasant hotel is on a quiet side street between République and the Gare de l'Est. Most of the rooms have been refurbished recently and are modern and clean. The lobby contains a soda dispenser and an elevator is available.

NEAR THE GARE ST-LAZARE

Hôtel de Parme. 61 rue de Clichy, 75009 Paris. ☎ **01-48-74-40-41.** Fax 01-53-21-91-84. 36 units, 11 with shower only, 16 with bathroom (tub or shower). 180F ($30) single/double with sink only, 230F ($38) single/double with shower only, 250F–280F ($42–$47) single/double with bathroom; 300F ($50) triple with bathroom. Breakfast 30F ($5). MC, V. Métro: Place Clichy, Trinité, or Liège.

In a middle-class neighborhood north of central Paris's grand monuments, this is a well-managed place. It has a kindly English-speaking manager on site, M. Cornilleau, as well as clean rooms done with floral wallpaper and colorful curtains. Because of its location away from the usual tourist traffic, it often has vacant rooms when other hotels are fully booked. Paying for a room with a bath comes with an unexpected benefit: double-glazed windows that block out street noise. The hotel is only a 15-minute walk from the Roissy Bus Terminal at Opéra (the Roissy bus is the most practical and least expensive way to go from Charles de Gaulle Airport to the center of Paris).

IN THE FAUBOURG ST-GERMAIN

In the 18th century, Parisian aristocrats built elegant *hôtels particuliers* (mansions) west of boulevard St-Germain in what soon became the *quartier chic par excellence.* Those mansions still stand, now usually occupied by embassies and ministries.

Though you'll find plenty of fine restaurants as well as *épiceries* (food shops), *pâtisseries* (pastry shops), and *boulangeries* (bakeries), this is the most expensive neighborhood in the city. Bargains are few and far between.

Hôtel de Nevers. 83 rue du Bac, 75007 Paris. ☎ **01-45-44-61-30.** Fax 01-42-22-29-47. 11 units, all with bathroom (shower or tub). MINIBAR TV TEL. 390F ($65) single with shower; 420F ($70) twin with shower; 410–450F ($68–$75) double with shower or tub. Continental breakfast 30F ($5). No credit cards. Métro: Rue-du-Bac.

This building is one of the oldest in a historically important neighborhood. Between 1627 and 1790, it functioned as a convent for the Soeurs de la Recollette before they were disbanded by the Revolution. (Look for the religious plaque on the stone wall opposite the front desk.) The building is now classé, which means that any restoration must respect the original architecture. That precludes an elevator, so you'll have to climb the never-ending but beautiful staircase. The rooms, cozy and pleasant, contain a mishmash of antique and reproduction furniture. Nos. 10 and 11 are especially sought after because of their terraces overlooking either a corner of rue du Bac or a rear courtyard. In 1996, many rooms were upgraded with new fabrics and wall coverings.

A GAY & LESBIAN HOTEL

Hôtel Central. 33 rue Vieille-du-Temple, 75004 Paris. ☎ **01-48-87-99-33.** Fax 01-42-77-06-27. 7 units, 1 with bathroom (shower). TEL. 450F ($75) single; 535F ($89) double. Breakfast 35F ($7). MC, V. Métro: Hôtel-de-Ville.

As the only gay hotel conveniently in the heart of the Marais, this is a good port of entry into the city's gay scene, with a friendly staff ready to point out clubs, restaurants, and bars. The rooms are on the third, fourth, and fifth floors of an 18th-century building that contains **Le Central,** a relaxed gay bar. Though the rooms are serviceable and clean, with double-glazed windows, new beds and new carpets would definitely be in order. Since the reception closes at 5pm, guests are issued their own front door key and can come and go as they please. There's also a cozy first-floor salon to unwind and meet others. What you're paying for is privacy and a comfortable, secure environment, but you could find spiffier rooms elsewhere.

YOUTH HOSTELS

Paris has plenty of youth hostels *(auberges de jeunesse)* and *foyers* (literally "homes") to accommodate the hordes of young travelers who descend every summer. Quality differs greatly from place to place, but the superior hostels offer excellent value. Many welcome travelers regardless of age.

RESERVATIONS SERVICES   If you arrive in the city late in the day and don't want to start calling up or going to hostels that may already be full, it's a good idea simply to head for one of the offices of **OTU (Organization du Tourism Universitaire) Voyages,** 119 rue St-Martin, 4e (☎ **01-40-29-12-12;** Métro: Rambuteau; RER: Châtelet–Les Halles), across from the Centre Pompidou. It maintains access to 30 inexpensive hotels or student dorms throughout Paris, each of which houses students and low-budget travelers. You'll be offered a space wherever it's available, costing 90F ($15) per person, breakfast included. Lodgings are in basically furnished rooms that contain two, three, or four beds; though they're scattered throughout Greater Paris, they're accessible via the city's subway system.

   Another clearinghouse for securing cost-conscious lodgings is the **BVJ (Bureau Voyages Jeunesse) Club,** 20 rue Jean-Jacques Rousseau, 75001 Paris (☎ **01-53-00-90-90;** fax 01-53-00-90-19; Métro: Les Halles or Louvre-Rivoli). It controls access to two budget hotels and will secure reservations, if rooms aren't fully booked or under renovation, at either of them. The larger of the two lies upstairs from the organization's headquarters (above) and has 200 beds in 45 units. The organization's **annex** at 44 rue des Bernardins, 75005 Paris (☎ **01-43-29-34-80;** Métro: Maubert-Mutualité), with 150 beds in 54 units, tends to book many of its lodgings on long-term bases to students at Paris universities, but often has some kind of bed available for short-term stays of a night or two. Rooms in the annex have private facilities (toilet and shower) in each room, but rooms in the hotel on rue Jean-Jacques Rousseau have toilets and showers in the hall. With breakfast included, they cost 120F ($20) per person (130F/$22 for a single room). Neither of the hotels accepts credit cards, and bookings are most easily (and reliably) done through the main office.

Auberge Internationale des Jeunes. 10 rue Trousseau, 75011 Paris. ☎ **01-47-00-62-00.** Fax 01-47-00-33-16. 50 units, 22 with bathroom (shower). E-mail: aijaijparis.com. Internet: www.aijparis.com. 81F–91F ($14–$15) per night, including bed, bedsheet, and breakfast. AE, MC, V. Métro: Ledru-Rollin.

Next to place Bastille and its Opéra, this hostel was entirely renovated in the mid-1990s and offers a higher level of comfort than most Paris hostels. Rooms contain two to six beds for the most part; all rooms for five and six guests have a bathroom inside; some with four beds have a bathroom. Common showers and toilets are on each floor. The hostel is open 24 hours and has an Internet connection at a charge of 1F (20¢) per minute.

WORTH A SPLURGE

Hôtel Abbatial St-Germain. 46 bd. St-Germain, 75005 Paris. ☎ **01-46-34-02-12.** Fax 01-43-25-47-73. 43 units, all with bathroom (tub). A/C MINIBAR TV TEL. 490F–660F ($82–$110) single; 660F–820F ($111–$137) double; 950F ($158) triple. AE, MC, V. Métro: Maubert-Mutualité. RER: St-Michel.

In the early 1990s, this hotel was upgraded into the streamlined and comfortable place you see today. Its name derives from its position across from the Abbaye St-Nicolas du Chardonnet, and from its fifth and sixth floors you get sweeping views as far as the Panthéon and Notre-Dame. A tiny elevator carries you to the simple but comfortable rooms. Many have floral wallpaper and curtains; others, to a lesser degree, are more modern, with solid colors. Each contains a safe, and streetside windows have double glazing.

✪ **Hôtel St-Louis Marais.** 1 rue Charles-V, 75004 Paris. ☎ **01-48-87-87-04.** Fax 01-48-87-33-26. 15 units, all with bathroom (tub). TEL. 510F ($85) single; 610F–710F ($102–$118) double. Breakfast 40F ($7). MC, V. Métro: Sully–Morland, Bastille, or St-Paul.

This is a bit more dowdy but much more charming than many of its more modern competitors. The four-story building (no elevator) was built as a convent for the Celestines, a Benedictine order. The guest rooms contain antique and semiantique furnishings and beamed ceilings. Those looking for a small hotel with a cultivated atmosphere will like this place.

4 Great Deals on Dining

In the current economic environment, Parisians are scrutinizing prices as carefully as they scrutinize the wine list. Eat how they eat and you'll save money. They start the day with a light breakfast, usually consisting of a *café au lait* and a croissant or a buttered baguette called a *tartine.* Unless breakfast is included in the price of your hotel room, go to a sidewalk cafe and stand at the counter. The experience is inimitably Parisian and the price will be about 40% to 50% lower at the counter than if you sit down and have a waiter serve you.

Lunch is an important meal in Paris, and you may wish to make it the main meal of the day. You'll notice that the majority of restaurants, bistros, and cafes offer a fixed-price lunch on weekdays called a *menu du jour* or *formule,* a two- or three-course meal that sometimes includes wine. The fixed-price meal can be a terrific bargain, allowing you to eat at otherwise unaffordable restaurants. A few places offer the same fixed-price menu at dinner, but in most the dinner menu is more expensive, though still cheaper than ordering à la carte. An alternative is the *plat du jour* or *plat garni,* a main-course platter garnished with vegetables and little extras. It's usually made with the freshest and most seasonal ingredients and is cheaper than a full-course *menu du jour,* though less filling.

A Parisian *Pique-nique*

One of the best ways to save money and also to participate in Parisian life is to picnic. Go to a *fromagerie* and purchase some cheese; to a *boulangerie* for a baguette or two; to a *charcuterie* for some pâté, sausage, or salad; and to a *pâtisserie* for some luscious pastries. Add a friendly bottle of Côtes du Rhone—it usually goes well with picnics—and you'll have the makings of a delightful and typically French meal that you can take to the nearest park. Pretend you're in Manet's *Déjeuner sur l'herbe* and enjoy!

Most restaurants in Paris are open for lunch noon to 2:30pm and for dinner 7 to 10pm. For a quick meal outside these times, go to a cafe: However, choose one carefully. Prime locations or famous literary cafes carry higher price tags. Most cafes offer reasonably priced omelets, sandwiches, soups, or salads. Omelets come plain with just a sprinkling of herbs or filled with cheese, ham, or other hearty additions. Onion soup is a traditional Parisian dish, and you may see *soupe de poisson* (fish soup) on the menu. Another cafe favorite is the *croque monsieur,* a grilled ham sandwich covered with melted cheese, or a *croque madame,* the same dish topped with an egg. Or try a *salade Niçoise,* a huge bowl filled with lettuce, boiled potato, tuna, hard-boiled egg, capers, tomatoes, olives, and anchovies. These dishes make a light, pleasant meal for 35F to 65F ($6 to $11). If you want a free glass of water (as opposed to its bottled counterpart), ask for *une carafe d'eau* ("ewn *kah*-rahf doh").

IN THE LATIN QUARTER

✪ **La Petite Hostellerie.** 35 rue de la Harpe (just east of bd. St-Michel), 5e. ☎ **01-43-54-47-12.** Fixed-price meal 55.70F ($9) at lunch, 59F–89F ($10–$15) at dinner. Tues–Sat noon–2:30pm and 7–10:30pm. AE, DC, MC, V. Métro: St-Michel or Cluny–La Sorbonne. FRENCH.

This place has three dining rooms: a usually crowded ground-floor one and two larger (seating 100) upstairs ones with attractive 18th-century woodwork. People come for the cozy ambiance and decor, decent French country cooking, polite service, and excellent prices. The 59F ($10) menu has a surprising variety of choices. You can begin with *soupe à l'oignon,* follow with paella or *boeuf bourguignon,* and finish with a pleasant crème caramel. The house wine is a reasonable 54F ($9) a bottle.

Le Grenier de Notre-Dame. 18 rue de la Bûcherie (near Notre-Dame and bd. St-Michel), 5e. ☎ **01-43-29-98-29.** Fixed-price menus 75F ($13), 78F ($13), and 105F ($18); main courses 53F–90F ($9–$15). AE, V. Daily noon–3pm and 7–11:30pm. Métro: Maubert-Mutualité or St-Michel. FRENCH/VEGETARIAN.

This earthy arts-oriented hideaway claims to be one of only five vegetarian restaurants in Paris. It prides itself on specifying (in French and English) which dishes contain light doses of eggs or dairy products, which have a hint of fish (in some cases only a calamari ring or two), and which are vegan (no dairy, eggs, or animal by-products). Favorite dishes are *cassoulet végétarien* (white beans, onions, tomatoes, soy sausage), vegetarian moussaka (with lentils substituted for lamb), and a tofu-like dish not served anywhere else in Paris, *escalope de seitan* (like a meat loaf, made from two kinds of organic flour and boiled for 5 hours). The desserts often verge on the surreal, like seaweed flan.

✪ **Restaurant Perraudin.** 157 rue St-Jacques, 5e. ☎ **01-46-33-15-75.** Plats du jour 59F ($10); 3-course lunch 63F ($10); main courses 59F ($10). No credit cards. Tues–Fri noon–2:15pm; Mon–Sat 7:30–10:15pm. Métro: Luxembourg. BISTRO.

Getting the Best Deal on Dining

- Fill up at lunch when you can get a three-course prix-fixe meal for a fraction of the price you'd pay at dinner.
- Stop at sidewalk booths where you can buy inexpensive sandwiches and crêpes.
- Choose a sidewalk cafe for breakfast, unless the meal is included in the price of your room.
- Order the *plat du jour*—an ideal money-saving choice for lunch or dinner.
- Avoid the huge markup on bottled water by ordering *une carafe d'eau*—tap water.
- Note that it's less expensive to have coffee or a drink standing at a counter rather than sitting at a table.

This ever-popular restaurant with its red-check tablecloths and lace lamp shades has been the haunt of students, professors, and editors for years. The lunch menu offers a choice of three appetizers, two main courses, and cheese or dessert. A typical menu might offer a green salad or tomatoes and mozzarella as an appetizer, ham with endives or roast beef as a main course, then baba au rum or a fruit tart for dessert. Classic dishes like salmon with a sorrel sauce, duck confit, steak au poivre vert, and gigot d'agneau with a gratin Dauphinois are on the à la carte menu. Lunchtime only, Mme Perraudin provides a quarter-liter of red wine for 10F ($2). Go early or you'll have to wait.

IN ST-GERMAIN

✪ **A la Bonne Crêpe.** 11 rue Grégoire-de-Tours, 6e. ☎ **01-43-54-60-74.** Three-course lunch with crêpe main course 50F ($8); crêpes à la carte 14F–49F ($2–$8). No credit cards. Mon–Sat noon–2:30pm and 7–11pm. Métro: Odéon. FRENCH/BRETON.

The region of Brittany is known for its crêpes and ciders, and in this 30-seat restaurant (Paris's oldest crêperie, opened in 1946) you can combine these goodies into lunch or dinner. Savory crêpes filled with cheese, meat, seafood, or other hearty ingredients make the main course, and sweet crêpes filled with jam or chocolate are a fine dessert. The cider is the alcoholic kind, Brittany's answer to beer. Rue Grégoire-de-Tours is a tiny street beginning between nos. 140 and 142 bd. St-Germain and going north toward the Seine.

✪ **Au Pied de Fouet.** 45 rue de Babylone, 7e. ☎ **01-47-05-12-27.** Main courses 45F–65F ($8–$11). No credit cards. Mon–Fri noon–2:30pm and 7–9:30pm, Sat noon–2:30pm. Métro: Vaneau. FRENCH.

This is one of the smallest (30 cramped seats) restaurants in the neighborhood, with one of the longest histories and some of the most reasonable prices. Halfway between the ritzy faubourg district and St-Germain-des-Prés, it attracts locals and students with big appetites and lean pockets. Don't expect a leisurely meal at this place, as food and drink are consumed faster than at more expensive competitors. The dishes are solid, unpretentious, and straightforward, including such staples as *blanquette de veau* (veal in white sauce), *petit salé* (a savory stew made from pork and vegetables), roasted salmon in tarragon sauce, and sole meunière.

✪ **Au Vieux Casque.** 19 rue Bonaparte, 6e. ☎ **01-43-54-99-46.** Reservations recommended. Menu du jour, wine included, 98F ($16); plats du jour 46F–60F ($8–$10); à la carte dishes 38F–70F ($6–$12). V. Mon–Sat 7–11:15pm. Métro: St-Germain-des-Prés or Mabillon. FRENCH.

Street Eats

In Paris, you can find a large variety of very affordable street food sold everywhere from the Latin Quarter to outside the grands magasins on the Right Bank. Tasty sandwiches, crêpes, frites, and (in cold weather) delicious roasted chestnuts are just a few of the items available. The crêpes are especially good—freshly made and filled with your choice of ingredients: cheese, ham, egg (or a combination of these); chocolate and nuts; apricot jam; or some other treat.

Au Vieux Casque has lots of atmosphere, boasting a wood-and-stucco ground-floor dining room, a stone-vaulted cellar, and an upstairs room with rough-hewn beams. You can see the chef at work on the ground floor, preparing updated classics a cut above those at similar places—try a delicate tomato salad to start, followed by a turkey cutlet in cream sauce with rice; then finish with Camembert, fruit, or a dessert.

Bistro Mazarin. 42 rue Mazarine, 6e. ☎ **01-43-29-99-01.** Reservations recommended. Main courses 55F–65F ($9–$11). AE, MC, V. Daily noon–3pm and 7:30pm–midnight. Métro: Odéon. FRENCH.

This bistro bustles and vibrates, and just about everyone inside seems associated with the shops or universities of the historic and highly commercial neighborhood around it. In either of two dining rooms whose wood paneling has been congenially battered over the years, you can order from a spectrum of dishes known since childhood to almost everyone born in France. Examples are petit salé of pork, prepared like a stew; beef bourguignon; a midwinter selection of fresh oysters; veal chops sautéed with butter and lemon sauce; and a satisfying combination of lentils with charcuterie and herbs. Everything can be washed down with reasonably priced local wines. Some tables are outdoors.

Così. 54 rue de Seine, 6e. ☎ **01-46-33-35-36.** Sandwiches 32–48F ($5–$8). Daily noon–midnight. No credit cards. Métro: Odéon. SANDWICHES.

The New Zealand owner of Così is passionate about opera and Italian bread. While you decide whether to stuff your sandwich with baked salmon, roasted eggplant, smothered onions, roast beef, or mozzarella and tomatoes, focaccia-style bread is baking in the oven and opera melodies drift through the two-story shop. With moist, chewy bread and tasty fillings, the sandwiches make a fine light meal. Add soup, a glass of wine, and a slice of the sinful chocolate cake and you'll have a small but perfect feast. You can take your food out or eat upstairs.

Le Petit Vatel. 5 rue Lobineau, 6e. ☎ **01-43-54-28-49.** Fixed-price menu 60F ($10); main courses 45F–55F ($8–$9). MC, V. Tues–Sat noon–3pm and 7pm–midnight. Métro: Mabillon or Odéon. MEDITERRANEAN/SOUTHWESTERN FRENCH.

Since 1914 (and through a changing collection of owners) this has remained one of Paris's most charming cost-conscious eateries. With hanging lamps and a handful of photos commemorating earlier incarnations, it contains only 22 seats (plus a few on the sidewalk in summer) in a pocket-size dining room. The daily specials are based on unfussy dishes reflecting the traditions of Toulouse and France's Mediterranean coast and include several versions of robust soup; a Catalan platter (pamboli) that includes slices of grilled bread garnished with country ham and mountain cheese, spicy tomato sauce, and olive oil; Catalan-style rabbit; and beef with carrots or boeuf bourguignon. The place is crowded thanks to its no-nonsense prices and rib-sticking cuisine.

✪ **Le Polidor.** 41 rue Monsieur-le-Prince, 6e. ☎ **01-43-26-95-34.** Two-course weekday lunch menu 55F ($9); dinner menu 100F ($17). No credit cards. Mon–Sat noon–2:30pm and 7pm–12:30am; Sun 7–11pm. Métro: Odéon. BISTRO.

An institution in Paris for about 150 years, this is the quintessential Left Bank bistro, perpetually crowded with people sitting elbow to elbow. The cooking is just like home—if your home is administered by a stern French grandmother who insists on the correct preparation of recipes belonging to her grandmother. Blanquette de veau, boeuf bourguignon, ragoût of pork, and gigot d'agneau flageolets won't set the world of gastronomy on fire, but you won't be disappointed either. For weekday lunches you can get a quarter-liter of wine for 7F ($1).

Restaurant Orestias. 4 rue Grégoire-de-Tours, 6e. ☎ **01-43-54-62-01.** Three-course menu 44F ($7) lunch/dinner, except Fri–Sat after 8pm. Mon–Sat noon–2:30pm and 5:30–11:30pm. MC, V. Métro: Odéon. GREEK/FRENCH.

The waiters in this folksy restaurant welcome you as though you were their long-lost relatives from Greece. Seated at long wooden tables under beamed ceilings, you can satisfy the most ravenous hunger with heaping portions of food. The kitchen turns out basic Greek dishes like stuffed grape leaves with salad, souvlaki, and baklava, as well as roast chicken, lamb chops, and steak with potatoes, peas, and rice. You can't expect frills and thrills at these prices, but the ingredients are fresh and the dishes are cooked correctly.

Thoumieux. 79 rue St-Dominique, 7e. ☎ **01-47-05-49-75.** Reservations recommended. Main courses 70F–120F ($12–$20); fixed-price menu 82F ($14). AE, MC, V. Mon–Sat noon–3:30pm and 6:45pm–midnight; Sun noon–midnight. Métro: Invalides. SOUTH-WESTERN FRENCH.

Thoumieux was opened in 1923 by a family whose origins lay in the southwest of France, and today it's maintained with the same style by descendants of the founder. In an art deco setting, you'll dine in one of three dining rooms. Menu items include a gigantic cassoulet, confit of duckling in the style of Toulouse, *boudin* (blood sausage), filet of beef with peppercorns, and a dish favored by the French but not by many others, calf's head ravigote. You might settle for *blanquette de veau* (veal in white sauce) instead.

NEAR THE HOTEL DE VILLE

✪ **Trumilou.** 84 quai de l'Hôtel-de-Ville, 4e. ☎ **01-42-77-63-98.** Reservations recommended Sat–Sun. Fixed-price menus 65F–80F ($11–$13); main courses 65F–102F ($11–$17). MC, V. Daily noon–3pm and 7–11pm. Métro: Hôtel-de-Ville. FRENCH.

This is one of the most popular of the restaurants surrounding Paris's Hôtel de Ville (town hall) with an unusual decor that includes a rustic collection of farm implements and memorabilia. The tables are closely crowded and the staff is jovial. Prices have remained steady here, as the owner confides, "because of our current economic crisis." The cuisine is tried and true, with examples like poulet (chicken) provençal, sweet-breads "grand-mère," duckling with plums, stuffed cabbage, and blanquette de veau.

NEAR THE CENTRE POMPIDOU

Dame Tartine. 2 rue Brise Miche, 4e. ☎ **01-42-77-32-22.** Platters 37F–40F ($6–$7). MC, V. Daily noon–midnight. Métro: Rambuteau. FRENCH.

This place is like a busy cafe where patrons happen to want something more substantial than a lump of sugar to go with their *café.* Crowded and cheerful, "The Dame" faces the whimsical Stravinsky Fountain outside the Beaubourg. It emphasizes simple but generous platters that might include chicken curry, chicken with cinnamon sauce, ham steak, fried fillet of fish with tartar sauce, and various salads. Most are served with bread, with the expectation that you'll create your own open-faced sandwich with the ingredients on your platter, perhaps accompanying it with glasses of beer or wine. The place is noisy, youthful, and breezy, usually filled with students counting their francs.

ON THE CHAMPS-ELYSEES

Chez Clément. 123 av. des Champs-Elysées, 8e. ☎ **01-40-73-87-00.** Reservations recommended. Main courses 45F–120F ($8–$20). MC, V. Daily 11am–1am. Métro: George-V. FRENCH.

It's called "The Impossible Dream": a new cheap restaurant on the "main street" of Paris. Its low prices and generous portions are especially impressive considering the staggeringly expensive rent this restaurant is forced to pay because of its location. The place prides itself on well-prepared platters of standard French food whose presentation and flavors rarely vary. The menu offers everything from a platter of cheeses, which makes a minimeal when accompanied with a salad, to a generously proportioned mixed grill (grande rôtisserie) combining steak, chicken, and pork with mashed potatoes. Fresh oysters might precede any of the main courses.

EAST OF THE OPERA GARNIER

✪ **Chartier.** 7 rue du Faubourg-Montmartre, 9e. ☎ **01-47-70-86-29.** Three-course menu, wine included, 79F ($13); à la carte dishes 30–45F ($5–$8). V. Daily 11:30am–3pm and 6–10pm. Métro: Rue-Montmartre. FRENCH.

At the turn of the century, Chartier was a "bouillon" or cantine for workers. Workers have been replaced by visitors from all parts of the globe who come more for the ambiance than the food. The dark wood, mirrors, and hazy lighting in the spacious hall create a wonderful sense of intrigue that has been captured in several French films. The food is, as the French say, "correct"—nothing more, nothing less. There are about 100 items on the menu, including 16 main courses like poulet rôti, a variety of steaks and frites, and turkey in cream sauce. Prices are low enough that a three-course repast is easy on the budget, even if you don't choose the fixed-price meal.

Restaurant Lou Cantou. 35 Cité d'Antin, 9e. ☎ **01-48-74-75-15.** Three-course menu, wine included, 59.50F ($10); plat du jour 41F ($7). No credit cards. Mon–Sat 11:30am–3pm. Métro: Chausée-d'Antin. FRENCH.

If you'd like to fuel up quickly, cheaply, and in pleasant surroundings, this homey bistro will do the job. Lace curtains, flowers, plants, and copper pots on the wall create an inviting space that attracts a middle-management crowd for lunch. The fixed-price menu includes a large choice of entrees and *plats*. None is a culinary miracle, but they do provide a simple and satisfying meal. To find Cité d'Antin, look for the passage at 61 rue de Provence.

AROUND THE LOUVRE

Osaka. 163 rue St-Honoré, 1e. ☎ **01-42-60-64-29.** Lunch menu 58F ($10); soups 42F–55F ($7–$9). MC, V. Wed–Mon noon–2pm and 7–10pm. Métro: Palais-Royal. JAPANESE.

Steps from the Louvre and the Palais Royal off place André-Malraux, this restaurant offers hearty noodle soups that make a one-dish meal. You select your soup from pictures on the wall, tell the cashier your choice, and take a seat at the counter. The giant steaming bowls contain a hard-boiled egg, Japanese vegetables, and whatever meat, fish, or vegetables you've selected. Adjacent to the "soup room," a sushi bar offers a lunch menu of raw fish for 80F ($13). Both rooms are jammed at lunch, mostly with Japanese—a testament to the authenticity of the cuisine.

Universal Restaurant. 99 rue de Rivoli, 1er (entrance rue de Rivoli or from the Louvre). ☎ **01-47-03-96-58.** Main dishes from 25F ($4); 3 courses à la carte 45F–50F ($7–$8). V. Mon, Wed, Thurs, and Sat 8am–11pm; Tues, Fri, and Sun 8am–10pm. Metro: Palais-Royal–Musée-du-Louvre. FRENCH CAFETERIA/INTERNATIONAL.

Next to the inverted pyramid in the Galerie Carrousel du Louvre, this busy cafeteria offers a rich assortment of ethnic and French specialties at unbeatable prices. Lunch is a madhouse as hungry hordes load up their trays from stands offering Spanish tapas, Chinese lo mein, pasta salad, Mexican burritos, or all-American hamburger and fries. Other counters display Lebanese food, roast chicken, salads, muffins, ice cream, cheese, and crêpes. Though the ambiance is hardly relaxing (signs ask you not to "install yourself" at the tables), it's a quick place to fortify yourself between bouts with the Louvre.

IN THE MARAIS

Le Petit Gavroche. 15 rue Ste-Croix-de-la-Bretonnerie, 4e. ☎ **01-48-87-74-26.** Three-course menu 48F ($8) at lunch, 50F ($8) at dinner. AE, V. Mon–Fri noon–3pm and 7–11:30pm, Sat 7–11:30pm. Métro: Hôtel-de-Ville. FRENCH.

This is an easygoing spot to pop into for a sturdy feed. In true bistro style, the menu is on a chalkboard and you eat at solid wood tables. The decor runs to stuffed hens and fluorescent lighting. Get here early for lunch, since it's very popular with old-timers who take 2-hour lunches. The food isn't bad for the price; try the steamed mussels with fries or the goulash with noodles, followed by a lemon tart.

Les Temps des Cerises. 31 rue de la Cerisaie, 4e. ☎ **01-42-72-08-63.** Lunch 68F ($11). No credit cards. Mon–Fri 7:45am–8pm (lunch 11:30am–2:30pm). Closed Aug. Métro: Bastille or Sully–Morland. FRENCH.

This bistro is charged with history, for it's been in business since 1900 in an 18th-century building that once served as a convent. It's a classic French bar/bistro, with mosaic tile floor, pewter bar, and posters and other art covering the walls. Locals gather to chat and hang out over a glass of wine or coffee. It's always packed at lunch, but it's a bargain and worth a little crowding. There's a choice of menus (which don't include a beverage) that might tempt you with anything from pâté and egg mayonnaise to start to paupiette of salmon with citron-butter sauce or steak with shallot sauce and braised endive to follow. The wines can be expensive, but you can always select one of the chalkboard specials or the inexpensive house wine. There are no meals served after lunchtime, but you can graze on bread and paté, cheese or *charcuterie* while you sip your wine.

Marais Plus. 20 rue des Francs-Bourgeois, 3e. ☎ **01-48-87-01-40.** Pots of tea 25F ($4); salads 55F–70F ($9–$12); tartes and tourtes 50F–55F ($8–$11). AE, MC, V. Daily 10am–7:30pm. Métro: St-Paul. FRENCH.

This is more of a cultural icon than a restaurant, as it's vastly different from most of the other food emporiums in the Marais. It combines a bookstore (focusing almost entirely on French-language art and children's books) with a tearoom dispensing light food. The menu choices are limited but fresh and flavorful: salads, croissants, pastries, *café au lait* or tea, and *tartes* and *tourtes* (open-faced or pastry-wrapped minipies) whose ingredients change daily. Tartes are sugared and tourtes salted. Versions with mozzarella and/or herbs, spinach, salted ham, and mushrooms are the most popular and the best. The only drawbacks are the hours (if you want dinner you'll have to go early) and the limited menu. The crowd is young, sophisticated, and good-natured.

NEAR THE EIFFEL TOWER

✪ **Le Café du Commerce.** 51 rue du Commerce, 15e. ☎ **01-45-75-03-27.** Three-course fixed-price menu 85F–115F ($14–$19); main courses 55F–91F ($9–$15). AE, DC, MC, V. Daily noon–midnight. Métro: Emile-Zola, Commerce, or La Motte–Picquet. FRENCH.

Le Café is one of the best bargains in this area of unpretentious stores and busy streets. It contains dozens of plants and photos of the various writers who wrote manuscripts on its premises. The tables are scattered over three floors, illuminated from an overhead atrium. The menu items are old-fashioned, with no attempts at modernity or high style. You can choose from warm goat cheese on a bed of lettuce, *poulet sauce estragon* (chicken tarragon), duck breast with green-peppercorn sauce, sole meunière, or escalope of salmon with sage sauce. Crème caramel or chocolate mousse makes for a satisfying dessert.

NEAR THE GARE DU NORD

✪ **L'Alsaco.** 10 rue Condorcet, 9e. ☎ **01-45-26-44-31.** Three-course menu 87F ($15) at lunch, 95F ($16) at dinner. AE, V. Mon–Fri noon–2pm and 7:30–11pm; Sat 7:30–11pm. Métro: Anvers or Poissonnière. ALSATIAN.

When the winter chill (which can last through spring) seeps into your bones, the best way to thaw out is to dig into a plate of steaming *choucroute* topped with sausage and cuts of ham. The sauerkraut served in the back room of this wine bar comes from the Alsatian village of Krautergersheim and is as aromatic as any you'll find in Paris. For only 49F ($8) you get a hearty platter topped with three different sausages that goes well with a stein of Alsatian beer.

PICNICKING

For a truly French *pique-nique*, the magic words are *charcuterie, épicerie, boulangerie,* and *pâtisserie* (butcher shop, grocery store, bakery, and pastry shop). *Charcuterie* used to refer to a butcher who specialized in pork, but today it refers to a gourmet store selling cold meats, pâtés, salads, breads, rolls, cakes, and pastries—all delectably displayed.

The best place to eat your picnic is in the nearest park. My favorite is the Jardin des Tuileries and Parc Monceau, on the Right Bank, but equally charming are place des Vosges in the Marais, with handsome benches; the vast Jardin du Luxembourg on the Left Bank; and the Parc du Champ-du-Mars by the Eiffel Tower. There are many more intimate spots—so many that it's not hard to find a pleasant spot to enjoy a meal *en plein air.*

WORTH A SPLURGE

Aux Charpentiers. 10 rue Mabillon, 6e. ☎ **01-43-26-30-05.** Three-course fixed-price meal 122F ($20) at lunch, 155F ($26) at dinner; à la carte dishes 90F–189F ($15–$32). AE, DC, MC, V. Daily noon–3pm and 7–11:30pm. Métro: Mabillon. MASSIF CENTRAL.

The walls of this 170-seat bilevel restaurant are decorated with photographs and plans of carpentry, including models of wooden vaults and roof structures. The 155F ($26) dinner menu offers a choice of four appetizers, such as warm Lyon sausage with potato salad or hare pâté flavored with sweetened onions and oranges. There follows a choice of five main courses that may be chicken breast with tarragon or daube of beef provençal with zesty orange confit. The desserts may include soufflé glacé au Grand Marnier. Other à la carte dishes range from roasted Bresse chicken to grilled filet mignon. (The fixed-price menu at lunch doesn't include wine, though it is included in the fixed-price dinner.)

✪ **Bofinger.** 5–7 rue de la Bastille, 4e. ☎ **01-42-72-87-82.** Three-course menu including half bottle of wine 169F ($29). AE, MC, V. Mon–Fri noon–3pm and 6:30pm–1am, Sat–Sun noon–1am. Métro: Bastille. ALSATIAN.

Bofinger opened in 1864 as a brasserie specializing in the cuisine of France's German-influenced Alsace region, and it's now one of the best-loved restaurants in the city. Classified as a *Monument Historique,* its belle époque decor—dark wood, gleaming brass, bright lights, glass ceiling, and waiters with long white aprons—will transport you back to the 19th century. Ladies should be sure to visit the elaborately tiled ladies room—it's one of a kind. The menu features many Alsatian specialties, like choucroute (sauerkraut), and is also famous for oysters, foie gras, and seafood platters. And the prices are actually quite moderate for Paris.

5 Seeing the Sights

SIGHTSEEING SUGGESTIONS

IF YOU HAVE 1 DAY   Start early by having coffee and croissants at a cafe. Then begin at Kilometer 0: All distances in France are measured from the square in front of **Notre-Dame,** on the Ile de la Cité. From here, cross the **River Seine** to the **Louvre.** Select a few rooms in a particular collection for your first visit, for this is one of the world's largest and finest museums, and it would take months to see it in its entirety. Have lunch in the inexpensive Universal Restaurant in the Louvre.

From the museum, stroll through the **Jardin des Tuileries** to **place de la Concorde** and then walk up the **Champs-Elysées** to the **Arc de Triomphe.** Note that Métro Line 1 runs in a straight line from the Louvre to the Arc de Triomphe (Métro: Charles-de-Gaulle–Etoile), or you can climb aboard bus no. 73 at the Concorde and ride up the Champs-Elysées to the Arc de Triomphe.

From the Arc de Triomphe, walk down avenue Kléber to place du Trocadéro for some splendid views of the **Eiffel Tower** (bus nos. 22 and 30 also go to Trocadéro as well as the Métro Line 6). Visit the tower and then head for the Left Bank. You can catch the RER at Champ-de-Mars, southwest of the Eiffel Tower on the Seine (a long walk), to the St-Michel station in the heart of the **Latin Quarter.** Or you can take bus no. 63 from Trocadéro, which drops you off at the **St-Germain-des-Prés church.** Stroll down the boulevard St-Germain-des-Prés to **place St-Michel** (or vice versa if you've taken the train) and detour into the maze of streets that lie between the boulevard and the Seine. This is an excellent area for dinner.

IF YOU HAVE 2 DAYS   On Day 1, follow the above from **Notre-Dame** to the **Arc de Triomphe** but take a little more time in the **Louvre.** From the Arc de Triomphe, either walk south on avenue Marceau or take bus no. 92 to Alma-Marceau and board the Bateaux-Mouches for a **Seine boat ride.** Afterward, walk up posh avenue Montaigne to the Champs-Elysées and take Métro Line 1 to St-Paul, in the heart of the **Marais;** walk east on rue St-Antoine and turn left on rue de Brague to see Paris's oldest square, the aristocratic **place des Vosges.**

Explore the Left Bank on Day 2. Start at the **Eiffel Tower** and stroll past the **Invalides,** with the Tomb of Napoléon, through the **faubourg St-Germain,** a district of elegant 18th-century mansions (the **Musée Rodin** and **Musée d'Orsay** are here). Head back to the Latin Quarter for the evening.

IF YOU HAVE 3 DAYS   Combine the above with visits to **Père-Lachaise cemetery** and **Montmartre** and **Sacré-Coeur.** You'll also have time to explore a park: either the **Jardin du Luxembourg** on the Left Bank or **Parc Monceau** on the Right Bank.

A Museum Pass Tip

La Carte Musées et Monuments is available at any of the museums honoring it or at branches of the Office de Tourisme de Paris (see "Visitor Information," earlier in this chapter). It offers free entrance to the permanent collections of 65 monuments and museums in Paris and the Ile de France. The cost of a 1-day pass is 70F ($12), a 3-day pass 140F ($23), and a 5-day pass 200F ($33).

IF YOU HAVE 5 DAYS   Five days is a sensible amount of time to stay in Paris, and if you have a week or 10 days, so much the better. You'll probably have time to see **Sainte-Chapelle** and the **Conciergerie** on the Ile de la Cité; explore more museums; and visit **Versailles, Fontainebleau, Chartres,** or **Giverny** outside the city.

THE TOP MUSEUMS

✪ **Musée du Louvre.** 34–36 quai du Louvre, 1er. ☎ **01-40-20-51-51** for recorded message, 01-40-20-53-17 for information desk, or 01-49-87-54-54 to order tickets. Internet: www.louvre.fr. Admission 45F ($8) before 3pm, 26F ($4) after 3pm and Sun; free for ages 17 and under. Free for everyone first Sun of every month. Mon (limited rooms) and Wed 9am–9:45pm, Thurs–Sun 9am–6pm. 90-minute English-language tours leave Mon and Wed–Sat at various times for 38F ($6) adults, 22F ($4) ages 13–18, free with museum ticket for age 12 and under. Métro: Palais-Royal or Musée-du-Louvre.

The overall excellence of the collection, the enormous quantity of works displayed, and the abundance of recognizable masterpieces make the Louvre one of the world's top museums. It can be exhausting as well as exhaustive, but the 90-minute guided tour will cover the most popular works and give you a quick orientation to the museum's layout.

If you choose to go it alone, try to zero in on a particular department, collection, or wing. The museum is divided into seven departments: Egyptian antiquities; Oriental antiquities; Greek, Etruscan, and Roman antiquities; sculptures; paintings; graphics and the graphic arts; and art objects. The departments are spread across three wings: **Sully, Denon,** and **Richelieu.**

First-timers usually head to the three most famous works: *Mona Lisa, Winged Victory of Samothrace,* and *Venus de Milo.* Finding your way is easy; the route is clearly marked by signs and the great flow of other visitors carries you along like a cork on a wave.

On the route from *Winged Victory* to *Mona Lisa* you'll pass David's vast *Coronation of Napoléon* opposite his languid *Portrait of Madame Récamier.* Stop and admire Ingres's *Grand Odalisque.* In the Salle des Etats, Leonardo da Vinci's *La Gioconda (Mona Lisa)* is the center of attention, with camera clickers crowding around like crazed paparazzi. The secret of her tantalizing smile is a technique known as *sfumato,* blending the borders of the subject into the background. The artist blurred the outlines of her features so as to make the corners of her mouth and eyes fade away, making her expression ever changeable and eternally mysterious.

The 1993 inauguration of the Richelieu Wing opened several acres of new exhibition space, allowing display of some 12,000 works of art. Before heading into these galleries, look in at the adjoining Cour Marly, the glass-roofed courtyard that houses the rearing Marly Horses by Coustou. For a change of pace, see the apartments of Napoléon III, decorated and furnished in over-the-top Second Empire style (open mornings only).

The enormous **I. M. Pei glass pyramid** that serves as the museum's entrance was a controversial undertaking supported by President Mitterrand during the last decade.

Some Louvre Tips

Long waiting lines outside the Louvre's pyramid entrance are notorious, but here are some tricks for avoiding them:

- Enter via the underground shopping mall Carrousel du Louvre at 99 rue de Rivoli.
- Enter directly from the Palais-Royal–Musée du Louvre Métro station.
- Buy a Carte Musées et Monuments (Museum and Monuments Pass) allowing direct entry through the priority entrance at the Passage Richelieu, 93 rue de Rivoli.
- Order tickets by phone at the number above, have them charged to your Visa or MasterCard, and then pick them up at any FNAC store, which also gives you direct entry through the Passage Richelieu.

While many admired the audacious design, others feared its modernism would clash with the palace's classical lines. Like other monuments that initially faced strong opposition, the pyramid has gradually won over most critics. Whether by day when the pyramid gathers and reflects the sunlight or by night when the courtyard sparkles with artificial light, the monument has taken its place among the beauties of Paris.

✪ **Musée d'Orsay.** 62 rue de Lille/1 rue de Bellechasse, 7e. ☎ **01-40-49-48-14,** or 01-40-49-48-48 for information desk. Admission 40F ($7) adults, 30F ($5) ages 18–24, and Sun; free for age 17 and under. Tues–Wed and Fri–Sat 10am–6pm, Thurs 10am–9:45pm, Sun 9am–6pm (June 20–Sept 20 opens at 9am). Métro: Solférino. RER: Musée-d'Orsay.

More than a decade ago, a brilliantly renovated train station and the best art of the 19th century were combined to create one of the world's great museums. For years, Paris's collections of 19th-century art were distributed among the Louvre, the Musée d'Art Moderne, and the very crowded rooms of the small Musée du Jeu de Paume, with its unsurpassed impressionist masterpieces. In 1986, these collections were transferred to the Orsay, an ornate turn-of-the-century train station. Thousands of paintings, sculptures, objets d'art, items of furniture, architectural displays, and even photographs and movies illustrate the diversity and richness of 19th-century art, including not only impressionism but also realism, postimpressionism, and art nouveau.

There are three floors of exhibits. On the ground floor is Manet's *Olympia* and other works of early impressionism, but I always head to the upper level, which contains Renoir's *Le Moulin de la Galette,* Manet's *Déjeuner sur l'herbe,* Degas's *Racing at Longchamps,* Monet's "Cathedrals," *Whistler's Mother,* and a whole roomful of van Goghs. There are also works by Gauguin, Toulouse-Lautrec, Pissarro, Cézanne, and Seurat.

Besides exhibiting astounding art, the Musée d'Orsay is a great place in which to spend an entire afternoon. Its restaurant and cafe are quite pleasant, and the bookstore and gift shop have an excellent selection.

✪ **Musée Picasso.** In the Hôtel Salé, 5 rue de Thorigny, 3e. ☎ **01-42-71-25-21.** Admission 30F ($5) adults, 20F ($3) students/ages 19–24 and Sun, free for age 18 and under. Apr–Sept Wed–Mon 9:30am–6pm; Oct–Mar Wed–Mon 9:30am–5:30pm. Métro: Chemin-Vert, St-Paul, or Filles-du-Calvaire.

The Hôtel Salé, a renovated mansion in the Marais, houses the world's greatest collection of Pablo Picasso's works. After his death in 1973, the artist's estate arranged to donate this enormous collection in lieu of French inheritance taxes, which were also enormous. The spectacular collection includes more than 200 paintings, almost 160

Adieu, Pompidou—For Now

What has been called "the most avant-garde building in the world," the **Centre Pompidou,** place Georges-Pompidou or plateau Beaubourg (☎ **01-44-78-12-33**), closed in late 1997 for extensive renovations.

The dream of former president Georges Pompidou, this center for 20th-century art (designed by Renzo Piano) opened in 1977 and immediately became the focus of loud controversy: Its bold exoskeletal architecture and the brightly painted pipes and ducts crisscrossing its transparent facade were considered jarring in the old Beaubourg neighborhood. Perhaps the detractors were right all along—within 20 years the building began to deteriorate so badly that a major restoration was called for.

The original plan was to keep the center open while work progressed, but the insurance company didn't like that idea. However, parts will remain open, so if you're interested call the number above to see what's open. The grand reopening is scheduled for December 31, 1999, to usher in the millennium.

sculptures, and 88 ceramics, as well as more than 3,000 prints and drawings—but only a fraction are on display at any given time. Besides Picasso's own paintings, sculptures, ceramics, engravings, and sketches (numbering in the thousands), the museum displays works by the artist's favorite painters, including Corot, Cézanne, and Matisse.

Musée Carnavalet. 23 rue de Sévigné, 3e. ☎ **01-42-72-21-13.** Admission 35F ($6) adults, 25F($4) ages 18–25/over 60, free for age 17 and under. Tues–Sun 10am–5:40pm. Métro: St-Paul, then walk east on rue St-Antoine and turn left on rue de Sévigné.

In the Marais, this is also known as the Musée de l'Histoire de Paris, and it details the city's history from prehistoric times to the present. Paintings, signs, items of furniture, models of the Bastille, and Marie Antoinette's personal items are all on display. The most intriguing salons depict events related to the Revolution: a bust of Marat, a portrait of Danton, a replica of the Bastille. The museum is housed in two splendid mansions: the Hôtel Le Peletier de St-Fargeau and the Hôtel Carnavalet, once the home of Mme de Sévigné, the 17th-century writer of masterful letters.

Musée de l'Orangerie des Tuileries. Place de la Concorde, 1er. ☎ **01-42-97-48-16.** Admission 30F ($5) adults, 20F ($3) ages 18–25 and Sun, free for age 17 and under. Wed–Mon 9:45am–5:15pm. Métro: Concorde.

Since 1984, the Orangerie has housed the renowned Jean Walter and Paul Guillaume art collection. It was sold to the French state by Domenica Walter, who had married both men. The collection, though comprising fewer than 150 paintings from impressionism to the 1930s, is remarkable. Among the painters represented are Cézanne, Renoir, Rousseau, Matisse, Derain, Picasso, and Soutine. The lower floor contains the most incredible display of Monet's *Nymphéas* anywhere, two oval rooms that are wrapped around with almost 360° of water lilies that Monet painted especially for the Orangerie. The effect is like being in the gardens at the artists' home in Giverny.

Musée Marmottan–Claude Monet. 2 rue Louis-Boilly, 16e. ☎ **01-42-24-07-02.** Admission 40F ($7) adults, 25F ($4) students; free for age 8 and under. Tues–Sun 10am–5:30pm. Métro: La Muette.

On the edge of the Bois de Boulogne, this jewel contains a veritable cache of Monets that were donated to the Academy des Beaux-Arts by Monet's son. Among them are the *Impression at Sunrise* that gave its name to the impressionist movement, *The Houses of Parliament,* and *Water Lilies,* plus numerous paintings of Giverny.

Paris

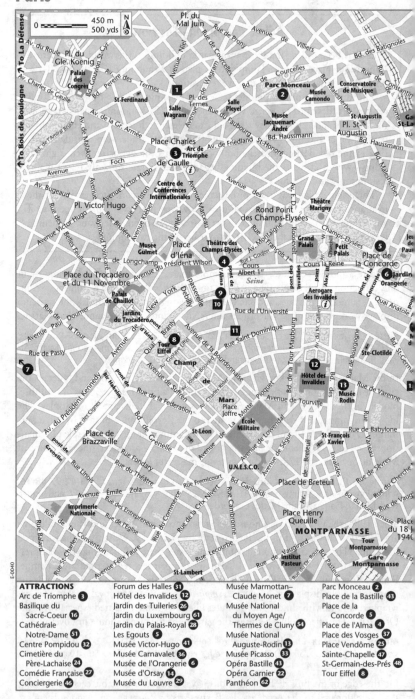

690

Getting the Best Deal on Sightseeing

- Purchase La Carte Musées et Monuments (see "Paris Deals & Discounts," earlier in this chapter) if you plan to visit many museums. Especially the 3- or 5-day pass will save you lots of francs, in both Paris and the Ile de France.
- Take one of the regular buses that tour monumental Paris for a fraction of the price charged by bus-tour companies. A 50-minute ride on bus no. 95 takes you from Tour Montparnasse; past St-Germain-des-Prés, the Louvre, the Palais Royal, and the Opéra; and all the way to Montmartre. Get off at the Caulincourt stop and you can walk the rest of the way up the hill for a panoramic view from Sacré-Coeur. This view is more interesting than the expensive look from the Eiffel Tower.
- Take one of the free guided tours of Notre-Dame, the best way to learn about this monument. Ask at the information booth to the right as you enter. Tours in English are Wednesday and Thursday at noon and Saturday at 2:30pm.
- Note that it won't cost you a franc to explore Paris's streets. Walk along the quays of the Seine and browse through the shops and stalls; each street opens onto a new vista. If you're an early riser, a walk through Paris at dawn can be memorable; you'll see the city come to life as shopfronts are washed clean, cafes open, and vegetable vendors arrange their produce.
- Be aware that the spacious forecourt of the Centre Pompidou, place Georges-Pompidou, is a free "entertainment center" featuring mimes, fire-eaters, would-be circus performers, and sometimes first-rate musicians. The Pompidou may now be closed, but the action here hasn't change.
- For a free look at some of the most stunning interiors in Paris, check out the churches—some even boast masterpieces, like those of Delacroix at St-Sulpice and the Rouault etchings at St-Severin.
- Spend an afternoon in a park or garden sampling true Parisian life at no cost. These are more than places to relax: They're sights in their own right, especially the Bois de Boulogne, Jardin des Tuileries, Jardin du Luxembourg, and Jardin du Palais-Royal. Or follow in the footsteps of Marcel Proust and explore the Parc Monceau.
- Museum-hop on Sunday and take advantage of reduced-price admission. However, remember that crowds of others will be doing the same thing.

Musée National du Moyen Age/Thermes de Cluny. 6 place Paul-Painlevé, 5e. ☎ **01-53-73-78-00.** Admission 30F ($5) adults, 20F ($3) ages 18–24 and Sun, free for age 17 and under. Wed–Mon 9:15am–5:45pm. Métro: Cluny–La Sorbonne.

This is Paris's museum of medieval art. Wood and stone sculptures, brilliant stained glass and metalwork, and rich tapestries (including the famous 15th-century *Lady and the Unicorn*, with its representation of the five senses) are among the exhibits. The Hôtel de Cluny, in which the museum is housed, is one of the city's foremost examples of medieval architecture. Some parts date back to Roman times, and you can see the ruins of thermal baths.

✪ **Musée National Auguste-Rodin.** In the Hôtel Biron, 77 rue de Varenne, 7e. ☎ **01-44-18-61-10.** Admission 28F ($5) adults, 18F ($3) ages 18–26 and Sun, 5F ($1) for the garden only, free for age 17 and under. Apr–Sept Tues–Sun 9:30am–5:45pm; Oct–Mar Tues–Sun 9:30am–4:45pm. Métro: Varenne.

Ile de la Cité & Ile St-Louis

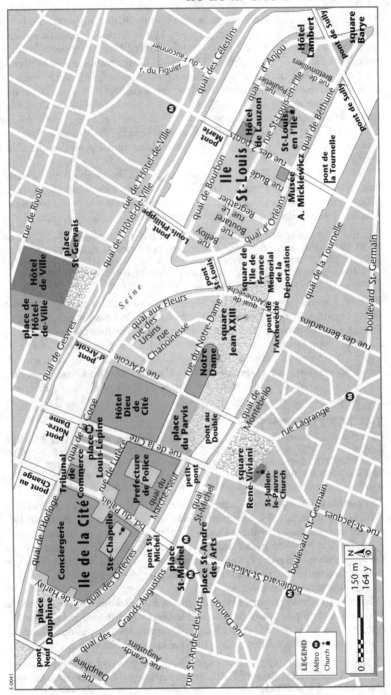

The extraordinary ability of Rodin to breathe life into marble and bronze makes this museum a standout in a city full of great art. This wide-ranging collection offers a superlative insight into Rodin's genius and includes all his greatest works, many of which you can see in the garden for only 5F ($1). My favorite is *The Burghers of Calais,* a harrowing commemoration of the siege of Calais in 1347, after which the triumphant Edward III of England kept the town's six richest burghers as servants. Also in the garden is *The Thinker,* "primal, tense, his chin resting on a toil worn hand," wrote Helen Keller. "In every limb I felt the throes of emerging mind." The *Gates of Hell* is a portrayal of Dante's *Inferno.* Intended for the Musée des Arts Decoratifs, these massive bronze doors weren't completed until 7 years after the artist's death.

Inside is the stunning *The Kiss,* whose lovers appear to be emerging from the marble into life. Upstairs are two versions of the celebrated and condemned nude of Balzac, his bulky torso rising from a tree trunk. Look also for the few works by Camille Claudel, Rodin's mistress and a brilliant sculptor herself.

Cité des Sciences et de l'Industrie. 30 av. Corentin-Cariou, La Villette, 19e. ☎ **01-40-05-81-00.** Internet: www.cite-sciences.fr. Admission to the exhibits, including the Argonaut, 50F ($8), 35F ($6) after 4pm, free for under age 7; to the Geode, 57F ($9.50); cinaxe, 34F ($6). Three-in-one ticket 124F ($21). Entrance to the Cité des Enfants 25F ($4). Tues–Sat 10am–6pm, Sun 10am–7pm. Métro: Porte-de-la-Villette.

Built as an abattoir, this structure was converted into a museum complex of extraordinary ambition. At the **Explora,** view exhibits, shows, and models and play interactive games demonstrating scientific techniques. Subjects include the universe, space, Earth, the environment, computer science, and health. The planetarium is also in the Explora. You'll find an adventure playground for kids 3 to 12 and the submarine the *Argonaut* to explore. In the **Géode,** four to six films are shown on a huge hemispheric screen that enfolds the audience in the action. At the **cinéaxe,** you'll experience breathtaking simulations.

THE TOP CHURCHES

✪ **Cathédrale Notre-Dame.** 6 place du parvis Notre-Dame, 4e. ☎ **01-42-34-56-10.** Cathedral, free; crypt, 32F ($5) adults, 21F ($3.65) ages 12–25. Cathedral, daily 8am–6:45pm (closed Sat 12:30–2pm); Crypt, Apr–Sept daily 10am–6pm, Oct–Mar 10am–5pm; museum, Wed and Sat–Sun 2:30–6pm; treasury, Mon–Sat 9:30am–5:30pm. Six masses are celebrated on Sun, 4 on weekdays, and 1 on Sat. Métro: Cité or St-Michel. RER: St-Michel.

The Gothic loftiness of Notre-Dame dominates both the Seine and the history of Paris. It was begun in 1163, completed in the 14th century, pillaged during the Revolution, and restored by Viollet-le-Duc in the 19th century. Polyphonic music developed here, and Napoléon audaciously crowned himself emperor in this sanctuary. But for all its history, it's the art of Notre-Dame that still awes. Built in an age of illiteracy, the cathedral retells the stories of the Bible in its portals, paintings, and stained glass; its three rose windows are masterful.

For a look at the upper parts of the church, the river, and much of Paris, climb the 387 steps to the top of one of the towers. The south tower (on the right as you face the cathedral) holds Notre-Dame's 13-ton bell, rung on special occasions. The cathedral's museum features exhibits dealing with the history of Notre-Dame.

✪ **Sainte-Chapelle.** Palais de Justice, 4 bd. du Palais, 1er. ☎ **01-53-73-78-51.** Admission 32F ($5) adults, 21F ($3.50) ages 12–25, free for under age 12. Combined ticket Sainte-Chapelle–Conciergerie 50F ($8). Apr–Sept daily 9:30am–6:30pm; Oct–Mar daily 10am–5pm. Closed major holidays. Métro: Cité or St-Michel. RER: St-Michel.

Notre-Dame de Paris

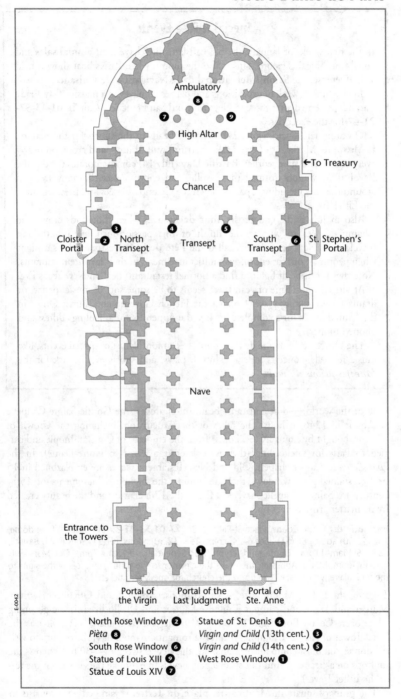

Ambulatory

8

7 High Altar **9**

←To Treasury

Chancel

3 **4** **5**

Cloister
Portal **2** North
Transept Transept South
Transept **6** St. Stephen's
Portal

Nave

Entrance to
the Towers

1

Portal of
the Virgin Portal of the
Last Judgment Portal of
Ste. Anne

North Rose Window **2**	Statue of St. Denis **4**
Pièta **8**	*Virgin and Child* (13th cent.) **3**
South Rose Window **6**	*Virgin and Child* (14th cent.) **5**
Statue of Louis XIII **9**	West Rose Window **1**
Statue of Louis XIV **7**	

E-0042

Special & Free Events

In the first weeks of January, the big Parisian stores have their **annual sales** and you'll find bargains galore. This is also the month when Paris's boat show is held at La Défense: the **Salon International de la Navigation de Plaisance.**

In late June, a week of expositions and parties climaxes in a massive **Gay Pride Parade,** patterned after those in New York and San Francisco. Call ☎ **01-43-57-21-47** for the exact date.

On Summer Solstice (June 21), everyone heads to the streets for the **Fête de la Musique.** Musicians of every caliber strum, wail, thump, and croon on nearly every square and street corner. **Bastille Day** (July 14) commemorates the day the Revolutionary mob stormed the Bastille, and enormous celebrations are held around the city, including a parade down the Champs-Elysées and fireworks near the Eiffel Tower.

Also in July is the end of the **Tour de France,** when thousands crowd the Champs-Elysées to witness the finish of this passion-inspiring month-long bicycle race. New Year's Eve is called the **Fête de St-Sylvestre,** and it's a night when people go out for enormous multicourse meals in their favorite restaurants. Note that it can be difficult to find a normal restaurant meal on New Year's Eve.

At virtually any time of year, there seems to be some sort of music, dance, or drama festival taking place. Contact the French Government Tourist Office in the United States for a complete list (see the Appendix for a mailing address and phone number).

The Office de Tourisme de Paris publishes a monthly list of special events, like music festivals, concerts, opera, exhibits, plays, and sports events. Ask for the *Manifestations du mois.*

One of the world's oldest and most beautiful churches, the Gothic Sainte-Chapelle was built in 1246 to house the relics of the Crucifixion, including the Crown of Thorns, bought by Louis IX (St. Louis) from the emperor of Constantinople and carried to Paris for safekeeping (they were later transferred to Notre-Dame). In the *chapelle haute* (upper chapel), Old and New Testament scenes are emblazoned in 15 perfect stained-glass windows that are among the highest achievements of 13th-century art. Sainte-Chapelle survived a fire in the 17th century and the beauty created by its master artisans lives on.

Basilique du Sacré-Coeur. Place St-Pierre, 18e. ☎ **01-53-41-89-00.** Basilica, free; dome, 15F ($2.50) adults, 8F ($1) ages 6–24; crypt, 15F ($2.50) adults, 8F ($1) ages 6–24. Basilica, daily 6:45am–11pm. Dome and crypt, Apr–Sept daily 9:15am–7pm; Oct–Mar daily 9:15am–6pm. Métro: Abbesses, then take the elevator to the surface and follow the signs to the funiculaire, which takes you up to the church for one Métro ticket.

Topping the hill of Montmartre, where composers Berlioz and Offenbach, writers Murger and Tzara, and painters Toulouse-Lautrec and Utrillo lived, is the gleaming white Sacré-Coeur. Built from 1876 to 1919, the church is nearly as familiar as the Eiffel Tower or Arc de Triomphe. It too is a romantic symbol of Paris. Be sure to visit the dome: You must climb lots of stairs, but the view is sweeping—30 miles across the rooftops on a clear day. And this spectacular view is free (unlike the view from the top of the Eiffel Tower).

The primary square in Montmartre, **place du Tertre,** is jammed with tourists in search of stereotypical Paris who are hassled by artists demanding their permission for a portrait. It has become a tawdry trap, but the side streets are worth exploring and so are the **vineyard** that still produces wine and the **museum** on rue Cortot. The **Cimetière du Montmartre** holds the remains of several illustrious writers, painters, and musicians, like Zola, Stendhal, Fragonard, Degas, Berlioz, Délibes, and Offenbach.

TWO PARIS ICONS

Arc de Triomphe. Place Charles-de-Gaulle–Etoile, 16e. ☎ **01-43-80-31-31.** Admission 35F ($6) adults, 23F ($4) ages 12–25, free for under age 12. Apr–Sept daily 9:30am–11pm; Oct–Mar daily 10am–10:30pm. Closed major holidays. Métro: Charles-de-Gaulle–Etoile.

The world's largest triumphal arch was commissioned by Napoléon in honor of his Grande Armée and its 128 victories. The arch was far from done by the time the imperial army had been swept from the field at Waterloo and wasn't completed until 1836. Although it has come to symbolize the greatness of France and its spirit (or, as Victor Hugo described it, a "stone built on glory"), it has also witnessed some of the country's defeats, as when German armies marched through the arch and down the Champs-Elysées in 1871 and again in 1940. Beneath the arch, under a gigantic tricolor flag, burns an eternal flame honoring France's Unknown Soldier, buried here in 1920 in memory of those who lost their lives in World War I. On August 25, 1944, Gen. Charles de Gaulle paid homage here before parading down the Champs-Elysées. Several notable 19th-century sculptures cover the arch, like Rude's *La Marseillaise,* seen on the Champs-Elysées side, and his relief, *Departure of the Volunteers.*

To reach the stairs and elevators that climb the arch, take the underpass (via the Métro entrances). From the top, 162 feet and 284 steps high, you can see in a straight line the Champs-Elysées, the obelisk in place de la Concorde, and the Louvre. On the other side is the Grande Arche de La Défense, a multipurpose structure shaped like an open cube so large that Notre-Dame could fit beneath it.

Tour Eiffel. Parc du Champ-de-Mars, 7e. ☎ **01-44-11-23-23.** Internet: www.tour-eiffel.fr. Admission 20F ($3) for elevator to 1st level (188 ft.), 42F ($7) to 2nd level (380 ft.), 59F ($10) to highest level (1,060 ft.). Reduced admission for under age 12. Walking up the stairs to 1st and 2nd levels 14F ($2). Sept to mid-June daily 9:30am–11pm; late June–Aug daily 9am–midnight. Fall and winter, stairs open only to 6:30pm. Métro: Trocadéro, Bir-Hakeim, or Ecole-Militaire. RER: Champs-de-Mars.

Built as a temporary structure to add flair to the 1889 Universal Exhibition, the Eiffel Tower managed to survive and become the soaring symbol of Paris. Praised by some and damned by others (like writers Guy de Maupassant and Georges-Charles Huysmans, who called it "a hollow candlestick"), the tower created as much controversy in its time as I. M. Pei's Louvre pyramid did in the 1980s. As the new millennium approaches, a huge panel counts down each day to the year 2000.

Take the Métro to Trocadéro and walk from the Palais de Chaillot to the Seine to get the full effect of the tower and its surroundings. Besides panoramic views (especially when the Trocadéro fountains are in full play), you get a free show from the dancers and acrobats in front of the Palais de Chaillot.

The tower has elevators in two of its pillars. Expect long waits. The best view is from the top level, where historians have re-created the office of engineer Alexandre-Gustave Eiffel. The tower has several restaurants and bars.

The vast green esplanade beneath the Eiffel Tower, the **Parc du Champ-de-Mars,** extends all the way to the 18th-century Ecole Militaire (Military Academy) at its southeast end. Now a formal lawn, it was once a parade ground for French troops.

OTHER HISTORIC SITES

✪ **Cimetière du Père-Lachaise.** 16 rue du Repos, 20e. ☎ **01-43-70-70-33.** Free admission. Mar 15–Nov 5 Mon–Fri 8am–6pm, Sat 8:30am–6pm, Sun 9am–6pm; Nov 6–Mar 14 Mon–Fri 8am–5:30pm, Sat 8:30am–5:30pm, Sun 9am–5:30pm. Métro: Père-Lachaise.

In eastern Paris, Père-Lachaise is the city's most famous cemetery and one of the world's most beautiful, with a profusion of sculpture along shady lanes. The illustrious men and women buried here include greats from the worlds of art, literature, and music: Molière, Ingres, Balzac, Chopin, Bizet, Wilde, Bernhardt, Proust, Modigliani, Apollinaire, Isadora Duncan, Colette, Stein and Toklas, Piaf, Jim Morrison, and Simone Signoret, to name only a few. A map of the cemetery with many famous marked grave sites is given free at the entrance.

Conciergerie. 1 quai de l'Horloge, Ile de la Cité, 1er. ☎ **01-53-73-78-50.** Admission 32F ($5) adults, 21F ($3.50) ages 12–25, free for under age 12. Combined ticket Sainte-Chapelle–Conciergerie 50F ($8). Apr–Sept daily 9:30am–6:30pm; Oct–Mar daily 10am–5pm. Métro: Cité, Châtelet-les-Halles, or St-Michel. RER: St-Michel.

Most of this building dates from the 14th century when King Philippe le Bel decided to extend the ancient Capetian palace that once stood here. Later, this building's prisons were used as holding cells for the Revolution's tribunals. Marie Antoinette was held here before her execution; others imprisoned here prior to execution included Robespierre and Danton. You can visit the renovated cells where these unfortunates spent their last days and hours and marvel at the vagaries of fate.

Les Egouts (The Sewers of Paris). Pont de l'Alma, 7e. ☎ **01-53-68-27-81.** Admission 25F ($4) adults, 20F ($3) students/over age 60, 15F ($2.50) ages 5–12. May–Oct Sat–Wed 11am–5pm; Nov–Apr Sat–Wed 11am–4pm. Closed 3 weeks in Jan. Métro: Alma-Marceau. RER: Pont de l'Alma.

Those who have read Victor Hugo's *Les Misérables* or seen old movies of World War II Resistance fighters may want to visit the sewers of Paris—not as beautiful as the city aboveground but enormously interesting. Paris's sewer system is actually an engineering marvel, laid out under Napoléon III by Belgrand, at the same time as the *grands boulevards* were being laid out under the direction of Baron Haussmann. If the mechanical guts of a great city interest you, get in line for a visit on one of the few afternoons when a glimpse is offered. Remember that the temperature is substantially cooler down under.

✪ **Hôtel des Invalides (Napoléon's Tomb).** Place des Invalides, 7e. ☎ **01-44-42-37-72.** Admission 37F ($6) adults, 27F ($4.50) ages 12–18, free for age 11 and under. Apr–Sept daily 10am–6pm (Tomb of Napoléon, 10am–7pm June–Sept); Oct–Mar daily 10am–5pm. Closed Jan 1, May 1, Nov 1, and Dec 25. Métro: Latour-Maubourg, Invalides, or Varenne.

Louis XIV built this majestic building as a hospital and home for wounded war veterans. These functions are still performed here, and there's office space for numerous departments of the French armed forces. But most visitors come to see the **Tomb of Napoléon,** a great porphyry sarcophagus lying beneath the golden dome of the Invalides. The emperor's body was transferred to this monumental resting place in 1840, almost 2 decades after his death on the remote South Atlantic island of St. Helena, where he was in exile.

If you like military lore, you'll want to visit the **Musée de l'Armée,** one of the greatest army museums in the world. It features thousands of weapons from prehistory to World War II. You'll see spearheads and arrowheads, suits of armor, cannons, battle flags, booty, and all sorts of military paraphernalia.

Panthéon. Place du Panthéon, 5e. ☎ **01-43-54-34-51.** Admission 32F ($5) adults, 21F ($3.50) ages 12–25, free for under age 12. Apr–Sept daily 9:30am–6:30pm; Oct–Mar daily 10am–6:15pm. Métro: Cardinal-Lemoine or Maubert-Mutualité.

For Diana Fans

Place de l'Alma (Métro: Alma-Marceau) has been turned into a tribute to the late Diana, Princess of Wales, who was killed in an auto accident August 31, 1997, in the nearby underpass. The bronze flame in the center is a replication of the flame in the Statue of Liberty and was a 1989 gift by the *International Herald Tribune* to honor Franco-American friendship. Many bouquets and messages are *still* placed around the flame, which seems to have come to represent the princess.

This neoclassical building with a huge dome was originally a church: It was commissioned by Louis XV in thanksgiving for his having recovered from a serious illness and called the Eglise Ste-Geneviève (after Paris's patron saint). Following the Revolution, it was renamed the Panthéon and rededicated as a necropolis for France's secular heroes. In the crypt beneath the dome are the tombs of Voltaire, Jean-Jacques Rousseau, Victor Hugo, Louis Braille (inventor of the reading system for the blind), Emile Zola, and other outstanding figures. In the spring of 1995 the ashes of the scientist Marie Curie were entombed at the Panthéon, "the first lady so honored in our history for her own merits," in the words of the late president François Mitterrand. Most recently, French writer/politician/adventurer André Malraux was honored by a tomb here. A pendulum suspended from the central dome re-creates Jean Bernard Foucault's 1851 demonstration proving the rotation of the earth.

AVANT-GARDE ARCHITECTURE

Musée de la Musique. 221 av. Jean-Jaurès, 19e. ☎ **01-44-84-45-00,** or 01-44-84-44-84 for ticket sales/information. Internet: www.cite-musique.fr. Museum, 35F ($6) adults, 25F ($4) students, 10F ($2) ages 6–18; visit with commentary, 60F ($10) adults, 45F ($7.50) students, 20F ($3) ages 6–18; free for age 5 and under. Métro: Porte-de-Pantin.

Of the half a dozen *grands travaux* conceived by the Mitterrand administration, this testimony to the power of music has been the most widely applauded and is the most ethereal and innovative. At the city's northeastern edge, in what used to be a rundown neighborhood, it incorporates a network of concert halls, a library/research center for the categorization and study of all kinds of music, and a museum, scattered over many floors of the complex and providing a showcase for musical instruments from the 17th through the 20th centuries.

Designed as an interconnected complex of bulky postcubist shapes by noted architect Christian de Portzamparc, the Cité has targeted as its audience Paris's growing low-income multicultural population. Its directors envision it as eclectic and multinational, with archives documenting such musical forms as folk songs from Brittany and Siberia, classical music from North Africa, jazz, and unusual interpretations of French baroque.

The Cité also presents a regular schedule of concerts, with prices ranging from 80F to 160F ($13 to $27).

La Grande Arche de La Défense. 1 place du Parvis de La Défense, 92040 Paris La Défense. ☎ **01-49-07-27-57.** Admission 40F ($7) adults, 30F ($5) under age 18/over age 65, free for under age 6. Daily 10am–6pm. Métro: Grande-Arche-de-La-Défense. RER: La Défense.

This 35-story arch completes the great design conceived by Le Nôtre in the 17th century that envisaged a continuous line of perspective running from the Arc de Triomphe du Carrousel in the courtyard of the Louvre, down the avenue des Champs-Elysées, and through the Arc de Triomphe to La Défense. The Arche was built in 1989 to Johan Otto von Spreckelsen's design as the architectural centerpiece of the suburb of La Défense.

By the way, the netting you'll see is there to catch any pieces of the facade that might decide to fall down. Several chunks of stone have already done so, and the netting was added to protect passersby.

HISTORIC SQUARES

Serene and rational yet intimate and endearing, ✪ **place des Vosges** in the Marais (Métro: St-Paul, then walk east on rue St-Antoine and turn left on rue de Brague) is Paris's oldest and most beautiful square. Henri IV planned it in the early 17th century on the spot where Henri II had been killed in a tournament. Originally known as place Royale, it retains its royal heritage in the white fleurs-de-lis crowning each row of rose-pink brick houses. After the Revolution, it became place de l'Indivisibilité and later place des Vosges, in honor of the first département of France that completely paid its taxes. Among the famous figures connected with the square are Mme de Sévigné, who was born at no. 1 bis, and Victor Hugo, who lived at no. 6 for 16 years and whose house presently contains the Musée Victor-Hugo.

The fashionable promenades and romantic duels of the 17th century are long gone, and antiques dealers, booksellers, and cafes compete today for your attention. Children play and older residents chat—all in all, an affable slice of Parisian life.

Place Vendôme (Métro: Opéra) features some of the most fashionable addresses in Paris. Here you'll find the Hôtel Ritz and such luxurious stores as Van Cleef et Arpels. The column in the center was commissioned by Napoléon to honor those who fought and won the Battle of Austerlitz, and 1,200 captured Austrian cannons were melted down and used in its construction. Among the square's famous residents was Chopin, who died at no. 12 in 1849.

Place de la Bastille (Métro: Bastille) is where on July 14, 1789, a mob attacked the Bastille prison and began the Revolution (there were only a handful of prisoners inside at the time). Nothing remains of the Bastille built in 1369. The best-known prisoner held here was the "Man in the Iron Mask," whose identity was never revealed. In the center of the square is the Colonne de Juillet (July Column), crowned by a figure of Liberty and honoring the memory of Parisians killed in the uprisings of 1830 and 1848. Today this area is dominated by the Opéra Bastille.

PARKS & GARDENS

Formerly a forest and a royal hunting preserve, the **Bois de Boulogne** (☎ 01-40-67-90-82; Métro: Les-Sablons, Porte-Maillot, or Porte-Dauphine) in the 16e arrondissement is Paris's largest park. Napoléon III donated the bois to the city and Baron Haussmann, his town planner, created the Service Municipal des Parcs et Plantations to help transform it into a park. Today it's a vast reserve of more than 2,200 acres with jogging, horseback riding, bicycle trails (you can rent a bike there), two lakes for boating, the famous Longchamp and Auteuil racecourses, the beautiful Jardin Shakespeare in the Pré Catelan, and the Jardin d'Acclimatation, a children's amusement park (Admission 12F [$2]). Bois de Boulogne is open all night. Other parks are closed 9pm to 7am.

The **Jardin des Tuileries,** between the Louvre and place de la Concorde, 1er (☎ 01-44-50-75-01; Métro: Tuileries or Concorde), was laid out in the 1560s by Catherine de Medici, wife of Henri II, to accompany her Palais des Tuileries (which was burned to the ground in 1871 and never rebuilt). A century later, Le Nôtre, creator of French landscaping, redesigned it in the classical style. Today it's a restful green space adorned with statues, including beautiful Maillols in the midst of Paris. Its odd name comes from the clay earth of the land here, once used to make roof tiles called *tuiles.* There are free guided visits of the gardens (in French) Wednesday, Friday, and Sunday at 3pm. Call ☎ **01-42-96-19-33** for details.

Commissioned by the widow of Henry IV, the Italian-born Marie de Medici, the ✪ **Jardin de Luxembourg** (Métro: Odéon; RER: Luxembourg) is one of Paris's best-loved and most evocative parks. Set to the south of the Latin Quarter, it's popular with students and a favorite of children, who love the *parc à jeux* (playground) and the randomly scheduled *théâtre des marionettes* (puppet theater). Rigidly symmetrical, with complicated networks of gravel-covered paths, the park contains pools, fountains, and statues of queens and poets who include Baudelaire and Verlaine. There are also spaces for the many games of boules conducted here by longtime cronies enjoying the air, light, and trees.

The park's centerpiece is the Palais de Luxembourg, 15 rue de Vaugirard, 6e, one of Paris's most outstanding examples of Renaissance architecture. Most of its interior is devoted to the meeting rooms of the French Senate and so is off-limits to the public—except on the first Sunday of the month, when there are guided visits. You must reserve at least 2 weeks in advance, however. For information, call ☎ **01-44-61-20-89.**

It's hard to believe that the quiet **Jardin du Palais-Royal** (Métro: Louvre), sheltered between three covered arcades behind Cardinal Richelieu's Palais Royal, was once the site of dramatic events that launched the Revolution; it was also a veritable pleasure garden during the 18th century, filled with gambling dens and more lascivious attractions. Today the garden's most controversial aspect is the prison-striped columns built in 1986 by sculptor Daniel Buren. Note Pol Bury's steel-ball sculptures decorating the fountains.

Of Paris's parks and squares, the English-style **Parc Monceau** (☎ **01-42-27-08-64;** Métro: Monceau or Villiers; Bus: 30 or 94) is the most romantic. A favorite of Proust, it contains a number of odd features, including a pyramid, ancient columns, and several tombs of unknown origin. The park is in the heart of a well-heeled residential district, and some nearby streets (like rue Rembrandt and avenue Velázquez) feature handsome buildings. Two excellent small museums are in this area: the **Musée Nissim de Camondo,** 63 rue de Monceau, 8e (☎ **01-53-89-06-40**), with an extraordinary collection of 18th-century furniture and decorative arts; and the **Musée Cernuschi,** 7 av. Velázquez, 8e (☎ **01-45-63-50-75**), specializing in Chinese art from its origins to the 14th century.

ORGANIZED TOURS

BUS TOURS   Paris is the perfect city to explore on your own, but if your time or legs don't permit, consider taking an introductory bus tour. The most prominent company is **Cityrama,** 4 place des Pyramides, 1er (☎ **01-44-55-60-00;** Métro: Palais-Royal–Musée-du-Louvre). Its 2-hour orientation tour costs 150F ($25), whereas longer tours are 290F ($48) for a half day and 500F ($83) for a full day. Half-day tours to Versailles at 195F to 320F ($33 to $53) and half-day tours to Chartres at 265F ($44) represent good value and remove at least some of the hassle associated with visiting those monuments. I recommend you avoid the company's nighttime tours of Paris, as they tend to be expensive, tame, and touristy.

In the 1990s, the same entity that maintains Paris's network of Métros and buses, the **RATP** (☎ **01-36-68-77-14**), initiated motorized transport exclusively as a means of appreciating the visual grandeur of Paris. Known as the **Balabus,** a wordplay on the French phrase *se ballader par bus* ("go out for a drive by bus"), it's a program with a fleet of big-windowed orange-and-white motorcoaches whose one drawback is their limited operating hours—Sunday noon to 8pm and the afternoons of some national holidays. Itineraries run in both directions between the Gare de Lyon and the Grand Arche de La Défense. Three Métro tickets will carry you along the entire route. You'll recognize the bus, and the route it follows, by the "Bb" symbol emblazoned across its side and along signs posted beside the route.

BOAT TOURS Among the most favored ways to see Paris is by the **Bateaux-Mouches** (☎ 01-40-76-99-99, or 01-42-25-96-10 for reservations; Métro: Alma-Marceau), sightseeing boats that cruise up and down the Seine. They sail from the pont de l'Alma on the Right Bank. March to mid-November, departures are usually on the hour and half hour, and in winter there are 5 to 16 cruises per day, depending on demand. The voyage lasts 1¼ hours and costs 40F ($7) per adult; seniors 65 and up and ages 5 to 13 are charged 20F ($3), and those 4 and under ride free. **Bateaux-Parisiens** (☎ 01-44-11-33-44 for reservations) offer similar tours at similar prices and leave from the pont d'Iéna on the Left Bank.

Another option is the **Batobus** (☎ 01-44-11-33-44), ferryboats that operate daily April to September on an east-west trajectory along the Seine, stopping at five points en route: the Eiffel Tower, the Musée d'Orsay, the Louvre, Notre-Dame, and the Hôtel de Ville. Fares between any two stops are 20F ($3) per person, though I consider the Batobuses an expensive way to cross a river that's already crisscrossed with an impressive network of bridges. More appealing is to pay 60F ($10) per adult or 30F ($5) for ages 3 to 11 for a day ticket that allows you to enter and exit from the boats as many times as you like (and ride as long as you like) during any single day.

6 Shopping

Paris is at the forefront of the world of fashion and design, and you can visit (if not purchase anything in) the boutiques of some of the great designers. Try strolling along **rue du Faubourg St-Honoré** and **avenue Montaigne** for starters—but remember to dress with style if you wish to enter these shops; otherwise, the salespeople may not be at their friendliest.

FASHION

For "Yves Saint Laurent on a budget," try your luck at **Le Mouton à Cinq Pattes,** 19 rue Grégoire-de-Tours, 6e (☎ 01-43-29-73-56; Métro: Odéon), known for its selection of discounted *dégriffées* merchandise (clothes with the label cut out), many from name designers. The stock changes frequently, but avoid the free-for-all madhouse on Saturday. Men, women, and children can be smartly attired here at a good price. Try also **Réciproque,** 89–123 rue de la Pompe, 16e (☎ 01-47-04-30-28; Métro: Victor-Hugo), for those who like their couture haute but their prices low. There are several branches: No. 92 specializes in leather, for example. Every big designer is carried, along with discounted shoes, accessories, menswear, and wedding gifts. Everything has been worn, but some items have been worn only on runways or during photo sessions.

DEPARTMENT STORES

Paris's great department stores, the *grands magasins,* sell all sorts of French goods. Though expensive, they're experienced at helping with VAT refunds (see "Special Discounts," earlier in this chapter). Try **Galeries Lafayette,** 64 bd. Haussmann, 9e (☎ 01-42-82-34-56; Métro: Chaussée d'Antin; RER: Auber), and **Au Printemps,** 64 bd. Haussmann, 9e (☎ 01-42-82-50-00; Métro: Havre-Caumartin; RER: Auber). These attractive stores are directly behind the Opéra Garnier.

For inexpensive groceries, toiletries, clothes, and housewares, Parisians usually head to the nearest **Monoprix** or **Prisunic.** Near the Opéra you'll find a Monoprix at 21 av. de l'Opéra (☎ **01-42-61-78-08**) and Prisunic at 102 rue de Provence (☎ **01-42-82-43-39**), but there are dozens of other outlets around the city.

The largest department store is **La Samaritaine,** 19 rue de la Monnaie, 1er (☎ 01-40-41-20-20; Métro: Pont-Neuf or Châtelet–Les Halles), between the Louvre and pont Neuf. It's housed in four buildings with art nouveau touches and has an art deco facade on quai du Louvre. The fifth floor of store no. 2 has a fine inexpensive restaurant; look for signs to the panorama, a free observation point with a superb view.

BOOKSTORES

Paris has several English-language bookstores carrying American and English books and maps and guides. Try **Brentano's,** 37 av. de l'Opéra, 2e (☎ **01-42-61-52-50**; Métro: Opéra), or **Galignani,** 224 rue de Rivoli, 1er (☎ **01-42-60-76-07**; Métro: Tuileries). **W. H. Smith,** 248 rue de Rivoli (☎ **01-44-77-88-99**; Métro: Concorde), offers Paris's largest selection of paperbacks in English. On the Left Bank are **Shakespeare & Company,** 37 rue de la Bûcherie, 5e (☎ **01-43-26-96-50**; Métro/RER: St-Michel), a spin-off of Sylvia Beach's famous literary meeting place, and **Village Voice,** 6 rue Princesse, 6e (☎ **01-46-33-36-47**; Métro: Odéon), which specializes in quality fiction.

MARKETS

For a real shopping adventure, come to the vast **Marché aux Puces de Clignancourt,** 17e (Métro: Porte-de-Clignancourt). The Clignancourt flea market, as it's commonly known, features several thousand stalls, carts, shops, and vendors selling everything from used blue jeans to antique paintings and furniture.

More comprehensible, and certainly prettier, is the **Marché aux Fleurs** (Métro: Cité), the flower market in place Louis-Lepine on the Ile de la Cité. Come Monday to Saturday 8am to 4pm to enjoy the flowers, whether you buy anything or not; on Sunday it becomes the Marché aux Oiseaux, an equally colorful bird market. It's held Saturday, Sunday, and Monday 7:30am to 7pm. *Note:* Watch out for pickpockets.

7 Paris After Dark

Nightlife in Paris is bewilderingly diverse. If you speak French, the wonders of the world of French theater are yours. Opera, ballet, and classical music performances are world-class. Movie listings are incredibly varied, and there are numerous bars and dance clubs.

Several local publications provide up-to-the-minute listings of performances and other evening entertainment. Foremost is *Pariscope: Une Semaine de Paris,* a weekly guide with thorough coverage of movies, plays, ballet, art exhibits, clubs, and so on. You can buy it at any newsstand for 3F (60¢).

For half-price theater tickets, go to the **Kiosque-Théâtre** at the northwest corner of the Madeleine church (Métro: Madeleine). You can buy tickets only for that same day's performance. It's open Tuesday to Saturday 12:30 to 8pm and Sunday 12:30 to 4pm. There are also **ticket counters** in the Châtelet–Les Halles Métro Station and at Gare Montparnasse.

Students with an ISIC card can often get last-minute tickets at a discount by applying at the box office an hour before curtain time.

THE PERFORMING ARTS

THEATER The classics of Molière, Racine, and other French playwrights are staged marvelously at the 300-year-old refurbished **Comédie-Française,** 2 rue de Richelieu, 1er (☎ **01-44-58-15-15;** Métro: Palais-Royal–Musée-du-Louvre). Schedules are varied with the addition of more modern works and plays translated from other languages. Prices average 30F to 225F ($5 to $38), with last-minute seats even cheaper. The box office is open daily 11am to 6pm (closed August to September 15). You can buy tickets up to 2 weeks in advance. *Pariscope* has full listings of other theaters.

OPERA & DANCE The city's principal opera stage is the **Opéra Bastille,** on place de la Bastille, 12e (☎ **01-44-73-13-00** for opera/concert tickets, 01-43-43-96-96 for tape-recorded program information, 01-47-42-53-71 for ballet tickets, 01-44-73-13-99 for information; Métro: Bastille). Opened to commemorate the 1989 bicentennial of the Revolution, this modernistic performance center was designed by the Uruguayan–Canadian architect Carlos Ott and has brought new life to the Bastille neighborhood. Tickets are 60F to 635F ($10 to $106). The box office is open daily 11am to 6pm.

The **Opéra Garnier (Palais Garnier),** place de l'Opéra, 9e (☎ **01-40-01-17-89;** Métro: Opéra), is the premier stage for dance and once again for opera. Because of the competition from the Opéra Bastille, the original opera has made great efforts to present more up-to-date works, including choreography by Jerome Robbins, Twyla Tharp, Agnes de Mille, and George Balanchine. This rococo wonder was designed as a contest entry by the young architect Charles Garnier in the heyday of the empire. The facade is adorned with marble and sculpture, including *The Dance* by Carpeaux. Months of painstaking restorations have returned the Garnier to its former glory: The boxes and walls are once again lined with flowing red damask, the gilt is gleaming, the ceiling (painted by Marc Chagall) has been cleaned, and a new air-conditioning system has been added. Opera tickets are 60F to 610F ($10 to $102) and dance tickets 30F to 380F ($5 to $63). The box office is open daily 11am to 6pm.

CLASSICAL MUSIC More than a dozen Parisian churches regularly schedule free or inexpensive organ recitals and concerts, among them the **Eglise St-Sulpice,** 6e (☎ **01-46-33-21-78;** Métro: St-Sulpice); **Eglise St-Eustache,** rue du Jour, 1e (☎ **01-42-36-31-05;** Métro: Châtelet–Les Halles); and the **American Church,** 65 quai d'Orsay, 7e (☎ **01-40-62-05-00;** Métro: Invalides). Concerts are held regularly at the splendid **Sainte-Chapelle,** 4 bd. du Palais, 1e (☎ **01-53-73-78-51;** Métro: Cité or St-Michel; RER: St-Michel), which cost 80F to 150F ($13 to $25).

Other concerts are held in halls throughout the city. The Orchestre de Paris plays in the **Salle Pleyel,** 252 rue du faubourg St-Honoré, 8e (☎ **01-45-61-53-00;** Métro: Ternes), with tickets at 50F to 350F ($8 to $58); the **Théâtre du Châtelet,** 1 place du Châtelet, 1er (☎ **01-40-28-28-98,** or 01-42-33-00-00 for recorded information; Métro: Châtelet), with tickets from 80F to 580F ($13 to $97); and the **Cité de la Musique,** 221 av. Jean-Jaurès, 19e (☎ **01-44-84-45-00,** or 01-44-84-44-84 for ticket sales/information; Métro: Porte-de-Pantin), with concerts at 75F to 100F ($13 to $17). *Pariscope* carries full listings.

VARIETY THEATER One of the most legendary mass-market theaters in Paris is the **Folies-Bergères,** 32 rue Richer, 9e (☎ **01-44-79-98-98;** Métro: Cadet or Rue-Montmartre). Don't expect the naughty and slyly permissive skin-and-glitter revue that used to be the trademark of this place. In 1993 all that ended with a radical restoration of the theater and a reopening under new management. Today it's a conventional 1,600-seat theater presenting musicals. A recent production was the French version of *Fame*. Shows are presented Tuesday to Sunday at 9pm, with matinees Saturday and Sunday at 3pm. After the opening curtain, late-comers aren't allowed inside. Tickets cost 130F to 350F ($22 to $58).

JAZZ & SALSA CLUBS

Parisians seem to have an insatiable craving for American music, especially jazz, and so Paris has a very vibrant jazz scene. Look through current listings in *Pariscope* for the jazz masters you admire.

The **Caveau de la Huchette,** 5 rue de la Huchette, 5e (☎ 01-43-26-65-05; Métro/RER: St-Michel), is Paris's jazz club of long standing, popular with foreigners and locals of all ages. Programming runs to the happy sounds of swing and boogie-woogie. It's open Sunday to Thursday 9:30pm to 2:30am and Friday and Saturday 9:30pm to 4am. The cover is 60F ($10) Sunday to Thursday, 70F ($12) Friday and Saturday, and 55F ($9) weekdays for students under 25.

In 1999, **New Morning,** 7–9 rue des Petites-Ecuries, 10e (☎ 01-45-23-51-41; Métro: Château-d'Eau), celebrates its 18th anniversary as the capital's most enduring citadel of jazz. Cairo-born Eglai Fahri, the city's "madame of jazz," presides over the club, where concerts usually start after 9pm and the cover is 110F to 190F ($18 to $32). New Morning attracts all the jazz greats, such as John Scofield. The program changes nightly.

Au Duc des Lombards, 42 rue des Lombards, 1er (☎ 01-42-33-22-88; Métro: Châtelet), is crowded, noisy, and smoky but presents some of the most interesting jazz around. Artists begin playing Tuesday to Sunday at 10pm and continue (with breaks) for 5 hours. Their repertoire ranges from free jazz to hard bop. The cover runs 80F to 100F ($13 to $17).

Paris hasn't quite replaced jazz with salsa, but salsa clubs are sprouting up yearly. In spite of its tattered premises, the best venue is **Les Etoiles,** 61 rue du Château-d'Eau, 10e (☎ 01-47-70-60-56; Métro: Château-d'Eau). The cover is 120F ($24), but it's a really good deal because dinner is included. For live nightclub entertainment and dinner, this is an astonishing bargain on the Paris after-dark circuit. This quintessential music hall has been around since 1856, but today it rocks with the sound of salsa bands. The food is almost exclusively Cubano. The club is open Thursday to Tuesday 9pm to 4am.

BARS

Stylish but easygoing, the **Lizard Lounge,** 18 rue du Bourg-Tibourg, 4e (☎ 01-42-72-81-34; Métro: Hôtel-de-Ville), is a pleasant Marais place to hang out with an arty, international crowd after dinner. You could also come early for a light meal prepared in the open kitchen. The heavy-gauge steel balcony overlooking the main bar offers a chance for a quiet conversation, while the recently refurbished basement has a DJ Wednesday to Saturday spinning dance music. It's open daily noon to 2am.

Nightlife is exploding in east Paris, especially along rue Oberkampf, and **Café Charbon,** 109 rue Oberkampf, 11e (☎ 01-43-57-55-13; Métro: Parmentier), is in the heart of it. This turn-of-the-century dance hall was restored a few years ago and has become the hottest spot in Paris for people who like people and don't mind being crowded. With high ceilings, hanging lamps, and walls that alternate mirrors, wood, and hand-painted murals, the spacious interior is vaguely art nouveau, which you can barely perceive through the bustle and haze. During the day or early evening it's a relaxed place to hang out, chat, or read a newspaper. After about 9pm the music gets louder, the long wood bar and banquettes fill up, and you'll be lucky to get in let alone get a seat. The cafe is open daily 9am to 2am.

DANCE CLUBS

The clubs of Paris are among the hippest/chicest in the world. At present, many Parisian circles seem to favor salsa, rap, reggae, and Eurodisco, and they fastidiously extol the virtues of going out on weeknights, to avoid the suburban crowds who come into the city on Friday and Saturday. The later you go, the better. But everything can change overnight.

Edith Piaf used to perform at ✪ **Le Balajo,** 9 rue de Lappe, 11e (☎ **01-47-00-07-87;** Métro: Bastille), but now the music is rap, reggae, and salsa combined with the musette of yesteryear. The international crowd is racially mixed, fun, hip, and wild. Ages are from 18 to 80, with the Sunday afternoon *bal musette* drawing older crowds. The best nights/mornings are Monday/Tuesday and Thursday/Friday. Sometimes there are live bands. Everybody dances together, and there's very little posing. It really gets going around 3am. Cover is 50F to 100F ($9 to $17), including one drink, and it's open daily from 10pm.

Le Rex Club, 5 bd. Poissonnière, 2e (☎ **01-42-36-83-98;** Métro: Bonne-Nouvelle), is known for its tea dances for an older crowd (40 to 65) who appreciates tangos and waltzes, with occasional 1970s disco. But after 11pm, Rex emulates the techno-grunge clubs of London, with an international crowd in the 18-to-30 age range. A revolving host of deejays keeps the music hot and loud. Rex is open Tuesday and Thursday to Saturday 1:45 to 9pm and 11:30pm to 6am; the cover is 50F to 80F ($8 to $13).

The capital's stellar rock club is **Bus Palladium,** 6 rue Fontaine, 9e (☎ **01-53-21-07-33;** Métro: Blanche or Pigalle). This temple to music is set in a single room, and does it ever rock, with the sounds from the 1950s to the 1990s. This is certainly a place to play the mating game if you're 25 to 35. The club is open Tuesday to Saturday 11pm to 6am; the cover is 100F ($17) for men on Tuesday, Friday, and Saturday and 100F ($17) for women only on Friday and Saturday.

GAY & LESBIAN CLUBS

Gay life is centered around Les Halles and Le Marais, with the greatest concentration of clubs, restaurants, bars, and shops between the Hôtel-de-Ville and Rambuteau Métro stops. See the "Networks & Resources" box, earlier in this chapter, for a list of magazines to check out for the latest clubs.

Le Queen, 102 av. des Champs-Elysées, 8e (☎ **01-53-89-08-90**), may be artfully blasé and disorganized, but it's certainly the queen of the night in gay Paree. Follow the flashing purple sign on the "main street of Paris," near the corner of avenue George-V, to the epicenter of gay nightlife. The place is often mobbed, mainly with gay men and, to a lesser degree, chic women who work in the fashion and film industries. Look for drag shows, muscle shows, striptease, and everything from 1970s disco nights (Monday) to Tuesday-night foam parties in summer, when cascades of mousse descend onto the dance floor. The cover is 50F ($8) Monday and 100F ($17) Friday and Saturday; other nights are free. Le Queen is open daily from midnight.

Banana Café, 13 rue de la Ferronnerie, 1er (☎ **01-42-33-35-31;** Métro: Châtelet–Les Halles), is one of the most popular gay bars in the Marais. On two floors of a 19th-century building, it has walls the color of an overripe banana, dim lighting, and a well-known happy hour when the price of drinks is reduced daily 7 to 10pm. The street level features just a bar. The cellar level contains music alternating between a live pianist and recorded disco. Thursday to Saturday, go-go dancers perform from spotlit platforms in the cellar. The place is open daily 4:15pm to 6am.

Open Café, 17 rue des Archives, 4e (☎ **01-42-72-26-78;** Métro: Hôtel-de-Ville), is hot, hot, hot right now with a casually chic crowd that has virtually commandeered this corner of rue des Archives and rue Ste-Croix-de-la-Bretonnerie. Floor-to-ceiling windows and subtle neon bathe the spacious interior with light, and there are tables inside and out to accommodate the crush. Though busy all day, the scene really gets going around "happy hour" (6 to 8pm), when you get two beers for the price of one. It's open daily 10am to 2am.

L'Entr'acte, 25 bd. Poissonnière, 2e (☎ 01-40-26-01-93; Métro: Rue-Montmarte), has made a spectacular comeback and is now the hippest lesbian dance club in Paris. Its decor is like a 19th-century French music hall, and the venue, as the French say, is "cool," with all types of cutting-edge music. Don't show up until after midnight. The presence of men is discouraged. What to do if you're a gay male? Go to the side entrance with a "separate but equal facility," Le Scorp (same address; ☎ 01-40-26-28-30), where les mecs gais (gay guys) are welcomed. Both clubs are open Tuesday to Sunday 11:45pm to 5am, with no cover.

8 Side Trips: The Ile de France

After exploring Paris's wealth of treasures, you may be tempted to venture outside the city for a look at the attractions in the surrounding area, known as the Ile de France. All the following are easily reachable by car or public transport from Paris and make great day trips.

VERSAILLES

Louis XIV, who reigned from 1643 to 1715, commissioned the ✪ Château de Versailles (☎ 01-30-84-74-00) and its vast grounds and gardens. Construction lasted for 50 years, and the result is simply astounding. Fourteen miles southwest of Paris, Versailles is one of France's great attractions.

Guided tours take you through parts of the château. Highlights include the Royal Apartments and the famous Hall of Mirrors, where the armistice ending World War I was signed. Save time for the Grand Trianon, the royal guesthouse, and the Petit Trianon, loved by Marie Antoinette. The gardens at Versailles, with their fabulous system of waterworks, are marvelous. Water shows called *grands eaux* are played May to September on Sunday afternoon, and there's also one night show per month, with the fountains illuminated. For schedules, ask at the tourist office in Paris or at the tourist office in the town of Versailles, 7 rue des Réservoirs (☎ 01-39-50-36-22), a short walk from the palace.

It's open Tuesday to Sunday: May to September 9am to 6:30pm and October to April 9am to 5:30pm. Entrance to the château is 45F ($7.50) until 3:30pm, when the price is reduced to 35F ($6). Entrance to the Grand Trianon is 25F ($4), reduced to 15F ($2.50) after 3:30pm; admission to the Petit Trianon is 15F ($2.50), lowered to 10F ($2) after 3:30pm. Students pay the reduced rate all day.

To get there, catch RER Line C5 at the Gare d'Austerlitz, St-Michel, Musée-d'Orsay, Invalides, Pont de l'Alma, Champ-de-Mars, or Javel station and take it to the Versailles Rive Gauche station, from which there's a shuttle bus to the château. The 14F ($2) trip takes 35 to 40 minutes. A regular train also leaves from Gare St-Lazare for the Versailles Rive Gauche RER station. By car, take the périphérique (ring road around Paris) to exit N10, which will take you straight to Versailles.

CHARTRES

"For a visit to Chartres, choose some pleasant morning when the lights are soft, for one wants to be welcome, and the Cathedral has moods, at times severe." Thus wrote Henry Adams in *Mont St-Michel and Chartres,* and, yes, the cathedral may at times

A Dining Tip

To save money on food, I recommend packing a light picnic before you leave Paris. These side trips are all major attractions where, except for Disneyland, available meals are expensive and not very good. Giverny, Versailles, and Vaux-le-Vicomte have cafeterias, but all offer the possibility of outdoor dining. At Versailles you can eat in one of the world's most magnificent gardens, at Fontainebleau you can eat along a canal with ducks and swans gliding by, and in Chartres look for the Parc André-Gagnon, a few minutes' walk northwest of the cathedral.

have severe moods—gray and cold like winter weather in the Ile de France region—but it's always astoundingly beautiful, with its harmonious architecture and lofty stained-glass windows.

The ✪ **Cathédrale Notre-Dame de Chartres,** place de la Cathédrale (☎ 02-37-21-56-33), is one of the greatest architectural and spiritual statements of the Middle Ages. It survived both the Revolution, when it was scheduled for demolition, and the two World Wars, when its famous stained glass was carefully removed and stored in nearby caves to prevent damage from gunfire and bombs. Light filtering through the red and blue stained glass onto the cold gray stonework of the cathedral is often cited as among the most mystical experiences of a trip to Europe. Even if your time is limited, save some for a stroll through the winding narrow streets of the tranquil town of Chartres.

Admission to the cathedral is free. It's open daily: April to September 7:30am to 7:30pm and October to March 7:30am to 7pm. Take one of the excellent **guided tours** (30F/$5)—especially those by Englishman Malcolm Miller (☎ 02-37-28-15-58). Mr. Miller gives tours daily except Sunday at noon and 2:45pm April to November and is sometimes available in winter as well.

More invigorating is a climb up winding staircases to the soaring **tower,** where the views of the building's meticulously crafted stone, lead, and copperwork are enhanced by sweeping panoramas over the town. The tower is open daily: April to September 9:30am to 5:30pm and October to March 10 to 11:30am and 2 to 4:30pm. Admission is 25F ($4) adults and 15F ($2.50) seniors/students/children.

Trains run frequently from Paris's Gare Montparnasse to Chartres. A round-trip ticket costs around 142F ($24), and the trip takes about an hour each way. For additional information about the cathedral, the town, and the surrounding region, drop into the Chartres **Office de Tourisme** on place de la Cathédrale (☎ 02-37-21-50-00). By **car,** take A10/11 southwest from the périphérique and follow the signs to Le Mans and Chartres (the Chartres exit is clearly marked).

FONTAINEBLEAU

Napoléon called **Fontainebleau,** 37 miles south of Paris, the house of the centuries. Much of French history has taken place within its walls, perhaps no moment more memorable than when Napoléon stood on the horseshoe-shaped exterior staircase and bade farewell to his army before his departure into exile on Elba. That scene has been the subject of many paintings, including Vernet's *Les Adieux.*

Napoléon joined in the grand parade of French rulers who used the palace, now known as the **Musée National du Château de Fontainebleau** (☎ 01-60-71-50-70) as a resort, hunting in its magnificent forest. Under François I the hunting lodge here was enlarged into a royal palace, much in the Italian Renaissance style. The style got botched up, but many artists, including Cellini, came from Italy to work for the French monarch. Under François I's patronage, the School of Fontainebleau (led by

Versailles

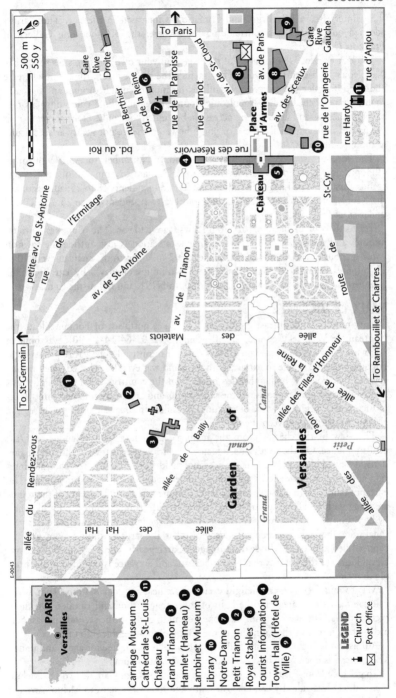

the painters Rosso Fiorentino and Primaticcio) increased in prestige. These artists adorned one of the most outstanding rooms here: the 210-foot-long **Gallery of François I.**

You can wander around much of the palace on your own, visiting sites that evoke Napoléon's 19th-century heyday. They include the throne room, the room where he abdicated his rulership of France, his offices, his monumental bedroom, and his bathroom. Some of the smaller Napoleonic Rooms, especially those containing his personal mementos and artifacts, are accessible by guided tour only. Don't forget to visit the gardens and, especially, the carp pond; however, they're not nearly as spectacular as those at Versailles.

The interior is open Wednesday to Monday: November to April 9:30am to 12:30pm and 2 to 5pm and May to October 9:30am to 5pm. Admission for the grands appartements is 35F ($6) adults and 23F ($4) students 18 to 25; admission for the Napoleonic Rooms is 16F ($3) adults and 12F ($2) students 18 to 25. Age 17 and under enter free.

Trains to Fontainebleau depart from Paris's Gare de Lyon. The trip takes 35 to 60 minutes and costs 47F ($8). The Fontainebleau station is just outside the town in Avon, a suburb of Paris; a local **bus** makes the 2-mile trip to the château every 10 to 15 minutes Monday to Saturday (every 30 minutes Sunday). By **car,** from the *périphérique*, take A6 south from Paris, exit onto N191, and follow the signs.

VAUX-LE-VICOMTE

Twenty-nine miles southeast of Paris and 12 miles northeast of Fontainebleau, the **Château de Vaux-le-Vicomte,** 77950 Maincy (☎ **01-64-14-41-90**), was built in 1656 for Nicolas Fouquet, Louis XIV's finance minister. Louis wasn't pleased that Fouquet was able to live so extravagantly here and was even less pleased when he discovered that Fouquet had embezzled funds from the country's treasury. Fouquet was swiftly arrested, then Louis hired the same artists and architects who had built Vaux-le-Vicomte to begin the task of creating Versailles. If you visit both you'll see the striking similarities between them.

The view of the château from the main gate will reveal the splendor of 17th-century France. On the south side, a majestic staircase sweeps toward the formal **gardens,** designed by Le Nôtre. The **grand canal** divides the greenery. The château's interior, now a private residence, is furnished and decorated with 17th-century pieces. The entrance hall leads to 12 state rooms, including the oval rotunda. Many of the rooms are hung with Gobelin tapestries and decorated with painted ceiling and wall panels by Le Brun, with sculpture by Girardon. A tour of the interior includes Fouquet's personal suite, the huge basement with its wine cellar, the servants' dining room, and the copper-filled kitchen. A **Musée d'Equipages (Carriage Museum)** is housed in the stables. Hours are the same as that of the château, and entrance is included in the price of admission.

May to mid-October, **candlelight evenings** are held Saturday 8:30 to 11pm, when you can visit the château by the light of more than a thousand candles. On those evenings, the Carriage Museum stays open to midnight. On the second and last Saturday of each month the fountains of the 13 main pools bubble 3 to 6pm.

Admission is 56F ($9) adults and 46F ($8) ages 6 to 15; free for age 5 and under. The château is open March to November daily 10am to 6pm.

To get here from Paris, take a 45-miniute **train** ride from Gare de Lyon to Melun, then a direct **bus** ride. By **car,** take A6 south and follow the signs to Melun. Arriving at Melun, follow N36 in the direction of Meaux and you'll see signs to the château.

GIVERNY: IN THE FOOTSTEPS OF MONET

Even before you arrive at ✪ **Giverny,** 50 miles northwest of Paris, it's very likely you'll already have some idea of what you're going to see, since Claude Monet's paintings of his garden are known and loved throughout the world.

Monet moved to Giverny in 1883, and the water lilies beneath the Japanese bridge in the garden, as well as the flower garden, became his regular subjects until his death in 1926. In 1966, the Monet family donated Giverny to the Academie des Beaux-Arts in Paris, perhaps the most prestigious fine-arts school in France, and they subsequently decided to open the site to the public. It has since become one of the most popular attractions in France, but even the crowds can't completely overwhelm the magic of this place.

Though the gardens are lovely year-round, they're usually at their best in May and June and in September and October. Should you yearn to have them almost to yourself, you should plan to be at the gates some morning when they first open. For more information, call ☎ **02-32-51-28-21.**

April to October, the gardens are open Tuesday to Sunday 10am to 6pm. Admission to the house and gardens is 35F ($6) adults, 25F ($4) students, and 20F ($3) ages 7 to 12; admission to the gardens only is 25F ($4).

Trains leave the Gare Saint Lazare in Paris approximately every 45 minutes for Vernon, the town nearest the Monet gardens. The round-trip fare is roughly 134F ($22). From the station, **buses** make the 3-mile trip to the museum for 12F ($2) or you can go on foot—the route along the Seine makes for a nice walk. If you're coming by **car,** take autoroute A13 from Porte d'Auteuil to Bonnieres and then D201 to Giverny.

DISNEYLAND PARIS

This entertainment park, 20 miles east of Paris, about halfway between Charles de Gaulle and Orly airports, opened in April 1992 as Euro Disney—now it's called, unofficially at least, **Disneyland Paris** (☎ **01-64-74-30-00**). One-fifth the size of Paris, it features 39 attractions in five entertainment lands: Main Street U.S.A., Frontierland, Adventureland, Fantasyland, and Discoveryland. The latest feature is Space Mountain, which catapults riders from a cannon on Earth through the Milky Way to the moon. Outside the park are hotels, a 27-hole golf course, pools, tennis courts, restaurants, and a Congress Center.

Admission to the park for 1 day, depending on the season, is 160F to 200F ($27 to $33) adults and 130F to 155F ($22 to $26) ages 4 to 11; age 3 and under enter free. Admission for 2 days is 305F to 385F ($51 to $64) adults and 250F to 300F ($42 to $50) children. The peak season is mid-June to mid-September as well as Christmas and Easter weeks. Entrance to Festival Disney (the consortium of shops, dance clubs, and restaurants) is free, though there's usually a cover for the dance clubs.

Disneyland Paris is open June 12 to September 12, daily 9am to 11pm; September 13 to June 11, Monday to Friday 10am to 6pm and Saturday and Sunday 9am to 8pm. Hours, however, vary with the weather and season, so call the number above before setting out.

The resort is linked to the **RER commuter express** rail network (Line A), which maintains a stop within walking distance of the park. In Paris, board at Charles-de-Gaulle–Etoile, Châtelet–Les Halles, or Nation. Get off at Line A's last stop, Marne-la-Vallée/Chessy, 45 minutes from central Paris. The fare is 38F ($6) one-way or 76F ($13) round-trip. Trains run every 10 to 20 minutes, depending on the time of day. If you're **driving,** take A4 east from Paris and get off at exit 14. Guest parking at any of the thousands of spaces begins at 40F ($7) per day. Interconnected moving sidewalks speed up pedestrian transit from the parking areas to the entrance. Parking is free for guests of any of the resort's hotels.

22 Prague & the Best of Bohemia

by John Mastrini

Prague is a perfect end-of-millennium destination—here you'll find the triumphs and tragedies of 10 centuries spiked with the peculiarities of post-Communist reconstruction. Almost 75 years after Franz Kafka's death, Prague's mix of the melancholy and the magnificent, the shadows and the fog of everyday life set against some of Europe's most spectacular architecture, still confounds all who live or visit here. Its tightly wound brick paths have felt the hooves of kings' horses, the jackboots of Hitler's armies, the heaving tracks of Soviet tanks, and the shuffle of students in passive revolt. The six-centuries-old Charles Bridge is today jammed with visitors and executives looking for memories or profits from a once-captive city now enjoying yet another renaissance. Too bad mindless graffiti now blights almost every glimpse of this magnificent city.

The combination of a turbulent past, pristine architecture, and a promising future gives Prague an eclectic energy. Its rebirth has come with the labor pains of inflation, traffic jams, people jams, and ever-present pounding construction crews. The Czechs' 7-year post-Communist shopping spree came to a bitter end in the spring of 1997, as a ballooning trade deficit caused the Czech crown to plummet. So as of this writing, the new exchange rates make many things more than 20% cheaper for most foreign visitors than they were in 1996. Prague remains a great value.

REQUIRED DOCUMENTS American, British, and Canadian citizens need only passports for stays under 30 days. All children, even infants, are required to have a passport.

OTHER FROMMER'S TITLES For more on Prague, see *Frommer's Prague & the Best of the Czech Republic, Frommer's Gay & Lesbian Europe,* or *Frommer's Europe.*

1 Prague Deals & Discounts

SPECIAL DISCOUNTS

Prague's public transportation system of subways, buses, and trams is fast, efficient, and affordable, and it's even more of a deal when you buy one of the passes available: A **1-day pass** good for unlimited rides is 70Kč ($2.10), a **3-day pass** 180Kč ($5), a **7-day pass** 250Kč ($8), and a **15-day pass** 280Kč ($9). If you're staying for more than 2 weeks, buy a **monthly pass** for 380Kč ($12).

Budget Bests

In Prague, **private rooms** are always the best buy—a double may cost 750Kč to 1,500Kč ($23 to $45). Compare that to 2,500Kč ($76) or more for a double in a full-service hotel. But for a special affordable getaway, the **Pension Větrník** (☎ 02/2051 3390), is hard to beat with its friendly country setting, large made-to-order breakfasts, and clay tennis court available when the weather permits.

The city's **walks,** affordable **cultural events,** and cheap, world-renowned **Bohemian beer** make it one of Europe's bargains. Many restaurants are in a budget traveler's range, especially **pubs** that provide a hearty meal at a price locals demand.

Prague's **museums and galleries** are inexpensive, with admission fees less than $2 and many with student discounts and free days.

Public transportation fares are still incredibly low, and the best draws—**Charles Bridge,** the **Prague Castle gardens and courtyards, Old Town Square,** and the area around them—are free for the walking.

For food, look no further than the local *hospoda* (beer pub), using the rule that the farther it is from the city center and the less English spoken, the cheaper it'll be. You can find a special dining discount during the lunch hour at **U Čížků** on Charles Square (☎ 02/298 891), where the menu is half price before 5pm, bringing most main courses down to below $5.

Also note that students receive discounted admission at most sightseeing attractions.

WORTH A SPLURGE

If you can afford a splurge, I suggest you fully experience the baroque elegance of Prague by seeing most any production at the **Estates' Theater (Stavovské Divadlo).** The most sought-after ticket is Mozart's *Don Giovanni,* usually on the program at least twice a month in its original home for as little as 250Kč ($8) or as much as 2,000Kč ($61), depending on whether the official box office is sold out and you have to seek tickets through one of the private agencies.

2 Essentials

ARRIVING

BY PLANE   Prague's freshly reconstructed **Ruzyně Airport** (☎ 02/2011 1111), 12 miles west of the city center, has a bank for changing money (usually daily 7am to 11pm), several car-rental offices (see "Getting Around," below), and a luggage storage office charging 60Kč ($1.80) per item per day. The official VW airport **taxis** parked in front of the terminal cost about twice the price of the rickety Škodas and Ladas taxis waiting on the edges of the terminal.

CSA, the Czech national airline, operates an **airport shuttle** to and from its main office in downtown Prague, every 30 minutes from 7:30am to 7:30pm. The **CSA main office** is at Na Celnici 5 (☎ 02/2431 4270). The shuttle costs 30Kč (90¢) per person.

The not-too-inconvenient public transport option is a combination of **city bus no. 119,** which delivers you from just outside the airport baggage claim to the **Dejvická metro station** (Line A). It costs only 12Kč (36¢), but the bus makes many stops. Travel time is about 40 minutes.

What Things Cost in Prague	U.S. $
Taxi from Ruzyně Airport to center city	15.00
Metro, tram, or public bus to anywhere in Prague	0.30
Local telephone call	0.10
Double room at Pension Větrník (inexpensive)	60.60
Double room at Hotel Betlem Club (moderate)	110.00
Double room at Hotel Orion (inexpensive)	65.00
Lunch for one at most pubs (inexpensive)	3.00
Dinner for one, without wine, at U Čížků (moderate)	14.00
Dinner for one, without wine, at Avalon (inexpensive)	9.00
Half liter of beer in a pub	0.90
Coca-Cola in a restaurant	1.00
Cup of coffee	1.05
Roll of ASA 100 film, 36 exposures	7.50
Admission to National Museum	.25
Movie ticket	2.45
Ticket to National Theater Opera	7.50–20.00

BY TRAIN   Of the two central rail stations, **Hlavní nádraží,** Wilsonova třída, Praha 2 (☎ **02/2461 1111**), is the grander and more popular; however, it's also seedier. The basement holds a 24-hour luggage storage counter charging 20Kč (60¢) per bag per day. Though cheaper, the nearby lockers aren't secure and should be avoided. Beneath the main hall are surprisingly clean public showers that are a good place to refresh yourself for just 40Kč ($1.20); they're open Monday to Friday 6am to 8pm, Saturday 7am to 7pm, and Sunday 8am to 4pm. On the second floor is the train information office (marked by a lowercase "i"), open daily 6am to 10pm; and on the top floor is a tattered restaurant recommendable only to the famished. From the main train station it's a 5-minute stroll to the "top" end of Wenceslas Square or a 15-minute walk to Old Town Square. Metro Line C connects the station to the rest of the city. Metro trains depart from the lower level, and city-center no-transfer tickets, costing 6Kč (20¢), are available at the newsstand near the metro entrance. Taxis line up outside the station day and night.

   Nádraží Holešovice, Partyzánská at Vrbenského, Praha 7 (☎ **02/2422 4200**), usually serves trains from Berlin and other points north. Though it isn't as centrally located as the main station, its more manageable size and position at the end of metro Line C make it almost as convenient.

BY BUS   The **Central Bus Station Praha–Florenc,** Křižíkova 5, Praha 8 (☎ **02/2421 1060**), is a few blocks north of the main rail station, and most local and long-distance buses arrive here. The adjacent Florenc metro station is on metro Lines B and C. Smaller depots are at **Želivského** (metro Line A), **Smíchovské nádraží** (metro Line B), and **Nádraží Holešovice** (metro Line C).

VISITOR INFORMATION

Those arriving via train at either of the two primary stations (Hlavní or Holešovice—see above) will find the greatest success obtaining information from **AVE Ltd.**

A Taxi Warning

Most of Prague's taxi drivers will take advantage of you; obtaining an honestly metered ride from the airport is close to impossible. The fare from the airport to Wenceslas Square *should* be no more than about 400Kč ($12). If you pay this, you're exceedingly lucky. More likely the fare will be $15 or even more.

(☎ **02/2422 3226** or 02/2422 3521; fax 02/549 743; e-mail: avetours@avetours. anet.cz; www.ave.anet.cz), an accommodations agency that also distributes printed information. The two train station offices are open daily 6am to 11pm.

Čedok, Na příkopě 18, Praha 1 (☎ **02/2419 7111**), once the country's official state-owned visitors bureau, is now a traditional travel agency. Like others in town, it prefers selling tickets and tours to dispensing free information. The company also books rail tickets and accepts major credit cards. The office is open Monday to Friday 8:30am to 6pm and Saturday 9am to 2pm.

The city's **Cultural and Information Center,** on the ground floor of the remodeled Municipal House (Obecní dům), náměstí Republiky 5, Praha 1 (☎ **02/2200 2100;** fax 02/2200 2636; e-mail: od@monet.cz), is a new attempt at visitor-friendly relations, offering advice, tickets, souvenirs, refreshments, and rest rooms. It's open daily 9am to 5pm.

CITY LAYOUT

The **river Vltava** bisects Prague. **Staré Město (Old Town)** and **Nové Město (New Town)** are on the east (right) side of the river, while the **Hradčany (Castle District)** and **Malá Strana (Lesser Town)** are on the west (left) bank.

After the castle that hovers over the city, bridges and squares are the most prominent landmarks. **Charles Bridge,** the oldest and most famous of those spanning the Vltava, is at the epicenter and connects Old Town with Lesser Town and the Castle District. Several important streets radiate from Old Town Square, including fashionable **Pařížská** to the northwest, historic **Celetná** to the east, and **Melantrichova,** connecting to **Wenceslas Square (Václavské náměstí)** to the southeast.

On the west side of Charles Bridge is **Mostecká,** a 3-block-long connection to **Malostranské náměstí,** Malá Strana's main square. Hradčany, the Castle District, is just northwest of the square, while a second hill, **Petřín,** is just southwest.

FINDING AN ADDRESS   You should know that *ulice* (abbreviated ul.) means "street," *třída* means "avenue," *náměstí* (abbreviated nám.) is a "square" or "plaza," a *most* is a "bridge," and *nábřeží* is "quay." In Czech, none of these are capitalized. In addresses street numbers follow the street name (like Václavské nám. 25).

Each address is followed by a district number, such as Praha 1 (Praha means "Prague" in Czech). Praha 1 is the oldest and most historically concentrated district, encompassing Staré Město (Old Town), the Hradčany (Castle District), and Malá Strana (Lesser Town). Praha 2 is mostly Nové Město (New Town). The remaining eight districts are more remote and contain few major attractions.

GETTING AROUND

BY METRO, BUS & TRAM   Prague's Communist-built public transport network is a vast—and usually efficient—system of subways, trams, and buses. You can ride a maximum of four stations on the metro or 15 minutes on a tram or bus, without transfers, for 8Kč (25¢); kids 5 and under are free. This will usually suffice for trips in the historic districts. Rides of more than four stops on the metro or longer tram or bus rides, with unlimited transfers for up to 1 hour after your ticket is validated, cost 12Kč (35¢). You can buy tickets from coin-operated orange machines in metro stations or at most newsstands marked TABÁK or TRAFIKA. Hold on to your ticket (which you must validate at the orange or yellow stamp clocks in each tram or bus when you get on board or at the entrance to the metro) during your ride—you'll need it to prove you've paid if a ticket collector asks.

If you're caught without a valid ticket, you'll have to pay a 200Kč ($6) fine to a plainclothes ticket controller on the spot (the fine will probably double before this book goes to press). Make sure he or she shows you a very official-looking badge.

A **1-day pass** good for unlimited rides is 70Kč ($2.10), a **3-day pass** 180Kč ($5), a **7-day pass** 250Kč ($8), and a **15-day pass** 280Kč ($9). If you're staying for more than 2 weeks, buy a **monthly pass** for 380Kč ($12). You can buy the day passes at the "DP" windows at any metro station, but the photo ID monthly pass is available only at the Dopravní podnik (transport department) office on Na bojišti, near the I. P. Pavlova metro station (☎ **02/9619 1111**).

Metro trains operate daily 5am to midnight and run every 3 to 8 minutes. On the three lettered lines (A, B, C) the most convenient central stations are Můstek, at the foot of Václavské náměstí (Wenceslas Square); Staroměstská, for Old Town Square and Charles Bridge; and Malostranská, serving Malá Strana and the Castle District.

The 24 **electric tram** (streetcar) lines run practically everywhere. There's always another tram with the same number traveling back. You never have to hail trams, for they make every stop. The most popular, no. 22 (the "tourist tram" or "pickpocket express"), runs past top sights like the National Theater and Prague Castle.

To ride the **bus,** you have to buy the same tickets as for other modes in advance and validate them upon boarding. Regular bus and tram service stops at midnight, after which selected routes run reduced schedules, usually only once per hour. If you miss a night connection, expect a long wait for the next.

BY FUNICULAR The cog railway makes the scenic run up and down Petřín Hill every 15 minutes or so from 9:15am to 8:45pm, with an intermediate stop at the Nebozízek Restaurant in the middle of the hill overlooking the city. It requires the same 12Kč ticket as other public transport. The funicular departs from a small house in the park just above the middle of Újezd in Malá Strana.

BY TAXI Avoid taxis. If you must, you can hail one in the streets or in front of train stations, large hotels, and popular attractions, but be forewarned that many drivers simply gouge unsuspecting tourists. In late 1996, to let the market decide, the city canceled price regulations on taxis. But instead of creating price competition, it started a turf war between cab companies vying for the best taxi stand spots. The best fare you can hope for is 17Kč (50¢) per kilometer, but twice or three times that isn't rare. The rates are usually posted not on the exterior of the car but on the dashboard, making it too late to haggle once you're in and on your way. Negotiate a price and have it written down before getting in. Better yet, go on foot or by public transport. Somewhat reputable companies with English-speaking dispatchers are **AAA Taxi** (☎ **02/342 410** or 02/3399); **RONY Taxi** (☎ **02/692 1958** or 02/430 403); and the unfortunately named **ProfiTaxi** (☎ **02/6104 5555** or 02/6104 5550). Get a receipt (and send it to the mayor).

BY RENTAL CAR Not only budget travelers but also most any travelers will find driving in Prague not worth the money or effort. The roads are frustrating and slow and parking is minimal and expensive. If you want to rent a car to explore the environs, try **Europcar/InterRent,** Pařížská 28, Praha 1 (☎ **02/2481 0515** or 02/2481 1290), open daily 8am to 8pm. Also there's **Hertz,** Karlovo nám. 28, Praha 2

Prague Metro

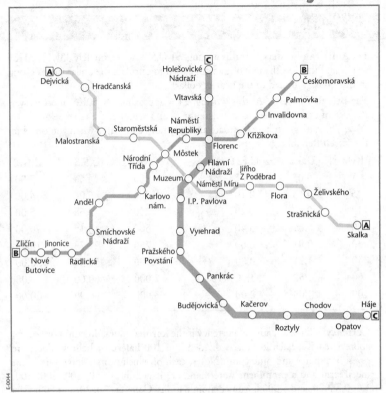

(☎ **02/291 851** or 02/290 122), and **Budget,** at Ruzyně Airport (☎ **02/316 5214**) and in the Hotel Inter-Continental, náměstí Curieových, Praha 1 (☎ **02/231 9595**).

Local Czech car-rental companies sometimes offer lower rates than the big international firms. Compare **A Rent Cars,** Opletalova 33, Praha 1 (☎ **02/2422 9848**), and **SeccoCar,** Přístavní 39, Praha 7 (☎ **02/684 3403**).

FAST FACTS: Prague

American Express For travel arrangements, traveler's checks, currency exchange, and other member services, visit the city's sole office at Václavské nám. 56 (Wenceslas Square), Praha 1 (☎ **02/2421 9992;** fax 02/2422 7708), open daily 9am to 7pm. To report lost or stolen cards, call ☎ **02/2421-9978.**

Baby-sitters If your hotel can't recommend a sitter, phone **Affordable Luxuries,** Štěpánská 15, Praha 1 (☎ **02/2166 1319** or 02/2166 1266), an American-owned company that provides various child-minding services. Make reservations far in advance. The fee is 180Kč ($5) per hour.

Business Hours Most **banks** are open Monday to Friday 8:30am to 6pm, but some also open Saturday 9am to noon. Business **offices** are generally open Monday to Friday 8am to 6pm. **Pubs** are usually open daily 11am to midnight. Most **restaurants** open for lunch noon to 3pm and for dinner 6 to 11pm; only a few stay open later.

The Czech Koruna

For American Readers   At this writing, $1 U.S. = approximately 33Kč (or 1Kč = 3¢), and this was the rate of exchange used to calculate the dollar values given in this book (rounded to the nearest dollar).

For British Readers   At this writing, £1 = approximately 50Kč, and this was the rate of exchange used to calculate the pound values in the table below.

Note: The rates given here fluctuate and may not be the same when you travel to the Czech Republic.

Kč	U.S.$	U.K.£	Kč	U.S.$	U.K.£
1	0.03	0.02	150	4.54	3.00
5	0.15	0.10	200	6.06	4.00
10	0.30	0.20	250	7.58	5.00
20	0.61	0.40	500	15.15	10.00
30	0.91	0.60	750	22.73	15.00
40	1.21	0.80	1,000	30.30	20.00
50	1.52	1.00	2,000	60.60	40.00
100	3.03	2.00	3,000	90.90	60.00

Currency   The basic unit of currency is the **koruna** (plural, **koruny**) or **crown,** abbreviated **Kč.** Each koruna is divided into 100 **haléřů** or **hellers.** There are seven banknotes and nine coins. Notes, each of which bears a forgery-resistant metal strip and a prominent watermark, are issued in 20, 50, 100, 200, 500, 1,000, 2,000, and 5,000 koruny denominations. Coins are 10, 20, and 50 hellers and 1, 2, 5, 10, 20, and 50 koruny.

Currency Exchange   Banks generally offer the best exchange rates. Don't hesitate to use a credit or debit card to draw cash for the best rates. **Komerční banka** has three Praha 1 locations with ATMs accepting Visa, MasterCard, and American Express: Na Příkopě 33, Národní 32, and Václavské nám. (☎ **02/2442 1111** for all branches). The exchange offices are open Monday to Friday 8am to 5pm, but the ATMs are accessible 24 hours.

Dentists & Doctors   If you need a doctor or dentist and your condition isn't life-threatening, you can visit the **Polyclinic at Národní,** Národní 9, Praha 1 (☎ **02/2207 5120;** for emergencies, ☎ 02/0600 111, operator ☎ 140 533), during walk-in hours daily 8am to 5pm. Dr. Stránský is an Ivy League–trained straight-talking physician. For **emergency medical aid,** call the **Foreigners' Medical Clinic,** Na Homolce Hospital, Praha 5 (☎ **02/5292 2146** or 02/5292 2191 after hours).

Embassies   The **U.S. Embassy,** Tržiště 15, Praha 1 (☎ **02/5732 0663**), is open Monday to Friday 8am to 11:30am and 2:30 to 4pm. The **Canadian Embassy,** Mickiewiczova 6, Praha 6 (☎ **02/2431 1108**), is open Monday to Friday 8:30am to noon and 2 to 4pm. The **U.K. Embassy,** Thunovská 14, Praha 1 (☎ **02/5732 0355**), is open Monday to Friday 9am to noon. You can visit the **Australian Honorary Consul,** Na Ořechovce 38, Praha 6 (☎ **02/2431 0743**), on Monday to Thursday 8:30am to 5pm and Friday 8:30am to 2pm.

Emergencies   You can reach Prague's **police** and **fire** services by dialing ☎ **158** from any phone. To call an **ambulance,** dial ☎ **155.**

Hospitals   Particularly welcoming to foreigners is **Nemocnice Na Homolce,** V úvalu 84 (Motol), Praha 5 (☎ **02/5292 2146** or 02/5292 2191 after hours). The English-speaking doctors can also make house calls. See "Dentists & Doctors" above for more. In an emergency, dial ☎ **155** for an ambulance.

Laundry   Laundry Kings, Dejvická 16, Praha 6 (☎ **02/312 3743**), was Prague's first American-style coin-operated self-service Laundromat.

Luggage Storage & Lockers   The **Ruzyně Airport Luggage Storage Office** never closes and charges 60Kč ($1.80) per item per day. Left-luggage offices are also available at the main train stations, **Hlavní nádraží** and **Nádraží Holešovice.** Both charge 20Kč (60¢) per bag per day and are technically open 24 hours, but if your train is departing late at night, check to make sure someone will be around. Luggage lockers are available in all of Prague's train stations, but avoid them.

Mail   Post offices are plentiful and normally open Monday to Friday 8am to 6pm. Mailboxes are orange and usually attached to the sides of buildings. Mail can take up to 10 days to reach its destination.

The **Main Post Office (Hlavní pošta),** Jindřišská 14, Praha 1, 110 00 (☎ **02/2422 8856**), a few steps from Václavské náměstí, is open 24 hours. You can receive mail here, marked Poste Restante and addressed to you, care of this post office.

Pharmacies   The most central pharmacy *(lékárna)* is at Václavské nám. 8, Praha 1 (☎ **02/2422 7532**), open Monday to Friday 8am to 6pm. The nearest emergency (24-hour) pharmacy is at Palackého 5, Praha 1 (☎ **02/267 814**). If you're in Praha 2, there's an emergency pharmacy on Belgická 37 (☎ **02/ 258 189**).

Police   In an emergency, dial ☎ **158.**

Rest Rooms   Toilets are located in every metro station and are staffed by cleaning personnel who usually charge 3Kč (9¢) and dispense a few precious sheets of toilet paper. Restaurants and pubs around all the major sights are usually kind to nonpatrons who wish to use their facilities. Public toilets are clearly marked with the letters "WC."

Safety   In Prague's center you'll feel generally safer than in most Western cities, but don't walk alone at night around Wenceslas Square—one of the main areas for prostitution and where a lot of unexplainable loitering takes place. All visitors should be watchful of pickpockets in heavily touristed areas, especially on Charles Bridge, in Old Town Square, and in front of the main train station. Be especially wary in crowded buses, trams, and trains. Don't keep your wallet in a back pocket and don't flash a lot of cash or jewelry.

Taxes   A 22% **value-added tax (VAT)** is built into the price of most goods and services rather than being tacked on at the register. Most restaurants also include VAT in the prices on their menus. If they don't, that fact should be stated somewhere on the menu.

Telephone   You can get **directory assistance** in English by dialing (without charge) ☎ **0149.** For **information on services** and rates, dial ☎ **0139.** Dial tones are continual high-pitched beeps that sound something like busy signals in America.

There are two kinds of **pay phones.** The first accepts coins and the other operates only with a phonecard, available from post offices and news agents in denominations ranging from 50Kč to 500Kč ($1.50 to $15). The minimum cost

Country & City Codes

The **country code** for the Czech Republic is **420.** The **city code** for Prague is **2;** use this code if you're calling from outside the Czech Republic. If you're within the Czech Republic but not in Prague, use **02.** If you're calling within Prague, simply leave off the code and dial the regular phone number.

of a **local call** is 2Kč (6¢). Coin-op phones have displays telling you the minimum price for your call, but they don't make change, so don't load more than you have to. You can add more coins as the display nears zero. Phonecard telephones deduct the price of your call from the card. If you're calling home, get a phonecard with plenty of points, as calls run about 42Kč ($1.30) per minute to the United States and 25Kč (50p) to the United Kingdom. **Long-distance phone charges** are higher in the Czech Republic than they are in the United States, and hotels usually add their own surcharge, sometimes as hefty as 100% to 200%, which you may be unaware of until you're presented with the bill. Ask before placing any call from a hotel. Charging to your phone credit card from a public telephone is often the most economical way to call home.

A fast, convenient way to call the United States from Europe is via services like AT&T USA Direct. This bypasses the foreign operator and automatically links you to an operator with your long-distance carrier in your home country. The access number in the Czech Republic for **AT&T USA Direct** is ☎ **0042 000 101,** for **MCI CALL USA** ☎ **0042 000 112, and for Sprint Express USA** ☎ **00 420 87187.** Canadians can connect with **Canada Direct** at ☎ **00 420 00151,** and Brits can connect with **BT Direct** at ☎ **00 420 04401** or **Mercury Call UK** at ☎ **00 420 04450.** From a pay phone in the Czech Republic, your local phone card will be debited only for a local call.

Tipping   Rules for tipping aren't as strict in the Czech Republic as they are in the United States. At most restaurants and pubs, locals just round the bill up to the nearest few koruny. When you're presented with good service at tablecloth places, a 10% tip is proper. Washroom and cloakroom attendants usually demand a couple of koruny, and porters in airports and rail stations usually receive 20Kč (60¢) per bag. Taxi drivers should get about 10%, unless they've already ripped you off.

3 Accommodations You Can Afford

Prague pensions are much cheaper than hotels, but they're pricey compared with similar Western B&Bs. Still, those listed below give good value. Do be aware that with the rapid changes in the Czech economy, rates can often fluctuate as the forces of supply and demand battle to find their balance, and exchange rates fluctuate wildly.

Rooms in private homes or apartments offer a budget stay with usually a little more privacy than hostels, but if you don't like feeling as if you're invading somebody else's home and simply want a bed, Prague has several relatively clean dorm-type hostels. Full-service hotels have improved in the face of heavier international competition, but room rates still exceed those in many Western European hotels of similar or better quality.

If you show up at a hotel and think rooms are going empty, you can always negotiate the price before committing. Use the lack of amenities in specific rooms as a reason for the lower rate or ask if you can get a better rate for staying a few nights.

A Telephone Warning

Be aware that the Czech Republic is going through a massive overhaul of its telephone network, and phone numbers can change overnight without notice.

Note: You can find the lodging choices below plotted on the map included in "Seeing the Sights," later in this chapter.

ROOM-FINDING SERVICES   Expect to pay between 750Kč and 1,500Kč ($23 and $46) for a single and 1,500Kč and 6,000Kč ($45 and $182) for an apartment for two. Rental agencies include my favorite, **AVE Ltd.** (☎ **02/2422 3226** or 02/2422 3521; fax 02/549 743; e-mail: avetours@avetours.anet.cz; www.ave.anet.cz), located at Ruzyně airport; at the main train station, Hlavní nádraží; and at the north train station, Nádraží Holešovice—see "Visitor Information," earlier in this chapter. After placing several friends and colleagues with AVE, I've yet to hear a complaint. There's also the **Prague Accommodation Service,** Haštalské nám., Praha 1 (☎ **02/231 0202;** fax 02/231 6640); **Top Tour,** Rybná 3, Praha 1 (☎ **02/232 1077;** fax 02/2481 1400); and the former-Communist bureau **Čedok,** at Na Příkopě 18 and at Václavské nám. 24, Praha 1 (☎ **02/2419 7111;** fax 02/232 1656).

IN STARÉ MĚSTO (OLD TOWN)

✪ **Betlem Club.** Betlémské nám. 9, Praha 1. ☎ **02/2421 6872.** Fax 02/2421 8054. 22 units, all with bathroom. MINIBAR TV TEL. 3,300Kč ($100) double. Rates include breakfast. No credit cards. Metro: Národní třída.

The location is fantastic, opposite Bethlehem Chapel, where 15th-century Protestant leader Jan Hus preached to the masses. Several restaurants and bars are on this quiet square, and Charles Bridge, Wenceslas Square, and Old Town Square are within easy walking distance. The Betlem feels more like a private pension than a central-city hotel, with small rooms that don't encourage extended lounging; about half are decorated in 1970s Czech style, while the others are more contemporary, with black lacquer pieces. Breakfast is served in a vaulted medieval cellar.

NEAR STAROMĚSTSKÉ NÁMĚSTÍ (OLD TOWN SQUARE)

Dům krále Jiřího. Liliová 10, Praha 1. ☎ **02/2422 2013.** Fax 02/2422 1983. 8 units, all with bathroom. 1,100Kč ($33) single; 2,200Kč ($66) double. Rates include breakfast. AE, MC, V. Metro: Staroměstská.

The "House at King George's" is above two pubs on a narrow side street. The recently remodeled rooms have a bit more charm than before but are still pretty bare. The ceilings are high, and the dark wooden furniture is a great leap forward. Charles Bridge is a few dozen steps and a swing to the left from the pension, but this narrow alley has become more like Bourbon Street than the Royal Route. Ask for a room in back if you want to deaden the pub clamor.

Pension Unitas. Bartolomějská 9, Praha 1. ☎ **02/232 7700.** Fax 02/232 7709. 32 units, none with bathroom. 1,020Kč ($30) single; 1,200Kč ($36) double. No credit cards. Metro: Staroměstská.

Between Old Town Square and the National Theater, the Unitas is a pension-hotel, converted from a building of holding cells of the secret police. It sounds ominous, but the Unitas, now run by an order of nuns, offers sparse accommodations at an unbeatable location for the price. Smoking and drinking are banned. The upstairs rooms are brighter, though you might like to stay down in Cell P6, once occupied by dissident playwright Václav Havel, now president of the country.

Getting the Best Deal on Accommodations

- Note that in Prague you can find the best value in the center of the city by staying in one of the numerous pensions or hotels near náměstí Míru, just a few blocks above Wenceslas Square.

- Avoid anything that resembles a Western-style full-service hotel—most often they have Europe-standard rates with Warsaw Pact–standard furnishings and service.

- Try the pension and apartment locator service at AVE Ltd. (see above)—it represents a wide range of accommodations at various prices and has a good reputation for the honesty of its referrals.

- Don't be afraid to rent a room away from the old quarters of town, especially if it's close to a metro stop. The farther away from the center, the lower the rates will be, and the metro connections are fast and affordable.

NEAR NÁMĚSTÍ MÍRU

✪ **Flathotel Orion.** Americká 9, Praha 2. ☎ **02/691 0209.** Fax 02/691 0096. 19 units, all with bathroom. TV TEL. 2,130Kč ($65) double; 2,960Kč–3,890Kč ($90–$118) suite. Breakfast 110Kč ($3.35). Metro: Náměstí Míru.

The best family value close to the city center, the Orion is an apartment hotel with each unit boasting a well-equipped kitchen. In this friendly neighborhood, you'll find fruit and vegetable shops and corner groceries around náměstí Míru, up the street. All rooms are either one- or two-bedroom flats, sleeping up to six. They're comfortable but not imaginative, bordered in pale blue with black leather armchairs and dark wooden bed frames. The baths are basic and modern, much like the kitchens. The only extra outside the rooms is a Finnish sauna.

Pension City. Belgická 10, Praha 2. ☎ **02/691 1334.** Fax 02/691 1240. 19 units, 7 with bathroom. TEL. 1,500Kč ($45) double without bathroom, 2,300Kč ($67) double with bathroom. Rates include breakfast. AE, MC, V. Metro: Náměstí Míru.

The City offers clean, characterless rooms, with typical dark wood-veneer furniture and Communist-era Day-Glo orange interiors. However, they're large and expandable into triples or quads with an extra charge for additional people. TVs cost extra. The best thing about the City is that it's (like the Orion) around the corner from the pub Na Zvonařce (see "Great Deals on Dining," later in this chapter).

Warning 1: The prices should remain affordable, but the exact rate depends on the daily koruna/German mark exchange rate. *Warning 2:* The City has been waiting for its phone numbers to change for a while. If you can't get through, check with AVE Ltd. (see above). *Warning 3:* There's a restaurant, but I don't recommend it beyond the breakfast buffet.

ON VÁCLAVSKÉ NÁMĚSTÍ (WENCESLAS SQUARE)

Hotel Evropa. Václavské nám. 25, Praha 1. ☎ **02/2422 8117.** Fax 02/2422 4544. 87 units, 20 with bathroom; 3 suites. 2,160Kč ($65) double without bathroom, 2,800Kč ($85) double with bathroom; from 4,700Kč ($142) suite. Rates include continental breakfast. AE, MC, V. Metro: Můstek.

Rebuilt in its original turn-of-the-century style, the Evropa, in the heart of Wenceslas Square, has an ornate art nouveau facade that recalls more glorious years. Seats on the ground-floor cafe terrace are coveted—for style and people-watching, not food or service. The guest rooms range from adequate to shabby, with none matching the grandeur of the public areas. The best are front-facing doubles, half a dozen of which have balconies overlooking Václavské náměstí.

NEAR NÁMĚSTÍ REPUBLIKY

Hotel Axa. Na poříčí 40, Praha 1. ☎ **02/2481 2580.** Fax 02/232 2172. e-mail: axapraha@mbox.vol.cz. 131 units, all with bathroom. TV TEL. 3,250Kč ($98) double. Rates include continental breakfast. MC, V. Metro: Náměstí Republiky or Florenc.

The Axa added private baths and the prices have jumped, but it's still one of the most affordable central rests. The beds are loudly upholstered particle board, and the lobby feels like a hospital's. However, you'll find a six-lane 25-meter pool used for local competitions as well as a fitness center with weight machines, free weights, a sauna, and a solarium. This place may be better cast as a rehabilitation center.

IN MALÁ STRANA (LESSER TOWN)

Hostel Sokol. Hellichova 1, Praha 1. No phone. 100 beds. 190Kč ($8) per person. No credit cards. Open June–Sept. From Malostranská metro station, walk up Letenská, cross Malostranská náměstí, and continue along Karmelitská. Turn left onto Hellichova, and the hostel is 1 block ahead on your right.

Though this is one of Prague's best-located hostels, the Sokol does have its drawbacks. The rooms are packed with 10 to 12 beds each, they charge an extra 20Kč (60¢) if you return after 12:30am, and cleanliness is suspect. In the heart of Malá Strana, a short walk from Charles Bridge, it's a great base for exploring—and for finding a more suitable place. The hostel is closed daily 10am to 3pm.

OUTSIDE THE CITY CENTER

✪ **Pension Větrník.** U Větrníku 40, Praha 6. ☎ **02/2051 3390.** Fax 02/361 406. 6 units, all with bathroom. TV TEL. 2,000Kč ($61) double. Rates include large made-to-order breakfast. MC. Metro: Line A to Dejvice station, then tram 1, 2, or 18.

The mostly scenic half-hour tram ride from the city center (or metro/tram combo) takes you to a secret country hideaway. After getting off the tram, walk behind a bunch of large concrete dorms to find a restored 18th-century white windmill house. It made for the most romantic pension stay for my wife, Hana, and me. Once you buzz at the metal gate (avoid the buzzer for the door to the family residence), Miloš Opatrný will greet you in decent English, along with Arnošt, a lovable St. Bernard known in these parts as spokesdog for a Swiss insurance company. Arnošt will help show you through lush gardens and the tennis court into a quaint guesthouse, where a stone staircase leads to spacious rooms with big beds, open-beam ceilings, and modern amenities. The baths are roomy, with huge stand-up showers, and the windows are shuttered and boast flower boxes.

Opatrný, a former foreign service chef, takes pride in whipping up a traditional Czech country dinner and serving it personally in a small medieval stone cellar with a fire. If the guests don't mind, Arnošt adds atmosphere near the fireplace on a cold night. There's a patio for drinks outside. You can't get more romantic than this, especially for the price.

Strahov Hostels. Spartakiádní, Praha 6. ☎ and fax **02/2051 3431.** 1,500 beds. 250Kč–300Kč ($10–$12) per person. No credit cards. From Dejvická metro station, take bus no. 143, 149, or 217 to Strahov Stadium.

Across from the giant Strahov Stadium, these hostels were built to house competitors for Olympic-style games that were held before the fall of Communism. Today, these dozen concrete high-rises are students' homes throughout the school year and budget hotels in summer. Most rooms are doubles, none have a private bath, and all are open 24 hours.

WORTH A SPLURGE

Hotel Kampa. Všehrdova 16, Praha 1. ☎ **02/5732 0404.** Fax 02/5732 0262. 85 units, all with bathroom. TEL. 3,550Kč ($107) double. AE, MC, V. Metro: Malostranská, then no. 12 or 22 tram to Hellichova stop.

As one of the quaintest, quietest, and most affordable ways of staying on the left bank, the Kampa occupies what was once an armory, built at the beginning of the 17th century, now at the edge of Prague's riverside park. The rooms were renovated in 1992. The singles are incredibly simple, furnished with just a single-size bed and a stand-alone wardrobe. The doubles are larger and marginally nicer. There's no decoration on most walls, and the baths are compact.

4 Great Deals on Dining

The true Czech dining experience can be summed up in three native words: *vepřo, knedlo, zelo*—pork, dumplings, cabbage. Menus are packed with meat, meat, and more meat. When prepared with care and imagination, the standard fare can be hearty and satisfying, though you should ingest it when you can follow the meal with a short nap to aid digestion. With new restaurants pouring in, it's getting easier to eat lighter in Prague.

Avoid imported foods—always more expensive and less fresh than locally produced items. Look for fixed-price menus, two-for-one specials, and offers in English-language newspapers. Don't eat anything without seeing the price. Some places gouge for nuts or other on-table premeal snacks.

THE PICK OF THE PUBS

If what you want is really Czech and pretty cheap, try most any *hostinec* or *hospoda* (pub). The farther out of the city center, the cheaper they'll be. Most have a hearty goulash or pork dish with dumplings and cabbage, usually for 80Kč to 120Kč ($2.40 to $3.60), and after you wash it down with Czech beer you won't care about the food anyway (for the best beers, see the box "We're Here for the Beer," later in this chapter). In the city center, pub meals cost maybe 10% or 20% more, but the food tends to be better.

NEAR OLD TOWN SQUARE

Krušovická Pivnice. Široká 20, Praha 1. ☎ **02/231 6689.** Main courses 60Kč–130Kč ($1.80–$3.95). No credit cards. Daily 11am–midnight. Metro: Staroměstská. CZECH.

Across Pařížská from the Jewish Quarter's synagogues is one of the last *hospůdka* that still evokes the old days. Veteran Prague hands recall the Krušovické beer here used to be just 3Kč (9¢) a pint. While the price has grown to 18Kč (55¢), it's still one of the city center's cheapest draws. For nostalgia, the unkempt look takes you back to the pre-Revolution era, when competition for atmosphere didn't matter. The place still serves a pretty decent svíčková (slices of roast sirloin in a creamy sauce flavored with roasted vegetables).

✪ **Pivnice Radegast.** Templová 2, Praha 1. ☎ **02/232 8069.** Main courses 55Kč–120Kč ($1.70–$3.60). AE, MC, V. Daily 11am–midnight. Metro: Můstek or Náměstí Republiky. CZECH.

The raucous Radegast dishes up Prague's best pub *guláš* in a single, narrow vaulted hall. The namesake Moravian brew seems to never stop flowing from its taps. The Radegast attracts a good mix of visitors and locals and a somewhat younger and upwardly mobile crowd than the other two pub choices in the neighborhood.

Getting the Best Deal on Dining

- Don't come to Prague for its cuisine, but do come for its beer and eat where you drink it. The food won't be stunning, but it'll be filling and usually cheap. For more on Czech beer, see the box "We're Here for the Beer," later in this chapter.

- Stick to Czech cuisine and steer away from Asian fare. The more the menu varies from pork, cabbage, and dumplings (with the exception of pizza), the higher the price will be. And remember that the farther from the Castle or Old Town you go, generally the cheaper your meal will be.

- Be on the lookout for fixed-price menus, two-for-one specials, and deals in the local English-language newspapers.

- Watch for on-table add-ons like almonds, olives, and appetizers—you might get a shock when the bill comes.

U medvídků. Na Perštýně 7, Praha 1. ☎ **02/2422 0930.** Main courses 80Kč–250Kč ($2.40–$8). AE, MC, V. Daily 11am–11pm. Metro: Národní třída. CZECH.

Bright and noisy, the House at the Little Bears serves a better-than-average *vepřo, knedlo,* and *zelo* with *two colors* of cabbage. The pub on the right after entering is half as cheap and more lively as the restaurant to the left. It's a hangout mixing locals, German tour groups, and foreign journalists because it serves the original Czech Budweiser beer, the genuine article. In high season, an oompah band plays in the beer wagon in the center of the pub.

Near Náměstí Míru

✪ **Na Zvonařce.** Šafaříkova 1, Praha 2. ☎ **02/691 1311.** Main courses 50Kč–120Kč ($1.50–$3.60). V. Mon–Fri 11am–11pm, Sat–Sun noon–11pm. Metro: I. P. Pavlova. CZECH.

The best pub choice outside the city center, the pub At the Bellmaker's in Vinohrady has a huge menu, probably the best all-around pub food in town and super Pilsner Urquell beer. During summer it's hard to get a table on the patio, but take one if you can.

Worth a Splurge

✪ **Restaurant U Čížků.** Karlovo nám. 34, Praha 2. ☎ **02/298 891.** Reservations recommended. Main courses 180Kč–330Kč ($5–$10). AE, MC, V. Daily noon–10pm. Metro: Karlovo Náměstí. CZECH.

Officially a restaurant, not a pub, this cozy cellar cum hunting lodge on Charles Square has the warmth of a 19th-century Bohemian country inn complete with horned trophies on the walls. The fare is purely Czech, and the massive portions of game, smoked pork, and other meats are the perfect match for the huge mugs of Pilsner beer. A little more extravagant than a pub, this still excellent value earns this pioneer a star.

THE BEST NONPUB MEALS
Near Prague Castle

Saté Grill. Pohořelec 3, Praha 1. ☎ **02/2051 4552.** Main courses 50Kč–100Kč ($1.50–$3). No credit cards. Daily 12:30–10pm. Tram: 22. INDONESIAN.

A lunchtime savior just beyond the foreign ministry (černinský Palac) west of the Castle, the Saté has made quite a business out of its simple Indonesian dishes at simple

A Dining Warning

Be sure to check restaurant bills carefully, as there are many shifty waiters. Also be aware that the taxi driver afterward could really take you for a ride—monetarily speaking.

prices. The unassuming storefront on the same side as the Swedish Embassy doesn't scream out to you, so look closely. The pork saté comes in a peanut sauce along with a hearty noodle Migoreng. The casual dining room eagerly welcomes foot-dragging visitors in search of a bite and a rest.

IN MALÁ STRANA (LESSER TOWN)

✪ **Avalon Bar & Grill.** Malostranské nám. 12, Praha 1. ☎ **02/530 276.** Main courses 120Kč–250Kč ($4.45–$9). AE, MC, V. Daily 11am–1am. Metro: Malostranská. AMERICAN.

A California theme restaurant, this place is both authentic and unique (for Prague), not just someone's idea of West Coast kitsch. It was enormously popular when it opened in 1994, and locals now count on its overstuffed sandwiches, grilled chicken, burgers, potato skins, and buffalo wings. On Saturday and Sunday 11am to 4pm, American-style brunches include eggs, bacon, and pancakes.

NEAR VÁCLAVSKÉ NÁMĚSTÍ (WENCESLAS SQUARE)

Gany's. Národní třída 20, Praha 1. ☎ **02/297 223.** Main courses 100Kč–200Kč ($3–$6). AE, DC, MC, V. Daily 8am–11pm. Metro: Můstek. CZECH/INTERNATIONAL.

A big, breezy upstairs hall, Gany's is great for a coffee, an inexpensive pretheater meal, or an upscale game of pool. The fabulous art nouveau interior, with huge original chandeliers, buzzes with local coffee talk, shoppers, business lunchers, and students. Starters include smoked salmon, battered and fried asparagus, and ham au gratin with vegetables. Main dishes range from trout with horseradish to beans with garlic sauce. Avoid the always overcooked pastas and stick to the basic meats and fish. In the snazzy billiards parlor in back you can have drinks and light meals.

NEAR OLD TOWN SQUARE

Klub architektů. Betlémské nám. 5a, Praha 1. ☎ **02/2440 1214.** Reservations recommended. Main courses 70Kč–130Kč ($2.10–$3.95). AE, MC, V. Mon–Sat 11am–midnight. Metro: Národní třída. CZECH/INTERNATIONAL.

Tucked into the alcoves of a 12th-century cellar across the courtyard from Jan Hus's Bethlehem Chapel, this eclectic clubhouse for the city's progressive architects' society is the best nonpub value in Old Town. While seated among the exposed air ducts and industrial swag lights hovering above the tables in the stone dungeon, you can choose from baked chicken, pork steaks, pasta, stir-fry chicken, and even vegetarian burritos. The large portions and variety will satisfy a range of tastes. The wicker seating in the courtyard makes a summer night among the torches enjoyable, though the alfresco menu is limited.

Oscar's. Týn 1, Praha 1. ☎ **02/2489 5404.** Main courses 150Kč–300Kč ($4.50–$9). AE, MC, V. Daily 11am–12:30am; brunch Sun from 10am. Metro: Můstek. AMERICAN/SPORTS BAR.

You're greeted downstairs by the life-size statue of the world's most famous anatomically incorrect statuette—the restaurant's namesake. And the Oscar goes to . . . Inside is more sports bar than Spago, with a lineup of ribs, nachos, burgers, and even a few Czech standbys. This space is more comfortable for watching that can't-miss game on satellite TV.

Quick Bites

The Czech-style delicatessen **Obchod čerstvých uzenin,** Václavské nám. 36, Praha 1 (no phone), is on the ground floor of Wenceslas Square's Melantrich Building. The front of the shop is a takeout deli offering dozens of cooked and smoked meats, sausages, and salami. In the back, it serves goulash, cooked meats, sausages with mustard and a slice of dense bread, and cheap beer. You have to eat standing up, but prices are pure Czech. Expect to pay about 60Kč ($1.80) for a plate of meat and a beer. It's open Monday to Friday 7am to 7pm and Saturday and Sunday 9am to 7pm. No credit cards are accepted. Vegetarians will like **Country Life,** Melantrichova 15, Praha 1 (☎ 02/2421 3366), a health-food store offering a strictly meatless menu also served to go. You'll find tofu, tomato, cucumber, and shredded cabbage salads; zesty wheat bread pizzas topped with red peppers, garlic, and onions; and vegetable burgers on multigrain buns with garlic-yogurt dressing. Selections are 40Kč to 75Kč ($1.20 to $2.70). It's open Monday to Thursday 9am to 6:30pm and Friday 9am to 3pm. No credit cards. And in a pinch, there's always numerous **McDonald's,** including two at the top and bottom of Wenceslas Square (nos. 56 and 9), one at Vodičkova 15 just off the square, and one at Mostecká 21 about 100 meters after you get off Charles Bridge in Malá Strana. **KFC** is at Vodičkova 32, Wenceslas Square 56, and Kaprova 14 near Old Town Square. There's a **KFC/Pizza Hut** combo at Na Poříčí 42, next to the Hotel Axa, with an upstairs play area for kids.

✪ **Pizzeria Rugantino.** Dušní 4, Praha 1. ☎ **02/231 8172.** Individual pizzas 90Kč–150Kč ($2.75–$4.55). No credit cards. Mon–Sat 11am–11pm, Sun 6–11pm. Metro: Staroměstská. PIZZA.

Generous iceberg-lettuce salads front the best selection of individual pizzas in Prague. The wood-fired stoves and hand-made dough result in a crisp and delicate crust on which a multitude of cheeses, vegetables, and meats can be placed. The Diabolo with fresh garlic bits and very hot chiles goes nicely with a cool salad and a pull of Krušovice beer. The constant buzz, no-smoking area, and heavy childproof wooden tables make this a family favorite.

WORTH A SPLURGE

✪ **Fakhreldine.** Klimentská 48, Praha 1. ☎ **02/232 79 70.** Main courses 250Kč–350Kč ($8–$11). AE, DC, MC, V. Daily noon–midnight. Metro: Florenc. LEBANESE.

This outlet of London's popular Lebanese restaurant delivers a quality exotic menu in a simply elegant dining room. Entrees includes charcoal-grilled lamb, marinated veal, and steaks. But you can put together a mix of appetizers to form a fantastic variety of tastes to constitute a meal. These include raw lamb, grilled Armenian sausages, the spicy eggplant dish babaganoush, and Lebanese cream cheese. Three kinds of baklava and cardamom-scented coffee await the final course. Service is sharp and attentive.

CAFE SOCIETY
IN STARÉ MĚSTO (OLD TOWN) & JOSEFOV

Kavárna Obecní dům. In the Municipal House, náměstí Republiky 5, Praha 1. ☎ **02/2200 2100.** Cakes and coffees around 30Kč (90¢). No credit cards. Daily 7:30am–11pm. Metro: Náměstí Republiky. LIGHT FARE.

Of all the beautifully restored spaces in the Municipal House, the kavárna might be its most spectacular room. Lofty ceilings, marble accents and tables, an altarlike mantle at the far end, huge windows, and period chandeliers provide the awesome setting for coffees, teas, and other drinks along with pastries and light sandwiches. Here you can spend a true turn-of-the-century afternoon.

✪ **Kavárna Slavia.** Národní at Smetanovo nábřeží, Praha 1. ☎ **02/6115 2579.** Coffees and pastries 15Kč–25Kč (45¢–76¢); salad bar and light menu items 40Kč–120Kč ($1.20–$3.65). Daily 8am–midnight. Metro: Národní třída.

The Kavárna Slavia reopened in late 1997, saved from the dead after a half decade's absence prolonged by a Boston real estate speculator who was sitting on the property. President Havel, a Slavia regular when it was a dissident hangout, intervened, and after a long legal battle, the Slavia reopened on the Velvet Revolution's eighth anniversary. "A small victory for reason over stupidity," Havel called it. The restored art deco room recalls the place's 100 years as the rendezvous for the city's cultural and intellectual corps. The Slavia still has its relatively affordable menu of light fare served with the riverfront views of Prague Castle and the National Theater.

NEAR NÁMĚSTÍ MÍRU

Fondue. Slezská 20, Praha 2. ☎ **02/2425 0459.** Reservations suggested. Main courses 100Kč–350Kč ($3–$11). AE, MC, V. Daily 11:30am–1am. Metro: Náměstí Míru. FONDUE.

Once you claw through the dour ground-level bar and wind down a narrow staircase, this cook-it-yourself joint makes for a congenial meal in a pleasant earthy cellar. Choose from a variety of meats, including game, which you can sear on a hot stone, or order the Primator (Swiss cheese) or sweet-and-sour mix fondue for a bucket-o'-fun for two. The chocolate dessert fondues are certainly tempting. Radegast, a sometimes hard-to-find Moravian beer, and Irish Guinness are on tap.

✪ **Radost F/X Café.** Bělehradská 120, Praha 2. ☎ **02/2425 4776.** Main courses 60Kč–150Kč ($1.80–$4.55). MC, V. Daily 11am–5am. Metro: I. P. Pavlova. VEGETARIAN.

En vogue and vegetarian, Radost is a clubhouse for the hip new Bohemians, with plenty of Americans and others lingering too. The veggie burger is well seasoned and substantial on a grain bun, and the soups (like lentil and onion) are light and full of flavor. Saté vegetable dishes, tofu, and huge Greek salads round out the health-conscious menu. Avoid the poorly crusted pizzas. The dining area is a dark rec room with upholstered armchairs, chaise longues, 1960s couches, and coffee tables (from which you eat). Too cool.

5 Seeing the Sights

SIGHTSEEING SUGGESTIONS

Prague's intrigue comes from its outdoor sights—the architecture, the atmosphere, the shadows—best enjoyed by an aimless wander through the city's heart. If you have the time and energy, try taking a broad view of the grand Prague Castle and the Old Town skyline (best from Charles Bridge) at sunrise, then at sunset. You'll see two completely different cities.

Except for the busy main streets, where you may have to dodge traffic, this is an ideal city for walking. Actually, its the only way to truly explore it. Many of the oldest areas are walking zones, with motor traffic restricted. Wear comfortable, preferably flat, shoes. The crevices between the bricks in the streets have been known to eat stiletto heels.

IF YOU HAVE 1 DAY   In order to digest enough of Prague's wonders, do what visiting kings and potentates do on a 1-day visit: Walk the **Royal Route** from the top of the Hradčany hill (tram no. 22 or a taxi is suggested for the ride up unless you're very fit) and tour **Prague Castle** in the morning. After lunch, stroll across **Charles Bridge,** on the way to the winding alleys of **Old Town (Staré Město).**

IF YOU HAVE 2 DAYS   Spend Day 1 as above. On Day 2, explore the varied sights of **Old Town, Lesser Town,** and the **Jewish Quarter (Josefov)**—what you didn't have time for the day before. Wander and browse through numerous **shops** and **galleries** offering the finest Bohemian crystal, porcelain, and modern artwork, as well as top **boutiques, cafes,** and **restaurants.**

IF YOU HAVE 3 DAYS   Spend Days 1 and 2 as above, except go lighter on touring Prague Castle to begin the first day (your ticket for Prague Castle is good for 3 days). On Day 3, after seeing what you held over from the first day at the castle, visit the National Art Gallery at **Šternberk Palace,** the **Strahov Monastery** with its ornate libraries, and the **Loreto Palace** with its peculiar artwork.

IF YOU HAVE 5 DAYS OR MORE   Spend Days 1 to 3 as above. Beyond Day 3, try touring one of the many other museums or galleries or venture out of the city center. Visit the old southern citadel over the Vltava, **Vyšehrad,** where you get a completely different view of the city you've explored the past 3 days.

Beyond Prague's borders are easy day trips, such as an excursion to **Karlštejn Castle,** the most visited attraction outside Prague; **Karlovy Vary; Český Krumlov; Telč;** or **České Budějovice.**

PRAGUE CASTLE & CHARLES BRIDGE

Dating from the 14th century, ✪ **Charles Bridge (Karlův most),** Prague's most celebrated structure, links Prague Castle to Staré Město. For most of its 600 years, the 1,700-foot-long span has been a pedestrian promenade, though for centuries walkers had to share the concourse with horse-drawn vehicles and trolleys. Today, the bridge is filled with folks walking among folksy artists and busking musicians.

The best times to stroll across the bridge are in early morning or around sunset, when the crowds have thinned and the shadows are more mysterious. But you'll be crisscrossing the bridge throughout your stay.

✪ **Pražský Hrad (Prague Castle).** Hradčanské nám., Hradčany, Praha 1. ☎ **02/2437 3368.** Grounds, free. Combination ticket to four main castle attractions (St. Vitus Cathedral, Royal Palace, St. George's Basilica, Powder Tower), 100Kč ($3.05) adults, 50Kč ($1.50) students without guide; 150Kč ($4.55) adults, 100Kč ($3.05) students with English-speaking guide. Castle, daily 9am–5pm (to 4pm Nov–Mar). Metro: Line A to Malostranská or Hradčanská.

The huge hilltop complex known collectively as **Pražský Hrad (Prague Castle)** encompasses dozens of houses, towers, churches, courtyards, and monuments. A visit to the castle could easily take an entire day or more. Still, you can see the top sights— St. Vitus Cathedral, the Royal Palace, St. George's Basilica, the Powder Tower, plus Golden Lane—in the space of a morning or an afternoon.

St. Vitus Cathedral (Chrám sv. Víta), constructed in A.D. 926 as the court church of the Přemyslid princes, was named for a wealthy 4th-century Sicilian martyr and has long been the center of Prague's religious and political life. The key part of its Gothic construction took place in the 14th century under the direction of Mathias of Arras and Peter Parler of Gmuend. In the 18th and 19th centuries, subsequent baroque and neo-Gothic additions were made. In 1997, Pope John Paul II visited Prague to honor the 1,000th anniversary of the death of 10th-century Slavic evangelist St. Vojtěch. He conferred the saint's name on the cathedral along with St. Vitus's, but officially the Czech state calls it just St. Vitus.

The ✪ **Royal Palace (Královský palác),** in the third courtyard of the castle grounds, served as the residence of kings between the 10th and the 17th centuries. Vaulted Vladislav Hall, the interior's centerpiece, was used for coronations and special occasions. Here Václav Havel was inaugurated president. The adjacent Diet was where the king met with advisers and where the supreme court was held. You'll find a good selection of guidebooks, maps, and other related information at the entrance.

St. George's Basilica (Kostel sv. Jiří), adjacent to the Royal Palace, is Prague's oldest Romanesque structure, from the 10th century. It was also Bohemia's first convent. No longer serving a religious function, the building now houses a museum of historic Czech art.

Golden Lane (Zlatá ulička) is a picturesque street of tiny 16th-century servants' houses built into the castle fortifications. The houses now contain shops, galleries, and refreshment bars. In 1917, Franz Kafka lived briefly at no. 22.

The **Powder Tower (Prašná věž a.k.a. Mihulka)** forms part of the northern bastion of the castle complex just off the Golden Lane. Originally a gunpowder storehouse and a canon tower, it was turned into a laboratory for the 17th-century alchemists serving the court of Emperor Rudolf II.

Getting Tickets: Tickets are sold at the **Prague Castle Information Center** (☎ 02/2437 3368), in the second courtyard after passing through the main gate from Hradčanské náměstí. The center also arranges tours in various languages and sells tickets for individual concerts and exhibits held on the castle grounds.

THE TOP MUSEUMS

Bertramka (W. A. Mozart Museum). Mozartova 169, Praha 5. ☎ 02/543 893. Admission 50Kč ($1.50) adults, 30Kč (90¢) students. Daily 9:30am–6pm. Tram: 2, 6, 7, 9, 14, or 16 from Anděl metro station.

Mozart loved Prague, and when he visited he often stayed with the family who owned this villa, the Dušeks. Now a museum, the villa contains displays that include his written work and harpsichord. There's also a lock of Mozart's hair, encased in a cube of glass. Much of the Bertramka villa was destroyed by fire in the 1870s, but Mozart's rooms, where he finished composing *Don Giovanni,* have miraculously remained untouched.

The Jewish Museum in Prague. Maisel Synagogue, Maiselova (between Široká and Jáchymova), Praha 1. ☎ 02/2481 0099. Combined admission to all museum parts 450Kč ($14) adults, 330Kč ($10) students. May–Oct tours for groups of 10 or more on the hour starting 9am (last tour 4pm). Nov–Apr tours leave whenever enough people gather in same language. Metro: Staroměstská.

The Jewish Museum is the organization managing all the Jewish landmarks in Josefov, which forms the northwest quarter of Old Town. The organization provides guided package tours as part of a comprehensive admission price, with an English-speaking guide. The package includes the **Ceremonial Hall, Old Jewish Cemetery, Old-New Synagogue, Pinkas Synagogue, Klaus Synagogue,** and **Maisel Synagogue.**

The Maisel Synagogue serves as the exhibition space for the Jewish Museum. In October 1994, the State Jewish Museum closed; the Torah covers, 100,000 books, and other exhibits once housed there were given to the Jewish community, who then proceeded to return many items to synagogues throughout the country. Most of Prague's ancient Judaica was destroyed by the Nazis during World War II. Ironically, those

Prague Castle

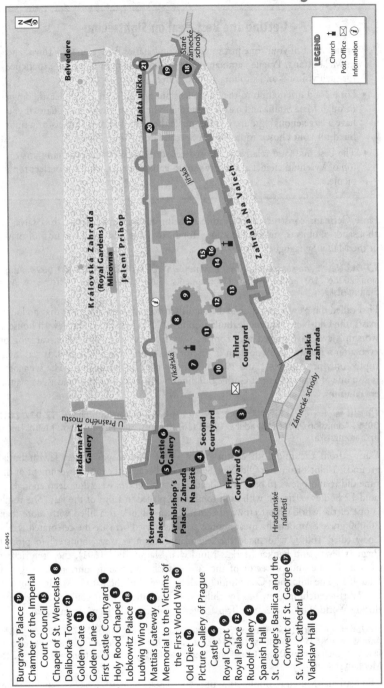

Getting the Best Deal on Sightseeing

- Spend most of your time just wandering on Charles Bridge, in Old Town, and in Malá Strana. Prague's ambiance and architecture offer a unique experience for each visitor—and strolling around is free.

- For a good orientation to the city, take tram no. 22 from Prague Castle down through Malá Strana and past the National Theater to Wenceslas Square. If you have a large enough group, you can make the trip affordably in a historic tram hired for your chosen route (see "A Special Group Tour," below).

- The best free (and relatively tourist-free) scenic view is from the ramparts on top of Vyšehrad citadel at the city's south end. The park within is perfect for a picnic.

---

same Germans constructed an "exotic museum of an extinct race," thus salvaging thousands of objects, such as the valued Torah covers, books, and silver now displayed at the Maisel Synagogue.

✪ **Old-New Synagogue (Staronová synagóga).** Červená 2. ☎ **02/2481 0099.** Admission 200Kč ($6) adults, 100Kč ($3) students. Sun–Fri 9am–6pm. Metro: Line A to Staroměstská.

First called the New Synagogue to distinguish it from an even older one that no longer exists, the Old-New Synagogue, built around 1270, is Europe's oldest Jewish house of worship. Jews have prayed here continuously for more than 700 years, carrying on even after a massive 1389 pogrom in Josefov that killed over 3,000 Jews. It was interrupted only between 1941 and 1945 because of the Nazi occupation. The synagogue is also one of Prague's largest Gothic buildings, with vaulted ceilings and Renaissance-era columns.

✪ **Old Jewish Cemetery (Starý židovský hřbitov).** U Starého hřbitova. ☎ **02/ 2481 0099.** Admission 250Kč ($8) adults, 190Kč ($6) students. Sun–Fri 9am–6pm. Metro: Line A to Staroměstská.

Dating from the mid-15th century, this is one of Europe's oldest Jewish burial grounds, 1 block from the Old-New Synagogue. Because the local government of the time didn't allow Jews to bury their dead elsewhere, graves were dug deep enough to hold 12 bodies vertically, with each tombstone placed in front of the last. The result is one of the world's most crowded cemeteries: a 1-block area filled with more than 20,000 graves. Among the most famous persons buried here are the celebrated Rabbi Loew (died 1609), who made the legendary Golem (a clay "monster" to protect Prague's Jews), and banker Markus Mordechai Maisel (died 1601), then the richest man in Prague and protector of the city's Jewish community during the reign of Rudolf II. The adjoining **Ceremonial Hall** at the end of the path is worth a look for the heart-wrenching drawings by children held at the Terezín concentration camp during World War II (see "Side Trips," later in this chapter for more on Terezín).

National Museum (Národní muzeum). Václavské nám. 68, Praha 1. ☎ **02/2423 0485.** Admission 40Kč ($1.20) adults, 15Kč (45¢) students, free for under age 6. Free for everyone first Mon each month. Daily 10am–6pm; closed first Tues each month. Metro: Line A or C to Muzeum station.

The National Museum, dominating upper Václavské náměstí, looks so much like an important government building that it even fooled the Communists, who fired on it during their 1968 invasion. If you look closely you can still see shell marks. The second oldest museum in the Czech lands, this neo-Renaissance-style museum opened in 1893. On the first floor is an exhaustive collection of minerals, rocks, and meteorites from the Czech and Slovak Republics. Only 12,000 of the museum's collection of more than 200,000 rocks and gems are on display, all neatly arranged in old wooden cases.

Šternberk Palace Art Museum (Šternberský palác). Hradčanské nám. 15, Praha 1. ☎ **02/2051 4599.** Admission 70Kč ($2.10) adults, 40Kč ($1.20) students/children. Tues–Sun 10am–6pm. Metro: Line A to Malostranská or Hradčanská.

The jewel in the National Gallery crown, the gallery at Šternberk Palace, adjacent to the main gate of Prague Castle, displays a wide menu of European art throughout the ages. It features six centuries of everything from oils to sculptures. The permanent collection is divided chronologically into pre–19th-century art, 19th- and 20th-century art, and 20th-century French painting and sculpture. The collection includes a good selection of cubist works by Braque and Picasso. Temporary exhibits, like Italian Renaissance bronzes, are always on show.

Veletržní Palace. Veletržní at Dukelských hrdinů 47, Praha 7. ☎ **02/2430 1111.** Admission 80Kč ($2.40); family pass 120Kč ($3.65). Tues–Sun 10am–6pm (Thurs to 9pm). Metro: Line C to Vltavská or tram 17.

This remodeled 1925 palace, built for trade fairs and reopened in December 1995, now holds the bulk of the National Gallery's collection of 20th-century works by Czech and other European artists. Three atrium-lit concourses provide a comfortable setting for some catchy and kitschy Czech sculpture and multimedia works.

Alas, the best cubist works by Braque and Picasso, Rodin bronzes, and many other primarily French pieces have been relegated to a poorly lit chalky section on the second floor. Several sections are devoted to peculiar but thought-provoking works from Czech artists that show how creativity still flowed under the weight of the Iron Curtain. Many traveling foreign temporary exhibits are shown on the first floor.

MORE ATTRACTIONS

Chrám sv. Mikuláše (Cathedral of St. Nicholas). Malostranské nám. Praha 1. Free admission. Daily 9am–5pm. Metro: Line A to Malostranská.

This church is critically regarded as one of the best examples of the high baroque north of the Alps. K. I. Dienzenhofer's 1711 design was augmented by his son Krystof's 260-foot-high dome, which dominates the Malá Strana skyline and was completed in 1752. While Prague's smog has played havoc with the building's exterior, its gilded interior is stunning. Gold-capped marble-veneered columns frame altars packed with statuary and frescoes.

Estates' Theater (Stavovské divadlo). Ovocný trh 1, Praha 1. ☎ **02/2421 4339.** Metro: Line A or B to Můstek.

The theater was completed in 1783 by the wealthy Count F. A. Nostitz, and Mozart staged the premier of *Don Giovanni* here in 1787 because he said the conservative patrons in Vienna didn't appreciate him or his passionate and often shocking work. "Praguers understand me," Mozart was quoted as saying. Czech director Miloš Forman returned to his native country to film his Oscar-winning *Amadeus*, shooting the scenes of Mozart in Prague with perfect authenticity at the Estates' Theater.

The theater doesn't have daily tours, but tickets for performances—and the chance to sit in one of the elegant private boxes—are usually available. Tour events are occasionally scheduled, and individual tours can be arranged by calling the city heritage group **Pražská vlastivěda** at ☎ **02/2481 6184.**

Prague

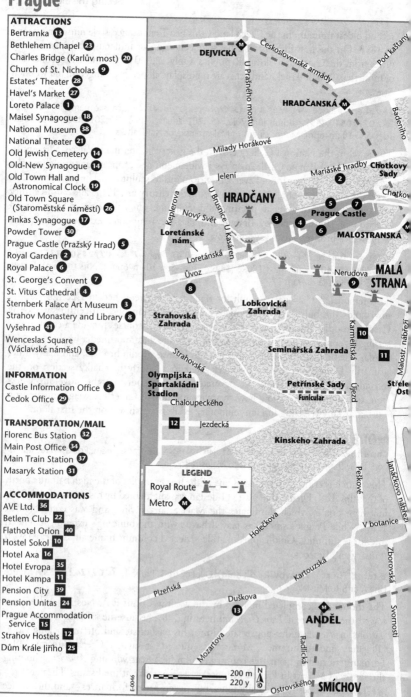

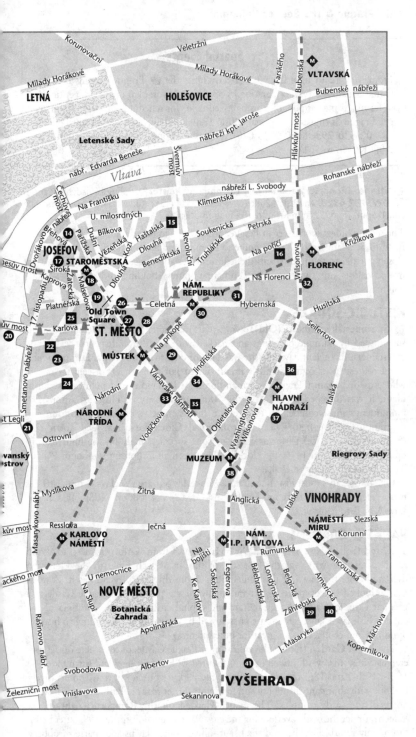

Special Events

From May 12 to June 2, 1999, the city hosts the ✪ **Prague Spring International Music Festival,** celebrating its 53rd year. If you plan to attend, get tickets as far in advance as possible through Čedok, or for schedules and tickets contact the Prague Spring International Music Festival, Hellichova 18, 11800 Praha 1 (☎ **02/530 293;** fax 02/536 040). Tickets for concerts range from 250Kč to 2,000Kč ($8 to $61).

✪ **Strahov Monastery and Library (Strahovský klášter).** Strahovské nádvoří, Praha 1. ☎ **02/5732 0828.** Admission 20Kč (60¢) adults, 5Kč (15¢) students. Tues–Sun 9am–noon and 1–5pm. Tram: 22 from Malostranská metro station.

The second oldest monastery in Prague, Strahov was founded high above Malá Strana in 1143 by Vladislav II. It's still home to Premonstratensian monks, a scholarly order closely related to the Jesuits, and their dormitories and refectory are off-limits. What draws visitors are the monastery's ornate libraries, holding more than 125,000 volumes.

HISTORIC SQUARES

✪ **Staroměstské náměstí (Old Town Square)** is the city's most celebrated square, surrounded by baroque buildings and packed with colorful craftspeople, cafes, and entertainers. In ancient days, the site was a major crossroads on central European merchant routes. In its center stands a **memorial to Jan Hus,** the 15th-century martyr who crusaded against Prague's German-dominated religious and political establishment; it was unveiled in 1915 on the 500th anniversary of Hus's execution. The monument's most compelling features are the asymmetry of the composition and the fluidity of the figures. The **Astronomical Clock (orloj)** at Old Town Hall (Staroměstská radnice) performs a glockenspiel spectacle daily on the hour 8am to 8pm. Constructed in 1410, the clock has long been an important symbol of Prague. Take the metro to Staroměstská.

One of the city's most historic squares, **Wenceslas Square (Václavské náměstí)** has thrice been the site of riots and revolutions—in 1848, 1968, and 1989. Take metro Line A or B to Můstek.

PARKS & GARDENS

Vyšehrad, Soběslavova 1 (☎ **02/296 651;** Tram: 3 from Karlovo náměstí to Výtoň south of New Town), was the first seat of the first Czech kings in the Přemyslid dynasty before the dawn of this millennium. From this spot, legend has it, Princess Libuše looked out over the Vltava valley toward the present-day Prague Castle and predicted the founding of a great state and capital city. Within the confines of the citadel, lush lawns and gardens are crisscrossed by dozens of paths leading to historic buildings and cemeteries. It's great for quiet picnics.

The **Royal Garden (Královská zahrada)** at Prague Castle, once the site of the sovereigns' vineyards, was founded in 1534. Dotted with lemon trees and surrounded by 16th-, 17th-, and 18th-century buildings, the park is consciously and conservatively laid out with abundant shrubbery and fountains. Enter from U Prašného mostu street north of the castle complex. The castle's **Garden on the Ramparts (Zahrada na Valech),** under the castle overlooking the city, was reopened in spring 1995 after being thoroughly refurbished. Beyond the beautifully groomed lawns and sparse shrubbery is a tranquil low-angle view of the castle above and one of the best views of Prague below. Enter the garden from the south side of the castle complex below Hradčanské náměstí. These gardens are open Tuesday to Sunday 9am to 5pm.

A SPECIAL GROUP TOUR

If you're traveling in a large group and really want a unique sightseeing experience, why not rent your own classic trolley? With enough people it really can be affordable thanks to the **Historic Tram Tour (Elektrické dráhy DP)**, Patočkova 4, Praha 6 (☎ and fax **02/312 3349;** Metro: Hradčanská, then tram 1, 8, or 18 two stops west).

If you send a fax with details 1 day ahead, the city transport department will arrange a private tour using one of the turn-of-the-century wooden trams that actually traveled on regular lines through Prague. Up to 24 people can fit in one car, which sports wooden-planked floors, cast-iron conductor's levers, and the "ching-ching" of a proper tram bell.

It costs 2,500Kč ($75) per hour. Up to 60 people can fit into a double car for 3,000Kč ($94) per hour. You can also order a cold smorgasbord with coffee, beer, champagne, a waiter to serve, and an accordion player if you wish. You can choose the route the tram takes—the no. 22 route is best.

6 Shopping

BEST BUYS

Czech porcelain, glass, and cheap but well-constructed clothing draw hoards of day-trippers from nearby Germany. In no sector of the economy has the change from communism to capitalism been more apparent than on the shopping front. Craft and specialty shops abound, and you can find good deals in street markets, art studios, and galleries. Shops lining the main route **from Old Town Square to Charles Bridge** are great for browsing. For clothing, porcelain, jewelry, garnets, and glass, stroll around **Wenceslas Square and Na příkopě,** the street connecting Wenceslas Square with náměstí Republiky.

SELECT SHOPS & MARKETS

Bohemian glass, porcelain, jewelry, and other specialty items can be packed and shipped directly from **Exclusive,** Vodičkova 28, Praha 1 (☎ **02/2416 2586;** Metro: Line A to Můstek or Museum). At **Cristallino,** Celetná 12, Praha 1 (☎ **02/261 265;** Metro: Náměstí Repubiky), you'll find a good selection of stemware and vases in traditional designs. The shop's central location belies its excellent prices.

Havelský trh (Havel's Market), Havelská ulice, Praha 1 (Metro: Line A to Můstek), is on a short street running perpendicular to Melantrichova, the main route connecting Staroměstské náměstí with Václavské náměstí. This open-air market (named well before a Havel became president) features dozens of private vendors selling seasonal home-grown fruits and vegetables. Other goods, including flowers and cheese, are also for sale. Since this place is designed primarily for locals, the prices are exceedingly low by Western European standards. The market is a great place to pick up picnic supplies and is open Monday to Friday 7am to 6pm.

BOOKSTORES

The largest English-language bookshops are **The Globe,** Janovského 14, Praha 7 (☎ **02/6671 2610;** Metro: Vltavská); **Big Ben Bookshop,** Malá Štupartská 5, Praha 1 (☎ **02/231 8021;** Metro: Můstek); and **U Knihomola,** Mánesova 79, Praha 2 (☎ **02/627 7770;** Metro: Jiøiho z Poděbrad).

7 Prague After Dark

Prague's nightlife has changed completely since the Velvet Revolution—for the better if you plan to go clubbing, for the worse if you hope to sample the city's classical offerings. Still, seeing *Don Giovanni* in the Estates' Theater, where Mozart first premiered it, is worth the admission. Ticket prices, while low by Western standards, have become prohibitively high for the average Czech. However, you'll find the exact reverse in the rock and jazz scene. Dozens of clubs have opened, and world-class bands are finally playing in Prague on their European tours.

Turn to the *Prague Post* for listings of cultural events and nightlife around the city; it's available at most newsstands in Old Town and Malá Strana.

Once in Prague, you can purchase tickets at theater box offices or from any one of dozens of agencies throughout the city center. Large centrally located agencies are the **Prague Tourist Center,** Rytířská 12, Praha 1 (☎ 02/2421 2209; Metro: Můstek), open daily 9am to 7pm; **Bohemia Ticket International,** Na příkopě 16, Praha 1 (☎ 02/2421 5031; Metro: Můstek); and **Čedok,** Na příkopě 18, Praha 1 (☎ 02/2481 1870; Metro: Můstek).

THE PERFORMING ARTS

Though there's plenty of music year-round, the symphonies and orchestras all come to life during the ✪ **Prague Spring Music Festival,** a 3-week series of concerts featuring the country's top performers, as well as noted guest conductors and soloists and visiting symphony orchestras. For more details, see the box "Special Events," earlier in this chapter.

The Czech Philharmonic Orchestra and Prague Symphony Orchestra usually perform at the **Rudolfinum,** náměstí Jana Palacha, Praha 1 (☎ 02/2489 3352; Metro: Staroměstská). The Czech Philharmonic is the traditional voice of the country's national pride, often playing works by Dvořák and Smetana; the Prague Symphony often ventures into more eclectic territory. Tickets range from 100Kč to 600Kč ($3.05 to $18).

In a city full of spectacularly beautiful theaters, the massive pale-green **Estates' Theater (Stavovské divadlo),** Ovocný trh 1, Praha 1 (☎ 02/2421 5001; Metro: Line A or B to Můstek), is one of the most awesome. Built in 1783 and site of the premiere of Mozart's *Don Giovanni* (conducted by the composer), the theater now hosts many of the classic productions of European opera and drama. Simultaneous English translation, transmitted via headphone, is available for most plays. Tickets cost 200Kč to 1,000Kč ($6 to $33).

Lavishly constructed in the late Renaissance style of northern Italy, the gold-crowned **Národní divadlo (National Theater),** Národní 2, Praha 1 (☎ 02/2491 3437; Metro: Národní třída), overlooking the Vltava River, is one of Prague's most recognizable landmarks. Completed in 1881, the theater was built to nurture the Czech National Revival—a grassroots movement to replace the dominant German culture with that of native Czechs. Today's classic productions are staged in a larger setting than at the Estates' Theater, but with about the same ticket prices.

The National Theater Ballet performs at the National Theater. The troupe has seen most of its top talent go West since 1989, but it still puts on a good show. Some critics have complained that Prague's top company has been performing virtually the same dances for many years and they're in serious need of refocusing. Choreographer Libor Vaculík has responded with humorous and quirky stagings of off-the-wall ballets like *Some Like It Hot* and *Psycho.* Tickets cost 200Kč to 600Kč ($6 to $18).

Laterna Magika, Národní třída 4, Praha 1 (☎ **02/2491 4129;** Metro: Národní třída), is a performance-art show based in the new wing of the National Theater. The multimedia show, which combines live theater with film and dance, was once considered on the radical edge. The shows are not for those easily offended by nudity. Tickets are 400Kč ($12).

THE CLUB & MUSIC SCENE

Prague's club and music scene is limited but lively. Rock acts have a local garage-band sound but are adding more sophisticated numbers to their gigs. Many venerable jazz groups who toiled in the underground caverns are finding a new audience in visitors who stumble on their clubs.

ROCK & DANCE CLUBS   At **Lávka,** Novotného lávka 1, Praha 1 (☎ **02/2421 4797;** Metro: Staroměstská), straightforward dance hits attract one of Prague's best-looking young crowds. Because of its location next to the Staré Město foot of Charles Bridge, Lávka also attracts a lot of less-well-dressed visitors. Open 24 hours, the club is one of the nicest in town, offering a large bar, a good dance floor, and fantastic outdoor seating in warm months. Cover is 50Kč to 100Kč ($1.50 to $3.05).

Popular with a mixed gay and model crowd, **Radost F/X,** Bělehradská 120, Praha 2 (☎ **02/251 210;** Metro: I. P. Pavlova), is built in the American mold. A subterranean labyrinth of nooks and crannies has a pulsating techno-heavy dance floor with good sight lines for wallflowers. Radost, extremely stylish and self-consciously urban, is open daily 9pm to 5am. Cover is usually about 50Kč ($1.50).

One of the city's most unusual venues, **Roxy,** Dlouhá 33, Praha 1 (☎ **02/2481 0951;** Metro: Náměstí Republiky), is a subterranean theater with a wraparound balcony overlooking a concrete dance floor. The club is ultra-downscale and extremely popular on Friday and Saturday. Persian rugs and lanterns soften the atmosphere but don't improve the lousy acoustics. Acid jazz, funk, techno, ambient, and other danceable tunes attract an artsy crowd. Arrive after midnight. It's open Tuesday to Saturday 8pm to 6am. The cover is 50Kč ($1.50), more for concerts.

JAZZ CLUBS   Relatively high prices guarantee the small **AghaRTA Jazz Centrum,** Krakovská 5, Praha 1 (☎ **02/2421 2914;** Metro: Muzeum), a predominantly foreign crowd. Upscale by Czech standards, the AghaRTA regularly features some of the best music in town, from standard acoustic trios to Dixieland, funk, and fusion. Hot Line, the house band led by the AghaRTA part-owner and drummer extraordinaire Michael Hejuna, regularly takes the stage with its keyboard-and-sax Crusaders-like sound. Bands usually begin at 9pm. The club is open Monday to Friday 4pm to 1am and Saturday and Sunday 7pm to 1am. Cover is 60Kč to 100Kč ($1.80 to $3.05).

The **Reduta Jazz Club,** Národní 20, Praha 1 (☎ **02/2491 2246;** Metro: Národní třída), is a smoky subterranean room that looks exactly like a jazz cellar should. An adventurous booking policy, which even included a saxophone gig with a U.S. president in 1994, means that different bands play almost every night. Music usually starts around 9:30pm. It's open Monday to Saturday 9pm to midnight. Admission is usually 100Kč ($3.05).

BARS & BEER HALLS   For Czech pubs, see "Great Deals on Dining," earlier in this chapter. At **Molly Malone's,** U Obecního Dvora 4, Praha 1 (☎ **02/231 6222;** Metro: Staroměstská), Guinness is on tap and you'll find worn-out Pogues CDs and a warm fireplace. Pub meals are served daily noon to 8pm, and the place is open Sunday to Thursday noon to 12:30am and Friday and Saturday 2pm to 1:30am. Hidden on an Old Town back street, the loud and lively **Chapeau Rouge/Banana Cafe,** Jakubská

We're Here for the Beer

While most post-Communist Czechs aren't very religious, one thing that elicits a piety unseen in many orthodox countries is *pivo* (beer). The golden nectar has inspired some of the most popular Czech fiction and films, poetry and prayers. For many, getting it straight from the tap is the best reason to visit Bohemia.

Czechs have brewed beer since the 9th century, but the golden lager *(lexák)* known around the world as Pilsner was born in 1842 in the western Bohemian town of Plzeň (Pilsen in German). Before then, beers and ales carried a murky, dull body, but the Pilsner method kept the brew bright and golden. What's unique here, experts say, is the exceptionally light and crisp hops grown on vines in the western Bohemian region of Žatec.

Czechs drink more beer per capita than any people in the world—320 pints of brew each year, according to industry studies, compared with 190 pints for Americans.

The debate over which Czech beer is best rages on, but here are some top contenders, all readily available in Prague (each pub or restaurant usually will flaunt its choice on the front of the building):

Budvar: The original "Budweiser," a semisweet lager that hails from České Budějovice.

Gambrinus: The best-selling domestic label, direct from the Pilsner Breweries, smooth and solid, not too bitter.

Pilsner Urquell: The more familiar, bitter brother of Gambrinus, packaged mostly for export.

Staropramen: The flagship label from Prague's home brewery is a hardy standby and easiest to find.

Krušovice: A favorite with American expatriates bred on light beer—heavy, somewhat sweet, yet with a spicy aroma that surrounds the back of your gullet.

2, Praha 1 (no phone; Metro: Staroměstská), has twin bars, industrial metal wall sconces, plank floors, and a good sound system playing contemporary rock. It sells four types of beer on tap and features regular drink specials. Open daily noon to 5am, it's busy and fun—if you avoid the headache-inducing concoctions from the frozen drink machine.

GAY & LESBIAN BARS For details on the gay and lesbian community, call the **SOHO Infocentrum** at ☎ 02/2422 0327. For a stylish place to dance, try **Radost F/X** (see above). Lesbians should look for **"A" Klub,** Milíčova 32, Praha 3 (no phone; Metro: Flora, then tram 9). This sharply decorated bar is covered with the works of female artists and sports cushy chairs and couches. Friday is only for women. Men are allowed on other nights, but only in the company of a woman. There's dancing and relaxed chat here daily 6pm to 6am. Cover is 25Kč (75¢).

Borsalino, Husitská 7, Praha 3 (☎ 02/627 8971; Metro: Florenc, then bus no. 133 to Husitská), is a multiactivity venue formerly known as Aqua Club 2000, and it attracts a mixed gay and lesbian crowd. This has become Prague's transvestite paradise, with weekend shows touted for their precision and authenticity. On the premises is a sauna and a disco. Open midnight to 4am (disco 9pm to 4am), Borsalina charges a cover of 30Kč (99¢) Monday to Wednesday and 80Kč ($2.40) Thursday to Saturday.

Just across the tracks from the main train station is the **Fire Club,** Seifertova 3, Praha 3 (no phone; Metro: Hlavní nádraží), which used to be the rock palace Alterna

Komotovka. It has been transformed to a wild pink-and-neon cavern serving an almost exclusively gay crowd and the original Budweiser on tap. It's open Friday and Saturday 9pm until whenever they feel like closing. No cover.

8 Side Trips: The Best of Bohemia

The rush of visitors into the new Czech Republic has been concentrated in Prague, but there are several destinations in the outlying regions worthy of attention. You can book train tickets and check schedules in Prague at **Čedok,** Na příkopě 18, Praha 1 (☎ **02/2419 7111**). Čedok also arranges tours with guides in several languages.

Thirty miles northwest of Prague is the ✪ **Terezín** concentration camp. At the so-called Paradise Ghetto, there were no gas chambers, mass machine-gun executions, or medical testing. Terezín wasn't used to exterminate the Jews, gays, Gypsies, and political prisoners it held. The Nazis used it as a transit camp. About 140,000 people passed though the gates; more than half ended up at Auschwitz or Treblinka. Prague-based **Wittman Tours** (☎ **02/25 12 35**) offers a bus tour to Terezín that costs 1,000Kč ($30). Call for tour times. To arrange a guide at Terezín, contact the **Town Information Center** on náměstí čs. Armady 84 (☎ **0416/92 369**). Expect to pay about 50Kč to 150Kč ($1.50 to $4.55) per person. However, the best way to see Terezín is with the **Matana** travel agency. The all-day tour includes lunch, a documentary, and transportation and is well worth 1,050Kč ($32), slightly less for students or children.

KARLŠTEJN CASTLE

The most popular day trip from Prague, the spectacular Romanesque ✪ **Karlštejn Castle,** 18 miles west of Prague, was founded in 1348 by Charles IV. However, it's more spectacular outside than inside since vandalism has forced the closure of several of its finest rooms.

ARRIVING   Trains leave from Prague's Smíchov Station (at the Smíchovské nádraží metro stop) hourly and take about 45 minutes. One-way second-class fare is 22Kč (67¢). If you **drive,** leave Prague from the southwest along Hwy. 4 in the direction of Strakonice and take the Karlštejn cutoff, following the signs. It'll take 30 minutes.

SEEING THE CASTLE   **The walk up the hill to Karlštejn, along with the view, makes the trip worthwhile. When you do reach the top, take some time to look out over the town and down the Well Tower. You then need to decide if the 100Kč ($3.05) tour is worth it. Be prepared: The **Holy Rood Chapel, famous for the more than 2,000 precious and semiprecious inlaid gems adorning its walls, and the **Chapel of St. Catherine** are closed. What is open are several rooms, most in the south palace. But the tour isn't a total waste of time. The **Audience Hall** and the **Imperial Bedroom** are impressive, despite being stripped of the original furnishings. Admission is 100Kč ($3.05) adults and 50Kč ($1.50) children. It's open daily: May, June, and September 9am to noon and 12:30 to 6pm; July and August 9am to noon and 12:30 to 7pm; and November and December 9am to noon and 1 to 4pm.

ACCOMMODATIONS   **For romance, head to the ✪ **Hotel Mlýn, 267 27 Karl-štejn (☎ **0311/94 194;** fax 0311/94 219). On the river's edge opposite the castle, the Mlýn is a reasonably priced country inn. Its 15 rooms are a bit small but quaint and nicely decorated. At the patio bar and restaurant, you can relax and enjoy the soothing river sounds. Rates are 600Kč ($18) single, 900Kč ($27) double, and 1,700Kč ($52) suite. Breakfast is 280Kč ($9), and Visa and MasterCard are accepted. Take the bridge across the river that leads to the rail station and turn left at the first street.

DINING   The ✪ **Restaurace Blanky z Valois,** on the main street, tries for a Provençal feel. While this cozy place doesn't exactly take you to France, the covered patio (where all but two of the eight or so tables are located) can be romantic. The food is a cut above the standard, with wild game like rabbit, boar, and venison the specialty. Main courses are 150Kč to 320Kč ($4.55 to $10); MasterCard and Visa are accepted. The restaurant is open daily 11am to 10pm.

ČESKÝ KRUMLOV

If you have time for only one excursion, make it ✪ **Český Krumlov,** 12 miles southwest of České Budějovice (see below) and 104 miles south of Prague. It's a living gallery of elegant Renaissance-era buildings housing cafes, pubs, restaurants, shops, and galleries. In 1992, UNESCO named it a World Heritage Site.

ARRIVING   The only way to reach Český Krumlov by **train** from Prague is via České Budějovice, a slow ride that'll deposit you at a station far from the town center. It takes 3½ hours; the fare is 136Kč ($5) first class or 96Kč ($3.55) second. From České Budějovice, it's about a 45-minute **drive** to Krumlov, depending on traffic. Take Hwy. 3 leading from the south of České Budějovice and turn onto Hwy. 159. The roads are clearly marked, with several signs directing traffic to the town. From Prague, it's a 2-hour drive.

The nearly 3-hour **bus** ride from Prague usually involves a transfer in České Budějovice. The fare is 125Kč ($4.15), and the bus station in Český Krumlov is a 15-minute walk from the main square.

SEEING THE SIGHTS   The town is split into the **Inner town** and **Latrán,** which houses the castle. Begin at the **Okresní Muzeum (Regional Museum)** (☎ 0337/711 674) at the top of Horní ulice, containing artifacts and displays relating to Český Krumlov's 1,000-year history. The highlight is a giant model of the town. Admission is 20Kč (60¢), and it's open Tuesday to Sunday 10am to 12:30pm and 1 to 6pm.

Across the street is the **Hotel Růže (Rose),** once a Jesuit student house. Built in the late 16th century, the hotel and the prelature next door show Gothic, Renaissance, and rococo influences. Don't be afraid to walk around and even ask questions at the reception desk. Continue down the street to the impressive Late Gothic **St. Vitus Cathedral.** Be sure to climb the tower for its spectacular view.

Continue down the street to **náměstí Svorností.** Few buildings show any character, making the main square of such an impressive town a bit disappointing. The **Radnice (Town Hall),** at náměstí Svorností 1, is one of the few exceptions. Its Gothic arcades and Renaissance vault inside are beautiful. From the square, streets fan out in all directions. Take some time just to wander through them. As you cross the bridge and head toward the castle, you'll see immediately to your right the former **hospital and church of St. Jošt.** Founded at the beginning of the 14th century, it has since been turned into apartments.

The second largest castle in Bohemia (after Prague Castle), the ✪ **Český Krumlov Château** was built in the 13th century. There's a long climb up. First greeting you will be a round 12th-century **tower,** with a Renaissance balcony, and then you'll pass over the moat, now occupied by two brown bears. Next is the **Dolní Hrad (Lower Castle)** and then the **Horní Hrad (Upper Castle).** The château is open April to October, exclusively by 1-hour guided tour. Most tours are in Czech or German. If you want an English-language tour, arrange it ahead by calling ☎ 0337/711 465. Past the main castle building, you can see one of the more stunning views of Český Krumlov from **most Na Plášti,** a walkway that doubles as a belvedere.

The castle hours are Tuesday to Sunday: May to August 7:45am to noon and 12:45 to 4pm, September 8:45am to noon and 12:45 to 4pm, and April and October

8:45am to noon and 12:45 to 3pm. The last entrance is 1 hour before closing. The tour is 100Kč ($3.05) adults and 50Kč ($1.50) students.

DINING   Open daily 7am to 11pm, **Rybařská Bašta Jakuba Krčína**, Kájovská 54 (☎ **0337/671 83**), specializes in freshwater fish, with main courses at 120Kč to 300Kč ($3.65 to $9). Trout, perch, pike, and eel are sautéed, grilled, baked, and fried in a variety of herbs and spices. Venison, rabbit, and other game are also available, along with roast beef and pork cutlet. Reservations are recommended, and American Express, MasterCard, and Visa are accepted.

ČESKÉ BUDĚJOVICE

The fortress town of **České Budějovice,** 92 miles south of Prague, was born in 1265, when Otakar II decided that the intersection of the Vltava and Malše rivers would be the site of a bastion to protect southern Bohemia. Though Otakar was killed in battle in 1278 and the town was subsequently ravaged by the rival Vítkovic family, the construction of České Budějovice continued, eventually taking the shape originally envisaged.

In the 15th century, the Hussite revolution swept across southern Bohemia, with one exception—České Budějovice. It developed into one of Bohemia's wealthiest and most important towns, reaching its pinnacle in the 16th century. This rise made České Budějovice an architecturally stunning place. Today it's the hometown of the original Budweiser brand beer.

ARRIVING   Daily **express trains** from Prague make the trip in about 2½ hours. The fare is 124Kč ($4.59) first class or 88Kč ($3.25) second. Several **express buses** run from Prague's Florenc station each day and take 2 hours. If you're **driving,** leave Prague to the south via the main D1 expressway and take the cutoff for Hwy. E55, which runs straight to České Budějovice. The trip takes about 1½ hours.

SEEING THE SIGHTS   At the town center is the large cobblestone **náměstí Přemysla Otakara II,** with the ornate **Fountain of Sampson,** an 18th-century water well that was once the town's principal water supply, plus baroque and Renaissance buildings. On the southwest corner is the baroque **Town Hall,** built between 1727 and 1730. On top, the larger-than-life statues represent the civic virtues: justice, bravery, wisdom, and diligence. A block northwest is the **Černá věž (Black Tower),** whose 360 steps are worth the climb to get a bird's-eye view. This 232-foot-tall 16th-century tower was built as a belfry for the adjacent **St. Nicholas Church.** You shouldn't miss its flamboyant baroque interior.

On the town's northern edge is where **Budějovický Budvar** (☎ **038/770 5111**), the original brewer of Budweiser beer, has its only factory. Established in 1895, Budvar draws on more than 700 years of the area's brewing tradition to produce one of the world's best beers. Trolley-bus nos. 2, 4, 6, and 8 stop by the brewery, costing 6Kč (18¢). You can hop a cab from the town square for about 100Kč to 150Kč ($3.35 to $4.45). Tours can be arranged by phoning ahead, but only for groups. If you're alone or with only one or two others, ask a concierge at one of the bigger hotels (I suggest the Zvon) if he or she can put you in with an already scheduled group.

Only 8 kilometers north of town is the 141-room ✪ **Hluboká nad Vltavou,** once the home of the Schwarzenberg family. The distance is short enough to make a pleasant bike trip from the city or a quick stop on the way to or coming from Prague. The castle is open April to October, Tuesday to Sunday 10am to 5:30pm. Tours in English run at 11am and 2 and 4pm and cost 60Kč ($1.80). If you're driving from České Budějovice, take Hwy. E49 north and then Hwy. 105 just after leaving the outskirts. For cyclists or those driving who prefer a slower, more scenic route, take the road that runs behind the brewery; it passes through the village of Obora. From the

13th century, Hluboká has undergone many face-lifts, but none that left as lasting an impression as those by the Schwarzenbergs. In the mid-19th century, they remodeled the castle in the neo-Gothic style of England's Windsor Castle. The **Alšova Jihočeská Galerie (Art Gallery of South Bohemia),** in the riding school, houses Bohemia's second largest art collection.

DINING   The **Rybářsky Sál,** in the Hotel Gomel, Míru třída 14 (☎ **038/289 49**), is a popular place known for four freshwater fish: carp, trout, perch, and pike. Chicken Kiev and other "turf" dishes are also served. Main courses run 110Kč to 290Kč ($3.35 to $9). Or you can try the **Myslivecky Sál** in the same hotel for wild game and more meat-laden dishes at similar prices. American Express, Diners Club, MasterCard, and Visa are accepted, and they're open Monday to Thursday 6am to 10pm and Friday and Saturday 6am to 11pm.

KARLOVY VARY (CARLSBAD)

Charles IV's discovery of **Karlovy Vary,** 75 miles west of Prague, reads like a 14th-century episode of *The Beverly Hillbillies.* According to local lore, the king was out huntin' for some food when up from the ground came abubblin' water. Charles set to work building a small castle in the area, naming the town that evolved around it Karlovy Vary (Charles's Boiling Place). The first spa buildings were built in 1522, and before long notables like Peter the Great, Bach, Beethoven, Freud, and Marx were showing up.

ARRIVING   *Avoid the train from Prague,* which takes over 4 hours. If you're arriving from another direction, Karlovy Vary's main train station is connected to the town center by bus no. 13. Frequent **express buses** arrive from Prague's Florenc station to Karlovy Vary's náměstí Dr. M. Horákové in about 2½ hours. They leave from platform 21 or 22 daily at 7, 9, and 9:40am, noon, and 4pm. Take a 10-minute walk or local bus no. 4 into the town center. You must have a ticket (6Kč/15¢) to board local transportation; buy these tickets at the main station stop or, if you have no change, at the kiosk across the street during regular business hours.

The nearly 2-hour **drive** from Prague to Karlovy Vary is easy. Take Hwy. E48 from the western end of Prague and follow it straight through to Karlovy Vary.

SEEING THE SIGHTS   The pedestrian promenades, lined with turn-of-the-century art nouveau buildings, turn strolling into an art form. Nighttime walks take on an even more mystical feel as the sewers, the river, and the many major cracks in the roads emit steam from the hot springs running underneath.

A good place to start is the **Hotel Thermal** at the north end of the old town's center. The 1960s glass, steel, and concrete Thermal sticks out like a sore Communist thumb amid the rest of the town's 19th-century architecture. Nonetheless, here you'll find the town's only centrally located outdoor public pool and the hotel's upper terrace, boasting a truly spectacular view.

As you enter the heart of the town on the river's west side, you'll see a white wrought-iron gazebo, the **Sadová Kolonáda,** adorning a beautiful park, the **Dvořakový Sady.** Continue on and about 100 meters later you'll come to the **Mlýnská Kolonáda.** This long, covered walkway houses several springs, which you can sample free 24 hours a day. Bring your own cup or buy one just about anywhere to sip the waters. When you hit the river bend, you'll see the majestic **Church of St. Mary Magdalene** overlooking the **Vřídlo,** the hottest spring. Housing Vřídlo, which blasts some 50 feet into the air, is the glass building where the statue of Soviet cosmonaut Yuri Gagarin once stood. (Gagarin's statue has since made a safe landing at the Karlovy Vary airport.) Now called the **Vřídelní Kolonáda,** the structure, built in 1974, houses several hot springs you can sample free daily 7am to 8pm. The building also holds the Kuri-Info information center.

Heading away from the Vřídelní Kolonáda are Stará and Nova Louka streets, which line either side of the river. Along **Stará (Old) Louka** are several fine cafes and glass and crystal shops. **Nova (New) Louka** is lined with hotels and the historic town's main theater, built in 1886. Both streets lead to the **Grandhotel Pupp.** Once catering to nobility from all over central Europe, the Pupp still houses one of the town's finest restaurants, the Grand, while its grounds are a favorite with the hiking crowd.

Atop the hill behind the Pupp is the **Diana Lookout Tower.** Footpaths lead to the tower through the forests and eventually spit you out at the base, as if to say, "Ha, the trip is only half over." The five-story climb up the tower tests your stamina, but the view of the town is more than worth it. For those who aren't up to the climb just to get to the tower, a cable car runs up every 15 minutes daily 7am to 7pm.

DINING   The ✪ **Vinarna Karel IV,** Zámecký vrch 3 (☎ **017/322 7255**), is the perfect place to sit out on a warm summer night; this is one of Vary's most satisfying restaurants, with main courses at 110Kč to 260Kč ($3 to $8). Reservations are recommended. American Express, MasterCard, and Visa are accepted, and it's open daily noon to 1am.

23

Rome & Environs

by Patricia Schultz

Rome is opera, grand and comic, soap and buffo. As majestic as its ancient empire and nerve-wracking as a freeway at rush hour, the city can be seductive, charming, sophisticated, infuriating, and slapstick, in rapid succession. Federico Fellini seems still to be directing his city in its mondo bizzarro.

Classical antiquities, crumbling medieval structures, exuberant baroque churches, impressive statues, and splashing fountains mix with high-tech boutiques and artisans' shops. Yet the more the Eternal City changes, the more it stays the same. The latest political scandals add to the confusion of Italy's future, especially now that the European Community is scrutinizing its every move. Rome has finally started to employ major plans to celebrate the Papal Jubilee Year 2000, when more people are expected to visit Rome and the Vatican than now live in all Italy (58 million), and the country is making real efforts to clean up graft and payoffs. "Everything's so clean now that no one knows how to do anything," a Roman has remarked. Rome is scrambling to finish renovations and cosmetic touch-ups, and 1999 may see much of it under wraps and behind scaffolding. The upside is that, without the crowds expected for 2000, you should be able to enjoy extended museum hours and special events and concerts being given a test run.

But Rome is still Rome—if more frenetic and noisy and traffic-clogged than ever. Yet the new floodlighting of buildings at night is spectacular, the streets are cleaner, the food is forever wonderful, and the piazzas clear out as families still feast away each Sunday afternoon. It was one of the world's first tourism meccas and continues to be one of the globe's greatest destinations. It wasn't built in a day, nor can it be seen or easily understood even if that coin in the fountain guarantees multiple returns. *Roma, non basta una vita!* Rome, a lifetime is not enough.

REQUIRED DOCUMENTS Italy requires all non–European Union visitors to carry a passport, but it doesn't require visas from U.S., Canadian, Australian, or New Zealand travelers.

OTHER FROMMER'S TITLES For more about Rome, see *Frommer's Rome, Frommer's Italy, Frommer's Italy from $50 a Day, Frommer's Gay & Lesbian Europe, Frommer's Europe,* or *Frommer's Food Lover's Companion to Italy.*

Budget Bests

Rome is very expensive in the usual sense, but lovers of art and antiquity will find many of the best things are free. Even the **Vatican Museums** are free if you go on the last Sunday of the month. The Forum and Colosseum aren't free, but thanks to the Renaissance popes, Rome is a city where much of the best art was commissioned for **churches** and **piazzas.** You can see the greatness of Michelangelo, Bernini, Borromini, Caravaggio, and so many others by simply entering a church or strolling through a piazza. The antiquity of Rome and its importance as *caput mundi,* the one-time capital of Western civilization, is evident around every corner. The **Pantheon** still charges no admission, and it's one of the world's most majestic buildings.

1 Rome Deals & Discounts

SPECIAL DISCOUNTS

FOR EVERYONE   Discount books and passes that other countries have in abundance are less often seen in Italy, but always check with the tourist office to see if new passes have been issued. In general, keep your ID with you and ask at museums whether student or senior discounts apply. Stop at the English-speaking **Enjoy Rome** (see "Visitor Information," below), fast becoming a clearinghouse for budget and not-so-budget travelers. Its staff finds and books rooms free of charge and gives advice on other travel plans in and outside Rome.

The **very low season** runs from the second week of November until Christmas and from January 7 to just before Easter. Though it can be cold in Rome in January, the air is brisk enough for easy walking and the city is occupied mainly by Italians. Mid-January to mid-March in 1998, airfares with major international carriers reached a remarkable low of $295 round-trip between New York and Milan or Rome, and this fare is often repeated in the very low season. You must check with the airlines daily, however, as a limited number of seats are sold at these prices. August is also low season (though that doesn't apply to airfares) and can have its pluses too, if hot weather (and a general lack of air-conditioning; Rome prefers merely to shut down, and this means stores and restaurants) isn't daunting. Many hotels reduce their rates then, when politicians, businesspeople, and international visitors head to the shore. Three- and four-star hotels often reduce rates dramatically.

Tour operators often give great independent package prices on hotels, airfare, transfers, and helpful advice. If you book ahead, you can often get great value. Ask your travel agents about Central Holidays (CHT), Perillo Tours, and TWA, among others.

If your Italian is pretty good, check the weekly supplements for the Rome daily paper, *Il Messaggero,* or Rome's Thursday supplement, *Trova Roma,* in *La Repubblica.* They list music events, including church concerts, many of which are free—though a donation is appreciated. Two English-language publications, *Metropolitan* and *Wanted in Rome,* are published twice a month, with listings of cultural events and short-term apartment rentals.

FOR STUDENTS   Many places in Rome reduce rates for students. If you need help leaving Rome, visit the **Centro Turistico Studentesco (CTS),** via Genova 16 (☎ **06/4-67-9271**), off via Nazionale. It sells the **Carta Verde,** allowing discounted plane, train, bus, and boat journeys for travelers 26 and under. CTS is open Monday to Friday 9am to 1pm and 3 to 7pm and Saturday 9am to 1pm. Take your photo ID.

What Things Cost in Rome	U.S. $
Taxi from airport to city center	39.30
Express train from airport to central Stazione Termini	7.30
Taxi from train station to piazza di Spagna	6.60
Public bus or subway (Metropolitana)	.85
Local telephone call	.10
Double room at the Excelsior (deluxe)	350.00
Double room at the Venezia (splurge)	134.85
Double room with bath at Kennedy (moderate)	98.30
Double room without bath at Papà Germano (budget)	39.30
Continental breakfast	
at any cafe/bar (standing at bar)	1.95
at most hotels	3.95
Lunch for one at Fiaschetteria Beltrame (moderate)	16.75
Lunch for one at Il Delfino (elegant self-service) (budget)	11.25
Dinner for one, with wine, at El Toulà (deluxe)	95.50
Dinner for one, without wine, at La Carbonara (splurge)	23.00
Dinner for one, without wine, at Polese (moderate)	16.85
Dinner for one, without wine, at the L' Insalata Ricca (budget)	11.00
Pint of beer (at the Fiddler's Elbow)	3.35
Glass of house wine (at La Vineria, standing)	1.10
Coca-Cola to take out	1.40
Cup of coffee (cappuccino) standing at bar	1.10
Roll of ASA 100 color film, 36 exposures	4.50
Joint admission to the Vatican Museums and the Sistine Chapel	8.40
Movie ticket	5.60
Cheapest opera ticket (student, at Terme di Caracalla)	11.25

WORTH A SPLURGE

Don't be discouraged by the hefty 15,000L ($8) joint admission to the **Vatican Museums** and **Sistine Chapel,** one of the most expensive museum admissions in Italy. Those with international student ID cards (ISIC) pay 10,000L ($6). And on the last Sunday of each month it's free for everyone, and at times it'll seem like everyone turns up. While this is one of Italy's most expensive attractions, it's also one of the most fascinating and important—and worth every lira. Economize somewhere else.

Rome is filled with good **trattorias** and **pizzerias,** many with outdoor dining areas in warm months. Plan on enjoying at least a few truly Roman meals, even if you need to scrimp at other times. Pizza by the slice *(pizza al taglio)* is a delicious alternative for lunch that'll leave ample lire for dinner.

2 Essentials

ARRIVING

BY PLANE Most international flights land at **Leonardo da Vinci Airport,** also known as **Fiumicino** (☎ **06/6-59-51**) after the city where it's located, 18 miles from downtown. Immediately after Passport Control (but before the baggage carousels), you'll see a *cambio* (bank) window at the right that changes money at surprisingly good rates; it's open daily 7:30am to 11pm. The lire you'll get when exchanging depends on the rate that day minus the commission charged. Cambios with signs that say NO FEE or NO COMMISSION generally give a lower exchange rate. By the time you arrive, a private **Hotels Reservation agency** should be open in the main hall; the 7,500L ($4.20) charge per person for a two-star hotel (it increases with the category of hotel) is deducted from the bill upon check-in at the hotel. An affiliate office has opened in the main Stazioni Termini train station. In the main arrivals hall you'll find a luggage-storage office, open 24 hours and charging 5,000L ($2.80) per bag per day.

There's a **train station** in the airport terminal. Express trains to Rome's central Stazione Termini take about 30 minutes for 15,000L ($8) one-way. An alternative train making local stops (Trastevere, Tiburtina, Ostiense) is almost as frequent and costs 7,000L ($3.95) one-way. Generally used by Romans living in these neighborhoods, it's not practical for most visitors. If you've boarded it by mistake, note that it terminates at Ostiense, where you have to change to a subway to Stazione Termini, a journey of about an hour with walking and stairs involved, frustrating for the heavy-laden.

The average price for a **taxi** ride to/from the airport is about 70,000L ($39) (from the airport to downtown, pay the meter plus 11,500L/$6; to the airport, pay the meter plus 14,000L/$8). Taxis line up in front of the arrivals terminal.

Charter flights sometimes land at the smaller **Ciampino Airport** (☎ **06/79-49-41**). Blue **COTRAL buses** leave this airport every half an hour or so and deposit you at Anagnina station, the last stop on the red Line A of the Metropolitana (subway). From there, take the **subway** to Rome's central rail station (Termini stop) or beyond. The complete journey takes about 45 minutes and costs 1,500L (85¢).

BY TRAIN Most Rome-bound trains arrive at the sprawling silver **Stazione Termini**, located on piazza dei Cinquecento. The official **Azienda di Promozione Turistica (A.P.T.)** staffs an information office in the station's main hall (☎ **06/487-12-70**), usually open daily 8:15am to 7:15pm. Be sure to pick up a free map and other information booklets. Don't expect this office to help with your hotel reservation, a service that has been picked up by a privately owned agency simply known as Hotel Reservations; the new office is in the station at the head of Tracks 8 and 9 (booking fees are deducted from your hotel stay upon check-in). The main tourist office isn't far away (see "Visitor Information," below), and you might stop there instead if you have time. A new addition to the station at the northern Metropolitana entrance is **Drugstore Termini,** a mall with grocery shops and lingerie and books and more, but no drugstore. For a *farmacia* (drugstore), cross the street at the left of the train station to find **Piram,** via Nazionale 228 (off piazza Repubblica), open 24 hours.

The two huge identical-looking exits on either side of the main hall may possibly be closed off in the future, directing all traffic out the principal exit straight ahead. But at press time this plan has been put on hold (any future plans haven't been reflected in my directions). For hotels designated below as "to the left of the station," head toward Track or Platform (Binario) 22 and via Giolitti; for hotels "to the right of the station toward via Marsala," head toward Track or Platform (Binario) 1.

The entrance to the **Metropolitana,** Rome's two-line subway, is down two separate sets of stairs (each marked by an illuminated white "M" surrounded by a red circle pointing the way) within the train station. Most of the city's **buses** begin their journeys in piazza dei Cinquecento, in front of the train station. You'll also find the **taxi** line here.

A Train Station Warning

In Stazione Termini, you'll almost certainly be approached by touts claiming to work for a tourist organization. They really work for individual hotels (not always the most recommendable) and will say almost anything to sell you a room. Unless you know something about Rome's layout and are savvy, it's best to ignore them.

Be aware of all your belongings at all times and be sure to keep your wallet and purse away from professionally experienced fingers. Never leave your bags unattended for even a second, and while making phone calls or waiting in line, make sure your attention doesn't wander from any bags you've set by your side or on the ground. Be aware if someone asks *you* for directions or information, it's meant to distract you and easily will.

There's a *cambio* near the train information office (below) that offers pretty good rates. Banks in Rome are closed much of the afternoon, but here the window remains open 8:30am to 7:30pm. There are two ATMs *(bancomat)* here: Before leaving home, check to make sure your PIN will be compatible with overseas codes.

In the station's massive outer hall is the **Informazioni Ferroviarie,** whose staff answers questions about train times, and nearby is a perpetually crowded bank of ticket windows. *Agenzie viaggi e turismo* (travel agents) in Rome, some of whom are in piazza Esedra nearby, sell tickets as well for no extra cost and minus the time you'll spend standing in lines. Allow ample time for these lines if you do intend to buy any tickets here before hopping on a train.

VISITOR INFORMATION

For those arriving by train, the most convenient **information office** is the one in the main hall (the one for years near Track 3 has been relocated here—see above). If you're not overloaded with luggage, go to Rome's main **Azienda di Promozione Turistica (A.P.T.),** via Parigi 5 (☎ **06/4889-9255;** fax 06/58-82-50), open Monday to Saturday 8:15am to 7:15pm. It distributes brochures, but the supply varies with the season; it no longer offers a free hotel reservation service. To reach this office from the train station, exit through the front doors, cross the enormous bus lot called piazza dei Cinquecento, walk through piazza della Repubblica (with a central fountain), look ahead for the Grand Hotel, and turn right past it onto via Parigi.

You can find new **information kiosks** in three locations: one at largo Goldoni, where via Condotti meets via del Corso (☎ **06/687-50-27**); one near the Colosseum at largo Ricci (☎ **06/678-09-92**); and one on via Nazionale at the Palazzo delle Esposizioni (☎ **06/474-59-29**). On Tuesday to Saturday 10am to 6pm and Sunday 10am to 1pm, they'll give details on happenings and practical information on opening hours and addresses.

Enjoy Rome, via Varese 39 (☎ **06/445-18-43;** fax 06/445-07-34; E-mail: fulang@flashnet.it; www.enjoyrome.com), was begun by a wonderful young couple, Fulvia and Pierluigi, with a simple but very bright idea, and it's the answer to many travelers' dreams. In their accommodating English-speaking, visitor-friendly office near the station, they dispense information on just about everything in Rome and are far more pleasant and organized than the government-run Board of Tourism. They also find hotel rooms at rock-bottom to moderate prices (hostels to three-star hotels) free of charge. Summer hours are Monday to Friday 8:30am to 7pm and Saturday 8:30am to 1:30pm; winter hours are Monday to Friday 8:30am to 1:30pm and 3:30 to 6pm.

CITY LAYOUT

Though you'll need a good map to find your way along the winding streets in the center of Rome, the basic design of the visitor's city is pretty simple. Once you locate the enormous white-marble "wedding cake" **monument to King Victor Emanuel** you'll be on your way. It stands at the south end of via del Corso, on **piazza Venezia.** Facing the monument, bear left for the **Forum** and the **Colosseum,** just behind and below. Bear right for the **Capitoline Museums,** behind and up a set of monumental stairs.

Conversely, with your back to the monument, to your left up ahead west of via del Corso is the section where the **Pantheon** and **piazza Navona** are neighborhood luminaries. A hard left leads you along **corso Vittorio Emanuele II** to the impressive church of **Sant'Andrea del Valle** of *Tosca* fame. A left after the church leads you to **campo de' Fiori, piazza Farnese,** the **Tiber River** (Tevere), and (on the other side of the river) the area known as **Trastevere** (literally, "across the Tiber").

Backtrack to piazza Venezia for just a minute to simplify your approach to the atmospheric old **Ghetto:** Take that same left on corso Vittorio Emanuele II (you're calling it corso Vittorio by now), but turn left as soon as you reach **largo di Torre Argentina** and keep heading straight to **via Portico d'Ottavia.** The Ghetto skirts the Tiber River.

For the **Vatican,** make no turns off the corso Vittorio, continuing straight across the eponymous bridge. Take the more scenic routes along dei Coronari to the north or via Giulia to the south, crossing at ponte Sant'Angelo when you have more time.

Back at the Vittorio Emanuele monument (with your back to it), look straight ahead toward **piazza del Popolo,** at the opposite (and north) end of via del Corso—a half hour's stroll. For the **Fontana di Trevi,** proceed along the Corso about halfway to piazza del Popolo, then turn right after about 6 blocks at via delle Muratte until you hear the sensual rush of water. It's always a shock to have the fountain jump out at you without a spacious expanse of surrounding piazza as you'd expect. Farther north along via del Corso, a right on via Condotti will take you to **piazza di Spagna** and the fabled **Spanish Steps.** This section is where Armani meets Krizia and Ferragamo, so prepare to window-shop.

To the northeast of the Vittorio Monument is the **Stazione Termini,** the main rail station, on piazza dei Cinquecento; it marks the eastern edge of the visitor's city. The broad, busy **via Nazionale** begins at **piazza della Repubblica,** just a short walk away, and stretches down to **piazza Venezia** (where the Vittorio Emanuele monument is located).

GETTING AROUND

Rome isn't a pedestrian's paradise (except for Sunday and August). It's spread out and crowded with cars, buses, and Vespas. Sidewalks are extremely narrow, if they exist at all. Still, the heart of Old Rome, around the Spanish Steps, piazza Navona, and campo de' Fiori, is a joy to wander through. Try it from 1:30 to 3pm, when all Romans and sensible visitors are enjoying lunch. This is the best time for bicycles too.

Free basic orientation maps are distributed by the tourist office. For an exact map showing every *vicolo* (alley) and piazza, you'll need to buy the heavy *StradaRoma 1999* (19,000L/$11) or ask at your hotel to photocopy the pages you need from *Tuttacittà,* an extremely detailed map supplement distributed with the Rome phone directory (and hard to come by). You'll also need (if you plan to use the bus system extensively) the *Roma Metro-Bus Map 1999,* published by Editrice Lozzi for 7,000L ($3.95) and usually carried by newsstands.

BY SUBWAY Rome's **Metropolitana** subway system (operating daily 5:30am to 11:30pm) has two lines that cross the city in roughly an X shape. They both stop at Stazione Termini, the only place they intersect. They connect most of the city's major hubs, though neither goes anywhere near Trastevere. Line A (red) is the most useful to the average visitor, for it stops at piazza della Repubblica, piazza Barberini (at the foot of via Veneto), piazza di Spagna, piazza del Popolo (Flaminio), and (crossing under the river) the Vatican (Ottaviano). In the opposite direction from Termini, Line A travels southeast past piazza San Giovanni to the Catacombs and other outlying sights. Line B (blue), meanwhile, heads southwest of Termini by way of via Cavour and the Colosseum (Colosseo); northeast of Termini it heads into the suburbs—the reason the Metro was originally built.

Tickets cost 1,500L (85¢) each, and you can buy them at *tabacchi* (tobacco shops), at many newsstands, and from machines in the stations. A **Roma Metro Bus ticket** is good for 75 minutes of travel on all buses, urban trains, and one Metro ride. All tickets must be stamped at the machines at the back of the bus or in the subway. To be caught without a stamped ticket means a 50,000L ($28) fine on the spot. Romans buy monthly passes and therefore don't need the daily stamp. You can also buy a **1-day pass,** good on all buses and the Metropolitana, for 6,000L ($3.40) or a **1-week pass** for 24,000L ($14).

BY BUS & STREETCAR There are three major drawbacks to Rome's bus and streetcar system: traffic, crowds, and petty thieves. Downtown congestion can be so bad you're sometimes better off on foot. When navigating this sprawling city by bus, remember **bus no. 64.** This notorious albeit indispensable line, sometimes called "the pickpocket bus," begins behind the train station's ticket booth, travels along via Nazionale, passes through piazza Venezia, and continues across the heart of the Old City along via Vittorio Emanuele, ending just off St. Peter's Square. In recent years, Rome has finally deigned to put plainclothes cops on this line, but don't bet your wallet on it. Keep everything inside your clothes or, in summer, in a safety wallet, available at luggage stores.

Bus no. 492 also makes the Termini–Vatican trip, on a longer route, by way of piazza Barberini, piazza Colonna, piazza Venezia, largo di Torre Argentina, and piazza Navona; **bus no. 492**'s western terminus is piazza Risorgimento, up via della Porta Angelica from the entrance to piazza San Pietro (St. Peter's Square) and convenient to the Vatican Museums. Other key lines from the station are **no. 27,** which travels to the Colosseum, and **nos. 75 and 170,** which cross the river into Trastevere. But confirm these numbers by reading the signs at the bus stop.

You can buy tickets from machines at major bus stations. However, these machines often refuse all but mint-condition bills and also higher-denomination bills, though the machine says it takes them. (The new "advantage" is you can be told in English on the computer screen that you can't get a ticket. Italians are better at ideas than at follow-up.) If the machine doesn't work, look for newsstands or *tabacchi* (tobacco shops) that carry the sign ATAC (the bus company) and buy several at once or a pass. The Metropolitana entrance at the via Cavour entrance to Termini station has a live

A Bus Warning

Note that as this book went to press, a good portion of Rome's public bus system was scheduled to be renumbered and rerouted: The bus numbers I've given as part of the directions to sites of interest are likely to have changed by the time you arrive, since 50% of central Rome's system will be affected.

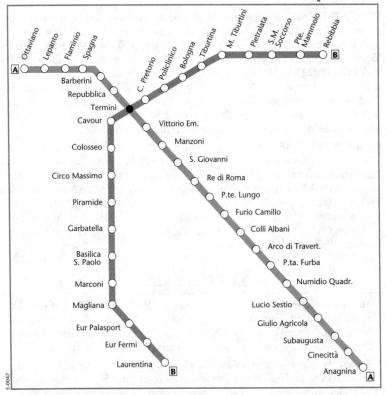

Rome Metropolitana

Ottaviano · Lepanto · Flaminio · Spagna · C. Pretorio · Policlinico · Bologna · Tiburtina · M. Tiburtini · Pietralata · S.M. Soccorso · Pte. Mammolo · Rebibbia

A

B

Barberini
Repubblica
Termini
Cavour · Vittorio Em.
Colosseo · Manzoni
Circo Massimo · S. Giovanni
Piramide · Re di Roma
Garbatella · P.te. Lungo
Basilica · Furio Camillo
S. Paolo · Colli Albani
Marconi · Arco di Travert.
Magliana · P.ta. Furba
Eur Palasport · Numidio Quadr.
Eur Fermi · Lucio Sestio
Laurentina · Giulio Agricola
B · Subaugusta
Cinecittà
Anagnina
A

person selling tickets. Go for it. The **bus information window** in front of Stazione Termini is open daily 7am to 7pm. ATAC's information number is ☎ **167/43-17-84** (daily 9am to 1pm and 2 to 5pm). With a pass you can enter buses at the front instead of the back, a help when buses are crowded (all day, except 2 to 3pm). Everyone exits from the middle door.

The **bus fare** is 1,500L (85¢); tickets must be stamped in the red boxes at either end of the bus. Easiest is to buy 10 or so at a time or a **week's pass** for all lines (24,000L/$14). See Roma Metro Bus ticket information under "By Subway," above.

BY TAXI Taxi fares begin at 4,500L ($2.50) for the first 3 kilometers (1.86 mi.) and click upward by 1,300L (75¢) for each extra kilometer (0.62 mi.). There's a 5,000L ($2.80) supplement for all night rides (10pm to 7am), a 2,000L ($1.25) add-on for travel on Sunday and holidays, and 2,000L ($1.10) extra per bag. If you order a taxi by phone, the meter goes on when they receive the call, not when you begin riding— the meter can easily be at 10,000L ($6) before you slip into the back seat. The ride from the airport to central Rome is about 70,000L ($39). Though Romans rarely tip, taxi drivers have come to expect a 10% tip from foreigners.

Beware of unmetered cabs, which are illegal and unlicensed and charge sometimes exorbitant uncontrolled rates. To call a taxi, dial ☎ **3570,** 88177, or 4994. Now you can occasionally hail cabs in the street but more frequently find them at stands marked TAXI in major piazzas. You can also ask a hotel or coffee bar employee to call for you. Give them 2,000L ($1.10) for their trouble.

BY RENTAL CAR   Renting a car to get around Rome is pointless; some will say a nightmare. Parking spots are scarce and only cars with special permits may enter the historic center. For day trips out of the city, try **Hertz** at ☎ **06/474-03-89** or **Avis** at ☎ **06/481-76-20.** Rent your car before leaving home, if possible. **Maiellano,** in New York (☎ **800/223-1616**), has a long tradition of car rental in Italy at competitive rates. Don't get the smallest—it's tiny and performs sluggishly on the autostrada. Air-conditioning and automatic transmission cost a substantial amount extra and must be requested well in advance, especially for summer rental. Pick up the car when leaving Rome outside of town at the airport, to save combating city traffic.

BY BICYCLE   Traffic, crazy drivers, bumpy cobbled streets, and the often over-looked fact that Rome was built on seven hills make cycling somewhat unnerving. For those who insist, areas like the large Villa Borghese park can be singular experiences for bike lovers. **I Bike Rome,** via Vittorio Veneto 156 (☎ **06/322-52-40**), rents bikes for 5,000L ($2.80) per hour or 38,000L ($21) per week. It's open daily 9am to 8pm. Mopeds cost 30,000L ($17) for 4 hours or 45,000L ($25) per day, and the more pow-erful Vespas are substantially more. Check the tourist offices or your hotel for other locations. Prices vary, but not by much.

FAST FACTS: Rome

American Express   The office at piazza di Spagna 38 (☎ **06/6-76-41**) exchanges traveler's checks (no fee) and is open Monday to Friday 9am to 5:30pm and Saturday 9am to 12:30pm; the ATM outside accepts American Express cards. It also cashes personal checks and accepts mail for clients.

Banks   Standard bank hours are Monday to Friday 8:30am to 1:30pm, then about 2:45 to 3:45pm; only a few banks are open Saturday, and then usually mornings only. There's a *cambio* (currency exchange) in the train station that's usually open Monday to Saturday 8:30am to 7:30pm and Sunday 8am to 2:15pm. When using a cambio, a commission will be deducted: Be sure to know what your change should be and count it before leaving the window. Many new cambios have opened in Rome, and though most are honest, you should be aware of the others. An excellent, reliable one is **EuroCambio,** via Francesco Crispi 92, open daily 8:30am to 2pm and 3 to 6pm. Hotels and restaurants also cash trav-eler's checks, but at a far lower rate. You can get Visa and MasterCard (Eurocard) cash advances at banks displaying their sign. Banks in the Cirrus network may have ATM *(bancomat)* access. For any ATM access, check with your cards first before leaving home: The PINs in Italy may not always be compatible with yours. Many ATMs accept dollars and other banknotes of foreign currencies that they'll exchange for lire.

Business Hours   In summer, most **businesses and shops** are open Monday to Friday 9am to 1pm and 4 to 8pm; on Saturday shops are open only in the morning. Mid-September to mid-June, most shops are open Tuesday to Saturday 9am to 1pm and 3:30 or 4:30 to 7:30pm; on Monday in winter shops don't open until the afternoon. In Rome, as throughout the rest of Italy, just about every-thing except restaurants is closed on Sunday. Most **restaurants** serve noon to 3pm and 7:30 to 11pm, slightly later than northern Italian cities.

Currency   The Italian unit of currency is the **lira (L),** almost always used in the plural form, **lire.** The lowest unit of currency is the silver 50L coin. New coins are small as American dimes, but many of the larger ones are still in circulation.

The Italian Lira

For American Readers At this writing, $1 = approximately 1,780L (or 100L = 5¢), and this was the rate of exchange used to calculate the dollar values given in this chapter (rounded to the nearest dollar if more than $5).

For British Readers At this writing, £1 = approximately 3,032L (or 100L = 3.3p), and this was the rate of exchange used to calculate the pound values in the table below.

Note: Exchange rates fluctuate regularly and may not be the same when you travel to Italy.

L	U.S.$	U.K.£	L	U.S.$	U.K.£
1,000	.56	.32	10,000	5.61	3.29
2,000	1.12	.65	15,000	8.42	4.94
3,000	1.68	.98	20,000	11.23	6.59
4,000	2.24	1.31	30,000	16.85	9.89
5,000	2.80	1.64	40,000	22.47	13.19
6,000	3.37	1.97	50,000	28.08	16.49
7,000	3.93	2.92	75,000	42.13	24.73
8,000	4.49	2.30	100,000	56.17	32.98
9,000	5.05	2.96	150,000	84.26	49.47

There's a silver 100L piece, a "gold" 200L coin, and a combination silver-and-gold 500L coin. Notes come in the following denominations: 1,000L, 2,000L, 5,000L, 10,000L, 50,000L, 100,000L, and 200,000L. Occasionally you'll come across a grooved token with a pictogram of a telephone on it. A remnant of Italy's old pay-phone system, which is gradually being phased out, the telephone *gettone* is worth 200L (11¢), the price of a phone call (public phones now accept coins and telephone cards).

Doctors & Dentists For a list of English-speaking doctors and dentists, consult your embassy or consulate. At the private (and expensive) **Salvator Mundi Hospital,** viale Mura Gianicolensi 67 (☎ 06/58-89-41), or the **Rome American Hospital,** via Emilio Longoni 69 (☎ 06/2-25-51), you're certain to find English-speaking doctors and staff.

Embassies The embassy of the **United States,** via Veneto 121 (☎ 06/4-67-41), is open Monday to Friday 8:30am to 5:30pm. The embassy of the **United Kingdom** is at via XX Settembre 80a (☎ 06/482-54-41); the embassy of **Canada** is at via Zara 30 (☎ 06/44-59-81); the embassy of **Australia** is at via Alessandria 215 (☎ 06/85-27-21); and the embassy of **New Zealand** is at via Zara 28 (☎ 06/440-29-28)—these are all open Monday to Friday about 9:30am to 12:30pm and 2 to 4pm. Different departments (visa, lost passports) keep different hours; call ahead to make certain.

Emergencies In Rome and throughout Italy, dial ☎ 113 for the **police.** For a fire, call ☎ 115. For **First Aid** (Pronto Soccorso), call ☎ 118. For a **Red Cross ambulance,** dial ☎ 5510.

Holidays Italy is a Catholic country and its calendar is packed with feast days and national holidays. Among them are New Year's Day (January 1), Epiphany (January 6), Easter Sunday and Monday (varies), Liberation Day (April 25),

Country & City Codes

The **country code** for Italy is **39**. The **city code** for Rome is **06**; use this code when you're calling from outside Italy, within Rome, and within Italy.

Labor Day (May 1), Feast of the Assumption (August 15), All Saints' Day (November 1), Feast of the Immaculate Conception (December 8), and Christmas and Santo Stefano (December 25 and 26). The city of Rome honors its patron saints, Peter and Paul, on June 29.

Laundry   Onda Blu, one of the few self-service laundries in Rome, has a number of bright and cheerful locations: Check the one south of the station (Metropolitana: Vittorio Emanuele) at via Lamarmora 10 (☎ **06/44-64-172**). It costs 12,000L ($7) to wash and dry 6½ kilos (14¼ lb.). Ask at your hotel if there are any closer alternatives at competitive rates.

Mail   Rome's **main post office** is at piazza San Silvestro 19, near piazza di Spagna. For *francobolli* (stamps), visit Windows 22 to 24, on the right as you enter. You can also buy stamps at face value at almost all *tabacchi* (tobacco stores, bars selling cigarettes indicated by a "T" posted outside). For foreign mail, many Romans prefer to use the more efficient postal service in Vatican City, on the left side of piazza San Pietro when facing the church (even the Vatican resorts to the Italian postal system for domestic mail). You must buy Vatican stamps and post mail within the Vatican in special blue post boxes: It's said that 4 to 5 days are shaved off transatlantic deliveries compared to the notoriously sluggish Italian mail, particularly bad in July to September (before, during, and following the annual August shutdown).

Tax   The **value-added tax (IVA in Italy)** is already included in the price of most products and services. The tax is refundable to non-EU citizens who spend more than 300,000L ($169) net in any one store, whether paid for by cash, traveler's check, or credit card. For details, see "Shopping," later in this chapter.

Telephone   There are two types of **public pay phones** in regular service. The first accepts coins or special grooved tokens *(gettoni),* which you'll sometimes (rarely these days) receive in change. The second operates with a **phonecard** (to buy one, ask for a *scheda* or *carta telefonica*), available at *tabacchi* and bars in 5,000L ($2.80) and 10,000L ($6) denominations; break off the perforated corner of the card before using it and insert arrow end first. Local phone calls cost 200L (11¢). To make a call, lift the receiver, insert a coin or card (arrow first), and dial.

To make **collect calls** to the United States, or with your calling card, phone AT&T's USA Direct at ☎ **06/172-10-11,** MCI's Call USA at ☎ **06/172-10-22,** or US Sprint at ☎ **06/172-18-77.** You can also call ☎ **06/172-10-01** for Canada, ☎ **06/172-10-61** for Australia, and ☎ **06/172-00-44** for the United Kingdom.

Tipping   In cafes, it's customary to leave 200L (11¢) or 300L (16¢) in coins on the counter with your empty espresso cup. If you've been sitting down, 500L (28¢) is more like it. If service is exceptional, an additional tip of 5% or more is appropriate, though not expected. In restaurants, tipping isn't expected, though Italians will leave 2,000L to 5,000L ($1.10 to $2.80) if they've enjoyed the meal and service. For taxis, tip up to 10%—service isn't included in their fares.

3 Accommodations You Can Afford

The American hotel/motel, with identical rooms and sparkling baths, doesn't exist in Rome. The budget hotels are usually what were formerly called *pensiones* and occupy one or two floors of a building, often without elevators. Most have undergone extensive renovations, but these old palazzi won't have the fresh look of the American scene—wherein lies much of their character. (But you won't be within a stone's throw of the Colosseum and the Sistine Chapel in America, either.) Rooms vary, often enormously, in quality; if your room isn't what you want, you could ask for another and might get it, if available. Rome's prices are heading north each year, and sometimes, with the best of planning, even experienced travelers must grin and bear it when rooms are dark, light bulbs dim, beds lumpy, and baths anything from ancient and spacious to brand new and minuscule.

You can get some of the most attractive prices in modern hotels before you leave through a tour operator like **Central Holidays,** 206 Central Ave., Jersey City, NJ 07307 (☎ **800/935-5000**). Travel agents can supply details. Off-season, Central Holidays has offered a double at three-star hotels for under $50 per night, with breakfast, tax, and tips included when part of a package deal. Hotels closer to the city center, like the Visconti Palace, are priced at about double this but still a percentage of their rack rates in high season.

You can book the budget hotels in advance (by fax) through **Enjoy Rome,** via Varese 39 (☎ **06/445-18-43;** fax 06/445-07-34). Most of the budget pensiones are near the rail station, an area that has improved enormously in the last year as Rome gets ready for the Jubilee Year 2000. There are fewer budget accommodations now than ever because old pensioni/hotels that once had rooms without baths have installed tiny modular shower/toilet combos and then upped their prices, graduating from one to two and even three stars. It's an easy walk to the Enjoy Rome office from the station, and if you haven't reserved ahead the staff can help with one-star (and higher) bookings free of charge.

From January 8 (immediately after Epiphany, January 6) to just before Palm Sunday is low season, as is August, for Europeans seek the sea in that month and Rome's heat (and the general absence of air-conditioning) reaches its maximum. The station-area hotels I've listed are all reasonably comfortable and of good value but rarely have air-conditioning. If you must arrive without a reservation, try to arrive early; the best places fill up by around midday.

Note: You can find the lodging choices below plotted on the map included in "Seeing the Sights," later in this chapter.

TO THE RIGHT OF THE TRAIN STATION

The two neighborhoods on either side of Stazione Termini have improved greatly recently and some streets are now attractive. The best-looking area is ahead and to your right as you exit the station on the via Marsala side. Most budget hotels here occupy a floor or more of a palazzo, and the entries are often drab. Don't go with your first impression: Upstairs they're often charming or at least clean and livable. If none of my hotels are available, ask for the booklet *Roma con poca spesa (Budget Rome)* at one of the tourist offices (above) or stand in line at the station's **Hotel Reservations office.** And try the English-speaking **Enjoy Rome** (above)—the staff can be very helpful for the least expensive accommodations available for no booking charge.

Bolognese. Via Palestro 15 (1st–3rd floors), 00185 Roma. ☎ and fax **06/49-00-45.** 21 units, 18 with bathroom. 45,000–50,000L ($25–$28) single without bathroom, 60,000L ($34) single with bathroom; 70,000L ($39) double without bathroom, 90,000–95,000L ($51–53)

A Train Station Warning

In 1998, the station's two side exits were to have been closed off permanently, prompting all traffic to use one principal exit straight ahead after exiting from the tracks. At press time, this complicated scheme had been put on indefinite hold and isn't reflected in the information I've provided.

double with bathroom; 100,000L ($56) triple without bathroom, 130,000L ($73) triple with bathroom; 150,000L ($84) quad with bathroom. Ask about rates for suites for families. No credit cards. Exit the station by Track 1, turn left, and walk along via Marsala, which becomes via Volturno; after 3 blocks, turn right on via Montebello; the hotel is 4 blocks ahead past the corner of via Palestro.

When owner Giorgio Calderara isn't carefully watching his hotel and ensuring his guests' happiness, you'll find him painting in a closet-size studio—all the canvases in the halls and rooms are his. The hotel has a lot of funny charm, and three rooms have balconies with neighborhood views, including wash on the line. It's very clean, homey, and cheerful. Suites with sitting rooms for large families or groups are available.

Corallo. Via Palestro 44 (6th floor), 00185 Roma. ☎ and fax **06/445-63-40.** 11 units, all with bathroom. TV TEL. 70,000L ($39) single; 120,000L ($67) double; 150,000L ($84) triple. Rates include breakfast. No credit cards. Exit the station by Track 1, walk straight for 4 blocks along via Marghera, and turn left onto via Palestro; the hotel is 2 blocks ahead (take the back elevator up to the reception desk).

This is a classic family-run place, where uncurbed finances and attention were invested in a 1997 renovation. The result is a hotel that belongs in a far classier neighborhood, but its location here guarantees low rates that are a rarity in Rome. The ever-professional and courteous Toni Cellestino or his wife is always on hand to make sure you're properly cared for. This place has unusual charm, thanks to the proprietors and amenities and attention to detail not always found at these rates (like a new breakfast room and the use of fresh flowers). Some rooms have balconies, with charming views of a typical Roman neighborhood.

Fawlty Towers. Via Magenta 39, 00185 Roma. ☎ and fax **06/445-03-74.** 15 units, 4 with shower only, 4 with bathroom. 55,000L ($31) single without bathroom, 70,000L ($39) single with bathroom; 80,000L ($45) double without bathroom, 95,000L ($53) double with shower only, 110,000L ($62) double with bathroom; 110,000L ($62) triple with shower only, 120,000L ($67) triple with bathroom; 30,000L ($17) per person in dorm-style quad without bathroom, 35,000L ($20) per person in dorm-style quad with bathroom. No credit cards. Turn right outside the station onto via Marghera, then left onto via Magenta.

It's not Torquay, but it's nearly as amusing as the British TV show (no Manuel, though). The offspring of the Enjoy Rome owners, this homey spot is part hostel, part budget hotel, and caters to a young (at heart, they say) crowd. There's a lounge with satellite TV, a rooftop terrace, and an international English-speaking staff that keeps it all in good order with an upbeat atmosphere. You can rent by the bed in a multi-share quad. Reservations in high season are a must.

Marini. Via Palestro 35 (3rd floor), 00185 Roma. ☎ **06/444-00-58.** 10 units, none with bathroom. 30,000L ($17) single; 50,000L ($28) double; 80,000L ($45) triple; 25,000L ($14) per person in shared room. No credit cards. Head up via Marghera, which begins opposite the north side of the station, then walk up 4 blocks to via Palestro and turn left; the hotel is on the left side of via Palestro between via San Martino della Battaglia and via Gaeta.

The Marini's rooms are as spartan as those at the Katty across the hall (a 1998 renovation didn't add baths), but with high ceilings they're a bit brighter and feel less like a dorm. The amiable owner, Antonia Marini, is welcoming and speaks working

Getting the Best Deal on Accommodations

- Remember to make reservations, which usually require a night's deposit. During late spring and summer, these are a necessity. Faxing is better than calling, since the return fax can be used as your confirmation.
- Note that if you arrive without a reservation, head to the Hotel Reservations office at the airport or in the train station. The tourism offices no longer offer this service.
- Take advantage of Enjoy Rome, which can be a great help to backpackers and other seekers of cheap rooms or rooms to share, as well as conventional (more expensive) hotels.
- Ask for a student discount or off-season rates if you're traveling out of season or in August.
- For those hotels that do accept credit cards, ask if they'll discount the room rate if you pay with cash or a traveler's check.

English. The prices here are nearly identical to the Katty's, and Antonia never puts more than three guests in a room. The building has no elevator and this place won't win any design awards, but you'll have the privacy of a room with a door for only a few dollars more than hostel rates.

✪ **Papà Germano.** Via Calatafimi 14A (about 8 blocks from the station), 00185 Roma. TV TEL. ☎ **06/48-69-19.** 16 units, 7 with bathroom. 40,000L ($23) single without bathroom; 70,000L ($39) double without bathroom, 80,000L ($45) double with bathroom; 90,000L ($51) triple without bathroom, 100,000L ($56) triple with bathroom; 25,000L ($14) per person in shared room. 10% reduction Nov–Mar. AE, MC, V. Exit the station by Track 1, turn left, and walk along via Marsala, which becomes via Volturno; turn right onto via Calatafimi, and the hotel will be half a block ahead on your left.

He tops the list in about every budget travel guide (they're framed near his tiny reception desk), but the owner, Gino, insists that word of mouth is his best advertising. This place is a standout, mostly because of him. He loves his job, offering advice, books, maps, and so on. The modern and airy rooms are kept spotless, and a 1996 refurbishment is still evident; perks like hair dryers and satellite TV are unusual at this price level. Solo budget travelers take note: He's also one of the few hoteliers in Rome who rents by the bed when possible at hostel rates in a far more delightful and superior environment. Perhaps the one drawback is that because the place is so small, noise carries far—don't expect to sleep late (however, this is true in most of Rome and certainly in this neighborhood). There's no curfew, but don't forget to ask for the outside key.

✪ **Romae.** Via Palestro 49, 00185 Roma. ☎ **06/446-35-54.** Fax 06/446-39-14. E-mail: htlromae@flasnet.it. 20 units, all with bathroom. TV TEL. 120,000L ($67) single; 160,000L ($90) double; 200,000L ($112) triple. Free for under age 6. Rates include continental breakfast. AE, MC, V. Parking in nearby garage 40,000L ($19). Exit the station by Track 1, walk straight ahead for 4 blocks along via Marghera, and turn left onto via Palestro; the hotel is 3 blocks ahead on your left.

This represents one of Rome's best values. The reception area contains a small espresso bar/lounge, and each sparkling-clean room has a bath with a hair dryer. All the rooms are simple, fresh and crisp, but those on the fourth floor are particularly recommendable. The young progressive-minded owners, Francesco and Lucy Boccaforno, have added ceiling fans and room safes. They speak excellent English and are proud to call this place home (they live with their mother and three young children, making this a nice atmosphere for traveling families—the Boccafornos will even arrange for baby-sitting).

TO THE LEFT OF THE TRAIN STATION

In the area to the left of the station, as you exit, the streets are wider, the traffic is heavier, and the noise level is higher than in the area to the right. This area off via Giolitti is being redeveloped, and now most streets are in good condition. There are a few that need improvement. The hotels I list are in safe areas, but caution at night is a given.

✪ **Bel Soggiorno.** Via Torino 117, 00184 Roma. ☎ **06/488-17-01.** Fax 06/481-57-55. 17 units, all with bathroom. MINIBAR TV TEL. 118,000L ($66) single; 160,000L ($90) double; 210,000L ($118) triple; 260,000L ($146) quad. Rates include breakfast. Half-pension also available. *For Frommer's readers:* Ask about the 10% discount if payment is made half in cash and half with credit card. AE, DC, MC, V. Metropolitana: Repubblica. Walk straight ahead of the station to piazza della Repubblica and turn left on via Nazionale; turn left onto via Torino, the 1st cross street.

Though the entrance isn't very attractive and the closed tin-box elevator isn't for claustrophobics, once you're inside this old-fashioned hotel you'll love it. A rooftop terrace with lounge chairs and umbrellaed tables overlooks the principal piazza della Repubblica and the Baths of Diocletian. The high-ceilinged rooms are nicely decorated and airy. The breakfast/dining room is dignified and opens onto a second but smaller terrace. The hotel is convenient to a subway line and will appeal to older travelers who appreciate the stately hotels of yesteryear. Renovations scheduled for 1999 will hopefully freshen things up while leaving that air of refinement.

Cortorillo. Via Principe Amedeo 79a (5th floor), 00185 Roma. ☎ **06/446-69-34.** Fax 06/44-54-769. 16 units, all with bathroom. 110,000L ($62) single; 160,000L ($90) double; 215,000L ($121) triple. Discounts during slow periods. Rates include breakfast. AE, MC, V. Exit the station by Track 22, turn left, walk half a block, and turn right onto via Gioberti (Bar Tavola Calda Etna is on the corner); after 2 blocks, turn left onto via Principe Amedeo; when you reach no. 79a, take the stairs on the right side of the courtyard.

Signora Iolanda Cortorillo is delighted to have celebrated her silver anniversary in this book—she's as gracious as she was more than 25 years ago. One of my least expensive listings (with elevator) is scheduled to upgrade to two stars with renovations taking place between November 1998 and January 1999. Even before the renovations, the rooms were spacious and clean, overlooking the interior courtyard, which makes them feel peaceful despite the noisy neighborhood. Signora Cortorillo speaks hardly a word of English, though her daughter is almost always there to help. La Signora still cooks dinner for 15,000L to 20,000L ($8 to $11)—with advance notice, of course.

✪ **Di Rienzo.** Via Principe Amedeo 79a (2nd floor), 00185 Roma. ☎ **06/446-71-31.** 20 units, 10 with bathroom. 70,000L ($39) single without bathroom, 80,000L ($45) single with bathroom; 77,000L ($43) double without bathroom, 94,000L ($53) double with bathroom. Inquire about triple/quad rates. Breakfast 15,000L ($8). Discounts up to 55% during slow periods. V. See the directions for Cortorillo, above.

Owner Balduino di Rienzo, with his wife and three daughters, hosts budget-minded travelers in what's certainly one of Rome's best rock-bottom pensiones, particularly during slow season, when his rates match those of the local hostel. When you inquire about his prices he's proud to say, "Little, very little." A shy, pleasant man, he speaks enough English to check you in and out, with his daughter often at hand for the big questions. His back-to-basics rooms are generally spacious and clean, with modern baths; some have balconies over the quiet courtyard. Unhurried renovations have been subtly improving this pleasant spot.

Elide. Via Firenze 50 (1st floor), 00184 Roma. ☎ **06/474-13-67.** Fax 06/489-04-318. 14 units, 9 with bathroom. TEL. 65,000L ($37) single without bathroom; 97,000L ($55) double without bathroom, 126,000L ($71) double with bathroom; 120,000L ($67) triple without bathroom, 160,000L ($90) triple with bathroom; 200,000L ($112) quad with bathroom. Breakfast 10,000L ($6). V. From the station, walk straight ahead to piazza della Repubblica, exiting it on via Nazionale; via Firenze is the 2nd street on the right.

This remarkable place is operated by one of Rome's friendliest families—appropriately named the Romas. The floors and the new modern baths always sparkle, and the prices are surprisingly low. They even try to change the wallpaper and paint the ceilings every year, which is quite an undertaking for such a small and inexpensive place. Ask for room no. 16 or 18, each with a unique carved and painted wooden ceiling. Everyone gets to enjoy the similarly decorated breakfast room.

Giuggiu'. Via del Viminale 8 (2nd floor), 00184 Roma. ☎ and fax **06/482-77-34.** 12 units, 9 with bathroom. 55,000L ($31) single without bathroom; 80,000L ($45) double without bathroom; 95,000L ($53) double with bathroom; 135,000L ($76) triple with bathroom. Continental breakfast 8,000L ($4.50). No credit cards. Exit the station by Track 22, turn right, and walk about 4 blocks with the bus lot on your right; turn left on largo di Villa Peretti; the hotel will be 2 blocks ahead on your left, at the head of via del Viminale.

A neon sign sticks out over the slightly forbidding entrance, though once you're inside, owner Mr. Chindamo and his family will make you feel at home. This small pensione (with elevator) boasts 14-foot ceilings and medium-size rooms that show some wear, but that's easily enough overlooked at these rates. The location is good, in a safe neighborhood a block from the Teatro dell'Opera.

Kennedy. Via Filippo Turati 62–64, 00185 Roma. ☎ **06/446-53-73.** Fax 06/44-65-417. E-mail: Hotelkennedy@micanet.it. 51 units, all with bathroom. A/C TV TEL. 120,000L ($67) single; 175,000L ($98) double; 199,000L ($112) triple; 320,000L ($180) quad. Rates include buffet breakfast. AE, DC, MC, V. Exit the station from Track 22, walk 1 block to via Filippo Turati, and turn left.

You'll find this shining good-value hotel in an otherwise dull neighborhood. The Sasson family never stops: Every year another floor is renovated and another project polishes the hotel's image. The five-story building (with elevator) has modern, colorful, and upbeat rooms; half boast views of ancient Roman walls or a neoclassical aquarium. There's even a small bar with coffee and juice free all day. The prices above apply to high season, which the owners define as the end of March to June and September to the first week of November. Otherwise, ask for low-season discounts, which can be steep in late autumn and winter.

NEAR THE COLOSSEUM

Perugia. Via del Colosseo 7, 00184 Roma. ☎ **06/679-72-00.** Fax 06/678-46-35. 11 units, 7 with bathroom. TEL. 70,000L ($39) single without bathroom, 90,000L ($51) single with bathroom; 95,000L ($53) double without bathroom, 125,000L ($70) double with bathroom. Extra bed 35% more. AE, DC, MC, V. Metropolitana: Colosseo, then turn right down via dei Fori Imperiali and right again onto the 1st small street, via del Tempio della Pace; after a 3rd right, at the intersection with via del Colosseo, the hotel is just ahead on your left).

Location is everything for the four-floor Perugia (no elevator). A short walk from the Colosseum in a quiet neighborhood, this budget place has spruced up considerably in the last year. All baths have windows, and the basic rooms are airy. One top-floor room even boasts a small terrace with a partial view of the Colosseum. The owners are nice and their prices are relatively low for this location between the Roman Forum and the Colosseum, an irresistible draw for ancient history buffs.

NEAR CAMPO DE' FIORI

This medieval area of *Vecchia Roma* (Old Rome) around campo de' Fiori and its vegetable-and-flower market is wonderfully atmospheric (and lively at night), historic, and well located. From here you can walk to the Pantheon, the Trevi Fountain, and even the Spanish Steps, as well as the Forum. Transportation is nearby, as a main bus terminal is at largo di Torre Argentina.

✪ **Campo de' Fiori.** Via del Biscione 6, 00186 Roma. ☎ **06/6880-6865** or 06/687-48-86. Fax 06/687-60-03. 27 units, 14 with shower only, 4 with bathroom. TEL. 140,000L ($79) double without bathroom, 160,000L ($90) double with shower only, 200,000L ($112) double with bathroom. Ask about single rates. Triple rates are double rates plus 35,000L–50,000L ($20–28) for 3rd bed. Rates include continental breakfast. 10% discount in Aug and Feb. MC, V. Bus: 64 from the train station to largo di Torre Argentina, then continue west—the direction the bus was going—along corso Vittorio Emanuele; after 3 blocks, turn left onto via Paradiso, a small street that spills into piazza Paradiso and continues as via del Biscione to the hotel; it's a 7-block walk.

They've mastered the art of the unique at this hotel in the heart of the historic district. Almost all the rooms are small, in a different whimsical or regional style—such as the Tuscan room, with the occasional gaudy detail. The rooms without bath have more average furnishings, minichandeliers over the beds, and floral wallpaper. Half a dozen rooms enjoy a view of campo de' Fiori, and all guests have access to the pocket-size roof garden with inspiring views of the rooftops as far as St. Peter's, helping to justify why this hotel continues to raise its rates. The hotel has no elevator, but you'll be able to make Rome's most elegant climb: There are few windows on the way up the marble stairs, but colorful floral scenes have been painted to brighten the ascent. Ten newly acquired apartments at 250,000L ($140) are a door or two away, complete with living rooms, baths, and small kitchens.

Piccolo. Via dei Chiavari 32, 00186 Roma. ☎ **06/6880-2560** or 06/689-23-30. 16 units, 10 with bathroom. TEL. 100,000L ($56) single without bathroom, 120,000L ($67) single with bathroom; 120,000L ($67) double without bathroom, 140,000L ($79) double with bathroom; 130,000L ($73) triple without bathroom, 150,000L ($84) triple with bathroom. Breakfast 7,000L ($3.95). AE, MC, V. Bus: 64 to largo di Torre Argentina, then walk west—the direction the bus was going—for 2 blocks and turn left onto via dei Chiavari; the hotel is 3 blocks ahead on your right.

You enter this smart family-run hotel through a contemporary cast-iron gate that contrasts well with the small old-fashioned stone street in front. A marble-lined entrance leads up to the first-floor reception and rooms that won't disappoint. The recently redecorated guest quarters are spacious (the singles are much larger than most), with spotless baths, and there's a small bar. The Piccolo is a star in one of Rome's top locations, where you'll want to spend time wandering even if you're not checked in here. Don't forget the 1am curfew.

Smeraldo. Vicolo dei Chiodaroli 11, 00186 Roma. ☎ **06/687-59-29.** Fax 06/6880-5495 or 06/689-21-21. 35 units, 24 with bathroom. A/C TV TEL. 90,000L ($51) single without bathroom, 130,000L ($73) single with bathroom; 125,000L ($70) double without bathroom, 160,000L ($90) double with bathroom; 150,000L ($84) triple without bathroom, 190,000L ($107) triple with bathroom. Breakfast 10,000L ($6). AE, MC, V. Bus: 64 from the train station to largo di Torre Argentina, then turn left onto via di Torre Argentina; take the 2nd right, via di S. Anna, and tiny vicolo dei Chiodaroli is just ahead on your left.

Success hasn't spoiled this four-story hotel (with elevator), whose location and moderate prices have steadily drawn return guests, so reserve ahead. It's a good value in Old Rome's most charming area, off campo de' Fiori. There's a modern reception with granite floors, but the rooms are simple, pleasant, and well cared for, so you shouldn't mind if they're small. Though this is one of Rome's liveliest neighborhoods at night, rooms overlooking an interior courtyard are especially quiet. Some fourth-floor rooms have small balconies. My only caveat: Avoid the hotel's breakfast and enjoy your meal somewhere in this warren of picturesque streets for half the price and twice the pleasure.

NEAR PIAZZA DI SPAGNA

The stylish streets at the foot of the Spanish Steps boast labels from Armani to Valentino. In the grid fanning out from there, a few hotels and trattorie still lure the frugal. Quasi-traffic-free via del Corso is Rome's catwalk for the daily ritual, the early-evening *passaggiata*, a human river that sweeps up the young and old (mostly young) from piazza del Popolo to piazza Venezia. During the day, it passes as a miracle mile of shops. The closer you get to the Spanish Steps, the higher the stratosphere.

Brotzky. Via del Corso 509, 00186 Roma. ☎ and fax **06/361-23-39**. 23 units, all with bathroom. TV. 85,000L ($48) single; 145,000L ($81) double, 180,000L ($101) double with TV. No credit cards. Metropolitana: Flaminio. Cross piazzale Flaminio, pass through the ancient gates to the city to piazza del Popolo, then head south on via del Corso.

After a few shaky years, the Brotzky is making a comeback. All the rooms are being renovated, and the process is expected to be complete by the end of 1999. The panoramic terrace opened on the fifth floor in the summer of 1997 for snacks and drinks. Some of the rooms have good views along via del Corso (a few have small balconies), but the Corso can be noisy when Vespas race along. This location is ideal, between the Spanish Steps and piazza del Popolo. There's a pay phone for guests' use at the reception.

✪ **Suisse.** Via Gregoriana 54, 00187 Roma. ☎ **06/678-36-49**. Fax 06/678-12-58. 15 units, 10 with bathroom. TEL. 115,000L ($65) single without bathroom, 135,000L ($76) single with bathroom; 140,000L ($79) double without bathroom, 190,000L ($107) double with bathroom; 265,000L ($149) triple with bathroom. Rates include breakfast. MC, V (for partial bill). Metropolitana: Spagna (via Gregoriana leads down from the top of the Spanish Steps) or Barberini.

The name's reference to Switzerland purposefully (and deservedly) implies the emphasis on efficiency, maintenance, and cleanliness at this ex-pensione. A favorite that's always full (reserve ahead) despite prices beginning to reflect the neighborhood's expensiveness, its rooms are simple and attractive, a mix of old-fashioned and modern. Some overlook fashionable via Gregoriana, running down from the top of the Spanish Steps and the fabled Hotel Hassler, but rooms in back are quieter. A warning to those arriving with luggage by subway: If you get off at the Spagna stop, you'll have to hike to the top of the Spanish Steps (not for the weak of knee). At the top, take in the view before turning right to head down via Gregoriana. Better yet: Splurge on a taxi from the train station.

NEAR PIAZZA NAVONA

✪ **Abruzzi.** Piazza della Rotonda 69, 00186 Roma. ☎ **06/679-20-21**. 25 units, none with bathroom. 93,000L ($52) single; 130,000L ($73) double. Ask about single rates. No credit cards. Bus: 64 to largo di Torre Argentina, then walk 4 blocks north along Minerva or via di Torre Argentina; the hotel is ahead, in front of the Pantheon.

Unbelievably, this unremarkable budget hotel (though with ever-increasing rates) directly overlooks the magnificent Pantheon and the adjacent piazza (known as piazza della Rotonda or piazza della Pantheon)—the only reason I give the place a star. Many of the basic rooms overlook the piazza ("Rome's Living Room"); but with no air-conditioning, these rooms are noisy until the wee hours, so many guests opt for the quieter (and cheaper) rooms in back. The four floors are filled with medium-size rooms, most with queen-size beds. The staff can be jaded. For breakfast, head around the corner to the revered Tazza d'Oro at via degli Orfani 84, known to offer Rome's best cup of coffee.

Navona. Via dei Sediari 8, 00186 Roma. ☎ **06/686-42-03**. Fax 06/6880-3802. 22 units, 10 with bathroom. 85,000L ($48) single without bathroom, 95,000L ($53) single with bathroom;

125,000L ($70) double without bathroom, 140,000L ($79) double with bathroom. Air-conditioning 25,000L ($14) per day. Rates include continental breakfast. No credit cards. Bus: 64 to largo di Torre Argentina. Via dei Sediari is a small street between piazza Navona and the Pantheon, best reached from piazza S. Andrea della Valle; walk a long block north on corso Rinascimento and turn right onto via dei Sediari; the hotel is ahead on your right.

Wrapping an open courtyard, this pretty first-floor pensione is full of character a stone's throw away from the eponymous piazza (to the west) and the Pantheon (to the east). Recent renovations have made many of the rooms comfortable if not stylish (courtyard rooms are quieter). The hotel occupies a grand 15th-century palace and holds architectural surprises at every turn. The baths are fully tiled, and the high ceilings with wooden beams lend an open feel. Not all rooms have air-conditioning, so specify when reserving. The helpful owners, the Australian-born Natale family, host a fair number of American and Australian students, so there's always youthful atmosphere.

NEAR CASTEL SANT'ANGELO

Near the Vatican, across the river from the historic center, the hotels here are a good bet for quiet and a local charm often missing from lodgings in more bustling areas.

✪ **Florida.** Via Cola di Rienzo 243, 00192 Roma. ☎ **06/324-18-72.** Fax 06/324-18-57. 9 units, 7 with bathroom. TV TEL. 65,000L ($37) single without bathroom, 110,000L ($62) single with bathroom; 95,000L ($53) double without bathroom, 145,000L ($81) double with bathroom; 180,000L ($101) triple with bathroom; 210,000L ($118) quad with bathroom. Breakfast 11,000L ($6). Off-season discounts Aug and Jan 8–Feb; discounts for stays of more than 6 nights. AE, MC, V. Metropolitana: Ottaviano. Bus: 492 from Stazione Termini.

Occupying two floors of a building on a busy retail thoroughfare that sees little tourism, this hotel is quite a find. Newly and tastefully redecorated throughout, this pretty pensione boasts cheerful prints and sparkling baths with lots of goodies. The earnest English-speaking management aims to please and usually does. The bar is a pleasant place to relax after a day's touring. If you plan on visiting during the hot months, inquire about the status of the air-conditioning, which was being added room-by-room at press time.

✪ **Forti's Guest House.** Via Fornovo 7, 00192 Roma. ☎ **06/321-22-56.** Fax 06/321-22-22. 30 units, 17 with bathroom. TEL. 75,000L ($42) single without bathroom, 85,000L ($48) single with bathroom; 100,000L ($56) double without bathroom, 135,000L ($76) double with bathroom; 135,000L ($76) triple without bathroom, 182,000L ($102) triple with bathroom. Rates include buffet breakfast. AE, DC, MC, V. Metropolitana: Lepanto. Walk down viale Giulio Cesare toward the river and take the 1st left onto via Fornovo.

Virginia-born and -raised Charles Cabell has made this homey spot a long-cherished haven for return American guests who enjoy the comfy reliability of the place and whose word-of-mouth keeps it full. The rooms are cheery, comfortable, and newly furnished. On the outer edge of what's generally considered tourist territory, it's still within striking distance of major sites, a 15-minute walk from piazza del Popolo, across the Tiber. Mr. Cabell, who's been at the helm for over 35 years, knows Rome better than the Romans, a keen insider's knowledge he gladly shares with guests.

NEAR THE VATICAN

Adriatic. Via Vitelleschi 25, 00193 Roma. ☎ **06/6880-8080.** Fax 06/68-93-552. 32 units, 26 with bathroom. TEL. 90,000L ($51) single without bathroom, 120,000L ($67) single with bathroom; 120,000L ($67) double without bathroom, 160,000L ($90) double with bathroom; 160,000L ($90) triple without bathroom, 215,000L ($121) triple with bathroom. Air-conditioning 30,000L ($17) per day; TV 20,000L ($11) per day. AE, MC, V. Bus: 64 from the train station to borgo Sant'Angelo; near St. Peter's, pass under the nearby portal, then continue 1 block along via Porta Castello until you reach via Vitelleschi, where you turn left.

Lanfranco Mencucci, his wife, and his son, Marino, take great pride in their hotel and see to it that their modern rooms and baths are kept clean and attractive. Not all rooms are equipped with air-conditioning or TVs, so make your request when booking or on arrival. There's a small terrace with fruit trees and a rose trellis off the reception area. The four-floor hotel (with elevator) is in the heart of the Vatican area, only slightly closer to Castel Sant'Angelo (a view enjoyed from four rooms with balconies; ask about their availability) than to St. Peter's Square, just a few blocks' walk.

Bramante. Vicolo delle Palline 24, 00193 Roma. ☎ **06/66880-64-26.** Fax 06/687-98-81. E-mail: bramante@excalhq.it. 20 units, 11 with bathroom. TV TEL. 97,000L ($55) single without bathroom, 132,000L ($74) single with bathroom; 132,000L ($74) double without bathroom, 176,000L ($99) double with bathroom; 178,000L ($100) triple without bathroom, 237,000L ($133) triple with bathroom; 297,000L ($167) quad with bathroom. Rates include breakfast. AE, DC, MC, V. Bus: 64 from the station to piazza Leonina (San Pietro) stop. Follow Vecchio Passetto in the direction of Castel Sant'Angelo and after the 2nd archway you'll find the hotel's narrow street.

In a charming building begun in the 16th century, this place is clean, comfortable, and about as close to the Vatican as you can get, in a neighborhood that still exudes an Old Roman spirit. The top floors have nice beamed ceilings, and other details hint of the palazzo's early beginnings as the home of Domenico Fontana, one of the principal architects of Vatican City. The ivy-covered breakfast terrace has a view of the Colonnato del Vaticano, the special escape wall connecting the Vatican with the Castel Sant'Angelo.

A CONVENT HOTEL

With prices in Rome continuing to rise, convents that rent rooms are becoming the best bet for those who don't mind the curfew. Some are in wonderful locations and all offer good value. They're booked up for months in advance by pilgrim groups around Easter. Single men and women or married couples are accepted. Here's my favorite:

Convento Santa Francesca Romana. Via dei Vascellari 61, 00153 Roma. ☎ **06/581-21-25.** 42 units, all with bathroom. 90,000L ($51) single; 130,000L ($73) double; 160,000L ($90) triple; 180,000 ($101) quad; 205,000L ($115) quint. Rates include breakfast. V. Bus: 170 to viale Trastevere; cross the viale and walk through piazza Sonnino to via Buco on the right, which becomes via Salumi, which leads to via dei Vascellari.

This lovely convent in Trastevere, home of a local saint and today's Sisters of Our Lady of Fatima, has been offering shelter to pilgrims as an innlike *casa di coglienza* for years. It's managed today by a group of affable young men who have seen to a recent upgrading that included a general sprucing up and, most notably, the addition of baths to all rooms. For these simple and reliably clean rooms, some with views of Trastevere street life, you'll find prices that approach many of the more conventional hotels above. Still, it's a great location for those who want to see an authentic Roman neighborhood at work and play, and the once-confining curfew has been extended to 1am. With dozens of rooms, there's often room at the inn.

WORTH A SPLURGE

Venezia. Via Varese 18, 00185 Roma. ☎ **06/445-71-01** or 06/446-36-87. Fax 06/495-76-87. E-mail: venezia@flashnet.it. 60 units, all with bathroom. A/C MINIBAR TV TEL. 177,000L ($99) single; 240,000L ($135) double; 326,000L ($183) triple. Rates include breakfast. *For Frommer's readers:* Ask about discounts. AE, DC, MC, V. From the train station, walk 3 blocks up via Marghera (begins opposite the exit by Track 1) to its intersection with via Varese; the hotel is on the left.

Swiss expatriate Rosemarie Diletti and her daughter, Patrizia, have beautified this unique 18th-century building with personal touches. Antiques, rugs, and historic pieces fill the ample-size rooms of a class-act hotel. Several top-floor accommodations have sunny balconies, and all have Murano-glass chandeliers and hair dryers. The staff is fluent in English and exceedingly helpful. At breakfast, look forward to a huge buffet, which usually includes fruit from the owner's garden. The Venezia is close enough to the train station to be convenient, but it's in a quiet neighborhood. If there are no vacancies, you'll be just as happy if you stay at the owners' second property south of piazza Repubblica, northwest (and equidistant) of the station.

4 Great Deals on Dining

Roman cooking is often overlooked by food critics. It's simple, wholesome, and inventive, with an unusually large selection of fresh vegetables. Of course, the city has restaurants from most of Italy's regions, but to ignore the food of Rome and the region of Lazio (sometimes called Latium in English) is to miss a very tasty opportunity.

The vegetable dishes are memorable, especially *carciofi all giudea* (baby Jerusalem artichokes flattened and fried crisp), simple salads of fresh local greens (endivelike *puntarella* comes only from the surrounding hills), and *fiori di zucca* (delicate zucchini flowers fried crisp sometimes with a jolt of anchovy paste or mozzarella inside). Vegetarians can be well satisfied in Italy, where a nationwide emphasis on freshness is imperative. For pasta, try *penne all'arrabbiata* (pasta in a fiery tomato sauce with sharp pecorino cheese); *spaghetti alla carbonara* (in a sauce of diced Italian bacon or pancetta, whipped eggs, and grated Parmesan); *penne all'amatriciana* (in a hearty tomato sauce with Italian bacon bits, onions, and a pinch of hot pepper, with pecorino); and the famous *fettuccine Alfredo* (egg noodles in a rich sauce of cream, butter, and Parmesan cheese) that's far more popular with foreigners than locals. Romans like their salt, perhaps more than in any other region. If you'd like the kitchen to abstain, ask the waiter for *"senza sale"* (without salt) or *"con poco sale"* (with little salt) and hope for the best.

In spring, lamb is the thing—especially *abbacchio al forno con patate* (roast baby lamb with potatoes)—and in fall, *porchetta* (pork roasted with wild fennel, rosemary, and garlic) is found everywhere, especially in the towns around Rome at fall festivals. Veal is typically Roman and *saltimbocca alla romana* (with ham and sage in a marsala sauce) is commonly found.

Pizza originated south of here in Naples, but it's a delicious Roman dish; ovens are often fired up only in the evening. The ubiquitous *menu turistico* or *menu del giorno* (tourist menu) is an all-inclusive fixed-price meal that's usually 12,500L to 21,000L ($7 to $12)—it consists of a pasta course *(primo)*, a main course *(secondo)*, a vegetable side dish *(contorno)*, bread, cover and service charges, and often wine and dessert or fruit. The one disadvantage is that you'll usually be offered only a limited selection of ordinary, sometimes uninteresting dishes.

Tramezzini are a visitor's dream—delicious, inexpensive, found everywhere, and easy to pack for a piazza picnic or train ride. Like giant tea sandwiches, these triangular crustless delights are stuffed with anything good imaginable. They're made for midmorning coffee breaks, so you find the freshest ones piled high in the morning at just about any coffee bar (called bar, not cafe, in Italian unless there are tables outside in a usual piazza location). Quality varies; they should look fresh and usually are, but anything with tuna or mayonnaise (two of the more commonplace ingredients) that looks a little tired should be avoided, especially at the end of a hot summer's day. You tell the cashier you want *un tramezzino* or *due tramezzini* and a cafe (espresso) or

---

A Dining Note

Pane e coperto ("bread and cover charge"), from 1,000L to 3,000L (55¢ to $1.70) per person, is an inexpensive but unavoidable menu charge that'll be new to most travelers. For better or worse, it's a charge you'll have to pay at restaurants simply for the privilege of eating there. Also note that a *servizio* (tip) of 10% to 15% will often be added to your bill or included in the price, though patrons often leave an extra 1,000L to 3,000L (55¢ to $1.70) as a token.

---

cappuccino, and so forth, then pay. *Caffè* (coffee) always means a demitasse of espresso until modified to *caffè-latte* (with warm milk sometimes on the side) or cappuccino. Then give the receipt *(scontrino)* to the barman. Leave a 100L, 200L, or 500L (5¢, 11¢, or 30¢) piece as a tip.

OFF VIA NAZIONALE

Pizzeria Est! Est! Est! Via Genova 32 (off via Nazionale). ☎ **06/488-11-07.** Pizza 8,000L–12,000L ($4.50–$7). Cover and service included. No credit cards. Tues–Sun 6:30–11:30pm. Metropolitana: Repubblica. Take a left off via Nazionale onto via Genova. PIZZA.

Open since the turn of the century, this is Rome's oldest pizzeria. Is it the best? Only you can judge. The decor hasn't changed much in more than 90 years despite a recent face-lift—you still eat at wooden tables astride antique woodwork served by starched, elderly waiters. Though it's not Rome's cheapest pizzeria, it's certainly the most storied and may be the best in a central but otherwise lackluster neighborhood.

NEAR PIAZZA NAVONA & LARGO DI TORRE ARGENTINA

✪ **Cul de Sac.** Piazza Pasquino 73 (off the south end of piazza Navona). ☎ **06/68-80-10-94.** Wines 3,000L–10,000L ($1.70–$6) by the glass; primi 9,000L–13,000L ($5–$7). MC, V. Tues–Sun 12:30–3pm; daily 6:30pm–12:30am. WINE BAR.

With over 1,400 wines, Rome's first wine bar is still a magnet for informal but delightful meals in one of the most colorful neighborhoods. A dozen carefully chosen reds and whites from Italy's regions change regularly for by-the-glass tastings, as does a savory menu whose simplicity compliments but never overshadows the importance of the wines. Rustic pâtés made on the premises are followed by a handful of primo choices like polenta with porcini mushrooms, French-influenced zuppa di cipolla (onion soup), or even fresh escargots. Assortments of sausages and salamis or cheeses are 12,500L ($7) each and constitute the one picnic-simple meal I dream of when I'm away from Rome too long.

Dar Filettaro a Santa Barbara. Largo dei Librari 88 (just off via de' Giubbonari). ☎ **06/696-40-18.** Cod fillets 5,000L ($2.80) each. No credit cards. Mon–Sat 5–10pm. SALT COD.

A true local favorite near campo de' Fiori, Dar Filettaro offers only one item: baccalà, or deep-fried salt-cod fillets, an age-old Roman specialty. The house wine, a good vino bianco from nearby Frascati, accompanies the dinner served on paper placemats to a cross-section of senators and market vendors (no one gets to linger, with the few tables forever in demand). This charming old place is set in a piazza crowned by the lovely, ever-closed Santa Barbara church. The tiny spot is worth a peak at least; these old Roman holes-in-the-wall are disappearing fast, and this one is a beloved institution.

Er Grottino. Via dei Baullari 25–27. ☎ **06/6880-3618.** Pizza 9,000L–12,000L ($5–$7); pasta courses 10,000L ($6); main courses 16,000L ($9) and up. DC, MC, V. Wed–Mon

---

Getting the Best Deal on Dining

- To eat well, learn the basic Italian food and wine vocabulary so that you don't rely on a poorly and unimaginatively translated English menu.
- If possible, avoid buying hotel breakfasts, usually expensive and unsatisfying. At a cafe/bar, you can stand at the counter for a delicious cappuccino and fresh *cornetto* (croissant) plain or filled with jam or *panna* (cream) for 3,000L to 4,500L ($1.70 to $2.50).
- Choose either lunch or dinner for true dining (lunch is the most important meal in Rome, dinner usually lighter) and use the other for pizza by the slice, sandwiches, or takeout meals.
- Take advantage of the all-inclusive fixed-price meals known as the *menu turistico* and *menu del giorno* if it looks interesting; the choice of dishes is often limited and not always the most authentic or imaginative.
- Be aware that in bars and cafes there's a difference between prices *alla banca* (at the bar) and *alla tavola* (at a table). Sit-down prices on all items are at least twice those if you stand at the bar.
- Try dining in a self-service pizzeria or *rosticceria*, an Italian cafeteria—there's no language barrier and turnover usually guarantees freshness.
- Cafe/bars are great budget refuges for lunch and are used by many Romans— the long lunch and siesta isn't an option for the average office worker.

---

noon–3:30pm and 5pm–midnight. Bus: 64 to Palazzo Cancelleria, 2 stops beyond largo di Torre Argentina, heading toward the Vatican. ROMAN.

Near campo de' Fiori, this little grotto has a good menu. Penne all'arrabbiata is a fiery beginning, softened with *scamorza* (a mozzarella-like cheese deep-fried) or saltimbocca for a second course. There's good pizza too, with toppings like *funghi* (mushrooms), *salsicce* (sausages), *alici* (anchovies), or *caperi* (capers). Try a fresh green salad of *puntarella*, a flavorful curlicue green found only in the hills outside Rome in late winter and early spring and spiked with anchovy-laced dressing.

Il Delfino. Corso Vittorio Emanuele 67 (just past largo di Torre Argentina). ☎ **06/686-40-53.** Menu turistico 17,000L ($10); pizza 8,000L–12,000L ($4.50–$7); pasta courses 7,000L–9,000L ($3.95–$5); meat courses 10,000L–15,000L ($6–$8). AE, DC, MC, V. Daily 7am–9pm. Metropolitana: Argentina. Bus: 64 from the train station or piazza Venezia to largo di Torre Argentina. ITALIAN.

Rome's biggest tavola calda (self-service restaurant) offers an exceptional selection of salads, pastas, and pizza available all day (in most pizzerias the ovens are fired up only for dinner). It's a cheery place, with polished green stone floors and piped-in pop music and less of a fast-food atmosphere than many of the newer self-services. Sustained success has spawned an extension next door at no. 69. Romans pretend to disdain it, but you'll note they make up the majority of the return patrons. Delfino's English/American crowd often heads here for the breakfast of two eggs, bacon, toast, juice, and coffee for 10,000L ($6).

Le Maschere. Via Monte della Farina 29. ☎ **06/687-94-94.** Pizza 9,500L–14,000L ($5–$8); pasta courses 9,000L–12,000L ($5–$7); meat and fish courses 12,000L–27,000L ($7–$15). AE, DC, MC, V. Tues–Sun 7pm–midnight. Bus: 64 from the train station to largo di Torre Argentina. CALABRIAN.

This 17th-century cellar restaurant looks like a southern Italian festival, decorated with folk art, spicy salamis, and wine jugs. It's a good place to try spicy southern Italian food (and an expansive antipasto table), which will bring back delicious recollections of Sunday afternoon dinners if you were blessed with a grandmother from Calabria. On weekends there's music, and a few tables are set outside in summer in a tiny piazza. It's a very good value and a relaxed place to have nothing more than a pizza and a beer and soak up some southern hospitality. Everyone heads over to piazza Navona for the de rigueur after-dinner gelato or campo de' Fiori for a glass of wine and a shot of nightlife color.

✪ **L'Insalata Ricca.** Largo dei Chiavari 85. ☎ **06/6880-3656.** Pasta courses 7,000L–11,000L ($3.95–$6); meat courses 8,000L–15,000L ($4.50–$8); salads 6,000L–10,000L ($3.40–$6). AE. Thurs–Tues noon–3pm and 7–11:30pm. Bus: 64 from the train station to the 1st stop after largo di Torre Argentina. ITALIAN.

The selection of second courses may be relatively limited, but you can always find at least 10 salads, 8 unique and delicious first courses, and a handful of daily specials. Save money by ordering just a pasta dish and salad, enough to satisfy the heartiest appetite, at about 16,000L ($11). The management boasts that the trattoria was created to provide a place where diners could order just one course or a salad without raising any eyebrows. Though it's no longer bargain basement, there's always a line for the excellent food served at this one-room restaurant. It's a no-smoking locale, a remarkable rarity in Rome.

There are now also **L'Insalata Ricca 2,** piazza Pasquino 72, near piazza Navona, off via Santa Maria dell'Anima (☎ **06/6880-7881**), with less of a fast-food approach to dining, and **L'Insalata Ricca 3,** via del Gazometro 62 (☎ **06/57-51-76;** Metropolitana: Piramide).

Pizzeria Baffetto. Via del Governo Vecchio 114 (at the corner of via Sora, near piazza Navona, behind the Chiesa Nuova). ☎ **06/686-16-17.** Meals 7,000L–11,000L ($3.95–$7). No credit cards. Daily 6:30pm–1am. PIZZA.

If you want to see young Rome, plan to have an informal (if not exactly leisurely) dinner in the city's most famous pizzeria. The two plainly decorated floors of sometimes communal tables are always crowded, thanks to the reputation of the Baffetto's first-rate thin-crusted pizzas and delicious calzones. In good weather, the crowd spills out to a few streetside tables. If you're in a hurry or especially hungry, arrive to grab a table as soon as it opens or prepare for a line. The service is often impersonal and lightning quick and so is the turnover.

Polese. Piazza Sforza Cesarini 40 (off corso Vittorio Emanuele, between piazza di Chiesa Nuova and the Tiber). ☎ **06/686-17-09.** Pizza 9,000L–12,000L ($6–$7); pasta courses 10,000L–15,000L ($6–$8); meat courses 12,000L–18,000L ($7–$10). AE, DC, MC, V. Wed–Mon 12:30–3pm and 7pm–midnight. ROMAN.

The large menu changes regularly—the last time I visited they were featuring no fewer than 12 pastas and soups and 15 second-course selections. The menu isn't translated, but most of the waiters speak English. You can order specialties like *fettuccine alla Sforza* (with a sauce of cream and porcini mushrooms), *fracostine di vitello alla fornata* (oven-roasted veal with potatoes), and *abbacchio al forno* (milk-fed roast baby lamb). The Polese remains busy year-round, with tables out on the charming tree-shaded piazza in summer. This is an excellent medium-price selection, where you can spend about 35,000L to 40,000L ($20 to $23) for a plentiful, hearty meal with wine. Pizza is a popular option and will cost much less.

Trattoria Da Luigi. Piazza Sforza Cesarini 24 (off corso Vittorio Emanuele, between piazza di Chiesa Nuova and the Tiber). ☎ **06/68-64-777.** Pasta courses 8,500L–12,000L ($4.75–$7); meat courses 11,500L–17,000L ($6–$20). AE, DC, MC, V. Tues–Sun noon–3pm and 7pm–midnight. ROMAN.

On the same square as the Polese (above), this place is similarly priced and just as popular and well known. Also like its nearby competitor, it has alfresco dining in summer and white canvas umbrellas over the tables. It's kept darker and more romantic inside, though, and is tastefully decorated with old theater posters and mirrors advertising various English liquors. Visitors and expatriates seem to prefer this place, while more Italians can be found at the Polese. They don't seem to mind if you order only a pasta dish; I especially recommend the penne alla vodka in a rich tomato-cream sauce with only a subtle hint of vodka.

NEAR THE COLOSSEUM

Taverna dei Quaranta. Via Claudia 24 (at the far side of the Colosseum, a half-moon turn from the Colosseo Metro stop near piazza Celimontana). ☎ **06/700-05-50.** Pasta courses 8,000L–12,000L ($4.50–$7); entrees 10,000L–18,000L ($6–$10). AE. Mon–Sat noon–3pm and 7–11pm (open Sun June–Sept). Metropolitana: Colosseo. ITALIAN.

Tastefully decorated (Piranesi prints) in its three rooms (one above) and cool in its outside tree shade, this (together with Pasqualino, below, a pasta-lover's preference) is the best place to relax after visiting the Colosseum. Traditional Roman fare includes olives stuffed with meat, gnocchi with Gorgonzola, and fresh fish that takes top billing on Tuesday and Friday. A good chianti house wine (or beer from the tap) and homemade desserts make it a great choice.

✪ **Trattoria Da Pasqualino.** Via dei Santi Quattro 66 (1 block from the Colosseum toward San Giovanni in Laterano). ☎ **06/700-45-76.** Pasta courses 7,000L–11,000L ($3.95–$6); entrees 9,000L–18,000L ($5–$10). AE, DC, MC, V. Tues–Sun noon–3pm and 7:30pm–midnight. Metropolitana: Colosseo. Follow via dei Fori Imperiali past the Colosseum and, just before it turns into via Labicana, turn right, then take the 2nd left. ITALIAN.

The well-known 100-year-old Da Pasqualino boasts a remarkable location. Yet despite the restaurant's proximity to Rome's famous arena, the prices are remarkably reasonable, the ambiance is typical and homey, and the portions are generous. This is a de rigueur stop for pasta lovers: There are over 20 types (fettuccine, penne, pappardelle, bucatini) and as many kinds of sauces (you can't go wrong asking for the day's homemade special). The waiters have an easy familylike rapport with the patrons, all of whom seem to be loyal regulars.

NEAR THE TREVI FOUNTAIN

Visitors flock by the busload to throw their loose lire into the dazzling baroque Trevi Fountain to ensure their return to Rome, as legend has it. Be sure to see it lit at night. (However, note that it might be behind scaffolding to repair a botched repair job.)

Ristorante/Tavola Calda Al Picchio. Via del Lavatore 39–40. ☎ **06/678-99-26.** Menu turistico (with 6 options, including wine) 18,000L–23,000L ($10–$13); pasta courses 6,000L–9,000L ($3.35–$5); entrees 7,000L–12,000L ($3.95–$7). AE, DC, MC, V. Jan–Feb Tues–Sun noon–3:30pm and 6–10:30pm; Mar–Dec daily, same hours. Facing the fountain, take the street on your right. ITALIAN.

Typical of this area that lives for tourism, this big foreigner-friendly restaurant is a bit more pleasant than its tourist-trap neighbors, despite the first impression given by six *menus turisticos* translated in six languages. The tables under a long barrel vault are more reminiscent of a Czech beer hall than an Italian eatery, but if you prefer, they offer a self-service rosticceria with counter seating. In summer, the air-conditioning is a lure, but serious palates won't be wooed by this brazen paean to those happy with a plate of spaghetti. Stick with the simple stuff and expect no culinary awards.

NEAR PIAZZA DEL POPOLO

Gran Sasso (da Ugo). Via di Ripetta 32. ☎ **06/321-48-83.** Pasta courses 7,000L–10,000L ($3.95–$6); main courses 6,000L–19,000L ($3.40–$11). AE, MC, V. Sun–Fri noon–3:30pm and 7–11pm. Metropolitana: Spagna or Flaminia. ABRUZZESE.

The owner, Giuseppe, is young and *simpatico* and has learned from generations of relatives how to run a trattoria with reasonable prices while his talented mother continues to run an admirable kitchen. Gran Sasso is a modest, friendly place with interesting paintings, which is appropriate, as it's near the Art Institute (Belle Arti). The true amatriciana sauce is made here, from his Amatrice mother's recipe (Amatrice is now part of Lazio but was formerly in Abruzzo, a neighboring region), smothering a dish of traditional penne-like bucatini pasta. Patrizia will recommend the specials of the house, like excellent eggplant parmigiana, roast meats, and fresh fish on Friday, an old Roman culinary tradition that originated from religious dictates. Desserts are also homemade, and Americans who think they're connoisseurs of apple pie *(torta di mele)* should sample it here. Top it off with the restaurant's own after-dinner amaro.

IN TRASTEVERE

Trastevere is the artists' and writers' quarter. Everyone has his or her own favorite trattoria in Trastevere: Ask a dozen Romans and you'll get a dozen must-visit addresses.

Da Corrado. Via delle Pelliccia 39. ☎ **06/580-60-04.** Pasta courses 7,000L–9,500L ($3.95–$5); entrees 9,000L–19,000L ($5–$11). No credit cards. Tues–Sat noon–3pm and 7:30–11pm. ROMAN.

In the neighborhood known for colorful restaurants, Da Corrado's atmosphere comes in spades from its everyday regularness. There's no sign outdoors for this quintessential working-class place on a characterful street between piazza Santa Maria in Trastevere and the river, well known because it reliably serves good pastas, meats, and salads along with generous amounts of wine and spirits. The repartee is sometimes heated, often humorous, and always part of the fun. There's no menu, and the bill is usually totaled on your paper tablecloth. This is as local as they come, a place you'd return to regularly if you came back in your next lifetime as a Roman.

Da Giovanni. Via della Lungara 41 (near ponte Sisto). ☎ **06/68-61-514.** Pasta courses 6,000L–9,000L ($3.40–$5); main courses 6,000L–10,000L ($3.35–$6). No credit cards. Mon–Sat noon–3pm and 7–10pm. ROMAN.

This is one of those inexpensive, authentic neighborhood finds everyone tried to keep out of the guidebooks—to no avail. Visitors on the hunt for simple food and local color now help fill the two tiny rooms otherwise filled with neighborhood patrons. It's a plain worker's restaurant, once very popular with starving artists, where you'll want a glass of red house wine and the homemade pasta—nothing complex or too sophisticated but never disappointing. The dishes are traditional Roman fare, hearty and cheap. The waiter tells you what's offered in Italian, but they'll usually try to track down a menu for first-timers.

✪ **Il Fontanone.** Piazza Trilussa 46 (just across ponte Sisto). ☎ **06/581-73-12.** Reservations suggested. Pasta courses 9,000L–12,000L ($5–$7); main courses 12,000L–16,000L ($7–$9). AE, DC, MC, V. Wed–Mon noon–2:30pm and 7–10:45pm. ROMAN.

This is one of the last of the old-fashioned favorites where locals and visitors rub elbows happily. The place is decorated in a rustic style (with alfresco dining in summer), and the third-generation owner, Pino, makes sure everything is country fresh. The pasta menu is extensive; the house special, fettuccine alla Fontanone, combines fresh tuna with garlic, mushrooms, and tomatoes. Or have Rome's classic amatriciana sauce on pasta—a simple tomato sauce with a smoky hint of Italian bacon, a local staple. Also recommendable are the osso buco and grilled chicken dishes. The antipasto table is a treat, always freshly prepared. The desserts are few but homemade. This is a great area to take an after-dinner stroll: Head to Trastevere's nighttime hub, piazza di Santa Maria.

Trattoria Mario. Via del Moro 53. ☎ **06/580-38-09.** Menu turistico 17,000L ($10); pasta courses 6,000L–9,000L ($3.40–$5); meat courses 7,000L–11,000L ($3.95–$6). AE, DC, MC, V. Mon–Sat noon–4pm and 6:30pm–midnight. Bus: 170 from the train station or piazza Venezia to the 1st ponte Garibaldi stop, then turn right onto via del Moro and walk toward ponte Sisto, looking for the trattoria halfway down on the left. ROMAN.

The savior of struggling artists and other low-budget folk, this charming place, decorated with the work of neighborhood artists, has been operated by three generations of Mario's family; it offers one of Rome's better food values. The 17,000L ($10) menu turistico is the cheapest outside the train station's vicinity and full of variety. The à la carte menu is equally attractive and quite varied. If you feel a splurge coming on, you can have game or other specialties here without pawning your jewels.

NEAR THE VATICAN

Taverna-Ristorante Tre Pupazzi. Via Borgo Pio 183 (at the corner of via Tre Pupazzi). ☎ **06/686-83-71.** Menu turistico (including dessert) 21,000L ($12); pizza 9,000L–12,000L ($5–$7); pasta courses 8,000L–16,000L ($4.50–$9); entrees 11,000L–22,000L ($6–$12). AE, MC, V. Mon–Sat noon–3:30pm and 7pm–midnight. Borgo Pio is 2 short blocks from, and parallel to, via della Conciliazione, at the corner of vicolo del Campanile. ROMAN/ABRUZZESE.

Around since 1625, this cozy and charming taverna has come highly recommended over the centuries from nearby hoteliers and loyal Roman patrons. Its 21,000L ($13) menu turistico is acceptable considering the delightful atmosphere and proximity to St. Peter's. Service is courteous but can be slow. It serves pizza not only late at night but also at lunch—a rarity in Rome.

NEAR STAZIONE TERMINI

This area is much improved, and you can dine here without worry (don't let down your normal city precautions). If you want a tourist menu, you'll see it posted in the window of any number of neighborhood trattorias. Two choices stand out: one a must-visit for wine lovers, the other an old-time standby that accomplishes the impossible task of keeping out-of-towners and locals equally satisfied.

Trattoria-Pizzeria La Reatina. Via San Martino della Battaglia 17. ☎ **06/49-03-14.** Pizza 7,000L–10,000L ($3.95–$6); pasta courses 8,000L ($4.50); entrees 8,000L–11,000L ($4.50–$6). AE, DC, MC, V. Sun–Fri noon–3pm and 6:30–11:30pm. Via San Martino della Battaglia runs between piazza Indipendenza and viale Castro Pretorio; the restaurant is on the right, past the intersection with via Villafranca. ROMAN.

A few blocks' walk east of the station and in an area studded with many budget hotels, La Reatina is a good pizzeria or trattoria choice for the area. There's no menu turistico, but with the moderate à la carte prices you'll have no trouble putting together an inexpensive meal with limited lire—a dinner of lasagna, veal scaloppine, and salad shouldn't be more than 20,000L ($11). Don't expect much in the way of atmosphere, just hearty, inexpensive food and a satisfied local crowd. Pizza is served, but only in the evening.

✪ **Trimani il Wine Bar.** Via Cernaia 37/b (northeast of Piazza Repubblica). ☎ **06/44-69-661.** Wines 4,000L–16,000L ($2.25–$9) by the glass; primi 10,000L–12,000L ($6–$7); main courses 12,000L–24,000L ($7–$14). AE, MC, V. Mon–Sat 11:30am–3pm and 6pm–midnight. Metropolitana: Repubblica. WINE BAR.

Founded in 1821, the Trimani wine shop (around the corner on via Goito no. 20) is Rome's oldest, best stocked, and most respected *enoteca*. In 1992, the Trimani family's decision to open this elegant wood-paneled wine bar was a sure-fire winner, spawning a number of competitors who don't come close to the selection of wines and interesting turnout you'll find here. This stylish but informal niche inauspiciously located near the train station area comes as a surprise, as does the quality of the untypically Roman menu that changes as regularly as the wine selection. Over 30 reds and whites (mostly of Italian provenance but with French choices as well) can be sampled by the glass, plus 15 sweet or dessert wines. Pair them with a limited but delicious choice of soups, crostini, pastas (homemade gnocchi with Gorgonzola makes a frequent appearance), or meat or fish entrees and you have an interesting menu meant to enhance but not overshadow the wine-lover's experience.

PICNICKING

Piazza Vittorio Emanuele, near the train station, is the principal open-air daily food market, where herbs and spices join the usual products. Plans to renovate this area include an eventual closing date for this market, which is apparently to be a gentrification casualty. However, it's still open now—but watch your wallet. There's another **open-air food market** near the train station on the right side on via Montebello, on the 2 blocks between via Volturno and via Goito, open year-round Monday to Saturday 6am to 2pm. The **morning market** in campo de' Fiori is especially characteristic and photogenic. It's one of the most interesting places in Old Rome and is one big glorious photo opportunity. You can buy almost anything, from cheese and olives to T-shirts and luggage—though the produce and flowers are the features with a supporting cast of merchants and local shoppers to round out the scenario. And there are numerous *panetterie, pasticcerie,* and *salumerie* in storefronts lining the piazza and some of the side streets to complete your picnic shopping.

A stylish food store/rosticceria, **Volpetti,** via della Scrofa 31–32, near the intersection with via dei Portoghese (☎ **06/686-19-40**), is great for a hot or cold takeout meal (spit-roasted chicken, oven-roasted potatoes with rosemary). They now have a small *tavola calda/caffeteria* dining room, making dining in situ possible. Prices aren't low here, but you save by buying small quantities of exactly what you want, choosing from an array of pastas and sliced roasted meats.

The **Villa Borghese,** Rome's only downtown park, is the most obvious "green" choice to take your fixings for an imperial picnic. But if you've packed an easy sandwich and juice, pull up one of the stone benches in **piazza Navona** or contemplate the timelessness of the Pantheon from the steps of the **fountain** that sits in front of it. Though the temptation may be great, don't eat or drink on the Spanish Steps or you could be fined (the police will most likely issue nothing more than a stern warning). But do come and sit for a moment at any time of the day—from the high steps for one of the world's great views or from any of the lower steps for unrivaled people-watching.

WORTH A SPLURGE

Fiaschetteria Beltrame. Via della Croce 39 (at Via Bocca di Leone off Via del Babuino). No phone. Pasta courses 14,000L ($8); main courses 16,000L–22,000L ($9–$12). No credit cards. Daily 12:15–3pm and 7:30–11pm. Metropolitana: Spagna; via della Croce begins at piazza di Spagna, at the corner where the Mondi shop is located. ROMAN.

The sketches on the wall were done by artists who frequent this rustic place that's been serving Roman specialties for more than a century. It's so well known among the city's artists and intellectuals that there's neither a menu nor a sign (other than FIASCHETTERIA, referring to its distant beginnings as a wine shop) out front. You'd hardly expect this small place of half a dozen tables and nondescript decor to figure on my short list of splurges. But Beltrame is a beloved old-timer that's proudly indifferent to its ultra-chic neighbors. The contrast created by this unpretentious eatery adored by those who can afford to eat anywhere is almost amusing.

✪ **La Carbonara.** Piazza Campo de' Fiori 23. ☎ **06/68-64-783.** Reservations recommended. Primi 12,000L–15,000L ($7–$8); entrees 14,000L–25,000L ($8–$14). Wed–Mon 12:30–3:30pm and 6–11:30pm. AE, DC, MC, V. ROMAN.

This has always been a quintessential Roman dining experience. First, there's the unrivaled location of its umbrellaed tables set in one of Rome's (or Italy's) most special piazzas. Even once the daily market closes (having supplied the kitchen with its freshest pickings), there's still much crumbling opera-set ambiance to absorb and local action to watch. Then there's the unchanging menu whose specialty of spaghetti alla carbonara is said to have originated here—certainly there's no one who prepares it better (but make sure someone orders the wonderful gnocchi made fresh daily and sauced with either a simple tomato recipe or the exotic *tartufo nero,* black truffle). There's also no better place to try stuffed zucchini flowers *(zucca di fiori),* lightly fried just right. A groaning table of antipasto usually presents artichokes and eggplant prepared in a number of ways. You needn't walk far to **La Vineria** (also known as Da Giorgio), in the piazza at no. 15, a hangout for the wine-loving circuit who wouldn't think of heading home without stopping by for a tipple.

5 Seeing the Sights

All roads led to Rome for a reason. Its position as one of the most influential centers of Western civilization is but one of many strata making it one of the world's most fascinating cities. You can see the Vatican's influence and its effect on art and architecture well outside Vatican City. And the exuberant nature of the baroque period is equaled nowhere else: Bernini made Rome a magnificent stage.

You can best see all this grandeur on Sunday, when the cars have gone to grandma's for lunch, when a stroll through the empty streets is a joy. This can also be true during August, when heat and Ferragosto (the national vacation period) send the Fiats and Vespas to the mountains or sea. The evening *passeggiata* (stroll) is made more pleasant by car-free streets like via del Corso and piazza di Spagna. At night, piazza Navona is enchanting, with Bernini's fountain floodlit at its center and lovely palazzi surrounding it.

SIGHTSEEING SUGGESTIONS
IF YOU HAVE 1 DAY Rome wasn't built in a day, so don't expect to see it all that quickly either. You'll just have to make the choice of a classical tour of its antiquities, highlighted by the **Colosseum** and **Forum,** a spiritual and artistic tour that includes **St. Peter's** and the **Vatican** area (the Vatican Museums are closed on Sunday, except for the last Sunday of the month), or an architectural and cultural visit through the historic center's tangle of streets, encompassing the **Spanish Steps,** the **Pantheon, piazza Navona,** and the **Trevi Fountain,** among other sites. Early risers in search of local color may want to see the market come to life at **campo de' Fiori**—take your camera.

IF YOU HAVE 2 DAYS Spend Day 2 at whichever place—the **Forum/Colosseum, St. Peter's/Vatican City,** or the **historic center**—you weren't able to get to on your first day.

IF YOU HAVE 3 DAYS What should you not miss once you've glimpsed Rome's best-known areas? The twin museums on the **Capitoline Hill** are a must-see, followed

A Sightseeing Note

Just about all the sights of significance, except the Vatican, the Colosseum, the Forum, and many churches, are closed Monday. In the last few years, summer has seen some museums, like the Galleria Borghese, enjoy viewing hours until as late as 11pm. Check upon your arrival with the tourism office.

by the **Etruscan Museum** at the Villa Giulia and the newly renovated **Galleria Borghese** in the Villa Borghese park. If you'd prefer to wander through the neighborhoods *(rioni)*, the streets around **campo de' Fiori** and **piazza Farnese** are fascinating, especially the artisan shops and old-time shops.

IF YOU HAVE 5 DAYS   If you've seen the major and less major sights, leave the city to explore **Tivoli** or **Ostia Antica.** You might even consider a full-day trip to **Pompeii.**

ST. PETER'S & THE VATICAN

In 1929, the Lateran Treaty between Pope Pius XI and the Italian government created the **Vatican,** the world's smallest sovereign independent state. It has only a few hundred citizens and is protected (theoretically) by its own militia, the curiously uniformed (some say by Michelangelo) Swiss guards.

The only entrance to the Vatican for the casual visitor is through one of the glories of the Western world—**piazza San Pietro (St. Peter's Square),** at the end of via della Conciliazione, the journey's end for millions of pilgrims each year. As you stand in the huge piazza—holding 300,000 is no problem for it—you'll be in the arms of an ellipse partly enclosed by a majestic Doric-pillared colonnade that reaches out to embrace the faithful. Atop the colonnade stands a gesticulating crowd of some 140 saints. Straight ahead is the facade of **St. Peter's Basilica** (Sts. Peter and Paul are represented by individual statues in front of the basilica, Peter carrying the Keys to the Kingdom), and to the right, above the colonnade, are the dark brown buildings of the **papal apartments** and the **Vatican Museums.** However, note that at presstime the basilica's facade was marred by scaffolding to get it ready for 2000. In the center of the square is an Egyptian obelisk, brought from the ancient city of Heliopolis on the Nile delta, that once adorned the nearby Nero's Circus. Flanking the obelisk are two 17th-century fountains that add the sound and sight of sparkling water. You can reach piazza San Pietro on bus no. 23, 30, 32, 49, 51, or 64.

On the left side of the piazza is the **Vatican Tourist Office** (☎ **06/6988-4466** or 06/6988-4866), open Monday to Saturday 8:30am to 7pm. It sells maps and guides, accepts reservations for tours of the Vatican Gardens (below), points you in the right direction for papal audience tickets, and tries to answer any questions you might have. A shuttle bus leaves from in front of this office for the entrance to the Vatican Museums (below) daily every 30 minutes 8:45am to 1:45pm in summer and 8:45am to 12:45pm in winter; the fare is 2,000L ($1.10). (Take it: It's a long and generally uninteresting walk; from the bus's route you'll pass through some of the Vatican's lovely gardens.) The post office and rest rooms are adjacent.

Separating the Vatican from the secular world on the north and west are 58 acres of carefully tended gardens filled with winding paths, brilliantly colored flowers, groves

A St. Peter's Warning

A dress code for men and women prohibiting shorts, bare arms and shoulders, and skirts above the knee is strictly enforced at all times in the basilica. You also must remain silent and cannot take photographs.

Rome

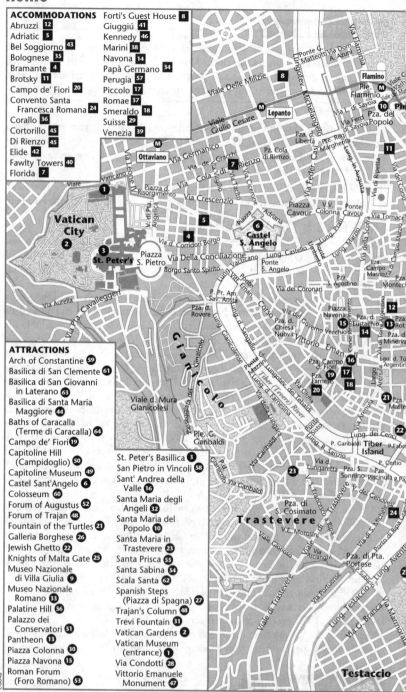

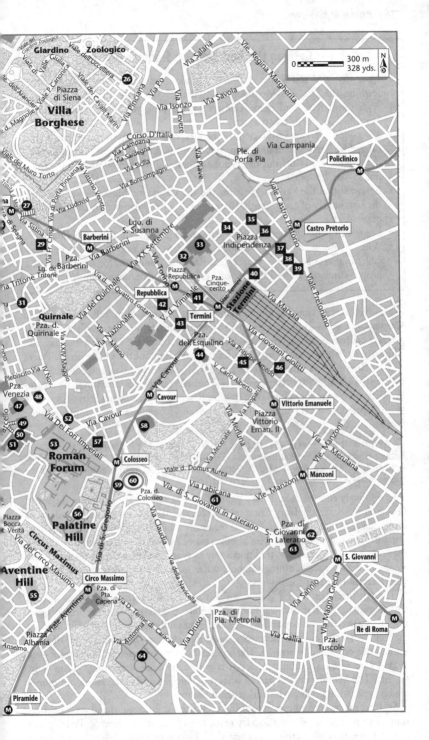

Getting the Best Deal on Sightseeing

- Note that the best value in Rome is undoubtedly found by walking and learning the bus and Metropolitana systems. (But remember that the bus system will have undergone changes by the time you arrive—see "A Bus Warning," earlier in this chapter.)
- For a good overview of the city, try the inexpensive 3-hour organized bus tour offered by ATAC, the transit company, for 15,000L ($8). It leaves from piazza dei Cinquecento, in front of Stazione Termini, daily at 3:30pm (winter and holidays at 2:30pm).
- Be aware that the Vatican Museum and the Capitoline Museums are free on the last Sunday of each month. But crowds can put a damper on an otherwise brilliant idea.
- Enjoy a free church concert—they're given frequently, especially at holidays.
- When in Rome, do like the Romans do and set up camp in one of the cafe tables in piazza Navona or piazza della Rotonda (Pantheon) for some priceless people-watching, all for the price of a *gelato* or late-afternoon Campari.

---

of massive oaks, and ancient fountains and pools. If you want to walk in the **Vatican Gardens,** guided tours of the Vatican City grounds are the only sort available—public access is otherwise not allowed. March to October, tours leave Monday, Tuesday, and Thursday to Saturday at 10 or 11am from the Vatican Tourist Office on St. Peter's Square; November to February, tours run only Tuesday, Thursday, and Saturday. The tour costs 16,000L ($9). Reservations are required year-round; in summer, it's recommended you reserve several days in advance. Reservations can be made in person only (with a passport or ID in hand), and payment is required when you make the reservation.

✪ **Basilica di San Pietro (St. Peter's Basilica).** Piazza San Pietro (St. Peter's Square). Piazza/basilica, free; to ascend the cupola, 5,000L ($2.80) on foot, 6,000L ($3.40) with elevator halfway. Basilica, Mar–Sept daily 7am–7pm (to 6pm Oct–Feb). Elevator/stairs up the cupola, Mar–Sept daily 8am–6pm (to 5pm Oct–Feb).

The absolutely enormous St. Peter's Basilica is the second largest church in the world (a pale contender in the Ivory Coast recently became the largest, though attendance is somewhat less) and the spiritual center for nearly a billion Catholics. Along the central aisle, markers indicate the size of other major cathedrals in the world—and how they dwarf by comparison. A traditional way to grasp its vast expanse is to stand next to one of the cherubs adorning the holy water fonts near the entrance and measure your forearm next to a cherub foot.

Though there has been a church on this site since the 4th century—as long as Christianity has been the official Roman religion—the present structure wasn't begun until the early 16th century and wasn't completed until more than 100 years later. To the right as you enter is Michelangelo's magnificent *Pietà*—he sculpted four of these statues, this one when he was 25. The sculpture is now protected by bulletproof glass since 1978, when a madman attacked it with a hammer, screaming, "I am Jesus Christ." The Madonna's face, part of what was damaged during the attack but immediately repaired, is celebrated for its ethereal beauty.

St. Peter's is meant to be awe-inspiring, a church for processions and great celebrations. The *pontificale,* or main Sunday mass, takes place at 10:30am. St. Peter's tomb is said to be beneath Bernini's celebrated 17th-century *baldacchino,* the decorative

Vatican City

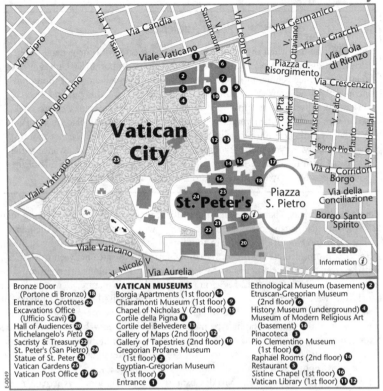

Bronze Door (Portone di Bronzo) **18**	**VATICAN MUSEUMS**	Ethnological Museum (basement) **2**
Entrance to Grottoes **24**	Borgia Apartments (1st floor) **14**	Etruscan-Gregorian Museum (2nd floor) **6**
Excavations Office (Ufficio Scavi) **21**	Chiaramonti Museum (1st floor) **9**	History Museum (underground) **4**
Hall of Audiences **20**	Chapel of Nicholas V (2nd floor) **15**	Museum of Modern Religious Art (basement) **14**
Michelangelo's *Pietà* **23**	Cortile della Pigna **8**	Pinacoteca **3**
Sacristy & Treasury **22**	Cortile del Belvedere **13**	Pio Clementino Museum (1st floor) **6**
St. Peter's (San Pietro) **24**	Gallery of Maps (2nd floor) **12**	
Statue of St. Peter **24**	Gallery of Tapestries (2nd floor) **10**	Raphael Rooms (2nd floor) **14**
Vatican Gardens **25**	Gregorian Profane Museum (1st floor) **1**	Restaurant **5**
Vatican Post Office **17** **19**	Egyptian-Gregorian Museum (1st floor) **7**	Sistine Chapel (1st floor) **16**
	Entrance **1**	Vatican Library (1st floor) **11** **12**

bronze canopy above the papal altar. Downstairs, you'll find the tombs of a number of popes and saints.

You can climb to the **cupola** for a breathtaking view of the Vatican complex and the rest of Rome. The entrance is at the far right end of the church as you enter. Be aware, though: There are still 330 steps after the elevator has taken you to the end of its line. Those in good shape will find it worth the climb.

✪ **Vatican Museums.** Viale Vaticano. ☎ **06/6988-3333.** Admission 15,000L ($8). Free for everyone the last Sun of each month. Mar 16–Oct 31 Mon–Fri 8:45am–4:45pm and Sat 8:45am–1:45pm; rest of the year Mon–Sat 8:45am–1:45pm. Last entrance 1 hour before closing. Closed Jan 6, Feb 11, Easter Mon, Ascension Day, May 1, Corpus Christi, June 29, Aug 15, Nov 1, and Dec 8. Metropolitana: Ottaviano, then about a 6-block walk to the entrance. Bus: 492 from the train station and Old City area.

The Vatican is home to a brilliant collection of artistic and historic treasures. The 4½ miles of corridors forming the Vatican Museums complex will take you through five outstanding museums, the breathtaking Raphael Rooms, and Fra Angelico's only work in Rome, all culminating in the unparalleled Sistine Chapel (see separate entry below). At the entrance you'll see a floor plan of four color-coded tours you may follow, depending on your interests and the amount of time you can spend. You'll also find a rest room, gift shop, and cafeteria.

You enter the museums through a series of long corridors hung with tapestries from the Raphael School. At the end of these halls commence the famous **Raphael Rooms.** Commissioned in the 16th century by Pope Julius II as the embellishment of what

Papal Audiences

Each Wednesday when the pope is in Rome, he speaks with the general public. Private audiences are reserved for figures of global importance: Unless you're related to Prince Rainier of Monaco, expect to join a small crowd of thousands. People of all religions are welcome. The regular time for this public session is 11am—usually 10am in summer. However, this can change from week to week, so be sure to check when you arrive. Audiences generally take place in the Paul VI Hall of Audiences or outside in St. Peter's Square during the warmer months; again, check when you pick up your tickets. Reserve free tickets in advance at the **Vatican City Prefecture Office** through the bronze door at the right side of the square, open Monday to Friday 9am to 1:30pm (☎ **06/698-830-17**).

were once his private chambers when the brilliant young artist was still a young man (25 when he first began), these salons are covered with frescoes glorifying the papacy.

The grim *Incendio di Borgo* (Fire in the Borgo), created from a sketch by Raphael, in the first room, depicts a 9th-century conflagration in the area between the Vatican and the river that was extinguished by Pope Leo IV's miraculous intervention. The second room, the Stanza della Segnatura (Room of the Signature; it was here that papal bulls were signed), is the most important and includes Raphael's depiction of *Truth* (on the wall in front of you as you enter). Clockwise, the other scenes are *Goodness, Theology,* and *Beauty.* Raphael painted himself into *Truth*—he's the man in the black cap in the lower right corner. Plato stands at the center, alongside Aristotle. And in the lower left corner of *Theology,* look for the old St. Peter's Basilica.

The third room, the Stanza di Eliodoro, shows the pope asking Attila the Hun to cease and desist in A.D. 410. The Sala di Costantino, the final room, was actually completed by students of Raphael after his death. Notice that these less skilled painters used black to signify shadowing, whereas the master employed darker shades of the same color.

Following the Raphael Rooms you'll come upon the somber, contemplative, and more formal **Cappella di Beato Angelico,** a small chapel decorated with the only work of Fra Angelico in Rome. In fact, the scenes in his work look more like Florence and Tuscany than Rome, a testament to the artist's homesickness.

If you're interested in the Vatican's **Museum of Modern Religious Art,** visit this collection now, before descending to the Sistine Chapel—the Vatican traffic cops operate a one-way museum because it's mobbed most of the year. The collection—55 rooms' worth—was commissioned by Pope Paul VI, who feared the religious artistic tradition was fading and was the first to extend the 18th- and 19th-century cutoff for artwork displayed at the Vatican. Twelve of the 55 rooms are dedicated to American artists.

The complex also includes an **Egyptian Museum,** with relics from the Roman conquest of that kingdom; an **Etruscan Museum,** with choice items on a par with the collection at the Villa Giulia; and the excellent **Pio-Clementine Museum,** dedicated to classical sculpture. The last's statue collection, many Roman copies of Greek works, shouldn't be missed. The partially preserved Greek statue from the 1st century B.C., the *Belvedere Torso,* became a model for Renaissance art students, including Michelangelo. The *Laocoön,* struggling with the snake; *Sleeping Ariadne; Augustus of Prima Porta;* and many others are exceptional and often immediately recognizable.

In the 18 rooms that make up the **Pinacoteca (Picture Gallery),** look for the *Angel Musician,* part of a Melozzo da Forli fresco. It's been reproduced widely in these days of endless angel fascination. The round painting of the *Virgin and Child* by Pinturic-chio, Caravaggio's *Descent from the Cross,* and Guido Reni's fine *St. Jerome* (San Giro-lamo) are among the treasures. Raphael's *Transfiguration,* often reproduced, was finished by followers of the maestro after his death. Nearby is his *Madonna de Foligno,* in which the Virgin and Child rest on a cloud of angels while St. Francis and John the Baptist look on. Leonardo da Vinci's *Saint Jerome and the Lion* is one of his few works in Rome.

❂ **Capella Sistina (Sistine Chapel).** Vatican Museums, viale Vaticano. The Sistine Chapel is part of the Vatican Museums complex (above) and can be seen only during a visit to the museums; it can be reached only at the end of any of the four itineraries. There's no short-cut, except for a sprint through the art-draped halls, bypassing the crowds.

The Sistine Chapel ceiling, completely restored from 1985 to 1992, to the horror of some and enormous admiration of others, contains some of history's most powerful painting. The Technicolor hues that've emerged after the painstaking cleaning still cause heated debate: Did the restorers take too much off? Depends on which art critic you read. Because Michelangelo was a sculptor (and one who undertook the papal com-mission under protest—ironic, as the Sistine Chapel became his greatest legacy), his artistic vision of the body differed from that of the average painter. A look at the earlier Botticelli works along the wall demonstrates this abruptly (the ceiling was done later).

The Sistine Chapel wasn't built as a chapel at all but was meant to be a vault—note its rectangular shape. It's here that the school of cardinals still meet to elect a pope and from here that smoke, black for no agreement or white to say *Habemus papem* (We have a pope), is sent up from a stove at the back. Pope Sixtus IV commissioned the early Renaissance wall frescoes by Ghirlandaio and Signorelli and other masters of the day; the left wall shows the story of Moses, while the right details the life of Jesus. Sixtus IV's successor and nephew, Pope Julius II, still wasn't pleased with the look, so he commanded Michelangelo to connect the two walls in 1508 by means of the 15,000-square-foot ceiling. It was a grueling 4-year labor during which Michelangelo worked mostly alone to create over 300 figures; it permanently damaged the Floren-tine artist's eyesight (he was then in his mid-30s) and tested his patience as the pope kept urging him to finish.

Each scene on the ceiling displays a different day in the Creation, as told in the book of Genesis. The most notable panels are the expulsion of Adam and Eve from the Garden of Eden and the world-recognized creation of man, where God's out-stretched hand imbues Adam with spirit. Others uphold the tremendously powerful Last Judgment, also done by Michelangelo, commissioned years later by Pope Paul III, as the chapel's crowning glory; it's to your right as you enter the chapel behind the altar. Michelangelo was then in his 60s and in a darker mood. Look for the face of Michelangelo at the bottom right, holding his own skin—presumably the way he felt after 7 years of endless arguments with the pope and breathing plaster dust. It's nice to know that even the great bow to self-publicity.

No flash photography is allowed, there are no guided tours (briefings are conducted in the halls and museum rooms preceding the chapel), and no loud talking is per-mitted inside the chapel. A few much coveted benches line the walls; no sitting on the altar steps is permitted. Despite the crowds, visitors are left to stay as long as they like; you may find yourself transfixed and lingering for a good deal of time. These may be the most memorable moments of your trip.

Castel Sant'Angelo. Lungotevere Castello. ☎ **06/687-50-36.** Admission 8,000L ($4.50) adults, free for seniors 60 and over/age 17 and under. Daily 9am–7pm; check hours. Closed 2nd and 4th Wed of each month. Metropolitana: Ottaviano. Bus: 23, 46, 49, 62, 64, 87, 98, 280, or 910.

A Sistine Chapel Tip

To get the best view of the Sistine Chapel's ceiling, bring along binoculars.

On the banks of the Tiber, connected to the Vatican by a wall that includes a secret escape tunnel, stands the imposing cylindrical Castel Sant'Angelo. The ponte Sant'Angelo, the pedestrians-only bridge leading to it (designed by Hadrian), sets the stage for something extraordinary. Ten 17th-century angels, each carrying a symbol of Christ's Passion, grace the expanse of the bridge: They're from Bernini's workshop. Built by the emperor Hadrian in A.D. 123 as his mausoleum, the Castello has subsequently served as a fortress in the Middle Ages, a prison (Renaissance sculptor/goldsmith Cellini was incarcerated here for embezzlement), and, most notably, a papal refuge. Highlights of the fortress are the weapons and suits of armor exhibits, the Pauline Hall, the Perseus Room, and the Library. At the top you'll find dazzling panoramic views (also available from the outdoor tables of the roof's sandwich bar) and an impressive statue of St. Michael the Archangel.

THE FORUM, THE COLOSSEUM & NEARBY

✪ **Foro Romano (Roman Forum) and Palatine Hill.** Via dei Fori Imperiali. ☎ **06/699-01-10.** Forum/Palatine Hill, 12,000L ($7) adults, free for seniors 60 and over/age 17 and under. Apr–Sept Mon–Sat 9am–6pm, Sun 9am–1pm; Oct–Mar Mon–Sat 9am–3pm, Sun 9am–1pm. Closed Jan 1 and May 1. Metropolitana: Colosseo. Bus: 27, 81, 85, 87, or 186.

The Roman Forum, in noble ruins, evokes the centuries when Rome ruled the world as *caput mundi*. To appreciate it fully, buy a copy of the small red book called *Rome Past and Present* (Vision Publications), sold in bookstores or on stands near the site. Its plastic overleafs show you the elaborate way things were 2,000 years ago.

Excavations started in the 19th century, but much of the Forum, like the Colosseum, had been stripped centuries ago when being used extensively as a quarry. Overturned columns, discarded fragments, and vanished temples call for a powerful imagination to evoke the Forum as it was in its glory days. Long the seat of commerce, government, and religion, the Forum drew all of Rome to its marbled porticoes to discuss the business of the Republic and was the principal marketplace for farmers and merchants. Temples to Vesta, Janus, and Saturn drew the faithful. (Remember that the Forum stays open during the long Roman lunch, when most things are closed, but beware of the summer heat.) You may enter from via dei Fori Imperiali and leave at the far side and proceed past the Arch of Constantine to the Colosseum (or vice versa).

Once you're in the Forum, it makes most sense for you to take a counterclockwise path. To your right you'll see the **Temple of Antonino and Faustina,** named for the emperor and his wife who adopted Marcus Aurelius; it was later converted into a church. The **via Sacra** begins here and continues to the left through the Roman Forum. It was through here that emperors proceeded to the cheers of the crowds.

Farther along you'll see remains of the **Basilica Aemilia,** built in 179 B.C. Fire and vandals destroyed much of it. The faint green stains in the nave were caused by copper coins burning when the Goths attacked. Basilicas were primarily business marts, almost convention centers, where those from the outer reaches could come to transact legal and commercial matters. They were large and airy, with two aisles usually. Cambios changed money from the empire's far corners. The area in front of the basilica is part of the original Forum, built in the 8th century B.C. by Etruscan kings, the pre-Roman race who first drained the marshes and began construction.

Ancient Rome & Environs

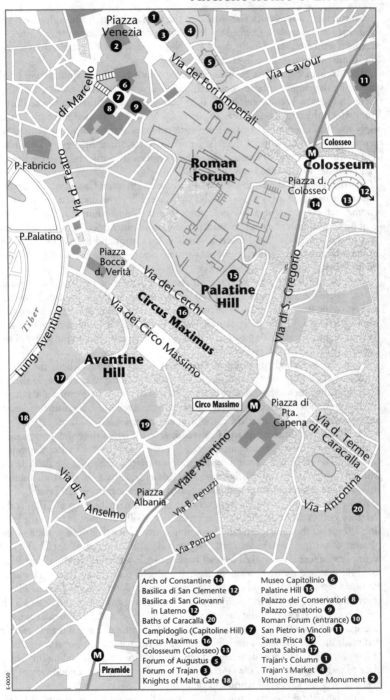

Continuing counterclockwise, you'll see the **Curia (Senate Building),** where over 600 senators met and determined the legal issues of the empire, often with the help of augurs (fortune-tellers). Nearby, the Lapis Niger, a sacred black marble slab, marked the Tomb of Romulus, the legendary founder of Rome.

The **Arch of Septimius Severus** was erected in A.D. 203 in appreciation of his extending the empire as far as Mesopotamia. (One son, Caracalla, murdered another, Geta, in order to become emperor.) At its back are the stairs that led to the Rostra, from which the crowd was addressed; some say Marc Antony used it for his famous elegy to Julius Caesar. Nearby you'll see eight columns of the **Temple of Saturn** (5th century B.C.), alleged site of the wild Saturnalia celebrations held every December. The **Column of Phocas** commemorates the Byzantine emperor who gave the Roman Pantheon to the pope and dates to A.D. 608.

Another **basilica,** similar to the first, was dedicated to Julius Caesar, which the man himself inaugurated in 54 B.C., while his star was still high, thanks to his victory over Pompey (an event that signaled the beginning of the Roman Empire). The three elegant 40-foot columns beyond are perhaps the most photographed sight in the Forum, part of the temple dedicated to the heavenly twins Castor and Pollux (the Dioscuri) in the 6th century B.C. Roman troops saw them before a major battle and attributed their victory to them.

Temples to Roman gods abound, but the most famous is the round **Temple of Vesta,** where the Vestal virgins lived and tended the flame that represented the eternalness of the state. The vestals were powerful and revered, but as a 7-year honor that would become a 30-year obligation, it was one not aspired to by every young girl. Those caught dallying with men met the same burial alive as those found guilty of letting the flame expire.

At the far end stands the **Arch of Titus,** built in A.D. 81 to celebrate the sack of Jerusalem (A.D. 70), and you can see in its friezes the sacred objects, among them a seven-branched menorah, that were brought back as spoils of war. Beyond and outside the Forum stands the largest and best preserved—the **Arch of Constantine.** Its reliefs are very well done and depict the emperor doing brave deeds, of course.

The **Basilica of Maxentius and Constantine,** to the left of the entrance, was massive and contained the enormous statue you'll see fragments of in the Capitoline Museum. The emperor Constantine was victorious over Maxentius at the Battle of the Milvian Bridge in Rome. Michelangelo and other architects of the 16th century studied these impressive ruins and incorporated some elements into St. Peter's.

Above the Forum, accessible from stairs or the road near the Arch of Titus, is the **Palatine Hill** (hold on to your Roman Forum ticket, offering joint entry to the Palatine). Rome was built on seven hills, beginning with this one. For those who know the pleasure of ruins (or who've watched every episode of Robert Grave's *I, Claudius* and want to see where Livia worked her evil ways; Caligula was murdered here), the Palatine Hill is magic for its views alone. Its tall umbrella pines bring Respighi's wistful *Pines of Rome* to mind. If you've taken the road, you'll soon reach the **Domus Flavia (Flavian Palace),** with a peristyle of columns surrounding an octagonal fountain. This was the official residence of the emperors, completed about A.D. 92. You can continue through these ruins, which only occasionally give a glimpse of the grandeur in marble that made up the Palatine. To the left is the **Domus Augustana,** the imperial residence of Domitian. The **Hippodrome** beyond was probably the emperor's riding ring and a place to watch games. From the far end of the Palatine you'll have a good view of the field that was the **Circus Maximus,** of Ben Hur fame.

At the far right side of the Farnese Gardens you'll see signs for the **House of Livia,** down the stairs. Some of the frescoes are in miraculous condition, similar to those uncovered in Pompeii. Farther along is the **Temple of Magna Mater** (191 B.C.), which reflects the cult of Cybele, the Great Mother, whose center was in Asia. Farther along stand the circular huts where Romulus and Remus lived. These legendary founders of Rome may be more fact than fiction, for archaeologists have dated the area at the mid–8th century B.C., when the twins were supposed to have lived. Now have an easy walk through the **Farnese Gardens,** first laid out in the 16th century and still lovely in spring and summer. From its balustrade you'll have a wonderful view of the Forum. Take the stairs down and exit beyond the Arch of Titus.

✪ **Colosseo (Colosseum) and Fori Imperiale (Imperial Forums).** Piazzale del Colosseo, via dei Fori Imperiali. ☎ **06/700-42-61.** Colosseum, street level of interior, free; upper levels, 8,000L ($4.50). Summer Mon–Tues and Thurs–Sat 9am–7pm (to 3pm winter). Metropolitana: Colosseo.

Every major city has at least one icon that symbolizes it: In Rome it's the **Colosseum,** a mammoth remnant from the 1st century A.D., the empire's golden age. It was commissioned by Vespian in A.D. 72, inaugurated by Titus in A.D. 80, and used at its peak during the days of Domitian. It was in this 50,000-seat stadium that Christians were said to be thrown to the lions and gladiators fought each other or wild beasts, legends considered unfounded by some historians. It was also flooded and used for mock naval battles. Much of the Colosseum's interior destruction came from its being used for centuries as a quarry for other construction projects. Its rich marble facade was stripped away to build palazzi and churches. (Much of Rome was regularly rearranged and recycled that way.) The original "floor" is also gone, revealing the labyrinthine underground network where prisoners, animals, and general provisions were kept.

To clamber up to the higher levels, go to the stairway to the left as you face the main entrance. In recent years, various of the three upper levels have been closed for reconstruction and reinforcement, part of a $25-million restoration sponsored by the Bank of Rome. Also, night illumination has given the structure a new mystery, making it impressive from far off in the glow of its three tiers of open arches. Parts of it will remain closed as it rushes toward a completion for 2000. Even if you see it only from the outside, it'll be worth it. Check with the tourist office for closing times if you plan an afternoon visit.

The **Imperial Forums of Augustus and Trajan:** If you walk away from the Colosseum on via Alessandrina, you'll find Augustus's Forum on the right and Trajan's on the left. Both are across via dei Fori Imperiale from the Roman Forum. Neither is open to the public, except by a guided tour, which is a recommended thing for those interested in classical history—buy tickets at the entrance at via IV (Quattro) Novembre 94. Admission to Trajan's Market is 4,000L ($2.25), but you can see the basic structure from the sidewalk above.

Trajan's Forum is the highlight of this imperial walk, with 25 standing columns, including the intricately carved **Colonna Traiano (Trajan's Column).** A stunning series of bas-reliefs winds up the monumental pillar, depicting the emperor's military career from the crossing of the Danube (bottom) on up to the deportation of the Dacian population. It's worth carrying your binoculars to see, especially when it's floodlit at night.

Via dei Fori Imperiali ends at **piazza Venezia,** dominated by the ostentatious 19th-century **Vittorio Emanuele Monument,** the "wedding cake monument," where Italian soldiers keep watch around the clock over the grave of Italy's unknown soldier, lit by an eternal flame. Nothing is more disturbing to some than this white marble typewriter-shaped monument amid Rome's honey tones, though over the years Roman's have grown accustomed to its facade.

✪ **Museo dei Conservatori and Museo Capitolino.** Capitoline Hill, piazza del Campidoglio. ☎ **06/6710-2071.** Piazza, free; museums, 10,000L ($6) for both, free for seniors 60 and over/age 18 and under. Free for everyone the last Sun in each month. Piazza, daily 24 hours. Both museums, Tues–Sun 9am–7pm. Bus: 46, 89, 92, 94, or 716.

The smallest of Rome's seven hills, the Capitoline was the political and religious center of the imperial city, and for many centuries since it has been home to Rome's Palazzo Senatorio (city hall). The hill's sweeping monumental steps, designed by Michelangelo, lead from piazza Venezia up to this majestic plateau and provide the most impressive approach, while the back side of the summit enjoys a terrific view of the Forum below—especially beautiful on a moonlit night. For the best view, walk up the graded steps beginning to the right around the Victor Emmanuel monument. The nongraded steps alongside were created for pilgrims to ascend on their knees to the Church of the Aracoeli at the top.

Crowning the top is a perfectly proportioned small square also designed by Michelangelo (said to be the inspiration for New York City's Lincoln Center for the Performing Arts). On one side is the **Palazzo dei Conservatori,** on the right as you reach the top, and opposite it is the **Museo Capitolino** (both said to be based on plans designed by Michelangelo but mildly disputed by historians). In the latter, the classical sculpture is some of the world's most impressive. The bronze equestrian statue of Marcus Aurelius was once the centerpiece of the piazza, creating a particular harmony. Dating to the 2nd century A.D., it was the only bronze statue to have survived since antiquity. It's now restored and has its own quarters in the museum (a replica is being made to replace it in the square).

Among the many statues of note within is that of the famous 5th-century B.C. bronze she-wolf *(Lupa Capitolina)* to which the twins, Romulus and Remus, were later additions (and the symbol of ancient Rome). You'll want to see the busts of the Caesars, the bronze *Boy with a Thorn* (Spinario), the *Dying Gaul,* the *Capitoline Venus,* and some fine mosaics from Hadrian's villa. A **Pinacoteca (Picture Gallery)** contains paintings mostly from the 16th and 17th centuries, including works by Caravaggio, Rubens, and Titian. In the Palazzo dei Conservatori's courtyard, the hand, head, and other body parts of the colossal statue of Constantine are arranged here and there. The head of Constantine measures 8 feet 6 inches and originally looked down from the Basilica of Maxentius in the Forum.

Chiesa di San Pietro in Vincoli (St. Peter in Chains). Piazza di San Pietro in Vincoli 4a. ☎ **06/488-28-65.** Free admission. Daily 7am–12:30pm and 3:30–6pm. Metropolitana: Piazza Cavour (then walk left across via Giovanni Lanza to via di Monte Polacco, trudge up the 3 endless flights of stairs that are this street, and turn right at the top; after a few hundred yards you'll come on a piazza and the church to the left) or Colosseo (then walk up largo Polveriera and go left on via Eudossiana to the church).

The chains that shackled St. Peter in Palestine can be seen behind glass under the high altar of this church. The church's chief attraction isn't the chains, however, but Michelangelo's *Moses,* complete with a marvelously carved waist-length beard. It was to sit on top of the tomb of Pope Julius II that was never completed: You'll find it on the right as you face the altar. Moses, whose horns were a sign of strength and authority (or rays of light according to others), was to have been one of 44 statues for the pope's magnificent tomb and is held by art historians as being one of his masterpieces. Michelangelo was largely responsible for Jacob's wives, *Rachel* (left of Moses) and *Leah* (on the right), which aren't exciting and are usually ignored.

Basilica di San Giovanni in Laterano (St. John in Lateran). Piazza San Giovanni in Laterano 4. Free admission. Summer daily 7am–6:45pm (to 5:45pm winter). Metropolitana: San

Giovanni, then walk through the portal at the walls of Rome and the church will come into sight.

One of Rome's four major basilicas, San Giovanni is the city of Rome's own cathedral, where the pope, as bishop of Rome, comes to celebrate mass on certain holidays. (The Vatican, or the Holy See, is its own country, not legally part of Rome or of Italy.) Indeed, the crimson building to the right as you face the church was the papal residence from the 4th to much of the 14th centuries. The impressive 18th-century facade was considerably damaged in 1993 by a terrorist bomb (said to be linked to the 1993 bombing of Florence's Uffizi), much of which has since been repaired. The interior was entirely remodeled in the baroque era by Borromini, who, in his zeal, is said to have destroyed frescoes by Giotto, a fragment of which you can still see since restoration uncovered it in 1952. The enormous bronze doors in the entrance came from the Curia in the Roman Forum. The Gothic baldacchino presides over what's believed to be the preserved heads of Sts. Peter and Paul, the patron saints of Rome. The adjoining baptistery's octagonal form became the prototype for baptisteries in Italy. It was built in the 4th century over the site of the first Christian baptism in Rome. The church's 13th-century cloisters have some lovely mosaics attributed to the local Cosmati marble guilds famous for their outstanding craftsmanship in the 12th and 13th centuries.

Santuario Scala Santa (Sanctuary of the Holy Staircase). Piazza San Giovanni in Laterano. ☎ **06/704-94-619.** Free admission. Daily 6:15am–12:30pm and 3–7pm. Metropolitana: San Giovanni, then walk through the portal in the walls of Rome and the church will come into sight.

The building off to the left and across the street as you exit the Basilica of San Giovanni in Laterano houses the Holy Stairs (Scala Santa), traditionally identified as the original 28 marble steps from Pontius Pilate's villa—now covered with wood for preservation—that Christ is said to have climbed the day he was condemned to death. According to a medieval tradition, they were brought from Jerusalem to Rome by Constantine's mother, Helen, in 326, and the stairs have been in their present location since 1589. Today pilgrims from all over the world come here to climb the steps on their knees. This is one of the holiest sites in Christendom, though some historians say the stairs may date only to the 4th century A.D.

Basilica di San Clemente. Piazza di San Clemente, via San Giovanni in Laterano. ☎ **06/704-51-018.** Main church, free; excavations, 3,000L ($1.70). Mon–Sat 9am–12:30pm and 3:30–6pm, Sun 10am–12:30pm and 3:30–6pm. Metropolitana: Colosseo, then a long block up via Labicana; it's a 10-minute walk from the Basilica di San Giovanni in Laterano.

A visit to the several descending layers of San Clemente (named for the fourth pope [A.D. 88–97], a convert from Judaism who was martyred under Hadrian) will give you a cross-section of early Christian Rome. Beneath this well-preserved 12th-century structure are the remains of two earlier structures, from the 4th and 1st centuries A.D., respectively. In the upper church, note the elaborate screen before the choir, marked with the monogram of John II (533–535). Don't miss the twisting papal candlestick, an example of 12th-century mosaic work by the local Cosmati family, and the delicate mosaics of the apse; the *Triumph of the Cross* is one of the most significant works.

The 15th-century frescoes of St. Catherine, in her chapel off the left nave, are the treasured work of Masolino responsible for the Brancacci Chapel in Florence. The church on the first level below was mentioned by St. Jerome in 392 and was the site of 5th-century papal councils. The fresco of the legend of San Clemente shows the saint being carried out of persecution's way, rolled up and disguised as a column. At the bottom you'll also see fascinating sculpture from the ancient pagan temple to the

Special & Free Events

There are two special times to be in Rome: **Easter** and **Christmas.** If you plan to visit at these holiest of times, especially Easter, make reservations *far* in advance. At Easter, you'll find balmy weather, flowers everywhere, and music in many churches; at Christmas, piazza Navona becomes the venue for the annual Christmas fair, whose stalls sell a roster of holiday-related toys and sweets but particularly *presepi* (Christmas cribs) that you'll see set up around town and in churches until Epiphany (January 6). The most artistically crafted ones still come from Naples, where craftspeople have carried on the tradition for centuries.

A beautiful **Rose Festival** is held on the Aventine Hill in early May. If you're planning to visit during the Jubilee Year 2000, you'd better reserve as soon as possible, at least for Christmas or Easter.

Rome has more "special events" now than ever before and will at least until the **Papal Jubilee Year 2000.** The tourist sources and newspapers have current details on art shows, concerts, and so forth. Check for extended evening hours—until 11pm—for the principal museums, such as the Galleria Borghese: They take place in high season and are announced only at the last minute.

god Mithras (a Persian god of the Sun and once a chief rival of Christianity) that was on the site, especially the dramatic altar, on which Mithras is seen slaying the bull. The church is under the care of Irish priests, and there's a mass in English at 10am the third Sunday of every month.

THE PANTHEON

✪ **The Pantheon.** Piazza della Rotonda. ☎ **06/6830-0230.** Free admission. July–Sept daily 9am–6pm (light permitting); Oct–June Mon–Sat 9am–4:30pm, Sun 9am–1pm. Bus: 64, 170, or 175 to largo di Torre Argentina (cross corso Vittorio Emanuele II and walk up via de' Cestari to piazza della Rotonda).

The Pantheon is one of the world's finest buildings, and you can marvel at its sheer power and simplicity in every light, dawn to moonlight. Inside it's a marvel of harmony and architectural ingenuity. The original building, built by Marcus Agrippa during the reign of Augustus Caesar (around 27 B.C.) as a temple to all the gods, was rectangular. All but the front columns and portico were destroyed by fire, and when it was rebuilt by Hadrian (A.D. 118–125), it took on its present round form. The diameter of 142 feet is equal to the height, meaning that a perfect sphere could potentially fit in its interior. The great bronze doors, as well as 13 of the 16 enormous columns holding up the temple's front porch, are original. The 28-foot *oculus* (open center) of the dome is its only source of light—a symbolic link between the temple and the heavens. Its miraculous state of preservation is due to its conversion to a church in 608. It's still officially a church, something easy to overlook. The great artists Raphael Sanzio (and his official mistress) and Annibale Carracci are buried here, as are two kings of Italy.

IN THE VILLA BORGHESE

✪ **Galleria Borghese.** Piazzale del Museo Borghese. ☎ **06/854-85-77.** Admission 12,000L ($7). Tues–Sat 9am–5pm, Sun 9am–1pm. Bus: 910 from the train station or 56 from piazza Barberini or piazza Venezia, to the park entrance closest to the museum. From the Villa Giulia, walk around behind the museum along viale delle Belle Arti, past the Modern Art Museum on your left, and straight into the heart of the park on viale di Villa Giulia; when you get to the top of the hill, you'll see a path branching off to the left and a sign directing you to the Galleria Borghese; this pleasant 20-minute amble looks longer on a map than it actually is.

At the opposite end of the Villa Borghese park from the Villa Giulia's Etruscan Museum (below) is the magnificently restored Galleria Borghese. An agonizingly long restoration begun in 1985 was finished to great fanfare in 1997, and again its excellent collection of paintings and sculpture is on display—for an admission that's now three times what it was before restoration. The ground floor houses a selection of world-class sculpture, with masterpieces like Bernini's dramatic *Rape of Persephone*, *David*, and *Apollo and Daphne*, said to be his finest. The figure of Daphne shows the youthful Bernini's genius for capturing the moment in sculpture, the metamorphosis, as Daphne begins to sprout leaves, turning into a tree. A more recent addition is Canova's early 19th-century erotic sculpture of Princess Pauline Borghese (Napoléon Bonaparte's sister). It was considered a scandal in its time—but then so was Pauline. The Quadreria, or picture collection, for years housed in Trastevere, has now been returned here. Among the notable works are Raphael's *Descent from the Cross* and paintings by Titian, Caravaggio, Botticelli, and Rubens.

✪ **Museo di Villa Giulia (Etruscan Museum).** Piazzale di Villa Giulia 9. ☎ **06/320-19-51.** Admission 8,000L ($4.50). Tues–Sat 9am–7pm, Sun 9am–1pm. Metropolitana: Flaminio, then bus no. 48 or a good 30-minute walk. Bus: 910 from the train station or 48 from the Flaminio Metropolitana stop.

This museum containing the world's most important collection of Etruscan art and artifacts gets a star for its interest to those drawn to the days before the sun rose on the Roman Empire. Scholars agree that the Etruscans brought a highly developed culture, as evidenced by their advanced art and sculpture. They're believed to have ruled Rome for a century or more beginning in the 7th century B.C. (their origins can be traced to the 9th century B.C. farther north, in Lazio and Tuscany), and since little remains of their architecture, destroyed by the Romans, these objects rescued mainly from their tombs prove they were a sophisticated race and passed many of their religious and political customs onto the early Romans. The museum is set in a 16th-century villa at one end of the Villa Borghese (Rome's main urban park) that was built as a summer villa for Pope Julius III; Michelangelo is said to have contributed to its design.

The museum offers a stunning window into the Etruscan civilization, mostly in the form of pottery (downstairs), though there's also a fine collection of bronze implements (upstairs), plus several outstanding larger sculpted pieces. The highlights of the first floor are the two figures of Apollo in Room 7 and the Sarcofago degli Sposi in Room 9, a remarkably well-preserved terra-cotta sarcophagus with a half-reclining married couple on top. Among the most impressive pieces upstairs is a 2-foot-tall bronze figure from Veio di Monterazzano.

NEAR THE TRAIN STATION
Chiesa di Santa Maria degli Angeli (St. Mary of the Angels). Piazza della Repubblica. ☎ **06/488-08-12.** Free admission. Daily 7:30am–noon and 4–6:30pm.

Michelangelo converted part of the ancient Roman Baths of Diocletian into this 16th-century church around the corner and adjoining the **Museo Nazionale Romano delle Terme,** with a fine archaeological collection. Its airy interior and beautiful marble floors are surrounded by huge paintings that would be the pride of any city less rich in great art.

Basilica di Santa Maria Maggiore (St. Mary Major). Piazza Santa Maria Maggiore. ☎ **06/48-31-95.** Free admission. Summer daily 7am–8pm (to 7pm winter). Only a short walk from Stazione Termini, the church can be entered from piazza Santa Maria Maggiore at the front or from via Cavour in the back.

One of the seven pilgrimage churches in Rome and one of Rome's four major basilicas, St. Mary Major houses relics of what's said to be the Holy Crib below the altar (exhibited at Christmastime) and a prized 5th-century triumphal arch above. Its other features include two richly decorated chapels—the right one in high Renaissance style, the left one baroque, a period when the basilica and facade were heavily rebuilt. The stunning 13th-century mosaic in the apse of the Coronation of the Virgin Mary is some of the oldest and finest in Rome. The gold-coffered ceiling is decorated with gold said to be brought back from the New World by Columbus. The basilica's origin was in a dream of Pope Liberius (352–66) in which the Virgin Mary showed the pontiff where to build a church by causing snow to fall, outlining the precise site of the basilica (on August 5, mind you) on Esquiline Hill. Each year on that day there's a celebration with flower petals thrown to represent the summertime snowfall.

PIAZZAS & FOUNTAINS

More than any other Italian city, Rome is known for its exuberant piazzas and fountains; they're among the Eternal City's greatest gifts to the traveler. ✪ **Piazza Navona** is a famous long ellipsis that's quintessentially baroque in feeling, yet its shape reflects its original use as Domitian's stadium in ancient Rome when it was flooded for the emperor's "nautical games" and mock sea battles. Now it's the loveliest place to stroll without cars buzzing around; to enjoy unparalleled people-watching, a coffee, or a gelato; or to watch the locals teach their children to ride bikes or parade their prams. At Christmas, a fair takes over, enlivening the piazza's wintry look. Of the piazza's three fountains, the central one is a triumph of Bernini (1651): the **Fontana dei Fiumi (Fountain of the Rivers),** an ancient Egyptian obelisk surrounded by figures representing the rivers of the four continents, the Ganges, Plate, Nile, and Danube. Local legend goes that some are shielding their faces from the nearby Church of Sant'Agnese in Agone, standing before it on the west side of the piazza and built by Bernini's rival, Borromini, but records show that the church's facade was designed by Borromini only after the completion of the fountain.

A must-not-skip visit to piazza Navona is often linked with a stroll through nearby ✪ **piazza Pantheon** (also called piazza della Rotonda), in the same high-real-estate niche due to the proximity of the country's Parliament and Senate buildings (and politicos with healthy expense accounts). Stop for a gelato or iced tea here, if only to sit on the worn steps of its small fountain as countless students have done before you over the millennium.

✪ **Campo de' Fiori,** evocative of medieval Rome, is famous for its chaotic morning fruit-and-vegetable market. Overlooking the colorful scene is the haunting statue of Giordano Bruno, who was burned here at the stake in 1601 for heresy (and daring to imply the earth revolved around the sun). Stroll around this piazza and its surrounding warren of streets to savor the villagelike character of Old Rome. Tall palm trees give a tropical air to elegant ✪ **piazza di Spagna,** boasting honey, cream, russet, and apricot tones. The newly restored **Spanish Steps** rise in three (for the Trinity) graceful tiers to the church of Trinità dei Monti at the top, from which you can enjoy a magnificent panorama, especially in late afternoon. At the foot of the steps is the city's best window-shopping.

For centuries, the northern gate to the city for Europe's carriage travelers and pilgrims and the first glimpse they'd get of Rome, **piazza del Popolo** is presided over by an obelisk more than 3,000 years old, brought from Egypt by Augustus. (However, at press time the piazza was under scaffolding and boarded up for renovations.) The lovely church of Santa Maria del Popolo, begun in 1472, and its two Caravaggios is at its northern curve, from which you can look back and see the twin churches at the opposite side. The piazza is known for the Dal Bolognese restaurant, whose outdoor tables are still frequented by the film and well-heeled set, and its two historical and fashionable outdoor cafes, the Rosati and Canova, where fresh *cornetti* (croissants) and cappuccino are an excellent way to begin a day. **Piazza Santa Maria in Trastevere** is the heart and soul of the popular Trastevere neighborhood, popular day and night. Its attraction is the sparkling facade of 13th-century mosaics that glitter in the sunlight or moonlight. You can have an expensive dinner at Sabatini's or an inexpensive ice cream here while drinking in the view and wandering the side streets.

In front of St. Peter's Basilica in Vatican City, the vast **piazza San Pietro** is partly enclosed by a triumphant colonnade. Here pilgrims by the multitude look up at the basilica, listen to the pope's Sunday message at noon, or watch for the lights in his apartment above the right arm of the piazza. Dozens of statues, including those of the city's patron saints Peter and Paul and two symmetrical sparkling fountains, are the adornments. In 1765, Piranesi designed the harmonious **piazza dei Cavalieri di Malta** on Aventine Hill, but few appreciate it, as everyone flocks to look through the bronze keyhole through which you can see St. Peter's across the Tiber, perfectly framed. It's worth a stop when visiting the Aventine.

The movie *Three Coins in the Fountain* ensured fame for the high baroque **Fontana di Trevi,** where everyone converges (beginning with large tour groups and the round-the-clock Roman gadabouts who have made cruising a full-time job here) to toss a coin over the left shoulder to be sure to return to Rome. Nicola Salvi designed it in 1762 for Pope Clement XII, a theatrical flight-of-fancy backdrop, along one side of a palazzo tucked away in a tiny piazza. Neptune is flanked by Tritons who symbolize a rough sea and a tranquil sea. Come at night, when it's gorgeously floodlit, but don't try to play Anita Ekberg, who took a late-night dip in *La Dolce Vita,* or you'll get yourself arrested. (However, note that it might be behind scaffolding to repair a botched repair job.)

From a design by Giacomo della Porta, the 16th-century **Fontana della Tartarughe (Fountain of the Turtles),** in the small piazza Mattei in the Ghetto's warren of winding streets, is the most delicate and graceful in Rome. Taddeo Landi sculpted the four slender boys, each nudging a turtle to take a drink from the water. Porpoises were added during the following century, possibly by Bernini.

THE APPIAN WAY & THE CATACOMBS

Of all the roads that led to Rome, **via Appia Antica,** built in 312 B.C., was the reigning leader. It eventually stretched all the way from Rome to the seaport of Brindisi, through which trade with the colonies in Greece and the East was funneled. According to Christian tradition, it was along the Appian Way that an escaping Peter encountered the vision of Christ, which caused him to go back into the city to face subsequent martyrdom.

Of the Roman monuments on via Appia Antica, the most impressive is the **Tomb of Cecilia Metella,** within walking distance of the catacombs (continue southeast from the catacombs). The cylindrical tomb honors the wife of one of Julius Caesar's military commanders from the Republican era. Why such an elaborate tomb for such an unimportant person? Cecilia Metella happened to be singled out for enduring fame because her tomb has remained and the others have decayed.

Along the Appian Way, the patrician Romans built great monuments above the ground and Christians met in the catacombs beneath the earth. You can visit the remains of both today. In some dank, dark grottoes (never stray too far from either your party or one of the exposed lightbulbs), you can still discover the remains of early

Christian art. Of the catacombs open to the public, those of St. Callixtus and St. Sebastian are the most important.

"The most venerable and most renowned of Rome," said Pope John XXIII of the ✪ **Catacombe di San Callisto (St. Callixtus),** via Appia Antica 110 (☎ **06/513-6725**). The founder of Christian archaeology, Giovanni Battista de Rossi (1822–94), called them "catacombs par excellence." They're the first cemetery of the Christian community of Rome, burial place of 16 popes in the 3rd century. They bear the name of St. Callixtus, the deacon Pope St. Zephyrinus put in charge of them and who was later elected pope (217–222) in his own right. The complex is a network of galleries stretching for nearly 12 miles, structured in five levels and reaching a depth of about 65 feet. There are many sepulchral chambers and almost half a million tombs. Paintings, sculptures, and epigraphs (with such symbols as the fish, anchor, and dove) provide invaluable material for the study of the life and customs of the ancient Christians and the story of their persecutions.

Entering the catacombs, you see at once the most important crypt, that of the nine popes. Some of the original marble tablets of their tombs are still preserved. The next crypt is that of St. Cecilia, the patron of sacred music. This early Christian martyr received three ax strokes on her neck, the maximum allowed by Roman law, which failed to kill her outright. Farther on, you'll find the famous Cubicula of the Sacraments with its 3rd-century frescoes.

Admission is 8,000L ($4.50) adults and 4,000L ($2.25) children 6 to 15; children 5 and under are free. The catacombs are open Thursday to Tuesday 8:30am to noon and 2:30 to 5pm (to 5:30pm in summer). Take bus no. 218 from piazza San Giovanni in Laterano to Fosse Ardeatine and ask the driver to let you off at the Catacombe di San Callisto.

Today the tomb of St. Sebastian is in the basilica, but his original tomb was under it in the **Catacombe di San Sebastiano,** via Appia Antica 136 (☎ **06/785-0350**). From the reign of Valerian to the reign of Constantine, the bodies of St. Peter and St. Paul were hidden in the catacombs, which were dug from tufo, a soft volcanic rock. The big church was built here in the 4th century. The tunnels here, if stretched out, would reach a length of 7 miles. In the tunnels and mausoleums are mosaics and graffiti, along with many other pagan and Christian objects from centuries even before the time of Constantine.

Admission is 8,000L ($4.50) adults and 4,000L ($2.25) children 6 to 15; children 5 and under are free. The catacombs are open Friday to Wednesday 8:30am to noon and 2:30 to 5:30pm (to 5pm in winter). For bus transportation, see above.

PARKS & GARDENS

Rome is a city of stone and stucco, not of green. Those who need a fix of fresh air should venture into the **Villa Borghese,** Rome's urban park, on the north side of the Old City. You'll find some of the best views over Rome from the edge of the park, as well as countless hills and trees and a duck pond. Bicycling, tennis, horseback riding, rowboating, and jogging are popular. The park is best approached from the Spagna or Flaminio Metropolitana station, on the south and west sides of the park, or by taking bus no. 910 from the station or bus no. 56 from piazza Barberini or piazza Venezia, to the east side of the greenlands.

On the **Aventine Hill,** south of the Circus Maximus, May ushers in a brilliant display of roses. The orange trees alongside the Aventine church of Santa Sabina are lovely in season. While there, enjoy the simple beauty of the early Christian churches on the Aventine, Santa Sabina, Santa Prisca, and Santa Saba. From the Circo Massimo

Metropolitana stop, walk along via del Circo Massimo and up the hill about midway along, at piazza La Malfa, or take bus no. 94 and get off up the hill, at Santa Prisca.

ORGANIZED TOURS

Secret Walks, viale Medaglie d'Oro 127 (☎ **06/3972-8728**), offers a wide variety of theme walks and bike tours by English-speaking foreign residents for about 25,000L ($14). If your Italian is reasonably good, read *Il Messaggero,* a Rome daily paper, for listings of special tours. Two Anglo-American papers, *Wanted in Rome* and *Metropolitan,* also list English tours periodically—as well as much more of interest to the English-speaking community. A number of interesting 3-hour walking tours of different themes leave daily, organized by **Enjoy Rome** (see "Visitor Information," earlier in this chapter), costing 30,000L ($17) for those over 26 and 25,000L ($14) for those under 26.

Slightly less expensive (and with five stops for those who'd rather walk less) is the **no. 110 Tourist Bus,** a city tour provided by ATAC, Rome's bus line. Tours leave from piazza dei Cinquecento, near the rail station, one each day (3:30pm summer or 2:30pm winter), last 3 hours, and cost 15,000L ($8). Buy tickets at the ATAC information booth in front of Stazione Termini in piazza dei Cinquecento.

For the standard bus tour, **American Express** (see "Fast Facts: Rome," earlier in this chapter) and **Carrani** (☎ **06/488-0510**) offer a medley of sights in town and day trips to Tivoli, Assisi (even Florence and Tuscany), and other spots. Tours can waste a lot of time waiting at hotels for clients and in traffic. Alas, you're not always better off on your own as connections to these destinations farther afield may be problematic and time-consuming. A good example is the 1-day bus trip to Pompeii: It can be a killer but a worthwhile one for those interested in classical history. For those with a few days to spare, take the train to Naples and then catch the hydrofoil to Capri in the Bay of Naples or head farther south to the fabled Amalfi Coast, including a trip to Pompeii along the way. The agency **Enjoy Rome** (see "Visitor Information," above) makes the 1-day sprint from Rome to Pompeii as inexpensive and painless as possible with an 8:30am-to-5:30pm round-trip daily tour by air-conditioned minivan (fitting eight passengers), costing 60,000L ($34). The trip is 3 hours one-way, and an English-speaking driver and loads of maps and materials help you bone up on the ancient wonders that await. You're on your own once you reach the archaeological site and there's no imposed restaurant lunch: That's what keeps their prices the lowest around. During the high season, be ready for crowds and temperatures at a consistent high.

6 Shopping

RECOVERING VAT

The **value-added tax (IVA in Italy)** is included in the stated price of all consumer goods and most services. The average tax is 19%, but it can go as high as 35% on some luxury items. Non-EU visitors are entitled to a refund of the tax paid if you spend more than 300,000L ($169) in any one store. Note the TAX-FREE FOR TOURISTS sign in the windows of many stores. Ask them for your tax-free shopping forms, which they'll fill out. Present the form and the goods bought at Customs before check-in (to show that the unused goods are accompanying you out of the EU). Ideally, the Tax-Free booth at the airport will give you a cash refund on the spot or a charge-account credit, if you prefer. More probably, they'll insist on mailing it to your address abroad, a procedure that can take many weeks and sometimes months.

BEST BUYS

The streets around **piazza di Spagna** are the most fashionable and thus expensive. Along these streets, particularly **via Condotti,** you'll find the best Italian and international names in clothing, accessories, and jewelry. Prices in this high-rent neighborhood are stratospheric, albeit similar to what you'd pay for the same designer names elsewhere. However, if you want to buy that Armani or Ferragamo, come in January/February and July/August, when the prices are a fraction of those in the States—not that this fraction means inexpensive, but it often means a very good value. Ferragamo maintains a store in the duty-free area at Rome's airport. Their classic pumps are available there at great savings, if you have heavy local taxes at home.

The medium range isn't a bargain in Italy, but you might find something different from your selections back home. Among Rome's less expensive shopping streets are **via Cola di Rienzo** near the Vatican, **via Nazionale,** and **via del Corso.** The department stores, such as **Rinascente** at piazza Colonna and the less-fashionable **Upim** on via del Tritone, are handy, as you can browse without the attendance of a sales clerk, but don't expect give-away prices. Finally, **Old Rome,** particularly north of piazza Venezia and between piazza Navona and the Trevi Fountain, is the place to wander for handcrafts and one-of-a-kind shops. T-shirts can be found everywhere, perhaps cheapest at 5,000L to 10,000L ($2.80 to $6) outside the Santa Anna gate at the Vatican (off the right of the piazza, when facing San Pietro). There are a few stalls around the **campo de' Fiori** market as well.

MARKETS

You can find everything from 17th-century candelabra and antique doorknockers to 5,000L ($2.80) pirated cassettes and 20,000L ($11) knock-off shoes at Rome's largest, oldest, and seemingly endless **flea market** at Porta Portese in Trastevere. Countless vendors and just plain folks set up shop every Sunday 6 or 7am to 1 or 2pm. Most of the wares (mostly clothes) are pretty chintzy and of little interest, but the market is a sight in and of itself. Stands with old books, prints, and baubles are the most interesting. Be sure to keep an eye out for pickpockets—Gypsies and other thieves flock here.

The best of the many markets specializing in flowers and produce is on picturesque **campo de' Fiori.** The rambunctious and colorful market, crammed with fresh fruit and vegetables, meat, fish, cheese, T-shirts, luggage, and flowers, is open Monday to Saturday 7 or 8am to 1 or 2pm. In spring and fall, look for untrimmed artichokes on long stalks. Autumn brings Muscat grapes and porcini mushrooms the size of Frisbees. Any season warrants a visit.

A handful of **pushcarts** offering used books, etchings, lithographs, art reproductions, antique jewelry, and one-of-a-kind items sets up Monday to Saturday 9am to about 6pm (to 4:30pm winter) at piazza Borghese, near ponte Cavour. To find them, walk out via Condotti from piazza di Spagna and continue for 2½ blocks past via del Corso on via della Fontanella Borghese.

Piazza Vittorio Emanuele, south of Stazione Termini, is the site of Rome's biggest daily open-air food market, open Monday to Saturday 8am to 2pm. The area is up for gentrification, so you might want to see it before it closes.

BOOKSTORES

The daily *International Herald Tribune* and assorted magazines in English can be found at larger newsstands. The widest selection of books is at the **Economy Book** and **Video Center,** via Torino 136 (☎ **06/474-68-77**). **Books on Italy,** via Giub-bonari 30, near campo de' Fiori (☎ **06/654-52-85**), has a wonderful selection of used and out-of-print books. Write for a catalog or call for an appointment. Ever a charmer is the **Lion Bookshop,** via del Babuino 181 (☎ **06/322-58-37**), specializing in British books and children's amusements; you can pick up a classic, a travel book, poetry, or a thriller.

The gay bookstore **Libreria Babele,** via Paola 44 (☎ **06/687-66-28**), sells a gay map of Rome. For women, the **Virginia Woolf Center,** via Lungara 1a in Trastevere (☎ **06/686-42-01**), is a main clearinghouse for information.

7 Rome After Dark

Un Ospite a Roma, available free from the concierge desks of top hotels, is full of cur-rent details on what's happening around town. *Trova Roma,* a weekly listings maga-zine inserted in the Thursday edition of *La Repubblica* newspaper, is indispensable for its movie, music, art, opera, and dance coverage; most newsstands stock extra, free copies in case you weren't able to pick it up on Thursday. The minimagazines *Metro-politan* and *Wanted in Rome* have listings of jazz, rock, and such and give an inter-esting look at expatriate Rome. The daily *Il Messaggero* lists current cultural news, especially in its Thursday magazine supplement, *Metro.*

OPERA & BALLET

Open-air opera and ballet at the **Terme di Caracalla (Baths of Caracalla),** via delle Terme di Caracalla, are among Italy's great summer events. (If you have the Three Tenors video, you can see how atmospheric a setting it is, amid the ruins of this one-time ancient Roman spa.) Usually two operas and a ballet are put on each July and August, with shows three or four times a week—however, at press time it was uncer-tain if performances of anything would ever again be given at the baths. The *Aïda* pro-duction, once Caracalla's most memorable, is no longer performed due to structural damage. Alternating with performances at the Stadio Olimpico has proven successful, and you may see more performances taking place at the far less evocative stadium, built for the 1960 Olympics. Exceptions may be made for the Papal Jubilee Year 2000, however. Visit the opera's Web site at **www.themix.it** for updates. Tickets are 25,000L to 65,000L ($14 to $37) for the opera or 20,000L to 55,000L ($11 to $31) for the ballet.

The main opera house ticket office, on via Firenze, on the block between via Nazionale and via del Viminale (☎ **06/48-17-003** for information), is open Tuesday to Sunday 10:40am to 5pm; the box office at the Terme is open 8 to 9:30pm on performance days. Take bus no. 93 from the train station to the Terme.

If there are no summer performances scheduled at the Terme di Caracalla when you visit, you can attend a performance at the **Teatro dell'Opera,** via Firenze 72 (☎ **06/48-16-01**), a plain white building almost remarkable for its stalwart facade. The opera season runs December to May or June. Tickets are 15,000L to 100,000L ($8 to $56). The box office is open Tuesday to Saturday 10am to 4pm and Sunday 10am to 1pm.

Check the daily papers for **free church concerts,** especially near Christmas or Easter.

LIVE-MUSIC CLUBS

Rome sports a fair variety of small jazz clubs with frequent performances by local and international musicians (you'll find most of them listed in the entertainment sections of Italian newspapers).

One favorite is **St. Louis Music City** (aka Jam Session Music), via del Cardello 13a (☎ **06/474-50-76**). A cavernous club with a jazz stage, this place also has a restaurant area and a pool table. Entrance is free, but you must become a club member first, a formality that'll set you back 10,000L ($6) for the season. If you sit at one of the tables near the stage, expect to pay 8,000L to 12,000L ($4.50 to $7) per drink. Happy hour is 8 to 9:30pm. There's live music almost every night from 10:30pm or so (closed Monday). Via del Cardello is halfway between the Colosseum and via Cavour.

Big Mama, vicolo San Francesco a Ripa 18 (☎ **06/581-25-51**), off via San Francesco a Ripa in Trastevere, has a good selection of sounds from jazz, rock, and R&B, but blues is the big draw to this smoky venue (Chet Baker used to perform here). There's a cover of 20,000L ($11) for the season, which permits free entrance except for major acts, which cost an extra 20,000L ($11). It's open September to May, Tuesday to Saturday 9pm to 1:30am.

Maybe it was first sparked off by the popularity of Antonio Banderas, but the most popular beat in Rome is still Latin. A longtime favorite is the tiny **Yes, Brazil,** via San Francesco a Ripa 103 (☎ **06/581-62-67**), close to the Big Mama (above). Small, crowded, and palmy, with good tropical drinks, it's open October to May, Monday to Saturday 9pm to 2:30am. There's no cover. See also **Caffè Latino** under "Dance Clubs," below.

CAFES & GELATERIAS

When in Rome, do as the Romans do: Enjoy a leisurely dinner at some hidden-away trattoria's outdoor tables, then while away the rest of the night at a cafe in a peaceful neighborhood.

The outdoor cafes on the pedestrians-only **piazza della Rotonda,** in the Pantheon's shadow, are some of the best places to be on warm summer nights. The price for a drink at an outdoor table (consider it rent) is a steep 5,000L ($2.80), though. The long oval **piazza Navona,** with the splendidly baroque fountain in the center, is nearby and another popular choice for nighttime hanging-about.

The **Spanish Steps** on piazza di Spagna are almost a sight in and of themselves. There are no cafes actually on the staircase, but on warm summer nights the place buzzes with the sounds of (mostly) young people from all over the world sitting around, hanging out, and generally having a good time. And from piazza di Spagna it's pleasant to stroll over to the **Fontana di Trevi,** a tiny cafe-free piazza.

Of the cafes near the Spanish Steps, the **Antico Caffè Greco,** via Condotti 86 (☎ **06/6791-70-00**), is the standout, the oldest in Rome. The waiters in tailcoats and the small rooms give it a turn-of-the-century (and earlier—it was founded in 1760) appeal, as in the days of habitués like Keats and Goethe and their compatriots. Now modern tourists crowd the worn marble-topped tables while locals crowd the front bar section Monday to Saturday 8am to 8:40pm. The **Caffè Gelateria Fontana di Trevi,** piazza Fontana di Trevi 90 (no phone), serves the richest cornetto this side of Sicily— it's a chocolate-covered croissant stuffed with whipped cream, chocolate cream, or custard. Small pizzas and sandwiches are also sold. Summer hours are daily 7am to 2am; winter hours are Thursday to Tuesday 7am to midnight. Also for ice cream, try **Gelateria Trevi,** via del Lavatore 84 (☎ **06/679-20-60**), south of the Trevi Fountain. This old-fashioned place is famous for its zabaglione semi-freddo (of mousselike consistency) and its good range of ice creams. In summer, it's open daily 11am to midnight (to 11pm in winter).

But Romans take their gelato seriously, and if you do too, head for the famous **Gelateria Tre Scalini,** piazza Navona 28 (☎ **06/880-19-96**). It's the place everyone wanders to after dinner, for a dessert and maybe an amaretto in the light of Bernini's fountain. If you're still budget-minded, have your ice cream standing up, always the cheaper position, or strolling around the square. This place is famous for the tartufo, a mound of bittersweet chocolate chips held together by a smidgen of chocolate ice cream crowned with whipped cream. In summer, it's open Thursday to Tuesday 8am to 1:30am (to 1am winter).

BARS

Several of Rome's favorite watering holes are along popular **via del Governo Vecchio,** a charming narrow back street near piazza Navona. All are equally cozy and small, such as the favorite **Enoteca il Piccolo,** nos. 74–76 (☎ **06/880-17-46**), open daily 10am to 2am. This imminently strollable neighborhood offers a number of subdued, comfortable places to sit and leisurely enjoy a few drinks or wine by the glass (like prosecco, a dry, lightly sparkling white wine from the Veneto). Snacks are also available in these wine bars (like Cul de Sac—see "Great Deals on Dining," earlier in this chapter). Most bars along this street are open nightly to 1 or 2am. You'll pay for the ambiance, often a stylish one; consider it a cover charge for the local color.

For a budget drink and a look at what most Romans consider the city's nightlife, you can't do better than **La Vineria** (also known as Da Giorgio), campo de' Fiori 15 (☎ **06/654-32-68**), an authentic wine store/bar specializing in small glasses of prosecco (sparkling wine) for 1,500L to 2,000L (85¢ to $1.10). Its legion patrons stand along the long bar or sit on adjacent wooden benches, invariably spilling out into the piazza. La Vineria is open Monday to Saturday 9:30am to 1pm and 5pm to 1am. A bit wilder on campo de' Fiori is **The Drunken Ship,** at nos. 20–21 (☎ **06/683-00-535**), where a younger crowd finds beer, bagels, nachos, and American music (no surprise here that the owner and staff are an affable set of Americans). It's open daily 5pm to 2am, but in summer opens at noon for brunch that can be enjoyed at a few outdoor tables.

Ironically, in a wine-revered culture, the Irish pub is more popular than ever. Among many are the **Fiddler's Elbow,** which has lasted many a year at via dell'Olmata 43, near piazza Santa Maria Maggiore and the train station (☎ **06/487-21-10**). Open 5pm to midnight, it's a pub where spontaneous singing is the thing (must be the Guinness). The **Guinness Pub,** via Muzio Clemente 12 (☎ **06/3218-4240**), has less Irish an air usually, but it serves up that frothy brew nicely. Live music is offered downstairs. It's near the ponte Cavour across the Tiber. Near the Stazione Termini, **Julius Caesar,** via della Fossa 16 (☎ **06/689-34-26**), has a happy hour 9 to 10pm with low-ticket beer and pizzas. The music is *loud.* It's open to 2am, unusual for Rome.

GAY & LESBIAN BARS

One of the most popular (though out of the way) gay bars/discos is **L'Alibi,** via Monte di Testaccio 40 (☎ **06/574-34-48**), spread over two stories (in summer there's also a great roof terrace), with a mixed crowd. It's open Tuesday to Sunday 11pm to 4am, with a 15,000L ($8) cover. In this same area of Testaccio is **Radio Londra** (see below), with a mixed crowd.

An American runs what was Rome's first gay bar, the very popular **Hangar,** via Selci 69 (☎ **06/488-13-97**), near the Forum. There's no cover. **Angelo Azzuro,** via

A Nightlife Note

A neighborhood with an edge, Testaccio is radical chic—don't wander around alone. The area still has a way to go before regentrification. However, Testaccio is the place to ask about what's hot in Rome when you arrive, as crowds are fickle.

Cardinal Merry del Val 13 (☎ **06/580-0472**), in the heart of Trastevere, is another hot spot. It's open Friday to Sunday, with a 20,000L ($11) cover on Saturday. For women, the **Time Cafe,** via di Monte Giordano, near piazza Navona (☎ **06/6830-7051**), seems to have a Sunday appeal.

Two English-speaking gay and lesbian organizations can be found in Rome: **ARCI-Gay,** via Primo Acciaresi 7 (☎ **06/4173-0752**), and **Circolo Mario Mieli,** via Ostiense 202 (☎ **06/54-13-985**). Both are helpful with political and social information. Helping with travel plans locally and throughout Italy and passing as a local info office for gays and lesbians is the English-speaking **Zipper Travel Agency,** via Castelfidardo 18, 2nd floor (☎ **06/488-2730;** fax 06/488-2729; E-mail: zipper.travel@ flashnet.it). Note that it may have moved by the time you arrive.

DANCE CLUBS

Stylish dancers, private dancers, and celebs are found at the restored **Jackie O,** via Boncompagni 11, off via Veneto (☎ **06/488-57-54**), and the old favorite **Gilda,** via Mario de' Fiori 97, near the Spanish Steps (☎ **06/678-48-38**). Gilda has an older crowd that doesn't seem to mind the cover and one drink charge of about 35,000L to 40,000L ($22 to $25). The nightclub part opens at midnight; earlier there's a pricey bar/restaurant. In summer it's a younger crowd at **Gilda on the Beach** at Fregene, near Rome, open Tuesday to Saturday 11pm to 4am. Check the magazine *Metropolitan* to see what entertainers are in town.

Young Rome heads toward the Testaccio neighborhood at night for dancing at crazy **Radio Londra,** via di Monte di Testaccio 18 (☎ **06/574-34-48**); slightly older sibs go to the **Caffè Latino,** a converted warehouse on via di Monte di Testaccio 96 (☎ **06/574-40-20**), to hear jazz and watch the video at the club that put this neighborhood on the map. This is also the setting for sophisticated **Spago,** via di Monte Testaccio (☎ **06/574-49-99**), where young upwardly mobile Romans dance to disco. This area has so many clubs now that you can mambo from one to another.

8 Side Trips: Tivoli, Ostia Antica & Pompeii

TIVOLI

The most popular half-day excursion, just 20 miles east of Rome (though traffic can make it a 1-hour trip), **Tivoli** (or Tibur to the ancient Romans) holds two major sites of interest. Tivoli is accessible by a **bus** marked AUTOBUS PER TIVOLI, which leaves every 15 to 20 minutes from via Gaeta just west of via Volturno, near Stazione Termini; the fare is 5,000L ($2.80) each way. The bus goes to the Villa d'Este; from there bus no. 2 or 4 (check for possibly changing bus numbers) goes to the Villa Adriana. There's **train** service to Tivoli but the bus is easier, more frequent, and less expensive.

The main attraction of the **hilltop town,** itself pleasant for strolling and cafe lingering, and the favorite of children and adults alike is the **Villa d'Este** (☎ **0774/2-20-70**) and its delightful water park tiered down a steep hillside. Built in the mid-16th century by the extravagant Cardinal Ippolito d'Este, son of Lucrezia Borgia (and grandson of the infamous Borgia Pope Alexander VI), it was a Renaissance playground and gives a peak into the frivolous luxuries the princes of the church allowed themselves. Those looking for a refreshing respite from the heat and stone of Rome revel in its 500 fountains, conduits, and waterfalls (a good number of which still work). Amazingly, these waterfalls operate entirely by gravity—quite an engineering feat for its day or any day—and are at the mercy of occasional and seasonal low-pressure periods.

The Renaissance villa is highlighted by an open loggia that's the starting point for an amble downward past moss-covered grottoes, under tree-shaded paths, and along the park's highlight, the **Viale delle Cento Fontane,** whose 100 fountains have led some people to proclaim this one of the world's most beautiful gardens.

About 2½ miles southwest of the town of Tivoli is the much older **Villa Adriana (Hadrian's Villa)** (☎ **0774/53-02-03**), a collection of replicas of all the beautiful places the emperor Hadrian had seen in the ancient world. It has been compared to a kind of Roman San Simeon and was built between A.D. 118 and 134 for the use of Hadrian's court with the purpose of escaping the threat of malaria and the discomfort of Rome's summer. The emperor enjoyed it for only 4 years before his death. A scale model of the entire city is at the entrance.

Both the Villa d'Este and the Villa Adriana are open daily 9am to an hour before sunset. Entrance is 10,000L ($6) for the Villa d'Este and 8,000L ($4.50) for the Villa Adriana. Some strenuous walking is called for at the Villa d'Este, and nonskid shoes are advised against potentially slippery walkways.

OSTIA ANTICA

An astonishingly well-preserved ancient Roman city, ✪ **Ostia Antica** was once the busy commercial seaport and military base of Rome. In a pastoral setting, the ruins of Ostia help capture the essence of Imperial Rome in the middle of its heyday. Founded in the 4th century B.C., it was gradually abandoned in the 4th and 5th centuries A.D. when the harbor was silted up, reducing it to a breeding bed of malaria. Once a flourishing city of 100,000, it eventually followed Rome into decline.

Ostia is especially worth visiting if you won't have a chance to visit Pompeii, for here you'll see an ancient city preserved in its entirety, in a smaller, parklike setting, with such dazzling details of Roman architecture as mosaic floors, marble walls, a few wall paintings—details by and large missing from the Roman Forum. Ostia is now inland (a full 1.9 mi. from the sea), and wasn't excavated until before World War II on orders of Mussolini.

Ostia Antica is open daily: March to September 9am to 7pm (the rest of the year to 5pm). Last entrance is 1 hour before closing, and admission is 12,000L ($7).

With numerous Metro connections and just 16 miles southwest of Rome, Ostia is Rome's most convenient day trip. To get there, take the **Metropolitana** Line B to the Magliana station and transfer there to a suburban **Lido train** connecting with Ostia Antica in half an hour. When you arrive, walk across a bridge over a highway and continue straight in that direction for 5 to 10 minutes.

FARTHER AFIELD TO POMPEII

Once a thriving city of 30,000, the Roman colony of **Pompeii** (*Pompei* in Italian) was virtually buried alive in A.D. 79 when nearby Mt. Vesuvius erupted, burying it beneath 20 feet of scalding cinder and volcanic ash (not lava as is commonly thought). It was "rediscovered" in the 16th century, but systematic digs didn't begin until 1860. Today, some two-thirds of the 160-acre site have been excavated, though work goes on. Much of the remarkable frescoes, mosaics, and statuary you've seen photographed has wound up in Naple's Museo Archeologico Nazionale, but enough has been left in situ to make these Europe's fascinating and best-preserved 2,000-year-old ruins.

Day-long trips from Rome to Pompeii (150 miles southeast) were always doable but were exhausting and, in the competent hands of a number of major agencies like American Express and Carrani (see earlier in this chapter), too expensive at a minimum of 150,000L ($84). Going solo meant catching the 2-hour express train to Naples and connecting with the local Circumvesuviana train to Pompeii—a 4-hour adventure if all went smoothly (it rarely did).

Enjoy Rome has now launched a daily air-conditioned minivan that whisks eight passengers from Rome to the gates of Pompeii in 3 hours. For details, see "Organized Tours," earlier in this chapter.

Salzburg & Environs

by Beth Reiber

Salzburg, surrounded by magnificent Alpine scenery, boasts one of the world's most striking cityscapes—a medieval fortress perched above a perfectly preserved baroque inner city filled with architectural wonders. Like most European cities, it's divided by a river—in this case, the Salzach. The names of the town and river derive from the region's salt mines, which brought Salzburg fame and fortune and are now popular attractions. With only 150,000 inhabitants, Salzburg is also one of Europe's leading cultural centers, especially for classical music. Mozart was born here, and Salzburg boasts one of the grandest music festivals in the world. A short journey by train or car from Munich, it's a very convenient and worthwhile stop for anyone traveling from Germany to Vienna or Italy.

REQUIRED DOCUMENTS   See chapter 28 on Vienna.

OTHER FROMMER'S TITLES   For more on Salzburg, see *Frommer's Austria, Frommer's Munich & the Bavarian Alps, Frommer's Europe,* or *Frommer's Europe's Greatest Driving Tours.*

1 Salzburg Deals & Discounts

SPECIAL DISCOUNTS

There are discounts on **museum admissions** and reduced **cable-car fares** granted to students and children under 15, provided you can show proof of age (passport) or an International Student ID Card. These reductions vary from 20% to 50%. Anyone age 26 and under can buy heavily reduced **rail and flight tickets** by contacting **Ökista,** Wolf-Dietrich-Strasse 31 (☎ **0662/88 32 52**), open Monday to Friday 9:30am to 5:30pm.

If you're staying on the outskirts of Salzburg and planning to visit most of the city's attractions, invest in the **Salzburg Card.** Purchase of this card allows you unlimited use of the city's public transportation system and includes admission to the city's top attractions (see "Essentials," later in this chapter).

WORTH A SPLURGE

Salzburg is famous for its **music,** presented throughout the year in a number of festivals and concerts. Tickets aren't always inexpensive and aren't even always available unless you order months in advance. But it's worth the effort and the money, considering that you're in one of

---

Budget Bests

In Salzburg, you'll find open-air food and drink stalls—called *Imbisse* or *Würstelbude*—practically everywhere. They sell wieners, hamburgers, sandwiches, *leberkäse*, soft drinks, and canned beer for much less than restaurants charge. You'll find a convenient imbiss in the center of the Altstadt (Old City) at Alter Markt, selling würste (sausages), french fries, and drinks. It's open year-round, Tuesday to Saturday 5pm to midnight and Sunday 2pm to midnight. On the other side of the Salzach River, on Linzergasse, is another imbiss selling würste, Wiener schnitzel, grilled chicken, *leberkäse,* and *gulasch* soup. It's open Monday to Friday 9am to midnight and Saturday, Sunday, and holidays 10am to midnight. On a rainy or cold day, the **self-service counters** in university cafeterias (known as mensas), department stores, and butcher shops are great money savers.

Be sure to visit the **City Tourist Office,** Mozartplatz 5 (☎ **0662/84 75 68**), for up-to-date information on such free events as concerts or folklore evenings that may take place during your stay. During summer, for example, there are free brass-band concerts in the Mirabellgarten on Wednesday at 8:30pm and Sunday at 10:30am. There are also free concerts throughout the school year given by students at the music school Mozarteum.

---

the music capitals of the world. For more information, see the "Special & Free Events" box and "Salzburg After Dark," later in this chapter.

2 Essentials

ARRIVING

BY PLANE   The **Salzburg Airport W. A. Mozart,** Innsbrucker Bundesstrasse 95 (☎ **0662/8580-0**), a mile southwest of the city, is larger than Innsbruck's and much smaller than Munich's. Daily flights go to/from Frankfurt, London (Gatwick), Amsterdam, Berlin, Brussels, Hamburg, Rome, Paris, Zurich, and Vienna. Bus no. 77 takes you to Salzburg's main train station for 22S ($1.75); taxis charge about 160S ($13) for the same trip.

BY TRAIN   Salzburg is about 1½ to 2 hours from Munich by train and about 3 hours from Vienna. Trains arrive at the **Hauptbahnhof** (main train station), on the right bank of the city center at Südtirolerplatz (☎ **0662/1717**). Buses depart from Südtirolerplatz to various parts of the city, including the Old City (Altstadt) across the river. It's about a 20-minute walk from the Hauptbahnhof to the heart of the Altstadt.

BY CAR   If you come by car, ask at your hotel where the nearest garage is located. Street parking (metered) is not only costly but also practically impossible to find, especially on the left bank with its narrow streets and pedestrians-only zones. Note that if you're staying at one of the hotels in the inner city's several pedestrian zones, you can still drive to your hotel for check-in. In the Altstadt you're required to stop at a ticket booth to obtain permission to drive to your hotel. In any case, once there, ask the hotel where you should park. You can reach most of Salzburg's sights on foot.

VISITOR INFORMATION

There's a small **tourist information kiosk** on Platform 2a of the Hauptbahnhof, Südtirolerplatz (☎ **0662/88 9 87-340**), where you can purchase a city map for 10S (80¢) or make hotel reservations by paying a deposit of 7.2% of your first night's payment. In addition, there's a service charge of 30S ($2.40) for two people; for three or

What Things Cost in Salzburg	U.S. $
Taxi from airport to the train station or hotel	12.80
Public transportation (bus or trolley bus)	1.20
Local telephone call (per minute)	.16
Double room at the Goldener Hirsch (deluxe)	376.00
Double room, with continental breakfast, at Trumer Stube (moderate)	100.00
Double room, with continental breakfast, at Pension Sandwirt (budget)	38.40
Lunch for one, without wine, at Sternbräu (moderate)	13.00
Lunch for one, without wine, at Mensa im Mozarteum (budget)	4.40
Dinner for one, without wine, at Stiftskeller St. Peter (deluxe)	25.00
Dinner for one, without wine, at Wienerwald (moderate)	10.00
Dinner for one, without wine, at Wilder Mann (budget)	7.00
Half liter of beer	2.30
Glass of wine (an eighth of a liter)	2.20
Coca-Cola (in a restaurant)	2.00
Cup of coffee with milk (in a restaurant)	2.95
Roll of ASA 100 color film, 36 exposures	5.60
Admission to Mozart's Birthplace	5.60
Movie ticket (depends on where you sit)	4.80–7.20
Orchestra concerts (in the Festspielhaus)	21.60

more, 60S ($4.80). The office is open daily: 9am to 9pm in summer and 8:45am to 7:45pm in winter.

A larger **City Tourist Office (Fremdenverkehrsbetriebe der Stadt Salzburg)** is in the heart of the Old City at Mozartplatz 5 (☎ **0662/88 9 87-330**), open May to September, daily 9am to 8pm; in winter, Monday to Saturday 9am to 6pm. The office also books hotel rooms, sells city maps, stocks brochures, and sells sightseeing, concert, and theater tickets. Be sure to pick up a free copy of *Veranstaltungen,* a monthly brochure that lists the concerts in Salzburg's many music halls. In addition, *City Journal* is an annual magazine published in German and English with information on musical events, special celebrations, and exhibitions, and other new tourism-type developments in Salzburg. Further information is available on the Internet at **www.salzburginfo.or.at** or via e-mail at **tourist@salzburginfo.or.at.**

CITY LAYOUT

Most attractions are on the left bank of the Salzach River, in the **Altstadt (Old City).** Much of the Altstadt is now a pedestrian zone, including Getreidegasse with its many shops, Domplatz, and Mozartplatz. The Altstadt is where you'll find such attractions as Mozarts Geburtshaus (Mozart's Birthplace), the Festival House complex, the cathedral, the Catacombs of St. Peter, the Haus der Natur (Museum of Natural History), and Salzburg's landmark, the **Hohensalzburg.** In fact, it's this fortress, towering above the Altstadt on a sheer cliff, that makes Salzburg so beautiful, even from afar. It's lit up at night, making a walk along the **Salzach River** one of the most romantic in Austria.

The **Hauptbahnhof** is on the opposite (right) side of the Salzach River, about a 20-minute walk from the Altstadt. This part of the city is newer and contains the Mirabellgarten and a number of nearby hotels and shops, just a short walk across the river from the Altstadt.

GETTING AROUND

Walking around Salzburg, especially in the Altstadt with its many pedestrian zones, is a pleasure. In fact, because Salzburg is rather compact, you can walk to most of its major attractions. One of the best walks is along the top of Mönchsberg from Café Winkler to the fortress, about a 30-minute stroll through woods and past medieval villas, with panoramic views.

BY PUBLIC TRANSPORTATION A quick, comfortable public transport system is provided by 12 **bus lines,** charging 22S ($1.75) per ticket if purchased from the driver. You can save money, however, by buying tickets in advance from one of the more than 100 tobacco shops throughout the city, marked with a sign that says TABAK TRAFIK. There are also ticket machines located at some of the major bus stops. Tickets come in blocks of five, with each one costing only 15S ($1.20). Be sure to validate advance-purchase tickets yourself by inserting them in the stamping machine inside the bus. Both the 22S and 15S tickets are good for a single journey, including transfers to reach your final destination.

If you think you'll be traveling a lot by bus, you might consider buying a **Netzkarte (Network Ticket),** also available in blocks of five; each ticket costs 32S ($2.55) and is valid for 24 hours upon stamping it for the first ride. For more information about Salzburg's public transportation system, call ☎ **0662/62 05 51-553** or 0662/87 21 45.

Another option is the **Salzburg Card,** which serves as a ticket for unlimited use of the city's public transport facilities and also includes admission to most of the city's attractions, including Mozart's Birthplace and Residence, the Hohensalzburg Fortress, the state rooms at the Residenz, Hellbrunn Palace, Haus der Natur, the Toy Museum, and more. The card, which you can purchase at any tourist information office, most hotels, and at all branches of Salzburger Sparkasse, is available as a 24-hour card for 200S ($16), a 48-hour card for 270S ($22), or a 72-hour card for 360S ($29).

BY TAXI The average taxi fare from the train station to a hotel or private home within the city limits is 100S to 170S ($8 to $14) and 160S ($13) to the airport. Fares start at 33S ($2.65); from 10pm to 6am, fares start at 43S ($3.45); luggage is an extra 10S (80¢) per piece. In and around the Altstadt you'll find convenient taxi stands at Hanuschplatz, Residenzplatz, and the Mönchsberg Lift; on the opposite side of the river you'll find stands at the train station, Makartplatz, and Auerspergstrasse. To phone for a taxi, call ☎ **8111** or 1715.

BY BICYCLE Biking is becoming more and more popular, evident from the more than 90 miles of bike paths through the city and surrounding countryside. If you feel like a long ride, try the bike path beside the Salzach River that goes all the way to Hallein, 9 miles away. Serious cyclists may want to buy the pamphlet *Salzburg Radkarte* at the tourist office for 89S ($7). Although only available in German, it marks biking routes through the city. You can rent bikes year-round at the **Hauptbahnhof** (main train station) at Counter 3 (☎ **0662/8887-3163**). About 50 standard and mountain bikes are available (no racing bikes), ranging in price from 150S to 200S ($12 to $16) per day depending on the type of bike. If you have a Eurailpass or a ticket valid for that day, the cost is 90S to 160S ($7 to $13).

BY RENTAL CAR It's much less expensive if you arrange for car rental before arriving in Europe. If you need a car in Salzburg, go to **Hertz,** Ferdinand-Porsche-Strasse 7 (☎ **0662/87 66 74**), across from the train station near the Hotel Europa, or to its airport office (☎ 0662/85 20 86). The downtown office is open Monday to Friday 8am to 6pm and Saturday 8am to 1pm. Also nearby is **Avis,** Ferdinand-Porsche-Strasse 7 (☎ **0662/87 72 78**), open Monday to Friday 7:30am to 6pm and Saturday 8am to noon. Charges for a 1-day rental of an Opel Corsa or a Ford Fiesta, with unlimited mileage and 20% tax, are about 996S ($80). There are always special weekend prices and other promotions, so it pays to shop around.

FAST FACTS: Salzburg

American Express The office is on Mozartplatz (☎ **0662/80 80**), next to the tourist office. It's open Monday to Friday 9am to 5:30pm and Saturday 9am to noon. There's no commission charge here to cash American Express traveler's checks.

Baby-sitters Students at Salzburg's university earn extra money by baby-sitting. Call ☎ **0662/8044-6001,** Monday to Friday 10am to noon.

Banks Banks are generally open Monday to Friday 8:30am to 12:30pm and 2 to 4:30pm. You can also exchange money at a post office, including the **main post office,** Residenzplatz 9 (☎ **0662/84 41 27**), open Monday to Friday 7am to 7pm and Saturday 8 to 10am. If you need to exchange money outside these hours, try the **Wechselstube (Exchange Office)** (☎ **0662/87 13 77**) at the Hauptbahnhof, open daily 7am to 9pm in summer and 7:30am to 8:30pm in winter. You can also obtain cash from Diners Club, MasterCard, and Visa here. In the Altstadt, you can exchange money after banking hours at the Hotel Weisse Taube, across the square from American Express at Kaigasse 9, open Monday to Friday 6:30 to 8pm, Saturday noon to 8pm, and Sunday 9am to 8pm. There's also a money exchange machine at the Sparda Bank near the tourist office on Mozartplatz that will exchange $5, $10, $20, $50, and $100 notes for schilling and accept MasterCard and Visa.

Business Hours Shops are usually open Monday to Friday 8 or 9am to 6 or 6:30pm (some close for an hour or two at noon) and Saturday 8 or 9am to noon or 1pm. On the first Saturday of the month (called *langer Samstag*), many shops remain open until 5pm.

Consulates The consulate general of the **United States** is at Alter Markt 1–3 (☎ **0662/84 87 76**), open Monday, Wednesday, and Thursday 9am to noon. The consulate of the **United Kingdom** is at Alter Markt 4 (☎ **0662/84 81 33**), open Monday to Friday 9am to noon. Citizens of Australia and Canada should contact their respective embassies in Vienna (see "Fast Facts: Vienna" in chapter 28).

Currency See "Fast Facts: Vienna" in chapter 28.

Dentists & Doctors If you need a doctor or dentist, head to one of Salzburg's hospitals; the largest is **St.-Johannsspital,** Müllner Hauptstrasse 48 (☎ **0662/4482-0**). Or ask your hotel concierge for the address of the hospital closest to you or inquire at your consulate. If you need an English-speaking doctor during the weekend, call ☎ **141.**

Emergencies For the **police,** phone ☎ **133;** to report a **fire,** ☎ **122;** for an **ambulance,** ☎ **144.** For urgent medical assistance on the weekend (7pm Friday to 7am Monday) or public holidays, or an English-speaking doctor, contact the **Ärzte-Bereitschaftsdienst,** Dr.-Karl-Renner-Strasse 7, ☎ **141.**

A useful pharmacy is the 200-year-old **Alte Hofapotheke,** Alter Markt 6 (☎ **0662/84 36 23**), a wonderful old-world drugstore a few blocks from the Mozart house. It's open Monday to Friday 8am to 6pm and Saturday 8am to noon. The names and addresses of pharmacies that are open on Saturday afternoon, Sunday, and holidays are posted in every pharmacy window.

Holidays Holidays celebrated in Salzburg are New Year's Day (January 1), Epiphany (January 6), Good Friday, Easter Monday, Labor Day (May 1), Ascension Day, Whitmonday, Corpus Christi, Feast of the Assumption (August 15), Austria Day (October 26), All Saints' Day (November 1), Feast of the Immaculate Conception (December 8), and Christmas (December 25 and 26).

Hospitals Hospitals in Salzburg include **St.-Johannsspital,** Müllner Hauptstrasse 48 (☎ **0662/4482-0**); **Unfallkrankenhaus (Accident Hospital),** Dr.-Franz-Rehrl-Platz 5 (☎ **0662/6580-0**); **Hospital of the Barmherzigen Brüder,** Kajetanerplatz 1 (☎ **0662/80 88**); and **Diakonissen Krankenhaus im Diakonie-Zentrum,** Guggenbichlerstrasse 20 (☎ **0662/6385-0**).

Laundry There's a self-service laundry east of Mirabellgarten on the right side of the Salzach: **Norge Exquisit,** Paris-Lodron-Strasse 16 (☎ **0662/87 63 81**), open Monday to Friday 7:30am to 6pm and Saturday 8am to noon. It charges 110S ($9) for 7 kilos (15½ lb.) of clothing washed and dried, including detergent.

Mail The **main post office (Hauptpostamt)** is in the center of the Altstadt at Residenzplatz 9, 5010 Salzburg (☎ **0662/84 41 21-0**). It's open Monday to Friday 7am to 7pm and Saturday 8 to 10am. Have your mail sent here Poste Restante. There's a **branch post office** beside the train station on Südtirolerplatz (☎ **0662/88 9 70-0**), open daily from 6am to 11pm. Postcards to North America cost 13S ($1.05), as do airmail letters weighing up to 20 grams.

Police The emergency number for the **police** is ☎ **133.**

Tax Government tax and service charge are already included in restaurant and hotel bills. If you've purchased goods for more than 1,000S ($80) from any one store, you're entitled to a refund of part of the value-added tax (VAT); see "Shopping," later in this chapter.

Telephone Telephone booths are painted either silver with a yellow top or green and are found on major roads and squares. For **local calls,** use two 1-schilling coins (16¢) for each minute—insert more coins to avoid being cut off (unused coins will be returned).

Note that phone numbers are gradually being changed in Salzburg. If you have problems making a connection or need a number, dial ☎ **1611** for information. And if you come across a number with a dash, as in 6580-0, the number after the dash is the extension. Simply dial the entire number.

Because hotels add a surcharge to calls made from guest rooms, make your **international calls** from a post office. It costs 31.50S ($2.50) to make a 3-minute call to the United States Monday to Friday 8am to 6pm; after 6pm and on weekends the rate falls to 28S ($2.25) for 3 minutes. If you're going to make a lot of local calls or wish to make international calls from a pay phone, purchase

---

Country & City Codes

The **country code** for Austria is **43.** The **city code** for Salzburg is **662;** use this code when you're calling from outside Austria. If you're within Austria but not in Salzburg, use **0662.** If you're calling within Salzburg, simply leave off the code and dial only the regular phone number.

---

a telephone card from any post office, available in values of 50S ($4), 100S ($8), or 200S ($16); then insert the card into slots of special phones found virtually everywhere. Alternatively, the American Express office on Mozartplatz (see above) has a telephone and fax machine that accepts American Express, Diners Club, MasterCard, and Visa.

Tipping   A service charge is included in hotel and restaurant bills and taxi fares. It's customary, however, to round up to the nearest 10S for meals costing less than 100S ($8); for meals costing more than 100S, add a 10% tip. Likewise, if you're satisfied with the service, tip up to 10% of the bill in taxis and beauty salons.

3 Accommodations You Can Afford

Most of Salzburg's budget accommodations are on the outskirts of town and in neighboring villages, easily reached by bus in less than 30 minutes. The cheapest rooms are often those rented out in private homes, with a shared bathroom down the hall. However, they're usually clean and equipped with sinks.

A bit more expensive are bathroomless doubles in a small pension (often called a *gasthof* or *gästehaus*). Not surprisingly, prices are usually higher in more centrally located establishments. In addition, many of the higher-priced accommodations charge even more during peak season, including Easter, the end of May, July to September, and December to New Year's. In January, when tourism is at its lowest, some hotels close completely.

If the places we recommend below are full, the **Salzburg City Tourist Office** at the train station and on Mozartplatz will book a room for a 30S ($2.40) fee if there are two of you or a 60S ($4.80) fee for three or more, plus a deposit toward your first night's payment. In addition, **Bob's Special Tours,** Kaigasse 19 in the Altstadt (☎ **0662/84 95 110;** e-mail: bobs-special-tours@net4you.co.at), will book inexpensive accommodations, including rooms in private homes, for no charge.

If, however, you've already booked a room with one of my recommendations below, please honor the reservation by showing up. *A word of warning:* In summer, it's become common practice for some places to employ hustlers at the train station to recruit people fresh off the train. Some of these lodgings are so far out in the countryside that you may as well be in Germany; some recruiters even go so far as to claim that they represent accommodations that travelers may have already booked, only in the end to deliver them someplace else.

Note: You can find most of the lodging choices below plotted on the map included in "Seeing the Sights," later in this chapter.

PRIVATE HOMES
IN THE CITY

These accommodations are in private homes, which sometimes offer less privacy but are good opportunities for getting to know the Austrians. Note, however, that they all prefer guests who stay longer than 1 night and that you should call in advance to make sure they have an empty room.

A Telephone Warning

Remember that phone numbers are being changed in Salzburg. If you can't reach any of my recommended accommodations, dial ☎ **1611** for information.

Brigitte Lenglachner. Scheibenweg 8, 5020 Salzburg. ☎ **0662/43 80 44.** 8 units, 4 with bathroom. 290S ($23) single without bathroom; 480S ($38) double without bathroom, 550S ($44) double with bathroom; 690S ($55) triple without bathroom. Rates include continental breakfast and showers. 20S ($1.60) extra per person for 1-night stay. No credit cards. Walk from the Hauptbahnhof across the Salzach River via the Pioniersteg Bridge (about a 15-minute walk).

This small two-story cottage is owned by a traditional Austrian, who wears dirndl costumes and speaks English. Take a look through her guest book—it's chock full of praise. The rooms, all with sinks, are pleasant and spotless. There's also a double equipped with a bunk bed for 390S ($31). This place is popular, so reserve well in advance.

Trude Poppenberger. Wachtelgasse 9, 5020 Salzburg. ☎ **0662/43 00 94.** 3 units, none with bathroom. 290S ($23) single; 480S ($38) double. Rates include continental breakfast and showers. No credit cards. Walk from the Hauptbahnhof across the Salzach River via the Pioniersteg Bridge (about a 20-minute walk).

Frau Poppenberger offers three comfortable rooms, all of which open onto a balcony outfitted with tables, chairs, and mountain views. There are two bathrooms, and breakfasts feature homemade cakes. You can have your clothes washed here for 80S ($6) a load. Frau Poppenberger will pick you up at the train station, and she and her husband, both of whom speak English, will happily provide sightseeing information.

Maria Raderbauer. Schiesstattstrasse 65, 5020 Salzburg. ☎ **0662/43 93 63.** 5 units, 3 with bathroom. 300S ($24) single without bathroom; 560S ($45) double with bathroom; 840S ($67) triple with bathroom. Rates include continental breakfast and showers. No credit cards. Walk from the Hauptbahnhof across the Salzach River via the Pioniersteg Bridge (about a 20-minute walk).

This two-story house in a quiet neighborhood is surrounded by rose bushes and has sparkling clean rooms. The triple has a balcony as well as its own bathroom across the hall. Frau Raderbauer, who speaks English, will pick you up at the station.

Hilde Radisch. Scheibenweg 5, 5020 Salzburg. ☎ **0662/42 47 12.** 3 units, none with bathroom. 275S ($22) single; 450S ($36) double. Rates include continental breakfast and showers. No credit cards. Walk from the Hauptbahnhof across the Salzach River via the Pioniersteg Bridge (about a 15-minute walk).

Frau Radisch, a talkative octogenarian who worked many years in day care and loves children, has an ivy-covered two-story house with private guest parking space and a garden and serves homemade marmalade for breakfast. She has one single room without a sink and two doubles with sinks, including an apartment-size double perfect for families, complete with living room and two sleeping rooms, one with a double bed and the other with two singles (the extra charge for children varies with their ages). Rooms are adorned with such antiques as a coffee grinder and kitchen scales; a few of the beds even boast horse-hair-filled mattresses and down covers.

Rudy and Friedl Simmerle. Wachtelgasse 13, 5020 Salzburg. ☎ **0662/42 75 53.** 2 units, neither with bathroom. 420S ($34) double. Rates include continental breakfast. Showers 25S ($2). No credit cards. Walk from the Hauptbahnhof across the Salzach River via the Pioniersteg Bridge (about a 20-minute walk).

Getting the Best Deal on Accommodations

- Ask about the winter discounts offered by medium- and upper-range hotels.
- Some of the people who rent rooms in private homes will pick you up at the train station, saving you the cost of a taxi or bus ride.
- Lower prices are charged for accommodations in surrounding villages.
- If you're staying in the outskirts or a nearby village, save money on transportation and sightseeing by purchasing the Salzburg Card.
- Look for accommodations offering cooking facilities, which will help you save on dining bills.
- Ask whether there's an extra charge for taking a shower and whether breakfast is included in the room rates.
- Before making a call, find out whether there's a surcharge on local and long-distance calls.

The Simmerles are a retired couple who speak fluent English. Their two rooms—one with its own toilet and sink and the other with just a sink—are large and well furnished. Living here is like being their guest; breakfasts include cheese and cold cuts. If you come by taxi from the train station, the Simmerles will reimburse half the cost. This home is in the northwestern part of the city.

IN THE OUTSKIRTS

✪ **Blobergerhof.** Hammerauerstrasse 4, 5020 Salzburg. ☎ **0662/83 02 27.** Fax 0662/82 70 61. 6 units, all with bathroom. 350S ($28) single; 550S–600S ($44–$48) double; 750S–800S ($60–$64) triple. Rates include continental breakfast. MC, V. Bus: 1 from the Hauptbahnhof to Hanuschplatz, then 60 from Hanuschplatz to Hammerauerstrasse (about 17 minutes), then a couple of minutes' walk.

This picturesque Salzburg-style farmhouse with flower boxes is managed by a wonderful English-speaking mother and daughter who receive repeated kudos from readers. Its rooms are spacious and it's neat as a pin. They raise chickens, so you can always be assured of fresh eggs, and there's a fine restaurant across the street. They'll pick you up at the station and have bicycles available for guest use.

Gästehaus Gassner. Moosstrasse 126b, 5020 Salzburg. ☎ **0662/82 49 90.** 10 units, 1 with toilet only, 7 with bathroom. 250S ($20) single with toilet only, 350S–400S ($28–$32) single with bathroom; 440S ($35) double without bathroom, 500S–600S ($40–$48) double with bathroom. Rates include buffet breakfast. 10% extra per person for 1-night stay. MC, V. Bus: 1 from the Hauptbahnhof to Hanuschplatz, then 60 from Hanuschplatz to the Felleitner stop (10 minutes), in front of the house.

This modern home south of the city has well-furnished, spacious rooms, most with minibar, TV, phone, and cassette player with radio and alarm clock. In summer you can eat breakfast on the terrace. There's also a laundry room. It's sometimes possible for Frau Gassner, who speaks English, to pick you up at the station.

Elfriede Kernstock. Karolingerstrasse 29, 5020 Salzburg. ☎ **0662/82 74 69.** Fax 0662/82 74 69. 6 units, all with bathroom. 500S–600S ($40–$48) double; 750S ($60) triple; 1,000S ($80) quad. Rates include continental breakfast. AE, MC, V. Bus: 77 from the Hauptbahnhof to Karolingerstrasse, then a few minutes' walk.

On the western edge of town near the airport, this beautiful bungalow offers more privacy than most homes—guest rooms have their own entry, separate from the family's living quarters. Two of the rooms boast a small kitchen; one room has hand-painted furniture; another has a balcony (overlooking, unfortunately, a trucking company). The English-speaking Frau Kernstock has bicycles you can ride for free, and if she's not busy with guests, she'll pick you up at the bus stop if you call from the station.

Mathilde Lindner. Panoramaweg 5, 5300 Hallwang. ☎ **0662/45 66 81** or 0662/45 67 73. 8 units, none with bathroom. 160S–200S ($13–$16) per person. Rates include continental breakfast and showers. No credit cards. Bus: 1, 2, 5, or 6 from the Hauptbahnhof to Mirabellplatz, then 15 from Mirabellplatz to Kasern (15 minutes), then a 10-minute walk uphill. Train: From the Hauptbahnhof to Maria-Plain, a 4-minute ride.

This nice Alpine cottage is on top of a high hill northeast of Salzburg, with a great view of the mountains. Four rooms have access to a balcony, and there's a garden for sunbathing. The rooms, which must be reserved at least 1 day in advance, are furnished with wooden beds, wardrobes, chairs, tables, and sinks. If she has time, Frau Lindner will pick you up from the station; if you're arriving by car, take the Autobahn Nord exit. If you have a Eurailpass, you can ride for free on a local train (the Regionalzug) from the Salzburg Hauptbahnhof to Maria-Plain. Families are welcome.

Moser. Turnerbühlel 1, 5300 Hallwang. ☎ **0662/45 66 76.** 4 units, none with bathroom. 180S ($14) single; 340S–360S ($27–$29) double. Rates include continental breakfast and showers. No credit cards. Bus: 1, 2, 5, or 6 from the Hauptbahnhof to Mirabellplatz, then 15 from Mirabellplatz to Kasern (15 minutes), then a 10-minute walk uphill. Train: From the Hauptbahnhof to Maria-Plain, a 4-minute ride.

Frau Moser's husband is a hunter, as is evident from the more than 100 sets of antlers decorating the walls of this home. Not far from Frau Lindner's (above), it also offers a great view of Salzburg, and its upper-priced doubles have their own balconies. The breakfast room has a panoramic view as well, and there's a terrace and garden. Free coffee and tea are available throughout the day. If you phone upon your arrival in Salzburg, she'll give instructions on how best to reach Kasern via a local train and will meet you at the Maria-Plain station.

Rosemarie Steiner. Moosstrasse 156c, 5020 Salzburg. ☎ **0662/83 00 31.** 6 units, all with bathroom; 1 apt. TV. 300S ($24) single; 520S ($42) double; 600S ($48) apt for 2, extra person 100S ($8). Rates include continental breakfast. No credit cards. Bus: 1 from the Hauptbahnhof to Hanuschplatz, then 60 from Hanuschplatz to Kaserer (about 20 minutes), then a couple minutes' walk.

This modern three-story house south of town offers a communal kitchen and adequately furnished clean rooms, three with balconies. The apartment features a living room, sleeping room, bathroom, and kitchen. The owner, who speaks English, is happy to give sightseeing advice.

✪ **Eveline Truhlar.** Lettensteig 11, 5082 Fürstenbrunn. ☎ **06246/73 377.** Fax 06246/73 377 4. 1 rm, without bathroom. 300S ($24) double. Rates include continental breakfast and showers. No credit cards. Bus: 1 from the Hauptbahnhof to Hanuschplatz, then 60 from Hanuschplatz to the last stop in Fürstenbrunn.

Eveline's double room, with a bathroom across the hall and free use of the family kitchen, is a good choice for young people in search of inexpensive accommodations. The owner, who has managed Bob's Special Tours for 20 years, speaks excellent English, will pick you up at the station, and knows Salzburg in and out. This is one of the best bargains around, and the tiny village of Fürstenbrunn should appeal to those who enjoy the countryside and walks through the woods.

HOTELS & PENSIONS
IN OR NEAR THE ALTSTADT

✪ **Amadeus.** Linzer Gasse 43–45, 5020 Salzburg. ☎ **0662/87 14 01** or 0662/87 61 63. Fax 0662/87 14 017 or 0662/876 16 37. E-mail: walkets@ping.at. 30 units, 27 with bathroom. TV TEL. 420S–500S ($34–$40) single without bathroom, 520S–850S ($42–$68) single with bathroom; 580S–780S ($46–$62) double without bathroom, 860S–1,500S ($69–$120) double with bathroom; 1,300S–1,950S ($104–$156) triple with bathroom. Rates include buffet breakfast and showers. AE, DC, MC, V. Free limited parking. Bus: 1, 2, 5, 6, or 51 from the Hauptbahnhof to Makartplatz.

This small hotel (with elevator) has a great location in the city center, just across the river from the Altstadt and within walking distance of almost everything. You have your choice of rooms facing either the street or a beautiful and peaceful cemetery (where Mozart's wife is buried). Recently renovated, the rooms are pleasant and have cable TV and hair dryers. The buffet breakfasts are substantial, offering eggs, cereals, and cold cuts, and for active guests, the hotel offers paragliding trips and free in-line skates (the nearby Salzach is great for a run). The higher prices in each category are for the peak tourist season, including mid-July to September; discounts are available for stays of 3 nights or more, as well as when you pay with cash in low season.

✪ **Bergland.** Rupertgasse 15, 5020 Salzburg. ☎ **0662/87 23 18-0.** Fax 0662/87 23 18-8. E-mail: pkuhn@sol.at. Internet: www.sol.at/bergland. 17 units, 3 with shower only, 12 with bathroom. TEL. 480S ($38) single with shower only, 560S ($45) single with bathroom; 640S ($51) double without bathroom, 860S–920S ($69–$74) double with bathroom; 1,060S ($85) triple with bathroom. Rates include buffet breakfast and showers. MC, V. Free parking. Closed mid-Nov to mid-Dec.

This pleasant pension, owned by the Kuhn family for more than 80 years, is on three floors of a postwar modern building on a residential street about a 10-minute walk across the river from the Altstadt. It has a cozy bar/lounge with a piano and guitar, plus a small English library. Adorning the walls is original artwork by English-speaking Peter Kuhn. The rooms are spotless and cheerfully decorated with Scandinavian furniture; the bathrooms were recently remodeled. Most rooms have cable TV with CNN and radio. The pension rents bikes and is located about a 12-minute walk south of the Hauptbahnhof.

✪ **Chiemsee.** Chiemseegasse 5, 5020 Salzburg. ☎ **0662/84 42 08.** Fax 0662/84 42 08-70. 6 units, all with shower only. 450S–480S ($36–$38) single; 750S–880S ($60–$70) double. Rates include continental breakfast. Additional person 200S ($16). MC, V. Bus: 5, 6, 51, or 55 from the Hauptbahnhof to Mozartsteg, then a 2-minute walk.

In the Altstadt, this tiny pension is a true find and is owned by Veronika Höllbacher, a Salzburg native who speaks English and gained experience running a restaurant before recently acquiring the pension. The house itself is 1,000 years old—note how worn the stone stairway is. The reception and small but pleasant breakfast room are up on the first floor, while guest rooms are on the third (no elevator). The rooms are simple but clean, with prices based on the room size and season. Because Chiemsee has only six rooms, it's best to reserve well in advance.

Junger Fuchs. Linzer Gasse 54, 5020 Salzburg. ☎ **0662/87 54 96.** 17 units, none with bathroom. 240S–300S ($19–$24) single; 380S–440S ($30–$35) double; 500S–550S ($40–$44) triple. No credit cards. Bus: 1, 2, 5, 6, or 51 from the Hauptbahnhof to Makartplatz.

This is the inner city's cheapest pension and looks as if it's been here forever. The old stone stairway (no elevator) is narrow and probably medieval; the rooms date from this century but look no less weary. Though bare, small, and simple, the accommodations are adequate, with a sink, hooks to hang up your coat, a bed, and a table. Some may smell of cigarette smoke, so it wouldn't hurt to ask to see your room first. Basically, this is just a cheap place to sleep in a convenient location, across the river from the Altstadt.

Wallner. Aiglhofstrasse 15, 5020 Salzburg. ☎ **0662/84 50 23.** Fax 0662/84 50 23-3. 18 units, 4 with shower only, 10 with bathroom. TEL. 360S ($29) single without bathroom, 420S ($34) single with shower only, 500 S ($40) single with bathroom; 580S ($46) double without bathroom, 680S ($54) double with shower only, 800S ($64) double with bathroom; 980S ($78) triple with bathroom; 1,180S ($94) quad with bathroom. Rates include continental breakfast and showers. No credit cards. Bus: 2 or 77 from the Hauptbahnhof to Aiglhof, then a 5-minute walk.

On the opposite side of Mönchsberg from the Altstadt, not far from the Augustiner-bräu brewery and beer garden, this 40-year-old pension is now managed by the original owner's daughter. It consists of two buildings; the one in back is very quiet. The simple accommodations include a four-bed room, with two sleeping quarters, good for families.

NEAR THE TRAIN STATION

Auerhahn. Bahnhofstrasse 15 (a 10-minute walk north of the Hauptbahnhof), 5020 Salzburg. ☎ **0662/45 10 52.** Fax 0662/45 10 52-3. 16 units, all with bathroom. TV TEL. 540S–650S ($43–$52) single; 900S–980S ($72–$78) double; 1,000S ($80) triple. Rates include buffet breakfast. AE, DC, MC, V.

This small well-furnished hotel is across from a secondary rail track (used once or twice a day, causing little noise). It's been owned by the same family for more than 30 years (the proprietress speaks fluent English), with a pleasant restaurant and outdoor terrace serving typical Austrian food, popular with locals. The rooms are upstairs, along corridors that have a hunting lodge feel, with heavy beams and *bauernmöbel* (wooden furniture gaily painted Austrian style). Recently renovated, all rooms are modern, with spotless tiled bathrooms, wood furniture, and cable TVs. The only disadvantage to staying here is that it's a bit far from the Altstadt.

IN THE OUTSKIRTS

✪ **Fürstenbrunn.** Fürstenbrunnerstrasse 50, 5082 Fürstenbrunn. ☎ **06246/73 342.** 11 units, all with bathroom. 380S–400S ($30–$32) single; 600S ($48) double; 790S ($63) triple; 900S ($72) quad. Rates include continental breakfast. No credit cards. Bus: 1 from the Hauptbahnhof to Hanuschplatz, then 60 from Hanuschplatz to Fürstenbrunn (about 20 minutes).

In a quiet location 5 miles south of Salzburg at the foot of Untersberg mountain, this is a cheerful guesthouse with plants in the hallway, large immaculate rooms, and gaily painted wooden furniture *(bauernmöbel)*. Owners Manfred and Heidelinde Schnöll speak some English and will pick you up at the train station. The restaurant, Gasthof Schnöll, serves lunch and dinner, has an outdoor beer garden, and is popular with locals.

Helmhof. Kirchengasse 29, 5020 Salzburg. ☎ and fax **0662/43 30 79.** 16 units, 12 with bathroom. TEL. 360S–380S ($28.80–$30.40) single without bathroom, 460S–490S ($37–$39) single with bathroom; 620S–680S ($50–$54) double without bathroom, 740S–890S ($59–$71) double with bathroom. Rates include continental breakfast and showers. No credit cards. Bus: 2 from the Hauptbahnhof to Rudolf-Biebl-Strasse, then 29 to Schmiedingerstrasse.

In Liefering on the northeastern edge of town, this pension may still have rooms when others in the town center are booked up. This attractive country house has a red roof, green shutters, balconies off most rooms, and flowers on the windowsills. The owner speaks English, and there's a tiny outdoor pool. The higher rates above are for peak season.

✪ **Parkpension Kasern.** Wickenburgallee 1, 5028 Salzburg. ☎ **0662/45 00 62.** Fax 0662/45 40 81. 14 units, all with bathroom. TV. 500S–650S ($40–$52) single; 800S–1,100S

($64–$88) double. Rates include continental breakfast. Extra person 200S ($18). MC, V. Bus: 1, 2, 5, or 6 from the Hauptbahnhof to Mirabellplatz, then 15 from Mirabellplatz to Kasern (about 15 minutes).

This is a lovely country house in a park on the town's northern outskirts. Built in 1870 as a private mansion, it's now in its fourth generation of owners and features exquisite artistry throughout. Most rooms are large, with tall ceilings and antique furniture; six modern rooms were recently added. All have cable TVs, and cooking facilities can be arranged for longer stays. There's a fine garden where you can sit in summer. The proprietor Felicitas Eichhausen and her husband speak excellent English.

✪ **Schiessling.** Anif 17, 5081 Salzburg. ☎ **06246/72 4 85.** 12 units, 2 with bathroom. 220S–250S ($18–$20) single without bathroom, 275S–300S ($22–$24) single with bathroom; 350S–385S ($28–$31) double without bathroom, 450S–500S ($36–$40) double with bathroom. Rates include continental breakfast and showers. No credit cards. Bus: 55 from the Hauptbahnhof to the Anif Hotel Friesacher (20 minutes).

This spotless pension in the village of Anif, south of Salzburg, offers three rooms in a former farmhouse and dairy, with the rest in a more modern structure across the street. Breakfast is served in a pleasant room with a terrace. Anif is known for its *heurige* (wine taverns), so there's more to do here in the evening than in most small villages. This pension is one of the best budget accommodations near Salzburg; the higher prices in each category are for stays of only 1 night.

A YOUTH HOSTEL
✪ **Yoho International Youth Hotel.** Paracelsusstrasse 9, 5020 Salzburg. ☎ **0662/87 96 49.** Fax 0662/87 88 10. 130 beds. 190S ($15) per person double; 170S ($14) per person quad; 150S ($12) dorm bed. Showers 10S (80¢). No credit cards. Walk 10 minutes south of the train station.

This is the best budget choice in town. It's centrally located (a 15-minute walk to the Altstadt), and there's no age limit. There are four doubles; the rest are quads and dorm-style rooms with six to eight beds each. All rooms have sinks, lockers are available, and there's a coin-operated laundry. Curfew is at 1am; the hotel bar is open until midnight and serves breakfast and dinner. *The Sound of Music* is shown free daily at 1:30pm. The only drawback is that you can only reserve a bed 1 day in advance of arrival, so call early in the morning. The young staff members speak English.

WORTH A SPLURGE
✪ **Trumer Stube.** Bergstrasse 6, 5020 Salzburg. ☎ **0662/87 47 76** or 0662/87 51 68. Fax 0662/87 43 26. E-mail: hotel.trumer-stube@eunet.at. 22 units, all with bathroom. TV TEL. 480S–680S ($38–$54) single; 780S–1,250S ($62–$100) double; 1,100S–1,600S ($88–$128) triple; 1,300S–1,800S ($104–$144) quad. Rates include continental breakfast. AE. Bus: 1, 2, 5, 6, or 51 from the Hauptbahnhof to Mirabellplatz.

This is a great place for a splurge, just across the river from the Altstadt and only a 5-minute walk from Mozart's Birthplace. Ideal for couples and families, it's owned by the charming Hirschbichlers, both of whom speak English and are eager to give sightseeing tips, secure concert tickets, make restaurant and guided tour reservations, and whatever else guests desire. The pension was recently renovated (with an elevator) and the rooms are spotless and cozy. The above prices reflect both the low- and high-season rates for each category.

✪ **Wolf.** Kaigasse 7, 5020 Salzburg. ☎ **0662/84 34 53-0.** Fax 0662/84 24 23-4. 15 units, all with bathroom. TV TEL. 640S–930S ($51–$74) single; 980S–1,630S ($78–$130) double. Rates include buffet breakfast. AE. Bus: 5, 6, 51, or 55 from the Hauptbahnhof to Mozartsteg, then a 2-minute walk.

This small hotel, in the heart of the Altstadt, has one of the best locations, in a quiet pedestrian zone at the foot of the Hohensalzburg Fortress. The structure itself is a national monument and dates from the 14th century, evident in such architectural details as arched ceilings in the breakfast room, but otherwise everything is supermodern with all the conveniences, including an elevator. Every room is unique, some with antiques and others with modern furniture. The owner wears dirndl costumes and speaks excellent English. The highest prices are for July to September.

4 Great Deals on Dining

You'll find Salzburg's inexpensive restaurants on both banks of the Salzach, and many are conveniently clustered in and around the Altstadt. Most feature specialties typical of Austria and southern Germany, like *leberknödelsuppe* (soup with liver dumplings), *knoblauchsuppe* (garlic soup), *bauernschmaus* (a combination dish of pork, ham, sausage, dumplings, and sauerkraut), *tafelspitz* (boiled beef with vegetables), *gulasch* (Hungarian stew), *leberkäse* (German meat loaf), or *Wiener schnitzel* (breaded veal cutlet). The only real Salzburg dish is *Salzburger nockerl*, a soufflé made of eggs, flour, butter, and sugar. When served at your table it looks like a blimp, too big to possibly eat it all, but as soon as you dig in the air escapes and it becomes more manageable. Try it at least once while in Salzburg.

LOCAL BUDGET BESTS

Mensa in der Hochschule Mozarteum. Mirabellplatz 1. ☎ **0662/87 35 06** or 0662/80 44-6930. Fixed-price meals (for nonstudents) 43S–55S ($3.45–$4.40). No credit cards. Mon–Fri 11:30am–2pm. Closed July 7–15, Sept 1–16, and Dec 21–Jan 7. Bus: 1, 2, 5, 6, or 51 from the Hauptbahnhof to Mirabellplatz. AUSTRIAN.

This student *Mensa* (cafeteria), in the Mozarteum music school, serves two fixed-price meals to both students and nonstudents, though students pay about 10S (80¢) less than the prices above. The menu changes daily, with several other main dishes and side dishes available in addition to the fixed-price meals. It's on the right side of the Salzach near the beautiful Mirabell Garden, between the train station and the Altstadt, less than a 10-minute walk from each. The only problem is that the Mensa, in a basement, is a bit difficult to find. Enter the Mozarteum through the Aicherpassage off Mirabellplatz; if you get lost, ask a student for directions.

✪ **Uni-Cafe Toskana, Mensa der Universität.** Churfürststrasse and Sigmund-Haffner-Gasse (between Alter Markt and Domplatz). ☎ **0662/8044-69 09.** Fixed-price meals 33S–44S ($2.65–$3.50) for students, 43S–55S ($3.45–$4.40) for nonstudents. No credit cards. Mon–Fri 11:30am–2pm. Closed Dec 21–Jan 6 and Feb. AUSTRIAN.

This student *Mensa*, with a courtyard entrance, is conveniently located in the center of the Altstadt and is by far one of the cheapest places for a meal in Salzburg. It offers two complete meals daily, with slightly higher prices for nonstudents. Although the fixed-price meals are served only during the hours above, the cafe itself is open Monday to Thursday 8am to 6pm (to 4pm in winter) and Friday 8am to 3pm, serving a few sandwiches, frankfurters, soup, desserts, coffee, and other drinks.

IN OR NEAR THE ALTSTADT

✪ **Augustiner Bräustübl Mülln.** Linderhofstrasse or Augustinergasse 4 (north of Mönchsberg). ☎ 0662/43 12 46. Meals 50S–100S ($4–$8). No credit cards. Mon–Fri 3–10:30pm, Sat–Sun and holidays 2:30–10:30pm. Bus: 1, 2, 5, or 6 from the Hauptbahnhof to Mirabellplatz, then 27 from Mirabellplatz to Augustinergasse; or 1 from the Hauptbahnhof to Hanuschplatz, then 27 from Hanuschplatz to Augustinergasse. AUSTRIAN.

Getting the Best Deal on Dining

- Try the daily specials called *Tagesgericht*, usually complete meals offered at discount prices.
- Take advantage of butcher shops and food departments of department stores, which usually offer such take-out food as German meat loaf and grilled chicken.
- Eat lunch at a student cafeteria *(Mensa)*, where nonstudents pay slightly higher prices for bargain meals.
- Dine at an inexpensive *imbiss*, or food stall, selling sausages, snacks, and beer.
- Ask whether there's an extra charge for each piece of bread consumed and whether your main course comes with vegetables or side dishes.

This is a great place for a meal, offering both an outdoor beer garden and huge beer halls upstairs. Known among locals as Augustinerbräu Müllnerbräu (because of the area, Müllner, 10 minutes from the Altstadt), this is a brewery where the star of the show is the brew. A half liter costs 28S ($2.25); a liter goes for 56S ($4.50). You can bring your own food, but there are also various counters selling sausages and cold cuts, cheese, pretzels, bread, hamburgers, grilled chicken, soup, salads, boiled pork with horseradish, beef with creamed spinach and potatoes, and more. Pick and choose and create your own dinner. It's a crowded, noisy place, as a brewery should be; it can also be smoky.

Bärenwirt. Müllner Hauptstrasse 8. ☎ **0662/43 03 86.** Meals 95S–170S ($8–$14). AE, DC, MC, V. Thurs–Tues 11:30am–2:30pm and 5:30–9pm. Bus: 1 from the Hauptbahnhof to Hanuschplatz, then 27, 49, or 95 from Hanuschplatz to Bärenwirt. AUSTRIAN.

Facing Müllner on the bank of the Salzach River, within an 8-minute walk from the center of the Altstadt, this cozy restaurant with wood-paneled walls and wooden tables and benches is one of Salzburg's oldest restaurants, established 300 years ago. It's a typical *gaststätte* (neighborhood family-owned inn) where most customers are regulars, the owner doubles as the main chef, and his English-speaking wife is the charming hostess, dressed in a traditional dirndl. Specialties on the English menu include the homemade *sülze* and *spinach-nockerl* (homemade green noodles with ham and cheese). In summer, treat yourself to homemade apple strudel on the little terrace overlooking the Salzach.

✪ Gasthaus Wilder Mann. Getreidegasse 20 or Griesgasse 17. ☎ 0662/84 17 87. Meals 60S–150S ($4.80–$12). No credit cards. Daily 11am–9pm (last order). Closed Sun in winter. Bus: 1 from the Hauptbahnhof to Hanuschplatz. AUSTRIAN.

This simple, popular restaurant has wooden tables, a wood-plank floor, and antlers on the wall. This is where the locals come to drink, eat, and gossip, and you may be the only non-Salzburger around. The menu lists *bauernschmaus, gulasch, bratwurst, Wiener schnitzel*, turkey with mushroom sauce, and pork chops, with most meals costing less than 100S ($8). Watch for the reasonable daily specials. It's conveniently located in a narrow passageway between Getreidegasse and Griesgasse, in the Altstadt.

Schwaighofer. Kranzlmarkt 3. ☎ **0662/84 27 09.** Main courses 75S–110S ($6–$9). No credit cards. Mon–Sat 9am–6:15pm, Sun and holidays 10am–5pm. Bus: 1 from the Hauptbahnhof to Hanuschplatz. AUSTRIAN.

This Austrian-style deli in the middle of the Altstadt offers more than 20 kinds of salad (sold by weight) and main courses like *gulasch, schweinebraten* with salad, *tafelspitz*, stuffed green peppers, and other Austrian specialties that change daily. Look for the outside blackboard with an English menu. It's a tiny place, with just a few seats in the back and a small side room where you can eat your meal.

Spaghetti & Co. Getreidegasse 14. ☎ **0662/84 14 00.** Pizza and pasta 60S–110S ($4.80–$9). AE, DC, MC, V (only on orders costing more than 300S/$24). Daily 11am–11pm. Bus: 1 from the Hauptbahnhof to Hanuschplatz. PASTA/PIZZA.

Near Mozart's Birthplace in the middle of the Altstadt, this is one branch of a chain of spaghetti parlors offering more than a dozen spaghetti dishes, as well as more than 20 kinds of pizza (you can also create your own), lasagna, soups, and salads. It also has a do-it-yourself salad bar, with a large plate costing 76S ($6).

✪ **Sternbräu.** Getreidegasse 34–36 or Griessgasse 23. ☎ **0662/84 21 40.** Meals 90S–195S ($7–$16). No credit cards. Daily 11:30am–10:45pm. Bus: 1 from the Haupt-bahnhof to Hanuschplatz. AUSTRIAN.

This is one of Salzburg's best moderately priced restaurants, a huge place with seating both inside and in a courtyard garden (a great place for a beer). The menu is exten-sive, including Austrian favorites like *bauernschmaus, Wiener schnitzel* with fries and salad, *tafelspitz,* rump steak with herb butter and salad, pork cutlet, fresh fish, and grilled steak.

Stiegl-Keller. Festungsgasse 10. ☎ **0662/84 26 81.** Main courses 85S–150S ($7–$12). AE, DC, MC, V. Daily 10am–10pm. Closed Oct–Apr. Bus: 5, 6, 51, or 55 from the Hauptbahnhof to Mozartsteg. AUSTRIAN.

Carved out of the foot of the mountain below the fortress, just a few hundred yards uphill from Residenzplatz, the Stiegl-Keller has been popular for its picturesque beer garden overlooking the Altstadt since 1820. It serves hearty Austrian fare, along with mugs of Stiegl beer.

Wienerwald Restaurant. Griesgasse 31. ☎ **0662/84 34 70.** Meals 64S–120S ($5–$10). AE, DC, MC, V. Daily 10am–midnight. Bus: 1 from the Hauptbahnhof to Hanuschplatz. AUSTRIAN.

This place has rooms decorated like those in a Swiss chalet, with comfortable seating. There are more than 300 restaurants of this chain in Austria, Germany, and Switzer-land, where the specialty is spit-roasted chicken. An especially good deal is the quarter grilled chicken, which together with a side dish costs 70S ($6). There's also a salad bar. It's popular with families and has a no-smoking section and an English menu.

NEAR THE HAUPTBAHNHOF

Interspar Restaurant. Südtirolerplatz 11 (in the Forum Am Bahnhof shopping center). ☎ **0662/45 84 66-851.** Meals 60S–85S ($4.80–$7). No credit cards. Mon–Fri 8am–7pm, Sat 8am–5pm. AUSTRIAN.

This self-service restaurant, across from the train station and to the right of the bus terminal, is up on the first floor of a small shopping complex. It offers two fixed-price meals daily, which can range from Wiener schnitzel with a side dish to salmon steak with broccoli and potatoes, as well as a salad bar and other choices in main courses. On weekdays, meals are half price after 6pm. A good place for a quick, inexpensive meal.

Rosenkavalier. In the Hauptbahnhof, Südtirolerplatz. ☎ **0662/87 23 77-15.** Meals 80S–135S ($6.40–$11). AE, MC, V. Daily 11am–7pm. AUSTRIAN.

Normally I avoid restaurants in train stations, but this is a notable exception. Ensconced in the grand Marble Hall (and not to be confused with the cheaper Salzburger Stüberl next door), it's a very civilized establishment, with high ceilings and a turn-of-the-century atmosphere embellished with white tablecloths and softly playing piano music. The English menu is fairly standard, including salads, soups, and such Austrian specialties as boiled beef, Wiener schnitzel, and *gulasch,* as well as spaghetti and daily specials. The main dishes come with a salad or potatoes, making them complete meals.

CAFES & *KONDITOREIS*

Salzburg is famous for its coffeehouses and pastry shops, where you can linger over pastry and coffee or a glass of wine, read the newspapers available (including the *International Herald Tribune*), and watch the passersby. In summer, many cafes have outdoor seating. If you prefer, get some pastries to go and eat them on a park bench or in your hotel.

Café Bazar. Schwarzstrasse 3 (on the right side of the Salzach River near the Staatsbrücke). ☎ **0662/87 42 78.** *Melange* (large coffee with milk) 37S ($2.95); desserts 30S–65S ($2.40–$5.20). No credit cards. Mon 10am–6pm, Tues–Sat 7:30am—11pm. COFFEEHOUSE/SNACKS.

This coffeehouse features chandeliers and large windows affording views of the river, with outdoor seating in summer. It's popular with locals, from students of the nearby Mozarteum to older people perusing the daily newspaper. In addition to coffee and desserts, it serves snacks and daily specials.

Café Tomaselli. Alter Markt 9. ☎ **0662/84 44 88.** *Melange* 37S ($2.95); desserts 25S–60S ($2–$4.80). No credit cards. Mon–Sat 7am–9pm, Sun 8am–9pm. COFFEEHOUSE.

Established in 1705, the Tomaselli is still going strong. It's so popular that you may have to wait to get a seat. In summer, extra chairs are placed out on the cobblestone square. Have a *melange* and dessert or choose from the pastry tray or the display case. There's also wine, beer, soft drinks, and snacks, plus ice cream in summer.

Café Winkler. Mönchsberg (take the lift from Gstättengasse 13, costing 27S/$2.15 one-way). ☎ **0662/84 77 38.** Large espresso or coffee 36S ($2.90); desserts 42S–98S ($3.35–$8). AE, MC, V. Tues–Sun 11am–11pm (open daily in August). COFFEEHOUSE/RESTAURANT.

Its meals are too high for our budget, but for the price of a coffee and perhaps dessert you are treated to one of the best views of Salzburg. Located atop Mönchsberg, Café Winkler overlooks the rooftops of the Altstadt and beyond. Although the lift is the easiest and fastest way to reach the cafe, you can also hike here from the Festung Hohensalzburg or from Augustinergasse (near the Augustiner Bräustübl Mülln brewery).

PICNICKING

In the Altstadt, a wonderful place for inexpensive food is **Schwaighofer,** Kranzlmarkt 3 (☎ **0662/84 27 09**), a tiny hole-in-the-wall described above and offering food for both indoor consumption and takeout. There are also many *imbisse* (see "Budget Bests," at the beginning of the chapter). If it's a nice day, you may want to join the other sun worshipers on the benches in the **Mirabellgarten** or along the **Salzach River.** Another good place is at the **Augustiner Bräustübl Mülln,** a brewery with an outdoor beer garden, described above.

WORTH A SPLURGE

✪ **Stiftskeller St. Peter.** St. Peter-Bezirk 1 (near St. Peter's Monastery at the foot of the Mönchsberg). ☎ **0662/84 84 81.** Main courses 105S–180S ($8–$14); Mozart Dinner Concert 530S ($42). AE, DC, MC, V. Daily 11:30am–2pm and 6–10:30pm. AUSTRIAN.

This is probably Salzburg's most popular first-class restaurant. It's under the management of St. Peter's Monastery and was first mentioned in documents dating from 803, making it Europe's oldest restaurant. There are various dining rooms, each unique but all with a medieval ambiance. The English menu lists international food as well as local specialties, like fresh trout, boiled beef with chives, veal ragoût, beef gulasch, and numerous daily specials. Its traditional desserts are great—try the *Salzburger nockerl.* For a real splurge, there's the Mozart Dinner Concert, held in the restaurant's elegant Baroque Hall and featuring music of Mozart played by musicians in period costumes and a three-course meal based on traditional 17th- and 18th-century recipes. Festivities begin at 8pm March to December, usually every Sunday, Tuesday, Wednesday, and Thursday at 8pm (nightly in August).

5 Seeing the Sights

SIGHTSEEING SUGGESTIONS

IF YOU HAVE 1 DAY   Start the morning with a tour of the **Hohensalzburg Fortress** and its museums. You might want to take the funicular up the hill, then walk back down into the city (about a 20-minute walk). Spend the afternoon in the **Altstadt,** strolling through its pedestrian lanes. Be sure to see **Mozart's Birthplace** on Getreidegasse, Salzburg's most picturesque street. Notice the many wrought-iron shop signs: In the days when many people were illiterate, they served a useful purpose. Other places to visit are the **Dom** and the beautiful **cemetery at St. Peter's.** Top off the day with a beer at **Augustiner Bräustübl Mülln.** In the evening, take a **river stroll** along the Salzach, where you'll have a view of the fortress, all lit up.

IF YOU HAVE 2 DAYS   To the above, add the **Hellbrunn Palace,** 3 miles south of the city (open only April to October). Its park with the trick fountains is unique. Try to include a visit to the **Haus der Natur (Museum of Natural History),** one of the best of its kind in the world; the **Residenz State Rooms;** the **Traditional Salzburg Costumes Museum;** or the **Toy Museum**—all in the Altstadt. In late afternoon, take the lift (elevator) to the **Café Winkler.** It's worth the trip to the top just for the view, the best in all Salzburg. If you feel like a hike, walk from the Café Winkler along the ridge to the **fortress** in about half an hour, with great photo opportunities along the way. In the evening, you may want to get dressed up and attend one of Salzburg's many musical events, such as a **concert in the fortress,** its **festival houses,** the **Mozarteum,** or the **Residenz.**

IF YOU HAVE 3 DAYS   Spend Days 1 and 2 as above. On Day 3, head for **Untersberg,** a mountain 7 miles south of Salzburg, where you'll have a lovely view of the city and the Alps. In the afternoon, take a stroll through the **Mirabellgarten,** topping it off with a sauna or swim at the adjoining **Kurhaus.**

IF YOU HAVE 5 DAYS   Consider taking **Bob's Bavarian Mountain Tour** (see "Organized Tours," below), a 4-hour guided (in English) excursion covering the major *Sound of Music* film locations and a visit to **Berchtesgaden.** Another interesting option is to take a do-it-yourself excursion to the village of **Hallein** with its **salt mines** and historic city center.

MOZART'S BIRTHPLACE & RESIDENCE

✪ **Mozarts Geburtshaus (Mozart's Birthplace).** Getreidegasse 9. ☎ **0662/84 43 13.** Admission 70S ($6) adults, 55S ($4.40) seniors/students, 25S ($2) ages 15–18, 20S ($1.60) ages 6–14, 170S ($14) families; combination ticket (birthplace and residence), 110S ($90) adults, 85S ($7) seniors/students, 30S–40S ($2.40–$3.20) children, 260S ($30) families.

Getting the Best Deal on Sightseeing

- Buy the Salzburg Card—available for 200S ($16) for 24 hours, 270S ($22) for 48 hours, or 360S ($29) for 72 hours—which offers unlimited public transportation and free entry into Salzburg's major sights and museums.
- Get a combination ticket for both the Mozart Birthplace and Residence—great for Mozart fans.
- Walk to the fortress instead of paying for a ticket on the funicular.

July–Aug daily 9am–7pm; Sept–June daily 9am–6pm (you must enter 30 minutes before closing). Bus: 1 from the Hauptbahnhof to Hanuschplatz; or 5 or 6 from the Hauptbahnhof to Rathausplatz.

This is the most heavily visited attraction in Salzburg. Wolfgang Amadeus Mozart was born in this third-floor apartment in 1756 and lived here with his family until 1773. The museum contains his clavichord, Hammerklavier (he started composing when he was 4), and the violin he played as a boy. A plaque marks the spot where his cradle stood. Of the several paintings of Amadeus, his sister Nannerl, and his family, only one is known to be a true likeness of the musical genius—the unfinished one by the piano, done by his brother-in-law. Another is thought to be of the musician when he was 9. In addition to the rooms where the family lived, there are a few adjoining rooms decorated in the style of a typical burgher's house in Mozart's time. There are also changing exhibitions related to Mozart's works.

✪ **Mozart-Wohnhaus (Mozart Residence).** Makartplatz 8. ☎ **0662/88 34 54-40.** Admission 70S ($6) adults, 55S ($4.40) seniors/students, 25S ($2) ages 15–18, 20S ($1.60) ages 6–14, 170S ($14) families; combination ticket (birthplace and residence), 110S ($9) adults, 85S ($7) seniors/students, 30S–40S ($2.40–$3.20) children, 260S ($30) families. July–Aug daily 9am–6pm; Sept–June daily 10am–6pm (you must enter 1 hour before closing). Bus: 1, 5, 6, or 51 from the Hauptbahnhof to Makartplatz.

Whereas Mozart's Birthplace is rather austere in its furnishings, this residence strives to chronicle the musician's life and the influence his family—particularly his father—had on his career, making it more worthwhile for those who know little about the genius's life. A teenage Mozart and his family moved from their small home on Getreidegasse to this more spacious and elegant residence in 1773, dating from 1617 and formerly used for dancing classes for the aristocracy. Amadeus lived here until 1780, composing symphonies, serenades, piano and violin concertos, and sacred music. His father died here in 1787. Today the residence, heavily damaged during World War II and completely rebuilt, contains a museum dedicated to Mozart and his family, along with furniture of the period and original music scores. Best, however, are the earphones visitors receive that are automatically activated by the various displays, complete with music, and a movie depicting the child prodigy's life in Salzburg and his tours of Europe.

CASTLES & PALACES

✪ **Festung Hohensalzburg (Hohensalzburg Fortress).** Mönchsberg 34. ☎ **0662/84 24 30** for fortress; **0662/82 58 58** for Welt der Marionetten. Fortress grounds and *Sound and Vision Show*, 35S ($2.80) adults, 20S ($1.60) children, 90S ($7) family; conducted tour and Burgmuseum and Rainermuseum, 35S ($2.80) adults, 20S ($1.60) children, 90S ($7) family; Welt er Marionetten, 35S ($2.80) adults, 30S ($2.40) seniors, 25S ($2) students and children. Conducted tours, July–Aug daily 9:30am–5:30pm; Apr–June and Sept–Oct daily 9:30am–5pm; Nov–Mar daily 10am–4:30pm. Fortress grounds, July–Sept daily

8am–7pm; Apr–June and Oct daily 9am–6pm; Nov–Mar daily 9am–5pm. Welt der Marionetten, July–Aug daily 10am–6pm; Apr–June and Sept–Oct daily 10am–5pm. Rainermuseum closed Oct–Apr. Take the funicular (59S/$4.70 one-way or 69S/$6 round-trip adults; 32S/$2.55 and 37S/$2.95, respectively, children; price includes admission to fortress), or a 30-minute walk from the Altstadt.

Dominating the city from its perch upon a cliff is this impressive medieval fortress/castle, built between the 11th and the 17th centuries as a residence for the prince-archbishops who ruled Salzburg for more than 500 years. It has the honor of being both the largest completely preserved fortress in central Europe and Europe's largest fortress from the 11th century. It contains the State Rooms of the former archbishops and two related museums, which can be visited only by joining a 40-minute tour, conducted in both German and English. I highly recommend taking the tour, not only because there's otherwise very little to do here but also because you'll learn a lot about medieval Salzburg in the process. The tour takes you through dark corridors and unfurnished chambers, including a dismal torture chamber filled with hideous instruments of pain. You'll also see the archbishops' living quarters, with their carvings of gold leaf and a late Gothic porcelain stove dating from 1501, the most valuable item in the fortress, as well as a huge open-air barrel organ dating from 1502, once used to signal the daily opening and closing of the city's gates. The tour concludes at the **Burgmuseum (Fortress Museum),** with a historical overview of the fortress with displays of weapons used in peasant revolts, furniture from the 14th and 15th centuries, and a macabre collection of medieval torture devices. The other museum, the **Rainermuseum,** is a military museum displaying armor, swords, uniforms, and other related items.

If you don't take the tour, the base admission price allows you to wander through the fortress grounds, courtyards, and viewing platforms and includes entrance to the *Sound and Vision Show,* a multimedia presentation of the history of the fortress. Also on fortress grounds is the **Welt der Marionetten (World of the Marionettes),** a newly opened museum with more than 120 marionettes from around the world, including marionettes from Salzburg's own famous marionette theater, with descriptions of how they operate. There is also a tavern in the fortress.

The easiest way to reach the fortress is by funicular, which includes base admission to the fortress grounds. If you're on a tight budget, you might wish to approach on foot. A path leading from the Altstadt and winding up the hill, offering changing vistas on the way, makes for a pleasant walk. As an alternative, you may wish to go up by funicular and descend on foot.

Residenz. Residenzplatz 1. ☎ **0662/80 42-27 61** for state rooms; **0662/84 04 51** for residenzgalerie. State Rooms tours, 50S ($4) adults, 40S ($3.20) seniors and students, 20S ($1.60) children; Residenzgalerie, 50S ($4) adults, 40S ($3.20) seniors and students, 15S ($1.20) children; combination ticket (State Rooms and Residenzgalerie), 80S ($7) adults, 70S ($6) seniors and students. State Rooms tours, July–Aug daily, on the hour and half hour, 10am–4:30pm (last tour); Sept–June Mon–Fri at 10am, 11am, noon, 2pm, and 3pm, also on weekends in May, June, Sept, Oct, and Dec. Residenzgalerie, daily 10am–5pm (closed Wed Oct–March).

The 180-room baroque Residenz, in the heart of the Altstadt, dates from the mid–12th century but was rebuilt extensively during the 16th, 17th, and 18th centuries, offering you a journey through 200 years of classical architecture. It served as the official residence of the archbishops when it was deemed safe for them to move down from the fortress into the city (after you've toured both places, you won't blame them for preferring the more elegant Residenz). Forty-minute guided tours (in

Salzburg

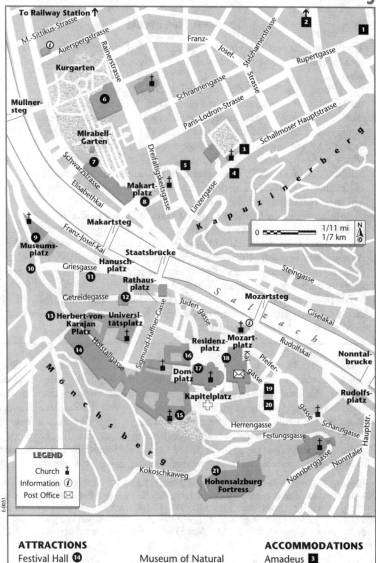

LEGEND

Church †
Information ⓘ
Post Office ✉

E-0051

ATTRACTIONS

Festival Hall ⑭
Glockenspiel ⑱
Hohensalzburg
  Fortress ㉑
Mönchsberg Lift ⑩
Mozart Birthplace ⑫
Mozart Residence ⑧
Mozarteum ⑦
Mirabell Palace ⑥

Museum of Natural
  History ⑨
Residenz ⑯
Salzburg Cathedral ⑰
St. Peter's Church ⑮
St. Peter's Cemetery ⑮
Toy Museum ⑬
Traditional Salzburg
  Costumes ⑪

ACCOMMODATIONS

Amadeus ③
Bergland ❶
Chiemsee ⑲
Junger Fuchs ④
Trumer Stube ⑤
Wolf ⑳

Yoho International
  Youth Hostel ❷

Special & Free Events

Throughout the year Salzburg hosts annual music festivals. The year kicks off with **Mozart Week** at the end of January, followed by the **Salzburg Easter Festival.**

July brings the **Sommer Szene Festival,** an international festival honoring dance, with an emphasis on avant-garde dance productions. The city's most famous spectacle is the **Salzburger Festspiele,** which is held from the end of July to the end of August and has a history stretching back 70 years. Tickets are hard to come by and impossible to get once the festival is under way. To find out what's being performed, contact the Salzburg Festival, Postfach 140, 5020 Salzburg (☎ **0662/8045**). Among the highlights are Mozart's operas, Hugo von Hofmannsthal's *Everyman,* performances of the Salzburg Marionette Theater, and guest philharmonic orchestras.

Autumn brings the **Salzburg Cultural Days,** a 2-week musical event held in October with more opera and concerts given by renowned national orchestras. International jazz stars dazzle with 4 days of concerts and jam sessions at the **Autumn Jazz Festival,** held in early November. Since these festivals are popular, make hotel reservations at least a month or two in advance if you wish to visit Salzburg during these times, especially in August.

For **free concerts,** your best bet is the **Hochschule Mozarteum,** where concerts are given regularly by students. In summer, free brass-band concerts are held in Mirabell Garden on Wednesday at 8:30pm and Sunday at 10:30am.

German only) take you through more than a dozen *Residenz Prunkräume* (State Rooms), including the throne room (the most beautiful room), the bedroom of the archbishop, the library, and other chambers, most with inlaid wooden floors, marble portals, frescoes, and precious furniture. Be sure, too, to visit the **Residenzgalerie,** a 15-room gallery of European art from the 16th to the 19th centuries. It includes works by Dutch, French, Italian, and Austrian baroque artists, including Rembrandt, Rubens, Brueghel, Friedrich Loos, Ferdinand Georg Waldmüller, and Hans Makart. Also of special interest are paintings depicting Salzburg through the centuries.

Hellbrunn Palace. 3 miles south of the city. ☎ **0662/82 03 72.** Palace, 30S ($2.40) adults, 20S ($1.60) students and children; trick fountains, 70S ($6) adults, 35S ($2.80) students and children; combination ticket, 90S ($7) adults, 45S ($3.60) students and children. Tours, Apr and Oct daily 9am–4:30pm (last tour); May–Sept daily 9am–5:30pm (last tour), with evening tours July–Aug 6–10pm. Closed Nov–Mar. Bus: 55 from the Hauptbahnhof to Hellbrunn (a 20-minute ride).

Built as a hunting lodge and summer residence for Salzburg's prince-bishops in the 17th century, this Italian Renaissance-style country villa is an impressive example of the wealth and comfort enjoyed by absolute rulers during the Renaissance. The most unique and intriguing features are its water gardens—dozens of trick fountains and water sprays hidden in its large baroque gardens, complete with mysterious grottoes and mythical statues. This is probably the only conducted tour in Europe in which laughing, running, and hiding are expected (you almost invariably get doused). Tours of the palace last about 20 minutes, while those of the garden last about 40 minutes.

While you're here, you may wish to visit the nearby **Volkskundemuseum (Folklore Museum),** in the Monatsschlösschen on Hellbrunn Hill, open daily April to October 9am to 5pm and costing 20S ($1.60) for adults, 15S ($1.20) for seniors, and 10S (80¢) for students and children. Not far away is the **Hellbrunn Zoo,** popular for its petting zoo and its free-flying griffin vultures, which breed and live in the nearby mountains but come to the zoo to feed. Worth a visit if you have kids, it's open daily from 8:30am, with different closing hours throughout the year (☎ 0662/82 01 76 for exact closing times), and costs 70S ($6) for adults and 30S ($2.40) for children.

CHURCHES

Catacombs of St. Peter's Church. St. Peter-Bezirk 1. ☎ 0662/84 45 78-0. Church and cemetery, free; catacombs tour, 12S (95¢) adults, 8S (65¢) seniors, students, and children. Church, daily 9am–5pm. Catacombs tour, May–Sept daily on the hour 10am–5pm; Oct–Apr infrequently 10:30am–3:30pm. Bus: 1 from the Hauptbahnhof to Hanuschplatz, then walk to the end of Sigmund Hafnergasse, turn left to Domplatz, and the church is next to the Dom.

This church in the Altstadt, located at the foot of Mönchsberg, has a lovely rococo interior and is surrounded by one of the most picturesque cemeteries I've ever seen, beautifully arranged and worth a walk through. At the entrance to the catacombs (against the cliff) are two of the cemetery's most important tombs—those of Mozart's sister, Nannerl, and Haydn's brother, Johann Michael Haydn. You might wish to join a guided tour of the catacombs (usually conducted in German but sometimes in English). You'll visit two rooms carved in the face of the cliff, the first dating from A.D. 250 and built by Roman Christians for secret religious ceremonies. *Be forewarned:* There are a lot of stairs on this 20-minute tour. In winter, tours are given infrequently, so check the notice board at the entrance for the next one. (*Note:* There has also been talk of discontinuing the tours entirely.)

Dom (Salzburg Cathedral). Domplatz. ☎ 0662/84 41 89. Dom, free (donations appreciated); Dom museum, 70S ($6) adults, 50S ($4) seniors and students, 25S ($2) children. Dom, daily 9am–7pm (to 5pm in winter); Dom museum, mid-May to mid-Oct Mon–Sat 10am–5pm, Sun 1–6pm. Closed mid-Oct to mid-May. Bus: 1 from the Hauptbahnhof to Hanuschplatz, then walk to the end of Sigmund Hafnergasse, turn left, and you've reached Domplatz.

Salzburg's Cathedral, in the center of the Altstadt, was first built in the 8th century but destroyed by fire in the 16th. The present Dom, commissioned by Archbishop Wolf-Dietrich and designed by the Italian architect Santino Solari, is the finest example of an early baroque building north of the Alps. This is where Mozart was baptized and engaged as a court organist, and it's famed for its three bronze doors and 4,000-pipe organ. Treasures of the Dom are on display in the museum to the right of the front door, but it is only worth visiting if you're interested in religious art.

MUSEUMS

Bürgerspital Spielzeug Museum (Toy Museum). Bürgerspitalgasse 2. ☎ 0662/84 75 60. Admission (including the puppet show) 30S ($2.40) adults, 10S (80¢) students and children. Tues–Sun 9am–5pm. Bus: 1 from the Hauptbahnhof to Hanuschplatz.

Housed in the former Salzburg Municipal Hospital, this delightful museum displays every conceivable sort of toy—from a hand-carved Noah's Ark to a merry-go-round, from model trains to dolls and dollhouses, cutouts, and cardboard theaters—all dating from the 16th century to the present. There's also folk art and temporary exhibits, and puppet shows for children are held every Tuesday and Wednesday at 3pm (in German only). You'll see more adults than children here.

Haus der Natur (Museum of Natural History). Museumsplatz 5. ☎ 0662/84 26 53. Admission 55S ($4.40) adults, 30S ($2.40) students and children. Daily 9am–5pm. Bus: 1 from the Hauptbahnhof to Hanuschplatz, then turn right onto Griesgasse and at the end of it is Museumsplatz.

On five floors in 80 exhibition rooms, practically everything that lives or grows is brilliantly displayed. Exhibits include model dinosaurs and other prehistoric animals; the twin roots of a fir tree hundreds of years old; live tarantulas; a rock crystal weighing 1,360 pounds; abnormalities like a calf with two legs, a chicken with four legs, and a deer with three legs; a giant model of a DNA molecule; models of the Saturn V rocket; and pieces of moon rock donated by President Nixon in 1973. There's also an aquarium with fresh- and seawater animals, as well as an exhibition on sharks and other ocean inhabitants and the Reptile Zoo with 200 scaly creatures. Without a doubt, this is one of the best natural history museums in Europe, and kids love it. Unfortunately, the descriptions are only in German.

Salzburger Trachten—Einst und Jetzt (Traditional Salzburg Costumes—Then and Now). Griesgasse 23. ☎ **0662/84 31 19.** Admission 30S ($2.40) adults, 20S ($1.60) students and children. Mon–Fri 10am–noon and 2–5pm, Sat 10am–noon. Bus: 1 from the Hauptbahnhof to Hanuschplatz, then turn right onto Griesgasse and the museum will be on your left.

Those who plan to buy dirndls (or lederhosen, sweaters, hats, and jackets) should come here first: Traditional Salzburg dress from the 18th to the 20th centuries is on exhibit, including garments from the baroque and Biedermeier periods and everyday and festive clothing worn today. Be sure to get the sheet in English that describes the various costumes.

Stiegl's Brauwelt. Bräuhausstrasse 9. ☎ **0662/83 87-1492.** Admission (including two pints of beer or a soft drink, a pretzel, and souvenir) 96S ($8) adults, 86S ($7) seniors and students, 50S ($4) children. Wed–Sun 10am–5pm. Bus: 1 or 2 to Bräuhausstrasse, or 27 to Rochusgasse.

Located on the western edge of town near the airport and housed in the former malt house of the Stiegl Brewery, Austria's oldest private brewery, this museum recounts the 500-year history of the brewery's history, shows the brewing process, and imparts information on beer-brewing nations around the world. (Did you know, for example, that the United States is the largest beer producer in the world?) Displays are in German only, but ask for the English translation at the ticket counter. At the end of your self-guided tour, stop by the pub where you have your choice of two pints of beer (included in the admission price). My recommendation is *Paracelsus Naturtrüb*, brewed in the basement of the museum and available only here.

A PANORAMIC VIEW

Mönchsberg and Café Winkler. Mönchsberg. ☎ **0662/84 77 38.** Mönchsberg Lift (elevator), 16S ($1.30) one-way and 27S ($2.15) round-trip adults, 9S (70¢) one-way and 14S ($1.10) round-trip children. Elevator, Mon 9am–7pm, Tues–Sun 9am–11pm. Café, Tues–Sun 11am–11pm (daily in August). Bus: 1 from the Hauptbahnhof to Hanuschplatz; the Lift is at Gstättengasse 13.

Salzburg's other conspicuous hilltop building is Café Winkler, which contains a cafe and sits high above the city. The best reason for coming here, however, is the view— Salzburg's most impressive. In front of you are all the churches, a stretch of the Salzach River, and the Hohensalzburg Fortress. Also of interest is the *Sattler Panorama*, a huge 360° mural of Salzburg, painted in 1825, that was taken throughout Europe as proof that Salzburg was a beautiful city worthy of a visit.

If you feel like a **hike,** take the path that skirts the top of the ridge to the fortress, about a 30-minute walk. Café Winkler can be reached via the Mönchsberg Lift, an elevator that whisks visitors to the top. The elevator is at Gstättengasse 13, and departs at least every 15 minutes.

PARKS & GARDENS

The town's most famous garden, now a public park, is the **Mirabellgarten,** on the river's right bank. Designed in the 17th century in baroque style with statues, marble vases designed by Fischer von Erlach, fountains, and ponds, it offers a great view of the Hohensalzburg Fortress. In the middle of the grounds is a palace built by Archbishop Wolf-Dietrich for his mistress (she bore him 14 children), now used for concerts, weddings, and administrative offices. The park is a popular place for a stroll, and its benches are always occupied with office workers and older people catching a few rays. The Orangerie is free, and in spring the garden comes alive with about 17,000 tulips. A small open-air cafeteria sells beverages and snacks. Adjoining the garden is the **Kurpark,** a tree-lined area with a small hill called Rosenhügel (a good spot for taking snapshots) and an indoor pool and spa center.

ORGANIZED TOURS

In a city as small as Salzburg that can be so pleasurably covered on foot, it really isn't necessary to spend money on a tour. For a quick overview of what the city has to offer, however, you might wish to join the 1-hour walking tour offered in German and English by the Salzburg Tourist Office. Departing daily at 12:15pm from the tourist office on Mozartplatz, it costs 80S ($6).

Otherwise, the primary reason for booking a bus tour is to visit out-of-town sights. For readers planning more than a 2-day stay, here's some excursions to consider:

Bob's Special Tours, in the Altstadt at Kaigasse 19 (☎ **0662/849 51 10**), has specialized in English-language tours for more than 20 years and offers two 4-hour tours. The "*Sound of Music* Tour" includes a short city tour and takes in most of the major film locations, including Leopoldskron Palace (which served as the von Trapp film home), the lake district where the opening scene was filmed, and the Hellbrunn Palace with its gazebo. The "Bavarian Mountain Tour" includes some *Sound of Music* sights, as well as Berchtesgaden in Germany (passport required) and a choice of either the Hallein salt mine or Hitler's Eagles Nest. Both tours depart daily at 9am and 2pm, with pickup at any guesthouse or hotel in Salzburg, and last approximately 4 hours. In addition, a skiing tour is also offered January to March at 8:30am daily, including transportation, a guide/instructor, and possibilities for skiing, snowboarding, ice skating, and indoor swimming (lift tickets, rentals, and admissions cost extra). Each of the three tours costs 350S ($28) adults, 320S ($26) students, and 290S ($23) children; a 10% reduction is given to those who book tours directly at the Kaigasse 19 office, open Monday to Friday 9am to 6pm and, in summer, also on Saturday 9am to 2pm. The tours are small and personable, in buses that seat 8 to 20.

Another tour company is **Salzburg Sightseeing Tours,** Mirabellplatz 2 (☎ **0662/88 16 16**), the first company to offer a *Sound of Music* tour (its bus even appeared in the film)—it still offers a 4-hour "The Most Unique *Sound of Music* Tour" in English for 350S ($28) adults and 170S ($14) children, with departures daily at 9:30am and 2pm. In addition to a variety of city tours, it also offers several excursions into the countryside. Most interesting, perhaps, is the daily 4-hour trip to the salt mines in Hallein, which includes a cable-car ride to the mines, a visit to an open-air reconstructed Celtic village, and an excursion through the mines, all for 490S ($39) adults and 340S ($27) children. For real *Sound of Music* fans, another option is the "Follow Maria's Footsteps Tour," which allows participants to join both the "*Sound of Music* Tour" and the "Salt Mine Tour" (the real Maria spent some time in Hallein) at a reduced rate of 690S ($55) adults and 400S ($32) children. Participants can do both tours in 1 day or on separate days. *Special note:* Readers who present this book are entitled to a 10% discount on the "*Sound of Music* Tour"; students and families receive further reductions on all tours except the Hallein "Salt Mine Tour." Prices for all tours include hotel pickup and all admission prices.

6 Shopping

Austrian artisanship is of high quality, with correspondingly high prices for sweaters, dirndls, leather goods, jewelry, and other local goods, including chocolates. Most shops are concentrated in the Altstadt along Getreidegasse and Alter Markt, as well as across the river along Linzergasse.

If you make purchases that total more than 1,000S ($80) in one store on any given day, you're entitled to a refund of the 13% **value-added tax (VAT).** Ask the store clerk for a U-34 form or a Tax-free Shopping Cheque, which you present to Customs upon departing the last European Union country on your way home. If, for example, you're flying back to the United States from Frankfurt, present your U-34 form or Cheque, receipt from the shop, and the goods purchased to the Customs officer at the Frankfurt airport. Then go to the Tax-Free Shopping counter for an immediate refund, minus a handling fee.

Salzburg has two well-known markets. The **Grünmarkt (Green Market)** is held in the Altstadt, in front of the Universitäts church on Universitätsplatz (behind Mozart's Birthplace). It features stalls selling vegetables, fruit, flowers, and souvenirs, as well as a stand-up food stall selling sausages. It takes place Monday to Friday 6am to 7pm and Saturday 6am to 1pm. On the other side of the river, in front of St. Andrew's Church near Mirabellplatz, is the **Schrannenmarkt.** This is where Salzburg's housewives go to shop and socialize, purchasing vegetables, flowers, bread, and even traditional handicraft products. It's held every Thursday (on Wednesday if Thursday is a public holiday) 6am to 1pm.

7 Salzburg After Dark

As the birthplace of Mozart and site of the Salzburg Festival (see the "Special & Free Events" box, earlier in this chapter), the city boasts a musical event almost every night of the year. To find out what's going on where, stop by the **City Tourist Office,** Mozartplatz 5 (☎ **0662/88 987-330**), to pick up a free copy of the monthly brochure *Veranstaltungen.*

The cheapest way to secure theater tickets is by purchasing directly at the theater box office. Otherwise, the **Salzburg Ticket Service,** which charges a 20% commission, is at the City Tourist Office on Mozartplatz (☎ **0662/84 03 10**). Selling tickets for all concerts, it's open in summer Monday to Friday 9am to 6pm and Saturday 9am to noon; in winter Monday to Friday 10am to 4pm and Saturday 9am to noon; and mid-July to August daily 9am to 7pm.

For the Salzburg Festival, you must book tickets months in advance.

THE PERFORMING ARTS

OPERA, DANCE & MUSIC The **Festspielhaus,** Hofstallgasse 1 (☎ **0662/80 45-0;** Bus: 1 from the Hauptbahnhof to Herbert-von-Karajan-Platz, or 5, 6, or 51 from the Hauptbahnhof to Rathausplatz), is where opera, ballet, and concerts are performed and major events of the Salzburg Festival take place. Performances are in the 1,324-seat Kleines Haus (Small House) or the 2,170-seat Grosses Haus (Large House), and it's best to buy tickets in advance; for the Salzburg Festival, months in advance for major performances. The box office for the Salzburg Festival is at Herbert-von-Karajan-Platz (☎ **0662/84 45 01**). It's open Monday to Friday 9:30am to 3pm, except from July 1 to the start of the festival, when it's open Monday to Saturday 9:30am to 5pm, and during the festival, when it's open daily 9:30am to 5pm. For orchestra concerts, given September to June, you'll find the box office at

Kulturvereinigung, Waagplatz 1A (☎ **0662/84 53 46**), near the tourist office. It's open Monday to Friday 8am to 6pm; performances are usually at 7:30pm. Tickets for orchestra concerts are 270S to 560S ($22 to $45); during the Salzburg Festival tickets range from 50S to 4,200S ($4 to $336).

Orchestra concerts and chamber music are presented in the **Mozarteum,** Schwarzstrasse 26 (☎ **0662/87 31 54;** Bus: 1, 5, 6, or 51 from the Hauptbahnhof to Makartplatz). The Mozarteum is on the river's right bank, near Mirabellgarten; its box office, open Monday to Thursday 9am to 2pm and Friday 9am to 4pm, is in the Mozart-Wohnhaus, Theatergasse 2. Performances are at 11am and/or 7:30pm, with most tickets ranging from 140S to 650S ($11 to $52). The **Hochschule Mozarteum (University of Music and Dramatic Art),** Mirabellplatz 1 (☎ **0662/88 908-0**), sometimes features **free student concerts.**

At the **Salzburger Mozart-Serenaden,** held in the Gothic Hall of St. Blasius Church, in the Altstadt at Bürgerspital 2 (☎ **0662/43 68 70;** Bus: 1 to Bürgerspitalplatz), Mozart's famous chamber music is performed together with other works from the Viennese classical period by chamber ensembles two or three times a week at 7:30 or 8:30pm, with more performances during Advent and in summer. Tickets run 330S to 380S ($26 to $30).

The **Salzburger Schlosskonzerte (Salzburg Palace Concerts)** take place year-round in the Mirabell Palace, Mirabellplatz (☎ **0662/84 85 86;** Bus: 1, 5, 6, or 51 from the Hauptbahnhof to Mirabellplatz [Mirabell Palace]). The chamber-music series presents mostly Mozart's music, as well as music by Mozart contemporaries and others, including works by Haydn, Beethoven, Schubert, and Vivaldi. Concerts, generally at 8pm Saturday and Sunday and often during the week as well, are held in intimate baroque surroundings, much as they were in Mozart's time. The box office, at Griesgasse 6, is open Monday to Friday 9am to 1pm and 2 to 5pm; performances are almost daily at 8 or 8:30pm. Tickets are 330S to 360S ($26 to $29).

Salzburg's landmark, the **Hohensalzburg Fortress,** Mönchsberg 34 (☎ **0662/82 58 58;** take the funicular from Festungsgasse), features concerts called the **Festungskonzerte** in the medieval Prince's Chamber, performed by the Salzburger Mozart-Ensemble, as well as guest musicians. The box office, at A.-Adlgasser-Weg 22, is open daily 9am to 9pm; performances are given almost daily at 8 or 8:30pm. Tickets are 360S or 420S ($29 to $34).

THEATER   Comedies, dramas, and musicals are performed at the **Salzburger Landestheater,** Schwarzstrasse 22 (☎ **0662/87 15 12;** Bus: 1, 5, 6, or 51 from the Hauptbahnhof to Makartplatz), as well as ballet, operas, and operettas. During August the theater takes part in the Salzburg Festival. The Landestheater has a central location on the river's right bank, just south of Mirabellgarten. The box office is open Tuesday to Friday 10am to 1pm and 5:30 to 7pm and Saturday 10am to 1pm; performances are usually Tuesday to Sunday at 7 or 7:30pm. Tickets are 205S to 615S ($16 to $49) for opera and 180S to 530S ($14 to $42) for musicals.

Next door, the **Salzburger Marionettentheater,** Schwarzstrasse 24 (☎ **0662/87 24 06;** Bus: 1, 5, 6, or 51 from the Hauptbahnhof to Makartplatz), was founded in 1913 and is one of Europe's largest and most famous marionette theaters. The company has toured the world. Using recordings made by top orchestras and singers, it presents operas and operettas Easter to September, during Christmas, and the last 2 weeks in January, including *The Magic Flute, Die Fledermaus, The Barber of Seville, The Marriage of Figaro,* and *Don Giovanni.* The box office is open Monday to Saturday 9am to 1pm and 2 hours before the start of each performance; performances are usually Monday to Saturday at 7:30pm, with occasional 4pm matinees in July and August. Tickets run 250S to 480S ($20 to $38).

DINNER SHOWS

For a real splurge, you might consider combining dinner with the music of Mozart. At the **Stiftskeller St. Peter** (see the dining section of this chapter), the **Mozart Dinner Concert** features music of Mozart played by musicians in period costumes and a three-course meal based on traditional recipes from the 17th and 18th centuries. Festivities, costing 530S ($42) per person, begin at 8pm March to December, usually every Sunday, Tuesday, Wednesday, and Thursday at 8pm (nightly in August). In addition, **Candlelight Dinner & Mozart Concert shows** are held year-round at the **Hohensalzburg Fortress,** with dinner beginning between 5:30 and 6:30pm (depending on the time of year) and concerts beginning 2 hours later. This culinary musical experience costs 590S ($47). For more information, contact the Salzburger Festungskonzerte box office at A.-Adlgasser-Weg 22 (☎ **0662/82 58 58**).

Capitalizing on Salzburg's movie fame with highlight tunes from *The Sound of Music,* the **New *Sound of Music* Show** (☎ **0662/83 20**) takes place daily mid-May to October at 7:30pm at the Stieglkeller, Festungsgasse 10. Under the direction of pianist/entertainer Franz Langer, the show includes melodies from the film, folksongs and dances from the Salzburger province, as well as a 10-minute documentary of the von Trapp family. The price of the dinner and show is 520S ($42); just the show, 360S ($29).

BARS

The **Augustiner Bräustübl Mülln,** Augustinergasse 4 (☎ **0662/43 12 46;** Bus: 27 from Mirabellplatz or Hanuschplatz to Augustinergasse), known as *Augustinerbräu* or *Müllnerbräu,* is one of the cheapest places in town for a brew, with seating either in its beer garden or in one of its massive dining halls. There are also counters selling sausages, pretzels, and other foods that go well with beer, which goes for 28S ($2.25) a half liter. The place is open Monday to Friday 3 to 10:30pm and Saturday, Sunday, and holidays 2:30 to 10:30pm.

Rockhouse, Schallmooser Hauptstrasse 46 (☎ **0662/88 49 14;** Bus: 29 to Canavalstrasse), is an alternative music venue that includes a cafe, open Monday to Saturday 6pm to 2am (also on Sunday when there's a concert), and a tunnel-shaped concert hall featuring local and international bands playing rock, jazz, funk, blues, and techno pop, with concerts three or four times a week. Occupying an 1842 building that formerly served as a wine and ice cellar, this is a welcome addition to the Salzburg music scene. Cover ranges from 80S to 250S ($6 to $20).

8 Side Trips: Untersberg & Hallein

UNTERSBERG

Untersberg, the mountain dominating Salzburg, reaches 6,115 feet above sea level, 7 miles south of the city in St. Leonhard. Visiting Untersberg is certainly worth the extra money and may very well be one of the highlights of your stay, especially if this is your only excursion into the Alpine scenery. To get there, take bus no. 55 from the train station or Mozartsteg to St. Leonhard, the last stop, and change to the cable car to ride to the mountaintop. From there, you'll have a glorious view of Salzburg and the Alps. A marked path leads to the peak in about 20 minutes (bring good walking shoes if you plan to hike); if you prefer, you can sit in the restaurant there and enjoy the view.

The round-trip fare for the **cable car** (☎ **0662/87 12 17** or 06246/72 4 77) is 205S ($16) adults and 105S ($8) children. The cable car operates daily: July to September 8:30am to 5:30pm (to 8pm on Wednesday), March to June and October 9am to 5pm, and mid-December to February 10am to 4pm. Closed November to beginning of December. Closed for maintenance 2 weeks in April.

HALLEIN

Hallein, 10 miles south of Salzburg, is famous for its **salt mines**—the **Salzbergwerk** (☎ **06245/852 85-15**)—on a mountain called Dürrnberg. Discovered by Celtic settlers as early as 500 B.C., the mines subsequently gave Salzburg both its name and its fortune. Today they're open to the public in the form of a 1-hour guided tour (in German and English), conducted by a uniformed miner. He'll give you a coverall to protect you from the cold, humidity, and dirt, then send you off on a mine train and swift double chutes that deposit you at the bottom of the mountain, where you'll take a small boat over a natural subterranean lake and watch a short film on the history and development of salt mining and production. Kids love this tour (they must be at least 4 to participate), and be sure to wear good hiking shoes. Cost of the tour is 180S ($14) adults, 160S ($13) seniors/students, and 90S ($7) children. Tours are given daily: mid-April to mid-October 9am to 5pm and in winter 11am to 3pm.

Before or after touring the mines, be sure, too, to visit the nearby **Keltendorf** (☎ **06245/852 85-22**), a reconstructed open-air Celtic village depicting life in the area 2,500 years ago, complete with a reconstructed **prince's tomb** discovered on Dürrnberg. It's open the same hours as the salt mines and costs 20S ($1.60) for adults (15S/$1.20 if you're also visiting the mines), half price for children.

In **Hallein,** a quaint village of 20,000 residents with a pedestrians-only city center (Zentrum), you might wish to expand your knowledge of the region's first settlers by visiting the **Keltenmuseum (Celtic Museum),** Pflegerplatz 5 (☎ **06245/807 83**), which displays many archaeological finds around Dürrnberg. May to October it's open daily 9am to 5pm and costs 40S ($3.20) adults, 30S ($2.40) seniors/students, and 10S (80¢) children.

To visit Hallein, take an early **train** from Salzburg, about a 25-minute ride. To reach the salt mines, follow signs from the train station to the Salzbergbahn **cable car** (about a 10-minute walk, on the other side of the Salzach River), which costs 110S ($9) round-trip adults and 55S ($4.40) children. Note, however, that the funicular is closed in winter and **buses** from the Hallein train station to the salt mine are infrequent (at last check, buses departed at 9:55am, 11:50am, 12:50pm, and 1:50pm); otherwise, take a **taxi** from the station or join an organized group tour, described earlier in this chapter.

For more information about Hallein, contact the **Hallein Tourist Office,** in the city center in the Sparkasse bank at Unterer Markt 1 (☎ **06245/853 94**), open Monday to Friday 9am to 4:30pm (in summer, also Saturday 9am to noon).

DINING   One of the best and most colorful places for a meal in Hallein is in the **Stadtkrug,** in the city center near the tourist office at Bayerhammerplatz 1 (☎ **06245/830 85**). Very popular with the locals, with seating outside in the square in summer, it offers Austrian and vegetarian meals and pizza, costing 64S to 142S ($5 to $11). Monday to Friday, it also offers a great fixed-price lunch, including an all-you-can-eat salad bar, for 90S ($7). It's open daily 11am to 2pm and 5pm to midnight (closed Saturday in winter). No credit cards are accepted. A couple minutes' walk from the train station, **Gasthof Hager,** Bundesstrasse Süd 10 (☎ **06245/804 71**), offers Austrian specialties in a rustic setting, with most meals costing 150S to 200S ($12 to $16). It's open daily 11:30am to 2pm and 5 to 10pm (closed Wednesday in winter). American Express, MasterCard, and Visa are accepted.

25

Seville & Andalusia

by Herbert Bailey Livesey

Images of Andalusia are the ones that flare in the mind when we think about Spain: villages of white houses covering hillsides like masses of huge sugar cubes; the rapid-fire of heels and castanets marking the ragged passion of the flamenco and the cool whirl of the *sevillanas;* tawny rolling plains ranked with olive trees and sectioned with wheat fields; Granada's Sierra Nevada, with peaks high enough to hold snow throughout the year; and beaches clogged with northern Europeans basting themselves from April to October.

Eight centuries of the Moors bestowed the region with castles, mosques, and imperial cities. And the conquistadors, their galleons brimming with plunder, arrived to build palaces for themselves and their patrons. Modern bullfighting was born in Andalusia, where matadors are still heroes.

Here an ancient titled aristocracy contrives to keep a low profile while a new monied elite doesn't, flaunting 200-foot yachts in the harbors of the Costa del Sol. Both largely ignore their impoverished fellow citizens, who suffer a 25%-plus unemployment rate. The former maintain manor houses on great estates and mansions in the hills overlooking the Mediterranean harbors; the latter, well inland, scrape subsistence from ancestral plots subdivided over generations. Traffic chokes the coastal roads, while those of the isolated interior are among the few signs that humans have even passed through. Despite these and other inequities, Andalusians are among the most welcoming of Spaniards.

Seville is the de facto capital of the region of Andalusia, a belt of eight provinces sweeping across the lower rim of Iberia from Portugal and the Atlantic to the southeast corner of the peninsula, where it rounds into the Mediterranean. Often deemed the most Spanish of cities, Seville can, in certain quarters, seem a living repository of the Iberian culture, still rooted in an earlier time. The country's fourth largest city, it feels smaller, perhaps because all the tourist sites are packed into a confined district. And commerce has always appeared to be well down on the list of *Sevilleno* concerns.

However, that started changing when the last Socialist government came to power. Its Seville-born prime minister saw to it that a new high-speed train was built between his hometown and Madrid, cutting travel time from 7 hours or more to 2½. He maneuvered a world's fair, Expo '92, for the city and arranged for an impressive new rail station, a revamped airport, and six futuristic bridges to be added. At

Budget Bests

The evening *paseo,* when everyone gets out of the house to walk the streets and plazas and promenades, is free and a true Spanish experience. One of the best places to join in is along the river between the Isabel II and San Telmo bridges.

Andalusia lays claim to the invention (disputed by Madrid) of the delicious bar snacks called *tapas.* Three or four of them, or a couple of the larger portions called *raciónes,* washed down with wine or beer, can constitute a satisfying, inexpensive meal.

Traditional months for **sales** *(rebajas)* are January, February, and July, with prices that usually decrease as those months go by.

---

about the same time, an astonishing deficiency was rectified when an opera house was built for the town that nurtured Carmen, Don Juan, and a certain barber.

REQUIRED DOCUMENTS   See chapter 18 on Madrid.

OTHER FROMMER'S TITLES   For more on Seville, see *Frommer's Barcelona, Madrid & Seville; Frommer's Spain; Frommer's Europe;* or *Frommer's Europe's Greatest Driving Tours.*

1 Seville Deals & Discounts

SPECIAL DISCOUNTS

If you're staying long enough to take full advantage of it, the 10-ride pass called the *bonobús* costs 615P ($4.25), a saving of 50% over the same number of single-ride tickets.

An **International Student Identity Card (ISIC)** is often necessary to obtain discounts on travel, lodging, and admission to museums. Youth hostal cards are issued at **Viajes TIVE,** Jesús de Veracruz 27 (☎ **95/490-60-22**). Visitors 65 or over can obtain **half-price tickets** on rail travel from the city.

WORTH A SPLURGE

The **Alfonso XIII,** San Fernando 2 (☎ **95/422-28-50**), is one of the most expensive hotels in Spain. But take in the atmosphere of the mock-Mudejar 1929 palace with a predinner drink in the courtyard (have dinner elsewhere).

Andalusia is the birthplace of the music and dance called **flamenco,** and Seville is the place to experience it. The cover charge for a midnight show is steep, but it at least includes the first drink. Sip slowly and enjoy.

2 Essentials

ARRIVING

BY PLANE   Less than 8 miles from downtown, on the Seville–Carmona road, **Aeropuerto San Pablo** (☎ **95/451-53-20**) was expanded and renovated for Expo '92. Flights from North America and most other international cities connect through Madrid's Barajas airport. There are direct flights to other Iberian cities, though, including to/from Barcelona, Lisbon, Palma de Mallorca, Santiago de Compostela, and the Canary Islands. While a **taxi** is the easiest way into town, costing only about $13, there's a **bus** that goes to Puerta de Jerez for 775P ($5) roughly on the hour 6:30am to 10:30pm.

What Things Cost in Seville	U.S. $
Taxi from the railroad station to the center	12.90
Bus ticket	.90
Half-hour buggy ride	25.00–35.00
Local telephone call	.15
Double room at the Hotel Alfonso XIII (luxury)	424.80
Double room at the Hotel San Gil (moderate)	117.90
Double room at the Hostal Goya (budget)	38.60
Lunch for one, without wine, at Casa Robles (moderate)	17.25
Lunch for one, without wine, at San Marco (budget)	8.90
Dinner for one, without wine, at Egaña Oriza (deluxe)	45.80
Dinner for one, without wine, at Rio Grande (moderate)	18.95
Dinner for one, without wine, at El Puerto (budget)	10.35
Glass of wine or beer	.65–1.35
Coca-Cola	1.10
Cup of coffee	.85
Admission to the Alcázar	4.15
Movie ticket	4.50
Ballet ticket	20.70

BY TRAIN The **Estación Santa Justam,** Avenida Kansas City (☎ 95/454-02-02), built for Expo '92, now receives all passenger trains. The most desirable of the two long-distance services is the ultra-high-speed **AVE trains,** using French technology and running along seamless tracks laid in 1991. It reduced the travel time between Madrid and Seville, with a stop in Córdoba, from over 7 hours to 2½; there are 5 to 7 trips each way daily. **TALGO trains** are older, make more stops, and take almost three times as long to complete the same route. Ten daily trains connect Seville and Córdoba, 50 minutes by AVE or 1½ hours by TALGO. Three trains run daily between Granada and Seville, taking 4 to 5 hours. Frequent buses, marked C1 and C2, make the run to the older main bus station at Prado de San Sebastián, with stops along the way. Turn left when exiting the station and walk down to the bus stop on Avenida Kansas City.

For more info and/or to book tickets on the Internet, try **www.raileurope.com** or **www.renfe.com** (the Spanish railroad company).

BY BUS Buses serving Andalusia arrive and depart at the **bus terminal** (☎ 95/441-71-11) at Prado de San Sebastián on Calle José María Osborne, within walking distance or a short taxi ride east of downtown. Most long-distance lines pick up and discharge passengers at the new **Plaza de Armas terminal,** at the east end of the Chapina Bridge. Several private companies provide frequent service from Cádiz, Córdoba, Granada, Jerez de la Frontera, Madrid, and other cities in the region. Except for the AVE train, buses are nearly always cheaper and faster than trains. Comforts and conveniences vary from one bus company to another, however. One prominent company is **Alsina** (☎ 95/441-88-11).

BY CAR Divided highways connect Seville with Jerez, Cádiz, Granada, and Málaga. The two principal routes from Madrid aren't as direct as might be wished, one of them

via Mérida, the other by way of Ciudad Real and Córdoba. They have four-lane seg-
ments only for parts of the way, but they're maintained well and traffic usually isn't too
heavy. If you arrive by car, I strongly recommend you park the car at your hotel or
in a garage and not use it again until you're ready to leave or want to drive into the
countryside.

VISITOR INFORMATION

The **Oficina de Informácion del Turismo** (☎ **95/422-14-04**) is at Avenida de la
Constitución 21B, a block southwest of the Alcázar. It has English-speaking attendants and is open Monday to Saturday 9am to 7pm and Sunday and holidays 10am
to 2pm.

CITY LAYOUT

Occupying both banks of the **Guadalquiver River,** navigable by fairly large ships to a
point just south of the center, Seville's buildings have a golden cast, turned russet at
sunset. Most of its attractions and desirable hotels are in the larger, eastern portion of
the city, dominated by the **cathedral,** the third largest in Europe, and its bell tower,
the **Giralda,** part Muslim and part Christian and therefore a fitting symbol of the city.

Immediately south of the cathedral is the **Alcázar,** a palace built for Pedro the Cruel
in the 14th century, and to the east the pedestrian maze of streets of the atmospheric
old Jewish quarter known as the **Barrio de Santa Cruz.** Guarding the river is the
12th-century **Torre de Oro (Tower of Gold),** which dominates the promenade above
the water. These monuments, with the riverside **Plaza de Toros,** form an inverted triangle that's the *centro histórico* (historic center), a logical area in which to find lodging,
since the city's worthiest *barrios* and architectural relics can all be reached from there
on foot.

South of the triangle lie the **gardens** of the Alcázar, and a few blocks farther is the
Parque María Luisa, a refuge shaded by hundreds of trees and containing some
remaining structures of a 1929 exposition, notably the **Plaza de España,** with its semi-
circular canal. The neighborhood north of the triangular old city is **El Arenal.** Along
its narrow streets are many shops and cafes; especially popular is **Calle Sierpes.** Over
toward the river is the **Museo de Bellas Artes,** facing a pleasant square.

On the opposite bank, primarily between the Isabel II and San Telmo bridges, is
Triana. Long identified as a Gitano (Gypsy) quarter, it's more notable for its many
restaurants and *tapas* bars, especially those along **Calle Betis,** bordering the river.

GETTING AROUND

By far the best way to explore the city is by walking, and there are plenty of cafes,
parks, plazas, and benches on which to rest, especially in the Barrio Santa Cruz and
along both sides of the river.

BY TAXI   The principal attractions occupy a fairly compact area, so taxis aren't an
unreasonable expense for getting to the more distant points. At night, they're almost
essential, given the unfortunately high level of street crime. Cabs are metered. Some
are minivans; all are white, with a diagonal yellow stripe on the side. The meter starts
at 129P (90¢) and clicks at 2P per nanosecond, so even a fairly short ride can quickly
mount to 500P ($3.45).

A single male passenger is usually expected to sit in front with the driver—such are
the egalitarian notions of the local culture. *Sevillano* cabdrivers have a genetic predis-
position to avoid direct routes, stretching even short drives by at least a few extra
blocks. Alas, unless you speak Spanish *and* know well Seville's welter of one-way
streets, there isn't much you can do to challenge the practice.

You can hail a cab on the street, but at night they're often hard to find. Restaurants and hotel *conserjes* will summon taxis for you, or you can call for one at ☎ **95/ 458-00-00** or 95/462-22-22.

BY BUS   Due to the many narrow or one-way streets, the orange city buses follow complicated routes that aren't easy to master. A one-ride fare costs 125P (85¢). If you find them useful, the 10-ride *bonopass* costs only 615P ($4.25). The *bonopass* can be purchased at tobacconists, newsstands, and booths near major stops marked TUSSAM.

BY CARRIAGE   Horse-drawn carriages muster around the edges of the Plaza Virgen de los Reyes, on the east side of the cathedral. They're an expensive way to get about, and undeniably touristy, but might serve as a one-time treat just to see the sights. The signs that once posted fares in both English and Spanish seem to have disappeared, but be sure to check whether new ones have been installed. Expect to pay about 4,350P ($30) for a 45-minute ride. At slow times, it might be possible to haggle a discount.

BY CAR   I don't recommend driving in Seville. Apart from a few wide boulevards, most of the streets of the city are narrow and many follow confusing one-way patterns. Parking is extremely limited, and even moving cars are a favorite target of Seville's rapacious criminal set. To rent cars for side trips to central and southern Andalusia, there's a **Hertz** at Av. República 3 (☎ **95/427-88-87**) and an **Avis** at Av. de la Constiución 15B (☎ **95/421-65-49**), with branch offices for each at the airport.

FAST FACTS: Seville

American Express   The office is in the **Hotel Inglaterra,** Plaza Nueva 7 (☎ **95/421-16-17**), open Monday to Friday 9:30am to 1:30pm and 4:30 to 7:30pm and Saturday 9am to noon.

Baby-sitters   Called *canguros* in Spanish, baby-sitters are often available through *conserjes* in the larger hotels. In family-run hostals, sons or daughters might oblige.

Business Hours   The traditional **siesta period** has greater justification in southern Spain, where the midday sun is fierce for 6 months. Most **offices** are open Monday to Friday 9am to 7pm, with a long lunch break 1:30 or 2pm to 4 or 5pm; in summer, offices often close for the day at 3pm. **Banks** are usually open Monday to Friday 9am to 2pm and Saturday 9am to 1pm. **Shops and many attractions** open at 10am, close for siesta 1:30 or 2pm to 4:30 or 5pm, and then stay open to 8pm.

Consulates   The **United States** consulate is at Paseo de las Delicias 7 (☎ **95/423-18-83**), open Monday to Friday 10am to 1pm and 2 to 4:30pm. The **Canadian** consulate is at Avenida de la Constitución 30 (☎ **95/422-94-13**), open Monday to Friday 9:30am to 1pm. The consulate of the **United Kingdom** is at Plaza Nueva 8 (☎ **95/422-88-75**), open Monday to Friday 8am to 3pm.

Crime   In a region with an unemployment rate topping 25%, Seville suffers an unenviable reputation as Spain's most crime-ridden city. While it must be hastily added that the strong chances are you'll encounter no unpleasantness, you should observe the usual urban cautionary measures. Cars, parked or moving, are particular targets. Leave nothing of value in view or in the trunk for any longer than absolutely necessary. Some experts suggest leaving the glove box open and empty so that thieves won't break windows. Keep purses and cameras firmly in hand when riding in the car, for criminals are known to rush out to cars stopped at

The **country code** for Spain is **34.** The **city code** for Seville is **5;** use this code when you're calling from outside Spain. If you're within Spain but not in Seville, use **95.** If you're calling within Seville, simply leave off the code and dial only the regular phone number.

traffic lights, reach in the window, and snatch whatever comes to hand. Keep the car doors locked while driving. For further hints, see "Fast Facts: Barcelona" in chapter 6.

Currency   See "Fast Facts: Madrid" in chapter 18.

Currency Exchange   You can change money at banks advertising *cambio.* A standard commission is charged, which makes cashing traveler's checks in small denominations expensive. Increasingly, **ATMs** are favored by travelers, for the rates applied are usually the best available at the time of exchange. Some U.S. banks charge excessive fees for this service, however, so check before leaving. ATMs accept either major credit cards or cash withdrawal cards in the Cirrus and Plus systems. If a machine rejects your card, often for unspecified "technical reasons," don't be alarmed. Assuming you have sufficient cash or credit in your account, the next ATM down the street will most likely honor your card.

Dentists & Doctors   For bilingual dental or medical attention, ask the hotel *conserje* for referrals or contact your consulate (several are listed above).

Emergencies   For the **police,** dial ☎ 091 (Policia Nacional) or 092 (Policia Municipal); to report a crime, go to the **station** at Paseo de las Delicias s/n (☎ 95/461-54-50). For **medical emergencies,** go to the Hospital Universitario y Provincial, Avenida Doctor Fedriani s/n (☎ 95/455-74-00).

Holidays   For a list of national holidays, see "Fast Facts: Madrid" in chapter 18.

Laundry   Even inexpensive hotels charge exorbitant fees for laundry. Take soiled clothes to a Laundromat, such as **Lavandería Robledo,** F. Sanchez Bedoya 18 (☎ 95/421-81-23).

Post Office   The main post office, **Correos,** is at Avenida de la Constitución 32 (☎ 95/421-95-85), open Monday to Friday 8:30am to 8:30pm and Saturday 9:30am to 2pm.

Telephone   The minimum charge for **local telephone calls** is 25P (15¢). Many hotels and hostals tack on a hefty surcharge for long-distance calls. Most public phones have clear instructions in English. Place at least 50P worth of coins in the rack at the top and let them roll in as required (you'll need many more 100P coins for long-distance calls). Many phones provide on-screen instructions in four languages and accept the **Tarjeta Telefónica,** a phonecard that comes in denominations of 1,000P or 2,000P ($7 or $14). You can buy the card at post offices, *estancos* (tobacconists), and the *Locutorio Público* (phone office) at Calle Sierpes 11, near Calle Rafael Padura. See chapter 18 on Madrid for more details.

Tipping   See "Fast Facts: Madrid" in chapter 18.

3 Accommodations You Can Afford

Virtually all Seville hotels and other lodgings observe three pricing seasons: the lowest in January, February, July, and August; the medium months of March, June, and

September to December; and the high holidays period of April to May, when Semana Santa (Holy Week) and the secular Fería de Abril are observed. A doubling of prices from the low months to April isn't unusual, and some of the lowliest of hostals even *triple* their rates. In the listings below, the price ranges are from low to medium months; expect to pay more in April and May. Reservations for Semana Santa and the Fería need to be made as much as a year in advance. Some hotels have significantly lower weekend rates, but you nearly always must make a specific request for them. (Note that hostals aren't youth hostels, though they are popular with young travelers. While they don't have all the conveniences of a conventional hotel, they're usually family-run and more personal.)

Air-conditioning is more common in lower-priced Andalusian hotels than in northern parts of the country, due to temperatures that often exceed 100°F in summer and can be almost as uncomfortable in April or October.

Note: You can find most of the lodging choices below plotted on the map included in "Seeing the Sights," later in this chapter.

IN THE BARRIO DE SANTA CRUZ

Arias. Mariana de Pineda 9 (2 short blocks east of Plaza de la Contratación), 41004 Sevilla. ☎ **95/422-68-40.** Fax 95/421-83-89. 15 units, all with bathroom. A/C TEL. 4,230P–6,850P ($29–$47) single; 5,350P–8,560P ($37–$59) double. AE, DC, MC, V.

Hidden on a quiet pedestrian lane touching the Alcázar wall, this hostal has three floors of dimly lit rooms that are clean, cool retreats from the Seville summer. Eight have TVs and only a few have windows. Some are barely large enough for the bed, but others contain two doubles; nos. 22 and 32 are the largest. The convivial owner speaks English.

Goya. Mateos Gagos 31 (1 block north of the cathedral), 41004 Sevilla. ☎ **95/421-11-70.** Fax 95/456-29-88. 20 units, 16 with shower and sink only. 3,900P–4,000P ($27–$28) single without shower; 5,600P ($39) double without shower, 6,300P ($43) double with shower. No credit cards.

This place is pretty barebones (no phones, TVs, air-conditioning) but not without the measure of charm provided by antiques and the dadoes of *azulejos* in public areas. Some rooms, including no. 20, are of good size, and there's a lounge with leather chairs and sofas. Best of all, apart from the rates, is the location, at the edge of the Barrio de Santa Cruz, 5 minutes from the Alcázar.

✪ Laurel. Plaza de los Venerables 5, 41004 Sevilla. ☎ **95/421-07-59.** Fax 95/421-04-50. 21 units, all with bathroom. A/C TV TEL. 5,000P–7,000P ($35–$48) single; 7,500P–9,500P ($52–$66) double. AE, DC, MC, V.

Touristy, yes; trashy, no. Sooner rather than later, every visitor comes on this atmospheric restaurant in the heart of the Barrio, with squat little tables out beside the orange trees. Most are unaware there's also a spiffy little hotel behind the tavern. The rooms are immaculate and of good size, with marble floors. *Tapas* in the bar all go for 225P ($1.55), and main dishes in the charming dining room are 1,300P to 2,500P ($9 to $17).

Monreal. Rodrigo Caro 8 (2 short blocks off Mateos Gago), 41004 Sevilla. ☎ **95/421-41-66.** 20 units, 12 with bathroom. A/C. 2,500P ($17) single without bathroom; 3,800P ($26) double without bathroom, 6,000P ($41) double with bathroom. AE, MC, V.

The rooms vary greatly: No. 315, for example, has only a sink but a big brass double bed and a little balcony with a table and chairs. Others have fetching rooftop views, and some have glimpses of the Giralda. The pretty lobby leads to a ground-floor restaurant in back. Prices jump to 10,000P ($68) during the high holidays.

Getting the Best Deal on Accommodations

- First and foremost, don't plan to go to Seville in April, when prices are doubled or even tripled over those charged in February.

- Know that discounts are often available for stays of a week or more.

- Don't accept the first rate quoted. Ask if cheaper rooms are available, especially in off-season.

- Ask if service and taxes are included in the tariff.

- Be aware that some of the larger budget hotels drop their prices 15% to 20% on weekends, so planning a visit to include Friday to Sunday can save serious money. Ask when reserving ahead.

Murillo. Lope de Rueda 7–9, 41004 Sevilla. ☎**95/421-60-95.** Fax 95/421-96-16. 27 units, all with bathroom. A/C TEL. 3,700P–4,500P ($26–$31) single; 6,200P–7,800P ($43–$54) double. AE, DC, MC, V.

Expect Ye Olde Spain kitsch-o-rama, with clunky suits of armor, overwrought carved friezes, coffered ceilings, and even little painters' palettes dangling from the room keys. For all that, the rooms are comfortable, the staff is pleasant, and the deep-Barrio location is amusing. The closest you can get by cab is the Plaza Santa Cruz, so walk the last 2 blocks following the signs and they'll send a cart for your luggage (assuming you can leave someone to watch your bags).

IN THE HISTORIC CENTER

Becquer. Reyes Católicos 4 (2 blocks east of the river), 41001 Sevilla. ☎ **95/422-89-00.** Fax 95/421-44-00. 120 units, all with bathroom. A/C TV TEL. 10,400P ($72) single; 13,000P ($90) double. AE, DC, MC, V.

The location is great—near both the Maestranza and the Museo de Bellas Artes and within walking distance of the Triana *tapas* district. This is also one of the easiest hotels to find when arriving by car in this vehicularly challenged city, and it even has a garage (1,300P/$9 per night). The rooms are of decent size and comfortable for the price, if bland. There's no restaurant, but plenty of cafes are nearby. Prices drop 18% on weekends.

Ducal. Plaza de la Encarnación 19, 41003 Sevilla. ☎ **95/421-51-07.** Fax 95/422-89-99. 51 units, all with bathroom. A/C TEL. 4,500P–6,860P ($31–$47) single; 6,700P–11,400P ($46–$79) double. AE, DC, MC, V.

Not an ounce of charm can it claim, so don't ask. But the staff is open and helpful, and the location is equidistant from just about everything you might want to see. The rooms are larger than these prices usually provide, with marble floors and tiny desks; some have double beds. The steepest prices above are for the April events.

París. San Pedro Mártir 14 (1 block south of the Museo de Bellas Artes), 41004 Sevilla. ☎ **95/422-98-61.** Fax 95/421-96-45. 15 units, all with bathroom. A/C TV TEL. 3,500P–5,000P ($24–$35) single; 5,000P–6,000P ($35–$41) double. MC, V.

Almost new (1991), on a quiet essentially pedestrian street, this conscientious little hostal is a pretty good deal even when the rates get jacked up to 9,000P ($63) during the April holidays. The singles are closet-size and the triples a little snug for any but very close friends or families, but the furnishings are new, including desks, and many rooms have double beds. Most look out into the light-filled center atrium rather than the street. The owners also have a couple of humbler hostals nearby if this one's full.

Puerta de Triana. Reyes Católicos 5 (2 blocks east of the river), 41001 Sevilla. ☎ **95/421-54-04.** Fax 95/421-54-01. 62 units, all with bathroom. A/C TV TEL. 6,500P–7,000P ($45–$48) single; 10,000P–10,500P ($69–$72) double. AE, DC, MC, V.

The windows of some rooms face one of the city's broadest avenues, and a few have small balconies. The decor skews toward the florid, and some mattresses are overdue for replacement. Most rooms are of decent proportion, though, and the baths have hair dryers. Prices jump 50% for the April season.

Sevilla. Daoiz 5 (behind the Iglesia de San Andrés), 41003 Sevilla. ☎ **95/438-41-61.** 35 units, all with bathroom. TEL. 3,745P–7,490P ($26–$52) single; 5,885P–11,235P ($41–$78) double. MC, V.

Though not a first choice, this is a place to remember when an empty bed is hard to find. Fronting a quiet triangular square, it's as old-fashioned as they come, with chipped paint on the moldings and a formidable brass-and-glass chandelier in the lobby. There's no restaurant, but you can have breakfast in the dignified bar on the opposite side of the plaza. The higher prices above are for the April to May holidays.

IN EL ARENAL

✪ **Simón.** García de Vinuesa 19 (west of Av. de la Constitución), 41001 Sevilla. ☎ **95/422-66-60.** Fax 95/456-22-41. 29 units, all with bathroom. A/C TEL. 5,500P–6,500P ($38–$45) single; 7,500P–10,500P ($52–$72) double. AE, DC, MC, V.

A converted 18th-century mansion barely half a block from the cathedral, this may be the top budget hotel in the area. A little paint here and there would help, but several of the baths have been renovated, some receiving hair dryers, and the walls are often covered all the way to the high ceilings with *azulejos*. Several connecting units share baths and sitting rooms—good for families or two couples traveling together at 10,700P to 14,000P ($74 to $97). The commodious inner court has lots of cushy chairs for meeting friends. This is one of the few places that keeps its price increases under 20% during spring's high holidays.

IN LA MACARENA

✪ **Baco.** Plaza Ponce de León 15, 41003 Sevilla. ☎ **95/456-50-50.** Fax 95/456-36-54. 25 units, all with bathroom. A/C MINIBAR TV TEL. 6,500P ($45) single; 9,000P ($62) double. AE, DC, MC, V.

Apart from April and May, when the above rates nearly double, you can't do better than the Baco at twice the price. Iridescent tiles, polished marble, buffed woods, and glistening brass are generously deployed on all three floors (with elevator), including in the upscale *charcutería* and accomplished **El Bacalao** *tapas* bar/restaurant (open Sunday) on the ground floor. Breakfast nooks occupy the landings upstairs. The baths have hair dryers and showers that produce more than dribbles.

WORTH A SPLURGE

✪ **Las Casas de la Judería.** Callejón de Dos Hermanas 7 (off Plaza Santa María La Blanca), 41004 Sevilla. ☎ **95/441-51-50.** Fax 95/442-21-70. 56 units, all with bathroom. A/C MINIBAR TV TEL. 7,500P–8,500P ($52–$59) single; 12,000P–14,500P ($83–$100) double; 14,000P–25,000P ($97–$172) suite. Breakfast buffet 1,200P ($8). AE, DC, MC, V.

About half the units in this row of noble 16th-century residences are suites, typically small bedrooms with larger sitting areas. While the exteriors, up a cobblestone lane from a discreet archway, hint at Seville's Moorish past, as do the ochre-and-white interior patios and splashing fountains, the suites bespeak a less distant Victorian era. You receive alert but understated attention from the staff, many of whom speak some English. The higher rates above are increased only for Semana Santa and Fería de Abril.

San Gil. Parras 28 (around the corner from the Basílica de la Macarena), 41002 Sevilla. ☎ **95/490-68-11.** Fax 95/490-69-39. 36 units, all with bathroom. A/C MINIBAR TV TEL. 11,500P–14,200P ($79–$98) single; 13,500P–17,100P ($93–$118) double; 20,100P–24,000P ($139–$166) suite. Rates include breakfast. AE, DC, MC, V.

At the northern edge of La Macarena, near the 12th-century walls of the Moorish Almoravid dynasty, this 1901 mansion in the Sevilleno style was converted to a first-class hotel in time for Expo '92. Tiles are applied lavishly, and the open interior court has a small grove of trees, including three olive, two orange, and one lemon, all bearing fruit much of the year. The principal luxury afforded is elbow room, with 5 suites and 14 duplexes with terraces. Some have minimal kitchenettes. Figure about 3,000P to 4,000P ($21 to $28) extra per person during April. Buses to the center stop near the walls, a better transportation choice than the elusive cabs.

4 Great Deals on Dining

Seville pronounces itself the birthplace of that greatest of Spanish culinary inventions, *tapas*. Never mind that the claim is disputed by Madrid. It was here, boosters insist, that a canny tavern-keeper first placed a slab of bread over a cup of wine to keep the flies out; here that one of his competitors laid a slice of ham or cheese or a bit of fish on the bread as incentive to drink at his place. Inevitable evolution from these modest gastronomic innovations led to *tabernas* and *mesónes* all over Spain, their bars lined with dozens of bowls and platters of flavorful fare.

There are hundreds of *tapas*-bilities. Some characteristic of Andalusia are *coquinas* (thumbnail-size clams tossed briefly in hot garlic oil), *pescado frito* (lightly breaded and fried fish, baby squid, and other sea creatures), *cabrillas* (snails), *pincho moruno* (small marinated and grilled kebabs), *bienmesabe* (fish chunks marinated in lemon juice, then floured and fried), *cabo de toro* (stewed bull's tail), and *almejas a la marinera* (clams in tomato sauce). Because they're such a staple, these treats often come in three sizes: *tapa* (small), *media ración* (about twice as much), and *ración* (slightly smaller than a full main course). This allows budget travelers to control both portions and total costs, keeping in mind that certain delicacies almost always cost the world. Beware, on that count, *angulas* (baby eels), *percebes* (goose barnacles), *langosta* (spiny lobster), and *bogavente* (clawed lobster). Of course, if you're in a mood for a splurge, the reason these items are so costly is that they're both rare and very tasty.

Most restaurants post their menus out front, at least the à la carte offerings if not the fixed-price *menú del día* that most make available. The latter usually includes soup or an appetizer, a main course, and dessert, and often bread and a beverage. Of course, this will be comprised of items from the cheaper end of the card, but they're usually at least satisfactory. By the way, the only sure way to get vegetables with your meal is to order them as a first course. Even then, they're likely to be cooked with bits of ham or pork fat. *Ensalada mixta* (mixed green salad) is a logical flesh-free alternative.

Contrary to what many visitors expect, service is usually swift. Unless you purposely slow the pace, you might well be served your entire three-course meal in under 30 minutes. On the other hand, once you sit down, the table is yours. No one will try to move you along, and *Sevillenos* often linger for 2 hours or more. The bill usually isn't presented until you ask for it, which might require repeated efforts.

IN THE BARRIO DE SANTA CRUZ

Don Raimundo. Argote de Molina 26 (at Francos). ☎ **95/422-33-55.** Main courses 1,500P–2,500P ($10–$17); *menú del día* 2,500P ($17). AE, DC, MC, V. Daily 12:30–4pm and 7:30pm–midnight. SPANISH.

A Dining Tip

There are worse ideas than making most or even all your meals of *tapas* while here. (Most of my restaurant recommendations have *tapas* bars in front of their dining rooms.) Seville's restaurants aren't noted for their culinary achievements. You can dine perfectly well, but rarely memorably, an experience restricted to fewer restaurants than you can count on one hand, namely the Egaña Oriza, the Florencia, and the formal dining room of the Taberna del Alabardero.

In this bewitching profusion of mismatched tiles, stained-glass panels, suits of armor, rococo chandeliers, and molded terra-cotta, all lit by a hooded fireplace that's in action when there's even a hint of chill in the air, the food tends to be a distant second attraction. It's actually quite satisfactory, as it happens, some of it allegedly based on recipes developed at the time of the Moors. Game stews and casseroles are tops in the cooler months, switching to lighter fish dishes when they crank up the air-conditioner during the long summer. At least stop in for a look and a *copa de tinto* (a small glass of red wine) in the bar. Its signs are affixed to a ruined building next door, but go up the vine-covered alley next to it.

La Judería. Cano y Cueto 13 (near the north end of the Jardines de Murillo). ☎ **95/ 441-20-52.** Main courses 1,400P–2,800P ($10–$19); *menú del día* 2,200P ($15). AE, DC, MC, V. Tues–Sun 12:30–5pm and 7:30pm–12:30am. SPANISH.

The sizable interior accommodates a large bar and dining room, done with brick arches in vintage Mudejar style but quite new. The tables are less closely arranged than the norm. Offerings are true to local tradition, like the consommé with an egg yolk plopped in the middle and the *cabo de toro* (four stewed sections of bull's tail with more bone and fat than meat, but in a thick rich sauce meant for sopping up with bread). The house wine is a good Rioja from Bodegas Montecillo, and a complimentary glass of icy fruit liqueur comes with coffee. You may also be treated (or subjected) to a pair of strolling musicians in velvet doublets. Service is adroit.

Modesto. Cano y Cueto 5 (at the north end of the Jardines de Murillo). ☎ **95/441-68-11.** Main courses 950P–4,500P ($7–$31); *menú del día* 2,200P ($15). AE, DC, MC, V. Thurs–Tues 8am–2am. SPANISH.

A happy cacophony prevails here. Though it has a dining room upstairs and a terrace out front, the identity of this busy operation is as *tapas* emporium extraordinaire. Most items are cooked to order, but since seafood dominates, it arrives quickly. *Fritura modesto* is a tumble of lightly fried shrimp, onions, and peppers for 1,150P ($8). A heap of dozens of *coquinas* (tiny clam nubbins smaller than peas) are cooked in sweet oil with slivers of garlic; half portions are 615P ($4.15) and full *raciónes* are 850P to 1,850P ($6 to $13).

IN THE HISTORIC CENTER

✪ **Taberna del Alabardero.** Zaragoza 20 (west of Plaza Nueva). ☎ **95/456-06-37.** Main courses 2,300P–3,200P ($16–$22); *menú del día* Mon–Fri 1,450P ($10), Sun–Sat 1,550P ($11). AE, DC, MC, V. Daily 8am–2am (cafetería), 1–4pm and 9pm–midnight (dining room). NEW SPANISH.

There are choices in this gloriously restored 18th-century mansion. Up top are seven enchanting rooms for rent (16,000P/$110 double), in the middle is a romantic white-and-gold formal restaurant, and on the ground floor are two gracious uncrowded rooms where imaginative *tapas*, snacks, and light meals are served from early morning until well after midnight. Upstairs, about $50 brings you superlative food equal to the

---

Getting the Best Deal on Dining

- Take advantage of the two- or three-course *menú del día* offered at lunch in most restaurants and at dinner in some.
- Eat and drink at the bar. Many restaurants have two prices for the same items: standing and sitting.
- Substitute a few of the bar snacks called *tapas* or a couple of the larger portions, *raciónes*, and pay far less than for a conventional meal.
- Keep an eye out for places that serve *platos combinados*—usually meat or fish with two vegetables and sometimes bread and a beverage. It's often advertised in the window.

---

best the city has to offer. Downstairs, eat well for a fifth as much. The *menú* there has over half a dozen choices for each of its three courses.

IN EL ARENAL

Bodegón Torre del Oro. Santander 15 (east of Paseo de Colón). ☎ **95/422-08-80.** Main courses 500P–2,300P ($3.45–$16); *menú del día* 1,500P ($10). AE, DC, MC, V. Daily 7am–4pm and 8pm–1am. SPANISH.

Take your own crowd to this cavernous alternative to the usual *tapas* dispenser. The room is about the size of a high school gym—one-third is the bar, one-third low bare tables for *tapas*, and one-third a sea of full-size tableclothed ones for regular meals. A long card lists *tapas* for only 200P ($1.35) each. The high ceiling and many fans keep smoke at untroublesome levels, except on those rare occasions when the place fills up, usually Sunday and fiesta days.

✪ **Casa Robles.** Alvarez Quintero 58 (near the cathedral). ☎ **95/456-32-72.** Main courses 950P–2,300P ($7–$16); *menú del día* 2,500P ($17). AE, DC, MC, V. Daily 1–4:30pm and 8pm–1am. SPANISH.

This is as fancy as affordable restaurants get in Seville, with serious young waitpeople in black vests and bow ties, and even bowls of flowers in the rest rooms. It's one of the old quarter's most attractive settings, especially the dining rooms upstairs and down, with academic paintings of matadors and genre scenes and vases of daisies on cream tablecloths (there's also a bar and tables out on the street). The kitchen strays somewhat from its traditional leanings, assembling ingredients with a refined eye. A first course of *verduras* (vegetables), for example, combines gently sautéed cauliflower, carrots, potatoes, and squash with disks of fresh duck liver, imparting an unusual creamy finish. Go for the *pescaito frito* to see how good this Andalusian standard can be.

IN LA MACARENA

Don Fadrique. Don Fadrique 7–9. ☎ **95/490-40-90.** Main courses 1,450P–2,100P ($10–$15); *menú del día* 1,700P ($12). AE, DC, MC, V. Daily 1:30–4:30pm and 8:30pm–midnight. SPANISH.

If you've come to see La Muralla—the Arab walls at the north end of the city—this is near the west end, facing the park in front of Parliament. The interior strives for an elegance it doesn't attain, but the service is agreeable and the kitchen competent. The meal starts with what the French call an *amuse-bouche*, a bite or two of something tasty, a bit of fish or a meatball or two. Typical of the meal to follow is *mero* (grouper) in a sauce of roasted peppers and tomatoes, with boiled potatoes on the side. Hardly adding to the mood are Bob Dylan and the Platters on the stereo.

IN TRIANA

All the following recommendations are on Calle Betís between the San Telmo and Isabel II bridges, bordering the west bank of the Guadalquivir.

El Puerto. Betís s/n. ☎ **95/427-17-25.** Main courses 950P–1,300P ($7–$9); *menú del día* 1,500P ($10). MC, V. Tues–Sun 1–4pm and 8pm–midnight. Closed Jan. SPANISH.

Next door to the better-known Río Grande (below), this earthy bar/restaurant has its own shaded dining terrace, the same view of the Torre del Oro, and significantly lower prices. *Tapas* cost 200P to 760P ($1.35 to $5), and the *menú* is only slightly more than half that of its neighbor. Avoid the gloomy dining room.

Kiosco de las Flores. Plaza del Altozano s/n. ☎ **95/433-38-98.** Main courses 500P–1,200P ($3.45–$8). Tues–Sun noon–4pm and 8pm–midnight. MC, V. SPANISH.

Squeezed up against the stairs giving egress to the west end of the Isabel II Bridge, this started out in 1930 as no more than an open-air stand. It has expanded somewhat, with a fleet of tables spreading out from the L-shaped bar onto the sidewalk and under an adjoining tented area. (Tables are reserved for eaters, not drinkers.) Fried and grilled fish and shellfish (shrimp, squid, shark) are featured and can be preceded with bowls of *gazpacho*. The anchor of the north end of the Calle Betís *tapeo*, Las Flores is a must stop.

La Albariza. Betis 6 (near Puente Triana). ☎ **95/433-20-16.** Main courses 600P–2,000P ($4.15–$14). MC, V. Tues–Sun noon–5pm and 8pm–midnight. SPANISH.

Upended black barrels serve as stand-up tables in the front bar, buttressing the place's self-description as a *bodega* (a wine bar or cellar), though most customers seem to order beer. The starring edible is *jamón Ibérico*, the very best air-cured ham, hand-sliced to order. Be careful, though, for that undeniable treat can easily cost more than a full meal in the welcoming sit-down salon in the rear. Back there, lamb chops and swordfish occupy diners' attention.

San Marco. Betis 68 (near Troya). ☎ **95/428-03-10.** Main courses 995P–1,290P ($7–$9); pastas and pizzas 650P–1,175P ($4.50–$8). AE, V. Tues–Sun 1–4:30pm and 8:30–1am. ITALIAN.

While the crowd skews to the hormonal side of 30, with university students much in evidence, this breezy trattoria also draws seniors and kids in substantial numbers. Billed as a pizzeria, it tosses together many interesting combos, including a toothsome mix of clams, mussels, and shrimp. But there are as many pastas on offer and many familiar Italian meat dishes. This isn't to be confused with the more ambitious and pricier restaurant of the same name at Calle Cuna 6, flagship of a small chain.

Río Grande. Betis 70. ☎ **95/427-39-56.** Main courses 1,600P–2,200P ($11–$15); *menú del día* 2,750P ($19). AE, DC, MC, V. Daily 1–5pm and 8pm–1am. SPANISH.

Renowned for its unobstructed views of the skyline of the historic quarter, this ever-green standby at the west end of the San Telmo Bridge has a windowed dining room and bar and sprawling terrace to take it all in—the Torre del Oro, the Giralda, the sightseeing boats, and the opposite promenade. The panorama justifies prices that would otherwise be a little high for food that's, in general, only okay. Expect no innovation—just dawdle over an icy pitcher of *sangría* and a plate of *paella de maríscos*.

PICNICKING

Gather picnic makings at **Horno de San Buenaventura,** at the corner of Avenida de la Constitución and Calle García de Vinuesa, opposite the cathedral. Apart from a variety of ready-made sandwiches, it has sumptuous displays of pastries, cold cuts,

Savor a Sherry

One of the three most important wine-producing districts in Spain is just 55 miles south of Seville. Jerez de la Frontera is famous for its sherries, fortified wines with a distinctive taste that has yet to be successfully imitated anywhere else. It comes in several classifications, largely based on relative sweetness. *Fino,* possessed of an almost dusty dryness, is most often drunk chilled as an aperitif, especially with *tapas. Manzanillas,* softer but still dry, is also popular with appetizers. *Amontillados* and *olorosos* are full-bodied, almost syrupy, and higher in alcoholic content, more likely ordered as digestifs, and the sweet Bristol creams are best with desserts.

breads, cheeses, wines, and assorted tapas. The logical places to take your selections are near Plaza de España in **Parque María Luisa,** a 15-minute walk south, or to a bench or on the wall along the **Paseo Alcalde Marques del Contadero,** bordering the river.

WORTH A SPLURGE

Enrique Becerra. Gamazo 2 (2 blocks south of Plaza Nueva). ☎ **95/421-30-49.** Main courses 1,650P–2,100P ($11–$15). AE, DC, MC, V. Mon–Sat 1–5pm and 8pm–midnight. SPANISH.

Named for the owner who transformed the 19th-century building, this place has a friendly *tapas* bar inside the door and dining rooms in back and up the stairs. The greeting of the host and his minions is persuasively (if professionally) welcoming, and they watch out for you as the meal progresses. The main room has massive dark beams supported by ancient columns, with tables at a decent distance from each other, providing some insulation from the foreign businesspeople who sometimes appear. Waiters stop by with baskets of good assorted breads, and meals proceed through Andalusian dishes of little imagination but considerable expertise. You do have to choose carefully to keep the total cost under 5,000P ($35), but you're unlikely to be disappointed.

La Albahaca. Plaza de Santa Cruz 12. ☎ **95/422-07-14.** Main courses 1,750P–3,300P ($12–$23); *menú del día* 3,500P ($24). AE, DC, MC, V. Mon–Sat noon–4pm and 8pm–midnight. BASQUE/SPANISH.

On a corner of a quiet and attractive square in the Barrio Santa Cruz, this elegant little manse dates only from 1929 but looks much older. High ceilings, many antiques and paintings, arched windows, and extensive use of *azulejos* make this one of the most idyllic dining settings in Seville. In concert with the creative ministrations of the restless young Basque chef, this all makes a most desirable place for a farewell dinner or an amorous proposal. The menu is adjusted seasonally, but look for such intriguing dishes as vegetables *escabeche* with oysters or medaillons of goose liver puddled with honey vinaigrette. Service is discreet.

5 Seeing the Sights

SIGHTSEEING SUGGESTIONS

IF YOU HAVE 1 DAY   After checking into your hotel, climb the Giralda tower of the **cathedral** for a panoramic view of the city. Afterward, descend for a look at the cathedral itself. Assuming sufficient daylight is left, walk 1 block south to visit the **Alcázar.** At dusk and into the evening, stroll along **Calle Betís,** sampling *tapas* in the many bars between the Isabel II and the San Telmo bridges and stopping to gaze at the spires of the old town in the fading light.

IF YOU HAVE 2 DAYS   Spend Day 1 as above. On Day 2, consider a splurge on a **buggy ride** to gain a city overview. Alternatively, follow the walking tour outlined at the end of this section. After lunch and perhaps a brief siesta to escape the heat, visit the refurbished **Museo Provincial de Bellas Artes,** then walk west to the river and stroll down the palm-lined **promenade** on the east bank of the river.

IF YOU HAVE 3 DAYS   Spend Days 1 and 2 as above. In the morning on Day 3, take the short drive to **Itálica,** the Roman ruins northwest of the city, then continue to **Carmona,** an attractive hill town 22 miles to the east with Roman and Moorish ruins. The modern but evocative **Parador de Carmona** is the place for lunch. Return to Seville, perhaps to take in a flamenco *tablao* after a late dinner.

IF YOU HAVE 5 DAYS   Spend Days 1 to 3 as above. On Day 4, make the hour-long journey south to the sherry-producing town of **Jerez de la Frontera** to tour the wine cellars. On Day 5, kick off the attractions not yet seen in Seville, perhaps the outlying **Convento de Santa Paula** and the **Casa de Pilatos,** the **Archivo General de Indias,** or the Murillo paintings in the **Hospital de la Santa Caridad.** Have a picnic lunch in the **Parque María Luisa** near the Plaza de España.

THE TOP ATTRACTIONS

In other Spanish cities, most attractions are closed Monday. But in Seville, the cathedral, Giralda, Hospital de los Venerables, Universidad, and Hospital de la Caridad are all open. Remember that most attractions observe the afternoon siesta.

✪ **Alcázar.** Plaza del Triunfo. ☎ **95/422-71-63.** Admission 600P ($4.15) adults, free for seniors/students/age 12 and under. Tues–Sat 9:30am–4pm, Sun and holidays 10am–1pm.

Also known by the plural Reales Alcázares in a nod to the presence of bits and pieces of an earlier Almohad palace and to the additions of later Christian kings, most of what's now on view was commissioned by Pedro the Cruel in the 14th century. An admirer of Moorish architecture, he hired Arab craftsmen to design and decorate the complex. Arab residents who chose to stay in Spain after their former rulers were vanquished were called Mudejar, and that name was given to the style they developed for their new masters.

Islam didn't allow them to create images of human or animal forms, so they carved intricate stylized floral motifs and intertwined Arabic script in the plaster and woodwork of walls and ceilings. One may wonder if the Christian royal residents knew that much of that scrollwork constituted huzzahs to the glories of Allah. Isabel I received her New World explorers here, and Holy Roman Emperor Carlos V added his own lavish apartments.

You enter through the **Puerta del León** on the south side of the Plaza del Triunfo. When lines are long at the counter, the nearby machines dispense tickets. After the entry is a long courtyard with trees and low sculptured hedges, and through the arched wall at the end is the larger **Patio de la Montería.** On the right is the **Cuarto del Almirante (Admiral's Apartment),** ordered built by Isabel to house the administrators of the explorations of the New World. Behind it is her own abode while in Seville, the **Casa de la Contratación.** The rooms in both are notable for their *artesonado* ceilings and extensive tile murals, but they've been closed to the public for years, in part because they serve as occasional residence to the present king and queen.

Enter the palace proper through the **Puerta Principal** in the Mudejar facade on the far side. Inside is the **Patio de las Doncellas (Maidens),** extensively appointed with

A Sightseeing Tip

Almost everything is closed January 1, Good Friday, May 1, and December 26, and hours are highly unpredictable during Holy Week and the Fería de Seville in the spring. Be sure to check museum hours before setting out, particularly at the smaller ones. They change seasonally and often for no obvious reasons.

tiles, richly carved plasterwork, and scalloped arches supported by twined columns. Through the bank of arches to the right is the entrance to the **Salón de Embajadores (Hall of Ambassadors).** Look up: Its most compelling feature is the domed ceiling of elaborately carved and gilded wood.

Continuing through the palace, you'll find it interesting to contemplate the harmonious arrangements of slender pillars around reflecting pools. With their sprays of horseshoe arches, they can be interpreted as representations of palms around desert oases, a harkening to the North African origins of the Mudejar artisans. After a banquet hall and the apartment of Felipe II, the dainty **Patio de las Muñecas (Courtyard of the Dolls)** is another highlight. These were the royal bedrooms, named for the delicate carved heads that adorn one of the arches.

Descend then to the vaulted subterranean **baths,** surviving from a 12th-century Arab structure. From there, passageways lead to the **Salones de Carlos V,** notable for their 16th-century Flemish tapestries. Adjacent to the apartments are **gardens** where the Holy Roman emperor walked.

✪ **Catedral.** Plaza del Triunfo, Avenida de la Constitución. ☎ **95/421-49-71.** Admission 700P ($4.80) adults, 200P ($1.35) seniors/students, free for age 12 and under. Mon–Sat 10:30am–5pm, Sun 2–7pm.

The third largest church in Europe, after St. Paul's in London and St. Peter's in Rome, this Gothic extravaganza was begun in 1401 and took centuries to complete. It replaced a former mosque that had been used as a Catholic church since the Reconquest of Seville in 1248. Expansive though it is, and intended to erase the memory of Islam, the builders retained the minaret, which constitutes the lower portion of the adjoining **Giralda bell tower** (see below), and the adjacent **Patio de los Naranjos (Court of the Orange Trees),** on the north side.

Primarily Gothic in design, and one of the last major buildings to adhere to that style, it does blend in Renaissance elements, a result of the long construction period. Long-voiced claims that the cathedral contains Columbus's remains are suspect, despite the presence of a monumental tomb at the end of the south transept, with four larger-than-life bronze figures shouldering a casket. It's more certain that the grave in the floor by the main door contains his son, Fernando. The cathedral is also the final resting place of Alfonso X, Fernando III, and Pedro the Cruel and his mistress, María de Padilla.

The door in the west facade, on Avenida de la Constitución, is often closed, so go directly to the entrance called the **Puerta del Lagarto** at the base of the Giralda. The interior is vast, with nearly 40 columns that used to be all but swallowed up in the murk by the ceiling. (New lights have taken away much of the former gloom.) The columns delineate the nave with double aisles to either side and chapels lining the walls. Sunlight illuminates 75 stained-glass windows, a few of which date from the 15th century. At the far end of the north side, the **second chapel** contains two paintings by Seville's most celebrated artist, Murillo. In the **Sala Capitular (Chapter House)** at the east end are several more of his canvases, notably the large *Conception* above the throne.

Getting the Best Deal on Sightseeing

- University students and visitors 65 and older should have proof of identity and age to claim the lower and sometimes free admission available to them.
- Note that several of the smaller special-interest museums are free to all.
- One of the best sightseeing bargains is simply taking a bench along the esplanade on the east bank of the Guadalquivir and watching the evening *paseo,* after work and before dinner, when all Sevillanos go out for their evening stroll.

Nearby is the **Sacristía Mayor,** housing the cathedral treasury and its prodigious collection of religious objects and paintings, including two virgins by Zurbarán. And the adjacent chapel leads to the **Sacristía de los Cálices,** with paintings by Goya and Murillo.

✪ **Giralda.** Plaza Virgen de los Reyes. Admission 600P ($4.15) adults, 200P ($1.35) seniors/students. Mon–Sat 10:30am–5pm, Sun and holidays 10:30am–1:30pm and 2–4pm.

The square rosy tower at the northeast corner of the cathedral began (in 1198) as the minaret of the mosque that was replaced by the church. Though it progresses from the austere stonework of the fundamentalist Almohads in control at its inception to the decorative brick latticework and pointed arches of the middle section and culminating in the comparatively florid Renaissance-influenced upper floors and bell chamber, it's surprisingly harmonious visually and serves as the most recognizable symbol of Seville. On the very top is a large weathervane in the shape of an angel, *Faith,* which moves in the wind despite its heft.

The structure is 322 feet high. Determined visitors can take the ramp inside up to a **viewing platform** at the 230-foot level. There's no equal overlook of the city.

At the foot of the Giralda is a doorway that opens onto the **Patio de los Naranjos (Court of the Orange Trees),** the only other surviving part of the mosque that stood here. Around the corner, on the north side, is an elaborate 16th-century Mudejar gate and portal, the **Puerta del Perdón.**

Torre del Oro. Paseo de Cristóbal Colón (at Almirante Lobo). ☎ **95/422-24-19.** Admission 100P (70¢). Tues–Sat 10am–2pm, Sun 11am–1pm.

This 12-sided sentinel tower at the east end of the San Telmo Bridge has long since lost the sheathing of gold ceramic tiles that may have inspired its name, but it was here to welcome the treasure galleons returning from the New World. Built during the period of the 13th-century Almohad dynasty, it was an important link in their defensive system, connecting with the Alcázar to the east and by a heavy chain across the Guadalquivir to a similar tower (no longer extant) on the opposite side. The slender turret atop the main structure was added in the 18th century. Subsequently used as a prison and a gunpowder magazine, it now houses a modest maritime museum, the **Museo Náutico,** its entrance marked by a brace of cannon. There are good views from the top.

MORE ATTRACTIONS

Ayuntamiento (City Hall). Plaza Nueva s/n. Free admission with passport.

The west side of the City Hall, facing the Plaza Nueva, presents a graceful uncluttered visage. But go around to the Plaza de San Francisco and discover a diametrically opposite mode of decoration. This side is as florid and overwrought as the other is austere.

Seville

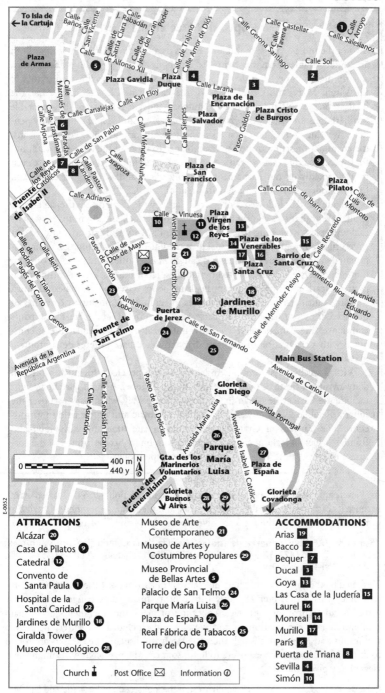

ATTRACTIONS

Alcázar 20
Casa de Pilatos 9
Catedral 12
Convento de Santa Paula 1
Hospital de la Santa Caridad 22
Jardines de Murillo 18
Giralda Tower 11
Museo Arqueológico 28

Museo de Arte Contemporaneo 21
Museo de Artes y Costumbres Populares 29
Museo Provincial de Bellas Artes 5
Palacio de San Telmo 24
Parque María Luisa 26
Plaza de España 27
Real Fábrica de Tabacos 25
Torre del Oro 23

ACCOMMODATIONS

Arias 19
Bacco 2
Bequer 7
Ducal 3
Goya 13
Las Casa de la Judería 15
Laurel 16
Monreal 14
Murillo 17
París 6
Puerta de Triana 8
Sevilla 4
Simón 10

Church ✝   Post Office ✉   Information ⓘ

847

Special & Free Events

Two of the most Spanish of folkloric events occur in Seville in early spring. Both are unforgettable. **Semana Santa** is the Holy Week preceding Easter, with solemn nightly processions led by massive floats bearing polychromed statues of the Virgin Mary, saints, and stages of the Passion of Christ. Called *pasos,* the floats represent 52 neighborhood churches and are maintained by venerable brotherhoods known as *las cofradías.* The *pasos* are both led and followed by penitents wearing conical hoods, masks, and robes in various hues. For Americans, the costumes present a troubling resemblance to those of the Ku Klux Klan, but these preceded that racist organization by centuries. Joining the columns are even more markedly devout participants carrying thick candles, dragging chains and heavy wooden crosses, even a few insistent on self-flagellation.

Semana Santa is followed 2 or 3 weeks later by the **Fería de Seville,** an annual secular event that had its origins in a long-ago livestock auction but is now a virtually sleepless week-long party. Its focus is a tent city laid out on a grid of dirt streets in a fairground on the west side of the Guadalquivir. Behind its giant illuminated gateway are over a thousand canvas *casetas* (little houses), some of them humble, others elaborate, erected by families, labor unions, clubs, and political parties. Nearly all of them have music, from boom boxes to live orchestras; most welcome outsiders. The populace dresses in traditional Andalusian costumes of flounced dresses or flat-brimmed hats with bolero jackets and form-fitting pants and dances the flamenco-like *sevillanas* until near dawn. A similar event, combined with a celebration of the grape harvest, takes place in Jerez de la Frontera in early September.

With 2 weeks to get around Andalusia, only a penchant for misfortune will deny a visitor a **fiesta** or two between May and October. A small sampling might include the **Cruces de Mayo** in Córdoba in early May, when patios all over the Judería are ablaze with flowers; the **festival of music and dance** held in various courts and gardens of Granada's Alhambra in late June and early July; and Ronda's principal **fería** in early September, with bullfights performed in the costumes of Goya's time and robust flamenco competitions.

Its Plateresque style, in vogue at the time of construction (1534), was so named because its carvings of cherubs, portrait busts, and medallions entwined with vine and floral motifs resembled the intricate silverwork (*plata,* "silver") of the period.

Casa Lonja/Archivo General de Indias. Avenida de la Constitución s/n (south of the cathedral). ☎ **95/421-12-34.** Admission 600P ($4.15) adults, 200P ($1.35) seniors/ students. Mon–Fri 10am–1pm.

Designed by the royal favorite, Juan de Herrera (El Escorial was also his commission— see "Side Trips" in chapter 18), this 16th-century financial exchange was later converted to an archive for a priceless collection of maps and documents from Spain's exploration and exploitation of the New World. Included are letters penned by Columbus and Magellan, though those are rarely on display. The exhibits are rotated to minimize damage from exposure to light, so it can't be predicted what might be on view at any given time.

Casa de Pilatos. Plaza Pilatos 1 (slightly west of the intersection of Recaredo and Luis Montoto). ☎ **95/422-50-55.** Admission 1,000P ($7). Daily 9am–6pm.

Said to be modeled in part on the house of Pontius Pilate in Jerusalem, this mansion with its expansive courtyard is more clearly an example of the blending of Mudejar, Gothic, and Renaissance styles. Inside are many gleaming *azulejos* and *artesonado* ceilings, as well as the delicately carved stucco associated with Moorish palaces. Among the artworks displayed are Greek and Roman statuary and paintings by mostly second-tier artists, not counting Goya. Despite all this, the stiff entrance fee is enough to buy a good lunch, so you may want to skip a tour.

Hospital de la Santa Caridad. Temprado 3. ☎ **95/422-32-22.** Admission 200P ($1.35). Mon–Sat 10am–2pm and 3:30–6pm.

At the end of the small park running east from the riverbank is the attractive facade of this 17th-century refuge for the poor. Don Miguel de Mañara purportedly was responsible for the building and its charitable activities. The nobleman may have been a model for the semifictional lothario Don Juan, and this institution is thought to be either his atonement for his past debauchery or a monument to the dead wife he deeply loved. One of Mañara's close friends was the Sevilleno artist Murillo, and several of the paintings in the Baroque chapel inside are his. Find it by turning left after entering the red-and-ochre patio.

La Maestranza (Plaza de Toros). Paseo de Cristóbal Colón s/n. ☎ **95/422-45-77.** Admission variable for bullfights, 300P ($2.05) for tours. Tours (except on bullfight days) Mon–Sat 10am–1:30pm.

Apart from the function for which they were built, bullrings rarely qualify as sightseeing attractions. This is one of the exceptions, both for the pleasing visual aspect of its perfect oval surmounted by graceful arches and for its age. Only the 17th-century plaza in the Andalusian hill town of Ronda competes in accumulated years. Obviously, the best times to see it are during *corridas,* especially those mounted during the Fería de Abril; the season runs late March to early October. It can seat fewer than 13,000 aficionados, so even the cheapest seats most distant from the ring have clear views. But if that spectacle is distasteful to you or merely too expensive, there are 15- to 20-minute tours on non-bullfight days.

Museo Arqueológico. Plaza de América s/n, Parque María Luisa. ☎ **95/423-24-01.** Admission 250P ($1.70) adults, free for seniors/students. Mon–Sat 9am–8pm, Sun 9am–2pm.

This richly embellished building in María Luisa Park, from the 1929 Exposition, now houses a collection of artifacts from archaeological sites around the province of Seville, especially Roman Itálica, but also of Paleolithic, Carthaginian, Greek, and Arab origin. Included are housewares, tools, jewelry, ceramics, and sculptures. One arresting exhibit is a mosaic depicting a generously endowed Hercules in danger of being groped by eager sirens. You'll find an interesting but fairly modest array, but coming here might be worth it if you also drop by the **Museo de Artes y Costumbres Populares** (☎ **95/423-25-76**), directly opposite at the same south end of the park. Admission to the Museum of Popular Arts and Costumes is 250P ($1.70), and it's open Tuesday to Sunday 9:30am to 2:30pm.

Museo de Arte Contemporáneo. Santo Tomás 5. ☎ **95/421-58-30.** Free admission. Tues–Fri 10am–9pm, Sat–Sun 10am–2pm.

Misleading name aside, this museum actually focuses most of its attention on popular arts and crafts, on country furniture and wagons, farm implements and saddles, folk costumes, and examples of the "suits of light" worn by matadors. In the basement of the mock-Mudejar building (1914) are larger contraptions of rural life, including a blacksmith's oven and a wine press.

Itálica: To See or Not to See

A little over 5 miles northwest of Seville is the town of Santiponce and the remains of the Roman city of Itálica. I mention it here only because it appears in virtually all the tourist literature and is a prominent outing by tour companies. Though it's easy to reach by bus from the Empresa Casal company's stop opposite the Plaza de Armas station, my recommendation is not to bother going, except, perhaps, as a brief stop on the way to somewhere else, like the far more appealing town of Carmona. Many of the most interesting architectural fragments and artifacts have been moved to Seville's archaeological museum, and nearly all the ancient buildings have been scavenged over the centuries for construction materials. What remains—some mosaic floors, paving stones, and crumbled portions of an amphitheater that once held 25,000—requires a vivid imagination on the part of visitors.

✪ **Museo de Bellas Artes.** Plaza de Museo 9. ☎ **95/422-07-90.** Admission 250P ($1.70). Tues 3–8pm, Wed–Sat 9am–8pm, Sun 9am–3pm.

Seville's most important art museum is modest by Barcelona's or Madrid's standards, but it definitely deserves a visit. This former 17th-century convent faces a pretty park with a prominent statue of Bartolomé Estéban Murillo, the native son of whom Seville is most proud. Highlights of the collection are canvases by Murillo, El Greco, Velázquez, and Zurbarán, whose influence on Murillo is evident. Look for the Virgin and Child called *La Servilleta,* named not for the subjects but for the legend that Murillo painted it on a napkin. The 14 galleries on two floors contain sculptures and paintings by many lesser-known but worthy artists of the School of Seville, notably Juan de Valdés Leal, and range from the Middle Ages to the early 20th century.

Real Fábrica de Tabacos/Universidad. San Fernando s/n (between Puerta de Jerez and Menéndez Pelayo). Free admission.

The prototype of the fiery Carmen of operatic legend worked in this 18th-century *fábrica de tabacos* (tobacco factory). It looks far too grand to have served that function, but in any event it's now part of the city's university.

STROLLING AROUND THE BARRIO DE SANTA CRUZ

Maps of the ancient Jewish quarter are hopelessly short on labels and details, so this route can help you negotiate its maze of alleys and narrow lanes. The *barrio* isn't too large, though, so even if you get lost, walk a few short blocks in almost any direction and you'll emerge from the pedestrian-only neighborhood into the rumble of the larger city of cars, trucks, and commerce.

Start in front of the cathedral's main entrance, on the **Plaza de la Virgen de los Reyes.** With your back to the church, walk across the square, past the ornate fountain in the middle, and into Calle Mateos Gogo. Orange trees line the street and its cafes and souvenir shops. After 2 blocks, note the yellow-ochre building with a sign reading MESÓN DEL MORO. Turn right.

This is the **Barrio de Santa Cruz,** with the winding streets and whitewashed houses that have been characteristic of southern Spain since the 700-year Moorish occupation. It was the *Judería,* a thriving Jewish community, until the Inquisition. Palms, bougainvillea, and citrus trees cast cooling shadows over its patios and pocket plazas. Cars are banned from much of the area. Restaurants set tables outdoors beside

A Walking Warning

When walking, especially in the barrio, keep a wary eye on the ground. Apart from the fact that pooper-scooper laws have yet to be imposed, ripe oranges falling from the many trees to the street can be a squishy hazard to dignity, if not to body parts.

bubbling fountains. Gated but open doorways invite visitors to peek in at tiled and planted inner courts.

Bear left at the end of the block, then turn right onto Calle Santa Teresa. At no. 8 is the **Casa-Museo Murillo,** one of several small galleries in a city that has only one midsize art museum. It's open Tuesday to Saturday 10am to 2pm and 5 to 8pm and Sunday 10am to 2pm and charges 250P ($1.70) admission.

Continue along until the street opens onto the **Plaza de Santa Cruz.** The small park in the center has a wrought-iron Victorian whimsy incorporating the shapes of saints, winged creatures, and dragons to form a lamp and cross. Note the restaurant **La Albahaca** and the flamenco club **Los Gallos,** both of which are recommended in this chapter.

Bear right around the plaza, past the club, and turn right past the sign for the **Hotel Murillo,** quickly entering the Plaza Alfaro. To the left, tall trees mark the edge of the **Jardines de Murillo,** a park with extensive horticultural displays beneath jacarandas and banyans. The street at the opposite corner is bordered by part of a **fortification** dating from the 9th century, the early years of the Moorish occupation.

Walk down that street. On the right, homeowners often leave their front doors open (behind locked iron gates) so that passersby can look into the **patios** and see their *azulejos* (ceramic tiles) and luxuriant potted plants. The second building has a plaque high up on the wall honoring Washington Irving, who lived here in 1828 during his brief diplomatic career. Turn right into the narrow Justino de Neve, with its herringbone brick paving. This soon ends in the **Plaza de los Venerables.**

To the right is one of my recommended hotel/restaurants, the **Hostería del Laurel;** straight ahead is the **Hospital de Venerables Sacerdotes** (☎ 95/456-26-96), now an art gallery with an inner court lined with *azulejos.* It's open daily 10am to 2pm and 4 to 8pm; admission is 500P ($3.45). Exit the plaza down the alley left of the Hospital and soon you'll reach the smaller **Plaza Doña Elvira.** Surrounded by orange trees arching over benches, the square can be a bit bedraggled, in part because it's heavily used as a late-night gathering place of young people who drink, flirt, and play their guitars.

Cross diagonally to the opposite corner, past another restaurant and up the alley called Calle Rodrigo Caro. It makes a sharp left turn, passing an upscale shop of leather goods and fragrances, then makes another right into the much larger **Plaza de Alianza.** Near the middle of the plaza is a fountain often in need of maintenance and on the left is the wall of the Alcázar. At the right corner is a shop called **Estudio John Fulton.** An American drawn to Spain by his dream of becoming a matador, he stayed on after his time in the bullring and pursued a career as a painter, writer, and photographer. He died early in 1998. James Michener discussed Fulton at considerable length in his book *Iberia.*

Pass the fountain and turn left down the wide staircase into Calle Joaquín Romero Murube. The Alcázar wall makes that turn too, now with the pointed crenellations typical of Arab fortresses. The street empties into the **Plaza del Triunfo.** The cathedral is now on your right. Walk straight ahead and turn left at the next corner. The entrance to the **Alcázar** is up ahead.

ISLA DE LA CARTUJA: SITE OF EXPO '92

No longer an island, thanks to landfill over the centuries, this flat tract delineated by two branches of the Guadalquivir was best known as home to the 15th-century **Monasterio de Santa María de las Cuevas** (☎ 95/448-06-11) and as a temporary residence of Christopher Columbus. After the monks were driven from the monastery by the French in 1835, it was converted to a ceramics factory. Otherwise largely undeveloped, the land was eventually designated as the site of Expo '92. Six new bridges of strikingly different design now provide access, as did a *teleférico* (cable-car system) that's no longer operational. A luxury hotel provided housing for expense-account visitors to the fair, and the various national and regional pavilions provided miles of futuristic skyline. Ambitious plans to create theme parks devoted to culture, science, and technology haven't jelled, however. At least not at press time. It's open Tuesday to Sunday: October to March 11am to 7pm (April to September to 9pm). Admission is 300P ($2.05).

PARKS & GARDENS

The western edge of **Parque María Luisa** runs along the edge of the river south of the **Palacio de San Telmo** and once constituted the bulk of the palace's estate. It served as the principal site for pavilions and other buildings erected for the 1929 Ibero-American Exposition. Several of these structures remain, most notably the neo-Renaissance government house that forms a semicircle around the **Plaza de España,** bordered by a half-moon canal and featuring an ornate fountain. Considerable renovations have been necessary to maintain the tile-covered bridges and balustrades. Boats can be rented to paddle about the canal. At the south end of the park is the **Plaza de America,** bordered by the **Museo de Artes y Costumbres Populares** and the **Museo Arqueológico** (see above).

ORGANIZED TOURS

For a quick city overview, **Seville Tour** (☎ 95/421-41-69) is at least satisfactory, using wheeled conversions of antique trams. The tours leave every 45 minutes 10am to 6:15pm from stops at the Torre del Oro, Plaza de España, and Monasterio de la Cartuja. Guides divest themselves of spiels that might as well have been recorded, but the tours hit the high points and provide enough familiarization for you to then set out on your own. No reservation is required—just show up. The fare is 1,300P ($9) adults and 800P ($6) seniors/students/children. Look around for the discount coupons at hotel desks and the tourist offices that take 300P ($2.05) off.

Longer, more informative tours are offered by **Visitours,** Avenida de los Descubrimientos s/n, Isla de la Cartuja (☎ 95/446-09-85). Morning and afternoon tours, 3 to 4 hours long starting at 9 or 9:30am and 3 or 3:30pm, are comprehensive, with frequent stops and knowledgeable commentary. Prices, however, are steep at 4,900P to 6,900P ($34 to $48). Regarding Visitours' excursions to Granada, Córdoba, Ronda, Jerez de la Frontera, and Cádiz—they're carefully planned, professional in tone and preparation, and expensive. For example, the long day trip to Granada and back is 13,750P ($95). Your call. (If you do go to Jerez with Visitours, try to make it on a Thursday, when there's a riding exhibition of the famous Andalusian horses.)

6 Shopping

BEST BUYS

Start looking along **Calle de las Sierpes,** the pedestrian "Street of the Snakes" running from Plaza Magdalena Campaña to the top of Plaza San Francisco. It's lined with mostly medium-priced shops selling clothing, electronics, jewelry, silverware, and leather goods. Bargains are elusive. Items that almost qualify, at least for those who are interested, are handmade ceramics (bowls, plates, pitchers, tureens) decorated with intricate floral traceries, largely blue on white. **Martián,** Sierpes 74 (☎ **95/421-34-13**), has a substantial selection.

For more ceramics in a greater variety of styles and shapes, including distinctive Moroccan varieties, cross the river via the Puente Isabel II to the Plaza del Altozano. Turn right on Calle San Jorge and ahead on the left are **Ceramica Santa Ana** (☎ **95/433-33-04**) at no. 31 and **Ceramica Ruiz** at no. 27, both with large stocks. Between them is a narrow lane, **Calle Antillano Campos,** with still more ceramics sellers. If you'd prefer antique or older-looking ceramics, seek out **Populart,** Pasaje de Vila 4 (no phone), in the Barrio Santa Cruz. Shopkeepers almost never agree to ship ceramics purchases, but they'll wrap them carefully for carrying by hand, almost certainly safer than trusting the Spanish postal service.

If Seville suggests fans to you, check out **Casa Rubio,** Sierpes 56 (☎ **95/422-68-72**). Past the north end of Sierpes, over to the left, is the local branch of the preeminent national department store, **El Corte Inglés,** Plaza del Duque 10 (☎ **95/422-19-31**). Next to it is a branch of **Marks & Spencer,** Plaza del Duque 6 (☎ **95/456-49-49**). The other big guy in the area is the new **Virgin Megastore,** Sierpes 81 (☎ **95/421-21-11**), purveyor of CDs, videos, and computer games and software.

A FLEA MARKET

On Sunday morning in working-class La Macarena, a 5-block tree-shaded concourse called the **Alameda de Hercules** is the site of a crowded flea market that makes no concession to tourism. Walk among eight-track players, cleavers, hubcaps, Peruvian sweaters, jars of marinated olives, sunglasses, canaries, videos, comic books, chandeliers, voltage meters, African carvings, hand-cranked sewing machines, lawn jockeys, carved canes—you name it. If you find something that piques your acquisitive impulse, be prepared to bargain. The two tall columns marking the southern end of the promenade are Roman, holding aloft statues of Caesar and Hercules.

7 Seville After Dark

A monthly giveaway magazine available at many hotel desks and the tourist office, *El Giraldillo* has comprehensive information about cultural and popular events taking place in Seville and other Andalusian cities. It's in Spanish but not difficult to figure out. A larger-format magazine called *Welcome & Olé* (also free) is in both Spanish and English but is advertiser driven and provides coverage only of Seville. Often found in the same places as those two publications is **?***Que Hacer? (What's On?),* a monthly listing of folkloric and cultural events throughout Andalusia.

THE PERFORMING ARTS

Spain's performing artists and organizations draw increasingly enthusiastic attention from audiences and critics around the world. Two of the fabulously successful Three Tenors are, after all, Spaniards. Many of these groups and individuals, including celebrated rock bands and pop singers as well as ballet companies and symphonies, make Seville a stop on their tours. Curiously, Seville, the city that inspired a score of operas by Bizet, Verdi, Mozart, and others, had no proper venue for staging them until very recently. Again Expo '92 provided the motivation to erase this lack, a need addressed by the stunning new Teatro de la Maestranza.

OPERA, DANCE & CLASSICAL MUSIC

Until the new opera house opened, the **Teatro Lope de Vega,** Avenida María Luisa s/n (☎ 95/423-1835), was the principal performance space. It's still important, hosting traveling companies of considerable variety, from dramatic productions to jazz to musicals like *West Side Story.* Curtain times are usually at 9pm, but be sure to check ahead. Similar diversity is provided at the **Teatro Central,** Isla de la Cartuja s/n (☎ 95/459-08-53).

Dominating these and other, lesser venues is the ✪ **Teatro de la Maestranza,** Paseo de Colón 22 (☎ 95/422-65-73), 2 blocks south of the Plaza de Toros that bears the same name and employs a similar, if austere, circular design. Home to the Real Orquestra Sinfónica de Seville, it seats 1,800 for varied seasons of symphonic and chamber concerts, ballet, opera, and the Spanish form of operetta called *zarzuela.* You can buy tickets at the box office daily 11am to 2pm and 5 to 8pm; prices vary with the attraction.

FLAMENCO

By most accounts, the profoundly Andalusian art form of flamenco degraded into commercialized pap long before any current viewers were around to judge for themselves. Blame it on Franco or on the homogenizing influences of mass tourism, but flamenco as it's now performed throughout the land of its birth rarely displays the authentic spontaneity and passion said to have informed it in the dim past. Even in Seville, performances are more often coolly choreographed rather than improvised and are too often allowed to descend into the travesty of audience participation.

To gain a hint of what flamenco once must have been, go late, after the tour groups have left and the performers have worked up a sweat. Watch carefully the older dancers, often a little thick around the waist but still able to bring fire to their twirling, twisting, foot-stamping performances, electrified by the kind of staccato hand-clapping you must be born Spanish to master.

On one of the most attractive squares of the Barrio Santa Cruz is **Los Gallos,** Plaza de Santa Cruz 11 (☎ 95/421-69-81), routinely deplored as a tourist trap. That assessment is difficult to dispute, but things usually get better after midnight, and you get to be seated close to the action. The cover (including the first drink) is 3,000P ($21). Quite similar but a little more expensive is **El Arenal,** Rodo 7 (☎ 95/421-64-92). The cover (including the first drink) is 3,800P ($26). **El Patio Sevilleno,** Paseo de Cristóbal Colón 11 (☎ 95/421-41-20), isn't a traditional *tablao* like the previous two places. It's a theatrical production rounding up several forms of folkloric and classical music and dance, carefully rehearsed. That said, you can have a pleasant evening here. The cover (including the first drink) is 3,700P ($26).

TAPAS & COCKTAILS

A *Sevilleno* evening inevitably starts with a *tapeo*—the traditional walkabout called a *paseo* combined with stops at several bars for *tapas.* This segues into drop-ins at *barres de la noche* ("bars of the night") that emphasize drinks, mingling, and music over food. As weekends approach, these are often followed, well after midnight and even 2am, by visits to rock clubs or discos.

Calle Mateos Gago, leading east from the cathedral and into the **Barrio de Santa Cruz,** is lined with pizzerias, *cervecerías,* and bars that clog on weekend evenings. **Bodega Belmonte,** Mateos Gago 24 (☎ 95/421-40-14), is easily the classiest stop on this strip, its bar surrounded on three sides by rows of bottles from every wine-producing region of the country. Appetizing *tapas* are available, if secondary to the opportunity for an informal tasting of wines, 10 of which you can have by the glass.

There's no accounting for the huge popularity of the unremarkable **Bodega Santa Cruz,** Rodrigo Caro 1 (☎ 95/421-32-46), except that it provides plastic glasses to take beer into the street, where hundreds of young people gather Friday and Saturday nights. (When you order a drink at the bar, the first question is, "In here or outside?") *Montaditos* are the favorite snacks, round toasted rolls with a dozen fillings.

A few steps away and a little less frenetic, **Queipiriña,** Rodrigo Caro 3 (☎ 95/456-36-72), is a long room of tile dadoes and high beams with a lengthy card of good *tapas.* A bartender/deejay spins tunes that go as far back as Bill Haley and the Comets and stop somewhere around mid-Springsteen. The university-age crowd comes more for talk than the food. From there, follow the throngs (for safety, if nothing else) into the heart of the Barrio and the convivial **Casa Román,** Plaza de los Venerables (☎ 95/421-64-08). Patrons surge through in waves, snaffling up plates and sandwiches of ham and sausage. Your consumption is chalked directly on the bar. Watch out for the Ibérico ham, a *ración* of which costs 1,800P ($12). Next you'll find what every major Spanish city seems to have at least one of: a mansion transformed into an extravagantly plush cocktail lounge. **Abades,** Abades 1 (☎ 95/455-15-69), centers on a courtyard with a burbling fountain, wicker chairs, and settees in conversational clusters. Food doesn't figure in the equation, so drink prices are hefty. It's worth it, especially when in the company of a romantic significant other.

As I've said, Seville claims the honor of inventing *tapas,* and chauvinistic food historians insist that the specific place of birth was **El Rinconcillo,** Gerona 40–42 (☎ 95/422-31-83). That was in 1670, they say, which also makes this one of the country's oldest *tabernas.* The *tapas* on the short list are only average, but that doesn't stop the hordes who course through its two rooms every day but Wednesday. It's in the lee of the colorful Iglesia de Santa Catalina, which faces the Plaza Ponce de León.

Much of the early *tapas* and later drinking action takes place in **Triana** along Calle Betis, the street that follows the west bank of the river. Several likely places are recommended under "Great Deals in Dining," including El Puerto, Kiosco de las Flores, and La Albariza. Scattered among them are several others: **El Mero**, **Los Chorritos,** and **Los Maestrantes.**

GAY & LESBIAN BARS

With a large transient population of university students, many of them foreign, and the inevitable conflict with a socially conservative moral tone, Seville's gay scene is elusive, even ephemeral. Bars and clubs open suddenly and close as quickly, sometimes moving a few buildings or blocks and opening again with different names. A short street that usually rewards a little judicious bar-hopping is **Calle Trastamara,** bordering the east side of the Plaza des Armas bus station.

Nearby, a more established area is around the intersection of **Paseo Cristóbal Colón** and **Reyes Católicos,** near the eastern end of the Puente Isabel II. One of the louder and therefore more obvious possibilities is **Isbillya,** Paseo Colón 2. Under another name less than a year ago, it now has a "laser juke" that plays rock of all shadings for the dance floor in back and the video in front. Around the corner is **To Ca Me,** Reyes Católicos 25, which caters to a mixed but largely gay crowd.

LIVE-MUSIC CLUBS

While Seville isn't yet a routine stop on the international tours of superstars like the Stones or Elton John, those performers who do drop in often use the open-air **El Auditoro,** on the Isla de la Cartuja, or the soccer stadium, **Estadio Ramón Sánchez Pijuan.** Lesser-known bands are usually booked into warehouse spaces in the industrial parks to the north and east of center city. Keep an eye out for posters and leaflets announcing their appearances.

Jazz remains an enthusiasm, evidenced by the **Festival Internacional de Jazz** held in early November. More prominent combos and bands appear at the **Teatro Central,** Isla de la Cartuja (☎ **95/446-07-80**), or the **Teatro Lope de Vega,** Avenida María Luisa s/n (☎ **95/458-09-53**). Otherwise, watch for the programs of the **Club de Jazz** of the Universidad de Seville. Admission is as little as 300P ($2.05). Established jazz clubs that frequently stray into blues and related forms are **Café Lisboa,** Alhóndiga 43; **Café Pavana,** Betis 40; **Blues Box,** Levies 18; and **Blue Moon,** Cavestany s/n.

8 Side Trips: The Best of Andalusia

Andalusia is the Florida of Europe. Millions of Germans, Dutch, French, Scandinavians, and British go straight from their charter flights into anonymous package hotels and theme restaurants that struggle valiantly to replicate the *Wiener schnitzels, broodjes,* and bangers-and-mash these people just left behind. The lard-pale northerners are here to chase golf and tennis balls, drink in bars self-segregated by national groups, and get themselves all-over tans by next Sunday. For local color, maybe they'll drive to a nearby hill town and take a ride on an ersatz donkey taxi. They might as well be in Orlando.

At least that's the drill along the Costa del Sol in all but the deepest winter. But the Sun Coast is just the thin edge of a region staggeringly rich in history, art, architecture, folklore, and culture. An hour or two inland from the international resorts of Marbella and Torremolinos are whitewashed villages clinging to peaks and cliffs and wonders of the Western world like the Mosque of Córdoba and the fabulous Alhambra of Granada. A comprehensive network of bus routes provides good connections with all but the more remote villages. Trains are less useful, except between Madrid and Málaga and Seville and Córdoba.

Andalusia is comprised of eight provinces occupying the entire southern rim of Spain, from Portugal in the west to the southeastern point of the Iberian peninsula. That's over 372 miles, about two-thirds of which, from Huelva, west of Seville, to Granada, is served by a new *autopista,* a fast but expensive toll highway. The coastal road from Almeria to Algeciras is free but far slower, passing through dozens of coastal villages and the housing developments called *urbanizaciónes,* with traffic at its worst April to September. Secondary roads are far easier to traverse, apart from the likelihood of spending time behind slow-moving trucks.

Seville, the region's capital, deserves at least 2 or 3 days and can serve as a base for day trips to nearby Carmona, Jerez de la Frontera, Arcos de la Frontera, Córdoba, Ronda, and Granada.

JEREZ DE LA FRONTERA: THE HEART OF SHERRY COUNTRY

A swift 1-hour drive or bus ride south of Seville on the A-4 autopista (55 miles), Jerez is at the heart of the vinicultural district that produces Spain's most distinctive wine, sherry. The "de la Frontera" appendage refers to the period when it marked the western frontier of the shrinking Muslim empire. Though Jerez is pronounced "*hair*-eth" by Spaniards, the tongue-tangled British vintners who took such a liking to the unusual fortified wines produced here somehow managed to utter it as "sherry."

Those English families and their descendants contributed a number of stately homes and many of the over 20 *bodegas* (wineries) that constitute most of the reasons for a visit. Their names, familiar to wine lovers, appear on many bottle labels, including Harvey (as in Harvey's Bristol Cream), Sandeman, and Williams and Humbert, alongside Pedro Domecq and González. Most of them accept visitors with

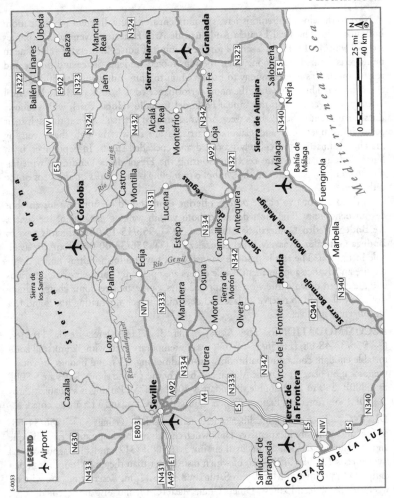

varying degrees of enthusiasm on guided tours of their *bodegas,* capped by tastings that are sometimes free. You can get information about the tours and other attractions at the **tourist office,** Alameda Cristina 7 (☎ **956/33-11-50**), open Monday to Friday 9am to 2pm and 5 to 7pm and Saturday 9am to 2pm.

Jerez is surrounded by vineyards planted on slopes of the chalky white soil *(albariza)* that helps impart the distinctive tastes of the several styles of sherry. The city itself is a gracious, rather subdued place, of a largely harmonious mien, notably around the central **Plaza Mamelón** and the palms of the **Plaza Arenal.** Near the latter square is a partly restored 12th-century **Alcázar,** Alameda Vieja s/n (☎ **956/33-11-50**), which incorporates a mosque that was made into a church after the Christian Reconquest and has now been restored to its original appearance. It's open Monday to Friday 10am to 2pm and 4 to 6pm; admission is free. North of the Plaza Mamelón is the **Museo de Los Relojes,** Cevantes s/n (☎ **956/18-21-00**), an antique clock museum housed in a former palace. For obvious reasons, try to be there at noon. It's open Monday to Saturday 10am to 2pm and admission is 300P ($2.05).

Next to the clock museum is Jerez's monument to a quite different preoccupation: horsemanship. The **Real Escuela Andaluza de Arte Ecuestre,** Avenida de Abrantes s/n (☎ **956/31-11-11**), is a school for the training of horses in dressage. The time to be there is Thursday at noon, when the four-footed students dance and prance and rear to music. It's open Monday to Friday 11am to 1pm. Admission is 450P ($3.10) every day but Thursday, when the noon performance costs 1,900P ($13). In late April or early May each year is the annual **Fería del Caballo (Horse Fair),** which follows the similar event in Seville by a week or two. Purebred Arabians are put through their paces in competitions and elaborate carriages are drawn through the streets by matched teams of immaculately groomed and cockaded steeds. In September, both horse flesh and harvest are celebrated during the **Fiesta de la Vendimia,** with flamenco contests, parades, and the symbolic trampling of the grapes on the steps of the cathedral.

Visits to one or two of the *bodegas* offering tours should be sufficient for any but devout oenophiles. The most desirable, both within walking distance of the center, are **Bodega Pedro Domecq,** San Ildefonso 3 (☎ **956/15-15-00**), which is next to **Bodega González Byass,** Manuel González s/n (☎ **956/34-00-00**). Tours are available in English. The rub is that the *bodegas* don't have uniform visiting hours. Some require an advance appointment, while others are open only during restricted periods and are closed down entirely on unexpected days. Some are free; some charge admission. So call ahead to reserve a place and determine which fluctuating hours and fees are currently in effect.

ACCOMMODATIONS The **Avila,** Avila 3, 11140 Jerez de la Frontera (☎ **956/33-48-08;** fax 956/33-68-07), is a contemporary hotel with 32 units, all comfortable enough, containing bathrooms, air-conditioning, TVs, and phones. Its convenient location places it near the Alcázar and both of the *bodegas* above. Rates are 5,800P to 8,800P ($40 to $61) double. Breakfast is 400P ($2.75). Parking is available nearby at 900P ($6). American Express, Diners Club, MasterCard, and Visa are accepted.

DINING Given the high caliber of its kitchen, **Gaitán,** Gaitán 3 (☎ **956/34-58-59**), is uncommonly inexpensive. The owner/chef draws his inspiration from Basque and Andalusian recipes. Squid in their ink is 1,700P ($12) and the ragout of veal sweetbreads 1,750P ($12), both of which taste better than they may sound. It's open daily 1:30 to 4pm and Monday to Saturday 8:30 to 11pm. Reservations are wise on weekends. American Express, Diners Club, MasterCard, and Visa are accepted.

ARCOS DE LA FRONTERA

Only 20 miles northeast of Jerez is one of the largest and most striking of Andalusia's famed "White Villages" *(Pueblos Blancos).* A narrow granite ridge erupts from a valley of rolling fields, its spiked high end rearing over 200 feet above the Guadalete River. The visual impact of the setting is best experienced when approaching the town from the east on Route 344, but it's easy to appreciate from any direction why the Arabs chose it as a defensible outpost. Whitewashed houses and honey-colored churches crowd the summit.

If you're driving up, following signs to the *parador,* the road soon takes a 45° angle, narrowing as it goes until it seems that another coat of paint on either the car or the encroaching walls will result in an immovable crush. At that last instant, the street takes a sharp right under an arch and then into the relative expanse of the **Plaza del Cabildo** (aka Plaza de España).

On the square are a **tourist office** (☎ **956/70-22-64;** open Monday to Friday 10am to 1:30pm and 5 to 7pm, Saturday 10am to 2pm, and Sunday 11am to 1:30pm), an especially attractive unit of the state-run *parador* chain, and the

Plateresque **Iglesia de Santa María** (open daily 10am to 1pm and 4 to 7pm), built primarily in the 15th and 16th centuries, with an incomplete tower from the 18th century. But the reason to make this steep climb by car or on foot (only for the fit) is the **belvedere** that affords a magnificent view of the river and valley. Look *down* at falcons and other birds wheeling about on the updrafts and fluttering into their nests in the cliff. Afterward, continue along the main street for peeks at narrow lanes largely unchanged since their medieval beginnings.

The **Parador de Arcos de la Frontera** (☎ **956/70-05-00**) isn't too expensive, but if its rates of 16,500P ($114) for a double seem too high, consider at least a drink on the balcony terrace or lunch in its dining room to take in that vista. Dining hours are daily 1:30 to 4pm and 8 to 10:30pm, and American Express, Diners Club, MasterCard, and Visa are accepted. Trains don't stop in Arcos, but buses do.

ACCOMMODATIONS A block beyond the *parador,* deep in the old town, is the **Marqués de Torresoto,** Marqués de Torresoto 4, 11630 Cádiz (☎ **956/70-07-17;** fax 956/70-11-16). With 15 air-conditioned units, all with bathrooms, TVs, and phones, this is the best budget alternative. Rates are 8,000P to 9,200P ($55 to $63), and American Express, Diners Club, MasterCard, and Visa are accepted.

DINING Apart from the *parador* restaurant, consensus favors the dining room of **El Convento,** Maldonado 2, a few doors away from the hotel above (☎ **956/70-11-17**). Andalusian meals averaging about 3,000P ($21) are served on a charming patio. It's open daily 1 to 4pm and 8:30 to 11pm and accepts American Express, Diners Club, MasterCard, and Visa.

CARMONA

Only 21 miles east of downtown Seville, Carmona sprawls across the top of a mesa rising above the otherwise flat plains of the Guadalquivir and the N-IV to Córdoba. Preceded by Iberians and Carthaginians, the Romans took over and called it Carmo, leaving just west of town a necropolis with origins in the 2nd century B.C.; it contains 800 tombs. The Arabs had their turn and erected three *alcázares* (fortresses). The town survived a year-long siege by Fernando III in 1247, an earthquake in 1504 that destroyed the fortress, and the assault of the rebel general Franco, who massacred hundreds of its citizens during the Spanish Civil War. Despite all this, it remains a fine example of white Andalusian hill towns.

You enter through the double-arched **Puerta de Seville,** erected by the Romans and embellished by the Moors. The cobblestone street climbs past mansions and churches in every style and agglomeration (from Mudejar to Gothic to the florid later stages of Renaissance and Baroque), but the dominant visual impression is of white stucco houses. At dusk, shepherds and their dogs gently urge their flocks of sheep and goats through the narrow streets and farmers return from the fields below to the dull clang of church bells.

Architectural highlights include the old High Renaissance **Ayuntamiento (Town Hall)** on the Plaza de San Fernando, which is enclosed by 17th-century mansions; the 15th-century **Iglesia de Santa María,** built over the remains of a mosque on Calle Martin López; and the **Alcázar del Rey Pedro,** an early Arab fortress that was transformed into a palace by Pedro the Cruel in the 14th century. Teetering at the lip of the plateau, its shards and crumbling walls now contain a modern *parador.*

The **tourist office** (☎ **95/419-09-55**) is now at the Puerta de Seville. Its staff may be able to help with lodging, for though the *parador* and the luxury Casa de Carmona are delightful, their rates are high and budget accommodations are few. My recommendation is either to return to Seville for the night or continue on N-IV to Córdoba, 65 miles northeast.

CÓRDOBA

The road from Seville borders the Guadalquivir, once navigable all the way to the ocean but now so shallow and silted that cattle graze on its sidebars. A still-used Roman bridge crosses the river, connecting the uninteresting new city on the south bank to the expansive Moorish quarters on the north.

At that point rises the perimeter wall of one of the most extraordinary sites in Spain, the ✪ **Mezquita,** a great mosque of immoderate but singularly graceful proportions. While you walk up along the west wall on Calle de Torrijos, the building appears pockmarked and battered, with failed intrusions, overlays, and bricked-up doors and windows both Arabic and Spanish. The wonder of it isn't revealed until later. Soon there's a portal in the wall—but for the full effect, continue to the corner, turn right, and enter beneath the Renaissance bell tower **Torre del Alminar,** through the 14th-century Mudejar **Puerta del Perdón,** and into the **Patio de los Naranjos.** In this traditional arrangement, Muslim worshipers undertook ritual washing at the fountains beneath the orange trees before entering the mosque proper, on the far side of the courtyard.

At this writing, the ticket booth is against the north wall, over to the left after passing through the Puerta del Perdón. Its position and admission policies are changed with some frequency, as are entrances, due to both ongoing restorations and repairs and continued efforts at crowd control. When I was there, entrance fees were 750P ($5) over age 13 and 375P ($2.60) ages 8 to 13; free for under age 8. Admission to the patio is free. Hours during most of the year are 10am to 6pm, with last tickets sold at 5:30pm.

Walk straight across the patio from the Puerta del Perdón to enter the original section of the mosque. Pause a moment to let your eyes adjust to the gloom, alleviated on sunny days by shafts of light from skylights and narrow windows. Soon you'll be able to comprehend the numbing vastness of the space and the unique way it has been formed.

A flat roof covers nearly 8 acres of floor space. It's supported by what's routinely described as a "forest" of some 850 pillars stretching off into the murk at the distant corners. Those columns (the exact number isn't known) support double arches, some of which have scalloped edges and all of which bear alternating bands of white stone and brick. The pillars are made from a variety of materials, including marble, granite, onyx, limestone, and even wood. No two are exactly alike.

Walk straight across from the entrance to the south wall, glancing to the left and right. The stunning magnitude of the building will become even more obvious. Directly ahead is the most dazzling component, commissioned by the second caliph to order an expansion of the mosque: the ✪ **Mihrab,** the holiest place, glowing in the shadows. Golden, glittery mosaic tiles encase the triple-domed enclosure known as the *maksourah,* reserved for the supreme ruler. The Mihrab itself is in a niche off this vestibule, its entrance formed by marble columns supporting entwined arches. The whole gleams like jewels cast on black velvet. Its beauty is enough to make even the faithful excuse the fact that, due to an ancient miscalculation, the Mihrab is oriented to the south rather than to the east and Mecca.

If you turn left (east), a far less felicitous element will make itself glaringly apparent. It's a **cathedral,** the reason of the official designation of this edifice as the **Mezquita-Catedral** and a grotesque tribute to Gothic-Baroque excess plunked in the middle of a monument characterized by structural lightness and spare decoration. In the early 16th century, bishops of the Church Triumphant obtained the permission of Carlos V to convert this Muslim house of worship into a cathedral. One might forgive its almost unimaginable desecration if the cathedral exemplified *good* Baroque style, but this accretion of marble saints, coffered ceilings, rampant cheribum, and curls of stucco, alabaster, and jasper would stand as a visual insult almost anywhere. When Carlos V saw the structure he authorized, he said, in effect: "What you have made here may be found in many places, but what you have destroyed is to be found nowhere else in the world."

In the bishops' defense, had they not imposed this cathedral and incorporated the rest of the mosque by closing off the once-open sides and building ancillary chapels, the entire Muslim structure might've been razed, as were so many others in the wake of the Christian Reconquest. And the Moors were hardly pure of heart, given that many of those 800-plus pillars were scavenged from Roman temples, Visigothic churches, and various pagan North African and Turkish sites.

Continue past the cathedral proper into the extension ordered by caliph Alhaken II in the mid-10th century to find a small **archaeological museum** displaying relics of the Visigothic church that once stood at this spot. The exit (at this writing) is up to the left.

You've just been exposed to manifestations of two of Spain's great religions, so it's appropriate that evocative hints of the third are close at hand. Take the street leading off from the northwest corner of the Mezquita into the quarter known as the ✪ **Judería,** the ancient Jewish *barrio.* After a short block of gaudy souvenir shops, turn right on Calle Deanes and, a few steps later, onto Calle Almanzor Romero. Most of the modest whitewashed homes here date from the 18th century, but they resemble the older Córdoba and a few predate the 1492 expulsion order of Queen Isabel and King Fernando.

Turn left into the Plaza Cardenal Salazar and into the connecting Plazuela de Maimónides, passing the **Museo Municipal Taurino,** a bullfighting museum open Tuesday to Saturday 10am to 2pm and 6 to 8pm and Sunday 10am to 3pm; admission is 425P ($2.95), except Tuesday, when it's free. Around to the right, in the small Plaza Tiberiades, is a **statue of Moses Maimónides.** Given the bitter antipathies among the three creeds in the modern era, it's difficult to imagine the relative tolerance displayed by the ruling Muslims of his time toward the Jews in their midst. But in 12th-century Córdoba, and in his sojourns around the Mediterranean after Islamic sufferance broke down, Maimónides achieved high honor as a physician, theologian, law scholar, and philosopher.

Not far beyond the statue at Calle Judios 20 is the entrance to **La Sinagoga,** one of only three intact synagogues remaining in Spain. It dates from the 14th century and has Middle Eastern embellishments in its intricately carved plasterwork; on the walls are Hebrew quotations from the Psalms. The building consists of a small square room, above which is the *ezrat nashim,* the segregated balcony for women and girls. No longer used for worship, La Sinagoga is open Tuesday to Saturday 10am to 2pm and 3:30 to 5:30pm and Sunday 10am to 1:30pm; admission is 50P (35¢).

Apart from the Mezquita-Catedral, there are relatively few monuments of note. This is a city with a densely textured history but not much else to show for it. You might wish to seek out the **Alcázar,** Amador de los Ríos s/n (☎ **957/42-01-51**). Two blocks southwest of the Mezquita, its most notable attractions are its gardens and Arab baths, supplemented by mosaics from an earlier Roman palace. Admission is 425P ($2.95), and it's open Tuesday to Saturday 10am to 2pm and 6 to 8pm and Sunday 9:30am to 3pm.

The ideal time to be in Córdoba is May, a month of many celebrations, especially the **Festival de los Patios.** At that time, residents of the Judería dress up the court-yards of their houses with thousands of plants and blooms, vivid against their blazing white walls, *azulejos,* and terra-cotta floors. The results are there for all to admire, as even normally closed patios are opened to curious passersby. Visitors invited to enter are expected to smile often at the hosts and to shower them with compliments. It's also customary to contribute a 50P coin or two to the discreet little basket or plate to help defray the cost of the displays.

Córdoba is the only intermediate stop on the high-speed AVE train between Madrid and Seville, placing it 1¾ hours from Madrid and 45 minutes from Seville. A taxi ride from the railroad station to the Mezquita is about 450P ($3.10). Once you're there, you can reach all the city's major sights on foot. Buses operated by several companies between Córdoba and Seville make the trip in 2 to 3 hours.

ACCOMMODATIONS   While you can easily do Córdoba as a day trip from Seville, it's an agreeable city to wander and absorb at leisure, so you may want to stay overnight. Among the most impressive budget hotels is **González,** Manriquez 3, 14003 Córdoba (☎ **957/47-98-19;** fax 957/48-61-87). Especially remarkable are its excellent location in the Judería, a short stroll from the Mezquita, and its ingratiating staff. The 16th-century mansion is pleasantly decorated in Andalusian style, with a dining courtyard and 17 air-conditioned units with phones. As at most Córdoba hotels, prices are highest during Holy Week and the annual Fería the last weekend in May. Those short periods aside, doubles go for 5,900P ($41) to 9,850P ($68). American Express, MasterCard, and Visa are accepted.

On the other side of the adjacent Plaza Juda Levi is the uncommonly appealing **Albergue Juvenil** (☎ **957/29-01-66;** fax 957/29-05-00), a member of Hostelling International. Large, well kept, and contemporary, it imposes a minimum of the kinds of rules and restrictions that can make hosteling a hassle. There's no curfew, and doubles with bathroom are available for 1,500P to 1,750P ($10 to $12) per person. No credit cards are accepted. Reservations are essential, especially April to October.

Up a street angling off the northeast corner of the Mezquita is **Los Omeyas,** Encarnación 17, 14003 Córdoba (☎ **957/49-22-67;** fax 957/49-16-59). Recently overhauled and much of it sheathed in marble, this crisply maintained hotel has 25 units, all with bathrooms, safes, TVs, air-conditioning, and phones; 7 have double beds, and all can be converted into triples by sliding in an extra bed. Breakfast is taken in the attractive patio or the Moorish-style bar. Doubles are 7,000P to 7,500P ($48 to $52), and American Express, MasterCard, and Visa are accepted.

DINING   Up an alley opposite the Mezquita's Puerta del Perdón is Córdoba's best-known restaurant, **El Caballo Rojo,** Cardenal Herrero 28 (☎ **957/47-53-75**). Claims that some of the recipes at "The Red Horse" are adapted directly from Sephardic and Moorish cookbooks may be exaggerated, but there's no doubt the Andalusian repertoire is adroitly executed. If the *menú del día* at 2,950P ($20) is too steep, step out of the hot sun into the cool ground-floor bar and order a beer to go with a sandwich or a couple of *tapas.* It's open daily 1 to 4pm and 8 to 11pm and accepts American Express, MasterCard, and Visa.

Adhering to the local style of setting out tables in an interior courtyard, the very new **Patio de la Judería,** Conde y Luque 6 (☎ **957/48-78-61**), observes the conventions of amiable service and a conservative menu. The owner acts as if he enjoys your company and wheels a portable heater over to your table if he thinks you might be chilly. When the sun is too harsh, he draws the shade over the patio. Try *salmorejo,* a Córdoba cousin of *gazpacho* that's a thick paste of cold tomato garnished with bits of ham and egg. There are *menús del día* of 975P and 1,200P ($7 and $8). It's open daily 1 to 4:30pm and 8:30 to 11pm and accepts MasterCard and Visa. In business since 1879, **Taberna Salinas,** Tundidores 3 (☎ **957/48-01-35**), is as atmospheric a tavern as can be found. Bullfighting memorabilia adorns the walls and wine casks are installed behind the bar. A list of *raciónes* suggests *gazpacho,* croquettes, and marinated anchovies, costing 600P to 750P ($4.15 to $5) each. Full meals in the adjoining dining room are equally inexpensive, served Monday to Saturday 11:30am to midnight. MasterCard and Visa are accepted.

RONDA

The road up to Ronda from the Costa del Sol used to be an impossibly narrow route, twisting 30 miles. It was widened and straightened about 10 years ago, though, so it needn't be feared by any but the severely acrophobic (who might want to approach from the less precipitous northern route nos. 339 and 341). Certainly the grandeur of the site is undeniable. The flat-topped cliff the city occupies is cleft across its breath by the narrow Guadalevin gorge, more than 490 feet deep, the two sides stitched together by an 18th-century bridge higher than it is long. The southern half of town dates from the Moors, while the bullring built in 1785 in the "new" section is claimed to be the country's oldest.

Parks and overlooks around the perimeter are the principal diversion, especially the **Alameda del Tajo** and its forever views, but the **Plaza de Toros** on Virgen de la Paz, with a baroque main portal and a neoclassical interior, is intriguing. It's open daily 10am to 7pm, and admission is 225P ($1.55). On the Moorish side, the 13th-century **Baños Árabes (Arab Baths)** are the sights to see. Alas, they've been closed for years for renovations. Check at the **tourist office** (☎ 95/287-12-72), a block south of the bullring, to find out if they've finally reopened. It's open Monday to Friday 10am to 2pm.

If you have a car, an excursion to the **Cuevas de Pileta** is worthwhile. They're 18 miles west of Ronda: Take Route 339 toward Jerez de la Frontera for 9 miles, then turn south at the sign for Montejaque along an usually deserted road for 9 miles. There's a climb from the parking lot, and tours, usually between 10am and 1pm and 3 to 5pm, are sporadic. Expect to wait for up to an hour, since the caretaker/guide locks the gate whenever he gathers enough people for a tour. For those who've never entered such a place, the black-and-red prehistoric drawings in these cathedral-size caves are startling, especially the etched fish that suggest an ocean once lapped at the base of this mountain. The fee for the guided tour, which leaves when there are enough people to justify it, is 800P ($6).

ACCOMMODATIONS & DINING   Meals at **Don Miguel,** Plaza de España 3 (☎ 95/287-10-90; fax 95/287-83-77), are spiced by the restaurant's position at the rim of the gorge, looking *up* at the bridge. The price exacted for that privilege is fairly high, with full meals around 3,500P ($24), so this is a good time to observe the strategy of avoiding appetizers and desserts and settling for a main course, which should keep the tab under 2,500P ($17). It's open daily 1 to 4:30pm and 8:30 to 10:30pm, with a 2-week vacation in January. American Express, Diners Club, MasterCard, and Visa are accepted. Don Miguel also offers 19 simple doubles at 9,000P ($62), all with bathrooms, TVs, and phones.

If your mood and credit-card balance are up to a special treat, the **Posada Real,** Real 42 (☎ 95/287-71-76; fax 95/287-83-70), is an underpublicized charmer of an old mansion a block from the old bridge. The 11 units (with air-conditioning, TVs, and phones) go for 14,000P to 16,500P ($97 to $114), and meals in its dining room average 3,000P ($21). Dining hours are Tuesday to Sunday 1:30 to 4:30pm and 8:30 to 11pm. American Express, Diners Club, MasterCard, and Visa are accepted.

Less expensive, under umbrellas on a terrace next to the Plaza de Toros, is **Jerez,** Paseo Blas Infante s/n (☎ 95/287-20-98). Stick to the *platos combinados* rather than

Granada's Alhambra

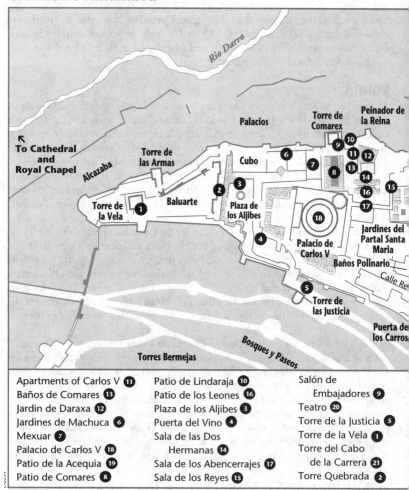

full meals and the cost should stay under 1,500P ($10). It's open daily 1 to 4:30pm and 8:30 to 11pm and accepts American Express, Diners Club, MasterCard, and Visa.

GRANADA

Even visitors intent on nothing more elevating than a sun-blasted, sangría-soaked week on the Costa del Sol should plan to make the short day trip to Granada (only 79 miles north). The ✪ **Alhambra,** after all, ranks with the Acropolis in visual and cultural impact. Floating above the city like a dream of palaces, its keeps and spires are sharp against the backdrop curtain folds of the **Sierra Nevada,** whose peaks are snow-capped into June. Unlike the Mezquita of Córdoba, the Alhambra ("ahl-*ahm*-bra") isn't a single structure but a regal compound of interlocking gardens, royal residences, pools, citrus groves, waterworks, fortifications, and places to worship two deities, complete with a supporting cast of hotels and restaurants.

SEEING THE ALHAMBRA   The cynosure is the **Palace of the Alhambra,** a series of connected structures and courtyards constituting the highest achievement of

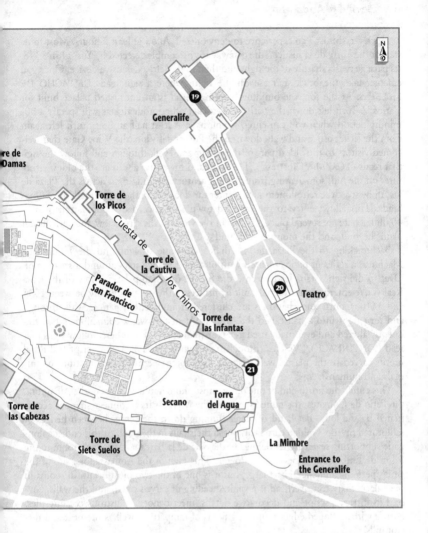

Islamic art in Iberia. Neglected and abused for centuries after the Christian Reconquest, it became a campground for Gypsies and brigands with little regard for the magnificence of their surroundings. American author/diplomat Washington Irving enjoyed a short residence here and wrote *Tales of the Alhambra*. Its popularity inspired the government to undertake restoration after 1828. Much of the palace's interior embellishment was lost, but enough remains to provide a sense of what must have been. This is all the more remarkable because the caliphs rarely built for posterity, evidenced by the fragile plaster ceiling decorations that resemble stalactites.

With its unchallenged stature as one of the great sights of Europe, the Alhambra is inevitably swamped with people, nearly 2 million each year. There's no hope of evading the throngs, but they do tend to thin at least a bit during the afternoon siesta period and the last couple of hours during the extended periods of summer. Getting to the ticket office at the stroke of 9am doesn't seem to make much difference, not with the first buses of the day arriving at the same time. This is unfortunate, for this garden of delights should be contemplated as was intended, in serenity.

However, this isn't an experience to deny oneself. Allow at least 2 hours. Most tours start at the Torre de la Justicia, the gateway to the complex erected by Yusuf I in 1348. Its passage twists sharply to the right and then to the left, a defensive device. Once you emerge, take the brick staircase on the right, where a sign reads DESPACHO DE BILLETES. At the top, the building looming ahead is an unfinished palace built for Carlos V. Turn left down the path to the ticket office. Your tickets will specify a 30-minute period when you can enter. If you have at least half an hour, turn left again from the ticket office and walk down to the Puerta del Vino, the Wine Gate that welcomed visitors to the oldest part of the Alhambra. Walk through and follow the sign that reads ALCAZABA ("fortress"). The walls and towers up ahead are the oldest structures on the hill, some dating from the 9th century. Angling right across the Plaza de los Aljibes past the refreshment kiosk, enter the doorway in the rose-tinted Torre Quebrada. This allows entry to the fortified town that once had a population of over 40,000. There are several places to take in the views of the city below, the agricultural plains beyond, and the mountains behind.

Backtracking to the Plaza de los Aljibes, continue straight into the Jardines de Machuca, a series of patios planted with olive and orange trees around a small pool. Over to the right, stairs lead up into the first of the Arab palaces. Most of the Casa Real you're entering was ordered built by princes of the Nasrid dynasty between 1335 and 1410. Courts and chambers are clustered around central patios. Walk through and turn right into a hall called the Mexuar. At first, it was a council chamber, frequently altered and eventually used as a Christian chapel. From here, follow signs that read CONTINUACIÓN VISITA, through rooms with reliefs of Arabic script and floral motifs carved in the plaster walls (Islamic law doesn't permit representations of animals and humans).

This enters the north end of one of the most photographed spaces in the Alhambra, the Patio de Comares, the famed Court of the Myrtles. Its rectilinear shape is accentuated by the long, flat band of water running down the center between hedges of sculptured myrtle. Golden carp lazily swish their tails in the pool. At this end, a colonnade supporting seven arches delineates the Sala de la Barca, a sort of anteroom to the Salón de Embajadores, beyond the loggia. This Hall of the Ambassadors, site of the emir's periodic audiences, isn't large, but it is one of the two most beautiful rooms in the palace. Sixty feet overhead is a vaulted ceiling of carved cedar, and the walls, covered in intricate script and decorative details, meet dadoes of lustrous ceramic tiles. Portals with scalloped edges frame fragments of ramparts as well as the near and distant hills.

Exiting the hall, walk on the left side of the pool. Near the end is a pair of doors leading to the famous Patio de los Leones, the Court of the Lions. In the center of the court are 12 stylized stone lions standing in a circle, bearing a large basin on their haunches. Jets of water arc from their mouths. A loggia of 124 marble pillars runs all around the courtyard, and protruding into the court at opposite ends are two pavilions with pyramidal cupolas above small pools. It's conjectured that these pillars and their intricately carved capitals were meant to represent the palm trunks and foliage of ancestral desert oases.

Around the court are several important chambers, including the Sala de los Abencerrajes, where a number of assassinations and executions took place; the Sala de los Reyes (Kings); and the Sala de las Dos Hermanas, named for the two marble slabs set into the floor. Exit through the small doorway with the pointed arch into a corridor with beams above and shuttered windows on the right. This takes you into a room that's obviously not Arabic. It's part of the apartments of Carlos V, adapted to the king's taste about 35 years after his grandparents conquered Granada in 1492.

Three centuries later, the apartment was lent to Washington Irving during his brief tenure as an American consular official in 1829.

Taking the staircase down to the Patio de Lindaraja, with orange and cypress trees, bear right into the Baños de Comares. These royal baths are closed part of the year to reduce wear and tear, but when open they reveal the cool vaulted chambers that remind some people of the sensuous orientalism depicted by European Romantic painters in the early 19th century. From there, proceed to the Jardín de Daraxa, the first of many terraced gardens to the east of the palace. Follow the CONTINUACÍON VISITA signs past the pools, rivulets, and gentle cascades that blend their gurgles with birdsong. Continuing, you'll reach the Torre del Cabo de la Carrera, literally the Tower of the End of the Track. It marks the edge of the palace grounds but not the end of the attraction. Up ahead is a viaduct spanning a deep ravine.

On the other side, a path leads up to the left toward the grounds of the summer residence of the Moorish kings, the **Generalife** ("hay-nay-ral-*ee*-fay"), which means "Gardens of Paradise." You'll find no palace up there, just many more luxuriant gardens of roses, geraniums, salvias, and oleander. But what draws attention and cameras is the narrow pool running more than 160 feet down the center of the **Patio de la Acequia,** for scores of high thin jets of water form a canopy above the length of the pool. You can hear the sound long before you can see the fountains, a fittingly musical denouement to this stroll among the playing grounds of the Moors.

All paths lead down to the bridge back across to the Alhambra grounds. After crossing the viaduct, turn left along a path partially bordered by cypress hedges. Soon, over to the right, you'll reach the **Parador de San Francisco,** highly popular but too expensive for these pages, unless you'll settle for a drink on the patio or lunch in the dining room. Continue down the street from the front of the *parador,* completing the circular tour. You might want to step into the **Palacio de Carlos V,** near the ticket office. Built in ponderous Spanish Renaissance style, it's in sharp contrast to the delicacy of the almost whimsical residences of the emirs. The circular opening in the roof was to be covered with a dome. The side galleries contain two small museums.

The visitor crush at the Alhambra has led the authorities to conduct ongoing experiments in crowd control. Micromanagement and calibrations lead to frequent changes, often unannounced, so flexibility is required regarding the following: At this writing, the Alhambra is open April to September Monday to Saturday 9am to 8pm and Sunday 9am to 6pm, plus Tuesday, Thursday, and Saturday 10pm to midnight; October to March, hours are daily 9am to 8pm, plus Saturday 8 to 10pm. When you get your ticket, you'll be assigned a specific 30-minute period. You must enter the Casa Real during that period or must purchase another ticket for a later period. Once inside, you can stay as long as you wish. Admission is 725P ($5), with 725P extra for the night visits. Sundays are free (and packed to the walls).

SEEING THE CITY   If you plan on staying overnight, there are lesser attractions to explore. First among them is the downtown **Catedral,** Plaza de la Lonja, Gran Vía de Colón 5 (☎ **958/22-29-59**). Queen Isabel and King Fernando ordered this splendid Renaissance-Baroque cathedral built after their victory over the Moors; the adjoining Flamboyant Gothic **Capilla Real (Royal Chapel)** became their final resting place. Admission to the cathedral is 250P ($1.70), the same for the chapel. Both are open daily 10:30am to 1:30pm and 4 to 7pm (to 6pm October to March).

Albaicín is the most picturesque quarter of the city, a largely residential district that most clearly evokes the period of transition from Islamic to Christian Granada. Twisting, narrow cobblestone streets of houses with terra-cotta roofs climb the hill opposite the Alhambra, north of the river Darro, northeast of the Plaza Nueva. Make your destination the **Mirador de San Nicolás,** near the church of that name, reached by the Cuesta del Chapiz. It should come as no surprise that I suggest you arrive at sunset for the best views of the city, the Alhambra, and the Generalife. *Warning:* Street crime is a problem in this quarter, usually of the snatch or grab variety, so keep tight control of your belongings.

Next to Albaicín is the heavily touted "Gypsy quarter" called **Sacramonte.** The hill it occupies is shot with caves, once inhabited as homes but most now unoccupied after severe flooding in 1962. A remaining few serve as troglodyte nightclubs. That romantic notion evaporates indoors. Strung with colored lights and furnished with stubby little tables and chairs, they function as primitive flamenco *tablaos.* With very rare exceptions, the performances of the featured singers, guitarists, and dancers are execrable. Still, once lured past the door, you might find it difficult to leave without parting with hefty wads of pesetas. You'll be pressed to tip the performers and to purchase shoddy cassettes, castanets, and vile sherry. Leaflets scattered around the city on *concerje* desks and any available flat surfaces urge you to join various "Granada by Night" tours of the "picturesque" caves. My heartfelt advice: Don't.

ACCOMMODATIONS & DINING   On the grounds of the Alhambra itself and only a few meters from the *parador,* the charmingly quirky **América,** Real de la Alhambra 53, 18009 Granada (☎ **958/22-74-71;** fax 958/22-74-70), is the top budget choice in the city. Pass through a sitting room/lobby of off-kilter antiques into the shaftlike courtyard for copious, homey meals at around 2,400P ($17). Upstairs are 13 doubles for about 12,000P ($83). Dining hours are Sunday to Friday 1 to 4pm and 8 to 10:30pm (closed mid-November to February). Reservations are suggested for both rooms and dining. American Express, Diners Club, MasterCard, and Visa are accepted.

Also on the Alhambra hill, but not in the complex proper, is the unpretentious **Guadalupe,** Avenida de los Alixares s/n, 18009 Granada (☎ **956/22-34-24;** fax 956/22-37-98). It's on the back road up and thus a little quieter than hotels downtown. All 42 units have air-conditioning, minibars, TVs, phones, and bathrooms; doubles are 7,500P ($52) off-season and 11,500P ($79) late spring through early fall. Some have views of the sierra. There's a bar and both a restaurant with a none-too-impressive continental menu and an informal *cafetería* featuring mostly Spanish selections. Dining hours are daily 1 to 4pm and 8 to 11pm. American Express, Diners Club, MasterCard, and Visa are accepted.

Down in the city, a few short blocks west of the cathedral, is the converted 19th-century mansion that's the **Reina Cristina,** Tablas 4, 18002 Granada (☎ **958/25-32-11;** fax 958/25-57-28). When the martyred poet García Lorca was on the lam during the Civil War, he hid out here for a while. It wasn't a luxurious stay, by the evidence, but the 40 units (with air-conditioning, baths, TVs, and phones) are adequate in comfort and the staff is pleasant. Doubles are 9,900P ($69). Simple meals in the dining room are about 1,700P ($12); dining hours are Tuesday to Sunday 1 to 4pm and 8:30 to 11pm. American Express, Diners Club, MasterCard, and Visa are accepted.

The location of **Macia,** Plaza Nueva 4, 18010 Granada (☎ **958/22-75-36;** fax 958/22-75-33), couldn't be better. It's on the square at the base of the main access road to the Alhambra, at the center of the downtown business district and only 5 or 6 blocks from the cathedral. None of the 40 units will knock your socks off, but they have air-conditioning, TVs, and phones and are at least functional. Doubles are 6,900P ($48). American Express, Diners Club, MasterCard, and Visa are accepted.

DINING   **Seville,** Oficios 14 (☎ **958/22-46-65**), has been around almost 70 years and is Granada's most reliable restaurant, for it neither excels nor disappoints. Out front is one of the city's best *tapas* bars, and it has four dining rooms and a terrace at which to sample Andalusian takes on monkfish, lamb, and chicken. Depending on your selections, a meal should be under 3,000P ($21), but if that's too much, make a meal of *tapas*. It's open daily 1 to 4pm and Monday to Saturday 8 to 11pm and accepts American Express, Diners Club, MasterCard, and Visa.

Choices are few in the Alhambra itself, apart from the several hotels, but the most obvious, **Polinarío,** Real de la Alhambra 3 (☎ **958/22-29-91**), isn't at all bad, given that every last visitor passes by and most stop in for a snack or drink. Opposite the Carlos V palace, it has a luncheon buffet costing 1,350P ($9) and an interior courtyard for dining. It's open daily 10am to 7pm, and no credit cards are accepted.

26 Stockholm & Environs

by Nikolaus Lorey

On a map, Stockholm appears cold and remote, a city disjointedly dotted across numerous islands, sliced up by icy arctic waters, and positioned as far north as Siberia. Yet to visit this breathtaking cosmopolitan city is to enter a romantic dream of old-world Europe. With remarkable grace, the Swedes have tamed their environment.

Up close, Stockholm is the most beautiful capital in Scandinavia; indeed, it's one of the most beautiful cities in the world. By day the narrow winding streets of Gamla Stan (Old Town) give way to the vast openness of Skansen. At night, world-class restaurants and glamorous clubs speak eloquently of the city's sophistication, and lights from some of Europe's grandest buildings beckon passersby across well-kept ocean inlets.

Not surprisingly, the Swedish mimic their environment. From afar, locals may appear reserved. However, when you delve into their culture and begin to meet the people, you'll find their openness, warmth, and hospitality boundless.

REQUIRED DOCUMENTS   Citizens of the United States, Canada, the United Kingdom, Australia, and New Zealand need only a passport to visit Sweden.

OTHER FROMMER'S TITLES   For more on Stockholm, see *Frommer's Scandinavia* or *Frommer's Europe.*

1 Stockholm Deals & Discounts

SPECIAL DISCOUNTS

FOR EVERYONE   Costing just 185KR ($25) for 1 day, 350KR ($47) for 2 days, or 470KR ($63) for 3 days, the **Stockholm Card** buys you unlimited rides on the public transport network, admission to most museums, free guided sightseeing tours, and a guidebook to Stockholm. You also get boat sightseeing at half price, plus a one-way ticket to Drottningholm Palace. Cards are sold at the tourist information counter at Sweden House and at Hotell Centralen at Central Station, and each is valid for one adult and two children 17 and under.

In addition, the city transportation network, SL, sells **day passes** for subways and buses, available at the SL Center (see "Visitor Information," below). A 1-day unlimited-use pass for the Stockholm area and the Djurgården ferries is 65KR ($9) and a 3-day pass is 120KR ($16).

Budget Bests

Opera and philharmonic tickets can be had practically for a song, and the city's many **playhouses** are reasonably priced. **Outdoor summer concerts** and other warm-weather events are usually free, as are a host of year-round **special events and activities.** During winter, open-air **ice skating** in the heart of the city is both exhilarating and inexpensive. Anytime, a **stroll along the waterfront** or a **walk through Old Town** is great fun and free.

Sweden's high taxes on alcohol are sobering. If you want to imbibe without taking out a mortgage, buy **duty-free alcohol** before entering the country. Ditto for tobacco. Overseas visitors may import up to 1 quart of alcohol and 200 cigarettes.

FOR STUDENTS & SENIORS   A valid student ID will get you discounts at some museums and at cultural events, such as the opera and ballet. Travelers age 65 and over receive most of the same discounts as students—and more. Take advantage of the reduced fares on subways and buses. The listings below have even more heartening discount news.

WORTH A SPLURGE

Stockholm County encompasses about 24,000 **small islands** that'll make you believe you're a million miles from anywhere. Most are uninhabited, a few were inhabited hundreds of years ago (and contain interesting ruins), while others are jammed every summer with vacationing city dwellers. The **Stockholm Information Service** (see "Visitor Information," later in this chapter) will help you plan an excursion, as either a day trip or an overnight stay. Ferries are usually frequent and cheap, hotels are more charming and less expensive than in the city, and camping is always free.

2 Essentials

ARRIVING

BY PLANE   Stockholm's **Arlanda Airport** is 28 miles north of town. Four rainbow-striped buses (☎ **08/600-10-00**) leave the airport every 10 to 15 minutes from 6:35am to 11pm, afterward according to the arrival times of specific flights. You want the one to Stockholm City. Take it to City Terminal. It costs 60KR ($8) for everyone except age 15 and under, who ride free with a parent. The journey takes 40 minutes. Taxis are available at the airport, but the ride into town will run about 360KR ($48).

You can change money at several places in the baggage-claim area, before you reach Customs (rates are reasonable, hours long). Adjacent red phones offer local calls for up to 3 minutes for 2KR (25¢). Beyond Customs, you'll find a post office, a bank, and representatives from most of the major car-rental companies. Downstairs is the 24-hour **Left-Luggage Office** (☎ **08/797-62-28**), charging 25KR ($3.35) per bag per day. Lockers cost 20KR to 25KR ($2.65 to $3.35).

Pick up a city map from the **information office** at the airport (☎ **08/797-61-00**), open 24 hours. If you need a brief rest before heading out, there are four day rooms with a bed, toilet, and shower at the airport.

BY TRAIN OR BUS   Stockholm's train station, **Central Station,** Vasagatan 14 (☎ **08/696-75-49;** T-Bana: Centralen), and bus station, **Cityterminalen (City Terminal),** Klarabergsviadukten 72 (☎ **08/762-59-97;** T-Bana: Centralen), are across from each other and are connected underground by escalators. The trilevel Central

What Things Cost in Stockholm	U.S. $
Taxi from Arlanda Airport to city center	$48.00
T-Bana from Central Station to an outlying neighborhood	1.90
Local telephone call	.25
Double room at the Grand Hotel (deluxe)	400.00
Double room without bath at the Queen's Hotel (moderate)	73.35
Double room without bath at the Tre Små Rum (budget)	66.00
Lunch for one, without wine, at Bistro Jarl (moderate)	12.00
Lunch for one, without wine, at Café Blå Porten (budget)	10.00
Dinner for one, without wine, at Stadhuskällaren (deluxe)	160.00
Dinner for one, without wine, at Michelangelo (moderate)	17.20
Dinner for one, without wine, at Nicki's Café (budget)	6.66
Pint of beer in a bar	5.35
Coca-Cola in a cafe	3.35
Cup of coffee in a cafe	2.15
Roll of ASA 100 color film, 36 exposures	6.40
Admission to the Vasa Museum	6.65
Movie ticket	10.00
Budget theater ticket	12.00

Station can be confusing; the more modern bilevel City Terminal is easy to maneuver through and seems more like an international airport than a bus station. It has an information desk to the left of the entrance, a money exchange window (look for the yellow-and-black sign), and a kiosk selling international newspapers.

Since neither the bus nor the train station is within walking distance of hostels or most budget hotels, you'll probably have to take the subway. You can connect directly to the subway system from the lower level of Central Station. Just follow the signs that say T-BANA or TUNNELBANA.

The ground level of the train station is home to the **tourist office** and the helpful **Hotell Centralen,** where you can book rooms (see "Accommodations You Can Afford," later in this chapter). Look for a sign with a white "i" on a green background pointing the way.

Baggage carts, lockers, and showers are available. The lockers cost 20KR or 25KR ($2.65 or $3.35), depending on size, for 24 hours, but it's much safer to use the **Resgods (Left-Luggage) Office** (☎ 08/762-25-49), which charges 40KR ($5.35) per bag per day. It's open daily 7am to 9pm.

Train tickets are sold on the ground floor; Tracks 1 to 9 are for trains heading north, and Tracks 10 to 18 for those heading south. The ground floor is also home to phones, train information (SJ Information), and a currency exchange called Forex, open daily 8am to 9pm (look for the big yellow-and-black sign).

There's a large market on the lowest level, along with clean bathrooms—there's a 5KR (65¢) charge to use them—and large showers, which cost 25KR ($3.35). An attendant is on duty.

For **train information** about rail service within Sweden, call ☎ 020/75-75-75; for **international rail service,** call ☎ 08/22-79-40. For **bus information,** call ☎ 08/700-51-47 or Swebus at ☎ 020/64-06-40; for **airport bus departures,** call

☎ **08/600-10-00.** If you're too loaded down to get to the airport bus from your hotel by local transportation (and vice versa), at this writing **Taxi Kurir** (☎ **08/30-00-00**) offers transport for 80KR ($11) that includes both taxi and bus fare—a great deal.

VISITOR INFORMATION

After getting settled in your room, your first stop in Stockholm should be **Sverige Huset (Sweden House),** Hamnagatan 27 (T-Bana: Kungsträdgården).

On the ground floor is the **Stockholm Information Service** (☎ **08/789-24-90**). Even if you desire no other information, get a free copy of *Stockholm This Week* for its lists of special and free events and good map. You can buy the Stockholm Card (see "Stockholm Deals & Discounts," earlier in this chapter) here, as well as city tour and archipelago excursion tickets. This office will reserve a hotel room for a 40KR ($5) service charge, plus a 10% deposit, or a youth hostel room for a 15KR ($2) service charge. The reservations desk can also book summer cottages and overnight packages and sell tickets to concerts and soccer games.

The 160-page *Discover Stockholm* book for 79KR ($11) is a good investment; a map of Stockholm and surrounding areas is 15KR ($2). You can also buy posters, cards, and gift items. There's a convenient bathroom on the premises, but you have to pay 5KR (65¢) to use it and someone must buzz you into it. The Stockholm Information Service is open June to August, Monday to Friday 9am to 6pm and Saturday and Sunday 9am to 5pm; September, Monday to Friday 9am to 6pm and Saturday and Sunday 9am to 3pm; and the rest of the year, Monday to Friday 9am to 6pm and Saturday and Sunday 10am to 3pm.

The **Swedish Institute Bookshop,** on the second floor of Sweden House (☎ **08/789-20-00;** fax 08/20-72-40), features an extensive collection of English-language books about Swedish life, plus coffee-table tomes, novels, records, cassettes, CDs, children's books, art books, and more. It's open Monday to Friday 9am to 6pm and Saturday 10am to 3pm.

Hotell Centralen, in the main hall of Central Station (☎ **08/24-08-80;** fax 08/791-86-66; T-Bana: Centralen), makes hotel reservations (see "Accommodations You Can Afford," later in this chapter) and distributes free maps. It's open May to September, daily 8am to 9pm; the rest of the year, Monday to Friday 8am to 5pm.

The **SL Center,** on the lower level of Sergels Torg in Norrmalm (☎ **08/686-11-97;** if it's busy, or if you need only info about times for buses, subways, and local trains, call ☎ 08/600-10-00; T-Bana: Centralen), offers information about local subway and bus transportation and sells a good transport map for 35KR ($4.65), as well as tickets for the system. It's open Monday to Friday 7am to 6:30pm and Saturday and Sunday 10am to 5pm.

CITY LAYOUT

Picture the city as the group of islands it is, even though bridges and tunnels connect them as one. Fortunately, only a handful of the thousands of islands in the archipelago are important for visitors. You'll find a reliable **free map** at the back of *Stockholm This Week.*

The heart of modern Stockholm, **Norrmalm** is actually on the mainland, in the northernmost part of the city center. It's where you'll arrive at the train station, shop, and probably find a hotel. **Drottninggatan,** the major pedestrian shopping street, runs approximately north-south and bisects Norrmalm. Along it are the important squares of **Sergels Torg** (the active center of Norrmalm) and **Hötorget,** home to the Åhléns and PUB department stores, respectively. Branching east from Sergels Torg is **Hamngatan,** a short street lined with chain-store outlets, the NK department store

(Sweden's largest), Sweden House (home of the Stockholm Information Service), and Kungsträdgården (half park, half street, and host to many free outdoor events). **Birger Jarlsgatan,** a few blocks east of Kungsträdgården, leads to the Royal Dramatic Theater and the American Express office and is filled with shops and cafes as far as **Sturegallerian,** the trendy shopping gallery at Stureplan.

Flanking Norrmalm on the east, the upscale **Östermalm** is home to the Royal Library, the Museum of History, shops, hotels, and restaurants. Due west of Norrmalm, **Kungsholmen** is home to Stockholm's striking City Hall, where the Nobel Prize banquet is held annually. In Swedish, **Gamla Stan** means Old Town, and on the city's maps this district's small island is always in the center. Pretty buildings, cobblestone streets, narrow alleys, and interesting shops provide a welcome counterpoint to Norrmalm's big-city landscape. Fast currents on either side of the island once forced sea merchants to portage their goods to vessels waiting on the other side. The paths these porters pounded are now the oldest extant streets and are well worth exploring.

South of Gamla Stan lies **Södermalm,** once considered the "bad" side of town. As the city has gentrified, Södermalm's rents have skyrocketed and chic restaurants, bars, and clubs have moved in. You might stay in one of Södermalm's budget hotels or private rooms, and you should visit the cliffs overlooking Stockholm Harbor. East of Gamla Stan, across a narrow channel, lies tiny, pretty **Skeppsholmen,** home to two popular youth hostels (and the Museum of Modern Art). The quiet streets on the island, as well as the islet connected to it, are perfect for strolling.

Farther east still is Stockholm's tour de force, the magnificent **Djurgården (Deer Garden),** which encompasses many of the city's top sights. This shady neck of land with lush oak groves would be any lumberjack's delight, but thankfully it's been protected for centuries by the government, which has maintained the area as a grazing ground for the king's deer. The *Vasa* Ship Museum and the massive outdoor Skansen folk museum are the area's top draws.

GETTING AROUND

Subways (called Tunnelbana) and buses are operated by SL, the city transportation network, and charge according to a zone system—the price increases the farther you go. Most places you'll visit in central Stockholm will cost 14KR ($1.85), payable at the Tunnelbana and bus entrance.

In addition to the **Stockholm Card,** which you can get at Sweden House and Hotell Centralen at Central Station, you can buy **day passes** at the SL Center (for more details on these, see "Stockholm Deals & Discounts," earlier in this chapter). People under 18 and seniors can buy half-price tickets for all forms of public transport. For more information, call ☎ **08/600-10-00.**

Walking is the best way to get to know the city. You'll have to explore Gamla Stan on foot, as cars are banned from most of the streets. Djurgården and Skeppsholmen are other popular haunts for strolling.

BY SUBWAY (TUNNELBANA OR T-BANA)   Stockholm is blessed with a fast, efficient, and far-reaching subway system called the T-Bana. Color-coded maps are on station walls and printed in most tourist publications. Timetables for each train are also posted. Many of the city's 100 subway stations are distinctive for the permanent artwork and other decoration they display. Especially eye-catching are Kungsträdgården, T-Centralen, Rådhuset, Solna, and Slussen.

One ticket costs 14KR ($1.85) and is good for 1 hour (use it as often as you want), or you can get a strip of 20 coupons for 95KR ($12.65). A 1-day **tourist card** for unlimited use in the Stockholm area is 60KR ($8) adults and 36KR ($4.80) seniors/children; a 3-day tourist card is 120KR ($16) adults and 60KR ($8)

A Note on the T-Bana

Most subway stops have several well-marked exits; save yourself time by checking your map and choosing the exit closest to your destination. Trains are shorter during less heavily trafficked periods, such as evenings, so stand toward the center of the platform for boarding.

seniors/children. Unlimited transportation is included in the cost of the Stockholm Card.

If you're paying with cash or using a strip ticket, pass through the gate and tell the person in the ticket booth where you're going. He or she will either ask for your fare or stamp your ticket. If you have a Stockholm Card, just flash it. Sometimes the ticket collector is absent; in these instances, few commuters wait for the collector to return—they just walk through.

BY BUS   Buses run where the subways don't, comprehensively covering the city. Enter through the front door and pay the driver, show your Stockholm Card, or have your strip ticket stamped. If you plan on taking the bus a lot, buy a transport map from the Stockholm Information Service or the SL Center (see "Visitor Information," above). Many buses depart from Normalmstorg, catercorner to Kungsträdgården and 2 blocks from Sweden House.

BY FERRY   Ferries run between Gamla Stan (and Slussen) and Djurgården year-round, providing the best link between these two. In summer, boats depart every 15 minutes 9am to midnight (to 10:40pm Sunday); in winter, daily 9am to 6pm. The ride costs 20KR ($2.65) adults, half price seniors and ages 7 to 18. Check with the Stockholm Information Service for more details.

BY TAXI   Beware! The meter starts at 25KR ($3.35), and a short ride can easily come to 60KR ($8), but the tip is included. You can order a cab by phone, but there may be an additional charge. Avoid gypsy cabs; always take one with a yellow license plate with the letter T at the end of the number. **Taxi Stockholm** (☎ 08/15-00-00) and **Taxi Kurir** (☎ **08/30-00-00**) are two companies with set prices. But always ask if there's an extra charge for a pickup. Taxi Kurir offers transport from your hotel to the airport bus that includes both the taxi and the bus fare for only 80KR ($11); for this service call ☎ **08/686-10-10.**

BY BICYCLE   Bicycling is a good way to explore Djurgården, and you can rent bikes from **Skepp o Hoj,** just to your right after you cross the bridge onto the island (☎ 08/660-57-57), May to August daily 9am to 9pm. It's most economical to rent for the day, at 100KR ($13) for 24 hours; or you can pay by the hour, at 40KR ($5) for the first hour and 35KR ($4.65) per hour thereafter. It also rents boats and skates.

BY RENTAL CAR   Unless you're planning an extended trip outside the city, you'll find that keeping a car is more trouble than it's worth. Most major U.S. car-rental firms, including Hertz and Avis, have counters at the airport and offices in Stockholm. Local companies are usually cheaper and are listed under "Biluthyrning" in the phone book and in the "Transportation" section of *Stockholm This Week.* Swedish law requires that motorists drive with their lights on day and night.

FAST FACTS: Stockholm

American Express   The Stockholm office gets a gold star from travelers for friendliness and helpfulness. It's at Magnus Ladulasgatan 5 (☎ **08/429-50-00;**

The Swedish Krona

For American Readers At this writing, $1 = approximately 7.50KR (or 1KR = 13¢), and this was the rate of exchange used to calculate the dollar values given in this chapter (rounded to the nearest dollar).

For British Readers At this writing, £1 = approximately 12KR (or 1KR = 8.3p), and this was the rate of exchange used to calculate the pound values in the table below.

Note: Exchange rates fluctuate from time to time and may not be the same when you travel to Sweden.

KR	U.S.$	U.K.£	KR	U.S.$	U.K.£
1	.13	.08	100	13.33	8.33
5	.67	.42	150	20.00	12.50
10	1.33	.83	200	26.67	16.67
15	2.00	1.25	250	33.33	20.83
20	2.67	1.67	300	40.00	25.00
25	3.33	2.08	400	53.33	33.33
30	4.00	2.50	500	66.67	41.67
40	5.33	3.33	600	80.00	50.00
50	6.67	4.17	700	93.33	58.33

T-Bana: Mariatorget), it can exchange money and hold or forward mail (see "Mail," below), and there's an ATM on site. The office is open Monday to Friday 9am to 5pm (to 6pm June to August) and Saturday 10am to 1pm. For 24-hour refund assistance, call ☎ **020/795-155.**

Banks Most banks in Stockholm are open Monday to Friday 9:30am to 3pm. Some in central Stockholm stay open to 5:30pm. Exchange rates rarely vary from bank to bank, but commissions do. These fees can be very high, around 35KR ($4.65) for a traveler's check transaction; however, you may often exchange up to six checks per transaction, so it's a good idea to change as much money as you think you'll need at one time. There may be no fee to change cash, but the rate is lower. Competitive rates are also offered by many post offices, including the main branch, which keeps long hours (see "Mail," below). The exchange window (Forex) at the train station is open daily 8am to 9pm. If you cash American Express traveler's checks at the American Express office there's no extra charge.

Business Hours Usually, **shops** are open Monday to Friday 9:30am to 6pm and Saturday 9:30am to 2pm. Larger **stores** may maintain longer hours Monday to Saturday and may open Sunday as well. Most **offices** are open Monday to Friday 9am to 5pm.

Currency You'll pay your way in Stockholm in **Swedish kronor (KR)** or **crowns** (singular, **krona**), sometimes abbreviated SEK, which are divided into 100 öre. Coins are minted in 50 öre, as well as 1KR, 5KR, and 10KR. Bills are issued in denominations of 10KR, 20KR, 50KR, 100KR, 500KR, and 1,000KR. For currency exchange, see "Banks," above, and "Mail," below.

Dentists Emergency dental care is available at **St. Eriks Hospital,** Fleminggatan 22 (☎ **08/654-11-17,** or 08/644-92-00 after 9pm: T-Bana:

Fridhelmsplan). Regular hospital hours for walk-ins are 8am to 7pm. At other times, call first.

Doctors   Normally, emergency medical care is provided by the hospital closest to the area you're staying in. For information, as well as advice regarding injuries, contact **Doctors on Duty** (☎ **08/644-92-00**). **City Akuten,** a privately run infirmary at Holländargartan 3 (☎ 08/411-71-77), can provide help, but at a cost of about 500KR ($67) a visit. Also check the phone directory under "Hälso-och sjukvaørd" (in the blue pages at the beginning of the Företag phone book) for clinics listed by neighborhood. You may be able to visit a local doctor for less money than the amount noted above.

Embassies   The embassy of the **United States** is at Strandvägen 101 (☎ **08/783-53-00;** T-Bana: Östermalmstorg); the embassy of **Canada,** at Tegelbacken 4 (☎ **08/453-30-00;** T-Bana: Centralen); the embassy of the **Republic of Ireland,** at Östermalmsgatan 97 (☎ **08/661-80-05;** T-Bana: Östermalmstorg); the embassy of the **United Kingdom,** at Skarpögatan 6–8 (☎ **08/671-90-00;** Bus: 69); and the embassy of **Australia,** at Sergels Torg 12 (☎ **08/613-29-00;** T-Bana: Hötorget). New Zealand doesn't maintain an embassy in Stockholm; inquiries should be made through the embassy of **New Zealand** in The Hague at ☎ **31-70/346-93-24.**

Emergencies   For police, fire department, or ambulance service, call ☎ **90-000.**

Holidays   Sweden celebrates New Year's Day (January 1), Epiphany, Good Friday, Easter and Easter Monday, May Day (May 1), Ascension Day (Thursday of the 6th week after Easter), Whitsunday and Whitmonday (also called Pentecost), Midsummer Day (the Saturday closest to June 24), All Saints' Day (the Saturday after October 30), and Christmas (December 24 to 26).

Hospitals   For the hospital closest to you, phone **Doctors on Duty** (☎ **08/644-92-00**) or visit **City Akuten,** Holländargartan 3 (☎ **08/11-71-02**), a privately run infirmary.

Laundry & Dry Cleaning   There's a self-service laundry, **Tvättomatten,** at Västmannagatan 61 (☎ **08/34-64-80;** T-Bana: Odenplan), beside the Hotel Gustav Vasa; it's open Monday to Friday 9am to 6pm and Saturday 10am to 2pm.

Mail   A central post office at Drottninggatan 53 (☎ **08/781-21-38;** T-Bana: Hötorget), 3 blocks from Sweden House, is open Monday to Friday 7am to 10pm and Saturday 10am to 7pm. The one in Central Station is open later. Most local post offices are open Monday to Friday 9am to 6pm and Saturday 9 or 10am to 1pm.

Pharmacy   For 24-hour service, go to **C. W. Scheele,** Klarabergsgatan 64 (☎ **08/454-81-30;** T-Bana: Centralen).

Police   For emergencies, dial ☎ **90-000.** For other matters, contact **Polishuset (Police Headquarters)** at Bergsgatan 52 (☎ **08/401-00-00**), open 24 hours.

Tax   A 21% **value-added tax (VAT)** is applied to entertainment, restaurants, and food; hotel rooms and other travel-related expenses are taxed 12%; and everything else is taxed 25%. You won't really have to worry about this, as the VAT is already added into the tag price of most store items, restaurant menus, and hotel tariffs. Many stores offer non-Scandinavian visitors the opportunity to recover the VAT on purchases over 100KR ($13). See "Shopping," later in this chapter.

Networks & Resources

STUDENTS Students who plan to study in Stockholm or elsewhere in Sweden can get a handbook about housing, health services, work permits, Swedish-language courses, sports, and social activities from the **Federation of Student Unions,** Körsbärsvägen 2 (Box 5903), 11489 Stockholm (☎ **08/674-54-00** or 08/674-54-44; T-Bana: Tekniska Högskolan). Call ahead for hours.

Kilroy Travels, Kungsgatan 4 (☎ **08/23-45-15;** T-Bana: Östermalmstorg), is the place for low-cost student air tickets; the maximum age for the latter is 34. It's usually open Monday to Friday 10am to 6pm. The office is 1 block from Birger Jarlsgatan at Stureplan. **Waastels Resor,** Stora Nygatan 37 (☎ **08/ 411-22-33;** T-Bana: Gamla Stan), offers discount rail and plane tickets for students to age 35 with valid ID. It's open Monday to Friday 9am to 6pm.

GAYS & LESBIANS Many local gays and lesbians gather at **RFSL-Huset,** Sveavägen 57 (☎ **08/736-02-12;** T-Bana: Rådmansgatan; Bus: 52). This large building is headquarters to most of Stockholm's gay and lesbian organizations and also houses a restaurant, disco, and bookstore. It's open Monday to Friday noon to 8pm.

In the complex, **Hus 1** (☎ **08/30-83-38**) is a casual eatery serving light fare like burgers, pasta, and fish-and-chips. If you're in the mood for a beer and a game of pool, that's possible too (see "Stockholm After Dark," later in this chapter). A disco in back is open Monday to Saturday 6pm to 3am and Sunday 6pm to midnight. The first Friday of the month is lesbian night, but men are still welcome at the bar. An admission of 60KR ($8) is charged Friday and Saturday. **Rosa Rummet (Pink Room Bookstore),** also in the complex (☎ **08/736-02-15**), has postcards and a good selection of Swedish- and English-language books on current gay issues. It's open Monday to Thursday noon to 8pm, Friday noon to 6pm, and Saturday and Sunday 1 to 4pm.

Hjarter Dam (Queen of Hearts), Polhemsgatan 23, near the City Hall (☎ **08/653-57-39;** T-Bana: Rådhuset), is a popular meeting place/cafe for gays and lesbians. It serves Swedish fare in informal, friendly surroundings.

Telephone **Local calls** cost 2KR (26¢) for the first few minutes, and 1KR more for every couple of minutes after that (depending on distance). Phones accept 1KR, 5KR, and 10KR coins. In Stockholm it's easier and definitely more convenient (though the cost is the same) to buy a phonecard, called a **Telekort,** from most any newsstand and use it in the growing number of phones that accept cards rather than coins.

The easiest way to make **international calls** to North America is via AT&T's USA Direct service. If you have an AT&T Calling Card, or call collect, you can reach an American operator from any phone by calling ☎ **020/795-611.** Alternatively, you can make international calls from the **TeleCenter Office** on the Central Station's ground floor (☎ **08/456-74-94**), open daily 8am to 9pm, except major holidays. A call to the United States or Canada costs 16.50KR ($2.20) per minute daily 10pm to 8am; rates fall to 12.50KR ($1.65) per minute 8am to 10pm (and all day Sunday). Long-distance rates are posted.

For **directory assistance,** dial ☎ **0018.** For directory listings or other information for Stockholm or other parts of Sweden only, dial ☎ **07975;** for other parts of Europe, dial ☎ **07977.**

Country & City Codes

The **country code** for Sweden is **46.** The **city code** for Stockholm is **8;** use this code when you're calling from outside Sweden. If you're within Sweden but not in Stockholm, use **08.** If you're calling within Stockholm, simply leave off the code and dial the regular phone number.

Tipping   A 10% service charge is routinely included in hotel and restaurant bills. Further tipping is unnecessary unless service is extraordinary; in that case, round up the amount (but only at dinner; in Stockholm it's never customary to tip at lunch).

3 Accommodations You Can Afford

Sure, you've heard about Stockholm's sky-high hotel prices. But less expensive options exist—so, armed with this guide, you're sure to find an affordable bed.

There's no budget hotel–packed street in the city. Budget hotels are few and far between and are listed below along with some alternatives. It's surprisingly common for Stockholm's city-dwellers to supplement their incomes by sharing their homes with visitors. Those who open their homes to foreigners are exceedingly friendly, well traveled, and interested in meeting new people, and they do a lot to ensure guests' comfort. There seems to be an unofficial network of private-room renters, so even if the home you phone is full, chances are good that the owners will refer you to a friend who has room.

Note: You can find the lodging choices below plotted on the map included in "Seeing the Sights," later in this chapter.

A DISCOUNTING SERVICE   On the ground level of Central Station, **Hotell Centralen** (☎ 08/789-24-25; fax 08/791-86-66) can sometimes offer cut-price rooms for same-day occupancy during slow periods. Of course, not all hotels discount rooms, but those that do usually lower their rates as the day wears on. The 40KR ($5) booking fee is waived if you book in advance by phone or fax. The office is open daily: June to August 7am to 9pm; May and September 8am to 7pm; and October to April 9am to 6pm.

A ROOM-FINDING SERVICE   **Hotelltjänst,** Vasagatan 15–17, 4th Floor, 11120 Stockholm (☎ **08/10-44-37, 57,** or **67;** fax 08/21-37-16), rents more than 50 rooms in private homes at excellent set rates. It's hard to beat the charge of 350KR ($47) single or 450KR ($60) double, with shared bath. There are no service fees, but you must stay 2 nights; ask for a place near a subway or bus stop (but first take a look at the private homes below). Hotelltjänst sometimes offers select hotel rooms at a discount often as much as 50% in summer. This can mean high-quality apartments for about 595KR ($79) single and 710KR ($95) double. You can reserve hotel rooms anytime in advance; private rooms, 10 days ahead. The office is 2 long blocks from Central Station; turn right when you get off the elevator. It's open Monday to Friday 9am to noon and 1 to 5pm. Ask for Gunnar Gustafsson, the man in charge.

PRIVATE HOMES

Call ahead to book a room and let the hosts know your arrival time so that they don't spend hours waiting for you.

Eivor Lichtsteiner. Bergsgatan 45, 11228 Stockholm. ☎ **08/746-91-66.** 2 units, neither with bathroom; 1 apt. 300KR ($40) single; 400KR ($53) double or apt. No credit cards.

T-Bana: Rådhuset; leave at the Police Huset exit, then turn left, slightly uphill, and the house is 3 minutes away.

The friendly and helpful Mrs. Lichtsteiner speaks six languages and writes books. Her rooms, two flights up from street level, have unpainted modern furniture and wall-to-wall carpeting and are decorated with plants and oil paintings, mostly horses. You have free use of the kitchen. This is a central, quiet, and safe area: The massive building complex across the street houses the Swedish police headquarters.

✪ **Eva Abelin.** Skeppargatan 49B, 11458 Stockholm. ☎ and fax **08/663-49-57.** 3 units, none with bathroom. 300KR ($40) single; 250KR ($33) per person double. Breakfast 40KR ($5). No credit cards. T-Bana: Östermalmstorg; take the Sibyllegatan exit and walk to Skeppargatan (less than 5 minutes) and turn left to the apartment building next to a flag shop.

This place has it all: a central location, elegant facilities, and an engaging, gracious host. Ms. Abelin, an avid art collector, rents a large double with a sink and TV, a smaller double across from the bathroom, and a single around the corner from the bath. All are comfortable, with plenty of light, a pleasing decor, interesting artwork, a writing table, a chest of drawers, and hanging space for clothes. The bathroom is large, with a big tub and a handheld shower. Guests enjoy sipping coffee and chatting at the kitchen table. It's convenient to walk to the attractions in Norrmalm and on to Djurgaørden from here.

✪ **Ingrid Ollén.** Störtloppsvägen 34, 12947 Stockholm. ☎ **08/646-68-68.** 2 units, neither with bathroom. 225KR ($30) single; 325KR ($47) double; 400KR ($53) triple. Breakfast 30KR ($4). No credit cards. T-Bana: Västertorp; exit the station following the arrow toward Störtloppsvägen, then turn left on that street and walk 2 blocks; when you reach the *apotek* (pharmacy), walk behind that building to find the entrance.

A 15-minute ride from the center in a pleasant neighborhood, this place offers two doubles (one with TV) with cooking privileges. One room is beside the full bathroom, the other beside the kitchen. Ms. Ollen is a retired nurse, not to mention a world traveler and an avid swimmer, who has welcomed people from 40 countries to her home. You can use the laundry for 25KR ($3.35), and there's an open-air pool nearby.

✪ **Pernilla Wilton.** Bastugatan 48A, 11825 Stockholm. ☎ **08/84-14-79** or 08/84-17-25. Fax 08/84-14-79. 1 unit, without bathroom. TV. 290KR ($39) single; 390KR ($52) double. No credit cards. T-Bana: Mariatorget; take the Torkel Knutssonsgatan exit.

On a quiet street on Södermalm, in one of the city's most attractive neighborhoods, Pernilla Wilton offers a spacious room with a full-size bed (more can be added to accommodate a family) and plenty of books and brochures to read. It's in a 19th-century house with a cozy Swedish ambiance and a view of Lake Malaren and the city, most notably the striking City Hall. You're assured a warm welcome and may use the kitchen. English and German are spoken. Gamla Stan is a 15-minute walk (or two T-Bana stops) away. Always call ahead to be sure the room is available and to get directions.

HOTELS

✪ **Hotell Örnsköld.** Nybrogatan 6, 11434 Stockholm. ☎ **08/667-02-85.** Fax 08/667-69-91. 27 units, 24 with bathroom. 275KR ($37) single without bathroom, 775KR–950KR ($103–$127) single with bathroom; 950KR–1,200KR ($127–$160) double with bathroom. Extra bed (up to 4) 200KR ($30). Rates include continental breakfast. Fri–Mon rates reduced by 20%. AE, DC, EURO, MC, V. T-Bana: Östermalmstorg; take the Linnegatan exit, take 2 long escalators, turn left, pass a florist, then take a short escalator, which leads to Nybrogatan; turn left, slightly downhill, and pass the red-brick Soluhall building; the hotel is right after McDonald's.

Getting the Best Deal on Accommodations

- Try renting a room in a private home—it will cost less than a hotel room and affords you the opportunity to get to know Swedish people in their own environment.
- Take advantage of a room-finding service that can find you cut-price rooms.
- Note that hostels are excellently priced, well-maintained, clean lodgings for people of all ages.

The basic rooms here are the best deal in all Stockholm, and the rooms with bathroom—spacious and soft-carpeted, with antique furniture, a color TV, a minibar, and a phone—are cheaper than most four-star hotels. You can walk to the city center in 5 minutes or to Central Station in 10. Börje Exstrand is the English-speaking owner/manager.

✪ **Lille Radmannen Hotel.** Rådmansgatan 67, 10430 Stockholm. ☎ **08/33-69-80.** Fax 08/32-50-32. 34 units, all with bathroom. TV. 950KR ($127) single; 1,150KR ($153) double/twin. Rates include buffet breakfast. AE, DC, MC, V. Extra bed (up to 4) 150KR ($20). T-Bana: Rådmansgatan; from the subway station, walk up the stairs to the street and then turn left. Bus: 69 to Tegnerlunden, in front of McDonald's; walk 30 yards, turn right, and you'll see the hotel.

This charming central hotel is managed by the equally charming Mona Erikson and Linda Lindau. The rooms have modern Scandinavian-style furniture and are housed in a three-story building, with an elevator; the reception is one flight up from street level. Free coffee- and tea-making facilities are available around the clock. It's in a quiet location where walking time to the city center is 10 minutes.

Tre Små Rum. Högbergsgatan 81, 11854 Stockholm. ☎ **08/641-23-71.** Fax 08/642-88-08. 6 units, none with bathroom. TV. 450KR ($60) single; 495KR double ($66); 550KR ($73) triple. Rates include continental breakfast. AE, MC, V. T-Bana: Mariatorget; turn right on Swedenborgsgatan and right again on Högbergsgatan, and the hotel is 3 blocks away.

Jakob Vunarndt, the enthusiastic young owner, got the idea for this hotel during his travels in Europe. Its motto is "cheap and clean." The place is modern, too, but not unlike a hostel: The rooms are small (and a bit claustrophobic and dark), though the beds are comfortable, and Jakob puts fruit in each room. You share two toilets and two large showers. The rooms book up quickly, so call ahead. Tre Små Rum is in a quiet neighborhood on Södermalm, near reasonably priced cafes and a laundry.

WEEKEND & SUMMER DISCOUNTS

Hotel Aldoria. St. Eriksgatan 38, 11234 Stockholm. ☎ **08/654-18-85.** Fax 08/652-29-63. 22 units, all with bathroom. TV TEL. 830KR ($111) single; 995KR ($133) double/twin; 1,260KR ($168) suite for 3; 1,500KR ($200) suite for 4. Rates include continental breakfast plus juice and cold cuts. Rates reduced about 20% on weekends (2 nights, Fri–Sun) and in summer. AE, DC, MC, V. Located 30 yards from Fridhelmsplan S-Torg station; take the Eriksgatan exit.

To enter the street door, push button B 0004 and take the elevator to the fifth-floor reception. The rooms are cozily furnished, impeccably clean, with soundproof windows and instant hot water. Friendly owner Wojtek Rybizki is from Poland. This place is recommended to all looking for a quiet location.

✪ **Hotell Anno 1647.** Mariagränd 3, 11646 Stockholm. ☎ **08/644-04-80.** Fax 08/643-37-00. 42 units, 29 with bathroom; 2 suites. TV TEL. Most days in summer and Fri–Sat year-round, 510KR ($68) single without bathroom, 790KR ($105) single with bathroom; 610KR

($81) double without bathroom, 1,090KR ($145) double with bathroom; 17,900KR ($239) suite. Sun–Thurs the rest of the year, rates are 35% higher. Rates include breakfast. AE, DC, EURO, MC, V. T-Bana: Slussen.

This pretty hotel has undergone many renovations since it was built in 1647. Though updating has made it more modern, the place still jealously guards its "country inn" roots. The rooms with bath are substantially nicer than those without, but hardwood floors and tasteful furnishings make them all more than adequate. A cafe serves lunch and snacks, and beer and wine are sold in the lobby. There's no elevator, so if you dislike stairs ask for a ground-floor room. (The no-smoking rooms, however, are on the fourth floor.) The hotel provides some excellent views of the harbor and Gamla Stan. The entrance is on narrow Mariagränd, off Götgatan, and is a block from the subway.

HOSTELS

Stockholm has four **International Youth Hostel Federation (IYHF) hostels,** offering excellently priced, well-maintained lodgings. Two, on Skeppsholmen, probably offer the best-located lodgings in the city (see the AF *Chapman,* below). All are similarly priced and offer lower rates to IYHF card carriers. If you aren't a member, you have to get a Welcome Card and pay an extra 35KR ($4.65) per night for up to 6 nights, after which you gain member status. Note that these hostels aren't just for young people.

✪ **AF** *Chapman.* Västra Brobänken, Skeppsholmen, 11149 Stockholm. ☎ **08/679-50-15.** Fax 08/611-71-55. 136 beds. 130KR ($17) per person with IYHF card, 170KR ($23) without IYHF card. Paper sheets 30KR ($4); towels 10KR ($1.35). Breakfast 45KR ($6). Maximum 5-night stay. EURO, MC, V. Closed mid-Dec to Apr 1. T-Bana: Kungsträdgården. Bus: 65 (to 6pm) to Skeppsholmen.

The fully rigged masts of this gallant tall ship are a Stockholm landmark. The vessel sailed under British, Norwegian, and Swedish flags for about half a century before permanently mooring on the island of Skeppsholmen and opening as a hostel in 1949. It's extremely popular, so arrive early to reserve a bed, especially in summer. The reception is open 7am to 2am. The rooms are closed daily 11am to 3pm for cleaning. You can buy disposable sheets, supply your own, or use a sleeping bag. There's no kitchen, laundry, or TV room, but you may watch TV across the street at the STF Vandrarhem (see below). Toilets and showers (only three for women) are in the corridor. Each room has a locker, but you must supply your own lock. The common area (and the cafe on the deck in summer) is conducive to meeting people.

Across the street is the **STF Vandrarhem/Hostel Skeppsholmen,** Västra Brobänken, Skeppsholmen, 11149 Stockholm (☎ **08/679-50-15;** fax 08/611-71-55), with 152 beds. This hostel provides more privacy than the *Chapman* and charges the same rates. Smoking isn't allowed; the curfew is at 2am. The reception desk is on the AF *Chapman.*

✪ **Columbus Hotell & Youth Hostel.** Tjärhovsgatan 11, 11621 Stockholm. ☎ **08/644-17-17.** Fax 08/702-07-64. 18 hotel units, none with bathroom; 100 hostel beds. Hotel, 480KR ($64) single; 320KR ($43) per person double; 276KR ($37) per person triple. Hostel, 310KR ($41) single; 175KR ($23) per person double; 135KR ($18) dorm bed. Breakfast 50KR ($7). Maximum 5-night stay in hostel. AE, DC, EURO, MC, V. T-Bana: Medborgarplatsen; walk 5 blocks east.

A hotel/hostel on the island of Södermalm, the Columbus is pretty and boasts a cordial staff. The hotel part consists of 18 rooms sharing a bathroom; each has a TV and phone. The hostel has rooms with two to eight beds each, lockers, and three showers for men and for women on each of the three floors. The public baths are passable but not sparkling. It has a small cafe serving beer and wine, a small kitchen, a secure baggage room, a room with a sun bed, and a summer outdoor cafe. A children's playground and an indoor pool are nearby. There's no curfew.

Hotel/Hostel *Gustaf AF Klint*. Stadsgårdskajen 153, 11645 Stockholm. ☎ **08/640-40-77** or 08/640-40-78. Fax 08/640-64-16. 32 cabins, none with bathroom. Hotel, 395KR ($53) single; 515KR ($69) double. Hostel, 140KR ($19) per person. Paper sheets 35KR ($4.65); cotton sheets 55KR ($7); towels 10KR ($1.35). Breakfast 40KR ($5). AE, DC, EURO, MC, V. T-Bana: Slussen; use the Södermalmstorg exit and take the stairs down to the riverbank; you'll see the ship to the right.

This floating hotel/hostel rigged with lights is on the riverbank across from Old Town. When the *Klint* served as a radar sounder mapping out the ocean floor, the officers lived in what's now the hotel (4 singles, 3 doubles), while the deckhands occupied what's now the hostel (10 doubles, 17 quads). The hotel is slightly more spacious than the hostel's cramped quarters; all the cabins are equipped with bunk beds. During summer, the ship's deck-top bar and cafe are open, with a lovely harbor view. Year-round, cheap dinners are served in a sometimes smoky pub.

WORTH A SPLURGE

✪ **Wellington Hotel.** Storgatan 6, 11451 Stockholm. ☎ **08/667-09-10.** Fax 08/667-12-54. 60 units, all with bathroom. TV TEL. Daily in summer and Sat–Sun year-round, 1,100KR ($147) single; 1,400KR ($187) double. Mon–Fri the rest of the year, 750KR–1,000KR ($100–$133). Rates include breakfast. AE, DC, EURO, MC, V. T-Bana: Öster-malmstorg.

Except for the special summer and weekend rates, this prize of a small hotel would far exceed budget status. Its staff is so friendly that guests often linger in the living room–like lobby chatting with them. From the comfortable rooms you can hear the soft sound of church bells on the hour. The free sauna is beautifully appointed, with a changing room, robes, towels, lotion and shampoo, shower, toilet, and sun bed. Add to that a breakfast room (with filling fare), concierge service, and two no-smoking floors. The top floors afford memorable views.

4 Great Deals on Dining

For those on a budget, meals can sometimes seem more like a chore than a delight. Food in Stockholm is priced higher than that in most other European cities, but in addition to good-value lunch specials (see below) there are a number of great budget places.

Though price limitations mean that you're unlikely to enjoy a full Swedish smörgås-bord, you can try other specialties, like *strömming* (herring), *ärtsoppa* (pea soup), eel, Swedish meatballs, dill meat fricassée, and *pytt i panna* (a simple tasty meat-and-potato hash).

If you're in Stockholm during the Christmas season, when tables are trimmed with traditional colorful holiday cutlery, be sure to sample ginger cookies and *glögg*, a potent traditional drink of fortified hot mulled wine with raisins and almonds. And don't forget to visit the Swedish pastry shops—some of the best in Europe.

Many restaurants compete for noontime midweek business with fantastic lunch specials. Most cost only 60KR to 90KR ($8 to $12), and unless otherwise noted, prices for all lunch specials here include a main course, salad, bread, and a nonalcoholic drink. Lunch is usually served 11am to 2pm (check the listings). Adjust your eating habits to take advantage of specials that make a large lunch considerably less expensive than dinner. If you don't see a daily special *(dagens rätt)* posted, ask for it. For dinner, look to pasta and pizza houses or one of a number of vegetarian restaurants. To save even more money, avoid alcohol; state control keeps prices extremely high.

It's not customary to tip in Swedish restaurants (a service fee has been incorporated into prices), but Swedes occasionally do tip at dinner for exceptional service. Even then, they simply round up the amount.

IN NORRMALM & ÖSTERMALM

Bistro Jarl. Birger Jarlsgatan 7. ☎ **08/611-76-30.** Fax 08/611-07-90. Lunch specials 60KR–80KR ($8–$11); main courses 90KR–180KR ($12–$24). AC, AE, DC, EURO, MC, V. Mon–Fri 11:30am–2:30pm and 5pm–1am, Sat 1pm–2am. T-Bana: Östermalmstorg. SWEDISH/FRENCH.

The lunch special here comes with homemade bread, a salad, and a main dish that's either meat, fish, or vegetarian. Homemade pies are available if you're still hungry after your meal. The elegant cafe has lace curtains, high ceilings, teardrop chandeliers, and linen tablecloths, and there are newspapers and backgammon for distractions. A new champagne bar was opened in 1997. Check the chalkboard menu for the day's offerings.

✪ **Café 24 Seats.** Jungfrugatan 6. ☎ **08/661-27-77.** Breakfast 30KR ($4); coffee and sandwich 29KR ($3.85); daily lunch 55KR ($7). No credit cards. Mon–Fri 9am–3pm. T-Bana: Östermalmstorg. LIGHT FARE.

This cozy place, managed by Michael and his niece, Maria, is popular among people working or living in the area. There are only 9 tables with 24 seats (hence the name) and white hanging lamps. The lunch special changes daily and may be spaghetti bolognese, fried or stewed chicken, or grilled sole—served with vegetables, bread, butter, and coffee. You may be the only non-Swede here, but if you're looking for a relaxing atmosphere this is the place to go.

Capri. Nybrogatan 15. ☎ **08/662-31-32.** Pizza 85KR ($11); pasta 95KR ($13); fish and meat dishes 145KR–200KR ($19–$27). Prices include bread, salad, and service. AC, AE, DC, EURO, MC, V. Mon–Fri 4:30pm–midnight, Sat noon–midnight, Sun 1–11pm. T-Bana: Östermalmstorg, then walk 2 blocks. ITALIAN.

Although this place also serves meat and fish, it's the extensive pasta and pizza menu, not to mention the courteous service and well-prepared dishes, that attracts budgeters. Capri's vaulted ceiling is reminiscent of Italy's Blue Grotto. If you come for dinner, look for the nightly special, usually less expensive than the regular menu.

✪ **City Lejon.** Holländargatan 8 (just off Kungsgatan, 1 block north of Hötorget Sq.). ☎ **08/23-00-80.** Meals 60KR–110KR ($8–$15); lunch specials from 50KR ($7). AE, EURO, MC. Mon–Fri 10:30am–9pm, Sat noon–6pm (lunch special Mon–Fri 10:30am–3pm). T-Bana: Hötorget. SWEDISH.

The lunch special here is one of the best values in town. This place bustles, mainly with local office workers. A continuous series of wooden doors covers the restaurant's walls, complemented by wooden tables and low-wattage stained-glass hanging lamps. The food here is good and filling, and the Wiener schnitzel and flank steak are particularly good.

Coffee House. Odengatan 45 (near Dobelnsgatan). ☎ **08/673-23-43.** Meals 16KR–58KR ($2.15–$8); lunch special 50KR ($7). No credit cards. Mon–Fri 7am–7pm (breakfast 7–10am), Sat–Sun 8am–6pm (breakfast 9–11am). T-Bana: Rådsmansgatan. LIGHT FARE.

This friendly place with a tiled floor and round tables fills with locals and the low hum of conversations. The lunch special, served 11am to closing, includes a sandwich, juice, and coffee. Quiche and large salads are also available, and good coffee or tea comes with a free refill (help yourself from the table inside the door). The Lebanese owners, the three Makdessi-Elias brothers, will make you feel most welcome. The homey atmosphere appeals to people of all ages.

Getting the Best Deal on Dining

- Note that lunch specials are large and considerably less expensive than dinner choices, so have your big meal at midday. You'll save money and fuel up for an afternoon of sightseeing.
- Always ask about a daily special *(dagens rätt)*—it may not always be posted.
- Try department-store cafeterias, pasta and pizza houses, and vegetarian restaurants for dinner—they're all great bargains.

✪ **Collage Restaurant.** Smalandsgatan 2 (at Nybrogatan, a few steps from the Royal Dramatic Theater). ☎ **08/611-31-95.** Reservations accepted. Lunch 60KR ($8); takeout lunch 53KR ($7); dinner (à la carte) about 89KR ($12). AE, DC, MC, V. Mon–Fri 11am–11pm, Sat–Sun 2pm–midnight. T-Bana: Östermalmstorg. INTERNATIONAL.

The Collage opened as a bilevel restaurant with 100 seats a few years ago and became an instant success, based on first-class food and a jolly atmosphere. During lunch on weekdays you'll hardly find a vacant seat, unless you show up at 11am sharp or make a reservation. A typical lunch menu consists of spareribs, steak, or fish, with fries and vegetables and a mixed salad. A "little menu" is offered 2 to 5pm (pasta with salad or goulash with rice) costing 40KR ($5). After 5pm, only à la carte meals are served. The walls are covered with funny signs, including one saying ST. JAMES'S GATE, HOME OF GUINNESS, 3,362 KM AWAY.

Hot WOK Cafe. Kungsgatan 44 (take the escalator down). ☎ **08/20-94-44.** Main courses 55KR–95KR ($7–$13). No credit cards. Mon–Fri 9:30am–6pm, Sat 9:30am–3pm. T-Bana: Hötorget. ASIAN.

The food is of top quality, and you won't find a seat (or at the other eight restaurants here, a real United Nations selection) unless you come before noon. It may be noisy, but it's one of the best budget choices in Stockholm. Twelve small tables face the open kitchen. The great fried noodles are 59KR ($8), the chicken surprise with rice is 69KR ($9), and the yellow prawns are 89KR ($12).

Leonardo. Sveavägen 55. ☎ **08/30-40-21.** Reservations recommended. Pizza and pasta 73KR–94KR ($10–$13); fish and meat dishes 158KR–200KR ($21–$27); lunch special (including bread, salad, espresso, and small glass of beer, juice, or soda) 69KR ($9). AE, DC, EURO, V. Mon–Fri 10:30am–11:30pm, Sat–Sun noon–11:30pm (lunch special 10:30am–2:30pm). T-Bana: Raødmansgatan, then walk half a block. Bus: 52 to Rådmansgatan. ITALIAN.

A refurbished Stockholm standard, it has gray-and-peach decor, sconces, mirrored walls, and a gleaming cappuccino machine. An authentic Italian staff and chef, a good menu, and great food are the real testaments to this trattoria's success. A special packs folks in at lunch, but to stay under budget at dinner you'll have to limit yourself to pasta and pizza (made with mozzarella and fresh tomatoes and supposedly the only oven pizza in Sweden); also take advantage of the chalkboard specials, from 69KR to 120KR ($9 to $16).

Masters Salad Bar. Vasagatan 40 (near Central Station). ☎ **08/10-23-30.** Sandwiches 15KR–35KR ($2–$4.65); salads 45KR–50KR ($6–$7); pasta dishes 45KR ($6). No credit cards. Mon–Fri 7am–7pm, Sat 9am–4pm. T-Bana: Central Station, then walk up Vasagatan and pass the red-brick post office. LIGHT FARE.

Here you'll find two tables, four chairs, and Stockholmers working or living in this busy part of town. About 90% of the food is for takeout: 35 kinds of sandwiches, 20 salads (with 5 dressings to choose from), and 6 pasta dishes. A best-seller is the quick light lunch (a sandwich or large salad, with bread and butter) for 45KR ($6). Masters is managed by a Greek family; it's very small, but the quality and variety of food are wonderful.

Örtagården (Herb Garden). Nybrogatan 31 (2nd floor). ☎ **08/662-40-51.** Reservations recommended at night. All-you-can-eat mini-smörgåsbord 70KR ($9) Mon–Fri 10:30am–5pm, 85KR ($11) Mon–Fri after 5pm and all day Sat–Sun. DC, EURO, MC, V. Mon–Fri 10:30am–9:30pm, Sat 11am–8:30pm, Sun noon–8:30pm. T-Bana: Östermalmstorg. VEGE-TARIAN.

Floral furniture, pastel-green woodwork, and a ceiling hung with glass chandeliers will have budget travelers convinced they're in the wrong place. However, Örtagården offers one of the best deals in town with its huge smörgåsbord and comfortable sur-roundings. Help yourself to the hot and cold dishes (including soup, salads, fruits, and fresh vegetables), take a seat in the pleasant dining room, and pay when you leave. Desserts cost extra but aren't expensive, and wine is served. Meat dishes are available at lunch only. At lunch and dinner a classical pianist performs. Örtagården is in the same building as the Östermalms food hall and a Chinese restaurant but with a sepa-rate entrance.

✪ **Teater Baren (Theater Bar).** Culture House, Sergels Torg 3 (2nd floor). ☎ **08/700-01-00.** Daily special 55KR ($7); salad buffet 55KR ($7); menu items 60KR–100KR ($8–$13). EURO, MC, V. Mon–Fri 11am–3pm, Sat–Sun 11am–5pm. T-Bana: T-Centralen; take the Sergels Torg exit. SWEDISH/VEGETARIAN.

This is a great place to come for lunch, for the food and the view, overlooking ani-mated Sergels Torg. Arrive before noon or after 1pm to avoid the crunch. The daily special includes a fish, meat, or vegetarian hot dish with bread, salad, soda or light beer, and coffee; if you want dessert, cookies are only 3KR (40¢) each. If you're hungry for veggies, try the outstanding salad bar. At the end of your meal, return your tray to the cart. There's really only one drawback: You have to pay 5KR (65¢) to use the toilet.

IN GAMLA STAN

Maharajah. Stora Nygatan 20. ☎ **08/21-04-04.** Main courses 59KR–99KR ($8–$13); lunch menu 50KR ($7). DC, EURO, MC, V. Mon–Fri 11am–11pm, Fri–Sat 11am–midnight, Sun 1–11pm. T-Bana: Gamla Stan. INDIAN.

A little removed from the heavily touristed areas of Gamla Stan, this is a quiet, pretty place with soft lighting and lots of woodwork. It serves standard Indian favorites—tandoori, curries, kebabs, vindaloo, and vegetarian dishes—along with a variety of wonderful breads, including nan, paratha, and chapati.

ON DJURGÅRDEN

✪ **Café Blå Porten.** Djurgårdsvägen 64. ☎ **08/662-71-62.** Meals 55KR–75KR ($7–$10). AE, DC, MC, V. Tues–Thurs 11am–9pm, Fri 11am–4:30pm, Sat–Sun 11am–5pm. Bus: 47 from Central Station. Ferry: From Slussen or Gamla Stan. LIGHT FARE.

There aren't many restaurants on this museum island, and those that are here cater almost exclusively to stranded tourists. This bohemian cafeteria-style cafe is an excep-tion, catering equally to students and art enthusiasts who visit the adjacent Liljevalch Art Gallery, where exhibits change every 12 weeks. The cafe has an inviting atmos-phere and serves soups, salads, quiche, and cold and hot meals, along with wine and beer. Sandwiches, cookies, fruit, and desserts, set on wooden tables, are also available. Café Blå Porten (it means Blue Door, and there is one) is beside the gallery, and in summer patrons spill out into the gallery's courtyard. It's particularly busy on weekends.

ON SÖDERMALM

Hannas Krog. Skanegatan 80. ☎ **08/643-82-25.** Reservations highly recommended. Main courses 85KR–165KR ($11–$22). AE, DC, EURO, MC, V. Mon–Fri 11am–3pm and 5pm–midnight, Sat–Sun 4pm–midnight. T-Bana: Medborgarplatsen. INTERNATIONAL.

On Södermalm, Stockholm's answer to New York's SoHo, Hannas Krog attracts a lively crowd. You can sit at the bar and chat with the locals and staff or opt to eat in one of the cozy dining areas. During summer, they open up the huge windows onto the street and provide outdoor seating. A second bar on the lower level has music, sometimes live; and across the street is Hannas Deli, an offshoot of the restaurant.

Strömmen. Södermalmstorg 1. ☎ **08/643-44-70.** Meals 40KR–120KR ($5–$16); lunch special 65KR ($9). AE, EURO, MC, V. Mon–Fri 7am–10pm, Sat noon–10pm, Sun noon–9pm. T-Bana: Slussen; take the Södermalmstorg exit. SWEDISH.

This is a coffee shop with a rooftop-restaurant view, and its perch above the harbor, in the freestanding blue building across the square from the Slussen T-Bana station, is one of the best in Stockholm. In addition to some of the cheapest dinner dishes in town, Strömmen serves breakfast, so if you're in the mood for an early morning walk across Gamla Stan to Södermalm, make this your goal for coffee and a roll. Lunch comes with bread, salad, and soda, coffee, or light beer, and every seat has a panoramic view.

FAST FOOD & PICNICKING

The high-quality fast-food eateries and fresh food markets around Hötorget Square are essential knowledge for budget travelers. Here you can buy picnic supplies, stop for a snack, or have a full meal.

On the south side of the square, enter through the glass doors of **Hötorgshallen** and take the escalator down to this great gourmet market. Hötorgshallen has been around since 1880 but was rebuilt in 1958; it houses 35 stands selling high-quality picnic supplies and prepared foreign foods like fresh breads, meats, fish, and cheeses. Head for the coffee bar or sample a falafel for about 30KR ($4). You can get fresh fish lunches and dinners—and sit down—at a popular spot called **Kajsas Fisk,** where the daily specials cost 55KR to 75KR ($7 to $10). By the escalator, **Piccolino Café** sells sandwiches. Hötorgshallen is open Monday to Friday 9:30am to 6pm and Saturday 9:30am to 3pm.

Fruits, vegetables, and a variety of other picnic supplies are available at the **outdoor market** on Hötorget Square itself. It's open Monday to Friday 9am to 6pm and Saturday 9am to 4pm.

The **Saluhall,** on Östermalmstorg at the corner of Nybrogatan and Humelgaørdsgatan, is the fanciest food market of the lot—and Sweden's oldest. Inside the striking brick building, nearly two dozen stalls, a few doubling as casual restaurants, offer high-quality fish, meats, cheeses, fresh produce, and Swedish specialties like biff Lindström (beef patties with capers and beets). Figure on spending 60KR to 110KR ($8 to $15). It's open Monday 10am to 6pm, Tuesday to Friday 9am to 6pm, and Saturday 9am to 3pm.

For picnic staples and general foods, try the supermarket in the basement of the **Åhléns department store,** on Drottninggatan (☎ **08/676-60-00**). Alternatively, **ICA** and **Konsum** are two of the largest supermarket chains around.

WORTH A SPLURGE

✪ **Le Bistrot de Wasahof.** Dalagatan 46 (across from Vasa Park). ☎ **08/32-34-40.** Reservations recommended. Dinner 78KR–205KR ($10–$27). AE, DC, EURO, MC, V. Mon–Sat 5pm–1am. T-Bana: Odenplan, then walk 2 blocks. SWEDISH/FRENCH/SEAFOOD/ITALIAN.

This bubbling bistro isn't tremendously above our budget and is recommended for a special night out. Just south of Odengatan, the restaurant is in an area known as Stockholm's "Off Broadway." The crowd is arty, the food tasty, and the atmosphere convivial. The paintings, from 1943, depict the life of the 18th-century Swedish musician Carl Michael Bellman. Seafood platters for one or two are available; try the oysters—they're imported from France and particularly popular. The menu changes monthly.

5 Seeing the Sights

In trying to decide what to see and do in Stockholm, keep in mind that the city's museums are busiest on weekends; most are closed Monday but stay open late on Thursday.

SIGHTSEEING SUGGESTIONS

IF YOU HAVE 1 DAY Start your day on Djurgården with a visit to the *Vasa* **Ship Museum** and the vast outdoor **Skansen folk museum.** After a picnic or a bite to eat in Café Blå Porten, in Djurgaørden, set your sights on **Gamla Stan (Old Town)** for an afternoon stroll (there are organized walking tours in summer; ask about them at the Stockholm Information Service). Take your time wandering around Stockholm's oldest streets and admiring the city's pretty port views.

IF YOU HAVE 2 DAYS Spend Day 1 as above. On Day 2, explore modern Stockholm's Norrmalm district. A visit to **Kungsträdgården** park is a must and in winter might include an ice-skating session. During summer, keep an eye out for the regularly scheduled special events. It's also easy to go from here to Kungsholmen and tour Stockholm's renowned **City Hall** or to either the **National Museum,** rich in Swedish and European art, or the **Museum of National Antiquities** and its impressive Gold Room.

IF YOU HAVE 3 DAYS Spend Days 1 and 2 as above. On Day 3, make the short trip to **Drottningholm Palace** to see the Swedish royal couple's house and gardens. Later, back in Stockholm's Old Town, compare Drottningholm with the older **Royal Palace** and visit **Storkyrkan,** Stockholm's cathedral and the oldest building in town.

IF YOU HAVE 5 DAYS Spend Days 1 to 3 as above. On Days 4 and 5, continue your museum-hopping at the **Millesgården,** the **Museum of National Antiquities,** the **National Art Museum,** and any other that might interest you. Then take an **archipelago cruise** or a trip to one of the many islands around the city.

ON DJURGÅRDEN

Many of Stockholm's best sights are clustered on Djurgården, the island that was once the king's hunting ground, east of Gamla Stan (Old Town). Beautiful, thick forests and sweeping harbor vistas gracefully combine with several well-designed attractions.

The most enjoyable way to get here in warm weather is by ferry from Gamla Stan. Buses and a trolley will also get you here; bus nos. 44 and 47 stop at the two top attractions, described below, and bus no. 69 will take you to the tip of the island and other attractions. It's also fun to take just for the inexpensive "unguided tour" it provides.

✪ **Vasamuseet (*Vasa* Museum).** Galärvet, Djurgården. ☎ **08/666-48-00.** Fax 08/666-48-88. Admission 50KR ($7) adults, 35KR ($4.65) students, 10KR ($1.35) ages 7–15; free for age 6 and under. MC, V. June 10–Aug 20 daily 9:30am–7pm; Aug 21–June 9 Thurs–Tues 10am–5pm, Wed 10am–8pm. Closed Jan 1, May 1, Dec 23–25, and Dec 31. Ferry: From Slussen (on Södermalm). Trolley: 7, departing in summer and on weekends year-round across from the Royal Dramatic Theater. Bus: 44, 47, or 69.

Getting the Best Deal on Sightseeing

- Ask about the discounted admission prices that are often available for students and seniors.
- Be aware that the Museum of Medieval Stockholm is free every late Wednesday afternoon and the Museum of Modern Art and Museum of Photography (at the same address) are half price on Thursday.
- Getting lost in Gamla Stan's timeless maze of car-free streets is one of Stockholm's greatest pleasures—and it's free.

When the warship *Vasa* set sail on its maiden voyage in August 1628, it was destined to become the pride of the Swedish fleet. But even before it reached the mouth of Stockholm harbor, the 64-cannon man-o'-war caught a sudden gust of wind and sank. Forgotten for centuries, the boat was discovered in 1956 by marine archaeologist Anders Franzén. Today this well-preserved wooden vessel is Stockholm's most frequently visited attraction.

It took 5 years and advanced technology to raise the fragile ship intact, but in 1961 the *Vasa* was reclaimed and placed in a temporary building. In 1988 it was moved into a stunning $35-million climate-controlled museum. Be sure to see the carvings on the bow and stern and the life-size replica of the ship's interior. An exhibit called "The Sailing Ship" displays one of the original six sails—they're the oldest existing sails in the world—and you can now view two of the original masts and two copies, along with the rigging. Both children and adults love the computer area, where they can try their hand at constructing a more stable version of the *Vasa*. Catch the 25-minute film about the warship, shown every hour on the hour. The museum has a good cafe, open daily 11am to 7pm.

✪ **Skansen.** Djurgården. ☎ **08/442-80-00.** Fax 08/442-82-80. Admission 30KR–55KR ($4–$7), depending on time of year and day of week; free for age 6 and under. Museum grounds, Jan–Feb and Nov–Dec daily 9am–4pm; Mar–Apr and Sept–Oct daily 9am–5pm; May–Aug daily 9am–10pm. Ferry: From Slussen (on Södermalm). Tram: 7, departing in summer and on weekends year-round across from the Royal Dramatic Theater. Bus: 44 or 47.

Founded in 1891, this wonderful 75-acre outdoor museum is home to over 150 buildings from the 16th to the early 20th centuries—it's a Swedish version of America's Colonial Williamsburg, displaying traditional Nordic log cabins and native stone houses in their original settings. Weather-beaten and imperfect, yet thoroughly charming, many of the buildings were transported from locations all across Sweden. Some cottages (rural dwellings and 18th-century town houses) maintain their original interiors, including painted wooden walls, fireplaces, spinning wheels, plates, and assorted folk decor. Craftspeople, using traditional tools and methods, demonstrate the former ways of farming, metalworking, typography, bookbinding, and 15 other trades.

The museum's buildings are interesting in and of themselves, but Skansen's real success is due to its peaceful surroundings on a naturally wooded peninsula. In addition, there's a particularly endearing zoo.

Restaurants (including Tre Byttor, which specializes in foods from olden times) and food stands are scattered throughout the area, but if the weather is nice it's fun to pack your own lunch and find a welcoming spot for a picnic. In summer, try your foot at

Stockholm

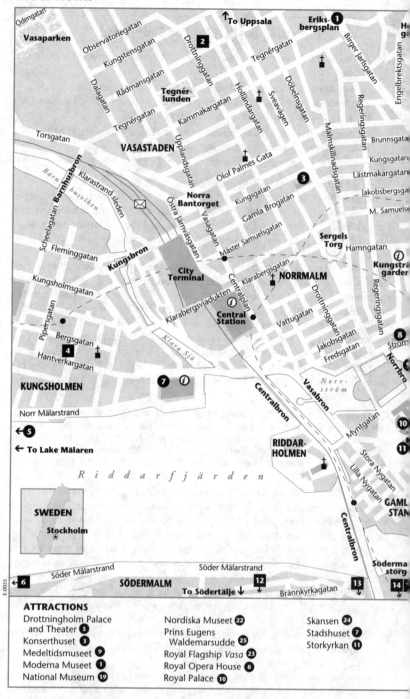

ATTRACTIONS

Drottningholm Palace
and Theater ⑤
Konserthuset ③
Medeltidsmuseet ⑨
Moderna Museet ①
National Museum ⑲

Nordiska Museet ㉒
Prins Eugens
Waldemarsudde ㉕
Royal Flagship *Vasa* ㉓
Royal Opera House ⑧
Royal Palace ⑩

Skansen ㉔
Stadshuset ⑦
Storkyrkan ⑪

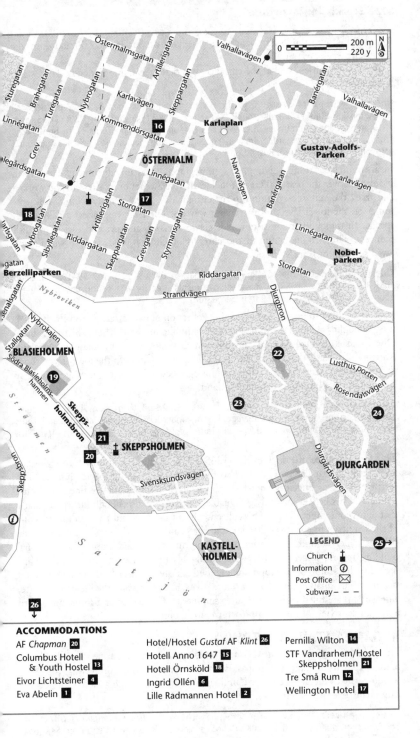

ACCOMMODATIONS

AF *Chapman* 20

Columbus Hotell
& Youth Hostel 13

Eivor Lichtsteiner 4

Eva Abelin 1

Hotel/Hostel *Gustaf* AF *Klint* 26

Hotell Anno 1647 15

Hotell Örnsköld 18

Ingrid Ollén 6

Lille Radmannen Hotel 2

Pernilla Wilton 14

STF Vandrarhem/Hostel
Skeppsholmen 21

Tre Små Rum 12

Wellington Hotel 17

folk dancing with the locals. Dances are scheduled on Sunday at 2:30 and 4pm, the rest of the week at 7pm.

A map of Skansen, sold at the entrance, will definitely come in handy. There's also a gift shop.

Nordiska Museet (Museum of Nordic History). Djurgårdsvägen 6–16. ☎ **08/666-46-00.** Admission 60KR ($8) adults, 40KR ($5) seniors, 30KR ($4) students, 10KR ($1.35) ages 7–15, free for age 6 and under. Tues–Wed and Fri–Sun 11am–5pm, Thurs 11am–8pm. Ferry: From Gamla Stan to Djurgården. Trolley: 7, departing in summer and on weekends year-round across from Norrmalmstorg. Bus: 47 or 69.

In an impressive stone building, this ethnographic museum documents changes in Nordic life over the past 500 years. You'll learn how Swedes lived, dressed, and worked and track the culture's evolution to the current day. Start with the Nordic folk costumes on the lower level and work your way up. The large cafe offers a daily lunch special. In the children's museum, kids get to dress up and pretend they're Swedish pioneers. The striking statue in the entry is of Gustav Wasa, by the well-known Swedish sculptor Carl Milles.

Thielska Galleriet (Thiel Gallery). Sjotullsbacken 6–8. ☎ **08/662-58-84.** Admission 40KR ($5.35) adults, 20KR ($2.65) seniors/students, free for age 6 and under. Mon–Sat noon–4pm, Sun 1–4pm. Bus: 69 from Sergelstorg.

Built as a gallery to house the burgeoning collection of banker/art patron Ernst Thiel, it was bought by Sweden and opened to the public in 1924, when Thiel went bust. One room is devoted to Carl Larsson, and there are works by Gauguin, Vuillard, Anders Zorn, Carl Wilhelmson, and Ernst Josephson. Climb to the tower room to see the two dozen Munchs and a fine archipelago view. On the grounds are works by Rodin and the Norwegian Gustav Vigeland.

Waldemarsudde. Prins Eugen's Väg 6. ☎ **08/662-28-00.** Admission 50KR ($7) adults, 30KR ($4) seniors/students, free for age 15 and under. MC, V. June–Aug Tues and Thurs 11am–5pm and 5–8pm, Wed and Fri–Sun 11am–5pm; Sept–May Tues–Sun 11am–4pm. Bus: 47.

This former palace of Prince Eugen (1865–1947) is known not only for its glorious architecture and palatial view but also for the artworks of the prince himself. The "artist prince," as Eugen is known, is said to have been among the finest landscape painters of his generation (this is arguable). The prince also bought art, particularly that of his contemporaries, and his collection of turn-of-the-century Swedish art is one of the country's finest; this collection and the prince's own work are exhibited in the palace's gallery annex. The principal rooms on the ground floor of the original building remain largely as they were during his life, while the two upper floors, including his studio on the top floor, are used mainly for special exhibits, which are a big draw. The small house adjacent to the palace has exhibits on the life of the prince. The gardens are filled with flowers and sculpture by Carl Milles and Rodin and afford a magnificent view of the sea approach to Stockholm.

IN GAMLA STAN (OLD TOWN)

Pretty shades of pastel separate the squat buildings along cobblestone streets in Gamla Stan. Exposed drainpipes run past wooden storm shutters protecting first-floor windows. Black metal streetlamps illuminate storefronts, and metal hooks for hoisting cargo hang over garret windows.

Medeltidsmuseet (Museum of Medieval Stockholm). Strömparterren. ☎ **08/20-61-68.** Admission 30KR ($4) adults, 20KR ($2.65) seniors/students age 18 and over, 5KR (65¢) ages 7–17, free for age 6 and under. Free for everyone late Wed afternoon. AE, MC, V.

July–Aug Tues–Thurs 11am–6pm, Fri–Mon 11am–4pm; Sept–June Tues and Thurs–Sun 11am–4pm, Wed 11am–6pm. T-Bana: Kungsträdgården or Gamla Stan, then go down the stairs in the middle of Norrebro, the bridge leading to Gamla Stan (or Norrmalm, depending on which way you're headed). Bus: 62 or 43.

Digging for a garage beneath the Parliament Building led to surprising archaeological finds and the creation of this museum (a recipient of the European Museum of the Year award), which shelters part of the city wall from around 1530 and a cemetery wall from around 1300, as well as myriad artifacts from 15th-century Stockholm. Particularly impressive are the vaulted passage leading from the entrance into the medieval city; an imaginative exhibit on spiritual life (you'll swear you're in a medieval cloister, with brick flooring, limestone pillars, and sandstone capitals); the *Riddarholm* ship (ca. 1520), excavated in 1930; and the eerie Gallows Hill, which reveals the way justice used to hold sway here. Plenty of skulls are displayed, many with a hole left by an arrow from a crossbow. A lot of texts are in English as well as Swedish.

Stockholms Slott (Royal Palace). Off Skeppsbron. ☎ **08/587-71-00.** Admission 50KR ($7) adults, 25KR ($3.35) students, free for age 6 and under. AE, MC, V. June–Aug daily 10am–1pm; Sept–May Tues–Sun noon–3pm. T-Bana: Gamla Stan.

A royal residence has stood on this spot for more than 700 years, and the existing palace, rebuilt between 1697 and 1754, reflects a time when Sweden flourished as one of Europe's major powers. Encompassing 608 rooms, it's used by the Swedish king for ceremonial tasks and state functions. The complex is huge and, though the massive stone facade is somewhat uninspired, the 18th-century **Royal Apartments** are grand, with flamboyantly painted ceilings, chandeliers, tapestries, and other royal riches on permanent display. (The apartments can close without notice for special occasions.)

Be sure to visit the **Royal Armory** (separate entrance and admission of 40KR/$5) to see the ceremonial armor for horses and riders, along with royal finery, including coronation robes and wedding costumes fit for a king (or queen), as well as the royal coaches (anyone who loves horses will be thrilled by a number of these exhibits). Forgo the **Royal Treasury** (separate entrance and admission) unless you have a thing for baubles; there are many stairs to maneuver for only two fairly small rooms.

At noon (1pm on Sunday) you can see the **Changing of the Guard** (free admission) in the palace courtyard. In summer, the spectacle includes the guards' parade and music.

Storkyrkan (Stockholm Cathedral). Trångsund (next to the Royal Palace). ☎ **08/723-30-00.** Cathedral, 10KR ($1.35) May–Sept, free the rest of the year; concerts, free–180KR ($24). Daily 9am–4pm (to 6pm in summer). T-Bana: Gamla Stan.

Founded in the 13th century, this church has seen some of Sweden's most important religious ceremonies, including coronations and royal marriages. As the oldest building in Stockholm still used for its original purpose, it bears testimony to the city's changing past. Every Saturday at 1pm and Sunday once or twice a month, concerts featuring the church's huge 18th-century organ are given here.

ON KUNGSHOLMEN

✪ **Stadshuset (City Hall).** Hantverksgatan 1. ☎ **08/5082-9095.** Stadshuset, 40KR ($5) adults, free for age 12 and under. Tower, 15KR ($2) adults, free for children. Tours, June–Aug daily at 10am, 11am, noon, and 2pm; Sept daily at 10am, noon, and 2pm; the rest of the year, daily at 10am and noon. Tower visits, May–Sept daily 10am–4:30pm (closed Oct–Apr). T-Bana: Rådhuset.

Stockholm's landmark City Hall is home to the annual Nobel Prize banquet and may be visited only by guided tour. The highlight is undoubtedly the **Golden Hall,** lavishly decorated with over 19 million 23-karat-gold tiles. Dinners honoring Nobel

Special & Free Events

The June **Midsummer Celebration** falls on the Friday nearest to the longest day of the year. Special events, most free, include folk music and dancing and fill the city's parks and other outdoor spaces. The 10-day **Stockholm Water Festival** in early August celebrates the element that makes Stockholm such a lovely city, where swimming and fishing in the center of town are longstanding traditions. Festivities include live entertainment, music, dancing, sporting events, fireworks, the world's largest crayfish festival, and the awarding of the Stockholm Water Prize—$150,000 in cash that goes to an individual or organization that has made an outstanding contribution to water conservation.

During summer, Norrmalm's park, **Kungsträdgården,** adjacent to Sweden House, comes alive almost daily with classical music concerts, rock bands, theater performances, and the like. During winter, an outdoor ice rink opens its gates here, providing some of the best inner-city skating anywhere. Summer also means frequent **free and almost-free concerts** in other parts of Stockholm. Folk dancing is performed Monday to Saturday evening and Sunday afternoon at the Skansen outdoor museum. Parkteatern (the Parks Theater) provides free open-air performances in the city's parks throughout summer.

The exciting week-long **Stockholm Open tennis championships** are held the last week of October or the first week of November in the Globe Arena. The **Nobel Prizes,** named after the Swedish inventor of dynamite, Alfred Nobel, are awarded on December 10 for excellence in physics, chemistry, medicine, literature, and economics.

Lucia, the festival of lights, is celebrated on December 13, the shortest day (and longest night) of the year. This is one of the most popular and colorful of all Swedish festivals, designed to "brighten up" an otherwise dark period. The festivities continue on the nearest Sunday, when a Lucia Queen is crowned with candles during a ceremony in Skansen. Concerts are held throughout the city from morning to night.

Finally, few locals miss the **Christmas Markets,** beginning 4 weeks before the holiday and held daily in the squares of Gamla Stan (Old Town) and every Sunday (on a much larger scale) in Skansen. Stalls are filled, selling handcrafts, gifts and other seasonal items, and traditional foods such as smoked reindeer meat, cloudberry jam, ginger cookies, and hot *glögg.*

Prize winners were originally held in this room, but swelling guest lists have forced the party to relocate to the even-larger **Blue Hall.** Marble floors, stone columns, and Gothic motifs make City Hall look and feel much older than its 70 years. In summer you may climb to the top of the distinctive tower, topped by three gleaming crowns.

IN NORRMALM & ÖSTERMALM

National Museum. Blasieholmskajen (at the foot of the bridge to Skeppsholmen). ☎ **08/666-42-50.** Admission 60KR ($8) adults, 40KR ($5) seniors/students, free for age 17 and under. AE, MC, V. Tues 11am–8pm, Wed–Sun 11am–5pm. T-Bana: Kungsträdgården.

Though it stocks masterpieces by stars like Rembrandt, Rubens, El Greco, and Renoir, this pleasant 206-year-old museum isn't labyrinthine like Paris's Louvre. There are English-language tours in summer, and the collection is well marked (in Swedish and English) and nicely displayed. Be sure to visit the third-floor gallery with mid-19th- to mid-20th-century Swedish painters, like Anders Zorn, Carl Larsson, and

Ernst Josephson. The third floor also houses works by Renoir, Degas, Rodin, and Corot, along with 16th- and 17th-century French, Italian, Flemish, and Dutch painters. The second-floor Department of Applied Arts features over 28,000 pieces of porcelain, glassware, silverwork, and jewelry.

✪ **Historiska Museet (Museum of National Antiquities).** Narvavägen 13–17. ☎ **08/783-94-00.** Admission 60KR ($8) adults, 50KR ($7) seniors/students, 30KR ($4) ages 7–15, free for age 6 and under. Tues–Wed and Fri–Sun noon–5pm, Thurs noon–8pm. T-Bana: Östermalmstorg. Bus: 44, 47, 56, or 69.

If you come for no other reason than to view the opulent **Gold Room,** a spiral gallery of gold and silver treasures, some dating from the 5th century—including the Dune Hoard, the largest medieval treasure in Scandinavia, consisting of 150 items that were probably buried in A.D. 1361—a visit here would be worthwhile. (Don't miss the 14th-century gold buckle the size of a small pizza.) The collection, complementing that of the Nordic Museum, shows daily life from the dawn of time to the Middle Ages.

Moderna Museet (Museum of Modern Art). Skeppsholmen. ☎ **08/666-42-50.** Admission 50KR ($7) adults, 30KR ($4) seniors/students, free for age 15 and under. Half price for everyone on Thurs. Tues–Thurs noon–7pm, Fri–Sun noon–5pm. T-Bana: Kungsträdgården. Bus: 65 to Skeppsholmen.

Conveniently open late three times a week, the Museum of Modern Art is an excellent choice for evening sightseeing, especially on Thursday, when the admission is half price (though, of course, there will be crowds). Housed in an impressive new building on the island of Skeppsholmen, the museum shows changing exhibits of Swedish and international contemporary art, along with works from the outstanding museum collections.

✪ **Hallwylska Museet (Hallwyl Museum).** Hamngatan 4. ☎ **08/666-44-99.** Admission 60KR ($8) adults, 20KR ($2.65) students, free for age 7 and under. AE, V. Tues–Sun noon–3pm; English-language tour Tues and Sun at 1pm. T-Bana: Kungsträdgården.

Stockholm's most eccentric museum is a magnificent turn-of-the-century residence filled with 70 years' worth of passionate collecting by Countess Wilhelmina von Hallwyl. On display is everything from buttons to Dutch and Swedish paintings, European china and silver, umbrellas, and weapons. The Hallwyls, who lived here from 1898 to 1930, had three daughters, one of whom, Ellen, became a sculptor and studied with Carl Milles; they had a modern bathroom before the king did. Admission to the house is by 1-hour guided tour only (tours are given on the hour). Arrive early—they book quickly.

ON SÖDERMALM
Katarina Elevator. Södermalmstorg, Slussen. Admission 10KR ($1.35) adults, free for age 6 and under. Mon–Sat 7:30am–10pm, Sun and holidays 10am–10pm. T-Bana: Slussen.

The Katarina Elevator itself isn't the attraction—it's the seven-story view it provides. Just over the bridge from Gamla Stan, the elevator lifts you to a perch high above the port. If you're feeling strong, take the stairs up the cliff behind the elevator, but don't miss this spectacular view of Stockholm.

ON LIDINGÖ
✪ **Millesgården.** Carl Milles Väg 2. ☎ **08/731-50-60.** Admission 50KR ($7) adults, 35KR ($4.65) seniors/students, 15KR ($2) ages 7–16, free for age 6 and under. May–Sept daily 10am–5pm; Oct–Apr Tues–Sun noon–4pm. T-Bana: Ropsten, then take a bus to Torsvik (pedestrians cannot cross the bridge on foot); from here, walk about 8 minutes, following the signs to the Millesgården (the entire trip will take about 40 minutes).

One of the greatest Swedish artists, sculptor Carl Milles (1875–1955) lived and worked in the United States from 1931 to 1951, when he returned to Stockholm to design and build a garden on a hill beside his home on Lidingö. The Millesgården is a little time-consuming to get to, but those who are eager enough will be rewarded with the opportunity to gaze at the artist's most important works, including the monumental *Hand of God,* overlooking all of Stockholm. In Milles's house, also open to the public, is his unique collection of medieval and Renaissance art and of art objects from ancient Rome and Greece.

PARKS & GARDENS

Parks are one of Stockholm's loveliest assets, and many have already been mentioned. Bring a picnic to **Skansen;** the wooded peninsula of **Djurg Waldemarsudde ården** and the **Millesgården** on the island of Lidingö are also excellent strolling grounds, as is the entire island of **Skeppsholmen.** In Norrmalm, take your lunch to the **Kungsträdgården,** a bustling urban park and the city's summer meeting place.

Tanto Lunden, with tiny cottages and carefully tended gardens near the city center, was created in 1919 so that city workers who couldn't afford a country home could still benefit from country living. The one-room cottages, which are rented from the city for 50 years, look more like dollhouses, with their equally tiny yards filled with birdhouses and compost heaps. To get here, take bus no. 43 or the T-Bana to Zinkensdamm. Zinkens Väg, where you'll find the Zinkensdamm Hostel and Hotel, dead-ends into Tanto Lunden; climb the wooden steps and enter a world in miniature. Don't overlook the delightful house at no. 69.

ORGANIZED TOURS

City Sightseeing (☎ 08/24-04-70) operates 3-hour bus tours of Stockholm year-round, leaving daily from the Opera House at 2pm, and also at 5pm mid-April to early October. The cost is 250KR ($33) adults and half price for ages 6 to 11. From early June to early August, 1-hour tours also leave from the Opera House at 10 and 11am, noon, and 2 and 3pm; the cost is 80KR ($11) adults and half price for ages 6 to 11. Ask about the combination excursions that include walking, touring by bus, and/or taking a boat.

Stockholm Sightseeing (☎ 08/24-04-70) provides boat tours of the city, departing from Strömkajen, in front of the Grand Hotel. (Locals insist that the best way to explore their city is by boat.) Get tickets at the kiosk topped with yellow flags with a red "S" on them. The company's "Under the Bridges of Stockholm" tour takes 2 hours and costs 130KR ($17) adults and half price for ages 6 to 15; it's offered mid-April to mid-December. The hour-long "Royal Canal Tour" runs mid-May to early September for 80KR ($11).

Strömma Sightseeing (☎ 08/23-33-75) offers a "Great Archipelago Boat Tour" with a guide from early June to mid-August at 65KR ($9) adults and half price for ages 6 to 11, except for evening cruises. The boat leaves from Nybroplan, in front of the Royal Dramatic Theater.

6 Shopping

A whopping 25% goods tax makes shopping in Sweden expensive, and you can get most items at home for less money. On the positive side, Swedish stores usually stock items of the highest quality. Favorite buys include crystal, clothing, and Scandinavian-design furniture.

Many stores offer **tax rebates** to visitors spending over 200KR ($27). When you make your purchase, ask the retailer for a Tax Free Check (valid for 1 month) and leave your purchase sealed until you leave the country. At any border crossing on your way out of Sweden (or at repayment centers in Denmark, Finland, or Norway), show both the check (to which you've added your name, address, and passport number) and the purchase to an official at the tax-free desk. You'll get a cash refund of about 16% to 18% in U.S. dollars (or any of seven other currencies) after the service charge has been deducted (remember not to check the purchase in your luggage until after you have received the refund). At Arlanda Airport there are separate booths for VAT purchases that are to be checked as baggage and those that are to be carried on the plane, so be sure to get in the right line. Also be sure to allow enough time before your flight in case there's a crowd. For more information, call ☎ **024/74-17-41.**

BEST BUYS

For the best shopping and window-shopping, stroll along the streets of **Gamla Stan** (especially **Västerlånggatan**), filled with boutiques, art galleries, and jewelry stores. Similarly winsome shops and galleries may be found along the **Hornsgats-Puckeln** (the Hornsgatan-Hunchback, a reference to the shape of the street), on **Södermalm.** Other streets that tempt browsing are **Hamngatan, Birger Jarlsgatan, Biblioteks-gatan,** and **Kungsgatan,** all in **Norrmalm.**

NK (Nordiska Kompaniet), Hamngatan 18–20 (☎ 08/762-80-00; T-Bana: Kungsträdgården), across from Sweden House, is the Harrods of Stockholm. The stunning department store, now actually an assortment of independent shops under one roof, is built around a four-story atrium, and the quality merchandise is beautifully displayed. There are several cafes. The ground-level information desk is quite helpful. For more reasonable prices, visit the **Åhléns City department store** (pronounced like Orleans), a block from Central Station at Klarabergsgatan 50 (☎ 08/676-60-00; T-Bana: Centralen). This is a good place to buy Swedish-designed crystal, ceramics, and gift items (all on the ground floor).

Gallerian, at Hamngatan 37 (T-Bana: Kungsträdgården), is a centrally located mall where you can buy luggage and day packs, toys, cheap postcards, and other items. Its upscale cousin, **Sturegallerian,** is at Stureplan 4 (T-Bana: Östermalmstorg). On Södermalm, near the Medborgarplatsen T-Bana station, is a fairly new mall called **Söderhallarna,** which consists of two buildings, the Saluhallen and the Björkhallen. It's the perfect place for those who like to combine shopping with dining out and movie-going.

The **Swedish Institute Bookshop,** on the second floor of Sweden House, Hamngatan 27 (☎ 08/789-20-00; T-Bana: Kungsträdgården), has a wealth of books about the art and culture of Sweden, CDs, cassettes, records, and children's books, including many by Astrid Lindgren. For toys, shop at **Stor & Liten,** in the Gallerian shopping center, Hamngatan 37 (☎ 08/23-13-90; T-Bana: Kungsträdgården), and **Leka Samman,** on Södermalm at Hornsgatan 50A (☎ 08/714-96-00; T-Bana: Hötorget).

For famous Swedish crystal and porcelain, visit **Duka,** at the Consert House, Kungsgatan 41, at Sveavägen (☎ 08/20-60-41; T-Bana: Hötorget). For handcrafts, including textiles, yarns, baskets, rugs, pottery, and items in wood and metal, browse through **Svensk Hemslöjd,** Sveavägen 44 (☎ 08/23-21-15; T-Bana: Hötorget), operated by the Swedish Handicraft Society.

If Scandinavian-design furniture, lamps, glass, ceramics, and the like intrigue you, don't miss **IKEA,** Kungens Kurva (☎ 08/744-83-00; T-Bana: Skärholmen). The store is 25 minutes from the city center and is served by a special free bus that leaves from Regeringsgatan 13 (opposite Fritzes bookshop) Monday to Friday 11am to 5pm (returning hourly on the half hour). The store doesn't accept credit cards.

7 Stockholm After Dark

Stockholm's "living arts" are well supported with state funds. As a result, the price of high-quality "serious" entertainment is extremely reasonable. Moreover, good public funding means that performing-arts houses don't have to rely on a conservative public—they can experiment with new and interesting ideas.

The city's concert hall, opera house, and theaters are closed in summer, but three deals are offered in their place. **Free open-air park performances** by Parkteatern (the Parks Theater) begin in June and continue throughout summer; **Sommarnättskonserterna (Summer Night Concerts),** on the main staircase of the National Museum, start in July and run to the end of August; and **folk dancing** at Skansen takes place Monday to Saturday at 7pm.

Also in summer, **jazz cruises** provide an exhilarating way to experience Stockholm from the water while enjoying upbeat entertainment under the stars.

Churches—the cathedral, on Gamla Stan; Jacob's Church, near the Opera House; and Hedvig Eleonora, in Östermalm, to name a few—often host free evening (and afternoon) concerts. Check the listings under "Music" in *Stockholm This Week* or look for announcements posted in front of individual churches.

On the late-night front, all is well. The nightlife in what once was a fairly staid capital has undergone a major change over the last decade or so. Today, late-nighters can engage in the city's thriving cafe culture, listen to live rock and jazz, and dance into the wee hours—usually at Kungsträdgården or on Gamla Stan or Södermalm.

Always check *Stockholm This Week* and local newspapers (especially *Dagens Nyheter* Thursday to Sunday) for details on upcoming events.

THE PERFORMING ARTS

Almost every capital has its national houses, where the biggest-budgeted performances are staged. But it's the proliferation of "alternative" theater and music that divides cities with great culture from all the rest. Stockholm is one such city, and you should try not to pass up an opportunity to visit one of its smaller playhouses. Check *Stockholm This Week* for a full list of current performances. Not many theaters are open in summer, but you'll find plenty of concerts.

The ✪ **Filharmonikerna i Konserthuset (Stockholm Concert Hall),** Hötorget 8 (☎ **08/786-02-00;** fax 08/20-05-48 for information, 08/10-21-10 for the box office; T-Bana: Hötorget), is home to the Royal Stockholm Philharmonic Orchestra, and performances are usually on Wednesday, Thursday, and Saturday from August to May, while touring companies sometimes light up the stage on other days throughout the year. Carl Milles's sculpture *Orpheus* is outside the building. The box office is open Monday to Friday noon to 6pm and Saturday 11am to 3pm. Tickets run 60KR to 350KR ($8 to $47); students/seniors get a 15% discount.

Berwaldhallen (Berwald Concert Hall), Strandvägen 69 (☎ **08/784-18-00;** Bus: 69, 56, or 76), an award-winning hexagonal structure built into a granite hillside, is home to the Stockholm Radio Symphony Orchestra and the Swedish Radio Choir. Call or check the entertainment section of local papers for a schedule and times for concerts. The box office, at Oxenstiernsgatan 20, is open Monday to Friday 11am to 6pm. Tickets run 40KR to 310KR ($5 to $41).

The **Engelska Teatern (English Theater Company),** Nybrogatan 35 (☎ **08/662-37-32;** T-Bana: Östermalmstorg), stages productions in English throughout the city. The office is open Monday to Friday 10am to 5pm; call for specific information. Tickets are 150KR to 200KR ($20 to $27). The **Kungliga Dramatiska Teatern (Royal Dramatic Theater),** on Nybroplan (☎ **08/667-06-80;** T-Bana:

Östermalmstorg), is one of the great playhouses of Europe. The plays performed here are almost exclusively in Swedish (with the exception of touring companies), but that shouldn't deter you. During summer the theater offers a daily guided tour for 25KR ($3.35) at 3pm; the rest of the year, at 5:30pm on Saturday only. It's usually closed for 2 weeks in summer. The box office is open Monday noon to 6pm, Tuesday to Saturday noon to 7pm, and Sunday noon to 4pm. Tickets run 90KR to 225KR ($12 to $30) for the large stage, 195KR ($26) for the small stage; age 16 and under pay half price; ages 20 to 26 and seniors get a 10% discount, but only on Sunday.

The **Operan (Royal Opera House)**, Gustav Adolfs Torg (☎ **08/24-82-40;** T-Bana: Kungsträdgården), built in 1898, houses the Royal Swedish Opera and the Royal Swedish Ballet. Most of the operas performed here are in the original language, with an emphasis on popular works like *La Traviata, Madame Butterfly,* and *Aïda.* The Royal Ballet presents classics like *The Nutcracker, Don Quixote,* and *Romeo and Juliet* as well as contemporary works. The season runs August to June. Call or visit the box office for a current schedule. The box office is open Monday to Friday noon to 7:30pm (to 6pm when no performance is scheduled) and Saturday noon to 3pm (later on performance days). Tickets run 100KR to 350KR ($13 to $47), with a 20% discount for students; there are some "listening seats" (no view, but not standing room) for 30KR ($4).

LIVE-MUSIC CLUBS

Stampen, Stora Nygatan 5 (☎ **08/20-57-93** or 08/20-57-94; T-Bana: Gamla Stan), a Stockholm tradition since 1968, is the city's lively center for jazz, soul, funk, blues, and rock, with two bands performing nightly. The upstairs stage is beneath a ceiling sporting a contra bass, a Christmas tree, a wooden sleigh, and other whimsical decor. The second stage is in the more subdued downstairs room where you can enjoy the music while dancing. Like many of the city's other live-music clubs, Stampen is in Gamla Stan. It's open Monday to Thursday 8pm to 1am, Friday and Saturday 8pm to 2am, and Sunday 1pm to 5am. Cover ranges from 60KR to 110KR ($8 to $15).

Engelen, Kornhamnstorg 59B (☎ **08/20-10-92;** fax 08/10-07-50; T-Bana: Gamla Stan), provides a stage for local bands nightly. The live music is upstairs 8:30pm to midnight, while dance discs spin below until 3am in Kolingen. The early to mid-20s crowd arrives before 10pm, especially on weekends, when it's packed. The cover usually isn't enforced until 9pm, so it pays in more ways than one to come early. It's open daily 5pm to 3am. The cover ranges from none (free before 9pm) to 100KR ($13).

Stockholm's futuristic **Globen (Globe Arena),** Johanneshov (☎ **08/725-10-00** for information, or 08/600-34-00 for the box office; T-Bana: Globen), measures 279 feet high by 361 feet wide and seats 16,000. It has hosted stars like Bruce Springsteen, Diana Ross, Liza Minnelli, and Luciano Pavarotti. If you're not a megaconcert fan, you might enjoy taking in an ice-hockey game here. The box office is open in summer, Monday to Friday 10am to 4pm; in winter, Monday to Friday 10am to 6pm and Saturday 10am to 3pm. Tickets run 240KR to 350KR ($32 to $47) for concerts and about 100KR ($13) for ice hockey.

In a house dating from 1769, **Kaos,** Stora Nygatan 21 (☎ **08/20-58-86;** fax 08/791-88-33; T-Bana: Gamla Stan), has been around for about 30 years and claims to be the oldest music club in Sweden. Visually and musically, there's definitely a sense of walking into the 1960s when you enter. The informal cafe/club has live music nightly. Sunday from 9pm on is dedicated to the blues, Wednesday is for boogie-woogie, and a free jam session is held at 2pm Saturday and Sunday. Several nights, especially on weekends, an additional stage is opened downstairs in the vaulted cellar, where a second band plays. There's no cover charge Sunday to Thursday and Friday and Saturday before 7:30pm; it's 15KR to 50KR ($2 to $7) Friday and Saturday after 7:30pm.

BARS

Because of the astronomical price of alcohol, most customers nurse their drinks for a long time and understanding waiters don't hurry you. For budget visitors, even a short hop to the local watering hole must be considered a splurge. With that in mind, here are some favorites:

The ◆ **Black & Brown Inn,** Hornsgatan 50B, on Södermalm (☎ **08/644-82-80;** T-Bana: Mariatorget), is the place to come when you're in the mood to sample many kinds of beer. Scottish and Irish music and classic hits play constantly in this landmark tavern. Fish-and-chips, burgers, and sausage with coleslaw and chips complement the beers. Prices are discounted 30% during happy hour (from opening to 7pm). It's open Monday to Wednesday 4pm to midnight, Thursday 4pm to 1am, Friday and Saturday 3pm to 1am, and Sunday 2 to 11pm.

Bakfickan (Back Pocket Bar), Operakällaren, Kungsträdgården (☎ **08/20-77-45;** T-Bana: Kungsträdgården), is a well-kept secret (from visitors anyway) that's as tiny as its name implies. Patrons sit around the bar (where service is quickest) or at bar stools along the tiled walls. The quietest time is 2 to 5pm. Good food is available all day and includes dishes like salmon or venison served with vegetables and bread. It's open Monday to Saturday 11:30am to midnight.

You'll have to fight local artists and journalists for a seat at the bar of Stockholm's oldest pub, **Tennstopet,** Dalagatan 50 (☎ **08/32-25-18;** T-Bana: Odenplan), with a bright red awning and equally red decor inside. There's a dart room in back and a couple of cozy tables in between it and the crowded bar area. It's open Monday to Thursday 3pm to 1am, Friday 3pm to 3am, Saturday 1pm to 3am, and Sunday 1pm to 1am.

A GAY & LESBIAN BAR/DISCO

Hus 1, Sveavägen 57 (☎ **08/30-83-38;** T-Bana: Rådmansgatan; Bus: 52), is a casual place housed in Stockholm's Gay Center (see the "Networks & Resources" box, earlier in this chapter), with soft lights and soft music. If you're hungry, there's plenty to eat: burgers, sandwiches, fish-and-chips, *pytt i panna* (Swedish stew), and steak, along with a daily pasta special. Food is served Sunday to Thursday 6 to 11pm and Friday and Saturday 6pm to midnight. Hus 1 also operates Wednesday to Saturday as the largest gay disco in the Scandinavian countries. Half a block from the Rådmansgatan T-Bana station on a pretty tree-lined street, it's open Monday to Saturday 6pm to 3am and Sunday 6pm to midnight. Admission of 60KR ($8) is charged Friday and Saturday.

DANCE CLUBS

Most of Stockholm's dance clubs are open for dinner; then there's a lull for a few hours before the diehards arrive around midnight. The nature of this scene requires a constant flow of new places, so ask around and check the listings in newspapers and magazines for the latest.

Café Opera, on Kungsträdgården, in the Opera House (☎ **08/411-00-26;** T-Bana: Kungsträdgården), is the most exclusive place in town, and even the bouncers are drop-dead gorgeous. While some people choose to eat the expensive dinners, the real socializing starts with the dancing after midnight. Drinks are appropriately expensive. To escape the frenzy for a while, turn right instead of left when you enter, pass through the Opera Bar, where artists and journalists gather, and make your way to the congenial Bacfickan, or Back Pocket Bar (see above). Café Opera is open Monday to Thursday 11:30am to 3pm and Friday to Sunday 11:30am to 4am. There's no cover before 11pm but 65KR ($9) 11pm to 3am.

The **Daily News Café,** on Kungsträdgården, behind the Opera House (☎ 08/ 21-56-55; T-Bana: Kungsträdgården), is just doors away from its rival, Café Opera (above). With an elaborate light show and good sound system, this place is more dance oriented than the Opera. The crowd doesn't arrive until late, and when they do you'll think you're in a New York City club. The drinks are ridiculously priced. There's live music upstairs and a disco downstairs; both get going around 10pm. It's open Wednesday to Saturday 7pm to 3am and Sunday 8pm to 3am. There's no cover on Wednesday, Thursday, and Sunday but 70KR ($9) on Friday and Saturday after 10pm.

At **Göta Källare,** in the Medborgarplatsen subway stop, on Södermalm (☎ 08/642-08-28; T-Bana: Medborgarplatsen, leave at the Folkimggatan exit, then turn right as you come up the stairs from the subway if you're coming from Norrmalm or Gamla Stan), well-dressed couples (most 40 to 60) who like to dance cheek-to-cheek congregate to enjoy the live bands, large dance floors, and Platters-style music. Live music for 45 minutes alternates with disco for 15 minutes, and food is served. You've got to be at least 25. It's open Monday to Saturday 8pm to 3am. The cover charge is 25KR ($3.35) Monday and Tuesday before 9:30pm or 85KR ($11) after; 50KR ($6.65) Wednesday and Thursday before 9:30pm or 85KR ($11) after; and 55KR ($7) Friday and Saturday before 9:30pm or 90KR ($12) after.

8 Side Trips: Palaces & Picturesque Towns

DROTTNINGHOLM

The palace of the present-day Swedish king Carl XVI Gustaf and Queen Silvia is open to visitors year-round. The 17th-century rococo structure is 7 miles from the city center (perfect for a half-day trip). In addition to the State Apartments, the palace grounds encompass a theater from 1766 and a beautiful Chinese Pavilion.

Drottningholm Slott (Drottningholm Palace) (☎ 08/402-62-80) was built for Sweden's Queen Eleonora in 1662. This four-story palace with two-story wings has often been referred to as "little Versailles." The interior dazzles with opulent furniture and art from the 17th to the 19th centuries, including painted ceilings framed by gold, chandeliers, and Chinese vases. Ample sculptured gardens surround the palace, and from time to time you may even spot the down-to-earth royal couple taking a stroll. Admission is 40KR ($5) adults and 20KR ($2.65) students. It's open May 11am to 4:30pm, June to August 10am to 4:30pm, and September noon to 3:30pm.

The **Drottningholm Court Theater** (☎ 08/759-04-06) is one of the world's oldest extant stages using the original backdrops and props; it stands exactly as it was on opening night in 1766. Eighteenth-century ballets and operas are still performed here, authentic down to the costumes. Inquire at the Stockholm Information Service for a schedule of the operas and ballets presented May to September. Even if no show is scheduled, visit the theater with a guided tour. Admission is 40KR ($5) adults and 20KR ($2.65) children. The theater is open daily: May to August noon to 4:30pm and September 1 to 3:30pm.

The **Kina Slott (Chinese Pavilion)** is near the end of the palace park. Many of Europe's grand old palaces were inspired by the exotic architecture of Asia. Constructed in Stockholm in 1753 as a royal birthday gift, it was quietly floated downriver so that it would surprise the queen when it arrived. Admission is 40KR ($5) adults and 20KR ($2.65) seniors/students. It's open daily: April and October 1 to 3:30pm, May to August 11am to 4:30pm, and September noon to 3:30pm.

There are two ways of reaching Drottningholm. The first, and more exciting, is **by steamboat,** which takes 50 minutes and costs 75KR ($10) round-trip adults or 50KR ($6.65) ages 6 to 11. Boats leave from Stadshusbron, beside Stockholm's City Hall, daily: early June to mid-August on the hour 10am to 4pm and at 6pm; May to early June and mid-August to early September 10am to 2pm (to 4pm on weekends). Contact Strömma Kanalbolaget at ☎ **08/23-33-75** (fax 08/20-50-31) for more information.

Stockholm Sightseeing (☎ **08/24-04-70**) offers round-trips to Drottningholm in turn-of-the-century boats. You can also take the T-Bana to Brommaplan, then connect to any Mälarö bus for Drottningholm.

MARIEFRED

A day trip to **Mariefred** on Lake Mälaren includes a boat ride, a pretty little town that's easy to explore on foot, an "old-time" train station and steam railway, a bookshop that's been around since 1897, and a castle with compelling nooks and crannies and a portrait collection from the 16th century to the present.

Gripsholm Castle (☎ **0159/101-94**), on a spit of land south of the town, is home to the National Portrait Gallery, with 1,200 of its 4,000 portraits on display. There's a multitude of rooms and portraits to see, outstanding among them the ceiling and paneling in Duke Karl's Chamber; the tiled fireplace in Princess Sofia Albertina's Study; the King's Bedchamber with a 17th-century ivory clock; the paneling and wall hangings in the Council Chamber; the White Drawing Room; the domed ceiling of Gustav III's Theater; the Sentry Corridor (a portrait of opera singer Jenny Lind hangs here); the Large Gallery (a portrait of Carl XVI Gustaf and his family hangs here, along with one of Lovisa Ulrika, whose attendants are depicted as hens); and the Tower Room, where you'll find modern portraits, including Dag Hammarskjöld, Greta Garbo, and Ingmar Bergman. Room 52 houses some compelling self-portraits.

A guidebook in English is helpful but costs about $5. Admission is 40KR ($5) adults and 20KR ($2.65) students/children. The castle and portrait gallery are open January to April, November, and December, Saturday and Sunday noon to 3pm; May to August daily 10am to 4pm; and September and October, Saturday and Sunday 10am to 3pm.

There are **shops,** an inviting cafe called **Konditori Fredman,** the **town hall** around the main square, and some **charming streets** to explore. **Gripsholms Vardshus,** an upscale hotel, has a public bar and a restaurant that serves substantial meals.

Many visitors never realize there's a **boardwalk** in Mariefred (walk in the opposite direction of the church and pier) leading past moored boats and houses with red-tile roofs peaking out to sea. There are benches where you can sit and gaze at the bullrushes, and beyond them, the church steeple and castle domes.

In summer, a coal-fired steamboat called the **SS *Mariefred,*** built in 1903, makes the trip to Mariefred from Stockholm; sit on the right side for the best views and photo ops. The trip, which offers splendid views of City Hall as the boat leaves Stockholm, takes a little more than an hour and costs 160KR ($21) round-trip, half price for age 15 and under. Snacks and drinks are served on board. In May and early June, the boat departs Stockholm at 10am Saturday and Sunday; mid-June to mid-August, it leaves Tuesday to Sunday at 10am. It returns from Mariefred at 4:30pm; double-check the departure time with the crew before you go exploring.

In summer, you may also travel to Mariefred **by train**—the last leg of the journey, from Läggesta to Mariefred (change trains at the small terminal called Läggesta Södra), is in a turn-of-the-century **steam-powered train.** For more information, call ☎ **08/669-88-50.**

SIGTUNA & UPPSALA

Another day-long getaway is to **Sigtuna.** This picturesque town was founded in A.D. 970 and has a beautiful waterfront walkway, historic ruins, a church, a museum, an old-fashioned cafe (**Tant Bruns Kaffestuga,** or "Auntie Brown's"), a revered hotel dating from 1907, a summer hostel, shops, and a helpful tourist office that serves coffee and cake. Plan to arrive at 10am, when the tourist office and cafes open. If you're pressed for time, do a quick transit by walking along **Storagatan** to the museum and hotel (pick up a map and information at the tourist office along the way), then double back following the waterfront walkway, head up to Town Hall Square, have coffee at Auntie Brown's, and visit St. Mary's Church and the ruins next to it.

You can get to Sigtuna on your Stockholm Card; take the train to Märsta, then change for the local bus, whose departure is coordinated with the train's arrival; the one-way trip takes about an hour. There's also a boat trip from Stockholm to Sigtuna in summer.

The university city of **Uppsala** is only 22 miles from Sigtuna, so you might want to take an extra day, hop on another bus, and visit it, notably the cathedral and the university grounds. If you do visit, be sure to have coffee and pastry at **Ofvandahls Café,** at Sysslomansgatan 3–5, a local tradition. A good and affordable accommodation choice in Uppsala is **Provobis Hotel Uplandia** (☎ **018/10-21-60;** fax 018/69-61-32), in the city center and near the tourist office; a double with breakfast is 1,380KR ($184) weekdays but only 690KR ($92) weekends. The trip between Sigtuna and Uppsala isn't covered on the Stockholm Card.

ARCHIPELAGO EXPLORATION

Greater Stockholm's beloved archipelago is 150 miles long and is made up of 24,000 nearby islands, starting just beyond Djurgaørden. If you want to explore the archipelago in depth, buy the **16-day ferry pass,** called a Batluffarkortet, for 250KR ($33).

If you don't have time to devote to island-hopping, consider an excursion of 1 or 2 days to **Finnhamm** (plenty of natural beauty, tranquillity, and a memorable youth hostel), **Sandhamm** (there's a town here that's popular with the yachting set; you can take the ferry one way and come back by bus), and **Utö** (famous for its bread). For a day's outing in summer, consider the **Feather Islands (Fjaderholmarna),** where there's an aquarium, a pub, a restaurant, a shop that sells smoked fish, and a building filled with handcrafts; locals pack a picnic when they go. The Stockholm Information Service can provide the particulars.

27

Venice & the Veneto

by Patricia Schultz

Prices can be double here what they are elsewhere in Italy—but this is Venice, *La Serenissima* (the Most Serene). For over a thousand years, people have flocked here because it's unlike any other city. They come to see the rio Frescada canal flowing past the houses with centuries-faded facades of muted reds and greens; to travel the truly grand Canal Grande as it winds past stately Gothic and Renaissance palazzi; to experience the unparalleled tranquillity of campo Santa Margherita, where only the sound of fruit vendors or children playing soccer pierces the stillness. And they come to ride the gondolas and *vaporetti* that ply the waters. Underneath its unique beauty and weathered decadence, Venice is a living city that seems almost too exquisite to be genuine, too fragile to survive the never-ending stream of tourism.

Venice was at the crossroads of the Eastern and Western worlds for centuries, resulting in an unrivaled heritage of art, architecture, and culture. It straddled the two worlds, and though traders and merchants no longer pass through as they once did, it nonetheless continues to find itself at a crossroads: an intersection in time between the uncontested period of maritime power that built it and the modern world that keeps it ever-so-gingerly afloat.

REQUIRED DOCUMENTS   See chapter 23 on Rome.

OTHER FROMMER'S TITLES   For more on Venice, see *Frommer's Portable Venice; Frommer's Italy; Frommer's Italy from $50 a Day; Frommer's Gay & Lesbian Europe; Frommer's Europe;* or *Frommer's Food Lover's Companion to Italy.*

1 Venice Deals & Discounts

SPECIAL DISCOUNTS

Anyone between 16 and 29 is eligible for a **"Rolling Venice" pass,** entitling you to discounts in museums, restaurants, stores, language courses, hotels, and bars across the city. Valid for 1 year, it costs 5,000L ($2.80) and can be picked up at a special "Rolling Venice" office set up in the train station during summer or at the **Assessorato alla Gioventù,** Corte Contarina 1529, off the Frezzeria (☎ **041/274-76-41**). The **Promove** organization is best known for its November to March hotel discounts (2-night minimum). Since Promove is represented by local travel agencies only, apply directly to **Intras Travel,**

Budget Bests

The **best free sight** in Venice is the city itself. While the crowds can be taxing in high season, there's something here you can't buy anywhere else—the quiet. You'll hear conversations going on in dozens of languages, but never an agitated automobile horn or a failing car muffler or an annoying Vespa motorbike.

Venice's many **festivals and special events** (see the box "Special & Free Events," later in this chapter) are also budget bests. Most of the revelry is free, and even at the Film Festival and the Biennale there are a number of inexpensive screenings and free exhibits.

You can always save money on food and drink by consuming them standing up at one of the city's ubiquitous **bars.** A 3,000L ($1.70) *panino* (sandwich) and a cappuccino at 2,000L ($1.10) make a quick and satisfying lunch. Prices double—at least—if you sit down.

piazza San Marco 72/B (☎ **041/522-48-70;** fax 041/528-63-47), or **Kele e Teo,** on the Mercerie 4930 (☎ **041/520-87-22;** fax 041/520-89-13).

WORTH A SPLURGE

The cost of life is significantly higher here than in any other city in Italy. But then again, this isn't really Italy. It's unique, magical, and worth every lira—but do plan cautiously.

When it comes to splurges, Venice's offerings are endless. Buying (but then having to carry home—be prepared) **champagne flutes from Murano** will mean you'll have instant heirlooms as well as a grand way to toast in 2000. Another great souvenir is an elaborate **Carnevale mask**—those from the Commedia dell'Arte are purely Venetian. And be sure to set aside some lire for a **Venetian dinner of quality fish.** It'll be costly but delicious and memorable.

Of course, Venice's top splurge opportunity is a world-famous **gondola ride.** Sure this may have become a touristy cliche, but it's also a perfect way to experience the essence of the city and see vignettes that are insightful, inspiring, and romantic.

2 Essentials

ARRIVING

BY PLANE Flights land at the **Aeroporto Marco Polo,** north of the city on the mainland (☎ **041/260-61-11**). The most fashionable and traditional way to arrive in piazza San Marco is by sea, so **Alilaguna** (☎ **041/522-23-03**) operates a *motoscafo* (shuttle boat) service from the airport with two stops (at Murano and the Lido for 8,500L/$4.80) before arriving after about 1 hour in piazza San Marco for 17,000L ($10). Call for the daily schedule of a dozen or so trips, which changes with the season and is coordinated with the principal arrival/departure of the major airlines (most hotels have the monthly schedule posted). A **private water taxi** is convenient but costly, about 110,000L ($62), and is worth considering if you're pressed for time, have an early flight, have a lot of luggage, or are traveling with a friend or two (or more).

There are two **bus** alternatives: The airport shuttle bus run by the Azienda Trasporti Veneto Orientale (ATVO) (☎ **041/520-55-30**) connects the airport with piazzale Roma. Buses leave for/from the airport about every hour, cost 5,000L ($2.80), and make the trip in 30 minutes. The slightly less expensive local ACTV bus no. 5 (☎ **041/52-87-886**) is 1,500L (85¢) per person. Buses leave for/from the airport and

What Things Cost in Venice	U.S. $
Water taxi (for journey of up to 7 minutes)	15.15
Public *vaporetto* boat (from any point in the city to any other point)	2.50
Local telephone call	.10
Double room with view of the Grand Canal at the Gritti Palace (deluxe)	500.00
Double room with view of the Grand Canal at the Locanda Sturion (splurge)	130.00
Double room without bathroom at the Albergo ai do Mori (budget)	73.00
Continental breakfast (cappuccino and croissant)	
standing at a cafe/bar	2.25
seated at a cafe/bar	4.50
per person at most hotels	4.50
Lunch for one at Trattoria Alla Madonna (moderate)	19.75
Lunch for one at any cafe in town (budget)	
standing at the bar	4.40
seated at a table	6.25
Pizza and a drink at most pizzerias, seated	6.90
Dinner for one, without wine, at Harry's Bar (deluxe)	80.00
Dinner for one, without wine, at Alla Madonna (moderate)	25.00
Dinner for one, without wine, at Vino Vino (budget)	12.00
Pint *(grande)* of beer at any cafe	3.75
Glass *(bicchiere)* of wine at any cafe	1.10
Coca-Cola	
takeout	1.70
seated at bar table	2.80
Cup of espresso (cappuccino slightly more) at any cafe	1.15
Drink at any outdoor cafe table in piazza San Marco	5.00
Roll of ASA 100 color film, 36 exposures	5.60
Joint ticket to the Palazzo Ducale and Correr Museum	7.85
Movie ticket	5.60
Least expensive ticket for a Vivaldi concert at the Church of Vivaldi	22.50

piazzale Roma hourly and can take up to 1 hour because of the frequent stops they make. For either of these, you'll have to walk from the final stop at the piazzale Roma bus stop to the nearby vaporetto stop for the final trip to your hotel; it's rare to see porters around who'll help with luggage.

BY TRAIN   Trains from all over Europe arrive at the **Stazione Venezia–Santa Lucia** (☎ **147-888-088** toll free from anywhere in Italy). To get there, all must pass through (though not necessarily stop at) a station marked VENEZIA–MESTRE. Don't be confused: Mestre is a charmless industrial city and the last stop on the mainland. Occasionally trains end in Mestre, in which case you have to catch one of the frequent 10-minute shuttle trains connecting Mestre with Venice; it's inconvenient (though easy enough), so when booking your ticket confirm that the final destination is Venezia/Stazione Santa Lucia.

At the far end as you come off the tracks at Santa Lucia, near the head of Track 7, is the *deposito bagagli* (luggage depot). If you're planning to look for accommodations or have packed so that you can bring the bare essentials with you to the hotel, you'll do well to leave your heavy gear here during your stay in Venice. The depot charges 5,000L ($2.80) per piece for every 12 hours and is open 24 hours. There's an Albergo Diurno (day hotel) at the far right side of the station as you face the tracks; it's open daily 7am to 8pm and charges 5,500L ($3.10) for a shower. The toilet is alongside Track 14.

The official city tourist board, **Azienda di Promozione Turistica (A.P.T.)** (☎ 041/529-87-27), operates an understaffed information office between the station's large front doors. It's open daily 8am to 7pm. The train information office (☎ 147-888-088 toll free from anywhere in Italy), marked with a lowercase "i," is also in the station's main hall. It's staffed daily 8am to 8pm.

Two banks for **currency exchange** *(cambio)* keep long hours (usually to 9pm) and compete with each other for business. Compare their rates and commission charges (often in fine print) before exchanging money. Finally, upon exiting the station you'll find the Grand Canal immediately in front of you, making a heart-stopping first impression. You'll find the docks for vaporetto Line 82 in front to your left; Lines 1 and 52 are to your right.

BY BUS   Though rail travel is more convenient and commonplace, Venice is serviced by long-distance buses from all over mainland Italy and some foreign cities. The final destination is piazzale Roma, where you'll need to pick up a vaporetto to connect you with stops in the heart of Venice and along the Grand Canal.

BY CAR   Arriving for a stay in Venice by car is problematic and expensive—and downright exasperating if it's high season and the parking facilities are full (they usually are). If you do arrive by car, do some research before choosing a garage—the rates vary widely. If you have reservations at a hotel, check before arriving: Most of them offer discount coupons for some of the parking facilities.

VISITOR INFORMATION

In addition to the one in the train station (see above), there's a **tourist office** in the Palazzina del Santi (☎ 041/522-63-56), between the small green park on the Grand Canal called the Giardini (or Giardinetti) Reali and the famous Harry's Bar. This is the new location for the office that was for years in a corner of piazza San Marco. It's open daily 9:30am to 6:30pm in summer and Monday to Saturday 9:30am to 3:30pm in winter. The staff is generally unwelcoming and most helpful if you need specific questions answered. Posters around town with exhibition and concert schedules are more helpful. Ask for a schedule of the month's special events and an updated list of museum and church hours, as these can change erratically and often.

CITY LAYOUT

Keep in mind as you wander seemingly hopelessly among the *calli* and *campi* that the city wasn't built to make sense (or appear impressive) to those on foot but rather to those plying its canals. No matter how good your map and sense of direction, time after time you'll get wonderfully lost and happen on Venice's most intriguing corners and vignettes.

Venice lies 2½ miles from terra firma, connected to mainland Mestre by the **ponte della Libertà.** Snaking through the city like an inverted S is the **Canal Grande**

A Note on Addresses

Within each sestiere is a most original system of numbering the palazzi, using one continuous string of 6,000 or so numbers. The format for addresses in this chapter is the official mailing address: the sestiere name followed by the building number in that district, followed by the name of the street or campo on which you'll find that address—for example, San Marco 1471 (salizzada San Moisé), 30121 Venezia. Be aware that San Marco 1471 may not be found close to San Marco 1475 and that many buildings aren't numbered at all.

(Grand Canal), the wide main artery of aquatic Venice. The "streets filled with water" are 177 narrow canals *(rios)* cutting through the interior of the two halves of the city, flowing gently by the doorsteps of centuries-old palazzi. They'd be endlessly frustrating to the landlubbing visitors trying to navigate the city on foot if not for the 400 foot-bridges that cross them, connecting Venice's 118 islands.

Only three bridges *(ponti)* cross the Grand Canal: **ponte degli Scalzi,** just outside the train station; the elegant white marble **ponte Rialto,** connecting the districts of San Marco and San Polo at the center of town; and the wooden **ponte Accademia,** connecting the campo Santo Stefano area of San Marco with the Accademia museum across the way in Dorsoduro.

Since 1711 the city has been divided into six *sestieri* ("sixths" or districts). **Cannaregio** stretches north and east, from the train station to the Jewish Ghetto and on to the vicinity of the Ca' d'Oro north of the Rialto Bridge. To the east beyond Cannaregio (and skirting the area north and east of piazza San Marco) is **Castello,** whose tony canalside "esplanade," riva degli Schiavoni, is lined with first-class and deluxe hotels. The central **San Marco** shares this side of the Grand Canal with Castello and Cannaregio, anchored by the magnificent piazza San Marco and the Basilica of San Marco to the south and the Rialto Bridge to the north; the most visited (and most expensive) of the sestieri, it's the city's commercial, religious, and political heart and has been for more than a millennium. **San Polo** is north of the Rialto Bridge, stretching west to just beyond campo dei Frari and campo San Rocco. **Santa Croce** is next, moving north and west, stretching all the way to piazzale Roma. Finally, the residential **Dorsoduro** is on the opposite side of the Accademia Bridge from San Marco. Most known for the Accademia and Peggy Guggenheim museums, it's the largest sestiere and is something of an artists' haven.

Venice shares its lagoon with several other islands. Opposite piazza San Marco and Dorsoduro is **La Giudecca,** a tranquil working-class place where you'll find the youth hostel and a handful of hotels (including the fabled Cipriani, one of Europe's finest) but mostly residential neighborhoods. The slim 7-mile-long **Lido di Venezia** is the city's beach; separating the lagoon from the sea and permitting car traffic, it's a popular summer destination for its concentration of seasonal hotels. **Murano, Burano,** and **Torcello** are popular destinations northeast of the city and easily accessible by public transport vaporetto. Since the 13th century, Murano has exported its glass products worldwide; it's an interesting day trip for those with the time, but you can do just as well in Venice's myriad glass stores. Burano was and still is equally famous for its lace, an art now practiced by so few island women that its prices are generally unaffordable. Torcello is the most remote and least populated. The 40-minute boat ride is worthwhile for history and art buffs who'll be awestruck by the Byzantine mosaics of the cathedral whose foundation dates to the 7th century, making this the oldest Venetian monument in existence.

A Few Notes on Getting Around

Be sure to pack light enough so that you can get you and your luggage to your hotel without despairing at the likely absence of a (costly) porter. This is especially important if you must deal with climbing stairs in an elevatorless hotel and/or navigating through the dreaded acqua alta floods.

Imagine yourself as a battery-operated toy car—when driven into a wall or other obstacle, it instantly turns and continues on its way. Time and again, you'll think you know where you're going, only to wind up on a dead-end street or at the side of a canal with no bridge to get to the other side. Just remind yourself that the city's physical complexity is an integral part of its charm and of the memorable experience Venice guarantees.

Take note, however, that with its countless stepped footbridges and almost no elevators in any buildings, Venice is one of the worst cities for the physically disabled.

Finally, the industrial city of **Mestre,** on the mainland, is the gateway to Venice and holds no reason to explore. In a pinch, its host of inexpensive hotels are worth consideration when Venice's hotels are full.

GETTING AROUND

The free map offered by the tourist office and most hotels has good intentions, but it doesn't even show, much less name or index, all the *calli* or streets and byways. For that, pick up a more **detailed map** *(pianta della città)* for sale at a number of bookstores or newsstands. How helpful the more elaborate maps can be is debatable—if you're lost, you're better off asking a Venetian to point you in the right direction.

As you wander, look for the ubiquitous yellow signs whose destinations and arrows direct you toward five major landmarks: Ferrovia (the train station), piazzale Roma, the Rialto (Bridge), (piazza) San Marco, and the Accademia (Bridge).

BY BOAT   The various sestieri are linked by a comprehensive vaporetto system of about a dozen lines operated by the **Azienda del Consorzio Trasporti Veneziano (ACTV),** calle Fuseri 1810, off the Frezzeria in San Marco (☎ **041/528-78-86**). Transit maps are more conveniently available at the tourist office (see above) and at most ACTV stations (be aware that vaporetto stops and lines were changed in 1994 and the occasional old map is still in circulation). It's easier to get around on foot; the vaporetti principally serve the Grand Canal (and can be crowded in summer), the outskirts, and the outer islands. The crisscross network of small canals is the province of delivery vessels, gondolas, and private boats.

The average fare on most boats is 4,500L ($2.50). Most lines run every 10 to 15 minutes daily 7am to midnight, then hourly until morning; most ticket booths have timetables posted. Note that not all stations sell tickets after dark; if you haven't purchased a pass, extra tickets, or a block of tickets, you'll have to settle up with the conductor on board (you'll have to find him—he won't come looking for you) or gamble on a 40,000L ($23) fine, with no excuses accepted if a surprise check finds you without a ticket.

Though the city, no larger than New York's Central Park, is easy to navigate on foot, boat lovers might want to consider the 15,000L ($8) **Biglietto 24 Ore** that entitles you to 24 hours of unlimited travel on any ACTV vessel (and is usually more than what you'd pay for a handful of tickets bought separately). The **Biglietto 3 Giorni,** covering 3 days of unlimited travel, isn't much of a savings either at 30,000L ($17), nor is the **Biglietto 7 Giorni** for 7 days at 55,000L ($31). The **Biglietto Isole,** valid for unlimited 1-day travel in one direction on Line 12 (which services Murano, Mazzorbo, Burano, and Torcello), is 5,000L ($2.80).

Just three bridges span the Grand Canal (plans for a fourth were once again pursued in 1996, but Venetians aren't holding their breath). To fill in the gaps, **traghetti gondolas** (oversized gondolas rowed by two standing gondolieri) cross the Grand Canal at seven or so intermediate points. You'll find a station at the end of any street named calle del Traghetto on your map (see map recommendation above) and indicated by a yellow sign with the black gondola symbol. The fare is 700L (40¢), which you hand to the gondolier when boarding. Most Venetians cross standing up.

BY WATER TAXI   *Taxi acquei* (water taxis) prices are high and not for visitors watching their lire. For journeys up to 7 minutes, the rate is 27,000L ($15); 500L (30¢) click off for each extra 15 seconds. There's an 8,500L ($4.80) supplement for service from 10pm to 7am and a 9,000L ($5) surcharge on Sunday and holidays; note that these two supplements can't be applied simultaneously. If they have to come get you, tack on another 8,000L ($4.50).

FAST FACTS: Venice

American Express   See "Currency Exchange," below.

Banks   Banks are normally open Monday to Friday 8:30am to 1:30pm and 2:35 to 3:35pm or 3 to 4pm; the American Express office (see "Currency Exchange," below) is open Saturday; some banks are open Saturday year-round (others in July or August only) and follow an 8:30 to 11:30am schedule. Both exchange offices (cambio) at the train station are open daily. Before leaving home, check with your bank for a listing of ATMs *(bancomat)* compatible with your bank card and make sure your PIN will be accepted in Italy, where the number of digits may differ.

Business Hours   Standard hours for **shops** are Monday to Saturday 9am to 12:30pm and 3 to 7:30pm. In winter, shops are closed Monday morning, while in summer it's usually Saturday afternoon they're closed. Most grocers are closed Wednesday afternoon throughout the year. In Venice and throughout Italy, just about everything is closed Sunday, though tourist shops in the San Marco area are permitted to stay open in high season. Restaurants are required to close at least 1 day per week *(il giorno di riposo),* but the particular day varies. Many are open for Sunday lunch but close for Sunday dinner and close Monday when the fish market is closed. Restaurants close 1 to 2 weeks for holidays *(chiuso per ferie)* sometime in July or August, frequently over Christmas, and sometime in January or February before the Carnevale rush.

Consulates   The **U.K. Consulate** is at Dorsoduro 1051 (☎ **041/522-72-07**), at the foot of the Accademia Bridge south of the museum; it's open Monday to Friday 9am to noon and 2 to 4pm. The **United States, Canada,** and **Australia** have consulates in Milan, about 3 hours away by train. The **U.S. Consulate** in Milan is at largo Donegani 1 (☎ **02/29-03-51**), open Monday to Friday 9am to 11am for visas only; from Monday to Friday it's also open for telephone service information 2 to 4pm. Along with **New Zealand,** they all maintain embassies in Rome (see "Fast Facts: Rome" in chapter 23).

Crime   Be aware of petty crime like pickpocketing on the crowded vaporetti, particularly the tourist routes where passengers are more intent on the passing scenery than watching their bags. Venice's deserted back streets were once virtually crimeproof; occasional tales of theft are circulating only recently.

Beware the Acqua Alta

Few cities boast as long a high season as Venice, beginning with the Easter period. May, June, and September are the best weather-wise and are thus the most crowded. July and August are hot—at times unbearably so (few of the one- and two-star hotels offer air-conditioning; when they do it costs extra).

The notorious acqua alta floods, a peculiarity related as much to the tides as to rainfall, can start as early as October, usually taking place November to March. Piazzas often flood—beginning with piazza San Marco, one of the city's lowest points—but usually recede after just an hour or two. Walkways are set up around town, but wet feet are a given.

Currency   See "Fast Facts: Rome" in chapter 23.

Currency Exchange   In addition to the banks mentioned in "Essentials," earlier in this chapter, you can change money commission-free at **American Express,** San Marco 1471, on Salizzada San Moisé (☎ **041/520-08-44**) (with your back to the Basilica di San Marco, exit the piazza by way of the arcade at the far left end; you'll see a mosaic American Express sign in the pavement pointing the way straight ahead). The office is open for banking in summer, Monday to Saturday 8am to 8pm (for all other services, 9am to 5:30pm); in winter, Monday to Friday 9am to 5:30pm and Saturday 9am to 12:30pm (for banking and other services). Be careful of the privately owned cambio around town whose boards boast good rates but whose commonly high commissions (sometimes as much as 10%) appear at the bottom in small print. They follow the same schedule as retail shops, not banks, often staying open during lunch.

Dentists & Doctors   For a short list, check with the consulate of the United Kingdom or the American Express office.

Emergencies   In Venice and throughout Italy, dial ☎ **113** to reach the police. Some Italians will recommend that you forgo the police and try the military-trained Carabinieri (☎ **112**). For an ambulance, phone ☎ **523-00-00.** To report a fire, dial ☎ **115.**

Holidays   See "Fast Facts: Rome" in chapter 23. Venice's patron saint, St. Mark, is honored on April 25.

Laundry   The self-service laundry most convenient to the train station is the **Lavaget** at Cannaregio 1269, to the left as you cross ponte alle Guglie from Lista di Spagna, open Monday to Friday 8:30am to 12:30pm and 3 to 7pm; the rate is about 16,000L ($9) for up to 4.5 kilos (10 lb.).

Mail   Venice's **Posta Centrale** is at San Marco 5554, on salizzada Fontego dei Tedeschi (☎ **041/271-71-11**), just off campo San Bartolomeo, in the area of the Rialto Bridge on the San Marco side of the Grand Canal. This office sells stamps at Window 12 Monday to Saturday 8:10am to 7pm (for parcels, 8:10am to 1:30pm).

If you're at piazza San Marco and need postal services, walk through sotto-portego San Geminian, the center portal at the opposite end of the piazza from the basilica on calle larga dell'Ascensione. This post office was closed for renovations at press time, and its scheduled reopening is the city's best-kept secret. Its usual hours are Monday to Friday 8:15am to 1:30pm and Saturday 8:15am to 12:10pm.

Country & City Codes

The **country code** for Italy is **39.** The **city code** for Venice is **041;** use this code when you're calling from outside Italy, within Venice, or from within Italy.

Pharmacies   Venice's many drugstores take turns staying open all night. To find out which one is on call in your area, ask at your hotel or dial ☎ **523-05-73.**

Police   In an emergency, dial ☎ **112** or **113.** For other business, dial ☎ **274-82-03.**

Rest Rooms   The use of the toilet in any bar is restricted to patrons; for the cost of an espresso or a mineral water you can use the services (there's usually only one to pick from unless you're lucky: *signori* means "men"; *signore,* "ladies"). Museums and galleries will also have facilities. Public toilets can be found at the train station; near the Giardinetti Reali park next to the tourist information office (Palazzina del Santi); on the southwest (Dorsoduro) side of the Accademia Bridge; next to the (closed) post office branch just west of piazza San Marco on calle larga dell'Ascensione; and off campo San Bartolomeo.

Tax & Tipping   See "Fast Facts: Rome" in chapter 23.

Telephone   See "Fast Facts: Rome" in chapter 23.

3 Accommodations You Can Afford

Hotels, like just about everything else, are more expensive here than in any other city in Italy, with no apparent upgrade in amenities. The least special of those listed below are clean and functional; at best they're charming and thoroughly enjoyable with the serenade of a passing gondolier thrown in. Some may even provide you with your best stay in Europe.

I strongly suggest that you reserve in advance once your itinerary is planned, regardless of the period. If you haven't booked, arrive as early as you can, definitely before noon. The tourist office in the train station will book rooms for you, but the lines are long and (understandably) the staff's patience is sometimes thin. If you're holding a Rolling Venice pass (see "Venice Deals & Discounts," earlier in this chapter), the small office in the Santa Lucia train station will help with reservations free of charge.

State-imposed ordinances have issued stringent deadlines for the updating of antiquated electrical, plumbing, and sewage systems—costly endeavors. To make up for this, small one- and two-star hotels then raise their rates, often applying for an upgrade in category for which they're now potentially eligible. However, the request can take years for approval. The good news is that now you'll have accommodations of a better quality; the bad news is that yesteryear's "finds" are slowly disappearing. The rates below were compiled in 1998. You can expect the usual increase of 4% to 8%, but you might be hit with an increase of as much as 20% if the hotel you pick is one that has been redone recently.

A few peculiarities about Venice hotels have everything to do with the fact that this unique city built on water doesn't consistently offer what you might take for granted: elevators, light, and spaciousness. Venice hotels have some of the smallest bathrooms I've ever seen, often closet-size rooms tacked on in the corner of a room not particularly large to begin with. Rooms can be dark and canal views are not half as frequent as we'd like them to be, and it's not unusual to have to hike to the fourth floor in the

---

A Note About Rates

Most hotels usually observe high- and low-season rates, though they're gradually adopting a single year-round rate. Even where it's not indicated in the listings, be sure to ask when you book or when you arrive at a hotel whether off-season prices are in effect. High season in Venice is approximately March 15 to November 5, with a lull during July and August. Some hotels close (sometimes without notice) from November or December until Carnevale, opening for about 2 weeks around Christmas and New Year's at high-season rates.

---

absence of an ancient building's elevator. This doesn't mean that a clean, welcoming, family-run hotel in an atmospheric neighborhood can't offer a memorable stay. Just don't expect the plush Danieli and Grand Canal vistas and you won't be disappointed.

Note: You can find the lodging choices below plotted on the map included in "Seeing the Sights," later in this chapter.

NEAR THE TRAIN STATION & ON LISTA DI SPAGNA

Albergo Adua. Cannaregio 233a (on Lista di Spagna), 30121 Venezia. ☎ and fax **041/71-61-84.** 22 units, 9 with bathroom. 80,000L ($45) single without bathroom, 125,000L ($70) single with bathroom; 95,000L ($53) double without bathroom, 160,000L ($90) double with bathroom; 128,000L ($72) triple without bathroom, 216,000L ($121) triple with bathroom. Low-season rates 10%–15% less. Breakfast 7,500L ($4.20). AE, MC, V. Vaporetto: Ferrovie. Exit the train station and turn left onto Lista di Spagna; the hotel is close on your right.

The Adua family has been in business more than 30 years—and has been included in this book nearly that long. At press time, they've received permission to renovate, which should be done by the time you arrive. The rates above reflect this renovation, but I wasn't able to see the finished work, so I'm not sure exactly what improvements are in store. Their comfortable-size rooms have appealed to all ages but were particularly popular with students who didn't mind the eclectic 1970s furnishings or rather creative pattern combinations. The private baths are new and attractive. Across the street is an independent palazzo managed by the Aduas with nine refurbished rooms sharing three baths; the rates are about the same as those above.

Albergo Santa Lucia. Cannaregio 358 (on calle della Misericordia), 30121 Venezia. ☎ **041/71-06-10.** ☎ and fax 041/71-51-80. 18 units, 8 with bathroom. TEL. 75,000L ($42) single without bathroom; 120,000L ($67) double without bathroom, 150,000L ($84) double with bathroom; 140,000L ($79) triple without bathroom, 180,000L ($101) triple with bathroom; 210,000L ($118) quad with bathroom. Rates include continental breakfast. AE, DC, MC, V. Closed Jan 7–Feb 10. Vaporetto: Ferrovie. Exit the train station and turn left onto Lista di Spagna. Take the second left onto calle della Misericordia.

This contemporary building with a garden-enclosed flagstone patio/terrace is one of the nicer choices in the train station area. Bordered by roses, oleander, and ivy, the patio is a lovely place to enjoy breakfast, served in an old-fashioned way, with coffee and tea brought in sterling silver pots (you're welcome to bring your own brown-bag lunch and enjoy it here). The friendly owner, Emilia Gonzato, oversees everything with pride and it shows: The large rooms are simple but bright and clean. She doesn't speak much English, but her son, Gianangelo, does.

Hotel Dolomiti. Cannaregio 72–74 (on calle Priuli), 30121 Venezia. ☎ **041/71-51-13.** Fax 041/71-66-35. 50 units, 20 with bathroom. TEL. 90,000L ($51) single without bathroom, 135,000L ($76) single with bathroom; 110,000L ($62) twin without bathroom, 165,000L ($93) twin with bathroom; 130,000L ($73) double without bathroom, 190,000L ($107)

Getting the Best Deal on Accommodations

- When booking your hotel, confirm whether breakfast is obligatory and, if not, what it costs; you might spend half as much at the neighborhood bar and possibly be more satisfied.
- If you haven't reserved, try to arrive in the city before noon, when it's more likely you'll find a budget room. If you're eligible, get a Rolling Venice pass for discounted rates (see "Venice Deals & Discounts," earlier in this chapter); the Rolling office will also help you with reservations for free.
- If the cheap accommodations have been snatched up, think about spending the night in Padova (Padua) if you're on a really tight budget, but incorporate the cost of a round-trip train ticket to Venice into your projected savings if you don't have a pass for unlimited train travel. Travel between the cities will be about 20 to 40 minutes.
- Check with Promove (see "Venice Deals & Discounts," earlier in this chapter) for off-season package deals that fit your budget. Remember that July and August, considered peak season elsewhere in parts of Italy, is low season here.
- When arranging for a room in person, always ask if the price quoted is the best available; in slow periods even during high season, hotels will often entice guests with discounted rates rather than have empty rooms, especially if you're standing in front of them fresh from the train station.
- If the hotels I've suggested are booked, check your luggage at the train station and wander the byways around the train station and the piazzale Roma area, the realm of one- and two-star hotels. Budget hotels closer to St. Mark's are fewer and far between.

---

double with bathroom; 162,000L ($91) triple without bathroom, 225,000L ($126) triple with bathroom; 192,000L ($108) quad without bathroom, 260,000L ($146) quad with bathroom. Inquire about low-season discounts. Rates include breakfast. MC, V. Closed Nov 15–Jan 31. Vaporetto: Ferrovia. Exit the train station, turn left onto Lista di Spagna, and take the first left onto calle Priuli.

For those who prefer to stay near the train station, this is an old-fashioned and reliable choice. Because it has large, clean but ordinary rooms spread over four floors (no elevator), your chances of finding availability are better at this family-owned hotel, one of the larger places I suggest. Sergio and Lorenzo, the efficient polylingual staff in the old-world lobby, supply weather forecasts, umbrellas, restaurant suggestions, and a big smile after a long day's meandering.

✪ **Hotel Geremia.** Cannaregio 290/A (on campo San Geremia), 30121 Venezia. ☎ **041/71-62-45.** Fax 041/52-423-42. 20 units, 14 with bathroom. TV TEL. *For Frommer's readers:* 75,000L ($42) single without bathroom, 120,000L ($67) single with bathroom; 90,000L ($51) double without bathroom, 140,000L ($79) double with bathroom; 180,000L ($101) triple with bathroom; 210,000L ($118) quadruple with bathroom. Ask about off-season rates. Rates include continental breakfast. AE, MC, V. Vaporetto: Ferrovie. Exit the train station, turn left onto Lista di Spagna, and follow it until you get to campo San Geremia; the hotel is on the left.

If this gem of a two-star hotel had an elevator and was in the high-rent San Marco district, it would cost twice what it does. Consider yourself lucky to settle into any one of the tastefully renovated rooms—ideally one of the seven overlooking the small campo (better yet, one of two top-floor rooms with a small private terrace for those who don't mind the hike up). All rooms have either blond-wood paneling with

---

A Note on Special Rates

In this chapter, several hotels, like the Geremia, offer special rates for Frommer's readers—look for these words in the rates listings. To avoid any confusion with the hotels, please make it clear upon booking or arrival (or both) that you're a Frommer's reader and are requesting the special rates. Note that a hotel's rates may have increased by the time you plan your trip, but it will still offer our readers a discount.

---

built-in headboards and closets or regular painted walls and deep green or burnished rattan headboards and matching chairs. The smallish bathrooms offer amenities like hair dryers and heated towel racks. A labor of love, this charming hotel is overseen by an English-speaking staff and owner/manager Claudio.

NEAR THE RIALTO BRIDGE

✪ Hotel Bernardi-Semenzato. Cannaregio 4366 (on calle de l'Oca), 30121 Venezia. ☎ **041/522-72-57.** Fax 041/522-24-24. Hotel, 18 units, 10 with bathroom; annex, 8 units, 1 with bathroom. A/C TV TEL. *For Frommer's readers:* 58,000L ($33) single without bathroom, 79,000L ($44) single with bathroom; 75,000L ($42) double without bathroom, 120,000L ($67) double with bathroom; 105,000L ($59) triple without bathroom, 130,000L ($73) triple with bathroom. Breakfast 6,000L ($3.40). Ask about off-season rates. MC, V. Closed Nov 20–Dec 10. Vaporetto: Ca' d'Oro; from the vaporetto stop, walk straight ahead to strada Nova, turn right in the direction of campo SS. Apostoli, and look for Cannaregio 4309, a stationery/toy store on your left; turn left on this narrow side street, calle Duca, then take the first right onto calle de l'Oca.

From the outside, this weather-worn palazzo doesn't hint of its top-to-toe 1995 renovation, which left hand-hewn ceiling beams exposed, air-conditioned rooms with coordinated headboard/spread sets, and bathrooms modernized and brightly retiled. The young and enthusiastic English-speaking owners, Maria Teresa and Leonardo Pepoli, aspire to three-star style and had just received a two-star rating at press time, but they're content to offer one-star rates (prices get even more interesting off-season). The addition of an annex *(dipendenza)* 3 blocks away offers the chance to feel more independent—as if you've rented an aristocratic apartment. Most of the large bathless rooms in the annex should have baths added by the time you arrive. For a look at one of the fabulous annex rooms, see the back cover of this book.

NEAR PIAZZA SAN MARCO

✪ Albergo ai do Mori. San Marco 658 (on calle larga San Marco), 30124 Venezia. ☎ **041/520-48-17** or 041/528-92-93. Fax 041/520-53-28. 11 units, 7 with bathroom. A/C TV TEL. 130,000L ($73) double without bathroom, 160,000L ($90) double with bathroom; 160,000L ($90) triple without bathroom, 210,000L ($118) triple with bathroom; 200,000L ($112) quad without bathroom, 300,000L ($169) quad with bathroom. Ask about singles and quints as well as off-season rates. MC, V. Vaporetto: San Marco; exit piazza San Marco underneath the Torre dell'Orologio clock tower; turn right at the Max Mara store and you'll find the hotel on the left.

Antonella, the young hands-on owner/manager of this super-central hotel, creates an efficient yet comfortable ambiance with special care given to Frommer's readers. The more accessible lower floors (there's no elevator and the hotel begins on the second floor) are slightly larger and offer rooftop views, but the somewhat smaller top-floor rooms boast views embracing San Marco's cupolas and the Torre dell'Orologio, whose two bronze Moors ring the bells every hour. The improvement-minded Antonella has recently added large double-paned windows to ensure quiet, and wonderfully firm mattresses. This place was great before, but its 1997–98 face-lift brought new lovely tiled bathrooms (with hair dryers), color TVs, and air-conditioning in all rooms, giving you value and amenities not easily found in these parts or at these prices. About those bells: One guest's romantic fantasy is another's nightmare (I lean toward fantasy—this is Venice, after all).

Albergo al Gambero. San Marco 4687 (on calle dei Fabbri), 30124 Venezia. ☎ **041/522-43-84** or 041/520-14-20. Fax 041/520-04-31. 27 units, 14 with bathroom. *For Frommer's readers:* 80,000L ($45) single without bathroom, 150,000L ($84) single with bathroom; 130,000L ($73) double without bathroom, 190,000L ($107) double with bathroom; 175,000L ($98) triple without bathroom, 255,000L ($143) triple with bathroom; 220,000L ($124) quad without bathroom, 320,000L ($180) quad with bathroom. Rates include continental breakfast. MC, V. Vaporetto: Rialto; from the vaporetto stop, head south on calle Bembo, which becomes calle dei Fabbri; the hotel is about 5 blocks ahead on your left.

One of central Venice's reliable budget hotels went upmarket with a 1998 renovation (not completed at press time) that'll lead to an upgrade in category and rates. But for the moment, pending bureaucratic approval, 1999 should provide redone Venetian-style rooms with new baths at extremely moderate rates. Though unable to see the finished product, I'm tempted to say that this will be a future Frommer's favorite: The owners have many years' experience in the local hotel and food industry, and they should handle this project competently and with professional style. Its location midway between piazza San Marco and the Rialto Bridge is enviable, and the rooms overlooking a small canal will enjoy the serenades of the passing gondoliers. At the ground-floor Bistrot de Venise (see "Great Deals on Dining," later in this chapter), hotel guests enjoy a 10% discount at lunch or dinner.

Hotel Gallini. San Marco 3673 (on calle della Verona), 30124 Venezia. ☎ **041/520-45-15.** Fax 041/520-91-03. TEL. 50 units, 40 with bathroom. *For Frommer's readers:* 100,000L ($56) single without bathroom, 145,000L ($82) single with bathroom; 150,000L ($84) double without bathroom, 205,000L ($115) double with bathroom; 270,000L ($152) triple with bathroom. Off-season rates about 10% lower. Rates include continental breakfast. AE, MC, V. Closed Nov 15–Carnevale. Vaporetto: Sant'Angelo; follow the zigzagging road south toward campo Sant'Angelo; exit the campo at the northeast end by taking calle de la Mandola; take a right at the Ottica optometrist onto calle dei Assassini, which becomes calle della Verona.

Though the La Fenice fire temporarily doused this neighborhood's spark, things have returned to normal and it's business as usual at the Gallini. The amiable Ceciliati brothers, Adriano and Gabriele, have been at the helm of this large family operation since 1952, so you can be assured that things run smoothly. This conveniently located base offers four floors (no elevator) of bright, spacious rooms and big modern baths: This is the largest of places I suggest in this neighborhood, so look here when the smaller options sell out. A smiling housekeeping staff seems to be forever cleaning, and rich-looking marble floors in green, red, or speckled black alternate with intricate parquet floors to lend an old-world air. Gondoliers' tunes waft up to the 10 rooms overlooking the narrow rio della Verona. A few rooms have air-conditioning (an extra 10,000L/$13 daily).

✪ **Hotel Locanda Remedio.** San Marco 4412 (on calle del Remedio), 30122 Venezia. ☎ **041/520-62-32.** Fax 041/521-04-85. 14 units, all with bathroom. A/C MINIBAR TV TEL. *For Frommer's readers:* 160,000L ($90) single; 200,000L ($112) double; 250,000L ($140) triple. Rates include breakfast. MC, V. Vaporetto: San Marco; exit piazza San Marco under the Torre dell'Orologio clock tower and turn right at the Max Mara store onto calle larga San Marco; at the Ristorante All'Angelo, turn left onto calle va al Ponte dell'Angelo and take the first right onto ramo del Anzolo; cross the small footbridge onto calle del Remedio and the hotel will be on your right.

Renato is of the new breed of Venice's young hotel owners/managers striving to create quality and charming lodgings at moderate rates. By Venetian standards, the hotel offers unusually large and quiet rooms in an ancient palazzo around the corner from one of St. Mark's busiest streets. Most of the rooms are on the second floor (one has lovely ceiling frescoes) off a ballroom-size corridor. Renato continues to upgrade—he has just modernized the small baths, put new carpeting in the rooms, and added a charming breakfast room.

✪ **Hotel Piave.** Castello 4838/40 (on Ruga Giuffa), 30122 Venezia. ☎ **041/528-51-74.** Fax 041/523-85-12. 13 units, 11 with bathroom. TV TEL. *For Frommer's readers:* 135,000L ($76) double without bathroom, 198,000L ($111) double with bathroom; 252,000L ($142) triple with bathroom; 288,000L ($162) quad with bathroom; 324,000 ($182) quad suite. Doubles for single occupancy are 30% off. Discount of 25% applied to all rooms off-season. Rates include continental breakfast. AE, DC, MC, V. Vaporetto: San Zaccaria; walk straight ahead on calle delle Rasse to the small campo SS. Filippo e Giacomo; exit the campo at the right and continue to campo San Provolo; here take a left, cross the first small footbridge, and follow the zigzagging calle that becomes Ruga Giuffa, a popular store-lined strip.

The Puppin family's small hotel is a delight at these prices: This level of graciousness coupled with the *buon gusto* in decor and ambiance isn't the average find in the two-star category. Most but not all rooms come with air-conditioning, so request this in advance. A discerning savvy crowd seems to have ferreted out this pretty spot, and its suites with corner kitchens are a great choice for families and traveling friends, so reserve far in advance. Its location on a busy store-lined calle a 10-minute walk north-east of piazza San Marco is worth searching out upon arrival and is easy to find once you get the hang of it. Convenient but blessedly not too touristy, this predominantly Venetian neighborhood boasts a pleasant everyday feel.

Locanda Casa Verardo. Castello 4765 (at the foot of ponte Storto), 30122 Venezia. ☎ **041/528-61-27.** Fax 041/523-27-65. 11 units, 9 with bathroom. TEL. 90,000L ($51) single without bathroom, 110,000L ($62) single with bathroom; 140,000L ($79) double without bathroom, 160,000L ($90) double with bathroom; 210,000L ($118) triple with bathroom; 270,000L ($152) quad with bathroom. Rates include continental breakfast. AE, DC, MC, V. Vaporetto: San Zaccaria; from the vaporetto stop, walk straight ahead on calle delle Rasse to campo SS. Filippo e Giacomo; cross the small campo to take calle Rimpeto la Sacrestia, which begins at Bar Europa; cross the first small bridge, ponte Storto, and you'll find the hotel on your left.

The Verardo promises a rare combination: a clean, welcoming, moderately priced oasis in a quiet but centralized (expensive) part of town convenient to St. Mark's Square. I reserve serving up star status as enthusiastic new owners, Massimo and Sandra, finish their first season in 1998 (look for that star next year) and iron out any beginners' wrinkles. The Verardo has long been a favorite, and they've improved on it with a total refurbishment (from the mattresses to the wiring and plumbing) and the addition of a breakfast terrace. Most baths will be redone by the time you arrive in Venice. Many of these fresh pastel-painted rooms could be called oversized and are especially appreciated by families.

Locanda Fiorita. San Marco 3457 (on campiello Novo), 30124 Venezia. ☎ **041/523-47-54.** Fax 041/522-80-43. E-mail: locafior@tin.it. 10 units, 8 with bathroom. TV TEL. 90,000L ($51) single without bathroom, 120,000L ($68) single with bathroom; 120,000L ($68) double without bathroom, 150,000L ($84) double with bathroom. Rates include continental breakfast. Extra bed 30% of room rate. AE, MC, V. Closed Jan 8–Feb 8. Vaporetto: Accademia; cross the Accademia Bridge and continue north to the large campo Santo Stefano; cross the campo and, at the far northern end, at the church, take a left at a flower stand; go up 3 steps to reach the raised campiello (small piazza), where you'll find the hotel.

New owners have created a cool and contemporary hotel in this Venetian red villa-like palazzo, parts of which date to the 1400s. The secular wisteria vine that partially covers its facade is at its glorious best in May or June. But this small hotel is an excellent choice year-round, whether for its simply furnished rooms with newly renovated baths (hair dryers are typical of the amenities that arrived with the new owners) or for its enviable location on a tiny picture-perfect campiello off the far grander and ever popular campo Santo Stefano (whose gelateria, Paolin, is always ranked as one of the city's best). Rooms 1 and 10 have their own little terraces beneath the lush wisteria pergola and overlook the campiello: They can't be guaranteed upon reserving, so ask when you get there. Air-conditioning is optional in most rooms for 20,000L ($11) daily.

NEAR THE ACCADEMIA (DORSODURO)

✪ **Hotel Galleria.** Dorsoduro 878a (at the foot of the Accademia Bridge), 30123 Venezia. ☎ **041/520-41-72** or 041/528-58-14. Fax 041/520-41-72. 10 units, 8 with bathroom. 75,000L ($47) single without bathroom; 110,000L ($69) double without bathroom, 140,000L ($88) double with bathroom; 190,000L ($119) triple with bathroom; 240,000L ($150) quad with bathroom. Rates include continental breakfast. AE, DC, MC, V. Closed Jan 10–30 and Dec 20–27. Vaporetto: Accademia; with the Accademia Bridge behind you, the hotel is just to your left next to the Totem Il Canale art gallery.

Step through this 17th-century palazzo's leaded-glass doors and ascend the narrow spiral staircase to the second-floor reception area. If you don't know any local aristocrats but have always dreamed of flinging open your windows to find the Grand Canal before you, check in here. But reserve way in advance—these are the cheapest rooms on the canal and the most charming at these rates, thanks to the new owners, Luciano Benedetti and Stefano Franceschini (who come with years of experience at the Lido's deluxe hotels). The baths are small but were redone in 1998. The one-floor hotel's location is unrivaled, with six rooms varying in size overlooking the canal; others have partial views that include the Accademia Bridge (that's the good news) over an open-air bar/cafe that can be annoying to noise-sensitive or jet-lagged guests (that's the bad) hoping to sleep before the bar closes for the night.

Hotel Messner. Dorsoduro 216–237 (on fondamenta Ca' Balà), 30123 Venezia. ☎ **041/522-74-43.** Fax 041/522-72-66. Main House, 11 units, all with bathroom; annex, 20 units, all with bathroom. A/C TV TEL (Main House). *For Frommer's readers:* Main House: 130,000L ($73) single with bathroom; 190,000L ($107) double with bathroom; 240,000L ($135) triple with bathroom; 270,000L ($152) quad with bathroom. Annex: 115,000L ($65) single with bathroom; 160,000L ($90) double with bathroom; 210,000L ($118) triple with bathroom; 230,000L ($130) quad with bathroom. Rates include continental breakfast. AE, DC, MC, V. Closed mid-Nov to mid-Dec. Vaporetto: Salute; follow the small canal immediately to the right of La Salute Church; turn right onto the third bridge and walk straight until you see the white awning just before reaching the rio della Fornace canal.

The Messner and the Alla Salute (below) are the best choices in the Guggenheim area (the choice of those in-the-know looking for a quiet alternative to St. Mark's), and at budget-embracing rates. The Messner is a two-part hotel consisting of the Casa Principale (Main House), where you'll find a handsome beamed-ceiling lobby and rooms in a stately 14th-century palazzo, and a 15th-century annex 20 yards away. With three rooms overlooking the picturesque rio della Fornace and closer attention to detail in the decor, the Main House is usually preferred, but you may opt for the annex's independence and lower rates. The similarly priced Alla Salute next door is an alternative when the Messner is full.

Pensione alla Salute (Da Cici). Dorsoduro 222 (on fondamenta Ca' Balà), 30123 Venezia. ☎ **041/523-54-04.** Fax 041/522-22-71. 40 units, 31 with shower only or with bathroom. TEL. 100,000L ($56) single without bathroom, 140,000L ($79) single with shower only; 130,000L ($73) double without bathroom, 190,000L ($107) double with bathroom; 190,000L ($107) triple without bathroom, 250,000L ($140) triple with bathroom. Ask about rooms sleeping 4–5. Discounts given in Mar, July, and Aug. Rates include continental breakfast. No credit cards. Often closes in Jan or Feb for repairs; call ahead. Vaporetto: Salute; facing La Salute church, turn right and head to the first small bridge; cross it and walk as straight ahead as you can to the next narrow canal, where you'll turn left (before crossing the bridge) onto fondamenta Ca' Balà.

An airy lobby with beamed ceilings and cool marble floors, a small but lovely terrace garden, and a cozy cocktail bar occupy the ground level of this converted 17th-century palazzo on the picturesque rio della Fornace. Upstairs, the rooms have high ceilings and huge windows, many large enough to accommodate families of four or even five. Breakfast is served in the garden in warm weather. Personal checks are accepted.

SUPERBUDGET CHOICES

With prices at an all-time high in Venice as compared to those in other Italian cities, the only accommodations in this category are church- or university-affiliated places or the local hostel. If the following are full, check with the tourist office for its more extensive listing (most operate in summer only).

Foresteria Domus Cavanis. Dorsoduro 896a (on rio Antonio Foscarini), 30123 Venezia. ☎ and fax **041/528-73-74.** 30 beds in single or double, none with bathroom. 40,000L ($23) single; 60,000L ($34) double. Discount for students ages 15–25. Continental breakfast 7,000L ($3.95); full board available. No credit cards. Closed Oct–May. Vaporetto: Accademia; veer left around the museum, then walk straight ahead on rio Antonio Foscarini; the Domus Cavanis will be halfway down on your right.

The location is the draw here, just behind the Accademia in the quiet, largely residential Dorsoduro neighborhood, a recommended escape from congested San Marco. The rooms in this converted dorm (open June to September only) are rather plain, the beds are narrow, and the place is popular with groups, but Padre Amedeo Morandi runs a top place with rock-bottom rates.

Foresteria Valdese. Castello 5170 (at the end of calle lunga Santa Maria Formosa), 30122 Venezia. ☎ **041/528-67-97.** Fax 041/523-97-45. 6 units, 2 with bathroom; 3 dorms (bunks sleeping 8, 11, or 16); 2 apts (sleeping 4–5) with bathroom. 40,000L ($23) per person double/triple; 28,000L ($16) dorm bed; 170,000L–180,000L ($96–$101) apt (minimum stay often required). Rates for rooms/dorms include breakfast. MC, V. Vaporetto: Rialto; head southeast to campo Santa Maria Formosa; look for the Bar all'Orologio, where calle lunga Santa Maria Formosa begins; the campo is about equidistant from piazza San Marco and the Rialto Bridge.

Those lucky enough to stay at this weathered yet elegant 16th-century palazzo will get a simple room in a charming ambiance at low prices. Since it's affiliated with Italy's Waldesian and Methodist church, the dorm-style rooms are often booked by church groups, though everyone is welcomed and an international and interreligious mix is often found. Each plainly furnished room opens onto a balcony overlooking a quiet canal. The frescoes that grace the high ceilings in the doubles and two of the dorms are by Bevilacqua, who decorated parts of the Correr Museum. The two four-room apartments, with kitchens, are the best budget choice for traveling families. The reception is open Monday to Saturday 9am to 1pm and 6 to 8pm and Sunday 9am to 1pm. Two new rooms (sleeping two or four) with baths were added in 1998.

Ostello Venezia. Giudecca 86 (on fondamenta Zitelle), 30133 Venezia. ☎ **041/523-82-11.** Fax 041/523-56-89. 270 beds (about 8–16 in each dorm). 25,000L ($14) dorm bed. Youth hostel card available on premises for 30,000L ($19), or you can buy a card on an installment basis for 5,000L ($2.80) per night for 6 nights. Rates include continental breakfast/sheets/showers. V. Closed Jan 15–Feb 1. Vaporetto: Zitelle, then it's a 1-minute walk to the right of the vaporetto stop.

Modern and efficiently run by Claudio Camillo, this is Venice's largest dorm. What's more, the view of the tip of Dorsoduro and piazza San Marco makes commuting to/from the eastern end of La Giudecca island a pleasure. Registration opens at 1pm. The rooms are closed 9:30am to 1pm all year, and the curfew is 11:30pm. This youth hostel is open to budget travelers of all ages. Add the 9,000L ($6) round-trip cost of the vaporetto to the cost of staying at this hostel. The ample lunch or dinner (14,000L/$8 for three courses and fruit) is one of the best values in town, and with notice, the kitchen will pack you a picnic for 10,000L ($6).

WORTH A SPLURGE

Hotel Campiello. Castello 4647 (on campiello del Vin), 30122 Venezia. ☎ **041/520-57-64.** Fax 041/520-57-98. 16 units, all with bathroom. A/C TV TEL. 150,000L ($84) single; 240,000L ($135) double; 300,000L ($169) triple. Rates about 25% lower off-season. Rates include continental breakfast. AE, DC, MC, V. Closed 2 weeks mid- to late Jan. Vaporetto: San Zaccaria; facing the large Hotel Savoia e Jolanda, take the narrow alley on its left, leading to the small campiello del Vin; the hotel is on your right.

Nestled on a tiny campiello just off the prestigious riva degli Schiavoni (the lagoonfront location of the legendary Danieli and other four- and five-star contenders) is this gem of a family-run hotel. The atmosphere is airy and bright, largely due to the seamless and smiling management of the Bianchini sisters, Monica and Nicoletta—as charming as they are efficient. The decor in the rooms and common areas is slowly being changed to traditional Venetian style, but there's nothing stuffy or staid here. The hotel exudes hospitality and good-quality service that surpasses its modest twostar category, and the location couldn't be finer.

Locanda Sturion. San Polo 679 (on calle del Sturion), 30125 Venezia. ☎ **041/523-62-43.** Fax 041/522-83-78. E-mail: sturion@tin.it. Internet: www.sayville.com\locanda-sturion. 11 units, all with bathroom. A/C MINIBAR TV TEL. *For Frommer's readers:* 171,000L ($96) single; 200,000L–310,000L ($112–$174) double without Grand Canal view, 230,000L–357,000L ($129–$201) double with Grand Canal view; 327,000L ($184) triple without Grand Canal view, 374,000L ($210) triple with Grand Canal view; 426,000L ($239) quad without Grand Canal view, 487,000L ($274) quad with Grand Canal view. Rates include continental breakfast. AE, MC, V. Vaporetto: Rialto; from the Rialto stop, cross the bridge, turn left at the other side, and walk along the Grand Canal; calle del Sturion will be the fourth narrow alley on the right, just before San Polo 740.

Though there's been a pensione on this site since 1290, a recent rebuilding has made the Sturion a lovely hotel managed by the charming Scottish-born Helen and coowner Flavia. It's perched four elevatorless flights (and 69 challenging steps—pack light!) above the Grand Canal—one of the less extravagantly priced places where you can savor a view of the bustling central waterway at the Rialto Bridge and your morning cappuccino. Only two rooms offer canal views, though the sunny breakfast room allows everyone to share the vista. The rest of the Venetian-style rooms have a charming view over the Rialto area rooftops. Management is smooth and professional while maintaining an ambiance that's both relaxed and enjoyable. Those not in shape won't consider the high-floor canal views worth the splurge if they view the stairs as a punishment and not as a chance to work off dinner.

4 Great Deals on Dining

Venice doesn't lack for restaurants, many of which specialize in Adriatic seafood and most of which serve mediocre fare to people they expect never to see again.

Spaghetti alle vongole (in clam sauce) can be wonderful if you choose the restaurant with care; the same holds for *seppie nere con polenta* (stewed cuttlefish in its own black

A Dining Note

Eating cheaply in Venice isn't easy, yet not at all difficult if you plan well and don't rely on the serendipity that may serve you well in other cities. Pizza is a southern specialty but has been readily adopted nationwide and represents a delicious way to save money. Standing at a bar, cafe, or rosticceria is uniformly less expensive than sitting down (where prices can sometimes double), even if it's not very relaxing for the weary.

"ink" over polenta, a thick traditional staple made from corn flour). *Bigoli in salsa* (homemade spaghetti-like pasta in a distinctive but not overpowering anchovy-and-onion sauce) is harder to find but also a regional specialty. Fresh, delicious grilled fish (*pesce alla griglia*) is readily available (*surgelato* on the menu indicates frozen fish) but expect to pay handsomely: The price on the menu commonly refers to the *etto* (per 100 g)—a fraction of the full cost (have the waiter estimate it before ordering). Finally, there's the ubiquitous *frittura mista* (or *fritto misto*), a mix of fried seafood (squid, mussels, clams, cuttlefish) whose success is in the freshness, quality, and variety of the fish and oil used. More earthly dishes are *risi e bisi* (rice with peas), *pasta e fagioli* (bean-and-pasta soup), and a delicious interpretation of *fegato alla veneziana* (liver and onions), which is heaven when prepared well.

With the exception of the first category of informal spots where grazing and light dining won't elicit nasty looks, the listings below give prices for a meal consisting of a first course *(primo)* like pasta, soup, or risotto and a main course *(secondo)* of fish or meat. Don't forget to add nominal charges for bread and cover *(coperto)*, service *(servizio)*, a salad or vegetable side dish *(contorno)*, and drink *(bevanda)*.

Venetians dine early compared to Romans and those in other points south: You should be seated by 7:30 to 8:30pm. Most kitchens close at 10 or 10:30pm, even though the restaurant may stay open until 11:30pm or midnight. Restaurants usually close for a week or two (or more) sometime in January or February before Carnevale and often for 2 to 3 weeks in August.

BUDGET BESTS

Venice offers countless neighborhood bars, cafes, and *bacari* (old-fashioned wine bars) where you can stand or sit with a *panino* (sandwich on a roll), *tramezzino* (triangle-shaped sandwich on sliced white bread), *toast* (here meaning a grilled ham-and-cheese sandwich), or a tasty variety of the local specialty *cichetti* (tapas-like finger foods like calamari rings, fried olives, and polenta squares). They'll cost 1,500L to 2,500L (85¢ to $1.40) if you stand at the bar, as much as double if you take a seat. Bar food is displayed in glass counters and usually sells out by late afternoon, so don't rely on this light grazing for dinner.

You'll find a concentration of popular well-stocked bars along the **Mercerie** shopping strip connecting piazza San Marco with the Rialto Bridge, the always lively **campo San Luca** (look for Bar Torino, Bar Black Jack, or the primarily pastry bar Rosa Salva), and **campo Santa Margherita.** Avoid the tired-looking pizza you'll find in most bars: Neighborhood pizzerias offer far more savory and fresher renditions for a minimum of 6,000L ($3.40), plus your drink and cover charge.

NEAR THE RIALTO BRIDGE (SAN POLO SIDE)

✪ **A Le Do Spade.** San Polo 860 (on sottoportego do Spade). ☎ **041/521-05-74.** Primi dishes 7,000L–12,000L ($3.95–$7); main courses 8,000L–12,000L ($4.50–$7). AE, V. Mon–Wed and Fri–Sat 9am–3pm and 5–11pm, Thurs 9am–3pm. Vaporetto: Rialto or San

Getting the Best Deal on Dining

- If you qualify for a Rolling Venice pass (see "Venice Deals & Discounts," at the beginning of this chapter), ask for the discount guide listing dozens of restaurants offering 10% to 30% discounts.
- Remember that standing up at a bar or cafe or rosticceria is uniformly less expensive than sitting down.
- Pizza may not be a local specialty, but it's certainly a delicious way to save money (or consider a picnic lunch in one of the piazzas), leaving more lire for dinner.
- Save your wine consumption for before or after dinner at a characteristic old bacaro (wine bar), not at the restaurant.
- Look for the words *servizio incluso* on your menu or at the bottom of your bill—you won't need to leave a 10% to 15% tip if service has already been included.
- Check out the breakdown of a *menu turistico* and determine just how hungry you are—you might spend less and be more satisfied with just pasta and a salad à la carte.
- Avoid surprises: Fish is the basis of Venice's traditional cuisine but will hike up your bill substantially. Have the waiter approximate the cost before you order, as the price usually appears per 200 grams (by the *etto*) on the menu.

Silvestro; at the San Polo side of the Rialto Bridge, walk away from the bridge and through the open-air market until you see the covered pescheria (fish market) on your right; take a left and then take the second right onto the sottoportego do Spade; walk 2 blocks and the wine bar is on your left. WINE BAR/VENETIAN.

Workers, fishmongers, and shoppers from the nearby Mercato della Pescheria (fish market) flock to this historic bacaro wine bar. There's color and bonhomie galore amid the locals here for their daily *ombra* (glass of wine)—a large number of excellent Veneto and Friuli wines are available by the glass. A counter is filled with cichetti (potato croquettes, fried calamari, polenta squares, cheeses). Unlike at most bacari, and a great stroke of luck for the foot-sore, this quintessentially Venetian cantina has added a number of tables and introduced a sit-down menu, accounting for my star here over its competitor, Cantina do Mori (below).

Cantina do Mori. San Polo 429 (on calle Galiazza). ☎ **041/522-54-01.** Sandwiches and cichetti bar food, 1,500L–2,500L (85¢–$1.40). No credit cards. Mon–Sat 9am–9pm. Vaporetto: Rialto; cross the Rialto Bridge to the San Polo side, walk to the end of the market stalls, turn left, then immediately right, and look for the small wooden cantina sign on the left. WINE BAR/SANDWICHES.

The most welcomed news I got during my 1998 trip to Venice was that this time-honored place (since 1462 the local watering hole of choice; Casanova was a habitué according to legend) was now open at lunch. Tramezzini are the fuel of Venice—sample them here where you're guaranteed fresh combinations of thinly sliced meats, tuna, cheeses, and vegetables, along with tapas-like cichetti. They're traditionally washed down with a small glass of wine, an ombra (shadow). Venetians stop to snack and socialize before and after meals, but if you don't mind standing (there are no tables) for a light lunch this is one of the best and most famous of the old-time bacari left. The locals wouldn't think of making a meal (preferably lunch) of this, but I always do. And now with a limited number of first courses like melanzane alla parmigiana

---

A Note on Fresh Fish

The fish merchants at the Mercato Rialto (Venice's main open-air market) take Monday off, which explains why so many restaurants are closed on Monday. Those that are open on Monday are selling Saturday's goods—beware!

(eggplant parmigiana) and fondi di carciofi saltati (lightly fried artichoke hearts), my obligatory stop here is more filling and fulfilling than ever.

Pizzeria da Sandro. San Polo 1473 (off campiello dei Meloni). ☎ **041/523-48-94.** Pizza 8,000L–14,000L ($4.50–$8); pasta dishes 8,000L–14,000L ($4.50–$8); main courses 12,000L–22,000L ($7–$12). AE, MC, V. Sat–Thurs noon–11pm. Vaporetto: San Silvestro; from the vaporetto stop, with your back to the Grand Canal, walk straight to the store-lined ruga Vecchia San Giovanni and take a left; follow the stream of people heading toward campo San Polo until you come upon campiello dei Meloni; the pizzeria is just beyond on your right. ITALIAN/PIZZERIA.

Like most pizzerias/trattorias, Sandro offers a dozen varieties of pizza (his specialty) as well as a full trattoria menu of pastas and entrees. But if you're looking for a 12,000L ($8) pizza-and-beer meal, this is a reliably good spot on the main drag linking the Rialto to campo San Polo (if you find yourself in campo San Polo—and you should, but not right now—you've gone too far). Italians like to carb out, and you won't raise any eyebrows if you order a pasta and pizza and pass on the meat or fish. There's communal seating at a few wooden picnic tables placed outdoors, with eight small tables inside.

OTHER CHOICES
NEAR THE RIALTO BRIDGE (SAN MARCO SIDE)

✪ **Ai Tre Spiedi.** Cannaregio 5906 (on salizzada San Cazian). ☎ **041/520-80-35.** Menu turistico with meat or fish entree 22,000L ($12); menu turistico with fish entree 30,000L ($38); primi dishes 7,000L–10,000L ($3.95–$6); main courses 16,000L–26,000L ($9–$15). MC, V. Tues–Sat noon–2:30pm and 7–9:30pm, Sun 12:30–3:30pm. Vaporetto: Rialto; on the San Marco side of the bridge, walk straight ahead to campo San Bartolomeo and take a left, following the stream of people past the post office, past the Coin department store, and past the San Crisostomo church on your right; cross the first bridge after the church, turn right at the toy store onto salizzada San Cazian, and the restaurant is on your right. VENETIAN.

Venetians bring their visiting friends here to make a *bella figura* (good impression) without breaking the bank, then swear them to secrecy. Rarely will you find as pleasant a setting and as appetizing a meal as in this casually elegant small trattoria with exposed-beam ceilings and some of the most reasonably priced fresh fish dining that'll keep meat-eaters happy as well. If you order à la carte, ask the English-speaking waiters to estimate the cost of your fish entree, since it'll typically appear priced by the etto (200 grams). This and Trattoria da Fiore (below) are the most reasonable choices for an authentic Venetian dinner of fresh fish; careful ordering needn't mean much of a splurge either. When they say it's fresh, you'll know it is.

Rosticceria San Bartolomeo. San Marco 5424 (on calle della Bissa). ☎ **041/522-35-69.** Menu turistico 17,000L–26,000L ($10–$15) in ground-floor dining room, 32,000L–42,000L ($18–$24) upstairs; pizzas and pasta courses 6,500L–8,000L ($3.65–$4.50) in ground-floor dining room, about 30% more upstairs; meat and fish courses 15,000L–23,000L ($8–$13) in ground-floor dining room, about 20% more upstairs. AE, MC, V. Thurs–Sun 9am–9pm. Vaporetto: Rialto; with the bridge at your back on the San Marco side of the canal, walk straight ahead to campo San Bartolomeo; take the underpass slightly to your left marked SOTTOPORTEGO DELLA BISSA; you'll come across the rosticceria at the first corner on your right. Look for Gislon (its old name) above the entrance. ITALIAN.

With long hours and a central location in the Rialto, this old-timer appears to be Venice's most popular rosticceria (and for good reason), so the continuous turnover guarantees fresh food. With a dozen pasta dishes and as many fish, seafood, or meat entrees, this place can satisfy any combination of culinary desires. Since the ready-made food is displayed under a glass counter, you don't have to worry about mis-translating—you'll know exactly what you're ordering. There's no coperto if you take your meal standing up or seated at the stools in the aroma-filled ground-floor eating area. For those who prefer to linger, head to the dining hall upstairs, though you can do much better than this institutional setting, which is best for a simple meal like pasta and a *contorno* (side dish).

Rosticceria Teatro Goldoni. San Marco 4747 (at the corner of calle dei Fabbri). ☎ **041/522-24-46.** Menu turistico 23,000L ($13); pizzas and pasta courses 8,000L–14,000L ($4.50–$8); combination salads 10,000L–15,000L ($6–$8); meat courses 8,000L–14,000L ($4.50–$8). AE, DC, V. Daily 8am–10pm (closed Wed Nov–Dec). Vaporetto: Rialto; walk from the San Marco side of the bridge to campo San Bartolomeo and exit it to your right in the direction of campo San Luca; the snack bar will be on your left. ITALIAN/INTERNATIONAL.

Bright and modern (though it has been here for over 50 years) and offering a wel-come seating area, this showcase of Venetian-style fast food tries to be everything: bar, cafe, rosticceria, and tavola calda on the ground floor and restaurant and pizzeria upstairs. A variety of sandwiches and pastries is displayed in a downstairs glass counter, and another has prepared foods (eggplant parmigiana, roast chicken, pasta e fagioli, lasagna) that'll be reheated when ordered; there are also dozens of pasta choices. A number of combination salads are a welcome concession to the American set and are freshest and most varied for lunch. This won't be your most memorable meal in Venice, but you won't walk away hungry, disappointed, or broke.

NEAR PIAZZA SAN MARCO

Alfredo Alfredo. Castello 4294 (on campo SS. Filippo e Giacomo). ☎ 041/522-53-31. Pasta dishes 8,000L–10,000L ($4.50–$6); main courses 8,000L–22,000L ($4.50–$12). No credit cards. Thurs–Tues 11am–2am. Vaporetto: San Zaccaria; from the riva degli Schiavoni waterfront, walk straight on calle delle Rasse to campo SS. Filippo e Giacomo. ITALIAN/INTERNATIONAL.

Though Alfredo Alfredo has a modern fast-food appearance and multiple-translation menu, rest assured of the reliability of this inexpensive spot and its rightful popularity with the 20- and 30-something set. You'll get no disparaging looks for ordering just pasta (homemade lasagna al forno is a specialty), any of the crêpes and omelets, or the unusual insalatoni (a number of chef's salad–type combinations with everything from olives and tuna to garbanzo or green beans and mozzarella). Don't confuse this with the other Alfredo, notorious for its fast food that could pass for airplane food without the airplane.

✪ **Bistrot de Venise.** San Marco 4687 (on calle dei Fabbri). ☎ 041/523-66-51. Appe-tizers and crêpes 8,000L–12,000L ($4.50–$7); pasta courses 12,000L–15,000L ($7–$8); pizza 8,000L–13,000L ($4.50–$7); main courses 18,000L–28,000L ($10–$16). MC, V. Wed–Mon 9am–1am. Vaporetto: Rialto; from the Rialto Bridge vaporetto stop, walk straight ahead on calle Bembo, which becomes calle dei Fabbri; the Bistrot is about 5 blocks ahead in the direc-tion of St. Mark's Square, on your left. VENETIAN/CONTINENTAL.

This relaxed traveler-friendly spot offers indoor (there's even a no-smoking section) and outdoor seating, young English-speaking waiters, and a varied eclectic (and generally inexpensive) menu. It's a popular meeting spot for Venetians and young artists, and you're made to feel welcome to sit and write postcards over a cappuccino, enjoy a simple lunch like risotto and salad, or dine when most of Venice is shutting down, lingering over an elaborate meal that may include dishes from 15th-century Venetian recipes (one of their more interesting specialties) or a large combination salad (insalatone). Create your own pizza, mixing and matching over 30 ingredients, or choose from a dozen entree or dessert crêpes. Peak in the back room to see what's going on—art exhibits, cabarets, live music, and poetry readings recall Paris in the old days.

Trattoria alla Rivetta. Castello 4625 (on salizzada San Provolo). ☎ **041/528-73-02.** Pasta courses 8,000L–14,000L ($4.50–$8); fish courses 10,000L–22,000L ($6–$12); other main courses 10,000L–15,000L ($6–$8). AE, MC, V. Tues–Sun noon–2:30pm and 7–10pm. Vaporetto: San Zaccaria; with your back to the water and facing the large Hotel Savoia e Jolanda, walk straight ahead to campo SS. Filippo e Giacomo; the canalside trattoria is literally tucked away next to a bridge just off the right side of the campo. SEAFOOD/VENETIAN.

Lively and frequented by gondoliers (always a reliable indicator of quality dining for the right price), merchants, and visitors who are drawn to its bonhomie and bustling popularity, this is one of the safer bets for Venetian cuisine and company in the San Marco area, a 10-minute walk east of the piazza. All sorts of fish—the specialty—decorate the window of this brightly lit place, where there's usually a short wait, even off-season.

NEAR LA FENICE OPERA HOUSE

Osteria alle Botteghe. San Marco 3454 (on calle delle Botteghe). ☎ **041/522-81-81.** Pizza 7,000L–14,000L ($3.95–$18); pasta courses 8,000L ($4.50); meat or fish dishes 14,000L ($8). DC, MC, V. Mon–Sat 11am–4pm and 7–10pm. Vaporetto: Accademia or Sant'Angelo; first find your way to campo Santo Stefano (follow the stream of people or ask); from the campo, take the narrow calle delle Botteghe at the Gelateria Paolin across from Santo Stefano church; the osteria is on the right. PIZZERIA/ITALIAN.

With a wide variety of tempting possibilities, this neighborhood favorite is a great choice for a pizza, a light snack, or an elaborate meal in informal surroundings. You can have stand-up cichetti and fresh sandwiches at the bar or windowside counter, while more serious diners can head to the tables in back to enjoy the dozen pizzas, tavola calda (a glass counter–enclosed buffet of prepared dishes like eggplant parmigiana, lasagna, and fresh cooked vegetables in season reheated when you order), or pastas.

✪ **Trattoria da Fiore.** San Marco 3561 (on calle delle Botteghe). ☎ **041/523-53-10.** Reservations suggested. Pasta dishes 9,000L–14,000L ($5–$8); fish and meat courses 18,000L–26,000L ($10–$15). AE, DC, MC, V. Wed–Mon noon–3pm and 7–10pm. Vaporetto: Accademia; cross the bridge to the San Marco side and walk straight ahead to the wide expanse of campo Santo Stefano; exit the campo at the northern end, take a left at the Bar/Gelateria Paolin onto calle delle Botteghe, and the trattoria is on your right. VENETIAN.

Don't confuse this trattoria with the well-known and expensive Osteria da Fiore. You might not eat better here, but it'll seem that way when your modest bill arrives. Start with the house specialty, pennette alla Fiore (with olive oil, garlic, and seven in-season vegetables), and you may be happy to call it a night. Or try the frittura mista, over a dozen varieties of fresh fish and seafood—a bargain at 20,000L to 25,000L ($11 to $14), depending on the day's ingredients. The *zuppa di pesce alla chef,* a delicious bouillabaisse-like soup, is stocked with mussels, crab, clams, shrimp, and tuna. At only 25,000L ($14), it doesn't get any better and is a meal in itself. You might want to come back some afternoon: This is a great place to snack or make a light lunch out of cichetti at the Bar Fiore next door (10:30am to 10:30pm).

✪ **Vino Vino.** San Marco 2007 (on ponte delle Veste). ☎ **041/523-70-27.** Pasta 8,000L ($4.50); main courses 8,000L–15,000L ($4.50–$8). AE, DC, MC, V. Wed–Mon 10am–midnight, Sat 10am–1am. Vaporetto: San Marco; with your back to the basilica, exit piazza San Marco through the arcade on the far left side; keep walking straight, pass American Express, cross over the canal, and, before the street jags left, turn right onto calle Veste; Vino Vino is just ahead, after a small bridge, and on your left. WINE BAR/ITALIAN.

Only a few years old, Vino Vino is already an institution, the informal wine-bar archetype offering well-prepared simple food to accompany an impressive selection of local and European wines sold by the bottle or glass. The Venetian specialties are written on a chalkboard but also usually displayed at the glass counter. After placing your order, settle into one of about a dozen wooden tables squeezed into two simple storefront-style rooms. You might eat better elsewhere, but not with this selection of wines. Come a bit early to avoid the inevitable crowd: Though the place is frequented for its late hours, the food usually runs out before closing. Venetians of all ages and social stations stop by for a chat over a glass of wine, not late dinners.

NEAR CAMPO DEI FRARI

Trattoria/Pizzeria San Tomà. San Polo 2864/A (on campo San Tomà). ☎ **041/523-88-19.** Pizza 8,000L–14,000L ($4.50–$8); piatto unico (combination meal) 15,000L ($8); menu turistico 20,000L ($11); pasta 8,000L–16,000L ($4.50–$9); main courses 12,000L–24,000L ($7–$14). DC, V. Wed–Mon 12:30–3:30pm and 6:30–11:30pm. Vaporetto: San Tomà; walk straight on calle del Traghetto; turn right and you'll be in campo San Tomà; the restaurant is on your left. ITALIAN/PIZZERIA.

Big appetites and big spenders can eat expensively here, but it's just as easy and enjoyable to spend surprisingly little. *Piatto unico* ("single course") meals are something unique here, the less expensive (13,000L/$7) being baked lasagna and a house salad and the more expensive (15,000L/$8) roast chicken and baked potatoes. San Tomà is as popular a pizzeria as it is a trattoria, and for a song you can enjoy the perfect pizza and glass of Veneto wine alfresco in this charming piazza.

BETWEEN THE ACCADEMIA & CAMPO SANTA MARGHERITA (DORSODURO)

Brasserie ai Pugni. Dorsoduro 2839 (at the foot of ponte dei Pugni). ☎ **041/523-98-31.** Menu turistici 10,000L, 12,000L, and 18,000L ($6, $7, and $10). AE, DC, MC, V. Tues–Sun noon–3pm and 7–11:30pm. Vaporetto: Ca' Rezzonico; walk due west toward campo San Barnabà; the restaurant is in front of the floating produce boat, a neighborhood fixture. ITALIAN/INTERNATIONAL.

Visitors seek out this no-frills canalside pub/bistro for the relaxed setting, and young locals for the unusual value for their money. With no cover and tax included, there are no hidden fees for simple but welcome meals even when you order à la carte or choose to linger over a beer. The most expensive menu turistico offers a daily pasta, *cotoletta alla milanese* (a northern Italian version of breaded Wiener schnitzel), and a house salad. If that's not reason enough to make a return visit, you can't leave Venice without experiencing this residential corner nestled between two lovely piazzas: the colorful campo San Barnabà and the far more expansive campo Santa Margherita. The area's pièce de résistance is the picturesque produce barge moored outside the pub—the last such floating market still used in Venice.

Taverna San Trovaso. Dorsoduro 1016 (on fondamenta Priuli). ☎ **041/520-37-03.** Menu turistico 26,000L ($15); pizzas and pasta courses 7,000L–14,000L ($3.95–$8); meat courses 10,000L–20,000L ($6–$11); fish courses 14,000L–25,000L ($8–$14). AE, MC, V. Tues–Sun noon–2:45pm and 7–10:30pm. Vaporetto: Rialto; walk to the right around the Accademia and take a right onto calle Gambara; when this street ends at a small canal, rio di San Trovaso, turn left onto fondamenta Priuli and the taverna is on your left. VENETIAN.

Wine bottles line wood-paneled walls and vaulted ceilings augment the sense of character in this cozy canalside tavern, always packed with an interesting mix of locals and first-timers. The menu turistico includes wine, an ample *frittura mista* (assortment of fried seafood), and dessert. Order à la carte from a variety of primi (first-course dishes; the gnocchi is homemade and makes a frequent appearance) or *secondi*—from a variety of pizzas to the local specialty of *fegato alla veneziana* (liver and onions) or simply grilled fish, the taverna's claim to fame. For a special occasion that'll test your budget but not bankrupt you, consider the fixed-price four-course menu at 65,000L ($37): It starts with a fresh antipasto of seafood followed by pasta and a fish entree (changing with the day's catch) and includes side dishes, dessert, and wine. While in the neighborhood, stroll along rio San Trovaso toward the Canale della Giudecca: On your right will be the squero di San Trovaso, one of the very few working boatyards that still makes and repairs the traditional gondolas.

PICNICKING

The enjoyable alternative of a picnic lunch allows you to indulge later with a fine dinner *alla veneziana* while observing the life of the city's few open piazzas or the aquatic parade on the Grand Canal. Doing your own shopping for food can be an interesting experience since there are few supermarkets as we know them.

Venice's principal open-air market is commonly referred to as the **Mercato Rialto** and is a sight to see. It has two parts, beginning with the fresh fruit and produce section, whose many stalls, alternating with souvenir vendors, unfold north on the San Polo side of the Rialto Bridge (behind these stalls are permanent food stores whose delicious cheese, cold cuts, and bread selections alone make the perfect lunch). At its farthest point is the covered fresh-fish market, picturesquely located on the Grand Canal opposite the magnificent Ca' d'Oro and still redolent of the days when it was one of the Mediterranean's great fish markets. The fruit and produce vendors are there Monday to Saturday 7am to 1pm, with a number who stay on in the afternoon; the fish merchants take Monday off and work on the other days in the mornings only.

Tuesday to Saturday 8:30am to 1 or 2pm, a number of open-air stalls selling fresh fruit and vegetables set up on spacious **campo Santa Margherita.** You should have no trouble filling out your picnic spread with the fixings available at the various shops lining the sides of the campo, including an exceptional *panetteria* (bakery), Rizzo Pane, at no. 2772; a fine *salumeria* (deli) at no. 2844; and a good shop for wine, sweets, and other picnic accessories next door. There's even a conventional supermarket, Merlini, just off the campo in the direction of the quasi-adjacent campo San Barnabà at no. 3019. This is also the area where you'll find Venice's **floating market,** operating from a boat moored just off campo San Barnabà at the ponte dei Pugni. This market is open Monday to Saturday 8am to 1pm and 3:30 to 7:30pm (closed Wednesday afternoon).

Alas, Venice doesn't have much in the way of green space for a picnic. An enjoyable alternative is to find some of the larger piazzas or campi that have park benches, and in some cases even a tree or two for shade, such as **campo Santa Margherita** and **campo San Polo.** For a picnic with a view, scout out the **Punta della Dogana** area near La Salute church for a prime viewing site across the Grand Canal from San Marco and the Palazzo Ducale; pull up a piece of the embankment and watch all the water activity. But perhaps the best picnic site is in a patch of sun on the **marble steps** leading down to the water of the Grand Canal, at the foot of the Rialto Bridge on the San Polo side.

WORTH A SPLURGE

✪ **Alla Madonna.** San Polo 594 (on calle della Madonna). ☎ **041/522-38-24.** Reservations required. Pasta 8,000L–16,000L ($4.50–$9); meat courses 12,000L–18,000L ($7–$10); fresh fish courses 9,000L–12,000L ($5–$7) per etto (200 grams). AE, MC, V. Thurs–Tues noon–3pm and 7–10pm. Vaporetto: Rialto; from the foot of the Rialto Bridge on the San Polo side of the Grand Canal, turn left and follow the canal; calle della Madonna (also called sottoportego della Madonna) will be the second calle on your right (look for the big yellow sign). VENETIAN.

This trattoria, packing them in for over 5 years, has it all: a location near the Rialto Bridge, five large dining rooms, an encouraging mix of locals and foreigners, a decor of high-beamed ceilings and walls packed with local artists' work, and—most important—a professional kitchen staff that prepares a menu of Venetian fish and seafood to perfection. With all this and (by Venetian standards) moderate prices to boot, it's no surprise that Alla Madonna is always jumping. (Don't expect the waiter to smile if you linger too long over dessert.) Most of the first courses are prepared with seafood, like spaghetti or risotto with *frutti di mare* (shrimp, clams, mussels) or pasta with *sepie* (cuttlefish), blackened from its own ink. Most of the special fish selections are best simply prepared *alla griglia* (grilled).

Trattoria da Remigio. Castello 3416 (on calle Bosello). ☎ **041/523-00-89.** Reservations required. Pasta courses 6,000L–10,000L ($3.40–$6); main courses 10,000L–20,000L ($6–$11). AE, DC, MC, V. Mon 1–3pm, Wed–Sun 1–3pm and 7–11pm. Vaporetto: San Zaccaria; follow riva degli Schiavoni east until you come to the white Chiesa della Pietà; turn left onto calle della Pietà, which jags left into calle Bosello; the restaurant is about 3 blocks ahead on your left. ITALIAN/VENETIAN.

Famous for its straightforward renditions of Adriatic classics, Remigio is the kind of place where you can order a simple plate of gnocchi alla pescatora (homemade gnocchi in tomato-based seafood sauce) and know it'll be buonissimo. The English-speaking head waiter, Pino, will talk you through the day's fish dishes (John Dory, sole, monkfish, cuttlefish); sold by the etto (200 grams), they're fresh and perfectly prepared, as is any antipasto. You'll even find a dozen meat possibilities. There are two pleasant but smallish dining rooms. Remigio's—less abuzz and more sedate than Alla Madonna (above)—is well known though not as easy to find, but just ask any local. It has been there forever, though it's looking fresh these days after a recent renovation.

5 Seeing the Sights

SIGHTSEEING SUGGESTIONS

IF YOU HAVE 1 DAY If you have just 1 day, I dare to suggest that you avoid the big draws: the Basilica di San Marco, Palazzo Ducale, Accademia, and Peggy Guggenheim Collection. Instead, wander among the **labyrinth of streets and passages,** because this ancient city "whose streets are filled with water" is its own most extraordinary attraction. For its weathered Oriental beauty, way of life, and Eastern/Western fusion of architecture and wealth of history, Venice has no match. Some of the residential neighborhoods off the beaten track are eastern **Castello** near the Arsenal, the **Ghetto** (once the Jewish quarter) in northern Cannaregio, and the island of **La Giudecca.** At some point, ride the **no. 1 vaporetto** line its full length from piazza San Marco to the Ferrovia (train station)—about 45 minutes each way. You'll cruise by the unbroken sequence of hundreds of proud palazzi lining the principal aquatic boulevard, as postcard perfect early in the morning as late in the afternoon; you might even do it again at midnight or after the city has gone to sleep and the quasi-traffic-free Grand Canal is illuminated by the moon.

IF YOU HAVE 2 DAYS   Once you've thoroughly taken in the city's best sight—itself—on Day 1, on Day 2 move on to the monumental sights. First has to be the magnificent **Basilica di San Marco** and its neighboring pink-and-white marble **Palazzo Ducale (Doges' Palace),** both on piazza San Marco. While you're on the piazza, take in the **Museo Correr** and ride the elevator to the top of the **Campanile di San Marco** for a terrific view of the city. If warm weather has arrived, so have the outdoor orchestras, one for each of the historic **cafes** lining the magnificent piazza San Marco.

IF YOU HAVE 3 DAYS   On Days 1 and 2 follow the above. Turn over Day 3 to Venice's art. In Dorsoduro, visit the **Accademia** for a look at the city's Renaissance heritage and the nearby **Collezione Peggy Guggenheim** for one of Europe's best displays of international 20th-century works. If you have the time and energy, take in either the **Ca' Rezzonico** (also in Dorsoduro) or the **Ca' d'Oro** (north of the Rialto Bridge)—either museum provides a look at the interior of one of the great palazzi gracing the Grand Canal. In between, make sure you stop for sustenance at any of the myriad **bacari** wine bars for the cichetti hors d'oeuvres and the colorful atmosphere.

IF YOU HAVE 5 DAYS   On Days 1 to 3, follow the above. For the sounds and smells of a Venice unchanged over the centuries, on Days 4 and 5 check out what's new at the Rialto by taking a stroll through the open-air produce market, the **Erberia,** and winding up at the weird and wonderful **Pescheria** (fish market). In Castello, visit the cavernous **Church of Santi Giovanni e Paolo** and the **Venetian Pantheon,** then repair to one of the small **outdoor cafes** for some piazza life. Alternatively, visit the **Scuola Grande di San Rocco** in San Polo on the other side of town—famous for its interior decorated with about 50 works by Tintoretto. Or if you're ready to expand your horizons, spend a day exploring the rest of the lagoon on islands like **Murano, Burano,** and **Torcello.**

THE BASILICA & THE PALAZZO DUCALE

✪ **Basilica di San Marco.** San Marco, piazza San Marco. ☎ **041/522-52-05.** Basilica, free; Museo Marciano (includes Loggia dei Cavalli), 3,000L ($1.70) adults, 1,500L (85¢) students; Tesoro (Treasury), 4,000L ($2.25) adults, 2,000L ($1.10) students; Pala d'Oro (altar screen), 3,000L ($1.70) adults, 2,000L ($1.10) students. Basilica, summer Mon–Sat 9am–5:30pm, Sun 2–5:30pm; winter Mon–Sat 9:30am–4:30pm, Sun 1:30–4:30pm; last entrance 30 minutes before closing time. Museo Marciano, summer Mon–Sun 10am–5pm; winter Mon–Sun 10am–4:30pm. Tesoro and Pala d'Oro, summer Mon–Sat 10am–5pm, Sun 1:30–5pm; winter Mon–Sat 10am–4:40pm, Sun 1:30–5pm. Vaporetto: San Marco.

Venice for centuries was Europe's principal gateway between the Orient and the West, so the style for the sumptuously Byzantine Basilica di San Marco, replete with five mosque-like bulbed domes, was borrowed from Constantinople (particularly, experts say, from Hagia Sofia). Legend has it that in 828 two merchants conspired to smuggle the remains of St. Mark the Evangelist from Alexandria by packing them in pickled pork, guaranteeing that Muslim guards would keep their distance. Thus, St. Mark replaced the Greek St. Theodore as Venice's patron saint and a small chapel was built in his honor. Through the subsequent centuries (much of what you see is from the 11th century), wealthy Venetian merchants and politicians vied with each other in donating gifts to expand and embellish this church, the saint's resting place, and, with the adjacent Palazzo Ducale, a symbol of Venetian wealth and power.

And so it is that San Marco earned its name as the Chiesa d'Oro (Golden Church), its cavernous interior exquisitely gilded with Byzantine mosaics added over some 7 centuries and covering every inch of the ceiling and pavements. For a close look at many of the most remarkable ceiling mosaics and for a better view of the Oriental carpet–like patterns of the pavements, pay the admission to go up to the galleries (entrance to the **Museo Marciano** is in the atrium). This is also the only way to the **Loggia dei Cavalli,** the open balcony running along the basilica's facade above the principal entrance, from which you can enjoy a closer look at the exterior. More important, it lets you mingle with the loggia's copies of the celebrated quadriga of gilded bronze horses (from the 2nd or 3rd century) brought here from Constantinople in 1204 with other booty from the Crusades; together with the Lion of St. Mark (a kind of mascot for the patron saint), they were a symbol of the unrivaled Maritime Republic. The recently restored originals have been moved inside to the otherwise not terribly interesting museum. A visit to the Loggia is a highlight, providing an excellent view of the piazza and what Napoléon called "the most beautiful salon in the world." The **Torre dell'Orologio (Clock Tower)** is to your right; its restoration (to be done by February 1999) was timed to coordinate with its 500-year anniversary; the **campanile (bell tower)** towers to your left, and beyond are the glistening waters of the lagoon.

The church's greatest treasure is the magnificent **Pala d'Oro,** an enamel- and jewel-encrusted golden altar screen created as early as the 10th century and embellished by master artisans between the 12th and 14th centuries. It's behind the main altar that covers the tomb of St. Mark. Also worth a visit is the **Tesoro (Treasury),** to the far right of the altar, with a collection of the Crusaders' plunder from Constantinople. Much of the Venetian fleet's booty has been incorporated into the basilica's interior and exterior in the form of marble, columns, capitals, and statuary. Second to the Pala d'Oro in importance is the 10th-century *Madonna di Nicopeia,* a bejeweled icon taken from Constantinople and exhibited in its own chapel to the left of the main altar.

Admission to the basilica is free but restricted, and there's often a line in high season—don't leave Venice without visiting its candlelit glittering interior, still redolent of Eastern cultures. In July and August (with much less certainty the rest of the year) there are free tours given Monday to Saturday by church-affiliated volunteers. They leave four or five times daily, beginning at 10:30am; groups gather in the atrium. Check the atrium for posters with schedules. The basilica is open Sunday morning for those wishing to attend mass; all others are strongly discouraged from entering during services (see hours above).

✪ **Palazzo Ducale and ponte dei Sospiri (Ducal Palace and Bridge of Sighs).** San Marco, piazza San Marco. ☎ **041/522-49-51.** Joint ticket with Museo Correr, 14,000L ($8) adults, 8,000L ($4.50) students. "Secret Trails" guided tours Thurs–Tues by reservations only, 10,000L ($6) adults, 6,000L ($3.40) students. Summer daily 8:30am–7pm (winter hours may vary); last entrance 1 hour before closing. Vaporetto: San Marco.

The Gothic-Renaissance **Palazzo Ducale,** the pink-and-white marble residence and government center of the doges (or "dukes," elected for life) who ruled Venice for centuries, stands between the Basilica di San Marco and the Bacino San Marco lagoon. After a succession of fires it was built and rebuilt in 1340 and 1424, forever expanding and transforming. The main entrance is at the 15th-century **Porta della Carta (Gate of Paper),** where the doges' proclamations were posted; it opens onto a splendid inner courtyard with a double row of Renaissance arches. Ahead you'll see Sansovino's enormous **Scala dei Giganti (Stairway of the Giants),** scene of the doges' lavish inaugurations and never used by mere mortals; it leads to wood-paneled courts and meeting rooms. The walls and ceilings of these rooms were richly

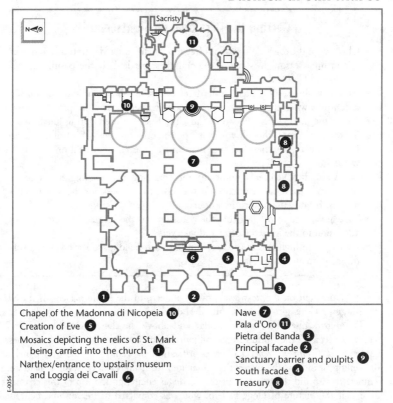

Chapel of the Madonna di Nicopeia **10**
Creation of Eve **5**
Mosaics depicting the relics of St. Mark being carried into the church **1**
Narthex/entrance to upstairs museum and Loggia dei Cavalli **6**

Nave **7**
Pala d'Oro **11**
Pietra del Banda **3**
Principal facade **2**
Sanctuary barrier and pulpits **9**
South facade **4**
Treasury **8**

decorated by Venetian masters like Veronese, Titian, Carpaccio, and Tintoretto to illustrate the history of the puissant Republic while impressing diplomats and emissaries from around the world with the uncontested prosperity and power it had attained.

If you want to understand something of this magnificent palace, the fascinating history of the 1,000-year-old Maritime Republic, and the intrigue of the government that ruled it, search out the infrared **audio tour** (at entrance: 6,000L/$3.40). Unless you can tag along with an English-language tour group, you may otherwise miss out on the importance of much of what you're seeing.

The first room you'll come to is the **Sala delle Quattro Porte (Hall of the Four Doors),** with a ceiling by Tintoretto. Foreign ambassadors were received in the **Sala del Collegio (College Chamber),** the next room, decorated with Tintorettos and 11 Veroneses. A right turn leads into one of the most impressive of the rooms, the richly adorned **Senato (Senate Chamber),** with Tintoretto's ceiling painting *The Triumph of Venice.* After passing again through the Sala delle Quattro Porte, you'll come to the Veronese-decorated **Stanza del Consiglio dei Dieci (Room of the Council of Ten,** the security police), where justice was dispensed. At times they were considered more powerful than the Senate and were feared by all. Just outside the adjacent chamber, the **Sala della Bussola (Compass Chamber),** notice the Bocca dei Leoni ("lion's mouth"), a slit in the wall into which secret denunciations of alleged enemies of the state were placed for quick action by the feared Council of Ten.

Getting the Best Deal on Sightseeing

- Check with the tourist office about free tours being offered (erratically and usually in high season) in some of the churches, particularly the Basilica di San Marco and Chiesa dei Frari.
- Note that almost all churches offer free admission—but don't show up during lunchtime, when they close for a few hours, reopening at 4 or 5pm.
- To fill the hours when the stores and churches are closed during lunch, head for the museums—though you won't be the only one with this brilliant idea. Recharge your batteries and take that tour of the Grand Canal on the no. 1 vaporetto.
- Be aware that Venice is notorious for changing the opening hours of its museums and even its churches. At the tourist office, ask for the season's current list of museum and church hours.
- Take advantage of the fact that the admission to the Palazzo Ducale includes admission to the Museo Correr and vice versa.
- Plan well: In high season the museum lines can be long, so leave yourself sufficient time once you're inside.

The main sight on the next level down—indeed, in the entire palace—is the **Sala del Maggior Consiglio (Great Council Hall).** This enormous space is made special by Tintoretto's huge *Paradiso* at the far end above the doge's seat. Measuring 23 feet by 75 feet, it's the world's largest oil painting on canvas; together with Veronese's gorgeous *Il Trionfo di Venezia* (The Glorification of Venice) in the oval panel on the ceiling, it affirms the power that emanated from the Council sessions held here. Tintoretto also did the portraits of the 76 doges encircling the top of this chamber; note that the picture of Doge Faliero, who was convicted of treason and beheaded in 1355, has been blacked out. Though elected for life since the 7th century, over time the doge became nothing but a figurehead: The power rested in the Great Council, comprised mostly of Venice's nobles and sometimes numbering well over 1,500 members.

Exit the hall via the tiny doorway on the opposite side of Tintoretto's *Paradiso* to find the enclosed **ponte dei Sospiri (Bridge of Sighs),** connecting the palace with the grim **Prigioni (Prisons).** The bridge took its current name in the 19th century, when visiting northern European poets envisioned the prisoners' final breath of resignation upon viewing the outside world one last time before being locked in their fetid cells. Some attribute the name to Casanova, who, after his arrest in 1755 (he was accused of spreading antireligious propaganda), crossed this very bridge. He was one of the rare few to escape alive, returning to Venice 20 years later.

Campanile di San Marco (Bell Tower). San Marco, piazza San Marco. ☎ **041/522-40-64.** Admission 6,000L ($3.40) adults, 3,000L ($1.70) students. June–Aug daily 9am–7:30pm; Sept–May daily 9:30am–4pm. Vaporetto: San Marco.

It's an easy elevator ride to the top of this 324-foot campanile for a breathtaking view of the lagoon, its neighboring islands, and the red rooftops and church domes. On a clear day you may even see the distant snowcapped Alps. Built in the 9th century, then rebuilt in the 12th, 14th, and 16th centuries, it collapsed unexpectedly in 1902, miraculously hurting no one. It was rebuilt exactly as before, using the same materials, even rescuing one of the five historic bells. Despite the scaffolding now enshrouding it (at press time), it's still open for business.

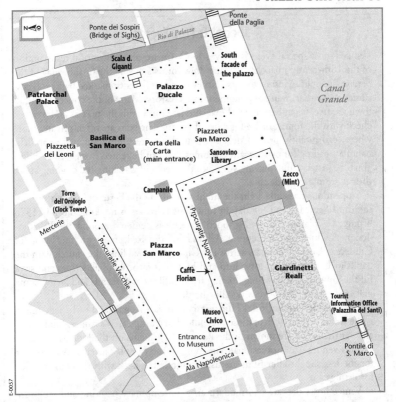

THE TOP MUSEUMS

✪ Galleria dell'Accademia. Dorsoduro, at the foot of the Accademia Bridge. ☎ **041/522-22-47.** Admission 12,000L ($7). Mon–Sat 9am–7pm, Sun 9am–2pm. Vaporetto: Accademia.

The Accademia is the treasure house of Venetian painting, which is exhibited chronologically from the 13th to the 18th centuries. There's no one hallmark masterpiece here; this is an outstanding and comprehensive showcase of works by all the great masters of Venice, the world's largest such collection. It includes the Bellini brothers and Carpaccio from the 15th century; Giorgione, Tintoretto, Veronese, and Titian from the 16th; and Piazzetta, Longhi, Canaletto, and Tiepolo from the 17th and 18th centuries. Most of all, though, the works open a window onto the Venice of 500 years ago. You'll see in the canvases how little Venice, perhaps least of any city in Europe, has changed. Housed in a deconsecrated church and an adjoining scuola (confraternity hall), this is Venice's principal picture gallery and one of the most important in Italy.

Admission is limited due to fire regulations and lines can be daunting, but come early (or show up at the end of the day), put up with the wait, and don't miss it.

Collezione Peggy Guggenheim. Dorsoduro 701 (on calle San Cristoforo). ☎ **041/520-62-88.** Admission 12,000L ($7) adults, 8,000L ($4.50) students. Wed–Mon 11am–6pm. Vaporetto: Accademia; walk around the left side of the Accademia, take the first left, and walk straight ahead following the signs—you'll cross a canal, then walk alongside another, until turning left when necessary.

Special & Free Events

Venice's most special event is the yearly ✪ **Carnevale,** a theatrical resuscitation of the 18th-century bacchanalia that drew tourists during the final heyday of the Serene Republic. Most of today's Carnevale-related events, masked balls, and costumes evoke that swan-song moment in its history. Many of the concerts around town are free, when baroque to Dixieland jazz music fills the piazzas and byways; check with the tourist office for a list of events. The balls are often private; those where (exorbitantly priced) tickets are available are sumptuous, with candlelit banquets calling for extravagant costumes that can be rented from special shops. You'll be just as happy having your face painted and watching the ongoing street theater from a ringside cafe.

Stupendous fireworks light the night sky during the **Festa del Redentore,** on the third Saturday and Sunday in July. This celebration marking the July 1578 lifting of a plague that had gripped the city is centered around the Palladio-designed Chiesa del Redentore (Church of the Redeemer) on the island of Giudecca. A bridge of boats across the Giudecca Canal links the church with the banks of Le Zattere in Dorsoduro and hundreds of boats of all shapes and sizes fill the Giudecca. It's one big floating feast until night descends and an awesome half-hour *spettacolo* of fireworks fills the sky.

The **Venice International Film Festival,** in late August and early September, is the finest summer celebration of celluloid in Europe after Cannes. Films from all over the world are shown in the Palazzo del Cinema on the Lido as well as at various venues—and occasionally in some of the campi. Ticket prices vary but for the less sought-after films are usually modest. Check with the tourist office for listings.

Venice hosts the latest in modern and contemporary painting and sculpture from dozens of countries during the prestigious **Biennale d'Arte,** an international modern-art show that fills the pavilions of the public gardens at the east end of Castello from late May to October of every odd-numbered year (1999 marks its 102nd anniversary). Many great modern artists have been "discovered" at this world-famous show. However, because of lack of funds and in-fighting, at press time it was likely the Biennale would be postponed until 2000 and then return to its original even-year schedule. For more details, contact the tourist office.

The **Regata Storica** that takes place on the Grand Canal on the first Sunday in September is an extravagant seagoing parade in historic costume as well as a genuine regatta. Just about every seaworthy gondola, richly decorated for the occasion and piloted by gondolieri in colorful livery, participates in the opening cavalcade. The aquatic parade is followed by three regattas that proceed along the Grand Canal. You can buy grandstand tickets through the tourist office, or you can come early and pull up a piece of embankment near the Rialto Bridge for the best seats in town.

April 25 is a local holiday, the feast day of St. Mark, beloved patron saint of Venice and of the ancient Serene Republic. A special high mass is celebrated in the Basilica di San Marco, roses are exchanged between loved ones, and a quiet air of *festa* permeates another closed-down town.

One of the world's most important collections of avant-garde painting and sculpture of the first half of the 20th century, this collection of painting and sculpture was assembled by the eccentric and eclectic American expatriate Peggy Guggenheim. She did a commendable job, with particular strengths in cubism, European abstraction, surrealism, and abstract expressionism since about 1910.

Among the major works are Magritte's *Empire of Light,* Picasso's *La Baignade,* Kandinsky's *Landscape with Church (with Red Spot),* Metzinger's *The Racing Cyclist,* and Pollock's *Alchemy.* The museum is also home to several haunting canvases by Max Ernst (once married to Guggenheim), Giacometti's unique figures, Brancusi's fluid sculptures, and numerous works by Braque, Dalí, Léger, Mondrian, Chagall, and Miró.

The 18th-century Palazzo Venier dei Leoni, never finished and thus its unusual one-story structure, was purchased by Guggenheim in 1949 and became her home in Venice until her death in 1979. The graves of her canine companions share the lovely interior garden with several sculptures, while the patio at the side of the Grand Canal, watched over by Marino Marini's *Angel of the Citadel,* is one of the best spots to linger. A new wing has opened across the inside courtyard, housing an interesting museum shop, temporary exhibit space, and a nice cafe/restaurant whose fresh sandwiches aren't cheap (8,000L to 18,000L/$4.50 to $10) but are worth the splurge to prolong your stay. Don't be shy about speaking English with the young staff working here on internship: Most of them are American.

OTHER MUSEUMS

Scuola Grande di San Rocco. San Polo 3058 (on campo San Rocco). ☎ **041/523-48-64.** Admission 8,000L ($4.50) adults, 6,000L ($3.40) students. Apr–Oct daily 9am–5:30pm; Nov–Mar daily 10am–4pm. Vaporetto: San Tomà; walk straight ahead on calle del Traghetto and turn right and then immediately left across campo San Tomà; walk as straight ahead as you can, on Ramo Mandoler, calle larga Prima, and finally salizzada San Rocco, which leads into the campo of the same name—look for the crimson sign behind the Frari Church.

This museum is a dazzling monument to Tintoretto—the largest collection of his work anywhere. The series of more than 50 dark and dramatic works took more than 20 years to complete, making this the richest of the many scuole (confraternity guilds) that once flourished in Venice. Begin upstairs in the **Sala dell'Albergo,** where the most notable of the enormous, powerful canvases is the moving *La Crocifissione* (The Crucifixion). In the center of the gilt ceiling of the **Great Hall,** also upstairs, is *Il Serpente di Bronzo* (The Bronze Snake). Among the eight paintings downstairs, each depicting a scene from the New Testament, the most noteworthy is *La Strage degli Innocenti* (The Slaughter of the Innocents).

Museo Correr. San Marco, west end of piazza San Marco. ☎ **041/522-56-25.** Joint ticket with Palazzo Ducale, 14,000 ($8) adults, 8,000L ($4.50) students. Summer daily 9am–7pm; winter Wed–Mon 9am–4pm; last entrance 45 minutes before closing. Vaporetto: San Marco.

This museum, which you enter through an arcade at the west end of piazza San Marco, opposite the basilica, is no match for the Accademia but does include some interesting scenes of Venetian life among its paintings and a fine collection of artifacts like coins, costumes, the doges' ceremonial robes and hats, and an incredible pair of 15-inch platform shoes that give an interesting feel for aspects of the day-to-day life in La Serenissima in the heyday of its glory. Bequeathed to the city by the aristocratic Correr family in 1830, it's divided into three sections: the History Section, the Painting Section, and the Museum of the Risorgimento. Of the paintings, Carpaccio's *Le Cortigiane* (The Courtesans) in Room 15 is one of the most notable.

Venice

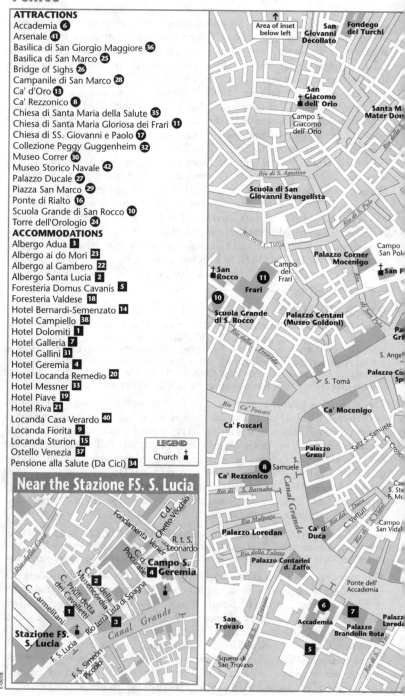

LEGEND
Church †

Near the Stazione FS. S. Lucia

E-0058

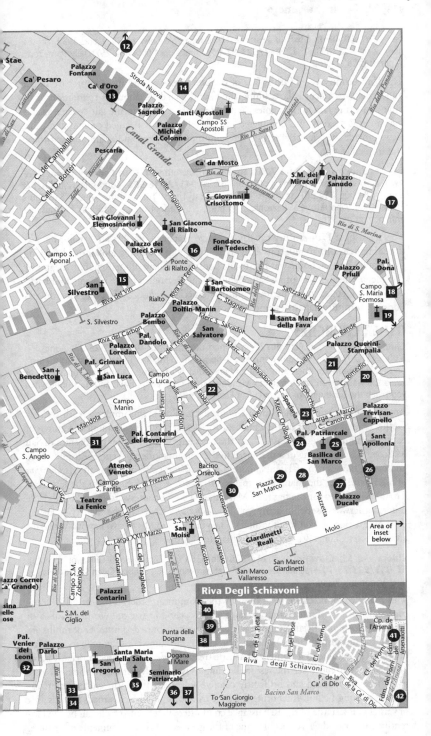

Ca' d'Oro (Galleria Giorgio Franchetti). Cannaregio between 3931 and 3932 (on the narrow calle Ca' d'Oro). ☎ **041/523-87-90.** Admission 4,000L ($2.25). Daily 9am–2pm. Vaporetto: Ca' d'Oro.

The 15th-century Ca' d'Oro is one of the best preserved and most impressive of the hundreds of patrician palazzi lining the Grand Canal. A laborious restoration of its pink-and-white facade (its name, the Golden Palace, refers to the gilt-covered facade that no longer exists) was completed in 1995. The ornate beamed ceilings and canal views provide the seignorial setting for sculptures, paintings, and an impressive bronze and iron collection.

Ca' Rezzonico (Museo del 700 Veneziano) Museum of 18th-Century Decorative Arts. Dorsoduro (on fondamenta Rezzonico). ☎ **041/24-18-506.** Admission 12,000L ($7) adults, 8,000L ($4.50) students. Summer Sat–Thurs 10am–5pm; winter Sat–Thurs 10am–4pm. Vaporetto: Ca' Rezzonico; go right, cross a foot bridge, and look for museum entrance on the left.

This handsome 17th-century canalside palazzo reopened in 1997 after major renovations. Freshened up to reflect its early days, it offers an intriguing look into what living in a grand Venetian home was like in the last sybaritic days of the Republic. Begun by Longhena, the architect of La Salute church, the Rezzonico home is a splendid backdrop for this collection of period paintings (especially works by Tiepolo, Guardi, and Longhi), furniture, tapestries, and artifacts.

OTHER CHURCHES

Chiesa dei Frari. San Polo 3072 (on campo dei Frari). ☎ **041/522-26-37.** Admission 3,000L ($1.70). Mon–Sat 9am–6pm, Sun 3–6pm. Vaporetto: San Tomà; walk straight ahead on calle del Traghetto, then turn right and immediately left across campo San Tomà; walk as straight ahead as you can, on Ramo Mandoler, then calle larga Prima, and turn right when you reach the beginning of salizzada San Rocco.

Around the corner from the Scuola Grande di San Rocco, this immense 13th-century Gothic church was built by the Franciscans. Together with the Dominican Church of Santi Giovanni e Paolo in Castello, it's the city's largest church after the Basilica di San Marco and is something of a memorial to the ancient glories of Venice. Austere inside and out, it houses two of Titian's masterpieces, the most striking being the *Assumption of the Virgin,* over the main altar. In his *Virgin of the Pesaro Family,* in the left nave, Titian's wife posed for the figure of Mary, then died soon afterward in childbirth. The other masterwork is Bellini's triptych *Madonna and Child,* in the sacristy (take the door on the right as you face the altar). The grandiose tombs of two famous Venetians are also here: Canova (d. 1822) and Titian (d. 1576).

Chiesa dei SS. Giovanni e Paolo. Castello 6363 (on campo Santi Giovanni e Paolo). ☎ **041/523-75-10.** Free admission. Mon–Sat 9am–noon and 3–6pm. Open Sun for services only. Vaporetto: Rialto.

This massive Gothic church was built by the Dominican order in the early 15th century and, with the Frari church in San Polo, is second in size only to the Basilica di San Marco. An unofficial Pantheon where 25 doges are buried (a number of tombs are part of the unfinished facade), the church, commonly known as Zanipolo in Venetian dialect, is also home to a number of artistic treasures. Visit the Cappella della Rosario off the left transept to see the restored ceiling canvases by Veronese. In the right aisle is the recently restored and brilliantly colored polyptych of St. Vincent Ferrer attributed to a young Bellini. Anchoring the large campo, a popular crossroads for this area of Castello, is a statue of the Renaissance condottiere Bartolomeo Colleoni by the Florentine master Andrea Verrocchio, one of the great equestrian monuments of its time.

Chiesa di Santa Maria della Salute. Dorsoduro, on campo della Salute. ☎ **041/522-55-58.** Church, free; sacristy, 2,000L ($1.10). Daily 9am–noon and 3–5:30pm. Vaporetto: Salute.

Referred to as La Salute, this 17th-century baroque jewel proudly reigns at this important point, almost directly across from piazza San Marco, where the Grand Canal empties into the lagoon. The first stone was laid in 1631 after the Senate decided to honor the Virgin Mary of Good Health (La Salute) for delivering Venice from a plague. They accepted the revolutionary plans of a relatively unknown young architect, Baldassare Longhena (he went on to design, among other projects in Venice, the Ca' Rezzonico). He dedicated the next 50 years to overseeing its progress (he died a year after its inauguration but 5 years before its completion).

CRUISING THE CANALS

A leisurely cruise along the ✪ **Canal Grande (Grand Canal)** from piazza San Marco to the Ferrovia (train station)—or the reverse—is one of Venice's must-do experiences. Hop on the no. 1 vaporetto in the late afternoon (it's open in the front: grab one of the outdoor seats), when the weather-worn colors of the former homes of Venice's merchant elite are warmed by the soft light and reflected in the canal's rippling waters and when the traffic of the city's main thoroughfare has eased somewhat. Some 200 palazzi, churches, and imposing Republican buildings from the 14th to the 18th centuries (many of the largest now converted into banks, museums, and galleries) line this 2-mile ribbon of water that loops through the city like an inverted S, crossed by only three bridges. It's the world's grandest Main Street.

A **gondola ride,** one of Europe's great traditions, really is as romantic as it looks. Though it's often quoted in print at differing "official" rates, expect to pay at least 120,000L ($67) for up to 50 minutes, with up to six passengers per vessel, and 60,000L ($34) for an extra 25 minutes. "Gondola by night" rates are 150,000L ($84), with 75,000L ($42) for an extra 25 minutes. But aim for late afternoon, when the light does its magic on the canals' reflections. If the price is too high, ask visitors at your hotel or others lingering about at the gondola stations if they'd like to share the cost. Establish the cost, time, and explanation of route (any of the back canals are preferable to the trafficked and often choppy waters of the Grand Canal) with the gondolier before setting off.

And what of the serenading gondolier immortalized in film? An ensemble of accordion player and tenor is so expensive it's shared among several gondolas traveling together. A number of travel agents around town book the evening serenades for 50,000L ($28) per person (see American Express in "Fast Facts: Venice," earlier in this chapter).

There are 12 gondola stations around Venice, including piazzale Roma, the train station, the Rialto Bridge, and piazza San Marco. There's also a number of smaller stations, with gondoliers standing alongside their sleek black boats looking for passengers.

ORGANIZED TOURS

Most of the centrally located travel agencies will have posters in their windows advertising half- and full-day walking tours of the city's sights. Most of these tours are piggybacked onto those organized by **American Express** (see "Fast Facts: Venice"), known for the best value for your money, and should cost the same, about 36,000L ($20) for a 2-hour tour and 65,000L ($37) for a full day, per person. Free organized tours of the basilica and some of the other churches can be erratic, as they're given by volunteers.

A visit to "The Islands of the Venetian Lagoon" includes a brief stop on Murano, Burano, and Torcello (see "Side Trips," at the end of this chapter) for about 25,000L ($14); it leaves from different booths on riva degli Schiavoni and from in front of La Zecca near the tourist office in Palazzina del Santi, just west of the Palazzo Ducale. However, I suggest that independent sightseers buy a special **1-day excursion ticket** (round-trip) on the no. 12 vaporetto for 10,000L ($6) and do it solo. The islands are small and easy to navigate, but check the schedule for the next island-to-island departure and eventually your return so that you don't spend most of your day waiting for connections.

6 Shopping

A mix of low-end trinket stores and middle-market to upscale boutiques line the narrow zigzagging **Mercerie** that runs north between piazza San Marco and the Rialto Bridge. More expensive clothing and gift boutiques make for great window-shopping on **calle larga XXII Marzo,** the wide street that begins west of piazza San Marco and wends its way to the expansive campo Santo Stefano near the Accademia. The narrow **Frezzeria,** also west of the piazza and not far from piazza San Marco, offers a grab bag of bars, souvenir shops, and tony clothing stores.

In a city that for centuries has thrived almost exclusively on tourism, remember this: Where you buy cheap, you get cheap. There are few bargains to be had, and there's nothing to compare with Florence's outdoor San Lorenzo Market; the nonproduce part of the **Rialto Market** is as good as it gets, where you'll find cheap T-shirts, plastic glow-in-the-dark gondolas, and tawdry glass trinkets. Venetians, centuries-old merchants, aren't known for bargaining. You'll stand a better chance when paying in cash or buying more than one.

If your bill at any one store totals 300,000L ($169), you're eligible for a **VAT (value-added tax) rebate** of approximately 19% (the VAT can vary according to the item). Ask the store for a formal receipt, and before leaving Italy or the European Union bring your receipt and purchase (the item must be available for inspection, so do this before check-in and allow sufficient time) to Italian Customs. The Customs agent will stamp your receipt and give you further directions (the stamped receipt gets sent back to the store and your reimbursement will either be credited against your credit card or sent to you by check; it can take months).

Venice is uniquely famous for several local crafts that have been produced here for centuries and are hard to get elsewhere: the **glassware** from the island of Murano, the delicate **lace** from Burano, and the *carta pesca* (papier-mâché) **Carnevale masks** you'll find in endless *botteghe* (mask shops), where you can watch artisans paint amid their wares.

Now here's the bad news: There's such an overwhelming sea of cheap glass gew-gaws that it becomes something of a turnoff (shipping and insurance costs make most things unaffordable; the alternative is to hand-carry something so fragile); there are so few women left on Burano willing to spend countless tedious hours keeping alive the

A Shopping Tip

If you have the good fortune of continuing on to Florence or Rome, then shop in Venice for clothing, leather goods, and accessories with prudence, as most things are more expensive here. However, if you happen on something that strikes you, consider it twice on the spot (not back at your hotel), then buy it. Don't plan on returning: In this web of alleys you may never find that shop again.

art of lace making that the few pieces you'll see not produced by machine in Hong Kong are sold at stratospheric prices; and most masks are mass-produced with little attention to quality or finish. Still, exceptions are to be found in all of the above, and when you find them you'll know.

7 Venice After Dark

Whatever time of year you're here, be sure to visit one of the tourist information centers for current English-language schedules of the month's special events (up-to-date listings are posted in the tourist offices and around town, but ask for a printed copy). The monthly *Ospite di Venezia* is distributed free and extremely helpful but is usually available only in the more expensive hotels. If you're looking for nocturnal action, you're in the wrong town. Your best bet is to sit in the moonlit piazza San Marco and listen to the orchestras, with the illuminated basilica before you—the perfect opera set.

THE PERFORMING ARTS

Venice has a long and rich tradition of classical music, and there's always a concert going on somewhere. Several churches regularly host classical music concerts (with an emphasis on the baroque) by local and international artists. This was, after all, the home of Vivaldi, and the ✪ **Chiesa di Vivaldi,** known officially as the Chiesa della Pietà, is the most popular venue for the music of Vivaldi and his contemporaries. A number of other churches (like **Santo Stefano, San Stae,** the **Scuola di San Giovanni Evangelista,** and the **Scuola di San Rocco**) also host concerts, but the Vivaldi Church, where the "red priest" was the choral director, offers perhaps the highest-quality ensembles (with tickets slightly more expensive). If you're lucky, they'll be performing *Le Quattro Staggioni* (The Four Seasons). Tickets are sold at the church's box office (☎ 041/52-31-096) on riva degli Schiavoni or at the front desk of the Metropole Hotel next door; they're usually 40,000L ($23) adults or 25,000L ($14) students. Information and schedules are available from the tourist office; tickets for most concerts should be bought in advance and are available from many hotels or travel agencies.

Close to the Rialto Bridge, the **Teatro Goldoni,** San Marco 4650/b, on calle Goldoni near campo San Luca (☎ **041/520-75-83**), is known for its theater season (October to May), which features well-known international productions, mostly in Italian. Tickets run 20,000L to 45,000L ($11 to $25). The box office is open Monday to Saturday 10am to 1pm and 4:30 to 7pm.

The city stood still in shock as the famous ✪ **Teatro La Fenice,** San Marco 1965, on campo San Fantin (☎ **041/78-65-62**), went up in flames in January 1996. For centuries it was the city's principal stage for world-class opera, music, theater, and ballet. Carpenters and artisans were on standby to begin working around the clock to re-create the teatro (built in 1836) according to achival designs; however, little progress has been made because political factions have been bickering over the bureaucracy involved. The Orchestra and Coro della Fenice honored the scheduled performances for the 1997 and 1998 seasons and should continue to do so for the future in the substitute venue, a year-round tent-like structure called the **PalaFenice** (☎ 147/88-22-11 within Italy or 6/326-580-10 from abroad) in the unlikely area of the Tronchetto parking facilities near piazzale Roma, convenient to many vaporetto lines. Tickets for the PalaFenice run 30,000L to 60,000L ($17 to $34). The box office is open Monday to Friday 9am to 6pm.

BARS & *BIRRERIE*

The **Devil's Forest Pub,** San Marco 5185, on calle Stagneri (☎ **041/520-06-23;** at the foot of the Rialto Bridge on the San Marco side of the Grand Canal is the important crossroads of campo San Bartolomeo; calle Stagneri begins at the right end of campo San Bartolomeo [with your back to the bridge, look for the Banca Commerciale Italiana on the corner]), and El Moro Pub (below) are the latest in the city's trend to imitate Anglo *birrerie*. But both pubs offer the outsider an authentic chance to take in the convivial atmosphere and find out just where Venetians do hang out. The crowd can be a bit younger at El Moro, where the older postuniversity types congregate at the bar. Both spots are popular for lunch with the neighborhood merchants and shop owners. The Devil's Forest is an ideal spot for relaxed socializing, a beer, and a host of games that include backgammon, chess, and Trivial Pursuit (this is a place to remember if the weather turns on you). A variety of simple pasta dishes and fresh sandwiches runs 6,000L to 10,000L ($3.40 to $6). It's open daily 10am to 1am.

Together with the Devil's Forest, the lively **El Moro Pub,** Castello 4531, on calle delle Rasse (☎ **041/528-25-73;** Vaporetto: San Zaccaria; facing the large Hotel Savoia e Jolanda, walk straight ahead on calle delle Rasse; the pub is on your left), is the biggest draw in town for its half-dozen beers on tap; a pint will cost 8,000L ($4.50). A long list of pub food has little to do with the expected British prototype: Here you'll find a number of pizzas (6,000L/$3.40 to 12,000L/$7), grilled panini (6,000L/$3.40 to 8,000L/$4.50), and insalatone ("big salads") (9,000L/$5 to 12,000L/$7). TVs sometimes transmit national soccer or tennis matches and the management welcomes those who linger, but sensitive nonsmokers won't want to. It's open Thursday to Tuesday 10am to 1am.

Good food at reasonable prices would be enough to regularly pack **Paradiso Perduto,** Cannaregio 2540, on fondamenta della Misericordia (☎ **041/72-05-81;** Vaporetto: Ferrovie; from the train station, walk along Lista di Spagna, past campo S. Geremia, and across the first bridge onto rio Terrà San Leonardo; turn left onto rio Terrà Farsetti, cross the bridge, turn right onto fondamenta della Misericordia, and the bar will be straight ahead on your left), but its biggest draw is the live jazz performed on a small stage several nights a week. Popular with Americans and other foreigners living in Venice, this bar was once largely devoid of tourists, primarily because of its hard-to-find location, but lately it looks as if the word is out. If you feel like eating, you'll find a good selection of well-prepared pizzas and pastas for under 10,000L ($6); arrive early for a table. It's open Thursday to Tuesday 7pm to 1 and sometimes 2am.

For just plain hanging out, at an even lower price and level of pretension, I'm fond of the **campo Santa Margherita,** a huge open piazza about halfway between the train station and Ca' Rezzonico—look for the popular Green Pub (no. 3053; closed Thursday), Bar Salus (no. 3112), Caffè/Bareto Rosso (no. 2963; closed Sunday). Late afternoons and early evenings, other popular squares that serve as meeting points for people before they disperse for other points are **campo San Bartolomeo,** at the foot of the Rialto Bridge, and the nearby **campo San Luca;** you'll see Venetians of all ages milling about in animated conversation, especially from 5pm until dinner when the campi empty out. **Campo Santo Stefano** is also worth a visit, to sit and sample the goods at the Bar/Gelateria Paolin (no. 2962; closed Friday), one of the city's best ice-cream sources and a good ringside seat for people-watching.

CAFES

Nightlife centers around the city's many bar/cafes in piazza San Marco, one of the world's most remarkable piazzas. The epicenter of life in Venice, it's also the most expensive and touristed place to linger over a Campari or cappuccino. The nostalgic 18th-century **Caffè Florian,** at San Marco 56a–59a, on the south side of the piazza (nearest the water), is the most famous (closed Wednesday in winter) and most theatrical inside; have a Bellini (prosecco and fresh peach nectar) at the back bar and spend half what you'd pay at an indoor table; alfresco seating is even more expensive when the band plays on but worth every lira for the million-dollar scenario.

On the opposite side of the square at San Marco 133–134 is the old-world **Caffè Lavena** (closed Tuesday in winter) and at no. 120 is **Caffè Quadri** (closed Monday in winter). At all spots, a cappuccino, tea, or Coca-Cola at a table will set you back about 9,000L ($6). But no one will rush you, and if the sun is warm and the orchestras are playing, I can think of nowhere else in the world I'd rather be. Around the corner (no. 11) and in front of the pink-and-white marble Palazzo Ducale with the lagoon on your right is the lesser-known, slightly less expensive **Caffè Chioggia** (closed Sunday). Come here at midnight and watch the Moors strike the hour atop the Clock Tower from your outside table, while the quartet or pianist plays everything from jazz to pop until the wee hours. I like the music more—no "Moon River" or "New York, New York."

THE GAY & LESBIAN SCENE
There isn't much gay nightlife in Venice, certainly nothing conspicuous. There is, however, a local division of a government-affiliated agency, **Arcigay Arcilesbica,** Campo S. Giacomo dell'Orio 1507, Santa Croce (☎ 041/72-11-97). It serves as a kind of home base for the gay community, with info on AIDS services, gay-friendly accommodations, and such. The best hours to call (it's hard to find) are Wednesday, Thursday, and Saturday 6 to 10pm.

DANCE CLUBS
Venice is a quiet town at night and offers little in the line of dance clubs. Evenings are best spent lingering over a late dinner, having a pint in a birrerie, nursing a slow glass of prosecco in one of the tony outdoor cafes in piazza San Marco, or in the popular after-hours places like Paradiso Perduto (above). Dance clubs barely enjoy their 15 minutes of popularity before changing hands or closing; some of those that have survived are open only in summer. Young Venetians tend to frequent the Lido or mainland Mestre, but if you really need that disco fix you're best off at Piccolo Mondo.

Piccolo Mondo, Dorsoduro 1056, near the Accademia (☎ 041/52-00-371; Vaporetto: Accademia; follow the narrow calle Gambara to the right of the museum; the club is on your right before you reach the canal), wears many hats. Self-billed as a disco/pub, it serves sandwiches during lunch to the tune of America's latest dance music and offers a happy hour in the late afternoon. But the only reason you'd want to come is if you want a disco night—the club is frequented mostly by curious foreigners and the young to not-so-young Venetians who seek them out. It's open daily: 10pm to 4am in summer and 10am to 4pm and 5 to 8pm in winter. There's live music and a 20,000L ($11) cover.

8 Side Trips: The Islands & the Veneto
MURANO, BURANO & TORCELLO
Venice shares its lagoon with three other principal islands: Murano, Burano, and Torcello. Guided tours of the three are operated by a few agencies, including the **Serenissima Company,** with departures from a dock between piazza San Marco and the Hotel Danieli, next to the wharf for the motonave to the Lido (☎ 041/522-85-38). The 4-hour 25,000L ($14) tours leave daily at 9:30am and 2:30pm (times change; check in advance).

You can also visit the islands on your own—conveniently and easily, as long as you check the vaporetto schedule so that you don't waste most of your day waiting for the next one. Vaporetto Lines 12 and 52 make the journey to Murano, and Line 12 continues on to Burano and Torcello.

MURANO   This island is famous for the products of its glass factories, but there's little to find in variety or prices that you won't find in Venice. A visit to the **Museo Vetrario (Museum of Glass Art)**, Fondamenta 8 (☎ **041/73-95-86**), will put the island's centuries-old legacy into perspective and is recommended for those considering major purchases. Hours are Thursday to Tuesday 10am to 5pm in summer (to 4pm in winter), and admission is 8,000L ($4.50) adults and 5,000L ($2.80) students. Dozens of *fornaci* (**furnaces**) offer free shows of mouth-blown glass-making almost invariably hitched to a hard-sell ("No obligation! Really!") tour of the factory outlet. These retail showrooms of delicate glassware can be enlightening or boring, depending on your frame of mind. Almost all the places ship, often doubling the price. On the other hand, these pieces are instant heirlooms.

BURANO   Lace is the claim to fame of tiny colorful Burano, for centuries kept alive by the wives of fishers who kept themselves busy with the time-consuming art while waiting for their husbands to return from the sea. The local government continues its attempt to keep the legacy alive with subsidized classes. Visit the **Lace Museum,** Scuola di Merletti, on piazza Galuppi (☎ **041/73-00-34**), to understand why anything so exquisite shouldn't be left to fade into extinction. It's open Wednesday to Monday 10am to 4pm, and admission is 5,000L ($2.80) adults and 3,000L ($1.70) children.

TORCELLO   Nearby Torcello is home to the special **Cattedrale di Torcello (Santa Maria Assunta),** whose foundation dates to the 7th century. The oldest church (or monument of any nature) in Venice, it's famous for its Byzantine mosaics rivaling those of St. Mark's. The cathedral is open daily 10am to 12:30pm and 2 to 5pm; admission is 1,500L (85¢). Also of interest is the adjacent **church dedicated to St. Fosca** and a small **archaeological museum;** the church's hours are the same as the cathedral's, and the museum is open Tuesday to Sunday 10am to 12:30pm and 2 to 5:30pm. Museum admission is 3,000L ($1.70) adults and 1,500L (85¢) children. Peaceful Torcello is uninhabited except for a handful of land-working families and is a favorite picnic spot (you'll have to bring the food from Venice, since on the island there are no stores and only one expensive restaurant). Once the tour groups have left, it offers a very special moment of solitude and escape when St. Mark's bottleneck becomes oppressive.

THE LIDO

Though only a 15-minute vaporetto ride away, Venice's **Lido beaches** aren't much to write home about. The Adriatic waters have had pollution problems and, for bathing and sun worshiping, there are much nicer beaches in Italy. But the parade of wealthy Italians and foreigners who frequent this *litorale* throughout summer is an interesting sight, though you'll find them at the elitist beaches affiliated with the deluxe hotels, such as the legendary Excelsior and the Des Bains.

There are a number of beach areas: the *spiaggia libera* (public beach) is called the **Bucintoro,** a 10-minute walk to the opposite end of Gran Viale Santa Maria Elisabetta (referred to as the Gran Viale) from the vaporetto station Santa Elisabetta; to the left of this is the **Veneziana Spiaggia** with umbrella and cabin rentals. At **San Nicolò,** a mile away, also reached by bus B, you'll have to pay 18,000L ($10) per person (standard at Italy's beaches) for use of the amenities and umbrella rental.

Vaporetto Lines 1, 6, 52, and 82 cross the lagoon to the Lido from the San Zaccaria–Danieli stop near San Marco. From the Lido–Santa Maria Elisabetta vaporetto stop, walk straight ahead along Gran Viale Santa Maria Elisabetta to reach the beach. Bus B goes to San Nicolò.

The Lido's big plus is wheels: those of cars and bicycles. Cars are permitted, though since it's flat country, biking is far more fun. You can **rent bikes** at a number of places along the Gran Viale Santa Maria Elisabetta for 5,000L to 6,000L ($2.80 to $3.40) per hour.

FARTHER AFIELD: PADUA, VICENZA & VERONA

Visitors venturing onto terra firma should include a night or more in any of the Veneto's towns before hurrying to Florence or Milan to catch a plane home. The "Veneto Arc" is highlighted by Padua, Vicenza, and Verona (east to west), all an easy round-trip from Venice.

Bus service exists among these towns, but train service is far more frequent. If you want to drive, take A4 (toward Milan) due west from Venice for all three towns.

PADUA

Padua, 26 miles west of Venice, is often used as a base for those visiting Venice but unable to find accommodations there: Express trains depart frequently, making the trip to/from Venice in under 30 minutes. It's not a bad choice, either, as a pleasant base for a day trip into Verona, 50 miles west of here. The hotels in Padua cost considerably less than Venice's while offering more amenities (there aren't many to choose from, so book in advance).

Padua is a vital city during the scholastic year, when its ancient university, where Dante and Copernicus once came to study, keeps the bars, cafes, and piazzas full. The university, founded in 1222, and the city flourished in the late Middle Ages and Renaissance as a center of learning and art. Padua's importance is evident by the presence of what art historians call the Sistine Chapel of northern Italy: the ✪ **Cappella degli Scrovegni (Arena Chapel or Scrovegni Chapel)** in piazza Ermitani off the Corso Garibaldi (☎ **049/820-45-50**). Giotto's recently restored vibrant frescoes depicting the New Testament revolutionized 14th-century painting, ending the period of medieval art and beginning that of the Renaissance; together with the seminal frescoes he'd later paint in St. Francis's Basilica in Assisi, these are the largest and best preserved of his work. The lines of art lovers in high season attest to it. A joint ticket with the adjacent **Museo Ermitani** (cloisters used as a civic museum, famous for its archaeological collection) is 15,000L ($8) adults and 10,000L ($6) students. They're open daily: February to October 9am to 7pm and November to January 9am to 6pm (Museo Ermitani closed Monday).

Paduans are enormously proud of their singular artistic treasure. They reserve the same feeling for "their" St. Anthony, the Portuguese-born monk who spent his final years in Padua (d. 1231) and for whom the enormous ✪ **Basilica di Sant'Antonio,** piazza del Santo, was built. Completed in 1307, its eight domes and elaborate interior embellishment recall Venice's Basilica di San Marco. The revered saint is said to be the patron of lost or mislaid objects, and the faithful flock here from around the world looking for everything from lost love to lost health. The tomb of "il Santo" is the undisputed highlight, always covered with flowers, photos, and notes of petition and gratitude. June 13 is his feast day, when his relics are paraded in a solemn procession. Admission is free, and the basilica is open daily 7:30am to 7:45pm in summer (to 7pm in winter).

You can also soak up much of the local spirit in the **Caffè Pedrocchi,** piazza Cavour. Opened in 1831 and called by many the world's most beautiful coffeehouse, it really is all about people-watching and paying 5,000L ($2.80) for the privilege of sitting with a Campari or iced tea for hours. It's open Tuesday to Sunday 9:30am to 8pm.

Trains from Venice to Padua run hourly. The fare is about 4,000L ($2.25), plus a 4,000L InterCity supplement if you take the fast train.

ACCOMMODATIONS The recently refurbished four-star ✪ **Hotel Majestic Toscanelli,** Via dell'Arco 2, 35122 Padova (☎ 049/66-32-44; fax 049/87-60-025), is in the pedestrians-only historical center. Rates for singles are 169,000L ($95), doubles 240,000L ($135), and triples 270,000L ($152), breakfast included. The place exudes old-world refinement in its 32 units (with bathrooms) as well as its common areas. American Express, Diners Club, MasterCard, and Visa are accepted.

You can spend far less at the **Hotel al Fagiano,** Via Locatelli 45, just west of piazza del Santo, 35122 Padova (☎ 049/87-50-073; fax 049/87-53-396). Of its 33 units, 30 are with sparkling new bathrooms. Those with bath are 85,000L ($48) single or 110,000L ($62) double. The few rooms without bathroom cost less.

DINING Easy-to-find **Brek,** piazza Cavour 20 (☎ 049/87-53-788), isn't dripping with atmosphere, but it's a large, pleasant spot whose consistent mixed-bag crowd makes sure that the quantity and variety of pastas, salads, and entrees are fresh and tasty. No credit cards are accepted, but with pastas approximately 5,000L ($2.80) and entrees never more than 8,000L ($4.50), you shouldn't go broke. It's open Saturday to Thursday 11:30am to 3pm and 6 to 10pm.

The **Osteria dei Fabbri,** Via dei Fabbri 13 (☎ 049/65-03-36), is one of the busier of the informal dining spots where students sit with suited managerial types and the occasional tourist squeezes in to sample the simple well-prepared menu. Regional specialties appear as daily-changing homemade pastas (10,000L/$6) or entrees (17,000L/$10). At this rustic old-fashioned tavern, a number of local vintages are available by the glass and after-midnight hours encourage one to linger amidst the bonhomie. American Express, Diners Club, MasterCard, and Visa are accepted, and the place is open Monday to Saturday noon to 3:30pm and 5:30pm to 1am.

VICENZA

It's just 20 miles west of Padua to **Vicenza** (46 miles west of Venice), a pilgrimage site for students and architecture lovers. Vicenza's most famous son and local boy wonder, Andrea di Pietro della Gondola (1508–80), better known as Palladio, was the most important and last great architect of the High Renaissance, and the concentration of his city palazzi and country villas in the surrounding hills have put Vicenza on the map.

If this is what draws you here, get thee to the **Tourist Information Office,** piazza Matteotti 12, next to the Teatro Olimpico (below) (☎ 0444/32-08-54), for a map of the city and his principal palazzi, as well as his Villas of the Veneto (Le Ville Venete). Organized tours of the latter are sometimes available, though information differs from season to season. The office is open Monday to Saturday 9am to 1pm and 2:30 to 6pm and Sunday 9am to 1pm.

Tony stores, gourmet shops, and a parade of well-heeled pedestrians makes a tool down the main drag, **Corso di Palladio,** a memorable passaggiata. A number of Palladio's (and his students') palazzi embellish the street, and a segue into the offshoot of **piazza dei Signori** will bring you to his magnificent bigger-than-life ✪ **"Basilica" Palladiana** (which isn't a church at all) on the site of the ancient Roman forum.

The most important site in town, Palladio's greatest work, is at the end of Corso Palladio: the ✪ **Teatro Olimpico,** piazza Matteotti (☎ 0444/32-37-81). It was completed by Palladio's pupil Scamozzi in 1583 and inspired by the theaters of antiquity.

Hours vary, so call ahead to check; admission is 5,000L ($2.80), which includes admission to the Museo Chivico (Municipal Museum) across the street, also by Palladio. This is the area of the Tourist Information Office (above), whose staff will direct you to the **Villa Rotonda** on the outskirts of town (and confirm its unpredictable visiting hours), one of the most perfect buildings ever constructed. You'll recognize it as the inspiration for Thomas Jefferson's Monticello and Chiswick House near London and countless other noble homes and government buildings around the globe. Farther afield are dozens of other villas, many along the Brenta Canal and belonging to the Palladian school of design.

Trains run hourly from Venice and Padua. The fare from Venice to Vicenza is about 6,200L ($3.50), plus a 4,500L ($2.50) InterCity supplement if you take the fast train. The fare from Padua to Vicenza is about 4,200L ($2.35), plus a 3,500L ($2) InterCity supplement.

DINING   The **Righetti,** piazza Duomo 3–4 (☎ **0444/54-31-35**), is warm and rustic inside. Homemade pastas of generous portions won't set you back more than 5,000L ($2.80), and with a few side dishes of fresh steamed or grilled vegetables you can call it a day. Entrees are 9,000L ($5) or less—prices are kept low (occasional grilled meat specialties may up your bill) because this is a self-service eatery, the best in town. No credit cards are accepted, and it's open Monday to Friday noon to 2:30pm and 7 to 10pm.

Operating since the early 1600s around the corner until a 1997 change of address, the ✪ **Trattoria Tre Visi,** off Corso Palladio 5 (☎ **0444/32-48-68**), is a local institution that prides itself on regional specialties (ignore the concessions to continental dishes), now in its "new" 17th-century home with an elegant alfresco courtyard. Homemade pastas don't exceed 12,000L ($7) and entrees are 25,000L ($14) or less. You won't be disappointed, especially if your splurge includes any of the fine Veneto wines or the house and regional specialty of *baccalà alla vicentina,* cod simmered for 48 hours in milk and olive oil with onions—far better sampled than described. American Express, Diners Club, MasterCard, and Visa are accepted. It's open Tuesday to Sunday 12:30 to 2:30pm and Tuesday to Saturday 7:30 to 10pm (closed May to October).

VERONA

At 70 miles west of Venice and 32 miles west of Vicenza, the Veneto's next most visited city is on the far side for a day trip except for the hardy and tireless. You'll most enjoy it if you can spend a night or two as there's much to be taken in other than its major sites.

Who doesn't know that **Verona** is the home of Romeo and Juliet? Amazingly, many don't realize that the chances of their being fictional figures are great. Regardless, Verona can be extra special, even magical, and why not believe that the star-crossed lovers existed? Local tourism authorities do everything to have you hope they did.

Verona reached a cultural and artistic peak under the puissant and often cruel della Scala (Scaligeri) dynasty that took up rule in the 1200s. In 1405, it surrendered to Venice, which remained in charge (hence the presence of St. Mark's winged lion about town) until the invasion of Napoléon in 1797. This was the city's heyday, and the magnificent palazzi, towers, churches, and piazzas you see are testimony to its influence and wealth.

On the former site of the Roman forum is the city's bustling marketplace, **piazza delle Erbe,** one of Italy's loveliest and most authentic (closed Sunday). Pull up a chair in any of the outdoor cafes—**Caffè Filippini** (no. 26) is the oldest and one of the most favored. Another magnet is the hole-in-the-wall stand-up pizzeria, **Da Aldo,** at no. 6. Sicilian-born Aldo sells pizza by the slice (2,500L/$1.40); a best-seller is the onion/pepper/potato/olive variety (closed Wednesday).

Behind the piazza is **piazza dei Signori (piazza Dante),** serene and elegant compared to the bustle of the piazza you've just left behind. Dante, whose 19th-century statue stands in the middle, found exile in Verona as a guest of the Scaligeri family, whose crenellated 13th-century palazzo frames one side of the piazza. The landmark **Antico Caffè Dante** offers outdoor tables and a chance to sit and take it all in (open daily, in summer to the wee hours). Just northeast of the piazza on Via delle Arche Scaligeri are the tombs of the Scaligeri family, which you can view only through the decorative ironwork gates.

There's no doubt that Verona's big draw is the ✪ **Casa di Giulietta (Juliet's House),** via Cappello 23, open Tuesday to Sunday 8am to 7pm. However, no one promises that she ever really existed except in the mind of Shakespeare (who, they say, never stepped foot in Italy despite the common placement of Verona, Venice, and so on in his settings). Don't pay the 5,000L ($2.80) to view the virtually empty 13th-century palazzo, but do try to catch the courtyard late in the afternoon during a quiet moment to see the famous balcony from which the young Veronese stole a few precious exchanges with her Romeo. The graffiti covering the palazzo walls (Gianni, ti adoro, M.) is moving and scrawled in a million languages.

The well-known opera season takes place every July and August in Verona's ancient amphitheater, the ✪ **Arena** in piazza Brà. It's Italy's best known and best preserved after Rome's Coliseum, built about A.D. 100 to accommodate more than 20,000 people. If you're in town during the season, even the opera-challenged should try to attend. Tickets vary according to weekday versus weekend rates, according to performance and cast (*Aida* is always the most sought after and expensive), and are subject to advance booking fees. Amazingly, the biglietteri (box office) is rather organized in helping you procure tickets in advance: call ☎ **045/80-051-51** or fax 045/80-13-287. Credit cards accepted by phone and fax.

Trains run hourly from Venice and Vicenza. The fare from Venice to Verona is about 10,800L ($6), plus a 7,000L ($3.95) InterCity supplement if you take the fast train. The fare from Vicenza to Verona is about 6,000L ($3.40), plus a 4,200L ($2.35) InterCity supplement.

ACCOMMODATIONS   The much-loved family-run **Locanda Catullo,** Via Catullo 1, 37121 Verona, is just north of the popular Principe V. Mazzini (☎ **045/80-02-786**). Only 4 of the 21 units have bathrooms. Those without cost 55,000L ($31) single and 80,000L ($45) double; those with bath are a bit more. Some rooms have a sink and some even have small terraces, but its the well-kept and tasteful ambiance that keeps the place full. No credit cards are accepted.

Spend a little more and check into the 1996-renovated **Hotel Aurora,** piazza delle Erbe 2 (☎ **045/59-47-17;** fax 045/80-10-860). Of the 19 rooms just two singles have been left without bathroom, costing 100,000L ($56). Doubles with bath can be adapted for single use at 150,000L ($84), and standard double occupancy with bath is 180,000L ($101); triples with bath are 225,000L ($126). Rates include breakfast and air-conditioning. Few of the rooms overlook the piazza and marketplace, but there's a lovely second-floor terrace. American Express, MasterCard, and Visa are accepted.

DINING   A favorite trattoria is the welcoming ✪ **Osteria dal Duca,** Via Arche Scaligeri 2, east of piazza dei Signori (☎ **045/59-44-74**). Legend goes that this 13th-century palazzo is the home of the Mantecchi (Montague) family. There's a daily-changing choice of 8 primi at 10,000L ($6) and 15 entrees from 15,000L to 20,000L ($8 to $11). The unusual *polenta tris* (polenta with gorgonzola cheese, mushrooms, and salami) and the vegetarian melanzane con pomodori (baked eggplant with fresh tomatoes) have long been house specialties. MasterCard and Visa are accepted, and it's open Monday to Saturday 12:30 to 2:30pm and 7 to 10:30pm (closed Saturday dinner June to September).

For an unrivaled setting and a great selection of more than 40 varieties, try **Pizzeria Impero,** piazza dei Signor 8 (☎ **045/80-3-160**). A full menu of changing homemade pastas and seafood is available, but you'd never know it to observe the quantity of pizza churned out by the wood-burning stoves. Pizzas range from 6,000L to 15,000L ($3.40 to $8). You're welcome to linger over a simple but memorable pizza and a beer in one of the world's great piazzas. June to September, it's open daily noon to 2am; the rest of the year, hours are Thursday to Tuesday noon to 3:30pm and 6pm to midnight. Diners Club, MasterCard, and Visa are accepted.

28

Vienna & Environs

by Beth Reiber

Being in Vienna makes me wish I had a time machine so that I could go back to the last half of the 18th century, when the city resounded with the music of Haydn and Mozart and Empress Maria Theresa ruled from Schönbrunn Palace. Or maybe the first decades of the 20th century would be better, when Freud was developing his methods of psychoanalysis, Klimt was covering canvases with his Jugendstil figures, and Vienna was whirling to Strauss waltzes.

But I'll settle gladly for Vienna today. Music is still the city's soul, the manifestation of its spirit—from chamber music and opera to jazz and alternative rock. The Habsburgs, Austria's rulers for six centuries, left a rich architectural legacy of magnificent baroque and rococo buildings and palaces, beautifully landscaped gardens, and fabulous art collections from the far corners of their empire.

Vienna, however, isn't resting on past laurels. After the Austro-Hungarian Empire was carved up following World War I, Vienna was a capital without an empire, and when the Iron Curtain descended after World War II, it was suddenly on the edge of Western Europe, far from other major capitals. Now that Eastern Europe has opened up and the emphasis has shifted farther east, Vienna is again in the center. A springboard for travel to and from Budapest, Prague, and beyond, Vienna has reblossomed into an international city.

REQUIRED DOCUMENTS Citizens of the United States, Canada, Australia, and New Zealand need only a valid passport for stays up to 90 days. British subjects need only an identity card.

OTHER FROMMER'S TITLES For more on Vienna, see *Frommer's Vienna & the Danube Valley, Frommer's Austria, Frommer's Europe,* or *Frommer's Europe's Greatest Driving Tours.*

1 Vienna Deals & Discounts

SPECIAL DISCOUNTS

FOR EVERYONE All **municipal museums** (including the residences of Mozart, Beethoven, Haydn, and Johann Strauss, and the Historical Museum of the City of Vienna) are free on Friday morning.

If you're interested in seeing the famous **Spanish Riding School,** consider going to one of the morning training sessions, when tickets cost 100S ($8). If you're willing to stand, you can see the **Vienna Boys' Choir** free (they perform at Sunday mass). And if you plan on

Budget Bests

The most wonderful thing you can do for yourself is go to a performance at the **Staatsoper (State Opera).** Standing-room tickets start at only $1.60, for which you're treated to extravaganzas held on one of Europe's most renowned stages. Even seat tickets aren't prohibitively expensive, starting at $8

The rest of Vienna is affordable too. Try to eat at least once at a *beisl,* a typical blue-collar pub, where you can get hearty home-cooked meals for as little as $8. But don't forget Vienna's wonderful **wine cellars,** where you can soak in the atmosphere for the price of a glass of wine.

And if you want to really save money, eat at a *würstelstand,* a sidewalk food stand selling various kinds of wurst and a roll for $2.40 to $2.80. They're all around the city and are as much a part of the Viennese scene as the opera house.

traveling a lot by public transportation, be sure to buy a **"strip ticket,"** or a **24-hour** or **72-hour ticket,** or perhaps even the **Vienna Card,** which gives discounts for both transportation and sightseeing (see "Getting Around, below").

FOR STUDENTS If you're a student with bonafide ID, you can save 50% or more off the **museum admissions** in Vienna. You can also obtain tickets to the **Staatsoper, Burgtheater,** or **Akademietheater** for as little as 50S ($4), but only if you can show current student status with a valid university ID card. Be sure to bring both your university card and an International Student Identity Card (ISIC).

If you've arrived in Vienna without an ISIC, you can get one at **Ökista,** where you can also purchase cheap airline and train tickets (for youths under 26). There are three locations: Türkenstrasse 6 (☎ 01/401 48 0; U-Bahn: U-2 to Schottentor), Karlsgasse 3 (☎ 01/505 01 28; U-Bahn: U-1, U-2, or U-4 to Karlsplatz), and Reichsratstrasse 13 (☎ 01/402 15 61; Tram: D, 1, or 2 to Burgtheater/Rathausplatz). All are open Monday to Friday 9am to 5:30pm.

2 Essentials

ARRIVING
BY PLANE Vienna's airport, **Schwechat,** also known as the Vienna International Airport (☎ 01/7007), is 11 miles southeast of the city center. A shuttle bus, the **Vienna Airport Line** (☎ 01/5800 2300), departs about every 20 minutes for the City Air Terminal, near the center of town next to the Hilton. The trip takes about 20 to 30 minutes, depending on traffic. From the City Air Terminal you can catch the U-Bahn (subway) at the Landstrasse station.

Less frequent are the shuttle buses to the Südbahnhof (a 20-minute trip) and the Westbahnhof (a 35-minute trip), Vienna's two train stations, with departures every hour. In any case, the cost of the shuttle bus to the City Air Terminal or the train stations is 70S ($5.60) one-way (60S/$4.80 one-way if the have the Vienna Card).

A cheaper alternative is to take Schnellzug (Rapid Transit) 7 from the airport to Wien Mitte, also in the center of town near the City Air Terminal and connected to the U-Bahn. The trip costs 34S ($2.70) one-way and takes approximately 30 minutes.

Taxis charge about 340S ($27) for the same trip. If you make arrangements a day in advance, however, **C & K Airport Service** (☎ 01/1731) will deliver you to or from the airport for 270S ($22) per person.

BY TRAIN Vienna has two main train stations, both with Tourist Information offices and currency exchange counters. If you're arriving from Germany, Switzerland,

What Things Cost in Vienna	U.S. $
Taxi from the airport to the city center	27.20
U-Bahn from Stephansdom to Schönbrunn	1.35
Local telephone call (1 min.)	.16
Double room at the Sacher (deluxe)	304.00
Double room at the Pertschy (moderate)	94.40
Double room at the Wild (budget)	55.20
Lunch for one, without wine, at Wienerwald (moderate)	8.00
Lunch for one, without wine, at the Naschmarkt (budget)	6.40
Dinner for one, without wine, at the Hauswirth (deluxe)	27.00
Dinner for one, without wine, at Gasthaus Witwe Bolte (moderate)	14.00
Dinner for one, without wine, at the Schnitzelwirt (budget)	8.00
Half liter of beer	2.80
Glass of wine (one-quarter liter)	2.25
Coca-Cola (in a restaurant)	2.00
Cup of coffee (in a restaurant)	2.55
Roll of ASA 100 color film, 36 exposures	5.60
Admission to Schönbrunn	7.20
Movie ticket (depends on where you sit)	5.50–8.00
Theater ticket (standing room at the Staatsoper)	1.60

France, Salzburg, or other points west or north, in most cases you'll arrive at the **Westbahnhof (West Station).** A subway line (U-3) connects the Westbahnhof with Stephansplatz in the center.

If you're arriving from the south or east—from Italy, Hungary, Greece, or countries of the former Yugoslavia—you'll most likely arrive at the **Südbahnhof (South Station).** Take Tram D from in front of the station if you're heading for the Ring and the city center. Tram no. 18 travels between the two stations.

It's unlikely you'll arrive at **Franz-Josefs-Bahnhof,** used primarily for local train traffic, but if you do, take Tram D for the Ring and the city center; Tram no. 5 travels to the Westbahnhof. The U-4 Friedensbrücke stop is about a 5-minute walk from the station.

For information on train schedules, call ☎ **01/1717.**

VISITOR INFORMATION

For a free map, brochures, and information on Vienna, including the current showings and times for the opera, theater, Spanish Riding School, and Vienna Boys' Choir, drop by the main office of **Vienna Tourist Information,** Kärntner Strasse 38 (☎ **01/211 14-0** Monday to Friday 8:30am to 4pm only; U-Bahn: U-1 or U-3 to Stephansplatz or U-1, U-2, or U-4 to Karlsplatz), on the corner of Philharmoniker Strasse, near the Sacher Hotel and the Staatsoper. It's open daily 9am to 7pm. Next door to the tourist office is the **Intropa travel agency** (☎ **01/51 514-245**), which sells theater tickets, books sightseeing tours, and exchanges money. In summer, it's open Monday to Friday 9am to 5:30pm, Saturday 9am to 3pm, and Sunday 10am to 3pm; in winter, Monday to Friday 9am to 5:30pm and Saturday 9am to noon.

If you're arriving at Vienna International Airport, there's a tourist office in the Arrivals Hall, open daily 8:30am to 9pm. A tourist office at the Westbahnhof is open daily 7am to 10pm, while another one at the Südbahnhof is open May to October, daily 6:30am to 10pm, and November to April, daily 6:30am to 9pm.

All Vienna Tourist Information offices will book hotel rooms for a 40S ($3.20) fee. Be sure, too, to pick up a free copy of *Wien Monatsprogramm*—it tells what's going on in Vienna's concert halls, theaters, and opera houses. If you're looking for detailed historical information on Vienna's many beautiful buildings, be sure to purchase a 50S ($4) English-language booklet called *Vienna from A to Z.* Its listings are keyed to the unique numbered plaques affixed to the front of every building of historic interest. You'll spot these plaques everywhere: They're heralded by little red-and-white flags in summer. By referring to the number on the plaque with the corresponding number in *Vienna from A to Z,* you'll have the English translations.

Additional information on Vienna via the Internet is available at **http://info.wien.at/.**

CITY LAYOUT

Vienna's **Altstadt (Old City)** is delightfully compact, filled with tiny cobblestone streets leading to majestic squares. In the center is **Stephansplatz,** with Vienna's most familiar landmark, Stephansdom (St. Stephen's Cathedral). From here it's a short walk to the Hofburg (official residence of the Habsburgs), the Kunsthistorisches Museum (Art History Museum), and the Staatsoper (State Opera). Kärntner Strasse, much of it pedestrian, is Vienna's main shopping street, leading from Stephansplatz past the Staatsoper to Karlsplatz.

Circling the Altstadt is "the Ring," as Vienna's **Ringstrasse** is commonly called. This impressive circular boulevard, 2½ miles long and 187 feet wide, was built in the mid-1800s along what used to be the city's fortifications (hence its shape as a circle around the Altstadt). Everything inside the Ring is known as the First Bezirk ("precinct," denoted by the 1010 postal code in addresses). The rest of Vienna is also divided into various precincts.

Trams run along the tree-shaded Ring, which is divided into various sections, including **Opernring** (home of the Staatsoper), **Kärntner-Ring, Burgring** (home of the Hofburg and Kunsthistorisches Museum), and **Schubert Ring.** Schönbrunn, Vienna's top sight, is a few miles southwest of the city center, easily reached by U-Bahn from Karlsplatz. **Mariahilfer Strasse,** lined with department stores, boutiques, and restaurants, stretches from the Kunsthistorisches Museum to the Westbahnhof and beyond.

GETTING AROUND

Vienna's transit network consists of five U-Bahn (subway) lines, trams, buses, and several rapid transit and commuter trains. The free map given out by the tourist office shows tram and bus lines, as well as subway stops, though you'll need a magnifying glass to read it. Luckily, most of Vienna's attractions are within walking distance of each other.

For information on Vienna's public transport system, visit the **Informationsdienst der Wiener Verkehrsbetriebe,** in the underground Opernpassage at Karlsplatz, in the U-Bahn station at Stephansplatz, or at the Westbahnhof U-Bahn station. All three are open Monday to Friday 6:30am to 6:30pm and Saturday, Sunday, and holidays 8:30am to 4pm. The staff can answer questions, such as which bus to take to reach your destination. You can also call ☎ **01/587 31 86** or 01/79 09-105.

A single ticket (good for the tram, bus, S-Bahn, or U-Bahn) costs 17S ($1.35) if bought in advance and permits as many transfers as you need to reach your destination as long as you keep moving in the same direction. You can buy advance tickets from machines in U-Bahn stations and ticket booths or from tobacconists. Tickets bought from bus or tram conductors, on the other hand, cost 20S ($1.60). I suggest that instead of single tickets you purchase the **Vierfahrtenstreifenkarte,** a strip ticket with either four rides for 68S ($5) or eight rides for 136S ($11). You must buy these in advance, either from ticket booths at Karlsplatz, Stephansplatz, and other major U-Bahn stations or from automatic machines at all U-Bahn and train stations (look for the VOR FAHRKARTEN sign).

In addition, there's a **24-hour ticket** available for 50S ($4), a **72-hour ticket** for 130S ($10), or an **8-day pass** for 265S ($21), which you can use for any 8 days, not necessarily in succession. You must validate all tickets yourself by inserting them into machines at the entryway of S-Bahn and U-Bahn platforms or on buses and trams. Children up to 6 can travel free, while those 7 to 14 travel for half fare, except on Sunday, holidays, and Vienna school holidays, when they travel free.

There are a couple of other options worth considering. If you're going to be in Vienna at least 3 days and plan on seeing the major sights, consider buying the **Vienna Card** for 180S ($14)—it allows unlimited transportation on Vienna's subways, buses, and trams for 72 hours and gives discounts of 10% to 50% for most of the city's attractions. You can purchase the Vienna Card at major hotels, Vienna Tourist Information, and transportation ticket booths.

An alternative is the Vienna Line's **Hop-On, Hop-Off,** a private bus line that travels to most of the city's major sights, including the State Opera and St. Stephen's Cathedral and outlying sights such as the Prater amusement park, KunstHausWien, and Schönbrunn and Belvedere palaces. Guided commentary is provided between each of the 13 stops, and you can get off and reboard as often as you like during a 2-day period. Tickets cost 220S ($18) adults and 120S ($10) children up to 12. For more information, see "Organized Tours," later in this chapter.

BY U-BAHN   The most important U-Bahn line for visitors is U-4, which stops at Karlsplatz before continuing to Kettenbrückengasse (site of Vienna's outdoor market and weekend flea market) and Schönbrunn. U-2 travels around part of the Ring, while U-1 has a station at Stephansplatz. U-4, U-2, and U-1 all converge at Karlsplatz. U-3 connects the Westbahnhof with Stephansplatz and beyond.

BY TRAM   Though the U-Bahn and buses are gradually taking over most of the tram routes, trams are still heavily used for traveling around the Ring (nos. 1 and 2) and for transportation between the Südbahnhof and the Ring (Tram D) and the Westbahnhof and Burgring (no. 58). Tram no. 18 travels between the Westbahnhof and the Südbahnhof.

BY BUS   Buses crisscross the entire city. Three buses (1A, 2A, and 3A) go through the inner city Monday to Saturday. For night owls, 22 buses operate throughout the night from Schwedenplatz to the suburbs (including Grinzing), with departures every half hour costing 25S ($2) one-way.

BY TAXI   If you need a taxi, you can call ☎ **31 300,** 81 400, 40 100, or 60 160. The base price is 26S ($2.10), plus 12S (95¢) for each extra kilometer. From 11pm to 6am and all day Sunday and holidays, the base fare is 27S ($2.15), plus 14S ($1.10) for each extra kilometer. Taxis called by phone cost an extra 26S ($2.10), while luggage is 13S ($1.05) extra.

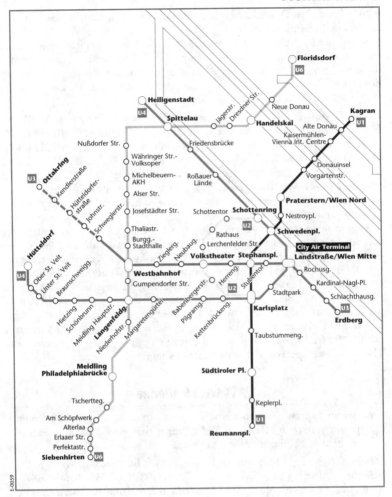

BY BICYCLE There are more than 350 miles of marked bike paths in Vienna. From May to September you may take bikes along for half fare in specially marked cars of the U-Bahn Monday to Friday 9am to 3pm and 6:30pm to the end of the day, Saturday after 9am, and all day Sunday and holidays. During the rest of the year, you can take your bike on the U-Bahn Saturday after 2pm and all day Sunday and holidays.

The most popular places for bike rentals and tours are at the amusement center of Prater and along the banks of the Donaukanal (Danube Canal), with several bike-rental agencies at both these spots open from about April to October. These include the **Radverleih Hochschaubahn** in Prater (☎ 01/729 58 88; U-Bahn: U-1 to Prater-stern); **Donauinsel** at the Floridsdorfer Bridge on the Danube Island (☎ 01/278 86 98; U-Bahn: U-6 to Handelskai); and **Radsport Nussdorf** on the Donau Canal near the boat dock in Nussdorf (☎ 01/37 45 98; Tram: D to Nussdorf). Near the center of town is **Radverleih City,** Kegelgasse 43, near the Hundertwasser Haus (☎ 01/713

93 95; Tram: N or O to Radetzkyplatz). Rentals begin at around 50S ($4) per hour or 200S ($16) for the whole day.

Rental bikes are also available year-round at the Westbahnhof and Südbahnhof train stations. If you have a Eurailpass or a valid train ticket for that day, the cost of a day's rental is 90S ($7); if you rent the bike after 3pm, you can also rent it for the next day at the same price. Otherwise, if you don't have a train ticket, bikes rent for 150S ($12) for 1 day. Mountain bikes cost more.

BY RENTAL CAR   Car-rental agencies include **Avis,** Opernring 3–5 (☎ **01/587 62 41;** U-Bahn: Karlsplatz); **Budget,** in the Hilton Air Terminal (☎ **01/714 65 65;** U-Bahn: Landstrasse/Wien Mitte); and **Hertz,** Kärntner-Ring 17 (☎ **01/512 86 77;** U-Bahn: Stephansplatz). Prices vary, but expect to pay about 996S ($80) per day for an Opel Corsa or a Ford Fiesta, including unlimited mileage and 20% tax. Weekend rates are always lower than weekday rates, there are almost always promotional bargains available, and smaller independent companies may offer better deals. It pays, therefore, to shop around.

Keep in mind that parking, especially in or near the First Precinct, is practically nonexistent, except for parking garages. Convenient garages in the First Precinct are **Parkgarage Am Hof** (☎ **01/533 55 71**), **Parkgarage Freyung/Herrengasse** (☎ **01/535 04 50**), and **Tiefgarage Kärntner Strasse** (☎ **01/587 17 97**). All are open 24 hours and charge 36S to 40S ($2.90 to $3.20) per hour; the U-Bahn stop for all is Stephansplatz. Since most of Vienna's attractions are easily reached on foot or by public transportation, an alternative is to leave your car at the **"Park & Ride" parking lot,** at the U-3 terminus on the corner of Franzosengraben and Erdbergstrasse (☎ **01/798 64 13**), open 24 hours and costing only 30S ($2.40) for the entire day. The U-3 subway gets you to the city center in 7 minutes.

FAST FACTS: Vienna

American Express   An office is at Kärntner Strasse 21–23 (☎ **01/51 540;** Stephansplatz), open Monday to Friday 9am to 5:30pm and Saturday 9am to noon. Its cash machine for American Express cards is open 24 hours.

Baby-sitters   For a baby-sitter in Vienna, call the **Baby-sitting Service** of the Austrian University Student Association (☎ **01/408 70 46-75** or 01/408 70 46-76), which takes calls Monday to Friday 9am to 2pm. Note that reservations are required at least 2 days in advance.

Banks   The main banks of Vienna are open Monday to Friday 8am to 12:30pm and 1:30 to 3pm (to 5:30pm Thursday). If you need to exchange money outside bank hours, you can do so at **Intropa,** beside Vienna Tourist Information at the corner of Philharmoniker Strasse and Kärntner Strasse, open in summer Monday to Friday 9am to 5:30pm, Saturday 9am to 3pm, and Sunday 10am to 3pm, and in winter Monday to Friday 9am to 5:30pm and Saturday 9am to noon. There are also money exchange counters at the Westbahnhof, open daily 7am to 10pm, and the Südbahnhof, open daily in summer 6:30am to 10pm and in winter 6:30am to 9pm, where you can also get cash advances for Diners Club, Master-Card, and Visa.

In addition, there are convenient automatic **money exchange machines** open 24 hours at Bank Austria in the heart of the city at Stephansplatz 2 (☎ **01/ 513-16-26-0;** U-Bahn: Stephansplatz) and at Bank Austria at Kärntner Strasse 32 (☎ **01/512 05 38;** U-Bahn: Stephansplatz), which will change U.S. $5, $10, $20, and $50 bills into Austrian currency. Note, too, that Bank Austria allows you to obtain cash from Visa credit cards. Creditanstalt, with convenient locations at Stephansplatz 7A and Kärntner Strasse 7, handles Diners Club and MasterCard.

Business Hours   Shop hours are generally Monday to Friday 9 or 9:30am to 6 or 7pm and Saturday 9am to 5pm. Shops outside the city center may close for lunch noon to 2 or 3pm.

Consulates   If you have questions or problems regarding American passports or visas, contact the consulate of the **United States,** in the Marriott Hotel at Gartenbaupromenade 2 (☎ **01/313 39;** U-Bahn: Stadtpark), open Monday and Friday 8:30am to noon and 1 to 3:30pm, Tuesday 8:30am to noon and 1 to 2pm, and Thursday 11am to noon and 1 to 3:30pm. The embassy of **Australia** is at Mattiellistrasse 2–4 (☎ **01/512 85 80;** U-Bahn: Karlsplatz), open Monday to Friday 9am to 12:30pm for visa applications and Monday to Thursday 2 to 5pm for matters such as lost passports. The consular and passport section of the embassy of **Canada,** at Fleischmarkt 19 with an entrance at Laurenzerbergstrasse 2 (☎ **01/531 38-0;** U-Bahn: Schwedenplatz), is open Monday to Friday 8:30am to 12:30pm and 1:30 to 3:30pm. The consulate of the **United Kingdom,** Jauresgasse 10 (☎ **01/716 13 5151;** Tram: 71 to Unteres Belvedere), is open Monday to Friday 9:15am to noon and (for British passport holders) 2 to 4pm.

Currency   The Austrian currency is the **schilling,** written **ASch, AS, ÖS,** or simply **S.** A schilling is made up of 100 **groschen** (which are seldom used). Coins are minted as 2, 5, 10, and 50 groschen, and 1, 5, 10, 20, 25, 50, 100, and 500 schilling (the 100S and 500S coins are for collecting and aren't circulated). Banknotes appear as 20, 50, 100, 500, 1,000, and 5,000 schilling.

Dentists   For a list of English-speaking dentists in Vienna, contact one of the consulates above. If you need dental assistance on a weekend or during the night, call ☎ **01/512 20 78** for a recorded message listing dentists with weekend or night emergency service.

Doctors   The consulates above have lists of English-speaking doctors in Vienna, or call the Doctors' Association at ☎ **1771** for a referral. If you need an emergency doctor during the night (daily 7pm to 7am) or on a weekend, call ☎ **141.** You can also call **First Care,** inside the Ring at Helferstorferstrasse 4 (☎ **01/0660-6125;** U-Bahn: Schottentor), a 24-hour doctor service. Call to make an appointment; doctors will also visit your hotel.

Emergencies   Dial ☎ **122** for the **fire department,** ☎ **133** for the **police,** ☎ **144** for an **ambulance,** and ☎ **1550** to find out which **pharmacy** has night hours. For medical emergencies, see "Dentists" or "Doctors," above, or "Hospitals," below.

Holidays   Vienna celebrates New Year's Day (January 1), Epiphany (January 6), Easter Monday, Labor Day (May 1), Ascension Day, Whitmonday, Corpus Christi, Feast of the Assumption (August 15), Austria Day (October 26), All Saints' Day (November 1), Feast of the Immaculate Conception (December 8), and Christmas (December 25 and 26).

Hospitals   The general hospital, the **Neue Allgemeine Krankenhaus,** at Währinger Gürtel 18–20 (☎ **01/40400-0**), is best reached by taking the U-Bahn (U-6) to the Michelbeuern/Allgemeine Krankenhaus station. Otherwise, free first-aid treatment is available 24 hours at the **Krankenhaus der Barmherzigen Brüder,** Grosse Mohren-Gasse 9 (☎ **01/21 12 10;** Tram: 21). A hospital to serve primarily needy people, it also dispenses medications free of charge.

The Austrian Schilling

For American Readers   At this writing, $1 = approximately 12.50S (or 1S = 8¢), and this was the rate of exchange used to calculate the dollar values given in ˙ this chapter.

For British Readers   At this writing, £1 = approximately 20.75S (or 1S = 5p), and this was the rate of exchange used to calculate the pound values in the table below.

Note: Exchange rates fluctuate from time to time and may not be the same when you travel to Austria.

S	U.S.$	U.K.£	S	U.S.$	U.K.£
1	.08	.05	200	16.00	9.64
5	.40	.24	300	24.00	14.46
10	.80	.48	400	32.00	19.28
15	1.20	.72	500	40.00	24.10
20	1.60	.96	600	48.00	28.92
25	2.00	1.20	700	56.00	33.73
30	2.40	1.45	800	64.00	38.55
40	3.20	1.93	900	72.00	43.37
50	4.00	2.41	1,000	80.00	48.19
100	8.00	4.82	1,250	100.00	60.24

Laundry   Ask the proprietor of your hotel for directions to the nearest self-service laundry. Otherwise, a convenient coin laundry is the **Münzwäscherei Margaretenstrasse,** Margaretenstrasse 52 (☎ **01/587 04 73**), open Monday to Friday 7am to 6pm and Saturday 8 to 11am. It costs 130S ($10.40) to wash and dry 6 kilos (13½ lb.) of laundry here, including detergent.

Mail   Most post offices in Vienna are open Monday to Friday 8am to noon and 2 to 6pm. The main post office, **Hauptpostamt 1010,** open 24 hours daily for long-distance phone calls, telegrams, and stamps, is in the heart of the city inside the Ring at Fleischmarkt 19 (☎ **01/51 509;** U-Bahn: Schwedenplatz), Vienna 1010. If you don't know where you'll be staying in Vienna, you can have your mail sent here Post Restante. Postcards sent airmail to North America cost 13S ($1.05), as do airmail letters weighing up to 20 grams.

Tax   Government tax and service charge is already included in restaurant and hotel bills. If you've purchased goods for more than 1,000S ($80), you're entitled to a refund of the 13% **value-added tax (VAT).** For more information, see "Shopping," later in this chapter.

Telephone   It costs 2S (15¢) to make a 1-minute local phone call (insert several 1S coins to ensure against being cut off—unused coins will be returned at the end of the call). If you come across a phone number with a dash at the end (such as 51553-0), it indicates an extension; treat it as you would any number and simply dial the whole number. Note that all phone numbers in Vienna are gradually being changed to seven digits (a process that will take years). If you come across a number in this book that has been changed, call information (dial ☎ **1611**) to inquire about the new number.

Country & City Codes

The **country code** for Austria is **43.** The **city code** for Vienna is **1;** use this code when you're calling from outside Austria. If you're within Austria but not in Vienna, use **01.** If you're calling within Vienna, simply leave off the code and dial only the regular phone number.

Hotels add a surcharge on calls made from their rooms, so you're best off going to a post office to make long-distance calls. It costs 31.50S ($2.50) to make a 3-minute call to the United States Monday to Friday 8am to 6pm; after 6pm and on weekends the rate falls to 28S ($2.25) for 3 minutes. An alternative to going to the post office is to buy a telephone card, available at any post office in values of 50S ($4), 100S ($8), and 200S ($16), which can be used in special phones found virtually everywhere (sometimes it's difficult nowadays to find a phone that will accept coins).

In recent years, special phones that accept credit/charge cards, including American Express, Diners Club, MasterCard, and Visa, have also made their appearance. You'll find one conveniently located on Stephansplatz behind Stephansdom and another one near the Vienna Tourist Information, just off Kärntner Strasse on Krugerstrasse.

Tipping   A 15% service charge is already included in restaurant bills, but it's customary to round off to the nearest 10S (80¢) on bills under 100S ($8). For more expensive meals, add 10%. The same rule applies to taxi drivers. Porters receive 20S ($1.60) per bag.

3 Accommodations You Can Afford

The largest concentration of budget accommodations is near the Westbahnhof train station and the university, west of the Ring and Altstadt. To save money, take a room without a private bath, but note that some places charge extra for showers in communal washrooms. Keep in mind also that some rates include breakfast whereas others don't—the room-only rate may end up being higher than rates that include showers and breakfast. The most expensive lodgings are those inside the Ring in the old city center. My recommendations include rooms in private homes, pensions (usually cheaper than hotels and sometimes cheaper than homes), and hotels.

And remember that if the accommodations are full, the **Vienna Tourist Information offices** will book a room for 40S ($3.20), including rooms in private homes. The busiest seasons in Vienna are May to mid-June; August and September; and the Christmas, New Year's, and Easter holidays. Reserve your room in advance if you plan on visiting at these times.

Note: You can find the city-center lodging choices below plotted on the map in "Seeing the Sights," later in this chapter.

PRIVATE HOMES
INSIDE THE RING

Adele Grün. Apt. 19, Gonzagagasse 1 (just off Franz-Josefs-Kai), Apt. 19, 1010 Wien. ☎ **01/533 25 06.** 4 units, none with bathroom. 500S ($40) single; 1,000S ($80) double; 1,200S ($96) triple. No credit cards. Rates include showers. U-Bahn: U-3 from the Westbahnhof to Stephansplatz, then U-1 from Stephansplatz to Schwedenplatz, then a 1-minute walk. Tram: D from the Südbahnhof to Oper, then 1 or 2 from Oper to Salztorbrücke; or D from Franz-Josefs-Bahnhof to Börserplatz, then 1 to Salztorbrücke.

Getting the Best Deal on Accommodations

- Be aware that accommodations outside the Ring are less expensive than those in the Old City.

- Note that accommodations offering cooking facilities can help save money on dining bills.

- Take advantage of winter discounts offered by some hotels and pensions, generally November to March (excluding the Christmas holidays).

- Inquire whether there's an extra charge for taking a shower and whether breakfast is included in the room rate.

- Ask whether a surcharge is added on local and long-distance phone calls.

In an elegant older building, up on the third floor (there's an elevator), the rooms here are pleasant and clean. There are two communal showers, one tub, and one toilet. Frau Grün, nearing 80, speaks English and is friendly.

Frau Hoffmann. Annagasse 3A (just off Kärntner Strasse), 1010 Wien. ☎ **01/512 49 04.** 2 units, 1 with shower only. 700S ($56) double without shower, 800S ($64) double with shower only. Rates include continental breakfast and showers. No credit cards. U-Bahn: U-3 from the Westbahnhof to Stephansplatz, then a 5-minute walk. Tram: D from the Südbahnhof or Franz-Josefs-Bahnhof to Oper, then a 3-minute walk.

Once a famous skater, Frau Hoffmann ran her establishment as a pension for more than 30 years but in 1988 decided to "retire" to private-room status; she prefers those who stay at least 2 nights. The rooms are enormous and the location, right off Kärntner Strasse and near the State Opera, can't be beat. Frau Hoffmann speaks English, serves big breakfasts, and gives advice on what to do in Vienna.

NEAR THE WESTBAHNHOF

If you're coming from the Südbahnhof, take Tram no. 18 to the Westbahnhof. From Franz-Josefs-Bahnhof, take Tram no. 5.

Hedwig Gally. Arnsteingasse 25 (off Mariahilfer Strasse, a 10-minute walk southwest of the train station), Apt. 10, 1150 Wien. ☎ **01/892 90 73** or 01/893 10 28. Fax 01/893 10 28. 7 units, 5 with shower only, 2 with bathroom; 7 apts. 260S ($21) single without bathroom, 300S ($24) single with shower only; 440S–460S ($35–$37) double without bathroom, 520S ($42) double with shower only, 600S–660S ($48–$53) double with bathroom; 600S ($48) triple without bathroom, 690S ($55) triple with shower only, 780S ($62) triple with bathroom. Rates include showers. Extra person 200S–210S ($16–$17). Breakfast 50S ($4). No credit cards. Free parking. Tram: 52 or 58 from the Westbahnhof to Kranzgasse (2 stops).

Frau Gally and her son, Martin, both of whom speak good English and dispense free city maps and sightseeing brochures, offer a variety of clean rooms, including one single, doubles with or without shower or bathroom, and even rooms and apartments with kitchens, some large enough for groups or families with children. Every room is equipped with a hot plate and utensils for cooking, as well as a sink with hot water. Satellite TV with CNN costs 40S ($3.20) per day (not available in all rooms). This place is good for longer stays.

F. Kaled. Lindengasse 42 (a 10-minute walk from the Westbahnhof and the Ring), 1070 Wien. ☎ and fax **01/523 90 13.** 5 units, 2 with bathroom. TV. 400S ($32) single without bathroom; 550S ($44) double without bathroom, 650S ($52) double with bathroom; 800S ($64) triple without bathroom. Rates include showers. Extra person 150S ($12). Breakfast 75S ($6). No credit cards. U-Bahn: U-3 to Neubaugasse. Tram: 5 to Lindengasse. Bus: 13A from the Südbahnhof to Mariahilfer Strasse.

A Telephone Number Tip

Vienna's phone system is being computerized, which means all households and businesses are gradually receiving new numbers. Though I've made every effort to be up-to-date, some phone numbers may no longer be current when you arrive. Call the information operator at ☎ **1611** if you have any problems.

Mr. Kaled, a young Tunisian with Austrian citizenship who speaks English, French, and German, offers spacious and spotless rooms, each with a radio/cassette player and cable TV. His partner, Tina, speaks excellent English and is happy to give sightseeing tips. All rooms face a quiet inner courtyard. Many readers have recommended this place.

Barbara Koller. Schmalzhofgasse 11 (a 10-minute walk from the train station, near Mariahilfer Strasse in the direction of the Ring), 1060 Wien. ☎ and fax **01/597 29 35.** 5 units, all with bathroom. 360S ($29) per person. Rates include continental breakfast. No credit cards. U-Bahn: U-3 to Zieglergasse (take the Webgasse exit). Tram: 18 from the Südbahnhof to the Westbahnhof.

This cheerful private home has its own stairway up to the first floor—look for the iron gate. The rooms wrap around an inner courtyard; they're large and spotless, with sturdy old-fashioned furniture, hair dryers, and safes. Though the charges are a bit higher than those at other nearby private homes, keep in mind that all rooms here have baths, some have refrigerators, and breakfast is included.

Irmgard and Sandy Lauria. Kaiserstrasse 77 (a 15-minute walk north of the Westbahnhof), 1070 Wien. ☎ **01/522 25 55.** 8 units, 3 with shower only. TV. 530S ($42) double without bathroom, 700S ($56) double with shower only; 700S ($56) triple without bathroom, 800S ($64) triple with shower only; 850S ($68) quad without bathroom, 940S ($75) quad with shower only. Rates include showers. MC, V. U-Bahn: U-6 from the Westbahnhof to Burggasse/Stadthalle (1 stop), then a 4-minute walk. Tram: 5 from the Westbahnhof or Franz-Josefs-Bahnhof to Burggasse. Bus: 13A from the Südbahnhof to Kellermann Gasse, then 48A from Kellermann Gasse to Kaiserstrasse.

Independent backpackers who don't like living in someone's house might prefer staying here, since Irmgard Lauria lives in an apartment in the same building. The atmosphere is laid-back and the rooms are cozy. Breakfast isn't served, but each room has plates and flatware and a hot-water kettle; there's also a communal refrigerator and toaster. The rooms are on the second floor, Apartment 8—but be sure to call first. For young travelers really counting their pennies, Frau Lauria also offers simpler accommodations in the same building, including rooms with bunk beds costing 480S ($38) for two and 600S ($48) for three, and a 25-bed **Panda Hostel** (☎ **01/522 78 88**), which sleeps four to eight in dorm-style rooms and costs 160S ($13) per person in summer and 110S ($9) in winter.

NEAR THE SÜDBAHNHOF

✪ **Frank Heberling.** Siccardsburggasse 42, Apt. 31, 1100 Wien. ☎ **01/607 21 17** or 01/604 02 29. 6 units, 1 with shower only. 450S ($36) double with/without shower; 130S ($10) per person in 4-bed dorm. Rates include showers. Breakfast 35S ($2.80). No credit cards. Tram: 6 from the Westbahnhof to Quellenplatz (4th stop after the underpath), or O from the Südbahnhof to Quellenplatz, then a 5-minute walk.

Be sure to call first, since the Heberlings are an older retired couple who live in a nearby building (in summer, Frau Heberling can usually be found at Apartment 31). The Heberlings, who prefer guests who stay more than 1 night, are warm and friendly and speak very good English. They'll give you a local map with directions on how to reach the city center, the closest laundry, and the like. The building is 100 years old but in excellent condition. Each room is actually a small apartment, comfortable if a bit plain, with a sink, a heater, and a sitting room in addition to a bedroom. Guests get breakfast in their rooms.

NEAR THE NASCHMARKT & KARLSPLATZ

Renate Gajdos. Pressgasse 28 (near the outdoor market and Karlsplatz, within a 10-minute walk of the Ring), 1040 Wien. ☎ **01/587 74 16.** 5 units, none with bathroom. TV. 450S ($36) single; 650S ($52) double; 900S ($72) triple. Rates include breakfast and showers. No credit cards. U-Bahn: U-6 from the Westbahnhof to Längenfeldgasse, then U-4 from Längenfeldgasse to Kettenbrückengasse. Bus: 13A from the Südbahnhof to Margaretenplatz, then 59A to Pressgasse.

Frau Gajdos has been in business more than 40 years. She lives on the first floor of a building just a stone's throw from the Naschmarkt outdoor market. Her young, energetic German hunting dog is likely to greet you at the door. One of the rooms here is a single and two others are joined, appropriate for families. The rooms are large, sunny, and well furnished, with cable TVs. The breakfast room is cheerful, with lots of interesting knickknacks on the shelves, so you have something to look at as you feast on Frau Gajdos's homemade marmalade along with yogurt, bread, cheese, and egg.

✪ **Renate Halper.** Straussengasse 5 (less than a 15-minute walk from the city center), 1050 Wien. ☎ **01/587 12 78.** 2 units and 1 apt, none with bathroom. TV. 500S ($40) single; 800S ($64) double; 400S ($32) per person in apt. No credit cards. Rates include breakfast and showers. U-Bahn: U-4 to Pilgramgasse; or U-3 from the Westbahnhof to Neubaugasse, then bus no. 13A (toward the Südbahnhof) to Ziegelofen Gasse. Bus: 13A from the Südbahnhof to Ziegelofen Gasse.

Renate Halper is a young, outgoing woman who speaks English fluently. She has even prepared for her guests a small booklet in English with information on nearby restaurants, directions to various sights, descriptions of Vienna's many kinds of coffee, and more. One room has furniture that used to belong to Renate's grandmother; another has a balcony. The apartment has its own kitchen.

✪ **Hilde Wolf.** Schleifmühlgasse 7 (a few minutes' walk from the Staatsoper and Karlsplatz), 1040 Wien. ☎ **01/586 51 03.** 4 units, none with bathroom. 395S ($32) single; 540S ($43) double; 790S ($63) triple; 1,025S ($82) quad. Breakfast 35S ($2.80). Showers 20S ($1.60). No credit cards. Tram: 6 from the Westbahnhof to Eichenstrasse (four stops), then 62 from Eichenstrasse to Paulanergasse; or D from the Südbahnhof or Franz-Josefs-Bahnhof to Oper, then 62 or 65 from Oper to Paulanergasse or bus no. 59A to Schleifmühlgasse.

English-speaking Frau Wolf and her husband, Otto, offer rooms literally large enough to dance in, with high ceilings typical of turn-of-the-century Viennese buildings and comfortable fin-de-siècle furniture. Frau Wolf, a retired teacher who loves children, welcomes families (and will even baby-sit), serves a lavish breakfast, and says that readers of this book can ask for second helpings of coffee, bread, butter, and marmalade. She'll also do laundry. Her first-floor apartment is near the outdoor market.

HOTELS & PENSIONS
INSIDE THE RING

City. Bauernmarkt 10 (just west of Stephansplatz), 1010 Wien. ☎ **01/533 95 21.** Fax 01/535 52 16. 19 units, all with bathroom. MINIBAR TV TEL. 630S ($50) single; 990S–1,200S ($79–$96) double. Winter discounts available. Rates include buffet breakfast. Extra person 300S ($24). AE, DC, MC, V. U-Bahn: U-1 or U-3 to Stephansplatz. Tram: D from the Südbahnhof to Oper; then bus no. 3A from Oper to Habsburgergasse.

Just a minute's walk from Stephansplatz, this small pension is in the house where the author Franz Grillparzer was born in 1791. It's on the second floor ("mezzanine level"), served by an ancient elevator. The rooms are rather plain but offer all the comforts; the tiny breakfast room is decorated with Klimt reprints. You can fuel up on the all-you-can-eat breakfast served until a late 11am (it can be delivered to your room). Though accommodations here are pricey, it may be worth it if you want to be in the heart of Old Vienna.

Dr. Geissler. Around the corner from the main post office (a 4-minute walk from Stephansplatz), Postgasse 14, 1010 Wien. ☎ **01/533 28 03** or 01/533 28 04. Fax 01/533 26 35. 32 units, 4 with shower only, 24 with bathroom. TV TEL. 550S–580S ($44–$46.40) single without bathroom, 800S–850S ($64–$68) single with shower only; 700S–780S ($56–$62) double without bathroom, 900S–980S ($72–$78) double with shower only, 1,180S ($94) double with bathroom. Winter discounts available. Rates include buffet breakfast and showers. AE, DC, MC, V. U-Bahn: U-1 or U-4 to Schwedenplatz. Tram: 1 or 2 to Schwedenplatz.

This pension, with a reception on the eighth floor (with elevator), has grown over the years, adding more rooms on more floors. The few rooms in the oldest, eighth-floor section, however, have the best views—you can even see the towers of Stephansdom. Otherwise, rooms are simple and slightly behind the times in decor. There's also a small dining area offering snacks as well as meals ordered in advance.

WEST OF THE RING

Adria. Wickenburggasse 23 (northwest of the Ring, a 20-minute walk from the city center), 1080 Wien. ☎ **01/402 02 38** or 01/408 39 06. Fax 01/408 39 06. 14 units, all with bathroom. MINIBAR TV TEL. 600S ($48) single; 860S–1,000S ($69–$80) double; 1,200S–1,300S ($96–$104) triple. Winter discounts available. Rates include buffet breakfast and showers. MC. Tram: D from the Südbahnhof to Schottentor, then a 10-minute walk; or 5 from the Westbahnhof or Franz-Josefs-Bahnhof to Lange Gasse.

This no-nonsense first-floor pension is simple and clean. It's owned by the English-speaking Mr. Hamde, a Jordanian who now has Austrian citizenship. All the high-ceilinged rooms have radios and cable TVs. The buffet breakfast is all-you-can-eat. Mr. Hamde also rents an apartment near the Südbahnhof and Belvedere; it comes complete with bathroom, kitchen, phone, and cable TV, and costs 500S to 650S ($40 to $52) for two persons per night depending on the length of stay, and 700S ($56) for three.

Astra. Alserstrasse 32, 1090 Wien. ☎ **01/402 43 54** or 01/408 22 70. Fax 01/402 46 62. 17 units, 2 with shower only, 15 with bathroom; 4 apts. TV TEL. 550S ($44) single with shower only, 700S ($56) single with bathroom; 800S ($64) double with shower only, 990S ($79) double with bathroom; 850S ($68) apt for 2, 1,200S ($96) apt for 3. Winter discounts available. Room (but not apt) rates include buffet breakfast. No credit cards. Crib available. U-Bahn: U-6 from the Westbahnhof to Alserstrasse. Tram: 5 from Franz-Josefs-Bahnhof to Spittalgasse/Alserstrasse, then a 5-minute walk. Bus: 13A from the Südbahnhof to Skodagasse (last stop).

Rooms in this first-floor pension are quiet and clean (all but one face away from the street). The manager is the friendly English-speaking Gaby Brekoupil. Most room TVs have cable, and the apartments come with a small kitchenette and TV, making them especially good for families or for longer stays.

Kugel. Siebensterngasse 43/Neubaugasse 46 (on the corner of Siebensterngasse and Neubaugasse), 1070 Wien. ☎ **01/523 33 55.** Fax 01/523 16 78. 38 units, 17 with shower only, 17 with bathroom. TV. 440S ($35) single without bathroom, 520S ($42) single with shower only, 620S ($50) single with bathroom; 620S ($50) double without bathroom, 780S

($62) double with shower only, 1,000S ($80) double with bathroom; 1,000S ($80) triple with shower only, 1,200S ($96) triple with bathroom. Winter discounts available. Rates include continental breakfast and showers. No credit cards. Closed Jan 7–Feb 4. Tram: 18 from the Westbahnhof (going toward Burggasse/Stadthalle) one stop, then 49 to Neubaugasse/Siebensterngasse; or D from Franz-Josefs-Bahnhof to Westbahnstrasse/Kaiserstrasse. Bus: 13A from the Südbahnhof to Kirchengasse.

The same family has owned this 140-year-old hotel since it opened; it's now in its third generation, soon to be passed on to the fourth. It shows its age, with small rooms and outdated wallpaper, but it has a good location and is adequate for the price. Only four rooms are without showers and/or toilets; showers were added as freestanding cabinets. In addition to singles, doubles, and triples, there are a few rooms large enough for four or five people.

Lindenhof. Lindengasse 4 (behind the Herzmansky department store), 1070 Wien. ☎ **01/523 04 98.** Fax 01/523 73 62. 19 units, 6 with bathroom. 370S ($30) single without bathroom, 470S ($38) single with bathroom; 620S ($50) double without bathroom, 840S ($67) double with bathroom; 930S ($74) triple without bathroom, 1,260S ($109) triple with bathroom. Winter discounts available. Rates include breakfast. Showers 20S ($1.75). No credit cards. U-Bahn: U-3 from the Westbahnhof to Neubaugasse. Bus: 13A from the Südbahnhof to Kirchengasse.

The owner of this pension is George Gebrael, an Armenian with Austrian citizenship who's married to a Bulgarian. Mr. Gebrael speaks seven languages, English among them, and his daughter and son attended an international school taught in English. The long corridor of this second-floor pension (with elevator) is filled with massive plants. Rooms come in various sizes and styles. Some are quite spacious and old-fashioned, with tall ceilings and beautiful wooden floors; some are smaller and have been remodeled with modern furniture. A few bathroomless rooms even have balconies.

Wild. Lange Gasse 10 (a 10-minute walk from the Ring), 1080 Wien. ☎ **01/406 51 74-0.** Fax 01/402 21 68. 21 units, 9 with shower only, 7 with bathroom. TEL. 490S ($39) single without bathroom, 590S ($47) single with shower only, 690S ($55) single with bathroom; 690S ($55) double without bathroom, 790S ($63) double with shower only, 990S ($79) double with bathroom. Rates include continental breakfast and showers. AE, DC, MC, V. U-Bahn: U-3 from the Westbahnhof to Volkstheater, then U-2 from Volkstheater to Lerchen-felderstrasse, then a 2-minute walk. Tram: D from Franz-Josefs-Bahnhof to Bellaria. Bus: 13A from the Südbahnhof to Piaristengasse.

Run by the friendly Frau Wild and her English-speaking son, Peter, this pension features refrigerators and cooking facilities and utensils on each floor, making it popular with students and for longer stays (spaghetti, says Frau Wild, is the most frequently cooked dish). The place started out more than 30 years ago with only one bed but now covers several floors, accessible by elevator. The rooms are clean and are slowly being renovated; those with a bathroom also boast a kitchen, cable TV with CNN, and minibar. Unfortunately, the pension has a tendency to overbook; extra guests are passed on to a nearby establishment. Insist on a room in this pension when making your reservation. A plus is that guests get shuttle service to/from the airport for 300S ($24) and to/from train stations for 100S ($8) per trip, regardless of how many people are in the van.

A YOUTH HOSTEL

Hostel Ruthensteiner. Robert-Hamerling-Gasse 24 (near the Westbahnhof), 1150 Wien. ☎ **01/893 42 02** or 01/893 27 96. Fax 01/893 27 96. E-mail: hostel.ruthensteiner@telecom.at. 11 units, none with bathroom; 30 dorm beds. 245S ($20) single; 470S ($38) double; 145S–169S ($12–$14) dorm bed. Rates include showers. Breakfast 25S ($2). No credit cards. U-Bahn: U-6 from Franz-Josefs-Bahnhof to the Westbahnhof. Tram: 18 from the Süd-bahnhof or 5 from Franz-Josefs-Bahnhof to the Westbahnhof, then a 5-minute walk.

This hostel, run by Erin and Walter Ruthensteiner (Erin is American), requires a membership card (though nonmembers can stay by paying an extra one-time fee of 40S/$3.20) and has no age limit or curfew. There is, however, a maximum stay of 4 nights. Single, double, and dorm rooms are available; in addition to the rates above, additional dorms are available in summer for 125S ($10) per person. All rooms have sinks, lockers, and bedside reading lights. You can cook your own food in the kitchen, and, even better, you can barbecue, eat, and play chess on the outdoor brick patio. Bikes are available May to September for 89S ($7) per day. Guests can use the computer for e-mail and the Internet.

WORTH A SPLURGE

✪ **Aviano.** Marco-d'Aviano-Gasse 1 (just off Kärntner Strasse), 1010 Wien. ☎ **01/512 83 30.** Fax 01/512 83 30-6. 17 units, all with bathroom. MINIBAR TV TEL. Summer, 880S ($70.40) single; 1,460S–1,560S ($116–$125) double. Winter, 770S ($62) single; 1,180S–1,260S ($94–$101) double. Rates include buffet breakfast. DC, MC, V. U-Bahn: U-3 from the Westbahnhof to Stephansplatz. Tram: 52 or 58 from the Westbahnhof to Burgring; or D from the Südbahnhof or Franz-Josefs-Bahnhof to Oper.

This centrally located, friendly pension offers elegant rooms decorated in Old Vienna Biedermeier style, as well as such modern conveniences as bidets and private safes. Some rooms also have radios, hair dryers, and hot plates, and some feature double-pane windows facing the famous shopping street, Kärntner Strasse. The reception is on the fourth floor. Summer-season rates are in effect from the end of March to November and during the Christmas/New Year's season.

✪ **Pertschy.** Habsburgergasse 5 (a few steps off Graben, near Stephansplatz), 1010 Wien. ☎ **01/534 49-0.** Fax 01/534 49-49. 43 units, all with bathroom. MINIBAR TV TEL. Summer, 880S ($70) single; 1,280S–1,560S ($102–$125) double. Winter, 770S ($62) single; 1,160S–1,360S ($93–$109) double. Rates include buffet breakfast. DC, MC, V. U-Bahn: U-1 or U-3 to Stephansplatz. Tram: D from the Südbahnhof to Oper, then bus no. 3A from Oper to Habsburgergasse.

This is a wonderful place for a splurge. It occupies the first several floors of an ancient "palais" built in 1725 and now an official historic landmark. The ceilings are high and vaulted, and the rooms are outfitted in updated Biedermeier style, complete with stucco ceilings, chandeliers, modern bathrooms, and satellite TV. Three rooms even have tile heaters—one is 200 years old. To get from room to room, you walk along an enclosed catwalk on a balcony that traces around a courtyard. As for the Pertschys, they lived in Canada for 10 years and have run this pension for more than 35 years—the whole family speaks perfect English. Summer-season rates are in effect from the end of March to November and during the Christmas/New Year's season.

4 Great Deals on Dining

Because many shops and businesses are inside the Ring and along Mariahilfer Strasse west of the Ring, many of Vienna's best-known restaurants are in these places too. You don't have to spend a lot of money to eat well, and there's enough variety to keep the palate interested.

Viennese cuisine is the culmination of various ethnic influences, including Bohemian, Hungarian, Croatian, Slovene, German, and Italian. At the top end of the price scale is wild game, followed by various fish, poultry, and beef dishes. Most restaurants serve complete meals, consisting of a main dish and one or several side dishes. Prices listed for each restaurant below, therefore, are usually for complete meals.

Dining Notes

The cheapest place for a meal is the *würstelstand* ("sausage stand"), which offers various types of drinks and sausages, most priced between 30S and 35S ($2.40 and $2.80). Convenient stands are those on Seilergasse (just off Stephansplatz), open Monday to Saturday 8am to 1am and Sunday 9am to 1am; on Kupferschmiedgasse (just off Kärntner Strasse), open daily 9am to 10pm; on Schwarzenbergplatz, open 24 hours; and at the Naschmarkt (see below).

Next on the economic ladder are self-service restaurants where you can create your own multicourse meal at very low prices. One of the most popular is the **Naschmarkt** chain of cafeterias. And *beisl* is the Austrian word for pub or tavern, many of which serve hearty and inexpensive meals.

For starters, you might try a soup like *griessnockerlsuppe* (clear soup with semolina dumplings), *leberknödlsuppe* (soup with liver dumplings), *rindsuppe* (beef broth), or *gulaschsuppe* (Hungarian goulash). Popular main courses are *bauernschmaus* (varied sausages and pork items with sauerkraut and dumplings), *tafelspitz* (boiled beef with vegetables), *Wiener schnitzel* (breaded veal cutlet), *schweinebraten* (roast pork), *spanferkel* (suckling pig), *backhendl* (fried and breaded chicken), and *gulasch* (stew). *Nockerl* are little dumplings, usually served with sauce. And then there are desserts. Vienna's *apfelstrudel* (apple strudel) is probably the best in the world. *Palatschinken* are light sugared pancakes; *kaiserschmarren* is a diced omelet, served with jam and sprinkled with sugar. A *sachertorte* is a sinfully rich chocolate cake.

And to top it all off you'll want coffee, of which there are at least 20 varieties. Introduced 300 years ago by the Turks during their unsuccessful attempt to conquer Vienna, coffee as served in Viennese coffeehouses has become an art form. Among the many kinds are the *kleiner schwarzer*, a small cup without milk; *kleiner brauner*, a small cup with a little milk; *melange*, a large cup with milk; *melange mit schlag*, coffee topped with whipped cream; *mokka*, strong black Viennese coffee; and *Türkischer*, Turkish coffee boiled in a small copper pot and served in a tiny cup. Coffee is always served with a glass of water.

Note: The hours given below are exactly the hours the doors remain open. Last orders are generally 1 hour before closing.

A LOCAL BUDGET BEST

Mensa. Technische Universität Wien, Turm B, Wiedner Hauptstrasse 8–19. ☎ **01/586 65 02** or 216 06 68. Fixed-price meals 35S–45S ($2.80–$3.60) students, 39S–49S ($3.10–$3.90) nonstudents. No credit cards. Mon–Fri 11am–2:30pm. Closed Dec 25–Jan 7. U-Bahn: U-1, U-2, or U-4 to Karlsplatz. AUSTRIAN.

Though technically for students, this cafeteria serves nonstudents for slightly more. It's on the first floor of a modern light green building not far from Karlsplatz and the Naschmarkt outdoor market. Four platters are usually available, from stews to grilled chicken or spaghetti. There are different counters for each, along with additional choices of soups and salad. Pay after choosing your food, and be sure to clear your tray when you're finished. You'll also find an inexpensive snack bar here. There's another **Mensa,** serving the Universität Wien (☎ **01/406 45 94**), on the seventh floor of the Neues Institutsgebäude at Universitätstrasse 7, near Schottentor just outside the Ring. It's open Monday to Friday 11am to 2pm and offers similar dishes at similar prices.

INSIDE THE RING

✪ **Bizi.** Rotenturmstrasse 4 (on the corner of Wollzeile, just north of Stephansplatz). ☎ **01/513 37 05.** Pizza and pasta 65S–80S ($5–$6); meat courses 85S–120S

Getting the Best Deal on Dining

- Take advantage of daily specials, often posted outside the door, which are complete meals at discount prices.
- Eat a quick meal at one of Vienna's many *würstelstände*, food stalls selling sausages and beer.
- Enjoy a few hearty meals in a *beisl*, a typical Viennese tavern that dishes out home-cooked food at low prices.
- Ask whether there's an extra charge for each piece of bread consumed and whether the main course comes with vegetables or a side dish.
- Note whether there's a table charge *(gedeck)*.

($7–$10). No credit cards. Daily 11am–11pm. U-Bahn: U-1 or U-3 to Stephansplatz. ITALIAN.

This popular self-service restaurant is my top choice for a quick, inexpensive, tasty meal inside the Ring. It offers a variety of pizza and pasta, like ravioli, gnocchi, tagliatelle, and tortellini, all with a choice of sauces. Pizza by the slice, which you can order to take out or to eat at one of the stand-up or sit-down tables, costs 28S ($2.25). There's also a salad bar (a large plate costs 58S/$4.65). The decor is upbeat and pleasant, with modern art on the walls, and there's even a no-smoking section.

Gösser Bierklinik. Steindelgasse 4 (just off Graben). ☎ **01/535 68 97.** Meals 95S–185S ($8–$15). AE, DC, MC, V. Mon–Sat 10am–11pm. Closed holidays. U-Bahn: U-1 or U-3 to Stephansplatz, then a 5-minute walk west. AUSTRIAN.

First mentioned in documents from 1406, this old building became a restaurant in the 17th century. Since 1924 it's been the property of Gösser Brewery, with dining spread among nine rooms on various floors. One room even displays a Turkish cannonball that hit the place 300 years ago when Vienna lay under siege. In this pleasantly decorated place, you can either splurge or eat lunch for under $10. Hearty dishes on the English menu include fresh fish, homemade *gulasch, bauernschmaus,* grilled duck, Wiener schnitzel, roast beef with onions, steak, and *tafelspitz.*

Naschmarkt. Schottengasse 1. ☎ **01/533 51 86.** Meals 70S–100S ($6–$8). DC, MC, V. Daily 10:30am–3:30pm. U-Bahn: U-2 to Schottentor-Universität or U-3 to Herrengasse. Tram: 1, 2, or D to Schottentor. AUSTRIAN.

Taking the name of Vienna's popular outdoor market, Naschmarkt is a popular lunchtime self-service cafeteria with a variety of Austrian dishes, salads (including a salad bar), soups, beer, desserts, and other items at very reasonable prices. Especially good are the daily specials, which may include schnitzel, schweinebraten, chicken, stews, fish, or spaghetti, along with one or two side dishes. The interior is modern and pleasant. A good old standby. You'll find another Naschmarkt just south of the Ring at Schwarzenbergplatz 16 (☎ 01/505 31 15), open Monday to Friday 6:30am to 10:30pm and Saturday, Sunday, and holidays 9am to 10:30pm.

Orpheus. Spiegelgasse 10 (parallel to Kärntner Strasse). ☎ **01/512 38 53.** Meals 95S–175S ($8–$14). MC. Sun–Thurs noon–11pm, Fri–Sat noon–midnight. U-Bahn: U-1 or U-3 to Stephansplatz. GREEK.

The walls in this popular place are a colorful blue and green, accentuated by black furniture. I recommend the Orpheus Plate for two, which comes with samplings of souvlaki, lamb cutlet, pork cutlet, and chicken breast. There's also the usual selection of moussaka, lamb, souvlaki, steaks, and fish, plus lunch specials Monday to Friday for less than 100S ($8).

Spaghetti & Co. Stephansplatz 7 (just north of Stephansdom). ☎ **01/512 14 44.** Pizza and pasta 75S–110S ($6–$9). AE, DC, MC, V. Daily 11am–11:30pm. U-Bahn: U-1 or U-3 to Stephansplatz. PIZZA/PASTA.

This conveniently located branch of a chain of spaghetti parlors offers more than a dozen kinds of spaghetti dishes, including one with chili sauce and one with salmon and mushrooms. It also offers half a dozen choices of lasagnas and gnocchi casseroles as well as pizza and salads, along with a salad bar. It's good for a fast, inexpensive sit-down meal.

۞ Stadtbeisl. Naglergasse 21 (just west of Graben). ☎ **01/533 35 07.** Meals 125S–230S ($10–$18). V. Daily 10am–11:30pm. U-Bahn: U-1 or U-3 to Stephansplatz, then a 5-minute walk west. AUSTRIAN.

In the heart of Old Vienna, this beisl has a history that stretches back to the early 1700s. Once under the ownership of a cloister that offered soup to the poor twice a week, the building has a cellar three stories deep—part of which consists of catacombs with underground passageways linked to Stephansdom and other parts of the inner city. You can visit the uppermost cellar with its arched ceilings and brick floor. The building has been a restaurant since 1745, with rooms resembling a hunting lodge. Antiques crowd the front room, while antlers decorate the back room. Traditional tiled stoves *(kachelofen)* heat the entire place. The English menu offers such standbys as Wiener schnitzel, tafelspitz, fish, and Cordon Bleu.

T.G.I. Friday's. Neuer Markt 8 (just off Kärntner Strasse). ☎ **01/513 77 89.** Meals 100S–220S ($8–$18). AE, DC, MC, V. Sun–Wed 11:30am–1am, Thurs–Sat 11:30am–2am. U-Bahn: U-1 or U-3 to Stephansplatz. Tram: 1, 2, or D to Oper. AMERICAN.

This American chain now claims more then 400 locations in more than 40 countries. Vienna's branch is one of the newest, and judging by the crowds, has firmly established itself as one of the best places inside the Ring for good American food and friendly service. Its ground floor serves as a large bar, while the first-floor restaurant offers casual dining in a rustic setting. The menu has everything from potato skins, nachos, and buffalo wings to sandwiches, burgers, pasta, steaks, ribs, chicken, and, my favorite, fajitas.

۞ Trzesniewski. Dorotheergasse 1 (just off Graben). ☎ **01/512 32 91.** Sandwiches 9S (70¢). No credit cards. Mon–Fri 8:30am–7:30pm, Sat 9am–5pm. U-Bahn: U-1 or U-3 to Stephansplatz. SANDWICHES.

This is one of the most popular cafeterias in all Vienna—and rightly so. This centrally located shop is so small that the mealtime line often snakes through the entire store; it's best to come during off-peak times. Trzesniewski is a buffet of small open-face finger sandwiches covered with such spreads as salami, egg salad, tuna fish, hot peppers, tomatoes, or a couple dozen other selections. Four sandwiches are usually enough for me, along with a *pfiff*, a very tiny beer (an eighth of a liter) for only 9S (70¢). Very Viennese in atmosphere, this place is highly recommended. You'll find a convenient branch west of the Ring at Mariahilfer Strasse 95 (☎ **01/596 42 91**), open Monday to Friday 8:30am to 7pm and Saturday 9am to 5pm.

Wienerwald. Annagasse 3 (just off Kärntner Strasse). ☎ **01/512 37 66.** Meals 70S–130S ($6–$10). AE, DC, MC, V. Daily 11am–11pm. U-Bahn: U-1 or U-3 to Stephansplatz; or U-1, U-2, or U-4 to Karlsplatz. Tram: 1, 2, or D to Oper. AUSTRIAN.

Wienerwald is a successful chain of grilled chicken restaurants found throughout Austria and Germany, with almost 20 locations in Vienna. The founder of the chain got the idea when he visited Munich's Oktoberfest after World War II and witnessed the huge consumption of chicken. One of the best deals is the quarter grilled chicken, which, when ordered with a side dish such as potato salad or sauerkraut, costs just 73S ($6). Other dishes on the English menu are soups, salads (including a salad bar), schnitzel, and chicken sandwiches. Other convenient branches are at Freyung 6 (☎ **01/533 14 20**) and Goldschmiedgasse 6 (☎ **535 40 12**), both inside the Ring; Mariahilfer Strasse 156 (☎ **01/89 23 306**); and Schönbrunner Strasse 244 (☎ **01/813 24 43**).

Wrenkh. Bauernmarkt 10 (just off Stephansplatz). ☎ **01/533 15 26.** Main courses 98S–175S ($8–$14). AE, DC, MC, V. Restaurant, Mon–Sat 11:30am–2:30pm and 6–11pm; bar, Mon–Sat 11am–11pm. U-Bahn: U-1 or U-3 to Stephansplatz. VEGETARIAN.

If you're vegetarian or simply tired of Austria's obsession with meat, head to this dark and romantic restaurant just off Stephansplatz and treat yourself to innovative dishes influenced by Mediterranean and Asian cuisine. You may wish to start with miso soup or tofu salad, followed by a main dish like zucchini risotto cooked with onions, garlic, herbs, parmesan, and smoked tofu; or spinach gnocchi and vegetables in a tomato sauce; or wild-rice risotto in a mushroom sauce. For a snack, try the delightful Appetizer Plate, a celebration of tastes and textures that two can share. The lunch menu is also a good deal, offering a choice of main dish and soup or salad for 98S ($8) or both for 127S ($10). An adjoining modern, sleek bar, open throughout the day, serves the same menu.

✪ **Zum Massinger.** Walfischgasse 8 (off Kärntner Strasse, near the Oper). ☎ **01/512 91 81.** Meals 80S–120S ($6–$10). No credit cards. Mon–Fri 11am–11pm. U-Bahn: U-1, U-2, or U-4 to Karlsplatz. Tram: 1, 2, or D to Oper. AUSTRIAN.

A typical neighborhood beisl, this family-run establishment (owner Alfred Massinger is almost always present) was for decades located just off Stephansplatz, where it was called Dom Beisl and was popular with the *fiaker,* the famous Viennese horse-carriage drivers stationed nearby. Recently ensconced in its new home near the opera house, it still offers the same hearty, home-cooked meals, including schweinebraten with *knödel* (dumplings), *bauernschmaus,* Wiener schnitzel, and *gulasch,* as well as daily specials.

WEST OF THE RING

Cafe Rudiger Hof. Hamburger Strasse 20 (west of Naschmarkt). ☎ **01/586 31 38.** Meals 70S–120S ($6–$10). No credit cards. Daily 10am–1am. Closed Jan and Feb. U-Bahn: U-4 to Kettenbrückengasse. AUSTRIAN.

This is a lovely place for a meal, snack, or drink after visiting the Naschmarkt (outdoor market). Owned by a charming woman who speaks fluent English, it occupies the first floor of an impressive art nouveau building. Its raised outdoor terrace is a popular meeting spot for young people on warm summer nights. In addition to regular dishes like Wiener schnitzel, turkey schnitzel, *gulasch, würstl* (sausages), and fish, it also offers two daily menus priced at 58S and 85S ($4.65 and $7).

Crêperie-Brasserie Spittelberg. Spittelberggasse 12 (north of Mariahilfer Strasse and west of the Natural History Museum). ☎ **01/526 15 70.** Meals 100S–175S ($8–$14). AE, DC, MC, V. Summer daily 6–11:30pm; winter Tues–Sat 6pm–11:30pm. U-Bahn: U-2 or U-3 to Volkstheater. Tram: 49 from Dr.-Karl-Renner-Ring to Spittelberg. FRENCH.

In what used to be Vienna's red-light district but has since become a small enclave of trendy restaurants, this casual yet upscale place has salads with a great selection of dressings, galettes stuffed with fillings like spinach or turkey, crêpes with sweet fillings, pasta, coq au vin, beef bourguignonne, baguettes, and vegetarian dishes. It's in a modernized old building, with hanging plants and lighting suspended from the super-tall ceiling. There's outdoor seating in summer.

✪ **Gasthaus Witwe Bolte.** Gutenberggasse 13. ☎ **01/523 14 50.** Meals 105S–250S ($8–$20). DC, MC, V. Jan–Feb Tues–Sat 5:30–11:30pm, Sun 11:30am–11:30pm; Mar–Dec daily 11:30am–11:30pm. U-Bahn: U-2 or U-3 to Volkstheater. Tram: 49 from Dr.-Karl-Renner-Ring to Spittelberg. AUSTRIAN.

Its facade is fancy baroque, but the interior consists of several small and simple rooms, where the emphasis is on home-cooked meals like *tafelspitz*, schnitzel, *schweinebraten*, and *gulasch*. There's also a wonderful outdoor dining area. The restaurant is next to the Crêperie-Brasserie Spittelberg (see above) on a narrow lamp-lit cobblestone street that centuries ago used to be the center of the red-light district. The empress Maria Theresa, a staunch Catholic, tried to curb prostitution here but had little success; according to local lore, her son, Josef II, fled through the door of this very house in 1778 disguised as a regular citizen.

Restaurant der Grieche. Barnabitengasse 5 (near Mariahilfer Strasse, half a block from the Gerngross department store and behind the Mariahilfer Church). ☎ **01/587 74 66.** Meals 105S–240S ($8–$19); fixed-price lunch 75S–85S ($6–$7); *gedeck* (table charge) 4S (30¢) at lunch, 10S (80¢) at dinner. MC, V. Daily 11:30am–2:30pm and 6–11:30pm. U-Bahn: U-3 to Neubaugasse. GREEK.

This modern restaurant has a garden for summer dining and a pleasant greenhouse for winter dining. In business more than 25 years, it attracts smartly dressed middle-age shoppers and business clientele, especially for its fixed-price lunch offered weekdays only. Retsina and domestic Greek wines are available, as well as gyros, *kleftiko* (lamb cooked with cheese and garlic), moussaka, shrimp, fish, souvlaki, lamb chops, and Greek salad. There's an English menu.

✪ **Schnitzelwirt.** Neubaugasse 52 (near the corner of Siebensterngasse). ☎ **01/523 37 71.** Meals 74S–120S ($6–$10). No credit cards. Mon–Sat 11am–10pm. Closed holidays. U-Bahn: U-3 to Neubaugasse, then a 3-minute walk. Tram: 49 from Dr.-Karl-Renner-Ring to Siebensterngasse. Bus: 13A to Siebensterngasse. AUSTRIAN.

Known also as the Gaststätte Helene Schmidt, this restaurant, specializing in variations of the schnitzel, has been one of Vienna's leading budget choices for years. Little wonder—the schnitzel are gigantic, covering the whole plate (you might consider sharing). Choices on the English menu include schnitzel Mexican style, Wiener schnitzel, and garlic schnitzel. It's a few blocks north of Vienna's popular shopping street, Mariahilfer Strasse. The place is often packed.

Shalimar. Schmalzhofgasse 11 (just south of Mariahilfer Strasse). ☎ **01/596 43 17.** Main courses 95S–190S ($8–$15); fixed-price meals 185S–250S ($15–$20); *gedeck* (table charge) 22S ($1.75) per person. AE, DC, MC, V. Daily 11am–2pm and 5:30–11pm. U-Bahn: U-3 to Zieglergasse. INDIAN.

This elaborately decorated Indian restaurant with outdoor seating offers tandoori chicken; curry dishes of chicken, pork, lamb, beef, and fish; and a variety of vegetarian dishes. Indian music plays in the background. There's a *gedeck* (table charge), but the food is good enough to warrant coming here. The fixed-priced meals are especially good values.

✪ **Tunnel.** Florianigasse 39 (behind the Rathaus, less than a 10-minute walk west of the Ring). ☎ **01/405 34 65.** Main dishes 40S–120S ($3.20–$10). No credit cards. Daily 9am–1am. U-Bahn: U-2 to Rathaus, then a 10-minute walk. Tram: 5. Bus: 13A. INTERNATIONAL.

This informal place is actually a restaurant/bar, with a live-music house in the basement. Catering to Vienna's large student population, it starts the day with huge breakfasts (like Arabian breakfast, granola, and omelets) and continues with sandwiches, salads, vegetarian dishes, pizza (the larger size is big enough for two), pasta, and

Coffeehouses Inside the Ring

As Paris has its sidewalk cafes, Vienna has its coffeehouses, institutions in themselves. All offer newspapers for leisurely perusal, and many also offer classical music. There are literally dozens of ways to order coffee (see the beginning of the "Dining" section). If all you're looking for is to fuel up with a cheap cup, look for the **Eduscho** chain. There's one at Graben 12 (U-Bahn: Stephansplatz), where a kleiner brauner costs 8S (65¢) and a cappuccino or melange costs 16S ($1.30). It's open Monday to Friday 8am to 6:30pm and Saturday 8am to 5pm. You can stand and sip your purchase at chest-high tables.

On a tiny street connecting Dorotheergasse and Bräunergasse (off Graben), the **Bräunerhof Cafe,** Stallburggasse 2 (☎ 01/512 38 93; U-Bahn: U-1 or U-3 to Stephansplatz), falls between Demel and Hawelka (both below) as far as style and decoration go. Rather than the dark-paneled walls of many older coffeehouses, this one has a bright and simple interior with gracefully arching lamps by Hoffmann. There are several expensive antiques shops in the area, and a trio entertains customers Saturday, Sunday, and holidays from 3 to 6pm. A melange here costs 32S ($2.55). It's open Monday to Saturday 7:30am to 8:30pm and Sunday and holidays 10am to 6pm.

Small, dark, and smoky, its walls covered with posters and placards, the **Cafe Hawelka,** Dorotheergasse 6 (just off Graben) (☎ 01/512 82 30; U-Bahn: U-1 or U-3 to Stephansplatz), attracts students, artists, writers, and other bohemian types. It's famous for its Buchtel, a pastry made fresh daily and available only after 10pm. I prefer this cafe to Demel, and its 37S ($2.95) for a melange is more acceptable. Hawelka is open Monday and Wednesday to Saturday 8am to 2am and Sunday and holidays 4pm to 2am.

Founded in 1785 by a pastry chef who later served as the pastry supplier to the royal family, **Demel,** Kohlmarkt 14 (☎ 01/535 17 17; U-Bahn: U-1 or U-3 to Stephansplatz), is Vienna's most expensive and most famous coffeehouse. Its elegant interior looks like the private parlor of a count. A small pot of coffee costs 50S ($4), worth the price just for the show of people and waitresses. Tortes and cakes start at 40S ($3.20). In apparent recognition of its high prices, Demel even accepts all major credit and charge cards. It's open daily 10am to 7pm.

Viennese pancakes. The eclectic menu also offers everything from hummus or gnocchi to moussaka or a dish of Asian vegetables. From 11:30am to 2:30pm there's a daily special for 45S ($3.60); bread is free with your meal. You can stay as long as you wish and can come for just a drink. This is a good place to visit with friends or write postcards.

PICNICKING

The best place for picnic supplies—and one of Vienna's most colorful attractions—is the **Naschmarkt,** a 5-minute walk southwest of Karlsplatz. Stalls in this open-air market sell fish, vegetables, fruit, meats, cheeses, Asian foodstuffs, Greek specialties, flowers, and tea. My Viennese friends say this is the best place to shop because of the freshness of the produce and the variety of goods, including exotic items. In between the food stalls are a number of stand-up fast-food counters where you can buy sausages, sandwiches, döner kebabs, beer, grilled chicken, and other ready-made foods. The Naschmarkt is open Monday to Friday 6am to 6:30pm and Saturday 6am to 5pm. It's between the Karlsplatz and Kettenbrückengasse U-Bahn stations.

As for picnic settings, Vienna's most accessible parks are the **Stadtpark** and the **Volksgarten,** both on the Ring. In addition, both Schönbrunn and Belvedere palaces have formal gardens. Keep in mind, however, that the Viennese are a bit stodgy and don't look kindly on people who wander off paths and sprawl on the grass. Some parks, in response to Vienna's younger generation, many of whom have staged sit-ins to protest the "Keep Off the Grass" rule, have finally opened designated *Liegewiesen* ("laying fields"). In any case, there are always lots of park benches. If you really want to get away from the city, take an excursion to the **Vienna Woods** or the **Danube** (see "Side Trips," at the end of the chapter).

WORTH A SPLURGE

A number of wine cellars under "Vienna After Dark" (later in this chapter) also offer meals. Though you can experience these places for the price of a drink, they're also great for a complete meal, which can cost $16 and up.

✪ **Restaurant Hauswirth.** Otto Bauergasse 20. ☎ **01/587 12 61.** Main courses 180S–270S ($14–$22). AE, DC, MC, V. Mon–Sat 11:30am–2pm and 6:30–10pm, Sun and holidays 6:30–10pm. U-Bahn: U-3 to Zieglergasse. AUSTRIAN.

Come to this refined restaurant, open since 1892, for an elegant dining experience, with chandeliers, fresh flowers, and a drawing room. It's like a restaurant from the turn of the century. In summer there's outdoor dining that still manages to maintain a high degree of elegance. The English menu, featuring light, original cuisine, changes to complement each season. In spring you may find fish; in summer, mushrooms and asparagus; and in autumn, wild game. The restaurant's own cellar, which you can visit on request, holds about 11,000 bottles of wine. The adjoining *beisl* offers lower prices for typical Viennese fare.

Wiener Rathauskeller. Rathausplatz. ☎ **01/405 12 10.** Reservations recommended Tues–Sat for the fixed-price meal. Main courses 140S–250S ($11–$20); fixed-price meal 410S ($33). AE, DC, MC, V. Mon–Sat 11:30am–3pm and 6–11pm. U-Bahn: U-2 to Rathaus. Tram: 1, 2, or D to Burgtheater/Rathausplatz. AUSTRIAN.

The Rittersaal (Knights' Hall), in the cellar of Vienna's City Hall, offers à la carte dining. The attractive decor features medieval-style murals on the vaulted ceilings, pink tablecloths, beautiful lamps, and flowers on every table. In the evenings there's live classical music. Farther down the hall, in the Grinzinger Keller, a fixed-price meal with traditional Viennese entertainment is offered from April to October, Tuesday to Saturday 8 to 11pm; call for reservations.

5 Seeing the Sights

Remember to purchase a copy of *Vienna from A to Z* for an explanation of the city's many historically important buildings. In addition, the *Wien Monatsprogramm* lists special exhibits in Vienna's museums and galleries. Both are available at Vienna Tourist Information offices.

SIGHTSEEING SUGGESTIONS

IF YOU HAVE 1 DAY Start the morning with a tour of Vienna's **Altstadt (Old City),** beginning at Stephansplatz. Here you'll find the towering **St. Stephen's Cathedral,** Vienna's most important Gothic building and best-known landmark. It has a 450-foot-high south tower with 343 spiral steps. You can climb them and be rewarded with a great view of the city. All around Stephansplatz is the Altstadt. Of particular beauty here are **Schönlaterngasse** and **Annagasse,** lanes reminiscent of an older

---

A Museum Note

Most museums are closed on January 1, Good Friday, Easter Sunday, May 1, Whitsunday, Corpus Christi, November 1 and 2, December 24 and 25, and for general elections. Exceptions are the Museum of Fine Arts, Schönbrunn Palace, the Hofburg, and the Imperial Burial Vault, which remain open on Easter Sunday and Whitsunday.

Vienna. Have coffee at one of the famous coffeehouses, then stroll down the **Kärntner Strasse** pedestrian shopping street for a look at modern Vienna.

After you've seen the inner city, hightail it to the palace and gardens of **Schönbrunn,** Vienna's most famous attraction, once the summer home of the Habsburg dynasty. Finish the day with a performance at the **opera** or **theater,** followed by a drink in one of Vienna's historic **wine cellars.**

IF YOU HAVE 2 DAYS   Spend Day 1 as above. On Day 2, head toward the **Hofburg,** the official residence of the Habsburgs, which now contains the imperial rooms, a silver collection, and a treasury with an astounding collection of riches. Nearby is the **Kunsthistorisches Museum,** a fine-arts museum with a great collection of old masters. If you have time, walk to the nearby **Imperial Crypts,** where the Habsburgs have been buried for the last 300 years. Spend the evening in **Grinzing** or one of Vienna's other **wine districts.**

IF YOU HAVE 3 DAYS   Spend Days 1 and 2 as above, then try to schedule some activities that occur only on certain days of the week, such as training sessions of the renowned **Spanish Riding School** or Sunday mass with the **Vienna Boys' Choir.** Other important sights are the **open-air market** at the Naschmarkt (on Saturday there's also a flea market) and **Belvedere Palace,** where you'll find galleries highlighting Austria's finest 19th- and 20th-century artists and other European masters. In the evening go to **Prater,** Vienna's old-fashioned amusement park.

IF YOU HAVE 5 DAYS   Spend Days 1 to 3 as above. On Day 4, explore your own special interests—visiting **composers' homes,** the **Museum of Military History,** the **Museum of Applied Arts,** or the **Historical Museum of the City of Vienna.** On Day 5, take a trip to Vienna's countryside. Popular destinations include the famous **Vienna Woods,** the extensive parklands along the **Danube** (where you can even go swimming in summer), and **Krems,** a jewel of a village on the Danube, about an hour's train ride from Vienna.

SCHÖNBRUNN & BELVEDERE PALACES

✪ **Schönbrunn.** Schönbrunner Schlossstrasse. ☎ **01/811 13 239.** Schönbrunn, 90S or 120S ($7 or $10) adults, 80S or 105S ($6 or $8) students, 45S or 60S ($3.60 or $4.80) ages 6–15. Wagenburg, 30S ($2.40) adults, 15S ($1.20) students, free for age 10 and under. Schönbrunn, Apr–Oct daily 8:30am–5pm; Nov–Mar daily 8:30am–4:30pm (closed Jan 1, Nov 1, Dec 25). Wagenburg, Apr–Oct daily 9am–6pm; Nov–Mar Tues–Sun 10am–4pm. U-Bahn: U-4 to Schönbrunn. Tram: 58 from anywhere along Mariahilfer Strasse to Schloss Schönbrunn.

A baroque summer palace with an astounding 1,441 rooms, the lovely Schönbrunn was built between 1696 and 1730 in the midst of a glorious garden. Empress Maria Theresa left the greatest imprint on Schönbrunn. In the course of having 16 children (one of whom was the ill-fated Marie Antoinette) in 20 years, running the country, and fighting a war for her right to sit on the Austrian throne, she found time to decorate and redesign the palace (1744–49), and it remains virtually as she left it. When the French besieged Vienna in the early 19th century, Napoléon was so impressed with

---

Getting the Best Deal on Sightseeing

- Keep in mind that all Vienna's municipal museums, including all the composers' homes and the Historical Museum of the City of Vienna, are free on Friday (excluding holidays) until noon.
- See the Spanish Riding School without spending a fortune by attending one of the morning training sessions.
- Note that the Vienna Card (costing 180S/$14) allows unlimited travel in the city for 3 days and offers reduced admission prices to the most important museums and attractions.

Schönbrunn that he occupied Maria Theresa's favorite rooms. Franz Josef I, who was born in the palace and reigned for 68 years, was the last emperor to live here. His wife, Elisabeth, popularly known as Sisi, was famed for her beauty (her hair reached to the ground), intelligence, and independent spirit. It was here, too, that Charles I, Austria's last emperor, abdicated and renounced the Imperial Crown.

You can tour the inside of the predominantly white-and-gilt palace on your own, choosing between the longer Grand Tour through 40 state rooms for 120S ($10) or the shorter Imperial Tour through 22 rooms for 90S ($7). Both tours include use of an English-language audio guide and allow you to see the private apartments of Emperor Franz Josef and Empress Elisabeth; Maria Theresa's nursery with portraits of her children; the Hall of Mirrors, where the 6-year-old Mozart played for Maria Theresa; the exotic Chinese Cabinets with inlaid lacquerware; the Hall of Ceremonies with a portrait of Maria Theresa; the Large Gallery, fashioned after a room in Versailles and used in a 1961 meeting between Kennedy and Khrushchev; and more. The Grand Tour then continues on through, among others, the Chinese Lacquered Room; the Napoleon Room, where Napoléon lived and his only legitimate son died; the delightful Porcelain Room, which served as Maria Theresa's study; and the Millions Room, decorated with 260 precious parchment miniatures brought from Constantinople and set under glass in the paneling. I recommend the Grand Tour, which takes approximately an hour. Though guided tours of the palace are available, they cost extra and are rarely in English. The audio guides are perfectly adequate.

In any case, even the self-guided tours are for a specific time, indicated on your ticket. If there's a long wait (possible in summer), you can always first explore the 500 acres of palace grounds, one of the most important baroque gardens in the French style. At the top of the hill opposite the palace is the **Gloriette,** a monument to soldiers. There's also the lovely Neptune Fountain, artificial Roman ruins, one of the world's oldest zoos, a butterfly house, and the **Palmenhaus,** built in 1883 as the largest greenhouse in Europe. Be sure, too, to visit the **Wagenburg,** a museum with 36 imperial carriages.

Österreichische Galerie Belvedere. Prinz-Eugen-Strasse 27 (Oberes Belvedere) and Rennweg 6a (Unteres Belvedere). ☎ **01/79 557-0.** Admission 60S ($4.80) adults; 30S ($2.40) seniors/students/children, free for age 14 and under. Tues–Sun 10am–5pm. Tram: D to Oberes Belvedere, or 71 to Unteres Belvedere.

The Belvedere is a light, airy baroque palace built in the early 1700s as a summer residence for beloved Prince Eugene of Savoy, who protected Austria from Turkish invasion. His reward was to be made minister of war and then prime minister by the emperor Charles VI. He never married, and when he died his estate fell to his heiress—"frightful Victoria," as the Viennese called her—who promptly sold it. The

Imperial Court acquired the buildings and gardens in 1752. It was here that Archduke Franz Ferdinand, heir to the throne, and his wife, Sophie, lived before taking their fateful trip to Sarajevo in 1914.

The Belvedere, which today houses the Austrian Gallery, is actually two palaces separated by a beautiful, formal garden. The **Oberes Belvedere** (the one closest to the Südbahnhof) is the more lavish of the two, up on a hill with a sweeping view of the city. Its Marble Hall, used for receptions and site of the 1955 treaty signaling the withdrawal of Allied troops from Austria, is the most magnificent room in the palace.

Today the Oberes Belvedere serves as a gallery for 19th- and 20th-century Austrian and international art, including Biedermeier paintings by Amerling and Waldmüller, works by Austrian painters at the turn of the century, and international art from the late 19th and 20th centuries, including impressionist and expressionist art. To make the most of your visit, consider renting an English-language audio guide for 40S ($3.20), which directs you to the most important works and puts them in historic perspective. Artists displayed include Renoir, Monet, Manet, Edvard Munch, van Gogh, Pissarro, Max Liebermann, and Lovis Corinth, as well as Austrian artists Hans Makart, Oskar Kokoschka (considered the leader of Austrian expressionism), Egon Schiele (a prolific artist who produced 330 oil canvases and more than 2,500 drawings and watercolors before dying at age 28), and Gustav Klimt. Two rooms are devoted to Klimt, considered the foremost representative of Viennese Jugendstil (art nouveau) painting, where you'll see his famous *Der Kuss* (The Kiss), *Judith* (the frame was made by his brother), and a portrait of Fritza Riedler.

A walk through the beautiful landscaped gardens brings you to the **Unteres Belvedere,** home of the Museum of Austrian Baroque, with its works from the 17th and 18th centuries, and the Museum of Medieval Austrian Art, which includes sculpture and panel paintings from the end of the 12th to the early 16th centuries. It's worth a walk through here even if you're not interested in the art, as the palace rooms are finer than the remodeled modern galleries of the Oberes Belvedere. Incidentally, next to the Unteres Belvedere is **SalmBräu,** a microbrewery serving Austrian fare and offering outdoor seating in a small courtyard.

THE HOFBURG PALACE COMPLEX

Hofburg Kaiserappartements (Imperial Apartments). Michaeler Platz 1 (inside the Ring, about a 7-minute walk from Stephansplatz; entrance via the Kaisertor in the Inneren Burghof). ☎ **01/533 75 70.** Admission 80S ($6) adults, 60S ($4.80) students, 40S ($3.20) children; combination ticket for Apartments and Silver Collection, 95S ($8) adults, 75S ($6) students, 50S ($4) children. Daily 9am–5pm. U-Bahn: U-1 or U-3 to Stephansplatz. Tram: 1, 2, 3, or J to Burgring.

The Hofburg was the Imperial Palace of the Habsburgs for more than six centuries, during which time changes and additions were made in several architectural styles: Gothic, Renaissance, baroque, rococo, and classical. The entire Hofburg occupies 47 acres; it's a virtual city within a city, with more than 2,600 rooms. Contained in the vast complex are the Imperial Apartments, the Imperial Silver Collection and the Treasury (both described below), the Spanish Riding School, and the Burgkapelle featuring Sunday masses with the Vienna Boys' Choir.

The Imperial Apartments, which served as the winter residence of the Habsburgs, may seem a bit plain if you've already seen the splendor of Schönbrunn, but I like the fact that you can wander on your own through the 22 rooms open to the public. You'll see the apartments of Franz Josef and his wife, Elisabeth, and of the tsar Alexander I of Russia. There are several portraits of a young Elisabeth (including one in Franz Josef's study), who came from the Wittelsbach family of Munich in 1854 to marry

Vienna

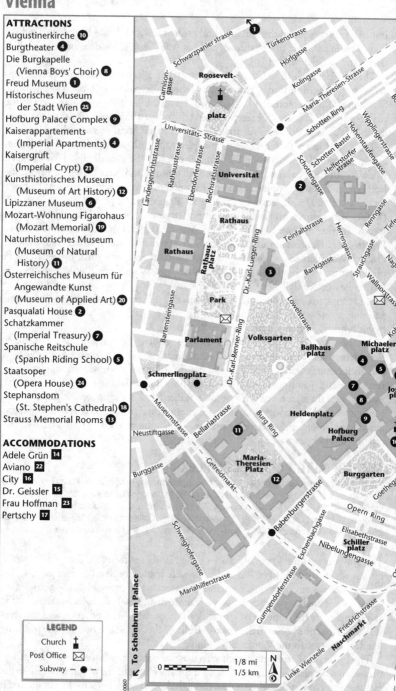

LEGEND
Church †
Post Office ✉
Subway ●—●

0   1/8 mi
     1/5 km

N

To Schönbrunn Palace

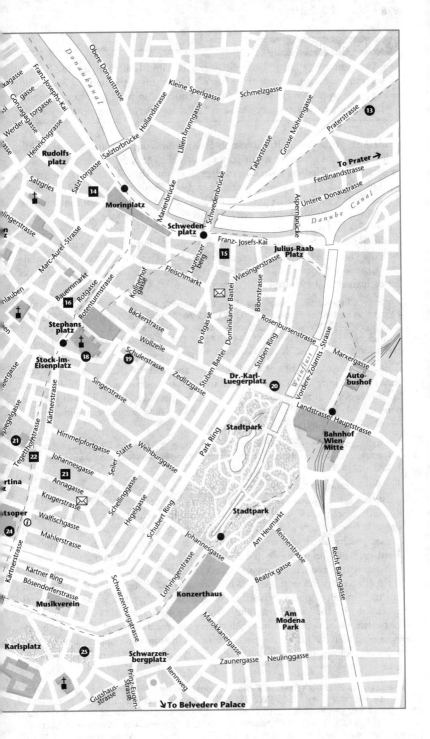

A Hofburg Palace Tip

If you've bought a combination ticket for the Silver Collection and the Imperial Apartments, be sure to tour the Silver Collection first—the Imperial Apartments exit is far away from the Silver Collection entrance, so you'd have to walk around the Hofburg to reenter to see the Silver Collection. Very inconvenient.

Franz Josef at the age of 16. Known as Sissi, she was talented, artistic, and slightly vain—she would no longer sit for portraits after the age of 30. She was an excellent rider, and in the Hofburg is her own small gymnasium, where she kept in shape (much to the disgust of the court, which thought it improper for a lady). Crown Prince Rudolf, son of Elisabeth and Franz Josef and the only male heir to the throne, committed suicide in a hunting lodge at Mayerling with his young mistress, Baroness Maria Vetsera. Elisabeth herself was assassinated in 1898 by an anarchist in Geneva. You'll also see the royal dining room laid out with the imperial place setting—notice how the silverware is placed only on the right side and is turned face down, according to Spanish court etiquette, which was the rage of the time. There are five wineglasses for each guest, and each napkin is 3.3 feet square.

Hofburg Silberkammer (Imperial Silver Collection). Michaeler Platz 1 (entrance via the Kaisertor in the Inneren Burghof). ☎ **01/533 75 70.** Admission 80S ($6) adults, 60S ($4.80) students, 40S ($3.20) children; combination ticket for Apartments and Silver Collection, 95S ($8) adults, 75S ($6) students, 50S ($4) children. Daily 9am–5pm. U-Bahn: U-1 or U-3 to Stephansplatz. Tram: 1, 2, 3, or J to Burgring.

This collection of royal silverware, dinnerware, and tableware, dating to the 15th century, provides insight into the imperial household and court etiquette. It displays items of daily use as well as valuable pieces, everything from cooking molds and pots and pans to table linens, elaborate centerpieces, crystal, silver serving sets, gilded candelabras, silverware, and porcelain table settings.

Schatzkammer (Treasury). Schweizerhof 1, Hofburg. ☎ **01/533 79 31.** Admission 80S ($6) adults, 50S ($4) seniors/students, free for age 9 and under. Wed–Mon 10am–6pm. Tram: 1, 2, D, or J to Burgring.

The Schatzkammer displays a stunning collection of the secular and ecclesiastical treasures of the Habsburgs. Its priceless imperial regalia and relics of the Holy Roman Empire include royal crowns inlaid with diamonds, rubies, pearls, sapphires, and other gems (such as the crown of Charlemagne), as well as swords, imperial crosses, jewelry, altars, christening robes, coronation robes, and other richly embroidered garments belonging to the Habsburgs. Two prized heirlooms are believed to have mystical and religious significance: the Agate Bowl, carved in Constantinople in the 4th century from a single piece of agate and once thought to be the Holy Grail; and the Ainkhörn, a huge narwhale tusk, considered a symbol of the unicorn and associated with the Virgin Mary and Christ. The Holy Lance was once thought to be the lance used to pierce Christ's side during the crucifixion; next to it is a reliquary containing what is regarded as a piece of the cross. Be sure to pick up the free English-language audio guide, which will guide you through the collections in about an hour.

Spanische Reitschule (Spanish Riding School). Hofburg, Josefsplatz. No phone. Regular Gala performances, seats 250S–900S ($20–$72), standing room 200S ($18); Classical Dressage to Music performances, 250S ($20), plus 22% commission; Morning Training Sessions, 100S ($8) adults, 30S ($2.40) children. Regular Gala performances, Mar–June and Sept to mid-Dec, most Suns at 10:45am and some Weds at 7pm; Classical Dressage to Music performances, Apr–June and Sept, most Sats at 10am; Morning Training Sessions, Mar–June, first 2 weeks in Sept, and mid-Oct to mid-Dec, Tues–Sat 10am–noon (except Sat when Classical Dressage to Music performances are held). U-Bahn: U-1 or U-3 to Stephansplatz.

This prestigious school has roots dating to more than 400 years ago when Spanish horses were brought to Austria for breeding; the baroque hall in which they now perform dates from the 1730s. The famous, graceful Lippizaner horses are a cross of Berber and Arabian stock with Spanish and Italian horses. They're born with dark coats that turn white only between ages 4 and 10. Their performances, with intricate steps and movements, are a sight to see, but cheaper and almost as good are the morning training sessions.

In fact, tickets for the regular Gala performances are so hard to come by that the training sessions may be your only option. If, however, you're determined to see a Gala performance, write several months in advance to Spanische Reitschule, Hofburg, 1010 Wien (fax 01/535 01 86). Otherwise, theater ticket and travel agencies (including American Express and Intropa, both on Kärntner Strasse) also sell tickets, for which you'll pay an extra 22% commission.

In addition to regular Gala performances, there are two kinds of training sessions. The more elaborate is the 1-hour "Classical Dressage to Music," which is kind of like a dress rehearsal. Tickets for these shows are available only through theater ticket or travel agencies, such as American Express. Otherwise, there are also cheaper regular Morning Training Sessions, with tickets sold directly in the inner courtyard of the Imperial Palace on a first-come, first-served basis the day of the session. You'll need to get there early and wait in line. Stop by the tourist office for a pamphlet with a current schedule.

Lipizzaner Museum. Reitschulstrasse 2, Stallburg, Hofburg. ☎ **01/526 41 84-30.** Admission 50S ($4) adults, 35S ($2.80) seniors/students/children. Daily 9am–6pm. U-Bahn: U-1 or U-3 to Stephansplatz.

If you can't get to a performance of the Spanish Riding School or you're a real horse fan, you might wish to visit the newly opened Lipizzaner Museum, located in the imperial stables of the Hofburg (off Michaelerplatz). Documenting the history of the famous white horses from their origins in the 16th century to the present, it displays paintings, photographs, uniforms, saddles, harnesses, and videos, but the highlight is the window allowing visitors to peer into the Lipizzaner stables.

Wiener Sängerknaben (Vienna Boys' Choir). Burgkapelle, Hofburg (entrance on Schweizerhof). Seats, 60S–310S ($4.80–$25); standing room free. Mass performed Sun and some religious holidays at 9:15am mid-Sept to June. Concerts performed Fri at 3:30pm in May, June, Sept, and Oct. U-Bahn: U-1 or U-3 to Stephansplatz.

The Vienna Boys' Choir was founded in 1498 to sing at church services for the Royal Chapel of the Imperial Palace. Both Joseph Haydn and Franz Schubert sang in the choir, which now consists of several choirs, two of which are usually on world tours. You can hear the Boys' Choir, accompanied by orchestra members of the Vienna State Opera, every Sunday and some religious holidays at 9:15am mass in the Burgkapelle of the Hofburg from January to June and mid-September to Christmas Day. Order seats at least 2 months in advance by writing to Hofmusikkapelle, Hofburg, 1010 Wien (fax 01/533 99 27-75). Don't enclose money or a check, but rather pick up your ticket at the Burgkapelle on the Friday preceding the performance 11am to 1pm or 3 to 5pm, as well as Sunday 8:15 to 8:45am. Unsold tickets go on sale at the Burgkapelle on Friday 3 to 5pm (it's wise to get there by 2:30pm).

Note: Standing room for mass is free, but there's room for only 20 people on a first-come, first-served basis—get there early if you're interested.

Another opportunity to hear the Vienna Boys' Choir is at performances given every Friday at 3:30pm at the Konzerthaus, Lothringerstrasse 20, in May, June, September, and October, during which mixed programs of motets and madrigals by old masters, waltz music, and folk songs are performed. You can get tickets, which cost 390S or 430S ($31 or $34), from hotels or from **Reisebüro Mondial,** Faulmanngasse 4 (☎ **01/588 04-141**).

THE TOP CHURCHES

Stephansdom (St. Stephen's Cathedral). Stephansplatz. ☎ **01/515 52-563.** Cathedral, free; south tower, 30S ($2.40) adults, 20S ($1.60) students, 10S (80¢) children; north tower elevator, 40S ($3.20) adults, 15S ($1.30) children; catacombs, 40S ($3.20) adults, 15S ($1.20) children; organ concerts, 100S ($8). Cathedral, Mon–Sat 9am–11:30am and 1–4:30pm, Sun 1–4:30pm; south and north towers, daily 9am–5:30pm; catacombs, Mon–Sat 10–11:30am and 2–4:30pm, Sun and holidays 2–4:30pm. U-Bahn: U-1 or U-3 to Stephansplatz.

In the heart of Old Vienna, Stephansdom is the city's best-known landmark. Constructed in the 12th century and then enlarged and rebuilt over the next eight centuries, it remains Vienna's most important Gothic structure. Its dimensions are staggering—352 feet long with a nave 128 feet high. The highest part is its 450-foot-high south tower, completed in 1433, with 343 spiral steps. This tower is open to the public (entrance outside the church on its south side) and affords one of the best views of the city. If you don't like to climb stairs, you can take an elevator (its entrance is inside the church) to the top of the north tower, which was never completed and is only about half as high as the south tower. May to November, there are organ concerts every Wednesday at 8pm. The cathedral catacombs contain copper urns bearing the intestines of the Habsburg family (their bodies are in the Imperial Burial Vault, while their hearts are in the Augustiner Church).

Kapuzinerkirche, with the Kaisergruft (Imperial Burial Vault). Neuer Markt 1 (inside the Ring, behind the Opera House on tiny Tegetthoffstrasse). ☎ **01/512 68 53-12.** Admission 40S ($3.20) adults, 30S ($2.40) seniors/students, 10S (80¢) age 13 and under. Daily 9:30am–4pm (you must enter by 3:40pm). U-Bahn: U-1 or U-3 to Stephansplatz.

Most visitors to Vienna feel duty-bound to make a pilgrimage to the Kapuziner Church, which contains the Imperial Burial Vault and the coffins of 136 Habsburg family members. Some of the coffins are elaborate, made of pewter and adorned with skulls, angels, and other harbingers of death. The biggest one belongs to Empress Maria Theresa and her husband and is topped with their reclining statues. It's surrounded by the coffins of their 16 children, many of whom died in infancy. The only non-Habsburg to be buried here was the governess to Maria Theresa and her children. Each coffin has two keys, which are kept in separate places. Only the embalmed bodies are contained inside; the intestines are kept in copper urns in the catacombs of Stephansdom, while the hearts are in the Augustiner Church.

THE TOP MUSEUMS

✪ **Kunsthistorisches Museum (Museum of Fine Arts).** Maria-Theresien-Platz. ☎ **01/525 24.** Admission 45S ($3.60) adults, 30S ($2.40) seniors/students/children, free to age 9 and under; special exhibits, 100S ($8) adults, 65S ($5) seniors/students/children. Tues–Wed and Fri–Sun 10am–6pm, Thurs 10am–9pm. U-Bahn: U-2 or U-3 to Volkstheater. Tram: 1, 2, 52, 58, D, or J to Burgring.

This great museum owes its existence largely to the Habsburgs, who for centuries were patrons and collectors of art. There are several collections, of which the Egyptian-Oriental Collection and the Picture Gallery are the most outstanding. Other displays

Special & Free Events

If you're coming to Vienna for the theater, avoid July and August—the Staatsoper, Volksoper, Burgtheater, and Akademietheater are all closed then. In addition, in July and August there are no performances of the Spanish Riding School (nor in January or February) or the Vienna Boys' Choir. However, Vienna's **Summer of Music** festival features many other events.

It's not surprising that many of Vienna's festivals and events revolve around music. The **Operetta Festival** in early February stages productions at the Volksoper. In February and March there's a **Haydn Festival,** followed by Osterklang (Sound of Easter Festival), with performances by famous orchestras the week leading up to Easter. The **Wiener Festwochen (Vienna Festival)** in May and June features primarily new and avant-garde theater productions, with guest companies performing in various languages, including English, as well as jazz and classical concerts and art exhibits. In June, the **Danube Island Festival** is a gigantic open-air party on the banks of the Danube, complete with rock, pop, and folk music and an evening fireworks display.

In July and August there's something going on almost every night. Vienna's **Klangbogen Wien (Rainbow of Music)** features about 150 concerts and events held at the city's most beautiful venues, including weekly operettas, classical concerts, and Viennese waltzes held at Schönbrunn Palace. Don't miss the open-air performances of **Mozart's operas** staged in front of the Roman Ruins in Schönbrunn Palace Park. Another popular event is the free **Festival of Music Films,** with evening open-air performances of famous orchestras and conductors shown on a giant screen in front of the Rathaus (City Hall) and stalls selling food from around the world.

The annual **Schubert Festival** is in November. December is the month of the outdoor **Christmas bazaar,** with stalls selling handcrafted items and decorations in front of the Rathaus, on Spittelberg, and on Freyung. Another popular winter event is the **Wiener Eistraum,** which features a large public ice-skating rink in front of the Rathaus, open the end of January to March daily 9am to 11pm; after 8pm it becomes an ice-skating disco.

---

feature coins and medals, as well as sculpture and applied arts from the medieval, Renaissance, and baroque periods.

The Picture Gallery, on the first floor, contains paintings by Rubens, Rembrandt, Dürer, Titian, Giorgione, Tintoretto, Caravaggio, and Velázquez. The high point of the museum is a room full of Brueghels, including the *Turmbau zu Babel* (Tower of Babel), *Die Jäger im Schnee* (The Hunters in the Snow—you can hardly believe it's not real), the *Kinderspiel* (in which children have taken over an entire town), and *Die Bauernhochzeit* (The Peasant Wedding—notice how the bride is isolated in front of the green cloth, barred by custom from eating or talking).

Heeresgeschichtliches Museum (Museum of Military History). Arsenal. ☎ 01/79 561-0. Admission 40S ($3.20) adults; 20S ($1.60) seniors/students/children. Sat–Thurs 10am–4pm. U-Bahn: U-1 to the Südbahnhof. Tram: D or 18 to the Südbahnhof. Bus: 13A to the Südbahnhof. Then it's a 10-minute walk through the Schweizer Garten.

Housed in a Moorish-Byzantine–style building constructed in the 1850s as part of the Vienna Arsenal, this museum has an admirable collection of weapons, uniforms, and memorabilia from the Thirty Years' War to the present. You'll find guns, sabers, planes, tanks, heavy artillery, and model ships. The most interesting room examines the start of World War I; it displays the automobile in which Archduke Franz Ferdinand and his wife, Sophie, were riding when they were assassinated and even the uniform the archduke was wearing.

Historisches Museum der Stadt Wien (Historical Museum of the City of Vienna). Karlsplatz 4. ☎ **01/505 87 47.** Admission 50S ($4) adults, 25S ($2) seniors, 20S ($1.60) students/children. Tues–Sun 9am–4:30pm. U-Bahn: U-1, U-2, or U-4 to Karlsplatz.

This museum is devoted to Vienna's 7,000 years of history, from the Neolithic period and the time of the tribal migrations, through the Middle Ages to the blossoming of Biedermeier and Jugendstil. There's armor, booty from the Turkish invasions, models of the city, furniture, glassware, and paintings by Klimt, Waldmüller, and Schiele, among others. One room is the complete interior of the poet Franz Grillparzer's apartment; another holds the living room of the architect Loos.

KunstHausWien. Untere Weissgerberstrasse 13. ☎ **01/712 04 91.** Admission 90S ($7) adults, 50S ($4) seniors/students, free for age 11 and under; temporary exhibits extra. KunstHausWien, daily 10am–7pm. Kalke Village, winter daily 10am–5pm; summer daily 9am–7pm. Tram: N or O to Radetzkyplatz.

One of the newer additions to Vienna's art scene, this is the brainchild of the painter/designer Friedensreich Hundertwasser, famous for his whimsical, fantastical, colorful, and thought-provoking paintings, prints, and architecture. Created from a former factory building of the Thonet Company (well known for its bentwood furniture), the museum houses approximately 300 of Hundertwasser's works, including paintings, prints, tapestries, and architectural models. Temporary shows feature the works of international artists. Typical of Hundertwasser, the building itself is one of the exhibits, a colorful protest against the mundane gray of modern cities.

The cafe here features 100 Thonet chairs and an uneven buckled floor, as well as a museum shop. Be sure to see the Hundertwasser Haus, a nearby apartment complex that Hundertwasser designed on the corner of Kegelgasse and Löwengasse in the mid-1980s (about a 4-minute walk from the KunstHausWien). On Kegelgasse is also Kalke Village, another Hundertwasser architectural conversion, this time a former stable and gas station turned into a small shopping complex of boutiques and a cafe.

Museum Moderner Kunst (Museum of Modern Art). Liechtenstein Palace, Fürstengasse 1. ☎ **01/317 69 00.** Admission 45S ($3.60) adults, 25S ($2) seniors/students, free for children. Tues–Sun 10am–6pm. Tram: D to Fürstengasse.

The city's Museum of Modern Art, housed in a baroque palace, displays international works from the 20th century. Included are works by Picasso, Juan Miró, Georg Baselitz, Jackson Pollock, Richard Estes, Malcolm Morley, Andy Warhol, Paul Klee, Wassily Kandinsky, and the Austrians Kolo Moser, Max Oppenheimer, Oskar Kokoschka, and Egon Schiele. The emphasis is on Viennese works since 1900, "classical modern" art from cubism to abstraction, and abstract and contemporary art since 1950. The permanent exhibitions are on the first and second floors. There are also temporary exhibits both here and at a second location, Museum des 20, Jahrhunderts, in the Schweizer Garten near the Südbahnhof.

✪ **Österreichisches Museum für Angewandte Kunst (Austrian Museum of Applied Arts).** Stubenring 5. ☎ **01/71136.** Admission 30S ($2.40) adults, 15S ($1.20) seniors/students/children, free for age 9 and under; during special exhibits, 90S ($7) adults, half price for seniors/students/children. Tues–Wed and Fri–Sun 10am–6pm, Thurs 10am–9pm. U-Bahn: U-3 to Stubentor. Tram: 1 or 2 to Dr.-Karl-Lueger-Platz.

Europe's oldest museum of applied arts, this is a fine collection of Austrian ceramics, furniture, silver, and jewelry, housed in a stately 19th-century building in Florentine

Renaissance style. Exhibits are arranged chronologically, from Romanesque to 20th-century design. It contains a fascinating collection of Viennese chairs from the 1800s (including Thonet) as well as designs of the Wiener Werkstätte, a remarkable work-shop founded at the turn of the century by Josef Hoffmann, Kolo Moser, and Fritz Waerndorfer. The museum's Jugendstil collections are particularly outstanding. There's also a room devoted to works from Asia, including lacquerware, porcelain, and Buddha statues, while another room shows the similarities between Eastern and Western art. At times, the museum hosts special exhibitions of experimental contem-porary art from around the world, during which a higher admission is charged. Amaz-ingly, this fascinating museum is rarely crowded.

Sigmund-Freud-Haus. Berggasse 19. ☎ **01/319 15 96.** Admission 60S ($4.80) adults, 40S ($3.20) students, 25S ($2) children, free for age 11 and under. Daily 9am–4pm. U-Bahn: U-2 to Schottentor, then a 10-minute walk. Tram: D to Schlickgasse.

Sigmund Freud lived and worked here from 1891 to 1938. This small museum doc-uments his life, with photographs of him, his mother, his wife, and others who influ-enced his life. A notebook in English identifies everything in the museum, with translations of passages written by Freud. To enter the house, you have to ring the doorbell and push the door at the same time.

AN AMUSEMENT PARK

Prater. Hauptallee. ☎ **01/512 83 14.** Park, free; amusement rides, charges vary. May–Sept daily 9am–midnight; Apr and Oct daily 10am–10pm; Nov–Mar daily 10am–6pm. U-Bahn: U-1 to Praterstern.

Prater is Vienna's amusement park, opened to the general public in 1766 on the former grounds of the emperor Maximilian II's game preserve. Most notable is its giant Ferris wheel, built in 1896 (then rebuilt after its destruction in World War II) and measuring 200 feet in diameter. There are also some 200 booths and attractions, including the usual shooting ranges, amusement rides, game arcades, and beer halls.

MEMORIALS TO VIENNA'S MUSICAL GENIUSES

If you're a fan of Mozart, Schubert, Strauss, Haydn, or Beethoven, you've certainly come to the right city. Here you'll find the houses where they lived, the cemetery where most of them are buried, and statues of these musical giants everywhere (espe-cially in the Stadtpark and the Burggarten).

In addition, you might like to see the interior of the **Staatsoper,** Opernring 2 (☎ **01/514 44-2955;** U-Bahn: U-1, U-2, or U-4 to Karlsplatz-Oper). Built from 1861 to 1869 and rebuilt after World War II, it's one of the world's finest opera houses (see "Vienna After Dark"). Alas, there are no performances during July and August, though other performances (such as concerts) are held here then, and tours of the Staatsoper are conducted throughout the year—check the board outside the entrance for a schedule of the day's tours, usually twice a day in winter and as many as five times a day in summer, in English and German. Tours, lasting about 35 minutes, cost 60S ($4.80) adults, 45S ($3.60) seniors, 30S ($2.40) students, and 20S ($1.60) children.

You can visit the apartments where the composers lived. Set up as memorials, they're a bit plain and unadorned, of interest only to devoted music fans. All the apartments are open the same hours (Tuesday to Sunday 9am to 12:15pm and 1 to 4:30pm) for the same charge (25S/$2 adults, 10S/80¢ students/children) and are free on Friday morning (except holidays).

Ludwig van Beethoven (1770–1827) came to Vienna from Germany when he was 22 and stayed in the city until his death. From 1804 to 1815 he lived on and off at the **Beethoven-Gedenkstätte,** in the Pasqualati House, Mölker Bastei 8 (☎ **01/535**

89 05; U-Bahn: U-2 to Schottentor; Tram: 1, 2, or D to Schottentor). Moody, rebellious, and eventually going deaf, he had habits so irregular (he sometimes played and composed in the middle of the night) that he was constantly being evicted from apartments all over Vienna. One landlord who loved him, however, was Mr. Pasqualati, who kept Beethoven's apartment free—no one else was allowed to live in it, even when the restless composer wasn't there. Beethoven composed his fourth, fifth, and seventh symphonies here. Adjoining is the Adalbert Stifter Memorial, with paintings and drawings. (You can visit other places where Beethoven lived: at Probusgasse 6 and the Eroica House at Döblinger Hauptstrasse 92.)

Inventor of the symphony, Joseph Haydn (1732–1809) bought the tiny **Haydn-Wohnhaus mit Brahms-Gedenkraum,** Haydngasse 19 (☎ **01/596 13 07;** U-Bahn: U-3 to Zieglergasse), in 1793 and lived here until his death. In addition to his letters, manuscripts, and personal mementos are two pianos and his death mask. There's also a memorial room to Brahms.

Born in Salzburg, Wolfgang Amadeus Mozart (1756–91) moved to Vienna in 1781 but moved around often, occupying more than a dozen apartments. Here at the **Figarohaus,** Domgasse 5 (just off Stephansplatz) (☎ **01/513 62 94;** U-Bahn: U-1 or U-3 to Stephansplatz), Mozart lived with his wife, Constanze, and son from 1784 to 1787. These were his happiest years. Here he wrote *The Marriage of Figaro* and received visits from Haydn and a 16-year-old Beethoven. Set in what used to be a wealthy neighborhood, the Figarohaus was already 200 years old when Mozart lived here. His apartment is on the first floor, which you can reach by walking through a tiny courtyard and up some dark stairs. Headphones with Mozart's music are available for self-guided tours. Mozart later lived in poverty and died a pauper.

Schubert's Birthplace, Nussdorfer Strasse 54 (☎ **01/317 36 01;** Tram: 37 or 38 to Canisiusgasse), is obviously where Franz Schubert was born in 1797, the 12th of 14 children. At that time, as many as 17 families occupied the modest two-story building. A versatile and prolific composer, Schubert is most famous for his songs but also wrote symphonies and chamber music. He died when he was only 31. You can also visit the place where he died, at Kettenbrückengasse 6.

The **Johann-Strauss-Wohnung,** Praterstrasse 54 (☎ **01/214 01 21;** U-Bahn: U-1 to Nestroyplatz), is where Strauss (1825–99) composed his famous "Blue Danube Waltz," which is probably better known than the Austrian national anthem. He lived here from 1863 to 1870.

Austria's largest cemetery, **Zentralfriedhof (Central Cemetery),** Simmeringer Hauptstrasse 234 (☎ **01/760 41;** Tram: 71 from Schwarzenbergplatz to the next-to-the-last stop), contains the graves of the Strausses (father and sons), Brahms, Schubert, Franz von Suppé, and Beethoven, as well as a commemorative grave for Mozart. To find the Graves of Honor, near the Dr. Karl Lueger Church where you'll find all the composers buried within a few feet of each other, walk straight ahead from the main entrance (Gate 2) on the large pathway—the graves are to the left just before the path ends at the church. Admission is free. It's open daily: summer 7am to 7pm and winter 8am to 5pm.

ORGANIZED TOURS

WALKING TOURS A number of walking tours are conducted in English. **Vienna Tourist Guides,** for example, offers guided walks through medieval Vienna, the Jewish quarter, and other parts of the city. It also conducts themed walks that center on Mozart and other famous musicians; the history of Jews in Vienna; Vienna at the turn of the century as expressed in textile, glass, and furniture design; the life and times of Sigmund Freud; and other topics. Tours (excluding entrance fees) cost 130S ($10) adults and 65S ($5) age 17 and under.

Pick up a brochure, *Walks in Vienna,* detailing the various tours, times, and departure points from the Vienna Tourist Board, Kärntner Strasse 38. No reservations are necessary for the tours, which last 1½ to 2 hours and are held throughout the year regardless of the weather.

BUS TOURS   A number of tour companies offer general city tours and specialized tours, which you can book at travel agencies and at top hotels. The oldest tour company is **Vienna Sightseeing Tours,** Stelzhamergasse 4 (☎ **01/712 46 83-0**), which offers various tours that include performances of the Spanish Riding School, the Vienna Boys' Choir Sunday mass performance in the Hofburg chapel, the Vienna Woods, the Mayerling hunting lodge where Crown Prince Rudolph and Baroness Maria Vetsera committed suicide, the wine-growing district of Grinzing, and more. A 3½-hour city tour, which includes a visit through Schönbrunn Palace, costs 390S ($31) adults and 160S ($13) children. Departure is from the Staatsoper or major hotels.

For those who prefer to go it alone but would like the convenience of door-to-door transportation with commentary along the way, there's the **Vienna Line's Hop-On, Hop-Off** (☎ **01/712 46 83-0**), a private bus line that travels to most of the city's major sights, including the State Opera and St. Stephen's Cathedral and outlying sights such as the Prater amusement park, KunstHausWien, and Schönbrunn and Belvedere palaces. There are 13 stops altogether, with guided commentary provided in between, and you can get off and reboard as often as you like during a 2-day period. If you wish, you can also stay on board and travel the entire 2½-hour circuit. April to October, buses arrive at each stop about every hour 9am to 5pm; November to March, every 2 hours 9am to 3pm. Cost of the ticket is 220S ($18) adults and 120S ($10) under age 12.

TRAM TOURS   May to September, 1-hour tours of Vienna via a 1929-vintage tram car are conducted Saturday at 11:30am and 1:30pm and Sunday and holidays at 9:30 and 11:30am and 1:30pm. Departure is from the Otto Wagner Pavilion on Karlsplatz; the cost is 200S ($16) adults and 70S ($6) children. For more information, contact the Vienna Tourist Information office.

BOAT TOURS   Boats cruise the Danube during the warmer months, departing from a pier next to the Schwedenbrücke (the U-Bahn station is Schwedenplatz), a 5-minute walk from Stephansplatz. One of the most popular is the Hundertwasser Tour offered by **DDSG** (☎ **01/588 80-0**), which departs Schwedenplatz May to September daily at 11am, 1pm, 3pm, and 5pm and October daily at 11am, 1pm, and 3pm. The 1½-hour cruises, aboard a boat designed by Hundertwasser himself, travels through Old Vienna on the Danube Canal to the KunstHausWien. The cost is 140S ($11) adults, 70S ($6) ages 10 to 15, and free for age 9 and under.

6 Shopping

Vienna is known for the excellent quality of its works, which of course don't come cheap. If money is no object, you may want to shop for petit-point items, hand-painted Augarten porcelain, gold or enamel jewelry, ceramics, and leather goods. Other popular items are suits made of Loden (the boiled and rolled wool fabric made into overcoats), and hats, as well as knitted sweaters.

Vienna's most famous shopping streets are inside the Ring in the city center, including the pedestrian Kärntner Strasse, Graben, Kohlmarkt, and Rotenturmstrasse. Mariahilfer Strasse west of the Ring also has department stores, boutiques, and specialty shops, like the Gerngross and Herzmansky department stores, and Generali-Center, a shopping mall.

RECOVERING VAT

If you make a purchase of more than 1,000S ($80) at any store on any given day, you're entitled to a refund of the 13% **value-added tax (VAT).** Ask the store clerk for a U-34 form or a Tax-free Shopping Cheque, which you present to Customs on departing the last European Union country on your way home. If, for example, you're flying back to the United States from Frankfurt, present your U-34 form or Cheque, receipt from the shop, and the goods purchased to the Customs officer at the Frankfurt airport. Then go to the Tax-Free Shopping counter for an immediate refund, minus a handling fee.

FLEA MARKETS

If you're in Vienna on a Saturday, head straight for the town's best-known flea market, held just past the Naschmarkt outdoor market on **Linke Wienzeile** near the Kettenbrücken U-Bahn station. This is the most colorful (and crowded) place to look for curios, antiques, old books, and junk. I've bought old coffee grinders here for almost everyone I know (though they aren't the bargain they were 15 years ago). Be sure to haggle. It's open Saturday about 8am to 6pm. It's also worth a trip to the adjoining **Naschmarkt,** Vienna's outdoor food-and-produce market, open Monday to Friday 6am to 6:30pm and Saturday 6am to 5pm (see "Great Deals on Dining," earlier in this chapter).

A **market for arts, crafts, and antiques,** held only from May to August, takes place Saturday 2 to 6pm and Sunday 10am to 6pm along the promenade of the Donaukanal at Franz-Joseph-Kai (near the Schwedenplatz U-Bahn station, north of Stephansplatz). From March to December, a small art and antiques market is held inside the Ring at Am Hof every Friday and Saturday 10am to 7pm, with about 40 vendors participating.

Finally, there's another wonderful market, the **Spittelberg Arts and Crafts Exhibition** (U-Bahn: U-2 or U-3 to Volkstheater; Tram 49 to Spittelberg), held daily in August and also in December until Christmas, with artists selling arts and crafts up and down the historic Spittelberg street, outside the Ring just west of the Kunsthistorisches Museum.

DEPARTMENT STORES

Vienna's main department stores are all conveniently located: **Gerngross,** Mariahilfer Strasse 38–48 (☎ **01/521 80-0;** U-3 to Neubaugasse); **Herzmansky,** Mariahilfer Strasse 26–30 (☎ **01/521 58-0;** U-3 to Neubaugasse); and **Steffl,** Kärntner Strasse 19 (☎ **01/514 31;** U-1 or U-3 to Stephansplatz).

7 Vienna After Dark

Everything in Vienna is somewhat theatrical, perhaps because of its majestic baroque backdrop. Small wonder that opera and theater reign supreme. It would be a shame if you came all this way without experiencing something that's very dear to the Viennese heart.

To find out what's being played on Vienna's many stages, pick up a copy of *Wien Monatsprogramm,* a monthly brochure available free at the Vienna Tourist Information office. In addition to its information of theatrical productions, concerts, events, and other programs, it lists places where you can buy tickets in advance, thereby avoiding the 22% surcharge at travel agencies. If you're a student under 27 with a current valid ID from your college or university, you can purchase tickets at reduced prices for the Staatsoper (Austrian State Opera) and Burgtheater on the night of the performance (a current student card from your university is required; an International Student Identity Card on its own won't be accepted as proof of status). Even if you're not a student, you can see the Burgtheater or Staatsoper for as little as 15S to 20S ($1.20 to $1.60) for standing-room tickets.

THE PERFORMING ARTS

For advance sales of tickets for the Burgtheater, Staatsoper, and several other state theaters, go to the **Bundestheaterkassen,** Goethegasse 1 (☎ **01/514 44-2959**), a minute's walk northwest of the Staatsoper. They go on sale a week before the performance. The Bundestheaterkassen is open Monday to Friday 8am to 6pm and Saturday, Sunday, and holidays 9am to noon (the first Saturday of the month 9am to 5pm). Tickets for individual theaters are available directly at each box office an hour before the performance, but only for that day's performance.

If you want to see a production at the Burgtheater, Staatsoper, or Volksoper, the Bundestheaterkassen should be your first stop. Otherwise, you can order tickets for these venues by credit card by calling ☎ **01/513 15 13** Monday to Friday 10am to 6pm and Saturday, Sunday, and holidays 10am to noon. Phone sales begin approximately 1 month before the day of performance and can be ordered by holders of American Express, Diners Club, MasterCard, and Visa. Note that standing-room tickets aren't sold in advance but only on the night of the performance.

OPERA & BALLET   One of the world's leading opera houses, the **Staatsoper,** Opernring 2 (☎ **01/514 44-2959** or 01/514 44-2960; U-Bahn: U-1, U-2, or U-4 to Karlsplatz-Oper), stages grand productions throughout the year, except in July and August. It's traditional to start off each year with the production of Johann Strauss's operetta *Die Fledermaus* in January, followed by a repertoire of 40 operatic works each season. Opera or ballet, accompanied by the Viennese Philharmonic Orchestra, is presented nightly September to June. A staff of about 1,200 people, including the stage crew, singers, and production workers, ensure that everything runs smoothly. At 5,300 square feet, the stage area is one of the largest in Europe and is even much larger than the spectator floor of the opera house, which holds 2,200 people—1,700 in seats and 500 in the standing-room sections. Thirty-five-minute tours are given almost daily throughout the year, two to five times a day (check the board outside the entrance for the times); the cost is 60S ($4.80) adults, 45S ($3.60) seniors, 30S ($2.40) students, and 20S ($1.60) children.

The cheapest way to see the opera house, however, and a performance to boot, is to purchase one of the 500 standing-room tickets available on the night of the performance. To do so, go to the Staatsoper at least 3 hours before the performance, stand in line, buy your ticket, and, once inside, mark your "seat" by tying a scarf to the rail. You can then leave and come back just before the performance. True seats range from 100S to 2,000S ($8 to $160) for most productions; standing room is 20S ($1.60) for the Galerie and Balkon (upper balconies) or 30S ($2.40) for the slightly better Parter-restehplatz (ground floor); unsold tickets are available to students with valid ID from their university for 50S to 120S ($4 to $10) on the performance night at the box office.

THEATER   Under the direction of Claus Peymann, the **Burgtheater,** Dr.-Karl-Lueger-Ring 2 (☎ **01/514 44-2959** or 01/514 44-2960; Tram: 1, 2, or D to Burgtheater), stages the great German classics as well as modern plays, from Friedrich

Schiller's *Wilhelm Tell* to Georg Büchner's *Woyzeck*. Actors consider an engagement here a highlight in their careers. Performances are given most evenings September to June. Seats are 50S to 500S ($4 to $40); standing room is 15S ($1.20) and student tickets are 50S ($4).

The **Theater an der Wien,** Linke Wienzeile 6 (☎ **01/588 30-265;** U-Bahn: U-1, U-2, or U-4 to Karlsplatz-Oper), and the **Raimundtheater,** Wallgasse 18–20 (☎ **01/599 77-27;** U-Bahn: U-3 to Westbahnhof), stage musicals. Both are part of the Vereinigte Bühen (United Theaters) under the direction of Rudi Klausnitzer. Previous productions have included *Les Misérables, The Phantom of the Opera, Freudiana, Beauty and the Beast, Kiss of the Spider Woman,* and *Dance of the Vampire.* Performances are given daily throughout the year. The box office for both, at Linke Wienzeile 6, is open daily 10am to 1pm and 2 to 6pm. In addition, a small kiosk called **Wien Ticket,** on Kärntner Strasse beside the Staatsoper, sells tickets for the Theater an der Wien and Raimundtheater at no extra commission. It's open daily from 10am to 7pm. Seats for Theater an der Wien start at 120S ($10) Sunday to Thursday and at 130S ($11) Friday and Saturday; standing-room tickets (available an hour before the performance) are 30S ($2.40). At Raimundtheater, prices begin at 130S and 140S ($10 and $11) respectively and standing-room tickets are 35S ($2.80).

The English-language **International Theatre,** Porzellangasse 8 (☎ **01/319 62 72;** U-Bahn: U-4 to Rossauer Lände), presents American and British plays, usually offering four productions a year and an annual presentation of Charles Dickens's *A Christmas Carol.* Performances are September to July, Tuesday to Saturday at 7:30pm. The box office is open Monday to Friday 11am to 3pm. Tickets run 220S to 280S ($18 to $22), or 140S ($11) students and seniors. And the **English Theater,** Josefsgasse 12 (☎ **01/402 12 60;** U-Bahn: U-2 to Rathaus), stages professional productions of both classic and contemporary plays, with performances usually Monday to Saturday throughout the year at 7:30pm. Tickets are 180S to 480S ($14 to $38), and its box office is open Monday to Friday 10am to 5pm.

CLASSICAL MUSIC   Be sure to check the *Wien Monatsprogramm* for a current listing of concerts. The **Vienna Hofburg Orchestra,** for example, presents waltz and operetta concerts every Tuesday and Saturday at 8:30pm May to October in the Festsaal of the Hofburg; every Wednesday at 8:30pm May to October (and Friday during May and June) it performs the music of Mozart and Strauss in the Konzerthaus, Lothringer Strasse 20. Tickets for both performances are 450S ($36). The **Vienna Mozart Orchestra,** dressed in period costumes, performs several nights a week in summer at various venues. A great place for free entertainment in July and August is in front of the Rathaus, where a giant screen presents performances of famous orchestras and conductors.

LIVE-MUSIC HOUSES

The **Metropol,** Hernalser Hauptstrasse 55 (☎ **01/407 77 407;** Tram: 43 from Schottentor to Elterleinplatz), has served as a mecca of the Viennese youth scene for more than a decade, with productions ranging from rock, new wave, jazz, and reggae concerts to cabaret. It's open Tuesday to Saturday from 8pm. Cover is 170S to 350S ($14 to $28). A couple of minutes' walk south of the Ring, **Papa's Tapas,** Schwarzenbergplatz 10 (☎ **01/505 03 11;** Tram: 1, 2, 71, or D to Schwarzenbergplatz), is a small basement place featuring blues, boogie woogie, country, and rock in a cozy setting. It's open Monday to Thursday 8pm to 2am and Friday and Saturday 8pm to 4am; concerts begin around 9pm. The cover charge is 70S to 150S ($6 to $12) for most bands.

The *Heurige*

Heurige are Viennese wine taverns featuring local Viennese wines (called *heurige* as well). Today there are about 400 families still cultivating vineyards in and around Vienna, spread over the wine-growing districts of Grinzing, Nussdorf, Stammersdorf, Heiligenstadt, Strebersdorf, Sievering, and Neustift, among others. Though most of the these districts are now within city limits, many have preserved their original village atmosphere.

Of these, Grinzing is probably the best known, with about 20 *heurige* clustered together along a charming main street lined with colorful, fairy-tale-like houses. Almost all *heurige* offer an outdoor wine garden for summer drinking, evening *heurigenmusik,* and a buffet with cold cuts, cheeses, salads, and meats like grilled chicken, smoked pork, and schweinebraten. You can expect to spend about 200S ($16) per person for a satisfying meal. Or, if you wish, you can buy a quarter-liter mug of wine and linger as long as you wish. Most *heurige* are open from 4pm to midnight, and although some are closed from November to March, you'll always find *heurige* that are open. Look for the sprig of pine, usually hung above the entrance, and a small plaque with EIGENBAU written on it, which means that the grower serves his or her own wine.

Although it's probably easiest to wander about and simply choose a *heuriger* that suits your fancy, for a specific recommendation you might try the **Altes Presshaus,** Cobenzlgasse 15 (☎ **01/320 23 93**), located uphill from the tram stop. Built in 1527, it's the oldest *heuriger* in Grinzing, with an interior filled with wood paneling and antique furniture and a pleasant garden terrace that blossoms throughout the summer. It's open March to December daily 4pm to midnight, with live music from 6:30pm. On the opposite end of the main road, downhill from the tram stop, is **Bach-Hengl,** Sandgasse 7–9 (☎ **01/320 24 39**). The Hengl family has been producing wine since 1137. This *heuriger* is open year-round daily 4pm to midnight, with live music from 7pm. Its cozy interior is great for cold winter nights. Families love the outdoor terrace, complete with a small play area for children.

Grinzing is only 5 miles from the city center. From Schottentor, take Tram no. 38 to the last stop, Grinzing, a 20-minute ride.

Rockhaus, Adalbert-Stifter-Strasse 73 (☎ **01/332 46 41;** Tram: 31, 32, or N; Bus: 11A or 35A), is one of Vienna's best-known venues for blues, rock, reggae, new wave, and hard rock. International groups provide the main entertainment, while Austrian musicians are usually the warm-up. Check the newspaper or *Wien Monatsprogramm* for current concerts. It's open Tuesday to Sunday; the bar opens at 6pm and concerts begin around 8pm. Cover is 80S to 150S ($6 to $12) for local bands and 150S to 300S ($12 to $24) for international bands.

The basement-level **Tunnel,** Florianigasse 39, behind the Rathaus near the university district (☎ **01/405 34 65;** U-Bahn: U-2 to Rathaus, then a 10-minute walk; Tram: 5; Bus: 13A), features live music nightly, from blues and rock to folk and jazz. Groups are mainly European, including bands from Eastern Europe. Free jam sessions are featured on Monday. If you're hungry, an inexpensive restaurant on the ground floor serves food until 1am. Tunnel's music venue is open daily 8pm to 2am (live music begins around 9pm); the cafe is open daily 9am to 2am. The cover charge is usually 30S to 70S ($2.40 to $6) Tuesday to Sunday (free after 11pm if there's room); Monday jam sessions are free.

BARS

HISTORIC WINE CELLARS   Since these wine cellars, all inside the Ring, may be crowded during mealtimes, you might consider coming for a drink early or late in the evening. Expect to pay about 30S ($2.40) for a glass of wine (a quarter liter).

With a history stretching back several centuries, the **Augustiner Keller,** Augustinerstrasse 1, a minute's walk from the opera (☎ **01/533 10 26** or 01/533 09 46; U-Bahn: U-1, U-2, or U-4 to Karlsplatz or U-1 or U-3 to Stephansplatz), does seem rather ancient, with wooden floors, a vaulted brick ceiling, and a long, narrow room. A *heuriger* (wine tavern) serving wine from its own vineyards, it offers traditional heurigenmusik daily starting at 6:30pm (no cover, but drink prices are higher). Its menu includes grilled chicken, pork cutlet, grilled shank of pork, tafelspitz, and apfelstrudel. It's open daily 3pm to midnight in winter and 11am to midnight in summer. **Melkerstiftskeller,** Schottengasse 3 (☎ **01/533 55 30**; U-Bahn: U-2 to Schottentor or U-3 to Herrengasse), is also a *heuriger* featuring wine from its own vineyards, served in historic vaulted rooms. The menu offers Wiener schnitzel, pork cutlets, and other typical Viennese cuisine, with most meals between 110S and 160S ($9 and $13). It's open Tuesday to Saturday 5pm to midnight.

On one of Vienna's venerable old squares in the heart of the city, the **Urbanikeller,** Am Hof 12 (☎ **01/533 91 02**; U-Bahn: U-1 or U-3 to Stephansplatz, or U-3 to Herrengasse), gets my vote for the most picturesque wine cellar. Founded in 1906, its dining room looks like the setting of some medieval movie, with stone walls, an arched ceiling, and heavy oak tables. There's live Viennese music from 7pm to midnight, making it a great place to stop for a late-night drink. Wine is a bit more expensive, but it's worth it. It's open daily 6pm to 1am; closed mid-July to mid-August.

Zwölf Apostelkeller, Sonnenfelsgasse 3 (☎ **01/512 67 77**; U-Bahn: U-1 or U-3 to Stephansplatz), is a huge wine cellar two levels deep. The vaulting of the upper cellar is mainly 15th-century Gothic, while the lower cellar is early baroque. Unlike the places above, it offers only a limited menu, so you can come here anytime just for drinks. Its Apostel wine is the specialty of the house. It's open daily 4:30pm to midnight.

IN VIENNA'S OLD QUARTER   Several of these bars are in Rabensteig, the old Jewish quarter. About a 3-minute walk north of Stephansplatz, it's one of Vienna's most popular nightspots, with several bars on Rabensteig, Seitenstettengasse, and other small pedestrians-only streets, in an area popularly referred to as the Bermuda Triangle.

Kaffee Alt Wien, Bäckerstrasse 9 (☎ **01/512 52 22**; U-Bahn: U-1 or U-3 to Stephansplatz), is a dimly lit, old cafe/bar in the heart of Old Vienna. It opened in 1936 and is popular with students, artists, and writers. Its tired walls are hidden under a barrage of posters announcing concerts and exhibitions. Come here in the afternoon to read the paper, write letters, and relax; late at night it can get so crowded it's hard to get through the door. It's open daily 10am to 2am.

Der Neue Engel, Rabensteig 5 (☎ **01/535 41 05**; U-Bahn: U-1 or U-4 to Schwedenplatz), boasts a modern, slightly theatrical interior with various levels of seating and artwork on the walls. Upstairs are billiard tables and a cocktail bar. It's open Monday to Thursday 5pm to 2am, Friday and Saturday 5pm to 3am, and Sunday 6pm to 1am. Across the street is tiny **Casablanca,** Rabensteig 8 (☎ **01/533 34 63**; U-Bahn: U-1 or U-4 to Schwedenplatz), which offers outdoor seating and the usual wine and beer, along with live music provided by local bands. It's open daily 6pm to 4am. Live music begins around 8:30pm nightly. There's a music charge of 21S ($1.70).

The fact that you can choose from among 50 kinds of beer makes **Krah Krah,** Rabensteig 8 (☎ **01/533 81 93;** U-Bahn: U-1 or U-4 to Schwedenplatz), one of the most popular and crowded bars in the area. Incidentally, "Krah Krah" is the sound a raven makes, referring to the street Rabensteig, which means Ravens' Path. It's open Monday to Saturday 11am to 2am and Sunday 11am to 1am.

Not far from the Bermuda Triangle, moored on the Donau Canal at Marienbrücke, is the **Classic Rock Cafe** (☎ **01/533 93 67;** U-Bahn: U-1 or U-4 to Schwedenplatz), which occupies a colorful turquoise-colored boat topped with an American flag. True to its name, it plays classic rock from the 1950s to the 1990s. Glitzy in decor and decorated with musical instruments and TV screens showing music videos, it offers a bar (check out the bar stools), restaurant, and, in summer, outdoor top-deck seating. An English menu lists American food from steaks to burgers, with most dishes under 120S ($10). Throughout the evening the staff bursts into song for short performances, mostly of Broadway hits. It's open Tuesday to Saturday 6pm to 2am.

GAY & LESBIAN BARS

Easy to spot with its pink-and-purple exterior, the **Rosa Lila Villa,** Linke Wienzeile 102 (☎ **01/586 81 50** for women, 01/587 17 78 for men; U-4 to Pilgramgasse), serves as Vienna's information center for gays and lesbians, dispensing information on cultural activities as well as advice and holding discussions and encounter groups. The center itself is open Monday to Friday 5 to 8pm. There's also a cafe called Willendorf, open daily 6pm to 2am.

Alfi's Goldener Spiegel, located near the Naschmarkt at Linke Wienzeile 46 with an entrance on Stiegengasse (☎ **01/586 66 08;** U-Bahn: U-4 to Kettenbrückengasse), is one of the most popular gay havens in Vienna, attracting a lot of foreigners. Attached to the bar is a restaurant serving Viennese food at moderate prices and specializing in Wiener schnitzel. Alfi's is open Wednesday to Monday 7pm to 2am. On the other side of Naschmarkt is the **Alte Lampe,** Heumühlgasse 13 (☎ **01/587 34 54;** U-Bahn: U-4 to Kettenbrückengasse), Vienna's oldest gay bar, open since the 1960s. Friday and Saturday, a mostly mature crowd listens to the same schmaltzy piano music that has been played here for years. It's open Sunday, Wednesday, and Thursday 6pm to 1am and Friday and Saturday 8pm to 3am.

DANCE CLUBS

The Atrium, Schwindgasse 1, just off Schwarzenbergplatz (☎ **01/505 35 94;** Tram: 1, 2, 71, or D to Schwarzenbergplatz), was in 1958 Austria's first disco and is still going strong as an international meeting place. A cavernous underground club of various rooms, it attracts people in their 20s, in part because of a reduced student admission and in part because of promotions and weekly specials. It's open Thursday 8:30pm to 2am and Friday and Saturday 8:30pm to 3:30am. The cover is 50S ($4); students pay 30S ($2.40).

Stars come alive as soon as you descend into the basement-level **Move,** Daungasse 1 (☎ **01/406 32 78** or 409 78 89; U-Bahn: U-2 to Rathaus or U-6 to Josefstädter Strasse, then a 10-minute walk; Tram: 43 or 44 to Skodagasse, or 5 or 31 to Laudongasse), with its black walls and thousands of orange and green neon dots. Holograms line the walls. It's open Sunday to Thursday 9pm to 4am and Friday and Saturday 9pm to 5am. The cover charge is 50S ($4), 20S ($1.60) of which goes toward the first drink; students pay 20S ($1.60), 10S (80¢) of which goes toward the first drink; women are admitted free Tuesday and Thursday.

P1 Discothek, Rotgasse 9, not far from Stephansplatz (☎ **01/535 99 95;** U-Bahn: U-1 to Stephansplatz), is one of Vienna's hottest and certainly most conveniently located dance clubs, popular with people in their 20s. This former film studio is huge, with a dance floor and enough room to accommodate 1,500. It opened in 1988 and attained instant fame when Tina Turner came here at the start of her European tour. Today it features hip hop on Tuesday, music from the 1970s and 1980s on Wednesday, house music on Thursday, house and trance music on Friday, and popular hits on Saturday. It's open Tuesday to Saturday 9pm to 5am. The cover is 60S ($4.80).

8 Side Trips: The Vienna Woods & Krems

For information on the Vienna Woods, Krems, and other destinations in the vicinity of Vienna, stop by the **Niederösterreich (Lower Austria) Touristik Information,** just off Kärntner Strasse not far from the Vienna Tourist Information office at Walfischgasse 6 (☎ **01/513 80 22-0**). It's open Monday to Friday 9am to 6pm.

THE DANUBE

How about a swim in the Danube? Actually, it's the Alte Donau (Old Danube), formerly a section of the Danube that has been sealed off and now serves as a recreational lake. You'll find numerous beaches, restaurants, paddleboats, rental bikes, and other facilities along its shores, but the largest and oldest beach is **Gänsehäufel,** actually an island in the Alte Donau and well known for its segregated nudist beach. To reach the Alte Donau and its many beaches, take U-Bahn U-1 to the Alte Donau station. Nearby is the 13-mile-long **Donauinsel (Danube Island),** sandwiched between the Donau and the Neue Donau (New Danube). It's the largest recreation area in Vienna's immediate vicinity, popular with joggers, cyclists, and strollers, and offers bathing opportunities right off its bank, making it the best bet for a quick getaway from city traffic. You can reach the Donauinsel by taking U-Bahn U-1 to the Donauinsel station (two stops before the Alte Donau station).

THE VIENNA WOODS

The **Vienna Woods (Wienerwald),** surrounding much of the city, provides the Viennese with a 540-square-mile natural playground right at their back door. The woods offer mile upon mile of hiking trails, views, solitude, and unique destinations. Many bus and tram lines end at the starting point of hiking routes. Among these, one of the quickest and most favored destinations is Kahlenberg, which affords great views over the whole city. To reach Kahlenberg, take U-Bahn U-4 to the last stop, Heiligenstadt.

Otherwise, the most popular destination in the Vienna Woods is undoubtedly **Baden,** famous since Roman times for its thermal baths. Its guests have included many royal and well-known figures, such as Maria Theresa, Napoléon, and Mozart. A village of 26,000 inhabitants about 16 miles south of Vienna, Baden boasts Biedermeier-era villas, patrician homes, squares, gardens, a casino, an outdoor swimming pool complete with a sandy beach and thermal bath, and an indoor public thermal bath. The village is especially popular with Austria's older generation.

From Vienna, Baden is easily reached by Schnellbahn (commuter train) in about 40 minutes, with departures from both Wien Mitte and Südbahnhof train station. For more information on Baden, contact the **Kur- und Bäderdirektion Baden,** Brusatti-platz 3 (☎ **02252/445 31-59**).

From Baden, one of the most picturesque excursions is through the **Helenental** to Mayerling. The Helenental is a river valley with steep, wooded hills rising above it, on which perch two ruined Gothic castles. Of all the names and destinations in the Vienna Woods, none evokes more images of a tragic past than **Mayerling** (☎ **02258/22 75**). It was here that Crown Prince Rudolf, the only male heir to the throne, committed suicide in a hunting lodge in 1889 with his mistress, Baroness Maria Vetsera. The lodge has since been replaced by a convent and a faux-Gothic church, open daily in summer 9am to 12:30pm and 1:30 to 6pm and in winter daily 9am to 12:30pm and 1:30 to 5pm, with 30-minute guided tours costing 20S ($1.60) and beginning daily at 10am. Buses bound for Mayerling depart from Baden's train station, reaching Mayerling 20 minutes later.

KREMS

Krems, 45 miles northwest of Vienna on the Danube, is a delightful medieval village with a 1,000-year history, making it one of the oldest towns in Austria. Today it encompasses Stein, once a separate village. Krem is a mellow town of courtyards, arched gateways, impossibly narrow cobbled lanes, and partially preserved town walls. It contains more than 700 buildings from the 12th to 19th centuries, showcasing styles ranging from Romanesque and Gothic to baroque and Renaissance.

In the fertile Wachau region of the Danube valley, Krems stretches narrowly along the river, terraced vineyards rising behind it. This is prime wine-making country, and Krems lives and breathes wine. Just as the Viennese flock to Grinzing and other suburbs to sample new wine in *heurige,* so the people of the Wachau come here to taste the local vintners' products, which appear in Krems earlier in the year. Krems is famous for two types of wine—classical Grüne Veltliner and Riesling—available at *heurige* throughout the village.

ARRIVING   From Vienna, **trains** depart from the Wien Franz-Josefs-Bahnhof at intervals of 60 minutes or less, arriving in Krems an hour later. In Krems, you can reach most city sights on foot; from the train station, the walk west along the Danube to Stein takes less than 30 minutes. Alternatively, you can rent bicycles at the train station for 90S ($7) per day, if you have a valid train ticket; otherwise, it costs 150S ($12).

One of your first stops should be the **Tourismusbüro der Stadt Krems,** about a 10-minute walk from the train station at Undstrasse 6 (☎ **02732/826 76**), reached by heading straight out of the station and turning left on Ringstrasse, then right on Reifgasse. April to October, it's open Monday to Friday 9am to 7pm and Saturday and Sunday 10am to noon and 1 to 7pm; November to March, Monday to Friday 9am to 6pm. In addition to obtaining a map and brochure on Krems, you can pay 40S ($3.20) for a "Kremsman," an audio guide in English that'll lead you through Krems and Stein in about 3 hours.

SEEING THE SIGHTS   For an overview of Krems and its history, visit the **Weinstadt Museum,** Körnermarkt 14 (☎ **02732/801 567**), located in the heart of Krems in a restored 13th-century Gothic Dominican monastery. Among its displays is a copy of a 32,000-year-old Venus statuette, Austria's oldest work of art to date. You'll also find Roman masks, an 18th-century wine press, festive and everyday clothing of the Wachau, and works by Martin Johann Schmidt, who lived in Stein and is recognized as one of Austria's most important baroque painters. Also of interest are the 16th-century cellar tunnels that have been excavated underneath the cloister. Apparently, Krems is riddled with tunnels, used primarily for the storage of wine. The museum is open March to October, Tuesday 9am to 6pm and Wednesday to Sunday 1 to 6pm. Admission is 40S ($3.20) adults, 30S ($2.40) seniors/students, and 20S ($1.60) children.

On the way to Stein lies the **Kunst.halle.Krems,** Steiner Landstrasse 8 (☎ **02732/826 69-14**). Occupying a converted 19th-century tobacco factory, it stages a variety of innovative art shows and concerts surprising for a town this size.

Admission costs vary; the hours are Tuesday to Sunday 10am to 6pm. Otherwise, the most interesting part of Krems today is what was once the little village of **Stein,** with narrow streets terraced above the river and flanked with impressive patrician homes. On Kellergasse you'll find one *heuriger* after the other, as well as a remnant of the old city wall. Be sure, too, to stroll down Krems's main pedestrian lane, **Obere and Untere Landstrasse,** marked by a tower gate. It's popular in summer for its kiosks that sell glasses of local wine.

From Krems, it's worth taking a short excursion across the Danube to the region's most striking structure, the **Stift Göttweig (Benedictine Monastery Göttweig)** (☎ **02732/846 63**), which spreads like a palace on the top of a hill and commands a breathtaking view of the Wachau region. To reach it, there's one city bus a day departing from the Krems train station at 1:35pm, with a return trip at 4:10pm. Alternatively, you can take a 10-minute train ride from Krems to Furth, followed by a 20-minute walk up a steep incline; a taxi from Krems to the monastery will run about 150S ($12). The monastery, which lies 164 feet above sea level and is home to about 20 monks, was founded in 1083 and rebuilt in its present baroque style in the 18th century. Rivaling the much better known Melk Monastery in size and splendor, Stift Göttweig contains an ornate abbey church, an original 11th-century medieval chapel, and an imperial wing with what is considered one of the most beautiful baroque staircases in Europe. It's open daily 10am to 6pm. Additionally, guided tours are available from mid-March to mid-November at 10 and 11am and 2, 3, 4, and 5pm. Tours last an hour and cost 70S ($6) adults and 40S ($3.20) children. Admission without a guided tour is 60S ($4.80) adults and 30S ($2.40) children.

ACCOMMODATIONS Try **Gästehaus Zöhrer,** on a hill above Krems at Sandgrube 1, 3500 Krems (☎ **02732/831 91**). Belonging to one of the oldest winegrowing families in Wachau (the Zöhrers have been vintners 700 years), this is also a *heuriger,* complete with outside terrace, making it a popular choice for wine tasters. Six units, with bathroom, TV, and phone, go for 410S to 440S ($33 to $35) single and 640S to 700S ($51 to $56) double. There are also three apartments sleeping two to four persons, with a small kitchen, costing 700S ($56) per day, plus a 300S ($24) final cleaning charge. Prices include breakfast; no credit cards are accepted. A rustic breakfast room with a brick floor and wooden beams overlooks a small vineyard and pool.

In the heart of Krems on its pedestrian lane is **Hotel-Restaurant Alte Post,** Obere Landstrasse 32 (☎ **02732/822 76**). With a 500-year-old history, it claims to be Krems's oldest inn. It offers 25 units (7 with shower only and 1 with bathroom). A single is 350S ($28) without bathroom or 480S ($38) with shower only. A double is 620S ($50) without bathroom, 740S ($59) with shower only, or 840S ($67) with bathroom and TV. Prices include breakfast and showers. No credit cards are accepted.

DINING The **Alte Post,** above, is also a good place for Austrian food, especially if you can get a table in its romantic inner courtyard. Expect to spend 130S to 180S ($10 to $14) for a meal. It's open Tuesday 11:30am to 2pm and Thursday to Monday 11:30am to midnight (closed January to mid-March). No credit cards are accepted. Another good choice is **Gozzoburg,** Margaretenstrasse 14 (☎ **02732/852 47**), in the heart of Krems near Hoher Markt. Very rustic, with a terrace overlooking the town and with exhibits by local artists, it offers Austrian meals for 75S to 200S ($6 to $16) and is open Wednesday to Monday 11am to 11pm. No credit cards are accepted.

Appendix

A European Tourist Offices

Here are the addresses, phone numbers, e-mail addresses, and Internet
Web sites for the tourist offices of the countries covered in this guide.

Note that the official Web site of the **European Travel Commission** is **www.visiteurope.com**.

AUSTRIAN NATIONAL TOURIST OFFICE

IN THE U.S. P.O. Box 1142, New York, NY 10108-1142
(☎ **212/944-6880**); 500 N. Michigan Ave., Suite 1950, Chicago, IL
60611 (☎ **312/644-8029**); P.O. Box 491938, Los Angeles, CA
90049 (☎ **310/478-8376**).

IN CANADA 1010 Sherbrooke St. W., Suite 1410, Montréal, PQ
H3A 2R7 (☎ **514/849-3709**); 2 Bloor St. E., Suite 3330, Toronto,
ON M4W 1A8 (☎ **416/967-3381**); Suite 1380, Granville Square,
200 Granville St., Vancouver, BC V6C 1S4 (☎ **604/683-5808**).

IN THE U.K. 30 St. George St., London W1R 0AL (☎ **0171/
629-0461**).

E-MAIL None.

WEB SITE www.anto.com

BELGIAN TOURIST OFFICE

IN THE U.S. 780 Third Ave., New York, NY 10017 (☎ **212/
758-8130**).

IN CANADA P.O. Box 760 NDG, Montréal, PQ H4A 3S2
(☎ **514/489-8965**).

IN THE U.K. 29 Prince St., London W1R 7RG (☎ **0171/
629-3777**).

E-MAIL belinfo@nyxfer.blythe.org

WEB SITE www.visitbelgium.com

BRITISH TOURIST AUTHORITY

IN THE U.S. 551 Fifth Ave., Suite 701, New York, NY 10176
(☎ **800/462-2748** or 212/986-2200); 625 N. Michigan Ave., Suite
1510, Chicago, IL 60611 (☎ **312/787-0464**).

IN CANADA 111 Avenue Rd., Suite 450, Toronto, ON M5R 3J8
(☎ **416/961-8124**).

IN AUSTRALIA Level 16, Gateway, 1 Macquarie Place, Sydney, NSW 2000 (☎ **02/9377-4400**).

IN NEW ZEALAND Suite 305, Dilworth Bldg., Customs and Queen streets, Auckland 1 (☎ **09/303-1446**).

E-MAIL travelinfo@bta.org.uk

WEB SITE www.vistibritain.com

CZECH TOURIST AUTHORITY

IN THE U.S. 1109 Madison Ave., New York, NY 10028 (☎ **212/288-0830**).

IN CANADA P.O. Box 198, Exchange Tower, 130 King St. W, Suite 715, Toronto, ON M5X 1A6 (☎ **416/367-3432**).

IN THE U.K. 95 Great Portland St., London W1M 5RA (☎ **0171/291-9920**).

E-MAIL nycenter@ny.czech.cz

WEB SITE wwwczech.cz/new_york

FRENCH GOVERNMENT TOURIST OFFICE

IN THE U.S. 444 Madison Ave., 16th Floor, New York, NY 10022 (☎ **212/838-7800**); 676 N. Michigan Ave., Suite 3360, Chicago, IL 60611 (☎ **312/751-7800**); 9454 Wilshire Blvd., Suite 715, Beverly Hills, CA 90212 (☎ **310/271-6665**). To request information at any of these offices, call the **France on Call hot line** at ☎ **900/990-0040** (50¢ per minute).

IN CANADA Maison de la France/French Government Tourist Office, 1981 av. McGill College, Suite 490, Montréal, PQ H3A 2W9 (☎ **514/288-4264**).

IN THE U.K. Maison de la France/French Government Tourist Office, 178 Piccadilly, London, W1V 0AL (☎ **0891/244-123**).

IN AUSTRALIA French Tourist Bureau, 25 Bligh St., Sydney, NSW 2000 (☎ **02/9231-5244**).

E-MAIL info@francetourism.com

WEB SITE www.fgtousa.org or www.francetourism.com

GERMAN NATIONAL TOURIST OFFICE

IN THE U.S. 122 E. 42nd St., 52nd Floor, New York, NY 10168 (☎ **212/661-7200**); 11766 Wilshire Blvd., Suite 750, Los Angeles, CA 90025 (☎ **310/575-9799**).

IN CANADA 175 Bloor St. E., North Tower, 6th Floor, Toronto, ON M4W 3R8 (☎ **416/968-1570**).

IN THE U.K. Nightingale House, 65 Curzon St., London, W1Y 8NE (☎ **0171/495-0081**).

IN AUSTRALIA Lufthansa House, 143 Macquarie St., 12th Floor, Sydney, NSW 2000 (☎ **02/9367-3890**).

E-MAIL gntony@aol.com

WEB SITE www.germany-tourism.de

GREEK NATIONAL TOURIST ORGANIZATION

IN THE U.S. 645 Fifth Ave., 5th Floor, New York, NY 10022 (☎ **212/421-5777**); 168 N. Michigan Ave., Suite 600, Chicago, IL 60601 (☎ **312/782-1084**); 611 W. 6th St., Suite 2198, Los Angeles, CA 90017 (☎ **213/626-6696**).

IN CANADA 2 Bloor St. W., Cumberland Terrace, Toronto, ON M4W 3E2 (☎ **416/968-2220**); 1233 rue de la Montagne, Suite 101, Montréal, PQ H3G 1Z2 (☎ **514/871-1535**).

IN THE U.K. 4 Conduit St., London W1R D0J (☎ **0171/734-5997**).

IN AUSTRALIA 51–57 Pitt St., Sydney, NWS 2000 (☎ **02/9241-1663**).

E-MAIL None.

WEB SITE www.hellas.de or www.greektourism.com

HUNGARIAN NATIONAL TOURIST OFFICE
IN THE U.S. 150 E. 58th St., New York, NY 10155 (☎ **212/355-0240**).

IN THE U.K. c/o Embassy of the Republic of Hungary, Trade Commission, 46 Eaton Place, London, SW1 X8AL (☎ **0171/823-1032**).

E-MAIL huntour@idt.net

WEB SITE www.hungarytourism.hu

IRISH TOURIST BOARD
IN THE U.S. 345 Park Ave., New York, NY 10154 (☎ **800/223-6470** or 212/418-0800).

IN CANADA 160 Bloor St. E., Suite 1150, Toronto, ON M4W 1B9 (☎ **416/929-2777**).

IN THE U.K. 150 New Bond St., London W1Y OAQ (☎ **0171/493-3201**).

IN AUSTRALIA 36 Carrington St., 5th Level, Sydney, NSW 2000 (☎ **02/9299-6177**).

E-MAIL info@irishtouristboard.com

WEB SITE www.ireland.travel.ie

ITALIAN GOVERNMENT TOURIST BOARD
IN THE U.S. 630 Fifth Ave., Suite 1565, New York, NY 10111 (☎ **212/245-4822**); 401 N. Michigan Ave., Suite 3030, Chicago, IL 60611 (☎ **312/644-0990**); 12400 Wilshire Blvd., Suite 550, Beverly Hills, CA 90025 (☎ **310/820-0098**).

IN CANADA 1 place Ville-Marie, Suite 1914, Montréal, PQ H3B 2C3 (☎ **514/866-7667**).

IN THE U.K. 1 Princes St., London W1R 8AY (☎ **0171/408-1254**).

E-MAIL None.

WEB SITE None.

MONACO GOVERNMENT TOURIST OFFICE
IN THE U.S. 565 Fifth Ave., New York, NY 10017 (☎ **800/753-9696** or 212/286-3330); 542 S. Dearborn St., Suite 550, Chicago, IL 60605 (☎ **312/939-7836**).

IN THE U.K. 3–8 Chelsea Garden Market, Chelsea Harbour, London, SW10 0XE (☎ **0171/352-9962**).

E-MAIL mgto@monaco1.org

WEB SITE www.monaco.mc/usa

NETHERLANDS BOARD OF TOURISM
IN THE U.S.   355 Lexington Ave., 21st Floor, New York, NY 10017 (☎ **212/ 370-7360**); 225 N. Michigan Ave., Suite 1854, Chicago, IL 60601 (☎ **312/ 819-0300**).

IN CANADA   25 Adelaide St. E., Suite 710, Toronto, ON M5C 1Y2 (☎ **416/ 363-1577**).

IN THE U.K.   18 Buckingham Gate, London, SW1E 6LB (☎ **0171/828-7900**).

E-MAIL   go2holland@aol.com

WEB SITE   www.goholland.com

PORTUGUESE NATIONAL TOURIST OFFICE
IN THE U.S.   590 Fifth Ave., New York, NY 10036 (☎ **212/354-4403**).

IN CANADA   600 Bloor St. W., Suite 1005, Toronto, ON M4W 3B8 (☎ **416/921-7376**).

IN THE U.K.   1–5 New Bond St., London, W1Y 0NP (☎ **0171/493-3873**).

E-MAIL   aavila@portugal.org

WEB SITE   www.portugal.org

SCANDINAVIAN TOURIST BOARDS
IN THE U.S.   P.O. Box 4649, Grand Central Station, New York, NY 10163 (☎ **212/949-2333** or 212/885-9700); 8929 Wilshire Blvd., Beverly Hills, CA 90211 (☎ **213/854-1549**).

IN THE U.K.   The **Danish Tourist Board,** 55 Sloane St., London SW1X 95Y (☎ **0171/259-5959**); the **Swedish Travel and Tourism Council,** 73 Welbeck St., London W1M 8AN (☎ **0171/724-5869**).

E-MAIL   info@gosweden.org

WEB SITES   www.visitdenmark.com or www.gosweden.org

SWITZERLAND TOURISM
IN THE U.S.   608 Fifth Ave., New York, NY 10020 (☎ **212/757-5944**); 150 N. Michigan Ave., Suite 2930, Chicago, IL 60601 (☎ **312/630-5840**); 222 N. Sepulveda Blvd., Suite 1570, El Segundo, CA 90245 (☎ **310/335-5980**).

IN CANADA   154 University Ave., Suite 610, Toronto, ON M5H 3Y9 (☎ **416/971-9734**).

IN THE U.K.   Swiss Centre, Swiss Court, London, W1V 8EE (☎ **0171/ 734-1921**).

E-MAIL   stnewyork@switzerlandtourism.com

WEB SITE   www.switzerlandtourism.com

TOURIST OFFICE OF SPAIN
IN THE U.S.   666 Fifth Ave., 35th Floor, New York, NY 10103 (☎ **212/265- 8822**); 845 N. Michigan Ave., Suite 915E, Chicago, IL 60611 (☎ **312/642-1992**); 8383 Wilshire Blvd., Suite 960, Beverly Hills, CA 90211 (☎ **213/658-7188**); 1221 Brickell Ave., Suite 1850, Miami, FL 33131 (☎ **305/358-1992**).

IN CANADA   102 Bloor St. W., 14th Floor, Toronto, ON M5S 1M9 (☎ **416/ 961-3131**).

IN THE U.K.   57 St. James's St., London SW1 (☎ **0171/499-0901**).

IN AUSTRALIA   203 Castlereagh St., Suite 21A (P.O. Box 675), Sydney, NSW 2000 (☎ **02/9264-7966**).

E-MAIL   oetny@here-i.com

WEB SITE   www.okspain.org

B Train Fares & Schedules

FARES

The expected cost of one-way second-class tickets for trips between the major cities of Europe for 1999 is shown below.

Amsterdam to: Paris, $71; Copenhagen, $150; London, $157 (via Brussels and Chunnel) or $135 (via Sealink); Vienna, $210; Brussels, $36; Frankfurt, $91; Rome, $263; Venice, $222.

Barcelona to: Marseille, $65; Nice, $79; Paris, $97; Rome, $114; Lourdes, $71.

London to: Brussels, $99 (via Chunnel) or $70 (via Sealink); Edinburgh, $119; Glasgow, $119; Dublin, $129; Paris, $99 (via Chunnel); Amsterdam, $157 (via Chunnel and Brussels) or $135 (via Sealink).

Madrid to: Barcelona, $45; Toledo, $6; Valencia, $34; Lisbon, $45; Paris, $122; Rome, $170; Seville, $58.

Munich to: Amsterdam, $171; Brussels, $159; Copenhagen, $233; Innsbruck, $31; Milan, $60; Naples, $101; Paris, $135; Rome, $85; Salzburg, $29; Venice, $56; Vienna, $63; Zurich, $74.

Paris to: Brussels, $60; Amsterdam, $72; Madrid, $122; Copenhagen, $215; Frankfurt, $83; Munich, $142; Zurich, $80; Rome, $164; Cannes, $95; Lourdes, $87; Marseille, $80; Nice, $95; Strasbourg, $55.

Rome to: Florence, $26; Naples, $15; Genoa, $35; Venice, $39; Milan, $42; Amsterdam, $263; Barcelona, $116; Brussels, $175; Frankfurt, $173; Geneva, $100; London, $228 (via Chunnel) or $217 (via Sealink); Madrid, $170; Munich, $89; Paris, $164; Vienna, $91; Trieste, $48; Zurich, $101.

SCHEDULES

The following rail schedules show the trains departing from major European cities. With few exceptions, only the major international expresses are listed. But not every international express is here, for many of these famous trains have only first-class accommodations. You can be sure that if a train is mentioned in *Frommer's Europe from $50 a Day*, it has second-class seats or couchettes.

These departure and arrival times are in effect between May 30 and September 25, 1999. The summer schedule in 2000 is valid from May 28 to September 23—and very few changes compared with 1999 are foreseen. Unless otherwise stated, these trains make their runs daily in all seasons. The abbreviation *lv* means "leaves"; *ar* indicates a train's arrival time. Usually, we'll give the train's departure time from all the cities in the country from which it sets out and provide its arrival in the various cities of the countries to which it goes.

CHUNNEL RAIL SERVICE BY *EUROSTAR*

With the opening of the Chunnel/Channel Tunnel in 1995, one of the greatest engineering projects became a reality. Travel time on the *Eurostar* train between London and Paris was reduced to 3 hours, and between London and Brussels to 4 hours. For

A Note on Train Times

The schedules for European trains are given in "military" time, based on a 24-hour clock. Since you'll be seeing this style in Europe, we've used it in this section. For example, 12:05am is 00:05, 1:44am is 01:44, 7am is 07:00, 7:15am is 07:15, noon is 12:00, 3pm is 15:00, 7pm is 19:00, and midnight is 24:00.

Eurostar fares and updated schedules for London, call ☎ **0233/617-575** or fax 00441/233-617-998; for Paris, call ☎ **01-45-82-50-50** or fax 01-21-00-69-00; for Brussels, call ☎ **02/224-8856.**

AMSTERDAM

For train information, call ☎ **20/624-83-91.**

Amsterdam–Hamburg–Copenhagen–Stockholm *(North-West Express)* Lv Amsterdam 19:00, ar Hamburg 02:22, ar Copenhagen 08:40, ar Stockholm 15:53.

Amsterdam–Cologne–Passau–Vienna *(Donauwalzer Express)* Lv Amsterdam 20:05, ar Cologne 22:44, ar Passau 07:35, ar Vienna 10:52.

Amsterdam–Cologne–Munich Lv Amsterdam 19:25, ar Cologne 22:00, ar Munich 06:30.

Amsterdam–London (via *Eurostar,* with train change in Brussels) Lv Amsterdam 09:30 and 14:30, ar Brussels (Gare du Midi) 12:31 and 17:31; lv Brussels (Gare du Midi) 13:01 and 17:54, ar London (Waterloo) 14:43 and 19:39.

Amsterdam–Brussels–Paris Lv Amsterdam 07:40, 09:40, and 17:40; ar Rotterdam 08:47, 10:24, and 17:40; ar Brussels (Gare du Midi) 10:32, 12:32, and 20:32; ar Paris 12:05, 14:08, and 22:05.

BARCELONA

For train information, call ☎ **3/478 5000.**

Barcelona–Geneva–Zurich *(Pau Casals Express)* Lv Barcelona Franca 20:15, ar Geneva 05:49, ar Zurich 09:17.

BRUSSELS

For train information, call ☎ **2/224-60-10.**

Brussels–Cologne–Vienna Lv Brussels (Gare du Midi) 19:17; lv Liège 20:23; ar Aachen 21:10, ar Cologne 22:20, ar Passau 04:37, ar Linz 07:40, ar Vienna (Westbahnhof) 09:43.

Brussels–London *(Eurostar)* Lv Brussels (Gare du Midi) 07:02, 17:54, and 21:01; ar London (Waterloo) 08:50, 19:39, and 22:43.

Brussels–Rotterdam–Amsterdam Lv Brussels (Gare du Midi) 08:07; lv Antwerp 08:46; ar Rotterdam 10:01, ar The Hague 10:20, ar Amsterdam 11:04.

Brussels–Paris Lv Brussels (Gare du Nord) 07:23, 10:32, 15:30, and 20:32; ar Paris 09:05, 12:05, 17:05, and 22:05.

Brussels–Luxembourg Lv Brussels (Gare du Midi) 05:21, 07:15, 09:21, and 19:11; ar Luxembourg 08:15, 09:49, 12:15, and 21:49 (18 daily connections).

COPENHAGEN

For train information, call ☎ **33-14-11-20.**

Copenhagen–Cologne–Paris Lv Copenhagen 07:55, ar Cologne 16:50, ar Aachen 18:03, ar Liège 19:30, ar Paris 22:03.

Copenhagen–Hamburg–Bremen–Amsterdam *(North-West Express)* Lv Copenhagen 20:18, ar Hamburg 02:07, lv Bremen 03:45, ar Amsterdam 09:54.

Copenhagen–Stockholm Lv Copenhagen 06:49 and 15:09, ar Stockholm 12:41 and 23:47.

Copenhagen–Munich Lv Copenhagen 18:18, ar Hamburg 01:50, ar Nuremberg 07:30, ar Munich 09:20.

INNSBRUCK

For train information, call ☎ **0512/1717.**

Innsbruck–Munich Lv Innsbruck 06:39, 08:37, and 16:37; ar Munich 08:30, 10:30, and 18:30.

Innsbruck–Salzburg Lv Innsbruck 07:33, 13:19, and 21:30; ar Salzburg 09:36, 15:29, and 23:29.

Innsbruck–Vienna Lv Innsbruck 09:30, 11:30, and 17:30; ar Vienna (Westbahnhof) 14:45, 18:45, and 22:45.

Innsbruck–Rome Lv Innsbruck 11:28 and 22:40; ar Rome (Termini) 19:50 and 8:15.

LONDON

London–Paris *(Eurostar)* A minimum of 5 daily departures 05:08 to 09:53, 12 departures 10:23 to 16:23, and 5 departures 17:50 to 19:53. For up-to-date departure and arrival times, call ☎ **035/881-881.** Travel time from Waterloo Station to Gare du Nord is 3 hours.

London–Brussels *(Eurostar)* 10 departures on weekdays, 8 on Sunday. Travel time to Gare du Midi is 4 hours.

London–Amsterdam (via *Eurostar)* Same departures as London–Brussels, with connecting train waiting in Brussels for Brussels–Amsterdam. Travel time to Centraal Station is 7 hours.

London–Copenhagen (via *Eurostar,* **with train change in Brussels)** Lv London (Waterloo) 12:27, ar Brussels (Gare du Midi) 16:10; lv Brussels (Gare du Midi) 18:47, ar Copenhagen 8:30.

London–Cologne–Vienna (via *Eurostar,* **with train change in Brussels)** Lv London (Waterloo) 14:23, ar Brussels (Gare du Midi) 18:02; lv Brussels (Gare du Midi) 19:17, ar Cologne 22:20, ar Vienna (Westbahnhof) 05:55.

London–Edinburgh Lv London (King's Cross) Monday to Saturday hourly 06:15 to 18:00, Sunday hourly 9:00 to 23:10. Travel time is an average 4½ hours.

MADRID

For train information, call ☎ **1/305-8544.**

Madrid–Bordeaux–Paris *(Francisco de Goya Express)* Lv Madrid (Chamartín) 19:25, ar Paris (Gare d'Austerlitz) 08:29.

Madrid–Lisbon *(Lusitania Express)* Lv Madrid (Atocha) 22:35, ar Lisbon 08:40.

MUNICH

For train information, call ☎ **089/194-19.**

Munich–Zurich *(Gottfried Keller Express)*   Lv Munich 12:15; lv Lindau 14:29; ar Zurich 16:26.

Munich–Florence–Rome *(Michelangelo Express)*   Lv Munich 09:29; lv Innsbruck 11:22; ar Verona 15:05, ar Florence 17:49, ar Rome 19:50.

Munich–Hamburg–Copenhagen   Lv Munich 19:50, ar Hamburg 04:00, ar Copenhagen 09:58 (sleepers and couchettes only).

Munich–Zurich *(The Bavaria)*   Lv Munich 18:15; lv Lindau 20:29; ar Zurich 22:23.

Munich–Innsbruck–Verona–Florence–Rome   Lv Munich 20:30; lv Innsbruck 22:22; ar Verona 02:08, ar Florence 04:08, ar Rome 08:15.

Munich–Venice   Lv Munich 11:30 and 23:40 (sleepers only); ar Venice 18:37 and 08:45.

NICE

For up-to-date rail information, call ☎ **04-93-87-60-60.**

Nice–Paris   Lv Nice 09:30 and 12:52 (both TGV trains), ar Paris (Gare de Lyon) 16:21 and 19:18.

PARIS

For train information on all six Paris train stations, call ☎ **01-45-82-50-50.**

Paris–Munich–Vienna–Budapest *(Orient Express)*   Lv Paris (Gare de l'Est) 17:49; lv Strasbourg 22:02, ar Karlsruhe 22:57, ar Munich 03:05, ar Salzburg 04:50, ar Vienna 08:30, ar Budapest 11:58.

Paris–Hamburg–Copenhagen *(Viking Express)*   Lv Paris (Gare du Nord) 16:55, ar Liège 19:33, ar Cologne 20:11, ar Hamburg 02:22, ar Puttgarden 04:50, ar Copenhagen 08:40.

Paris–Brussels–Amsterdam   Lv Paris (Gare du Nord) 06:55, 10:55, 15:55, 17:25, and 23:16; ar Brussels 8:28, 12:28, 17:23, 18:50, and 04:47; ar Amsterdam 11:07, 15:07, 20:07, 22:07, and 08:02.

Paris–London *(Eurostar)*   Lv Paris (Gare du Nord) 07:16, 09:10, 18:19, and 20:07; ar London (Waterloo) 09:09, 11:30, 20:13, and 22:13.

Paris–Barcelona *(Jean Miró Express)*   Lv Paris (Gare d'Austerlitz) 21:00, ar Barcelona 09:13.

Paris–Madrid   Lv Paris (Gare d'Austerlitz) 20:00, ar Madrid 08:55.

Paris–Luxembourg   Lv Paris (Gare de l'Est) 08:54, 10:54, and 17:17; ar Luxembourg 12:34, 14:35, and 20:52.

Paris–Rome   Lv Paris (Gare de Lyon) 20:03, ar Genoa 06:10, ar Rome (Termini) 10:05.

Paris–Geneva   Lv Paris (Gare de Lyon) 07:12, 10:18, 14:40, and 17:18 (TGV train); ar Geneva 10:55, 13:55, 18:19, and 20:57.

Paris–Nice   Lv Paris (Gare de Lyon) 11:24 and 15:18 (TGV train), ar Nice 18:44 and 22:31.

ROME

For train information, call ☎ **6/484972.**

Rome–Pisa–Paris *(Palatino Express)*   Lv Rome 19:05; lv Pisa 22:13; ar Paris (Gare de Lyon) 09:50 (sleepers and couchettes only).

Rome–Florence–Innsbruck–Munich   Lv Rome 18:20; lv Florence 20:35; lv Bologna 00:47; lv Verona 02:56; ar Innsbruck 06:37; ar Munich 08:30.

Rome–Florence–Venice–Trieste   Lv Rome 09:05, ar Florence 11:10, ar Venice 13:30, ar Trieste 15:49.

Rome–Florence   20 daily departures, including: Lv Rome 07:15, 08:20, 14:20, 18:00, and 20:20; ar Florence 09:50, 11:46, 17:45, 20:52, and 23:50.

Rome–Milan   21 daily departures, including: Lv Rome 09:50, 13:35, 15:20, and 17:30; ar Milan 15:40, 18:00, 20:00, and 23:59.

Rome–Naples–Messina–Palermo   Lv Rome 20:30; lv Naples 22:50; lv Messina 05:08; ar Palermo 08:25.

Rome–Lausanne–Geneva (with train change in Milan)   Lv Rome 08:35, ar Florence 10:19, ar Milan (Centrale) 13:00; lv Milan (Centrale) 13:25, ar Brig 15:55, ar Lausanne 17:56, ar Geneva 18:42.

SEVILLE
For train information, call ☎ **05/410-658.**

Seville–Barcelona   Lv Seville 09:40 and 21:10, ar Barcelona (Sants) 20:30 and 08:30.

Seville–Madrid   Lv Seville 09:00, 16:00 and 19:00; ar Madrid (Atocha) 11:30, 18:30, and 21:30.

Seville–Málaga   Lv Seville 08:15, 12:40, and 17:10; ar Málaga 11:05, 15:35, and 20:08.

STOCKHOLM
For up-to-date train information, call ☎ **8/227 940.**

Stockholm–Copenhagen   Lv Stockholm 06:12, 08:06, and 11:36; ar Copenhagen 13:14, 14:54, and 19:10.

Stockholm–Oslo   Lv Stockholm 07:18, 16:48, and 22:37; ar Oslo 13:25, 22:28, and 07:32.

VIENNA
For train information, call ☎ **1/1717.**

Vienna–Frankfurt–Brussels–London   Lv Vienna (Westbahnhof) 08:20, ar Passau 11:25, ar Cologne 18:05, ar Brussels (Gare du Midi) 20:06; lv Brussels (Gare du Midi) 21:01, ar London (Waterloo) 22:43.

Vienna–Munich–Paris *(Orient Express)*   Lv Vienna (Westbahnhof) 20:28; lv Salzburg 23:58; lv Munich 01:22; ar Strasbourg 05:58, ar Paris 10:23.

Vienna–Paris *(The Mozart)*   Lv Vienna 08:50, ar Paris 22:22 (via Munich and Strasbourg).

Vienna–Warsaw–Moscow   Lv Vienna (Südbahnhof) 00:06; Lv Warsaw 06:53; ar Minsk 20:48; ar Moscow (Kievskaya) 08:30.

Vienna–Venice   The *Romulus Express* (lv Vienna 07:30, ar Venice 15:50) is your best train for this trip, but three others leave Vienna daily for Venice, all departing from the Sudbahnhof: lv Vienna 12:55, 20:10, and 22:45; ar Venice 21:52, 04:14, and 08:30 (the last two trains, sleepers only).

C Average Travel Times by Rail

Amsterdam to
>   Berlin   8 hr. 30 min.
>   Cologne   3 hr.
>   Copenhagen   11 hr. 30 min.
>   Frankfurt   6 hr.
>   Munich   8 hr. 30 min.
>   Paris   4 hr. 15 min.
>   Zurich   10 hr.

Athens to
>   Munich   42 hr. 30 min.
>   Vienna   43 hr.

Avignon to
>   Barcelona   6 hr. 30 min.
>   Paris   3 hr. 30 min.

Barcelona to
>   Madrid   7 hr.
>   Paris   11 hr. 30 min.

Bath to
>   London   1 hr. 11 min.

Berlin to
>   Frankfurt   6 hr.
>   Munich   7 hr.
>   Paris   11 hr.
>   Prague   6 hr. 30 min.

Bern to
>   Interlaken   1 hr.
>   Milan   4 hr. 30 min.
>   Paris   4 hr. 30 min.
>   Zurich   1 hr. 30 min.

Bordeaux to
>   Paris   3 hr.

Brussels to
>   Frankfurt   5 hr. 30 min.
>   London   2 hr. 45min.
>   Paris   1 hr. 25 min.

Budapest to
>   Frankfurt   15 hr. 30 min.
>   Prague   9 hr. 30 min.
>   Vienna   4 hr.

Cannes to
>   Paris   6 hr.

Copenhagen to
>   Oslo   10 hr. 30 min.
>   Paris   15 hr.
>   Stockholm   8 hr.

Edinburgh to
>   London   4 hr.

Florence to
>   Geneva   8 hr.
>   Milan   3 hr.
>   Paris   12 hr. 30 min.
>   Rome   1 hr. 30 min.
>   Venice   3 hr.
>   Zurich   8 hr.

Frankfurt to
>   Munich   3 hr. 30 min.
>   Paris   6 hr. 15 min.
>   Prague   8 hr.
>   Salzburg   5 hr.
>   Vienna   8 hr.
>   Zurich   5 hr.

Geneva to
>   Milan   4 hr. 15 min.
>   Paris   3 hr. 30 min.
>   Venice   8 hr.

Glasgow to
>   London   5 hr. 5 min.

Granada to
>   Madrid   6 hr. 30 min.

Helsinki to
>   Stockholm   10 hr.

Innsbruck to
>   Munich   3 hr.
>   Vienna   8 hr.
>   Zurich   5 hr.

Lausanne to
>   Milan   4 hr. 30 min.
>   Paris   3 hr. 45 min.

Lillehammer to
>   Oslo   2 hr. 30 min.

Lisbon to
>   Madrid   10 hr.

London to
>   Paris   3 hr.

Luxembourg to
>   Paris   4 hr.

Luzerne to
>   Paris   7 hr. 30 min.
>   Venice   8 hr.

Lyon to
>   Nice   5 hr.
>   Paris   2 hr.

Madrid to
>   Malaga   7 hr.

Marseille to
>   Paris   4 hr. 15 min.

Milan to
>   Nice   5 hr.
>   Paris (day)   6 hr. 40 min.
>   Rome   5 hr.
>   Venice   3 hr.
>   Zurich   4 hr. 30 min.

Munich to
>   Paris   8 hr. 30 min.
>   Prague   7 hr. 30 min.
>   Rome   11 hr.
>   Salzburg   2 hr.
>   Venice   9 hr.
>   Vienna   4 hr. 45 min.
>   Zurich   5 hr.

Nantes to
>   Paris   2 hr.

Naples to
>   Rome   2 hr.

Nice to
>   Paris   6 hr. 30 min.
>   Rome   10 hr.
>   Venice   10 hr.

Oslo to
>   Stockholm   6 hr. 30 min.

Paris to
>   Rome   15 hr.
>   Salzburg   10 hr.
>   Strasbourg   4 hr.
>   Toulouse   5 hr.
>   Tours   1 hr.
>   Venice   12 hr. 15 min.
>   Vienna   13 hr. 30 min.
>   Zurich   6 hr.

Pisa to
>   Rome   4 hr.

Prague to
>   Vienna   5 hr.

Rome to
>   Siena   3 hr.
>   Venice   4 hr. 30 min.
>   Zurich   8 hr. 30 min.

Salzburg to
>   Vienna   4 hr.

Venice to
>   Vienna   8 hr.

Vienna to
>   Zurich   12 hr.

Index

Page numbers in italics refer to maps.

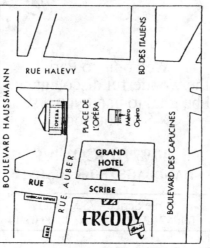

The English House

Please mention this coupon when you are making your dinner reservations. If you have any trouble with the validity of the coupon, please ask to speak to the manager.

The English House Restaurant Limited
3 Milner Street, London SW3
Tel: 0171/584-3002
Fax: 0171/584-2848

DeSelby's

**Open Monday – Friday, 5:30–11 p.m.
Saturday, noon to 11 p.m., and Sunday, noon to 10 p.m.**

The the DART to Dun Laoghaire station,
or take the 7, 7A, 8, or 46A bus.

Astor House Hotel

Phone: 0171/581-5888
Fax: 0171/584-4925

Rates include breakfast.
American Express, MasterCard, and VISA are accepted.

Take Tube to South Kensington.
Walk 3 blocks down Old Brampton Road
to Sumner Place (on your left).

Travel Certificate

5% Off
Any European Car Rental

Or

$20 Off
Any Air Fare To Europe

Or

$5 Off
Per Night, Any European Hotel

auto ⊕ europe.®

Contact Your Travel Agent

Reservations: 1-800-223-5555

www.autoeurope.com

FROMMER'S® COMPLETE TRAVEL GUIDES

(Comprehensive guides with selections in all price ranges—from deluxe to budget)

Alaska
Amsterdam
Arizona
Atlanta
Australia
Austria
Bahamas
Barcelona, Madrid & Seville
Belgium, Holland &
  Luxembourg
Bermuda
Boston
Budapest & the Best of
  Hungary
California
Canada
Cancún, Cozumel & the
  Yucatán
Cape Cod, Nantucket &
  Martha's Vineyard
Caribbean
Caribbean Cruises &
  Ports of Call
Caribbean Ports of Call
Carolinas & Georgia
Chicago
China
Colorado
Costa Rica
Denver, Boulder &
  Colorado Springs
England
Europe
Florida

France
Germany
Greece
Hawaii
Hong Kong
Honolulu, Waikiki & Oahu
Ireland
Israel
Italy
Jamaica & Barbados
Japan
Las Vegas
London
Los Angeles
Maryland & Delaware
Maui
Mexico
Miami & the Keys
Montana & Wyoming
Montréal & Québec City
Munich & the Bavarian Alps
Nashville & Memphis
Nepal
New England
New Mexico
New Orleans
New York City
Nova Scotia, New
  Brunswick &
  Prince Edward Island
Oregon
Paris
Philadelphia & the Amish
  Country

Portugal
Prague & the Best of the
  Czech Republic
Provence & the Riviera
Puerto Rico
Rome
San Antonio & Austin
San Diego
San Francisco
Santa Fe, Taos &
  Albuquerque
Scandinavia
Scotland
Seattle & Portland
Singapore & Malaysia
South Pacific
Spain
Switzerland
Thailand
Tokyo
Toronto
Tuscany & Umbria
USA
Utah
Vancouver & Victoria
Vermont, New Hampshire &
  Maine
Vienna & the Danube Valley
Virgin Islands
Virginia
Walt Disney World &
  Orlando
Washington, D.C.
Washington State

FROMMER'S® DOLLAR-A-DAY GUIDES

(The ultimate guides to comfortable low-cost travel)

Australia from $50 a Day
California from $60 a Day
Caribbean from $60 a Day
England from $60 a Day
Europe from $50 a Day
Florida from $60 a Day
Greece from $50 a Day
Hawaii from $60 a Day
Ireland from $50 a Day

Israel from $45 a Day
Italy from $50 a Day
London from $70 a Day
New York from $75 a Day
New Zealand from $50 a Day
Paris from $70 a Day
San Francisco from $60 a Day
Washington, D.C., from
  $60 a Day

FROMMER'S® MEMORABLE WALKS

Chicago
London

New York
Paris

San Francisco

FROMMER'S® PORTABLE GUIDES

Acapulco, Ixtapa/
  Zihuatenejo
Bahamas
California Wine
  Country
Charleston & Savannah
Chicago

Dublin
Las Vegas
London
Maine Coast
New Orleans
New York City
Paris

Puerto Vallarta, Manzanillo
  & Guadalajara
San Francisco
Sydney
Tampa Bay & St. Petersburg
Venice
Washington, D.C.

FROMMER'S® NATIONAL PARK GUIDES

Grand Canyon
National Parks of the American West
Yellowstone & Grand Teton

Yosemite & Sequoia/
  Kings Canyon
Zion & Bryce Canyon

THE COMPLETE IDIOT'S TRAVEL GUIDES
(The ultimate user-friendly trip planners)

Cruise Vacations
Planning Your Trip to Europe
Hawaii

Las Vegas
Mexico's Beach Resorts
New Orleans

New York City
San Francisco
Walt Disney World

SPECIAL-INTEREST TITLES

The Civil War Trust's Official Guide to
  the Civil War Discovery Trail
Frommer's Caribbean Hideaways
Israel Past & Present
New York City with Kids
New York Times Weekends
Outside Magazine's Adventure Guide
  to New England
Outside Magazine's Adventure Guide
  to Northern California

Outside Magazine's Adventure Guide
  to the Pacific Northwest
Outside Magazine's Guide to Family Vacations
Places Rated Almanac
Retirement Places Rated
Washington, D.C., with Kids
Wonderful Weekends from Boston
Wonderful Weekends from New York City
Wonderful Weekends from San Francisco
Wonderful Weekends from Los Angeles

THE UNOFFICIAL GUIDES®
(Get the unbiased truth from these candid, value-conscious guides)

Atlanta
Branson, Missouri
Chicago
Cruises
Disneyland

Florida with Kids
The Great Smoky
  & Blue Ridge
  Mountains
Las Vegas

Miami & the Keys
Mini-Mickey
New Orleans
New York City
San Francisco

Skiing in the West
Walt Disney World
Walt Disney World
  Companion
Washington, D.C.

FROMMER'S® IRREVERENT GUIDES
(Wickedly honest guides for sophisticated travelers)

Amsterdam
Boston
Chicago

London
Manhattan

New Orleans
Paris

San Francisco
Walt Disney World
Washington, D.C.

FROMMER'S® DRIVING TOURS

America
Britain
California

Florida
France
Germany

Ireland
Italy
New England

Scotland
Spain
Western Europe

WHEREVER YOU TRAVEL, *H*ELP IS NEVER FAR AWAY.

From planning your trip to

providing travel assistance along

the way, American Express®

Travel Service Offices are

always there to help.

American Express Travel Service
Offices are found in central locations
throughout Europe.

Travel

http://www.americanexpress.com/travel